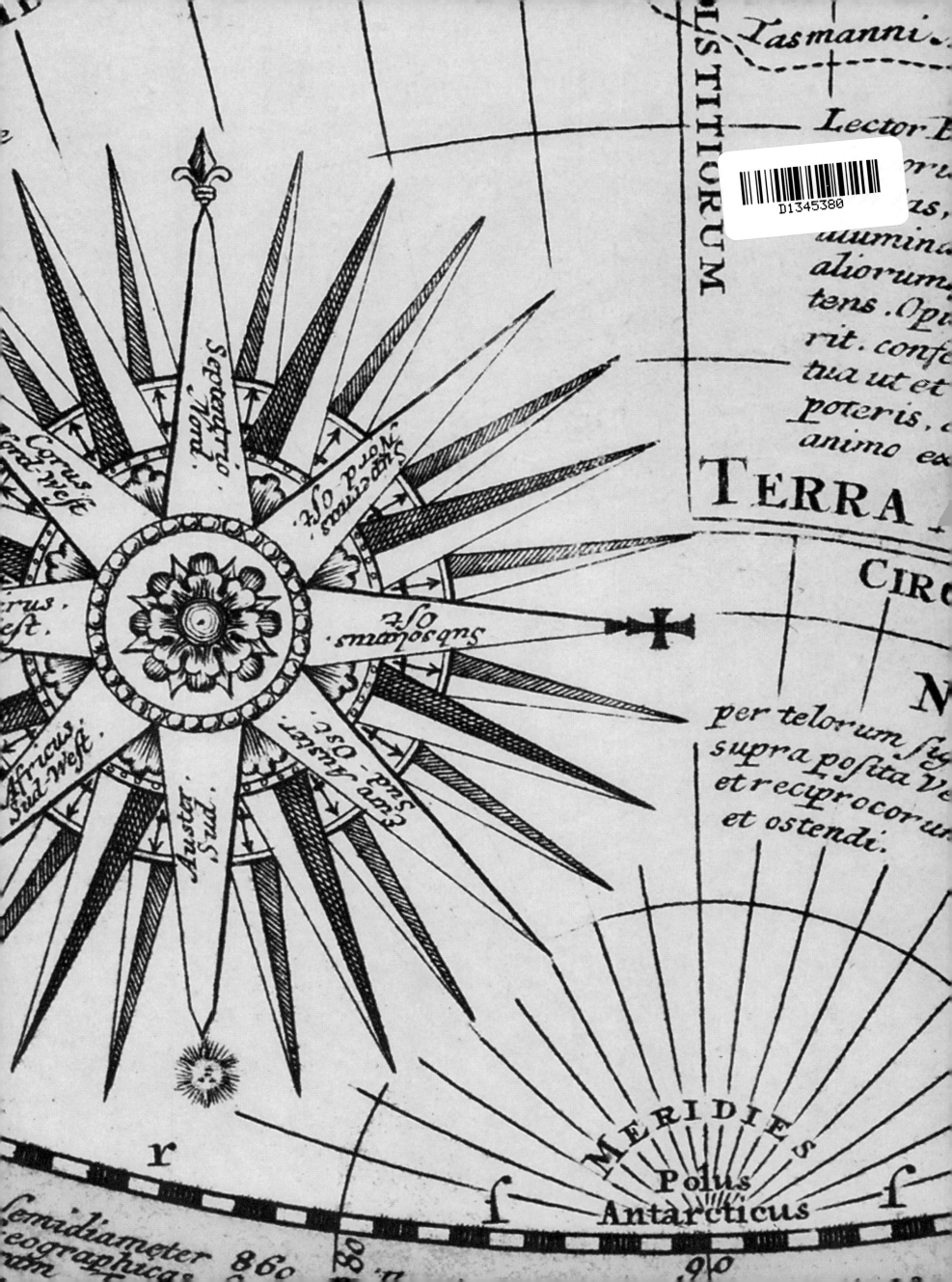

DK ATLAS OF WORLD HISTORY

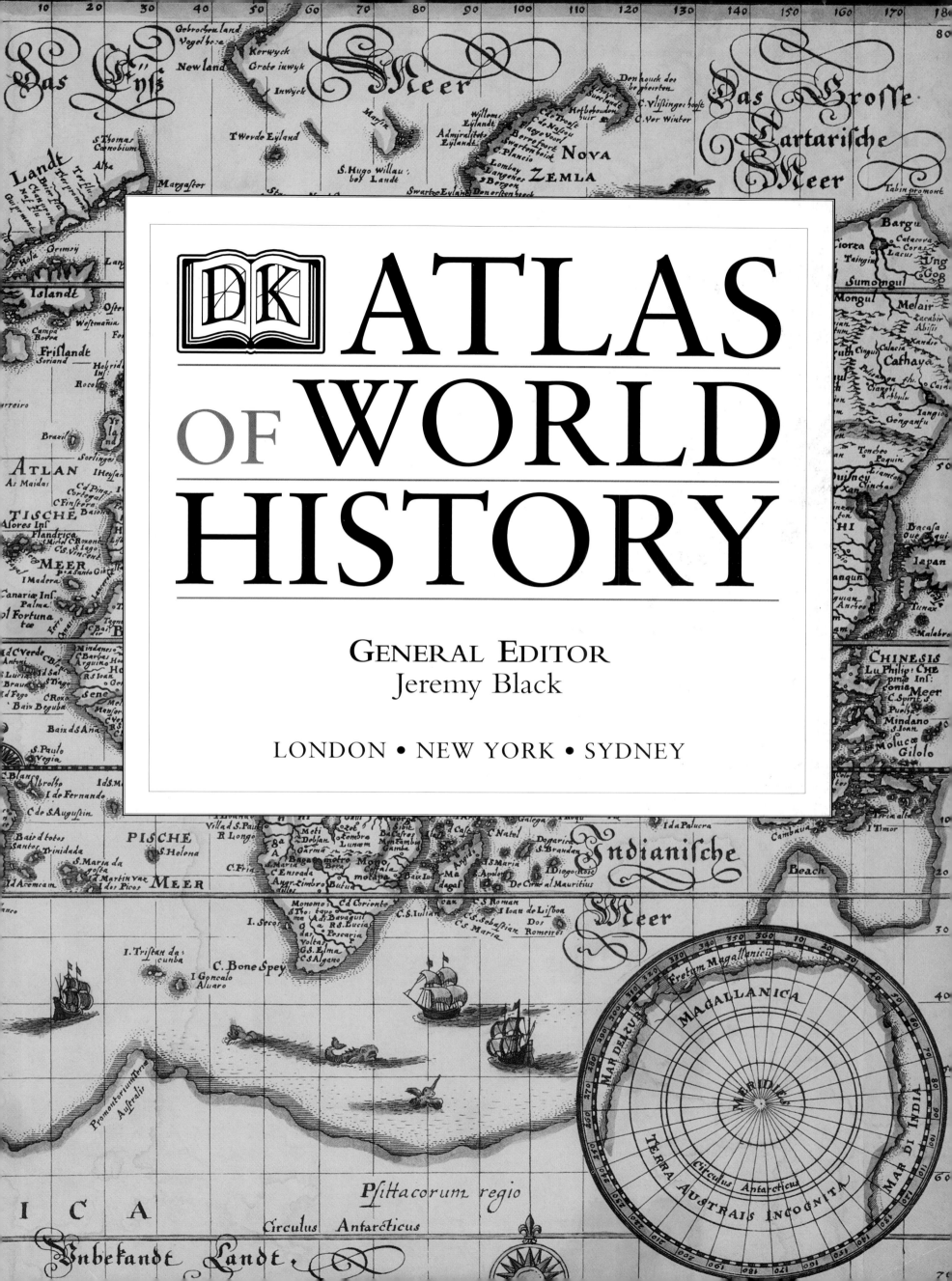

DK ATLAS OF WORLD HISTORY

GENERAL EDITOR
Jeremy Black

LONDON • NEW YORK • SYDNEY

A DORLING KINDERSLEY BOOK
www.dk.com

CONSULTANTS

GENERAL EDITOR Professor Jeremy Black, Department of History, University of Exeter, UK

WORLD HISTORY
Professor Jerry Bentley, Department of History, University of Hawaii, USA
Professor James Chambers, Department of History, Texas Christian University, USA
Dr John France, Department of History, University of Swansea, UK
Dr Guy Halsall, Department of History, Birkbeck College, London, UK
Dr Chris Scarre, Department of Archaeology, Cambridge University, UK
H. P. Wilmott, Royal Military Academy, Sandhurst, UK

NORTH AMERICA
Professor Donald S. Frazier, Department of History, McMurray University, Texas, USA
Professor Ross Hassig, Department of Anthropology, Oklahoma State University, USA
Dr Kendrick Oliver, Department of History, University of Southampton, UK
Professor George Raudzens, Department of History, Macquarie University, Sydney, Australia
Dr Brian Ward, Department of History, University of Florida, USA

SOUTH AMERICA
Dr Edwin F. Early, Department of Economics, University of Plymouth, UK
Dr Anthony McFarlane, Department of History, University of Warwick, UK
Dr Nicholas James, Cambridge, UK
Professor Neil Whitehead, Department of Anthropology, University of Wisconsin, USA

AFRICA
Professor John Thornton, Department of History, Millersville University, USA

EUROPE
Professor Richard Britnell, Department of History, University of Durham, UK
Dr Michael Broers, School of History, University of Leeds, UK
Professor Brian Davies, Department of History, University of Texas, San Antonio USA

EUROPE (continued)
Professor Michael Jones, Department of History, University of Nottingham, UK
Dr Don McRaild, Department of History, University of Sunderland
Dr Susan Rose, Department of History, Roehampton Institute, London, UK
Professor Peter Waldron, Department of History, University of Sunderland, UK
Dr Peter Wilson, Department of History, University of Sunderland, UK
Professor Spencer Tucker, Department of History, Virginia Military Institute, USA
Professor Edward M. Yates, Department of Geography, King's College, London, UK

WEST ASIA
Dr Ahron Bregman, Webster University, Regent's College, London, UK
Professor Ian Netton, School of Arabic Studies, University of Leeds, UK
Sajjid Rizvi, Department of Oriental Studies, Cambridge University, UK

SOUTH AND SOUTHEAST ASIA
Professor Joseph E. Schwartzberg, Department of Geography, University of Minnesota, USA
Dr Sunil Kumar, Department of Medieval History, University of New Delhi, India

NORTH AND EAST ASIA
Professor Gina Barnes, Department of East Asian Studies, University of Durham, UK

AUSTRALASIA AND OCEANIA
Dr Steven Roger Fischer, Institute of Polynesian Languages and Literatures, Auckland, New Zealand

The publishers would like to acknowledge additional contributions and advice from the following people: Professor Richard Overy, Professor Geoffrey Parker, Gordon Marsden, Professor Kenneth Kiple, Paul Keeler.

DORLING KINDERSLEY CARTOGRAPHY

EDITOR-IN-CHIEF Andrew Heritage

MANAGING EDITOR Lisa Thomas

SENIOR EDITOR Ferdie McDonald

PROJECT EDITORS Margaret Hynes, Elizabeth Wyse, Ailsa Heritage, Caroline Chapman, Debra Clapson, Wim Jenkins

ADDITIONAL EDITORIAL ASSISTANCE Louise Keane, Adele Rackley

SENIOR MANAGING ART EDITOR Philip Lord

PRINCIPAL DESIGNER Nicola Liddiard

PROJECT ART EDITORS Rhonda Fisher, Carol Ann Davis, Karen Gregory

CARTOGRAPHIC MANAGER David Roberts

SENIOR CARTOGRAPHIC EDITOR Roger Bullen

CARTOGRAPHIC DESIGN John Plumer

DIGITAL MAPS CREATED BY Rob Stokes

PROJECT CARTOGRAPHERS Pamela Alford, James Anderson, Dale Buckton, Tony Chambers, Jan Clark, Tom Coulson, Martin Darlison, Jeremy Hepworth, Chris Jackson, Julia Lunn, John Plumer, Alka Ranger, Ann Stephenson, Julie Turner, Peter Winfield

ADDITIONAL CARTOGRAPHY Advanced Illustration Ltd., Arcadia Ltd., Lovell Johns Ltd.

HISTORICAL CARTOGRAPHIC CONSULTANT András Bereznay

PICTURE RESEARCH Deborah Pownall, Louise Thomas

INDEXING Julia Lynch, Janet Smy, Jo Russ, Sophie Park, Ruth Duxbury, Zoë Ellinson

DATABASE CONSULTANT Simon Lewis

SYSTEMS MANAGER Philip Rowles

PRODUCTION David Proffit

First published in 1999 by Dorling Kindersley Limited, 9 Henrietta Street, London, WC2E 8PS

Copyright © Dorling Kindersley Limited, London 1999

Picture information: *p.1* Andreas Cellarius, rector of the Latin school at Hoorn in northern Holland, produced this map of the eastern hemisphere in 1708 as part of his exquisite atlas of the heavens, *Atlas Coelestis; seu Harmonia Macrocosmica.* The map illustrates the seasons of the year and the various climate zones from pole to pole. *pp.2–3* Produced in 1646, by Matthäus Merian, a Swiss engraver. The geography in the map is based on world maps using the influential Mercator projection, produced by the Dutch Blaeu family, a dynasty of master cartographers. *p.5* This 1598 Dutch engraving shows a cartographer at work, probably Rogerius Bullenius.

INTRODUCTION

WE SEE OURSELVES in the mirror of the past, and in this mirror we see how
we have created our world, and where we have come from. The *DK Atlas of
World History* offers a history of the world relevant as we start a new Millennium
and as we look back to consider how we have got here.

An international team of experts was assembled and
given the task of producing an atlas that would make
sense for all parts of the world. Unlike other works
of this type, we have sought to avoid a Eurocentric
approach to history. To achieve this, we have combined
a comprehensive global overview of world history
in Part One, with more detailed narratives of the
development of each of the world's regions in Part Two.

This is not the only new feature of this atlas. Again,
unlike most historical atlases, this is a work that puts
maps first. This is not simply a book with maps, but
represents an integrated cartographic approach. The maps
have been created using the most modern techniques
and accurate digital data, drawing on the established
state-of-the-art skills of DK as innovative map
publishers. In addition, the atlas includes numerous
examples of historical maps, setting past views of the
world in contrast with modern knowledge.

The atlas is structured so that readers can look at
history from a number of different angles: global,
thematic, regional, and chronological. This offers a rich
variety of approaches which allows the reader to form
a comprehensive picture of the past.

The inclusion of past maps, both European and non-
European, is valuable, as it reminds us that there are, and
have been, many different ways of describing the world.
Ours is not the only way to consider space, place, and
the world.

The pages in this atlas are portraits of an alien world.
A range of devices has been used to relate this lost realm
to our own: the distribution of sites and cultures, political
borders and structures, areas of cultural influence and
political control, with arrows indicating the movements

of peoples and the spread of technologies and ideas.
Frequently, explanatory annotations have been added to
the maps. Beyond the maps themselves, each page offers
texts, chronological timelines, and carefully chosen
pictures to built up as complete an impression of each
period or historical episode as possible. This is not
intended as a visual dictionary of dates – dates merely
provide the historian with a skeletal framework, signposts
on the journey into the past. *The DK Atlas of World
History* is, rather, about geography and about the
continuous processes of change.

Change through time is multi-faceted: political and
economic, demographic and social, cultural and
ecological. This atlas attempts to cover all these features,
although the extent to which historical developments
can be mapped varies, with to the quality and nature of
the sources and research available. Yet, benefiting from
a wide range of talent, this atlas pushes forward the
geography of the past as never before. It includes maps
of familiar episodes from history and many more never
previously described in cartographic form.

Mapping episodes through time demands dynamic
narrative tools. The digital mapmaking techniques used
in this atlas make it possible to offer exciting and
informative perspectives and projections. The earth can
be seen from any viewpoint, creating explanatory yet
accurate formats for the visualization of historical stories.
The rigid orthodoxy of the north-oriented map is, after
all, a relatively recent – and European – invention.

This atlas is produced with an awareness of the
relationship between geography and history. It is up-to-
date and of its time, not an atlas for all time, but the best
possible at the start of the new Millennium.

Jeremy Black, June 1999

CONTENTS

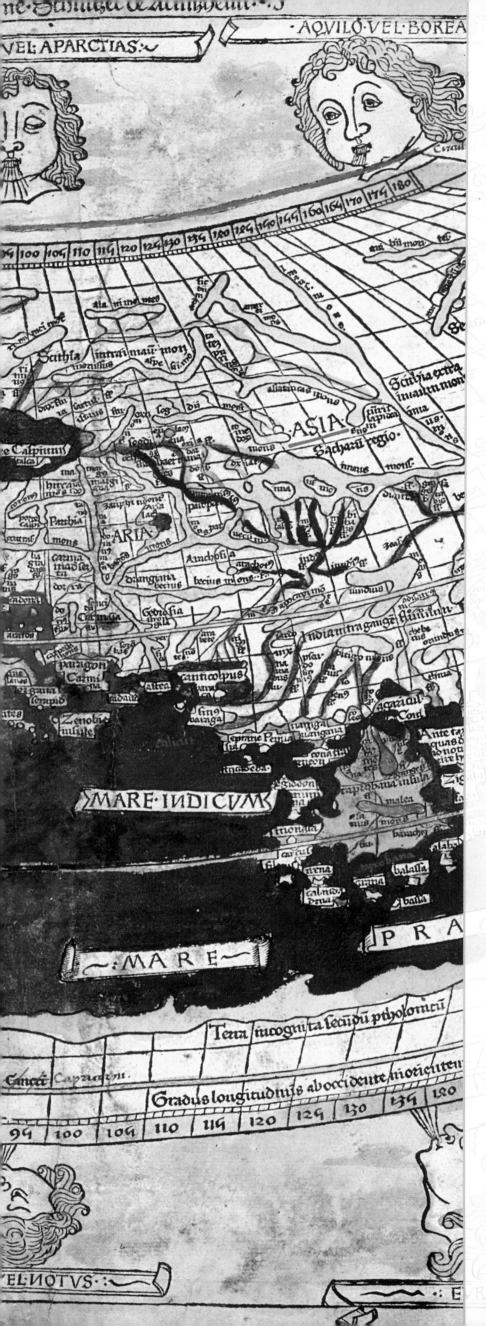

PART ONE

ERAS OF WORLD HISTORY

GLOBAL CITIZENS at the beginning of the 3rd millennium are uniquely able to regard their world both as a totality and as a sum of its constituent parts. The first section of this Atlas presents history on a global basis, comprising a series of chronological overviews of the world across the last twenty millennia. These maps portray the changing map of the world and its cultures from ancient times down to the present day, accompanied by summaries of regional developments. Features highlighting the main technological advances of the period are complemented by maps or views of the world produced at the time. Each overview is followed by pages which examine aspects of the changing global scene – political, economic, religious, or demographic – which had a global impact during that period.

The Greek polymath, Ptolemy wrote his famous *Guide to Geography* in the 2nd century CE, and his conclusions about the map of the world held sway until the 16th century. This woodcut map of the Ptolemaic world – incorporating Africa, Europe, and Asia – was published in 1486.

THE EARLY HISTORY OF HUMANITY

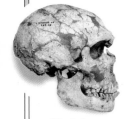

This skull comes from the Neanderthal burial site at La Ferrassie, southwest France.

THE AUSTRALOPITHECINES, OR SOUTHERN APES, which emerged in Africa c.4 million years ago, possessed many ape-like characteristics, but crucially had evolved the ability to walk upright. The oldest of these species, *Australopithecus afarensis*, which is represented by the find of a skeleton of a small adult female, known as 'Lucy', from the Hadar region of Ethiopia, may be ancestral to the earliest species of *Homo* (man), which emerged some 2.5 million years ago. The increased brain capacity of *Homo* was matched by the ability to make tools and control fire, vital cultural developments which enabled human ancestors to exploit a wide range of foods and colonize marginal environments. Fully modern humans, distinguished by their refined tool-making skills, resourcefulness, and ingenuity, were able to withstand the ravages of the last Ice Age and reach the most remote corners of the globe.

Neanderthals

The Neanderthals, a separate and distinct branch of the *Homo* genus, evolved in Europe and West Asia about 120,000 years ago, surviving until up to 35,000 years ago. They had powerful heavy skeletons, with a projecting jaw, and broad nose and brow ridge, and their brains were the same size as those of fully modern humans. They adapted to a wide range of habitats and harsh climates. Neanderthal burials are clear evidence that they had developed cultural rituals.

The Neanderthal burial at Kebana in Israel is c.60,000 years old. The discovery of burials, often with items intended to equip the deceased for the afterlife, led to a revision of the view that Neanderthals were both brutal and primitive.

Human ancestors

The genus *Australopithecus* evolved in eastern and southern Africa between 4 and 1.7 million years ago. Australopithecines were small and sturdy, with apelike bodies, but they had mastered bipedalism, as finds of fossilized footprints, at least 4 million years old, from Laetolil in Tanzania testify. Four major Australopithecine species, classified by variations in their skulls and teeth, have been identified. The earliest known fossils of the *Homo* genus date to 2.5 million years ago. They are distinguished by larger brain size, rounded skulls and a distinctively human formation to the hips and pelvis.

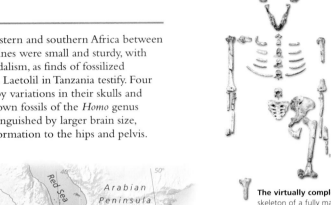

The virtually complete skeleton of a fully mature adult female, known as 'Lucy', found at Hadar in Ethiopia, is c.3.4 million years old and belongs to the oldest known species of Australopithecines.

Prehistoric technology

The first crucial development in the history of early technology was the appearance, about 1.3 million years ago, of stone handaxes, used for butchering hides, cutting wood, and preparing plant foods. Around 100,000 years ago, stone tools, shaped by striking flakes from the core, started to be made. Composite tools, where points, blades and scrapers, were mounted in wooden or bone hafts developed c.45,000 years ago.

Stone handaxes, such as these examples from Hoxne in eastern England dating to at least 100,000 years ago, were made by chipping away flakes to create a sharp cutting edge. They became standard implements throughout Africa, Asia, and Europe.

◀ ❶ Hominid ancestors

Australopithecus remains
- ◆ afarensis
- ◆ africanus
- ◇ boisei
- ◇ robustus

[Map of Africa with locations: Aramis, Sahara, Lake Chad, Nile, Red Sea, Arabian Peninsula, Lake Tana, Hadar, Ethiopian Highlands, Sudd, Omo, Ileret, West Turkana, Lomekwi, Allia Bay, Koobi Fora, Lothagam, Lake Rudolf, Chesowanja, Baringo, Lake Albert, Lake Kyoga, Lake Edward, Lake Victoria, Lake Kivu, Peninj, Olduvai Gorge, Laetolil, Equator, Congo Basin, AFRICA, INDIAN OCEAN, Lake Tanganyika, Lake Mweru, Lake Bangweulu, Malema, Lake Nyasa, Mozambique Channel, Zambezi, Cunene, Limpopo, Makapansgat, Kalahari Desert, Swartkrans, Kromdraai, Sterkfontein, Taung, Orange River, Drakensberg, ATLANTIC OCEAN, Tropic of Capricorn]

Recent discoveries of a new australopithecine (A.bahrelchazali) stretch the geographical range 3800 km west of Great Rift Valley

Find site of 'Lucy', skeleton of an adult female *Australopithecus afarensis*, dated to c.3.4 million years ago

Limited remains of first hominid *Australopithecus anamensis* dating to c.4.2 million years ago

First finds of *Australopithecus boisei* c.2.7–1.7 million years ago

500 km / 500 miles

The skull of the 'Taung child', is c.2.5 million years old. It was discovered in 1924 and revolutionized theories about human evolution.

The evolution of hominids

Hominid evolution is still a matter of dispute. The australopithecines, the earliest hominids, evolved some 4 million years ago. The oldest species (*Australophithecus afarensis*) may be ancestral to the earliest species of *Homo*, the precursors of modern humans, which evolved some 2.5 million years ago. Alternatively, *Homo* may have evolved separately.

By around 30,000 years ago, tools and weapons had become infinitely more sophisticated, adapted both the environment and methods of hunting, as demonstrated by the detailed carving and attention to function on these bone spearheads.

Human evolution

c.4.2 million years ago: *Australopithecus anamensis*: limited remains of bipedal hominid found on shores of Lake Rudolf	c.3 million years ago: *Australopithecus africanus*: notable for powerful build of upper body	c.2.5 million years ago: *Homo habilis*: large brain in relation to body size. Average male height, 1.32 m	c.2 million years ago: *Australopithecus robustus*: hand bones indicate anatomical ability to make stone tools	c.1 million years ago: Earliest evidence of the use of fire	c.900,000 years ago: Earliest evidence of hominids in Asia	c.120,000 years ago: Neanderthals: short-limbed, thick-bodied. Average male height, 1.65 m	c.35,000 years ago: First fully modern humans in Europe; disappearance of Neanderthals

4,000,000 BP	3,000,000 BP	2,000,000 BP	1,000,000 BP	present

| c.3.8 million years ago: *Australopithecus afarensis*: based on find of 'Lucy' skeleton at Hadar, Ethiopia. Average male height, 1.5 m | c.2.6 million years ago: *Australopithecus boisei* with massive chewing muscles. Earliest finds of stone stools | c.1.8 million years ago: *Homo erectus*: distinguished by long limbs. Average male height, 1.77 m | c.850,000 years ago: Hominids reach Europe from Africa | c.800,000 years ago: Archaic *Homo sapiens*: Average male height, 1.75 m | c.100,000 years ago: *Homo sapiens* (anatomically modern humans): earliest evidence in Africa |

The emergence of modern humans

The first representative of the *Homo* genus, *Homo habilis* ('handy man'), emerged about 2.5 million years ago and was distinguished by the ability to make and use tools. *Homo erectus*, which appeared about 1.7 million years ago, had a still larger brain capacity, tall, long-legged physique and ability to walk fully upright, and adapted successfully to a wide range of environments, spreading from Africa to Asia and Europe over the next million years. The earliest fossil remains of fully modern humans, *Homo sapiens sapiens,* found in Africa, date to c.100,000 years ago. Resourceful and inventive, modern humans colonized the most marginal regions, and became the sole surviving human species.

Fossils of *Homo habilis* were discovered in the Olduvai Gorge in the 1960s, and are dated to 2.5 million years ago.

The fossils found at Koobi Fora in Kenya, dating to 1.7 million years ago, are amongst the earliest finds of *Homo erectus*, and clearly demonstrate a marked increase in brain size.

Modern humans reached Europe from Africa c.35,000 years ago, and replaced the Neanderthal population. This skull was found at the site of Predmosti in eastern Europe.

SEE ALSO:

North America: pp.120–121

South America: pp.142–143

Africa: pp.160–161

Europe: pp.174–175

West Asia: pp.220–221

South and Southeast Asia: pp.240–241

North and East Asia: pp.258–259

Australasia and Oceania: pp.278–279

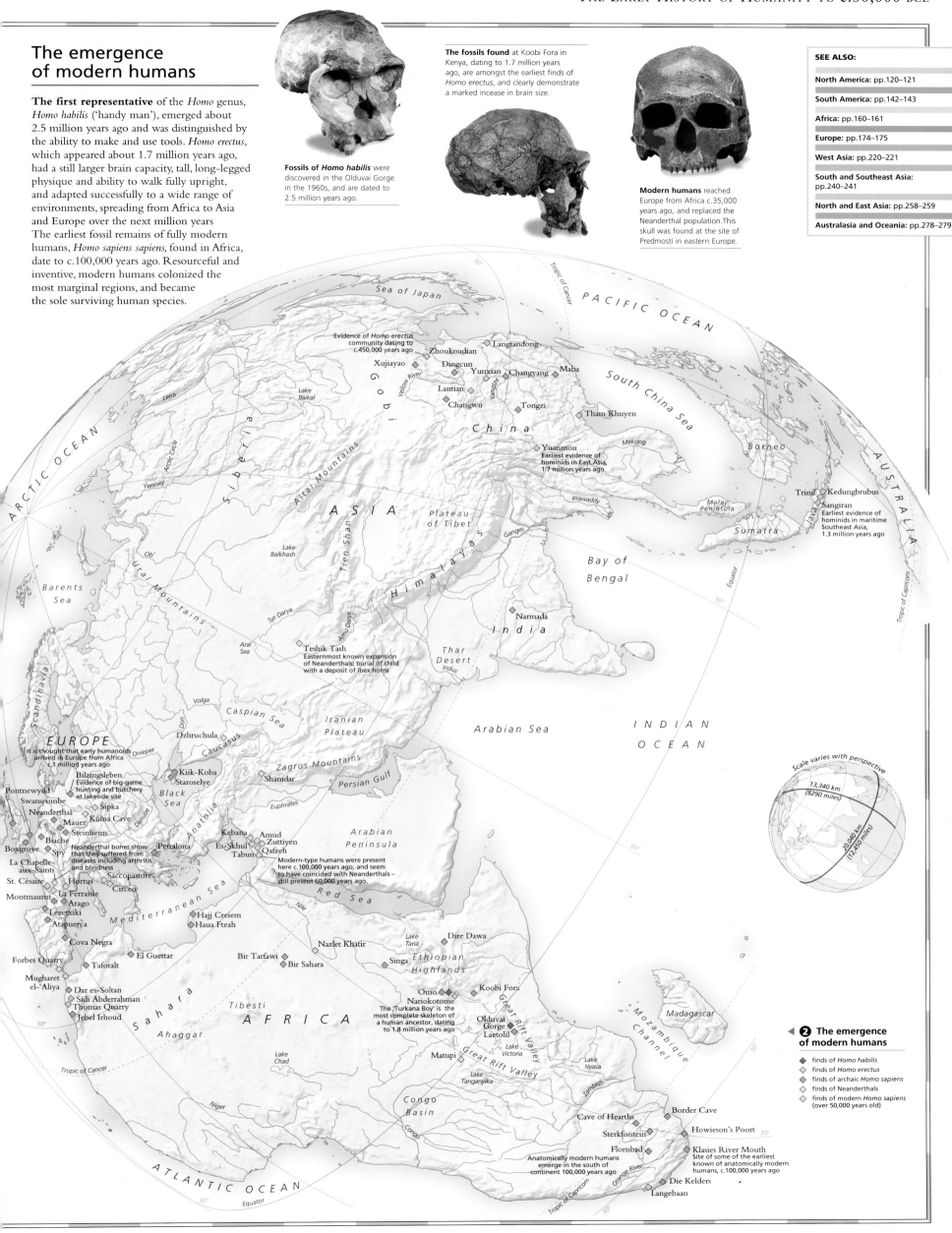

Evidence of *Homo erectus* community dating to c.450,000 years ago

Yuanmou Earliest evidence of hominids in East Asia, 1.7 million years ago

Sangiran Earliest evidence of hominids in maritime Southeast Asia, 1.3 million years ago

Teshik-Tash Easternmost known expansion of Neanderthals; burial of child with a deposit of ibex horns

EUROPE It is thought that early humanoids arrived in Europe from Africa c.1 million years ago

Bilzingsleben Evidence of big-game hunting and butchery at lakeside site

Neanderthal bones show that they suffered from diseases including arthritis and blindness

Modern-type humans were present here c.100,000 years ago, and seem to have coincided with Neanderthals – still present 60,000 years ago.

Nariokotome The 'Turkana Boy' is the most complete skeleton of a human ancestor, dating to 1.8 million years ago

Anatomically modern humans emerge in the south of continent 100,000 years ago

Klasies River Mouth Site of some of the earliest known of anatomically modern humans, c.100,000 years ago

Scale varies with perspective

13,340 km (8290 miles)

20,040 km (12,450 miles)

2 The emergence of modern humans

◆ finds of *Homo habilis*
◇ finds of *Homo erectus*
◇ finds of archaic *Homo sapiens*
◇ finds of Neanderthals
◇ finds of modern *Homo sapiens* (over 50,000 years old)

THE WORLD FROM PREHISTORY TO 10,000 BCE

FULLY MODERN HUMANS evolved in Africa between 200,000 and 100,000 years ago. With their tool-making skills and abilities to communicate and organize themselves into groups, these early hunter-gatherers were uniquely well-equipped to explore and settle new environments. By 30,000 years ago, they had colonized much of the globe. When the last Ice Age reached its peak, 20,000 years ago, they were forced to adapt; they refined their tool technology, enabling them to fully exploit the depleted resources, and used sturdy shelters and warm clothing to survive the harsh conditions. As the temperatures rose and the ice sheets retreated, plants and animals became more abundant and new areas were settled. By 9000 BCE larger populations and intense hunting had contributed to the near-extinction of large mammals, such as mastodons and mammoths. In the Near East, groups of hunter-gatherers were living in permanent settlements, harvesting wild cereals and experimenting with the domestication of local animals and the transition to agriculture was under way.

MESOLITHIC MAN AND THE ENVIRONMENT

Mesolithic peoples, whether semi-settled in one location or constantly on the move in search of food, would have carried a detailed mental map of important local landmarks. Precious water or food sources may have become centres of cultic activity, as in the rock painting below. Though its meaning is far from clear, the wavy vertical lines seem to represent cascades of water. The painting may even be a representation of a specific sacred site.

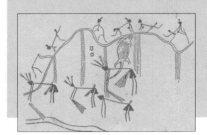

This painting discovered at Kalhotia in central India seems to show a lizard or crocodile, cascades, a stream, and people carrying bundles of stone-tipped arrows.

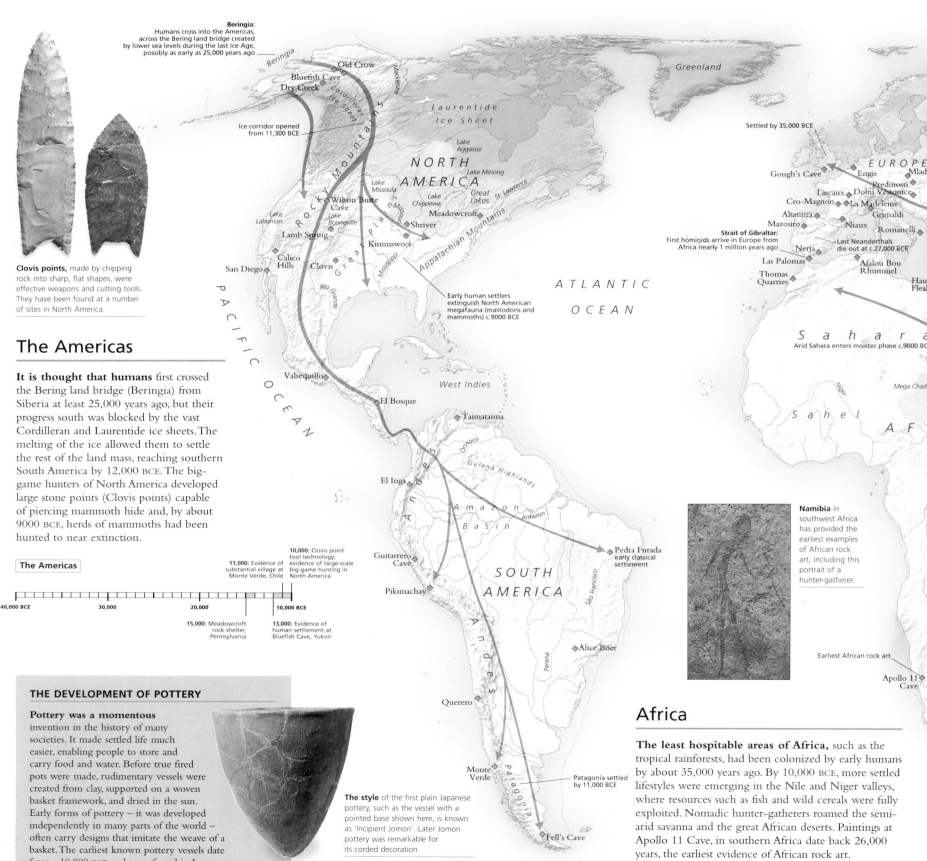

Clovis points, made by chipping rock into sharp, flat shapes, were effective weapons and cutting tools. They have been found at a number of sites in North America.

The Americas

It is thought that humans first crossed the Bering land bridge (Beringia) from Siberia at least 25,000 years ago, but their progress south was blocked by the vast Cordilleran and Laurentide ice sheets. The melting of the ice allowed them to settle the rest of the land mass, reaching southern South America by 12,000 BCE. The big-game hunters of North America developed large stone points (Clovis points) capable of piercing mammoth hide and, by about 9000 BCE, herds of mammoths had been hunted to near extinction.

The Americas

40,000 BCE — 30,000 — 20,000 — 10,000

15,000: Meadowcroft rock shelter, Pennsylvania

11,000: Evidence of substantial village at Monte Verde, Chile

13,000: Evidence of human settlement at Bluefish Cave, Yukon

10,000: Clovis point tool technology; evidence of large-scale big-game hunting in North America

THE DEVELOPMENT OF POTTERY

Pottery was a momentous invention in the history of many societies. It made settled life much easier, enabling people to store and carry food and water. Before true fired pots were made, rudimentary vessels were created from clay, supported on a woven basket framework, and dried in the sun. Early forms of pottery – it was developed independently in many parts of the world – often carry designs that imitate the weave of a basket. The earliest known pottery vessels date from c.10,000 BCE and were found in Japan.

The style of the first plain Japanese pottery, such as the vessel with a pointed base shown here, is known as 'Incipient Jomon'. Later Jomon pottery was remarkable for its corded decoration.

Namibia in southwest Africa has provided the earliest examples of African rock art, including this portrait of a hunter-gatherer.

Africa

The least hospitable areas of Africa, such as the tropical rainforests, had been colonized by early humans by about 35,000 years ago. By 10,000 BCE, more settled lifestyles were emerging in the Nile and Niger valleys, where resources such as fish and wild cereals were fully exploited. Nomadic hunter-gatherers roamed the semi-arid savanna and the great African deserts. Paintings at Apollo 11 Cave, in southern Africa date back 26,000 years, the earliest evidence of African rock art.

Portable art objects – sculptures and engravings of animals, like these reindeer, on bone and antler, or small stone slabs or plaques – were being produced in Europe by 25,000 years ago.

Europe

Settled by modern humans by about 35,000 BCE, Ice Age conditions over much of Europe tested their ingenuity; wood, bone, hide, and antler were all used to build a range of shelters, and new tools – bows and arrows, spear throwers, and harpoons – were used to hunt big game. As the climate stabilized, some sites were occupied year-round, while others were used by seasonal hunters.

West Asia

The world's earliest known burial, at Qafzeh Cave in Israel, dates back 100,000 years and is evidence that complex forms of social organization had already begun to evolve in this region. By 13,000 BCE people from Wadi en-Natuf, also in Israel, were intensively harvesting, grinding, and storing the abundant wild grains which grew there. It was in this region that agriculture was soon to develop.

This bone and shell necklace was one of the personal items found at a burial in Mugharet el-Kebara in Israel.

SEE ALSO:

North America: pp.118–119

South America: pp.144–145

Africa: pp.158–159

Europe: pp.174–175

West Asia: pp.220–221

South and Southeast Asia: pp.240–241

North and East Asia: pp.258–259

Australasia and Oceania: pp.280–281

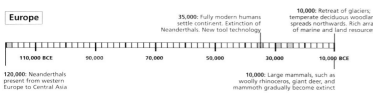

Europe

35,000: Fully modern humans settle continent. Extinction of Neanderthals. New tool technology

10,000: Retreat of glaciers; temperate deciduous woodland spreads northwards. Rich array of marine and land resources

120,000 BCE 90,000 70,000 50,000 30,000 10,000 BCE

120,000: Neanderthals present from western Europe to Central Asia

10,000: Large mammals, such as woolly rhinoceros, giant deer, and mammoth gradually become extinct

West and South Asia

100,000: World's first known burial at Qafzeh Cave, Israel

40,000: Neanderthals still present alongside modern humans in southwest Asia

13,000: Intensive harvesting of wild cereals by Natufian people, Israel

11,000: Dogs domesticated in Middle East; the world's first domesticated animals

110,000 BCE 90,000 70,000 50,000 30,000 10,000 BCE

45,000: Aurignacian flint tool technology developed in Israel and spreads across southern Europe

17,000: Evidence of wild cereal gathering in the Middle East

12,000: First use of grindstones in Middle East

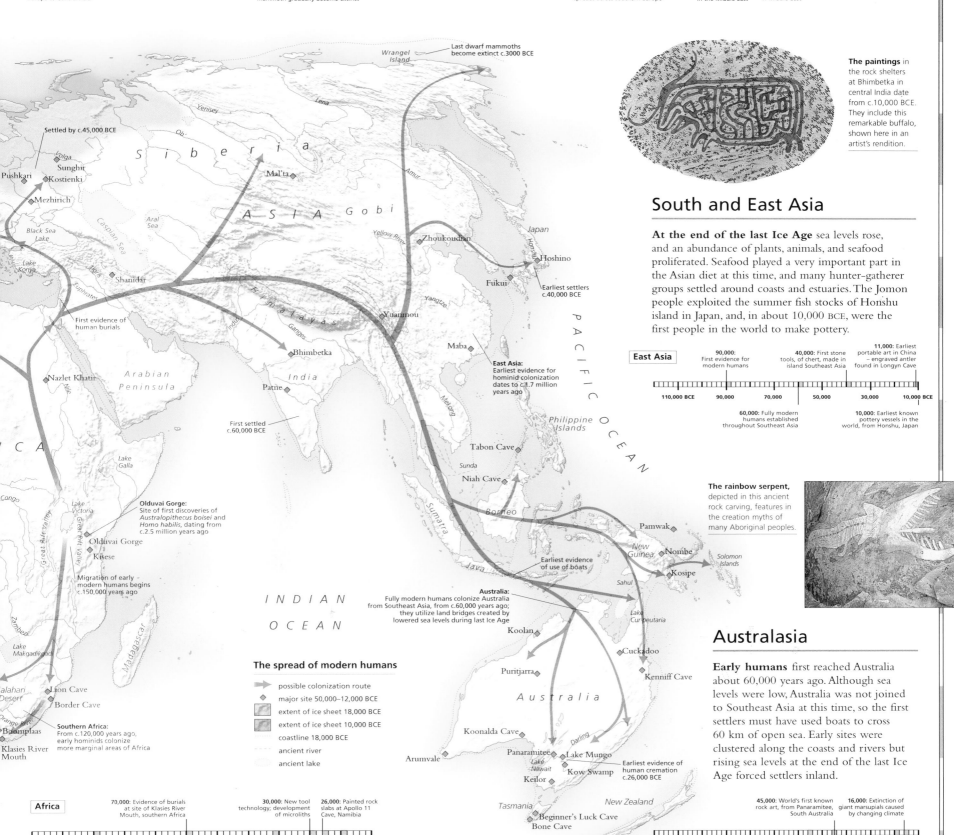

Last dwarf mammoths become extinct c.3000 BCE

The paintings in the rock shelters at Bhimbetka in central India date from c.10,000 BCE. They include this remarkable buffalo, shown here in an artist's rendition.

South and East Asia

At the end of the last Ice Age sea levels rose, and an abundance of plants, animals, and seafood proliferated. Seafood played a very important part in the Asian diet at this time, and many hunter-gatherer groups settled around coasts and estuaries. The Jomon people exploited the summer fish stocks of Honshu island in Japan, and, in about 10,000 BCE, were the first people in the world to make pottery.

East Asia

90,000: First evidence for modern humans

40,000: First stone tools, of chert, made in island Southeast Asia

11,000: Earliest portable art in China – engraved antler found in Longyn Cave

110,000 BCE 90,000 70,000 50,000 30,000 10,000 BCE

60,000: Fully modern humans established throughout Southeast Asia

10,000: Earliest known pottery vessels in the world, from Honshu, Japan

The rainbow serpent, depicted in this ancient rock carving, features in the creation myths of many Aboriginal peoples.

Australasia

Early humans first reached Australia about 60,000 years ago. Although sea levels were low, Australia was not joined to Southeast Asia at this time, so the first settlers must have used boats to cross 60 km of open sea. Early sites were clustered along the coasts and rivers but rising sea levels at the end of the last Ice Age forced settlers inland.

Settled by c.45,000 BCE

First evidence of human burials

First settled c.60,000 BCE

East Asia: Earliest evidence for hominid colonization dates to c.1.7 million years ago

Olduvai Gorge: Site of first discoveries of *Australopithecus boisei* and *Homo habilis*, dating from c.2.5 million years ago

Migration of early modern humans begins c.150,000 years ago

Southern Africa: From c.120,000 years ago, early hominids colonize more marginal areas of Africa

Earliest evidence of use of boats

Australia: Fully modern humans colonize Australia from Southeast Asia, from c.60,000 years ago; they utilize land bridges created by lowered sea levels during last Ice Age

Earliest evidence of human cremation c.26,000

The spread of modern humans

→ possible colonization route
◆ major site 50,000–12,000 BCE
▨ extent of ice sheet 18,000 BCE
▨ extent of ice sheet 10,000 BCE
—— coastline 18,000 BCE
—— ancient river
—— ancient lake

Africa

70,000: Evidence of burials at site of Klasies River Mouth, southern Africa

30,000: New tool technology; development of microliths

26,000: Painted rock slabs at Apollo 11 Cave, Namibia

110,000 BCE 90,000 70,000 50,000 30,000 10,000 BCE

100,000: Earliest evidence of modern humans in eastern and southern Africa

42,000: Red ochre being mined from Lion Cave, southern Africa; probably used for body decoration

20,000: Terracotta figurines from Algeria. Engraved objects from Border Cave, South Africa

45,000: World's first known rock art, from Panaramitee, South Australia

16,000: Extinction of giant marsupials caused by changing climate

110,000 BCE 90,000 70,000 50,000 30,000 10,000 BCE

Australasia

60,000: Settlement of Australia by groups from Southeast Asia

20,000: Settlement extends to southern coast of Tasmania

15

THE SETTLING OF THE GLOBE

This figure of a mammoth, carved from an animal's shoulder bone dates from the last Ice Age.

THE MELTING OF THE GLACIERS at the end of the last Ice Age radically transformed the global environment; as the climate changed, with warmer temperatures and increased rainfall, food sources became more abundant and diverse, and populations increased. Hunters and gatherers could use the technological and survival skills acquired during the Ice Age to colonize new areas and adapt to more plentiful food supplies. In many regions, hunters began to live together in larger, more sedentary communities, working co-operatively and evolving more specialized roles within the group. Rituals and symbols were used to reinforce group identity – the beginnings of truly modern behaviour.

Survival strategies

The rapidly changing environments of the postglacial world required a wide range of adaptations. In some regions, such as eastern Europe and North America, plentiful supplies of big game meant that hunters could depend on a specialized diet of mammoth, mastodon, or bison. In other regions, such as the fertile river valleys of the Middle East and North Africa, wild cereals – the ancestors of cultivated grains – were harvested. In Europe, a varied diet encompassed game, edible plants, and fish and shellfish, evidenced by deposits of discarded shells, or middens. Climate and local resources influenced the building of shelters; a wide range of materials was used, from mud and stone to timber and hides. Some shelters were portable, used by hunters following migrating herds; in other areas plentiful food supplies meant that permanent villages could be built.

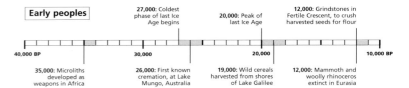

Early peoples	27,000: Coldest phase of last Ice Age begins	20,000: Peak of last Ice Age	12,000: Grindstones in Fertile Crescent, to crush harvested seeds for flour

40,000 BP — 30,000 — 20,000 — 10,000 BP

35,000: Microliths developed as weapons in Africa

26,000: First known cremation, at Lake Mungo, Australia

19,000: Wild cereals harvested from shores of Lake Galilee

12,000: Mammoth and woolly rhinoceros extinct in Eurasia

France

At Pincevent, in the Seine valley, hunters following migrating herds of reindeer camped from midsummer to midwinter in portable tents, made of wooden poles covered by animal skins.

Israel

The El Wad cave on the eastern Mediterranean coast was used as a shelter by hunters stalking fallow deer in the nearby hills. The site may have been used during the summer months. The cave has been occupied many times in the past 100,000 years.

Ukraine

On the treeless, windswept steppes of the Ukraine, mammoth-hunters, lacking wood, used the remains of their prey to build shelters. They constructed the walls from mammoth bones, which were then covered with animal hides, anchored down in high winds by heavy mammoth jawbones.

▼ ❶ **Different ways of life c.10,000 BCE**

☐ uninhabited and/or marginally inhabited areas

◇ early settlement site

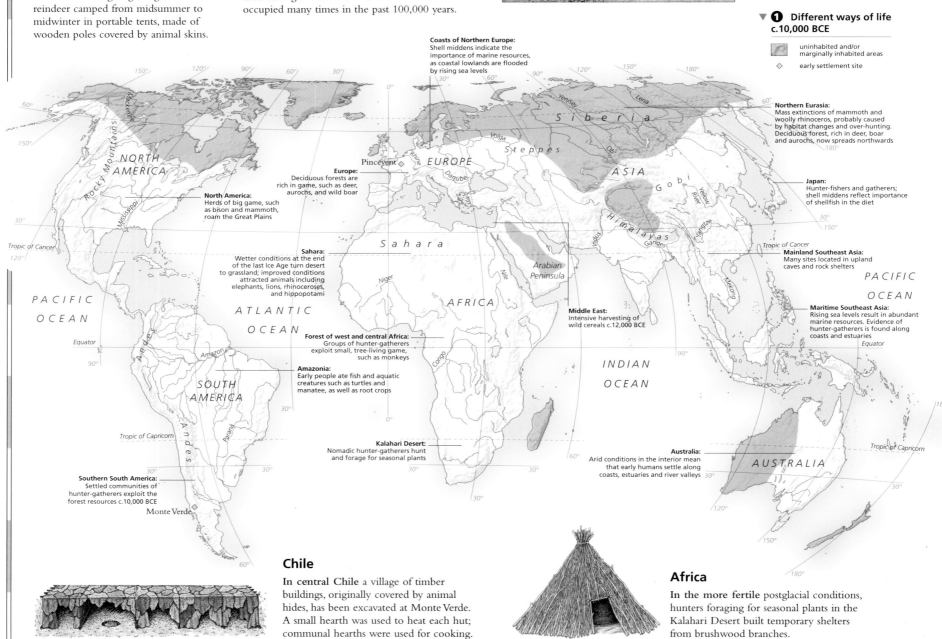

Coasts of Northern Europe: Shell middens indicate the importance of marine resources, as coastal lowlands are flooded by rising sea levels

Europe: Deciduous forests are rich in game, such as deer, aurochs, and wild boar

North America: Herds of big game, such as bison and mammoth, roam the Great Plains

Sahara: Wetter conditions at the end of the last Ice Age turn desert to grassland; improved conditions attracted animals including elephants, lions, rhinoceroses, and hippopotami

Forest of west and central Africa: Groups of hunter-gatherers exploit small, tree-living game, such as monkeys

Amazonia: Early people ate fish and aquatic creatures such as turtles and manatee, as well as root crops

Kalahari Desert: Nomadic hunter-gatherers hunt and forage for seasonal plants

Southern South America: Settled communities of hunter-gatherers exploit the forest resources c.10,000 BCE

Monte Verde

Northern Eurasia: Mass extinctions of mammoth and woolly rhinoceros, probably caused by habitat changes and over-hunting. Deciduous forest, rich in deer, boar and aurochs, now spreads northwards

Japan: Hunter-fishers and gatherers; shell middens reflect importance of shellfish in the diet

Mainland Southeast Asia: Many sites located in upland caves and rock shelters

Middle East: Intensive harvesting of wild cereals c.12,000 BCE

Maritime Southeast Asia: Rising sea levels result in abundant marine resources. Evidence of hunter-gatherers is found along coasts and estuaries

Australia: Arid conditions in the interior mean that early humans settle along coasts, estuaries and river valleys

Chile

In central Chile a village of timber buildings, originally covered by animal hides, has been excavated at Monte Verde. A small hearth was used to heat each hut; communal hearths were used for cooking.

Africa

In the more fertile postglacial conditions, hunters foraging for seasonal plants in the Kalahari Desert built temporary shelters from brushwood branches.

Palaeolithic art

The art of the last Ice Age and its aftermath, ranging from painted caves to engraved and finely carved objects and clay sculptures, is found in many parts of the world. Since much of this art is probably associated with religious rituals concerned with hunting, fertility, and the initiation of the young, it is a testament to the increasing complexity and sophistication of human society. One of the greatest flowerings of palaeolithic art is undoubtedly the extraordinary painted caves of southwestern Europe, but there is evidence of a wide range of different regional artistic traditions, from the ochre-decorated rock shelters of Kisesse in East Africa to the rock art of Bhimbetka in South Asia, which dates to the coldest phase of the last Ice Age.

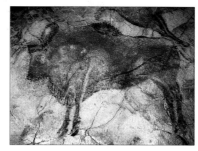

In the caves of southwest Europe, animals such as bison are depicted with grace and fluidity.

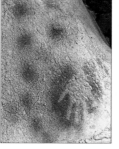

Hand stencils often dominate the part of the cave in which they are found. The red pigments could be made from either iron oxide or red ochre.

Hand paintings

Stencils of hands, made by blowing a spray of powdered pigment over the outstretched hand, are found on cave walls in both western Europe and Australia. The stencils may be associated with initiation rites – children's footprints have also been found in the European caves.

SEE ALSO:

North America: pp.116–117

South America: pp.140–141

Africa: pp.154–155

Europe: pp.170–171

West Asia: pp.216–217

South and Southeast Asia: pp.236–237

North and East Asia: pp.254–255

Australasia and Oceania: pp.276–277

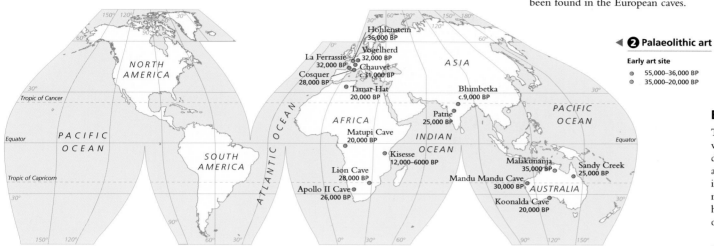

◀ **❷ Palaeolithic art**

Early art site
- ● 55,000–36,000 BP
- ○ 35,000–20,000 BP

European cave paintings

The caves of southwestern Europe, with their vibrant paintings of bison, deer, oxen, and horses, and bas-relief and clay sculptures, are unique. These images, often found in the darkest and most inaccessible parts of the caves, may have acted as forms of hunting magic or illustrated myths and traditions.

▼ **❸ Painted caves and rock art**

◇ important rock art site

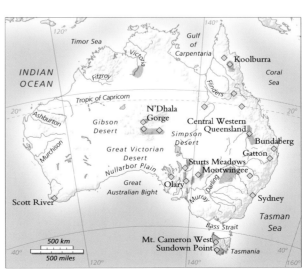

Portable art

Small plaques of engraved antler and bone, decorated ornaments of amber and ivory – including pendants and beads – and carved figurines of both animals and humans are found throughout Europe. Highly stylized female figurines *(right)* are possibly representations of the mother goddess, and may have been associated with fertility rituals.

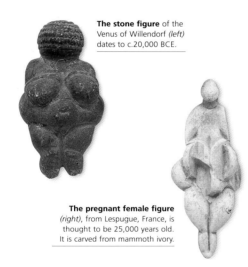

The stone figure of the Venus of Willendorf *(left)* dates to c.20,000 BCE.

The pregnant female figure *(right)*, from Lespugue, France, is thought to be 25,000 years old. It is carved from mammoth ivory.

❹ Venus figurines in Europe ▼

◇ important find of Venus figurines

Australia

The oldest rock engravings in the world, from Panaramittee, date to 45,000 BCE. Australian rock paintings and engravings are widespread; most designs are abstract, using lines, dots, crescents, and spirals. Some are thought to represent kangaroo and bird tracks.

Some of the earliest examples of Aboriginal rock carvings or petroglyphs – here in the form of circles and stars – are found at Wilpena Sacred Canyon in southern Australia.

▲ **❺ Australian rock art**

◇ Panaramittee style rock engraving

▨ major rock art region

Early examples of human art

45,000: Oldest rock engravings from Panaramittee, south Australia

40,000: Ostrich eggshells, engraved with abstract patterns, from central India

32,000: Carved ivory statuette from Hohlenstein-Stadel Cave, Germany, is one of world's earliest figurines

29,000: Caves at Kisesse, East Africa decorated with ochre-stained palettes

26,000: Oldest rock paintings in Africa, from Apollo II Cave, Namibia

25,000: Stylized female figurines found throughout Europe

20,000 BP: Limestone pebble with human head from Aq Kupruk in central Asia

17,000: Cave paintings produced at Lascaux

15,000 BP: Hand stencils found in Wargata Mina Cave, Tasmania

45,000 BP | 35,000 | 25,000 | 15,000 BP

THE WORLD 10,000 – 5000 BCE

IN THE MORE HOSPITABLE CLIMATE and terrain of the post-glacial world, groups of hunter-gatherers began to experiment with the domestication of wild cereals and animals. By 7000 BCE, farming was the main means of subsistence in West Asia, although hunter-gathering remained the most common form of subsistence elsewhere. Over the next 5000 years farming became established independently in other areas. The impact of the agricultural revolution on early societies was immense. Farming could support much larger populations, so settlement sizes increased significantly. Larger communities generated new demands and possibilities, and a class of specialized craftsmen evolved. Trade in raw materials and manufactured goods increased contact between farming communities. Communal ventures, such as irrigation, encouraged co-operation. All these developments paved the way for the much larger cities and states which were soon to follow.

THE FIRST USE OF METAL

The discovery that metals can be isolated from ore-bearing rocks by heating appears to have been made independently in West Asia and southeastern Europe between 7000–5000 BCE. Copper, gold, and lead, all soft metals that melt at relatively low temperatures, were the first metals in use. In early copper-using societies, most copper objects were decorative items that denoted the status of the owner: tools made from the new material could not compete with those of flint and stone.

This horned bull, fashioned from sheet gold is one of a pair from a rich set of grave goods unearthed at a cemetery in Varna, southeast Europe.

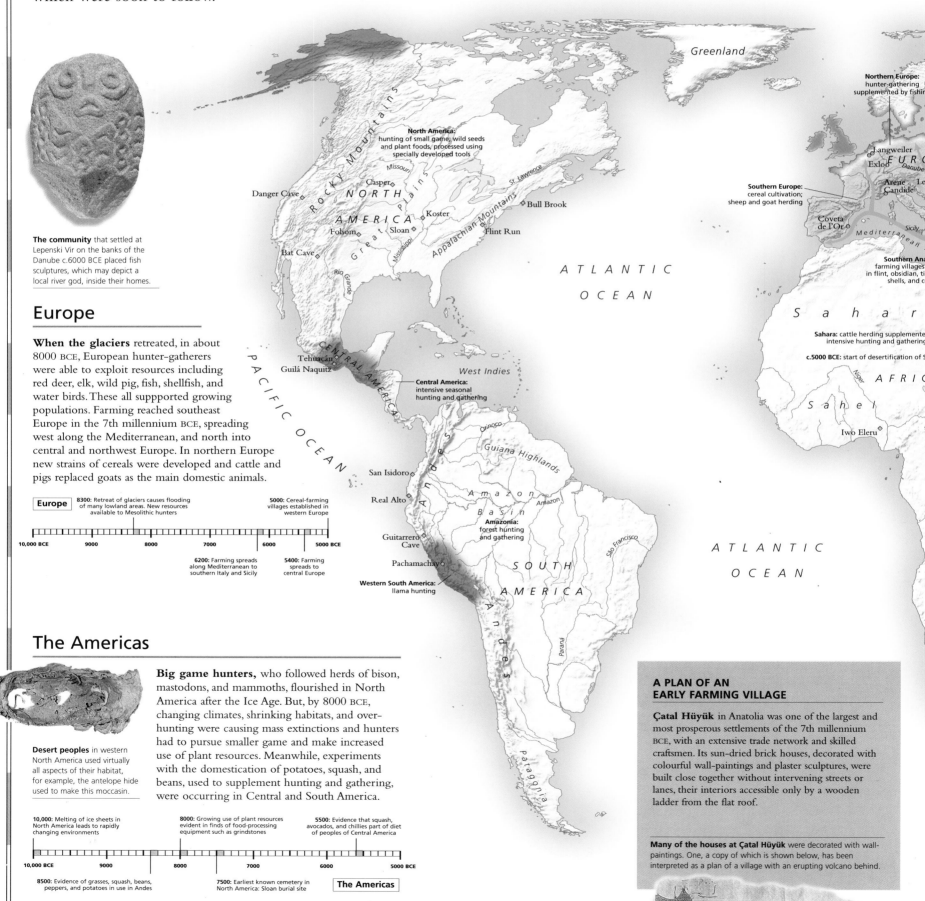

The community that settled at Lepenski Vir on the banks of the Danube c.6000 BCE placed fish sculptures, which may depict a local river god, inside their homes.

Europe

When the glaciers retreated, in about 8000 BCE, European hunter-gatherers were able to exploit resources including red deer, elk, wild pig, fish, shellfish, and water birds. These all supported growing populations. Farming reached southeast Europe in the 7th millennium BCE, spreading west along the Mediterranean, and north into central and northwest Europe. In northern Europe new strains of cereals were developed and cattle and pigs replaced goats as the main domestic animals.

Europe					
8300: Retreat of glaciers causes flooding of many lowland areas. New resources available to Mesolithic hunters				5000: Cereal-farming villages established in western Europe	
10,000 BCE	9000	8000	7000	6000	5000 BCE
		6200: Farming spreads along Mediterranean to southern Italy and Sicily	5400: Farming spreads to central Europe		

The Americas

Desert peoples in western North America used virtually all aspects of their habitat, for example, the antelope hide used to make this moccasin.

Big game hunters, who followed herds of bison, mastodons, and mammoths, flourished in North America after the Ice Age. But, by 8000 BCE, changing climates, shrinking habitats, and over-hunting were causing mass extinctions and hunters had to pursue smaller game and make increased use of plant resources. Meanwhile, experiments with the domestication of potatoes, squash, and beans, used to supplement hunting and gathering, were occurring in Central and South America.

10,000: Melting of ice sheets in North America leads to rapidly changing environments		8000: Growing use of plant resources evident in finds of food-processing equipment such as grindstones		5500: Evidence that squash, avocados, and chillies part of diet of peoples of Central America	
10,000 BCE	9000	8000	7000	6000	5000 BCE
8500: Evidence of grasses, squash, beans, peppers, and potatoes in use in Andes		7500: Earliest known cemetery in North America: Sloan burial site	The Americas		

Map labels

Greenland

Northern Europe: hunter-gathering supplemented by fishing

North America: hunting of small game; wild seeds and plant foods, processed using specially developed tools

Rocky Mountains · NORTH AMERICA · Great Plains · Appalachian Mountains · Missouri · Mississippi · St. Lawrence · Rio Grande

Danger Cave · Casper · Koster · Folsom · Sloan · Bat Cave · Flint Run · Bull Brook

Southern Europe: cereal cultivation; sheep and goat herding

Langweiler · Exloo · Danube · Arene Candide · Lepenski Vir · Coveta de l'Or · Sicily · EUROPE · Mediterranean Sea

Southern Anatolia: farming villages trade in flint, obsidian, timber, shells, and copper

ATLANTIC OCEAN

S a h a r a

Sahara: cattle herding supplemented by intensive hunting and gathering

c.5000 BCE: start of desertification of Sahara

AFRICA · S a h e l · Niger · Iwo Eleru

CENTRAL AMERICA · Tehuacán · Guilá Naquitz · West Indies

Central America: intensive seasonal hunting and gathering

PACIFIC OCEAN

Orinoco · Guiana Highlands · A m a z o n B a s i n · Amazon · Andes

San Isidoro · Real Alto · Guitarrero Cave · Pachamachay

Amazonia: forest hunting and gathering

Western South America: llama hunting

SOUTH AMERICA · São Francisco · Paraná · Patagonia

ATLANTIC OCEAN

A PLAN OF AN EARLY FARMING VILLAGE

Çatal Hüyük in Anatolia was one of the largest and most prosperous settlements of the 7th millennium BCE, with an extensive trade network and skilled craftsmen. Its sun-dried brick houses, decorated with colourful wall-paintings and plaster sculptures, were built close together without intervening streets or lanes, their interiors accessible only by a wooden ladder from the flat roof.

Many of the houses at Çatal Hüyük were decorated with wall-paintings. One, a copy of which is shown below, has been interpreted as a plan of a village with an erupting volcano behind.

West Asia

The world's earliest farmers settled in the fertile arc of land stretching from the Persian Gulf to the eastern Mediterranean. Large-seeded grains were domesticated in Jericho by 8000 BCE. Villages of mud-brick houses appeared in Anatolia, and in central Mesopotamia by the 7th millennium BCE and craftsmen were smelting copper and lead by 6000 BCE. By 5500 BCE the farmers of southern Mesopotamia were irrigating arid land to improve crop yields.

Terracotta figurines of goddesses with swollen abdomens were found at Çatal Hüyük, suggesting a fertility cult.

West Asia

9000: Wheat (einkorn) harvested in Mesopotamia

8000: First fully domesticated cereals harvested in Jericho

7000: Goat becomes main domesticated animal throughout region. Foundation of settlement of Çatal Hüyük, Anatolia

6000: At Hassuna in northern Mesopotamia; painted pottery and copper and lead smelting

6500: Earliest known Old World textiles (linen) from Çatal Hüyük

5500: Ubaid culture of southern Mesopotamia harnesses spring floods of Euphrates for irrigation

East Asia

In northern China, agriculture dates back to c.7000 BCE. At farming villages such as Banpo, millet was cultivated and kept in grain storage pits, and there is evidence that pigs and dogs were domesticated. In a separate development, rice cultivation was initiated in the lowlands of the Yangtze delta, probably by 6000 BCE. In Japan, the Jomon people lived by hunting, fishing, and gathering in the well-stocked mountains and coastal waters. Although the Japanese were making pottery by 10,500 BCE, their way of life would remain based on hunting and gathering for several thousand years.

The people of Banpo were producing and firing pottery such as this cord-scored amphora by the 5th millennium BCE.

East Asia

9000: Limestone caves in central China give evidence of hunting, fishing, and gathering way of life

c.5000: Hunting and fishing villages in Yangtze river delta begin cultivating rice

5000: Jade imported into northern Manchuria from Central Asia or Siberia

6500: 'Jomon' pottery spreads throughout southern Japanese archipelago

SEE ALSO:

North America: pp.120–121

South America: pp.144–145

Africa: pp.158–159

Europe: pp.174–175

West Asia: pp.220–221

South and Southeast Asia: pp.240–241

North and East Asia: pp.258–259

Australasia and Oceania: pp.280–281

South and Southeast Asia

The first South Asian farmers were cultivating wheat and barley in the fertile highlands of northern India by the 5th millennium BCE. At the same time there was a gradual transition from hunting to farming, primarily rice, to the south of the Ganges valley. In Southeast Asia, post-glacial rises in sea levels created many new islands and estuaries with a marked increase in maritime resources. By c.2000 BCE farming had gradually become established in this region.

South and Southeast Asia

7000: Evidence of drainage and cultivation in the highlands of New Guinea

6000: Pottery in grave goods from Mehrgarh indicates trade with Central Asia

6000: First pottery production in mainland Southeast Asia

At Mehrgarh in the Baluchi highlands, burials took place in open spaces within the settlement; the dead were often accompanied by personal ornaments including bone, shell, and limestone beads.

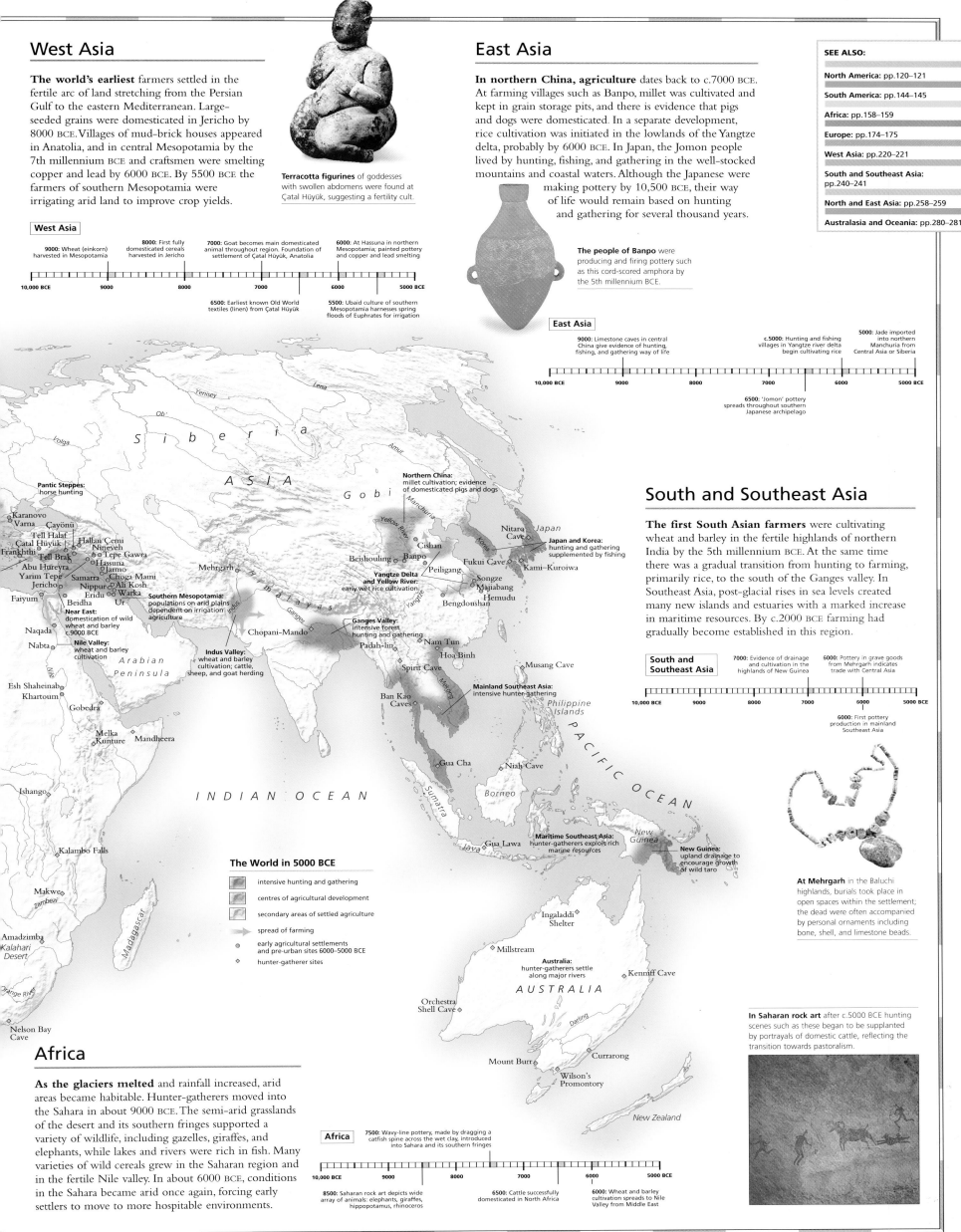

The World in 5000 BCE

- intensive hunting and gathering
- centres of agricultural development
- secondary areas of settled agriculture
- spread of farming
- early agricultural settlements and pre-urban sites 6000–5000 BCE
- hunter-gatherer sites

Africa

As the glaciers melted and rainfall increased, arid areas became habitable. Hunter-gatherers moved into the Sahara in about 9000 BCE. The semi-arid grasslands of the desert and its southern fringes supported a variety of wildlife, including gazelles, giraffes, and elephants, while lakes and rivers were rich in fish. Many varieties of wild cereals grew in the Saharan region and in the fertile Nile valley. In about 6000 BCE, conditions in the Sahara became arid once again, forcing early settlers to move to more hospitable environments.

Africa

7500: Wavy-line pottery, made by dragging a catfish spine across the wet clay, introduced into Sahara and its southern fringes

8500: Saharan rock art depicts wide array of animals: elephants, giraffes, hippopotamus, rhinoceros

6500: Cattle successfully domesticated in North Africa

6000: Wheat and barley cultivation spreads to Nile Valley from Middle East

In Saharan rock art after c.5000 BCE hunting scenes such as these began to be supplanted by portrayals of domestic cattle, reflecting the transition towards pastoralism.

THE ADVENT OF AGRICULTURE

Fragments of Egyptian wavy-line pottery, decorated with a fish spine from c.7000 BCE

THE APPEARANCE OF FARMING transformed the face of the Earth. It was not merely a change in subsistence – in many regions a necessity caused by over-hunting, limited natural resources and population growth – it also transformed the way in which our ancestors lived. Agriculture, and the vastly greater crop yields it produced, enabled large groups of people to live in permanent villages, surrounded by material goods and equipment. Specialized craftsmen produced these goods, supported by the community as a whole – the beginnings of social differentiation. These developments led ultimately to the emergence of the first cities, but in 5000 BCE only a limited number of regions were fully dependent on agriculture. In many parts of the globe, small-scale farming was being used to supplement hunting and gathering – the first steps in the gradual transition to the sedentary agricultural way of life.

The agricultural revolution

The advent of farming brought large groups of people together into settled communities. Not only could food production be made more efficient, but animals could be tended communally, and food surpluses used to support villagers through the winter months. Some members of the community were therefore able to develop craft skills, engage in long-distance trade, and experiment with technology, such as pottery kilns, gold, and copper metallurgy and, by c.5500 BCE, irrigation. But sedentary co-existence also exposed people to infectious disease; the settlement of Çatal Hüyük, for example, was plagued by malaria.

Stone querns, dating to about 6000 years ago, were used by farmers for grinding grain into flour, which could then be kept in storage pits.

Ways of life

The exceptional productivity of the major cultivated species, in particular cereals, was vital to the viability of early farming villages. Cereals can be kept as a year-round resource, providing a staple supplement to more seasonal foods, thus creating a total dependence on farming. An inevitable, and necessary, by-product of this settled way of life was pottery – pottery containers could be used for both storing and cooking the harvested food. The technique of hand-modelling and firing clay pots evolved independently in many regions. Moulds, wheels and kilns were later innovations, and became the province of specialized craftsmen.

The earliest pottery had a round-based shape (right), and was sometimes decorated with incisions or impressions. A characteristic later vessel from western Europe was the flat-based beaker (left), again decorated with incisions, In other regions of Europe, notably the southeast, painted decoration was also used.

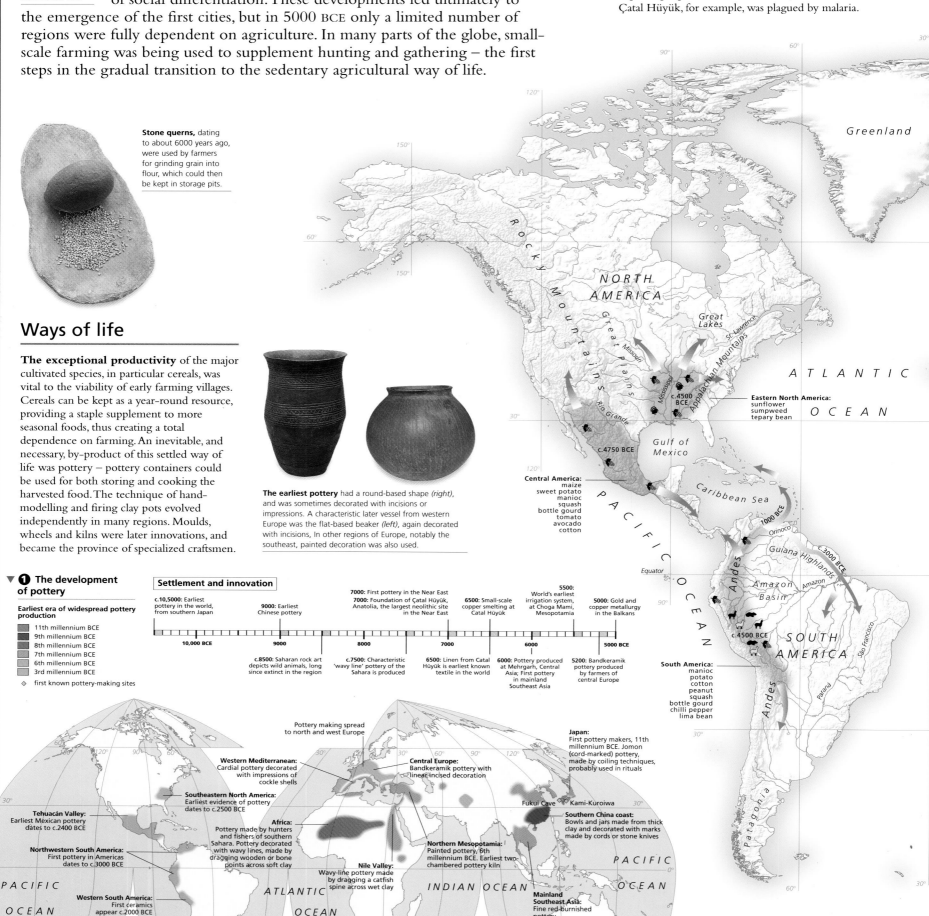

▼ **① The development of pottery**

Earliest era of widespread pottery production

- 11th millennium BCE
- 9th millennium BCE
- 8th millennium BCE
- 7th millennium BCE
- 6th millennium BCE
- 3rd millennium BCE

◇ first known pottery-making sites

Settlement and innovation

c.10,5000: Earliest pottery in the world, from southern Japan

9000: Earliest Chinese pottery

7000: First pottery in the Near East
7000: Foundation of Çatal Hüyük, Anatolia, the largest neolithic site in the Near East

6500: Small-scale copper smelting at Çatal Hüyük

5500: World's earliest irrigation system, at Choga Mami, Mesopotamia

5000: Gold and copper metallurgy in the Balkans

10,000 BCE ... **9000** ... **8000** ... **7000** ... **6000** ... **5000 BCE**

c.8500: Saharan rock art depicts wild animals, long since extinct in the region

c.7500: Characteristic 'wavy line' pottery of the Sahara is produced

6500: Linen from Çatal Hüyük is earliest known textile in the world

6000: Pottery produced at Mehrgarh, Central Asia; First pottery in mainland Southeast Asia

5200: Bandkeramik pottery produced by farmers of central Europe

Map labels

Greenland

NORTH AMERICA

ROCKY Mountains

Great Lakes

St. Lawrence

Great Plains

Appalachian Mountains

Missouri

Mississippi

Rio Grande

ATLANTIC OCEAN

c.4500 BCE

Eastern North America: sunflower sumpweed tepary bean

c.4750 BCE

Gulf of Mexico

Central America: maize sweet potato manioc squash bottle gourd tomato avocado cotton

Caribbean Sea

PACIFIC OCEAN

Equator

7000 BCE

Orinoco

c.3000 BCE

Guiana Highlands

Amazon Basin

Amazon

c.4500 BCE

Andes

SOUTH AMERICA

São Francisco

South America: manioc potato cotton peanut squash bottle gourd chilli pepper lima bean

Paraná

Andes

Patagonia

PACIFIC OCEAN

Lower globes

Pottery making spread to north and west Europe

Western Mediterranean: Cardial pottery decorated with impressions of cockle shells

Central Europe: Bandkeramik pottery with linear incised decoration

Japan: First pottery makers, 11th millennium BCE. Jomon (cord-marked) pottery, made by coiling techniques, probably used in rituals

Fukui Cave ● Kami-Kuroiwa

Tehuacán Valley: Earliest Mexican pottery dates to c.2400 BCE

Southeastern North America: Earliest evidence of pottery dates to c.2500 BCE

Africa: Pottery made by hunters and fishers of southern Sahara. Pottery decorated with wavy lines, made by dragging wooden or bone points across soft clay

Northwestern South America: First pottery in Americas dates to c.3000 BCE

Nile Valley: Wavy-line pottery made by dragging a catfish spine across wet clay

Northern Mesopotamia: Painted pottery, 6th millennium BCE. Earliest two-chambered pottery kiln

Southern China coast: Bowls and jars made from thick clay and decorated with marks made by cords or stone knives

Western South America: First ceramics appear c.2000 BCE

Mainland Southeast Asia: Fine red-burnished pottery

PACIFIC OCEAN

ATLANTIC OCEAN

INDIAN OCEAN

PACIFIC OCEAN

Domestication

Domestication, a process of selecting and propagating beneficial traits in wild crops, occurred independently in a number of areas at different times, principally in the subtropical zone. Each region developed a dependence on different staple crops: wheat and barley in the Middle East and South Asia; millet and rice in China and Southeast Asia; maize in the New World. Animals were also domesticated, and a process of selective breeding gradually enhanced useful traits. Sheep and goats, native to West and Central Asia, were domesticated for their meat, milk, hides and wool. Cattle were domesticated all over Eurasia, and eventually used to pull ploughs, thus increasing plant yields.

The early pastoral farmers of the Sahara made a number of paintings on rocks and in caves, depicting the animals they herded. Cattle are an important feature of these early paintings, some dating from 6000 BCE.

Wild einkorn has brittle stalks, which make it difficult to harvest and transport.

Domestic einkorn, has larger seeds and a tougher stalk than its wild form. It needs to be threshed in order for the seeds to disperse.

SEE ALSO:

North America: pp.120–121

South America: pp.144–145

Africa: pp.158–159

Europe: pp.174–175

West Asia: pp.220–221

South and Southeast Asia: pp.240–241

North and East Asia: pp.258–259

Australasia and Oceania: pp.280–281

c.9000: Einkorn wheat grown in northern Syria: first evidence of true cultivation

c.8500: Rice domesticated in southern China

c.7750: Broomcorn and foxtail millets domesticated on North China Plain

c.7000: Farming in northern India; barley is main crop

c.6500: Farming spreads to Balkans from Near East

c.6500: Cattle domesticated in Saharan region

c.6000: Farming spreads to Nile Valley from Near East

c.4750: First evidence of plant and animal domestication in Central America

c.4500: Cultivation of maize in eastern North America

c.4500: Evidence of agriculture in south-central Andes

c.4000: Plants domesticated in sub-Saharan Africa

Stages in domestication

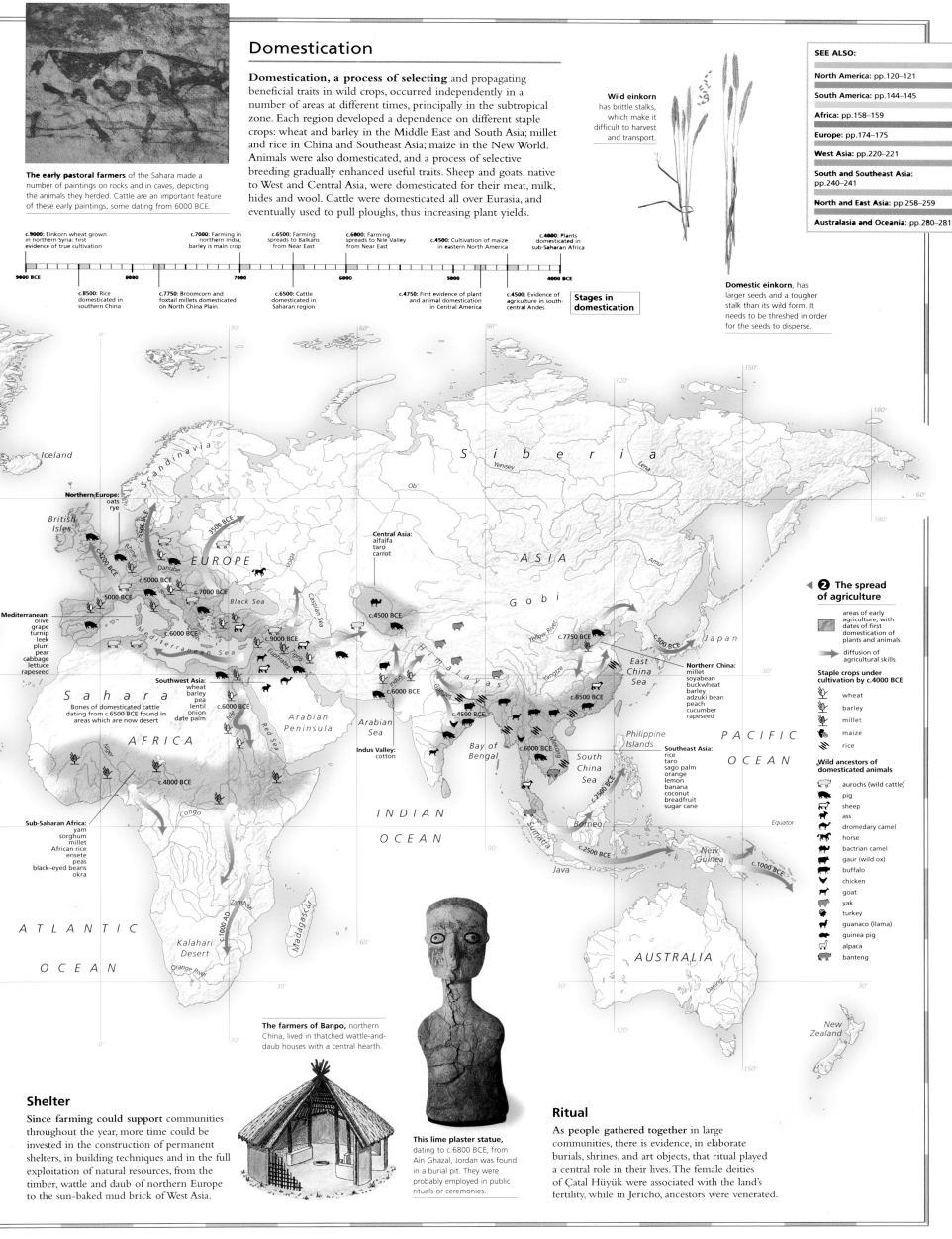

Northern Europe: oats, rye

Mediterranean: olive, grape, turnip, leek, plum, pear, cabbage, lettuce, rapeseed

Southwest Asia: wheat, barley, pea, lentil, onion, date palm

Sub-Saharan Africa: yam, sorghum, millet, African rice, ensete, peas, black–eyed beans, okra

Bones of domesticated cattle dating from c.6500 BCE found in areas which are now desert

Central Asia: alfalfa, taro, carrot

Indus Valley: cotton

Southeast Asia: rice, taro, sago palm, orange, lemon, banana, coconut, breadfruit, sugar cane

Northern China: millet, soyabean, buckwheat, barley, adzuki bean, peach, cucumber, rapeseed

❷ The spread of agriculture

areas of early agriculture, with dates of first domestication of plants and animals

diffusion of agricultural skills

Staple crops under cultivation by c.4000 BCE

wheat
barley
millet
maize
rice

Wild ancestors of domesticated animals

aurochs (wild cattle)
pig
sheep
ass
dromedary camel
horse
bactrian camel
gaur (wild ox)
buffalo
chicken
goat
yak
turkey
guanaco (llama)
guinea pig
alpaca
banteng

Shelter

Since farming could support communities throughout the year, more time could be invested in the construction of permanent shelters, in building techniques and in the full exploitation of natural resources, from the timber, wattle and daub of northern Europe to the sun-baked mud brick of West Asia.

The farmers of Banpo, northern China, lived in thatched wattle-and-daub houses with a central hearth.

This lime plaster statue, dating to c.6800 BCE, from Ain Ghazal, Jordan was found in a burial pit. They were probably employed in public rituals or ceremonies.

Ritual

As people gathered together in large communities, there is evidence, in elaborate burials, shrines, and art objects, that ritual played a central role in their lives. The female deities of Çatal Hüyük were associated with the land's fertility, while in Jericho, ancestors were venerated.

THE WORLD 5000–2500 BCE

THE FERTILE RIVER VALLEYS of the Nile, Tigris, Euphrates, Indus, and Yellow River were able to support very large populations, and it was here that the great urban civilizations of the ancient world emerged. Although cities developed independently in several regions, they shared certain characteristics. Urban societies were hierarchical, with complex labour divisions. They were administered, economically and spiritually, by an elite literate class, and in some cases, were subject to a divine monarch. Monuments came to symbolize and represent the powers of the ruling elite. Elsewhere, farming communities came together to create ritual centres or burial sites, while craftsmen experimented with new materials and techniques, such as copper and bronze casting, and glazed pottery. All these developments indicate that urban and non-urban societies were attaining a high degree of social organization.

EARLY PERCEPTIONS OF THE COSMOS

The stone circles and alignments of northwestern Europe are extraordinary prehistoric monuments which have mystified successive generations. Astronomical observations are central to the ritual purpose of these structures; at many monuments, stones are arranged to be illuminated by the Sun only on certain days, such as the winter solstice or midsummer's day.

central axis

Stonehenge became the preeminent ritual centre of southern Britain c.2500 BCE. The rising sun on midsummer's day shines along the central axis of the site, but little is known of the ritual enacted there.

WHEELED VEHICLES

The origin of the wheel is uncertain; humans probably first made use of rotary motion in log rollers, and then in the potter's wheel. Wheeled vehicles were known in southwest Asia by 3500 BCE – a Sumerian pictograph from this period depicts a sledge equipped with wheels – and their use had spread to Europe and India by 3000 BCE. Early vehicles were probably ox-drawn, two-wheeled carts, on wheels formed from planks of wood secured with crosspieces.

This ceramic model of a two-wheeled bullock cart is from a grave at Harappa in the Indus Valley.

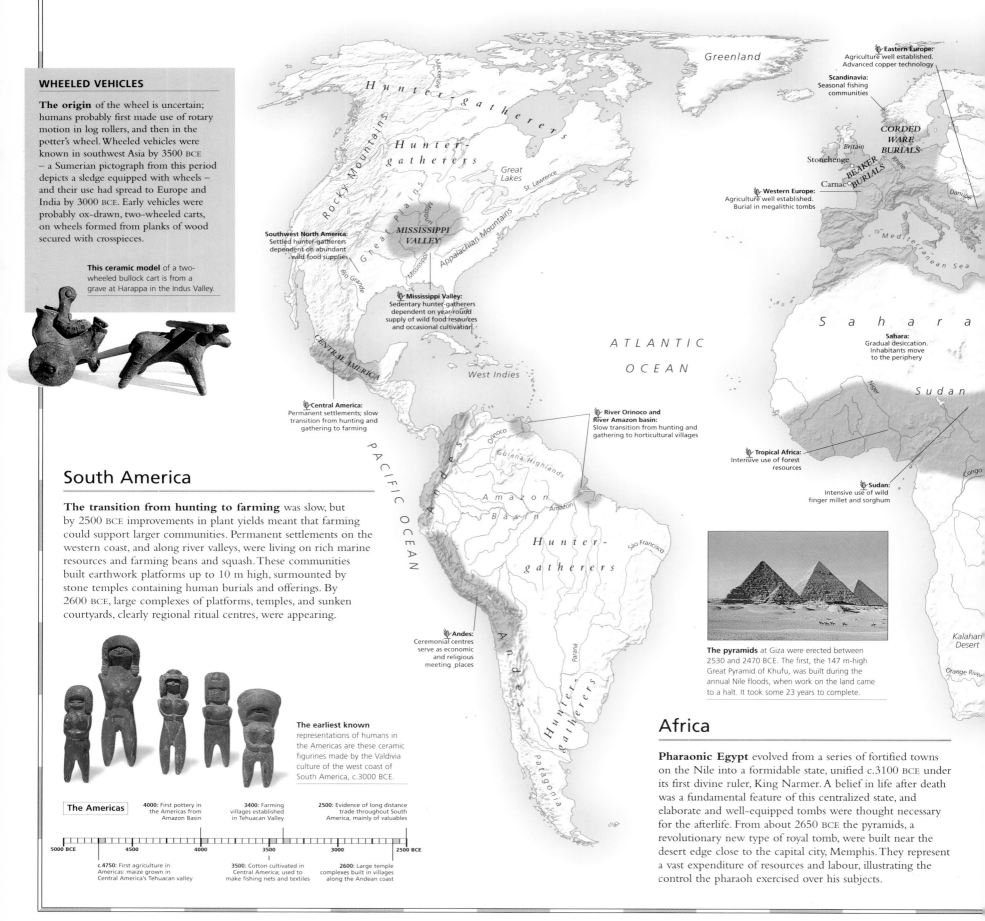

Southwest North America: Settled hunter-gatherers dependent on abundant wild food supplies

Mississippi Valley: Sedentary hunter-gatherers dependent on year-round supply of wild food resources and occasional cultivation.

Central America: Permanent settlements; slow transition from hunting and gathering to farming

River Orinoco and River Amazon basin: Slow transition from hunting and gathering to horticultural villages

Eastern Europe: Agriculture well established. Advanced copper technology

Scandinavia: Seasonal fishing communities

Western Europe: Agriculture well established. Burial in megalithic tombs

Sahara: Gradual desiccation. Inhabitants move to the periphery

Tropical Africa: Intensive use of forest resources

Sudan: Intensive use of wild finger millet and sorghum

Andes: Ceremonial centres serve as economic and religious meeting places

South America

The transition from hunting to farming was slow, but by 2500 BCE improvements in plant yields meant that farming could support larger communities. Permanent settlements on the western coast, and along river valleys, were living on rich marine resources and farming beans and squash. These communities built earthwork platforms up to 10 m high, surmounted by stone temples containing human burials and offerings. By 2600 BCE, large complexes of platforms, temples, and sunken courtyards, clearly regional ritual centres, were appearing.

The earliest known representations of humans in the Americas are these ceramic figurines made by the Valdivia culture of the west coast of South America, c.3000 BCE.

The pyramids at Giza were erected between 2530 and 2470 BCE. The first, the 147 m-high Great Pyramid of Khufu, was built during the annual Nile floods, when work on the land came to a halt. It took some 23 years to complete.

Africa

Pharaonic Egypt evolved from a series of fortified towns on the Nile into a formidable state, unified c.3100 BCE under its first divine ruler, King Narmer. A belief in life after death was a fundamental feature of this centralized state, and elaborate and well-equipped tombs were thought necessary for the afterlife. From about 2650 BCE the pyramids, a revolutionary new type of royal tomb, were built near the desert edge close to the capital city, Memphis. They represent a vast expenditure of resources and labour, illustrating the control the pharaoh exercised over his subjects.

The Americas					
	4000: First pottery in the Americas from Amazon Basin	**3400:** Farming villages established in Tehuacan Valley		**2500:** Evidence of long distance trade throughout South America, mainly of valuables	
5000 BCE	4500	4000	3500	3000	2500 BCE
	c.4750: First agriculture in Americas: maize grown in Central America's Tehuacan valley		**3500:** Cotton cultivated in Central America; used to make fishing nets and textiles	**2600:** Large temple complexes built in villages along the Andean coast	

Europe

Elaborate burials, from the megalithic tombs of northern Europe to the large cemeteries of central and eastern Europe, indicate an increasing level of social organization among the scattered farming communities of the European continent. By the 3rd millennium BCE small farming communities were gathering to build defensive enclosures and to create regional centres. Stone circles, such as Stonehenge, or stone avenues, such as Carnac, were major communal undertakings which acted as social, economic, and ritual centres.

Skara Brae is a magnificently preserved Stone Age village on the Orkneys. The village consists of one-room houses of undressed stone, with paved walkways between them and a drainage system.

Europe

5000 BCE	4500	4000	3500	3000	2500 BCE

4500: Large cemeteries, for example on the western coast of the Black Sea, contain rich burials with elaborate gold jewellery

3800: Ditched enclosures around settlements in central Europe create defended villages

3200: Stone circles and rows of standing stones built throughout northern and western Europe

c.5000: Metallurgy discovered in south-eastern Europe

c.4500: In western Europe, megalithic (large stone) chamber tombs, built as communal burial places

2900: Earliest burials containing Corded Ware pottery in northern and central Europe

East Asia

As the early farming villages of China became more prosperous, new skills emerged. Farmers of the Longshan culture of eastern China invented the potter's wheel and were making eggshell-thin vessels by 3000 BCE; 250 years later they were raising silkworms and weaving silk. By 3000 BCE there was a marked difference between rich and poor burials, and walled settlements were appearing. The more complex social organization that these developments indicate was soon to lead to China's first urban civilization, the Shang.

This Kui (a pitcher with three hollow legs) is typical of Longshan pottery from the late 3rd millennium BCE.

East Asia

5000 BCE	4500	4000	3500	3000	2500 BCE

c.4000: Planned villages in northern China, with distinct residential, workshop, and burial areas

3000: First evidence of farming (millet cultivation) in Korea

2500: Banshan culture of western China produces boldly painted burial urns

c.3000: Potter's wheel invented during formative phase of Longshan culture of eastern China

2750: First Chinese bronze artefacts

SEE ALSO:

North America: pp.120–121

South America: pp.144–145

Africa: pp.158–159

Europe: pp.174–175

West Asia: pp.220–221

South and Southeast Asia: pp.240–241

North and East Asia: pp.258–259

Australasia and Oceania: pp.280–281

South Asia

By 2500 BCE, an urban civilization had developed in the Indus Valley, dominated by Harappa and Mohenjo-Daro. At its height, the latter had a population of about 40,000. A network of residential streets, houses made with standardized bricks and sophisticated drains running into main sewers, overlooked by the 'citadel', the religious and ceremonial focus of the city. Merchandise was traded as far afield as Mesopotamia.

The Harappans developed a pictographic form of writing which they used mainly on sealstones.

South Asia

5000 BCE	4500	4000	3500	3000	2500 BCE

5000: Evidence of use of pottery vessels at Mehrgarh and other Indus Valley settlements

2500: True cities emerge in Indus Valley. Cultural uniformity throughout Indus plain. Evidence of trade links with Central Asia and Mesopotamia

4500: Introduction of irrigation techniques in Indus Valley increases size and prosperity of farming settlements

3500: Indus Valley lowlands settled by farmers; walled towns develop

The world in 2500 BCE

- transition from hunting and gathering to agriculture
- agricultural areas
- urban areas
- urban hinterland

The royal standard of Ur depicts the Sumerian ruler at war and in peacetime. The panels are crafted in lapis lazuli and shell from as far away as Afghanistan.

West Asia

Mesopotamia's fertile floodplains were the crucible of the urban revolution. Uruk, the first city-state, evolved c.3500 BCE. The early cities of Mesopotamia were built around the raised mud-brick temple complex. The temple administered much of the city's land and livestock and a priestly elite was responsible for recording and storing produce. The temple accounting system led to pictographic writing by c.3250 BCE.

Africa

5000 BCE	4500	4000	3500	3000	2500 BCE

3400: First walled towns appear in Egypt

3000: First evidence of hieroglyphic writing system

2530: Construction of Great Pyramid of Khufu, the largest of the Egyptian pyramids, at Giza

3100: King Narmer unifies Upper and Lower Egypt, and becomes first pharaoh. City of Memphis is founded

2650: The step pyramid of Zoser, the first Egyptian pyramid, is built at Saqqara

West Asia

5000 BCE	4500	4000	3500	3000	2500 BCE

c.3250: Pictographic clay tablets from Tell Brak: earliest evidence of writing

2500: City-states present throughout Mesopotamia and Levant

3500: Emergence of Uruk, the first city-state

2500: Rich array of grave goods at Royal Graves at Ur indicate extensive trade links

Map labels:
Hunter-gatherers, Lena, Ob', Yenisey, Siberia, Gobi, Amur, Volga, Livestock herding, PIT GRAVE CULTURE, Pontic Steppes: Cereal cultivation, Aral Sea, Caspian Sea, Black Sea, River Yenisey: Cereal cultivation, Yellow River Valley: Barley and millet cultivation, Hattushash, Mesopotamia, Tell Brak, Iranian Plateau: scattered trading cities, Japan: Hunter-gathering and fishing, Tigris, Euphrates, Susa, Uruk, Ur, SUMER, Mehrgarh, Mohenjo-Daro, Harappa, Yellow River, Korea, Japan, Yangshao, LONGSHAN CULTURE, Giza, Memphis, Saqqara, OLD KINGDOM OF EGYPT, INDUS VALLEY, Indus, Himalayas, Ganges, Yangtze, China, Yangtze Delta: Wet rice cultivation, Ganges Valley: Wet rice cultivation, Arabian Peninsula, Nile, Kachhi: Wheat and barley cultivation, Deccan: Cattle pastoralists, Mekong, Coastal Vietnam: Rice-farming villages, domesticated animals, bronze tools and ornaments, Philippine Islands, PACIFIC OCEAN, Upper Nile Valley: Wheat and barley cultivation, Sumatra, Borneo, Java, New Guinea, Maritime Southeast Asia: Slow transition from hunting and gathering to farming, Hunter-gatherers, Madagascar, Zambezi, INDIAN OCEAN, Hunter-gatherers Australia, Darling, New Zealand

TRADE AND THE FIRST CITIES

This Egyptian ivory label is inscribed with the name of King Djet (c.3000 BCE).

BY 2500 BCE, CITIES WERE ESTABLISHED in three major centres: the Nile Valley, Mesopotamia, and the Indus valley, with a scattering of other cities across the intervening terrain. The culmination of a long process of settlement and expansion – some early cities had populations tens of thousands strong – the first urban civilizations all relied on rich agricultural lands to support their growth. In each case, lack of the most important natural resources – timber, metal, and stone – forced these urban civilizations to establish trading networks which ultimately extended from the Hindu Kush to the Mediterranean. They imported a diverse range of goods: metals and precious stones, such as lapis lazuli, gold, and turquoise, met the demands of the growing social elites for luxury goods; diorite, limestone, and timber were needed for the monumental construction programmes which were an integral part of urban life. Where trading contacts led, cultural influence followed, and cities soon began to develop in the trading hinterlands of the Iranian Plateau and Anatolia.

Ur: a trading city

The ancient city of Ur, was the capital of a south Mesopotamian empire towards the end of the 3rd millennium. It was a major economic centre, with extensive trade links extending as far as Dilmun (Bahrain) and the cities of the Indus. Ships, laden with gold, copper, timber, ivory, and precious stones, had access to the Persian Gulf via canals which linked the city to the Euphrates. Archives of clay tablets record, in minute detail, transactions and ships' cargoes. The wealth this trade generated is reflected in the grandiose buildings which adorned the city, most notably the ziggurat dedicated to the city's deity, Ur-Nammu, and in the lavishly furnished burials of Ur's so-called 'Royal Graves'.

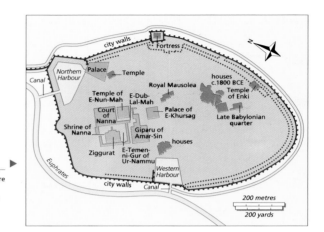

1 Ur

sacred enclosure
royal palace
other building
inner walls
outer walls

200 metres
200 yards

Cities and trade

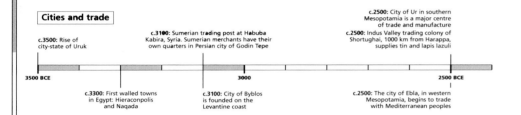

c.3500: Rise of city-state of Uruk

c.3100: Sumerian trading post at Habuba Kabira, Syria. Sumerian merchants have their own quarters in Persian city of Godin Tepe

c.2500: City of Ur in southern Mesopotamia is a major centre of trade and manufacture

c.2500: Indus Valley trading colony of Shortughai, 1000 km from Harappa, supplies tin and lapis lazuli

3500 BCE — 3000 — 2500 BCE

c.3300: First walled towns in Egypt: Hieraconpolis and Naqada

c.3100: City of Byblos is founded on the Levantine coast

c.2500: The city of Ebla, in western Mesopotamia, begins to trade with Mediterranean peoples

Transport

The long-distance trading networks of the ancient world required revolutionary developments in transport. Much of the trade was maritime; the cities of Mesopotamia all had access, via rivers and canals, to the Persian Gulf and Indus Valley, and there is ample evidence for trade along the Gulf coast and Arabian Sea to the mouth of the Indus. The timber boats of the Nile, depicted carrying great columns of granite and alabaster, are known from tomb reliefs, models and burials. Overland trade was dependent on newly-domesticated beasts of burden, such as asses and camels. Wheeled carts, pulled by oxen and bullocks, were also used.

A high-prowed reed boat can be seen on this impression from a cylinder seal from Uruk, dating to the 4th millennium BCE. The boat is being used to transport a priest or ruler, probably as part of a religious procession.

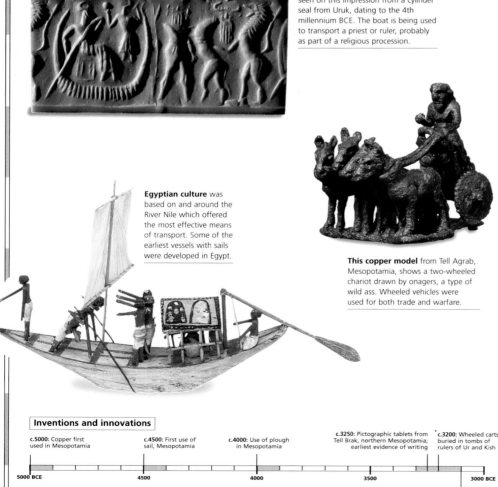

Egyptian culture was based on and around the River Nile which offered the most effective means of transport. Some of the earliest vessels with sails were developed in Egypt.

This copper model from Tell Agrab, Mesopotamia, shows a two-wheeled chariot drawn by onagers, a type of wild ass. Wheeled vehicles were used for both trade and warfare.

Levant: Coastal trade between Egypt and Mesopotamia

Egypt: The Nile enabled cargoes of precious metals and building materials to be shipped downriver from Nubia

Inventions and innovations

c.5000: Copper first used in Mesopotamia

c.4500: First use of sail, Mesopotamia

c.4000: Use of plough in Mesopotamia

c.3250: Pictographic tablets from Tell Brak, northern Mesopotamia; earliest evidence of writing

c.3200: Wheeled carts buried in tombs of rulers of Ur and Kish

5000 BCE — 4500 — 4000 — 3500 — 3000 BCE

c.3100: Development of cuneiform script in Mesopotamia. Experiments with bronze working

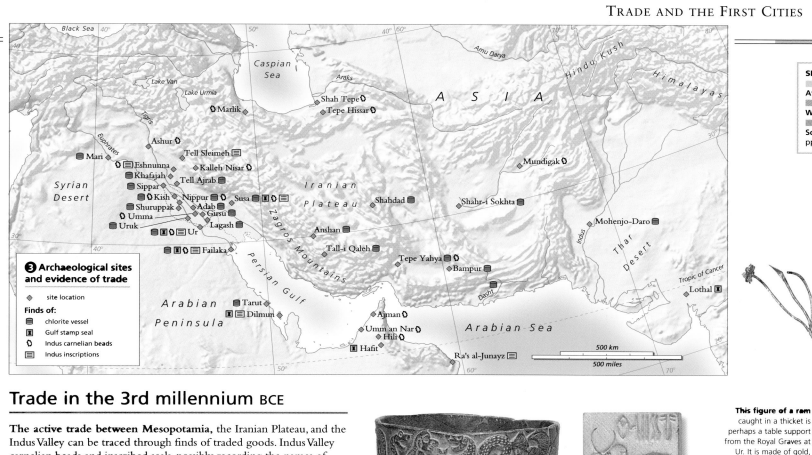

❸ Archaeological sites and evidence of trade

◆ site location

Finds of:
▭ chlorite vessel
▣ Gulf stamp seal
◊ Indus carnelian beads
▤ Indus inscriptions

SEE ALSO:

Africa: pp.158–159

West Asia: pp.174–175

South and Southeast Asia: pp.240–241

Trade in the 3rd millennium BCE

The active trade between Mesopotamia, the Iranian Plateau, and the Indus Valley can be traced through finds of traded goods. Indus Valley carnelian beads and inscribed seals, possibly recording the names of merchants, are found throughout southern Mesopotamia. Vessels made of chlorite schist, a soft mineral rock from southern Persia, are also found throughout the region. Dilmun (Bahrain) was an important Gulf entrepôt and trading post for copper from Oman, trading with both the main Mesopotamian ports of Ur and Lagash and the Indus Valley. Finds of Gulf stamp seals reflect the extent of Gulf trading contacts.

The Iranian Plateau was rich in chlorite schist, lapis lazuli, carnelian, gold, and silver. Imported chlorite, used to make this bowl from southern Persia, can be found throughout the region from Mari in the west to Mohenjo-Daro in the east.

Indus seals, used for securing bales of merchandise, have been found in Mesopotamia. The short inscriptions may record merchants' names.

This figure of a ram caught in a thicket is perhaps a table support from the Royal Graves at Ur. It is made of gold, silver, shell and lapis lazuli – evidence of Ur's thriving long distance trade links.

❷ Urban centres and trade routes 3500–2000 BCE

▱ zone of urban civilization
▱ trading hinterland
○ urban centres
— major trade route
···· modern coast where different
–––– modern river where different

Traded raw materials
▯ alabaster
▯ dolerite
▯ flint
▯ granite
▯ limestone
▯ steatite
▯ copper
▯ gold
▯ silver
▯ tin
● carnelian
● turquoise
● lapis lazuli
♣ timber

Iranian Plateau: Trading cities engaged in long distance trade with Mesopotamia and the Indus Valley

Oman: Coastal cities trade with both Mesopotamia and the Indus Valley

Seals were used by traders to record ownership. This inscribed seal from Mesopotamia, was used to roll out an impression on soft clay.

Only scribes were literate, and they became a privileged class in ancient cities. The Egyptian scribe Imhotep, for example, designed the pyramid at Saqqara.

Writing

Perhaps the single greatest innovation of urban civilization, writing evolved to record trading transactions. The first texts, from Mesopotamia and dating to the 4th millennium BCE, are receipts, showing symbols and numbers only; soon a pictographic script, where pictures represent words, developed and, in time, symbols came to be used for sounds (cuneiform). Specialized scribes became keepers of temple archives, responsible for libraries of clay tablets which recorded the detail of state-run temple economies. Writing soon transcended its business roots, and was used to codify laws, record myths, and preserve religious transactions. Writing equally old is now known from the royal tombs at Abydos in Upper Egypt.

Sumerian cuneiform writing is named after the wedge-shaped marks or incisions made with a stylus on soft clay tablets. *Cuneus* is Latin for a wedge.

THE WORLD 2500–1250 BCE

AS THE FIRST CITIES expanded and proliferated, states developed, populations grew, and economic pressures increased. Rivalry for territory and power made the early states increasingly militaristic, and warfare, weapons, and diplomacy are conspicuous in the archaeology of this period. As these early societies became more stratified, distinct classes – warriors, priests, scribes, craftspeople, labourers – began to emerge. The great wealth of rulers and the social elite is reflected in the rich array of grave goods found in their burials. Urban civilizations still covered only a tiny fraction of the Earth's surface; in Europe, scattered agricultural communities were becoming more sophisticated, developing metallurgy and trade, and beginning to compete for land and resources. Hunter-gatherer groups still thrived in many areas, and many islands in the Pacific were yet to be settled at this time.

SUN SYMBOLISM

Symbolic representations of the Sun, suggestive of life, fertility, and creation, are found in almost all cultures. During this period in Egypt, the sun god Ra was the dominant figure among the high gods, his enhanced status culminating in the brief solar monotheism under Pharaoh Akhenaton c.1350 BCE. In Scandinavia, ritual finds such as the sun chariot found in a bog at Trundholm (below) attest to monotheistic sun worship and fertility rites in the region during the Bronze Age.

This bronze wheeled model of a horse drawing a disc, which dates to c.1650 BCE, may depict the sun's progress across the heavens.

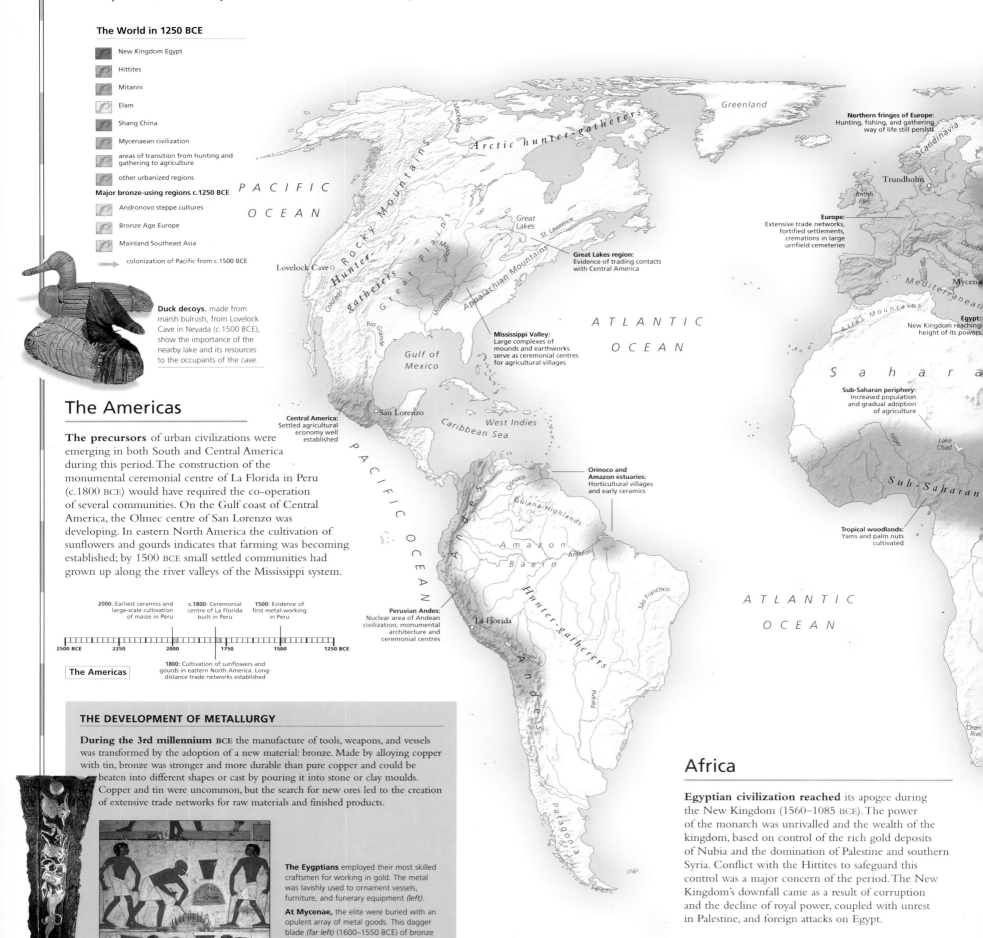

The World in 1250 BCE

- New Kingdom Egypt
- Hittites
- Mitanni
- Elam
- Shang China
- Mycenaean civilization
- areas of transition from hunting and gathering to agriculture
- other urbanized regions

Major bronze-using regions c.1250 BCE
- Andronovo steppe cultures
- Bronze Age Europe
- Mainland Southeast Asia
- → colonization of Pacific from c.1500 BCE

Duck decoys, made from marsh bulrush, from Lovelock Cave in Nevada (c.1500 BCE), show the importance of the nearby lake and its resources to the occupants of the cave.

Northern fringes of Europe: Hunting, fishing, and gathering way of life still persists

Great Lakes region: Evidence of trading contacts with Central America

Europe: Extensive trade networks, fortified settlements, cremations in large urnfield cemeteries

Egypt: New Kingdom reaching height of its powers

Mississippi Valley: Large complexes of mounds and earthworks serve as ceremonial centres for agricultural villages

Sub-Saharan periphery: Increased population and gradual adoption of agriculture

Central America: Settled agricultural economy well established

Orinoco and Amazon estuaries: Horticultural villages and early ceramics

Tropical woodlands: Yams and palm nuts cultivated

Peruvian Andes: Nuclear area of Andean civilization; monumental architecture and ceremonial centres

The Americas

The precursors of urban civilizations were emerging in both South and Central America during this period. The construction of the monumental ceremonial centre of La Florida in Peru (c.1800 BCE) would have required the co-operation of several communities. On the Gulf coast of Central America, the Olmec centre of San Lorenzo was developing. In eastern North America the cultivation of sunflowers and gourds indicates that farming was becoming established; by 1500 BCE small settled communities had grown up along the river valleys of the Mississippi system.

2000: Earliest ceramics and large-scale cultivation of maize in Peru

c.1800: Ceremonial centre of La Florida built in Peru

1500: Evidence of first metal-working in Peru

2500 BCE — 2250 — 2000 — 1750 — 1500 — 1250 BCE

The Americas

1800: Cultivation of sunflowers and gourds in eastern North America. Long-distance trade networks established

THE DEVELOPMENT OF METALLURGY

During the 3rd millennium BCE the manufacture of tools, weapons, and vessels was transformed by the adoption of a new material: bronze. Made by alloying copper with tin, bronze was stronger and more durable than pure copper and could be beaten into different shapes or cast by pouring it into stone or clay moulds. Copper and tin were uncommon, but the search for new ores led to the creation of extensive trade networks for raw materials and finished products.

The Eygptians employed their most skilled craftsmen for working in gold. The metal was lavishly used to ornament vessels, furniture, and funerary equipment (left).

At Mycenae, the elite were buried with an opulent array of metal goods. This dagger blade (far left) (1600–1550 BCE) of bronze inlaid with silver portrays a lion hunt.

Africa

Egyptian civilization reached its apogee during the New Kingdom (1560–1085 BCE). The power of the monarch was unrivalled and the wealth of the kingdom, based on control of the rich gold deposits of Nubia and the domination of Palestine and southern Syria. Conflict with the Hittites to safeguard this control was a major concern of the period. The New Kingdom's downfall came as a result of corruption and the decline of royal power, coupled with unrest in Palestine, and foreign attacks on Egypt.

Europe

European field systems and settlements, ranging from hillforts to island villages, indicate that increased pressures on land were causing conflict. New types of bronze weapons show the emergence of a warrior elite. The palace of Knossos on Crete marked the appearance of the first Mediterranean state, and on the mainland, the small, palace-based cities of Mycenaean Greece grew wealthy on east Mediterranean trade, but were all sacked or abandoned by the 12th century BCE.

Many aspects of Minoan life are depicted in the colourful frescoes at Knossos, a recurring theme being the acrobatic bull-leaping game on which a religious cult was possibly centred.

Europe

2300: Bronze technology reaches Europe	**2000:** Fortified settlements appear in central and eastern Europe	**1550:** Mycenaeans become dominant power on Greek mainland

2500 BCE — 2250 — 2000 — 1750 — 1500 — 1250 BCE

2000: Minoan civilization becomes established on island of Crete; palace of Knossos is built

1650: Linear A script comes into use on Crete

West Asia

Northern Mesopotamia was dominated by a number of city-states, such as Ashur and Mari, which centred on palaces and religious complexes. The palace administered each city's long-distance trade and tribute, and recorded these transactions on archives of clay tablets. In the 18th century BCE, the city-state of Babylon gained temporary control of the region. In central Anatolia, the Hittites ruled a powerful kingdom from their fortified citadel at Hattushash. Their attempts to gain contol over the wealthy trading cities of the Levant brought them into conflict with Egypt.

This gold figurine of a Hittite king dates to c.1400 BCE.

West Asia

2300: City-states of southern Mesopotamia temporarily united under Sargon of Agade	**1775:** Construction of palace of Zimri-Lim at Mari. Palace archive contained 17,500 clay tablets	**1650:** Emergence of Hittite kingdom, with capital at Hattushash	**1500:** Period of endemic warfare between Hittites, Egyptians, and Mitanni of northern Mesopotamia

2500 BCE — 2250 — 2000 — 1750 — 1500 — 1250 BCE

1760: City-state of Babylon gains political hegemony over northern Mesopotamia

1600: Phoenicians start to use Canaanite script – the first alphabetic script

1290: Battle of Kadesh: Egypt versus the Hittites

SEE ALSO:

North America: pp.120–121

South America: pp.144–145

Africa: pp.158–159

Europe: pp.174–175

West Asia: pp.220–221

South and Southeast Asia: pp.240–241

North and East Asia: pp.258–259

Australasia and Oceania: pp.280–281

East Asia

The urban civilization of Shang China developed in about 1800 BCE in the middle valley of the Yellow River. The Shang dynasty exercised an absolute power reflected in their incredibly rich burials. Yet this absolute power was based on the labour of farmers who cultivated beans and millet with tools of wood and stone. Elsewhere, in Southeast Asia, the transition to farming was slow, although agricultural villages in Thailand were producing bronze vessels using similar techniques to the Chinese.

Chinese mastery of bronze casting is evident in the exquisite vessels, created primarily for ceremonial use, that often accompanied the wealthy elite into the grave.

East Asia

1800: Emergence of Shang dynasty in middle valley of Yellow River	**1500:** Evidence of bronze-working in mainland Southeast Asia	**1400:** Anyang succeeds Zhengzhou as the Shang capital	

2500 BCE — 2250 — 2000 — 1750 — 1500 — 1250 BCE

2500: First domesticated animals and pottery in island Southeast Asia

1900 BCE: First Chinese city founded at Erlitou on the Yellow River

1800: First bronze vessels cast from ceramic moulds

1400: First written inscriptions appear on oracle bones, which were used in a process of divination

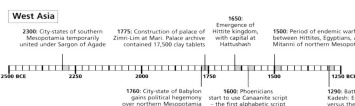

Map labels

Arctic hunter-gatherers

Siberia
Steppes

Yenisey
Lena
Ob'
Volga
Amur
Lake Baikal

Andronovo steppe cultures: Cattle herders and seasonal nomads

Aral Sea
Lake Balkhash

Gobi

China: Longshan groups form basis of Shang state c.1800 BCE

Japan

Anyang
Yellow River
Erlitou · Zhengzhou

Japan: Jomon hunter-gatherers living in villages

Black Sea
Caspian Sea

Troy · Hattushash
Anatolia
Knossos · Kadesh
Byblos · Nineveh · Ashur
Tyre
Jerusalem · Jericho
Babylon
El-Amarna
El-Lisht
Thebes

Iranian Plateau: Scattered trading cities

Himalayas
Indus
Ganges
Yangtze

Levant: City states repeatedly absorbed by neighbouring empires; Hittite Empire, Elam and Kingdom of Mitanni vying with Egypt for control of region

Arabian Peninsula

Deccan

Indus Valley: Disappearance of urban civilization; northwest India occupied by Aryan settlers

Ganges Valley: Rice-farming villages

Red River valley: Sophisticated bronze working; Dong Son drums

Pacific Ocean

Nile
Nubia

East Africa: Teff and ensete cultivation

pastoralists

Congo
Lake Victoria

Philippine Islands

Mainland Southeast Asia: Rice-farming villages, bronze tools and ornaments

Maritime Southeast Asia: Slow transition from hunting and gathering to agriculture

Mekong
Sumatra
Borneo
East Indies
Java
New Guinea
Bismarck Archipelago

Hunter-gatherers
Zambezi
Madagascar

Kalahari Desert

INDIAN OCEAN

Polynesian dispersal: Lapita population colonize the islands of Melanesia

When the Lapita people arrived in the western Pacific islands they were carrying a variety of food plants, the pig, and their distinctive style of pottery, the decoration of which was applied with short-toothed implements.

Hunter-gatherers
Australia
Darling

Oceania

One of the great population dispersals of the ancient world began c.1500 BCE, when the Lapita people, originally settlers from the East Indies, set off from New Guinea and the Solomons to explore and colonize the islands of the Pacific Ocean. The Lapita culture spread rapidly, reaching Tonga and Samoa, by 1000 BCE.

New Zealand

Egyptian agriculture centred on the cultivation of cereals, primarily emmer wheat and barley. The fertile soils of the Nile floodplain produced high annual yields and large surpluses were a major source of the state's weath.

Africa

1560: Rise of New Kingdom. New capital founded at Thebes	**1417:** Egyptian prosperity, power and prestige reach their high point under Amenophis III	

2500 BCE — 2250 — 2000 — 1750 — 1500 — 1250 BCE

2040: Egypt re-united under Middle Kingdom pharaohs after perod of dominance by nobles. New capital is founded at El-Lisht

1633: Much of Egypt ruled by the Hyksos, an Asiatic people

1350: Pharaoh Akhenaton introduces sun worship in Egypt

Oceania

c.2500: Dingo introduced to Australia, probably from Southeast Asia	**1500:** Lapita colonists start to colonize Pacific Ocean, reaching Tonga and Samoa by c.1000 BCE

2500 BCE — 2250 — 2000 — 1750 — 1500 — 1250 BCE

c.1600: Earliest examples of Lapita pottery in Bismarck Archipelago

27

THE GROWTH OF THE CITY

Pharaoh Akhenaten
(1379–1362 BCE) was
the founder of the new
city of El-Amarna.

OVER THE COURSE OF 2000 YEARS from c.3500 BCE, cities evolved in many different ways, reflecting the culture from which they emerged, outside pressures, and the preoccupations of their rulers. Yet, in a period of increasing social stratification, all cities represented the gulf between the ruler and the ruled, the sacred and the secular. They were physically, and symbolically, dominated by the palaces of the ruling elite, and by temples and religious precincts. The elaborate monuments of these early centres, clearly segregated from the houses and workshops of the labouring classes, symbolized the absolute power wielded by royal dynasties, priests, and the aristocracy. But the *status quo* was underpinned by a relentless quest for new territory and greater wealth; ultimately, this urge to expand was to evolve into imperialism.

The urban heartland

By 1250 BCE, zones of urbanism extended from the Mediterranean to China. The early expansion of urban civilization in southern Mesopotamia had created a swathe of cities, from Ur to Mycenae, which thrived on trade and contact, supplemented by the levying of taxes, tolls, and tribute. Rivalry for control of key cities, especially in the Levant, was endemic. While Egypt was also vying for political and economic control of the Levant, the cities of the Nile were stately religious and dynastic centres, adorned by magnificent temples, palaces, and cities of the dead. The distant cities of Shang China were strictly segregated – symbolic of a stratified society where the great wealth and luxury of the few rested on a simple farming base.

❷ Nippur

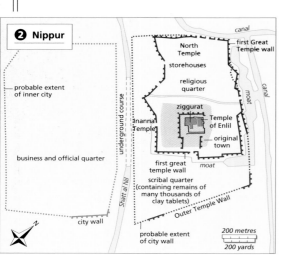

A ruler's power was legitimized by the foundation of cities and temples, as this sculpture of a Babylonian king carrying building materials shows.

Nippur

Centre of the worship of Enlil, the chief deity of the Sumerian pantheon, Nippur retained its importance over three millennia. Located on the Shatt al Nil, an ancient course of the Euphrates, the city was first occupied in c.4000 BCE. In c.2100 BCE, Ur-Nammu, ruler of the city-state of Ur, legitimized his role as Enlil's earthly representative by building the first temple and ziggurat to the deity. The temple was subsequently destroyed and rebuilt at least three times. The remains of the extensive religious quarter encompass a large scribal district as well as a temple to Inanna, queen of heaven.

A map of the city of Nippur – probably the oldest plan in the world – was found on a clay tablet from the site dating to c.1500 BCE. The two lines on the far left denote the River Euphrates; adjoining lines show one wall of the city.

① Urbanism 1250 BCE
- urban area of the Old World, c.1250 BCE
- area of secondary urbanization, with date
- extent of Indus civilization c.5000–2500 BCE
- ○ major city

Europe: Urbanism spreads in early centuries CE with Roman imperialism

Arabian Peninsula: Harsh desert terrain is sparsely populated by desert pastoralists

Sculpted lions flank the 'Lion Gate', a major entrance into the city of Hattushash. In the 14th century BCE the fortifications of Hattushash were extended and strengthened, as befitted its status as an important imperial capital.

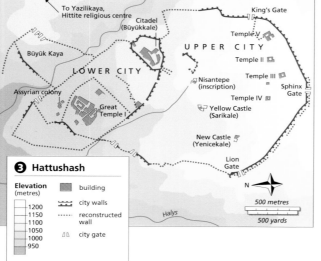

❸ Hattushash

Elevation (metres)	
1200	▨ building
1150	⌒ city walls
1100	⋯ reconstructed wall
1050	
1000	⌒ city gate
950	

Hattushash

The Hittite kingdom, which emerged from the conquest of a number of Anatolian city states in the 17th century BCE, adopted the site of Hattushash (Boğazköy) as its capital. Situated at the head of a fertile river valley, the citadel, Büyükkale, was the core of the old city. By c.1400 BCE the walls had been extended to encompass the 'Upper City', and Hattushash had been adorned with a series of grandiose monuments – five temples and a palace within the citadel with a large pillared audience hall and a royal archive of 3000 clay tablets. The city walls, which stood on stone-faced ramparts, with projecting towers and twin-towered gateways, made Hattushash one of the most strongly fortified cities in the Middle East.

The development of cities

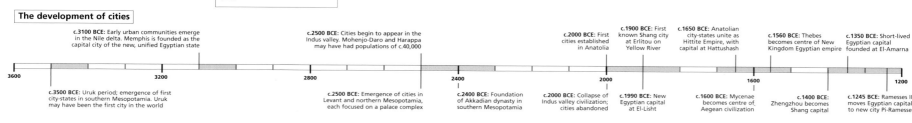

c.3100 BCE: Early urban communities emerge in the Nile delta. Memphis is founded as the capital city of the new, unified Egyptian state

c.2500 BCE: Cities begin to appear in the Indus valley. Mohenjo-Daro and Harappa may have had populations of c.40,000

c.2000 BCE: First cities established in Anatolia

c.1900 BCE: First known Shang city at Erlitou on Yellow River

c.1650 BCE: Anatolian city-states unite as Hittite Empire, with capital at Hattushash

c.1560 BCE: Thebes becomes centre of New Kingdom Egyptian empire

c.1350 BCE: Short-lived Egyptian capital founded at El-Amarna

c.3500 BCE: Uruk period; emergence of first city-states in southern Mesopotamia. Uruk may have been the first city in the world

c.2500 BCE: Emergence of cities in Levant and northern Mesopotamia, each focused on a palace complex

c.2400 BCE: Foundation of Akkadian dynasty in southern Mesopotamia

c.2000 BCE: Collapse of Indus valley civilization; cities abandoned

c.1990 BCE: New Egyptian capital at El-Lisht

c.1600 BCE: Mycenae becomes centre of Aegean civilization

c.1400 BCE: Zhengzhou becomes Shang capital

c.1245 BCE: Ramesses II moves Egyptian capital to new city Pi-Ramesse

Zhengzhou

The Shang dynasty ruled in the middle valley of the Yellow River from c.1800 BCE. Remains of Shang cities, rich tombs and luxury artefacts all indicate the presence of a highly sophisticated urban elite. Zhengzhou, one of successive Shang capitals, was founded c.1700 BCE. It consists of a roughly square enclosure, surrounded by 7 km-long, 10 m-high rammed earth walls. Within these walls stood the palace and ritual altar, dwelling places, storage pits for grain, pottery, and oracle bones (a means of divination, used by the Shang to consult their ancestors) and pits for human sacrifices. Outside the walls stood the residential areas, and specialist workshops producing fine artefacts in bone, bronze, and pottery.

④ Zhengzhou

- urban area
- building
- city wall
- pottery site
- bronze site
- distillery site

1 km
1 mile

SEE ALSO:

Africa: pp.158–159

Europe: pp.174–175

West Asia: pp.220–221

South and Southeast Asia: pp.240–241

North and East Asia: pp.258–259

Japan and Korea: Cities do not appear until 1st millennium CE

Gobi: Harsh and dangerous terrain, unfit for permanent settlement

Russian steppes: Populated by nomadic peoples, specializing in horse-rearing, cattle and sheep herding, supplemented by hunting

Takla Makan Desert: Trading posts develop on fringes of desert with opening of trans-Asian trade routes, c.1st century CE

Xi Jiang Delta: Urbanism slow to develop due to malarial infestation of low-lying swamps

Southern China c.600 BCE

Southeast Asia c.200 BCE

Indus valley: Urban civilization disappears c.2000 BCE, possibly due to a combination of environmental factors and invasion from the north by Aryan peoples

Ganges/Northern Deccan c.500 BCE

Maritime Southeast Asia: Cities do not appear until 1st millennium CE

Sri Lanka c.400 BCE

The major cities of Shang China lay on the edge of the North China Plain. This fertile area, rich in alluvium deposited by the Yellow River, provided the agricultural base for Shang civilization.

6670 km (4140 miles)

13,360 km (8300 miles)

Scale varies with perspective

El-Amarna

El-Amarna was built by the Egyptian pharaoh Akhenaten to honour his god, Aten, in the 14th century BCE, and was abandoned shortly after his death. The city stood on a cliff-encircled plain on the east bank of the Nile. The Great Temple of Aten dominated the city, while immediately to the south lay the palace, bisected by the Royal Road, running parallel to the Nile, which divided it into private and official quarters. Outlying residential areas contained many fine private houses, with gardens and pools, probably the homes of prominent courtiers, interspersed with the tightly-packed dwellings of the poor.

NORTH CITY

North Palace

northern tombs

desert altars

NORTH SUBURB

official residence of High Priest Panehsy

Great Temple of Aten

CEREMONIAL CENTRE

military post

records office

King's House

House of King's statue

Great Palace Coronation Hall

residential area

smaller Aten Temple

house of sculptor, Thutmose

SOUTH SUBURB

500 metres
500 yards

⑤ El-Amarna

- arable land
- unexcavated site
- urban area
- important building
- irrigation channel
- path

Akhenaten built El-Amarna to symbolize his rejection of Egyptian tradition. His successor, Tutankhamun, returned to Thebes *(left)* and re-opened the temples of the old gods.

This plaster fragment decorated the walls of Akhenaten's Great Palace. It shows two of the king's daughters; their distorted features are typical of the art of the period.

THE WORLD 1250–750 BCE

THE INEXORABLE RIVALRIES between the cities and states of the Old World and incursions by nomadic tribes created a shifting pattern of allegiance and control within West Asia. The Assyrians formed the world's first large empire, and ruled their territory with ruthless efficiency, utilizing cavalry and new iron technology to fashion more effective weapons and armour. In both Europe and Asia iron revolutionized weapons, tools, and agricultural implements. More efficient farming produced higher crop yields and supported larger populations. Long-distance trade networks disseminated political and cultural influences across Europe and along the Mediterranean shores, but many areas remained unaffected. The first major centres of the Americas, the Chavín in Peru and the Olmec in Central America, developed in isolation, evolving the art styles, religious motifs, and ceremonies which were to imbue the civilizations that succeeded them.

North America

The first great Mexican civilization, the Olmec, emerged in the coastal lowlands southwest of Yucatán in about 1200 BCE. The Olmec founded a number of ceremonial centres, notably at San Lorenzo and La Venta. They also established trade networks in commodities such as obsidian, jade, and basalt which extended far to the north and west. To the northeast, the peoples of the Adena culture, based along the Ohio River from about 1000–300 BCE, constructed burial chambers beneath earthen mounds.

At San Lorenzo, the Olmec sculpted remarkable stone monuments, including colossal basalt heads with characteristic flat faces, thickened lips, and protective helmets.

North America

1200: Olmec civilization, based at San Lorenzo, is flourishing

1000: Adena culture develops in middle Ohio River valley in eastern North America

1250 BCE — 1150 — 1050 — 950 — 850 — 750 BCE

1200: Town of Tlatilco is well established in the central Valley of Mexico

900: San Lorenzo is destroyed. Its leading role is taken over by La Venta

The World in 750 BCE

- Greek cities and territories
- Phoenician cities and territories
- small Chinese states under the Eastern Zhou dynasty

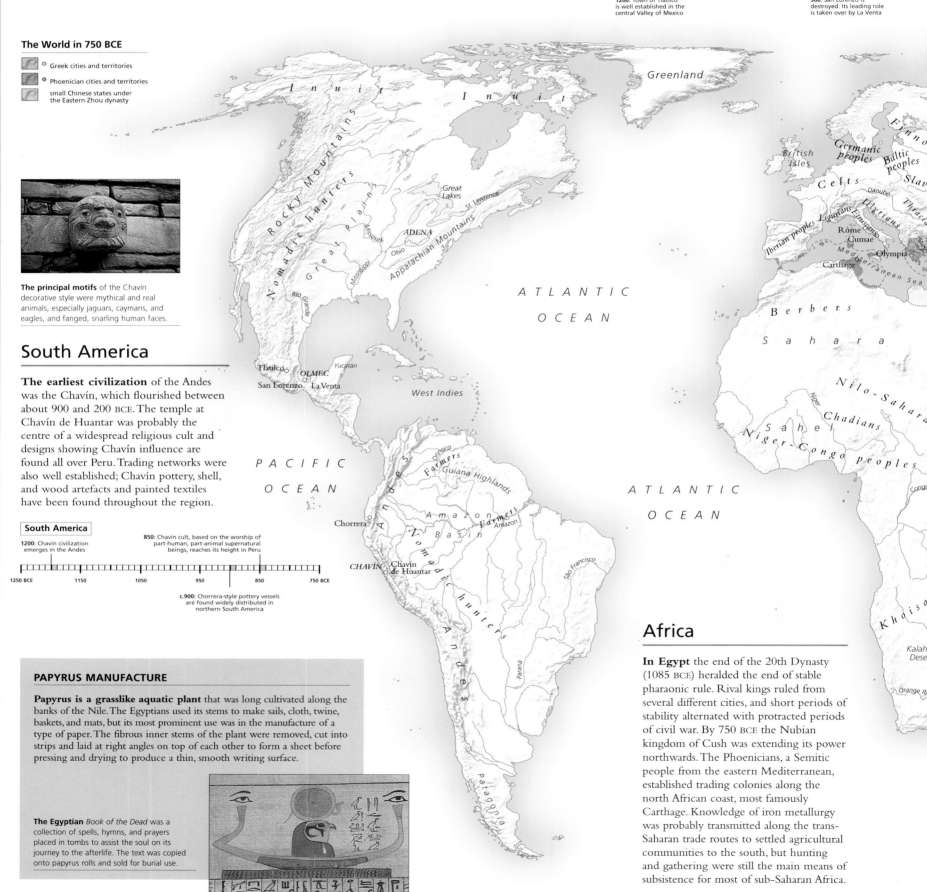

The principal motifs of the Chavín decorative style were mythical and real animals, especially jaguars, caymans, and eagles, and fanged, snarling human faces.

South America

The earliest civilization of the Andes was the Chavín, which flourished between about 900 and 200 BCE. The temple at Chavín de Huantar was probably the centre of a widespread religious cult and designs showing Chavín influence are found all over Peru. Trading networks were also well established; Chavín pottery, shell, and wood artefacts and painted textiles have been found throughout the region.

South America

1200: Chavín civilization emerges in the Andes

850: Chavín cult, based on the worship of part-human, part-animal supernatural beings, reaches its height in Peru

1250 BCE — 1150 — 1050 — 950 — 850 — 750 BCE

c.900: Chorrera-style pottery vessels are found widely distributed in northern South America

PAPYRUS MANUFACTURE

Papyrus is a grasslike aquatic plant that was long cultivated along the banks of the Nile. The Egyptians used its stems to make sails, cloth, twine, baskets, and mats, but its most prominent use was in the manufacture of a type of paper. The fibrous inner stems of the plant were removed, cut into strips and laid at right angles on top of each other to form a sheet before pressing and drying to produce a thin, smooth writing surface.

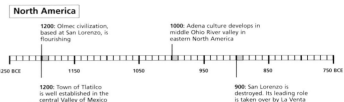

The Egyptian Book of the Dead was a collection of spells, hymns, and prayers placed in tombs to assist the soul on its journey to the afterlife. The text was copied onto papyrus rolls and sold for burial use.

Africa

In Egypt the end of the 20th Dynasty (1085 BCE) heralded the end of stable pharaonic rule. Rival kings ruled from several different cities, and short periods of stability alternated with protracted periods of civil war. By 750 BCE the Nubian kingdom of Cush was extending its power northwards. The Phoenicians, a Semitic people from the eastern Mediterranean, established trading colonies along the north African coast, most famously Carthage. Knowledge of iron metallurgy was probably transmitted along the trans-Saharan trade routes to settled agricultural communities to the south, but hunting and gathering were still the main means of subsistence for most of sub-Saharan Africa.

Europe

Independent city-states were founded throughout Greece and western Asia Minor. The establishment of trade links with Italy and the Levant increased prosperity and population and colonists began to build Greek trading cities along the shores of the Mediterranean. In Italy, the Etruscans built fortified hilltop cities and established extensive trade links with Africa and Europe. Iron metallurgy, established in Central Europe by 1000 BCE, had reached the British Isles by the 8th century. Iron was used to make sophisticated weapons and tools.

After the fall of Mycenean Greece in the 12th century, various powers vied for control of the east Mediterranean. Naval battles were fought between fleets of long, narrow oared vessels built for speed and manoeuvrability, such as the Greek galley depicted on this pot.

BABYLONIAN ASTRONOMY

The Babylonians were one of the earliest peoples to make a systematic, scientific study of the skies. Their records go back to c.1800 BCE and accumulated over centuries. By 1000 BCE they were able to predict lunar eclipses and within two or three hundred years, the path of the Sun and some of the planets had been plotted with considerable accuracy. These astronomical records contributed to the later flowering of western astronomy.

This bronze model of the solar system is from Lake Sevan in Armenia. It dates from 10th–9th century BCE.

SEE ALSO:

North America: pp.120–121

South America: pp.144–145

Africa: pp.160–161

Europe: pp.176–177

West Asia: pp.222–223

South and Southeast Asia: pp.240–243

North and East Asia: pp.258–259

Australasia and Oceania: pp.280–281

Europe

1150: Collapse of Mycenean Greece	**1000:** Colonists from mainland Greece settle coast of Asia Minor and islands of eastern Aegean	**900:** End of dark ages in Greece	**800:** Rise of Etruscan city-states in central Italy	**776:** First Pan-Hellenic athletics festival held at the Sanctuary of Zeus, Olympia	

1250 BCE — 1150 — 1050 — 950 — 850 — 750 BCE

1200: New Urnfield culture emerges in Danube area. Named after tradition of placing cremated ashes in urns in large communal burial fields

c.1000: Iron-working reaches Central Europe from the Near East

850: Earliest village on Rome's Palatine Hill

800: First phase of Celtic Iron Age named after cemetery at Hallstatt in Austria

West Asia

Power struggles between the established empires of the West Asia created opportunities for infiltration by barbarian tribes, such as the Medes, Chaldeans, Philistines, Hebrews, and Phrygians, who attempted to seize power. The Hebrews under King David briefly created a kingdom which united Palestine and Syria, but it collapsed after the rule of Solomon (966–926 BCE). From the 9th century BCE, the dominant power in the region was Assyria, originally based in the Tigris valley. By the 8th century BCE the Assyrian Empire, extended from the Levant to the Persian Gulf. Subject peoples were ruled by provincial governors and resistance was ruthlessly suppressed. Only the Armenian kingdom of Urartu remained beyond Assyrian control.

Assyrian kings ploughed the proceeds of their military conquests into the building of vast temples and palaces at Nimrud and Nineveh. Booty acquired during the campaigns, like this ivory panel of a sphinx, enriched many palace furnishings.

West Asia

1200: Collapse of the Hittite Empire	**c.1100:** Syria and Palestine settled by nomadic tribes	**c.1000:** King David unites Israel and Judaea, with its capital city at Jerusalem	**900:** Kingdom of Urartu established in Armenia resists Assyrian expansion	

1250 BCE — 1150 — 1050 — 950 — 850 — 750 BCE

c.1200: Jewish exodus from Egypt and settlement in Palestine

c.1000: Phoenicians dominate trade of Levant and develop an alphabetic script

950: Foundation of the Assyrian Empire

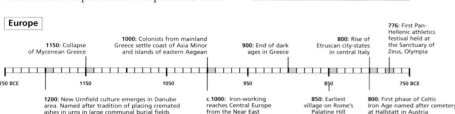

Zhou rulers maintained Shang cultural traditions, including ancestor worship. Food and drink were offered in bronze ritual vessels, often shaped into bizarre combinations of animal forms.

East Asia

In China the Zhou dynasty succeeded the Shang in the 11th century BCE, heralding a period of stability until the 8th century when central authority collapsed, former fiefs rose up against the Zhou, and China split into separate kingdoms. Bronze technology for weapons and ornaments reached the Korean peninsula from Manchuria in about 1000 BCE.

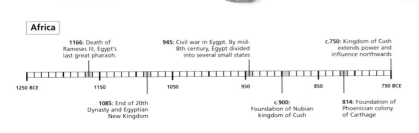

The need to preserve the body from decay – through mummification – was an integral part of the Egyptian belief in a life after death. This anthropomorphic case belonged to Shepenmut, Priestess of Thebes, who was buried around 800 BCE.

Africa

1166: Death of Rameses III, Egypt's last great pharaoh.	**945:** Civil war in Eygpt. By mid-8th century, Egypt divided into several small states	**c.750:** Kingdom of Cush extends power and influence northwards	

1250 BCE — 1150 — 1050 — 950 — 850 — 750 BCE

1085: End of 20th Dynasty and Egyptian New Kingdom

c.900: Foundation of Nubian kingdom of Cush

814: Foundation of Phoenician colony of Carthage

East Asia

1027: Zhou dynasty replaces Shang in China	**1000:** Chinese bronze casting reaches level of craftsmanship unrivalled elsewhere at this period	

1250 BCE — 1150 — 1050 — 950 — 850 — 750 BCE

c.1000: Wet rice cultivation introduced to Korea from China

c.770: Western Zhou period ends with collapse of centralized power

WRITING, COUNTING, AND CALENDARS

The Greek inscription
(above) is an offering of thanks to Asclepius, the god of healing.

THE INTERTWINED DEVELOPMENT of writing and counting was closely related to the advent of agriculture and the need to record and tally stored goods, livestock, and commercial transactions. The precursors of the first known writing and numerical systems were clay counting tokens, used in Sumeria from c.3400 BCE to record quantities of stored goods. They were eventually sealed in clay envelopes, and marked on the outside with signs indicating their contents – the first written symbols. Within a thousand years, writing and numerical systems had spread throughout West Asia (they evolved separately in China and Central America), bringing a revolutionary change in human consciousness. The ability to count in abstract enabled humans to measure, assess, record, and evaluate their world – calendrical systems, weights and measures, coinage, astronomical calculations, and geometry all followed. Writing became a powerful tool of government, a means of communicating over increasing distances, codifying laws, and recording myths and history.

The evolution and spread of major scripts

The earliest symbolic records, of economic transactions, were used in Sumeria from c.3400 BCE, and gradually evolved into a pictographic script, where pictures represented words. Cuneiform writing (made by impressing a wet clay tablet with a stylus) was used to record a variety of languages, and spread throughout West Asia. The system eventually became more complex, and written symbols also came to stand for concepts or sounds. Egyptian hieroglyphics probably developed under Sumerian influence, though the system was unique. Chinese pictographic writing developed independently, as did the Zapotec and Maya systems in Central America. Ugaritic alphabetic cuneiform (c.1400 BCE) was the precursor of the Phoenician alphabet, adapted by the Greeks in the 8th century BCE.

This inscription in Egyptian hieratic is a record of a trading transaction. Hieratic was a form of cursive script, written with ink and a reed brush.

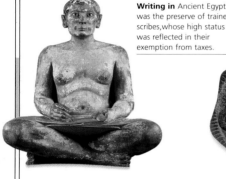

Writing in Ancient Egypt was the preserve of trained scribes, whose high status was reflected in their exemption from taxes.

This glyph from Central America, represents the word 'grass'.

Oracle bones, the earliest examples of writing from Shang dynasty China, record predictions made by interpreting cracks in the bones.

The inscriptions on this black basalt pillar are the most complete example of the lawcode of Hammurabi, king of Babylonia (c.1790–1750 BCE), who is depicted on the top of the pillar.

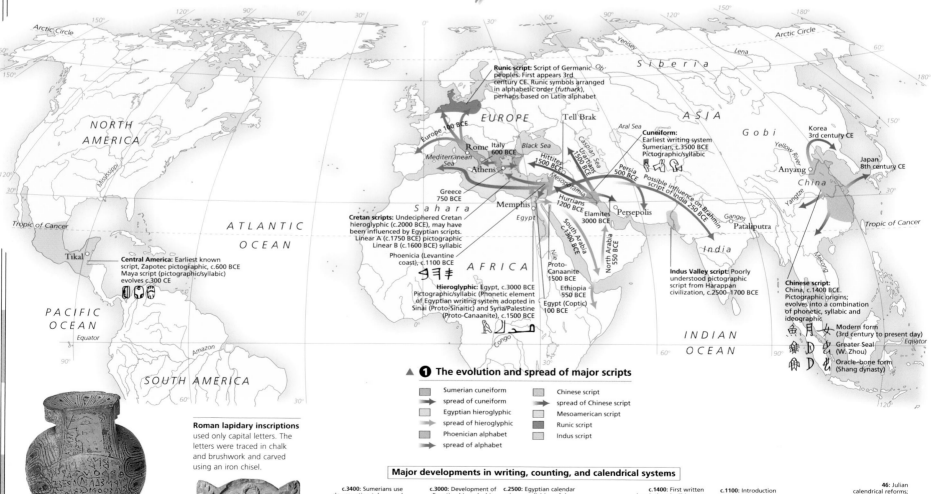

Runic script: Script of Germanic peoples. First appears 3rd century CE. Runic symbols arranged in alphabetic order (*futhark*), perhaps based on Latin alphabet

Cuneiform: Earliest writing system Sumerian, c.3500 BCE Pictographic/syllabic

Cretan scripts: Undeciphered Cretan hieroglyphic (c.2000 BCE), may have been influenced by Egyptian scripts. Linear A (c.1750 BCE) pictographic Linear B (c.1600 BCE) syllabic

Central America: Earliest known script, Zapotec pictographic, c.600 BCE Maya script (pictographic/syllabic) evolves c.300 CE

Hieroglyphic: Egypt, c.3000 BCE Pictographic/syllabic (Phonetic element of Egyptian writing system adopted in Sinai (Proto-Sinaitic) and Syria/Palestine (Proto-Canaanite), c.1500 BCE

Indus Valley script: Poorly understood pictographic script from Harappan civilization, c.2500–1700 BCE

Chinese script: China, c.1400 BCE. Pictographic origins; evolves into a combination of phonetic, syllabic and ideographic

Modern form (3rd century to present day)
Greater Seal (W. Zhou)
Oracle-bone form (Shang dynasty)

Europe 100 BCE
Rome Italy 600 BCE
Athens
Greece 750 BCE
Phoenicia (Levantine coast) c.1100 BCE
Proto-Canaanite 1500 BCE
Ethiopia 550 BCE
Egypt (Coptic) 100 BCE
Memphis
Egypt
Tell Brak
Hittites 1500 BCE
Hurrians 1200 BCE
Elamites 3000 BCE
Persepolis
Persia 500 BCE
South Arabia c.800 BCE
North Arabia 550 BCE
Urartians 1500 BCE
Possible influence on Brahmin script of India 250 BCE
Korea 3rd century CE
Japan 8th century CE
Anyang
China
Pataliputra
India

Tikal

▲ ❶ The evolution and spread of major scripts

Sumerian cuneiform
→ spread of cuneiform
Egyptian hieroglyphic
→ spread of hieroglyphic
Phoenician alphabet
→ spread of alphabet
Chinese script
→ spread of Chinese script
Mesoamerican script
Runic script
Indus script

Roman lapidary inscriptions used only capital letters. The letters were traced in chalk and brushwork and carved using an iron chisel.

This perfume jar from Corinth in Greece is inscribed in the alphabetic script which was adapted from the Phoenician, and used in Greece from the 8th century BCE.

Major developments in writing, counting, and calendrical systems

c.3400: Sumerians use clay counting tokens and first written symbols

c.3000: Development of Egyptian hieroglyphic writing system

c.2500: Egyptian calendar pioneers division of day into 24 units

c.1400: First written inscriptions in China, on Shang oracle bones

c.1100: Introduction of Phoenician alphabet

46: Julian calendrical reforms; 'Year of Confusion' is 445 days long

| 3500 BCE | 3000 BCE | 2500 BCE | 2000 BCE | 1500 BCE | 1000 BCE | 500 BCE | 1 CE |

c.3250: Earliest writing in the world; clay pictographic tablets from Tell Brak, Syria

c.2000: Appearance of Cretan hieroglyphic writing

c.600: First Greek coins
c.600: First Central American script (Zapotec)
c.500: First coins used in China

c.500: Hebrews evolve use of 7-day weeks

The Rhind mathematical papyrus
dates to c.1575 BCE. It demonstrates that the Egyptians had some understanding of the properties of right-angled triangles.

The evolution of numerical systems

Wooden tally sticks were used over 30,000 years ago, probably to record numbers of animals killed. From c.3400 BCE the Sumerians used clay counting tokens, of various sizes and shapes to represent order of magnitude, and evolved the first written numbering system. As humans count using their fingers and toes, most systems used base 10, while Mayans, Aztecs, and Celts chose base 20. The Sumerian and Babylonian use of base 60 (still evident in our use of 60 minutes and seconds, and 360 degrees) remains mysterious. Alphabetic counting systems, used by Greeks, Hebrews, and Arabs, wrote numbers by using letters. The concept of zero, and the positional numbering system, was an Indian invention.

This Babylonian mathematical text with cuneiform numbers dates to c.500 BCE. The use of the sexagesimal system was an important factor in the development of Babylonian astronomy.

SEE ALSO:

North America: pp.122–123

South America: pp.146–147

West Asia: pp.222–223

North and East Asia: pp.258–259

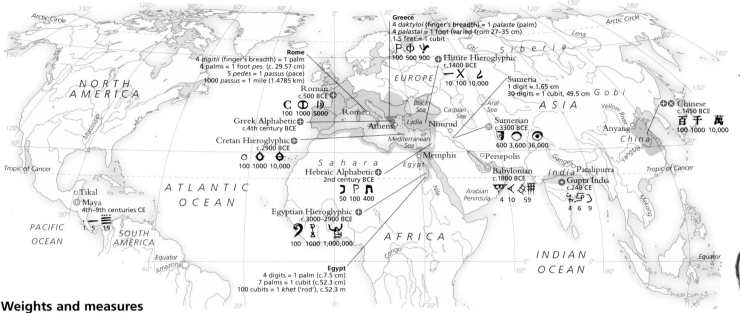

② The evolution of numerical systems

Earliest known date of counting system

Numerical system		Regions
additive		Roman
multiplicative		Hittite
positional		Egyptian
		Greek
Base		Hebraic
Base 10		Gupta India
Base 20		Chinese
Base 60		

Heracles is shown stringing a bow on this Theban coin (c.446–426 BCE).

This Athenian coin is known as a tetradrachm (479 BCE). The owl was a symbol of Athena.

Weights and measures

The parts of the body, such as the fingers, palms, and toes, were used by all ancient civilizations for shorter units of measurement. Greater distances reflect the nature of the civilization; the Roman *passus* (1.6 m) reflects the Romans' road system and marching armies, the Greek stadion originates in the length of an athletic race track.

Bronze scales, using a simple balance system, were used extensively in Ancient Rome. Weights were verified by officials.

Mesopotamian weights were calculated according to the sexagesimal system. This 1st-millennium relief from Nimrud, Iraq, shows tribute being weighed.

Coinage

As trade networks expanded, barter, which depended on long negotiations, became increasingly inconvenient. The need for an agreed system of equivalences of value led to the invention of coins, metal objects with a constant weight, marked with the official stamp of a public authority. The Greeks of Lydia developed the system in the 7th century BCE, and it was rapidly adopted elsewhere.

This early Egyptian counting stick was found with pieces of metal, used as money.

Fragments of a bronze Celtic lunisolar calendar have been found at Coligny, France. Pegs may have been inserted into holes to mark the passage of the days.

The evolution of calendrical systems

The development of calendars was linked to religion and the need to predict days of ritual significance, such as the summer solstice. Calendrical systems developed through astronomical observation and record-keeping, and were dependent on both writing and numeracy. All calendars had to resolve the incommensurate cycles of days, lunations and solar years, usually by intercalating extra days or months at regular intervals. Eras were assessed by different means, most commonly from the regnal years of monarchy, or from the year of birth of significant individuals, such as Buddha or Christ.

Light penetrates the neolithic tomb at Newgrange in Ireland at sunrise on 21 December, an example of the astronomical significance of many stone alignments.

The Babylonians made systematic observations of the setting and rising of the planet Venus at the city of Kish, recorded on the Venus tablet (c.1700 BCE).

③ The evolution and spread of calendrical systems

- lunar (months are kept in step with lunar cycle by intercalating days)
- solar (lunar cycle is ignored; years are kept in step with the Sun by intercalating days)
- lunisolar (month is geared to lunar cycle; extra months are intercalated to key year synchronized with sun)
- wandering year (fixed number of days; lunar and solar cycles abandoned)
- extent of Roman Empire in 2nd century CE

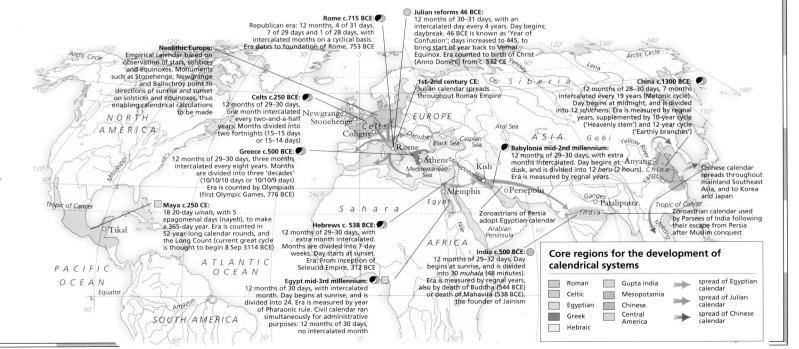

Core regions for the development of calendrical systems

Roman	Gupta India	spread of Egyptian calendar
Celtic	Mesopotamia	spread of Julian calendar
Egyptian	Chinese	spread of Chinese calendar
Greek	Central America	
Hebraic		

THE WORLD 750–500 BCE

THE CIVILIZATIONS OF EURASIA, although they only occupied a small portion of the Earth's surface, now lay in a more or less continuous belt from the Mediterranean to China. Both trade and cultural contact were well-established; understanding of iron metallurgy had spread from the Middle East as far as China, and by the 6th century BCE Chinese silk was beginning to appear in Europe, marking the beginning of 1,500 years of trans-Asian trade. All these civilizations, however, were increasingly subjected to incursions by tribes of nomadic pastoralists who were rapidly spreading across Central Asia, eastern Europe, and Siberia. By 500 BCE, the Classical Age in Greece – a high point in the history of western civilization – was beginning. It was to have a profound impact on European political institutions, art, architecture, drama, and philosophy. In 505 BCE, the *polis* of Athens initiated radical political reforms and became the birthplace of democracy.

Europe

As the city-states of Greece became more prosperous, their civic pride was expressed through magnificent buildings. Greek colonies, which stretched from the Black Sea to the Iberian Peninsula, were major trading centres, importing raw materials and food supplies in exchange for manufactures, such as pottery. The expanding European population moved into more marginal areas, using iron tools for land clearance and agriculture. Northern Europe was occupied by Celtic and Germanic peoples, whose tribal societies centred on princely graves and hill-top fortresses.

Revelry is a common theme in the tomb frescoes of the Etruscans, whose urban civilization reached its height in 6th-century BCE Italy.

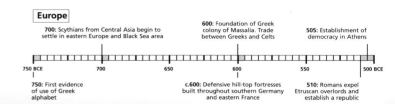

Europe

700: Scythians from Central Asia begin to settle in eastern Europe and Black Sea area

600: Foundation of Greek colony of Massalia. Trade between Greeks and Celts

505: Establishment of democracy in Athens

750 BCE   700   650   600   550   500 BCE

750: First evidence of use of Greek alphabet

c.600: Defensive hill-top fortresses built throughout southern Germany and eastern France

510: Romans expel Etruscan overlords and establish a republic

BABYLONIAN MAP

The earliest known graphic representations of parts of the Earth are the maps engraved by the Babylonians on clay tablets. On this tablet from around 600 BCE the Earth is depicted as a disc surrounded by water. The Euphrates River is shown as two curved lines and small circles carry the names of cities and adjacent countries in cuneiform script.

The Babylonians oriented their maps with Babylon at the centre.

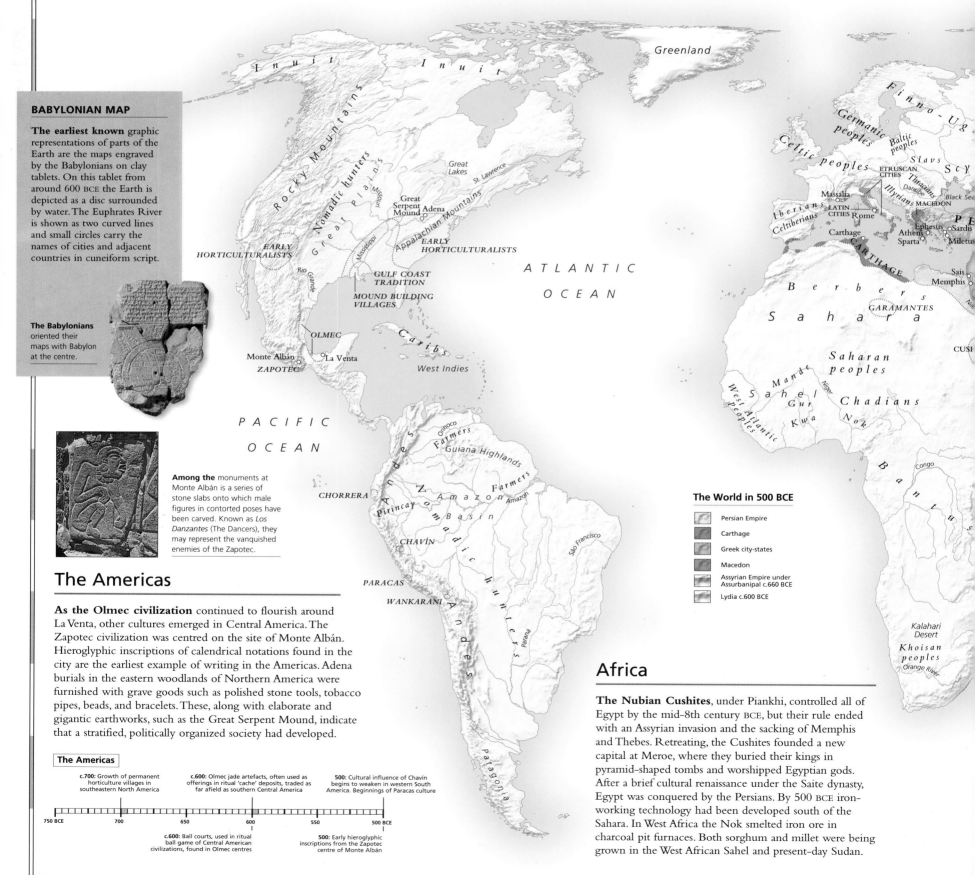

Among the monuments at Monte Albán is a series of stone slabs onto which male figures in contorted poses have been carved. Known as *Los Danzantes* (The Dancers), they may represent the vanquished enemies of the Zapotec.

The Americas

As the Olmec civilization continued to flourish around La Venta, other cultures emerged in Central America. The Zapotec civilization was centred on the site of Monte Albán. Hieroglyphic inscriptions of calendrical notations found in the city are the earliest example of writing in the Americas. Adena burials in the eastern woodlands of Northern America were furnished with grave goods such as polished stone tools, tobacco pipes, beads, and bracelets. These, along with elaborate and gigantic earthworks, such as the Great Serpent Mound, indicate that a stratified, politically organized society had developed.

The Americas

c.700: Growth of permanent horticulture villages in southeastern North America

c.600: Olmec jade artefacts, often used as offerings in ritual 'cache' deposits, traded as far afield as southern Central America

500: Cultural influence of Chavín begins to weaken in western South America. Beginnings of Paracas culture

750 BCE   700   650   600   550   500 BCE

c.600: Ball courts, used in ritual ball game of Central American civilizations, found in Olmec centres

500: Early hieroglyphic inscriptions from the Zapotec centre of Monte Albán

The World in 500 BCE

- Persian Empire
- Carthage
- Greek city-states
- Macedon
- Assyrian Empire under Assurbanipal c.660 BCE
- Lydia c.600 BCE

Africa

The Nubian Cushites, under Piankhi, controlled all of Egypt by the mid-8th century BCE, but their rule ended with an Assyrian invasion and the sacking of Memphis and Thebes. Retreating, the Cushites founded a new capital at Meroe, where they buried their kings in pyramid-shaped tombs and worshipped Egyptian gods. After a brief cultural renaissance under the Saite dynasty, Egypt was conquered by the Persians. By 500 BCE iron-working technology had been developed south of the Sahara. In West Africa the Nok smelted iron ore in charcoal pit furnaces. Both sorghum and millet were being grown in the West African Sahel and present-day Sudan.

THE FIRST COINS

The use of metals to make payments can be traced back more than 4000 years, but standardization and certification in the form of coinage did not arrive until the 7th century BCE. The first coins were issued by the Lydians of western Anatolia. They consisted of bean-sized pieces of electrum – a natural alloy of gold and silver – with punchmarks testifying to their weight and therefore their value in payments. By 570 BCE coinage had spread west to Greece and east to Persia. It was invented independently in China and India c.500 BCE.

The first Chinese coins, introduced c.500 BCE, were miniature bronze hoes or spades (*left*), copies of the tools that previously had been used for barter. Early Greek coins carried stamped designs, many derived from the animal world (*right*).

West Asia

Assyria's enemies united to overthrow the empire in 612 BCE, and for a brief period Babylon again enjoyed ascendancy in Mesopotamia. This changed with the arrival of the Medes and Persians, Indo-Europeans from Central Asia. In 550 BCE the Persian king, Cyrus the Great, defeated the Medes and united the two peoples, founding the Achaemenid Empire, which became the largest state the world had yet seen, stretching from the Nile to the Indus. A later Persian ruler, Darius I, consolidated imperial rule: subject peoples were divided into provinces, or satrapies; taxes were levied and the construction of the Royal Road from Sardis to Susa facilitated fast, efficient communications.

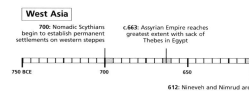

The king is the focus of the decoration of the palace at Persepolis, ceremonial capital of the Achaemenid Persians. Reliefs depict his court and processions of tribute-bearers from his empire.

West Asia

700: Nomadic Scythians begin to establish permanent settlements on western steppes
c.663: Assyrian Empire reaches greatest extent with sack of Thebes in Egypt
604: Nebuchadnezzar II rebuilds Babylon and captures Jerusalem
539: Cyrus takes Babylon, and Babylonian Empire, without bloodshed

750 BCE — 700 — 650 — 600 — 550 — 500 BCE

612: Nineveh and Nimrud are sacked by Babylonians and Medes; end of Assyrian Empire
c.550: Cyrus the Great of Persia defeats Medes and founds Achaemenid Empire
521: Persian Empire reaches greatest extent, under Darius I

East Asia

With the beginning of the Eastern Zhou period in 770 BCE, China experienced several centuries of conflict as many former vassals of the Zhou competed for supremacy. This was a period of technological and cultural change. The widespread use of iron tools improved the productivity of the land and led to a marked population increase. At the same time new ideas stimulated feverish intellectual debate. The teaching of Confucius was a practical, ethical guide to good government and social behaviour, whereas Taoism was a philosophy based on a mystical faith in natural forces.

During this period Chinese chariots were elaborately decorated to enhance their appearance in battle. This bronze bull's head chariot fitting is inlaid with gold.

East Asia

c.650: Introduction of iron technology to China. Silk painting, lacquerwork, and ceramics become highly skilled
605: Birth of Lao-tzu, founder of Taoism
551: Birth of Confucius
c.500: Bronze coinage introduced in China

750 BCE — 700 — 650 — 600 — 550 — 500 BCE

c.500: Iron-casting used to manufacture huge quantities of tools and weapons in China

In India, early traditions, dating back before 2000 BCE, evolved into Hinduism. This stone statue portrays an early deity, Surya, the sun god.

South Asia

From about 1500 BCE the peoples of central north India began to adopt a sedentary life and expanded eastwards to settle the Ganges plain. By the 7th century BCE, a patchwork of small states had emerged in northern India. Some were tribal republics, others absolute monarchies, but their common roots – apparent in the Hindu religion and the caste system – underpinned their religious and social organization. The Afghan region of Gandhara and the Indus Valley were absorbed into the Persian Empire in the late 6th century BCE.

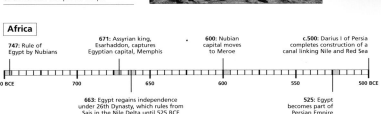

From Meroe, the Cushites were able to maintain their rule over the middle Nile until the 4th century CE, while Egypt suffered a series of invasions. This stone ram lies among the ruins of a Meroitic temple at Naqa.

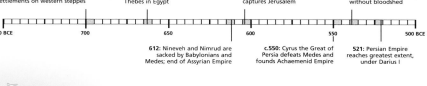

Africa

747: Rule of Egypt by Nubians
671: Assyrian king, Esarhaddon, captures Egyptian capital, Memphis
600: Nubian capital moves to Meroe
c.500: Darius I of Persia completes construction of a canal linking Nile and Red Sea

750 BCE — 700 — 650 — 600 — 550 — 500 BCE

663: Egypt regains independence under 26th Dynasty, which rules from Sais in the Nile Delta until 525 BCE
525: Egypt becomes part of Persian Empire

South Asia

c.600: 16 Aryan kingdoms are spread across northern India
c.540: Birth of Mahavira, founder of Jain religion

750 BCE — 700 — 650 — 600 — 550 — 500 BCE

c.566: Birth of Buddha, who forsakes life of a nobleman to seek enlightenment through asceticism and good conduct
533: Kingdom of Gandhara becomes satrapy of Persia

THE ORIGINS OF ORGANIZED RELIGION

The development of a priestly class, as here at Sumer, was central in the organization of religious practice as a core social activity.

THE 6TH CENTURY BCE has been called an axial period in the development of religion. Judaism, Hinduism, and Taoism were well established. Reformers such as Deutero-Isaiah, Mahavira, Siddhartha Gautama, and Confucius were at work. Around the Mediterranean, a melting-pot of local cults was forming the roots of European Classical civilization, while in the Americas the first urban cultures brought with them organized religion. And frequently, it was the adoption by political rulers of a particular religion which would ensure its longevity and evolution – as in Buddhism, Confucianism, and, later, Christianity – into a world religion.

The development of organized religion

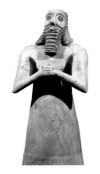

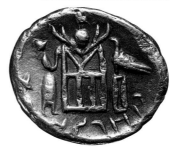

Zoroastrian worship focused on a supreme being, Ahura Mazda, who was widely worshipped at fire altars.

The development of organized religions was linked to the emergence of urban civilization. The earliest known state religion was that of Sumer in the 3rd millennium BCE, and the oldest coherent mythology was that of Egypt, from the 2nd millennium BCE. By the 1st millennium a range of common characteristics and practices had emerged from local cults to acquire the trappings of organized religion: shamans became priests; myth became doctrine; sacrifice became ceremony; ancestor worship was celebrated in increasingly rich and elaborate burial practices and grandiose monumental architecture.

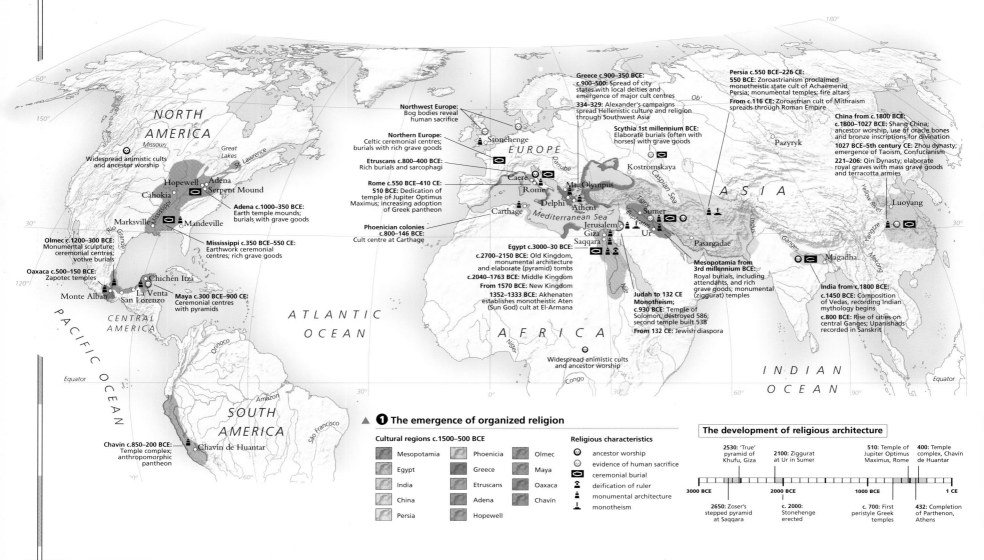

NORTH AMERICA
Widespread animistic cults and ancestor worship
Great Lakes
St Lawrence
Missouri
Hopewell
Adena
Serpent Mound
Cahokia
Adena c.1000–350 BCE: Earthwork temple mounds; burials with grave goods
Marksville
Mandeville
Mississippi
Rio Grande
Olmec c.1200–300 BCE: Monumental sculpture; ceremonial centres; votive burials
Mississippi c.350 BCE–550 CE: Earthwork ceremonial centres; rich grave goods
Oaxaca c.500–150 BCE: Zapotec temples
Chichén Itzá
Monte Albán
La Venta
San Lorenzo
Maya c.300 BCE–900 CE: Ceremonial centres with pyramids
CENTRAL AMERICA
PACIFIC OCEAN
ATLANTIC OCEAN
Orinoco
Amazon
SOUTH AMERICA
São Francisco
Chavín c.850–200 BCE: Temple complex; anthropomorphic pantheon
Chavín de Huantar
Equator
Northwest Europe: Bog bodies reveal human sacrifice
Northern Europe: Celtic ceremonial centres; burials with rich grave goods
Stonehenge
EUROPE
Etruscans c.800–400 BCE: Rich burials and sarcophagi
Rome c.550 BCE–410 CE: 510 BCE: Dedication of temple of Jupiter Optimus Maximus; increasing adoption of Greek pantheon
Caere
Rome
Danube
Phoenician colonies c.800–146 BCE: Cult centre at Carthage
Carthage
Delphi
Mt. Olympus
Athens
Mediterranean Sea
Greece c.900–350 BCE: c.900–500: Spread of city states with local deities and emergence of major cult centres
334–329: Alexander's campaigns spread Hellenistic culture and religion through Southwest Asia
Scythia 1st millennium BCE: Elaborate burials (often with horses) with grave goods
Kostromskaya
Caspian Sea
Ob'
Persia c.550 BCE–226 CE: 550 BCE: Zoroastrianism proclaimed monotheistic state cult of Achaemenid Persia; monumental temples; fire altars
From c.116 CE: Zoroastrian cult of Mithraism spreads through Roman Empire
Pazyryk
ASIA
Tigris
Euphrates
Sumer
Ur
Jerusalem
Giza
Saqqara
Nile
Egypt c.3000–30 BCE: c.2700–2150 BCE: Old Kingdom, monumental architecture and elaborate (pyramid) tombs
c.2040–1763 BCE: Middle Kingdom
From 1570 BCE: New Kingdom
1352–1333 BCE: Akhenaten establishes monotheistic Aten (Sun God) cult at El-Armana
Pasargadae
Indus
Mesopotamia from 3rd millennium BCE: Royal burials, including attendants, and rich grave goods; monumental (ziggurat) temples
Judah to 132 CE Monotheism; c.930 BCE: Temple of Solomon, destroyed 586; second temple built 538
From 132 CE: Jewish diaspora
AFRICA
Niger
Congo
Widespread animistic cults and ancestor worship
Ganges
Magadha
India from c.1800 BCE: c.1450 BCE: Composition of Vedas, recording Indian mythology begins
c.800 BCE: Rise of cities on central Ganges; Upanishads recorded in Sanskrit
China from c.1800 BCE: c.1800–1027 BCE: Shang China; ancestor worship, use of oracle bones and bronze inscriptions for divination
1027 BCE–5th century CE: Zhou dynasty; emergence of Taoism, Confucianism
221–206: Qin Dynasty; elaborate royal graves with mass grave goods and terracotta armies
Yellow River
Yangtze
Mekong
Luoyang
INDIAN OCEAN
Equator

1 The emergence of organized religion

Cultural regions c.1500–500 BCE

Mesopotamia, Egypt, India, China, Persia, Phoenicia, Greece, Etruscans, Adena, Hopewell, Olmec, Maya, Oaxaca, Chavin

Religious characteristics

- ancestor worship
- evidence of human sacrifice
- ceremonial burial
- deification of ruler
- monumental architecture
- monotheism

The development of religious architecture

3000 BCE – 2000 BCE – 1000 BCE – 1 CE

- 2650: Zoser's stepped pyramid at Saqqara
- 2530: 'True' pyramid of Khufu, Giza
- c. 2000: Stonehenge erected
- 2100: Ziggurat at Ur in Sumer
- c. 700: First peristyle Greek temples
- 510: Temple of Jupiter Optimus Maximus, Rome
- 432: Completion of Parthenon, Athens
- 400: Temple complex, Chavin de Huantar

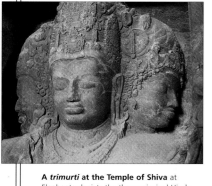

A *trimurti* at the Temple of Shiva at Elephanta depicts the three principal Hindu divinities, Shiva, Vishnu, and Brahma.

Early religion in South Asia

The religion of the ancient Aryan tribes is known largely from the hymns of the *Rig Veda*, and the *Vedas*, *Brahmanas*, and *Upanishads*. It focused on sacrifices to a pantheon of deities and semigods quite different to those of today. From its core region in Brahmavarta, Vedic Hinduism spread over much of India before the rise of Buddhism and Jainism, both of which developed in northeastern India in reaction to the excesses of Aryan religious practices. These faiths emphasized *ahimsa* (non-violence), meditation, and the suppression of desire for worldly possessions.

2 Religions of South Asia

- UDICHYA — broad cultural region recognised by ancient Aryans
- MAGADHA — other regions
- *Yamuna* — sacred river
- core area of Buddhism and Jainism
- Ashokan rock and pillar edicts

Early religion in South Asia

1400 BCE – 1000 – 600 – 200 BCE

- c.1550: Aryans overwhelm Indus valley civilization and settle northern India
- c.800: Rise of urban culture in Ganges valley
- c.600: Rise to dominance of Magadha
- 6th century: Life of Mahavira, founder of Jainism
- 566: Birth of Siddartha Gautama, founder of Buddhism
- 322: Chandragupta founds Mauryan dynasty
- 272–232: Reign of Ashoka, who promulgates Buddhism as state religion

Legendary descent of the Buddha from heaven
563: Birthplace
534: Great Renunciation
Kampilya
Samkashya
Kanauj
Lumbini
Shravasti
Kapilavatthu
Ayodhya
Kusinagara
483: Attainment of Nirvana
KOSHALA
Yamuna
Ganges
Vaishali
Pataliputra
Champa
Prayaga
Sarnath
MAGADHA
Nalanda
Kaushambi
Benares
Rajgir
Bodh Gaya
Gaya
ANGA
200 km
200 miles
528: Sermon in the Deer Park
528: Attainment of Enlightenment

500 km
500 miles
Taxila
UDICHYA
SAPTA SINDHAVA
Initial core Aryan region
BHARATA-VARSHA
Field of battle in epic Mahabharata war
KURU-KSHETRA
Hastinapura
Himalayas
Home city of Rama, hero of Ramayana epic
Area visited by Gautama Buddha and Mahavira
see inset
Yamuna
Ganges
Indus
Mathura
Ayodhya
Thar Desert
PRATICHYA
MADHYAMA-DISH
Kashi
Pataliputra
Rajagriha
MAGADHA
Brahmaputra
Later core Aryan region
Bodh Gaya
Core region of Mauryan Empire
PRACHYA
Ujjayini
Narmada
DAKSINA-PATHA
Deccan
Tamralipti
Godavari
Eastern Ghats
KALINGA
Bay of Bengal
Western Ghats
Krishna
Ashoka's bloody conquest of this region leads him to foreswear war and adopt Buddhism
Arabian Sea
Kaveri
Lanka (Simhala)
Anuradhapura

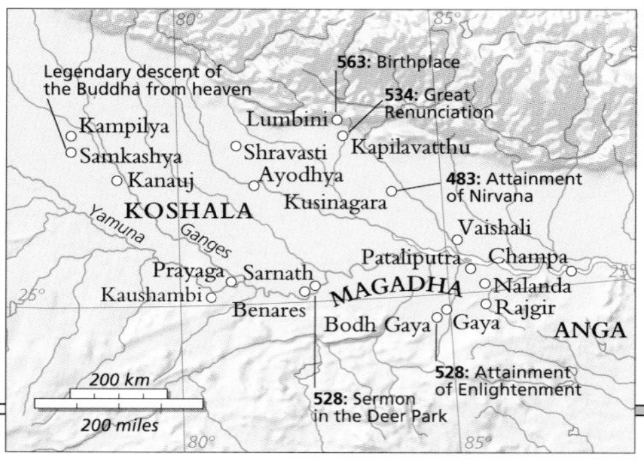

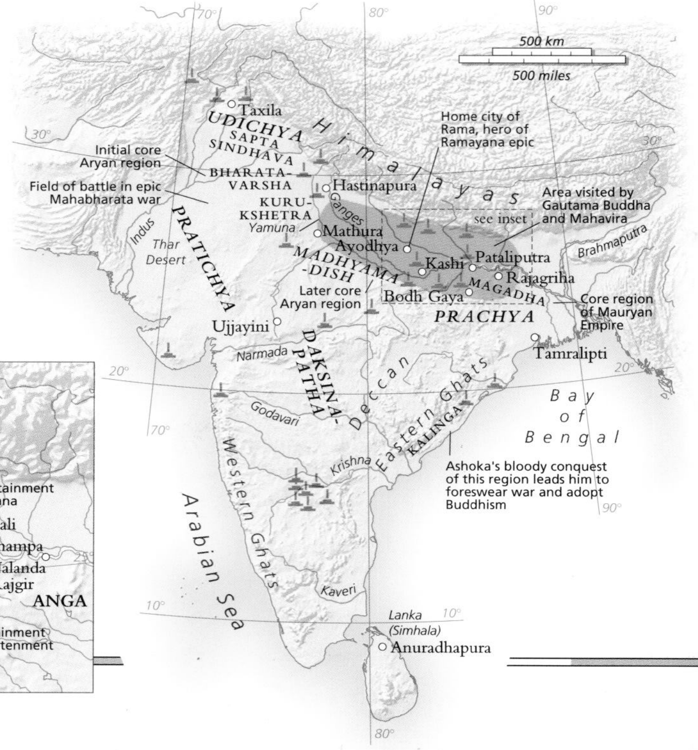

Religions of the Mediterranean

The Mediterranean world in the 1st millennium BCE was the home of a range of discrete cultures, each supporting its own religious beliefs. However, many of these shared striking similarities in mythology, the character and nature of their pantheons of gods, and in religious practice and observance. Rivalry, warfare, and trade created an interaction of influences and cross-fertilizations, and with the rise of Classical Greece, Hellenistic culture and then Rome, certain local beliefs and practices became widespread.

Zeus (Jupiter for the Romans) was the supreme Greek deity.

Greece

The Greek mythological pantheon, developed during the Mycenaean period, was described by writers such as Homer and became, during the Classic Greek period, a central force in Greek life. Each city-state worshipped favoured cults, but the emergence of oracles and other cult centres (such as Mount Olympus) codified a pan-Hellenic religious tradition which was spread widely by colonization and the campaigns of Alexander the Great *(see pp.40–41).*

SEE ALSO:

Africa: pp.160–161

Europe: pp.174–179

West Asia: pp.220–221

South and Southeast Asia: pp.242–243

North and East Asia: pp.258–259

❸ The Mediterranean cults ▶

Cult centres
- Egyptian
- Greek
- other

Ares   main divinity worshipped
→ spread of the cult of Cybele
→ spread of the Greek Pantheon
→ spread of Mithraism

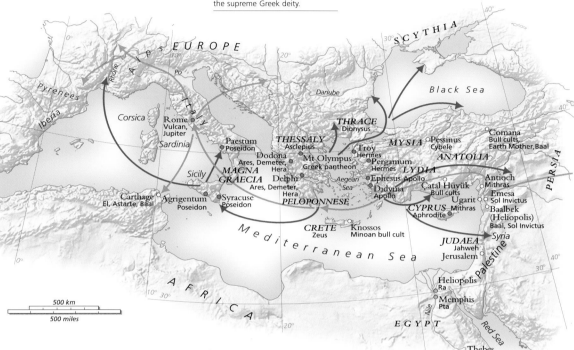

A dead man kneels before Anubis, goddess of mummification. Life after death was central to Egyptian theology, celebrated through a series of elaborate rituals.

The Jewish candelabra (menorah) symbolizes the eternal light (ner tamid) which burned in the first Temple of Solomon.

Judaism

Originating around 1200 BCE with the worship of Jahweh, Judaism remained almost unique in being monotheistic. Formalized as a state religion of Israel during the reign of David (c.1000 BCE), the religion survived exile and persecution to form the seedbed of Christianity.

This Mycenaean ritual sprinkler takes the form of a bull's head.

Egypt

A detailed mythology and pantheon permeated Ancient Egyptian life and thought, and is recorded abundantly in votive statuary and hieroglyphic tomb paintings. The hierarchy and character of Egyptian cosmology probably influenced the development of the Mycenaean and Greek pantheon.

Bull cults

Bull worshipping was widespread in the Mediterranean region, from Çatal Hüyük (c.7000 BCE) to the famous Minos cult in Crete (from c.2000 BCE); bulls also played a significant role in Egyptian and Greek mythology.

The demi-god Heracles (Hercules in Latin) formed part of the Greek mythological pantheon adopted by the Romans.

Rome

Rome's pantheon was largely adopted from that of Greece, although certain local cults gained popularity as the empire grew. One of the most widespread was that of Mithras, which spread from Persia to Syria, then throughout the empire; eventually the most influential was Christianity.

Taoism and Confucianism

Taoism developed during the Zhou dynasty as the most widespread of Chinese religions. Based on the worship of ancestors, nature spirits, and sacred places, it was codified by Lao-tzu (605–520 BCE). The philosopher Confucius (551–479 BCE) promulgated a system of filial observance, learning, obedience, and selflessness which became central to Chinese imperial policy and governance. Followers such as Mencius (c.370–300 BCE) ensured that his teachings survived the Warring States period (403–221 BCE).

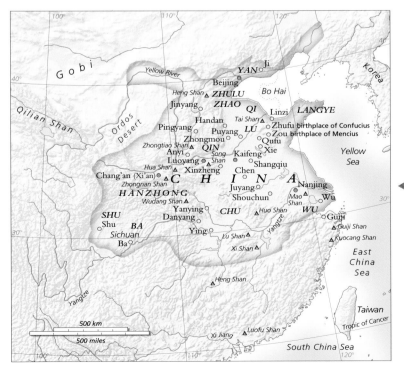

◀ ❹ Taoism and Confucianism

▨ Chinese cultural area c.220 BCE
YAN region associated with development of Taoism
▲ mountain sacred to Taoism

Centres of Confucianism
⊙ Imperial capital
● Qin state capital by c.220 BCE

The teachings of Confucius ensured that even the most lowly could, by ability, correct behaviour, and hard work, aspire to high office.

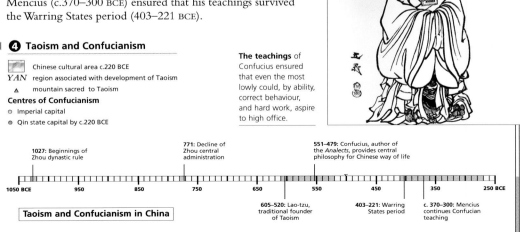

771: Decline of Zhou central administration

1027: Beginnings of Zhou dynastic rule

551–479: Confucius, author of the *Analects*, provides central philosophy for Chinese way of life

| 1050 BCE | 950 | 850 | 750 | 650 | 550 | 450 | 350 | 250 BCE |

Taoism and Confucianism in China

605–520: Lao-tzu, traditional founder of Taoism

403–221: Warring States period

c. 370–300: Mencius continues Confucian teaching

THE WORLD 500–250 BCE

THE 5TH CENTURY BCE was an age of enlightened and innovative thought. It was the climax of the Classical Age in Greece, a period that was remarkable for its art, philosophy, drama, architecture, and political theory. At the same time the Buddhist religion, based on the precepts of renouncing all material desires as practised by Siddhartha Gautama (c.566–486 BCE), was spreading throughout the Indian subcontinent. In China, the teachings of Confucius (551–479 BCE) were concerned with ethical conduct and propriety in human relations. Yet the ensuing centuries were a time of conflict and conquest. From 331–323 BCE Alexander the Great's military conquests created an empire which stretched from Macedon to the Indus. From c.272 BCE the emperor Ashoka absorbed most of the Indian subcontinent into his empire, while in China the Warring States period was a time of violent turmoil.

The shrine of Delphi was the site of the Pythian Games, one of four great athletic festivals that brought Greeks together at set intervals of years.

Europe

In the 5th century BCE, Greece reached the pinnacle of the Classical Age. Athens' conflict with Sparta in the Peloponnesian Wars weakened the Greek city-states, which in the 4th century fell to Philip of Macedon. Under his son, Alexander the Great, who conquered the Persian Empire, Greece became a great imperial power. In Italy, by 264 BCE, Rome was poised to become a world power.

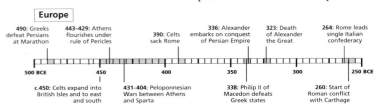

Europe

490: Greeks defeat Persians at Marathon	**443–429:** Athens flourishes under rule of Pericles	**390:** Celts sack Rome	**336:** Alexander embarks on conquest of Persian Empire	**323:** Death of Alexander the Great	**264:** Rome leads single Italian confederacy
500 BCE	450	400		300	250 BCE
c.450: Celts expand into British Isles and to east and south	**431–404:** Peloponnesian Wars between Athens and Sparta		**338:** Philip II of Macedon defeats Greek states	**260:** Start of Roman conflict with Carthage	

THE ARCHIMEDEAN SCREW

Named after Archimedes, the Greek mathematician (287–212 BCE), the Archimedean screw is one of the earliest devices for raising water. It was probably invented in the 7th or 8th century BCE in Mesopotamia. Consisting of a spiral screw revolving inside a close-fitting cylinder, it has been widely used over the centuries for irrigation and land drainage.

This Egyptian terracotta figurine from c.30 BCE shows a slave driving an Archimedean screw by means of a treadmill.

Textiles are one of the earliest and greatest art forms in the Andean region. This strikingly embroidered alpaca-wool piece shows the complex imagery of the Paracas culture.

The Americas

As the influence of Chavín culture waned, distinct local cultures began to emerge in South America. At Paracas in southern Peru cemeteries have been found containing thousands of mummified bodies, wrapped in coloured woven textiles, decorated with mythical beasts and deities which bear a strong Chavín imprint. In North America the Hopewell culture of the eastern woodlands succeeded the Adena, continuing earlier traditions of building elaborate burial mounds and large earthworks.

The Americas

c.500: Paracas culture of southern Peru, famed for brightly coloured textiles, emerges		**c.350:** Beginnings of Nazca culture in southern Peru		
500 BCE	450	400	350	300	250 BCE
	c.400: Early Zapotec culture flourishing around city of Monte Albán		**c.300:** Hopewell culture in eastern North America develops traditions of earlier Adena culture	

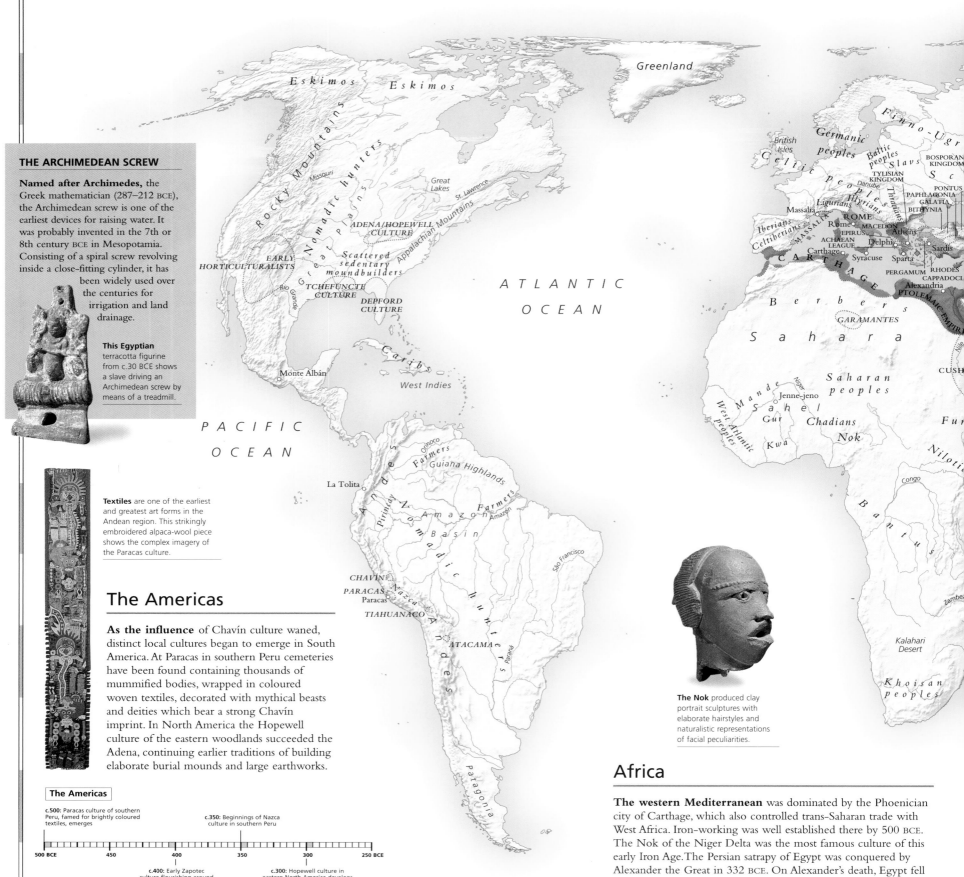

The Nok produced clay portrait sculptures with elaborate hairstyles and naturalistic representations of facial peculiarities.

Africa

The western Mediterranean was dominated by the Phoenician city of Carthage, which also controlled trans-Saharan trade with West Africa. Iron-working was well established there by 500 BCE. The Nok of the Niger Delta was the most famous culture of this early Iron Age. The Persian satrapy of Egypt was conquered by Alexander the Great in 332 BCE. On Alexander's death, Egypt fell to his successor, Ptolemy, who founded the Ptolemaic dynasty.

SEE ALSO:

North America: pp.120–121

South America: pp.144–147

Africa: pp.158–161

Europe: pp.176–179

West Asia: pp.222–223

South and Southeast Asia: pp.240–243

North and East Asia: pp.258–259

Australasia and Oceania: pp.280–281

MAPPING THE FIXED STARS

Ancient astronomers had noticed that the Sun, Moon, and planets did not remain stationary relative to the 'fixed' stars. Instead, over the course of a year, they seemed to pass through a region in the sky occupied by twelve specific constellations that we now call the zodiac, from a Greek term meaning 'circle of animals'. The zodiacal signs appear to have been a Babylonian invention: their first appearance is on a cuneiform horoscope from c.410 BCE.

The twelve signs of the zodiac border a procession of horses and musicians on this 4th-century BCE fresco from a Thracian tomb.

West Asia

In 490 BCE Darius I of Persia sent a punitive expedition against Athens and other cities that had helped Greek cities in Asia Minor to rebel, but it was defeated at Marathon. Over the next century, the Persian empire was weakened by strife and rebellion. In 331 BCE Alexander the Great of Macedon defeated Darius III and brought the Persian Empire to an end. In 323 BCE, Alexander's vast empire was divided among three successors. Most of West Asia became part of the Seleucid Empire. Small local kingdoms were ruled by ethnic or mixed Greek dynasties.

Following his untimely death at the age of 32, Alexander the Great remained a legendary figure in the ancient world. This detail of a 1st-century BCE mosaic from Pompeii shows the young king in battle against the Persians at Issus in 333 BCE.

West Asia

490: Persian expedition to Greece is defeated at Marathon

331: Alexander the Great's victory at the battle of Gaugamela brings Achaemenid Persian Empire to an end

276–272: Ptolemaic Empire expands into Syria during war with Seleucids

| 500 BCE | 450 | 400 | 350 | 300 | 250 BCE |

480: Darius I is succeeded by his son Xerxes who invades Greece, and is defeated at Salamis, Plataea, and Mycale

312: Seleucus gains control of Persia, Syria, and much of Asia Minor; founds the Seleucid dynasty

East Asia

From about 1000 BCE, nomads reared cattle, goats, and sheep, supplemented by farming and hunting, on the Russian steppe. Contemporary burial sites in the Altai Mountains contain leather, wood, fur, textiles, a wooden wagon, and tattooed bodies. Steppe chieftains may have acted as middlemen in trade between China and Europe. From 403–221 BCE, China was locked in internal conflict, with seven major states competing for supremacy. By the 4th century BCE the Qin were starting to assert control over the whole region.

Mythical combat was a favoured theme in the art of the hunting and herding peoples of the Altai region. On this wooden carving, a stag is gripped in the jaws of a griffin.

East Asia

c.450: Burials at Pazyryk and Noin Ula in Siberia give insight into life of steppe nomads

403: Beginning of Warring States period in China

c.350: The crossbow invented in China

256: Qin takes Luoyang area

| 500 BCE | 450 | 400 | 350 | 300 | 250 BCE |

c.480: Death of Confucius, who developed humanistic ethical system

400: Iron-working introduced to Korea

c.350: Qin state develops new political and economic system based on strict system of rewards and punishments

Ashoka recorded his understanding of the moral teachings of Buddhism by inscribing edicts on pillars and stones at suitable sites throughout India, including the Great Stupa at Sanchi.

South Asia

During the 5th century BCE the states of the Ganges plain were eventually absorbed into the kingdom of Magadha. Shortly after Alexander's invasion of northwest India in 327 BCE, Chandragupta Maurya seized the throne and began to expand the empire. By the time of Ashoka (297–232 BCE), the Mauryans ruled most of the subcontinent. Ashoka became repelled by warfare and converted to Buddhism, which, under his patronage, became a major force in India, and beyond.

South Asia

327: Alexander the Great occupies northwest India

260: Ashoka converts to Buddhism

| 500 BCE | 450 | 400 | 350 | 300 | 250 BCE |

320: Chandragupta Maurya controls Magadha kingdom and advances towards Indus and central India

272: Ashoka seizes throne and embarks on further imperial conquests

Africa

c.500: First iron-working in sub-Saharan Africa. Beginning of period of Nok culture in Niger Delta

332: Alexander the Great conquers Egypt. He lays the foundations of Alexandria

302: Ptolemy I declares himself king of Egypt. The Ptolemies took pharaonic titles and worshipped Egyptian deities

| 500 BCE | 450 | 400 | 350 | 300 | 250 BCE |

c.500: Iron-using Bantus begin to spread from Niger to East African lakes region and down west coast of Africa

c.250: Settlement of Jenne-jeno is founded on inland Niger Delta

The World in 250 BCE

- Qin Empire
- Carthage
- Massalia
- Greek city-states
- Macedon
- Mauryan Empire
- Seleucid Empire
- Ptolemaic Empire
- Empire of Alexander the Great 323 BCE

Map labels: Palaeosiberians, Yenisey, Lena, Samoyeds, Ob', Siberia, Steppes, Tungus, Amur, Turks, Altai Mountains, Pazyryk, Noin Ula, EMPIRE OF THE XIONGNU, Hun tribal confederacy, Gobi, Ainu, Japan, CHOSON, Korea, Xianyang, Luoyang, QIN EMPIRE, unified with Qin 221 BCE, Yangtze, Yellow River, GRAEGO BACTRIA, Bactra, Taxila, Tibetans, Himalayas, Ganges, MAURYAN EMPIRE, Pataliputra, Ujjain, Sanchi, Sinitic peoples, Mon-Khmer peoples, Chams, Mekong, Philippine Islands, PACIFIC OCEAN, SMALL STATES, Malays, Sumatra, Borneo, Java, New Guinea, Papuans, INDIAN OCEAN, Australian Aborigines, Darling, New Zealand, Madagascar, Meroe, Semites, HIMYARITES, Cushites, Arabs, Arabian Peninsula, SELEUCID EMPIRE, Persepolis, Babylon, Seleucia, Damascus, SYRIA, Gauganela, Antioch, ARMENIA, MEDIA ATROPATENE, Ecbatana, Caucasian peoples, Caspian Sea, Scythians, Volga, Samoyeds

THE EMPIRE OF ALEXANDER

Alexander the Great, (356–323 BCE), was king of Macedonia and conqueror of a great Afro-Eurasian empire.

THE CONQUESTS OF ALEXANDER took Greek armies to Egypt, Mesopotamia, the Hindu Kush, and India's western borders, and forced Achaemenid Persia, the most powerful empire in the world, into submission. This extraordinary and audacious military feat, accomplished in just ten years, was to create a truly cosmopolitan civilization. Hellenism permeated the cultures of West Asia: some Hellenistic kingdoms survived into the 1st century CE, while Greek remained the official language in many parts of West Asia until the 8th and 9th centuries CE; cities founded in the aftermath of Alexander's conquests, perpetuated the ideals of Greek civilization – some, such as Alexandria, Kandahar, and Tashkent, survive to this day. Ultimately, Alexander opened up new horizons; his followers encountered different peoples and cultures and established trade routes which linked the Mediterranean with East Africa, India, and Asia.

The battle between the Greeks and Persians is depicted with vigorous, high-relief realism on this sarcophagus, found at Sidon.

The conquests of Alexander

① The Empire of Alexander

Empire of Alexander

dependent regions

independent states

→ route of Alexander the Great

→ route of Nearchus

→ return route of Craterus

⚔ major battle

— Persian Royal Road

Alexander succeeded to the Macedonian throne after the assassination of his father, Philip, in 336 BCE. He crossed into Asia in 334 BCE, defeated the Persian provincial army at Granicus and liberated the old Greek cities of Asia Minor. After a brief sojourn in Egypt, he won a spectacular victory over the Persian emperor, Darius III, at Issus and pursued him into Persia, taking the cities of Babylon, Susa, and Persepolis. He pressed on to Bactria and Sogdiana, the eastern outposts of the Persian Empire, and crossed the Hindu Kush. At the River Hyphasis (Beas) his army refused to go further. He died in Babylon in 323 BCE, aged 32.

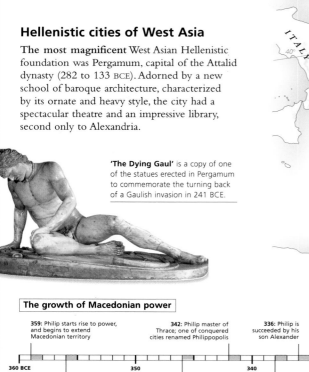

This 1st-century Roman mosaic (based possibly on a Macedonian original) shows Darius III, the Persian emperor, at the battle of Issus (333 BCE). His crushing defeat allowed Alexander to conquer the western half of the Persian Empire.

Hellenistic cities of West Asia

The most magnificent West Asian Hellenistic foundation was Pergamum, capital of the Attalid dynasty (282 to 133 BCE). Adorned by a new school of baroque architecture, characterized by its ornate and heavy style, the city had a spectacular theatre and an impressive library, second only to Alexandria.

'The Dying Gaul' is a copy of one of the statues erected in Pergamum to commemorate the turning back of a Gaulish invasion in 241 BCE.

Scale varies with perspective

3330 km (2070 miles)

8900 km (5530 miles)

Spring 333 BCE: Over 30 cities in Lycia surrender to Alexander; he reaches Gordium, where he cuts Gordian Knot, said to be sign he will rule all Asia

1 Oct 331 BCE: Alexander's second battle with Darius III, whose army includes elephants and scythe-wheeled chariots. Victory for Alexander signals effective end of Persian Empire

May 334 BCE: Alexander visits Troy, where he appropriates so-called sword of Achilles

Feb 324 BCE: Returns to Susa. Mass marriage of Greek soldiers to Persian Brides

Nov 333 BCE: Alexander's first meeting in battle with Darius III. Persian army taken by surprise, suffer heavy losses, and Darius flees

Nov 331 BCE: Following surrender of Babylon, Alexander enters city in triumph

10 Jun 323 BCE: Alexander dies in Babylon

Sep–Nov 332 BCE: Siege of key Persian fortress of Gaza. Alexander wounded by catapult bolt

Midwinter 331 BCE: Alexander visits oracle of Ammon at Siwa; kinship with Ammon-Zeus proclaimed

The growth of Macedonian power

359: Philip starts rise to power, and begins to extend Macedonian territory

342: Philip master of Thrace; one of conquered cities renamed Philippopolis

336: Philip is succeeded by his son Alexander

333: Persian king Darius III is defeated at Issus

326: Alexander reaches Taxila; prevented from advancing into India by revolt of his troops

360 BCE	350	340	330	320 BCE

359: Philip II takes title of king; birth of his son Alexander

346: War in central Greece ends in uneasy peace between Philip and Athens

338: Battle of Chaeronea; Philip II defeats Greek states

332: Alexander founds the city of Alexandria in northern Egypt

331: Decisive defeat of the Persians at battle of Gaugamela

323: Death of Alexander

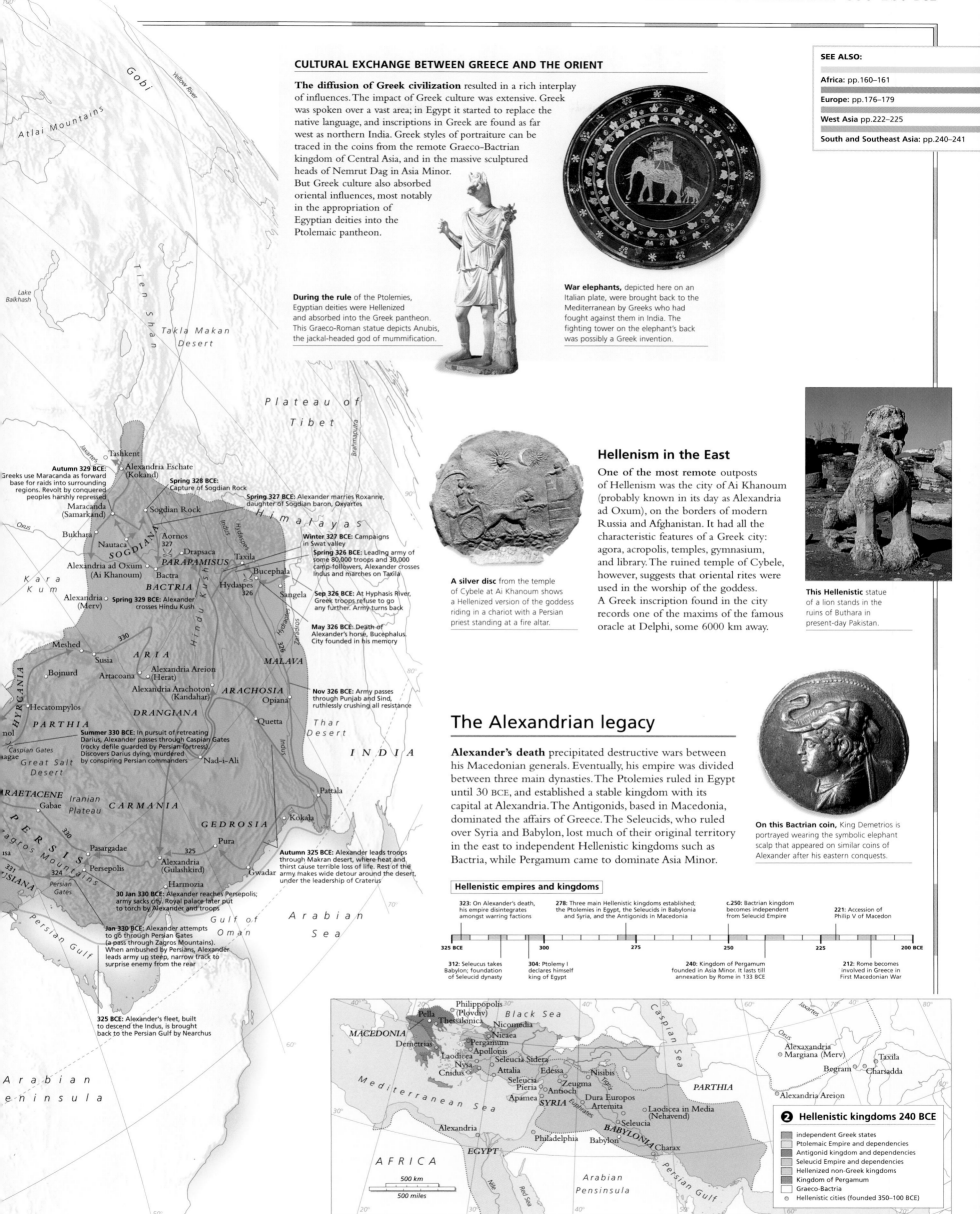

CULTURAL EXCHANGE BETWEEN GREECE AND THE ORIENT

The diffusion of Greek civilization resulted in a rich interplay of influences. The impact of Greek culture was extensive. Greek was spoken over a vast area; in Egypt it started to replace the native language, and inscriptions in Greek are found as far west as northern India. Greek styles of portraiture can be traced in the coins from the remote Graeco-Bactrian kingdom of Central Asia, and in the massive sculptured heads of Nemrut Dag in Asia Minor. But Greek culture also absorbed oriental influences, most notably in the appropriation of Egyptian deities into the Ptolemaic pantheon.

During the rule of the Ptolemies, Egyptian deities were Hellenized and absorbed into the Greek pantheon. This Graeco-Roman statue depicts Anubis, the jackal-headed god of mummification.

War elephants, depicted here on an Italian plate, were brought back to the Mediterranean by Greeks who had fought against them in India. The fighting tower on the elephant's back was possibly a Greek invention.

SEE ALSO:

Africa: pp.160–161

Europe: pp.176–179

West Asia pp.222–225

South and Southeast Asia: pp.240–241

Hellenism in the East

One of the most remote outposts of Hellenism was the city of Ai Khanoum (probably known in its day as Alexandria ad Oxum), on the borders of modern Russia and Afghanistan. It had all the characteristic features of a Greek city: agora, acropolis, temples, gymnasium, and library. The ruined temple of Cybele, however, suggests that oriental rites were used in the worship of the goddess. A Greek inscription found in the city records one of the maxims of the famous oracle at Delphi, some 6000 km away.

A silver disc from the temple of Cybele at Ai Khanoum shows a Hellenized version of the goddess riding in a chariot with a Persian priest standing at a fire altar.

This Hellenistic statue of a lion stands in the ruins of Buthara in present-day Pakistan.

The Alexandrian legacy

Alexander's death precipitated destructive wars between his Macedonian generals. Eventually, his empire was divided between three main dynasties. The Ptolemies ruled in Egypt until 30 BCE, and established a stable kingdom with its capital at Alexandria. The Antigonids, based in Macedonia, dominated the affairs of Greece. The Seleucids, who ruled over Syria and Babylon, lost much of their original territory in the east to independent Hellenistic kingdoms such as Bactria, while Pergamum came to dominate Asia Minor.

On this Bactrian coin, King Demetrios is portrayed wearing the symbolic elephant scalp that appeared on similar coins of Alexander after his eastern conquests.

Hellenistic empires and kingdoms

323: On Alexander's death, his empire disintegrates amongst warring factions

278: Three main Hellenistic kingdoms established; the Ptolemies in Egypt, the Seleucids in Babylonia and Syria, and the Antigonids in Macedonia

c.250: Bactrian kingdom becomes independent from Seleucid Empire

221: Accession of Philip V of Macedon

325 BCE — 300 — 275 — 250 — 225 — 200 BCE

312: Seleucus takes Babylon; foundation of Seleucid dynasty

304: Ptolemy I declares himself king of Egypt

240: Kingdom of Pergamum founded in Asia Minor. It lasts till annexation by Rome in 133 BCE

212: Rome becomes involved in Greece in First Macedonian War

Map labels (main map)

Gobi
Atlai Mountains
Yellow River
Tien Shan
Takla Makan Desert
Lake Balkhash
Plateau of Tibet
Brahmaputra
Jaxartes
Tashkent
Alexandria Eschate (Kokand)

Autumn 329 BCE: Greeks use Maracanda as forward base for raids into surrounding regions. Revolt by conquered peoples harshly repressed

Spring 328 BCE: Capture of Sogdian Rock

Spring 327 BCE: Alexander marries Roxanne, daughter of Sogdian baron, Oxyartes

Maracanda (Samarkand)
Oxus
Bukhara
SOGDIANA
Nautaca
Sogdian Rock
Aornos 327
Himalayas
Alexandria ad Oxum (Ai Khanoum)
Drapsaca
Taxila
PARAPAMISUS
Bactra
Bucephala
BACTRIA
Hydaspes 326
Kara Kum
Alexandria (Merv)
Hindu Kush
Sangela

Spring 329 BCE: Alexander crosses Hindu Kush

Winter 327 BCE: Campaigns in Swat valley

Spring 326 BCE: Leading army of some 80,000 troops and 30,000 camp-followers, Alexander crosses Indus and marches on Taxila

Sep 326 BCE: At Hyphasis River, Greek troops refuse to go any further. Army turns back

May 326 BCE: Death of Alexander's horse, Bucephalus. City founded in his memory

Meshed
ARIA
Susia
MALAVA
Bojnurd
Artacoana
Alexandria Areion (Herat)
Alexandria Arachoton (Kandahar)
ARACHOSIA
Hecatompylos
DRANGIANA
Opiana
PARTHIA
Quetta
nol
Thar Desert
INDIA
Nad-i-Ali

Summer 330 BCE: In pursuit of retreating Darius, Alexander passes through Caspian Gates (rocky defile guarded by Persian fortress). Discovers Darius dying, murdered by conspiring Persian commanders

Nov 326 BCE: Army passes through Punjab and Sind, ruthlessly crushing all resistance

Caspian Gates
aagae
Great Salt Desert
RAETACENE
Gabae
Iranian Plateau
CARMANIA
Pattala
Kokala
GEDROSIA
PERSIS
Pura
agros Mountains
Pasargadae
Alexandria (Gulashkird)
Persepolis
Gwadar
331
324
Harmozia
USIANA
Persian Gates
isa

Autumn 325 BCE: Alexander leads troops through Makran desert, where heat and thirst cause terrible loss of life. Rest of the army makes wide detour around the desert, under the leadership of Craterus

30 Jan 330 BCE: Alexander reaches Persepolis; army sacks city. Royal palace later put to torch by Alexander and troops

Jan 330 BCE: Alexander attempts to go through Persian Gates (a pass through Zagros Mountains). When ambushed by Persians, Alexander leads army up steep, narrow track to surprise enemy from the rear

Persian Gulf
Gulf of Oman
Arabian Sea

325 BCE: Alexander's fleet, built to descend the Indus, is brought back to the Persian Gulf by Nearchus

Arabian Peninsula

Inset map (Hellenistic kingdoms 240 BCE)

MACEDONIA
Philippopolis (Plovdiv)
Pella
Thessalonica
Black Sea
Nicomedia
Demetrias
Nicaea
Pergamum
Apollonis
Caspian Sea
Jaxartes
Oxus
Laodicea
Seleucia Sidera
Attalia
Edessa
Nysa
Nisibis
Alexaxandria Margiana (Merv)
Cnidus
Seleucia Pieria
Zeugma
Taxila
Antioch
Dura Europos
Begram
Apamea
Artemita
PARTHIA
Charsadda
Mediterranean Sea
SYRIA
Tigris
Euphrates
Laodicea in Media (Nehavend)
Alexandria Areion
Alexandria
Seleucia
Philadelphia
BABYLONIA
Babylon
Charax
AFRICA
EGYPT
Nile
Red Sea
Arabian Peninsula
Persian Gulf

❷ Hellenistic kingdoms 240 BCE

- independent Greek states
- Ptolemaic Empire and dependencies
- Antigonid kingdom and dependencies
- Seleucid Empire and dependencies
- Hellenized non-Greek kingdoms
- Kingdom of Pergamum
- Graeco-Bactria
- ○ Hellenistic cities (founded 350–100 BCE)

500 km
500 miles

THE WORLD 250 BCE – 1 CE

BY 1 CE HALF THE GLOBAL population, which had reached about 250 million, lived within three major empires, Rome, Parthia, and Han China. With the addition of the developing kingdoms of northern India and Southeast Asia, urban civilization now existed in a wide swathe across the Old World, from the Iberian Peninsula in the west to Korea in the east, surrounded by nomadic pastoralists, farmers, and increasingly marginalized hunter-gatherers. The opening up of the Silk Road in the 1st century BCE and the discovery of monsoon trade routes across the Indian Ocean led to an unprecedented degree of contact between empires, disseminating both religious and cultural influences. In the New World the increasingly sophisticated Nazca and Moche cultures were developing in Peru, while Teotihuacán in Mexico was poised to become one of the world's most populous cities.

Europe

The Ara Pacis (Altar of Peace) was set up in Rome in 9 BCE to commemorate the pacification of Gaul and Iberia by the Emperor Augustus.

Following the defeat of Carthage in the 2nd century BCE, Rome embarked on a programme of expansion, which extended control to Greek territories in the east and Gaul to the north. In the 1st century BCE, a period of civil wars and rule by military dictators threatened the unity of the growing empire. In 27 BCE Octavian assumed imperial power (and the title Augustus), reuniting the Roman world and ushering in two centuries of stability and prosperity.

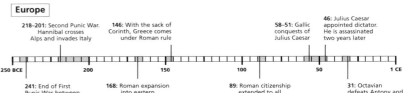

Europe

218–201: Second Punic War. Hannibal crosses Alps and invades Italy	**146:** With the sack of Corinth, Greece comes under Roman rule
241: End of First Punic War between Rome and Carthage	**168:** Roman expansion into eastern Mediterranean begins

58–51: Gallic conquests of Julius Caesar

46: Julius Caesar appointed dictator. He is assassinated two years later

89: Roman citizenship extended to all Italians

31: Octavian defeats Antony and Cleopatra at Actium

250 BCE — 200 — 150 — 100 — 50 — 1 CE

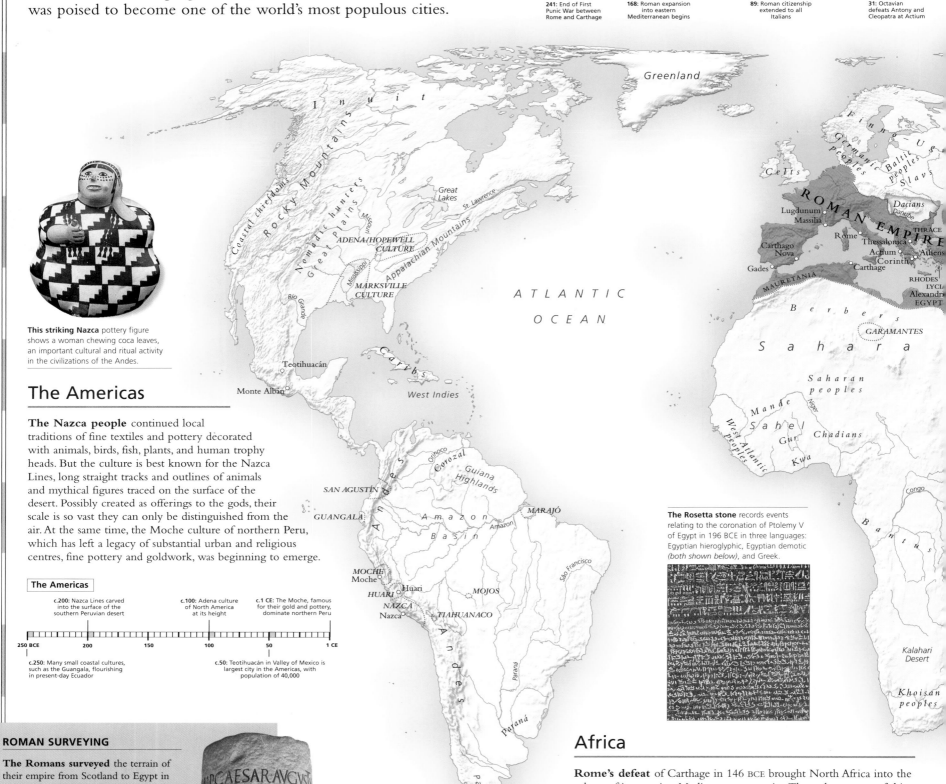

This striking Nazca pottery figure shows a woman chewing coca leaves, an important cultural and ritual activity in the civilizations of the Andes.

The Americas

The Nazca people continued local traditions of fine textiles and pottery decorated with animals, birds, fish, plants, and human trophy heads. But the culture is best known for the Nazca Lines, long straight tracks and outlines of animals and mythical figures traced on the surface of the desert. Possibly created as offerings to the gods, their scale is so vast they can only be distinguished from the air. At the same time, the Moche culture of northern Peru, which has left a legacy of substantial urban and religious centres, fine pottery and goldwork, was beginning to emerge.

The Americas

c.200: Nazca Lines carved into the surface of the southern Peruvian desert

c.100: Adena culture of North America at its height

c.1 CE: The Moche, famous for their gold and pottery, dominate northern Peru

250 BCE — 200 — 150 — 100 — 50 — 1 CE

c.250: Many small coastal cultures, such as the Guangala, flourishing in present-day Ecuador

c.50: Teotihuacán in Valley of Mexico is largest city in the Americas, with population of 40,000

The Rosetta stone records events relating to the coronation of Ptolemy V of Egypt in 196 BCE in three languages: Egyptian hieroglyphic, Egyptian demotic (both shown below), and Greek.

ROMAN SURVEYING

The Romans surveyed the terrain of their empire from Scotland to Egypt in order to build roads. The purpose of the roads was primarily military – to enable Roman legions to move quickly to troublespots within the empire – but they also carried local commercial traffic. Distances were measured in thousands of paces *(mille passuum)* – hence the word mile – and milestones were placed at regular intervals. The Roman mile was about 1540 metres (1680 yards).

This Roman milestone stood on the Via Aemilia, which ran in a straight line across northern Italy. The inscription records road repairs undertaken in the reign of Augustus (27 BCE–14 CE).

Africa

Rome's defeat of Carthage in 146 BCE brought North Africa into the sphere of its growing Mediterranean empire. Throughout most of this period, Egypt was ruled by the Ptolemies, whose introduction of Greek language and writing hastened the decline of Egyptian civilization. In 31 BCE, when Octavian defeated Antony and Cleopatra at the battle of Actium, Egypt became a Roman province destined to serve as Rome's granary. To the south the kingdom of Meroe prospered, exporting frankincense to Rome along the Red Sea. The Bantus continued their progress into southern Africa, introducing agriculture and iron-working.

West Asia

Following the secession of Bactria, Sogdiana, and Parthia from Seleucid rule in the mid-3rd century BCE, the nomadic Parthians took advantage of the upheaval to extend their territory. By the early 1st century BCE, their empire included Mesopotamia and stretched from Syria to Bactria. With their heavily armoured cavalry, the Parthians withstood the might of Rome at the battle of Carrhae (53 BCE), halting Rome's eastern expansion. The Parthian Empire lasted 500 years, growing wealthy from its control of the Silk Road linking China and Rome.

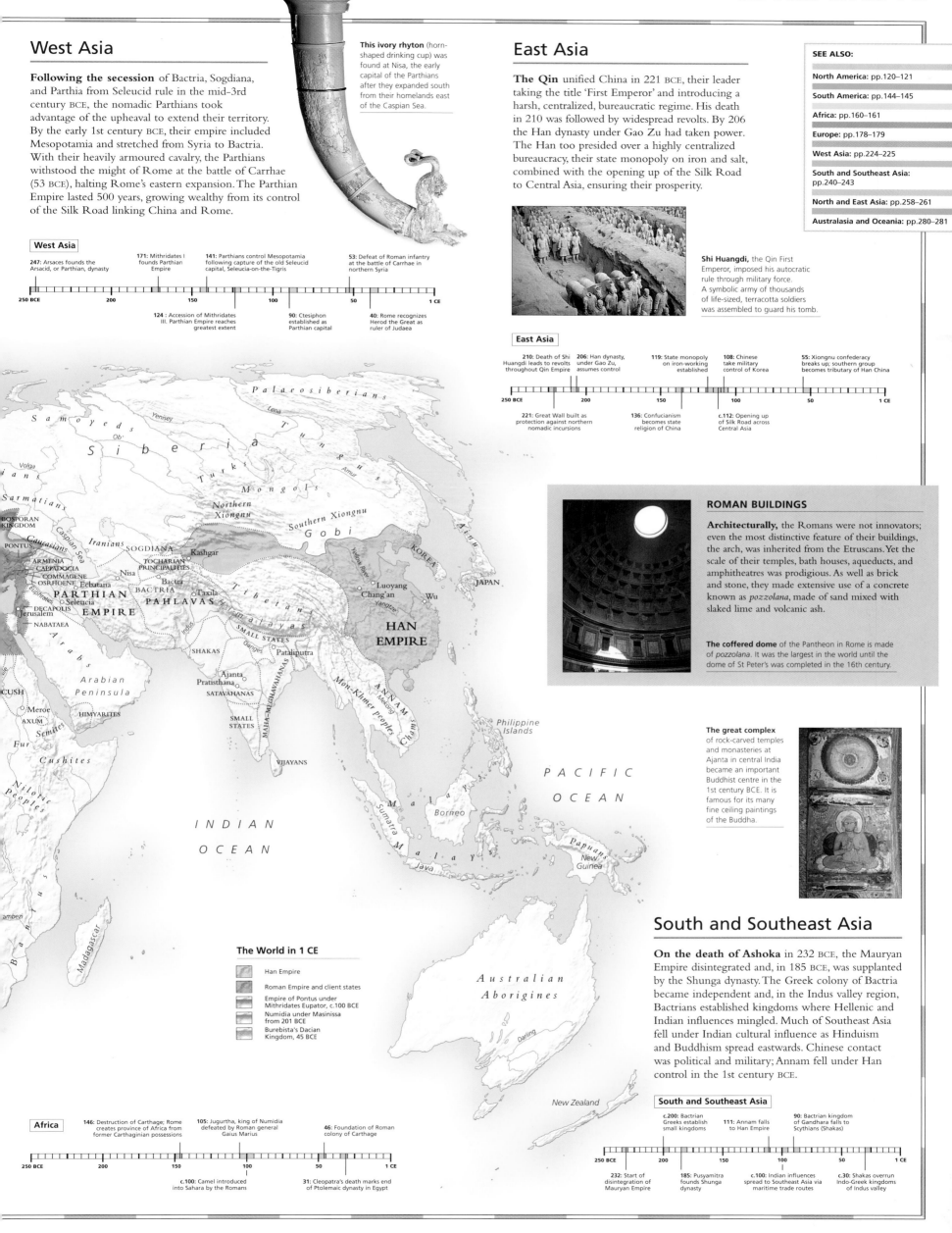

This ivory rhyton (horn-shaped drinking cup) was found at Nisa, the early capital of the Parthians after they expanded south from their homelands east of the Caspian Sea.

West Asia
247: Arsaces founds the Arsacid, or Parthian, dynasty
171: Mithridates I founds Parthian Empire
141: Parthians control Mesopotamia following capture of the old Seleucid capital, Seleucia-on-the-Tigris
53: Defeat of Roman infantry at the battle of Carrhae in northern Syria

250 BCE — 200 — 150 — 100 — 50 — 1 CE

124 : Accession of Mithridates III. Parthian Empire reaches greatest extent
90: Ctesiphon established as Parthian capital
40: Rome recognizes Herod the Great as ruler of Judaea

East Asia

The Qin unified China in 221 BCE, their leader taking the title 'First Emperor' and introducing a harsh, centralized, bureaucratic regime. His death in 210 was followed by widespread revolts. By 206 the Han dynasty under Gao Zu had taken power. The Han too presided over a highly centralized bureaucracy, their state monopoly on iron and salt, combined with the opening up of the Silk Road to Central Asia, ensuring their prosperity.

Shi Huangdi, the Qin First Emperor, imposed his autocratic rule through military force. A symbolic army of thousands of life-sized, terracotta soldiers was assembled to guard his tomb.

East Asia
210: Death of Shi Huangdi leads to revolts throughout Qin Empire
206: Han dynasty, under Gao Zu, assumes control
119: State monopoly on iron-working established
108: Chinese take military control of Korea
55: Xiongnu confederacy breaks up; southern group becomes tributary of Han China

250 BCE — 200 — 150 — 100 — 50 — 1 CE

221: Great Wall built as protection against northern nomadic incursions
136: Confucianism becomes state religion of China
c.112: Opening up of Silk Road across Central Asia

ROMAN BUILDINGS

Architecturally, the Romans were not innovators; even the most distinctive feature of their buildings, the arch, was inherited from the Etruscans. Yet the scale of their temples, bath houses, aqueducts, and amphitheatres was prodigious. As well as brick and stone, they made extensive use of a concrete known as *pozzolana*, made of sand mixed with slaked lime and volcanic ash.

The coffered dome of the Pantheon in Rome is made of *pozzolana*. It was the largest in the world until the dome of St Peter's was completed in the 16th century.

The great complex of rock-carved temples and monasteries at Ajanta in central India became an important Buddhist centre in the 1st century BCE. It is famous for its many fine ceiling paintings of the Buddha.

South and Southeast Asia

On the death of Ashoka in 232 BCE, the Mauryan Empire disintegrated and, in 185 BCE, was supplanted by the Shunga dynasty. The Greek colony of Bactria became independent and, in the Indus valley region, Bactrians established kingdoms where Hellenic and Indian influences mingled. Much of Southeast Asia fell under Indian cultural influence as Hinduism and Buddhism spread eastwards. Chinese contact was political and military; Annam fell under Han control in the 1st century BCE.

The World in 1 CE
- Han Empire
- Roman Empire and client states
- Empire of Pontus under Mithridates Eupator, c.100 BCE
- Numidia under Masinissa from 201 BCE
- Burebista's Dacian Kingdom, 45 BCE

Africa
146: Destruction of Carthage; Rome creates province of Africa from former Carthaginian possessions
105: Jugurtha, king of Numidia defeated by Roman general Gaius Marius
46: Foundation of Roman colony of Carthage

250 BCE — 200 — 150 — 100 — 50 — 1 CE

c.100: Camel introduced into Sahara by the Romans
31: Cleopatra's death marks end of Ptolemaic dynasty in Egypt

South and Southeast Asia
c.200: Bactrian Greeks establish small kingdoms
111: Annam falls to Han Empire
90: Bactrian kingdom of Gandhara falls to Scythians (Shakas)

250 BCE — 200 — 150 — 100 — 50 — 1 CE

232: Start of disintegration of Mauryan Empire
185: Pusyamitra founds Shunga dynasty
c.100: Indian influences spread to Southeast Asia via maritime trade routes
c.30: Shakas overrun Indo-Greek kingdoms of Indus valley

TRADE IN THE CLASSICAL WORLD

Fine Chinese silks from this period, lightweight and of high value, have been found throughout Eurasia, as far west as Egypt and Greece.

BY THE BEGINNING of the 1st millennium CE, a series of commercial and political networks had evolved which combined to form a nexus of trade which linked the eastern shores of the Atlantic Ocean, the Indian Ocean, and the western shores of the Pacific. At its extremes this network linked the Roman Empire, centred on the Mediterranean, and the land-based Han Empire of China. As the commercial and territorial influences of these two power bases spread beyond their political domains, so outlying regions were drawn into the web, from sub-Saharan Africa to the East Indies. However, the most important link to emerge was the Silk Road which spanned Asia, threading through the mountain ranges and deserts of the central Asian landmass, and along which a chain of powerful trading cities and states came into being.

Han China and the wider world

The Han Dynasty, which emerged to take over the territorial extent of the Qin Empire from 206 BCE, was largely self-sufficient. Trade was not regarded as an imperial concern, although desirable goods were drawn into Han markets by successive middlemen on the empire's fringes – spices from South and Southeast Asia, trepang and mother-of-pearl from the East Indies and, with the extension of the empire into Central Asia, the swift cavalry horses of Ferghana became highly prized. Conversely, Chinese products such as silk and lacquerware commanded high prices across Asia.

Decorated Han votive mirrors were used as diplomatic gifts by the Chinese, and have been found as far away as Siberia, the Caucasus, and southern Russia.

The nimble 'Horses of Heaven' from Ferghana provided the Chinese with the style of cavalry needed to keep the Xiongnu at bay.

Han trade
(in approximate order of value)

Exports	Imports
silk	horses
lacquerware	spices
	precious stones

The Classical world

Roman trade

Rome, in contrast to Han China, was an empire largely dependent on trade. Rome's imports were prodigious. A single currency, common citizenship, low customs barriers, and the development of a broadly secure network of roads, inland waterways, harbours, and sea-routes provided a hub of commerce which drew in produce from far beyond the imperial boundaries.

The popular Roman taste for combat with exotic wild animals in the arena saw bears, bulls, and boars being imported from northern Europe, lions and tigers from Asia, crocodiles from Egypt, and rhinoceros, hippopotami, and a variety of large cats from sub-Saharan Africa.

Roman trade
(in approximate order of value)

Exports	Imports
gold	food
silver	slaves
wine	animals
olive oil	spices
glassware	silk
	incense
	ivory
	cotton

The Romans built many ports and harbours around the Mediterranean, elaborate complexes with lighthouses and quays, which serviced the Roman maritime trading network.

Knowledge of Classical Eurasia

Although there is no evidence of direct contact between Rome and the Han Empire, there was extensive knowledge of the general shape of Classical Eurasia. The Greek geographer Strabo gave a detailed description of the known world in his 17-volume *Geography* (c.20 CE) and by 150 CE the Alexandrian Ptolemy's *Geography* formally laid out the topography of Eurasia. His world view (*below*) names Sinae (China), Taprobane (Sri Lanka), and Sera Metropolis (Chang'an).

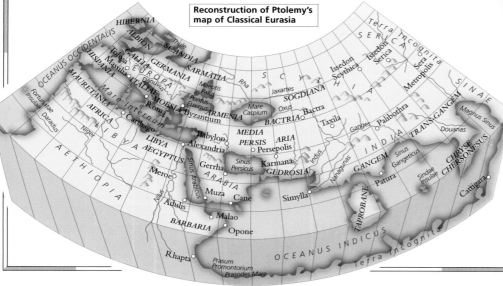

Reconstruction of Ptolemy's map of Classical Eurasia

Central Asian trade

The opening of the Silk Road saw the growth of a string of powerful cities and states which thrived, controlling the trade which passed through them. The greatest of these was the Parthian Empire of Persia (247 BCE–244 CE), while to the north Transoxiana, Bactria, and the Kushan Empire of modern Uzbekistan straddled the region in which the Silk Road converged and intersected with routes travelling north from India through the Hindu Kush, and on to the Caspian Sea and the river routes of Scythia.

The Silk Road

The campaigns by the Qin First Emperor, Shi Huangdi, and his Han successor Wudi against the nomadic Xiongnu opened a series of routes which traversed Central Asia, remaining the principal east–west trade route for centuries. The Silk Road linked Samarkand in the west with Anxi in the east; a summer route went north of the Tien Shan range, while the main route split to skirt the Takla Makan.

SEE ALSO:

Africa: pp.160–161

Europe: pp.180–181

West Asia: pp.224–225

South and Southeast Asia: pp.240–241

North and East Asia: pp.260–261

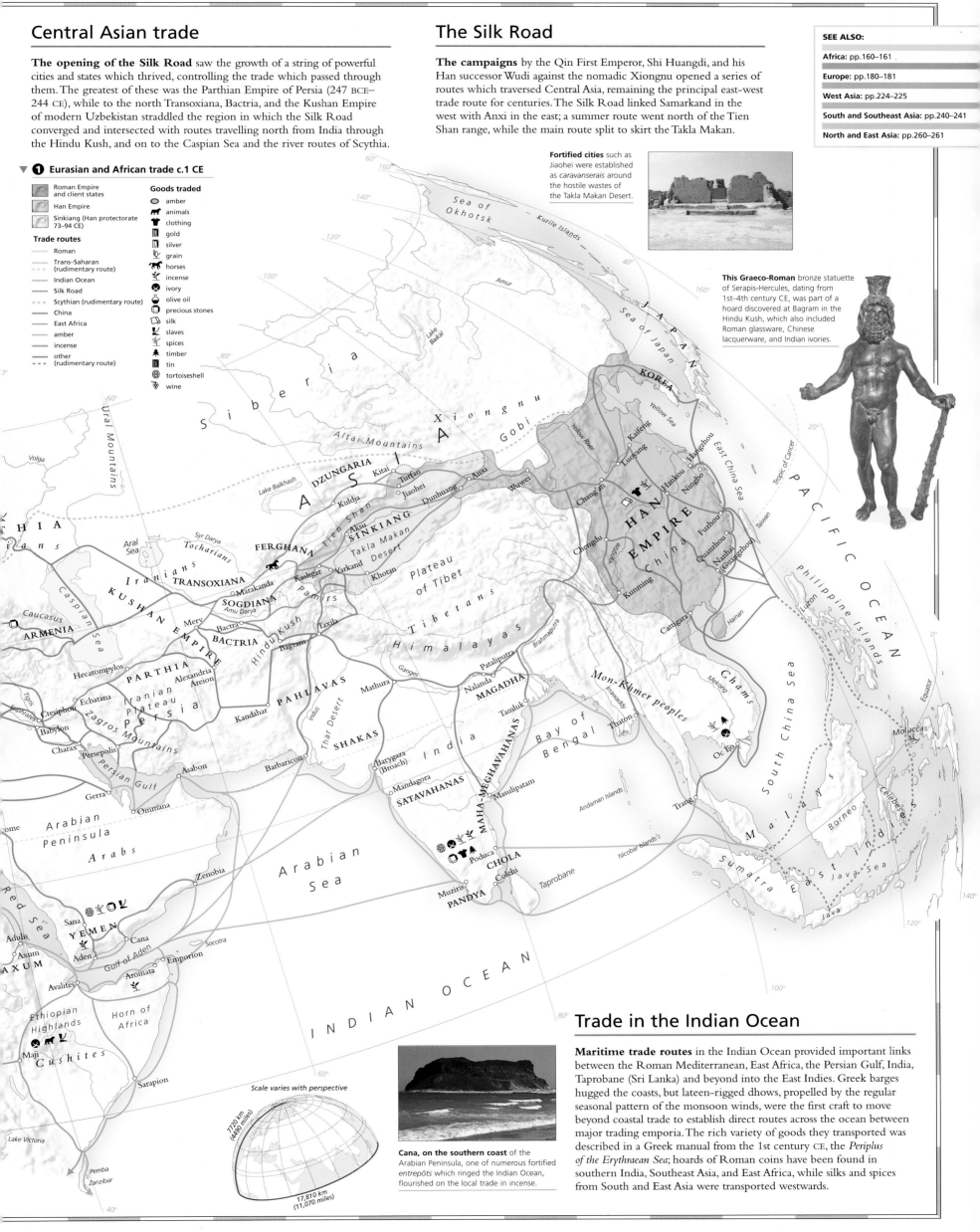

▼ ① Eurasian and African trade c.1 CE

Roman Empire and client states
Han Empire
Sinkiang (Han protectorate 73–94 CE)

Trade routes
Roman
Trans–Saharan (rudimentary route)
Indian Ocean
Silk Road
Scythian (rudimentary route)
China
East Africa
amber
incense
other (rudimentary route)

Goods traded
amber
animals
clothing
gold
silver
grain
horses
incense
ivory
olive oil
precious stones
silk
slaves
spices
timber
tin
tortoiseshell
wine

Fortified cities such as Jiaohei were established as *caravanserais* around the hostile wastes of the Takla Makan Desert.

This Graeco-Roman bronze statuette of Serapis-Hercules, dating from 1st–4th century CE, was part of a hoard discovered at Bagram in the Hindu Kush, which also included Roman glassware, Chinese lacquerware, and Indian ivories.

Cana, on the southern coast of the Arabian Peninsula, one of numerous fortified *entrepôts* which ringed the Indian Ocean, flourished on the local trade in incense.

Scale varies with perspective

770 km (4490 miles)

17,810 km (11,070 miles)

Trade in the Indian Ocean

Maritime trade routes in the Indian Ocean provided important links between the Roman Mediterranean, East Africa, the Persian Gulf, India, Taprobane (Sri Lanka) and beyond into the East Indies. Greek barges hugged the coasts, but lateen-rigged dhows, propelled by the regular seasonal pattern of the monsoon winds, were the first craft to move beyond coastal trade to establish direct routes across the ocean between major trading emporia. The rich variety of goods they transported was described in a Greek manual from the 1st century CE, the *Periplus of the Erythraean Sea*; hoards of Roman coins have been found in southern India, Southeast Asia, and East Africa, while silks and spices from South and East Asia were transported westwards.

THE WORLD 1–250 CE

AS THE EMPIRES OF THE OLD WORLD expanded, the protection of their borders and far-flung imperial outposts became an urgent priority. Increasing threats from the mounted nomadic pastoralists of Asia, the Germanic tribes of eastern Europe and the Berbers of northern Africa stretched resources to the limit, weakening Roman control, and leading to economic and social chaos. The empire of Han China collapsed in 220 CE, a victim of famine, floods, insurgency, and the growing power of regional warlords. By the early 3rd century CE, pressures on Rome's eastern borders precipitated a stormy century of civil wars, dynastic disputes, and army revolts. Against this troubled backdrop a new religion, Christianity, was beginning to spread throughout the Roman world. Originating with the teachings of Jesus of Nazareth in Palestine, the new religion proved remarkably resistant to Roman persecution.

Marcus Aurelius was one of the most conscientious Roman emperors: a Stoic philosopher and tireless campaigner on the German frontier.

Europe

In the 2nd century CE the Roman Empire stretched from West Asia to the Atlantic, united by one language, one coinage, and a system of well-paved roads, and protected by fortified frontiers. The empire prospered under strong emperors, but stresses began to appear. Conflict over the imperial succession undermined central authority, leading to civil wars between rivals, economic breakdown, and revolts by the army. Pressure on imperial frontiers, especially from the Germanic tribes to the east of the Rhine, stretched the empire's resources, leading to inflation, famine, disease, and lawlessness.

Europe

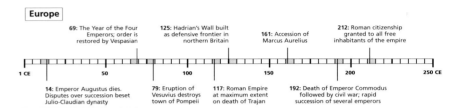

69: The Year of the Four Emperors; order is restored by Vespasian

125: Hadrian's Wall built as defensive frontier in northern Britain

161: Accession of Marcus Aurelius

212: Roman citizenship granted to all free inhabitants of the empire

1 CE — 50 — 100 — 150 — 200 — 250 CE

14: Emperor Augustus dies. Disputes over succession beset Julio-Claudian dynasty

79: Eruption of Vesuvius destroys town of Pompeii

117: Roman Empire at maximum extent on death of Trajan

192: Death of Emperor Commodus followed by civil war; rapid succession of several emperors

The most striking pottery of the early Andean civilizations was made by the Moche people. This vessel is shaped into a triple portrait of a fanged deity.

The Americas

The Moche culture of coastal Peru began to thrive in the 1st century CE, expanding through military conquest, and leaving substantial remains, such as temples of solid adobe brick. In Mexico, the vast metropolis of Teotihuacán controlled the production and distribution of obsidian throughout Central America. The city, laid out in a grid pattern on a north–south axis, housed a population of some 200,000. Ambitious projects at this time included the monumental Pyramid of the Sun, the largest structure in pre-Columbian America.

The Americas

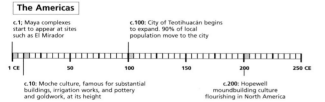

c.1: Maya complexes start to appear at sites such as El Mirador

c.100: City of Teotihuacán begins to expand. 90% of local population move to the city

1 CE — 50 — 100 — 150 — 200 — 250 CE

c.10: Moche culture, famous for substantial buildings, irrigation works, and pottery and goldwork, at its height

c.200: Hopewell moundbuilding culture flourishing in North America

The World in 250 CE

- Roman Empire
- Kushan power at peak under Kanishka, c.100 CE

THE FIRST PAPER

The traditional date for the invention of paper is 105 CE, but lightweight felted material for writing had been made in China for some time before then. The pulp was made of scraps of bark, bamboo, and hemp, finely chopped and boiled with wood ash. As techniques improved, paper replaced expensive silk and cumbersome wooden tablets.

A Chinese worker lifts a mesh screen covered with a thin layer of pulp that will drain and dry to form a sheet of paper.

Africa

Under Roman rule, Egypt experienced a remarkable economic recovery. As ancient Egyptian cults and traditions declined, Christianity found converts amongst the Egyptians. To the west, the Romans extended their control to the Berber kingdoms of Numidia and Mauretania. The fertile coastal plains were fully exploited, but the southern borders of Roman territory were under constant threat of Berber invasion. By 100 CE the Red Sea kingdom of Axum, its wealth based on control of the incense trade, had become a major power.

The ruined city of Petra contains remarkable rock-cut tombs. It was annexed by Rome in 106 as capital of the province of Arabia.

West Asia

In the 1st century CE the Parthian Empire was torn by internal dissent and dynastic struggles. Between 114 and 198, the Romans invaded three times, sacking the cities of Seleucia and Ctesiphon. In 224 Ardashir Papakan defeated his Parthian overlords and founded the Sassanian dynasty. He introduced a centralized administration, and transformed vassal kingdoms into provinces, ruled by Sassanian princes. His son Shapur repelled the Romans and made Sassanian Persia the most stable power of late antiquity.

East Asia

In 25 CE, after a brief interregnum, Han emperors regained control of China, but their rule depended on the support of powerful landowners. The capital moved to Luoyang, and eastern and southern China exerted greater political influence. In the early 3rd century the empire, beset by rebellions and feuds, collapsed. Regional warlords carved out three new kingdoms and China remained fragmented for over 300 years. With the decline of the Han, small local states, notably Koguryo and Silla, took control of Korea.

This model horse and trap was found among the goods in the grave of a high-ranking officer of the Han period.

West Asia

70: Romans suppress Jewish revolt and destroy temple in Jerusalem
c.150: Petra, a major trading post for incense, at height of prosperity
165: Avidius Cassius sacks Seleucia and Ctesiphon
224: Sassanians take over Parthian Empire

c.114: Trajan annexes Armenia, takes Seleucia and reaches Persian Gulf
c.132: Second Jewish revolt precipitates diaspora
197: Septimus Severus sails down Euphrates to invade Parthian Empire

East Asia

9: Wang Mang seizes throne, founding short-lived Xin dynasty
159: Han imperial family feuds hand effective power to court eunuchs
c.220: Collapse of Han dynasty; replaced by three kingdoms: Shu, Wu, and Wei

25: Han reassert control over China, but their power is limited
184: Rising of the Yellow Turbans, an insurgent group, in China
c.200: Emergence of native states in Korea

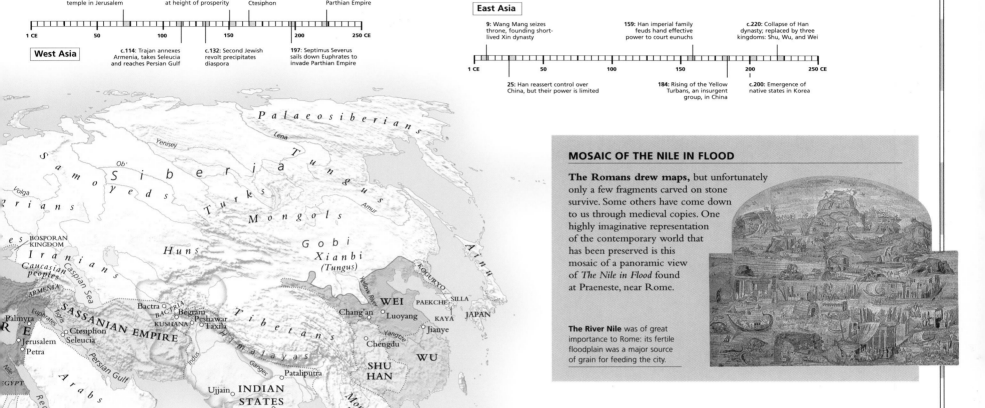

MOSAIC OF THE NILE IN FLOOD

The Romans drew maps, but unfortunately only a few fragments carved on stone survive. Some others have come down to us through medieval copies. One highly imaginative representation of the contemporary world that has been preserved is this mosaic of a panoramic view of *The Nile in Flood* found at Praeneste, near Rome.

The River Nile was of great importance to Rome: its fertile floodplain was a major source of grain for feeding the city.

South Asia

In the 1st century CE the nomadic Yuezhi were pushed westwards from the borders of China. One of the tribes, the Kushans, united the others, moved into Bactria, and from there expanded into northern India, founding their capital at Peshawar. The Kingdom of Kushana crumbled at the end of the 2nd century, when native peoples – the Tamils of southern India and the Satavahanas of the Deccan – were beginning to assert their power.

The Kushans' wealth came from their control of east–west trade routes. This ivory plaque was part of a famous hoard found at Begram, which contained artefacts from Rome, Africa, India, and China.

Egyptian mummy cases took on a curious hybrid appearance under Roman rule. The portrait on this 2nd-century example shows the Romans' Hellenistic taste in art.

Africa

c.50: Kingdom of Axum starts to emerge
c.100: Alexandria emerges as a centre of Christian scholarship, seat of one of the earliest Christian bishoprics
c.150: Christianity starts to spread westwards to Roman provinces of Numidia and Mauretania

44: Mauretania annexed by Rome
69: Romans defeat powerful Saharan kingdom of Garamantes, but do not absorb it into empire

South Asia

99: Indian embassy to court of Trajan in Rome, probably to announce Kushan conquests
c.102: Death of Kushans' greatest ruler, Kanishka
c.200: Cities appear for first time on Deccan plateau

c.60: Kushans, under Kadphises I, unite Yuezhi tribes and advance into northern India
c.150: Kushans become Persian vassals

THE EMERGENCE OF GLOBAL RELIGIONS

This 7th-century silver plaque from Hexham, England is thought to depict a Christian saint.

BY 250 CE CERTAIN OLD WORLD religions (*see pp.36–37*) had spread far beyond their areas of origin to become substantial bodies of faith. In the west, the Roman taste for monotheistic Mithraism, derived from Persian Zoroastrianism, spread throughout the empire, but in its wake the cult of Christianity was becoming firmly established. Further, the Roman suppression of the Jewish revolt in 132 CE had caused a diaspora through much of the empire. In South Asia, Hinduism became deeply rooted throughout the sub-continent as Dravidians and tribal peoples adopted the practices of their Aryan conquerors; meanwhile Buddhism was spread overland to Central Asia and China and beyond by missionaries of various sectarian schools.

Mithraism, Judaism, and Christianity

The worship of Mithras was arduous and limited to males; it was popular among the Roman legions, spreading to the corners of the empire. Its monotheism paved the way for Christianity which, in parallel to the Jewish diaspora, spread to centres throughout the empire. This was inaugurated by the missionary journeys of St. Paul, in the 1st century CE. By the time of Diocletian's persecutions (304 CE) centres had been established in Asia Minor, Mesopotamia, and around the Mediterranean. The fusion of Christian theology with the ethical concerns of Greek philosophy gave it intellectual respectability, and when Constantine (306–337) adopted the faith, Christianity became the official religion of the empire.

This 5th-century pottery amphora is decorated with two versions of the Christian cross, which became the most widely used symbol of the religion.

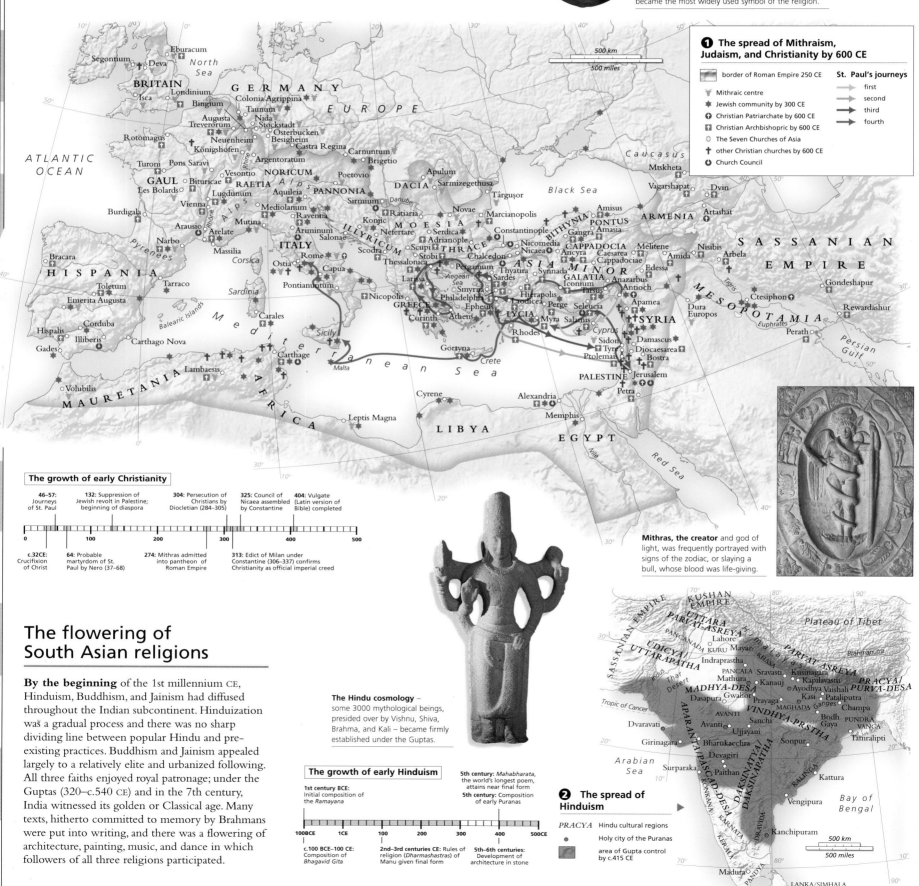

❶ The spread of Mithraism, Judaism, and Christianity by 600 CE

▨ border of Roman Empire 250 CE	**St. Paul's journeys**
⚐ Mithraic centre	→ first
✦ Jewish community by 300 CE	→ second
⊕ Christian Patriarchate by 600 CE	→ third
⊡ Christian Archbishopric by 600 CE	→ fourth
⊙ The Seven Churches of Asia	
✝ other Christian churches by 600 CE	
⊙ Church Council	

Mithras, the creator and god of light, was frequently portrayed with signs of the zodiac, or slaying a bull, whose blood was life-giving.

The growth of early Christianity

46–57: Journeys of St. Paul	**132:** Suppression of Jewish revolt in Palestine; beginning of diaspora	**304:** Persecution of Christians by Diocletian (284–305)	**325:** Council of Nicaea assembled by Constantine	**404:** Vulgate (Latin version of Bible) completed

0	100	200	300	400	500

c.32CE: Crucifixion of Christ	**64:** Probable martyrdom of St. Paul by Nero (37–68)	**274:** Mithras admitted into pantheon of Roman Empire	**313:** Edict of Milan under Constantine (306–337) confirms Christianity as official imperial creed

The flowering of South Asian religions

By the beginning of the 1st millennium CE, Hinduism, Buddhism, and Jainism had diffused throughout the Indian subcontinent. Hinduization was a gradual process and there was no sharp dividing line between popular Hindu and pre-existing practices. Buddhism and Jainism appealed largely to a relatively elite and urbanized following. All three faiths enjoyed royal patronage; under the Guptas (320–c.540 CE) and in the 7th century, India witnessed its golden or Classical age. Many texts, hitherto committed to memory by Brahmans, were put into writing, and there was a flowering of architecture, painting, music, and dance in which followers of all three religions participated.

The Hindu cosmology – some 3000 mythological beings, presided over by Vishnu, Shiva, Brahma, and Kali – became firmly established under the Guptas.

The growth of early Hinduism

1st century BCE: Initial composition of the *Ramayana*			**5th century:** *Mahabharata,* the world's longest poem, attains near final form **5th century:** Composition of early Puranas

100BCE	1CE	100	200	300	400	500CE

c.100 BCE–100 CE: Composition of *Bhagavid Gita*	**2nd–3rd centuries CE:** Rules of religion (*Dharmashastras*) of Manu given final form	**5th–6th centuries:** Development of architecture in stone

❷ The spread of Hinduism

PRACYA Hindu cultural regions
● Holy city of the Puranas
▨ area of Gupta control by c.415 CE

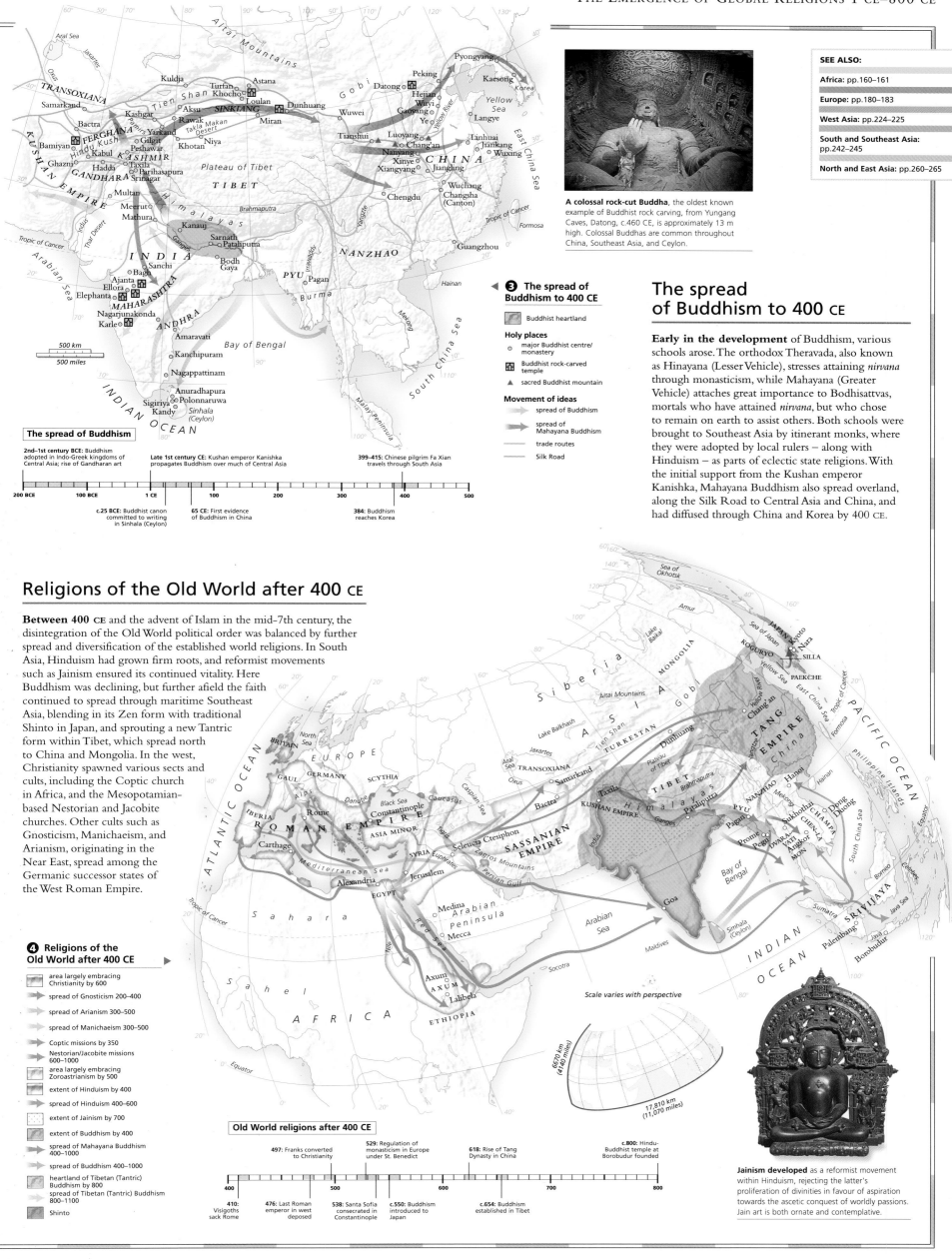

SEE ALSO:

Africa: pp.160–161

Europe: pp.180–183

West Asia: pp.224–225

South and Southeast Asia: pp.242–245

North and East Asia: pp.260–265

A colossal rock-cut Buddha, the oldest known example of Buddhist rock carving, from Yungang Caves, Datong, c.460 CE, is approximately 13 m high. Colossal Buddhas are common throughout China, Southeast Asia, and Ceylon.

❸ The spread of Buddhism to 400 CE

Buddhist heartland

Holy places
- ○ major Buddhist centre/ monastery
- ⊞ Buddhist rock-carved temple
- ▲ sacred Buddhist mountain

Movement of ideas
- → spread of Buddhism
- ⇒ spread of Mahayana Buddhism
- — trade routes
- — Silk Road

The spread of Buddhism

2nd–1st century BCE: Buddhism adopted in Indo-Greek kingdoms of Central Asia; rise of Gandharan art

Late 1st century CE: Kushan emperor Kanishka propagates Buddhism over much of Central Asia

399–415: Chinese pilgrim Fa Xian travels through South Asia

c.25 BCE: Buddhist canon committed to writing in Sinhala (Ceylon)

65 CE: First evidence of Buddhism in China

384: Buddhism reaches Korea

| 200 BCE | 100 BCE | 1 CE | 100 | 200 | 300 | 400 | 500 |

The spread of Buddhism to 400 CE

Early in the development of Buddhism, various schools arose. The orthodox Theravada, also known as Hinayana (Lesser Vehicle), stresses attaining *nirvana* through monasticism, while Mahayana (Greater Vehicle) attaches great importance to Bodhisattvas, mortals who have attained *nirvana*, but who chose to remain on earth to assist others. Both schools were brought to Southeast Asia by itinerant monks, where they were adopted by local rulers – along with Hinduism – as parts of eclectic state religions. With the initial support from the Kushan emperor Kanishka, Mahayana Buddhism also spread overland, along the Silk Road to Central Asia and China, and had diffused through China and Korea by 400 CE.

Religions of the Old World after 400 CE

Between 400 CE and the advent of Islam in the mid-7th century, the disintegration of the Old World political order was balanced by further spread and diversification of the established world religions. In South Asia, Hinduism had grown firm roots, and reformist movements such as Jainism ensured its continued vitality. Here Buddhism was declining, but further afield the faith continued to spread through maritime Southeast Asia, blending in its Zen form with traditional Shinto in Japan, and sprouting a new Tantric form within Tibet, which spread north to China and Mongolia. In the west, Christianity spawned various sects and cults, including the Coptic church in Africa, and the Mesopotamian-based Nestorian and Jacobite churches. Other cults such as Gnosticism, Manichaeism, and Arianism, originating in the Near East, spread among the Germanic successor states of the West Roman Empire.

❹ Religions of the Old World after 400 CE

- area largely embracing Christianity by 600
- spread of Gnosticism 200–400
- spread of Arianism 300–500
- spread of Manichaeism 300–500
- Coptic missions by 350
- Nestorian/Jacobite missions 600–1000
- area largely embracing Zoroastrianism by 500
- extent of Hinduism by 400
- spread of Hinduism 400–600
- extent of Jainism by 700
- extent of Buddhism by 400
- spread of Mahayana Buddhism 400–1000
- spread of Buddhism 400–1000
- heartland of Tibetan (Tantric) Buddhism by 800
- spread of Tibetan (Tantric) Buddhism 800–1100
- Shinto

Scale varies with perspective

6570 km (4140 miles)

17,810 km (11,070 miles)

Old World religions after 400 CE

497: Franks converted to Christianity

529: Regulation of monasticism in Europe under St. Benedict

618: Rise of Tang Dynasty in China

c.800: Hindu-Buddhist temple at Borobudur founded

| 400 | 500 | 600 | 700 | 800 |

410: Visigoths sack Rome

476: Last Roman emperor in west deposed

538: Santa Sofia consecrated in Constantinople

c.550: Buddhism introduced to Japan

c.654: Buddhism established in Tibet

Jainism developed as a reformist movement within Hinduism, rejecting the latter's proliferation of divinities in favour of aspiration towards the ascetic conquest of worldly passions. Jain art is both ornate and contemplative.

THE WORLD 250–500

BY 500, MIGRATIONS IN ASIA AND EUROPE had so weakened the civilizations of the Old World that only the East Roman Empire and Sassanian Persia survived. Asian nomads broke the power of the Chinese and destroyed India's Gupta Empire. The Huns even invaded Europe, where the Romans repulsed them, but only with the aid of their Gothic allies. Rome relied increasingly on the aid of the Goths and other Germanic peoples, who settled within the empire and, as central authority waned, carved out new kingdoms for themselves. In contrast to the collapsing empires of the Old World, the great urban civilizations of Central America, Teotihuacán, the Maya, and the Zapotecs, were beginning to flourish.

Much of the best late Roman sculpture is found in the carving of Christian scenes on sarcophagi.

Europe

In 284, **Diocletian** divided the Roman Empire into eastern and western halves. With the advent of Christianity and the establishment of Constantinople as a new capital in 324, the empire's centre of gravity shifted eastward. Meanwhile, Germanic and Slav peoples, living on Rome's northern borders, infiltrated imperial territory, at times peacefully, often by force. The Western Empire collapsed in 476 to be replaced by a series of Germanic kingdoms and the mantle of empire passed to Constantinople in the east.

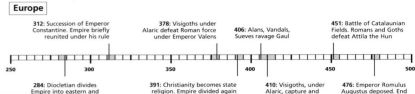

Europe

312: Succession of Emperor Constantine. Empire briefly reunited under his rule

378: Visigoths under Alaric defeat Roman force under Emperor Valens

406: Alans, Vandals, Sueves ravage Gaul

451: Battle of Catalaunian Fields. Romans and Goths defeat Attila the Hun

284: Diocletian divides Empire into eastern and western halves

391: Christianity becomes state religion. Empire divided again

410: Visigoths, under Alaric, capture and sack Rome

476: Emperor Romulus Augustus deposed. End of Western Empire

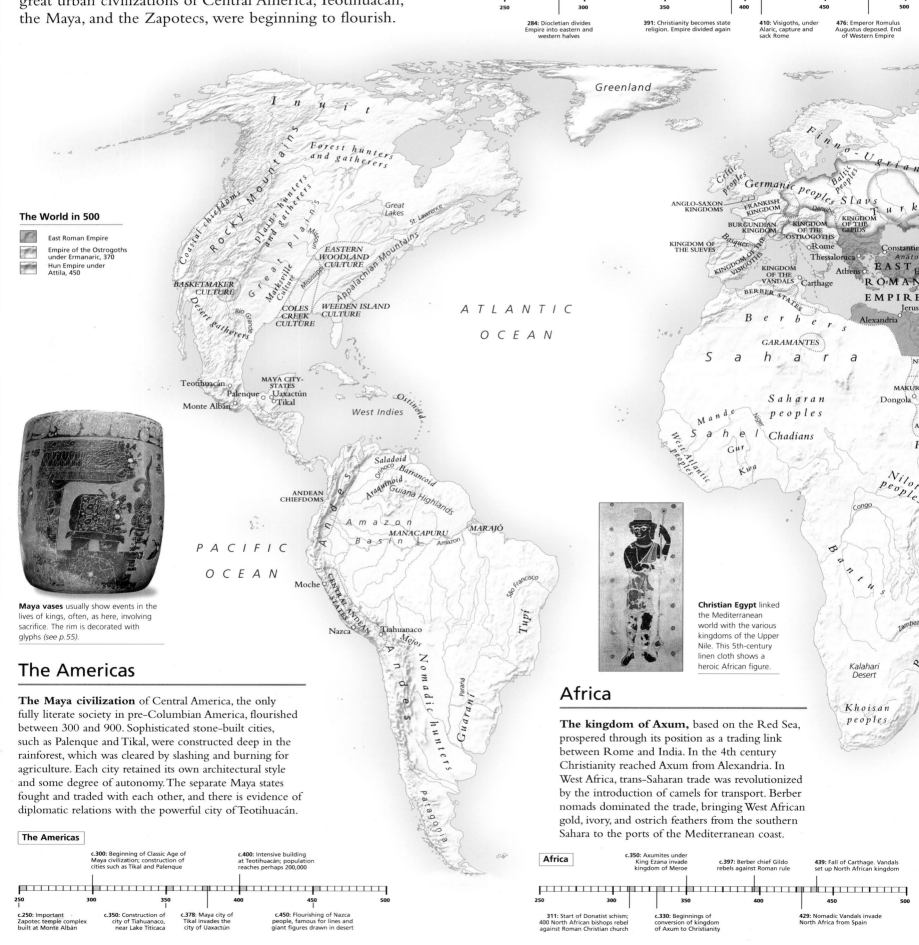

The World in 500

- East Roman Empire
- Empire of the Ostrogoths under Ermanaric, 370
- Hun Empire under Attila, 450

Maya vases usually show events in the lives of kings, often, as here, involving sacrifice. The rim is decorated with glyphs (see p.55).

Christian Egypt linked the Mediterranean world with the various kingdoms of the Upper Nile. This 5th-century linen cloth shows a heroic African figure.

The Americas

The Maya civilization of Central America, the only fully literate society in pre-Columbian America, flourished between 300 and 900. Sophisticated stone-built cities, such as Palenque and Tikal, were constructed deep in the rainforest, which was cleared by slashing and burning for agriculture. Each city retained its own architectural style and some degree of autonomy. The separate Maya states fought and traded with each other, and there is evidence of diplomatic relations with the powerful city of Teotihuacán.

The Americas

c.300: Beginning of Classic Age of Maya civilization; construction of cities such as Tikal and Palenque

c.400: Intensive building at Teotihuacán; population reaches perhaps 200,000

c.250: Important Zapotec temple complex built at Monte Albán

c.350: Construction of city of Tiahuanaco, near Lake Titicaca

c.378: Maya city of Tikal invades the city of Uaxactún

c.450: Flourishing of Nazca people, famous for lines and giant figures drawn in desert

Africa

The kingdom of Axum, based on the Red Sea, prospered through its position as a trading link between Rome and India. In the 4th century Christianity reached Axum from Alexandria. In West Africa, trans-Saharan trade was revolutionized by the introduction of camels for transport. Berber nomads dominated the trade, bringing West African gold, ivory, and ostrich feathers from the southern Sahara to the ports of the Mediterranean coast.

Africa

c.350: Axumites under King Ezana invade kingdom of Meroe

c.397: Berber chief Gildo rebels against Roman rule

439: Fall of Carthage. Vandals set up North African kingdom

311: Start of Donatist schism; 400 North African bishops rebel against Roman Christian church

c.330: Beginnings of conversion of kingdom of Axum to Christianity

429: Nomadic Vandals invade North Africa from Spain

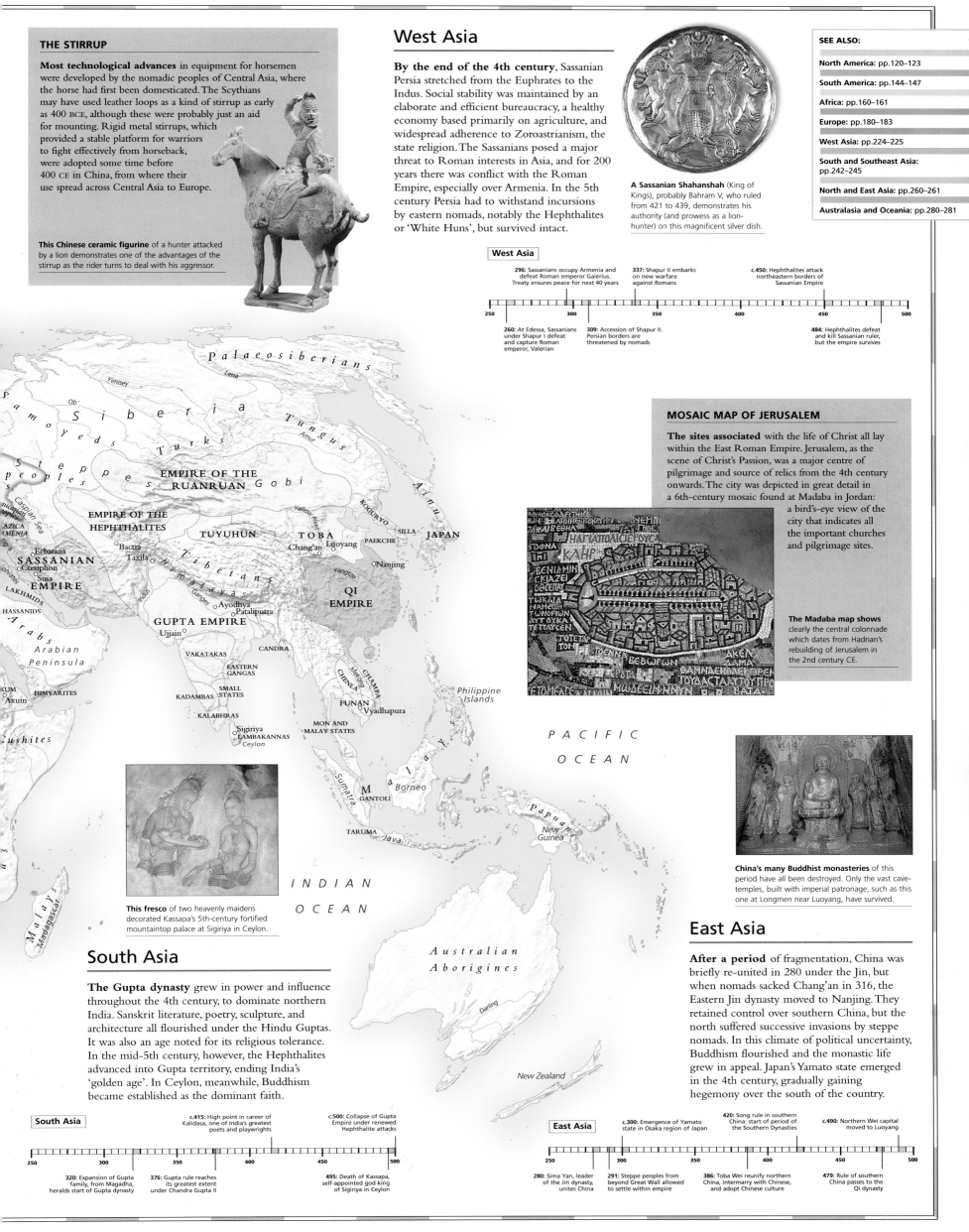

THE STIRRUP

Most technological advances in equipment for horsemen were developed by the nomadic peoples of Central Asia, where the horse had first been domesticated. The Scythians may have used leather loops as a kind of stirrup as early as 400 BCE, although these were probably just an aid for mounting. Rigid metal stirrups, which provided a stable platform for warriors to fight effectively from horseback, were adopted some time before 400 CE in China, from where their use spread across Central Asia to Europe.

This Chinese ceramic figurine of a hunter attacked by a lion demonstrates one of the advantages of the stirrup as the rider turns to deal with his aggressor.

West Asia

By the end of the 4th century, Sassanian Persia stretched from the Euphrates to the Indus. Social stability was maintained by an elaborate and efficient bureaucracy, a healthy economy based primarily on agriculture, and widespread adherence to Zoroastrianism, the state religion. The Sassanians posed a major threat to Roman interests in Asia, and for 200 years there was conflict with the Roman Empire, especially over Armenia. In the 5th century Persia had to withstand incursions by eastern nomads, notably the Hephthalites or 'White Huns', but survived intact.

A Sassanian Shahanshah (King of Kings), probably Bahram V, who ruled from 421 to 439, demonstrates his authority (and prowess as a lion-hunter) on this magnificent silver dish.

SEE ALSO:

North America: pp.120–123

South America: pp.144–147

Africa: pp.160–161

Europe: pp.180–183

West Asia: pp.224–225

South and Southeast Asia: pp.242–245

North and East Asia: pp.260–261

Australasia and Oceania: pp.280–281

West Asia

296: Sassanians occupy Armenia and defeat Roman emperor Galerius. Treaty ensures peace for next 40 years

337: Shapur II embarks on new warfare against Romans

c.450: Hephthalites attack northeastern borders of Sassanian Empire

260: At Edessa, Sassanians under Shapur I defeat and capture Roman emperor, Valerian

309: Accession of Shapur II. Persian borders are threatened by nomads

484: Hephthalites defeat and kill Sassanian ruler, but the empire survives

MOSAIC MAP OF JERUSALEM

The sites associated with the life of Christ all lay within the East Roman Empire. Jerusalem, as the scene of Christ's Passion, was a major centre of pilgrimage and source of relics from the 4th century onwards. The city was depicted in great detail in a 6th-century mosaic found at Madaba in Jordan: a bird's-eye view of the city that indicates all the important churches and pilgrimage sites.

The Madaba map shows clearly the central colonnade which dates from Hadrian's rebuilding of Jerusalem in the 2nd century CE.

This fresco of two heavenly maidens decorated Kassapa's 5th-century fortified mountaintop palace at Sigiriya in Ceylon.

China's many Buddhist monasteries of this period have all been destroyed. Only the vast cave-temples, built with imperial patronage, such as this one at Longmen near Luoyang, have survived.

South Asia

The Gupta dynasty grew in power and influence throughout the 4th century, to dominate northern India. Sanskrit literature, poetry, sculpture, and architecture all flourished under the Hindu Guptas. It was also an age noted for its religious tolerance. In the mid-5th century, however, the Hephthalites advanced into Gupta territory, ending India's 'golden age'. In Ceylon, meanwhile, Buddhism became established as the dominant faith.

South Asia

c.415: High point in career of Kalidasa, one of India's greatest poets and playwrights

c.500: Collapse of Gupta Empire under renewed Hephthalite attacks

320: Expansion of Gupta family, from Magadha, heralds start of Gupta dynasty

376: Gupta rule reaches its greatest extent under Chandra Gupta II

495: Death of Kassapa, self-appointed god king of Sigiriya in Ceylon

East Asia

After a period of fragmentation, China was briefly re-united in 280 under the Jin, but when nomads sacked Chang'an in 316, the Eastern Jin dynasty moved to Nanjing. They retained control over southern China, but the north suffered successive invasions by steppe nomads. In this climate of political uncertainty, Buddhism flourished and the monastic life grew in appeal. Japan's Yamato state emerged in the 4th century, gradually gaining hegemony over the south of the country.

East Asia

c.300: Emergence of Yamato state in Osaka region of Japan

420: Song rule in southern China: start of period of the Southern Dynasties

c.490: Northern Wei capital moved to Luoyang

280: Sima Yan, leader of the Jin dynasty, unites China

291: Steppe peoples from beyond Great Wall allowed to settle within empire

386: Toba Wei reunify northern China, intermarry with Chinese, and adopt Chinese culture

479: Rule of southern China passes to the Qi dynasty

MIGRATIONS AND INVASIONS

The half-Vandal general Stilicho was regent during the reign of the child emperor Honorius.

THE GERMANIC PEOPLES who migrated into the Roman Empire during the 5th century were seeking to share in the fruits of empire, not to destroy it. They were spurred to move west in search of land by a combination of factors: famine, population pressure, and the prospects of a better standard of living. Rome initially accepted 'barbarian' recruits into its depleted army as *foederati* (federates), and allowed them to retain their own leaders and laws. But when the Romans opposed the settlement of large groups or refused to reward them for their services, the results could be disastrous: campaigns of plunder, sacked cities, and the breakdown of imperial control.

Turmoil in Italy

From the late 4th century, the West Roman Empire was plagued by disputes over the imperial succession, which led to factionalism and civil wars. These were very destructive of Roman manpower and led to the recruitment of large numbers of barbarians under their own leaders. Emperors were often pawns in the power struggles of generals. Many of these, such as the half-Vandal Stilicho and the Suevian Ricimer, were of Germanic origin.

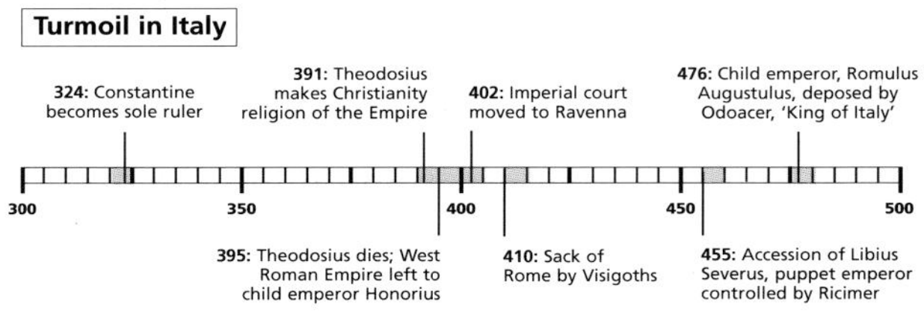

Honorius succeeded his father, Theodosius, as western emperor in 395 while still a child. He lived in comfortable seclusion while senior ministers governed.

Turmoil in Italy

324: Constantine becomes sole ruler	**391:** Theodosius makes Christianity religion of the Empire	**402:** Imperial court moved to Ravenna	**476:** Child emperor, Romulus Augustulus, deposed by Odoacer, 'King of Italy'

300 — 350 — 400 — 450 — 500

395: Theodosius dies; West Roman Empire left to child emperor Honorius

410: Sack of Rome by Visigoths

455: Accession of Libius Severus, puppet emperor controlled by Ricimer

The aims of the migrations

The peoples who invaded the Roman Empire in the 4th and 5th centuries were driven by a variety of motives. Some, like Alaric's Visigoths, sought official acceptance by the Roman authorities, others, such as the peoples of the Great Migration of 406, were intent on finding land anywhere and by any means. The only invaders bent purely on destruction and plunder were the Huns. As steppe nomads, the Huns' strength lay in their mobility and their skill with bow, lance, and sabre. They were able to smash the overstretched imperial defences, but were repulsed when Goths and Roman joined forces against them. The Romans relied more and more on Gothic military support and it was the Goths who emerged as the first inheritors of the Empire's western territories.

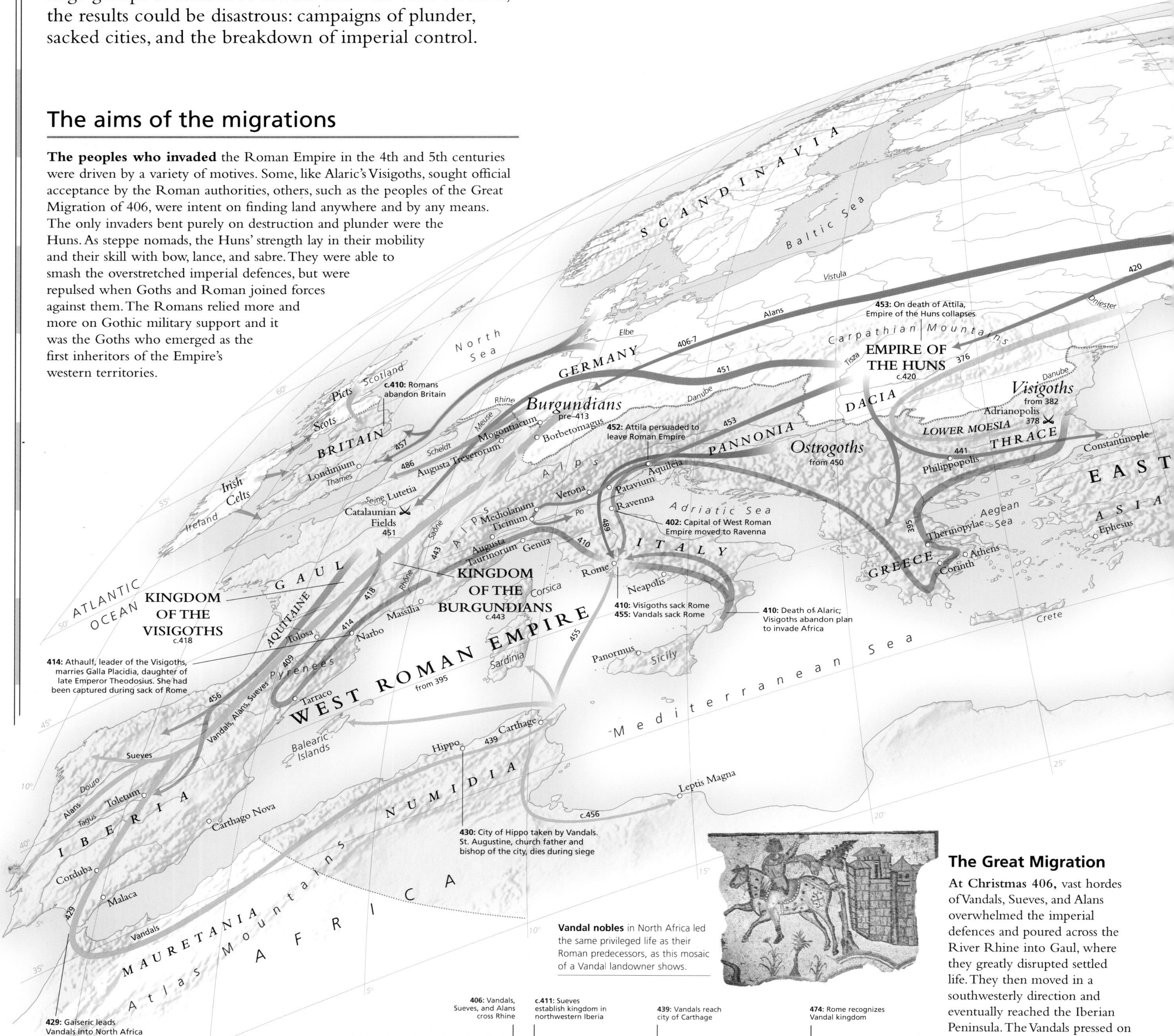

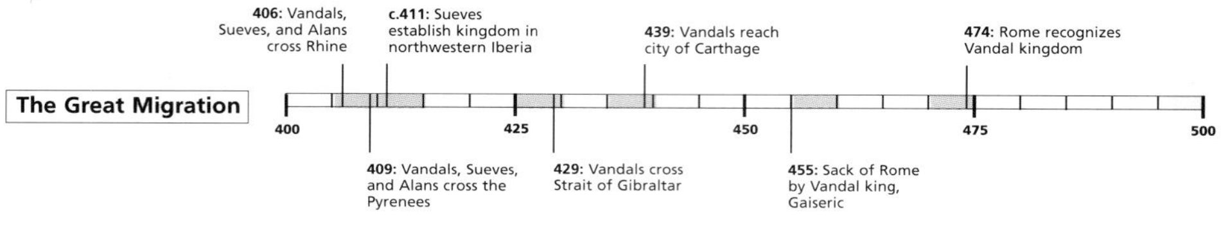

The Great Migration

At Christmas 406, vast hordes of Vandals, Sueves, and Alans overwhelmed the imperial defences and poured across the River Rhine into Gaul, where they greatly disrupted settled life. They then moved in a southwesterly direction and eventually reached the Iberian Peninsula. The Vandals pressed on to North Africa, crossing the Strait of Gibraltar in 429, while the Sueves and Alans set up kingdoms in Iberia.

Vandal nobles in North Africa led the same privileged life as their Roman predecessors, as this mosaic of a Vandal landowner shows.

The Great Migration

406: Vandals, Sueves, and Alans cross Rhine	**c.411:** Sueves establish kingdom in northwestern Iberia	**439:** Vandals reach city of Carthage	**474:** Rome recognizes Vandal kingdom

400 — 425 — 450 — 475 — 500

409: Vandals, Sueves, and Alans cross the Pyrenees

429: Vandals cross Strait of Gibraltar

455: Sack of Rome by Vandal king, Gaiseric

Map labels and annotations:

SCANDINAVIA

Baltic Sea

North Sea

GERMANY

Vistula

Alans

406-7

Elbe

Rhine

451

453: On death of Attila, Empire of the Huns collapses

Carpathian Mountains

EMPIRE OF THE HUNS c.420

376

420

Dniester

Danube

Visigoths from 382

DACIA

PANNONIA

Tisza

Adrianopolis

378

LOWER MOESIA

441

THRACE

Ostrogoths from 450

395

Constantinople

EAST

ASIA

Philippopolis

Thermopylae

Aegean Sea

Ephesus

GREECE

Corinth

Athens

Crete

c.410: Romans abandon Britain

Picts

Scots

Scotland

BRITAIN

Londinium

Thames

457

486

Augusta Treverorum

Irish Celts

Ireland

Scheldt

Meuse

Mogontiacum

Burgundians pre-413

Borbetomagus

452: Attila persuaded to leave Roman Empire

Danube

453

Alps

Seine

Lutetia

Catalaunian Fields 451

Loire

Saône

Augusta Taurinorum

Mediolanum

Ticinum

Po

Genua

Patavium

Aquileia

Verona

Ravenna

402: Capital of West Roman Empire moved to Ravenna

Adriatic Sea

KINGDOM OF THE BURGUNDIANS c.443

Corsica

Rome

ITALY

Neapolis

410: Visigoths sack Rome
455: Vandals sack Rome

410: Death of Alaric; Visigoths abandon plan to invade Africa

GAUL

ATLANTIC OCEAN

KINGDOM OF THE VISIGOTHS c.418

AQUITAINE

443

418

414

Tolosa

Narbo

Massilia

Rhône

410

WEST ROMAN EMPIRE from 395

455

Panormus

Sicily

Sardinia

456

409

Pyrenees

Vandals, Alans, Sueves

Tarraco

414: Athaulf, leader of the Visigoths, marries Galla Placidia, daughter of late Emperor Theodosius. She had been captured during sack of Rome

Balearic Islands

Carthage

439

Mediterranean Sea

Leptis Magna

Sueves

IBERIA

Douro

Alans

Toletum

Tagus

Carthago Nova

Corduba

Malaca

NUMIDIA

Hippo

c.456

430: City of Hippo taken by Vandals. St. Augustine, church father and bishop of the city, dies during siege

MAURETANIA

Atlas Mountains

AFRICA

429

Vandals

429: Gaiseric leads Vandals into North Africa

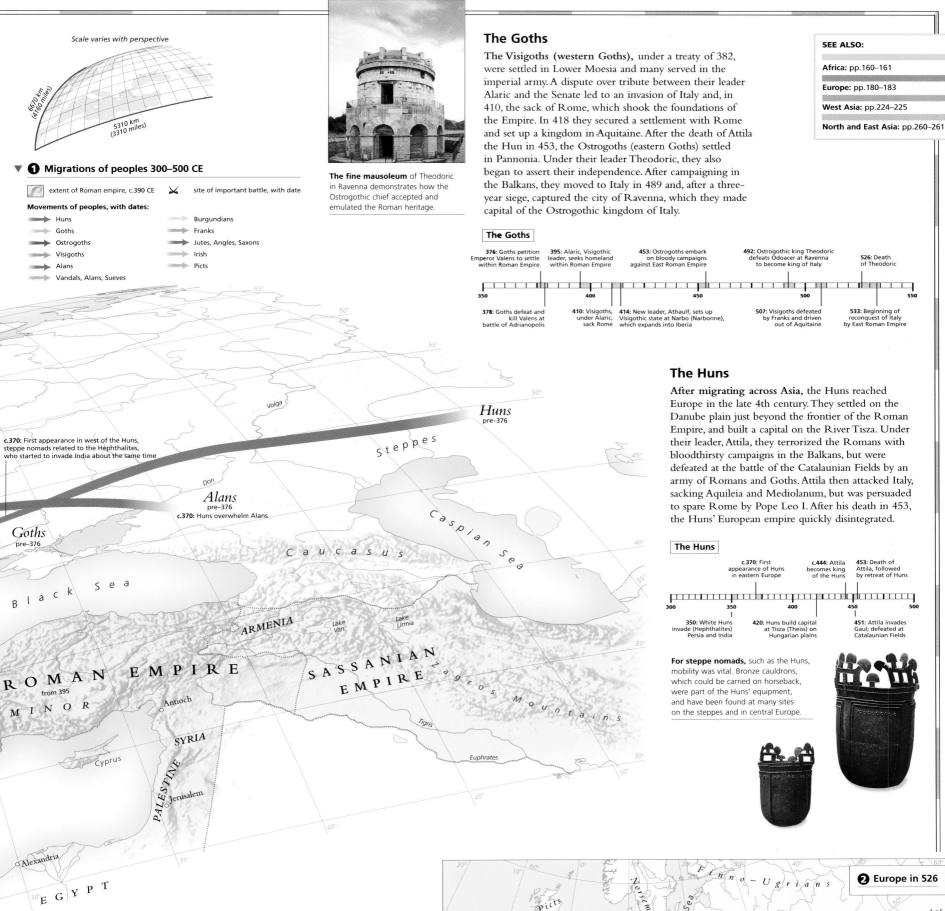

Scale varies with perspective

6670 km
(4160 miles)

5310 km
(3310 miles)

65°

60°

55°

50°

45°

40°

35°

30°

40°

35°

① Migrations of peoples 300–500 CE

▨ extent of Roman empire, c.390 CE	⚔ site of important battle, with date

Movements of peoples, with dates:

➤ Huns	➤ Burgundians
➤ Goths	➤ Franks
➤ Ostrogoths	➤ Jutes, Angles, Saxons
➤ Visigoths	➤ Irish
➤ Alans	➤ Picts
➤ Vandals, Alans, Sueves	

The fine mausoleum of Theodoric in Ravenna demonstrates how the Ostrogothic chief accepted and emulated the Roman heritage.

The Goths

The Visigoths (western Goths), under a treaty of 382, were settled in Lower Moesia and many served in the imperial army. A dispute over tribute between their leader Alaric and the Senate led to an invasion of Italy and, in 410, the sack of Rome, which shook the foundations of the Empire. In 418 they secured a settlement with Rome and set up a kingdom in Aquitaine. After the death of Attila the Hun in 453, the Ostrogoths (eastern Goths) settled in Pannonia. Under their leader Theodoric, they also began to assert their independence. After campaigning in the Balkans, they moved to Italy in 489 and, after a three-year siege, captured the city of Ravenna, which they made capital of the Ostrogothic kingdom of Italy.

SEE ALSO:

Africa: pp.160–161

Europe: pp.180–183

West Asia: pp.224–225

North and East Asia: pp.260–261

The Goths

376: Goths petition Emperor Valens to settle within Roman Empire

395: Alaric, Visigothic leader, seeks homeland within Roman Empire

453: Ostrogoths embark on bloody campaigns against East Roman Empire

492: Ostrogothic king Theodoric defeats Odoacer at Ravenna to become king of Italy

526: Death of Theodoric

350 — 400 — 450 — 500 — 550

378: Goths defeat and kill Valens at battle of Adrianopolis

410: Visigoths, under Alaric, sack Rome

414: New leader, Athaulf, sets up Visigothic state at Narbo (Narbonne), which expands into Iberia

507: Visigoths defeated by Franks and driven out of Aquitaine

533: Beginning of reconquest of Italy by East Roman Empire

The Huns

After migrating across Asia, the Huns reached Europe in the late 4th century. They settled on the Danube plain just beyond the frontier of the Roman Empire, and built a capital on the River Tisza. Under their leader, Attila, they terrorized the Romans with bloodthirsty campaigns in the Balkans, but were defeated at the battle of the Catalaunian Fields by an army of Romans and Goths. Attila then attacked Italy, sacking Aquileia and Mediolanum, but was persuaded to spare Rome by Pope Leo I. After his death in 453, the Huns' European empire quickly disintegrated.

The Huns

c.370: First appearance of Huns in eastern Europe

c.444: Attila becomes king of the Huns

453: Death of Attila, followed by retreat of Huns

300 — 350 — 400 — 450 — 500

350: White Huns (Hephthalites) invade Persia and India

420: Huns build capital at Tisza (Theiss) on Hungarian plains

451: Attila invades Gaul; defeated at Catalaunian Fields

For steppe nomads, such as the Huns, mobility was vital. Bronze cauldrons, which could be carried on horseback, were part of the Huns' equipment, and have been found at many sites on the steppes and in central Europe.

Map labels:

Volga

Huns pre–376

Steppes

Don

Alans pre–376

c.370: First appearance in west of the Huns, steppe nomads related to the Hephthalites, who started to invade India about the same time

c.370: Huns overwhelm Alans

Goths pre–376

Caucasus

Caspian Sea

Black Sea

ARMENIA

Lake Van

Lake Urmia

ROMAN EMPIRE
from 395

SASSANIAN EMPIRE

Zagros Mountains

MINOR

Antioch

Tigris

SYRIA

Cyprus

Euphrates

PALESTINE

Jerusalem

Alexandria

EGYPT

The inheritors of western Europe

The magnificent votive crown of the 7th-century king Reccesuinth illustrates the importance of Christianity in Iberia under the Visigoths. Their rule lasted from the 5th century to the Arab conquest of 711.

By 526, the waves of migrations had redrawn the map of western Europe. The Ostrogoths, under their charismatic leader Theodoric, controlled Italy, while the Visigoths had captured most of the Iberian Peninsula. The Vandals were established in North Africa, the Sueves in Galicia, and the Burgundians, who crossed the Rhine c.400, had settled in southeast France. The most enduring of the many Germanic kingdoms, however, would prove to be that of the Franks, founded in 456 by Clovis, which laid the foundations of modern France and Germany.

② Europe in 526

Map labels:

Finno-Ugrians

Picts

Norsemen

Baltic Sea

Turkic peoples

North Sea

Jutes

Angles

Saxons

Baltic peoples

Volga

Celts

Saxons

Angles

Jutes

Elbe

Rhine

Thuringians

Slavs

Caspian Sea

ATLANTIC OCEAN

Bretons

Meuse

Seine

KINGDOM OF THE FRANKS

Alemanni

Danube

Lombards

Dniester

Alans

Caucasus

Lyon

BURGUNDIAN KINGDOM

KINGDOM OF THE OSTROGOTHS

Milan

Gepids

Danube

Black Sea

KINGDOM OF THE SUEVES

Douro

Basques

Toulouse

Corsica

Ravenna

Rome

Constantinople

EAST ROMAN EMPIRE

SYRIA

SASSANIAN EMPIRE

Tagus

KINGDOM OF THE VISIGOTHS

Toledo

Balearic Islands

Sardinia

Sicily

Crete

Cyprus

KINGDOM OF THE VANDALS

Carthage

Mediterranean Sea

Arabian Peninsula

Berbers

Alexandria

AFRICA

EGYPT

Nile

500 km

500 miles

THE WORLD 500–750

THE RAPID RECOVERY of the ancient world from the onslaught of invading nomads is evident in the rise of two great empires in West Asia and China. The new religion of Islam was based on the teachings of Muhammad, an Arabian merchant from Mecca. Fired by a zeal for conquest and conversion, Islamic armies overran West Asia and North Africa, and by 750, had created an empire that stretched from the Indus to Spain. Under the Tang dynasty, Chinese civilization reached new heights; Tang control penetrated deep into Central Asia and Chinese cultural influence was widespread. In the Americas, the Maya remained the most advanced civilization, though their small city-states did not have the far-reaching influence of the great city of Teotihuacán.

The Byzantines were the champions of Christianity. This mosaic shows Emperor Justinian as God's representative on Earth.

Europe

The Franks became the most powerful of all Rome's Germanic successors. United under Clovis I, their overlordship was extended to the south of France and east of the Rhine. Constantinople was the Christian capital of the Byzantine Empire. The Emperor Justinian (527–65) reconquered North Africa and much of Italy, briefly creating an empire stretching from Spain to Persia. Over the next two centuries much of this territory was lost to Islam and, in the Balkans, to Slavic invaders.

Europe

500	550	600	650	700	750

527: Justinian becomes Byzantine emperor

597: Papal missionary Augustine converts the king of Kent to Christianity

674–78: Arabs besiege Constantinople, but fail to take it

732: Frankish leader Charles Martel defeats Arab armies at battle of Poitiers

511: Death of Frankish king Clovis

531: Frankish kingdom absorbs Burgundy

c.590: The Avars, nomads from the steppes, establish state on Hungarian plains

680: Bulgars invade Balkans

711: Muslim invasion of Spain

The World in 750

- Tang Empire
- Byzantine Empire
- Umayyad Caliphate
- Kök Türk Empire 551–572
- East Roman Empire 554–565
- Horsha's Empire c.640
- Avar Empire c.595

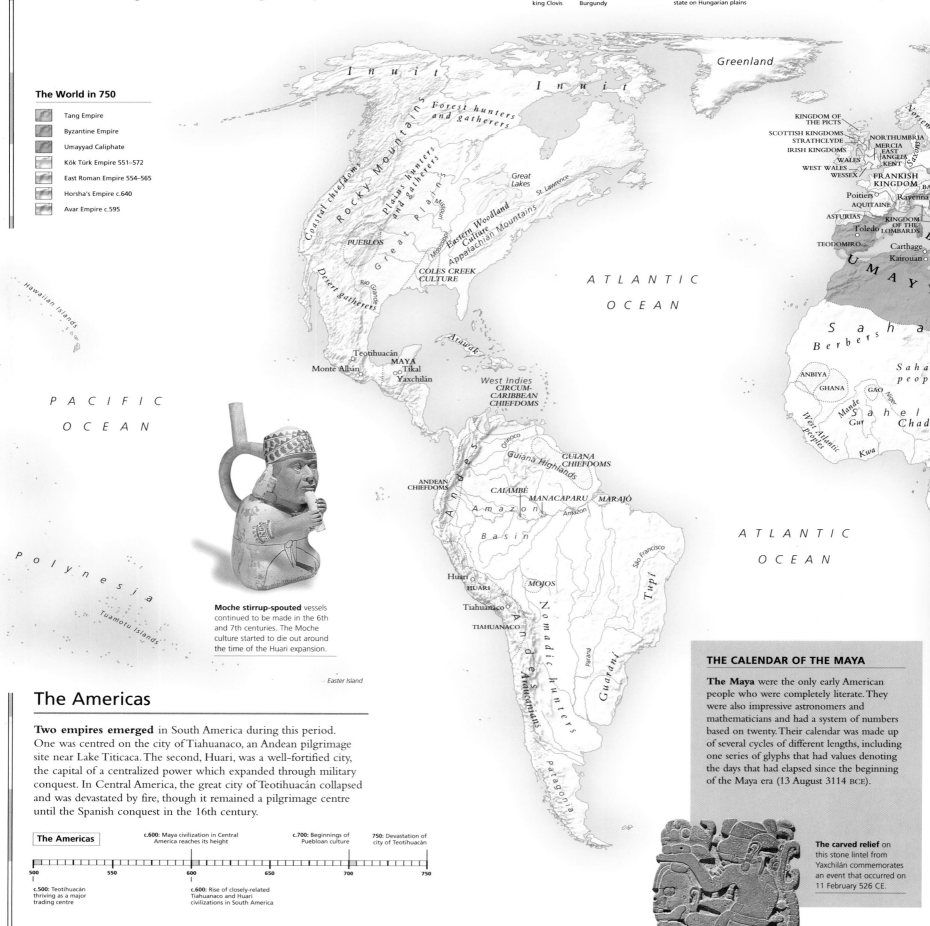

Moche stirrup-spouted vessels continued to be made in the 6th and 7th centuries. The Moche culture started to die out around the time of the Huari expansion.

The Americas

Two empires emerged in South America during this period. One was centred on the city of Tiahuanaco, an Andean pilgrimage site near Lake Titicaca. The second, Huari, was a well-fortified city, the capital of a centralized power which expanded through military conquest. In Central America, the great city of Teotihuacán collapsed and was devastated by fire, though it remained a pilgrimage centre until the Spanish conquest in the 16th century.

The Americas

500	550	600	650	700	750

c.600: Maya civilization in Central America reaches its height

c.700: Beginnings of Puebloan culture

750: Devastation of city of Teotihuacán

c.500: Teotihuacán thriving as a major trading centre

c.600: Rise of closely-related Tiahuanaco and Huari civilizations in South America

THE CALENDAR OF THE MAYA

The Maya were the only early American people who were completely literate. They were also impressive astronomers and mathematicians and had a system of numbers based on twenty. Their calendar was made up of several cycles of different lengths, including one series of glyphs that had values denoting the days that had elapsed since the beginning of the Maya era (13 August 3114 BCE).

The carved relief on this stone lintel from Yaxchilán commemorates an event that occurred on 11 February 526 CE.

The Dome of the Rock in Jerusalem was built in 692 over the ruins of the Jewish Temple. It is sacred to Islam as the site of Muhammad's journey to heaven.

West Asia

In the 7th century the whole of West Asia was overrun by Arabian armies, soldiers of Islam, inspired to conquer and convert by the new religion founded by Muhammad. They were able to exploit the weaknesses of the two great powers in the region, the Sassanians and the Byzantines. Sassanian Persia had reached its peak under Khosrau I (531–79), who invaded Byzantine Syria and captured Antioch. But continuing conflict with the Byzantines led to a crushing defeat at Nineveh in 628.

CLASSICAL ARAB WORLD MAPS

When the Arabs took over much of the Greek-speaking eastern Mediterranean, they seized on the Classical scholarship of Alexandria, including the famous *Geography* of Ptolemy (*see p.44*). Though no maps from this period survive, it seems that, while the map-making tradition died out in the west, it was kept alive by Arab scholars, albeit in the academic style of this later world map.

Al-Istakhri's world map, from the 10th century, uses a Ptolemaic projection, but with south at the top.

SEE ALSO:

North America: pp.122–123

South America: pp.142–145

Africa: pp.162–163

Europe: pp.182–185

West Asia: pp.226–227

South and Southeast Asia: pp.242–245

North and East Asia: pp.262–265

Australasia and Oceania: pp.280–281

West Asia

570: Prophet Muhammad born in Mecca
622: The Hegira: Muhammad and his followers move to Medina; start of Islamic era
656: Arabians overrun Persia
661: Start of Umayyad dynasty. Damascus is centre of Islamic empire
698: Arabs capture Carthage

500   550   600   650   700   750

531: Beginning of reign of Sassanian ruler, Khosrau I Anohshirvanh
628: Defeat of Sassanians by Byzantine emperor Heraclius
637: Arabian armies capture Sassanian capital, Ctesiphon
674–78: Arabian siege of Constantinople
711: Islamic armies cross the Strait of Gibraltar and conquer Spain

Tang ceramics were of very high quality. This 7th-century figurine portrays one of the celebrated Ferghana horses, prized for their speed.

East Asia

538: Buddhism reaches Japan
589: Turko-Chinese Sui reunite China
640: Tang armies reach Turfan in Central Asia
c.660: Tang forces in India and Central Asia
710: Nara becomes Japanese capital

500   550   600   650   700   750

c.550: Kök Türk (Blue Turks) establish vast Central Asian empire
617: Sui dynasty collapses; succeeded in 618 by Tang
645: Buddhism reaches Tibet
668: Korean peninsula united under Silla dynasty

East Asia

After centuries of conflict, China was united under the Sui dynasty (581–617), which was succeeded by the Tang in 618. Chinese territory was again extended into Central Asia, protectorates were set up as far afield as eastern Persia, and they gained control of much of the Silk Road. Chinese culture exerted a strong influence over surrounding areas; Buddhism reached Japan from China in about 538. Under Chinese influence, Japan underwent a series of social and political reforms: the abolition of slavery, the creation of a civil service, and the adoption of a modified form of written Chinese.

Oceania

The island of Fiji was first settled around 1500 BCE and it was there and in nearby islands that Polynesian culture developed. Descendants of these first settlers would eventually colonize the whole Pacific Ocean. The Polynesians sailed across the open ocean in twin-hulled outrigger canoes, using sails and paddles, with only their knowledge of the skies, winds, and ocean currents to guide them. By 400 CE they had reached Easter Island and the Hawaiian Islands, but did not colonize New Zealand until about 700.

Oceania

c.600: Polynesian colonists settle the Tuamotu Islands
c.650: Easter Islanders start to build *ahus*, sacred stone platforms
c.700: Polynesians reach North Island of New Zealand

500   550   600   650   700   750

This greenstone *heitiki* is a traditional ornament of the Maori, one of the most recent cultures of Polynesia.

THE IMPACT OF ISLAM

This richly-decorated copy of the Koran dates from 704.

THE RAPID SPREAD OF ISLAM was one of the most decisive developments of the medieval period. The Arabian Peninsula was conquered for Islam within ten years, and following the death of Muhammad in 632, the expansion of Islam continued unabated. By the early 8th century, Arab armies fired by the concept of *jihad* (holy war) had reached the borders of India in the east and were invading Spain in the west. With the establishment of the Abbasid Caliphate, by 750 the Muslim realm was second only to that of China in extent and cultural sophistication. The Caliphate controlled Eurasian trade on land and by sea – trade which would spread the faith further afield, deep into Africa, across the Indian Ocean and north into Central Asia, over the subsequent centuries.

The spread of Islam 623–751

The Great Mosque at Kairouan is one of the oldest surviving Islamic buildings. It was begun in 670, shortly after Arab armies had swept through the Byzantine possessions along the North African coast.

Muhammad's vision of the Archangel Gabriel in about 610 began a process of revelation, enshrined in the Koran, the Holy Book which lies at the heart of Islam. His opposition to polytheism and adherence to a strict code of observation and conduct led to hostility in Mecca, and his withdrawal to Medina (the Hegira) in 622. Here the first Muslim state was established. By 630, with an army of 10,000 followers, he re-entered Mecca, and began the conquest of Arabia. Conversion swelled the Muslim ranks, and Muhammad's work was continued after his death in 632 by his disciples. Within a century the heartland of Eurasia was dominated by Islam. Although Muslim warriors believed it their duty to conquer in the name of Islam, conquered peoples, especially Christians and Jews, were treated with tolerance.

The early history of the Caliphate

Muhammad's first successors – who became known as caliphs – were early disciples (Companions of the Prophet): Abu Bakr (632–34), 'Umar (634–44), and 'Uthman, who was murdered in 656. The authority of 'Uthman's successor Ali – Muhammad's cousin and son-in-law – was challenged by 'Uthman's family, the Umayyads. Ali was murdered in 661, and the Umayyads gained power as caliphs; their supporters were known as Sunnites. A minority of Muslims, however, known as Shi'a, saw the descendants of Ali (the Imams) as the true successors of the Prophet. This fundamental division within the faith continues to this day.

Harun al-Rashid, the great Abbasid caliph, reigned from 786 to 809. This illustration shows him in an episode from the *1001 Nights* with a barber in a Turkish Bath.

❶ The growth of the Islamic world

Muslim lands by 634	⚔ Muslim victory, with date
Muslim lands by 656	⚔ Muslim defeat, with date
Muslim lands by 756	649 date of Muslim conquest
→ Muslim raid, with date	Byzantine Empire c.610
• new city founded by Muslims	Sassanian Empire c.610
🏰 Muslim fortress	Frankish Empire c.610

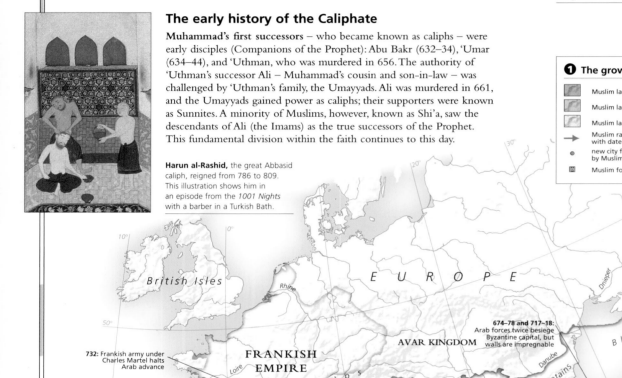

732: Frankish army under Charles Martel halts Arab advance

674–78 and 717–18: Arab forces twice besiege Byzantine capital, but walls are impregnable

732: Frankish army under Charles Martel halts Arab advance

711: Berber general Tariq leads troops across Strait of Gibraltar (Jabal al-Tariq, the Rock of Tariq)

695–97: Byzantines driven from Carthage

The spread of Islam

622: Beginning of Islamic calendar, marked by the Hegira of Muhammad

634: Caliphate of 'Umar (to 644)

641: Conquest of Egypt

644: Caliphate of 'Uthman (to 646)

661: Umayyad Caliphate (to 750)

670: Foundation of Kairouan

692: Dome of the Rock mosque in Jerusalem

732: Arab armies halted at Poitiers

751: Arab armies defeat Chinese on Talas River

762: Baghdad becomes Abbasid capital

632: Death of Muhammad; succession of Abu Bakr (to 634)

637: Conquest of Mesopotamia

656: Imamate of Ali (to 661)

664: Conquest of Kabul

711: Invasion of Iberian Peninsula by Tariq; rapid conquest of Visigothic kingdom

718: Christian victory at battle of Covadonga halts Muslim advance in Iberian Peninsula

744: Abbasid Caliphate established

756: Breakaway Umayyad Emirate established at Cordova (to 1031); claims status of caliphate in 928

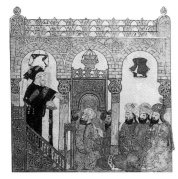

Preaching and teaching spread the Arabic language throughout the Islamic world. This 13th-century Persian illustration shows a preacher in the mosque at Samarkand.

The impact of the Islamic advance

Water-wheels for irrigation were introduced wherever the Arabs settled. This example stands at Hamah in Syria. The Arabs also introduced Asian fruits, such as peaches and apricots.

The Islamic imprint 1000–1200

By 1000, the Islamic world had become broadly divided into two caliphates: the Abbasids, based at Baghdad, and, in the west, the Umayyads (a branch of the Abbasids' predecessors), who ruled the Iberian Peninsula. So extensive were the Abbasid domains that many subsidiary rulers wielded local power in varying degrees and were able to found autonomous dynasties. Further, the movement of peoples into the Islamic world caused further decentralization of power. In the west, the Berbers gradually established a string of local dynasties along the Maghreb coast. The Shi'ite Fatimids emerged in North Africa, conquered Egypt, and claimed caliphate status, but the most significant blow to the Abbasid Caliphate was the invasion of the Seljuk Turks from Central Asia, who moved across southwest Asia, conquered Baghdad and drove back the frontiers of the Byzantine Empire, eventually occupying Anatolia.

SEE ALSO:

Africa: pp.162–163

Europe: pp.186–187

West Asia: pp.226–227

South and Southeast Asia: pp.242–243

2 The Islamic imprint c.800–1200

- Islamic world c.1000
- Abbasid Caliphate at its greatest extent c.800
- campaigns of Seljuk Turks
- campaigns of Berbers
- further expansion of Islam

ZIRIDS Muslim dynasty, with dates

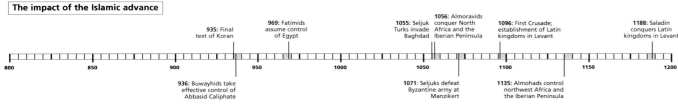

Timeline:
- 935: Final text of Koran
- 936: Buwayhids take effective control of Abbasid Caliphate
- 969: Fatimids assume control of Egypt
- 1055: Seljuk Turks invade Baghdad
- 1056: Almoravids conquer North Africa and the Iberian Peninsula
- 1071: Seljuks defeat Byzantine army at Manzikert
- 1096: First Crusade; establishment of Latin kingdoms in Levant
- 1135: Almohads control northwest Africa and the Iberian Peninsula
- 1188: Saladin conquers Latin kingdoms in Levant

800 | 850 | 900 | 950 | 1000 | 1050 | 1100 | 1150 | 1200

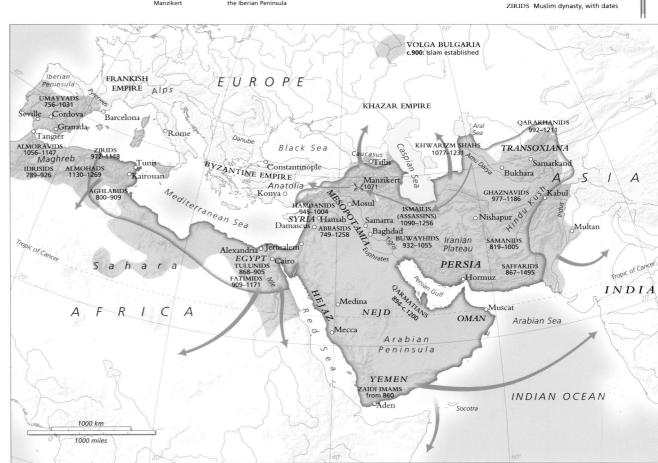

Samarra: an Islamic city

Founded by the Abbasid caliph al-Mu'tasim, Samarra was the Abbasid capital from 836–892, and grew to sprawl some 40 km (25 miles) along the east bank of the Tigris. The new city was based around earlier settlements; it was not walled, and was organized into residential cantonments arranged around central features such as palaces and mosques, and included luxurious facilities such as racetracks and a gigantic 30 sq km game reserve. Later caliphs added substantial areas, notably al-Mu'tasim's successor al-Mutawakkil, who built a new centre to the north, Ja'fariyya. The Abbasid court returned to its original capital at Baghdad after the death of the eighth caliph, al-Mu'tamid.

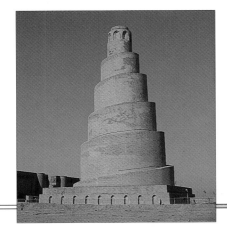

The spiral minaret of the Great Mosque of al-Mutawakkil at Samarra is one of the few standing remains of the city.

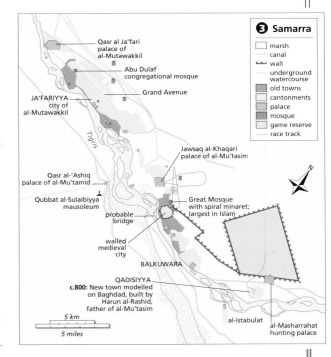

3 Samarra

- marsh
- canal
- wall
- underground watercourse
- old towns
- cantonments
- palace
- mosque
- game reserve
- race track

THE WORLD 750–1000

THE DISINTEGRATION OF GREAT EMPIRES and conflicts between warring dynasties were widespread throughout the 9th and 10th centuries. In Europe, Charlemagne was crowned western Emperor in 800, but his Frankish Empire was broken apart by disputes over inheritance. The Abbasid Caliphate, based in Baghdad, could not maintain central control over the vast Islamic world. New Islamic dynasties, such as the Fatimids of northern Africa, broke away from Baghdad's authority. In China, the mighty Tang Empire split into small warring states while in Central America, the Maya were in decline. In contrast to this political fragmentation, powerful new states developed in many parts of the world: the Khmers in Southeast Asia, Koryo in Korea, the Toltecs in Mexico, Ghana and Kanem–Bornu in Africa, and Kievan Rus in eastern Europe.

Europe

Charlemagne, king of the Franks, incorporated most of western Europe into a single dominion. After disputes over his inheritance, the kingdom was divided into three parts. Henry I, the Saxon successor, extended his influence over the German duchies, and conquered Italy. His son, Otto I, defeated the Magyars and was crowned Holy Roman Emperor. In the west, the Carolingian Empire and the British Isles fell prey to Viking raiders.

Ireland suffered badly from Viking raids in the 9th and 10th centuries, so monasteries built distinctive round towers, such as these at Glendalough, as lookouts and refuges.

Europe

752: Lombards capture Ravenna

774: Charlemagne defeats Lombards in Italy

800: Charlemagne crowned Holy Roman Emperor by the pope in Rome

827: Crete and Sicily occupied by Saracen (Arab) raiders

843: Treaty of Verdun divides Carolingian empire into three

884: Kiev becomes capital of new Russian state

885: Saxon ruler, Alfred the Great, reconquers London from Vikings

896: Danish raiders besiege Paris

955: Otto I defeats Magyars and halts expansion of Hungary

996: Start of war between Byzantines, led by Emperor Basil II, and Bulgaria

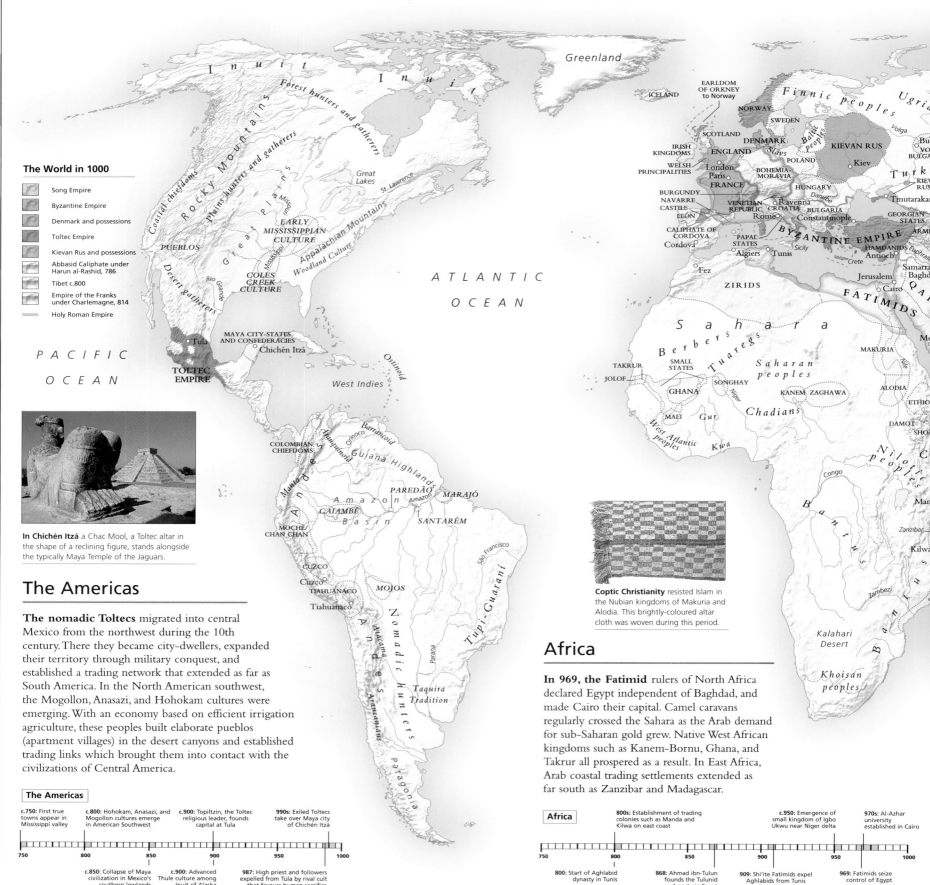

The World in 1000

- Song Empire
- Byzantine Empire
- Denmark and possessions
- Toltec Empire
- Kievan Rus and possessions
- Abbasid Caliphate under Harun al-Rashid, 786
- Tibet c.800
- Empire of the Franks under Charlemagne, 814
- Holy Roman Empire

In Chichén Itzá a Chac Mool, a Toltec altar in the shape of a reclining figure, stands alongside the typically Maya Temple of the Jaguars.

Coptic Christianity resisted Islam in the Nubian kingdoms of Makuria and Alodia. This brightly-coloured altar cloth was woven during this period.

The Americas

The nomadic Toltecs migrated into central Mexico from the northwest during the 10th century. There they became city-dwellers, expanded their territory through military conquest, and established a trading network that extended as far as South America. In the North American southwest, the Mogollon, Anasazi, and Hohokam cultures were emerging. With an economy based on efficient irrigation agriculture, these peoples built elaborate pueblos (apartment villages) in the desert canyons and established trading links which brought them into contact with the civilizations of Central America.

The Americas

c.750: First true towns appear in Mississippi valley

c.800: Hohokam, Anasazi, and Mogollon cultures emerge in American Southwest

c.850: Collapse of Maya civilization in Mexico's southern lowlands

c.900: Topiltzin, the Toltec religious leader, founds capital at Tula

c.900: Advanced Thule culture among Inuit of Alaska

987: High priest and followers expelled from Tula by rival cult that favours human sacrifice

990s: Exiled Toltecs take over Maya city of Chichén Itzá

Africa

In 969, the Fatimid rulers of North Africa declared Egypt independent of Baghdad, and made Cairo their capital. Camel caravans regularly crossed the Sahara as the Arab demand for sub-Saharan gold grew. Native West African kingdoms such as Kanem-Bornu, Ghana, and Takrur all prospered as a result. In East Africa, Arab coastal trading settlements extended as far south as Zanzibar and Madagascar.

Africa

800: Start of Aghlabid dynasty in Tunis

800s: Establishment of trading colonies such as Manda and Kilwa on east coast

868: Ahmad ibn-Tulun founds the Tulunid dynasty in Egypt

909: Shi'ite Fatimids expel Aghlabids from Tunis

c.950: Emergence of small kingdom of Igbo Ukwu near Niger delta

969: Fatimids seize control of Egypt

970s: Al-Azhar university established in Cairo

PRINTING IN CHINA

The Chinese had been experimenting with ways of reproducing writing and illustrations for centuries, before they made their greatest breakthrough under the Tang in the 8th century. Carving characters and pictures in reverse onto wooden blocks was a time-consuming process, but it allowed many hundreds of copies to made before the wood's surface became too worn. All kinds of documents – from religious texts to tax receipts – were printed by this method.

The earliest printed document that can be dated with certainty is *The Diamond Sutra*, a work of Buddhist doctrine printed on a scroll, produced in 868.

After the fervour of the 7th-century *jihads*, many Arab tribes subsequently turned against one another as they competed to rule the various parts of the Islamic world.

West Asia

The Abbasid dynasty came to power in 750. Though the arts, culture, and trade flourished under their rule, disagreements over the succession meant that their authority was not universally recognized. Even in Baghdad the caliphs became figureheads, real power being in the hands of Turkish mercenary or slave troops and Persian administrators. Under a new dynasty of Macedonian rulers (867–1081) the Byzantine Empire reached its apogee, and came into conflict with the Arabs to the east. Byzantine troops regained control of most of Anatolia and, in 969, reconquered Antioch.

SEE ALSO:

North America: pp.122–123

South America: pp.144–145

Africa: pp.162–163

Europe: pp.184–185

West Asia: pp.226–227

South and Southeast Asia: pp.244–245

North and East Asia: pp.262–265

Australasia and Oceania: pp.280–281

West Asia

750: Umayyad Caliphate is overthrown and succeeded by the Abbasid dynasty

786: Under Caliph Harun al-Rashid Baghdad becomes centre of arts and learning

863: Byzantines annihilate Arab forces to stem Muslim advance in Anatolia

945: Persian Buwayhids conquer Baghdad but allow caliph to reign as figurehead

976: Byzantine forces threaten to take Jerusalem

762: Abbasid capital founded at Baghdad

836: Baghdad terrorized by Turkish slave troops; Abbasid Caliph al-Mutasim builds new capital at Samarra

936: Caliphs of Baghdad lose effective power; caliphate under control of Turkish troops

ARAB STAR MAPS

Arab scientists and mathematicians were the finest in the world and their astronomers added greatly to our knowledge of the heavens during this period. As well as using the night sky to set a course at sea and help them cross the desert, the Arabs continued to name stars and map constellations in the tradition of Ptolemy and other Greek astronomers. Many stars, such as Aldebaran, Rigel, and Rasalgethi, are still known by their Arab names.

The constellation of Andromeda is one of many attractive illustrations in *The Book of the Fixed Stars* compiled by Abd al-Rahman ibn Umar al-Sufi in the 10th century. The individual stars forming the constellation are shown in red.

Buddhism affected all aspects of life in Tang China, the Buddha assuming Chinese features, as in this wall painting from Dunhuang.

This bronze of the god Shiva was made under the Chola dynasty. In this period cults of individual Hindu deities grew in popularity.

South and Southeast Asia

In the north, the Islamic kingdom of the Afghan ruler Mahmud of Ghazni stretched from the Oxus to the Indus, while states such as Gurjara-Pratiharas and the Buddhist Palas vied for the Ganges plain. To the south, the Tamil Cholas and the Chalukyas fought over the Godavari and Krishna rivers. Chola conquests expanded to include Ceylon and parts of the Malay Peninsula.

South and Southeast Asia

802: Angkorian dynasty founded by King Jayavarman II

889: Khmer King Indravarman I begins construction of Angkor

997: Mahmud of Ghazni extends rule into northwest India

c.800: Construction of Buddhist temple at Borobudur, Java

886: Chola dynasty rules much of southern India

c.900: Gurjara-Pratiharas dominates northern India

962: Foundation of Afghan Ghaznavid dynasty

East Asia

Threats of internal rebellion in the middle of the 8th century weakened the Tang dynasty's control of China. As a result the empire became more inward looking and the political and economic centre of gravity began to shift south to the Yangtze valley. The Tang dynasty eventually collapsed after massive peasant uprisings in the 9th century, and China split into ten separate states until 960–79, when it was reunified under the Song. Both Korea and Japan were governed by strong, centralized Buddhist dynasties.

East Asia

751: Defeat of Chinese by Muslim forces at battle of Talas River

794: Kyoto becomes capital of Japan

868: *The Diamond Sutra*, world's oldest surviving printed work

935: Foundation of kingdom of Koryo in Korea

979: Song establish power in China

756: Rebel general An Lushan captures Chang'an

763: Tang China is invaded by Tibetans

870s: Peasant uprisings throughout Tang China

907: End of the Tang dynasty

970: Paper money introduced by Chinese government

EXPLORERS OF THE OCEANS

The stylized image of a ship decorates this early Viking coin, which was minted at Hedeby in the 9th century.

IN THE 1ST MILLENNIUM CE, three peoples excelled all others as navigators of the world's oceans: the Vikings, the Arabs, and the Polynesians. The traders and raiders of Scandinavia created the fast, efficient Viking longship, which took them along the rivers of Russia to the Black Sea, and across the Atlantic Ocean to Iceland and North America. The Arabs were already accomplished seafarers; the discovery, in the 8th century, of the sea route to China via the Strait of Malacca heralded a new era of long-distance trade, and Arab ships sailed to the East Indies, East Africa, and China. Perhaps the most extraordinary seafarers of all were the Polynesians, who by 1000 CE had completed the colonization of all the islands of the Pacific.

These 12th-century walrus ivory chesspieces are from Lewis in the Outer Hebrides. The islands were settled by Norwegians in the 9th and 10th centuries, but remained a regular target for Viking raids.

NORTH AMERICA

Region visited for timber by Greenland settlers

St Lawrence

VINLAND

c.1000: Site of small Norse settlement, occupied for about 20 years

L'Anse aux Meadows

MARKLAND

Newfoundland

Most southerly region visited by Vikings – so named for vines growing there

800 km
800 miles

The Viking world

Harsh northern conditions drove the Vikings to sail in search of new lands and resources. At first they dominated their Baltic neighbours, taking tribute in the form of amber, wax, fish, ivory, and furs. Norwegians and Danes exploited weaknesses in France, England, and Ireland, using their fast, manoeuvrable longships to conduct lightning raids, exacting tribute, conquering, and colonizing. Eventually, in a quest for land, they crossed the Atlantic, reaching Iceland in 860 and Newfoundland c.1000. Swedish traders penetrated the navigable rivers of Russia to dominate the lucrative trade with Constantinople and the Arab world. Varangians (as these eastern Vikings were called) founded Kievan Rus, the first Russian state, and their fighting qualities were recognized by the Byzantine emperors, who employed them as their elite mercenary guard.

Viking longships were oar-powered, ranging from 16–30 m in length. Their light, flexible hulls 'rode' the waves and made them ideal for raiding in shallow, coastal waters.

Viking voyages

793: Vikings plunder island monastery of Lindisfarne off northeast coast of England

845: Vikings sack Paris; exact tribute from Franks

866: Vikings take York

c.900: Norwegians settle in Scotland and northwest England

c.1000: Voyages from Greenland to Newfoundland and coast of North America

700   800   900   1000   1100

c.789: First recorded Viking raid on England; first raids on Ireland and Scotland recorded in 795

839: Swedes travel through Russia to Constantinople

862: Novgorod founded by Rurik the Viking

c.930: Viking settlement of Iceland complete

986: Erik the Red begins settlement of Greenland

1042: End of Danish rule in England

The Polynesians

The first wave of colonization of the Pacific, between 2000 and 1500 BCE, took settlers from New Guinea and neighbouring islands as far as the Fiji Islands. From there, they sailed on to the Tonga and Samoa groups. In about 200 BCE, the Polynesians embarked on a series of far longer voyages, crossing vast tracts of empty ocean to settle the Marquesas, the Society Islands, Hawaii, Rapa Nui (Easter Island), and New Zealand. By about 1000 CE they had discovered almost every island in the Pacific. They sailed in double-hulled canoes, laden with seed plants, chickens, and pigs. The canoes could tack into the wind, and they probably navigated by observing the sun and the stars, the direction of prevailing winds, and the flight patterns of homing birds.

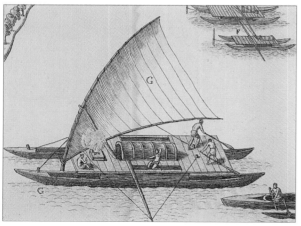

On their epic ocean voyages, the Polynesians used twin-hulled canoes, similar to the one in this 19th-century engraving, up to 30 m long. Canoes with an outrigger, attached to the hull and kept to windward for balance, were probably for inshore sailing and shorter voyages. Both types of vessel could be powered by oars or sails.

Polynesian voyages 1500 BCE–1000 CE

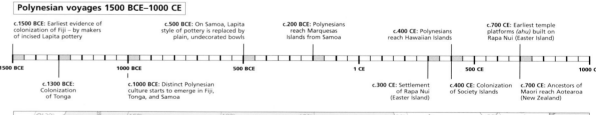

c.1500 BCE: Earliest evidence of colonization of Fiji – by makers of incised Lapita pottery

c.500 BCE: On Samoa, Lapita style of pottery is replaced by plain, undecorated bowls

c.200 BCE: Polynesians reach Marquesas Islands from Samoa

c.400 CE: Polynesians reach Hawaiian Islands

c.700 CE: Earliest temple platforms (ahu) built on Rapa Nui (Easter Island)

1500 BCE   1000 BCE   500 BCE   1 CE   500 CE   1000 CE

c.1300 BCE: Colonization of Tonga

c.1000 BCE: Distinct Polynesian culture starts to emerge in Fiji, Tonga, and Samoa

c.300 CE: Settlement of Rapa Nui (Easter Island)

c.400 CE: Colonization of Society Islands

c.700 CE: Ancestors of Maori reach Aotearoa (New Zealand)

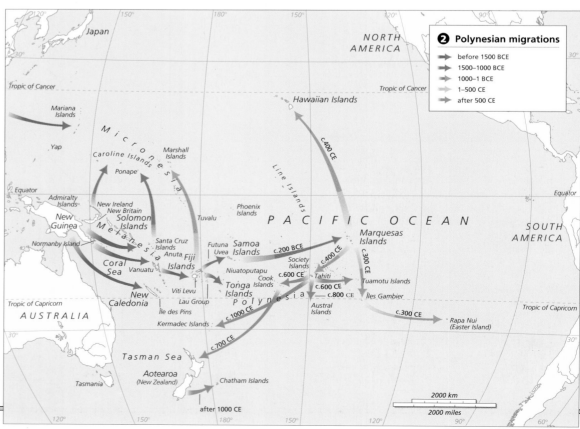

Japan

NORTH AMERICA

Tropic of Cancer

2 Polynesian migrations

— before 1500 BCE
— 1500–1000 BCE
— 1000–1 BCE
— 1–500 CE
— after 500 CE

Mariana Islands

Hawaiian Islands

Micronesia

Yap

Caroline Islands

Marshall Islands

Equator

Admiralty Islands

New Ireland

New Britain

Solomon Islands

New Guinea

Normanby Island

Melanesia

Santa Cruz Islands

Anuta

Tuvalu

Phoenix Islands

Line Islands

PACIFIC OCEAN

SOUTH AMERICA

Coral Sea

Vanuatu

Fiji Islands

Futuna

Uvea

Samoa Islands

c.200 BCE

Society Islands

Marquesas Islands

c.400 CE

c.300 CE

New Caledonia

Viti Levu

Lau Group

Île des Pins

Niuatoputapu

Tonga Islands

c.600 CE

Cook Islands

Tahiti

c.600 CE

Austral Islands

Tuamotu Islands

Îles Gambier

Polynesia

c.800 CE

Tropic of Capricorn

AUSTRALIA

c.1000 CE

Kermadec Islands

c.300 CE

Rapa Nui (Easter Island)

c.700 CE

Tasman Sea

Tasmania

Aotearoa (New Zealand)

Chatham Islands

after 1000 CE

2000 km
2000 miles

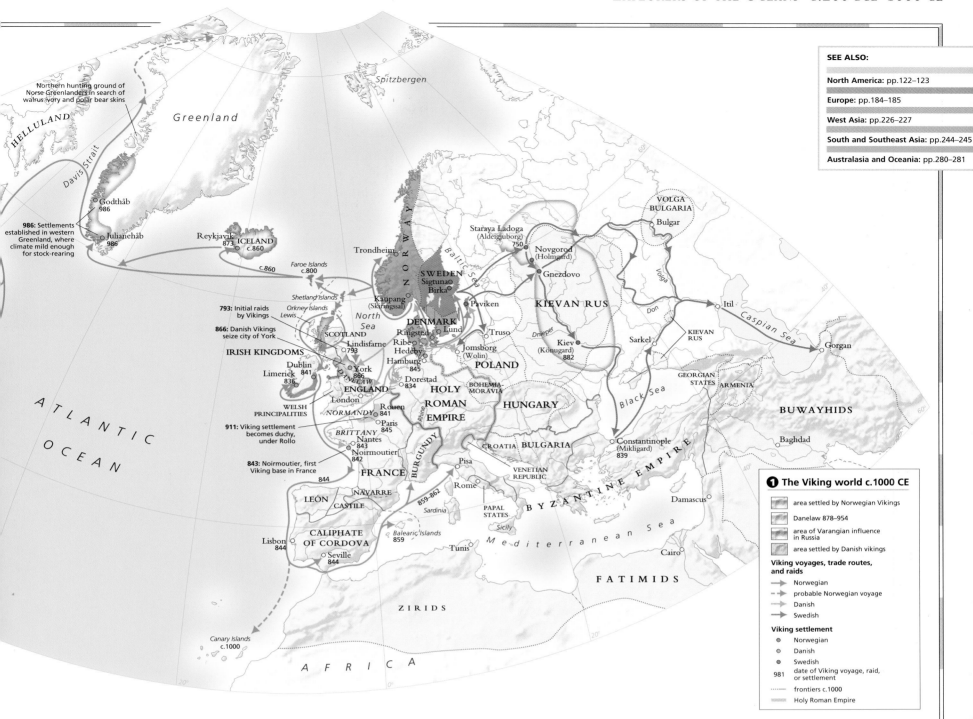

SEE ALSO:

North America: pp.122–123

Europe: pp.184–185

West Asia: pp.226–227

South and Southeast Asia: pp.244–245

Australasia and Oceania: pp.280–281

Northern hunting ground of Norse Greenlanders in search of walrus ivory and polar bear skins

986: Settlements established in western Greenland, where climate mild enough for stock-rearing

793: Initial raids by Vikings

866: Danish Vikings seize city of York

911: Viking settlement becomes duchy, under Rollo

843: Noirmoutier, first Viking base in France

❶ The Viking world c.1000 CE

- area settled by Norwegian Vikings
- Danelaw 878–954
- area of Varangian influence in Russia
- area settled by Danish vikings

Viking voyages, trade routes, and raids

- → Norwegian
- ⇢ probable Norwegian voyage
- → Danish
- → Swedish

Viking settlement

- ● Norwegian
- ● Danish
- ● Swedish
- 981 date of Viking voyage, raid, or settlement
- ···· frontiers c.1000
- ▬ Holy Roman Empire

Arab traders in the Indian Ocean

The Arabs used the wind systems of the monsoon to propel their ships eastward from the Persian Gulf in November and to return them westward in the summer. In the 8th century, Arab traders discovered the sea-route to Guangzhou (Canton) by way of the Malabar Coast, the Strait of Malacca, and Hanoi, a journey of 120 days, which nevertheless could take between 18 months and three years. The Arabs exported iron, wool, incense, and bullion in return for silk and spices. When the fall of the Tang Empire disrupted trade with China c.1000 CE, the Arabs turned to the East Indies, and Islam consequently became well established in the the islands of Southeast Asia. They also navigated the East African coast to Zanzibar and Madagascar, where they met the Malays who had colonized the island some 300 years earlier.

An Indian ship is depicted in an Arab manuscript of 1238. It has a square-rigged sail, suitable for running with the strong monsoonal winds, well known from the 1st century CE. The capacious hold could carry both passengers and cargo, essential for thriving Indian Ocean trade routes from the 8th century CE.

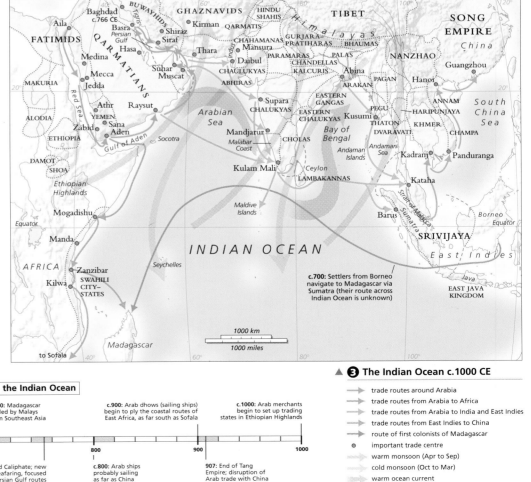

c.700: Settlers from Borneo navigate to Madagascar via Sumatra (their route across Indian Ocean is unknown)

▲ ❸ The Indian Ocean c.1000 CE

- → trade routes around Arabia
- → trade routes from Arabia to Africa
- → trade routes from Arabia to India and East Indies
- → trade routes from East Indies to China
- → route of first colonists of Madagascar
- ● important trade centre
- ⇒ warm monsoon (Apr to Sep)
- ⇒ cold monsoon (Oct to Mar)
- ⇒ warm ocean current

Arab and other traders in the Indian Ocean

c.632: Death of Muhammad begins the era of Arab expansion

c.700: Madagascar settled by Malays from Southeast Asia

c.900: Arab dhows (sailing ships) begin to ply the coastal routes of East Africa, as far south as Sofala

c.1000: Arab merchants begin to set up trading states in Ethiopian Highlands

756: Abbasid Caliphate; new interest in seafaring, focused on Persian Gulf routes

c.800: Arab ships probably sailing as far as China

907: End of Tang Empire; disruption of Arab trade with China

THE WORLD 1000–1200

IN MANY PARTS OF THE WORLD conflict over territory and religion was intense. This was a time when the Christian west was recovering from the tumult that followed the fall of Rome. As marginal land was cleared for agriculture, the population expanded. Trade routes crossed Europe and a mercantile economy developed and prospered. Yet the resurgence of Christian Europe brought it into direct confrontation with Islam when it launched the Crusades to regain the Holy Land. This ultimately proved a failure, but in Spain and Portugal the Christian reconquest made intermittent progress. To the east, the states of northern India fell to Muslim invaders, and Buddhism was finally driven from the sub-continent. In China the Song Empire shrank under pressure from powerful nomadic peoples to the north, such as the Xixia and the Jin.

The power of the Church was expressed in new cathedrals built first in the Romanesque and then in the Gothic style, typified by the soaring facade of Chartres.

Europe

The assimilation in the 11th century of Poland, Hungary, and the Scandinavian kingdoms into the realm of western Christianity brought it to a new peak of power and influence. As western Europeans began to wrest control of the Mediterranean from the Arabs and Byzantines, a new era of prosperity based on trade began. Italian merchants became middlemen in Byzantine trade, and north Italian towns, such as Venice, Genoa, and Pisa, prospered. Elsewhere, forests and marginal land were cleared for agriculture, populations grew, and new towns were founded.

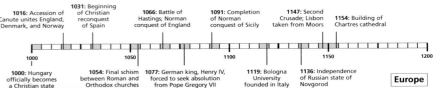

1016: Accession of Canute unites England, Denmark, and Norway	**1031:** Beginning of Christian reconquest of Spain	**1066:** Battle of Hastings; Norman conquest of England	**1091:** Completion of Norman conquest of Sicily	**1147:** Second Crusade; Lisbon taken from Moors	**1154:** Building of Chartres cathedral	

1000 — 1050 — 1100 — 1150 — 1200

1000: Hungary officially becomes a Christian state — **1054:** Final schism between Roman and Orthodox churches — **1077:** German king, Henry IV, forced to seek absolution from Pope Gregory VII — **1119:** Bologna University founded in Italy — **1136:** Independence of Russian state of Novgorod

Europe

AL-IDRISI'S WORLD MAP

Islamic geographers led the world in medieval times. Al-Idrisi (1100–65) was a Moroccan in the service of Roger II of Sicily. The island had been under Arab rule in the 10th century and became a meeting point of two cultures where much of the knowledge of the Islamic world was transmitted to the Christian west.

Al-Idrisi's map shows the lasting influence of Ptolemy (see p.44). However, he oriented his maps, as did most contemporary Islamic geographers, with the south at the top.

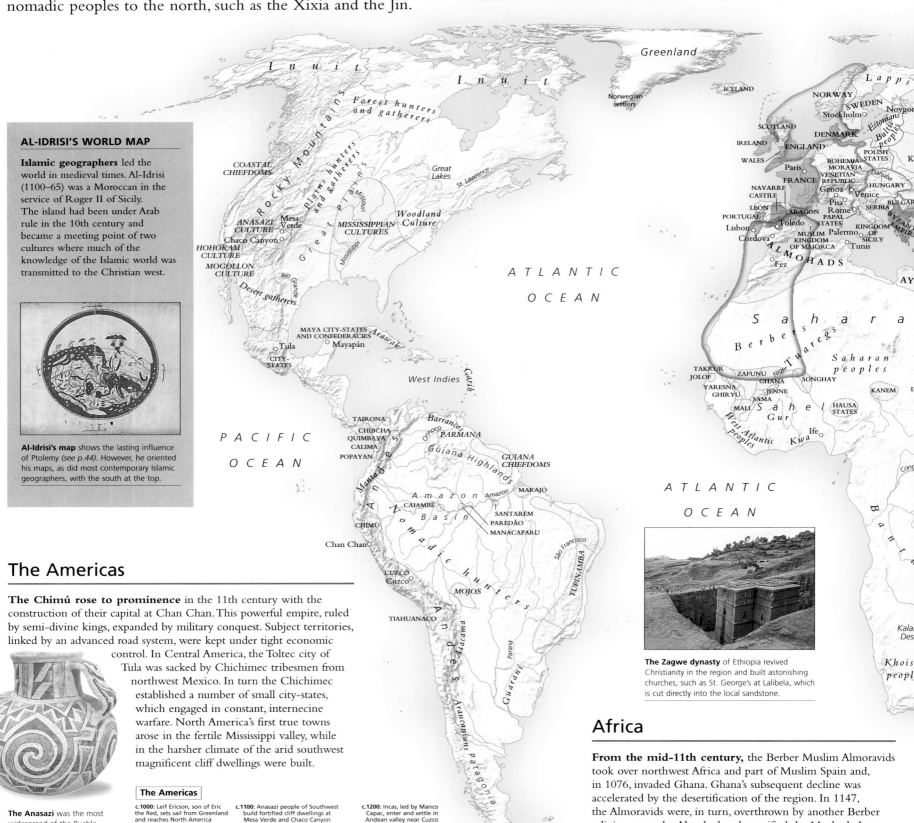

The Zagwe dynasty of Ethiopia revived Christianity in the region and built astonishing churches, such as St. George's at Lalibela, which is cut directly into the local sandstone.

The Americas

The Chimú rose to prominence in the 11th century with the construction of their capital at Chan Chan. This powerful empire, ruled by semi-divine kings, expanded by military conquest. Subject territories, linked by an advanced road system, were kept under tight economic control. In Central America, the Toltec city of Tula was sacked by Chichimec tribesmen from northwest Mexico. In turn the Chichimec established a number of small city-states, which engaged in constant, internecine warfare. North America's first true towns arose in the fertile Mississippi valley, while in the harsher climate of the arid southwest magnificent cliff dwellings were built.

The Anasazi was the most widespread of the Pueblo farming cultures of the American Southwest. Roads linked their impressive canyon villages, where they produced fine black and white pottery.

The Americas

c.1000: Leif Ericson, son of Eric the Red, sets sail from Greenland and reaches North America	**c.1100:** Anasazi people of Southwest build fortified cliff dwellings at Mesa Verde and Chaco Canyon	**c.1200:** Incas, led by Manco Capac, enter and settle in Andean valley near Cuzco

1000 — 1050 — 1100 — 1150 — 1200

c.1050: Settlements of mound-builders of Mississippi valley expand to become true towns — **1121:** Bishop Eirik visits North America from Greenland — **c.1175:** Toltec capital, Tula, is sacked by Chichimec

Africa

From the mid-11th century, the Berber Muslim Almoravids took over northwest Africa and part of Muslim Spain and, in 1076, invaded Ghana. Ghana's subsequent decline was accelerated by the desertification of the region. In 1147, the Almoravids were, in turn, overthrown by another Berber religious sect, the Almohads, who unified the Maghreb. In Ethiopia, a revival of Red Sea trade and the emergence of the Zagwe dynasty in 1150, led to a more expansionist, prosperous era. In Egypt, the military leader Saladin became ruler in 1174, ending the Fatimid dynasty and founding that of the Ayyubids.

WINDMILLS

Wind power had been harnessed in various different ways, notably in Persia and China, for grinding corn and raising water, but it was not until the 12th century that the windmill started to take on its familiar European form. The mills of northern Europe differed from earlier versions in that the shaft turned horizontally rather than vertically and the sails were turned so that they kept facing the wind. The first northern European mills were simple post-mills. These evolved gradually into bulkier tower mills with rotating caps.

In Europe windmills were used only for grinding corn up until the 15th century, as illustrated in this English woodcut from c.1340. Their power was then adapted for tasks such as land drainage, particularly in Holland.

SEE ALSO:

North America: pp.122–123

South America: pp.146–147

Africa: pp.162–163

Europe: pp.186–187

West Asia: pp.228–229

South and Southeast Asia: pp.244–245

North and East Asia: pp.262–265

West Asia

Byzantium's resurgence under Basil II did not last and in the 11th century most of the empire's Asian lands fell to the Seljuk Turks. The Islamic Turks, originally from Central Asia, established themselves in Baghdad in 1055. As 'men of the sword', they formed a partnership with the Persians and Arabs, the 'men of the law'. Tens of thousands of Europeans answered Pope Urban II's call in 1095 to recapture Jerusalem for Christendom. In 1099 the holy city was taken and the Crusaders set up states in Antioch, Edessa, Tripoli, and Jerusalem. In the following century, Muslim leaders, notably Saladin, founder of the Ayyubid dynasty in Egypt, embarked on a campaign of reconquest.

The capture of Antioch in 1098 was one of the first Christian successes on the First Crusade. The strongly fortified city held out for seven months.

West Asia

1055: Seljuk Turks capture Baghdad
1099: Jerusalem captured by Crusaders
1174: Founding of Ayyubid Sultanate in Egypt
1187: Saladin recaptures Jerusalem

1025: Death of great Byzantine emperor, Basil II
1071: Seljuk Turks defeat Byzantines at Manzikert
1144: Fall of Edessa to Muslims
1188: Crusader states reduced to coastal enclaves by Saladin

East Asia

By 1110, Song China was the most advanced, prosperous, and populous state in the world. However the Song alliance with the Manchurian Jin to dislodge the hostile Liao from their northern border, fatally weakened the Song Empire. The Jin overran northern China and the Song were forced to regroup in the southeast, defensive and hostile to outside influences. In Japan, the emperors lost power to the Fujiwara family in the mid-12th century. A period of violent inter-clan warfare followed, ending with the victory of the Minamoto clan.

This Song scroll gives a vivid depiction of the bustling street life and prosperity of Kaifeng in the 12th century. In 1105 the city's population had risen to 260,000.

East Asia

1005: Song China becomes subject state of northern Liao kingdom, with capital at Beijing
1125: Liao defeated by Jin from Manchuria
1191: Zen Buddhist order founded in Japan

c.1045: Movable type printing invented in China
1130: Song capital moves to Hangzhou
1192: Minamoto Yoritomo becomes Shogun and forms military government in Japan

The Khmer Empire was at its height in the 11th and 12th centuries. The artistic brilliance of the court, evident in these carvings decorating a temple at Angkor Wat, was in marked contrast to the conditions of the mass of the population.

South and Southeast Asia

Northern India was repeatedly invaded by the Ghazni Muslims of Afghanistan. In 1186 the last Ghazni ruler was deposed by the Turkish leader, Muhammad al Ghur, who continued to wage holy war in the region. Southeastern India was dominated by the Chola dynasty, who controlled the sea route between West Asia and China. The two most powerful states of Southeast Asia, the Khmer Empire and the kingdom of Pagan, both enjoyed an artistic golden age.

South and Southeast Asia

1014: Rajendra I becomes ruler of the Cholas of southeastern India
1018: Rajendra conquers Ceylon
1113: Accession of Suryavarman II, powerful warrior king of the Khmer
1152: Temple of Angkor Wat completed
1191: Muhammad al Ghur defeats Rajput clans

c.1000: First Muslim raids into northern India, led by Sultan Muhammad of Ghazni
1044: Establishment of first Burmese state at Pagan
1077: Chola merchants send embassy to China
1186: Raids by Muhammad al Ghur herald end of Buddhism in northern India

The World in 1200

- Byzantine Empire
- England and possessions
- Venetian Republic
- Holy Roman Empire
- Almoravid Empire 1120
- Great Seljuk Empire 1071
- possessions of Canute 1028–1035

Africa

1048: Fatimids lose control of Ifriqiya (Libya)
c.1110: Onset of serious desiccation of Sahel region
1147: Almohads established in Morocco and southern Spain
1171: Shi'ite Fatimid dynasty in Egypt suppressed by Saladin

1076: Ghana falls to Almoravids
1128: Almohads start takeover of Almoravid dominions
1150: Zagwe dynasty established in Ethiopia

Map labels

Palaeosiberians
Samoyeds
Ugrians
RUSSIAN PRINCIPALITIES
VOLGA BULGARIA
Turkic peoples
RUSSIAN PRINCIPALITIES
Siberia
Tungus
Yenisey
Lena
Ob'
Volga
Amur
Gobi
Mongols
KARA KHITAI EMPIRE
UIGHUR CITY-STATES
XIXIA
Manchuria
Liao
Yanjing
Beijing
KORYO
JAPAN
Kyoto
Constantinople
GEORGIA
DAGHESTAN
Manzikert
RUM
Edessa
LITTLE ARMENIA
ANTIOCH
CYPRUS
Bukhara
EMPIRE OF THE KHWARIZM SHAH
Kabul
KASHMIR
JIN EMPIRE
Kaifeng
Yellow River
TIBET
Himalayas
Baghdad
ABBASIDS
ALGHURIDS
GHURID EMPIRE
Delhi
PARAMARAS
Ganges
SMALL DYNASTIES
Yangtze
Hangzhou
SOUTHERN SONG EMPIRE
Jerusalem
TRIPOLI
Cairo
ID SULTANATE
Beduin
Red Sea
Mecca
OMAN
Arabian Peninsula
CAULUKYAS
YADAVAS
EASTERN GANGAS
KAKATIYAS
NANZHAO
PAGAN
Thais
ARAKAN
ANNAM
SILAHARAS
KADAMBAS
HOYSALAS
TELUGUCODAS
PANDYAS
CHOLAS
CERAS
Ceylon
SIMHALA
HARIPUNJAYA
KHMER
Angkor
CHAMPA
Mekong
MAKURIA
ALWA
ETHIOPIA
Lalibela
GOJJAM
DAMOT
IFAT
HARAR
SHOA
DAWARO
FETEGAR
Nilotic Peoples
Cushites
SWAHILI CITY-STATES
Zambezi
Malays
Madagascar
MAPUNGUBWE
INDIAN OCEAN
Philippine Islands
Borneo
SRIVIJAYA
Sumatra
Java
KEDIRI
Papuans
New Guinea
PACIFIC OCEAN
Malay Archipelago
Australian Aborigines
Darling
New Zealand
Maoris

THE AGE OF THE CRUSADES

The idealism of a devout Crusader is captured in this 13th-century drawing.

THE IDEA OF A HOLY WAR was never part of the doctrine of the early Christian church. This changed in 1095, when Pope Urban II made an impassioned speech at Clermont, urging French barons and knights to go to the aid of the beleaguered Christians of the Byzantine Empire. In return, they were promised indulgences. When they got to the Holy Land and captured Jerusalem in 1099, the aims of the Crusaders became rather less spiritual. Those rewarded with land tried to recreate the society of feudal Europe, but there was always a shortage of manpower to maintain the Crusader states in their precarious two centuries of existence. Nevertheless, the crusading ideal became firmly established in European consciousness and there were many subsequent expeditions to defend or recapture Jerusalem, but none was as successful as the first.

The most devout and determined of all the crusading kings of Europe was Louis IX of France (St. Louis). He sailed on two Crusades, once to invade Egypt, the second time to convert the King of Tunis. Both ended in disaster. In 1270, Louis and his men were struck down by disease as they camped before Tunis. Louis himself died. Here his coffin is being loaded on a ship to be carried back to France.

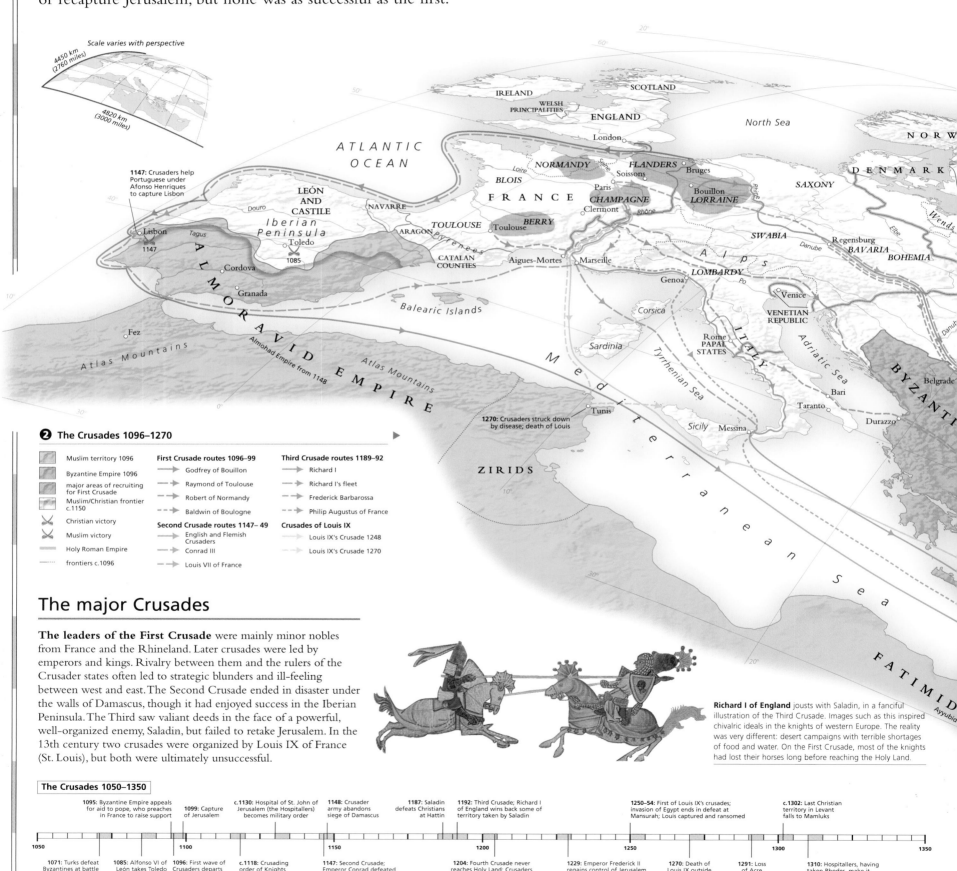

Scale varies with perspective

4450 km (2760 miles)
4820 km (3000 miles)

1147: Crusaders help Portuguese under Afonso Henriques to capture Lisbon

1270: Crusaders struck down by disease; death of Louis

❷ The Crusades 1096–1270

Muslim territory 1096	**First Crusade routes 1096–99**	**Third Crusade routes 1189–92**
Byzantine Empire 1096	Godfrey of Bouillon	Richard I
major areas of recruiting for First Crusade	Raymond of Toulouse	Richard I's fleet
Muslim/Christian frontier c.1150	Robert of Normandy	Frederick Barbarossa
Christian victory	Baldwin of Boulogne	Philip Augustus of France
Muslim victory	**Second Crusade routes 1147–49**	**Crusades of Louis IX**
Holy Roman Empire	English and Flemish Crusaders	Louis IX's Crusade 1248
frontiers c.1096	Conrad III	Louis IX's Crusade 1270
	Louis VII of France	

The major Crusades

The leaders of the First Crusade were mainly minor nobles from France and the Rhineland. Later crusades were led by emperors and kings. Rivalry between them and the rulers of the Crusader states often led to strategic blunders and ill-feeling between west and east. The Second Crusade ended in disaster under the walls of Damascus, though it had enjoyed success in the Iberian Peninsula. The Third saw valiant deeds in the face of a powerful, well-organized enemy, Saladin, but failed to retake Jerusalem. In the 13th century two crusades were organized by Louis IX of France (St. Louis), but both were ultimately unsuccessful.

Richard I of England jousts with Saladin, in a fanciful illustration of the Third Crusade. Images such as this inspired chivalric ideals in the knights of western Europe. The reality was very different: desert campaigns with terrible shortages of food and water. On the First Crusade, most of the knights had lost their horses long before reaching the Holy Land.

The Crusades 1050–1350

1095: Byzantine Empire appeals for aid to pope, who preaches in France to raise support
1099: Capture of Jerusalem
c.1130: Hospital of St. John of Jerusalem (the Hospitallers) becomes military order
1148: Crusader army abandons siege of Damascus
1187: Saladin defeats Christians at Hattin
1192: Third Crusade; Richard I of England wins back some of territory taken by Saladin
1250–54: First of Louis IX's crusades; invasion of Egypt ends in defeat at Mansurah; Louis captured and ransomed
c.1302: Last Christian territory in Levant falls to Mamluks

1050   1100   1150   1200   1250   1300   1350

1071: Turks defeat Byzantines at battle of Manzikert
1085: Alfonso VI of León takes Toledo
1096: First wave of Crusaders departs
c.1118: Crusading order of Knights Templar founded
1147: Second Crusade; Emperor Conrad defeated by Turks at Dorylaeum
1204: Fourth Crusade never reaches Holy Land; Crusaders take Constantinople
1229: Emperor Frederick II regains control of Jerusalem through diplomacy
1270: Death of Louis IX outside walls of Tunis
1291: Loss of Acre
1310: Hospitallers, having taken Rhodes, make it their headquarters

The boundaries of Christianity and Islam

In the 9th and 10th centuries, the boundaries between the Islamic and Christian worlds shifted very little. A new threat to Christianity came in the mid-11th century with the advance of the Seljuk Turks, newly converted to Islam, and effective rulers of the Abbasid Caliphate after reaching Baghdad in 1055. Following their victory over the Byzantines in 1071 at Manzikert, they won control of almost all Asia Minor, home to former Christian subjects of the Byzantine Empire. In the Iberian Peninsula, however, the Christian kingdoms won back land from the Muslims in the course of the 11th century.

SEE ALSO:

Africa: pp.162–163

Europe: pp.186–187

West Asia: pp.228–229

1 Islam and Christianity c.1090

- Muslim lands
- Greek Christians (Orthodox)
- Roman Church (under papal authority)
- Greek Christians in Muslim lands
- other Christians
- → direction of Muslim expansion
- → direction of Greek Christian expansion
- → direction of Roman Church expansion
- • city with important Jewish community

Godfrey of Bouillon leads the attack on Jerusalem in 1099. After all the hardship and the long journey there, the capture of the Holy City was hailed as a miracle. It was followed by the murder or brutal eviction of many of the city's Muslims and Jews.

Krak des Chevaliers was one of many heavily fortified Crusader castles. Manned by the Hospitallers, it held out against Saladin's forces, but fell to the Mamluks in 1271 after a month's siege.

Crusader states in the Levant

How the Crusaders' conquests should be ruled was not considered until after Jerusalem had fallen. The solution – a feudal kingdom of Jerusalem buttressed by the counties of Edessa, Tripoli, and Antioch – alienated the Byzantines, who had hoped to regain their former territories. Jerusalem was always a weak state with a small population, heavily dependent on supplies and recruits from western Christendom. When a strong Islamic ruler such as Saladin emerged, the colonists had little hope against a determined Muslim onslaught. They held on to the coast through the 13th century, but in 1291, Acre, the last major city in Christian hands, fell to the Mamluks of Egypt.

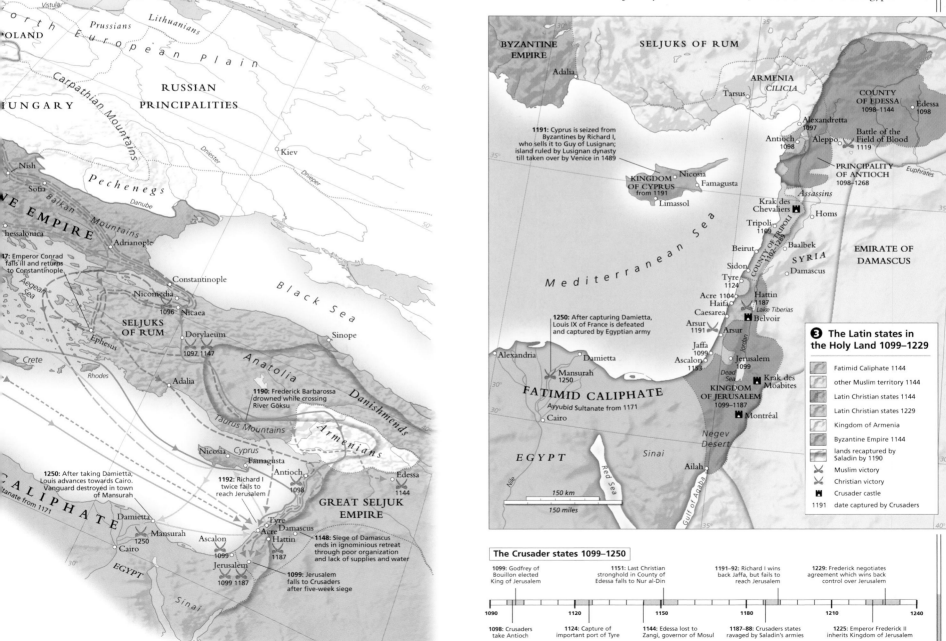

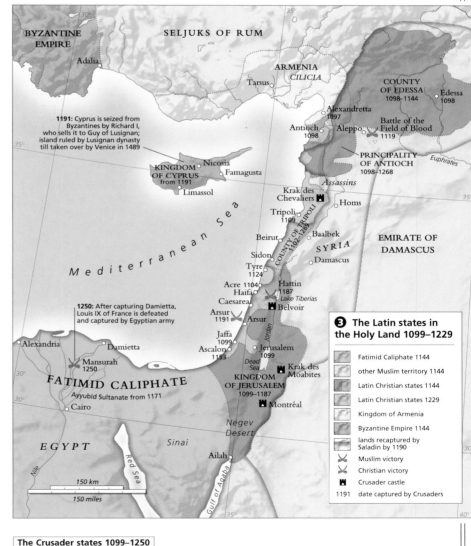

3 The Latin states in the Holy Land 1099–1229

- Fatimid Caliphate 1144
- other Muslim territory 1144
- Latin Christian states 1144
- Latin Christian states 1229
- Kingdom of Armenia
- Byzantine Empire 1144
- lands recaptured by Saladin by 1190
- ✗ Muslim victory
- ✗ Christian victory
- ⚑ Crusader castle
- 1191 date captured by Crusaders

1191: Cyprus is seized from Byzantines by Richard I, who sells it to Guy of Lusignan; island ruled by Lusignan dynasty till taken over by Venice in 1489

1250: After capturing Damietta, Louis IX of France is defeated and captured by Egyptian army

The Crusader states 1099–1250

1099: Godfrey of Bouillon elected King of Jerusalem	1151: Last Christian stronghold in County of Edessa falls to Nur al-Din	1191–92: Richard I wins back Jaffa, but fails to reach Jerusalem	1229: Frederick negotiates agreement which wins back control over Jerusalem

1090	1120	1150	1180	1210	1240

1098: Crusaders take Antioch	1124: Capture of important port of Tyre	1144: Edessa lost to Zangi, governor of Mosul	1187–88: Crusaders states ravaged by Saladin's armies	1225: Emperor Frederick II inherits Kingdom of Jerusalem

THE WORLD 1200–1300

IN THE 13TH CENTURY Mongol horsemen burst out of their central Asian homeland and conquered a vast swathe of the Eurasian landmass. By 1300, they had divided their conquests into four large empires that stretched from China to eastern Europe. Mongol campaigns brought devastation, particularly to China and the Islamic states of southwest Asia but, once all resistance had been crushed, merchants, ambassadors, and other travellers were able to move safely through the Mongol realms. Though the old political order of the Islamic world, centred on the Abbasid Caliphate and Baghdad, was swept away, the influence of Islam continued to spread as many Mongols adopted the religion. Powerful new Muslim states also emerged in Mamluk Egypt and the Sultanate of Delhi. Europe remained on the defensive in the face of the Mongols and Islam, but city-states such as Venice and Genoa prospered through increased trading links with the East.

The port of Venice was the richest city in western Europe. This illustration shows Marco Polo with his father and uncle setting off in 1271 on the first stage of their incredible journey to the court of the Great Khan.

Europe

The feudal monarchies of England and France consolidated large regional states, but conflict between popes and emperors prevented any similar process in Italy and Germany. In Spain, Christian forces took Córdoba and Seville, leaving only the small kingdom of Granada in Moorish control. In eastern Europe, the Mongols of the Golden Horde collected tribute from the Russian principalities. Western Europe, in contrast, prospered economically as Italian merchants linked northern lands to the commerce of the Mediterranean basin.

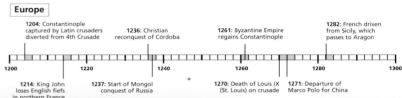

Europe

| 1204: Constantinople captured by Latin crusaders diverted from 4th Crusade | 1236: Christian reconquest of Córdoba | 1261: Byzantine Empire regains Constantinople | 1282: French driven from Sicily, which passes to Aragon |

| 1200 | 1220 | 1240 | 1260 | 1280 | 1300 |

| 1214: King John loses English fiefs in northern France | 1237: Start of Mongol conquest of Russia | 1270: Death of Louis IX (St. Louis) on crusade | 1271: Departure of Marco Polo for China |

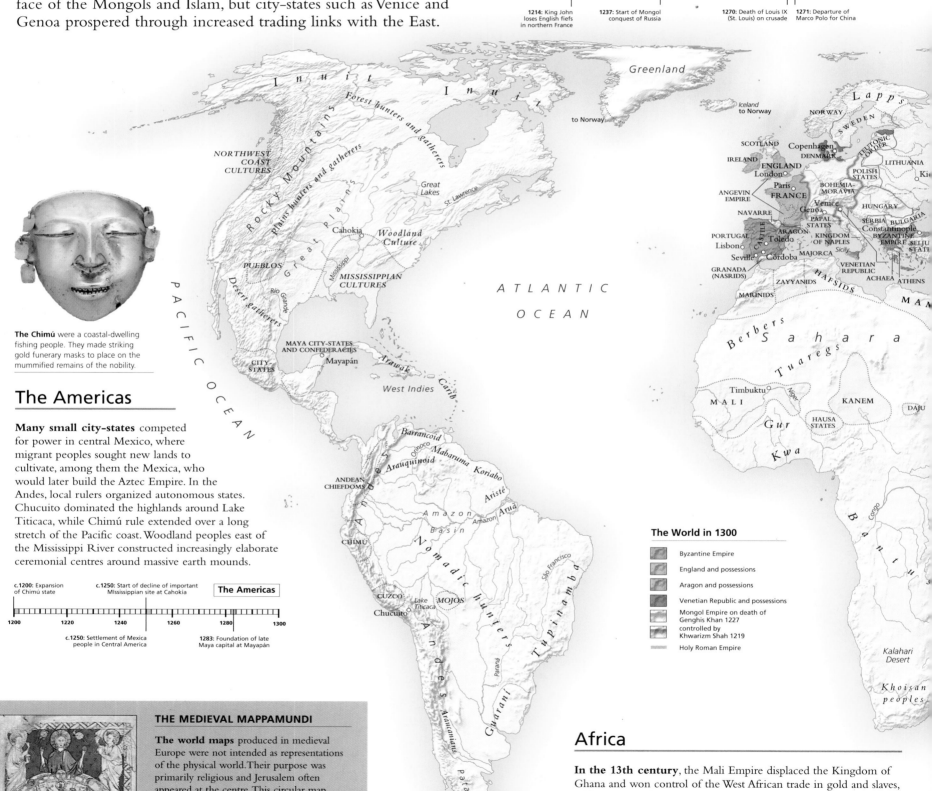

The Chimú were a coastal-dwelling fishing people. They made striking gold funerary masks to place on the mummified remains of the nobility.

The Americas

Many small city-states competed for power in central Mexico, where migrant peoples sought new lands to cultivate, among them the Mexica, who would later build the Aztec Empire. In the Andes, local rulers organized autonomous states. Chucuito dominated the highlands around Lake Titicaca, while Chimú rule extended over a long stretch of the Pacific coast. Woodland peoples east of the Mississippi River constructed increasingly elaborate ceremonial centres around massive earth mounds.

| c.1200: Expansion of Chimú state | c.1250: Start of decline of important Mississippian site at Cahokia | | **The Americas** |

| 1200 | 1220 | 1240 | 1260 | 1280 | 1300 |

| c.1250: Settlement of Mexica people in Central America | 1283: Foundation of late Maya capital at Mayapán |

The World in 1300

- Byzantine Empire
- England and possessions
- Aragon and possessions
- Venetian Republic and possessions
- Mongol Empire on death of Genghis Khan 1227
- controlled by Khwarizm Shah 1219
- Holy Roman Empire

THE MEDIEVAL MAPPAMUNDI

The world maps produced in medieval Europe were not intended as representations of the physical world. Their purpose was primarily religious and Jerusalem often appeared at the centre. This circular map, oriented with Asia at the top, is full of Christian symbolism and is decorated with grotesque faces and mythical beasts.

A 13th-century English psalter contains this tiny world map or *mappamundi*, which measures just 10 cm across.

Africa

In the 13th century, the Mali Empire displaced the Kingdom of Ghana and won control of the West African trade in gold and slaves, with caravans of as many as 25,000 camels crossing the Sahara to North Africa. Meanwhile, the Swahili city-states on the East African coast exported goods through the trading networks of the Indian Ocean. Rulers of Mali and the Swahili city-states adopted Islam and built mosques and religious schools. Islam did not reach central and southern Africa, but the trade it generated led to the establishment of wealthy inland states such as the Kingdom of Great Zimbabwe.

West Asia

In 1258 the Mongols sacked Baghdad and overthrew the Abbasid Caliphate. Their leaders established themselves as Il-Khans, nominally subordinate to the Great Khan in China. Their empire extended almost to the Mediterranean, where their westward expansion was halted by the Mamluks of Egypt. By 1300 most Mongols of the Il-Khanate had embraced Islam, as had many of their fellow Mongols of the Golden Horde. Meanwhile, the Seljuks and other Turkic peoples consolidated their position in formerly Byzantine territory by establishing regional states.

This lustre tile from 13th-century Persia is decorated with a verse from the Koran. The Mongols were too few to impose their beliefs on the peoples they conquered. Instead, many of them became Muslims.

THE MAGNETIC COMPASS

The Chinese had long known that a floating magnetized needle always points in the same direction. Their sailors started to make regular use of this fact in about 1100. By the 13th century, the magnetic compass was probably in widespread use among the Arab navigators of the Indian Ocean. In Europe, a written account of its principles appeared as early as 1190.

In the 13th century the Chinese simply floated a magnetized needle on water. This boxed compass is an early example.

SEE ALSO:

North America: pp.122–123

South America: pp.146–147

Africa: pp.162–163

Europe: pp.186–191

West Asia: pp.228–229

South and Southeast Asia: pp.244–245

North and East Asia: pp.262–265

West Asia

- **1219:** Mongol invasion of Khwarizm Empire
- **1260:** Battle of Ain Jalut; Mamluks defeat Mongol army north of Jerusalem
- **1299:** Osman founds Ottoman state among the small Seljuk states in western Turkey
- **1231:** Mongols reconquer resurgent Empire of the Khwarizm Shah
- **1258:** Sack of Baghdad and fall of Abbasid Caliphate; Hülegü founds Il-Khanate
- **1265:** Death of Hülegü
- **1295:** Conversion of the Il-Khan Ghazan to Islam

`1200 1220 1240 1260 1280 1300`

North and East Asia

Genghis Khan invaded northern China in 1211, but the Southern Song Empire fell only after a long campaign (1260–79) directed by Kublai Khan. China was the richest of all the Mongol conquests. Kublai became emperor and founded the Yuan dynasty. He appointed many foreigners to govern the empire and fostered both maritime and overland trade with other lands throughout East Asia. From Korea (Koryo) the Mongols made two failed attempts to invade Japan.

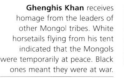

Ghenghis Khan receives homage from the leaders of other Mongol tribes. White horsetails flying from his tent indicated that the Mongols were temporarily at peace. Black ones meant they were at war.

North and East Asia

- **1206:** Temujin named Genghis Khan
- **1233:** Mongols take Jin capital, Kaifeng
- **1264:** Kublai elected Great Khan
- **1279:** Foundation of Yuan dynasty
- **1294:** Death of Kublai
- **1211:** Mongols begin conquest of northern China
- **1274:** First Mongol attempt to invade Japan
- **1292:** Departure of Marco Polo from China

`1200 1220 1240 1260 1280 1300`

South and Southeast Asia

In 1206 Qutb al-din, leader of the Islamic raiders who had terrorized northern India for the past 30 years, fixed the capital of a new sultanate at Delhi. The Sultanate suffered occasional Mongol raids, whereas the Mongols made repeated forays from China into Annam and Pagan, without ever gaining secure control of the region. They also launched a massive seaborne attack on Java, but their tactics were ineffective in the island's tropical jungles.

The spectacular royal enclosure of Great Zimbabwe was rebuilt many times between the 11th and the 15th century. The kings owed their wealth to trade in cattle, gold, and copper.

The Qutb Minar minaret rises beside the Quwwat-al-Islam mosque in Delhi. Begun in 1199, it became a powerful symbol of Islamic rule in northern India.

Africa

- **1228:** Start of collapse of Almohad Empire in North Africa
- **c.1250:** Building of stone mosques in Swahili city-states
- **1270:** Expansion of Christian Kingdom of Ethiopia
- **1230:** Establishment of the Mali Empire by Sundiata
- **1250:** Mamluk military caste takes over Egypt
- **1255:** Death of Sundiata
- **1269:** Marinids inflict final defeat on Almohads in Morocco

`1200 1220 1240 1260 1280 1300`

South and Southeast Asia

- **1206:** Foundation of Sultanate of Delhi
- **1258:** First Mongol expedition to Annam
- **1288:** Kublai Khan gives up attempt to subdue Annam and Champa
- **1293:** Failed Mongol invasion of Java

`1200 1220 1240 1260 1280 1300`

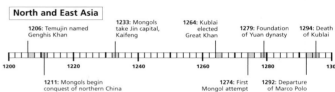

THE AGE OF THE MONGOLS

Genghis Khan – the title means 'universal ruler' – was born Temujin, son of a minor Mongol chief.

THE NOMADIC HERDSMEN of the Mongolian steppe traded livestock, horses, and hides with the settled agricultural civilization of China to the south, but relations between the two were usually marked by hostility and suspicion. By the 13th century, the Chinese empire had become weak and fragmented. Into this power vacuum burst the Mongols, a fierce race of skilled horsemen, their normally warring tribes united under the inspired leadership of Genghis Khan. Genghis did not seek war at all costs; he first gave his enemies a chance to submit – on his terms. If they refused, he unleashed a campaign of terror, sacking cities and massacring entire populations. Although at first the Mongols numbered no more than a million, their ranks were swelled by Turks, Arabs, and other subject peoples. Genghis's successors extended his conquests across Asia and deep into Europe, but his empire then split into four khanates. By 1400, the Mongols were a divided and weakened force and most of their conquests had been lost.

Genghis Khan, preceded by Jebe, one of his most trusted commanders, leads a cavalry charge. Jebe and another great general, Sübedei, made the astonishing raid into Russia in 1222 that first made Europe aware of the Mongols' existence.

Caravan routes across Central Asia thrived in the climate of law and order imposed by Mongol rule. This illustration from the Catalan Atlas of 1375 shows a group of European merchants riding along the Silk Road.

The Mongol peace

The Mongols' chief aim was always to exact tribute from conquered peoples, but they also brought long periods of peace; travellers were able to cross Eurasia in safety along the old Silk Road. In the reign of Genghis Khan's grandson Möngke (1251–59) it was said that a virgin with a pot of gold on her head could walk unmolested across his empire. The two most famous travellers to benefit from the Mongol peace were the Venetian merchant Marco Polo, who claimed to have spent 17 years in the employment of Kublai Khan, and Ibn Battuta, a Muslim legal scholar from Tangier in Morocco, who also travelled as far as China.

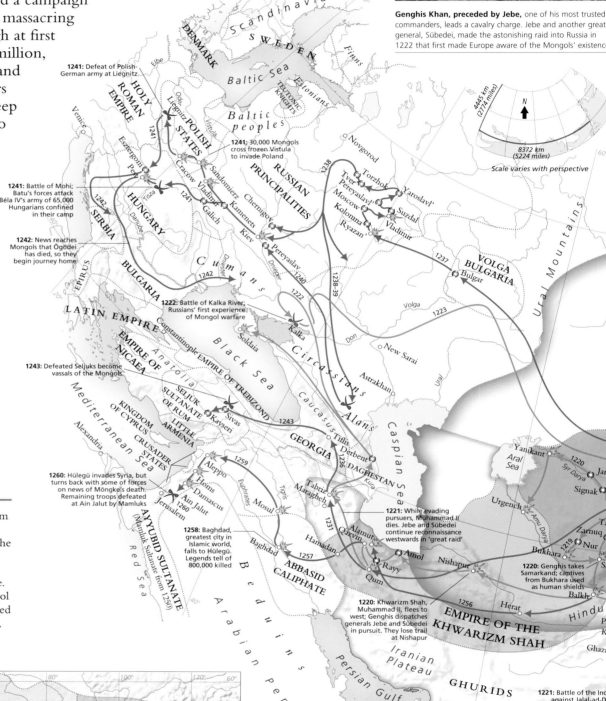

1241: Defeat of Polish-German army at Liegnitz.

1241: 30,000 Mongols cross frozen Vistula to invade Poland

1241: Battle of Mohi; Batu's forces attack Béla IV's army of 65,000 Hungarians confined in their camp

1242: News reaches Mongols that Ögödei has died, so they begin journey home

1222: Battle of Kalka River; Russians' first experience of Mongol warfare

1243: Defeated Seljuks become vassals of the Mongols

1260: Hülegü invades Syria, but turns back with some of forces on news of Möngke's death. Remaining troops defeated at Ain Jalut by Mamluks

1258: Baghdad, greatest city in Islamic world, falls to Hülegü. Legends tell of 800,000 killed

1221: While evading pursuers, Muhammad II continue reconnaissance westwards in 'great raid'

1220: Genghis takes Samarkand; captives from Bukhara used as human shields

1220: Khwarizm Shah, Muhammad II, flees to west; Genghis dispatches generals Jebe and Sübedei in pursuit. They lose trail at Nishapur

1221: Battle of the Indus against Jalal-ad-Din, son of Muhammad II

Scale varies with perspective

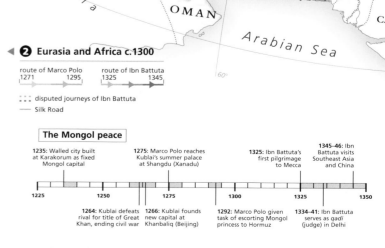

❷ Eurasia and Africa c.1300

route of Marco Polo 1271   1295 — route of Ibn Battuta 1325   1345

disputed journeys of Ibn Battuta

— Silk Road

The Mongol peace

1235: Walled city built at Karakorum as fixed Mongol capital

1275: Marco Polo reaches Kublai's summer palace at Shangdu (Xanadu)

1325: Ibn Battuta's first pilgrimage to Mecca

1345–46: Ibn Battuta visits Southeast Asia and China

1264: Kublai defeats rival for title of Great Khan, ending civil war

1266: Kublai founds new capital at Khanbaliq (Beijing)

1292: Marco Polo given task of escorting Mongol princess to Hormuz

1334–41: Ibn Battuta serves as qadi (judge) in Delhi

The Mongol conquests

In less than 20 years, in a series of conquests without parallel in history, Genghis Khan shattered the Muslim states of Central Asia, overran northern China, and sent troops on a lightning raid into Russia. Genghis's immediate successor was his third son Ögödei, whose reign as Great Khan saw the destruction of the Jin and Khwarizm empires, continued fighting with Song China, and an invasion of Europe that reached Hungary and Poland. The conquest of the Song was completed by Kublai Khan, a grandson of Genghis, who became emperor of China, while Kublai's brother, Hülegü, founder of the Il-Khanate, destroyed the Abbasid Caliphate, sacking the great Islamic city of Baghdad. The first setback to Mongol expansion came at the hands of the Mamluks, who, in 1260, prevented their advance into Egypt at Ain Jalut.

At the siege of Hezhou in 1258–59, Mongol horsemen tried unsuccessfully to cross the Yangtze on a pontoon of boats. The conquest of Song China was accomplished only after many protracted sieges.

Mongol conquests of the 13th century

1206: Mongols united by Genghis Khan
1211: First invasion of Jin Empire
1219: Genghis attacks Khwarizm
1227: Death of Genghis
1229: Ögödei elected Great Khan
1242: Batu founds Golden Horde
1260: Hülegü invades Syria; Mongols suffer first major defeat at Ain Jalut
1258: Sack of Baghdad
1279: Last Song resistance crushed
1281: Second failed invasion of Japan
1294: Death of Kublai

1200   1220   1240   1260   1280   1300

SEE ALSO:

Europe: pp.188–189

West Asia: pp.228–229

South and Southeast Asia: pp.244–245

North and East Asia: pp.262–265

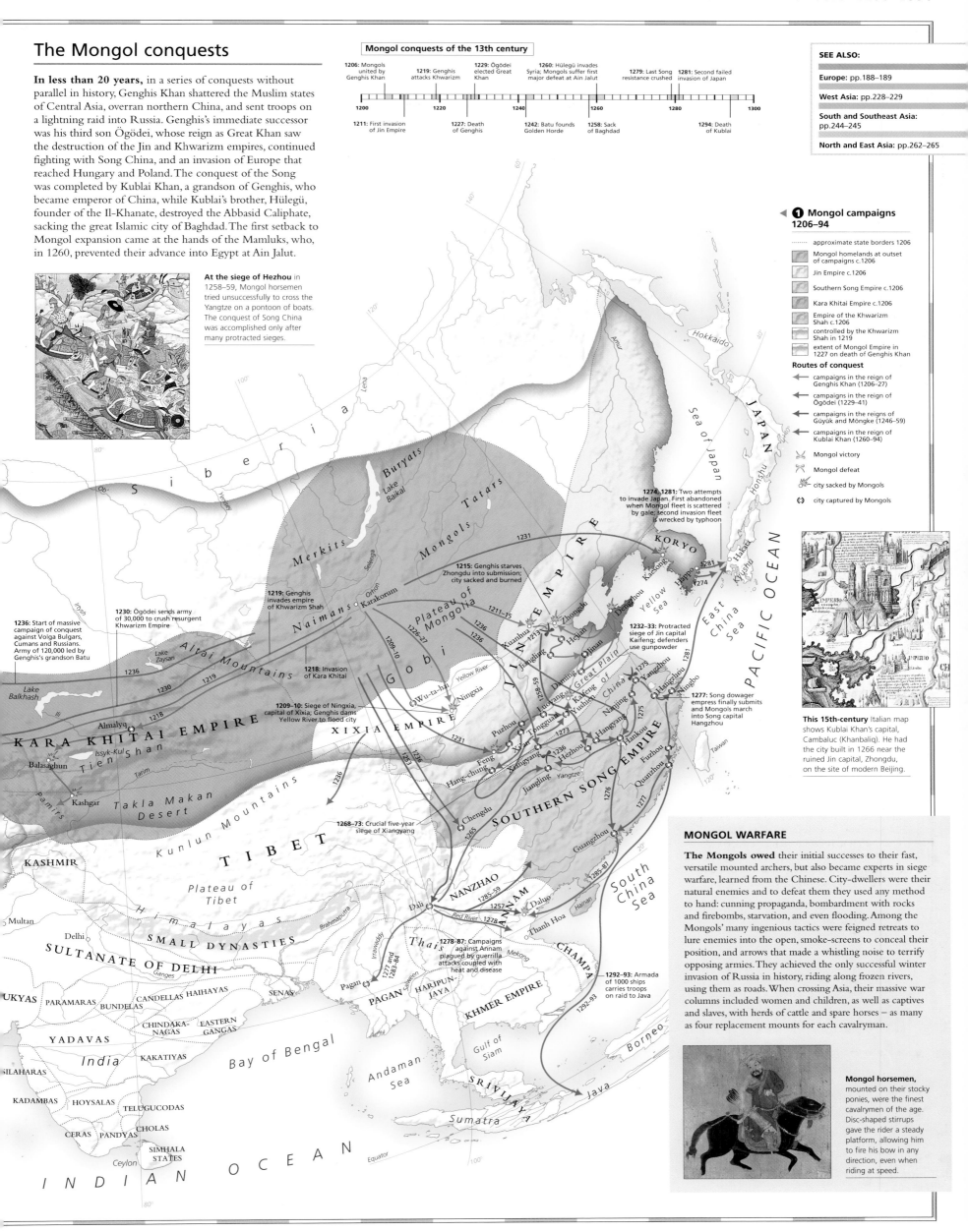

1 Mongol campaigns 1206–94

.... approximate state borders 1206
Mongol homelands at outset of campaigns c.1206
Jin Empire c.1206
Southern Song Empire c.1206
Kara Khitai Empire c.1206
Empire of the Khwarizm Shah c.1206
controlled by the Khwarizm Shah in 1219
extent of Mongol Empire in 1227 on death of Genghis Khan

Routes of conquest
→ campaigns in the reign of Genghis Khan (1206–27)
→ campaigns in the reign of Ögödei (1229–41)
→ campaigns in the reigns of Güyük and Möngke (1246–59)
→ campaigns in the reign of Kublai Khan (1260–94)
✕ Mongol victory
✕ Mongol defeat
☼ city sacked by Mongols
☼ city captured by Mongols

This 15th-century Italian map shows Kublai Khan's capital, Cambaluc (Khanbaliq). He had the city built in 1266 near the ruined Jin capital, Zhongdu, on the site of modern Beijing.

Map annotations

1236: Start of massive campaign of conquest against Volga Bulgars, Cumans and Russians. Army of 120,000 led by Genghis's grandson Batu

1230: Ögödei sends army of 30,000 to crush resurgent Khwarizm Empire

1219: Genghis invades empire of Khwarizm Shah

1218: Invasion of Kara Khitai

1209–10: Siege of Ningxia, capital of Xixia; Genghis dams Yellow River to flood city

1215: Genghis starves Zhongdu into submission; city sacked and burned

1232–33: Protracted siege of Jin capital Kaifeng; defenders use gunpowder

1274, 1281: Two attempts to invade Japan. First abandoned when Mongol fleet is scattered by gale; second invasion fleet is wrecked by typhoon

1277: Song dowager empress finally submits and Mongols march into Song capital Hangzhou

1268–73: Crucial five-year siege of Xiangyang

1278–87: Campaigns against Annam plagued by guerrilla attacks coupled with heat and disease

1292–93: Armada of 1000 ships carries troops on raid to Java

MONGOL WARFARE

The Mongols owed their initial successes to their fast, versatile mounted archers, but also became experts in siege warfare, learned from the Chinese. City-dwellers were their natural enemies and to defeat them they used any method to hand: cunning propaganda, bombardment with rocks and firebombs, starvation, and even flooding. Among the Mongols' many ingenious tactics were feigned retreats to lure enemies into the open, smoke-screens to conceal their position, and arrows that made a whistling noise to terrify opposing armies. They achieved the only successful winter invasion of Russia in history, riding along frozen rivers, using them as roads. When crossing Asia, their massive war columns included women and children, as well as captives and slaves, with herds of cattle and spare horses – as many as four replacement mounts for each cavalryman.

Mongol horsemen, mounted on their stocky ponies, were the finest cavalrymen of the age. Disc-shaped stirrups gave the rider a steady platform, allowing him to fire his bow in any direction, even when riding at speed.

THE WORLD 1300–1400

DURING THE 14TH CENTURY epidemics of bubonic plague swept across the Old World from China and Korea to the west coast of Europe. Dramatic demographic decline led to economic and social disruption that weakened states throughout Eurasia and North Africa. In addition, the onset of the so-called 'Little Ice Age', which would last till the 19th century, brought bad weather and poor harvests to many of the regions affected by plague. The Mongol empires, which had dominated Eurasia since the conquests of Genghis Khan in the 13th century, began to disintegrate, though the Khanate of the Golden Horde maintained its hegemony in southern Russia into the 15th century. In both China and Persia the Mongols were assimilated into the local population, but in China, a new dynasty, the Ming, introduced a Han Chinese aristocratic regime.

Europe

Europe struggled to recover from the social and economic disruption caused by the Black Death. Scarcity of labour led peasants and workers to seek improved conditions and higher wages, but landlords and employers resisted their demands, provoking many revolts in western Europe. France suffered too from the military campaigns of the Hundred Years' War, fuelled by the dynastic ambitions of English kings. Religious differences also brought disorder. Rival popes residing in Rome and Avignon both claimed authority over the Catholic church, while in England the Lollards challenged the authority and doctrine of the church itself.

The Black Death reached Europe from Asia in 1347. In three years it probably killed one third of the population. The fear it generated is captured in this image of Death strangling a plague victim.

Europe

- **1309:** Pope takes up residence at Avignon
- **1312:** Order of Knights Templar suppressed by pope
- **1337:** Beginning of the Hundred Years' War
- **1346:** English defeat French at Battle of Crécy
- **1347:** Arrival of bubonic plague in Italy
- **1358:** The Jacquerie, uprising against nobility in France
- **1378:** Beginning of Great Schism in Catholic church
- **1381:** Peasants' Revolt in England
- **1397:** Union of Kalmar; Norway, Denmark, and Sweden united under a single monarch

The World in 1400

- Ming Empire
- Byzantine Empire
- Ottoman Empire
- England and possessions
- Union of Kalmar
- Aragon and possessions
- Muscovy
- Genoa and possessions
- Burgundy and possessions
- Venetian Republic and possessions
- Habsburg possessions
- Luxembourg possessions
- Holy Roman Empire
- Tughluq's Empire 1335

THE CATALAN ATLAS

The Catalans were fine seamen who sailed regularly as far as the Black Sea and the Baltic. The Catalan Atlas of 1375 is a large world map on wooden panels, probably the work of the king of Aragon's mapmaker, Abraham Cresques, a Majorcan Jew. Most of the information for Europe is derived from the mariners' charts known as portolans that were used by Italian and Catalan ships' captains. The main source for China and the Far East, which are far less accurately mapped, is Marco Polo's account of his journeys (see p.68).

The Catalan map gives a comprehensive and accurate picture of the coastline and ports of Europe and North Africa.

Africa

The Islamic Mali Empire controlled the trans-Saharan caravan trade, using the profits to maintain a powerful army and dominate West Africa. Gold and slaves went north in exchange for salt, textiles, horses, and manufactured goods. Tales of the wealth of Mali spread to Europe and West Asia, especially after the ostentatious pilgrimage to Mecca made by one of the country's most powerful rulers, Mansa Musa. Many smaller states emerged in the region as rulers sought to ensure a regular supply of trade goods. The Swahili cities of East Africa were not hit by plague, but commercial traffic declined as their trading partners in Asia experienced social and economic disruption.

THE CANNON

The Chinese had a long tradition of using gunpowder weapons, including bamboo tubes that fired arrows and bullets. The English word 'cannon' comes from the Italian *cannone*, meaning a large bamboo cane. Metal cannon were probably first used in China, but by the early 14th century were in action across Asia and in most of Europe. The earliest metal cannons in Europe were forged, but these were superseded by much larger ones cast using the technology initially developed for making church bells.

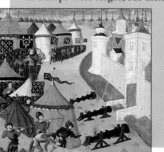

The cannon was primarily used as a siege weapon. Its effectiveness had a major influence on castle design.

West Asia

During the late 14th century the Turkish warrior chieftain Timur (Tamerlane), who claimed descent from Genghis Khan, carved out a vast central Asian empire, and built himself a magnificent capital at Samarkand. Timur invaded India and sacked the city of Delhi, and he was planning an invasion of China when he died in 1405. One other empire expanded during this period – that of the Ottoman Turks, who seized Anatolia and encroached on Byzantine holdings in southeastern Europe. By 1400 the once-mighty Byzantine Empire consisted of Constantinople and a few coastal regions in Greece and western Anatolia that maintained maritime links with the capital.

Timur's ambition and cruelty revived memories of Genghis Khan. He instilled fear into conquered peoples and opponents of his rule by building towers studded with the severed heads of his victims.

SEE ALSO:

North America: pp.122–123

South America: pp.146–147

Africa: pp.162–163

Europe: pp.188–191

West Asia: pp.228–231

South and Southeast Asia: pp.242–243

North and East Asia: pp.262–267

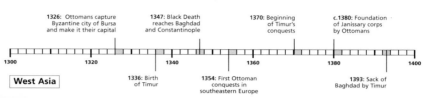

West Asia

1326: Ottomans capture Byzantine city of Bursa and make it their capital
1347: Black Death reaches Baghdad and Constantinople
1370: Beginning of Timur's conquests
c.1380: Foundation of Janissary corps by Ottomans
1336: Birth of Timur
1354: First Ottoman conquests in southeastern Europe
1393: Sack of Baghdad by Timur

1300 · 1320 · 1340 · 1360 · 1380 · 1400

East Asia

Plague, floods, and famine all contributed to the build-up of Chinese resentment at Mongol rule. Local uprisings became increasingly frequent, culminating in 1356 in a rebellion in southeastern China, which carried Zhu Yuanzhang, founder of the Ming dynasty, to power. War with the Mongols continued for some years, but the Chinese drove them back to their original homelands in the north. Japan had successfully resisted Mongol attempts at invasion, but their own Kamakura shogunate collapsed in 1333. The new shoguns of the Ashikaga family never succeeded in exercising the same degree of control over the country.

The Ming emperors restored Chinese values after a century of Mongol rule. This statue portrays a guardian of the spirit world.

East Asia

1335: Rebellions against Mongol rule in China
1351: Massive flooding of Yellow River
1392: Foundation of Yi dynasty in Korea
1336: Foundation of Ashikaga shogunate in Japan
1368: Establishment of the Ming dynasty

1300 · 1320 · 1340 · 1360 · 1380 · 1400

South and Southeast Asia

In India, the Sultanate of Delhi reached its greatest extent in the reign of Tughluq, but by the end of the century had lost control of most of the peninsula. The small kingdoms of mainland Southeast Asia all maintained diplomatic and commercial links with Ming China. The new Thai kingdom of Siam proved especially skilful in its dealings with its powerful neighbour to the north. During the 14th century island Southeast Asia fell increasingly under the influence of the Majapahit empire based in Java. A Javanese navy, financed by taxes levied on the lucrative trade in spices, patrolled the waters of the archipelago and controlled maritime trade.

The marble dome of Tughluq's mausoleum rises above the ramparts of the fortified city he built at Delhi in 1321.

Map labels:
Palaeosiberians, Samoyeds, Ugrians, Ostyaks, Siberia, Tungus, Yenisey, Ob', Lena, Amur, KHANATE OF THE GOLDEN HORDE, KHANATE OF THE OIRATS, Gobi, REBIZOND, Caspian Sea, Samarkand, CHAGATAI KHANATE, Beijing, Yellow River, KOREA, JAPAN, Ardabil, DULKADIR, Euphrates, Tigris, EMPIRE OF TIMUR, KASHMIR, TIBET, MING EMPIRE, Yangtze, Baghdad, Bedouins, Delhi, SHARQIS, MALLA, SMALL STATES, SHAN STATES, SHARIFS OF MEDINA, OMAN, SIND, SULTANATE OF DELHI, Ganges, BENGAL, CHIENGMAI, SHARIFS OF MECCA, Arabian Peninsula, KHANDESH, SMALL STATES, ARAKAN, LAOS, ANNAM, Mecca, BAHMANI KINGDOM, EASTERN GANGAS, TOUNGOO, Mekong, RASULIDS, TELINGANA, REDDIS, PEGU, SIAM, CAMBODIA, ETHIOPIA, VIJAYANAGAR, SUKHOTHAI, Ayutthaya, CHAMPA, IFAT, SMALL STATES, Philippine Islands, SIDAMA STATES, Cushites, PACIFIC OCEAN, SWAHILI CITY-STATES, MALAY STATES, Borneo, Malaya, Papuans, New Guinea, PAJAJARAN, MAJAPAHIT, Java, Bali, INDIAN OCEAN, Malays, Madagascar, Australian Aborigines, Darling, New Zealand, Maoris

Mansa Musa, ruler of Mali, is depicted on the Catalan Atlas of 1375. Europeans were in awe of his reported wealth and the splendour of his court.

Africa

1331: Ibn Battuta's voyage to the Swahili cities of East Africa
1344: Ethiopia at its height at death of ruler Amde Sion
c.1390: Formation of the kingdom of Kongo
1324: Pilgrimage to Mecca by Mansa Musa of Mali
1347: Marinids take Tunis
1352: Ibn Battuta's travels to the Mali Empire

1300 · 1320 · 1340 · 1360 · 1380 · 1400

South and Southeast Asia

1320: Muhammad ibn Tughluq succeeds to Sultanate of Delhi
1343: Majapahit Empire completes conquest of Bali
1378: Sukhothai becomes vassal of Siam and is gradually absorbed
c.1350: Founding of Ayutthaya, capital of new kingdom of Siam
1398: Delhi sacked by Timur

1300 · 1320 · 1340 · 1360 · 1380 · 1300

TRADE AND BIOLOGICAL DIFFUSION

CAMPAIGNS OF IMPERIAL EXPANSION, mass migration, cross-cultural trade, and long-distance travel all facilitated the spread of agricultural crops, domesticated animals, and diseases throughout much of the Old World. From 500 to 1500 CE, an array of historical processes helped introduce biological species to new regions and peoples. Chinese rulers extended their authority south of the Yangtze river; Muslim armies pushed into India, Persia, and North Africa; Bantu-speaking peoples migrated throughout most of sub-Saharan Africa; Muslim merchants pursued commercial opportunities throughout the Indian Ocean basin and across the Sahara; and missionaries, pilgrims, diplomats, administrators, and other travellers ventured throughout Eurasia and North Africa. Biological exchanges resulting from these changes profoundly influenced the development of societies throughout the eastern hemisphere.

The peripatetic black rat, at home in a wide range of human environments, was the host for plague-carrying fleas.

Skulls, crossbones, and other images of death were frequently represented in both religious and secular art during the period of the so-called 'Black Death'.

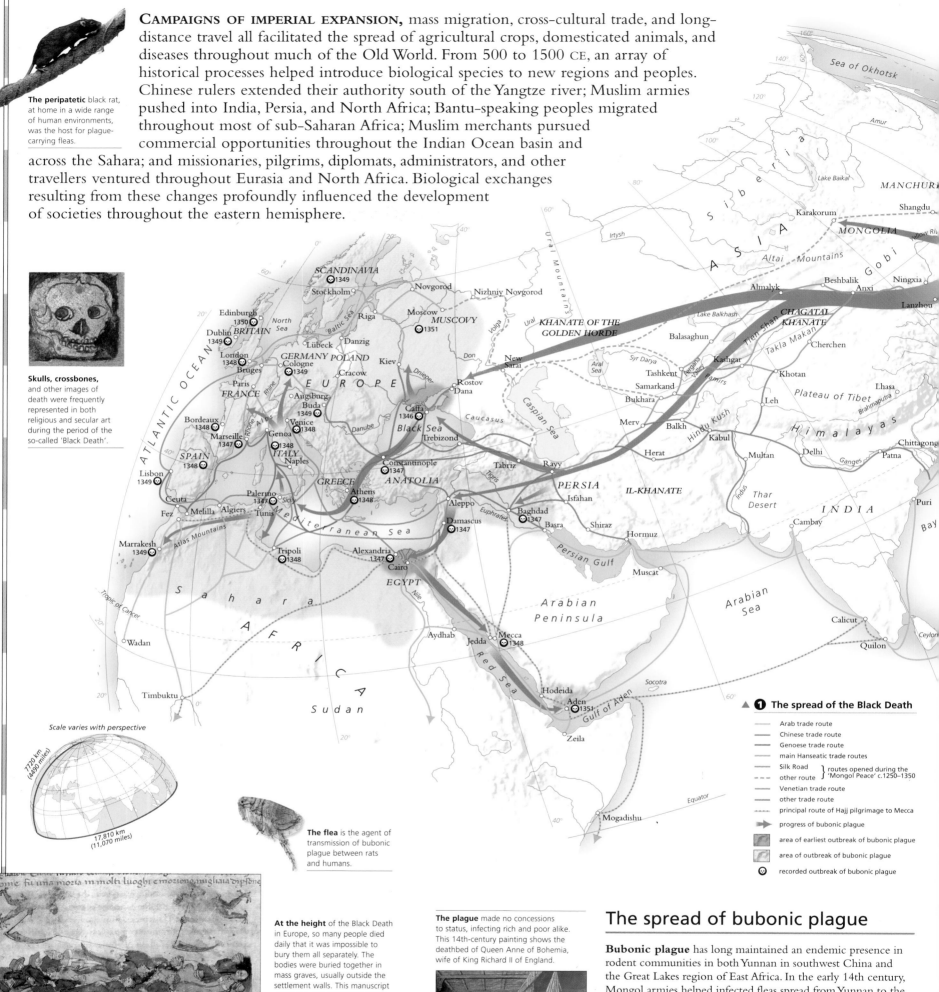

Scale varies with perspective

7720 km (4490 miles)
17,810 km (11,070 miles)

The flea is the agent of transmission of bubonic plague between rats and humans.

▲ ① The spread of the Black Death

- Arab trade route
- Chinese trade route
- Genoese trade route
- main Hanseatic trade routes
- Silk Road } routes opened during the
- other route } 'Mongol Peace' c.1250–1350
- Venetian trade route
- other trade route
- principal route of Hajj pilgrimage to Mecca
- ➤ progress of bubonic plague
- area of earliest outbreak of bubonic plague
- area of outbreak of bubonic plague
- ☻ recorded outbreak of bubonic plague

At the height of the Black Death in Europe, so many people died daily that it was impossible to bury them all separately. The bodies were buried together in mass graves, usually outside the settlement walls. This manuscript illustration shows plague victims carried off by agents of Death.

The plague made no concessions to status, infecting rich and poor alike. This 14th-century painting shows the deathbed of Queen Anne of Bohemia, wife of King Richard II of England.

The spread of bubonic plague

Bubonic plague has long maintained an endemic presence in rodent communities in both Yunnan in southwest China and the Great Lakes region of East Africa. In the early 14th century, Mongol armies helped infected fleas spread from Yunnan to the rest of China. In 1331 an outbreak of plague reportedly carried away 90% of the population in parts of northeast China, and by the 1350s there were widely scattered epidemics throughout China. From China, bubonic plague spread rapidly west along the Silk Roads of Central Asia. By 1346 it had reached the Black Sea. Muslim merchants carried it south and west to southwest Asia, Egypt, and North Africa, while Italian merchants carried it west to Italy and then to northern and western Europe, where it became known as the Black Death. Up to one-third of Europe's population is thought to have died in this one episode.

The spread of plague during the 14th century

1320: Outbreak of plague in Yunnan province
1330: Plague reaches northeastern China
1348: Black Death hits Greece, Italy, France, Spain, Britain, and North Africa
1351: Black Death reaches much of northern Europe

1310 — 1320 — 1330 — 1340 — 1350 — 1360

1320–30: Mongol armies help spread plague throughout China
1346: Plague reaches coast of Black Sea
1349: Black Death arrives in central Europe

The changing balance of world population

The spread of diseases and agricultural crops decisively influenced population levels throughout the Old World. In sub-Saharan Africa, for example, bananas grew well in forested regions that did not favour yams and millet, the earliest staples of Bantu cultivators. In 500 CE the population of sub-Saharan Africa was about 12 million, but following the spread of bananas it rose to 20 million by 1000 and 35.5 million by 1500. The spread of fast-ripening rice in China fuelled an even more dramatic demographic surge: from 60 million in 1000, when fast-ripening rice went north from Vietnam to the Yangtze river valley, the Chinese population climbed to 100 million in 1100 and 115 million in 1200. However, beginning in the 14th century, bubonic plague raced through densely-populated lands from China to Morocco, thinning human numbers with drastic effect. By 1400, China's population had fallen to about 70 million.

Many people were displaced by the depopulation of the Black Death and the societal changes that it wrought. Those reduced to begging often sought alms at the doors of churches or other religious foundations.

Some towns and villages suffered such depredations in population during the Black Death that they were abandoned by those who were left. The ruined church (*left*) is one of few remnants of the former village of Calceby, in the fenlands of eastern England.

② Distribution of world population c.1400 ▼

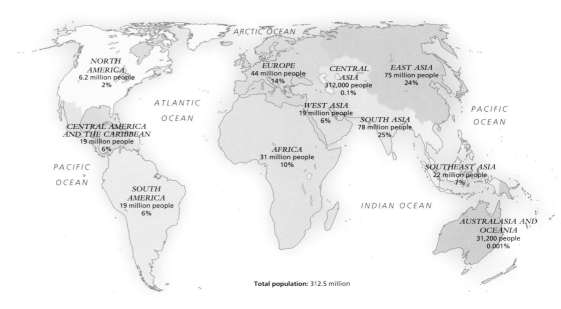

NORTH AMERICA
6.2 million people
2%

EUROPE
44 million people
14%

CENTRAL ASIA
312,000 people
0.1%

EAST ASIA
75 million people
24%

CENTRAL AMERICA AND THE CARIBBEAN
19 million people
6%

WEST ASIA
19 million people
6%

SOUTH ASIA
78 million people
25%

AFRICA
31 million people
10%

SOUTHEAST ASIA
22 million people
7%

SOUTH AMERICA
19 million people
6%

AUSTRALASIA AND OCEANIA
31,200 people
0.001%

Total population: 312.5 million

③ The diffusion of staple crops to c.1500 ▶

Original source areas (pre-700)
- bananas
- sugar cane
- cotton
- sorghum

Spread of crops c.700–1500
→ spread of bananas
→ spread of sugar cane
→ spread of cotton
→ spread of sorghum

Areas to which crops had spread by 1500
- bananas
- sugar cane
- cotton
- sorghum

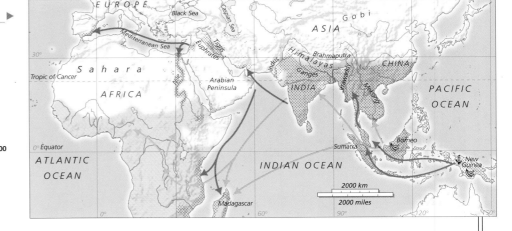

Sugar cane was taken westward to Europe from India from c.600 CE. This 16th-century engraving of a Sicilian sugar mill shows raw sugar being transformed into sugar loaves.

The diffusion of staple crops

A massive diffusion of agricultural crops took place between about 700 and 1400 CE. Most crops spread from tropical or subtropical lands in South and Southeast Asia to the more temperate regions of the eastern hemisphere. Many crops moved with the aid of Muslim merchants, administrators, diplomats, soldiers, missionaries, pilgrims, and other travellers who visited lands from Morocco and Spain to Java and southern China. Sugar cane, native to New Guinea, arrived in the Mediterranean basin as a result of this biological diffusion, along with hard wheat, aubergines, spinach, artichokes, lemons, and limes. Other crops that dispersed widely during this era included rice, sorghum, bananas, coconuts, watermelons, oranges, mangoes, cotton, indigo, and henna.

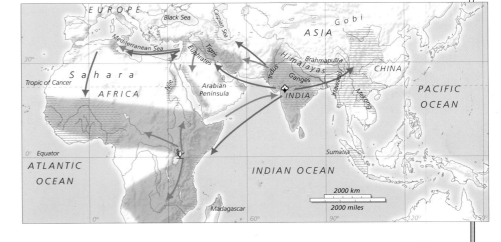

THE WORLD 1400–1500

BY 1500 MOST OF THE EASTERN HEMISPHERE had recovered from the depopulation caused by the Black Death in the 14th century. China began the 15th century by sponsoring naval expeditions in the Indian Ocean, but in the 1430s the Ming rulers ended these voyages and concentrated on their land empire. In southwest Asia, two Turkish peoples established strong empires – the Ottomans in Anatolia and the Safavids in Persia. European states, meanwhile, were starting to build central governments with standing armies and gunpowder weapons. In the course of the 15th century Portuguese mariners settled the Atlantic islands, explored the west coast of Africa, and completed a sea voyage to India. It was, however, a Spanish expedition under the Genoese Columbus that crossed the Atlantic to make contact with the Americas, where the Aztec and Inca empires ruled over complex organized agricultural societies.

North America

The Aztec Empire reached its height in the late 1400s, exacting heavy tribute from the small city-states it had conquered. Through trade, Aztec influence reached far beyond the borders of the empire, extending across most of Central America as far as the Pueblo farmers north of the Rio Grande. In the woodlands around the Mississippi River, mound-building peoples maintained sizeable communities based on the cultivation of maize.

Human sacrifice to the sun god Huitzilopochtli was the core of the Aztec religion. Thousands of prisoners might be killed in a single ceremony.

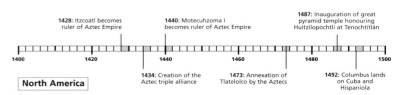

1428: Itzcoatl becomes ruler of Aztec Empire
1440: Motecuhzoma I becomes ruler of Aztec Empire
1487: Inauguration of great pyramid temple honouring Huitzilopochtli at Tenochtitlán

| North America |

1434: Creation of the Aztec triple alliance
1473: Annexation of Tlatelolco by the Aztecs
1492: Columbus lands on Cuba and Hispaniola

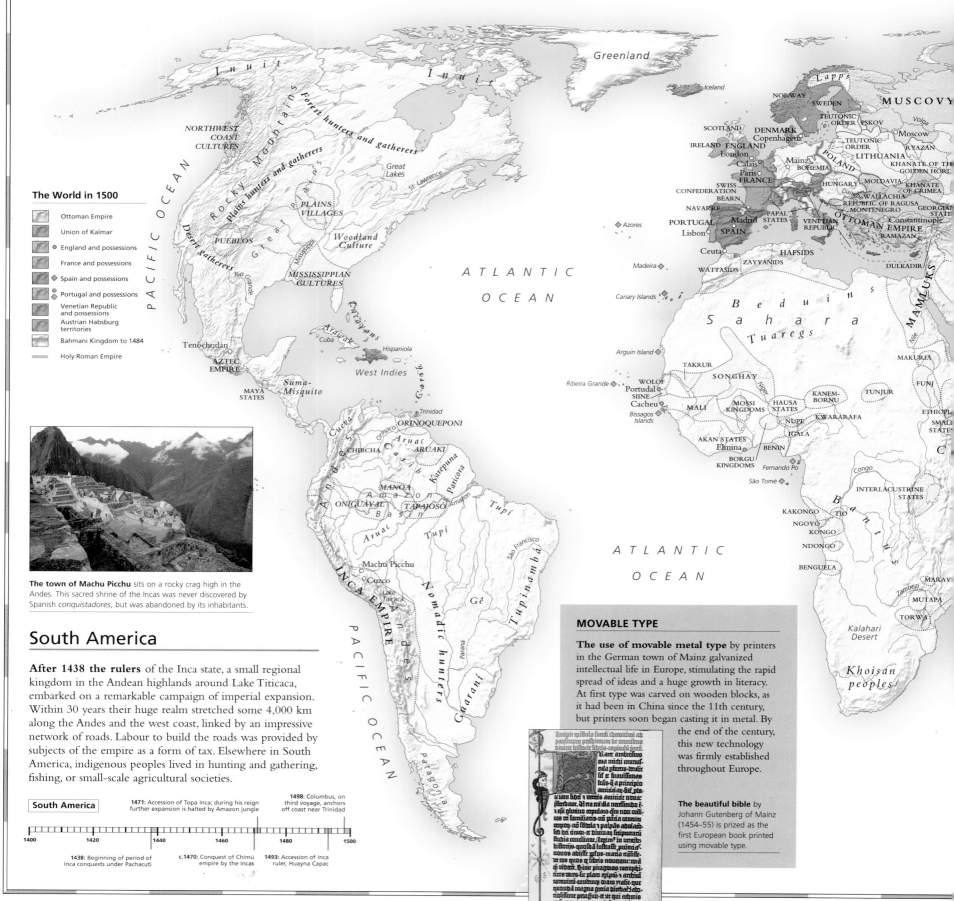

The World in 1500

- Ottoman Empire
- Union of Kalmar
- England and possessions
- France and possessions
- Spain and possessions
- Portugal and possessions
- Venetian Republic and possessions
- Austrian Habsburg territories
- Bahmani Kingdom to 1484
- Holy Roman Empire

The town of Machu Picchu sits on a rocky crag high in the Andes. This sacred shrine of the Incas was never discovered by Spanish *conquistadores*, but was abandoned by its inhabitants.

South America

After 1438 the rulers of the Inca state, a small regional kingdom in the Andean highlands around Lake Titicaca, embarked on a remarkable campaign of imperial expansion. Within 30 years their huge realm stretched some 4,000 km along the Andes and the west coast, linked by an impressive network of roads. Labour to build the roads was provided by subjects of the empire as a form of tax. Elsewhere in South America, indigenous peoples lived in hunting and gathering, fishing, or small-scale agricultural societies.

| South America |

1471: Accession of Topa Inca; during his reign further expansion is halted by Amazon jungle
1498: Columbus, on third voyage, anchors off coast near Trinidad

1438: Beginning of period of Inca conquests under Pachacuti
c.1470: Conquest of Chimú empire by the Incas
1493: Accession of Inca ruler, Huayna Capac

MOVABLE TYPE

The use of movable metal type by printers in the German town of Mainz galvanized intellectual life in Europe, stimulating the rapid spread of ideas and a huge growth in literacy. At first type was carved on wooden blocks, as it had been in China since the 11th century, but printers soon began casting it in metal. By the end of the century, this new technology was firmly established throughout Europe.

The beautiful bible by Johann Gutenberg of Mainz (1454–55) is prized as the first European book printed using movable type.

Europe

The 15th century saw the start of the Renaissance, a flowering of architecture, art, and humanist idealism inspired by Classical models. The city-states of Italy were the cultural leaders of Europe, but political power was shifting towards the 'new monarchs', who created strong, centralized kingdoms in England, France, and Spain. Poland dominated eastern Europe, but here the future lay with Muscovy, where Ivan III launched Russian expansion to the east and south and in 1472 assumed the title of 'tsar'.

Sixtus IV, elected in 1471, was typical of the popes of the Renaissance. A worldly, nepotistic prince, he commissioned great works of art and architecture, including the Sistine Chapel.

MARTIN BEHAIM'S GLOBE

Martin Behaim was a geographer of Nuremberg who visited Portugal and sailed down the west coast of Africa with Portuguese mariners in the 1480s. His globe, produced in 1490–92, is the oldest surviving globe in the world. Since he knew nothing of the existence of America, he depicted the island of 'Cipangu' (Japan) and the east Asian mainland directly across the Atlantic from western Europe.

Martin Behaim's globe gives a very good picture of how Columbus must have imagined the world before he set sail across the Atlantic Ocean.

SEE ALSO:

North America: pp.122–123

South America: pp.146–147

Africa: pp.162–163

Europe: pp.192–193

West Asia: pp.228–231

South and Southeast Asia: pp.244–245

North and East Asia: pp.264–267

Europe

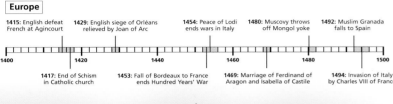

1415: English defeat French at Agincourt | 1429: English siege of Orléans relieved by Joan of Arc | 1454: Peace of Lodi ends wars in Italy | 1480: Muscovy throws off Mongol yoke | 1492: Muslim Granada falls to Spain

1417: End of Schism in Catholic church | 1453: Fall of Bordeaux to France ends Hundred Years' War | 1469: Marriage of Ferdinand of Aragon and Isabella of Castile | 1494: Invasion of Italy by Charles VIII of France

West Asia

When Timur died in 1405, his empire was divided among his four sons. After a series of quarrels, Shah Rukh, who inherited the eastern part, presided over an era of peace, in which the arts and architecture flourished. The Shaybanids, who expanded south across the Syr Darya, were descendants of Genghis Khan. However, a new power was rising that would eclipse the Mongol dynasties that vied to control Persia – the Shi'ite Safavids. In the west, the Ottoman Turks, led by Sultan Mehmed II ('the Conqueror') and aided by powerful cannons, took Constantinople in 1453 and put an end to the Byzantine Empire.

The fall of Constantinople removed the major Christian stronghold barring Islam's spread to the west. The small defending force of Byzantines and Italians was no match for the besieging army of 100,000.

West Asia

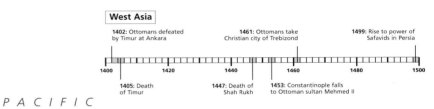

1402: Ottomans defeated by Timur at Ankara | 1461: Ottomans take Christian city of Trebizond | 1499: Rise to power of Safavids in Persia

1405: Death of Timur | 1447: Death of Shah Rukh | 1453: Constantinople falls to Ottoman sultan Mehmed II

This painting on silk shows the courtyards of the Forbidden City, the compound of the imperial palace at the centre of Beijing. The Ming capital was moved north from Nanjing to Beijing in 1421 during Yung Luo's campaign against the Mongols.

East and Southeast Asia

The Ming dynasty consolidated its hold on China, rebuilding the Great Wall to prevent raids by Mongol Oirats to the north. After Zheng He's epic, but costly, voyages in the Indian Ocean, the Ming rulers adopted a policy of self-sufficiency, discouraging travel and trade. In contrast to this defensive, inward-looking attitude, Southeast Asia thrived on trade. The most important entrepôt was Malacca. By 1500 its population was about 50,000, and it was reported that 84 languages could be heard in the city's streets.

Africa

Between the 1460s and 1490s the Songhay ruler Sunni Ali conquered Mali and took over the Saharan caravan trade. Meanwhile, the Portuguese explored the west coast, where African rulers, seeing opportunities for trade, laid the foundations for the small kingdoms of Akan and Benin. Sailors from the Swahili city-states in East Africa helped Vasco da Gama understand the local monsoon winds and complete his voyage to India.

This bronze statue of a Portuguese soldier was made in Benin, one of Portugal's West African trading partners.

Africa

1441: First shipment of African slaves to Portugal | 1464: Beginning of Songhay expansion under Sunni Ali

1415: Portuguese capture Ceuta in Morocco | c.1450: Eclipse of Great Zimbabwe by Mutapa empire | 1482: Fort of Elmina founded by Portuguese

East and Southeast Asia

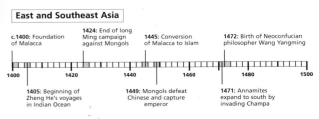

c.1400: Foundation of Malacca | 1424: End of long Ming campaign against Mongols | 1445: Conversion of Malacca to Islam | 1472: Birth of Neoconfucian philosopher Wang Yangming

1405: Beginning of Zheng He's voyages in Indian Ocean | 1449: Mongols defeat Chinese and capture emperor | 1471: Annamites expand to south by invading Champa

GLOBAL KNOWLEDGE

Knowledge of the world and its peoples was coloured by hearsay and travellers' tales.

THE GLOBAL WORLD VIEW is a relatively modern concept. The Americas were unknown to Old World Eurasia until 500 years ago, and each of the major cultural regions had discrete world views of varying extents. Each region had developed its own means of subsistence, and technologies which were direct responses to their immediate environment. In Eurasia, ideas, faiths, and technical achievements were spread by trade, migration, and cultural or political expansion; thus the imprint of Buddhism, Christianity, and Islam was widespread, and technical ideas as diverse as printing and gunpowder, originating in East Asia, had reached Europe. Mapping in one form or another was used by all cultures as a means of recording geographical information and knowledge, although pathfinding and navigation was usually a matter of handed-down knowledge, experience, and word of mouth.

❶ Global economies and technologies c.1500

Principal economies

	hunting and gathering		hand cultivation and hunting and gathering
	herding/pastoralism		slash and burn farming
	hand cultivation		terraced farming
	plough cultivation		uninhabited

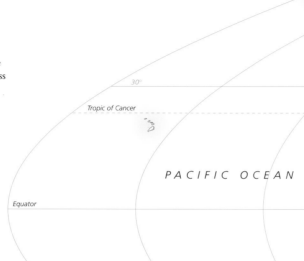

The Americas

Both the Aztecs of Central America and the Incas of the Andes were still in the process of consolidating their young empires when the first Europeans arrived. Although there is evidence in both regions of extensive trading contacts, geographical obstacles (deserts, jungle) and relative immaturity meant their worlds were closely defined.

❷ The Americas ▲

- Aztec Empire
- known world 1500
- Inca Empire
- known world 1500

The size of the globe

The rediscovery of Classical texts was an important stimulus to the development of technology, science, and the arts, which flowered in the European Renaissance. European cartographers began to build a more detailed world map, using the works of Classical geographers such as Strabo and Ptolemy. The voyage of Bartolomeu Dias (1487–88) around the Cape of Good Hope established the limits of Africa; but in 1492, when Columbus made landfall in the Caribbean four weeks after leaving the Canary Islands, he assumed he had reached China (Cathay) rather than the West Indies. Although the circumnavigation by Magellan and del Cano some 30 years later (1519–22) dispelled many uncertainties, the accurate charting of the world's oceans and coasts would not be completed until the 20th century.

◀ ❽ The Ptolemaic map of the world

◀ ❾ The Behaim map of the world 1492

→ Marco Polo 1271-75
Marco Polo assumed he had travelled 16,000 miles instead of 7000 miles

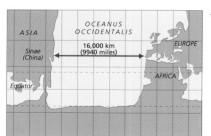

◀ ❿ The modern map of the world

Coasts charted by
- 1500
- 1600
- 1700
- 1800
- 1900

❶ Global economies and technologies c.1500

Significant technologies
▸ draft animals
- 🐃 buffalo
- 🐂 oxen
- 🐎 horse/mule
- 🐪 camel
- 🐘 elephant
- 🦙 llama/alpaca

▸ transport
- wheeled vehicles
- dragged vehicles

▸ hydraulics
- canals
- aqueducts
- irrigation

▸ architecture
- temporary shelters
- post and lintel
- barrel vaulting
- groyne vaulting

▸ navigation
- riverine
- coastal
- oceanic
- Ⓝ lodestone/compass

▸ warfare
- thrown missiles
- archery
- gunpowder

▸ power
- windmills
- watermills
- X technology not developed

▸ recording of knowledge
- knowledge recorded in writing
- knowledge preserved orally
- empirical cartographic tradition

The Muslim World

The most extensive and cosmopolitan of the Old World cultures, by 1500 Islam straddled large extents of three continents, stretching from the islands of the southwest Pacific to the shores of the Atlantic. Knowledge acquired from trade and travel underpinned much Muslim cultural hegemony and scholarship.

❸ The Muslim world ▲
- Muslim heartland
- known world 1500

❻ South Asia ▼
- South Asian states
- known world 1500

South Asia

In 1500, India was about to become subject to Muslim (Mughal) rule. Nevertheless its position on the crossroads of trade across the Indian Ocean, and overland routes from East and Southeast Asia, dated back many centuries, and its exports were known in Europe. Although essentially inward-looking, South Asian rulers and scholars had an extensive knowledge of the Old World.

Europe

By the end of the 15th century, Europe was poised on the brink of rapid territorial expansion. Technically sophisticated and resourceful, the Europeans had built up through trade and travel, a fairly detailed knowledge of much of the Old World, from coastal Africa, through Arabia and southern Asia, to China and the many islands of the East Indies.

⑤ Europe
- ■ Western Christendom
- □ known world 1492

East Asia

China, Korea, and Japan, although frequently isolationist – the Chinese 'Middle Kingdom' regarded itself, with some justification, as the most powerful in the world – had nevertheless acquired considerable knowledge of the Old World, illustrated by the ambassadorial voyages of the Ming admiral Zheng He throughout the Indian Ocean (1405–33).

④ East Asia
- ■ charted by Chinese c.1500
- □ known world c.1500

SEE ALSO:

North America: pp.118–119

South America: pp.142–143

Africa: pp.156–157

Europe: pp.172–173

West Asia: pp.218–219

South and Southeast Asia: pp.238–239

North and East Asia: 256–257

Australasia and Oceania: pp.278–279

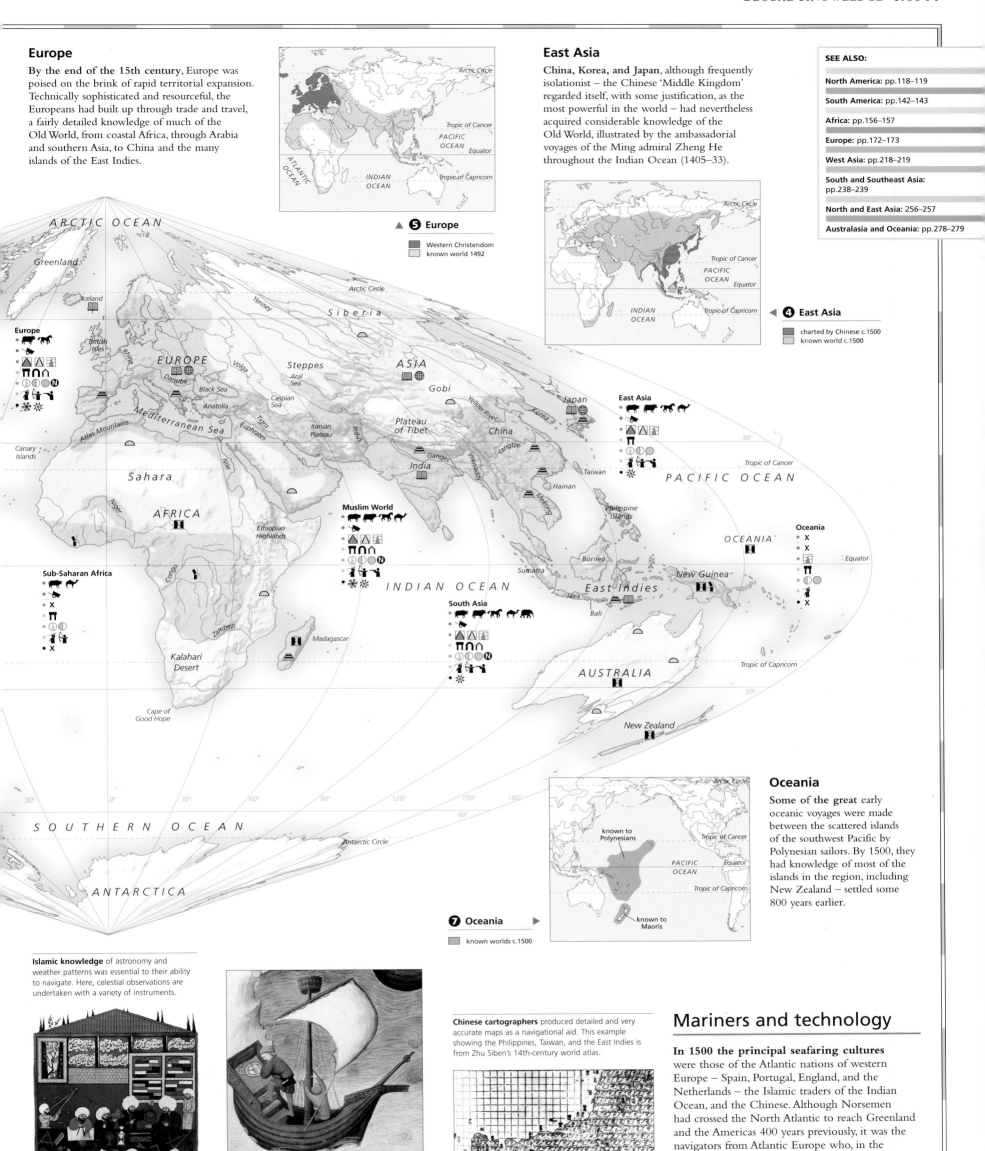

Oceania

Some of the great early oceanic voyages were made between the scattered islands of the southwest Pacific by Polynesian sailors. By 1500, they had knowledge of most of the islands in the region, including New Zealand – settled some 800 years earlier.

⑦ Oceania
- ■ known worlds c.1500

Islamic knowledge of astronomy and weather patterns was essential to their ability to navigate. Here, celestial observations are undertaken with a variety of instruments.

European navigators used an astrolabe, which gave an approximate position in relation to the position of the stars. For lunar and solar measures, an almanac was also necessary.

Chinese cartographers produced detailed and very accurate maps as a navigational aid. This example showing the Philippines, Taiwan, and the East Indies is from Zhu Siben's 14th-century world atlas.

Mariners and technology

In 1500 the principal seafaring cultures were those of the Atlantic nations of western Europe – Spain, Portugal, England, and the Netherlands – the Islamic traders of the Indian Ocean, and the Chinese. Although Norsemen had crossed the North Atlantic to reach Greenland and the Americas 400 years previously, it was the navigators from Atlantic Europe who, in the 15th century, began the systematic exploration of Atlantic island groups and the African coastline. When they sailed east into the Indian Ocean, they benefited from the superior local knowledge of Arab, and later, Chinese navigators.

THE WORLD 1500–1600

IN THE 16TH CENTURY Spain seized a vast land empire that encompassed much of South and Central America, the West Indies, and the Philippine Islands. Meanwhile, the Portuguese acquired a largely maritime empire stretching from Brazil to Malacca and Macao. Ferdinand Magellan, a Portuguese in the service of Spain, demonstrated that all the world's oceans were linked and sea lanes were established through the Indian, Atlantic, and Pacific oceans, creating for the first time a genuinely global trading network. Although the Portuguese traded with the Ming Empire and Japan, cultural contact between Europeans and East Asia was limited. In Africa, too, European impact barely extended beyond the coast. Missionaries took the Catholic faith to distant parts of the Spanish and Portuguese empires, but in Europe the church of Rome faced the threat of the Reformation, while Catholic kingdoms fought to stem Ottoman expansion in the Mediterranean and into the Habsburg lands of central Europe.

Europe

The Protestant Reformation dominated 16th-century Europe. Rulers in Scandinavia, England, Scotland, and many German states abandoned the Roman church and took over monasteries and the running of church affairs. In France Protestants fought Catholics in a debilitating round of civil wars (1562–98) and religion was a major factor in the Dutch revolt against Spanish rule in 1565. The kings of Spain championed Catholicism and promoted missions worldwide. In the east, Russia's tsars extended their empire to the Caspian Sea and western Siberia.

Spanish troops raid a convoy in a scene typical of the atrocities of the Dutch Wars of Independence.

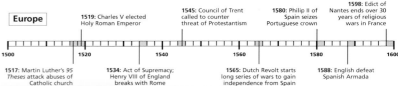

Europe					
	1519: Charles V elected Holy Roman Emperor	**1545:** Council of Trent called to counter threat of Protestantism	**1580:** Philip II of Spain seizes Portuguese crown	**1598:** Edict of Nantes ends over 30 years of religious wars in France	
1500	**1520**	**1540**	**1560**	**1580**	**1600**
1517: Martin Luther's 95 Theses attack abuses of Catholic church	**1534:** Act of Supremacy; Henry VIII of England breaks with Rome	**1565:** Dutch Revolt starts long series of wars to gain independence from Spain	**1588:** English defeat Spanish Armada	

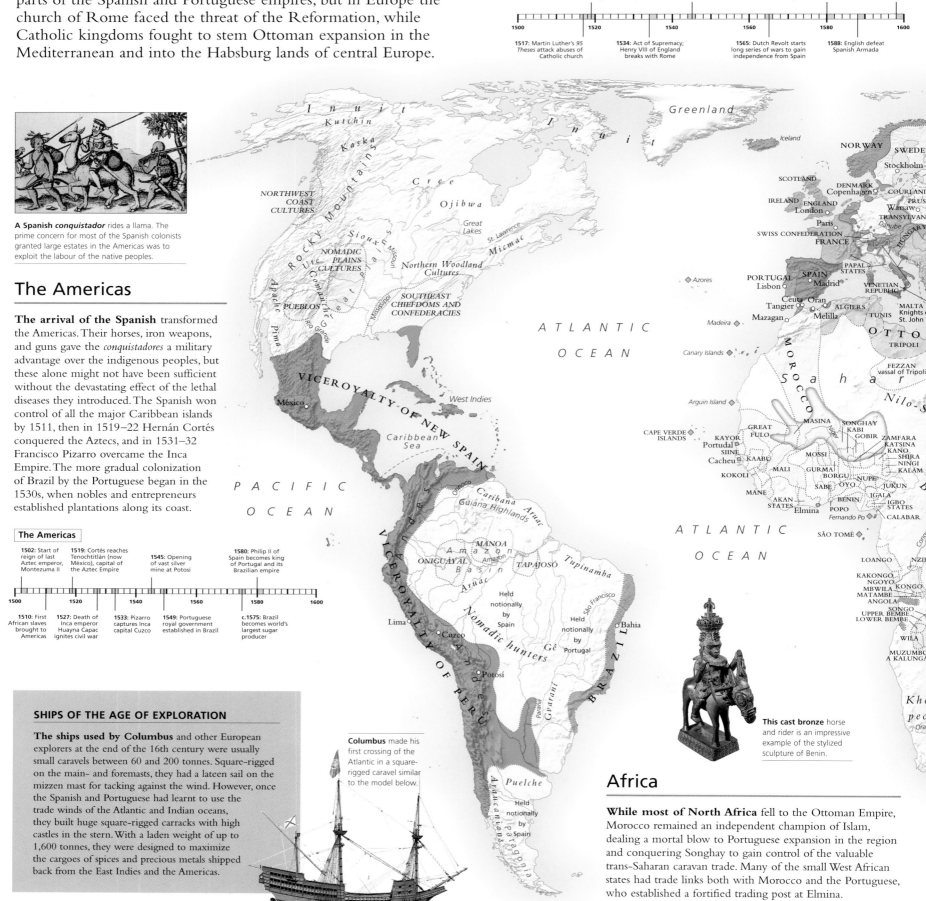

A Spanish *conquistador* rides a llama. The prime concern for most of the Spanish colonists granted large estates in the Americas was to exploit the labour of the native peoples.

The Americas

The arrival of the Spanish transformed the Americas. Their horses, iron weapons, and guns gave the *conquistadores* a military advantage over the indigenous peoples, but these alone might not have been sufficient without the devastating effect of the lethal diseases they introduced. The Spanish won control of all the major Caribbean islands by 1511, then in 1519–22 Hernán Cortés conquered the Aztecs, and in 1531–32 Francisco Pizarro overcame the Inca Empire. The more gradual colonization of Brazil by the Portuguese began in the 1530s, when nobles and entrepreneurs established plantations along its coast.

The Americas					
1502: Start of reign of last Aztec emperor, Montezuma II	**1519:** Cortés reaches Tenochtitlán (now México), capital of the Aztec Empire	**1545:** Opening of vast silver mine at Potosí	**1580:** Philip II of Spain becomes king of Portugal and its Brazilian empire		
1500	**1520**	**1540**	**1560**	**1580**	**1600**
1510: First African slaves brought to Americas	**1527:** Death of Inca emperor Huayna Capac ignites civil war	**1533:** Pizarro captures Inca capital Cuzco	**1549:** Portuguese royal government established in Brazil	**c.1575:** Brazil becomes world's largest sugar producer	

SHIPS OF THE AGE OF EXPLORATION

The ships used by Columbus and other European explorers at the end of the 16th century were usually small caravels between 60 and 200 tonnes. Square-rigged on the main- and foremasts, they had lateen sail on the mizzen mast for tacking against the wind. However, once the Spanish and Portuguese had learnt to use the trade winds of the Atlantic and Indian oceans, they built huge square-rigged carracks with high castles in the stern. With a laden weight of up to 1,600 tonnes, they were designed to maximize the cargoes of spices and precious metals shipped back from the East Indies and the Americas.

Columbus made his first crossing of the Atlantic in a square-rigged caravel similar to the model below.

This cast bronze horse and rider is an impressive example of the stylized sculpture of Benin.

Africa

While most of North Africa fell to the Ottoman Empire, Morocco remained an independent champion of Islam, dealing a mortal blow to Portuguese expansion in the region and conquering Songhay to gain control of the valuable trans-Saharan caravan trade. Many of the small West African states had trade links both with Morocco and the Portuguese, who established a fortified trading post at Elmina.

West Asia

In the 16th century the Ottoman Empire expanded into southwest Asia, North Africa, and southeastern Europe. The Ottoman navy was the pre-eminent power in the Mediterranean until its defeat by a Christian fleet at Lepanto in 1571 and Muslim vessels dominated the region's shipping. Ottoman rulers clashed constantly with the Safavids in Persia, and in the late 16th and early 17th centuries the two empires fought for control of Mesopotamia and the Caucasus. Many earlier Ottoman gains were reversed during the reign of Shah Abbas the Great, the Safavid ruler from 1588 to 1629.

Suleiman the Magnificent extended Ottoman rule far into southeastern Europe. In this miniature, he is seen receiving homage from his many Christian vassals.

West Asia

- **1507:** Portuguese victory over Ottoman and Arab fleet at Diu
- **1514:** Ottomans victory over Safavids at Chaldiran
- **1520:** Suleiman the Magnificent becomes Ottoman sultan
- **1526:** Battle of Mohács; Ottomans crush Hungarian army
- **1566:** Suleiman succeeded by Selim II
- **1571:** Battle of Lepanto; Ottoman navy defeated by united Christian fleet off Greek coast
- **1587:** Isfahan becomes capital of Safavid Empire
- **1588:** Abbas I the Great becomes Safavid shah

1500 — 1520 — 1540 — 1560 — 1580 — 1600

THE NEW WORLD BY ABRAHAM ORTELIUS

Abraham Ortelius was a mapseller from Antwerp whose *Theatrum Orbis Terrarum* of 1570 is considered the first modern atlas. He was not an original cartographer, but he travelled widely in search of reliable sources and his atlas sold well throughout Europe for over 40 years. His map of the New World was a fairly accurate summary of European explorers' knowledge of the Americas and the Pacific. The vast southern continent, *Terra Australis*, a relic of the Classical geography of Claudius Ptolemy, was a feature of most maps of the period. It includes Tierra del Fuego and part of the coast of New Guinea, but the rest is pure conjecture. Ortelius was a contemporary of Gerardus Mercator. Between them, the two great mapmakers did much to shift the centre of European cartography from Italy to the Low Countries.

The map gives a fairly accurate picture of Central America and the Caribbean; however many parts of America had still not been explored by Europeans at all.

SEE ALSO:

North America: pp.124–125

South America: pp.146–149

Africa: pp.162–163

Europe: pp.194–195

West Asia: pp.230–231

South and Southeast Asia: pp.244–247

North and East Asia: pp.264–267

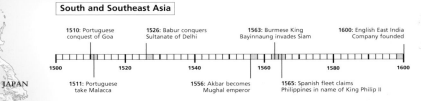

South and Southeast Asia

South and Southeast Asia

- **1510:** Portuguese conquest of Goa
- **1511:** Portuguese take Malacca
- **1526:** Babur conquers Sultanate of Delhi
- **1556:** Akbar becomes Mughal emperor
- **1563:** Burmese King Bayinnaung invades Siam
- **1565:** Spanish fleet claims Philippines in name of King Philip II
- **1600:** English East India Company founded

1500 — 1520 — 1540 — 1560 — 1580 — 1600

In 1523 the Chagatai Turk Babur invaded northern India, founding the Mughal dynasty of Islamic rulers. The empire was consolidated by Babur's grandson, Akbar. Mughal rulers concentrated on their land empire and agriculture, allowing the Portuguese to maintain coastal trading posts and a flourishing colony at Goa. Portugal also conquered Malacca and the 'Spice Islands' of the Moluccas. The dominant power in mainland Southeast Asia was Burma, which reached its largest extent under King Bayinnaung, who conquered Siam and Laos and installed puppet rulers.

The richest prize for European merchants in South and Southeast Asia was control of the valuable spice trade. This French illustration shows the pepper harvest in southern India.

The World in 1600

- Ming Empire
- Ottoman Empire
- Spain and possessions
- Portugal and possessions (ruled by Kings of Spain 1580–1640)
- England and possessions
- Austrian Habsburg territories
- France
- Denmark and possessions
- Venetian Republic and possessions
- United Provinces (fighting for independence from Spain)
- Dutch (United Provinces) possessions
- Mughal Empire at Akbar's accession, 1556
- under Burmese control, 1575
- Songhay to 1590
- Holy Roman Empire

Africa

- **c.1500:** Establishment of forest states of Oyo and Benin
- **1505:** First Portuguese trading posts in East Africa
- **1517:** Ottomans conquer Mamluks in Egypt
- **1546:** Songhay destroys Mali Empire
- **1570:** Establishment of Portuguese colony in Angola
- **1578:** Moroccans crush invading Portuguese
- **1591:** Songhay Empire falls to Morocco

1500 — 1520 — 1540 — 1560 — 1580 — 1600

Map labels: RUSSIAN EMPIRE, Moscow, Volga, Ob', Yenisei, Lena, Palaeosiberians, Samoyeds, Siberia, Yakuts, Tungus, Buryats, Amur, MONGOLIA in disintegration, Gobi, MANCHURIA, Yellow River, Beijing, KOREA, JAPAN, POLAND-LITHUANIA, MOLDAVIA, KHANATE OF CRIMEA, WALLACHIA, Constantinople, Turkic peoples, Caspian Sea, KHIVA, BUKHARA, CHAGATAI KHANATE, TIBET, MING EMPIRE, Yangtze, Macao, SAFAVID EMPIRE, Isfahan, Tigris, Euphrates, Mesopotamia, Caucasus, OTTOMAN EMPIRE, Hormuz, Muscat, OMAN, Arabian Peninsula, Beduins, Nile, BEDUINS, FUNJ, Saharan peoples, TUNJUR, AUSSA, ETHIOPIA, ADAL, HARAR, SMALL OROMO STATES, Socotra, Cushites, Bantus, Mombasa, MARAVI, LUNDU, MUTAPA, BUTUA, Sofala, Zambezi, Mozambique, Inhambane, Delagoa Bay, Malays, Madagascar, Mauritius, MUGHAL EMPIRE, Himalayas, Ganges, Agra, BHUTAN, ASSAMESE STATES, NEPALESE PRINCIPALITIES, SHAN STATES, Cambay, Diu, Surat, Damao, Bassein, Bombay, Chaul, AHMADNAGAR, Goa, BIJAPUR, GOLCONDA, BIDAR, Masulipatam, GONDWANA, ARAKAN, BURMA, TRAN NINH, ANNAM, LAOS, Mekong, SIAM, CAMBODIA, CHAMPA, Bhatkal, Mangalore, Cannanore, Calicut, Cochin, POLYGAR KINGDOMS, Negapatam, Jaffna, Quilon, Batticaloa, Colombo, CEYLON, Galle, PHILIPPINE ISLANDS, ATJEH, MALAY STATES, BRUNEI, SULU, SULTANATE OF JOHORE, Malacca, Malays, East Indies, Moluccas, Area under Portuguese influence, Amboina, New Guinea, Papuans, PACIFIC OCEAN, Scattered Spanish possessions, CHERIBON, MATARAM, BANTAM, Timor, INDIAN OCEAN, Australian Aborigines, Darling, Maoris, New Zealand

THE AGE OF EUROPEAN EXPANSION

The Portuguese, Vasco da Gama was the first European navigator to reach India by sea.

THE 16TH CENTURY saw the expansion of several of the great European nations far beyond their continental limits. Explorers searching for new sources of luxury goods and precious metals began to open up new territories which monarchs such as Philip II of Spain quickly built up into great empires in the 'New World'. The Spanish and Portuguese, inspired by the voyages of Columbus and da Gama, led the way, closely followed by the Dutch and the English. The explorers were aided by technological advances in shipbuilding, navigational equipment, and cartography. At the start of the 16th century, the Americas were virtually unknown to Europeans; by 1700, outposts of a greater European empire had been established almost everywhere the explorers landed.

European voyages of expansion and discovery

Spain and Portugal were the leaders of world exploration in the 16th century. In search of maritime trade routes to Asia, the Portuguese found sea lanes through the Atlantic and Indian oceans to India. By 1512, fortified trading posts were in place at Goa and Malacca, and they had reached the 'Spice Islands' of the Moluccas in eastern Indonesia. The Spanish, taking a westward route, found the Caribbean islands and the Americas instead. Magellan's three-year global circumnavigation revealed a western route through the Strait of Magellan and across the Pacific Ocean. English and French mariners sought northern passages to Asian markets and their voyages paved the way for the establishment of European settlements in North America.

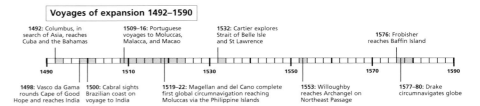

Voyages of expansion 1492–1590

1492: Columbus, in search of Asia, reaches Cuba and the Bahamas

1509–16: Portuguese voyages to Moluccas, Malacca, and Macao

1532: Cartier explores Strait of Belle Isle and St Lawrence

1576: Frobisher reaches Baffin Island

| 1490 | 1510 | 1530 | 1550 | 1570 | 1590 |

1498: Vasco da Gama rounds Cape of Good Hope and reaches India

1500: Cabral sights Brazilian coast on voyage to India

1519–22: Magellan and del Cano complete first global circumnavigation reaching Moluccas via the Philippine Islands

1553: Willoughby reaches Archangel on Northeast Passage

1577–80: Drake circumnavigates globe

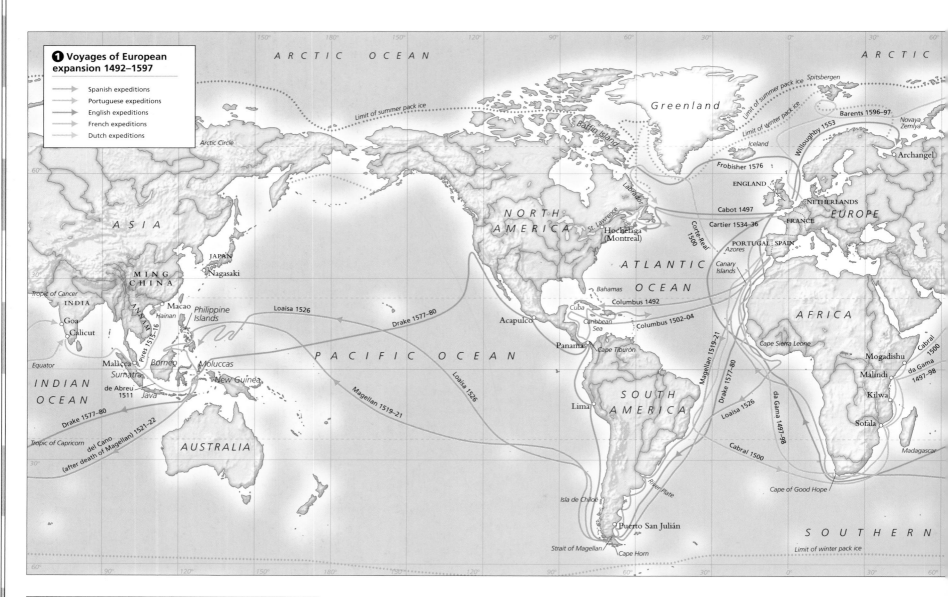

① Voyages of European expansion 1492–1597

→ Spanish expeditions
→ Portuguese expeditions
→ English expeditions
→ French expeditions
→ Dutch expeditions

EAST MEETS WEST

Europeans and the peoples they encountered in the East had much to learn from one another. Jesuit missionaries were particularly successful at establishing links between China and Japan and the West. During the 1580s, the Jesuit Matteo Ricci informed the Chinese emperor and his court about many European inventions. He presented them with elaborate clocks and taught them about astronomical equipment and weapons such as cannon. His primary purpose was to convert the Chinese to Christianity, using European scientific advances to demonstrate the superiority of European religion. Despite his efforts to accommodate Chinese culture – including the celebration of the mass in Chinese – large-scale conversion eluded him. But much future scientific endeavour was due to these cultural contacts: the revival of Chinese mathematics, the development of the suspension bridge, and early Western experiments in electrostatics and magnetism.

Magellan's global circumnavigation was so extraordinary that contemporary artists portrayed him abetted on his voyage by both the latest navigational technology and weaponry, and by mythical creatures such as monsters and mermaids. He was killed by hostile local people in the Philippine Islands in 1521.

The arrival of Portuguese merchants in Japan is shown below by a Japanese artist. From the mid-16th century, Portuguese traders provided a link between a hostile China and Japan and St. Francis Xavier began a mission to gain new Christian converts. They were soon perceived as a threat to Japanese security and ships which landed were ordered to be confiscated and their crews executed.

② Biological exchanges

Origin and movement of plants and animals

→ from Europe
→ from America
→ from Asia

Plants and animals

- bananas
- chilli peppers
- horses
- maize
- manioc
- peanuts
- potatoes
- rice
- sugar cane
- sweet potatoes
- tomatoes
- wheat
- yams

Diseases

➤ bubonic plague
➤ diphtheria, influenza, measles, smallpox, and whooping cough
➤ syphilis

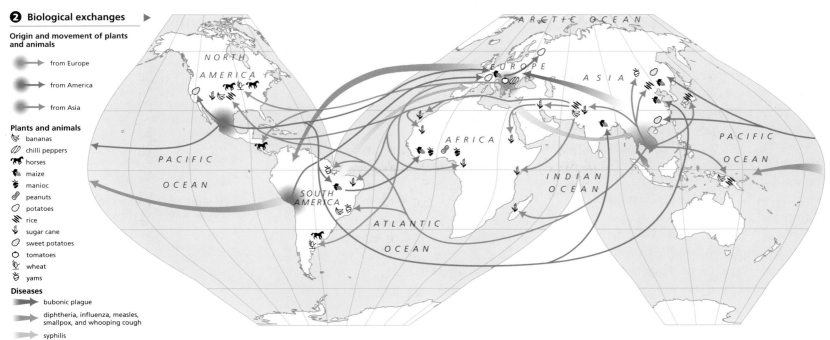

SEE ALSO:

North America:
pp.118–119, 122–123

South America:
pp.142–143, 148–149

Africa: pp.156–157, 162–163

South and Southeast Asia:
pp.238–239, 246–247

North and East Asia:
pp.256–257

Australasia and Oceania:
pp.278–279

Biological exchanges

European expansion had a profound biological impact. Travellers transported numerous species of fruits, vegetables, and animals from the Americas to Europe. At the same time, settlers introduced European species to the Americas and Oceania. Horses, pigs, and cattle were transported to the western hemisphere where, without natural predators, their numbers increased spectacularly. The settlers consciously introduced food crops, such as wheat, grapes, apples, peaches, and citrus fruits. Some plants, such as nettles, dandelions, and other weeds were inadvertently dispersed by the winds or on the coats of animals. European expansion also led to a spread of European diseases. Vast numbers of indigenous American peoples died from measles and smallpox, which broke out in massive epidemics among populations with no natural or acquired immunity. During the 16th century, syphilis – thought now to be the result of the fusion of two similar diseases from Europe and the New World – killed a million Europeans.

The plantain, a herb with medicinal properties, was known as 'Englishman's foot' by native North Americans who believed it would grow only where the English had trodden.

Many more indigenous Americans were killed by smallpox and measles than were slaughtered by the colonizers. Up to 90% of the total population may have perished from European diseases.

③ The Spanish Empire in 1600 ▶

☐ Spanish Empire
☐ Portugal and possessions annexed by Philip II of Spain in 1580

Trade
→ gold
→ silver
→ silk
→ spices

New Spain: conquered by Cortés in 1521, México, the former Aztec city of Tenochtitlán, became the centre of the Spanish Empire in North America.

South America: based around the city of Lima, the Viceroyalty of Peru was the centre of the Spanish Empire in South America.

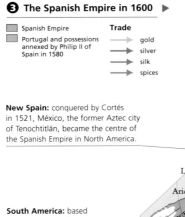

The Manila galleon: brought silver once a year from Acapulco in New Spain to Manila. The silver was used to buy silk, porcelain, and lacquerware which were transported back to New Spain and then to Spain.

The Philippine Islands: first discovered in 1521 by Magellan and claimed for Spain. A governorship and Spanish settlement of the Philippines began in 1565.

Europe: by 1600, the Spanish Empire in Europe included Portugal, Flanders, Naples, and Sicily.

The Treaty of Tordesillas (1494)
Under this treaty between Spain and Portugal, the yet-to-be-discovered world was divided, with Spain taking the western portion and Portugal the east. In 1529 a further treaty divided the eastern hemisphere.

The Spanish Empire

By the end of the 16th century the Spanish Empire included Central America, the West Indies, western South America, and most of the Philippine Islands. The need to safeguard the new lands, their precious natural resources and the new trading networks which evolved, led to the development of a colonial administration of unparalleled scope. Royal authority was vested in the twin institutions of *audiencias*, with political, administrative, and judicial functions, and a series of viceroys, who acted primarily as powerful governors, though they possessed no judicial powers. All information relating to government in the Spanish territories was controlled by specially created councils, the Council of Castile and the Council of the Indies, which met regularly to ensure communication between Spain and the distant possessions of the Spanish Empire.

The New World empire Philip II inherited from his father, Charles V, was greatly expanded after 1580 following the annexation of Portugal which added Brazil and the East Indies.

The Expansion of the Spanish Empire

1494: Treaty of Tordesillas divides western hemisphere between Spain and Portugal

1509: Spanish settlement of mainland Central America begins

1519–21: Cortés conquers Aztec Empire

1540s: Potosí becomes greatest single source of silver in the world

1564: System of Atlantic convoys established

1580: Union of Spanish and Portuguese crowns

1493: Columbus establishes first Spanish settlement in western hemisphere

1532–40: Pizarro conquers Inca Empire

1565–75: Spanish conquest of Philippine Islands

1571: Foundation of Manila

1590: Silver shipped to Manila almost equal in value to Atlantic trade

THE WORLD 1600–1700

DURING THE 17TH CENTURY Dutch, British, and French mariners followed Iberians into the world's seas. All three lands established colonies in North America, and all entered the trade networks of the Indian Ocean. British and French mariners searched for a northeast and a northwest passage from Europe to Asia and, although unsuccessful, their efforts expanded their understanding of the world's geography. Dutch incursions into the East Indies began to erode the dominance of the Portuguese empire in this region. Trade between Europe, Africa, North America, and South America pushed the Atlantic Ocean basin toward economic integration, while European trade in the Indian Ocean linked European and Asian markets.

Many European rulers believed that they governed by divine right. Louis XIV of France is here portrayed in a classical fashion which reflects both his supreme power and his belief in his godlike status.

Europe

The ramifications of the Protestant Reformation complicated political affairs in western and central Europe. The Thirty Years' War (1618–48) ravaged much of Germany, but the Peace of Westphalia that ended the war established a system of states based on a balance of power. This system did not eliminate conflict but maintained relative stability until the French Revolution. The Russian Empire expanded to reach the Pacific Ocean by the mid-17th century as Cossacks and other adventurers established forts throughout Siberia while searching for furs.

Europe

| 1618: Start of Thirty Years' War | 1643: Louis XIV becomes King of France | 1648: Thirty Years' War ended by Peace of Westphalia | 1682: Peter the Great becomes tsar of Russia |
| 1611: Accession of Gustavus Adolphus signals Swedish expansion | 1649: Execution of Charles I of England | 1683: Siege of Vienna ends in Ottoman defeat |

1600 1620 1640 1660 1680 1700

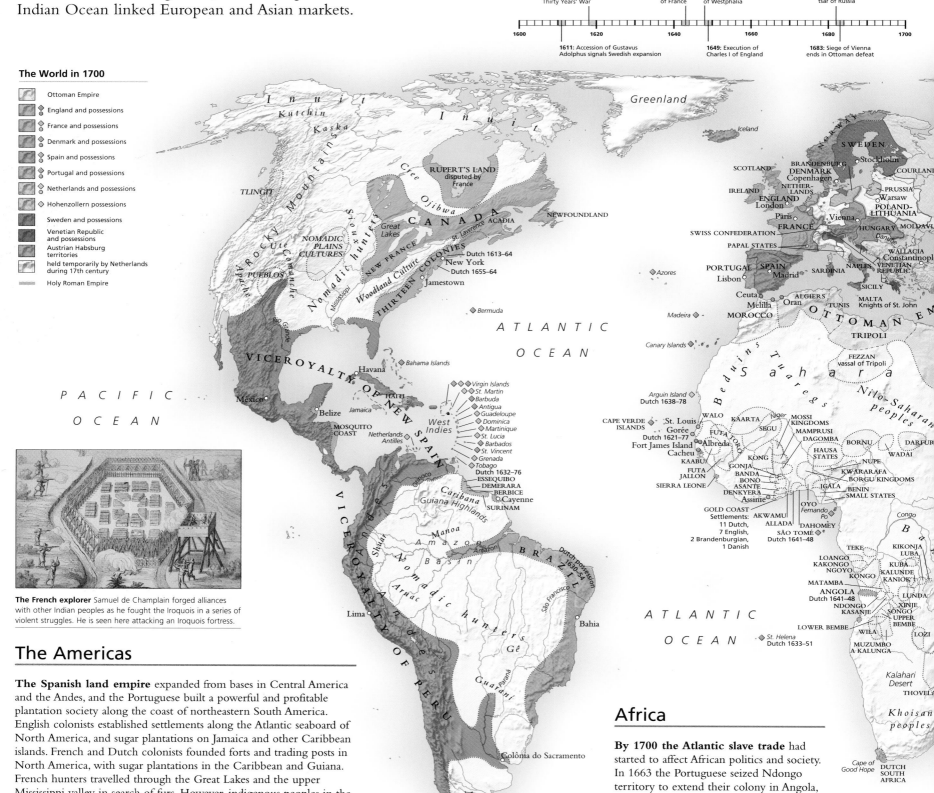

The French explorer Samuel de Champlain forged alliances with other Indian peoples as he fought the Iroquois in a series of violent struggles. He is seen here attacking an Iroquois fortress.

The World in 1700

- Ottoman Empire
- England and possessions
- France and possessions
- Denmark and possessions
- Spain and possessions
- Portugal and possessions
- Netherlands and possessions
- Hohenzollern possessions
- Sweden and possessions
- Venetian Republic and possessions
- Austrian Habsburg territories
- held temporarily by Netherlands during 17th century
- Holy Roman Empire

The Americas

The Spanish land empire expanded from bases in Central America and the Andes, and the Portuguese built a powerful and profitable plantation society along the coast of northeastern South America. English colonists established settlements along the Atlantic seaboard of North America, and sugar plantations on Jamaica and other Caribbean islands. French and Dutch colonists founded forts and trading posts in North America, with sugar plantations in the Caribbean and Guiana. French hunters travelled through the Great Lakes and the upper Mississippi valley in search of furs. However, indigenous peoples in the continental interior remained largely independent of European rule.

The Americas

| 1604–08: Foundation of French colony of Acadia | 1630: Beginning of Dutch conquest of Brazil | 1654: English seize Jamaica from Spain | 1695: Discovery of gold in Brazil |
| 1607: Foundation of English colony at Jamestown | 1630: Foundation of English Massachusetts Bay colony | 1664: English seizure of Dutch colony of New Amsterdam; renamed New York |

1600 1620 1640 1660 1680 1700

Africa

By 1700 the Atlantic slave trade had started to affect African politics and society. In 1663 the Portuguese seized Ndongo territory to extend their colony in Angola, and made frequent attempts to conquer Kongo. The African population was boosted by the introduction of food crops from the Americas, including manioc, maize, and peanuts, but this increase was offset by the export of two million slaves from Africa – mainly to the Americas – during the 17th century. States such as Asante, Dahomey, and Oyo raided their neighbours in search of slaves to exchange for European guns.

OPTICAL INSTRUMENTS

The development of telescopes and microscopes geatly advanced human knowledge of both distant objects and those too small to see with the naked eye during the 17th century. The refracting telescope, using a combination of lenses, was first used for observation of the Moon and distant universe by Galileo in 1609. Newton's reflecting telescope, using lenses and mirrors, gave a still clearer picture of the stars and planets. In 1683, Anton van Leeuwenhoek made the first high-powered precision microscope.

A model of Newton's reflecting telescope, made in 1668.

The Qing dynasty began their rule with great energy, encouraging many projects for the improvement of their new lands. These workers are building a new dyke constructed from timber and brushwood.

East Asia

In 1644 a Manchu army toppled the Ming dynasty, entered Beijing, and established the Qing dynasty (1644–1911). By the 1680s they had consolidated their hold on southern China, conquered the island of Formosa, and extended Chinese influence far into North and Central Asia. The Qing adapted to Chinese ways and largely preserved the Ming administrative structure. In Japan, the Tokugawa dynasty imposed a central government for the first time. Foreign trade was strictly controlled by both the Chinese and Japanese, confined mainly to Macao in China and Nagasaki in Japan.

SEE ALSO:

North America: pp.126–127

South America: pp.148–149

Africa: pp.164–165

Europe: pp.196–197

West Asia: pp.230–231

South and Southeast Asia: pp.244–245

North and East Asia: pp.268–269

Australasia and Oceania: pp.278–279

East Asia

1633: Closure of Japan by Tokugawa shoguns
1644: Manchu forces topple the Ming and establish the Qing dynasty
1683: Conquest of Formosa by Kangxi
1603: Establishment of Tokugawa dynasty in Japan
1654: Kangxi becomes Qing emperor
1689: Treaty of Nerchinsk between Russia and China; Russians withdraw from Amur basin

JOAN BLAEU'S EASTERN HEMISPHERE

During the 17th century, Dutch mariners and merchants pushed forward the boundaries of the world known to Europeans. Willem Blaeu and his son Joan were official cartographers to the Dutch East India Company (VOC), publishing maps and charts based on the most up-to-date and accurate information provided by explorers, as well as a series of world atlases.

The eastern hemisphere of Joan Blaeu's *Nova et accuratissima totius terrarum orbis tabula*, was first published in his *Atlas Major* in 1662. The map presents a familiar view of Africa, Europe, and most of Asia, although Australia is shown only sketchily.

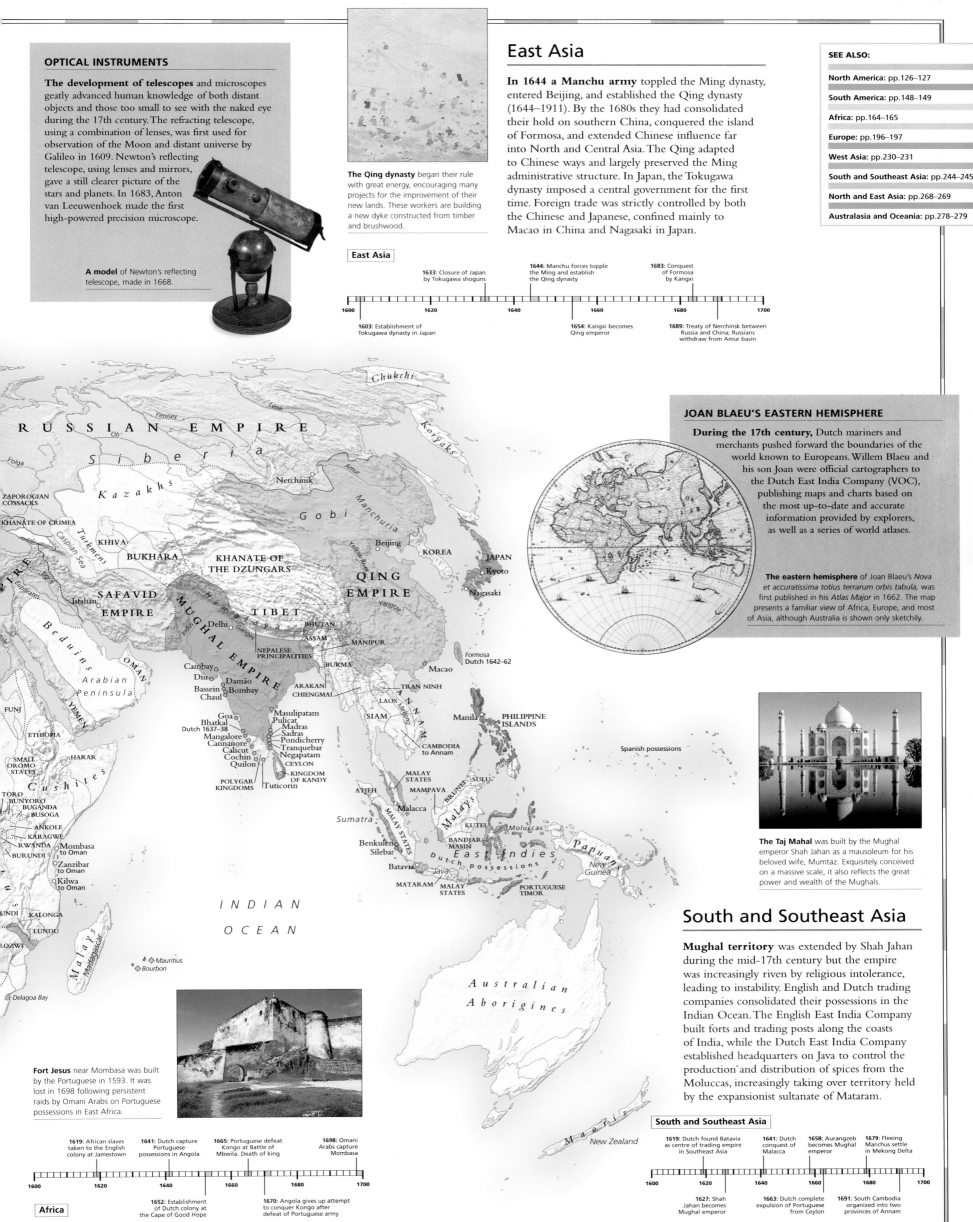

The Taj Mahal was built by the Mughal emperor Shah Jahan as a mausoleum for his beloved wife, Mumtaz. Exquisitely conceived on a massive scale, it also reflects the great power and wealth of the Mughals.

South and Southeast Asia

Mughal territory was extended by Shah Jahan during the mid-17th century but the empire was increasingly riven by religious intolerance, leading to instability. English and Dutch trading companies consolidated their possessions in the Indian Ocean. The English East India Company built forts and trading posts along the coasts of India, while the Dutch East India Company established headquarters on Java to control the production and distribution of spices from the Moluccas, increasingly taking over territory held by the expansionist sultanate of Mataram.

Fort Jesus near Mombasa was built by the Portuguese in 1593. It was lost in 1698 following persistent raids by Omani Arabs on Portuguese possessions in East Africa.

1619: African slaves taken to the English colony at Jamestown
1641: Dutch capture Portuguese possessions in Angola
1665: Portuguese defeat Kongo at Battle of Mbwila. Death of king
1698: Omani Arabs capture Mombasa
1652: Establishment of Dutch colony at the Cape of Good Hope
1670: Angola gives up attempt to conquer Kongo after defeat of Portuguese army

Africa

South and Southeast Asia

1619: Dutch found Batavia as centre of trading empire in Southeast Asia
1641: Dutch conquest of Malacca
1658: Aurangzeb becomes Mughal emperor
1679: Fleeing Manchus settle in Mekong Delta
1627: Shah Jahan becomes Mughal emperor
1663: Dutch complete expulsion of Portuguese from Ceylon
1691: South Cambodia organized into two provinces of Annam

TRADING IN HUMAN LIVES

Hugh Crow was a Liverpool trader who made a fortune from slaves in the early 19th century.

THE USE OF SLAVES seems to have been endemic in most human societies. Normally taken as prisoners of war, slaves were also acquired as a form of tribute. The establishment of European colonies and overseas empires between the 16th and 19th centuries saw the creation of a slave trade on an industrial scale, a commerce which laid the foundations for inter-global trading networks. Trading concerns such as the English and Dutch East India companies developed trade on a larger scale than ever before; but it was the need to supply labour for the plantations of the Americas which led to the greatest movement of peoples across the face of the earth.

The Atlantic slave trade

From the late 15th to the early 19th century, European merchants – especially the British and Portuguese – carried on a massive trade in African slaves across the Atlantic. As well as utilizing the established sources of slaves from the central and West African kingdoms, they also raided coastal areas of West Africa for additional supplies of slaves. European manufactured goods, especially guns, were exchanged for slaves destined to work as agricultural labourers on plantations in the Caribbean and the tropical Americas. Slaves transported to the western hemisphere may have numbered 12 million or more.

Conditions on the terrible 'Middle Passage' from the slave ports of West Africa to the New World improved little over the centuries, although the death rate declined because journey times decreased significantly. Between four and five million people are thought to have perished before reaching the Americas.

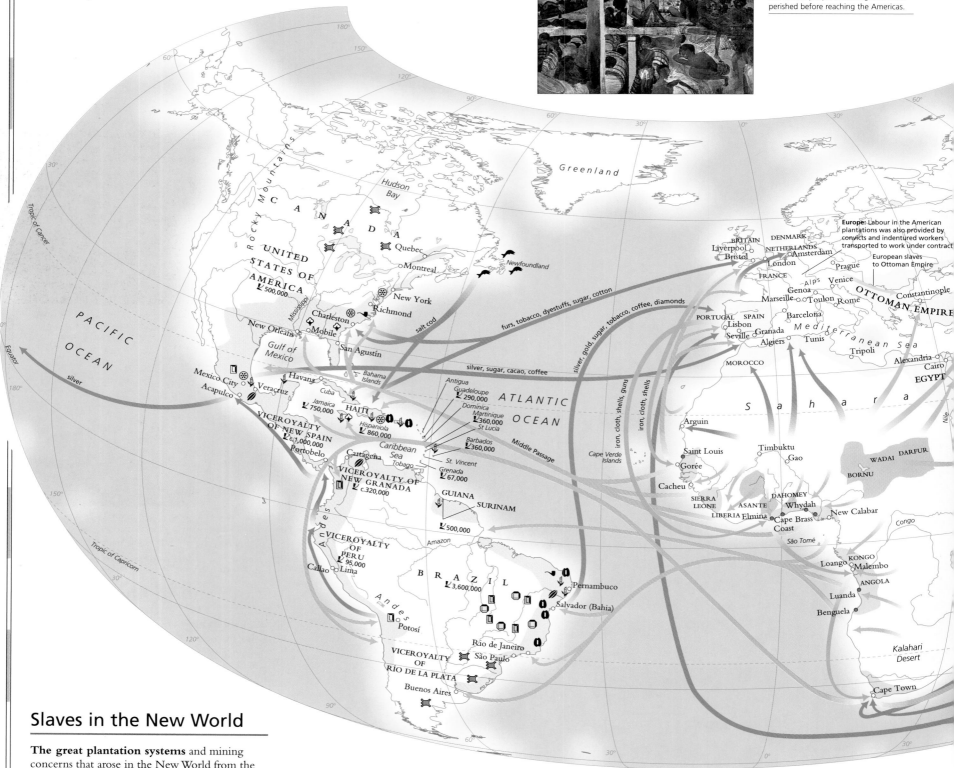

Slaves in the New World

The great plantation systems and mining concerns that arose in the New World from the 16th century onward demanded large reservoirs of labour. Though the Spanish and Portuguese initially used enslaved indigenous people, they soon required a more reliable source of labour. The Portuguese began bringing African slaves to the Caribbean and Brazil in the early 16th century. The cotton plantations of the southern US which boomed in the early 19th century were a key factor in sustaining the Atlantic trade.

Slaves planting sugar cane cuttings in specially-prepared plots on an Antiguan plantation in 1823 illustrate the labour-intensiveness of plantation agriculture. As European colonies, the Caribbean islands concentrated on cash crops such as sugar, coffee, and spices.

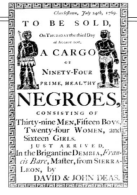

Slaves were sold at auction at ports such as Charleston. They swelled the population of southern North America: in the early 18th century, they comprised more than half of South Carolina's population

Other slave trades

By the 9th and 10th centuries, a number of complex slave-trading routes were in existence in Europe and the Near East. Viking and Russian merchants traded in slaves from the Balkans who were often sold to harems in southern Spain and North Africa. The Baghdad Caliphate drew slaves from western Europe via the ports of Venice, Prague, and Marseille, and Slavic and Turkic slaves from eastern Europe and Central Asia. In the 13th century, the Mongols sold slaves at Karakorum and in the Volga region. There was long-standing commerce in African slaves – primarily from East Africa before European mariners entered the slave trade. Between the 9th and 19th centuries Muslim merchants may have transported as many as 14 million across the Sahara by camel caravan and through East African ports, principally to destinations in the Indian Ocean basin.

This illustration from a 13th-century Arabic manuscript shows Africans and Europeans for sale at a slave market. Arab slave traders drew slaves from much of mainland Europe, Central Asia, and Africa.

SEE ALSO:

North America: pp.126–127, 130–131

South America: pp.148–149

Africa: pp.162–165

Slave trades

Timeline:

- **1479:** Treaty of Alcaçovas permits Portuguese importation of slaves into Spain
- **1502:** Introduction of African slaves to the Caribbean
- **1522:** First American slave revolt in Hispaniola
- **1685:** French Code Noir restricts slavery in French Caribbean colonies
- **1739:** Stono rebellion in South Carolina
- **1791:** Slave revolt in Haiti
- **1804:** Foundation of independent Haitian state
- **1807:** Slave trade outlawed in Britain
- **1850:** Effective end of slave trade in Brazil
- **1863:** Emancipation proclamation frees slaves in US
- **1867:** Last known arrival of a slave ship in Cuba

(1450 – 1900)

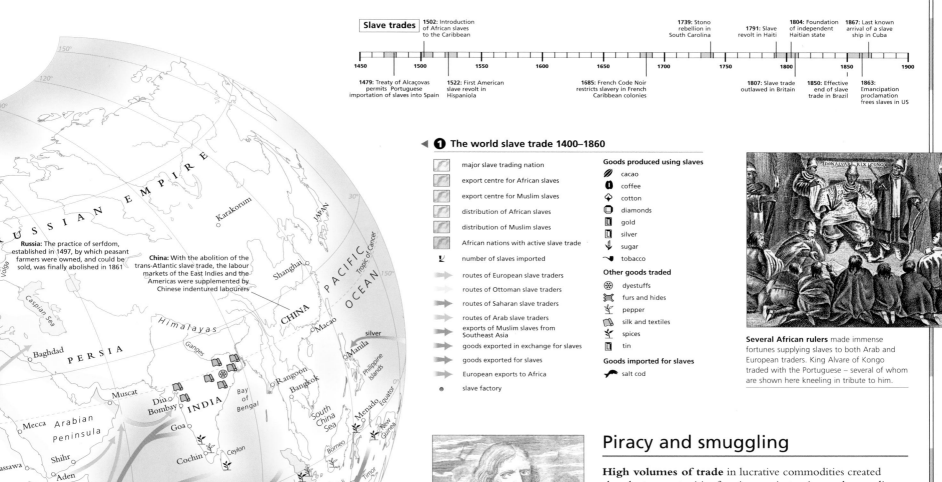

◀ ① The world slave trade 1400–1860

- ▨ major slave trading nation
- export centre for African slaves
- export centre for Muslim slaves
- distribution of African slaves
- distribution of Muslim slaves
- African nations with active slave trade
- ⟱ number of slaves imported
- ⟶ routes of European slave traders
- ⟶ routes of Ottoman slave traders
- ⟶ routes of Saharan slave traders
- ⟶ routes of Arab slave traders
- ⟶ exports of Muslim slaves from Southeast Asia
- ⟶ goods exported in exchange for slaves
- ⟶ goods exported for slaves
- ⟶ European exports to Africa
- ● slave factory

Goods produced using slaves
- cacao
- coffee
- cotton
- diamonds
- gold
- silver
- sugar
- tobacco

Other goods traded
- dyestuffs
- furs and hides
- pepper
- silk and textiles
- spices
- tin

Goods imported for slaves
- salt cod

Russia: The practice of serfdom, established in 1497, by which peasant farmers were owned, and could be sold, was finally abolished in 1861

China: With the abolition of the trans-Atlantic slave trade, the labour markets of the East Indies and the Americas were supplemented by Chinese indentured labourers

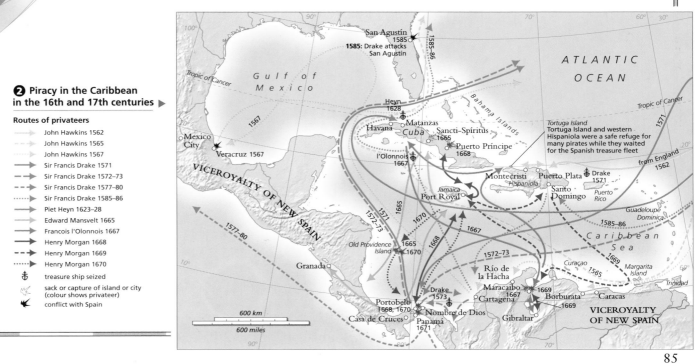

Several African rulers made immense fortunes supplying slaves to both Arab and European traders. King Alvare of Kongo traded with the Portuguese – several of whom are shown here kneeling in tribute to him.

Piracy and smuggling

High volumes of trade in lucrative commodities created abundant opportunities for piracy, privateering, and smuggling. Predators were most active in relatively unpoliced Caribbean and American waters. The numerous tiny islands, hidden harbours and dense, tropical vegetation – and the access it provided to valuable cargoes of sugar, rum, silver, and slaves – made the Caribbean a notorious hotspot for piracy and smuggling. Some predators were privateers who worked with the blessing of their home governments, such as Sir Francis Drake, but most maritime predators were freelance pirates, who selected their victims without discrimination.

Henry Morgan was a Welsh buccaneer who made a number of successful raids on Spanish ships and territory in the late 17th century – the most devastating being the destruction of Panamá in 1671.

This iron headcollar was one of number of cruel devices designed for the restraint of slaves.

② Piracy in the Caribbean in the 16th and 17th centuries ▶

Routes of privateers
- John Hawkins 1562
- John Hawkins 1565
- John Hawkins 1567
- Sir Francis Drake 1571
- Sir Francis Drake 1572–73
- Sir Francis Drake 1577–80
- Sir Francis Drake 1585–86
- Piet Heyn 1623–28
- Edward Mansvelt 1665
- Francois l'Olonnois 1667
- Henry Morgan 1668
- Henry Morgan 1669
- Henry Morgan 1670
- ⚓ treasure ship seized
- sack or capture of island or city (colour shows privateer)
- conflict with Spain

THE WORLD 1700–1800

FROM THE BEGINNING of the 18th century, new ideas in science, philosophy, and political organization fuelled change throughout the world. Popular reaction against the *ancien régime* in both France and North America led to the overthrow of the ruling governments. Improvements in agricultural techniques and land reform increased food production, and the population – especially in Europe – began to expand rapidly. Technological innovations in Europe led to the beginning of the Industrial Revolution and consequent urban growth. The expansion of European influence and territorial possessions throughout the world continued apace, with explorers charting the scattered islands of the Pacific and Britain establishing her power in India and Australia.

On 21 January 1793 the French king, Louis XVI was guillotined in front of a huge Parisian crowd. His wife, Marie Antoinette was executed later in the year.

Europe

Throughout Europe, government became more powerful, especially in the Russia of Peter the Great, and the Prussia of Frederick the Great. In France, Bourbon monarchy had reached its peak during the reign of Louis XIV (1643–1715). Revolutionary ideas unleashed by the 'enlightenment', combined with political relaxation, created an incendiary situation, leading in 1789 to the French Revolution whose effects reverberated throughout Europe.

Europe

1740: Prussia launches War of Austrian Succession and becomes major European power
1756–63: Seven Years' War in Europe
1774: Ottoman decline follows Treaty of Kuchuk Kainarji
1799: Coup brings Napoleon to power in France

1703: Foundation of St. Petersburg by Peter the Great
1715: Death of Louis XIV
1768: War between Russia and the Ottomans
1783: Russia conquers and annexes Crimea
1789: French Revolution begins

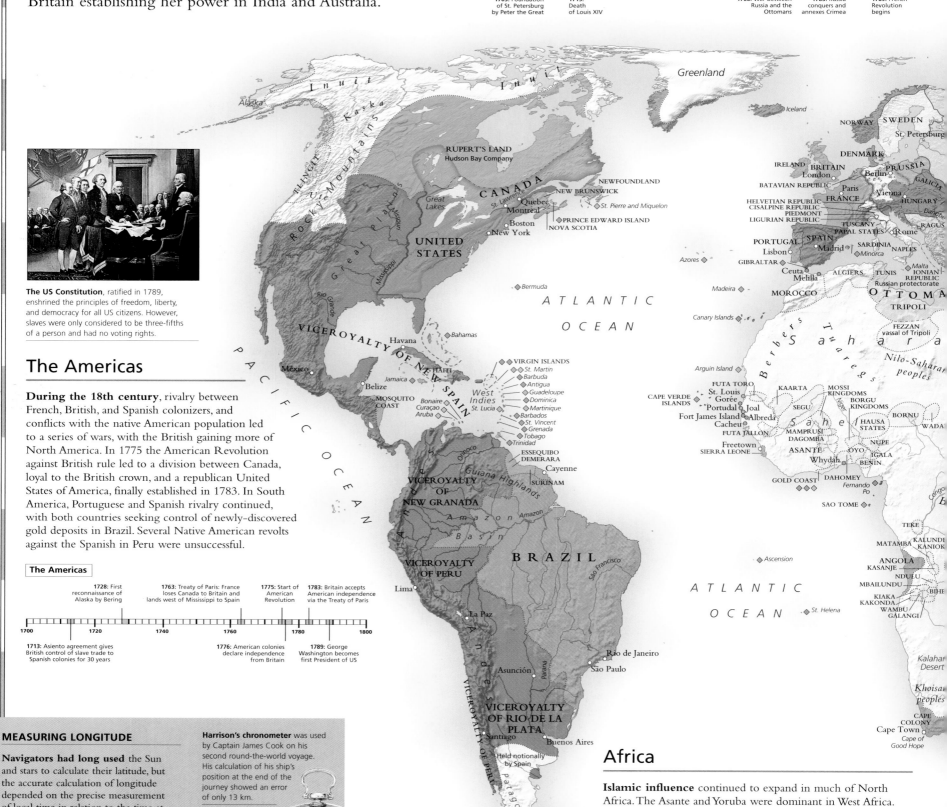

The US Constitution, ratified in 1789, enshrined the principles of freedom, liberty, and democracy for all US citizens. However, slaves were only considered to be three-fifths of a person and had no voting rights.

The Americas

During the 18th century, rivalry between French, British, and Spanish colonizers, and conflicts with the native American population led to a series of wars, with the British gaining more of North America. In 1775 the American Revolution against British rule led to a division between Canada, loyal to the British crown, and a republican United States of America, finally established in 1783. In South America, Portuguese and Spanish rivalry continued, with both countries seeking control of newly-discovered gold deposits in Brazil. Several Native American revolts against the Spanish in Peru were unsuccessful.

The Americas

1728: First reconnaissance of Alaska by Bering
1763: Treaty of Paris: France loses Canada to Britain and lands west of Mississippi to Spain
1775: Start of American Revolution
1783: Britain accepts American independence via the Treaty of Paris

1713: Asiento agreement gives British control of slave trade to Spanish colonies for 30 years
1776: American colonies declare independence from Britain
1789: George Washington becomes first President of US

MEASURING LONGITUDE

Navigators had long used the Sun and stars to calculate their latitude, but the accurate calculation of longitude depended on the precise measurement of local time in relation to the time at the Greenwich meridian. The invention by John Harrison of an accurate ship's chronometer in 1762 enabled navigators to calculate their position far more precisely, greatly reducing the risk of shipwrecks, and shortening journey times.

Harrison's chronometer was used by Captain James Cook on his second round-the-world voyage. His calculation of his ship's position at the end of the journey showed an error of only 13 km.

Africa

Islamic influence continued to expand in much of North Africa. The Asante and Yoruba were dominant in West Africa. But the slave trade which had flourished for centuries throughout much of Africa was internationalized and greatly magnified by European influence in this period. Over 13.5 million people left Africa as slaves during the 1700s. West Africans and Angolans were shipped to the New World – especially Brazil – and northern Africa traded with the Ottoman Empire. In southern Africa, Dutch and British colonists struggled for supremacy against organized Xhosa resistance.

CAPTAIN COOK'S MAP OF NEW ZEALAND

Until the 18th century Oceania and the South Seas remained a mystery to most navigators. The English sailor, Captain James Cook made three exploratory voyages to the South Pacific between 1768 and 1779. This map of New Zealand was made on Cook's first voyage. His ship, the *Endeavour*, traced the coast to make this remarkably accurate map.

Cook's map was the first accurate representation of New Zealand and copies were issued to map publishers all over Europe.

By the late 18th century, many Indian rulers such as the Nawab of Bengal had assigned administrative powers to the British.

South and West Asia

The Persians under Nadir Shah began to challenge the Ottomans and pushed eastward into Mughal India, even sacking the city of Delhi in 1739. By the middle of the 18th century, the Marathas were emerging as successors to the Mughals, but they were comprehensively defeated by an Afghan army at Panipat in 1761. By the end of the century, the British East India Company had established firm control over much of India via a series of effective military campaigns.

SEE ALSO:

North America: pp.126–129

South America: pp.148–149

Africa: pp.164–165

Europe: pp.198–201

West Asia: pp.230–231

South and Southeast Asia: pp.246–249

North and East Asia: pp.268–269

Australasia and Oceania: pp.282–283

South and West Asia timeline

1707: Death of Aurangzeb heralds decline of Mughal power in India
1736: Nadir Shah becomes Shah of Persia
1747: Foundation of Afghanistan by Ahmad Khan Abdali
1761: British destroy French power in India following seizure of Pondicherry
1799: Conquest of Mysore ends challenge to British power in southern India

1722–36: Subjugation of Afghans by Persia
1757: Robert Clive defeats Bengalis at battle of Plassey
1765: Bengal comes under British control
1775: First Anglo-Maratha war
1786: Start of Qadjar dynasty in Persia
1796: British conquest of coastal Ceylon

East Asia, Southeast Asia, and Oceania

The Qing dynasty extended its empire to include a protectorate over Tibet and the conquest of Xiankiang (Dzungaria) by 1760. By 1790, the Chinese population had virtually tripled to 300 million. Trade in tea, porcelain, and silk with Russia and the West boosted the economy and Manchu China was able to resist European incursion. The kingdoms of Southeast Asia were frequently at war, and subject to invasion by the Chinese, as with Burma in 1765–69. Though the Portuguese and Dutch had set up trading ports, much of the East Indies had yet to be formally colonized.

East Asia, Southeast Asia, and Oceania timeline

1716: Start of Kyoho era in Japan
1752: Start of Konbaung dynasty in Burma
1765–69: Manchus invade Burma
1768: Captain James Cook starts exploration of Pacific
1788: First British settlement at Botany Bay in Australia

1751: Tibet, Dzungaria, and the Tarim Basin overrun by the Chinese
1755: Alaungpaya founds Rangoon and reunites Burma
1774: Nguyen Anh becomes emperor of Vietnam

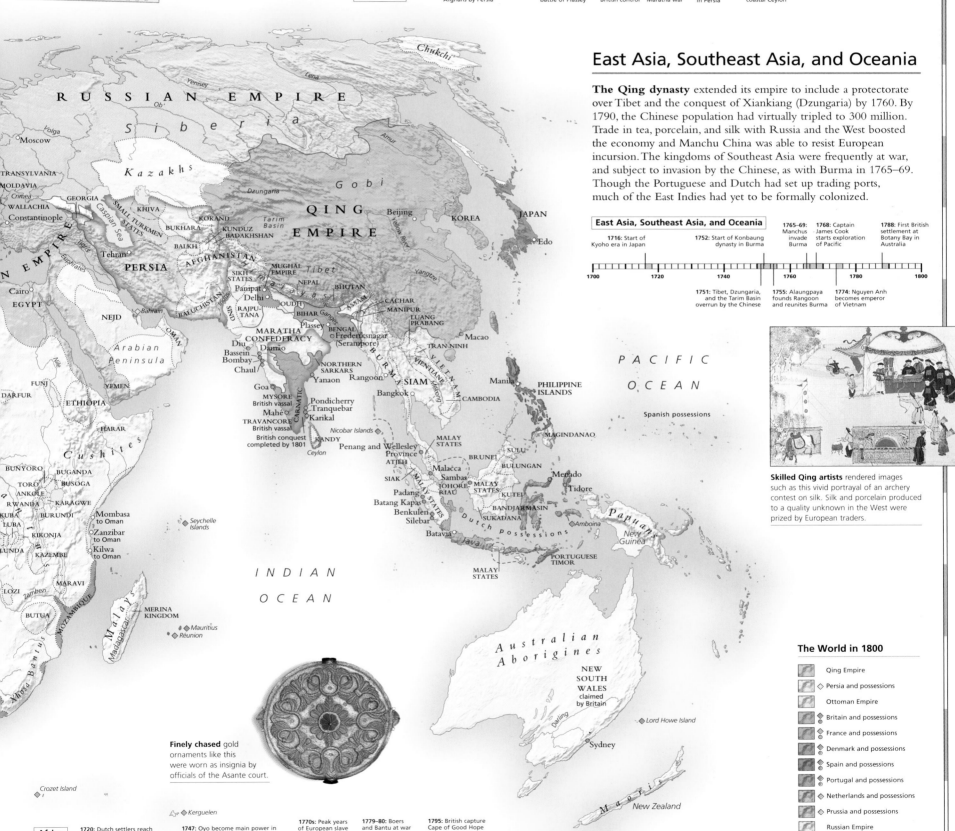

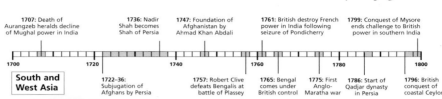

Skilled Qing artists rendered images such as this vivid portrayal of an archery contest on silk. Silk and porcelain produced to a quality unknown in the West were prized by European traders.

Finely chased gold ornaments like this were worn as insignia by officials of the Asante court.

The World in 1800

- Qing Empire
- Persia and possessions
- Ottoman Empire
- Britain and possessions
- France and possessions
- Denmark and possessions
- Spain and possessions
- Portugal and possessions
- Netherlands and possessions
- Prussia and possessions
- Russian Empire
- Austrian Habsburg territories
- Holy Roman Empire
- Persia on death of Nadir Shah 1747
- French possessions lost during 18th century

Africa timeline

1720: Dutch settlers reach Orange River from Cape
1747: Oyo become main power in Niger Delta after defeat of Dahomey
1770s: Peak years of European slave trade with Africa
1779–80: Boers and Bantu at war in southern Africa
1795: British capture Cape of Good Hope from the Dutch

1705: Foundation of Husaynid dynasty in Tunis, which rules until 1957
1730: Revival of ancient empire of Bornu in central Africa
1757: Muhammad III becomes Sultan of Morocco
1787: Settlement of first freed slaves from Britain at Freetown
1798: Occupation of Egypt by Napoleon Bonaparte

EMPIRE AND REVOLUTION

João V, king of Portugal from 1706–50, used most of the gold imported from his colonies in Brazil to finance his own grandiose building schemes.

RAPID POPULATION GROWTH, the creation of the first industrial societies, the maturing of Europe's American colonies, and new ideas about statehood and freedom of the individual, combined to create an overwhelming demand for political change in the late 18th century. Royal tax demands to finance expensive wars, and their often harsh attempts to control imperial subjects, became major focuses of discontent. The success of the Americans in their rebellion against British rule, and the total rejection of royal authority in favour of representative government during the French Revolution, had profound repercussions throughout Europe, with the revolutionary flame lit on numerous occasions from the 1790s onwards.

② An era of revolution 1768–1868 ▶

- area gaining independence from imperial control c.1750–1850
- area resisting imperial control or expansion c.1750–1850
- Britain and possessions
- Netherlands and possessions
- Spain and possessions
- France and possessions
- Portugal and possessions
- Denmark and possessions
- Russia and possessions
- △ independence achieved following war or revolution with date of independence
- European revolution or uprising 1750–1830 with date
- European revolution or uprising after 1830 with date
- area affected by 1848 revolutions
- important non-European uprising with date

War on a global scale

With the acquisition of new territories overseas during the 18th century, the major European powers often transferred their local conflicts to a far wider arena. The Seven Years' War (1756–63) was fought in the colonies as well as in Europe, with Britain able to take control of the Atlantic and defeat the French in North America. A few years later, however, French support for the American rebels and the resurgence of French naval power thwarted Britain's attempts to hold on to its American colonies. The position was reversed in India, where British victory at Plassey in 1757 gave her vital control of the state of Bengal, and enabled the rapid expansion of British India.

The signing of the Treaty of Paris in 1763 ended seven years of bitter fighting between Britain and France in North America. Great celebrations were held in London's Green Park to mark the agreement.

The export of European conflict

1743: King George's War between Britain and France in North America lasts until 1748	**1754:** French-Indian War between France and Indian allies and Britain	**1757:** British victory at battle of Plassey in northern India	**1760:** End of French resistance in North America; Britain gains control of much of French America

1740 — 1750 — 1760 — 1770

1744: Britain and France join Carnatic War in India	**1756:** Start of Seven Years' War in Europe parallels conflict in North America	**1758:** British take Senegal in West Africa from French; **1758–61:** British victorious over French at Fort St. David and Pondicherry in India	**1763:** Treaty of Paris ends Seven Years' War

① The European empires and the first world wars ▼

- Britain and possessions c.1750
- Dutch possessions c.1750
- Spain and possessions c.1750
- France and possessions c.1750
- Portugal and possessions c.1750
- Denmark and possessions c.1750
- Russia and possessions c.1750
- maximum area of French control in India c.1751
- ceded to Spain 1763
- ceded to Britain by 1766
- maximum area of British control in India by 1815
- ◇○ Dutch acquisition
- ◆○ British acquisition
- ◆○ French acquisition
- ◆○ Spanish acquisition
- ◆○ Portuguese acquisition
- ◇○ Russian acquisition
- ◆ Danish acquisition
- ✗ colonial conflict
- ✗ battle, with date

MEXICO △1821 including United Province of Central America

Gulf of Mexico

UNITED PROVINCES OF CENTRAL AMERICA △1823

REPUBLIC OF HAITI 1804 △

DOMINIC REPUBLI △1844

GREAT COLOMBIA △1822

PERU △1821

BOLIVIA △1825

CHILE △1818

UNITED PROVINCES OF LA PLATA △1816

PARAGUAY △1813

BRAZIL △1822 including Uruguay at date of independence

URUGUAY △1828

Patagonia

This American cartoon from 1774, shows Bostonians in revolt against the Stamp Act forcing tea into the mouth of a tax collector who has been tarred and feathered.

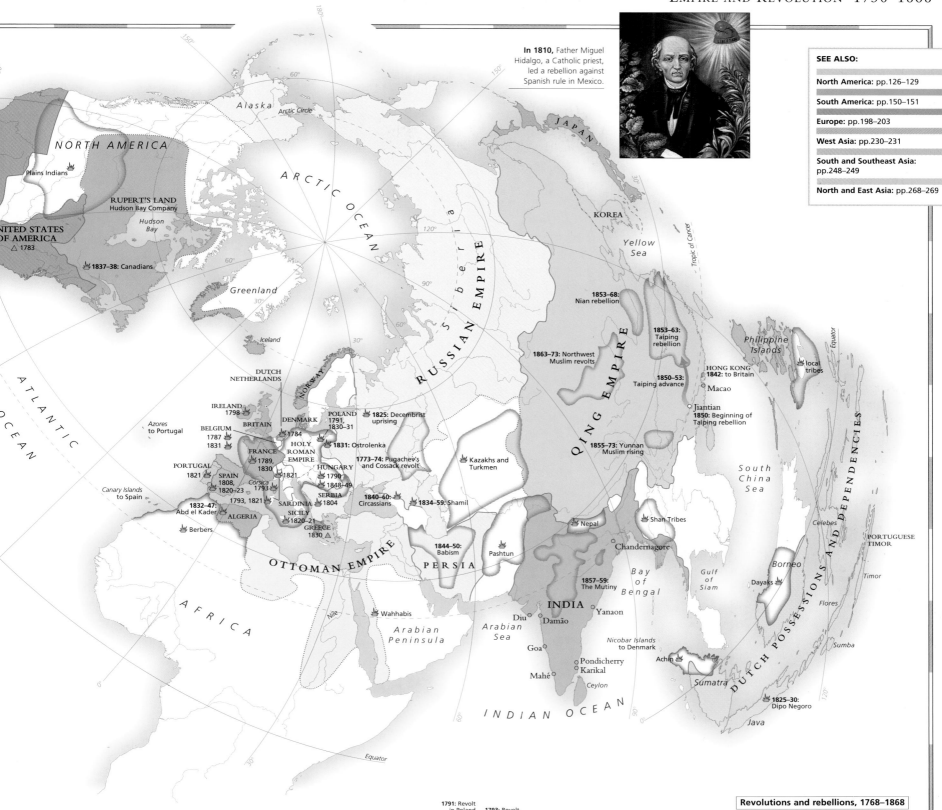

In **1810**, Father Miguel Hidalgo, a Catholic priest, led a rebellion against Spanish rule in Mexico.

SEE ALSO:

North America: pp.126–129

South America: pp.150–151

Europe: pp.198–203

West Asia: pp.230–231

South and Southeast Asia: pp.248–249

North and East Asia: pp.268–269

Map labels:

NORTH AMERICA
Alaska
Arctic Circle
Plains Indians
RUPERT'S LAND — Hudson Bay Company
Hudson Bay
UNITED STATES OF AMERICA △ 1783
1837–38: Canadians
Greenland
Iceland
ARCTIC OCEAN
ATLANTIC OCEAN
Siberia
RUSSIAN EMPIRE
Korea
Japan
Yellow Sea
Tropic of Cancer
1853–68: Nian rebellion
1853–63: Taiping rebellion
1863–73: Northwest Muslim revolts
QING EMPIRE
1850–53: Taiping advance
HONG KONG **1842:** to Britain
Macao
Philippine Islands
local tribes
Equator
1855–73: Yunnan Muslim rising
Jiantian **1850:** Beginning of Taiping rebellion
South China Sea
DUTCH NETHERLANDS
IRELAND 1798
NORWAY
DENMARK 1784
POLAND 1791, 1830–31 **1825:** Decembrist uprising
BELGIUM 1787 1831
BRITAIN
1831: Ostrolenka
HOLY ROMAN EMPIRE
FRANCE 1789, 1830
1773–74: Pugachev's and Cossack revolt
Kazakhs and Turkmen
PORTUGAL 1821
SPAIN 1808, 1820–23
Corsica 1793
HUNGARY 1790 1848–49
1821
1793, 1821
SARDINIA 1793, 1821
SERBIA 1804
1840–60: Circassians
1834–59: Shamil
1832–47: Abd el Kader
ALGERIA
SICILY 1820–21
GREECE 1830 △
1844–50: Babism
Pashtun
Berbers
OTTOMAN EMPIRE
PERSIA
AFRICA
Nile
Wahhabis
Arabian Peninsula
Arabian Sea
Diu
Damão
Goa
Mahé
Pondicherry
Karikal
INDIA
Yanaon
Nepal
Shan Tribes
Chandernagore
1857–59: The Mutiny
Bay of Bengal
Gulf of Siam
Borneo
Dayaks
DUTCH POSSESSIONS AND DEPENDENCIES
PORTUGUESE TIMOR
Timor
Celebes
Flores
Sumba
Ceylon
INDIAN OCEAN
Achin
Sumatra
1825–30: Dipo Negoro
Java
Equator
Azores to Portugal
Canary Islands to Spain
Nicobar Islands to Denmark

The era of revolution

The first serious challenges to absolutist monarchy and exploitative imperial rule came in the late 18th century, with Pugachev's revolt in Russia, the American Revolution against British colonial rule, and most influentially, the French Revolution of 1789. Uprisings continued in central and eastern Europe into the early 19th century, and the 1808 revolution in Spain spilled over into Spanish America, where a series of successful independence campaigns began in 1810. Periodic attempts to reastablish the old regime were continually met by risings, culminating in the 'year of revolutions' in 1848, when the fall of Louis Philippe in France inspired uprisings across most of Europe.

Revolutions and rebellions, 1768–1868

1773: Risings in southeast Russia led by Pugachev
1784: Risings in Dutch Netherlands
1791: Revolt in Poland
1791: Revolution in Haiti
1793: Revolt in Sardinia
1793: Rebellion in Corsica
1804: Revolt in Serbia
1810: Start of revolutions in Spanish America: by 1826 all Spanish colonies in South America have gained independence
1848: Year of revolution in Europe
1850s: Taiping rebellions and control in China

1768: Revolt in Geneva
1775: Start of American War of Independence
1789: Start of French Revolution
1790: Revolt in Hungary
1798: Revolt in Ireland
1808: Revolution in Spain
1850s: Muslim rebellions in China
1853–68: Nian rebellion in China

(Timeline: 1760 – 1780 – 1800 – 1820 – 1840 – 1860)

❸ The revolution in Haiti

Map labels:
Tortuga
Port-de-Paix
Le Cap
Fort Liberté (Fort Dauphin)
1802: French attack
Santiago
San Francisco de Macorís
1791: Slave revolt
1794: British attack
SAINT DOMINGUE
Gonâve
Jérémie
Port-au-Prince
Cayes
1801–02: Revolutionary invasion
SANTO DOMINGO
Hispaniola
Santo Domingo
ATLANTIC OCEAN
1790: border
1820: border between Haiti and Santo Domingo
Caribbean Sea
100 km
100 miles

Haiti: a post-revolutionary state

In 1791, fired by the French Revolution, slaves in the prosperous French colony of Saint-Domingue rebelled, and by 1794, slavery was abolished. In 1801, rebel forces entered Spanish Santo Domingo, briefly uniting the whole island. Intervention by British and French forces failed to stop Haiti declaring its independence in 1804.

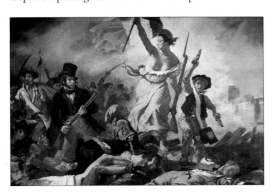

Delacroix's famous painting *Liberty on the Barricades,* became a banner of inspiration to French (and other European) revolutionary movements during the 19th century.

Toussaint l'Ouverture, a former slave, led the revolt of 1791, but did not declare Haiti fully independent. As a concession, he was appointed governor-general by the French in 1801. When French troops were sent to the island in 1802, Toussaint was forced to make terms with the commander of the invasion force. Subsequently betrayed, he died in prison in France in 1803.

THE WORLD 1800–1850

THE AFTERMATH OF THE FRENCH and American revolutions and the Napoleonic wars, led to a new nationalism and demands for democracy and freedom. The colonial regimes of South America were overthrown, and in Europe, Belgium and Greece gained independence. The US and northern Europe were transformed by the Industrial Revolution, as mass production and transportation led to an economic boom. There were mass movements of peoples to the expanding cities or to new lives abroad. Hunger for raw materials to feed industry and the desire to dominate world markets was soon to lead to unprecedented colonial expansion. In the US, Australia, and New Zealand, indigenous peoples were fighting a futile battle for lost territory.

A series of major innovations put Britain at the forefront of industrial development. The Nielsen hot blast process, invented in 1824, made iron smelting more efficient.

Europe

The Napoleonic Empire convulsed the established European order, abolishing states and national institutions. While liberals preached democracy, the ruling class responded with repressive measures to restrict freedom of speech and political expression. By the late 1840s civil unrest in the growing cities, bad harvests, and economic crisis, led to open rebellion. In 1848, Louis Philippe of France was forced to abdicate and revolution broke out throughout Europe.

Europe

1805: Defeat of Russia and Austria by France at Austerlitz
1815: New map of Europe drawn up at Congress of Vienna
1830: First wave of rebellions and social unrest in Europe
1845: Irish famine; 1,170,000 people driven to emigrate

1804: Napoleon becomes Emperor
1812: Napoleon's troops retreat from Moscow
1819: Carlsbad Decrees prohibit political meetings and censor press in German states
1831: Belgium becomes independent
1848: Rebellions throughout Europe are quickly suppressed

North America

The acquisition of new territories opened up the vast interior of North America to new settlement. Settlers pushing across the plains in search of fertile land and new wealth came into bloody conflict with native Americans who, equipped with both horses and guns, proved to be formidable foes. The mechanization of agriculture increased exports of wheat, tobacco, and cotton and as the economy prospered, cities expanded and immigrants arrived in great numbers.

The intensive plantation economy of the southern US was dependent on slave labour to pick cotton and harvest tobacco.

North America

1819: Parts of Spanish Florida conquered by US
1836: Texans rebel against Mexican rule and declare Republic of Texas
1849: Californian Gold Rush

1803: France sells territory between Mississippi and Rockies in Louisiana Purchase
1821: Mexico gains independence from Spanish colonists
1846–48: US victory in war with Mexico which cedes New Mexico and California to US

South America

When Spain was cut off from her colonies by the Napoleonic wars, nationalist forces took advantage of the resulting disorder and weakness of the colonial regimes. Argentina's struggle for independence was led by José de San Martín who marched an army across the Andes to liberate Chile and Peru from royalist control. Simón Bolívar led Venezuela and New Granada to independence, and helped found the new republic of Bolivia in 1825.

The Venezuelan Simón Bolívar (1783–1830) was known as the 'liberator of South America'.

South America

1810: Argentina declares independence from Spain
1821: Bolívar secures Venezuelan independence

1817: San Martín wins a decisive victory over the Spanish and liberates Chile
1822: Empire of Brazil becomes independent from Portugal

RAILWAYS

The steam locomotive was first developed in Britain in the early 19th century to haul heavy industrial loads. By 1830, engines were being used to pull carriages on iron rails and the first steam railway – the Stockton to Darlington – had opened. By 1850, railways had been built throughout Britain and were being introduced throughout its empire.

The steam engine, Locomotion, built by Robert Stephenson and Co. hauled the first train at the opening of the Stockton to Darlington railway in 1825.

Africa

In sub-Saharan west Africa several Islamic leaders waged *jihad* against neighbouring states. Under the Ottoman leader, Muhammad Ali, the viceroyalty of Egypt extended south to incorporate Sudan. The French invasion of Algeria in 1830 led to a war of resistance, led by Abd al-Qadir. In southeastern Africa, conflict broke out between different tribal groups (the *mfecane*) as natural resources became scarce. Shaka, the Zulu leader, established a united kingdom in southern Africa. In the late 1830s the 'Great Trek' of the Boers from Cape Colony extended European influence into the African interior.

Map labels

Alaska
Greenland
Iceland
HUDSON'S BAY COMPANY
CANADA
NEWFOUNDLAND
Great Lakes
St. Lawrence
Missouri
Chicago
Boston
New York
CAPE BRETON ISLAND
PRINCE EDWARD ISLAND
NOVA SCOTIA
NEW BRUNSWICK
St. Pierre and Miquelon
UNITED STATES OF AMERICA
New Mexico
California
Texas
Mississippi
Florida
Appalachian Mountains
Rocky Mountains
Rio Grande
MEXICO
México
Havana
Bermuda
Bahamas
CUBA
Jamaica
HAITI
DOMINICAN REPUBLIC
Puerto Rico
VIRGIN ISLANDS
St. Martin
Barbuda
Antigua
Guadeloupe
Dominica
Martinique
St. Lucia
Barbados
St. Vincent
Grenada
Tobago
Trinidad
Bonaire
Curaçao
Aruba
BRITISH HONDURAS
GUATEMALA
EL SALVADOR
HONDURAS
NICARAGUA
COSTA RICA
MOSQUITO PROTECTORATE
West Indies
VENEZUELA
NEW GRANADA
BRITISH GUIANA
DUTCH GUIANA
FRENCH GUIANA
Guiana Highlands
Orinoco
ECUADOR
Amazon Basin
Amazon
PERU
Lima
EMPIRE OF BRAZIL
BOLIVIA
São Francisco
Andes
PARAGUAY
ARGENTINE CONFEDERATION
CHILE
Paraná
Santiago
URUGUAY
Buenos Aires
Rio de Janeiro
São Paulo
Patagonia
FALKLAND ISLANDS
Hawaiin Islands
ATLANTIC OCEAN
PACIFIC OCEAN
Major areas of disputed/undecided status
NORWAY
BRITAIN
Manchester
Liverpool
London
DENMARK
PRUSSIA
NETH.
BELGIUM
WÜRTTEMBERG
BADEN
FRANCE
Paris
SWITZERLAND
SARDINIA
PORTUGAL
SPAIN
Lisbon
Madrid
TUSCANY
GIBRALTAR
Ceuta
Melilla
ALGERIA
French conquest in progress
Azores
MOROCCO
Madeira
Canary Islands
Arguin Island
Sahara
Berbers
Tuaregs
CAPE VERDE ISLANDS
FUTA TORO
St. Louis
Gorée
Bathurst
Cacheu
Bissau
FUTA JALLON
Freetown
LIBERIA
KAARTA
Medina
SEGU
MASINA
MOSSI KINGDOMS
MAMPRUSI
DAGOMBA
ASANTE
GOLD COAST
also some Dutch forts
BENIN
DAHOMEY
Whydah
Fernando Po
SAO TOME AND PRINCIPE
RIO MUNI
Libreville
DAMARGARAM
MARADI
GOBIR
SOKOTO
BORGU KIGDOM
IGALA
Ascension
ATLANTIC OCEAN
ST. HELENA

Superior firepower such as that displayed by the merchant steamer *Nemesis* enabled the British to overwhelm the wooden junks used by the Chinese in the first Opium War.

East and Southeast Asia

In the early 19th century, British merchants began to exploit the Chinese desire for Indian opium. As the trade flourished and the problem of opium addiction grew, the Chinese authorities attempted to stamp out the trade. The British objected and the first Opium War ensued. Japan, ruled by the inward-looking, Tokugawa shogunate for the last two centuries, remained closed to all foreigners, except a small Dutch trading community.

GEOLOGICAL MAPS

In the 19th century newly-discovered fossil remains were used to classify rocks and determine the sequence of geological strata. Geographical names were often used in the naming of rock types; for example, the Jura Mountains gave their name to the dinosaur-bearing Jurassic rocks.

Geologists used cross-sections to map the age of rocks. This one is taken from the Reverend William Buckland's *Bridgewater Treatise on Mineralogy and Geology.*

SEE ALSO:

North America: pp.128–131

South America: pp.150–151

Africa: pp.166–167

Europe: pp.200–205

West Asia: pp.232–233

South and Southeast Asia: pp.248–249

North and East Asia: pp.268–271

Australasia and Oceania: pp.282–285

East and Southeast Asia

1804: Russian envoy fails to agree commercial treaty with Japan

1819: Stamford Raffles, of the British East India company, founds Singapore

1837: Tokugawa Ieyoshi succeeds Ienari as Japanese shogun

1839–42: First Opium War in China

1800 — 1810 — 1820 — 1830 — 1840 — 1850

1802: Gia-Long proclaimed emperor of united Annam (Vietnam)

1834: Monopoly of China trade by East India Company abolished

1842: Treaty of Nanjing. Hong Kong ceded to British and five ports opened to foreign trade

Australasia and Oceania

New Zealand and Australia became British colonies in the first half of the 19th century. In Australia settlement spread from the penal colony at Port Jackson, now part of Sydney. As settlers founded towns at Adelaide, Melbourne, and Perth, they expropriated Aboriginal lands, and infected the people with fatal diseases, destroying local Aboriginal communities.

The Treaty of Waitangi allowed the Maori to maintain control over their lands while ceding the sovereignty of New Zealand to Britain, an unequal exchange which soon led to resentment and further wars.

Australasia and Oceania

1810: Kamehameha I unites Hawaiian islands

1825: Dutch annex western New Guinea

1840: British takeover of New Zealand under Treaty of Waitangi

1800 — 1810 — 1820 — 1830 — 1840 — 1850

1829: Britain annexes the whole continent of Australia

1835–36: British found Melbourne and Adelaide

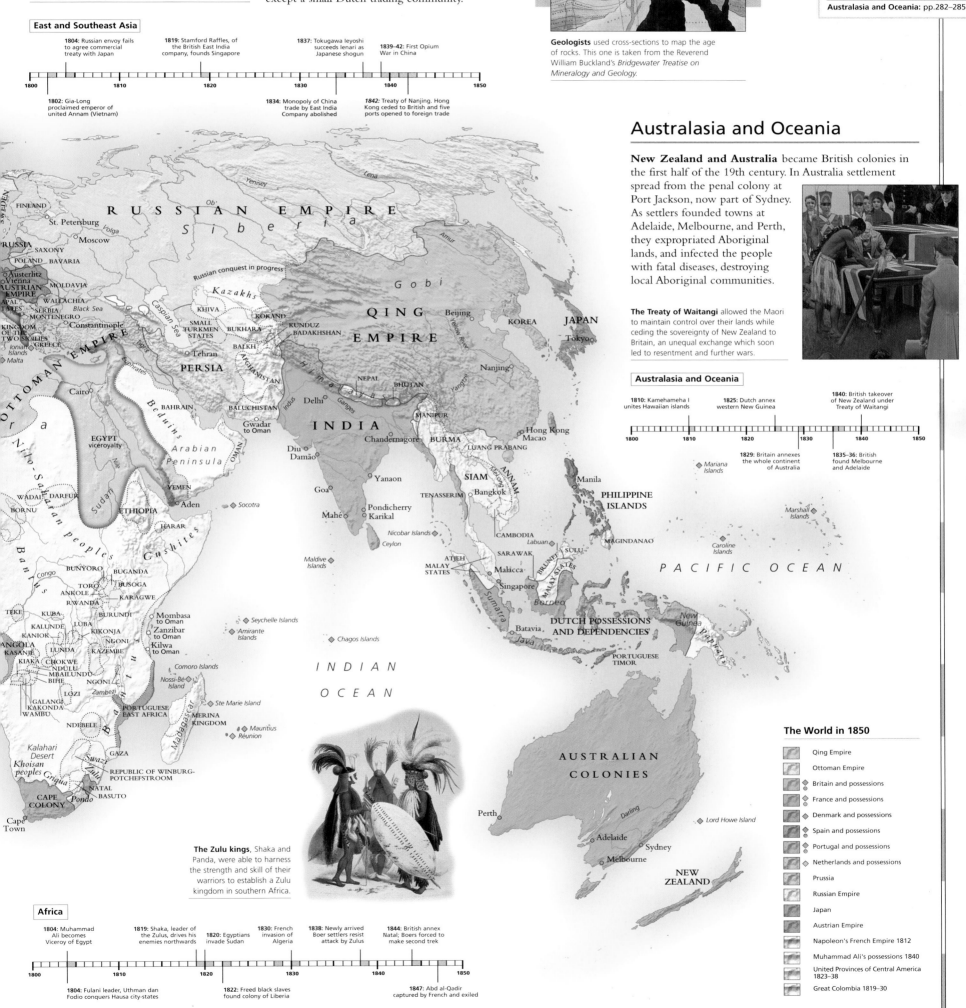

The Zulu kings, Shaka and Panda, were able to harness the strength and skill of their warriors to establish a Zulu kingdom in southern Africa.

The World in 1850

- Qing Empire
- Ottoman Empire
- Britain and possessions
- France and possessions
- Denmark and possessions
- Spain and possessions
- Portugal and possessions
- Netherlands and possessions
- Prussia
- Russian Empire
- Japan
- Austrian Empire
- Napoleon's French Empire 1812
- Muhammad Ali's possessions 1840
- United Provinces of Central America 1823–38
- Great Colombia 1819–30

Africa

1804: Muhammad Ali becomes Viceroy of Egypt

1819: Shaka, leader of the Zulus, drives his enemies northwards

1820: Egyptians invade Sudan

1830: French invasion of Algeria

1838: Newly arrived Boer settlers resist attack by Zulus

1844: British annex Natal; Boers forced to make second trek

1800 — 1810 — 1820 — 1830 — 1840 — 1850

1804: Fulani leader, Uthman dan Fodio conquers Hausa city-states

1822: Freed black slaves found colony of Liberia

1847: Abd al-Qadir captured by French and exiled

THE WORLD'S ECONOMIC REVOLUTION

Innovative new constructions of the late-19th century included the Eiffel Tower, built in 1889.

IN THE FIRST HALF of the 19th century, world trade and industry was dominated by Britain; by the 1870s the industrial balance was shifting in favour other nations, especially Germany, France, Russia, and the US, with rapid industrialization occurring throughout most of Europe by the end of the century. A stable currency, a standard (i.e. the price of gold) against which the currency's value could be measured, and an effective private banking system were seen as essential to the growth and success of every industrializing nation. The major industrial nations also began to invest heavily overseas. Their aims were the discovery and exploitation of cheaper raw materials, balanced by the development of overseas markets for their products.

The impact of the Industrial Revolution

The introduction of steam to ocean-going ships decreased journey times, and increased reliability because ships were no longer reliant on the wind.

World industrial output from 1870–1914 increased at an extraordinary rate: coal production by as much as 650%; steel by 2500%; steam engine capacity by over 350%. Technology revolutionized the world economy: the invention of refrigerated ships meant that meat, fruit, and other perishables could be shipped to Europe from as far away as New Zealand; sewing machines and power looms allowed the mass production of textiles and clothing; telephones, telegraphs, and railroads made communications faster.

The opening of the Suez Canal in 1869, linking the Red Sea to the Mediterranean, reduced the journey time from Europe to India by 50%.

By the 1880s almost all of the US was connected by long-distance rail networks including the Illinois Central Railroad (below).

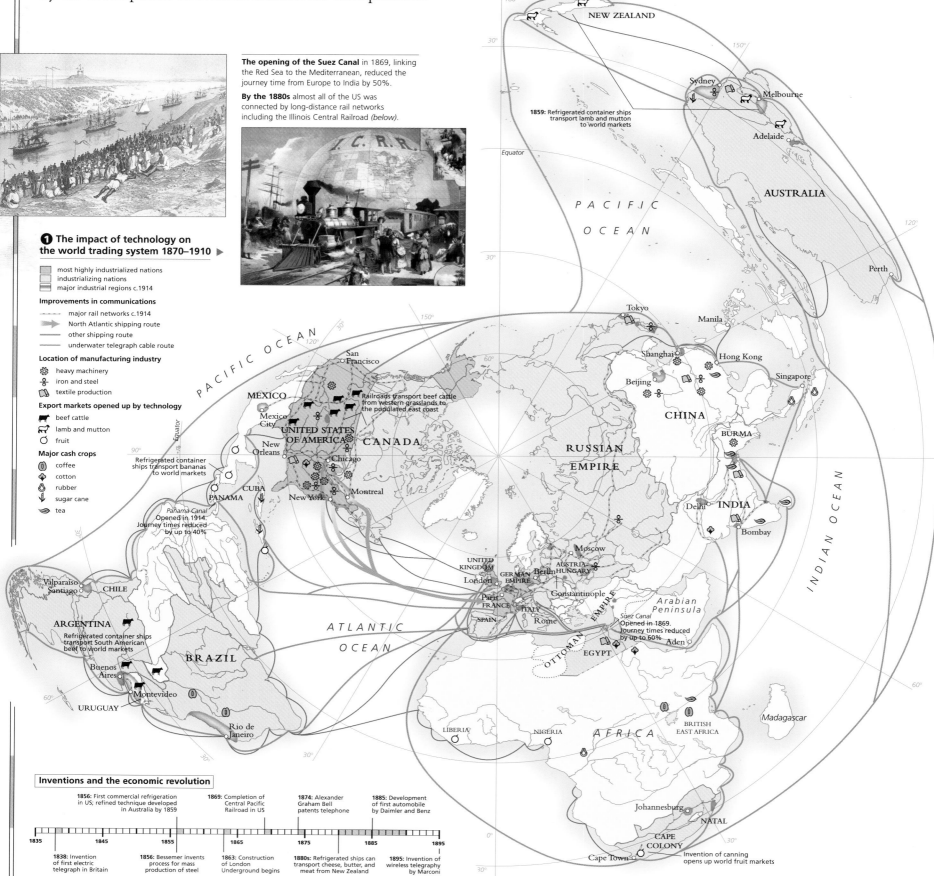

① The impact of technology on the world trading system 1870–1910 ▶

- most highly industrialized nations
- industrializing nations
- major industrial regions c.1914

Improvements in communications
- major rail networks c.1914
- North Atlantic shipping route
- other shipping route
- underwater telegraph cable route

Location of manufacturing industry
- heavy machinery
- iron and steel
- textile production

Export markets opened up by technology
- beef cattle
- lamb and mutton
- fruit

Major cash crops
- coffee
- cotton
- rubber
- sugar cane
- tea

1859: Refrigerated container ships transport lamb and mutton to world markets

Railroads transport beef cattle from western grasslands to the populated east coast

Refrigerated container ships transport bananas to world markets

Panama Canal Opened in 1914. Journey times reduced by up to 40%

Refrigerated container ships transport South American beef to world markets

Suez Canal Opened in 1869. Journey times reduced by up to 50%

Invention of canning opens up world fruit markets

Inventions and the economic revolution

1856: First commercial refrigeration in US; refined technique developed in Australia by 1859

1869: Completion of Central Pacific Railroad in US

1874: Alexander Graham Bell patents telephone

1885: Development of first automobile by Daimler and Benz

1835 1845 1855 1865 1875 1885 1895

1838: Invention of first electric telegraph in Britain

1856: Bessemer invents process for mass production of steel

1863: Construction of London Underground begins

1880s: Refrigerated ships can transport cheese, butter, and meat from New Zealand

1895: Invention of wireless telegraphy by Marconi

The great mineral rush

The search for new sources of minerals, both precious and functional, reached new heights of intensity in the industrial 19th century. New finds of gold and diamonds in the US, Canada, Australia, and South Africa fuelled the so-called gold and diamond rushes of the later 19th century. Though individuals could pan for gold in the Australian and North American rushes, the depth of gold and diamond deposits in South Africa meant that they could only be fully exploited with mechanical diggers owned by mining companies.

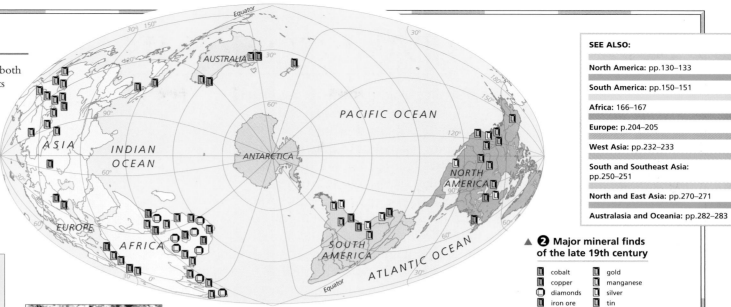

SEE ALSO:

North America: pp.130–133

South America: pp.150–151

Africa: 166–167

Europe: p.204–205

West Asia: pp.232–233

South and Southeast Asia: pp.250–251

North and East Asia: pp.270–271

Australasia and Oceania: pp.282–283

② Major mineral finds of the late 19th century

- cobalt
- copper
- diamonds
- iron ore
- gold
- manganese
- silver
- tin

③ The Yukon and Klondike gold rushes

- major gold strike
- settlement or fort

The Klondike and Yukon gold rushes

Gold was first discovered near the Pacific coast of Alaska in 1880 by the explorers Juneau and Harris. The mid-1890s saw frenzied activity along the Yukon river and its tributaries, with an influx of many thousands of prospectors into one of the world's most desolate regions. Though Dawson City and other settlements grew up to supply the miners, the boom had receded by 1899.

In the rush for instant riches miners such as this man, panning for gold in British Columbia in 1900, were prepared to undergo extreme hardship.

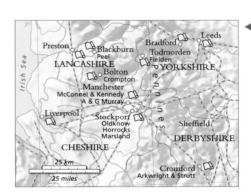

Boom towns sprang up rapidly during the Yukon gold rush. Such was the passion for gold that even the city streets were dug up by eager prospectors.

Gold and diamond rushes

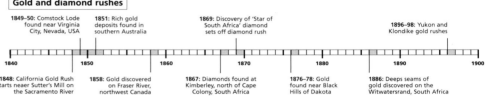

1849–50: Comstock Lode found near Virginia City, Nevada, USA	**1851:** Rich gold deposits found in southern Australia
1848: California Gold Rush starts neaer Sutter's Mill on the Sacramento River	**1858:** Gold discovered on Fraser River, northwest Canada

1869: Discovery of 'Star of South Africa' diamond sets off diamond rush

1867: Diamonds found at Kimberley, north of Cape Colony, South Africa

1876–78: Gold found near Black Hills of Dakota

1886: Deeps seams of gold discovered on the Witwatersrand, South Africa

1896–98: Yukon and Klondike gold rushes

The politics of cotton

In the 1870s woven cotton in India was still produced on a local scale, by individuals, rather than factories, and traded at local markets (above).

⑤ The politics of cotton ▼

- raw cotton from US to Britain
- cotton textiles to India
- raw cotton from India to Britain
- cotton producing region
- textile town
- major cotton-producing states

Cotton production was an early beneficiary of the Industrial Revolution. Eli Whitney's invention of the cotton gin led to a huge increase in the volume of cotton that could be processed; the invention of the power loom industrialized the weaving of cotton textiles. Britain's colonies in India and America supplied raw cotton for the cotton towns of Lancashire and Yorkshire; even with American independence, the Southern states continued to provide much of Britain's cotton. The economic and political importance of cotton to the US was reflected in the Confederate states' decision to use it as a bargaining tool during their struggle for international recognition following secession in 1861. The ploy failed as a strategy; during the Civil War, Britain turned to India for its raw cotton supplies. British cloth woven with Indian cotton was then exported back to India, a policy which benefited British producers, while keeping the Indian textile industry at a local level until the end of the 19th century.

◄ ④ The cotton towns of Lancashire and Yorkshire

- cotton town
- Peel textile firm
- major railway c.1850
- major canal

Cotton production in Lancashire

With plentiful water to power new machinery, Lancashire had developed as a major cotton-weaving centre by the late 18th century. Textile towns such as Stockport, Blackburn, and Cromford, often containing several firms, grew up in the area around Manchester, which acted as a major market for finished cloth.

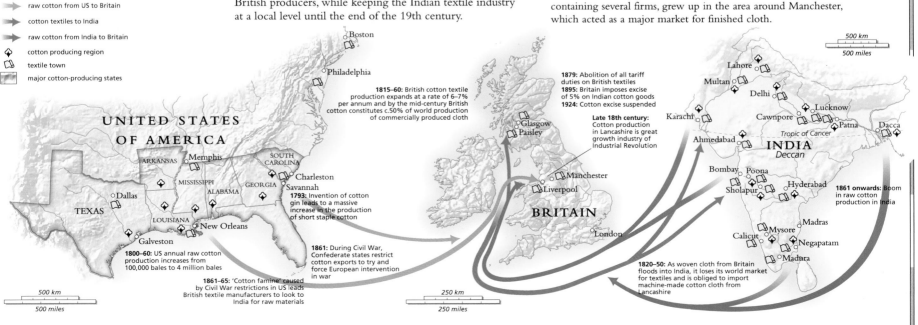

1815–60: British cotton textile production expands at a rate of 6–7% per annum and by the mid-century British cotton constitutes c.50% of world production of commercially produced cloth

1793: Invention of cotton gin leads to a massive increase in the production of short staple cotton

1800–60: US annual raw cotton production increases from 100,000 bales to 4 million bales

1861–65: 'Cotton famine' caused by Civil War restrictions in US leads British textile manufacturers to look to India for raw materials

1861: During Civil War, Confederate states restrict cotton exports to try and force European intervention in war

1879: Abolition of all tariff duties on British textiles
1895: Britain imposes excise of 5% on Indian cotton goods
1924: Cotton excise suspended

Late 18th century: Cotton production in Lancashire is great growth industry of Industrial Revolution

1861 onwards: Boom in raw cotton production in India

1820–50: As woven cloth from Britain floods into India, it loses its world market for textiles and is obliged to import machine-made cotton cloth from Lancashire

THE WORLD 1850–1900

BY 1900 THE EUROPEAN POPULATION had more than doubled to 420 million, while the population of the US had reached 90 million. Industry and commerce were booming, and both Europe and the US were traversed by railway networks. The major European powers were extending their economic and political influence to the very ends of the globe, while fierce rivalries and competition were being enacted on the international as well as the domestic scene. Within two decades the European powers had colonized virtually the whole of the African continent, the British had claimed India for the Crown, and the western powers had exploited the fatal weaknesses of China's crumbling Qing dynasty to penetrate deep into the heart of Asia.

Kaiser Wilhelm II was determined to establish Germany as Europe's leading military power.

Europe

The emergence of new states, the rise of nationalism, and growing economic and political power led to rivalry and conflict. Expansionist Russia's activities in the Balkans led in 1854 to the Crimean War, between a Franco-British-Turkish alliance and Russia. In 1870 Bismarck, prime minister of Prussia, goaded the French into war; the French defeat led to the collapse of the Second Empire, providing the final impetus to the creation of the new German and Italian nations.

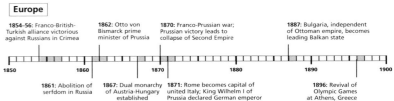

Europe

1854–56: Franco-British-Turkish alliance victorious against Russians in Crimea	**1862:** Otto von Bismarck prime minister of Prussia	**1870:** Franco-Prussian war; Prussian victory leads to collapse of Second Empire	**1887:** Bulgaria, independent of Ottoman empire, becomes leading Balkan state
1850 ... 1860 ... 1870 ... 1880 ... 1890 ... 1900			
1861: Abolition of serfdom in Russia	**1867:** Dual monarchy of Austria-Hungary established	**1871:** Rome becomes capital of united Italy; King Wilhelm I of Prussia declared German emperor	**1896:** Revival of Olympic Games at Athens, Greece

CAMPAIGN MAPS

During the American Civil War, new printing technology, combined with up-to-date information from correspondents on the battlefields allowed US newspapers to produce simplified campaign maps to explain the stages of the war to a fascinated public.

THE FIGHT AT CAMPBELL'S STATION.

This map shows the battle of Campbell's Station, Tennessee, as witnessed from the Union position by the *New York Tribune's* correspondent, Elias Smith.

The final push to populate the western US occurred in the latter half of the 19th century. Settlers and their wagon trains braved sometimes horrific conditions to claim new lands in the west.

The Americas

In 1861 seven southern states, fearful that the north was about to abolish slavery, left the Union and formed the Confederacy, beginning the Civil War, in which over 600,000 soldiers lost their lives. Following the Civil War the US became the fastest growing economy in the world, its population swollen by waves of immigrants. In South America, economic prosperity, especially from the export of meat and rubber, was enjoyed by the ruling elite, while border disputes bedevilled the new republics.

The Americas

	1864–70: Paraguayan War: Brazil, Argentina, and Uruguay defeat Paraguay	**1879–83:** War of Pacific; Chile, Peru, and Bolivia fight for control of Atacama Desert	
1861–65: US Civil War			
1850 ... 1860 ... 1870 ... 1880 ... 1890 ... 1900			
1858: Mexican Civil War between conservatives and liberals	**1867:** Canada becomes a British dominion	**1876:** Battle of Little Bighorn; Sioux warriors kill 250 US soldiers	**1898:** Spanish-American War. US occupies Cuba, and gains control of Philippines

The World in 1900

- Ottoman Empire
- Britain and possessions
- France and possessions
- Denmark and possessions
- Spain and possessions
- Portugal and possessions
- Netherlands and possessions
- German Empire and possessions
- Russian Empire and possessions
- Japan and possessions
- Italy and possessions
- US and possessions
- Confederate States 1861–65

East Asia

Agrarian unrest in China in the 1850s led to rebellion and famine. Western powers were quick to exploit internal dissent, carving out spheres of influence and annexing territory. A wave of xenophobia led to the Boxer Rebellion of 1900. Western troops were sent to China and concessions were extracted from the weak government. In Japan, the overthrow of the Tokugawa shogunate in 1868 was followed by industrial and economic modernization.

From the late 19th century, the newly-modernized Japan reopened its doors to foreign trade.

South Asia

By 1850 the British East India Company emerged as the major power on the sub-continent. Hostility to the British, combined with suspicions about their attitude to India's traditional faiths, led to the Mutiny of 1857–59. Following the Mutiny, the British took administrative control of India, developed an extensive railway network, and began to industrialize the Indian economy.

The railway station in Bombay was opened in 1887. The style and scale of the building reflected the great self-confidence of India's British rulers.

SEE ALSO:

North America: pp.128–133

South America: pp.150–151

Africa: pp.166–167

Europe: pp.202–207

West Asia: pp.232–233

South and Southeast Asia: pp.248–251

North and East Asia: pp.268–270

Australasia and Oceania: pp.282–285

East Asia

1850: Taiping Rebellion begins in Guangxi province
1860: British and French occupy Beijing
1871: Abolition of feudalism in Japan
1900: Boxer Rebellion: Christian missions and western legations attacked

1850 — 1860 — 1870 — 1880 — 1890 — 1900

1853: Rebels capture Nanjing – recaptured a year later
1868: Overthrow of Tokugawa shogunate
1877–79: Famine in northern China leaves at least 10 million dead
1894–95: Japanese overwhelm Chinese forces and annex Taiwan

South Asia

1878–79: Second Afghan War; British invade Afghanistan, which is coming under Russian influence
1885: Foundation of Indian National Congress

1850 — 1860 — 1870 — 1880 — 1890 — 1900

1857: Outbreak of Indian Mutiny
1876: Queen Victoria declared Empress of India, and a Viceroy appointed as her representative
1885–86: Third Burmese War leads to British annexation of Burma

THE TELEPHONE

The telephone was invented in 1876 by the Scottish-born inventor and speech therapist, Alexander Graham Bell. His device used a thin diaphragm to convert vibrations from the human voice into electrical signals. These were then reconverted into sound waves. Within a few years of its invention, the telephone had been installed in many city homes in Europe and the USA.

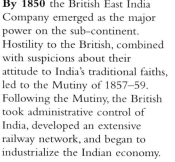

This view of Broadway in 1880 shows its skyline criss-crossed by telegraph and telephone wires.

Africa

In 1850 Africa was a patchwork of kingdoms and states, mostly unknown to Europeans. But, by 1900, the major European powers had seized virtually the entire continent. Rivalries between European nations were played out in Africa as colonizing countries raced for territory, raw materials, and new markets. In 1898, open war between France and the British in the White Nile region was only just averted. In 1899, the Boer War, a bitter struggle between the British and Afrikaaners, began.

By 1872, rich seams of gold- and diamond-bearing rock in Cape Colony were being heavily mined by European prospectors.

Africa

1869: Opening of Suez Canal
1880: White Boers have appropriated most habitable land in Cape Colony
1896: Abyssinia defeats Italians at Adowa
1899: Boer War begins

1850 — 1860 — 1870 — 1880 — 1890 — 1900

1863: Al-Hajj 'Umar clashes with French in Senegal valley and creates a Muslim empire
1879: Zulu War with British; Zulus defeated
1882: British invade and occupy Egypt
1893: French conquer Dahomey
1898: British and French clash at Fashoda

THE ERA OF WESTERN IMPERIALISM

THE LAST TWENTY YEARS of the 19th century saw unprecedented competition by the major European nations for control of territory overseas. The balance of imperial power was changing: having lost their American empires, Spain and Portugal were no longer pre-eminent. From the 1830s, France began to build a new empire, and Britain continued to acquire new lands throughout the century. Newly-unified Italy and Germany sought to bolster their nation status from the 1880s with their own empires. Africa was the most fiercely contested prize in this race to absorb the non-industrialized world, but much of Southeast Asia and Oceania was also appropriated in this period. Even the US, historically the champion of anti-colonial movements began to expand across the Pacific.

This *Punch* cartoon from 1890 depicts Germany as an eagle, with Africa as her prey. The caption reads, 'On the Swoop'.

Other nations were frequently critical of the behaviour of European imperialists in Africa. This German cartoon (*left*) has the caption: 'Even the lions weep at the way the native Africans are treated by the French'.

Many British officials in India maintained rituals of extreme formality (*below*), rather than adapting to native patterns of behaviour.

The scramble for Africa

The race for European political control Africa began in the early 1880s. The Berlin Conference of 1884–85, convened to discuss rival European claims to Africa, was the starting point for the 'scramble'. Some governments worked through commercial companies; elsewhere, land was independently annexed by these companies; sometimes Africans actually invited Europeans in. In most cases, however, European political control was directly imposed by conquest. By 1914, Africa was fully partitioned, along lines that bore little relation to cultural or linguistic traditions.

Colonial administrators often required extreme obeisance from the people they controlled. A local Moroccan sultan is shown here kneeling before a French colonel.

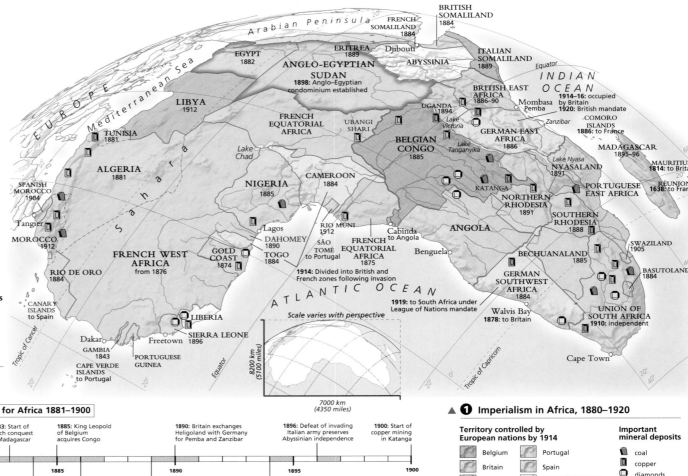

▲ ❶ Imperialism in Africa, 1880–1920

The scramble for Africa 1881–1900

1881: French occupation of Tunisia	1883: Start of French conquest of Madagascar

1885: King Leopold of Belgium acquires Congo

1890: Britain exchanges Heligoland with Germany for Pemba and Zanzibar

1896: Defeat of invading Italian army preserves Abyssinian independence

1900: Start of copper mining in Katanga

1882: Revolt in Egypt prompts occupation by British

1884: Germany acquires South West Africa, Togo, and Cameroon

1886: Germany and Britain divide up East Africa

1889: Establishment of first Italian colony in Eritrea
1889: Cecil Rhodes' British South Africa Company begins colonization of Rhodesia

1894: Uganda occupied by Britain

Territory controlled by European nations by 1914: Belgium, Britain, France, Germany, Italy, Portugal, Spain, nominally Ottoman, under British control

Important mineral deposits: coal, copper, diamonds, gold

The struggle for South Africa

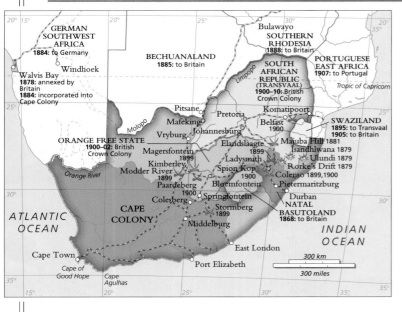

The British, with political control, the Afrikaners (Boers) – the first European settlers – and the Zulus all fought for control of South Africa in the 19th century. Seeking political autonomy, the Boers moved to found their own republics. The success of Transvaal, which grew rich from gold, led to annexation by Britain in 1877. British invasion of Zulu territory led to the First Zulu War, and British defeat, although this was swiftly reversed. In 1881, Boers in Transvaal rebelled against British rule, to set up the South African Republic. In 1899, the second Anglo-Boer war, broke out, lasting until 1902. The former Boer Republics became part of the British Empire as part of the Peace of Vereeniging.

It took more than 300,000 British soldiers five years to subdue 75,000 heavily-armed Boers, skilled in guerrilla and siege tactics, and with intimate knowledge of the terrain.

❷ The struggle for South Africa, 1854–1914

Cape Colony and Natal 1854; territory under British control 1895; South African Republic 1895; Orange Free State 1895; battle in Zulu wars

Boer War 1899–1902: Afrikaner (Boer) victory; British victory; Afrikaner sieges; Union of South Africa boundary 1910; railway

The struggle for South Africa 1871–1910

1871: Discovery of gold in Transvaal

1879: First Zulu War: British crushed at Isandhlwana but win at Ulundi

1902: Boers forced to surrender

1878: Transvaal annexed by Britain

1881: First Anglo-Boer War; British defeated at Majuba Hill; Transvaal reconstituted as South African Republic

1899: Start of Second Anglo-Boer War

1910: Formation of Union of South Africa with Afrikaners as majority white population

Imperialism in Southeast Asia

Though the Dutch East Indian Empire had existed since the early 17th century, much of Southeast Asia was not colonized until the mid-19th century. Moving east from India, British ambitions concentrated on Burma, the Malay Peninsula, and north Borneo. Renewed French interest in empire-building began in earnest with the capture of Saigon in 1858 following a concerted naval effort. By 1893, France controlled Tongking, Laos, Annam, and Cambodia, collectively known as Indo-China.

Imperialism in Southeast Asia 1858–1895

- **1855:** Start of British trade with Siam
- **1863:** French establish protectorate over Cambodia
- **1873:** Dutch attack on Achin sultanate
- **1884:** Annexation of northern New Guinea and Bismarck Archipelago by Germany
- **1886:** Britain annexes Upper Burma after Third Burmese War
- **1859:** Saigon captured by France
- **1859:** Timor divided between Netherlands and Portugal
- **1867:** French protectorate established in Cochin China
- **1874:** French protectorate established in Annam
- **1885:** French protectorate established in Tongking

SEE ALSO:

North America: pp.132–133

Africa: pp.166–167

Europe: pp.202–203, p.206

West Asia: pp.232–233

South and Southeast Asia: pp.250–251

North and East Asia: pp.268–271

Australasia and Oceania: pp.282–283

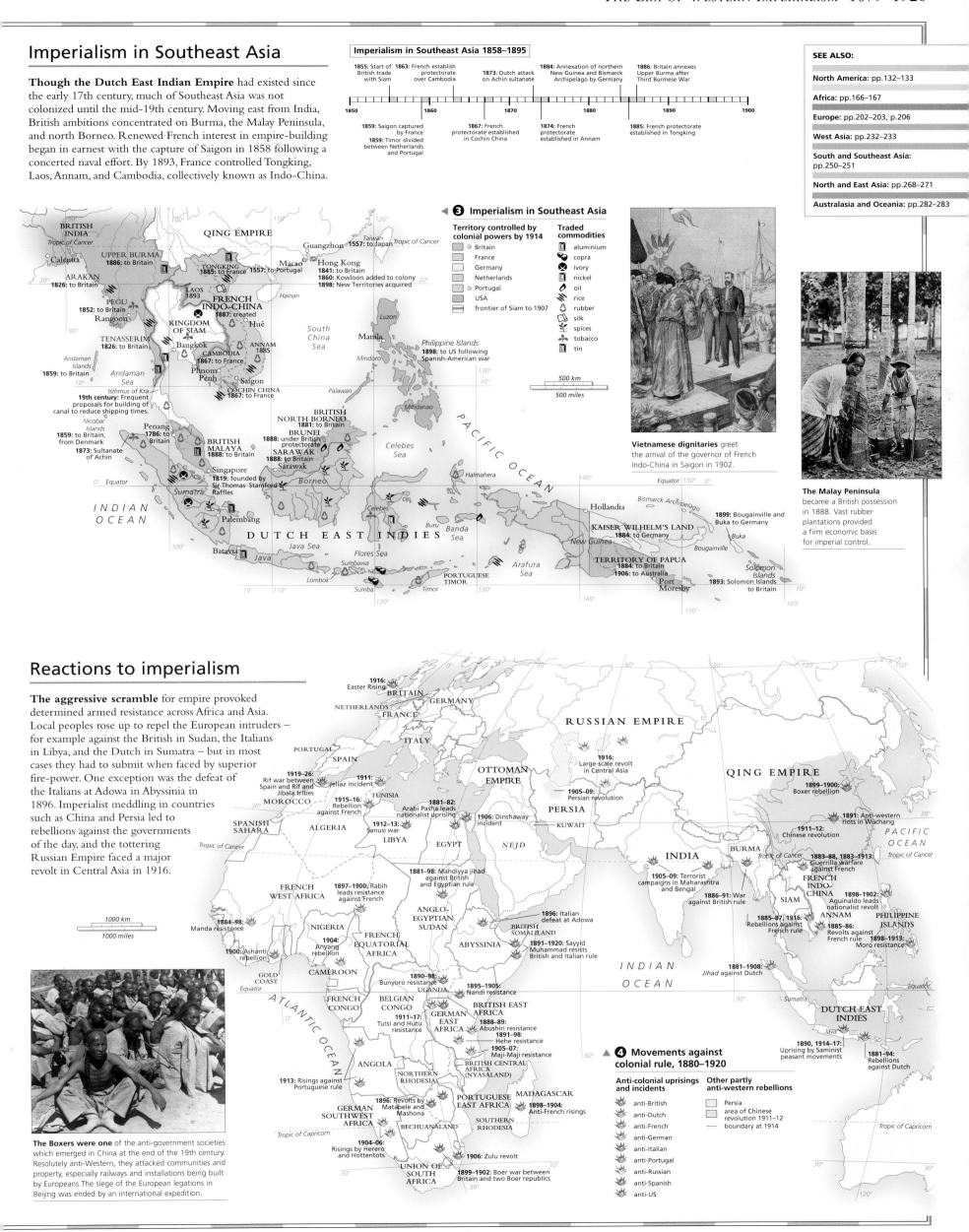

③ Imperialism in Southeast Asia

Territory controlled by colonial powers by 1914
- Britain
- France
- Germany
- Netherlands
- Portugal
- USA
- frontier of Siam to 1907

Traded commodities
- aluminium
- copra
- ivory
- nickel
- oil
- rice
- rubber
- silk
- spices
- tobacco
- tin

Philippine Islands 1898: to US following Spanish-American war

Vietnamese dignitaries greet the arrival of the governor of French Indo-China in Saigon in 1902.

The Malay Peninsula became a British possession in 1888. Vast rubber plantations provided a firm economic basis for imperial control.

Reactions to imperialism

The aggressive scramble for empire provoked determined armed resistance across Africa and Asia. Local peoples rose up to repel the European intruders – for example against the British in Sudan, the Italians in Libya, and the Dutch in Sumatra – but in most cases they had to submit when faced with superior fire-power. One exception was the defeat of the Italians at Adowa in Abyssinia in 1896. Imperialist meddling in countries such as China and Persia led to rebellions against the governments of the day, and the tottering Russian Empire faced a major revolt in Central Asia in 1916.

The Boxers were one of the anti-government societies which emerged in China at the end of the 19th century. Resolutely anti-Western, they attacked communities and property, especially railways and installations being built by Europeans. The siege of the European legations in Beijing was ended by an international expedition.

④ Movements against colonial rule, 1880–1920

Anti-colonial uprisings and incidents
- anti-British
- anti-Dutch
- anti-French
- anti-German
- anti-Italian
- anti-Portugal
- anti-Russian
- anti-Spanish
- anti-US

Other partly anti-western rebellions
- Persia
- area of Chinese revolution 1911–12
- boundary at 1914

THE WORLD 1900–1925

THE IMPERIAL AND MILITARY RIVALRY between Britain and France, and Germany and Austria-Hungary led, in 1914, to the First World War, which left millions dead and re-drew the map of Europe. The Habsburg and Ottoman empires broke up, leading to the emergence of a number of smaller nation states, while the end of the Ottoman Empire also created a territorial crisis in the Middle East. In 1917, the Russian Empire collapsed in revolution and civil war, to be transformed by the victorious Bolsheviks into the world's first Communist empire. US participation in the war confirmed its status as a world power, cemented by the central role played by President Wilson in the Versailles Settlement, and by the nation's increasing economic dominance.

German soldiers wearing gas masks emerge from a dug out. Troops on both sides endured terrible conditions in the trench warfare which dominated the war in France.

Europe

Most countries in Europe and their colonies took part in the First World War, which was fought on a scale unimagined in the 19th century. Years of rivalry between the major European powers, France, Britain and Germany had created an incendiary situation, finally touched off by a crisis in the Balkans. The Versailles Settlement of 1919 altered the balance of power in Europe irrevocably, setting up the conditions for a second European war 20 years later.

Europe

1905: Revolution in Russia; Norway becomes independent of Sweden
1910: Portuguese monarchy overthrown; republic proclaimed
1915–16: Thousands killed at Somme and Verdun, northern France
1917: Bolshevik Revolution in Russia
1920: Inauguration of League of Nations

1900   1905   1910   1915   1920   1925

1914: Assassination of Archduke Franz Ferdinand in Sarajevo precipitates start of First World War
1918: End of First World War
1919: Versailles Settlement creates a new European order

RADIO

Radio technology was first invented by Guglielmo Marconi in 1894. In 1901 he was able to send Morse Code messages across the Atlantic and by 1920 the first commercial radio station was set up in Pittsburgh, US. By the mid-1920s, radio was established as an immensely effective means of mass communication.

This radio, advertised using the famous fox terrier listening to 'His Master's Voice', dates from the 1920s.

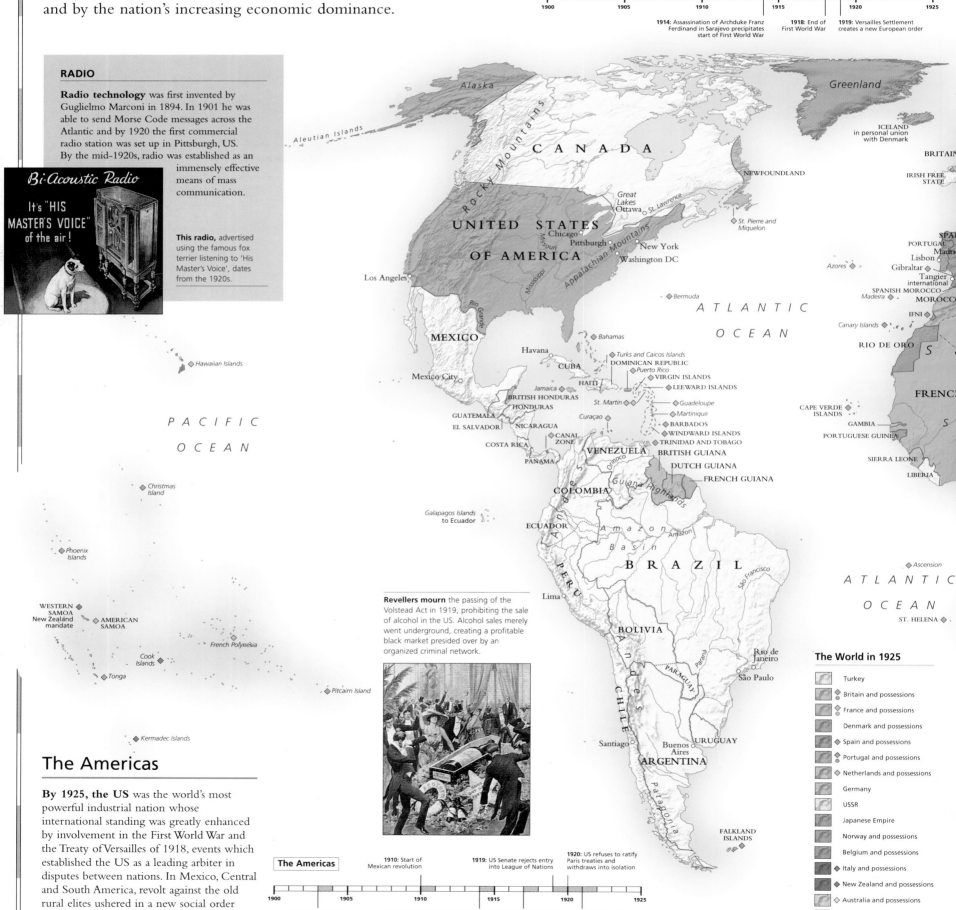

Revellers mourn the passing of the Volstead Act in 1919, prohibiting the sale of alcohol in the US. Alcohol sales merely went underground, creating a profitable black market presided over by an organized criminal network.

The World in 1925

- Turkey
- Britain and possessions
- France and possessions
- Denmark and possessions
- Spain and possessions
- Portugal and possessions
- Netherlands and possessions
- Germany
- USSR
- Japanese Empire
- Norway and possessions
- Belgium and possessions
- Italy and possessions
- New Zealand and possessions
- Australia and possessions
- US and possessions

The Americas

By 1925, the US was the world's most powerful industrial nation whose international standing was greatly enhanced by involvement in the First World War and the Treaty of Versailles of 1918, events which established the US as a leading arbiter in disputes between nations. In Mexico, Central and South America, revolt against the old rural elites ushered in a new social order and an increasingly urban society.

The Americas

1910: Start of Mexican revolution
1919: US Senate rejects entry into League of Nations
1920: US refuses to ratify Paris treaties and withdraws into isolation

1900   1905   1910   1915   1920   1925

1903: Panama Canal Zone ceded to US
1914: Opening of Panama Canal joins Atlantic and Pacific oceans
1917: US declares war on Germany and her allies
1921: US restricts immigration

Kemal Atatürk was the first leader of the new Turkish republic. From 1923–38 he radically overhauled Ottoman institutions to bring Turkey into the modern age.

West Asia

In 1918, the Ottoman Empire collapsed after more than 400 years. A new Turkish republic was inaugurated in 1923. In the post-war period much of the former Ottoman Empire, including Transjordan, Syria, and Iraq was controlled by Britain and France. A new Arab nationalism was becoming more strident, resulting in numerous political disturbances.

West Asia

1912–13: Ottomans lose most of their European lands in Balkan Wars
1915: Allied attack on Gallipoli
1917: Balfour Declaration commits to creation of Jewish state in Palestine

| 1900 | 1905 | 1910 | 1915 | 1920 | 1925 |

1908: Ottoman sultan deposed in Young Turk Revolution
1914: Ottomans ally with Germany and Austria after Britan, France and Russia declare war
1918: Collapse of Ottoman Empire
1923: Foundation of modern Turkey by Kemal Atatürk

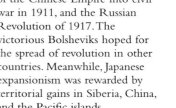

A Soviet propaganda poster encourages peasants to invest their savings in state projects. Much policy at this time was aimed at exerting control over the peasants.

Northeast Asia

Much of North and East Asia was destabilized by the collapse of the Chinese Empire into civil war in 1911, and the Russian Revolution of 1917. The victorious Bolsheviks hoped for the spread of revolution in other countries. Meanwhile, Japanese expansionism was rewarded by territorial gains in Siberia, China, and the Pacific islands.

Northeast Asia

1910: Japanese annexation of Korea
1914: Japan takes over many German colonies in the Pacific
1918–20: Japan occupies part of Manchuria and Siberia

| 1900 | 1905 | 1910 | 1915 | 1920 | 1925 |

1904–05: Russo-Japanese War; series of Russian defeats
1911: Qing dynasty overthrown by Sun Yat Sen's nationalists and Republic of China declared
1922: Washington Naval Agreement limits Japanese naval power in the Pacific

SEE ALSO:

North America: pp.132–133

South America: pp.152–153

Africa: pp.166–167

Europe: pp.206–207

West Asia: pp.232–233

South and Southeast Asia: pp.250–251

North and East Asia: pp.270–271

Australasia and Oceania: pp.284–285

ROAD MAPS

The growth in automobile use, a burgeoning road network and an increasingly mobile population, necessitated the creation of a new type of road map, more detailed than any made previously.

The cover of this 1920s road map emphasizes the link between car usage and leisure pursuits.

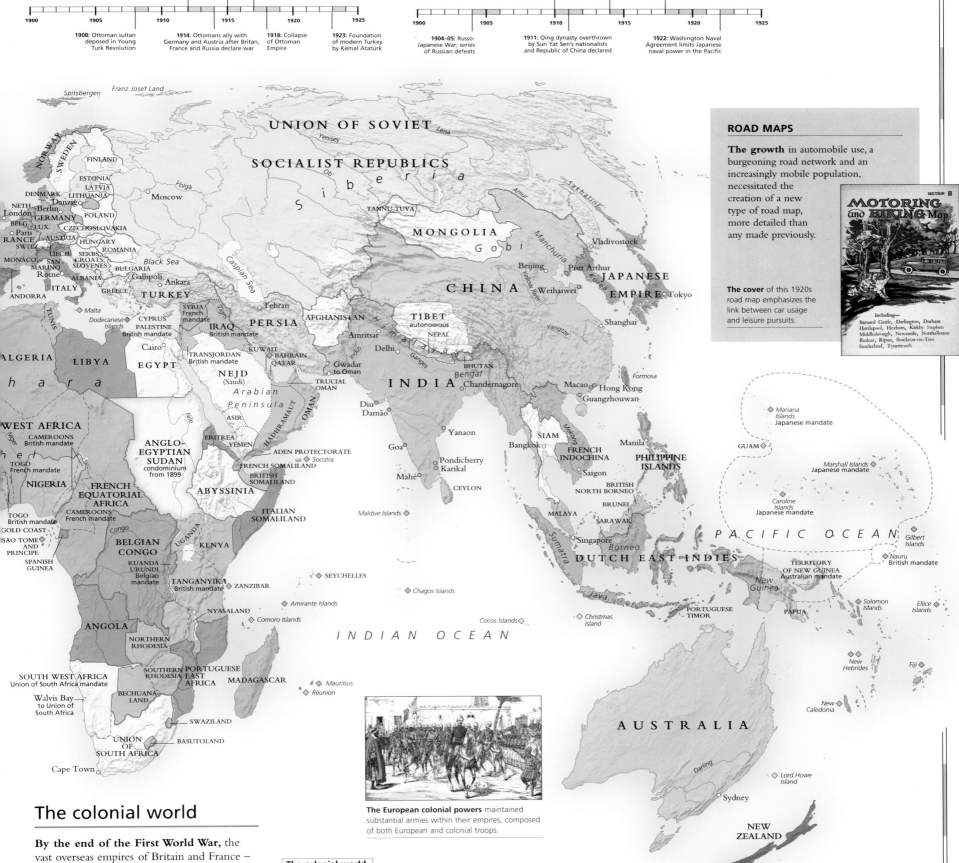

The European colonial powers maintained substantial armies within their empires, composed of both European and colonial troops.

The colonial world

By the end of the First World War, the vast overseas empires of Britain and France – which now included Germany's African lands – were becoming increasingly expensive and difficult to maintain. Colonialism was criticized by the US and the USSR, and independence movements developed in India and a number of African territories, alongside a growing nationalism in Southeast Asia.

The colonial world

1901: Commonwealth of Australia proclaimed
1904: Partition of Bengal: nationalist agitation in India
1910: Union of South Africa set up
1920: Mahatma Gandhi gains control of Indian National Congress

| 1900 | 1905 | 1910 | 1915 | 1920 | 1925 |

1902: End of Boer War in South Africa
1906: Foundation of All-India Muslim League
1911: Italian conquest of Libya
1919: Amritsar massacre leads to surge in Indian nationalism

GLOBAL MIGRATION

The Japanese shipping line *Osaka Shoshen Kaisha* carried thousands of immigrants to the US.

THE TECHNICAL INNOVATIONS of the Industrial Revolution made the 19th-century world seem a much smaller place. Railroads could quickly transport large human cargoes across continents, the Suez and Panama canals reduced travel times – sometimes by as much as 50%, and ships became larger, faster, and more seaworthy. The mechanization and centralization of industry required the concentration of labour on a scale never seen before. At the same time, the European imperial powers were exploiting their tropical possessions for economic benefit. Cash crops, grown on large plantations, needed a plentiful supply of labour as well. Political upheaval, wars, and economic hardship provided the most dramatic impetus to emigration – especially in the Russian Empire and Central Europe, and in southeastern China.

Migration in the 19th century

More than 80 million people emigrated from their country of origin during the 19th and early 20th centuries. Over half of them moved across the Atlantic to North and South America. The end of the American Civil War in 1865, and the opening up of Indian land to settlers saw the greatest period of immigration to the US and Canada. In the Russian Empire, movement was eastward from European Russia into Siberia and the Caspian region. Europeans moved south and east to take up employment in the colonies, while indentured labourers travelled to the Americas, Africa, and Southeast Asia.

Pogroms, or riots against Jews were frequent in late 19th-century Russia. Many fled following the riots; others were formally expelled from designated areas such as St. Petersburg *(above)*.

❶ World migration c.1860–1920 ▶

Transatlantic migration

➡ to North America
➡ to South America and the Caribbean
➡ to Europe from the Americas

Other European migration

➡ to Australia and New Zealand
➡ to North Africa

Asian migration

➡ to the Americas and Australia
➡ Russian migration into Siberia
➡ Indian inter-colonial migration

- - - transcontinental railroad
▨ major exporters of people
▨ major importers of people

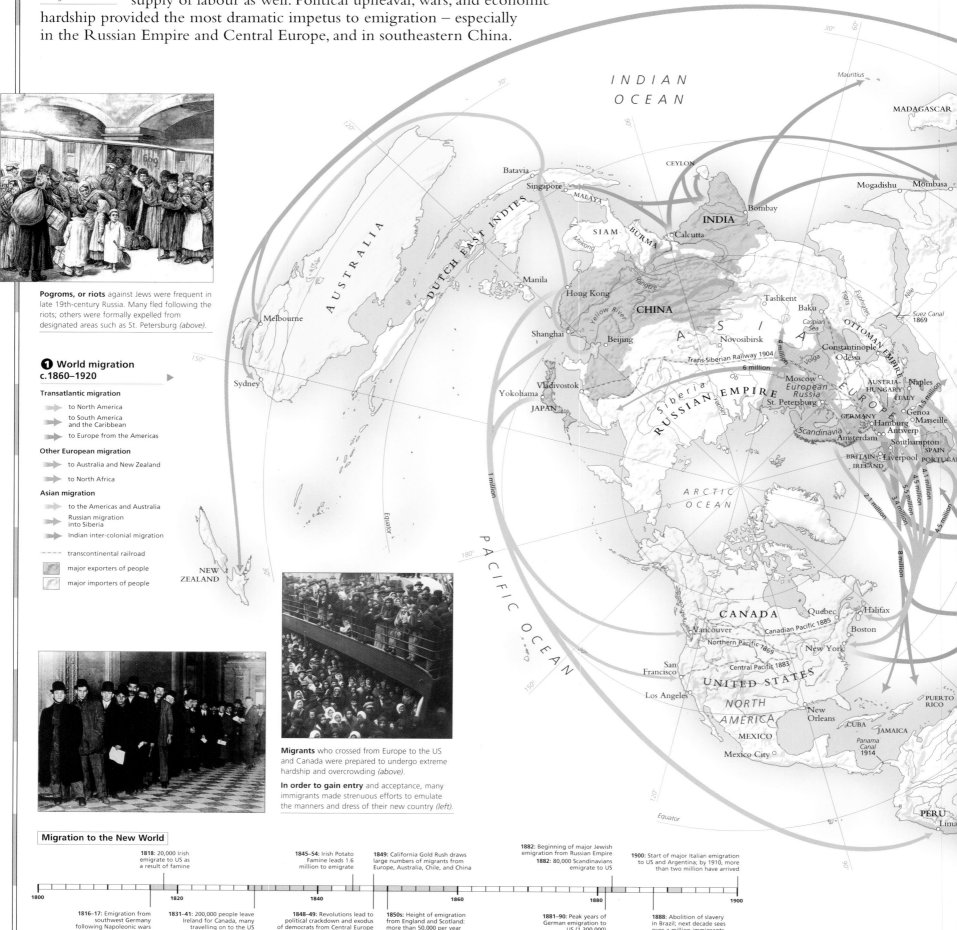

Migrants who crossed from Europe to the US and Canada were prepared to undergo extreme hardship and overcrowding *(above)*.

In order to gain entry and acceptance, many immigrants made strenuous efforts to emulate the manners and dress of their new country *(left)*.

Migration to the New World

1818: 20,000 Irish emigrate to US as a result of famine

1845–54: Irish Potato Famine leads 1.6 million to emigrate

1849: California Gold Rush draws large numbers of migrants from Europe, Australia, Chile, and China

1882: Beginning of major Jewish emigration from Russian Empire

1882: 80,000 Scandinavians emigrate to US

1900: Start of major Italian emigration to US and Argentina; by 1910, more than two million have arrived

| 1800 | 1820 | 1840 | 1860 | 1880 | 1900 |

1816–17: Emigration from southwest Germany following Napoleonic wars

1831–41: 200,000 people leave Ireland for Canada, many travelling on to the US

1848–49: Revolutions lead to political crackdown and exodus of democrats from Central Europe

1850s: Height of emigration from England and Scotland: more than 50,000 per year

1881–90: Peak years of German emigration to US (1,300,000)

1888: Abolition of slavery in Brazil; next decade sees over a million immigrants

➋ The great Jewish migration, 1880–1914 ▶

- ☐ major concentration of Jews in the Russian Empire (the 'Pale')
- ☐ region with emigrating Jewish population
- ☐ region with substantial Jewish immigration
- ✹ region where pogroms occurring
- ● gateway city
- ➡ Sephardic Jews
- ➡ Ashkenazi Jews
- 70,000 number of Jewish immigrants 1880–1914

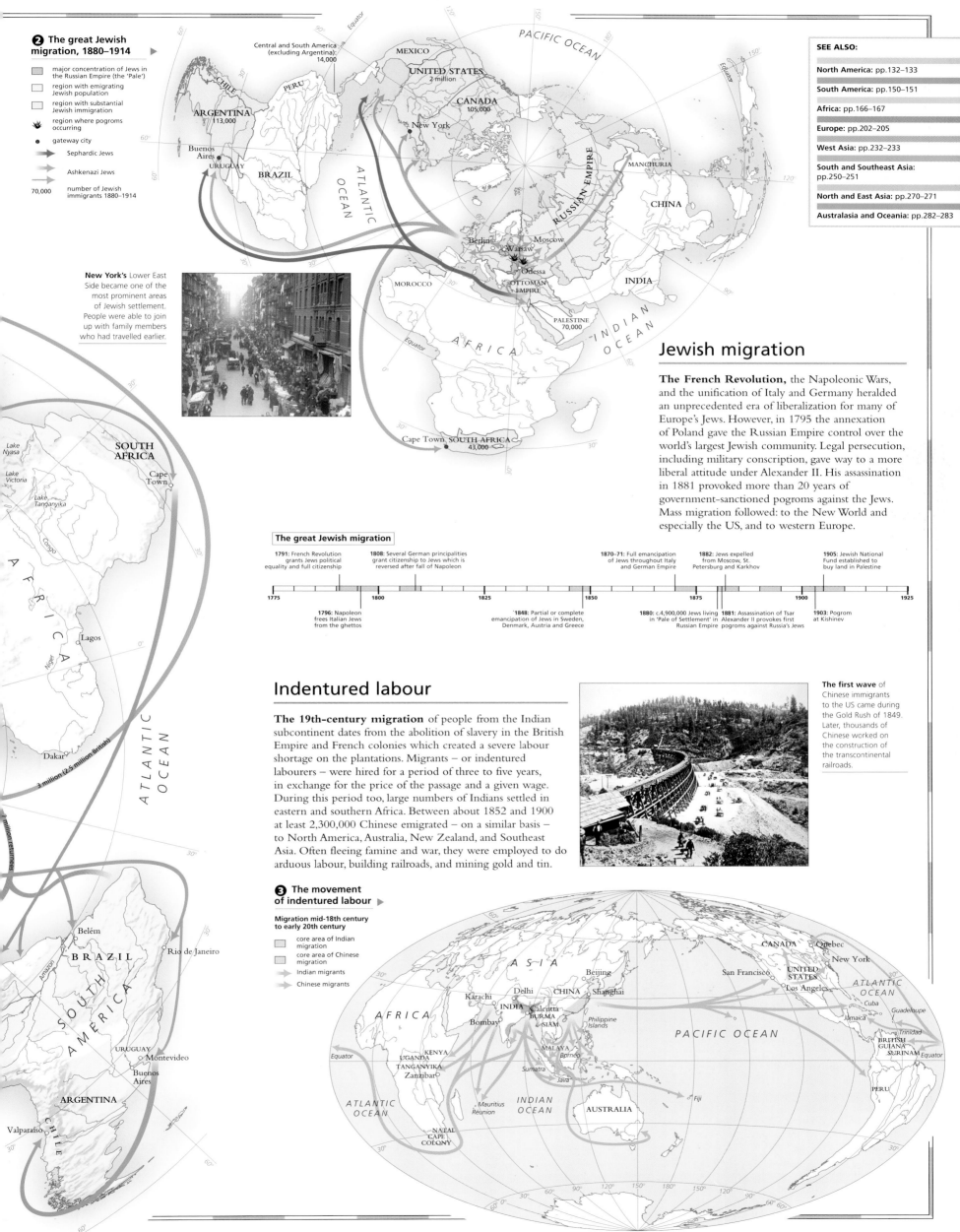

Central and South America (excluding Argentina): 14,000

MEXICO

UNITED STATES 2 million

CANADA 105,000

New York

CHILE

PERU

ARGENTINA 113,000

Buenos Aires

URUGUAY

BRAZIL

MANCHURIA

RUSSIAN EMPIRE

CHINA

Berlin   Moscow

Warsaw

Odessa

MOROCCO

OTTOMAN EMPIRE

INDIA

PALESTINE 70,000

AFRICA

Equator

Cape Town SOUTH AFRICA 43,000

SOUTH AFRICA

Cape Town

Lake Nyasa
Lake Victoria
Lake Tanganyika
Congo

AFRICA

Lagos
Niger

Dakar

3 million (2.5 million British)

7 million refugees

ATLANTIC OCEAN

Belém

BRAZIL

Rio de Janeiro

SOUTH AMERICA

Amazon

URUGUAY
Montevideo

Buenos Aires

ARGENTINA

Valparaíso

CHILE

New York's Lower East Side became one of the most prominent areas of Jewish settlement. People were able to join up with family members who had travelled earlier.

SEE ALSO:

North America: pp.132–133

South America: pp.150–151

Africa: pp.166–167

Europe: pp.202–205

West Asia: pp.232–233

South and Southeast Asia: pp.250–251

North and East Asia: pp.270–271

Australasia and Oceania: pp.282–283

Jewish migration

The French Revolution, the Napoleonic Wars, and the unification of Italy and Germany heralded an unprecedented era of liberalization for many of Europe's Jews. However, in 1795 the annexation of Poland gave the Russian Empire control over the world's largest Jewish community. Legal persecution, including military conscription, gave way to a more liberal attitude under Alexander II. His assassination in 1881 provoked more than 20 years of government-sanctioned pogroms against the Jews. Mass migration followed: to the New World and especially the US, and to western Europe.

The great Jewish migration

| 1791: French Revolution grants Jews political equality and full citizenship | 1808: Several German principalities grant citizenship to Jews which is reversed after fall of Napoleon | 1870–71: Full emancipation of Jews throughout Italy and German Empire | 1882: Jews expelled from Moscow, St. Petersburg and Karkhov | 1905: Jewish National Fund established to buy land in Palestine |

1775 — 1800 — 1825 — 1850 — 1875 — 1900 — 1925

1796: Napoleon frees Italian Jews from the ghettos

`1848: Partial or complete emancipation of Jews in Sweden, Denmark, Austria and Greece

1880: c.4,900,000 Jews living in 'Pale of Settlement' in Russian Empire

1881: Assassination of Tsar Alexander II provokes first pogroms against Russia's Jews

1903: Pogrom at Kishinev

Indentured labour

The 19th-century migration of people from the Indian subcontinent dates from the abolition of slavery in the British Empire and French colonies which created a severe labour shortage on the plantations. Migrants – or indentured labourers – were hired for a period of three to five years, in exchange for the price of the passage and a given wage. During this period too, large numbers of Indians settled in eastern and southern Africa. Between about 1852 and 1900 at least 2,300,000 Chinese emigrated – on a similar basis – to North America, Australia, New Zealand, and Southeast Asia. Often fleeing famine and war, they were employed to do arduous labour, building railroads, and mining gold and tin.

The first wave of Chinese immigrants to the US came during the Gold Rush of 1849. Later, thousands of Chinese worked on the construction of the transcontinental railroads.

➌ The movement of indentured labour ▶

Migration mid-18th century to early 20th century

- ☐ core area of Indian migration
- ☐ core area of Chinese migration
- ➡ Indian migrants
- ➡ Chinese migrants

ASIA

CANADA Québec

New York

UNITED STATES

San Francisco

Los Angeles

Beijing

CHINA Shanghai

Karachi
Delhi
INDIA Calcutta
Bombay BURMA
SIAM

Philippine Islands

PACIFIC OCEAN

ATLANTIC OCEAN

Cuba   Guadeloupe
Jamaica
Trinidad
BRITISH GUIANA
SURINAM Equator

PERU

AFRICA

KENYA
UGANDA
TANGANYIKA
Zanzibar

MALAYA
Borneo
Sumatra
Java

INDIAN OCEAN

Mauritius
Réunion

Fiji

AUSTRALIA

NATAL
CAPE COLONY

Equator

ATLANTIC OCEAN

THE WORLD 1925–1950

THOUGH THE PARTIES to the Versailles Treaty of 1919, which followed the First World War hoped for stability, the League of Nations, set up in 1919, proved ineffective. By 1939 expansionist nationalism in Germany, Italy, and Japan led once more to war on a massive scale. The Second World War devastated Europe, Asia, and the USSR, killing more than 50 million people – among them perhaps 21 million Soviet citizens and more than six million Jewish civilians. The real victors of the war were the US and the USSR, who emerged as the world's most powerful nations. The great empires of Britain and France began to fragment under the financial strain of war and the rise of independence movements in their territories, beginning with India in 1947.

Adolf Hitler used vast rallies such as this at Nuremberg to muster his followers and show the world the strength of his popular support.

Europe

Germany's humiliation at Versailles, alongside economic depression, created the conditions for a revival of aggressive German nationalism. In its efforts to create a greater Germany, Hitler's Nazi party seized much of continental Europe and launched a policy of genocide of European Jews. Only with US intervention and a resurgent Soviet Union was their advance finally halted.

Europe

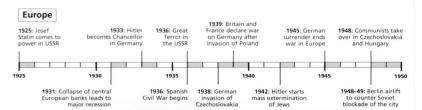

1925: Josef Stalin comes to power in USSR
1931: Collapse of central European banks leads to major recession
1933: Hitler becomes Chancellor in Germany
1936: Great Terror in the USSR
1936: Spanish Civil War begins
1938: German invasion of Czechoslovakia
1939: Britain and France declare war on Germany after invasion of Poland
1942: Hitler starts mass extermination of Jews
1945: German surrender ends war in Europe
1948: Communists take over in Czechoslovakia and Hungary
1948–49: Berlin airlift to counter Soviet blockade of the city

SCHEMATIC MAPS

The subway and metro maps produced in the 1930s are some of the simplest, yet most sophisticated maps ever produced. Using bold, clearly differentiated coloured lines for routes, and clear symbols to represent stations, they made no attempt to reproduce distances accurately, and showed direction only roughly. This schematic approach helped travellers to identify their destination and the quickest way to reach it.

The London Underground map devised by Harry Beck in 1931 and printed in 1933 is one of the most famous topological maps. Its design is based on electrical circuit diagrams.

Among the first to benefit from antibiotics were US troops wounded in the Pacific theatre of the Second World War.

The Americas

The Wall Street Crash of 1929 plunged the US into a severe depression. Only with the war effort was the economy rejuvenated: the mobilization of industry established the US as the world's leading military and industrial power. In South and Central America, a number of states sought to diversify their economies and gain control over valuable mineral reserves in neighbouring countries. The Chaco War between Bolivia and Paraguay was the most serious of these conflicts prior to the Second World War.

Eva Perón was the charismatic wife of the Argentinian president Juan Perón. Her immense popularity helped to mask the ruthlessness of his regime.

The Americas

1929: Wall Street Crash starts Great Depression
1930: Military revolution in Brazil
1932–35: Paraguay defeats Bolivia in Chaco War
1933: Roosevelt's New Deal begins
1941: US enters war following Japanese air attack on Pearl Harbor
1945: United Nations established in New York
1946: Juan Perón comes to power in Argentina
1947: Marshall Plan drawn up to aid recovery in western Europe

ANTIBIOTICS

The discovery of penicillin in 1928 led to the creation of antibiotics, powerful drugs which were able to combat epidemic diseases such as tuberculosis. Over-prescription has led to many bacteria developing antibiotic immunity, prompting a search for new agents to combat disease.

South and East Asia

Gandhi's strategy against British rule in India was based on non-violent civil disobedience.

Japanese expansionism during the 1930s led to war with China in 1937 and in 1941 Japan's bombing of Pearl Harbor forced US entry into the Second World War. Chinese Communist and Nationalist forces held the Japanese at bay; after the war the Communists overwhelmed their former allies. In India the move to independence became irresistible following the war. In 1947 the British withdrew and the separate nations of India and Pakistan were created.

Southeast Asia and Oceania

In 1942–42 Japanese forces rapidly overran European troops throughout Southeast Asia, in a campaign of 'liberation'. Their eventual defeat by Allied forces nevertheless precipitated a widespread reluctance to return to colonial rule among the peoples of the region.

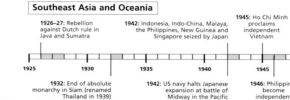

The mighty Japanese fleet was eventually destroyed by US planes launched from aircraft carriers.

SEE ALSO:

North America: pp.134–137

South America: pp.152–153

Africa: pp.168–169

Europe: pp.208–209

West Asia: pp.232–235

South and Southeast Asia: pp.250–251

North and East Asia: pp.272–273

Australasia and Oceania: pp.282–285

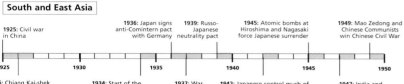

South and East Asia

- 1925: Civil war in China
- 1926: Chiang Kai-shek begins Chinese reunification
- 1934: Start of the Chinese Communists' 'Long March' to Yan'an
- 1936: Japan signs anti-Comintern pact with Germany
- 1937: War between China and Japan
- 1939: Russo-Japanese neutrality pact
- 1942: Japanese control much of South and East Asia; arrest of Congress leaders in India
- 1945: Atomic bombs at Hiroshima and Nagasaki force Japanese surrender
- 1947: India and Pakistan gain independence
- 1949: Mao Zedong and Chinese Communists win Chinese Civil War

Southeast Asia and Oceania

- 1926–27: Rebellion against Dutch rule in Java and Sumatra
- 1932: End of absolute monarchy in Siam (renamed Thailand in 1939)
- 1942: Indonesia, Indo-China, Malaya, the Philippines, New Guinea and Singapore seized by Japan
- 1942: US navy halts Japanese expansion at battle of Midway in the Pacific
- 1945: Ho Chi Minh proclaims independent Vietnam
- 1946: Philippines become independent
- 1949: Indonesia gains independence from the Dutch

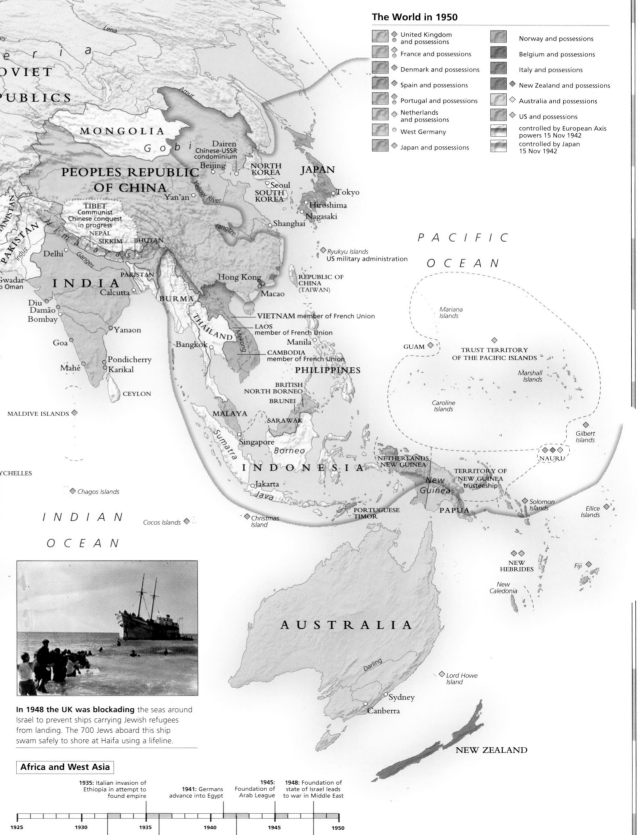

The World in 1950

- United Kingdom and possessions
- France and possessions
- Denmark and possessions
- Spain and possessions
- Portugal and possessions
- Netherlands and possessions
- West Germany
- Japan and possessions
- Norway and possessions
- Belgium and possessions
- Italy and possessions
- New Zealand and possessions
- Australia and possessions
- US and possessions
- controlled by European Axis powers 15 Nov 1942
- controlled by Japan 15 Nov 1942

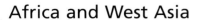

In 1948 the UK was blockading the seas around Israel to prevent ships carrying Jewish refugees from landing. The 700 Jews aboard this ship swam safely to shore at Haifa using a lifeline.

Africa and West Asia

At the end of the First World War Britain and France gained control over much of North Africa and West Asia – especially the oil-producing nations. In the Second World War the Horn of Africa and North Africa became battlegrounds; Italian and German forces were eventually defeated. A new state of Israel was proclaimed for the survivors of Nazi Germany's genocide of European Jews in 1948. Conflict over Israel's disputed territorial boundaries remained unresolved for over 50 years.

Africa and West Asia

- 1932: Foundation of kingdom of Saudi Arabia
- 1935: Italian invasion of Ethiopia in attempt to found empire
- 1936: Arab revolt in Palestine against Jewish immigration
- 1941: Germans advance into Egypt
- 1942: British halt German advance at battle of El Alamein
- 1945: Foundation of Arab League
- 1948: Foundation of state of Israel leads to war in Middle East
- 1948–49: National Party wins power in South Africa with a commitment to apartheid

THE SECOND WORLD WAR

Adolf Hitler's National Socialist (NAZI) party was underpinned by extreme nationalism and racism, enforced though a police state.

THE SECOND WORLD WAR was a protracted struggle by a host of Allied nations to contain, and eventually destroy, the political, economic, social, and territorial ambitions of the Axis, a small group of extreme right-wing nationalist states led by Germany and Japan. The struggle led to the mobilization of manpower and economic might on an unprecedented scale, a deployment of forces on land, sea, and air globally, and the prosecution of war far beyond the front line, deep into the civilian hinterland in all theatres. For these reasons it has been called a 'Total War'. Its human costs were enormous, variously estimated at between 50 and 60 million dead, and its conclusion – with the detonation of two atomic bombs over Japan – heralded the Nuclear Age.

The Second World War, 1939–41

Until May 1941 Japan and Germany fought and won localized conflicts: in a series of campaigns they conquered and denied isolated enemies the opportunity to gather support and mobilize potentially far superior resources. In summer 1941, with Britain isolated but for its empire, the German invasion of the Soviet Union and the Japanese move into Southeast Asia marked the point at which their separate conflicts changed and came together. Japan's provocation of the US and Germany's failure in Russia marked the end of Axis successes and the advent of global warfare.

The war to December 1941

Sep 1939: Invasion of Poland by Germany and Soviet Union
Jun 1940: Italy declares war on Britain and France
Jun 1941: Germany invades the Soviet Union (Operation Barbarossa)
Dec 1941: Japan attacks Pearl Harbor; US enters the war

Sep 1939: Britain and France declare war on Germany
Jun 1940: German troops enter Paris; fall of France
Jul–Oct 1940: Battle of Britain waged in air over southern England
Jul 1941: Soviet Union and Britain sign pact of mutual assistance
Dec 1941: Germany declares war on US

Japan's campaigns in Asia aimed to destroy British, US, and Dutch influence and create a 'Greater East Asian Co-Prosperity Sphere' in the region.

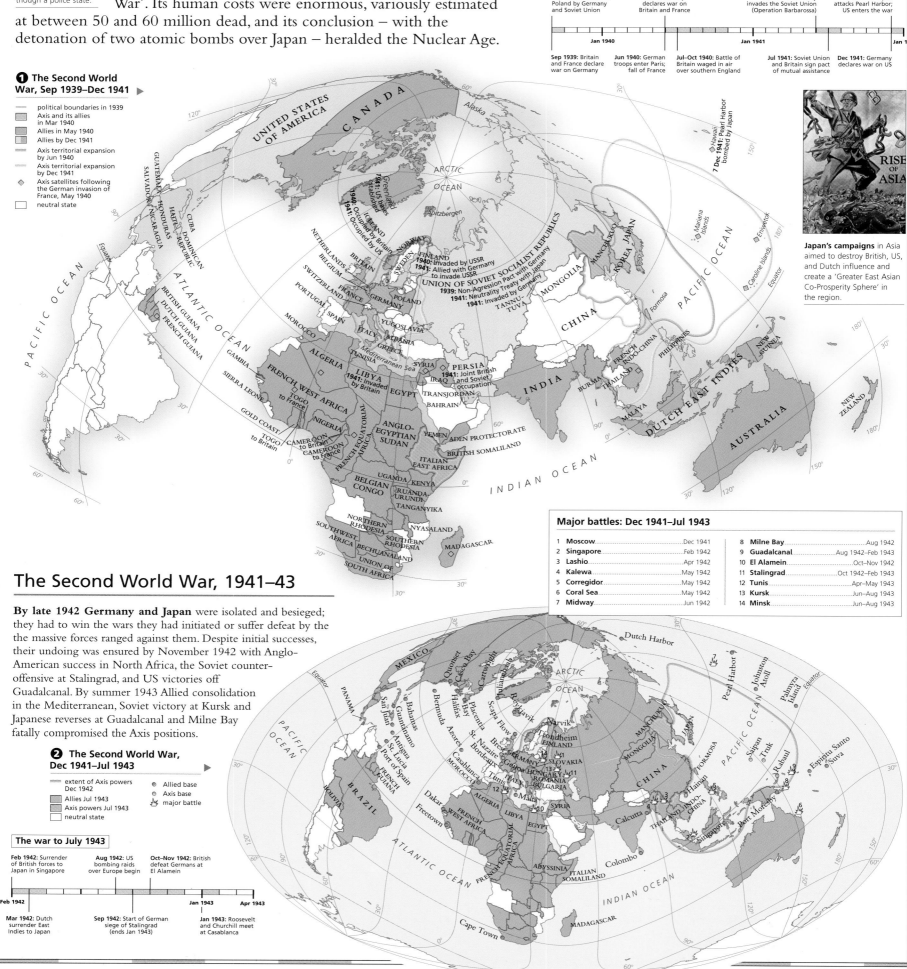

❶ The Second World War, Sep 1939–Dec 1941

— political boundaries in 1939
Axis and its allies in Mar 1940
Allies in May 1940
Allies by Dec 1941
Axis territorial expansion by Jun 1940
Axis territorial expansion by Dec 1941
◆ Axis satellites following the German invasion of France, May 1940
neutral state

The Second World War, 1941–43

By late 1942 Germany and Japan were isolated and besieged; they had to win the wars they had initiated or suffer defeat by the the massive forces ranged against them. Despite initial successes, their undoing was ensured by November 1942 with Anglo-American success in North Africa, the Soviet counter-offensive at Stalingrad, and US victories off Guadalcanal. By summer 1943 Allied consolidation in the Mediterranean, Soviet victory at Kursk and Japanese reverses at Guadalcanal and Milne Bay fatally compromised the Axis positions.

❷ The Second World War, Dec 1941–Jul 1943

— extent of Axis powers Dec 1942
Allies Jul 1943
Axis powers Jul 1943
neutral state
● Allied base
● Axis base
⚔ major battle

Major battles: Dec 1941–Jul 1943			
1 Moscow	Dec 1941	8 Milne Bay	Aug 1942
2 Singapore	Feb 1942	9 Guadalcanal	Aug 1942–Feb 1943
3 Lashio	Apr 1942	10 El Alamein	Oct–Nov 1942
4 Kalewa	May 1942	11 Stalingrad	Oct 1942–Feb 1943
5 Corregidor	May 1942	12 Tunis	Apr–May 1943
6 Coral Sea	May 1942	13 Kursk	Jun–Aug 1943
7 Midway	Jun 1942	14 Minsk	Jun–Aug 1943

The war to July 1943

Feb 1942: Surrender of British forces to Japan in Singapore
Aug 1942: US bombing raids over Europe begin
Oct–Nov 1942: British defeat Germans at El Alamein

Mar 1942: Dutch surrender East Indies to Japan
Sep 1942: Start of German siege of Stalingrad (ends Jan 1943)
Jan 1943: Roosevelt and Churchill meet at Casablanca

The Second World War, 1943–45

In 1943 Allied success was piecemeal and attritional; after June 1944 they achieved increasing depth of penetration and permanency of conquest. The Axis suffered escalating losses on the front line and in their heartlands. By August 1944 Germany's 'Fortress Europe' was breached by the Soviets in Central Europe, and by Anglo–American forces in Italy and Normandy, while US victory in the Philippine Sea fatally split Japan's 'Greater East Asian Co-Prosperity Sphere'. However, Axis tenacity and the Allied insistence upon unconditional surrender, meant that peace would only be achieved with the devastation of Europe and Japan.

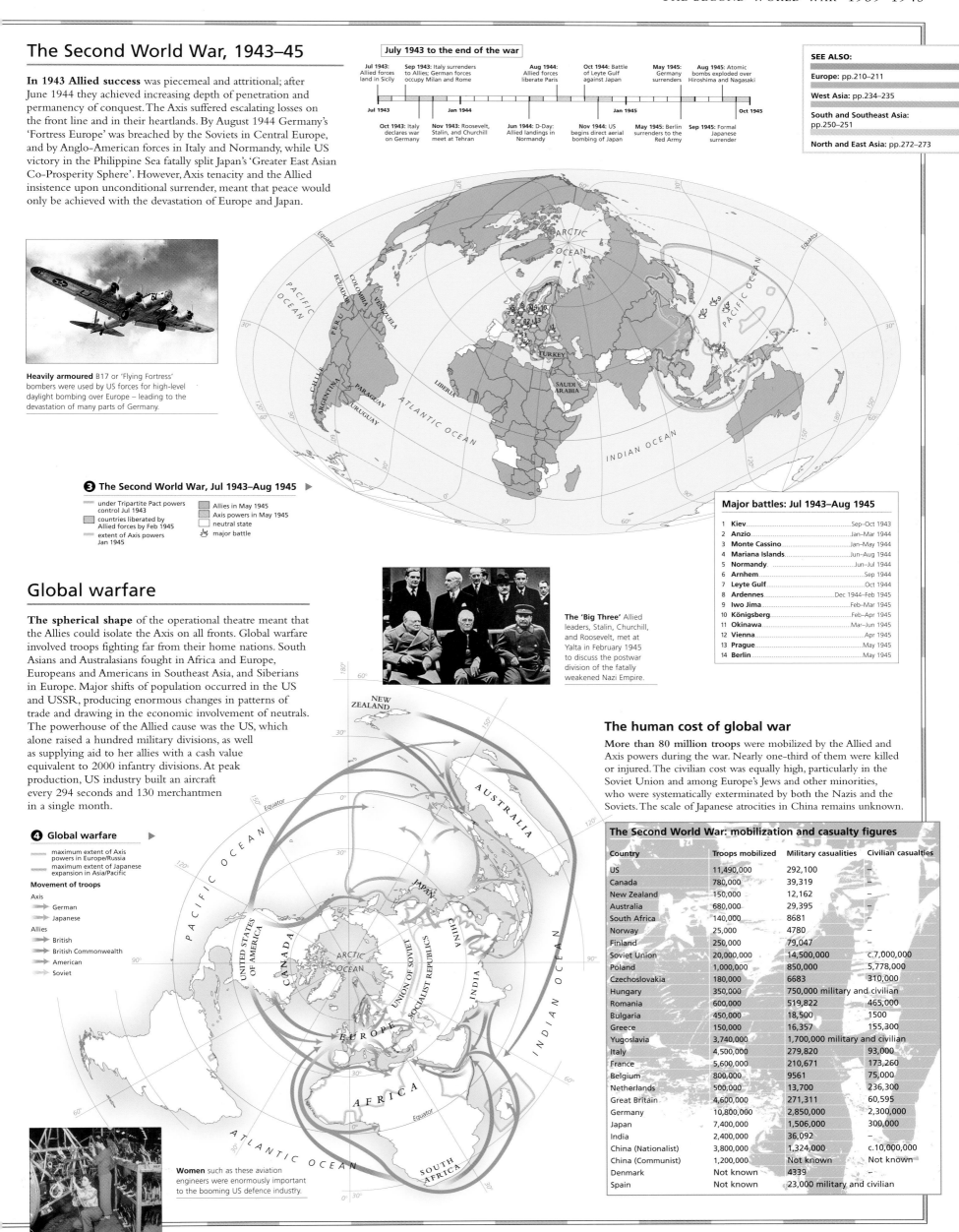

Heavily armoured B17 or 'Flying Fortress' bombers were used by US forces for high-level daylight bombing over Europe – leading to the devastation of many parts of Germany.

July 1943 to the end of the war

Jul 1943: Allied forces land in Sicily

Sep 1943: Italy surrenders to Allies; German forces occupy Milan and Rome

Aug 1944: Allied forces liberate Paris

Oct 1944: Battle of Leyte Gulf against Japan

May 1945: Germany surrenders

Aug 1945: Atomic bombs exploded over Hiroshima and Nagasaki

Jul 1943 — Jan 1944 — Jan 1945 — Oct 1945

Oct 1943: Italy declares war on Germany

Nov 1943: Roosevelt, Stalin, and Churchill meet at Tehran

Jun 1944: D-Day: Allied landings in Normandy

Nov 1944: US begins direct aerial bombing of Japan

May 1945: Berlin surrenders to the Red Army

Sep 1945: Formal Japanese surrender

SEE ALSO:

Europe: pp.210–211

West Asia: pp.234–235

South and Southeast Asia: pp.250–251

North and East Asia: pp.272–273

③ The Second World War, Jul 1943–Aug 1945 ▶

- under Tripartite Pact powers control Jul 1943
- countries liberated by Allied forces by Feb 1945
- extent of Axis powers Jan 1945
- Allies in May 1945
- Axis powers in May 1945
- neutral state
- major battle

Major battles: Jul 1943–Aug 1945

1	Kiev	Sep–Oct 1943
2	Anzio	Jan–Mar 1944
3	Monte Cassino	Jan–May 1944
4	Mariana Islands	Jun–Aug 1944
5	Normandy	Jun–Jul 1944
6	Arnhem	Sep 1944
7	Leyte Gulf	Oct 1944
8	Ardennes	Dec 1944–Feb 1945
9	Iwo Jima	Feb–Mar 1945
10	Königsberg	Feb–Apr 1945
11	Okinawa	Mar–Jun 1945
12	Vienna	Apr 1945
13	Prague	May 1945
14	Berlin	May 1945

Global warfare

The spherical shape of the operational theatre meant that the Allies could isolate the Axis on all fronts. Global warfare involved troops fighting far from their home nations. South Asians and Australasians fought in Africa and Europe, Europeans and Americans in Southeast Asia, and Siberians in Europe. Major shifts of population occurred in the US and USSR, producing enormous changes in patterns of trade and drawing in the economic involvement of neutrals. The powerhouse of the Allied cause was the US, which alone raised a hundred military divisions, as well as supplying aid to her allies with a cash value equivalent to 2000 infantry divisions. At peak production, US industry built an aircraft every 294 seconds and 130 merchantmen in a single month.

The 'Big Three' Allied leaders, Stalin, Churchill, and Roosevelt, met at Yalta in February 1945 to discuss the postwar division of the fatally weakened Nazi Empire.

④ Global warfare ▶

- maximum extent of Axis powers in Europe/Russia
- maximum extent of Japanese expansion in Asia/Pacific

Movement of troops

Axis
- German
- Japanese

Allies
- British
- British Commonwealth
- American
- Soviet

Women such as these aviation engineers were enormously important to the booming US defence industry.

The human cost of global war

More than 80 million troops were mobilized by the Allied and Axis powers during the war. Nearly one-third of them were killed or injured. The civilian cost was equally high, particularly in the Soviet Union and among Europe's Jews and other minorities, who were systematically exterminated by both the Nazis and the Soviets. The scale of Japanese atrocities in China remains unknown.

The Second World War: mobilization and casualty figures

Country	Troops mobilized	Military casualties	Civilian casualties
US	11,490,000	292,100	–
Canada	780,000	39,319	–
New Zealand	150,000	12,162	–
Australia	680,000	29,395	–
South Africa	140,000	8681	–
Norway	25,000	4780	–
Finland	250,000	79,047	–
Soviet Union	20,000,000	14,500,000	c.7,000,000
Poland	1,000,000	850,000	5,778,000
Czechoslovakia	180,000	6683	310,000
Hungary	350,000	750,000 military and civilian	
Romania	600,000	519,822	465,000
Bulgaria	450,000	18,500	1500
Greece	150,000	16,357	155,300
Yugoslavia	3,740,000	1,700,000 military and civilian	
Italy	4,500,000	279,820	93,000
France	5,600,000	210,671	173,260
Belgium	800,000	9561	75,000
Netherlands	500,000	13,700	236,300
Great Britain	4,600,000	271,311	60,595
Germany	10,800,000	2,850,000	2,300,000
Japan	7,400,000	1,506,000	300,000
India	2,400,000	36,092	–
China (Nationalist)	3,800,000	1,324,000	c.10,000,000
China (Communist)	1,200,000	Not known	Not known
Denmark	Not known	4339	–
Spain	Not known	23,000 military and civilian	

THE WORLD 1950–1975

WORLD POLITICS IN THE ERA following the close of the Second World War were defined by the tense relationship between the US and the USSR. The 'Cold War' between liberal-capitalism and Communism saw each side constantly attempting to contain and subvert the other. The Korean War (1950–55), the Cuban Missile Crisis of 1962, and the Vietnam War (1954–75), as well as many smaller conflicts – particularly in Central America and Africa – were all manifestations of the Cold War. Though no nuclear weapons were ever used in anger, both sides built up huge nuclear arsenals whose potential for mass destruction acted as a deterrent to conflict on a global scale.

Europe

During the Soviet era the May Day parade in Moscow's Red Square became the focus for the USSR's display of her military might. Weapons such as these ballistic rockets were wheeled through the streets.

The **1950s and 1960s** were a period of widespread prosperity and political stability in Western Europe, faltering only in the early 1970s. West Germany, banned from keeping an army, rebuilt its shattered economy and infrastructure with stunning success. Eastern Europe was overshadowed by Soviet Communism, which restricted both economic development and the personal freedom of its citizens.

Europe

1955: Warsaw Pact created as Soviet-bloc opponent of NATO

1957: Creation of European Economic Community (EEC)

1961: Berlin Wall separates East and West Berlin

1968: 'Prague Spring' reforms in Czechoslovakia crushed by USSR

1973: Oil crisis causes inflation and economic slowdown

1950 — 1955 — 1960 — 1965 — 1970 — 1975

1956: Hungarian revolt crushed by Warsaw Pact

1957: First artificial satellite, Sputnik II launched by USSR

1968: Student uprisings throughout Europe

1969: De Gaulle resigns after defeat in referendum on regional reform

SATELLITE IMAGERY

With space technology came the ability to keep artificial satellites in permanent orbit round the Earth. They are used to carry transmitters for telecommunications, as aids to navigation and as bases for space exploration. The data picked up by sensors can be digitally combined to create images of the Earth.

This satellite image of North and South America shows both vegetation cover and weather conditions at the time at which it was taken.

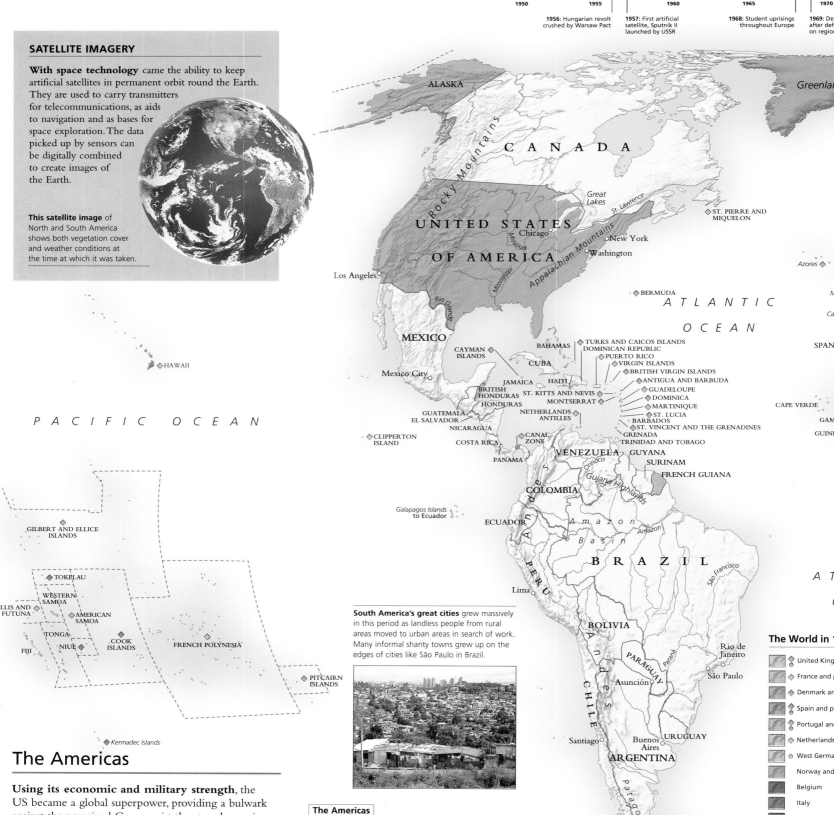

South America's great cities grew massively in this period as landless people from rural areas moved to urban areas in search of work. Many informal shanty towns grew up on the edges of cities like São Paulo in Brazil.

The Americas

Using its economic and military strength, the US became a global superpower, providing a bulwark against the perceived Communist threat and ensuring the world dominance of American popular culture. Many of the nations of Central and South America were ruled by military dictatorships which severely restricted the freedom of their citizens. Economic instability, high population growth – especially in urban areas – and high inflation were still major problems.

The Americas

1955: Argentinian leader Perón ousted by military coup. Remains out of power until 1973

1964: US Congress approves war with Vietnam

1969: NASA puts first humans on the Moon

1974: Resignation of Nixon following Watergate scandal

1950 — 1955 — 1960 — 1965 — 1970 — 1975

1959: Fidel Castro becomes Cuban leader; reorganizes economy along Soviet lines

1962: Cuban Missile Crisis

1967: Widespread protests against US involvement in Vietnam

1973: US backs coup against elected Marxist government in Chile

The World in 1975

- ◇ United Kingdom and possessions
- ◇ France and possessions
- ◇ Denmark and possessions
- ◇ Spain and possessions
- ◇ Portugal and possessions
- ◇ Netherlands and possessions
- ◇ West Germany
- Norway and possessions
- Belgium
- Italy
- ◇ New Zealand and possessions
- ◇ Australia and possessions
- ◇ US and possessions
- Biafra 1967–70
- Katanga 1960–63
- South Vietnam 1954–75

West and South Asia

Israel, supported by Western powers, fought a series of wars with its Arab neighbours to define its boundaries. The exploitation of extensive oil reserves brought immense wealth to the undeveloped Arabian Peninsula. Relations between India and Pakistan were strained by territorial disputes, and in 1971, the geographical separation of Pakistan proved unsustainable with East Pakistan becoming Bangladesh.

Intense rivalry between Israel and Egypt led in June 1967 to the Six Day War. Superior Israeli air power routed the Egyptian air force and the ground forces of Egypt, Jordan, Iraq, and Syria.

East and Southeast Asia

In China and mainland Southeast Asia, power passed to native Communist movements. Mao Zedong's Communist China became a superpower to rival the USSR, while the US intervened in Korea and Vietnam in response to the perceived threat of Communism. Japan began rebuilding its economy with American aid to become, by the mid-1970s, one of the world's richest nations. From 1950 onwards, mainland Southeast Asia was destabilized by Cold War-inspired conflict: in Laos, Vietnam, and Cambodia.

The political thoughts of Mao Zedong were published as the 'Little Red Book' and distributed to all Communist Party members.

West and South Asia

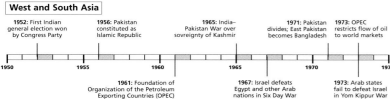

1952: First Indian general election won by Congress Party
1956: Pakistan constituted as Islamic Republic
1965: India–Pakistan War over sovereignty of Kashmir
1971: Pakistan divides; East Pakistan becomes Bangladesh
1973: OPEC restricts flow of oil to world markets

1950 — 1955 — 1960 — 1965 — 1970 — 1975

1961: Foundation of Organization of the Petroleum Exporting Countries (OPEC)
1967: Israel defeats Egypt and other Arab nations in Six Day War
1973: Arab states fail to defeat Israel in Yom Kippur War

East and Southeast Asia

1950: Outbreak of Korean War
1958: Start of Mao's 'Great Leap Forward' in China
1965: US troops sent to Vietnam – bombing of North begins
1975: US-backed South Vietnam regime falls

1950 — 1955 — 1960 — 1965 — 1970 — 1975

1954: Independence of Laos, Cambodia, and North and South Vietnam
1962: US military advisors sent to assist South Vietnamese regime
1966–70: Mao Zedong imposes Cultural Revolution in China

THE MICROCHIP

The miniaturization of transistors and other electronic components, allowed complete electronic circuits to be created on a single slice of silicon about the size of a human nail. The first microprocessor chip, the Intel 4004, was produced in the USA in 1971.

Most modern electronic devices use a number of integrated circuits like this.

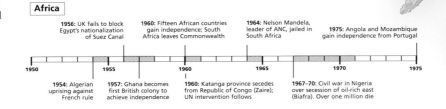

Africa's post-colonial era provided rich pickings for a series of corrupt military dictators such as President Mobutu, who ruled Zaire from 1965–97.

Africa

A succession of former colonies became independent from 1957 onwards; by 1975, 41 African counties had become independent. Few were fully prepared for the demands of independence and many countries remained pawns in the Cold War, armed by the opposing powers, and fighting wars on behalf of their conflicting ideologies.

Africa

1956: UK fails to block Egypt's nationalization of Suez Canal
1960: Fifteen African countries gain independence; South Africa leaves Commonwealth
1964: Nelson Mandela, leader of ANC, jailed in South Africa
1975: Angola and Mozambique gain independence from Portugal

1950 — 1955 — 1960 — 1965 — 1970 — 1975

1954: Algerian uprising against French rule
1957: Ghana becomes first British colony to achieve independence
1960: Katanga province secedes from Republic of Congo (Zaire); UN intervention follows
1967–70: Civil war in Nigeria over secession of oil-rich east (Biafra). Over one million die

THE COLD WAR

Spies, such as the Rosenbergs, executed in 1953 for passing US nuclear secrets to the USSR, were endemic during the Cold War.

FROM THE MEETING OF US AND SOVIET FORCES on the Elbe in April 1945 came a division of Europe and a confrontation between the former allies which would last for almost five decades. Defensive needs – for the US the security of Western Europe, for the USSR a buffer zone in Eastern Europe – appeared to each other offensive intents, overlaid by ideological, political, and economic rivalries. Thus the Cold War took shape, with the US committed to a policy of containment and attrition by all means just short of open conflict, and the USSR intent on supporting anti-Western revolutionary movements throughout the world. Strategic and armed stalemate gave rise to détente in the 1970s, but only the collapse of Soviet system in 1989–91 ended the Cold War.

The Cuban missile crisis 1961–62

The Cold War's most dangerous single episode arose from the Castro Revolution (1956–59) and subsequent US–Cuban estrangement. Castro's alignment with the Eastern bloc provided the USSR with an opportunity to offset its strategic inferiority by the creation of Cuban bases from which missiles could strike at the heart of continental USA. This was forestalled by a US blockade, and a stand-off following which the Soviets were forced to withdraw their missiles.

Cold warriors J. F. Kennedy and Nikita Khrushchev underestimated each other's strength and determination when they met in Vienna in 1961. By 1962 they had taken the world to the verge of nuclear conflict during the Cuban missile crisis.

Cold War crises 1956–64

1956–59: Cuban Revolution under Fidel Castro	Apr 1961: USSR launches first manned space flight	1962: Cuban missile crisis

1957: USSR launches first space satellite	1961: Increasing US involvement in Vietnam	1964: Kubrick's *Dr Strangelove* alerts public to dangers of Mutually Assured Destruction (MAD)

1956   1958   1960   1962   1964

Scale varies with perspective

4990 km (3100 miles)

4440 km (2760 miles)

★Apr 1961: CIA-backed invasion force of Cuban exiles aborted

2 The Cuban missile crisis 1961-62

- potential range of Soviet missiles (1100 miles)
- US blockade zone
- Soviet missile and jet base
- US air base
- US naval base

NATO and the Warsaw Pact

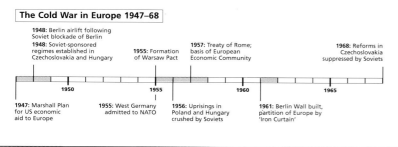

On 23 June 1948, the Soviet army blockaded the Western-controlled sectors of Berlin, forcing the Allied powers to mount a massive airlift to supply the beleaguered enclave.

Deepening US-Soviet hostility, plus Western Europe's patent inability to defend itself, led to the creation of the North Atlantic Treaty Organization (NATO) in April 1949; in effect, the US provided guarantee of Western Europe's security. The latter's continuing war-weariness saw a build-up of US forces in Europe, and contributed to the decision to permit West Germany to have armed forces, admitting the nation to NATO in 1955. This in turn prompted the USSR and its satellite countries in Eastern Europe to form the Warsaw Pact. The building of the Berlin Wall in 1960 consolidated the 'Iron Curtain' which divided Europe into two zones – East and West – until 1989.

The Cold War in Europe 1947–68

1948: Berlin airlift following Soviet blockade of Berlin			
1948: Soviet-sponsored regimes established in Czechoslovakia and Hungary	1955: Formation of Warsaw Pact	1957: Treaty of Rome; basis of European Economic Community	1968: Reforms in Czechoslovakia suppressed by Soviets

1950   1955   1960   1965

1947: Marshall Plan for US economic aid to Europe	1955: West Germany admitted to NATO	1956: Uprisings in Poland and Hungary crushed by Soviets	1961: Berlin Wall built, partition of Europe by 'Iron Curtain'

1953: Widespread uprisings; 1961: Berlin Wall built

1944–47: Civil war; 1953: Strikes and riots

1968: Widespread demonstrations; reformist government crushed

1956: Widespread uprising; government withdraws from Warsaw Pact, Russian invasion

1964: Nominal independence declared

1955: Allied occupied partition ends

1948: Tito splits from Soviet alliance; 1955: Détente

1968: Romania leaves Warsaw Pact

3 The Cold War in Europe

- original NATO members in 1949
- later NATO members (with dates)
- Warsaw Pact members in 1955
- neutral states

500 km

500 miles

① The alliances of the Cold War

US, allies, and satellite states	USSR and allies
US and original NATO 1949	USSR
later NATO	Warsaw Pact 1955
NATO dependencies 1960	Communist satellite states
other nations allied to the Western bloc by treaty	China
CENTO Pact 1959	major Soviet overseas base
major US and NATO overseas bases	Cold War flashpoint
	major US fleet

From the early 1960s the Western allies depended increasingly on long-range nuclear-powered submarines to deliver missiles in the event of war. With the development of Trident submarines in the 1980s the range extended to 7400 km, a key factor in the Strategic Arms Reduction (START) negotiations of 1982–91.

SEE ALSO:

North America: pp.138–139

South America: pp.152–153

Africa: pp.168–169

Europe: pp.212–215

West Asia: pp.234–235

South and Southeast Asia: pp.252–253

North and East Asia: pp.274–275

Australasia and Oceania: pp.284–285

Strategic manoeuvres in the Cold War

1947: Truman Doctrine seeks 'containment' of USSR
1949: Formation of NATO
1972: SALT I strategic arms limitation talks
1979: SALT II arms limitation agreement signed
1990: NATO and Warsaw Pact agree on conventional arms limitation in Europe

1945 1955 1965 1975 1985 1995

1945: Yalta Conference; division between Allies; origins of Cold War
1955: Formation of Warsaw Pact
1989–90: Collapse of Communism in Europe
1991: US and USSR sign START arms reduction treaty

The strategic balance

In the Cold War's first decade the US sought to contain the threat of global Communism by a series of regional treaties and alliances backed by economic and military strength. But by 1960, with a rift in Sino-Soviet relations splitting the Communist bloc, and as the simultaneous process of decolonization (endorsed by the US) deprived its European NATO allies of their global outreach, so the theatre of the Cold War shifted from Europe to the developing world. Here a series of conflicts from Cuba to Vietnam saw both the US and the Communist world frequently fighting a war by proxy.

The Korean War 1950–53

Reluctantly sanctioned by the USSR, North Korea's invasion of the south in June 1950 was immediately seen as a test of US global credibility. The challenge was initially countered by a US-led UN force, which was met in turn by Chinese intervention. Thereafter the front stabilized around the pre-war border. The US, confronted by the need to garrison Europe, and by a reluctance to carry the war beyond Korea's borders, accepted a policy of defensive self-restraint, which formed the basis of the Western Allies' Limited War doctrine.

The Korean War effectively ended in stalemate in July 1953, with the partition of Korea into a Communist North and a nominally democratic South along an armistice line, straddling the 38th parallel. This border has remained a heavily armed military frontier ever since. These South Korean troops were photographed in 1996.

④ The Korean War 1950–53

- area controlled by North Korean forces 15 Sep 1950
- front line 15 Sep 1950
- US forces 16 Sep–24 Oct 1950
- Chinese forces Oct 1950
- front line 24 Nov 1950
- front line 25 Jan 1951
- cease-fire line 27 Jul 1953

THE ARMS RACE

As the Cold War arms race began, the US held technological, numerical and positional advantages over the Soviet Union. In the 1960s, as US vulnerability increased, deterrence shifted from bombers to a triad built around submarine- and land-based intercontinental missiles (ICBMs). With the USSR acquiring ICBM capability by the late 1960s, both superpowers faced the future with secure second-strikes: MAD (Mutually Assured Destruction). This situation, and the development of multiple-warhead (MRV, MIRV) technology threatened a new round in the arms race. The 1970s saw ceilings on missile and warhead numbers, and anti-missile defences (ABM) were limited (SALT I in 1972, and SALT II in 1979). The brief period of détente gave way to perhaps the most dangerous phase of the Cold War, one that witnessed ABM revival with the Strategic Defence Initiative (SDI, Star Wars) which only ended with the collapse of the USSR in 1979.

The Angolan Civil War 1975–88

Ideological indoctrination by both East and West during the Cold War conflicts in the developing world was enforced irrespective of sex or age. The image of the child soldier is an enduring legacy of these conflicts in Africa.

By the 1970s Soviet naval and airlift capacity enabled it to give active support to anti-Western revolution globally. However, its major efforts in Africa, in Angola (1976–88) and Ethiopia (1977–89), were conducted by proxy via Cuba. In Angola, the three main organizations which had fought to end Portuguese rule were bitterly hostile to each other, and by 1975 there was a three-way civil war, the Marxist MPLA initially clearing the FNLA and UNITA from the north. The Soviets sustained the MPLA with Cuban troops, while the Western powers, through South Africa, secured southern borders in support of UNITA. The conflict lasted until 1988, the Cubans, MPLA and South Africa concluding an uneasy ceasefire. Throughout the struggle, UNITA dominated most of Angola through guerrilla warfare, but 50,000 Cuban troops ensured the survival of the MPLA.

⑤ The Angolan Civil War from 1975

- under FNLA control 1975
- under MPLA control 1975
- under UNITA control 1975
- area of MPLA control by mid-1976
- area under UNITA control by mid-1976
- Cuban troops and Soviet aid to MPLA from 1975
- area of effective South African occupation
- South African attacks in support of UNITA 1976–88
- limit of UNITA guerrilla activity 1976–92

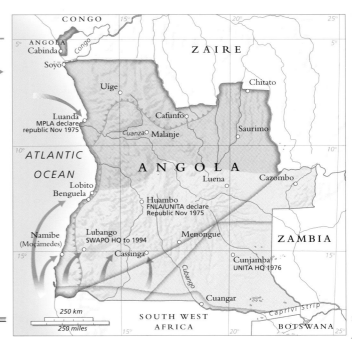

THE WORLD
THE MODERN AGE

WITH THE CLOSE OF THE COLD WAR IN 1989, a new world order emerged. Rivalry between the US and the USSR ended, as the latter broke up in 1991, and the former Eastern bloc was opened up to the West and free-market forces, although Russia itself suffered crises of confidence. In the Middle East, disputes between Israel and her neighbours remained unresolved, while Islamic fundamentalism in Iran, and Saddam Hussein's aggressive militarism kept much of the region on constant standby for war. In Southeast Asia, massive investment during the 1980s fed an economic boom which proved unsustainable, plunging the region into depression in the late 1990s. South Africa's all-embracing elections of 1994 were a triumph for democracy in Africa, but as the century closed, central Africa was becoming enveloped in regional war.

The Berlin Wall, hated symbol of division between East and West was torn down in 1989, and Germany's two halves were reunited the following year.

Europe

While Western Europe progressed towards economic and political unity under the European Union (EU), eastern Europe was still economically constrained by Soviet Communism. But in 1989 popular movements rejected Communism, fracturing first the Eastern bloc and in 1991 the USSR itself. The fragmentation boiled over into civil war, notably in Yugoslavia and Georgia, where conflicts were fuelled by ethnic nationalism.

Europe				
1985: Mikhail Gorbachev becomes Soviet leader; moves to end Cold War	**1990:** East and West Germany reunited	**1991:** Breakup of USSR	**1995:** Ceasefire agreed in Bosnia and Herzegovina; UN troops remain	

1975 — 1980 — 1985 — 1990 — 1995 — 2000

1975: General Franco dies in Spain. He is replaced by King Juan Carlos

1989: End of Communism in Poland, Hungary, Czechoslovakia, Romania, East Germany, and Bulgaria

1991: Start of civil war in Yugoslavia

REMOTE-SENSED MAPPING

The detailed data collected by sensor-bearing satellites can be used to map changing geographic patterns. Examples include climatic conditions, soils, vegetation, pollution, and levels of urbanization.

An infrared satellite image of Buenos Aires taken from a French *SPOT* satellite shows densely populated urban areas in blue, vegetation in red and water – including the River Plate – in black.

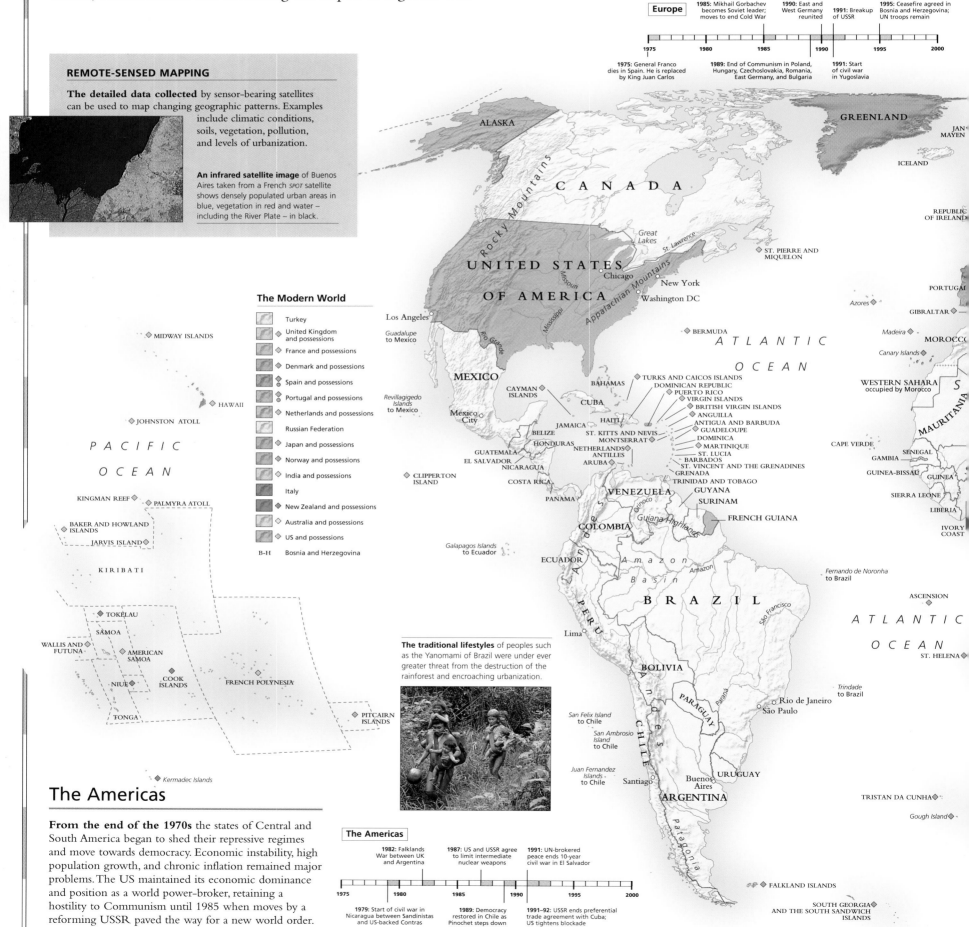

The Modern World

- Turkey
- United Kingdom and possessions
- France and possessions
- Denmark and possessions
- Spain and possessions
- Portugal and possessions
- Netherlands and possessions
- Russian Federation
- Japan and possessions
- Norway and possessions
- India and possessions
- Italy
- New Zealand and possessions
- Australia and possessions
- US and possessions

B-H Bosnia and Herzegovina

The traditional lifestyles of peoples such as the Yanomami of Brazil were under ever greater threat from the destruction of the rainforest and encroaching urbanization.

The Americas

From the end of the 1970s the states of Central and South America began to shed their repressive regimes and move towards democracy. Economic instability, high population growth, and chronic inflation remained major problems. The US maintained its economic dominance and position as a world power-broker, retaining a hostility to Communism until 1985 when moves by a reforming USSR paved the way for a new world order.

The Americas			
1982: Falklands War between UK and Argentina	**1987:** US and USSR agree to limit intermediate nuclear weapons	**1991:** UN-brokered peace ends 10-year civil war in El Salvador	

1975 — 1980 — 1985 — 1990 — 1995 — 2000

1979: Start of civil war in Nicaragua between Sandinistas and US-backed Contras

1989: Democracy restored in Chile as Pinochet steps down

1991–92: USSR ends preferential trade agreement with Cuba; US tightens blockade

West and South Asia

In 1979, an Islamic revolution led by the Ayatollah Khomeini overthrew the corrupt regime of the Shah of Iran. Iran became an Islamic state, vilifying the West, governed by religious laws and ruthlessly suppressing political opposition.

Conflict continued throughout the Middle East, paralleled by a resurgence of a more fundamentalist form of Islam, especially in Iran. This led in turn to a destabilization of much of the western region, affecting particularly Lebanon, nearby Iraq, and Syria, and leading to a number of wars. Disputes over the boundaries between Israel and her neighbours, and Palestinian self-government proved difficult to resolve.

West and South Asia						
	1980: Start of Iran–Iraq War	**1984:** Assassination of Indira Gandhi by Sikh bodyguards	**1989:** USSR withdraws from Afghanistan	**1990:** Iraqi invasion of Kuwait sparks Gulf War	**1995:** Israeli-PLO agreement extends Palestinian self-rule within the West Bank	
1979: Islamic revolution in Iran						

1975 — 1980 — 1985 — 1990 — 1995 — 2000

1977: Start of Middle East peace process
1979: Soviet invasion of Afghanistan
1988: End of Iran–Iraq War
1996: Taliban forces capture Kabul

East and Southeast Asia

From the late 1970s, China sought closer links with the West and began a programme of industrial expansion. Calls for greater democracy were halted in 1989 following the massacre of students in Tiananmen Square. The Japanese economy boomed and Pacific Rim economies such as South Korea, Taiwan, Singapore, and Indonesia saw unprecedented industrial growth until an economic collapse in the late 1990s.

Cheaper labour costs led many firms to relocate their production to factories in China and Southeast Asia during the 1980s. These women are making toys for a Western firm in a factory near Guangzhou.

East and Southeast Asia					
		1989: Crushing of pro-democracy demonstrators in Beijing		**1998:** Economic crisis in Indonesia leads to overthrow of government	

1975 — 1980 — 1985 — 1990 — 1995 — 2000

1975: Indonesia annexes East Timor
1979: Vietnamese invasion of Cambodia ousts Pol Pot
1997: Hong Kong returned to Chinese rule

SEE ALSO:

North America: pp.136–137

South America: pp.152–153

Africa: pp.168–169

Europe: pp.214–215

West Asia: pp.234–235

South and Southeast Asia: pp.252–253

North and East Asia: pp.274–275

Australasia and Oceania: pp.284–285

THE COMPUTER AGE

Computer technology has revolutionized the way in which business is conducted internationally. Information can be transmitted in seconds and decisions made with equal speed across continents and time zones.

Brokers in a dealing room have access to information from across the world via their computers.

Imprisoned from 1962–90 for his fight against apartheid, Nelson Mandela was finally able to vote for a democratic South Africa in 1994, becoming its first black premier.

Africa

In South Africa, the political violence of the mid-1980s gave way to the breakdown of apartheid, and, in 1994, to the first completely democratic elections. In East and Central Africa, inter-ethnic warfare in Somalia, Sudan, and Rwanda led to the displacement of millions, while in North Africa, Islamic fundamentalism became a destabilizing force.

Africa					
1975: Independence in Angola and Mozambique followed by civil wars		**1987:** Famine in Ethiopia	**1994:** Non-racial elections held in South Africa; Nelson Mandela wins presidency		

1975 — 1980 — 1985 — 1990 — 1995 — 2000

1986: US bombs Libya
1994: Massacre of 500,000 Tutsis by Hutu in Rwanda
1997: President Mobutu overthrown in Zaire

HIDDEN WORLDS OF TODAY

THE WORLD ECONOMY at the end of the 20th century was dominated increasingly by investment trends and corporate business strategies determined at trans-continental and global rather than national levels. The World Trade Organization (WTO) formed in 1995 and enshrining liberal free trade principles, found itself tackling disputes as likely to be between trade blocs as between individual countries. The phenomenon of globalization was made possible, and greatly reinforced, by digital technology and the rapid growth of telecommunications. At the same time, links of ethnic origin, cultural affinity or religious identity were the defining characteristics of communities transcending national boundaries – such as the Islamic world. Across Europe, the trend towards economic integration was accompanied by some devolution of government, to meet demands for autonomy within existing states.

The production of illegal drugs occurs globally. These examples of 'kif' and opium were made in Morocco.

The Greater African Nation

The African diaspora in the Americas, originating with the slave trade in the 16th–18th centuries, is today over 80 million strong. Only the Caribbean states have majority black populations, but African Americans in the US are the world's fourth largest black community and Brazil's population is also in the world top ten. The UK's black minority is a more recent result of post-war immigration, as is Portugal's. The black community has few political ties internationally, but a shared sense of identity and awareness of their African roots.

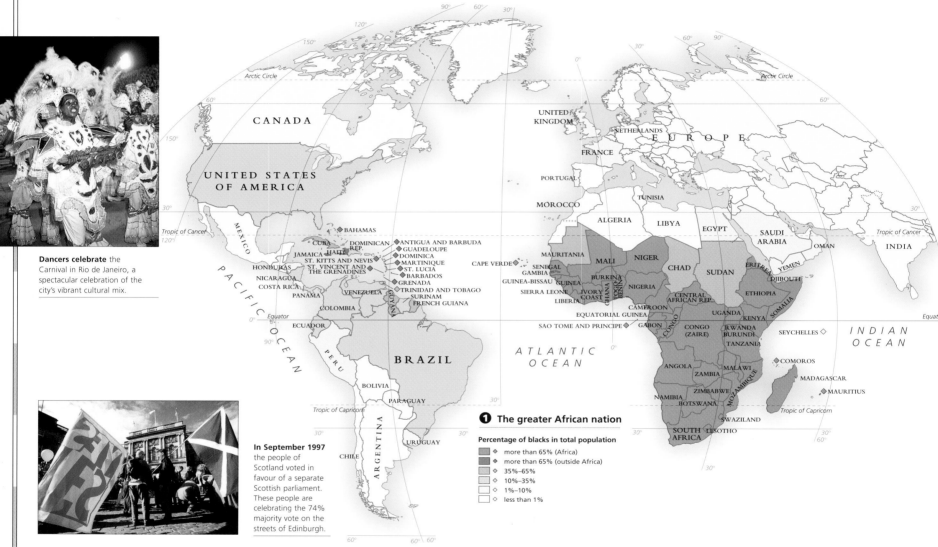

Dancers celebrate the Carnival in Rio de Janeiro, a spectacular celebration of the city's vibrant cultural mix.

In September 1997 the people of Scotland voted in favour of a separate Scottish parliament. These people are celebrating the 74% majority vote on the streets of Edinburgh.

❶ The greater African nation

Percentage of blacks in total population
- more than 65% (Africa)
- more than 65% (outside Africa)
- 35%–65%
- 10%–35%
- 1%–10%
- less than 1%

Devolution in Europe

Europe's new nation states of the 1990s emerged from the demise of the Soviet Union, the 'velvet divorce' of Czechs from Slovaks, and the bloody break-up of the former socialist Yugoslavia. Unresolved separatist aspirations persisted, notably among Albanian-speakers under Serbian rule in Kosovo, while Bosnia now barely exists beyond its separate Serb and Muslim-Croat 'entities'. Within the European Union, the archetype of 'supranational' integration, a federal system like Germany's gave substantial autonomy to state government. Belgium, riven by rivalries between the Flemish and the francophone Walloons, opted to devolve power to the regions – as did Spain, albeit not far enough for more militant Basques, while even centralist France held out special status plans for Corsica, and in Italy a separatist Northern League became a political force.

❷ Devolution and statehood in Europe
- new state since 1990
- a degree of devolution acknowledged
- substantial ethnic groups without their own state
- pressure for greater self-determination

Serbian persecution of ethnic Albanians in the Kosovo region of the rump state of Yugoslavia led, in early 1999 to air strikes against Serbia by NATO and the murder or exodus of hundreds of thousands of refugees, 'ethnically cleansed' from their former homes.

The pan-Islamic world

Sunni Islam is the dominant tradition in the Muslim world, under regimes ranging from secular states and conservative Gulf sheikdoms to the extreme militancy of the Afghani Taliban. Iran is the major contemporary Shi'a power – and the Iranian revolution the inspiration for Shi'a militancy elsewhere. Outside Iran, however, only Azerbaijan, Bahrain, and parts of Iraq have Shi'a majorities and even in Bahrain and Iraq it is Sunnis who hold power. Assad's regime in Syria is based on the Alawite minority, who follow a variant of Shi'a Islam.

The Muslim requirement for prayer to Mecca several times daily continues despite the restrictions posed by modern urban life. These Egyptian Muslims are praying in the middle of an Alexandria street.

SEE ALSO:

North America: pp.138–139

South America: p152–153

Africa: pp.168–169

Europe: pp.214–215

West Asia: pp.234–235

South and Southeast Asia: pp.252–253

North and East Asia: pp.274–275

❸ The pan–Islamic World

Percentage of Muslims in population
- 91–100%
- 51–90%
- 21–50%
- 6–20%
- 1–5%
- less than 1%

Official status of Islam
- ☪ formally designated Islamic republic
- ⬤ secular state where population is more then 50% Muslim
- 🏛 established religion is Islam
- ✳ membership of Organization of the Islamic Conference (OIC)
- ⚔ active conflict over militant Islam

THE WORLD WIDE WEB

Wide-area computer networking, developed originally for sharing information between academic institutions, expanded to become a worldwide Internet whose user numbers exploded in the 1990s. The big stimulus to its popular success was the creation of a graphical interface for 'surfing' hyperlinked sites on what became known as the World Wide Web. The opportunities for anonymity, the use of encrypted communications, and the problems of authentication and copyright protection posed great difficulties for policing and control.

This 'Internet Cafe' in Taiwan, offers diners access to the Internet while they eat.

The subterranean world of organized crime

Ease of travel and speed of communication encouraged the spread of organized crime syndicates far beyond national borders. As business became globalized, so too was corruption in business and finance; traditional criminal industries such as narcotics, prostitution, gambling, extortion, and money-laundering were transformed into global industries. Law enforcement had some successes in curtailing the Italian and US mafia, but the collapse of Communism in the Soviet Union created conditions in which a Russian mafia grew rapidly, becoming established across Eurasia and America. The big drug cartels, dealing in cocaine or heroin, fought for control of the production and distribution channels to the rich markets of North America and Europe. Profits, 'laundered' through other businesses and exploiting the confidentiality of banking systems, were used to acquire increasing political influence and protection.

❹ The world of organized crime

Narcotics production and trafficking
- cannabis production
- cocaine production
- heroin production
- heroin and cannabis production
- → heroin trafficking
- → cocaine trafficking
- → cannabis trafficking

Major centres for criminal organizations
- ◆ ● Mafia
- ◇ ○ Triads
- ⚗ major centre for drug-related crime
- ▭ drug transit centres
- — 'Golden Triangle'
- Ⓢ major centre for money laundering
- ⊘ murder rate greater than 8 per 100,000, with figure

Extent of international organized crime
- Italian Mafia
- Triads
- Jamaican Posses
- Russian Mafia
- Colombian cartels
- Japanese Yakuzas
- United States Cosa Nostra
- Turkish Mafia

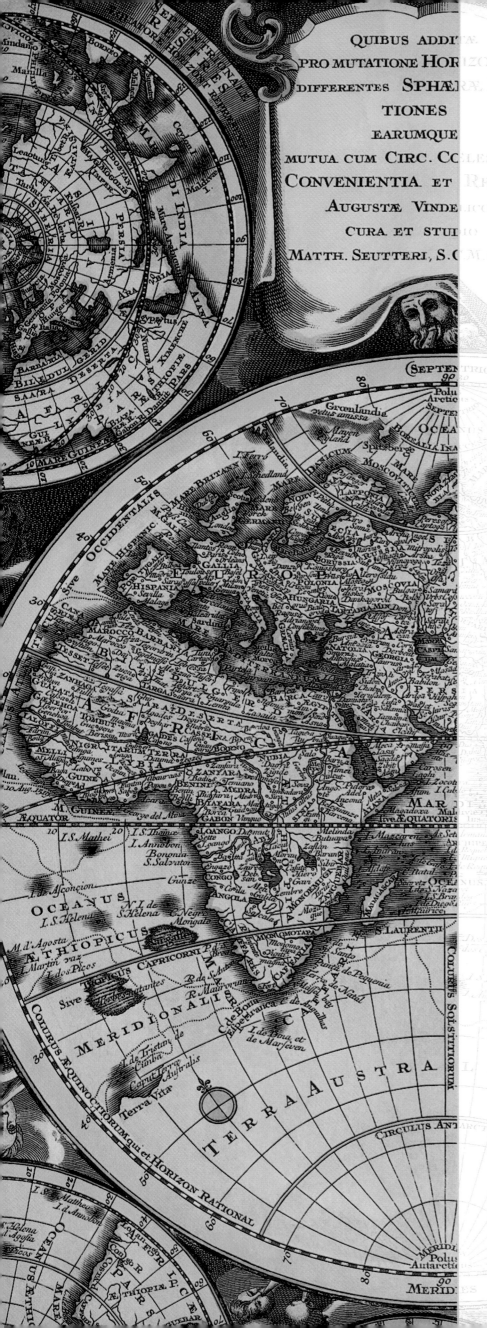

PART TWO
REGIONAL HISTORY

INHABITANTS OF EACH PART of the globe view the history of the world through the lens of their regional heritage. The second section of this atlas presents the chronological story of eight principal geographic regions: North America, South America, Africa, Europe, West Asia, South and Southeast Asia, North and East Asia and, finally, Australasia and Oceania. Each regional narrative is prefaced by a map which examines its historical geography. This is followed by pages covering the exploration and mapping of the area, showing how it came to be known in its present form. Thereafter, the maps are organized to present the continuous historical development of each region through time.

By the 18th century, the modern world map was clearly emerging. This map, produced by the Dutch cartographer, Matthias Seutter in 1730, combines a series of detailed projections of the various hemispheres, with compass points depicted as a variety of different windheads.

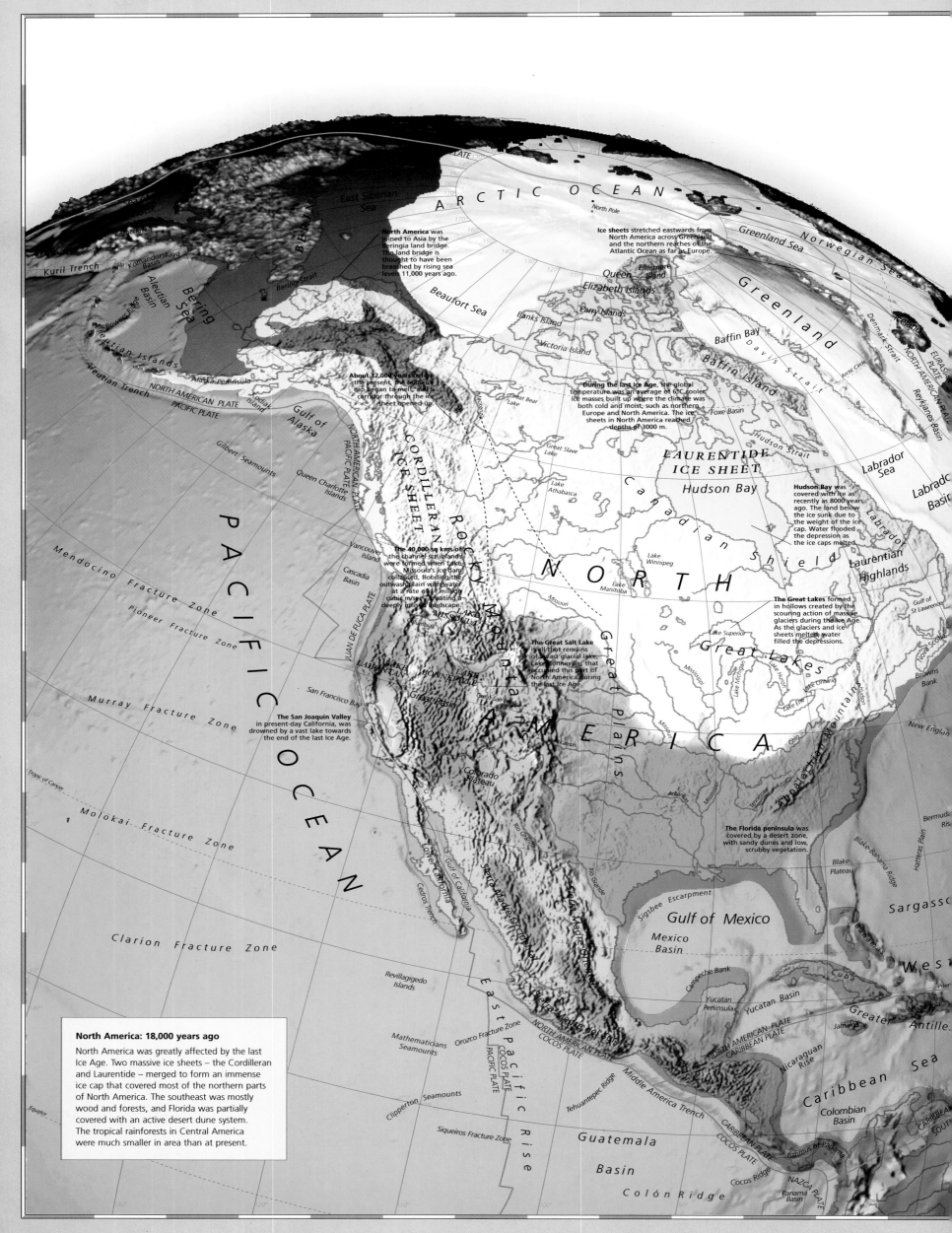

ARCTIC OCEAN

North Pole

North America was joined to Asia by the Beringia land bridge. The land bridge is thought to have been breached by rising sea levels 11,000 years ago.

Ice sheets stretched eastwards from North America across Greenland and the northern reaches of the Atlantic Ocean as far as Europe.

Norwegian Sea

Greenland Sea

Greenland

Denmark Strait

Iceland

NORTH AMERICAN PLATE

Reykjanes Basin

Queen Elizabeth Islands

Ellesmere Island

Baffin Bay

Davis Strait

Beaufort Sea

Banks Island

Barry Islands

Arctic Circle

Victoria Island

Foxe Basin

Baffin Island

Kuril Trench

Komandorskaya Basin

Kamchatka

East Siberian Sea

Siberia

BERING PLATE

150

170

160

140

130

120

Bowers Ridge

Aleutian Basin

Bering Strait

Bering Sea

Aleutian Islands

Aleutian Trench

Alaska Peninsula

NORTH AMERICAN PLATE

PACIFIC PLATE

Kodiak Island

Gulf of Alaska

Yukon

Mackenzie

Great Bear Lake

Hudson Strait

About 12,000 years before the present, the North ice cap began to melt and a corridor through the ice sheet opened up.

During the last Ice Age, the global temperature was an average of 6°C cooler. Ice masses built up where the climate was both cold and moist, such as northern Europe and North America. The ice sheets in North America reached depths of 3000 m.

LAURENTIDE ICE SHEET

Labrador Sea

Labrador Basin

Gilbert Seamounts

Queen Charlotte Islands

CORDILLERAN ICE SHEET

Great Slave Lake

Hudson Bay

Hudson Bay was covered with ice as recently as 8000 years ago. The land below the ice sunk due to the weight of the ice cap. Water flooded the depression as the ice caps melted.

Lake Athabasca

Canadian Shield

Laurentian Highlands

Gulf of St Lawrence

Vancouver Island

Cascadia Basin

ROCKY

NORTH AMERICAN PLATE

PACIFIC PLATE

Lake Winnipeg

NORTH

The 40,000 sq kms of the channel scrublands were formed when Lake Missoula's ice dam collapsed, flooding the outwash plain with water at a rate of 1 million cubic m/sec, creating a deeply incised landscape.

MOUNTAINS

Lake Manitoba

Missouri

Lake Superior

The Great Lakes formed in hollows created by the scouring action of massive glaciers during the Ice Age. As the glaciers and ice sheets melted, water filled the depressions.

Great Plains

Lake Michigan

Lake Huron

Lake Ontario

Lake Erie

Great Lakes

MENDOCINO FRACTURE ZONE

Pioneer Fracture Zone

San Francisco Bay

LAKE LAHONTAN

LAKE BONNEVILLE

Great Basin

Great Salt Lake

The Great Salt Lake is all that remains of a vast glacial lake, Lake Bonneville, that occupied this part of North America during the last Ice Age.

Columbia

Missouri

Arkansas

AMERICA

Ohio

New England

PACIFIC OCEAN

Murray Fracture Zone

The San Joaquin Valley in present-day California, was drowned by a vast lake towards the end of the last Ice Age.

Colorado Plateau

Rio Grande

Arkansas

Tennessee

Mississippi

Appalachian Mountains

Hudson

Browns Bank

Bermuda Rise

Molokai Fracture Zone

Tropic of Cancer

Lower California

Gulf of California

Cedros Trench

Sierra Madre Occidental

Sierra Madre Oriental

The Florida peninsula was covered by a desert zone, with sandy dunes and low, scrubby vegetation.

Sigsbee Escarpment

Blake Plateau

Blake-Bahama Ridge

Hatteras Plain

Sargasso

Clarion Fracture Zone

Revillagigedo Islands

Gulf of Mexico

Mexico Basin

Campeche Bank

Yucatan Peninsula

Yucatan Basin

Cuba

Greater Antilles

West

Mathematicians Seamounts

Orozco Fracture Zone

NORTH AMERICAN PLATE

COCOS PLATE

PACIFIC PLATE

East Pacific Rise

Middle America Trench

NAZCA PLATE

CARIBBEAN PLATE

Jamaica

Clipperton Seamounts

Tehuantepec Ridge

Guatemala Basin

Cocos Ridge

Isthmus of Panama

Nicaraguan Rise

Caribbean Sea

Colombian Basin

Panama Basin

Equator

Siqueiros Fracture Zone

Colón Ridge

North America: 18,000 years ago

North America was greatly affected by the last Ice Age. Two massive ice sheets – the Cordilleran and Laurentide – merged to form an immense ice cap that covered most of the northern parts of North America. The southeast was mostly wood and forests, and Florida was partially covered with an active desert dune system. The tropical rainforests in Central America were much smaller in area than at present.

Vegetation type

- ice cap and glacier
- tundra
- polar and alpine desert
- semi-desert or sparsely vegetated
- grassland
- forest or open woodland
- tropical rainforest
- temperate desert
- tropical desert
- coastline (present-day)
- coastline (18,000 years ago)

NORTH AMERICA
REGIONAL HISTORY

THE HISTORICAL LANDSCAPE

HUMANS FIRST ENTERED NORTH AMERICA FROM SIBERIA some 30,000 years ago. They migrated over the land bridge across the Bering Strait and, as the ice receded, moved south, into the rich gamelands of the Great Plains and onwards to eventually populate Central and South America. As the ice melted and sea levels rose, these early settlers and their new homeland became isolated from Eurasia, and would remain so until the second millennium CE. The low population level and abundance of foods meant that sedentary agricultural life evolved only sporadically, some groups sustaining a hunting and gathering way of life to the present day. During this period of isolation, unique ecological, genetic, and social patterns emerged which proved disastrously fragile when challenged by the first European colonists in the 15th century CE. Within 500 years the indigenous cultures of North America had been destroyed or marginalized by waves of migrants from the Old World who, with astonishing energy and ferocity, transformed the continent into the World's foremost economic, industrial, and political power.

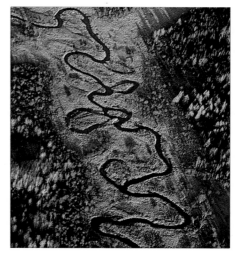

The gigantic basin drained by the Mississippi, spanning the entire tract between the Appalachians and the Rockies, provided a suitable environment for some of the first agricultural communities.

At the heart of the continent, it was the plains which provided homelands for Native North Americans, displaced and driven west by European immigrants.

The Central American mountain plateaux and uplands were where some of the earliest complex civilizations in North America developed. A combination of favourable climate and fertile land allowed plants to be cultivated and early agriculture to develop.

117

NORTH AMERICA
EXPLORATION AND MAPPING

Lewis (above) and Clark led an epic expedition to explore the west in 1805–06.

FOR MANY CENTURIES North America was untouched by contact with other continents. Viking seafarers en route from Iceland and Greenland made landfall at Newfoundland over 1000 years ago, but their settlements were short-lived and their area of operation quite limited. Not until the early 16th century was the presence of a vast continent across the Atlantic fully accepted, and knowledge about it remained fragmentary. Once Europeans began to investigate North America, they were able to draw heavily on information from indigenous peoples, and use their pre-existing trails to explore the continent.

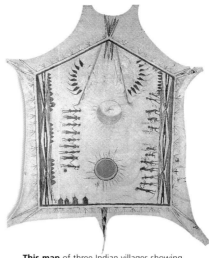

This map of three Indian villages showing their positions relative to the Sun and Moon was painted on a cured buffalo skin by members of the Qapaw tribe.

Native American maps

The indigenous peoples of North and Central America had detailed knowledge of the continent long before the first European expeditions. Much knowledge was undoubtedly passed on orally. But the location of early petroglyph maps carved on rocks suggests that they may have been produced as guides for travelling hunters, and to define territorial boundaries. Later maps – sometimes produced at the request of Europeans – reveal an intimate knowledge of the landscape and principles of space and distance. Several tribes used maps to show the long history of their tenure of the land when they were fighting for territory during the Indian removals of the 19th century.

Early European explorers

Though the first Europeans to visit North America were 10th-century Norsemen, European exploration began in earnest in the late 15th century when improvements in shipping made the longer exploratory voyages of Columbus and Cabot viable. By the mid-16th century Spanish-sponsored expeditions in search of gold and territory founded settlements in Florida, Central America, and the Caribbean, and explored the lands of the southeast and southwest. Meanwhile, English and French expeditions traced the Atlantic coast in detail, moving north in search of new routes to Asia.

① The first European explorers of North America

Norse expeditions
- Bjarni Herjolfsson 985–86
- Leif Eriksson 1003
- Thorvald Eriksson 1005–12

Spanish and Portuguese expeditions
- Christopher Columbus 1492–93
- Miguel Corte-Real 1501, 1502
- Christopher Columbus 1502–04
- Hernán Cortés 1519–21
- Juan Ponce de León 1513
- Panfilo de Narváez and Álvar Núñez Cabeza de Vaca 1528–36
- Francisco de Ulloa 1539–40
- Hernando de Soto 1539–43
- Francisco Vázquez de Coronado and Garcia Lopez de Cardeñas 1540–42
- Sebastián Vizcaíno 1602–03

English expeditions
- John Cabot 1497
- Martin Frobisher 1576–77
- Francis Drake 1579
- John Davis 1585–87
- Henry Hudson 1610–11

French expeditions
- Giovanni da Verrazano 1524
- Jacques Cartier 1535–36
- Samuel de Champlain 1604–07
- ○ European settlement 1608 and date of foundation

Map labels:
- 180°
- Iceland
- British Isles
- Arctic Circle
- Greenland
- Beaufort Sea
- Baffin Bay
- Mackenzie
- Great Bear Lake
- Gulf of Alaska
- Great Slave Lake
- Lake Athabasca
- **985:** Bjarni Herjolfsson sights land west and south of Greenland
- **1610:** Hudson reaches a 'spacious sea'
- Hudson Bay
- Labrador
- L'Anse aux Meadows c.1000
- **1497:** Cabot raises English flag on northern tip of Newfoundland
- **1535:** Cartier starts expedition into St. Lawrence River
- Newfoundland
- Rocky Mountains
- Lake Winnipeg
- Lake Superior
- Lake Huron
- Quebec 1608
- St. Lawrence
- Nova Scotia
- Great Plains
- Lake Michigan
- Lake Ontario
- Lake Erie
- Appalachian Mountains
- **1524:** Verrazano anchors close to present-day New York and is met by friendly native peoples
- **1579:** Drake sails north after raiding ports in Pacific South America. On landing near San Francisco Bay, he names the land New Albion
- Missouri
- Ohio
- Chesapeake Bay
- **1542:** Coronado's expedition sees vast herd of buffalo on Great Plains
- Jamestown 1607
- ATLANTIC OCEAN
- Tropic of Cancer
- Santa Fe 1609
- Arkansas
- Red River
- **1541:** Mississippi crossed for the first time by Europeans
- San Agustín 1565
- **1513:** de León's ships land at Florida, believing it to be an island
- **1492:** Christopher Columbus sights land now thought to be one of the Bahamian Islands
- Colorado
- Rio Grande
- Mississippi
- Lower California
- Sierra Madre Occidental
- Sierra Madre Oriental
- Bahamas
- Tropic of Cancer
- La Paz 1535
- Gulf of Mexico
- Cuba
- Santiago de Cuba
- San Juan 1509
- Hispaniola
- Santo Domingo 1496
- Lesser Antilles
- Tampico 1528
- Guadalajara 1531
- Tenochtitlan (Mexico City)
- **1521:** Cortés destroys Aztec capital Tenochtitlan
- Vera Cruz 1519
- Sierra Madre del Sur
- Greater Antilles
- Caribbean Sea
- PACIFIC OCEAN
- **1529–34:** Cabeza de Vaca and three men including African Estebán are only survivors of Narváez expedition after being enslaved by coastal Indians
- Acapulco 1565
- Isthmus of Panama
- **1513:** Vasco Núñez de Balboa is first explorer to sight Pacific Ocean
- SOUTH AMERICA
- 1000 km
- 1000 miles

This map of Florida and Chesapeake Bay (above) was painted in the late 16th century. The spatial relationships are very inaccurate, with the Caribbean islands depicted much too far to the north.

European explorers were astonished by the quantity of wildlife they encountered in North America (left). Fur-bearing animals such as beavers were quickly exploited for their pelts.

15th- and 16th-century European expeditions

- **1497:** Cabot lands on Newfoundland
- **1501:** Miguel Corte-Real enslaves 50 Indians from Beothuk
- **1524:** Verrazano sails up Atlantic coast as far as Nova Scotia
- **1539–43:** De Soto explores southeastern North America
- **1492:** Columbus lands in the Bahamas thinking he has reached Asia
- **1513:** Ponce de León traces coast of Florida
- **1528:** Cabeza de Vaca explores Gulf of Mexico and southwest
- **1534:** Cartier begins exploration of St. Lawrence

Timeline: 1490 · 1500 · 1510 · 1520 · 1530 · 1540

Exploring the eastern interior

The rich Atlantic fisheries and the bounteous wildlife of the northeast were magnets for European hunters and fishermen, and many of the earliest settlements were fur-trading posts. Samuel de Champlain, aided by Iroquois and Montagnais, explored the St. Lawrence and the Great Lakes, while Hudson and Davis ventured further west into Canada's great bays. Other expeditions were undertaken for missionary purposes, including Jolliet's Mississippian journey, where he was accompanied by Father Marquette. During the late 17th and early 18th centuries, several expeditions sought routes through the Appalachians, which would open up the Midwest to settlers.

One of America's great frontiersmen, Daniel Boone, is shown here leading a group of settlers through the Cumberland Gap, a pass through the Appalachian system which provided a route to the West.

By the late 17th century knowledge of the east coast of North America had improved significantly. This plate from Visscher's *Atlas Contractus* of 1671 shows the Atlantic coast from New England south as far as Chesapeake Bay. Detail of the lands further west and the Great Lakes remained limited.

❷ Journeys into the North American interior 1600–1775

British expeditions
→ John Smith 1608
⇢ Thomas Batts and Robert Fallam 1671
⇠ James Needham and Gabriel Arthur 1673
⋯ Dr Henry Woodward 1674, 1685

French expeditions
→ Samuel de Champlain 1609–16
⇢ Medart Chouart des Groseillers and Pierre-Esprit Radisson 1659–1660
⋯ Father Claude Allouez 1665–67
— Father Charles Albanel 1671–72
→ Louis Jolliet and Jacques Marquette 1672–73
→ René-Robert Cavelier Sieur de la Salle 1684–87
→ Louis Hennepin 1680
⋯ Chaussegros de Léry 1729

Dutch expeditions
→ Arnout Viele 1682–84
→ Johannes Rosebloom 1685–87

American expeditions
→ Christopher Gist 1750–51
⇢ Thomas Walker 1750
⋯ Daniel Boone 1769–71

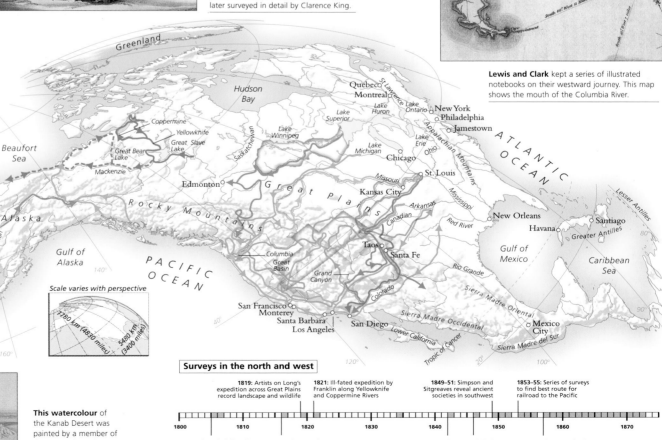

1671: Guided by Indians, Batts and Fallam become first Europeans to cross Appalachians and reach Mississippi watershed

1750: Walker reaches Cumberland Gap, the gateway to Kentucky

1607: Settlement founded by 120 colonists from England

17th- and 18th-century expeditions in eastern North America

1609–13: Champlain explores St. Lawrence and eastern Great Lakes	**1665–67:** Father Allouez explores Great Lakes	**1673:** Jolliet and Marquette explore Mississippi and Illinois Rivers	**1752:** John Finley realizes that Cumberland Gap is gateway to Kentucky lowlands
1600	1650	1700	1750
1607–08: John Smith leads colonizing expeditions in Virginia	**1673:** Needham and Arthur follow Occaneechee Path across Appalachians	**1682:** La Salle follows Mississippi to its mouth	**1729:** de Léry makes first proper survey of Allegheny and upper Ohio Rivers

Charting the West

The rapid expansion of the US created the need to survey and quantify the vast territories of the new nation. Lewis and Clark's famous cross-continental expedition was funded by Congress at the express request of President Jefferson. Fremont conducted his reconnaissance of the west under the auspices of the US Army's Corps of Topographical Engineers. The highly competitive railroad surveys of the 1850s were inspired by economic and political considerations, while Clarence King's survey of the western deserts was motivated primarily by scientific curiosity.

An illustration from Lieutenant Fremont's *Memoirs* shows members of his Great Basin survey team camped on the shores of the Pyramid Lake. The lake was later surveyed in detail by Clarence King.

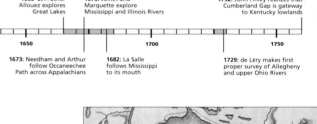

Lewis and Clark kept a series of illustrated notebooks on their westward journey. This map shows the mouth of the Columbia River.

❸ 19th-century exploration and surveys of the US and Canada

Individual expeditions
→ Meriwether Lewis and William Clark 1805–07
→ Lt. Zebulon M. Pike 1806–07
→ Major Stephen Long 1819–20
→ Lt. John Franklin 1820–21
⇢ Lt. John Franklin 1825–27
→ Lt. John C. Fremont 1842–44
→ Lt. William Emory 1846
→ Lt. James Simpson and Capt. Lorenzo Sitgreaves 1849–51
→ Lt. John Palliser 1857–59

Other expeditions and surveys
→ Russian expeditions to Alaska 1816–65
→ Western Railroad surveys 1853–55
→ Western Union Telegraph survey 1865–67
→ Canadian Yukon Exploring expedition 1887–89

Survey areas
■ Henry Hind 1857–58
■ George Wheeler 1867–72
■ Clarence King 1867–73

This watercolour of the Kanab Desert was painted by a member of the US Geological Survey team in 1880.

Scale varies with perspective

7780 km (4830 miles)
5480 km (3400 miles)

Surveys in the north and west

1819: Artists on Long's expedition across Great Plains record landscape and wildlife	**1821:** Ill-fated expedition by Franklin along Yellowknife and Coppermine Rivers	**1849–51:** Simpson and Sitgreaves reveal ancient societies in southwest	**1853–55:** Series of surveys to find best route for railroad to the Pacific	
1800	1810	1820	1830	1840 1850 1860 1870
1805–06: Lewis and Clark explore new land acquired in the Louisiana Purchase and reach Pacific coast	**1816:** Start of Russian exploration of Alaska	**1842:** Fremont begins series of expeditions to map American west and encourage settlement	**1846:** Emory surveys Spanish territory during Mexican War	**1857–72:** Wheeler produces first contour maps of southwest

EARLY PEOPLES OF NORTH AMERICA

The Hopewell produced beautifully-made grave offerings for burial with their dead, such as this hand, carved from a flat sheet of mica.

THE FIRST PEOPLE to settle North America are thought to have crossed over from Asia during the last Ice Age – more than 25,000 years ago. They probably spread out initially along the Pacific coast, only moving further north and southeast when the glaciers began to melt about 15,000 years ago. By about 11,000 BCE, significant hunting activities were taking place further south and many of the largest mammals, such as the woolly mammoth, may have become extinct through hunting. Once humans were established in Central America, they quickly became more sedentary, simple village structures evolving within a small time frame into far more complex societies. The archaeological evidence left by the Olmec and Zapotec in Central America, and the burial mounds of the Adena and Hopewell of the American southeast reveal sophisticated societies.

The hunter-gatherers

Hunter-gatherers recorded events in their lives on the walls of caves. This series of images from Cueva Flecha in Lower California, shows humans and animals pierced by spears – perhaps as a result of conflict with other groups in the area.

The first peoples of North and Central America banded together in egalitarian, extended-family groups, living by hunting and gathering. They eventually become specialized and adapted to the continent's various ecological niches: plains, mountains, deserts, woodlands, river valleys, and coastal areas. Specially-adapted spear points and other weaponry reveal the major prey species in different culture areas. The fine 'Clovis-pointed' spearheads were used by plains hunters to kill bison, barbed harpoon heads were developed by coastal peoples for spearing marine creatures; and darts with stone heads were thrown by the basin and mountain dwellers at the wildfowl which provided them with the bulk of their diet.

The first farmers

Agriculture in North America

emerged only gradually but proved revolutionary in its impact. Animal husbandry was largely absent, with only a few animals truly domesticated. In Central America, a few plants were cultivated as a supplement to hunting and gathering as early as 5000 BCE. New plants – especially maize, beans, and squash were brought under cultivation and soon offered a more secure food source. Hunting bands became seasonally sedentary and then semi-sedentary, until between 2500 and 1400 BCE Central America was dominated by settled horticultural villages. Further north, the earliest crops served initially as supplements rather than staples. Agriculture gradually became more important throughout the 1st millennium CE, with villagers becoming largely agricultural by the beginning of the 2nd millennium.

Maize and squash were first cultivated 7000 years ago. Through selective breeding, maize changed from a small grass with individual hulls over each seed, to a single husk over the entire ear which grew on a cob.

Dogs, honey bees, and turkeys were the first animals to be domesticated in North America – the latter spreading south into Central America 2000 years ago.

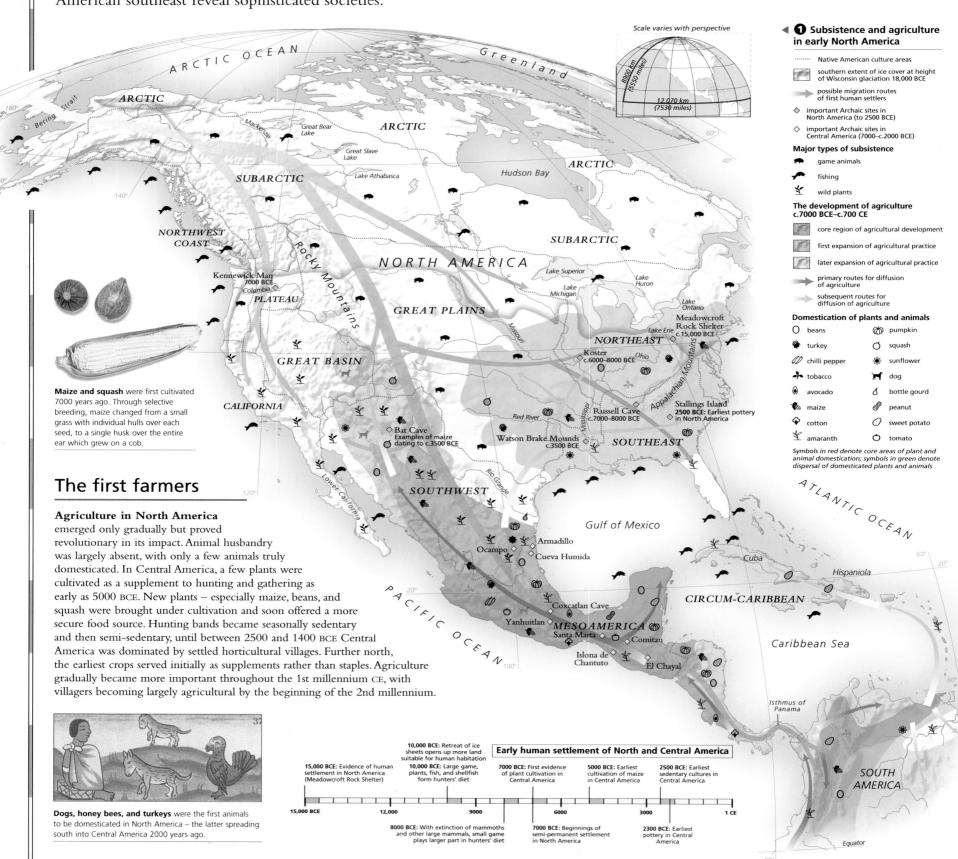

❶ Subsistence and agriculture in early North America

- ⋯⋯ Native American culture areas
- southern extent of ice cover at height of Wisconsin glaciation 18,000 BCE
- ➡ possible migration routes of first human settlers
- ◇ important Archaic sites in North America (to 2500 BCE)
- ◇ important Archaic sites in Central America (7000–c.2000 BCE)

Major types of subsistence

- game animals
- fishing
- wild plants

The development of agriculture c.7000 BCE–c.700 CE

- core region of agricultural development
- first expansion of agricultural practice
- later expansion of agricultural practice
- ➡ primary routes for diffusion of agriculture
- ➡ subsequent routes for diffusion of agriculture

Domestication of plants and animals

beans	pumpkin
turkey	squash
chilli pepper	sunflower
tobacco	dog
avocado	bottle gourd
maize	peanut
cotton	sweet potato
amaranth	tomato

Symbols in red denote core areas of plant and animal domestication; symbols in green denote dispersal of domesticated plants and animals

Map labels

ARCTIC OCEAN
Greenland
ARCTIC
ARCTIC
Bering Strait
Mackenzie
Great Bear Lake
Great Slave Lake
Lake Athabasca
Hudson Bay
ARCTIC
SUBARCTIC
SUBARCTIC
NORTHWEST COAST
Rocky Mountains
NORTH AMERICA
Lake Superior
Lake Michigan
Lake Huron
Lake Ontario
Lake Erie
Kennewick Man 7000 BCE Columbia
PLATEAU
GREAT PLAINS
Missouri
Meadowcroft Rock Shelter c.15,000 BCE
NORTHEAST
GREAT BASIN
Koster c.6000–8000 BCE Ohio
Appalachian Mountains
CALIFORNIA
Red River
Russell Cave c.7000–8000 BCE
Stallings Island 2500 BCE: Earliest pottery in North America
Bat Cave Examples of maize dating to c.3500 BCE
Watson Brake Mounds c.3500 BCE
Mississippi
SOUTHEAST
Lower California
SOUTHWEST
Rio Grande
Gulf of Mexico
ATLANTIC OCEAN
PACIFIC OCEAN
Ocampo
Armadillo
Cueva Humida
Cuba
Hispaniola
CIRCUM-CARIBBEAN
Coxcatlan Cave
Yanhuitlan
MESOAMERICA
Santa Marta
Comitan
Caribbean Sea
Islona de Chantuto
El Chayal
Isthmus of Panama
SOUTH AMERICA
Equator
Scale varies with perspective
8900 km (5530 miles)
12,070 km (7530 miles)

Early human settlement of North and Central America

15,000 BCE: Evidence of human settlement in North America (Meadowcroft Rock Shelter)

10,000 BCE: Retreat of ice sheets opens up more land suitable for human habitation

10,000 BCE: Large game, plants, fish, and shellfish form hunters' diet

7000 BCE: First evidence of plant cultivation in Central America

5000 BCE: Earliest cultivation of maize in Central America

2500 BCE: Earliest sedentary cultures in Central America

8000 BCE: With extinction of mammoths and other large mammals, small game plays larger part in hunters' diet

7000 BCE: Beginnings of semi-permanent settlement in North America

2300 BCE: Earliest pottery in Central America

15,000 BCE   12,000   9000   6000   3000   1 CE

Early civilizations of Central America

With the establishment of village life, the earliest complex settlements occurred in the tropical lowlands from the Gulf of Mexico across the Isthmus of Tehuantepec to the Pacific coast of present-day Guatemala. Increasingly sophisticated societies were made possible by new crops and productive soils. The Olmec civilization – widely regarded as the mother culture of Central America – emerged on the Gulf Coast c.1150 BCE and persisted as an important culture until 400 BCE. Slightly later than the Olmecs, the Valley of Oaxaca witnessed the development of a sophisticated society, and by 500 BCE, complex chiefdoms or early states dominated the three interconnected valleys of central Oaxaca. At their juncture, the Zapotecs built the hilltop city of Monte Albán which would dominate the region for over 1000 years. Further south, Kaminaljuyú emerged by c.500 BCE, but a nearby volcanic eruption c.250–200 BCE, and consequent mass migration, deprived the site of much of the population in the southern part of its trading area. In the highlands south of Yucatan, the Maya civilization was starting to emerge as early as 1000 BCE.

This Olmec ceremonial adze from La Venta is carved from the pale green jade typical of the site.

The Olmecs

The earliest civilization in Central America, the Olmecs initiated the Mesoamerican pantheon of gods, gave rise to kings and classes, and fought wars, as well as trading over vast distances and heavily influencing other cultures. They built elaborate platforms and mounds, made fine ceramics, worked precious stone, engaged in complex and sophisticated stone sculpture, established the Mesoamerican calendar, and invented the syllabary writing system. By 500–400 BCE, the Olmecs began withdrawing into their homeland and, though remaining an intellectually vibrant culture throughout the 1st millennium BCE, ceased to influence groups elsewhere directly.

❸ The heartland of the Olmecs

- ● important Olmec centre
- ⊕ Olmec sculpture site

(Map 3: The heartland of the Olmecs — sites include El Mesón, Nestepe, Isla de Tenaspi, Tres Zapotes (Thought to be last important Olmec centre), San Martín Pajapan, Llano del Jicaro, Los Soldados, La Venta (Became important Olmec site following demise of San Lorenzo), Laguna de los Cerros, Antonio Plaza, Arroyo Sonso, Cruz del Milagro, Tenochtitlán, San Lorenzo (Thrived between 1200 and 900 BCE – probably the earliest Olmec ceremonial centre), Potrero Nuevo, Estero Rabón, Los Idolos, Medias Aguas, Las Limas)

❷ Early civilizations of Central America

- area of Olmec influence
- area of Maya influence c.1000 BCE
- additional area of Maya influence c.800 BCE
- area of Zapotec influence

- ◇ site settled by, or influenced by the Olmecs
- ◆ other sites from formative period
- ➡ main Olmec trade routes

Mineral resources
- basalt
- obsidian
- iron ore (magnetite)
- serpentine
- green jade

(Map 2: Early civilizations of Central America — place names include Pavón, El Opéño, Chupicuaro, El Trapiche, El Viejon, Tlatilco, Cuicuilco, Tlapacoya, Remojadas, Gualupita, Cerro de las Mesas, Taxla, Chalcatzingo, Las Bocas, Tres Zapotes, Laguna de los Cerros, Capacha, Mezcala, Oxtotitlán Cave, San José Mogote, La Venta, San Lorenzo, Juxtlahuaca Cave, Monte Albán, Valley of Oaxaca, Cerro de la Bomba, Dainzú, San Jerónimo, Zanja, Boca de Río, Padre Piedra, Pijijiapan, Aquiles Serdán, Altamira, Izapa, San Isidro Piedra Parada, Kaminaljuyú, Copán, Yarumela, La Victoria, La Blanca, Abaj Takalik, Las Victorias, Ilopango, Chalchuapa, Yojoa, Los Naranjos, Playa de los Muertos, Dzibilchaltún, Chichén Itzá, Maní, Becan, Cuello, El Mirador, Uaxactún, Barton Ramie, Tikal, Xunantunich, Seibal, Altar de Sacrificios, Xoc, Santa Cruz, Chiapa de Corzo, Balancán)

Early civilizations of North and Central America

c.1150: Start of Olmec civilization	800: Evidence that Maya beginning to spread northward into Yucatan peninsula	500: Settlement of Monte Albán	400: Beginning of Olmec decline	
1200 BCE — **1000** — **800** — **600** — **400** — **200 BCE**				
1100: Establishment of Poverty Point in present-day Louisiana, an early non-agrarian settlement	700: Start of Adena culture		c.250: El Mirador, the largest early Maya city flourishing. Sites, such as Becan, fortified	

The moundbuilders of the eastern river valleys

The Adena culture was found in the upper Ohio valley as early as 700 BCE. Settlements were centred on burial mounds and extensive earthworks. Their grave goods included jewellery made from imported copper, carved tablets, and tubular pipes – which provide evidence of the early cultivation of tobacco *(see Map 1)*. The Hopewell culture had emerged by c.100 CE, and spread throughout the Mississippi Valley, sustained by small-scale agriculture. They created a complex and far-reaching trade network to source the many raw materials – including obsidian, quartz, shells, teeth, and copper – used in their characteristic animal and bird sculptures. Elements of Hopewell culture appear to have been adopted by many other Indian groups.

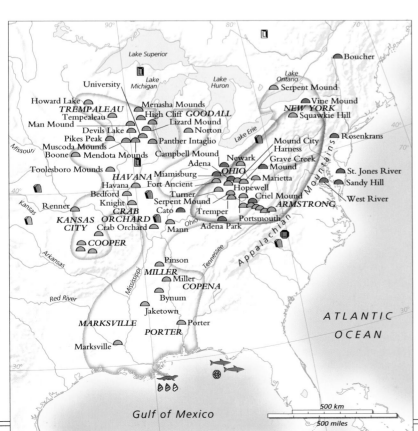

❹ Moundbuilders of eastern North America c.700 BCE–c.400 CE

- Adena heartland
- ⌂ Adena site
- Hopewell area of influence
- *OHIO* Hopewell cultural area
- ⌂ Hopewell burial mound site
- ⌂ effigy mound site

Resources traded by the Hopewell
- chert
- chlorite
- obsidian
- silver
- copper
- galena
- mica crystals
- olive shell
- tulip shell
- whelks
- turtle
- alligator
- barracuda
- shark

(Map 4: Moundbuilders of eastern North America — place names include University, Howard Lake, TREMPEALEAU, Tempealeau, Man Mound, Menasha Mounds, High Cliff, GOODALL, Lizard Mound, NEW YORK, Squawkie Hill, Vine Mound, Devils Lake, Pikes Peak, Norton, Rosenkrans, Muscoda Mounds, Panther Intaglio, Mound City, Harness, Boone, Mendota Mounds, Campbell Mound, Newark, Grave Creek Mound, St. Jones River, Toolesboro Mounds, Miamisburg, Adena, OHIO, Marietta, Sandy Hill, HAVANA, Havana, Fort Ancient, Hopewell, Bedford, Knight, Criel Mound, West River, Serpent Mound, Cato, ARMSTRONG, CRAB ORCHARD, KANSAS CITY, Crab Orchard, Tremper, Portsmouth, Mann, Adena Park, COOPER, Pinson, MILLER, Miller, COPENA, Bynum, Jaketown, Porter, MARKSVILLE, PORTER, Marksville, Serpent Mound, Boucher, Lake Superior, Lake Michigan, Lake Huron, Lake Ontario, Lake Erie, Appalachian Mountains)

The Hopewell produced many objects in the shape of animals including birds, beavers, and bears. The frog adorns a platform effigy pipe; tobacco was placed in a bowl in its back and inhaled through the hole in the front of the pipe.

CITIES AND EMPIRES

Hollow pottery dogs, typical of the highly realistic ceramics of western Mexico, are common grave offerings.

CENTRAL AMERICA was split into Mexican and Maya areas, between which there were some major differences, including languages, writing systems, and art and architectural styles. City-states dominated both areas: in the Maya area these tended to be small, multi-city regional polities or autonomous cities, while Mexico was dominated by a series of empires. The peoples of southern North America were turning to sedentary agriculture and establishing settled communities. Several overlapping cultures settled the desert southwest, including the Hohokam, Anasazi, and Mogollon. In the southeast, larger settlements in the Mississippi valley replaced the Hopewell by 800 CE.

Central American civilizations 400–1400

Teotihuacan emerged as the capital of the first major empire in the 1st century CE and influenced cities throughout Mexico and Guatemala, spreading ideas and innovations. The multi-ethnic city reached a population of 125,000–200,000 by 500,

exporting goods to the rest of Central America. By 550, Teotihuacan was in decline, and by 750, the city was largely abandoned. The resulting political vacuum encouraged the rise of several independent, fortified hilltop cities from about 650, including Cacaxtla and Xochicalco. All had extensive trade links and varying degrees of contact with other cultures. Centred at Tula, the Toltec Empire emerged in the 10th century. The Toltecs were traders, trading as far south as Costa Rica and north into the desert. Drought undermined Tula's agriculture and by 1168, it was abandoned.

Teotihuacan was centrally planned, laid out in a grid, and dominated by huge pyramids which would have held temples on their summits. It traded over much of Central America, dealing in obsidian products, ceramics, stone carvings, and featherwork.

These massive basalt figures stand on top of the central pyramid at Tula, the Toltec capital. The city reached a peak population of 60,000 inhabitants, with an equal number in the immediate hinterland.

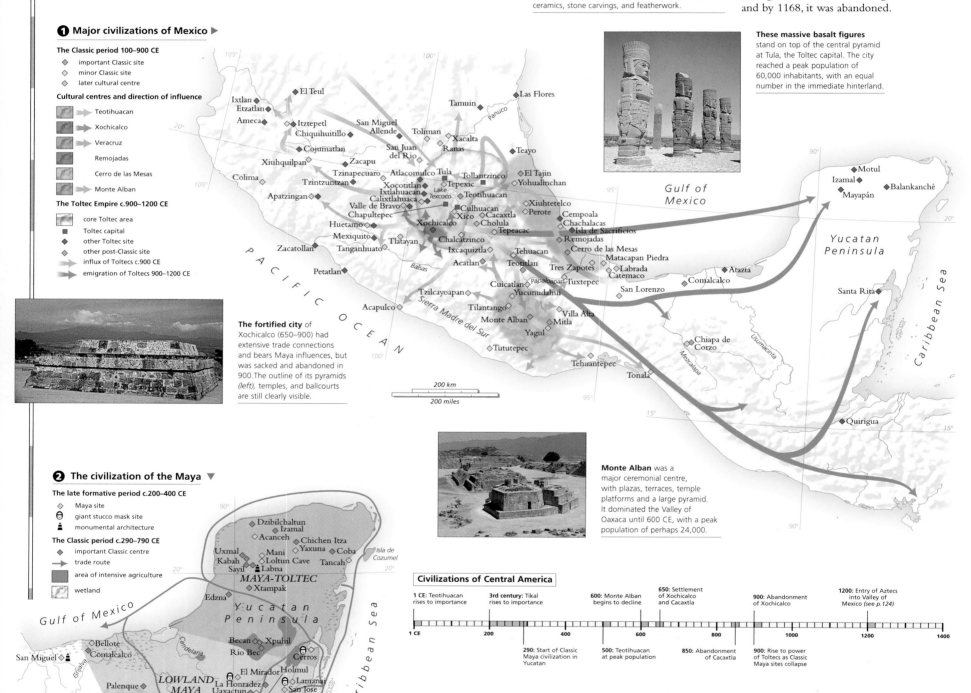

① Major civilizations of Mexico ▶

The Classic period 100–900 CE
◇ important Classic site
◇ minor Classic site
◇ later cultural centre

Cultural centres and direction of influence
→ Teotihuacan
→ Xochicalco
→ Veracruz
Remojadas
Cerro de las Mesas
→ Monte Alban

The Toltec Empire c.900–1200 CE
□ core Toltec area
■ Toltec capital
◆ other Toltec site
◆ other post-Classic site
→ influx of Toltecs c.900 CE
→ emigration of Toltecs 900–1200 CE

The fortified city of Xochicalco (650–900) had extensive trade connections and bears Maya influences, but was sacked and abandoned in 900. The outline of its pyramids *(left)*, temples, and ballcourts are still clearly visible.

Monte Alban was a major ceremonial centre, with plazas, terraces, temple platforms and a large pyramid. It dominated the Valley of Oaxaca until 600 CE, with a peak population of perhaps 24,000.

② The civilization of the Maya ▼

The late formative period c.200–400 CE
◇ Maya site
☉ giant stucco mask site
▪ monumental architecture

The Classic period c.290–790 CE
◇ important Classic centre
— trade route
▨ area of intensive agriculture
▨ wetland

Civilizations of Central America

1200: Entry of Aztecs into Valley of Mexico (see p.124)

1 CE: Teotihuacan rises to importance
3rd century: Tikal rises to importance
600: Monte Alban begins to decline
650: Settlement of Xochicalco and Cacaxtla
900: Abandonment of Xochicalco

290: Start of Classic Maya civilization in Yucatan
500: Teotihuacan at peak population
850: Abandonment of Cacaxtla
900: Rise to power of Toltecs as Classic Maya sites collapse

1 CE 200 400 600 800 1000 1200 1400

The city-states of the Maya

The jungle of Guatemala and Yucatan became the centre for the florescence of Maya civilization. Many city-states emerged, sometimes linked by elite marriages and sometimes by descent, but political ties were few and fleeting. The Classic Maya civilization is thought to be the first fully literate culture of the Americas, developing a hieroglyphic writing system. Classic Maya cities were characterized by their massive size and structural complexity. Following 700, many cities were abandoned and the focus of Maya civilization shifted to the northern lowlands.

The corbelled Arch of Labna in northern Yucatan dates from the late Classic period. Its intricate reliefs and massive size typify Maya archtecture during this period.

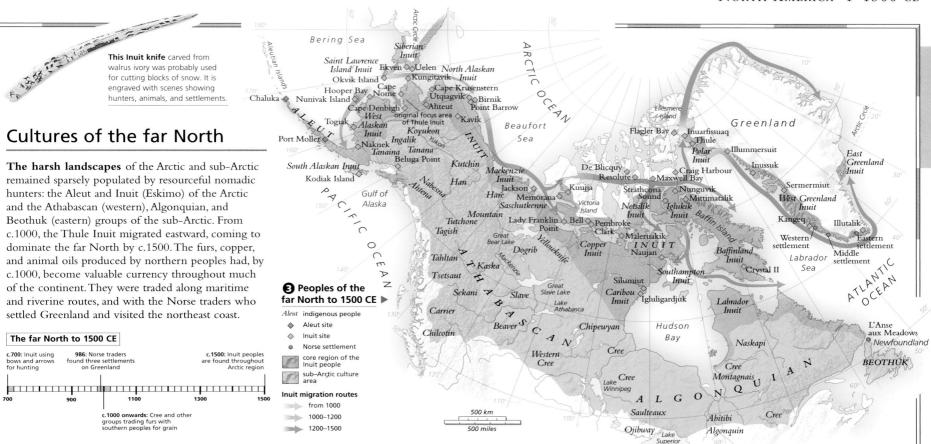

This **Inuit knife** carved from walrus ivory was probably used for cutting blocks of snow. It is engraved with scenes showing hunters, animals, and settlements.

Cultures of the far North

The harsh landscapes of the Arctic and sub-Arctic remained sparsely populated by resourceful nomadic hunters: the Aleut and Inuit (Eskimo) of the Arctic and the Athabascan (western), Algonquian, and Beothuk (eastern) groups of the sub-Arctic. From c.1000, the Thule Inuit migrated eastward, coming to dominate the far North by c.1500. The furs, copper, and animal oils produced by northern peoples had, by c.1000, become valuable currency throughout much of the continent. They were traded along maritime and riverine routes, and with the Norse traders who settled Greenland and visited the northeast coast.

The far North to 1500 CE

- **c.700:** Inuit using bows and arrows for hunting
- **986:** Norse traders found three settlements on Greenland
- **c.1500:** Inuit peoples are found throughout Arctic region
- **c.1000 onwards:** Cree and other groups trading furs with southern peoples for grain

③ Peoples of the far North to 1500 CE ▶

Aleut indigenous people
- ◆ Aleut site
- ◇ Inuit site
- ● Norse settlement
- core region of the Inuit people
- sub-Arctic culture area

Inuit migration routes
- → from 1000
- → 1000–1200
- → 1200–1500

The American Southwest

In the Southwest, sedentary ways of life increased throughout the 1st millennium CE, producing villages and cliff dwellings, such those of the Hohokam in Arizona, after 1000, and regional polities such as Chaco Canyon and Casas Grandes. The Hohokam developed irrigation systems to allow them to grow maize in the arid semi-desert and built multi-storey pueblos: storehouses and dwellings of stone or adobe sometimes with ball courts and low platform mounds. The Anasazi and Mogollon peoples left evidence of pueblos constructed for defensive purposes – probably to counter other hostile groups who entered the area from c.1300. Increasing aridity caused a decline in the southwest after 1250 leaving only dispersed puebloan groups.

The Mimbres branch of the Mogollon culture produced spectacular pottery, usually for burial purposes. The pots, adorned with geometric designs, were often ritually 'killed' by having a hole drilled through their base.

Settlement in the Southwest to 1500

- **100:** Emergence of Hohokam and Mogollon cultures
- **800:** Mimbres pottery starts to be made by Mogollon
- **1050:** Pueblos built for defensive purposes by Anasazi
- **1200:** Peak of importance of Chaco Canyon
- **c.950:** Flourishing pueblo culture in Southwest
- **1100:** Construction of the Cliff Palace at Mesa Verde
- **1350:** Most Anasazi pueblos abandoned – probably due to drought

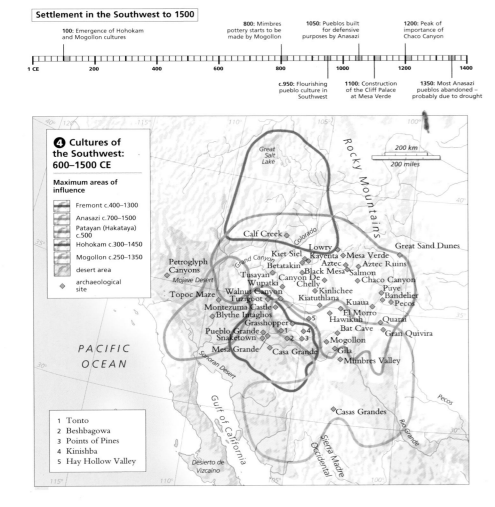

④ Cultures of the Southwest: 600–1500 CE

Maximum areas of influence
- Fremont c.400–1300
- Anasazi c.700–1500
- Patayan (Hakataya) c.500
- Hohokam c.300–1450
- Mogollon c.250–1350
- desert area
- ◆ archaeological site

1 Tonto
2 Beshbagowa
3 Points of Pines
4 Kinishba
5 Hay Hollow Valley

The American South and Mississippi Valley

In eastern North America there were improvements in agricultural technology, and crops such as beans and new varieties of maize were imported from Mexico. There was a developmental hiatus for about 400 years following the decline of the Hopewell trading empire but from c.800, settlements grew larger until, in around 1000, the Mississippian chiefdoms emerged, leading to more regional integration and significantly greater social differentiation. Many centres including sites such as Etowah and Moundville, became regional foci, with the largest being Cahokia, with a peak population of 15,000.

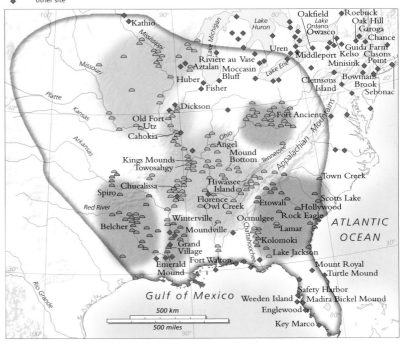

⑤ Mississippian cultures of eastern North America

Areas of influence and temple mound sites
- Middle Mississippian
- South Appalachian
- Fort Ancient
- extent of secondary Mississippian influence
- Plaquemine Mississippian
- Caddoan Mississippian
- Oneota
- ◆ other site

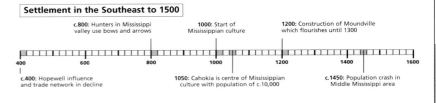

This sculpted soapstone pipe from the Spiro mound site is thought to depict a warrior beheading his victim.

Settlement in the Southeast to 1500

- **c.800:** Hunters in Mississippi valley use bows and arrows
- **1000:** Start of Mississippian culture
- **1200:** Construction of Moundville which flourishes until 1300
- **c.400:** Hopewell influence and trade network in decline
- **1050:** Cahokia is centre of Mississippian culture with population of c.10,000
- **c.1450:** Population crash in Middle Mississippi area

COMPETING EMPIRES

Quetzalcoatl, the god of wind, was one of a pantheon of gods worshipped by the Aztecs.

UNTIL THE EUROPEAN INCURSIONS of the late 15th century, North and Central America remained largely untouched by contacts with other continents. Spanish explorers and traders, seeking new routes and markets, first reconnoitred the Caribbean islands and Central America, returning later to claim Mexico, the Caribbean and much of the southern half of America as new territory for the Spanish crown. One of their most significant conquests was the Aztec Empire that dominated central Mexico. Elsewhere European impact was slight during the 16th century; they passed through, leaving little of their own cultures behind, save for animals, such as horses, that transformed native lives, and diseases that decimated populations.

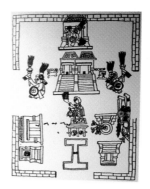

The Great Temple dominated the central plaza of Tenochtitlan. The northern temple (left) was dedicated to Tlaloc, god of rain and the southern temple (right) to the Aztec patron god of war, Huitzilopochtli.

The Aztec Empire

The Aztecs entered the already highly urbanized Valley of Mexico around 1200, establishing their island capital of Tenochtitlan on Lake Texcoco in 1325, and overthrowing their imperial masters, the Tepanecs, in 1428 to begin their own empire. By 1519, the Aztec Empire controlled most of central Mexico as well as the Maya areas of further east. The Aztecs presided over a collection of city-states which remained autonomous except for their tributary obligations to the Aztecs. The Aztec Empire maintained a state of constant military activity which served to provide a flow of tributes from neighbouring states.

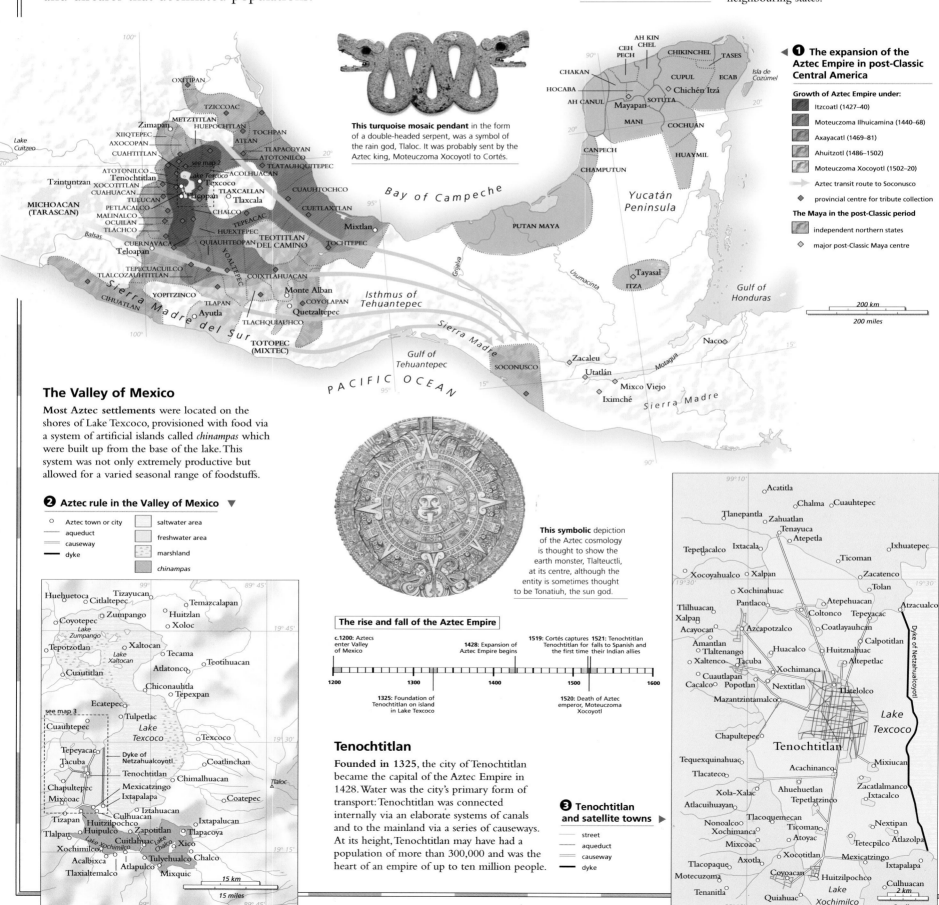

This turquoise mosaic pendant in the form of a double-headed serpent, was a symbol of the rain god, Tlaloc. It was probably sent by the Aztec king, Moteuczoma Xocoyotl to Cortés.

❶ The expansion of the Aztec Empire in post-Classic Central America

Growth of Aztec Empire under:
- Itzcoatl (1427–40)
- Moteuczoma Ilhuicamina (1440–68)
- Axayacatl (1469–81)
- Ahuitzotl (1486–1502)
- Moteuczoma Xocoyotl (1502–20)
- → Aztec transit route to Soconusco
- ◆ provincial centre for tribute collection

The Maya in the post-Classic period
- independent northern states
- ◇ major post-Classic Maya centre

The Valley of Mexico

Most Aztec settlements were located on the shores of Lake Texcoco, provisioned with food via a system of artificial islands called *chinampas* which were built up from the base of the lake. This system was not only extremely productive but allowed for a varied seasonal range of foodstuffs.

❷ Aztec rule in the Valley of Mexico
- ○ Aztec town or city
- aqueduct
- causeway
- ▬ dyke
- saltwater area
- freshwater area
- marshland
- chinampas

This symbolic depiction of the Aztec cosmology is thought to show the earth monster, Tlalteuctli, at its centre, although the entity is sometimes thought to be Tonatiuh, the sun god.

The rise and fall of the Aztec Empire

c.1200: Aztecs enter Valley of Mexico

1325: Foundation of Tenochtitlan on island in Lake Texcoco

1428: Expansion of Aztec Empire begins

1519: Cortés captures Tenochtitlan for the first time

1520: Death of Aztec emperor, Moteuczoma Xocoyotl

1521: Tenochtitlan falls to Spanish and their Indian allies

Tenochtitlan

Founded in 1325, the city of Tenochtitlan became the capital of the Aztec Empire in 1428. Water was the city's primary form of transport: Tenochtitlan was connected internally via an elaborate systems of canals and to the mainland via a series of causeways. At its height, Tenochtitlan may have had a population of more than 300,000 and was the heart of an empire of up to ten million people.

❸ Tenochtitlan and satellite towns
- street
- aqueduct
- causeway
- ▬ dyke

European exploration and conquest

The Spanish first visited the Gulf of Mexico and the Caribbean in the late 1400s and early 1500s, quickly conquering the West Indies whose people were enslaved or impressed into forced labour and devastated by European diseases such as smallpox. The first formal expedition to Mexico, led by Córdoba, reached the Yucatán Peninsula in 1517. In 1518, Grijalva landed on the Vera Cruz coast, trading with the natives and giving Aztec emissaries their first glimpse of Europeans. The rest of the 16th century saw the replacement of Indian leaders with Spanish, the substitution of Christianity for Indian religions, and the imposition of Spanish rule in Central America. Major entries were made into North America – in the southeast by expeditions, such as de Soto's in 1539–42, and in the southwest by Coronado in 1540, leading to the initial conquest of New Mexico and the founding of Santa Fe in 1609.

Some of the earliest evidence of Spanish incursions into Mexico and North America is in the form of religious buildings. The church of St. Francis at Tlaxcala dates from 1521.

Spanish colonizing expeditions in the New World

#	Expedition	Date
1	Sebastian de Ocampo	1508
2	Juan Ponce de León	1508 and 1512
3	Juan de Esquival	1509
4	Diego Velasquez	1511
5	Vasco Núñez de Balboa	1513–14
6	Pedrarias Dávila	1514–19
7	Hernández de Córdoba, Juan de Grijalva, Alonso Álvarez de Peneda and Francisco de Garay	1517–23
8	Pedrarias Dávila	1519
9	Hernan Cortés	1519
10	Gonzalo de Sandoval	1521
11	Luis Marín	1521–24
12	Francisco Orozco	1521
13	Francisco Gordillo and Pedro de Quexos	1521
14	Pedro de Alvarado	1522
15	Hernan Cortés	1522
16	Cristóbal de Olid	1522
17	Gil Gonzalez Dávila and Andres Nino	1522–23
18	Pedro de Alvarado	1523–24
19	Cristóbal de Olid	1524
20	Francisco Hernández de Córdoba	1524
21	Esteban Gomez	1524–25
22	Lucas Vázquez de Ayllón	1526
23	The Montejos	1527
24	Pánfilo de Narváez and Álvar Núñez Cabeza de Vaca	1528
25	Nuño de Guzmán and Cristóbal de Oñate	1529
26	Hurtado de Mendoza, Becerra, Grijalva, Cortés, Tapia, Ulloa, Alarcon	1532–42
27	Hernando de Soto	1539–42
28	Francisco Vásquez de Coronado	1540
29	The Montejos	1545
30	Francisco de Ibarra	1554
31	Pedro Menéndez de Avilés	1565
32	Juan de Oñate	1595
33	Sebastián Vizcaíno	1596

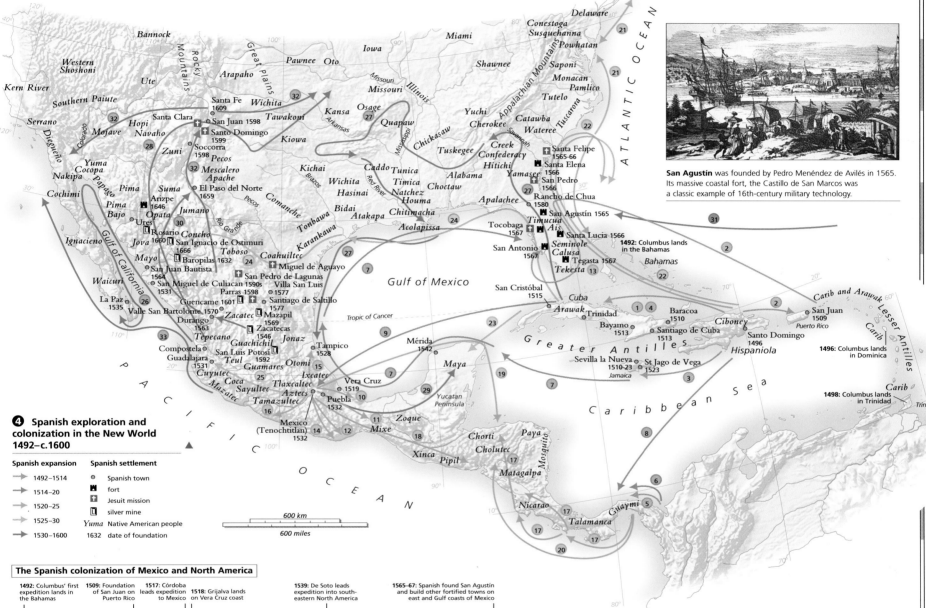

④ Spanish exploration and colonization in the New World 1492–c.1600

Spanish expansion		Spanish settlement	
→	1492–1514	○	Spanish town
→	1514–20	⌂	fort
→	1520–25	✝	Jesuit mission
→	1525–30	⬛	silver mine
→	1530–1600	*Yuma*	Native American people
		1632	date of foundation

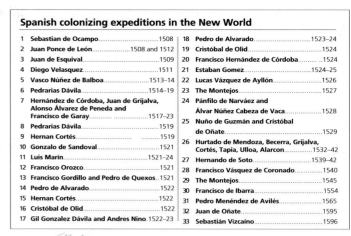

San Agustín was founded by Pedro Menéndez de Avilés in 1565. Its massive coastal fort, the Castillo de San Marcos was a classic example of 16th-century military technology.

The Spanish colonization of Mexico and North America

1492: Columbus' first expedition lands in the Bahamas
1496: Foundation of Santo Domingo on Hispaniola
1509: Foundation of San Juan on Puerto Rico
1517: Córdoba leads expedition to Mexico
1518: Grijalva lands on Vera Cruz coast
1519–21: Cortés' expedition into Mexico leads to collapse of Aztec Empire
1539: De Soto leads expedition into south-eastern North America
1540: Coronado leads expedition into south-western North America
1565–67: Spanish found San Agustín and build other fortified towns on east and Gulf coasts of Mexico
1560s: Jesuit missions established in the southeast (Florida) and in the southwest

1490 — 1510 — 1530 — 1550 — 1570

The conquest of the Aztecs

In 1519, **Hernan Cortés**, sponsored by the Governor of Cuba, landed on the Vera Cruz coast with about 450 soldiers. Forging alliances with the Totonacs and the Tlaxcaltecs he was able to seize the Aztec capital, Tenochtitlan in November 1519. Governor Velasquez then attempted to punish Cortés for disobeying his orders, sending a force to retrieve him which ultimately led to his being forced out of Tenochtitlan. But he was able to maintain his alliances with groups, such as the Chalcas and the Acolhua. In 1520 Cortés again led expeditions around the Valley of Mexico and beseiged Tenochtitlan, defeating the Aztecs in August 1521.

While Cortés claimed victory for Spain, the battles against the Aztecs were actually won by his tens of thousands of Indian allies. With several major allied groups, no one group was able to take power and Cortés reaped the benefits of what was in fact an Indian victory over Indians.

⑤ Cortés' invasion and conquest of Mexico, 1519–21

→ Cortés' march to Tenochtitlan, Apr–Nov 1519
→ retreat to Tlaxcala, 1520
→ final conquest of Tenochtitlan, 1520–21

FROM COLONIZATION TO INDEPENDENCE

George Washington, the first US president, came to prominence in the Anglo-French conflicts of the 1750s.

FROM THE EARLY 17TH CENTURY, British, French, and Dutch migrants settled along the Atlantic seaboard and in the Gulf of St. Lawrence. As they grew in numbers, they displaced native Indian peoples from their lands. Though the French were able to form mutually beneficial alliances with Indian peoples, relationships elsewhere were characterized by conflict, and by 1759, most of the surviving Indians had been driven westward. By the second half of the 18th century, the British emerged as the major political power in North America. By 1775, and with the elimination of French power in Canada, the American desire for self determination led to revolution, and the creation of an independent United States of America by 1783.

European colonial settlement 1600–1750

The site of Montreal was first visited by Jacques Cartier in 1535. In 1642, when this map was drawn, the first French settlement was set up.

During the 17th century, the British established a string of Atlantic colonies with a population that grew to about a million settlers, including African slaves. They produced export tobacco, timber, fish, and food, and ran a thriving colonial merchant fleet that dominated Atlantic trade, along with sugar colonies in the West Indies. To the north and west, a small number of French settlers forged strong alliances with native peoples, traded in fur, and established an arc of territories designed to stop further British expansion.

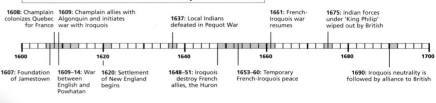

Settlement and conflict in 17th-century North America

1608: Champlain colonizes Quebec for France	**1609:** Champlain allies with Algonquin and initiates war with Iroquois	**1637:** Local Indians defeated in Pequot War	**1661:** French-Iroquois war resumes	**1675:** Indian forces under 'King Philip' wiped out by British

1600 — 1620 — 1640 — 1660 — 1680 — 1700

1607: Foundation of Jamestown	**1609–14:** War between English and Powhatan	**1620:** Settlement of New England begins	**1648–51:** Iroquois destroy French allies, the Huron	**1653–60:** Temporary French-Iroquois peace	**1690:** Iroquois neutrality is followed by alliance to British

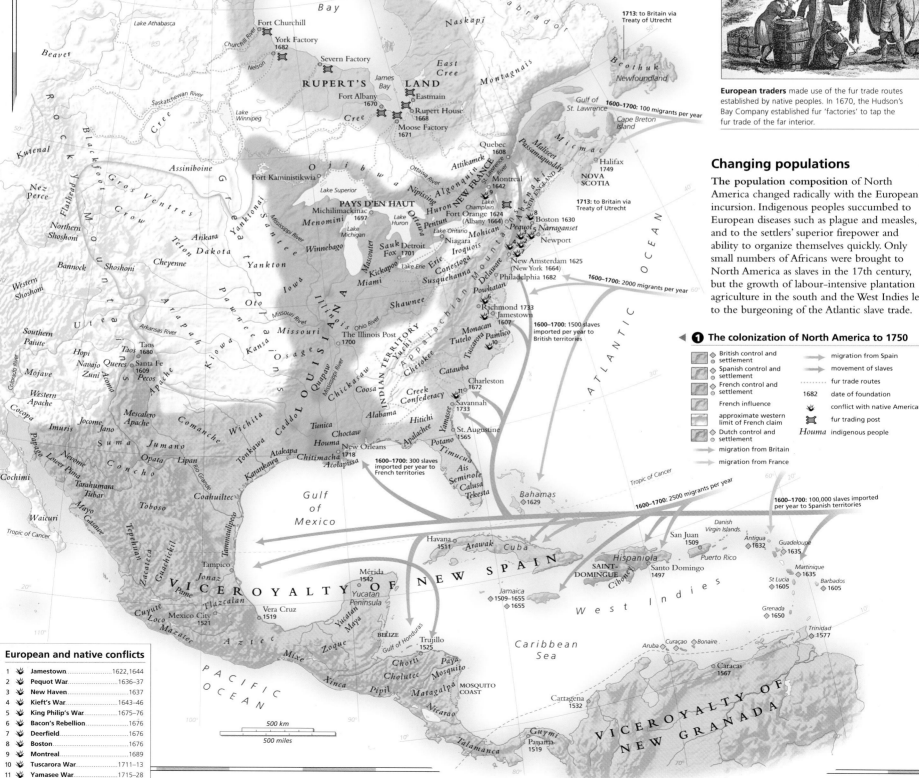

European traders made use of the fur trade routes established by native peoples. In 1670, the Hudson's Bay Company established fur 'factories' to tap the fur trade of the far interior.

Changing populations

The population composition of North America changed radically with the European incursion. Indigenous peoples succumbed to European diseases such as plague and measles, and to the settlers' superior firepower and ability to organize themselves quickly. Only small numbers of Africans were brought to North America as slaves in the 17th century, but the growth of labour-intensive plantation agriculture in the south and the West Indies led to the burgeoning of the Atlantic slave trade.

① The colonization of North America to 1750

- British control and settlement
- Spanish control and settlement
- French control and settlement
- French influence
- approximate western limit of French claim
- Dutch control and settlement
- migration from Britain
- migration from France
- migration from Spain
- movement of slaves
- fur trade routes
- 1682 date of foundation
- conflict with native Americans
- fur trading post
- *Houma* indigenous people

European and native conflicts

1	Jamestown	1622, 1644
2	Pequot War	1636–37
3	New Haven	1637
4	Kieft's War	1643–46
5	King Philip's War	1675–76
6	Bacon's Rebellion	1676
7	Deerfield	1676
8	Boston	1676
9	Montreal	1689
10	Tuscarora War	1711–13
11	Yamasee War	1715–28

500 km

500 miles

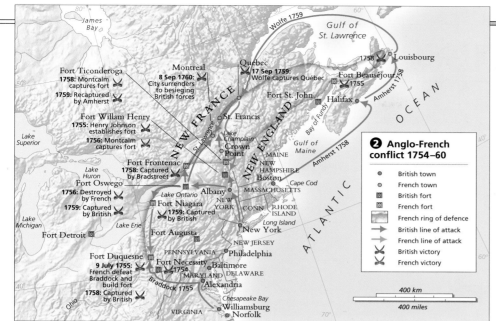

2 Anglo-French conflict 1754–60

- ● British town
- ● French town
- ▣ British fort
- ▣ French fort
- ⬚ French ring of defence
- → British line of attack
- → French line of attack
- ✕ British victory
- ✕ French victory

400 km
400 miles

Map labels (approximate): James Bay · Gulf of St. Lawrence · Wolfe 1759 · Louisbourg 1758 · Fort Ticonderoga 1758: Montcalm captures fort · 1759: Recaptured by Amherst · Montreal 8 Sep 1760: City surrenders to besieging British forces · Quebec 17 Sep 1759: Wolfe captures Quebec · Fort Beauséjour 1755 · Fort St. John · Halifax · Amherst 1758 · NEW FRANCE · Fort William Henry 1755: Henry Johnson establishes fort · 1756: Montcalm captures fort · Lake Superior · Lake Champlain · Crown Point · NEW HAMPSHIRE · MAINE · Bay of Fundy · Gulf of Maine · ATLANTIC OCEAN · Fort Frontenac 1758: Captured by Bradstreet · St. Francis · Lake Ontario · Lake Huron · Fort Oswego 1756: Destroyed by French · Fort Niagara 1759: Captured by British · Albany · NEW ENGLAND · Boston · MASSACHUSETTS · Cape Cod · Lake Michigan · Lake Erie · Fort Augusta · Fort Detroit · NEW YORK · CONN. · RHODE ISLAND · Long Island · New York · PENNSYLVANIA · Philadelphia · NEW JERSEY · Fort Duquesne 9 July 1755: French defeat Braddock and build fort · 1758: Captured by British · Fort Necessity 1754 · Braddock 1755 · Baltimore · MARYLAND · DELAWARE · Alexandria · Ohio · VIRGINIA · Chesapeake Bay · Williamsburg · Norfolk

Competition for North America 1690–1761

Conflict between France and Britain in North America at first mirrored the wars of Louis XIV in Europe in the 1690s. In the late 1730s Britain and Spain clashed in the Spanish colonies. Serious fighting between the British and French resumed in 1744–48, but the decisive struggle for the continent occurred between 1754–61. In July 1755, General Braddock, aided by provincial troops including George Washington, marched on Fort Duquesne but was repelled by the French. It took the full weight of the British army until 1759 to gain ascendancy over the French and their Indian allies. General Wolfe's capture of Quebec in September 1759 was followed by the surrender of Montreal. With peace agreed at the Treaty of Paris in 1763, Britain became the dominant colonial power in the New World.

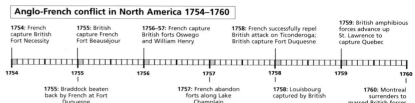

Anglo-French conflict in North America 1754–1760

1754	1755	1756	1757	1758	1759	1760
1754: French capture British Fort Necessity	1755: British capture French Fort Beauséjour	1756–57: French capture British forts Oswego and William Henry		1758: French successfully repel British attack on Ticonderoga; British capture Fort Duquesne	1759: British amphibious forces advance up St. Lawrence to capture Quebec	
	1755: Braddock beaten back by French at Fort Duquesne		1757: French abandon forts along Lake Champlain	1758: Louisbourg captured by British		1760: Montreal surrenders to massed British forces

The brief but fierce battle for Quebec in September 1759, claimed the lives of the commanders of both sides: the British General Wolfe (*left*), and the French Marquis de Montcalm the following day. Final victory belonged to the British who had been advancing up the Gulf of St. Lawrence for over a year.

The Revolutionary War 1775–1783

By the 1760s, the inhabitants of the British colonies had grown rapidly in population, wealth, and self-confidence and were increasingly resistant to conventional methods of colonial control, such as taxation. In addition, the British government was perceived to be keeping all the fruits of victory against the French for itself, including the Canadian fur trade and the western lands. In 1775, the first shots of the Revolutionary War were fired in Boston. Almost all of the early campaigns ended in stalemate: British forces were superior in numbers and weaponry, but the patriots gained support with every campaign as the struggle moved south. The American victory at Saratoga in 1777 convinced the French government to support the Americans with troops and ships. Later the Dutch and Spanish also joined against Britain. In 1781 George Washington forced General Cornwallis to surrender at Yorktown and the new nation was secure.

3 The American Revolutionary War

- ⬚ The Thirteen Colonies, 1775
- ⬚ The United States, 1783
- → British movements
- → French movements
- → US movements
- ✕ British victory
- ✕ French victory
- ✕ US victory
- ✕ indecisive outcome
- ▣ fort

Scale varies with perspective
1971 km (1230 miles)
1667 km (1040 miles)

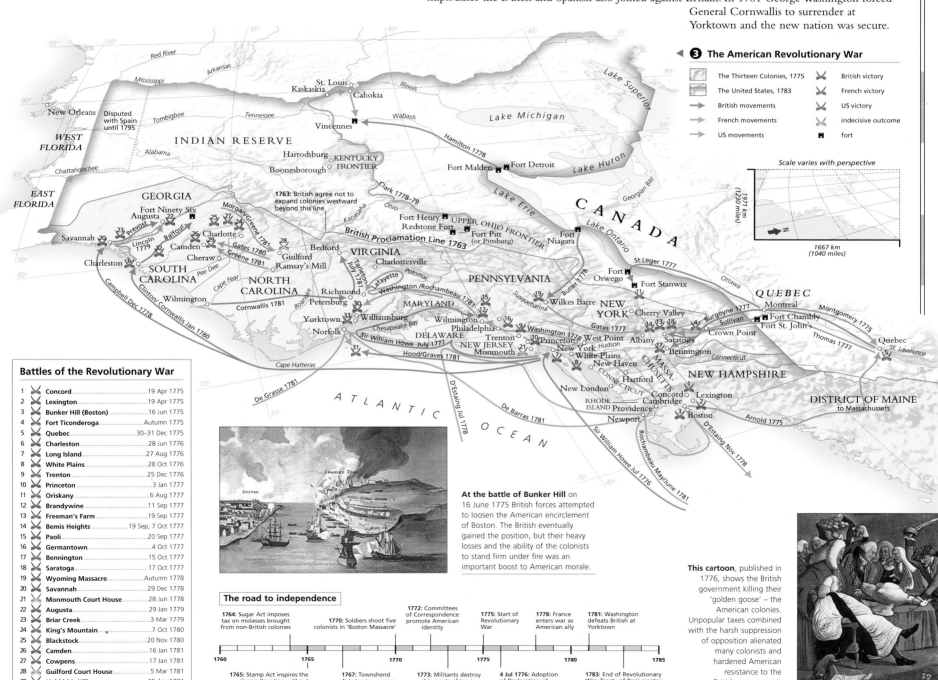

Battles of the Revolutionary War		
1	Concord	19 Apr 1775
2	Lexington	19 Apr 1775
3	Bunker Hill (Boston)	16 Jun 1775
4	Fort Ticonderoga	Autumn 1775
5	Quebec	30–31 Dec 1775
6	Charleston	28 Jun 1776
7	Long Island	27 Aug 1776
8	White Plains	28 Oct 1776
9	Trenton	25 Dec 1776
10	Princeton	3 Jan 1777
11	Oriskany	6 Aug 1777
12	Brandywine	11 Sep 1777
13	Freeman's Farm	19 Sep 1777
14	Bemis Heights	19 Sep, 7 Oct 1777
15	Paoli	20 Sep 1777
16	Germantown	4 Oct 1777
17	Bennington	15 Oct 1777
18	Saratoga	17 Oct 1777
19	Wyoming Massacre	Autumn 1778
20	Savannah	29 Dec 1778
21	Monmouth Court House	28 Jun 1778
22	Augusta	29 Jan 1779
23	Briar Creek	3 Mar 1779
24	King's Mountain	7 Oct 1780
25	Blackstock	20 Nov 1780
26	Camden	16 Jan 1781
27	Cowpens	17 Jan 1781
28	Guilford Court House	5 Mar 1781
29	Hobkirk's Hill	25 Apr 1781
30	Jamestown	6 Jul 1781
31	Virginia Capes	5 Sep 1781
32	Eutaw Springs	8 Sep 1781
33	Yorktown	19 Oct 1781

At the battle of Bunker Hill on 16 June 1775 British forces attempted to loosen the American encirclement of Boston. The British eventually gained the position, but their heavy losses and the ability of the colonists to stand firm under fire was an important boost to American morale.

The road to independence

1760	1765	1770	1775	1780	1785
	1764: Sugar Act imposes tax on molasses brought from non-British colonies	1770: Soldiers shoot five colonists in 'Boston Massacre'	1772: Committees of Correspondence promote American identity	1775: Start of Revolutionary War	1778: France enters war as American ally	1781: Washington defeats British at Yorktown
	1765: Stamp Act inspires the slogan 'taxation without representation is tyranny'	1767: Townshend Acts tax tea, paper, and other imports	1773: Militants destroy shipments of tea in 'Boston Tea Party'	4 Jul 1776: Adoption of Declaration of Independence	1783: End of Revolutionary War. Treaty of Paris creates new United States

This cartoon, published in 1776, shows the British government killing their 'golden goose' – the American colonies. Unpopular taxes combined with the harsh suppression of opposition alienated many colonists and hardened American resistance to the British government.

BUILDING NEW NATIONS

Thomas Jefferson was the principal author of the Declaration of Independence and the third US president.

BY 1783, THE NEWLY-FORMED United States of America had a draft constitution and a border which soon extended as far as the Mississippi, causing considerable alarm among its Indian, Spanish, and Canadian neighbours. In the War of 1812, Canada successfully fended off invasion by the United States, but remained fearful of the growing power to its south. In Mexico and Central America, Creole dissenters launched a disastrous war for independence from Spain starting in 1810. Mexico plunged into a bloody race war that killed hundreds of thousands and wrecked the colonial infrastructure. The nations of Central America and Mexico emerged independent during the 1820s, though greatly weakened from their former colonial status.

The growth of the US

The Louisiana Purchase of 1803 added to the US a huge swathe of western lands formerly controlled by France. After the War of 1812, all hope of annexing Canada was abandoned, and the US began the great push westward.

Settlers poured into the Great Plains, Oregon, and eventually the northern periphery of the Republic of Mexico, including Texas and California. The Santa Fe trail, open for trade by 1823, brought New Mexico under US influence. By mid-century, the US boasted an extensive communications network. Steamboat traffic dominated the riverine highway system, augmented by canals and railroads running cross-country.

The consolidation of western lands encouraged millions of pioneers to forge new lives in the West. The spirit of aggressive progress which drove settlers westward soon became known as 'manifest destiny'.

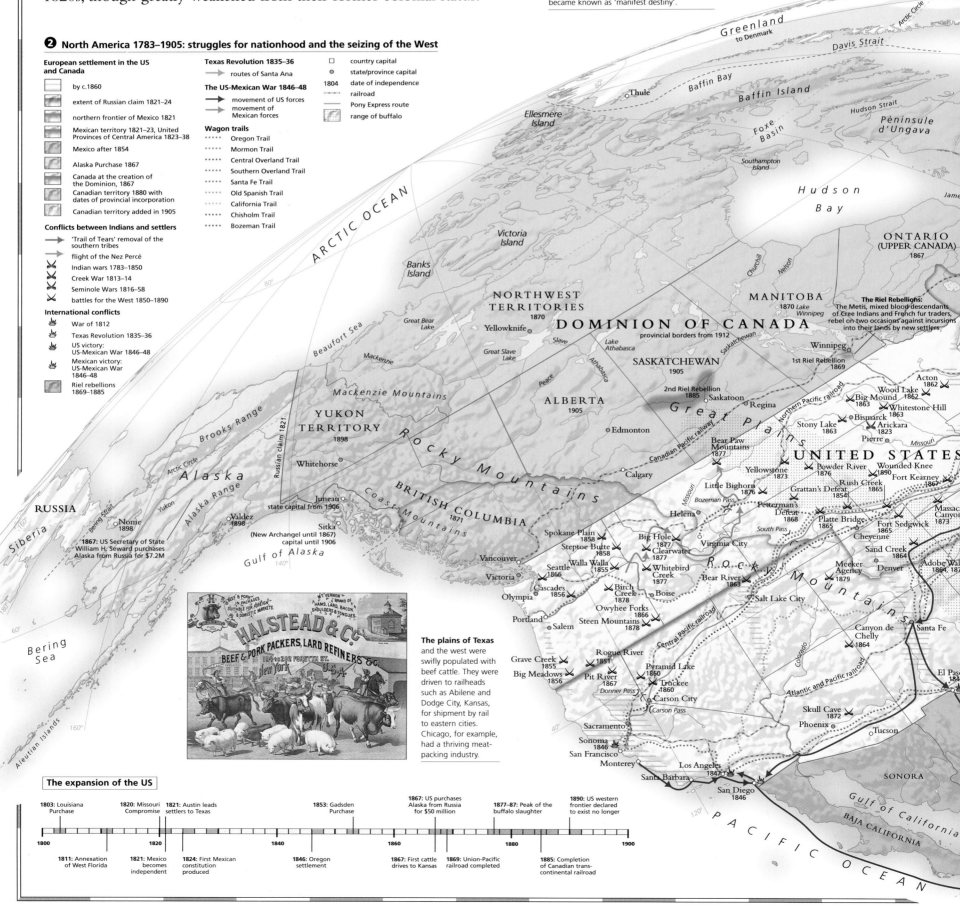

❷ North America 1783–1905: struggles for nationhood and the seizing of the West

European settlement in the US and Canada
- by c.1860
- extent of Russian claim 1821–24
- northern frontier of Mexico 1821
- Mexican territory 1821–23, United Provinces of Central America 1823–38
- Mexico after 1854
- Alaska Purchase 1867
- Canada at the creation of the Dominion, 1867
- Canadian territory 1880 with dates of provincial incorporation
- Canadian territory added in 1905

Conflicts between Indians and settlers
- 'Trail of Tears' removal of the southern tribes
- flight of the Nez Percé
- Indian wars 1783–1850
- Creek War 1813–14
- Seminole Wars 1816–58
- battles for the West 1850–1890

International conflicts
- War of 1812
- Texas Revolution 1835–36
- US victory: US-Mexican War 1846–48
- Mexican victory: US-Mexican War 1846–48
- Riel rebellions 1869–1885

Texas Revolution 1835–36
- routes of Santa Ana

The US-Mexican War 1846–48
- movement of US forces
- movement of Mexican forces

Wagon trails
- Oregon Trail
- Mormon Trail
- Central Overland Trail
- Southern Overland Trail
- Santa Fe Trail
- Old Spanish Trail
- California Trail
- Chisholm Trail
- Bozeman Trail

- country capital
- state/province capital
- 1804 date of independence
- railroad
- Pony Express route
- range of buffalo

The plains of Texas and the west were swiftly populated with beef cattle. They were driven to railheads such as Abilene and Dodge City, Kansas, for shipment by rail to eastern cities. Chicago, for example, had a thriving meat-packing industry.

The expansion of the US

1803: Louisiana Purchase	1820: Missouri Compromise	1821: Austin leads settlers to Texas		1853: Gadsden Purchase		1867: US purchases Alaska from Russia for $50 million	1877–87: Peak of the buffalo slaughter	1890: US western frontier declared to exist no longer
1800	**1820**		**1840**		**1860**		**1880**	**1900**
1811: Annexation of West Florida	1821: Mexico becomes independent	1824: First Mexican constitution produced		1846: Oregon settlement		1867: First cattle drives to Kansas	1869: Union-Pacific railroad completed	1885: Completion of Canadian trans-continental railroad

Territorial conflict and US expansion

Although involved in conflicts with Britain over the boundary with Canada, the US managed to solve these issues peacefully. A weak, divided Mexico however, feared US territorial demands, especially after President Andrew Jackson offered to purchase Texas. By 1835 the Texans had seceded. Suspicion between the US and Mexico turned quickly to crisis, and in 1846, to war. In 1848 Mexico yielded nearly half its territory to the US as terms of peace, and descended into civil war. The cession of the northern Oregon Country by Britain in 1846, and James Gadsden's 1853 purchase of 30,000 square miles south of the Gila river, from Mexico, completed the westward expansion of the US. The last piece of land added to the US was the northwestern territory of Alaska in 1867.

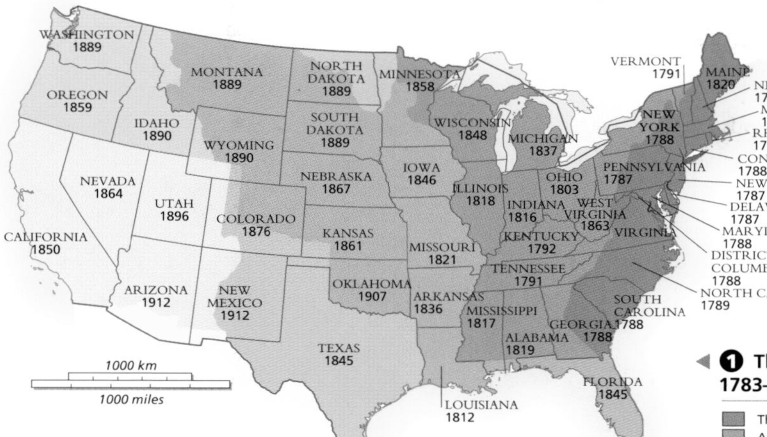

The destruction of the Indians

From the 1790s, Indians were removed westward in a migration forever afterwards known as the 'Trail of Tears' although some, like the Seminole in Florida, resisted stoutly. The settlement of the West from the 1860s was met with serious armed resistance from the Indians. With the final loss of their lands, Indian society was reorganized so as to eliminate native culture, and pave the way for their integration into the national population.

Sitting Bull (above), chief of the Teton Dakota, headed Sioux attempts to retain a homeland in the western lands and predicted the deaths of Custer and his men at the battle of Little Bighorn.

White Cloud (left) was chief of the Iowa tribe, who pursued a semi-sedentary agricultural existence alongside their hunting and battle activities. In 1836, the Iowa ceded their lands to the US and moved to a reservation on what is now the Kansas-Nebraska border.

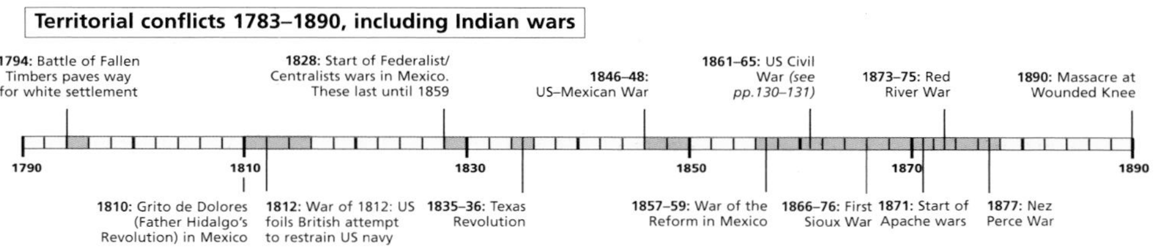

◀ ❶ The growth of the US, 1783–1896

- ☐ Thirteen Colonies 1776
- ☐ Addition of 1783
- ☐ Louisiana Purchase 1803
- ☐ Red River Cession 1818
- ☐ Purchase of Florida 1819
- ☐ Texas Annexation 1845
- ☐ Oregon Country Cession 1846
- ☐ Mexican Cession 1848
- ☐ Gadsden Purchase 1853
- 1812 date of admission to statehood
- — modern state boundary

Territorial conflicts 1783–1890, including Indian wars

1794: Battle of Fallen Timbers paves way for white settlement
1828: Start of Federalist/Centralists wars in Mexico. These last until 1859
1846–48: US–Mexican War
1861–65: US Civil War (see pp.130–131)
1873–75: Red River War
1890: Massacre at Wounded Knee

1790 — 1810 — 1830 — 1850 — 1870 — 1890

1810: Grito de Dolores (Father Hidalgo's Revolution) in Mexico
1812: War of 1812: US foils British attempt to restrain US navy
1835–36: Texas Revolution
1857–59: War of the Reform in Mexico
1866–76: First Sioux War
1871: Start of Apache wars
1877: Nez Perce War

Scale varies with perspective

8770 km (5450 miles)
12,230 km (7600 miles)

Texas Revolution 1835–36:
US settlers in Mexican province of Texas rebel, declaring independence from Mexico and driving out troops – led by General Santa Ana – sent in to quell the uprising

The US-Mexican War 1846–48:
Admission of Texas to the US in 1845 leads to war with Mexico. US quickly wins California and by 1848, Mexico has ceded 33% of its US territory for a fee of $15M

In the latter half of the 19th century, western Canada and the US prioritized the building of transcontinental railroads. These opened up the West to hunters who killed millions of buffalo for their hides, almost destroying the North American herd by the end of the century.

THE AMERICAN CIVIL WAR

Abraham Lincoln's 1863 Emancipation Proclamation freed the slaves of the south.

BETWEEN INDEPENDENCE in 1783 and 1860 there developed within the United States two very different, regional societies. In the North there emerged an industrialized society, committed to liberal banking and credit systems, and protective tariffs. The south was a less populous agrarian society opposed to the sale of public land in the Midwest, high duties, and restrictions upon the institution of slavery. Moreover, the libertarian North increasingly resented Southern political and judicial over-representation. The Democratic Party held the two parts together until 1859; its split, and the election of a president committed to opposing the spread of slavery, provoked the Union's collapse – even before Lincoln's inauguration, seven Southern states had seceded, and war became inevitable.

The cotton gin invented by Eli Whitney in 1793 enabled the swift processing of short-staple cotton. Cotton production increased massively in the Southern states with a resultant rise in the number of slaves required to work the burgeoning plantations.

An unequal nation

By 1860 the US was composed of 18 'free' states – mainly in the North, and 15 'slave' states – mainly in the South. On the issue of slavery, as well as economics, the expanding nation was divided. Industry and finance dominated the North which also had 71% of the population, 81% of bank deposits, 72% of railroad mileage and 85% of the country's factories. The South concentrated on farming, in particular on the production of cotton, tobacco, and sugar for export to Europe. In 1850 347,000 Southern families out of a total population of 6,000,000 were slave-owners. The West was developing an agricultural economy, but produced a greater variety of crops, and sold most of its produce to the northeast.

Industrial production fuelled the growth of Northern cities such as Chicago, seen here in the 1860s. The Southern states, largely dependent on agriculture, remained far less economically developed.

Compromises on the road to civil war

The addition of Missouri in 1820 was the first extension of Union territory west of the Mississippi. The question of whether slavery should be allowed in the new state was settled by the so-called Missouri Compromise, with an artificial limit of 36° 30' marking the boundary between slave and free territory. In 1854 the Kansas-Nebraska Act established two new territories and proposed to allow territorial legislatures to decide the issue of slavery. The Dred Scott decision of 1857 – whereby a slave who had been taken west by his master claimed that he was free because slavery was not legal in the new territory – led to the ruling that slavery could not be excluded from new territories.

⑥ The Civil War to the fall of Vicksburg Apr 1861–Jul 1863 ▶

- Union states 1861
- Confederate states 1861
- ▲▲▲ Union front line to Dec 1861
- ▲▲▲ Union front line to Dec 1862
- → Union movement
- → Confederate movement
- Union fort
- Confederate fort
- Union naval blockade
- ⚔ Union victory
- ⚔ Confederate victory
- 12 Apr 1865 date of battle or attack

① 1820: the Missouri Compromise

- free states
- free territories
- slave states
- territories where slavery legal

② 1850: a new compromise

- free states
- free territories
- slave states
- territories where slavery legal

③ 1854: the Kansas-Nebraska Act

- free states
- free territories
- slave states
- territories where slavery legal
- territories newly opened to slavery 1854
- area not subject to standard territorial laws

④ 1857: the Dred Scott decision

- free states
- slave states
- territories opened to slavery
- area not subject to standard territorial laws

⑤ North versus South: the state of the Union in 1861

- Union states
- Confederate states
- ⚓ slavery legal
- → major slave trade routes
- Jan 1861 date of secession from the Union

Resources and industry
- southern cotton belt
- northern corn belt
- coal
- iron ore
- precious metal
- textile production
- manufacturing city

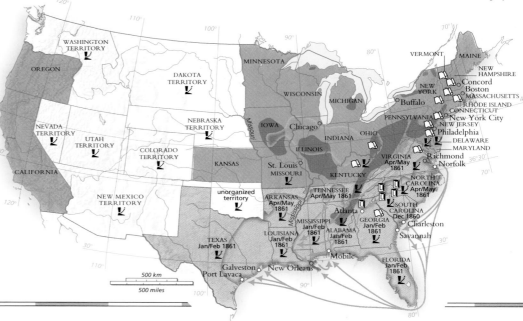

The Civil War 1861–65

In 1860, seven Southern states, fearing restrictions on slavery, seceded from the US. By 1861, they had been joined by four more and became known as the Confederacy. The remaining 23 so-called Union states remained loyal to the US. In April 1861, an attack on Fort Sumter in Charleston harbour started a war for which neither side was prepared. The Civil War became a war of exhaustion. The superior demographic, industrial, and positional resources of the North, combined with sea power that ensured the Confederacy's isolation, slowly destroyed the capacity and will of the Confederacy to wage war. The Confederacy rarely tried to carry the war to the North, meeting crushing defeat at Gettysburg in July 1863. For the most part it waged a defensive war in order to sap the will of the Union. Certainly by 1864 war-weariness had set in in the North, but the successes of the 1864 campaign ensured Lincoln's re-election and sealed the South's defeat.

The Civil War was the first war to be recorded using photography. Field photographers such as Matthew Brady were able to record the true horrors of battles such as Gettysburg, the dead from which are seen above.

The Civil War to the fall of Vicksburg

During 1861–62 Union forces lost a series of battles to an enemy with superior military skills. However, the Northern naval blockade began to cut off both Southern exports and essential supplies. With no Confederate offensive in the upper Ohio which might have split the Union, the North was able to undertake offensives against the Confederate capital, Richmond, and along the Tennessee and Mississippi. Repulsed before Richmond and obliged thereafter to move directly against the city, Union forces secured Memphis and New Orleans, capturing Vicksburg on 4 July 1863, to divide the Confederacy.

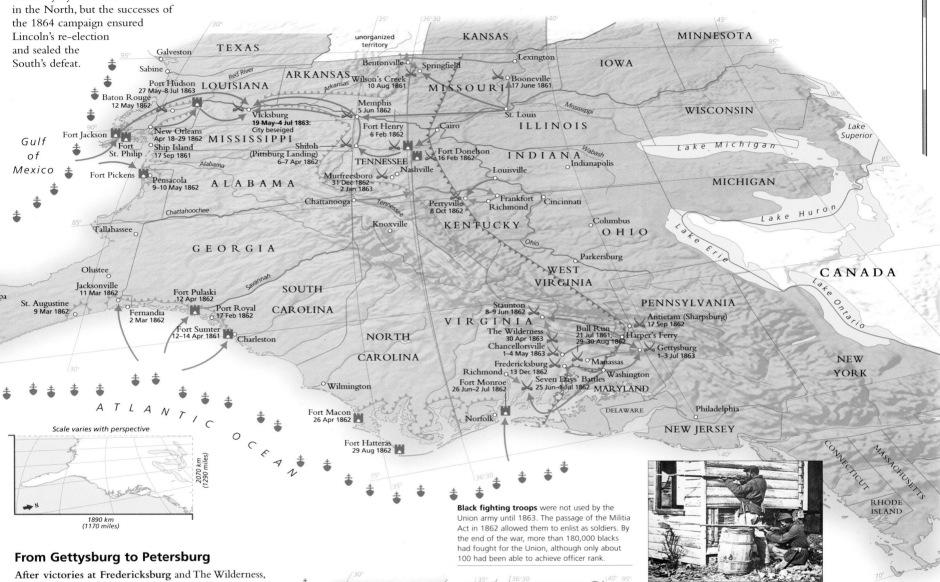

From Gettysburg to Petersburg

After victories at Fredericksburg and The Wilderness, the Confederate offensive into Pennsylvania was defeated at Gettysburg, on the same day as Vicksburg fell. Thereafter on the defensive, Confederate armies were increasingly outnumbered: with Grant's appointment as commander, they were also increasingly outfought. Grant undertook an offensive against Richmond that broke the Confederate freedom of action in a series of battles and the siege of Petersburg: at the same time Sherman's army broke into Georgia and South Carolina. With defeat in front of Petersburg, Confederate resistance collapsed in April 1865.

Black fighting troops were not used by the Union army until 1863. The passage of the Militia Act in 1862 allowed them to enlist as soldiers. By the end of the war, more than 180,000 blacks had fought for the Union, although only about 100 had been able to achieve officer rank.

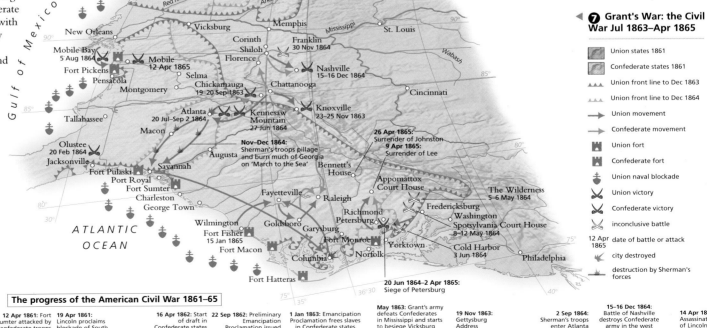

⑦ Grant's War: the Civil War Jul 1863–Apr 1865

- Union states 1861
- Confederate states 1861
- Union front line to Dec 1863
- Union front line to Dec 1864
- Union movement
- Confederate movement
- Union fort
- Confederate fort
- Union naval blockade
- Union victory
- Confederate victory
- inconclusive battle
- 12 Apr 1865 date of battle or attack
- city destroyed
- destruction by Sherman's forces

Ulysses S. Grant was appointed supreme commander of the Union forces in 1864.

The progress of the American Civil War 1861–65

12 Apr 1861: Fort Sumter attacked by Confederate troops
19 Apr 1861: Lincoln proclaims blockade of South
16 Apr 1862: Start of draft in Confederate states
22 Sep 1862: Preliminary Emancipation Proclamation issued
1 Jan 1863: Emancipation Proclamation frees slaves in Confederate states
May 1863: Grant's army defeats Confederates in Mississippi and starts to besiege Vicksburg
19 Nov 1863: Gettysburg Address
2 Sep 1864: Sherman's troops enter Atlanta
15–16 Dec 1864: Battle of Nashville destroys Confederate army in the west
14 Apr 1865: Assassination of Lincoln

15 Apr 1861: President Lincoln issues call for troops
6–7 Apr 1862: Battle of Shiloh: heavy casualties on both sides
1 May 1862: Union fleet captures New Orleans
13 Dec 1862: Severe Union defeat at Fredericksburg
3 Mar 1863: Draft law passed in North
1–3 Jul 1863: Confederate defeat at battle of Gettysburg
4 Jul 1863: Vicksburg captured by Union troops
15 Nov 1864: Sherman begins 'March to the Sea'
9 Apr 1965: Lee surrenders to Grant at Appomattox

NORTH AMERICA 1865–1920

THE NATIONS OF NORTH AMERICA focused on the development of their own resources after 1865. The US worked to reconstruct itself after the Civil War and like Canada, concentrated on the completion of transcontinental railroads to further exploit the continent's immense resources. Abroad, the US extended its influence in Central America and west across the Pacific, gaining new territory and economic advantage. In Mexico, Benito Juárez and his Republican forces felled the regime of Maximilian, ushering in a period of relative calm. Under Porfirio Díaz, Mexico attracted foreign investment and immigration, but its population remained brutally suppressed.

The Statue of Liberty came to symbolize the hope and freedom offered by the US.

Industrialization and urbanization

US manufacturing techniques and machinery were refined throughout the second half of the 19th century.

The growth of the railroads and industrialization transformed the North American landscape. The economic boom turned the continent into a magnet for immigration: thousands came to its shores seeking a better life. Inventions and innovations abounded; cities arose across the continent, supporting factories that had expanded rapidly because of the demands of the American Civil War. The new industrial cities became pressure cookers of societal and political discontent, with often bloody confrontations between organized labour, police, and even the military.

Theodore Roosevelt, president 1901–09, presided over the economic boom of the early 20th century.

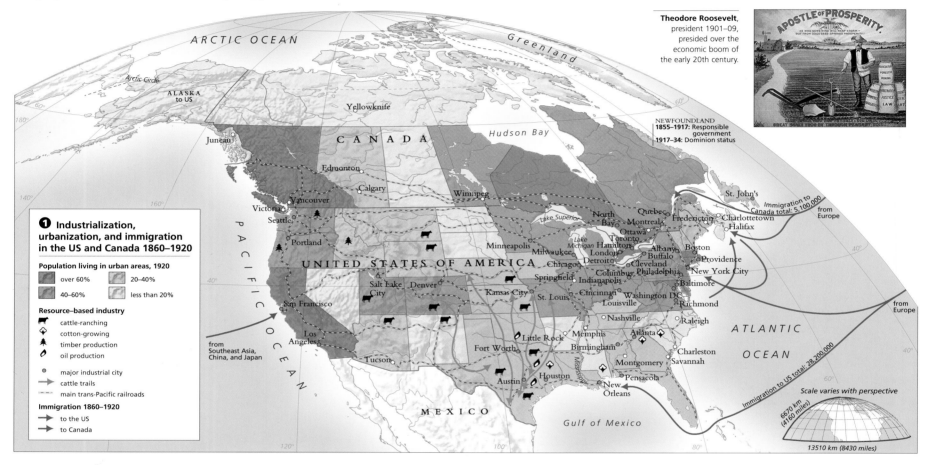

❶ Industrialization, urbanization, and immigration in the US and Canada 1860–1920

Population living in urban areas, 1920
- over 60%
- 40–60%
- 20–40%
- less than 20%

Resource–based industry
- cattle-ranching
- cotton-growing
- timber production
- oil production
- ○ major industrial city
- → cattle trails
- main trans-Pacific railroads

Immigration 1860–1920
- → to the US
- → to Canada

NEWFOUNDLAND
1855–1917: Responsible government
1917–34: Dominion status

Immigration to Canada total: 5,100,000 from Europe

Immigration to US total: 28,200,000 from Europe

Scale varies with perspective

13510 km (8430 miles)
6670 km (4160 miles)

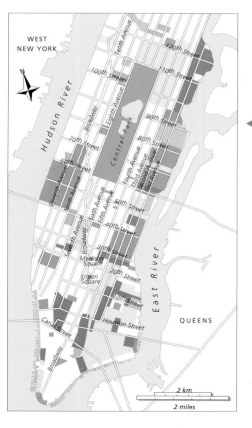

❷ Ethnic neighbourhoods in Manhattan c.1920
- African-American
- Chinese
- Czech, Hungarian
- French
- German
- Irish
- Italian
- Jewish
- Scandinavian, Finnish
- Syrian, Turkish, Armenian, Greek

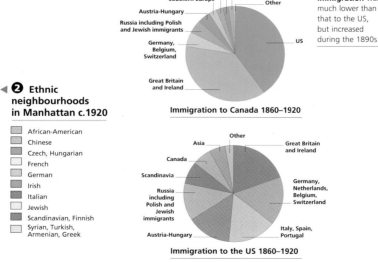

Immigration to Canada 1860–1920

Canadian immigration was much lower than that to the US, but increased during the 1890s.

Immigration to the US 1860–1920

The era of mass migration

During the 19th century nearly 50 million immigrants swelled the populations of Canada and the US. Immigration was initially from northern Europe: Germany, Scandinavia, Britain, and Ireland, but from the 1880s, the bulk of migrants came from eastern and southern Europe. Most settlers were lured by the economic opportunities offered by the Americas but others sought freedom from religious persecution and political uncertainty. After the First World War, immigration was severely curtailed.

The majority of new arrivals to the Americas were able to gain entry. Only about 2% were refused leave to stay.

New York

New York's Ellis Island was the point of entry for millions of immigrants between 1892 and 1920. Many people remained within the city, finding comfort and support in ethnic neighbourhoods which had grown up there. By the 1920s, the diversity of nationalities on Manhattan was a reflection of the diverse strains that made up the population of the US.

The US: 1865–1914

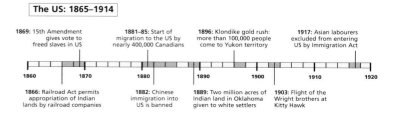

1869: 15th Amendment gives vote to freed slaves in US
1881–85: Start of migration to the US by nearly 400,000 Canadians
1896: Klondike gold rush: more than 100,000 people come to Yukon territory
1917: Asian labourers excluded from entering US by Immigration Act

1866: Railroad Act permits appropriation of Indian lands by railroad companies
1882: Chinese immigration into US is banned
1889: Two million acres of Indian land in Oklahoma given to white settlers
1903: Flight of the Wright brothers at Kitty Hawk

The Mexican Revolution 1910–20

Long-term government mismanagement of Mexico's natural resources, combined with political repression under Porfirio Díaz produced an explosive situation by 1910. Francisco Madero's *Plan de San Luis Potosí* called for a revolt against the government; revolutionary armies led by Pascual Orozco and Pancho Villa raided government garrisons in the north, while Emiliano Zapata waged a campaign against local political bosses in the south. From 1911–1915, Madero, Victoriano Huerta, Venustiano Carranza, and Eulalio Gutierrez all held the post of president but all failed to control the bloody anarchy which had been unleashed. The US, alarmed by the potential damage to its business interests, intervened militarily from 1915–17. In 1917, a new constitution was drawn up, which, while allowing the president dictatorial powers, gave the government the right to confiscate land from wealthy landowners, guaranteed workers' rights and limited the rights of the Catholic church.

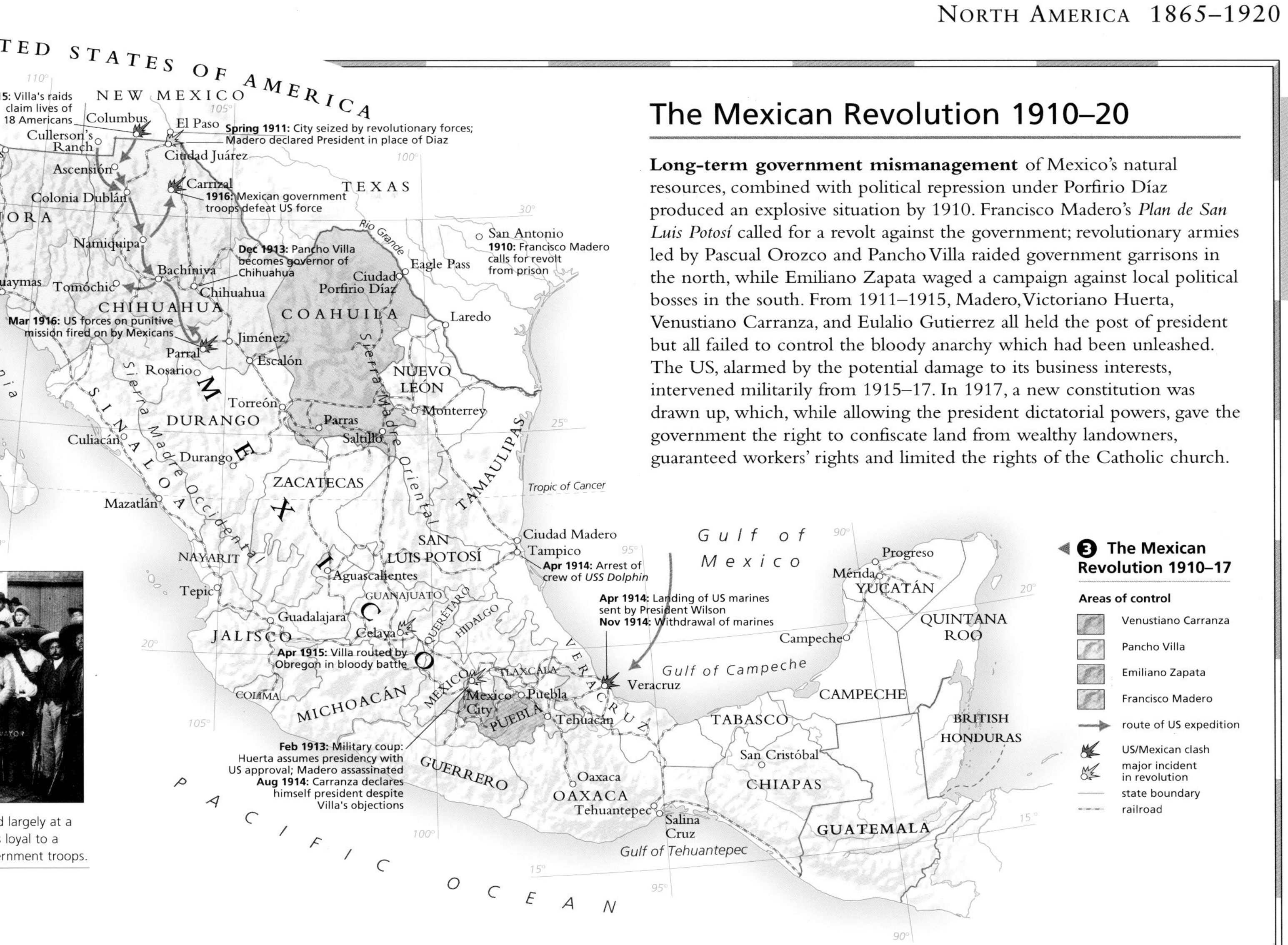

UNITED STATES OF AMERICA
ARIZONA
NEW MEXICO
TEXAS
1915: Villa's raids claim lives of 18 Americans
Columbus
El Paso
Spring 1911: City seized by revolutionary forces; Madero declared President in place of Diaz
Culleron's Ranch
Nogales
Ciudad Juárez
Ascensión
Colonia Dublán
Carrizal
1916: Mexican government troops defeat US force
SONORA
Namiquipa
Bachiniva
Dec 1913: Pancho Villa becomes governor of Chihuahua
Rio Grande
San Antonio
1910: Francisco Madero calls for revolt from prison
Eagle Pass
Guaymas
Tomóchic
Chihuahua
Ciudad Porfirio Díaz
CHIHUAHUA
COAHUILA
Laredo
Mar 1916: US forces on punitive mission fired on by Mexicans
Jiménez
Parral
Escalón
Rosario
NUEVO LEÓN
Monterrey
Torreón
DURANGO
Parras
Saltillo
Culiacán
Durango
SINALOA
Sierra Madre Occidental
Sierra Madre Oriental
TAMAULIPAS
ZACATECAS
Mazatlán
MEXICO
BAJA CALIFORNIA
Gulf of California
Tropic of Cancer
300 km
300 miles
Ciudad Madero
Tampico
Apr 1914: Arrest of crew of USS Dolphin
SAN LUIS POTOSÍ
NAYARIT
Aguascalientes
Tepic
GUANAJUATO
Guadalajara
QUERÉTARO
HIDALGO
JALISCO
Celaya
Apr 1915: Villa routed by Obregon in bloody battle
COLIMA
MICHOACÁN
MÉXICO
Mexico City
TLAXCALA
Puebla
PUEBLA
Tehuacán
VERACRUZ
Veracruz
Apr 1914: Landing of US marines sent by President Wilson
Nov 1914: Withdrawal of marines
Gulf of Mexico
Gulf of Campeche
Progreso
Mérida
YUCATÁN
Campeche
CAMPECHE
QUINTANA ROO
BRITISH HONDURAS
TABASCO
San Cristóbal
CHIAPAS
GUATEMALA
Feb 1913: Military coup: Huerta assumes presidency with US approval; Madero assassinated
Aug 1914: Carranza declares himself president despite Villa's objections
GUERRERO
Oaxaca
OAXACA
Tehuantepec
Salina Cruz
Gulf of Tehuantepec
PACIFIC OCEAN
3 The Mexican Revolution 1910–17
Areas of control
Venustiano Carranza
Pancho Villa
Emiliano Zapata
Francisco Madero
route of US expedition
US/Mexican clash
major incident in revolution
state boundary
railroad

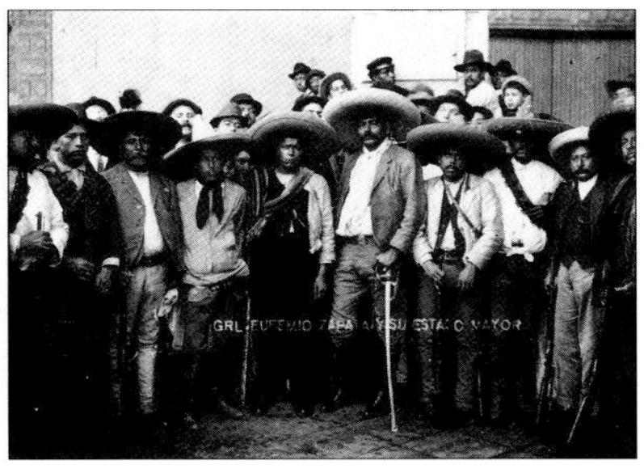

The Mexican revolution was conducted largely at a local level with bands of guerrilla fighters loyal to a factional leader waging war against government troops.

US imperial ambitions

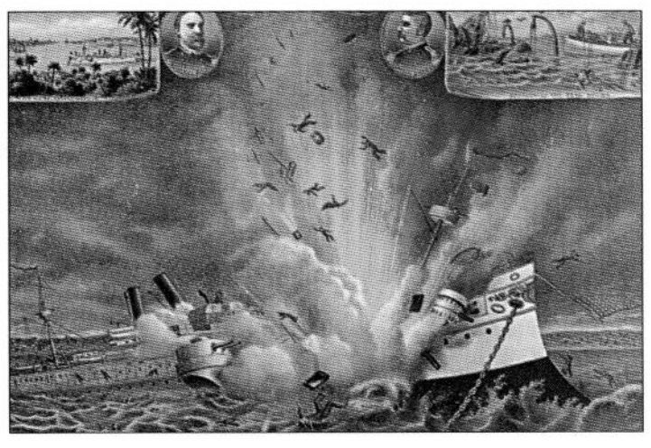

In 1898, the destruction of the *USS Maine* in Havana harbour with the loss of 266 of her crew, led to war between the US and Spain.

US expansion in the Pacific was fuelled partly by missionary zeal – especially in the case of the Philippines – and by a desire for access to the immense possibilities of the Chinese market. The US continued to dominate Latin American affairs, with frequent political and economic intervention becoming a feature of the relationship. The Spanish-American war resulted in Cuban independence and US control of Puerto Rico and the Philippines.

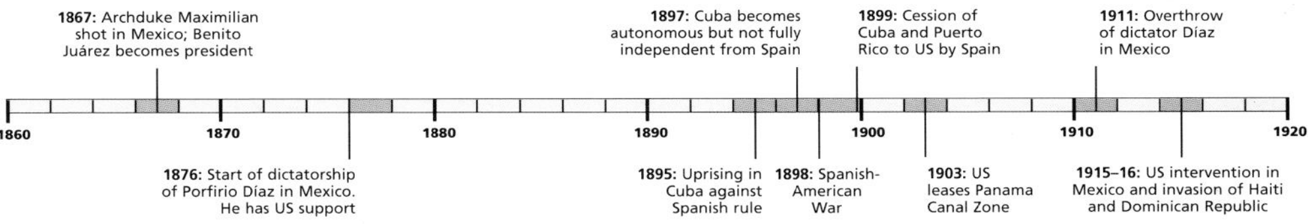

The US, Central America, and the Caribbean
1867: Archduke Maximilian shot in Mexico; Benito Juárez becomes president
1897: Cuba becomes autonomous but not fully independent from Spain
1899: Cession of Cuba and Puerto Rico to US by Spain
1911: Overthrow of dictator Díaz in Mexico
1860
1870
1880
1890
1900
1910
1920
1876: Start of dictatorship of Porfirio Díaz in Mexico. He has US support
1895: Uprising in Cuba against Spanish rule
1898: Spanish-American War
1903: US leases Panama Canal Zone
1915–16: US intervention in Mexico and invasion of Haiti and Dominican Republic

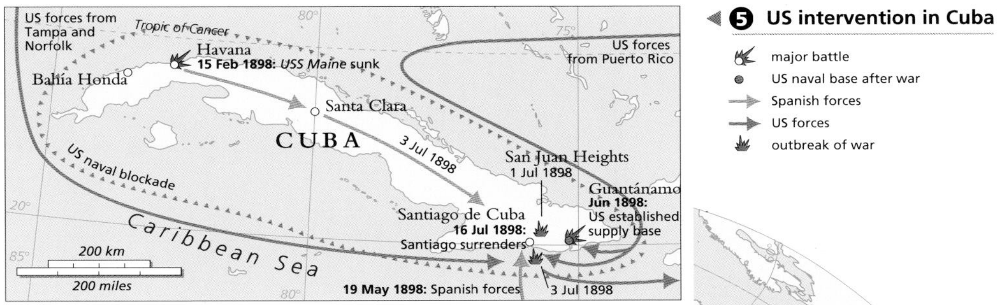

US forces from Tampa and Norfolk
Tropic of Cancer
Havana
15 Feb 1898: USS Maine sunk
Bahía Honda
Santa Clara
CUBA
US forces from Puerto Rico
3 Jul 1898
US naval blockade
San Juan Heights
1 Jul 1898
Guantánamo
Jun 1898: US established supply base
Santiago de Cuba
16 Jul 1898: Santiago surrenders
Caribbean Sea
200 km
200 miles
19 May 1898: Spanish forces
3 Jul 1898
5 US intervention in Cuba
major battle
US naval base after war
Spanish forces
US forces
outbreak of war

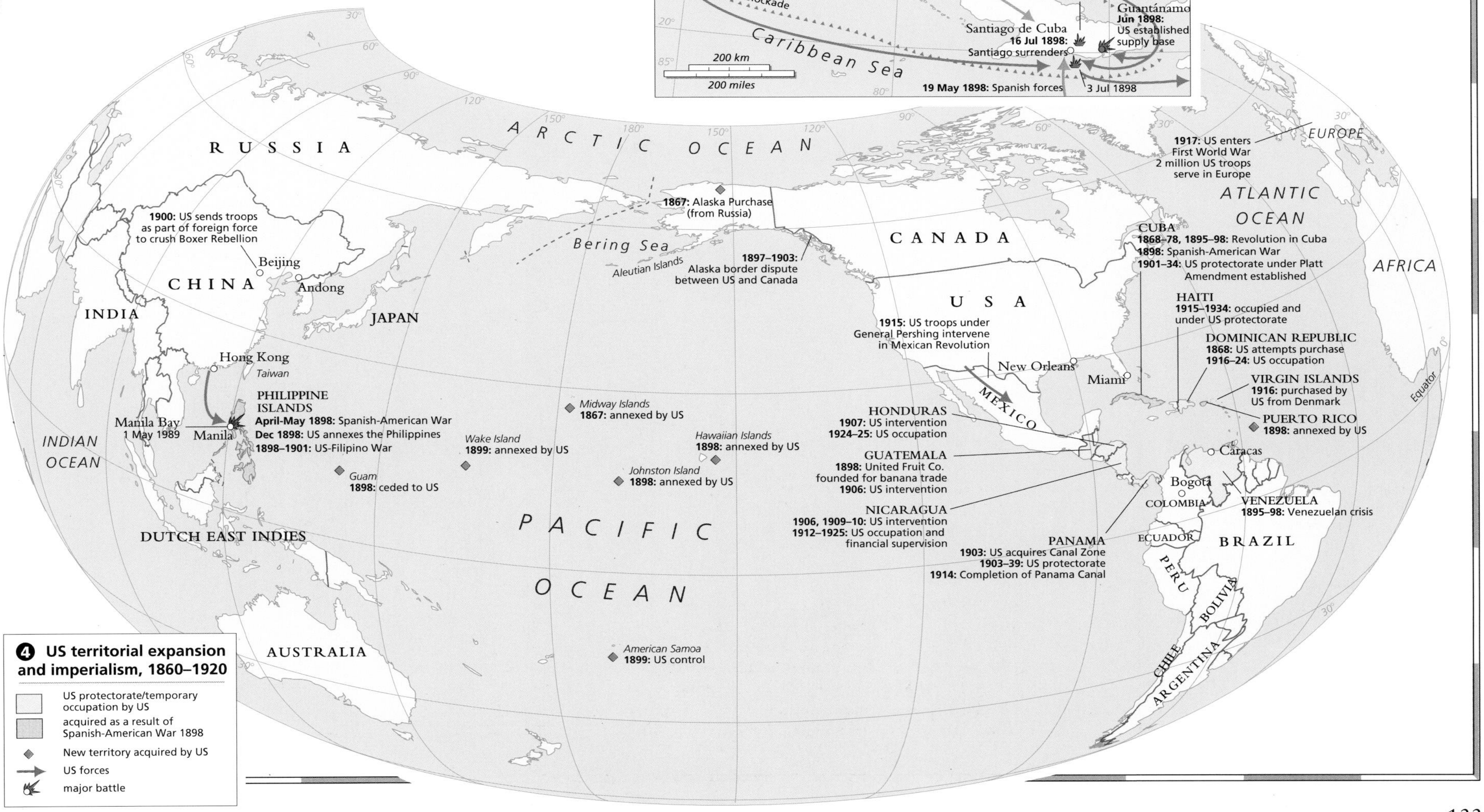

RUSSIA
ARCTIC OCEAN
EUROPE
1917: US enters First World War 2 million US troops serve in Europe
1867: Alaska Purchase (from Russia)
1900: US sends troops as part of foreign force to crush Boxer Rebellion
Beijing
CHINA
Andong
Bering Sea
Aleutian Islands
1897–1903: Alaska border dispute between US and Canada
CANADA
ATLANTIC OCEAN
CUBA
1868–78, 1895–98: Revolution in Cuba
1898: Spanish-American War
1901–34: US protectorate under Platt Amendment established
AFRICA
INDIA
JAPAN
USA
HAITI
1915–1934: occupied and under US protectorate
1915: US troops under General Pershing intervene in Mexican Revolution
DOMINICAN REPUBLIC
1868: US attempts purchase
1916–24: US occupation
Hong Kong
Taiwan
New Orleans
Miami
VIRGIN ISLANDS
1916: purchased by US from Denmark
PHILIPPINE ISLANDS
April–May 1898: Spanish-American War
Dec 1898: US annexes the Philippines
1898–1901: US-Filipino War
Manila Bay
1 May 1989
Manila
Midway Islands
1867: annexed by US
MEXICO
HONDURAS
1907: US intervention
1924–25: US occupation
PUERTO RICO
1898: annexed by US
Equator
INDIAN OCEAN
Wake Island
1899: annexed by US
Hawaiian Islands
1898: annexed by US
Caracas
Guam
1898: ceded to US
Johnston Island
1898: annexed by US
GUATEMALA
1898: United Fruit Co. founded for banana trade
1906: US intervention
Bogotá
COLOMBIA
VENEZUELA
1895–98: Venezuelan crisis
PACIFIC OCEAN
NICARAGUA
1906, 1909–10: US intervention
1912–1925: US occupation and financial supervision
ECUADOR
BRAZIL
DUTCH EAST INDIES
PANAMA
1903: US acquires Canal Zone
1903–39: US protectorate
1914: Completion of Panama Canal
PERU
BOLIVIA
AUSTRALIA
American Samoa
1899: US control
CHILE
ARGENTINA
4 US territorial expansion and imperialism, 1860–1920
US protectorate/temporary occupation by US
acquired as a result of Spanish-American War 1898
New territory acquired by US
US forces
major battle

AN ERA OF BOOM AND BUST

The NRA, set up in 1933, was the first New Deal recovery programme.

INVOLVEMENT IN THE FIRST WORLD WAR confirmed the US's position as a world power in the first quarter of the century. Immigration greatly magnified the population, but during the 1920s, laws were enacted to control the tide of European settlers. The economy grew quickly, but the boom proved vulnerable and in 1929 the stock market collapsed. Between 1930 and 1932, the number of unemployed rose from 4 million to between 12 and 15 million – 25% of the total workforce. The Republican government, which had promoted the boom and was blamed for the crash, was rejected by the electorate, leading to the political dominance of a Democrat, Franklin Delano Roosevelt for 13 years.

The industrial boom

The Model-T Ford was the first car to be built using production line techniques and initially produced only in black. By the 1930s, Henry Ford achieved his dream of 'a car so low in price that no man making a good salary will be unable to afford one'.

The early 1920s saw a massive growth in US production. Traditional industries such as iron and steel were in relative decline, but automobiles, petro-chemicals, construction, and the service industries grew rapidly, as did speculation on the stock market. But the boom was built on shaky foundations. High rates of small business failure in the 1920s gave the first signs of fragility and it was clear that production was outstripping consumption. Paper fortunes that had accrued in stocks and shares were wiped out by the Wall Street Crash of 1929.

The depression and the New Deal

The stock market crash of 1929 shattered millions of dreams and left many Americans destitute. Farmers were particularly hard hit, as banks withdrew funding, as were black people in both cities and rural areas. The Roosevelt administration devised a series of relief programmes known as the 'New Deal' to restart the economy and provide new jobs. Though millions of dollars of federal funding were spent on relief, 20% of Americans were still unemployed in 1939. Not until the Second World War did the economy recover.

The Works Progress Administration (WPA) provided work relief for 8.5 million unemployed. Projects included the building and repair of roads, bridges, schools, and hospitals.

① Major US industries c.1925

- iron and steel
- meat processing
- oil and gas
- textile production
- timber
- vehicle manufacture
- coalfield
- major industrial city

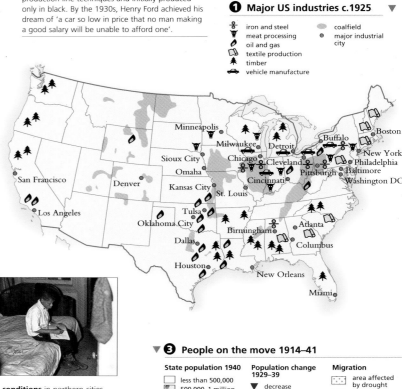

② The impact of the Great Depression 1933–34

Unemployed
- less than 10%
- 11–15%
- 16–25%
- over 25%

Families receiving relief
- less than 10%
- 10–15%
- over 15%

Living conditions in northern cities were often as poor as those that black southerners had left behind.

③ People on the move 1914–41

State population 1940
- less than 500,000
- 500,000–1 million
- 1–2 million
- 2–3 million
- 3–6 million
- over 6 million

Population change 1929–39
- ▼ decrease
- △ increase 0–10%
- △ increase 10–20%
- ▲ increase over 20%

Migration
- area affected by drought
- from the prairie states
- from Appalachia
- black migrants from south
- other

Migration in the US, 1914–41

Refugees from the Dust Bowl carry only the bare essentials as they walk towards Los Angeles in search of work (1939).

By the 1920s, more than 50% of Americans lived in urban areas. From 1917–20, more than 400,000 rural black southerners moved to northern cities and 600,000 more went in the 1920s. In the mid-1930s, farmers from the drought-affected prairie states abandoned their farms by the thousands and moved west – primarily to California's cities and valleys. Appalachia also saw a mass transference of people north to Indiana and Ohio and west to California.

The US 1914–1941

- **1917–20:** Start of migration of southern blacks to northern cities
- **1917:** US enters First World War
- **1918:** Armistice ends First World War
- **1919:** Influenza kills 500,000 Americans
- **1920:** American women granted the vote
- **1923:** More than 13 million cars on US roads
- **1923:** Republican Calvin Coolidge becomes president after death of Warren Harding
- **1928:** Republican Herbert Hoover elected president
- **1929:** Wall Street Crash: collapse of US stock market leads to prolonged depression
- **1930:** Introduction of Smoot-Hawley tariff leads to worsening of depression worldwide
- **1930–31:** Over 3000 bank failures
- **1932:** Democrat Franklin Roosevelt elected President
- **1933:** NRA (National Recovery Administration) set up to regulate wage levels and child labour
- **1934–36:** Mass migration of farmers from the Great Plains to California
- **1937:** Roosevelt attempts to 'pack' Supreme Court to ensure passage of New Deal legislation
- **1941:** Bombing of Pearl Harbor; US enters Second World War

1915   1920   1925   1930   1935   1940   1945

Popular culture in the US

Developments in technology during the First World War improved communications throughout the US. By the 1920s virtually all of the nation was connected to the Bell Telephone network. Radio sets enabled news and information to reach even isolated areas. The cinema became the first mass entertainment industry. From small beginnings in the early 1900s, by the 1930s the film industry in Hollywood was exporting its glamorous products worldwide. During the Depression, cheap cinema tickets kept audience numbers buoyant despite an initial downturn. Professional sports such as football, baseball, and boxing became of national interest for the first time, with huge attendances and highly-paid celebrities.

▼ **4** The major Hollywood studios in 1919

☆ Nestor
☆ Famous Players – Lasky Clater Paramount
☆ National Film Corporation of America
☆ Metro
☆ Chaplin
☆ Brunton
☆ Fox
☆ D.W. Griffith
☆ Vitagraph
☆ Mack Sennett
☆ Universal
☆ Ince
☆ Goldwyn

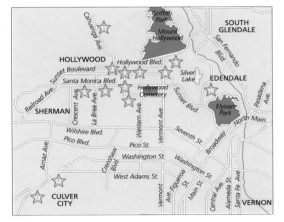

By 1919, most of the major film studios had established themselves to the north of Los Angeles. Hollywood became the heart of the world motion picture industry and a magnet for all aspiring film-makers.

Annual consumer expenditure on movie-going ($ millions)

720, 719, 482, 556, 676, 659, 809, 1275, 1450
1929, 1931, 1933, 1935, 1937, 1939, 1941, 1943, 1945

The growth in spending on cinema tickets reflected wartime prosperity.

Number of radio sets in the US (millions)

0.25, 12, 24
1921, 1930, 1935

By 1924, more than 2.5 million radios had been sold to American consumers.

Sales of records in the US ($ millions)

105.6, 92.4, 79.2, 68.2, 59.2
1921, 1922, 1923, 1924, 1925

The growth in popularity of the radio led to a dramatic decline in record buying: within five years sales had virtually halved.

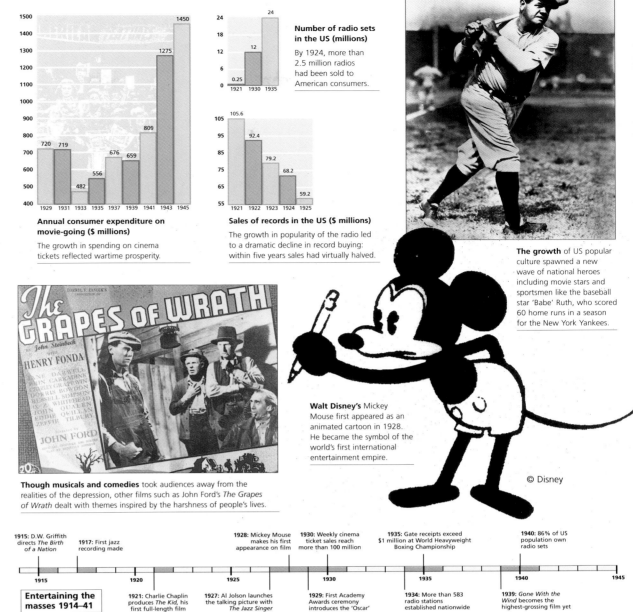

Though musicals and comedies took audiences away from the realities of the depression, other films such as John Ford's *The Grapes of Wrath* dealt with themes inspired by the harshness of people's lives.

The growth of US popular culture spawned a new wave of national heroes including movie stars and sportsmen like the baseball star 'Babe' Ruth, who scored 60 home runs in a season for the New York Yankees.

Walt Disney's Mickey Mouse first appeared as an animated cartoon in 1928. He became the symbol of the world's first international entertainment empire.

© Disney

Entertaining the masses 1914–41

1915: D.W. Griffith directs *The Birth of a Nation*
1917: First jazz recording made
1921: Charlie Chaplin produces *The Kid*, his first full-length film
1927: Al Jolson launches the talking picture with *The Jazz Singer*
1928: Mickey Mouse makes his first appearance on film
1929: First Academy Awards ceremony introduces the 'Oscar'
1930: Weekly cinema ticket sales reach more than 100 million
1934: More than 583 radio stations established nationwide
1935: Gate receipts exceed $1 million at World Heavyweight Boxing Championship
1939: *Gone With the Wind* becomes the highest-grossing film yet
1940: 86% of US population own radio sets

1915 1920 1925 1930 1935 1940 1945

THE FDR EFFECT

The political complexion of the US altered radically during the 1930s. Hoover's Republican party, so dominant at the height of the '20s boom, was routed by the Democrats in 1932. The patrician Franklin Delano Roosevelt attracted a 'New Deal coalition' of Blacks, women, labour groups, and southern whites which dominated American politics for over 30 years.

Roosevelt spoke regularly to the American people via his 'fireside chats' which were broadcast on national radio.

◀ **5** Presidential elections

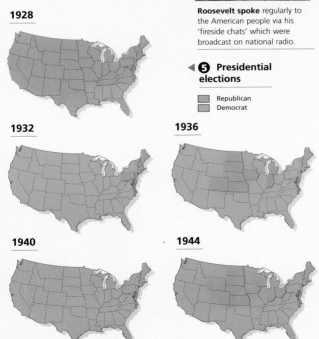

■ Republican
■ Democrat

1928
1932   1936
1940   1944

Intolerance

This period, particularly the 1920s, was marked by diverse displays of intolerance against perceived threats to the 'American Way of Life'. 'New' immigrants, black migration, the increased freedom of women, and economic instability all fuelled anxieties. The prohibition of alcohol, immigration 'Quota Acts', and the formation of the FBI in response to the 'Red Scare' of 1919–20 and the fear of Communism, were official responses to this new intolerance. Other – unofficial – reactions included race riots in the southern states and Midwest and the revival of the white supremacist Ku Klux Klan whose membership increased to more than two million in the 1920s.

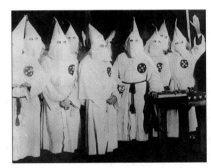

The growth of the Ku Klux Klan in this period was largely an expression of insecurity among small-town White Anglo-Saxon Protestants towards a multitude of apparent threats to their power and influence.

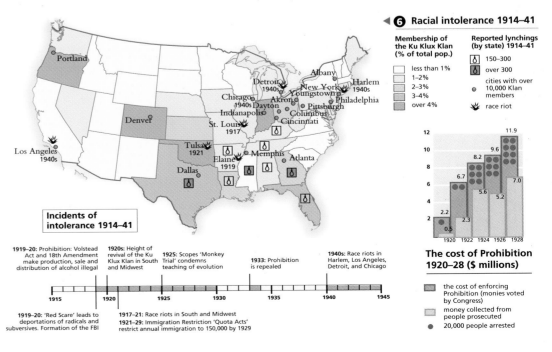

Incidents of intolerance 1914–41

1919–20: Prohibition: Volstead Act and 18th Amendment make production, sale and distribution of alcohol illegal
1919–20: 'Red Scare' leads to deportations of radicals and subversives. Formation of the FBI
1920s: Height of revival of the Ku Klux Klan in South and Midwest
1917–21: Race riots in South and Midwest
1921–29: Immigration Restriction 'Quota Acts' restrict annual immigration to 150,000 by 1929
1925: Scopes 'Monkey Trial' condemns teaching of evolution
1933: Prohibition is repealed
1940s: Race riots in Harlem, Los Angeles, Detroit, and Chicago

1915 1920 1925 1930 1935 1940 1945

◀ **6** Racial intolerance 1914–41

Membership of the Ku Klux Klan (% of total pop.)
☐ less than 1%
☐ 1–2%
☐ 2–3%
☐ 3–4%
☐ over 4%

Reported lynchings (by state) 1914–41
△ 150–300
△ over 300
● cities with over 10,000 Klan members
✦ race riot

The cost of Prohibition 1920–28 ($ millions)

0.5, 2.2, 2.3, 6.7, 5.6, 8.2, 5.2, 9.6, 7.0, 11.9
1920, 1922, 1924, 1926, 1928

■ the cost of enforcing Prohibition (monies voted by Congress)
☐ money collected from people prosecuted
● 20,000 people arrested

SOCIETIES IN TRANSITION

Martin Luther King harnessed the spontaneous protests of the 1950s to create a massive anti-racial movement.

IN THE 1950S, THE UNITED STATES was labelled 'the affluent society'. This phrase reflected the experience of unprecedented economic prosperity and social progress in the years since the Second World War ended the Great Depression. Most Americans enjoyed rising incomes on the back of the postwar boom. The quality of life was further enhanced by the availability of new consumer goods, new leisure opportunities, and suburban housing. The people of Mexico, Central America, and the Caribbean continued to have a much lower standard of living than the US and Canada. And within the US, itself, not all regions and social groups experienced equal advances in affluence and status.

Postwar prosperity in the US

The idealized family unit, headed by a male breadwinner, became a favourite image for advertisers and politicians during the 1950s.

The economic stimulus provided by the war and, later, the arms race with the Soviet Union were key factors in creating the affluence of the immediate postwar decades. As manufacturing switched to a peacetime mode, consumer durables flowed into the domestic marketplace. Consumerism generated a flourishing service sector. America's position at the hub of the international trading system gave her access to foreign markets and raw materials crucial to economic success. The boom ended in the early 1970s, with the Vietnam War and the energy crisis producing prolonged inflation and recession. Europe and Japan were also challenging American economic dominance.

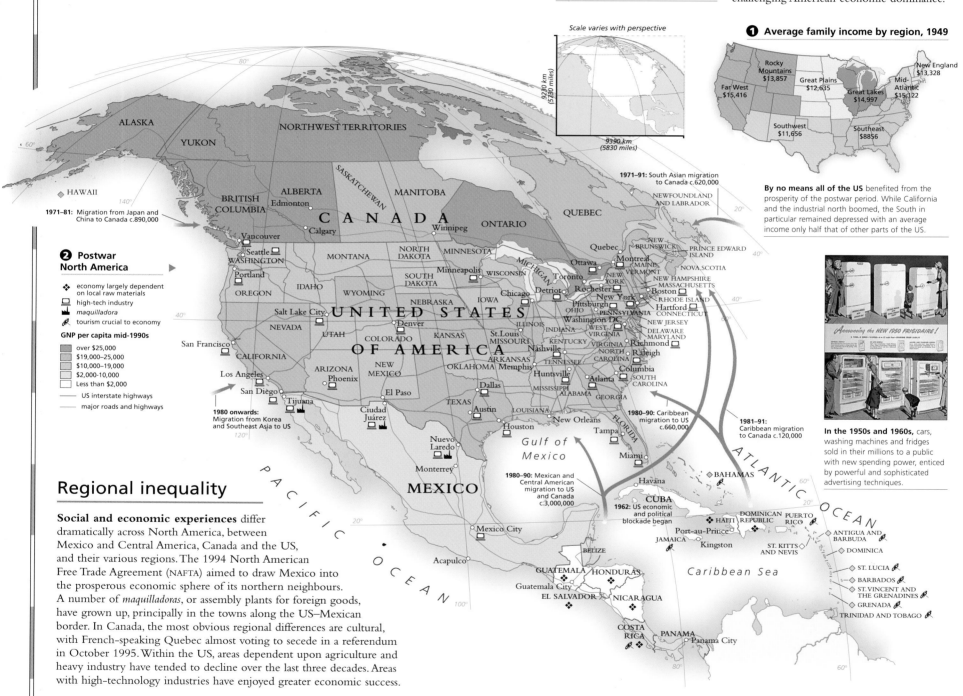

Scale varies with perspective

❶ Average family income by region, 1949

Rocky Mountains $13,857 · Great Plains $12,635 · Great Lakes $14,997 · New England $13,328 · Mid-Atlantic $15,122 · Far West $15,416 · Southwest $11,656 · Southeast $8856

By no means all of the US benefited from the prosperity of the postwar period. While California and the industrial north boomed, the South in particular remained depressed with an average income only half that of other parts of the US.

❷ Postwar North America

- ◈ economy largely dependent on local raw materials
- ▪ high-tech industry
- ▴ *maquilladora*
- tourism crucial to economy

GNP per capita mid-1990s
- over $25,000
- $19,000–25,000
- $10,000–19,000
- $2,000–10,000
- Less than $2,000

— US interstate highways
— major roads and highways

1971–81: Migration from Japan and China to Canada c.890,000

1971–91: South Asian migration to Canada c.620,000

1980 onwards: Migration from Korea and Southeast Asia to US

1980–90: Mexican and Central American migration to US and Canada c.3,000,000

1980–90: Caribbean migration to US c.660,000

1981–91: Caribbean migration to Canada c.120,000

1962: US economic and political blockade began

In the 1950s and 1960s, cars, washing machines and fridges sold in their millions to a public with new spending power, enticed by powerful and sophisticated advertising techniques.

Regional inequality

Social and economic experiences differ dramatically across North America, between Mexico and Central America, Canada and the US, and their various regions. The 1994 North American Free Trade Agreement (NAFTA) aimed to draw Mexico into the prosperous economic sphere of its northern neighbours. A number of *maquilladoras*, or assembly plants for foreign goods, have grown up, principally in the towns along the US–Mexican border. In Canada, the most obvious regional differences are cultural, with French-speaking Quebec almost voting to secede in a referendum in October 1995. Within the US, areas dependent upon agriculture and heavy industry have tended to decline over the last three decades. Areas with high-technology industries have enjoyed greater economic success.

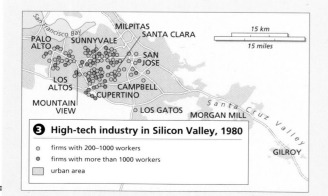

❸ High-tech industry in Silicon Valley, 1980
- ○ firms with 200–1000 workers
- ● firms with more than 1000 workers
- ▫ urban area

SILICON VALLEY

Without specific locational needs, many high-tech firms were able to site their businesses in non-urban areas in the South and West, helping to revitalize the economy of these regions. Silicon Valley near San Francisco, California, contains one of the world's highest concentrations of computing and electronic industries. Initially, many high-tech manufacturers relied upon contracts from the US military, but the age of the personal computer has allowed these manufacturers to play a key role in sustaining American exports and growth.

New high-tech industries including aerospace and electronics, as at Silicon Valley (right), grew up in the late 1970s to fill the gaps left by the decline of traditional US heavy industries.

Changes in urban life

As black Americans migrated from the rural South to urban centres in the 1940s and 1950s, many whites abandoned city life for the suburbs. These areas became increasingly detached from the cities; instead of petitioning for access to the cities' municipal facilities, postwar suburban residents fought fiercely against annexation proposals. The tax dollars of prosperous whites were no longer available to maintain the city infrastructure. The financial crisis was made worse by the decline of traditional US industries, and many of America's cities sank into crisis during the 1960s and 1970s. Housing stock deteriorated, roads were not repaired, and poverty, crime, and racial tension were common features of many urban areas in the US. Poverty was not confined to the inner cities: people in rural areas in the deep South, and the Appalachians were some of the most deprived in the US.

The centres of many of America's great cities declined physically as people move to the suburbs. Old housing stock was torn down but not replaced, and the infrastructure declined through lack of funding.

The new suburbs provided a safe haven away from the cities. Mortgage assistance was readily available to those wishing to move to suburban areas. Until the 1960s, money was siphoned into the suburbs by federal housing officials, who simultaneously denied loans to people still living in urban areas.

The growth of the suburbs

The 1950s saw the growth of suburban America. New construction techniques lowered the cost of new homes, and expressways improved access to and from urban centres. In the postwar era, cities like Chicago absorbed ever more of their surrounding areas.

④ Chicago: 1850–1969

Urban growth
- 1850
- 1875
- 1900
- 1925
- 1950
- 1969

LAKE COUNTY
McHENRY COUNTY
ILLINOIS
KANE COUNTY
DU PAGE COUNTY
Chicago
KENDALL COUNTY
WILL COUNTY
COOK COUNTY
Lake Michigan
INDIANA
LAKE COUNTY
PORTER COUNTY

20 km
20 miles

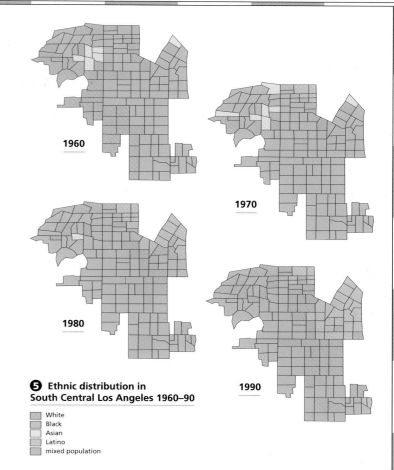

1960

1970

1980

1990

⑤ Ethnic distribution in South Central Los Angeles 1960–90

- White
- Black
- Asian
- Latino
- mixed population

Poverty and ethnic balance in inner city Los Angeles

Los Angeles demonstrates how wealth and poverty live separate lives in postwar urban America. The central neighbourhoods in an otherwise prosperous city have a massively disproportionate number of poor residents, with an ethnic mix in constant flux. In 1960, a substantial white population remained in South Central Los Angeles. By 1970, whites had largely left the area, which had a now predominantly black population. Twenty years later, Latinos formed a majority in many South Central neighbourhoods.

Civil Rights and other protest movements

1955: Bus boycott against segregation in Montgomery, Alabama

1961: Student freedom riders go into South to protest against segregation

1963: March on Washington led by Martin Luther King

1965: Voting Rights Act increases number of black voters; Watts Riots in Los Angeles

1968: Assassination of Martin Luther King sparks riots in 124 US cities

1970: Four students killed at Kent State University, Ohio in protest over US involvement in Cambodia

1955 — 1960 — 1965 — 1970 — 1975

1957: Martin Luther King heads coordinated resistance movement

1964: Civil Rights Act forbids segregation in public places

1966: Race riots in Atlanta

1968: Riots and protests follow Democrat rally in Chicago

1969: 250,000 people march on Washington in protest against war in Vietnam

1974: High Court gives go-ahead to busing for integration of US schools

In August 1969, 400,000 people gathered at a farm near Bethel in upper New York state to form the 'Woodstock Nation', a music festival which was also a celebration of peaceful, anti-establishment co-existence.

A woman prays for peace in Birmingham, Alabama, during a Civil Rights protest in May 1963, as fellow demonstrators dance and sing behind her.

⑥ Protest movements and urban unrest of the 1960s

- ☀ anti-war protest
- ✷ centre of civil rights activity
- 🌱 urban unrest/race riot

GEORGIA 28% 64% Percentage of the black population of voting age registered to vote: before the Voting Rights Act of 1965, in 1971

Blacks as a % of state population
- more than 30
- 20–30
- 15–20
- 7–15
- less than 7

Moves for freedom

The opportunities presented by postwar America were denied to many black Americans, particularly in the still-segregated South, where they were prevented by whites from voting. Inspired by decolonization movements abroad, and aided by a 1954 Supreme Court judgement that segregation was unconstitutional, black Americans began to challenge discrimination. In 1955, a bus boycott in Montgomery, Alabama forced the bus company to end segregation. The success inspired similar protests throughout the South. In 1964 and 1965, the US Congress passed legislation banning racial discrimination and protecting the democratic rights of all Americans. The 1960s also saw a rise in political consciousness among other groups; protests against the Vietnam War grew in number throughout the late 1960s, as did the movement for women's rights.

THE USA: GROWTH OF A SUPERPOWER

John F. Kennedy, a charismatic and popular US president, was assassinated in 1963.

THE JAPANESE ATTACK on Pearl Harbor in December 1941 and the subsequent US entry into the Second World War marked the beginning of a new era in America's role in the world. Thereafter, through alliances, military interventions, and trade, the United States exerted a powerful influence over the lives of other nations. While the US and Canada remained stable and prosperous, Central America and the Caribbean struggled for democracy and autonomy in the post–war period. Although challenged by the Cuban Revolution in 1959, the US continued to exercise power in the region, often through support for military dictatorships.

America and the world

During the Second World War, the US established a large number of military bases around the world. With the onset of the Cold War with the Soviet Union in the late 1940s, those bases had renewed importance. The Cold War also encouraged the Americans to form alliances with other nations. The North Atlantic Treaty Organization (NATO) was formed in 1949. After the Vietnam War, the US retreated from an active international role. The Soviet invasion of Afghanistan in 1979, however, revived the Cold War for another decade. With the collapse of the Soviet Union in 1991, the United States was left as the only superpower.

① Strategic alliances 1948–89

US collective defence treaties
- NATO from 1983
- Rio Treaty by 1975
- ANZUS Pact 1951
- Southeast Asia Collective Defence Treaty 1954
- Bilateral defence treaties (Japan 1960; South Korea 1953; Philippines 1951, Taiwan 1954)
- US troops on active service
- COMECON members
- other Communist states 1977
- Military Air Transit Rights, Eastern Hemisphere

US involvement in world affairs 1950–90

| 1950: Korean War | 1955: US intervention in Iran | 1958: Eisenhower Doctrine commits US to prevent spread of Communism in Middle East | 1973: US withdraws troops from Vietnam | 1979: Iran hostage crisis | 1990: US sends troops to The Gulf in response to Saddam Hussein's invasion of Kuwait |

| 1950 | 1960 | 1970 | 1980 | 1990 |

| 1950: Start of US involvement in Vietnam | 1961: Cuban Missile Crisis | 1973: US assists in right-wing coup in Chile | 1978: US-brokered peace deal between Egypt and Israel | 1983: US intervention in Grenada |

US involvement was crucial to Allied success in the Second World War, with campaigns in the Pacific and support both on the ground and in the air in Europe. At the end of the war, US troops liberated a number of Nazi concentration camps and prisoner-of-war camps (above).

US soldiers with a Viet Cong suspect during the Vietnam War (1950–73), the longest and most costly of US attempts to contain the perceived Communist threat during the Cold War.

US investment overseas

During the Cold War, investment overseas was seen as a way to bind other nations to the capitalist sphere. The Marshall Plan of 1948 aimed both to aid the postwar recovery of Western Europe and reduce the chances of Communist subversion. American firms also tried to secure access to valuable raw materials, most importantly oil in the Middle East. More recently, US companies sought to exploit cheap foreign labour by establishing factories overseas, threatening jobs at home.

◀ ② US investment overseas

US private direct investment abroad
- 1960
- 1984

0% 0% Soviet Union and Eastern Europe
33% 21% Canada
1% 3% Japan
21% 47% Western Europe
3% 7% Asia and Pacific (exc. Japan and Middle East)
3% 1% Middle East
28% 12% Central and South America and the Caribbean
2% 3% Africa (exc. South Africa)
1% 1% South Africa
3% 4% Australia and New Zealand

The decline of the Democratic South

The migration of Southern blacks to northern cities in the 1940s and 1950s killed off most of the remaining cotton plantations in the South, which had depended on their cheap labour, leading to a decline in the Southern economy. In the North, black Americans became an important political constituency. The Democratic Party tried to reconcile its desire for their votes with its desire for the continued support of white Southerners who traditionally voted Democrat. By the late 1960s, after the Civil Rights legislation of President Lyndon Johnson, many Southerners abandoned their traditional commitment to the Democratic Party.

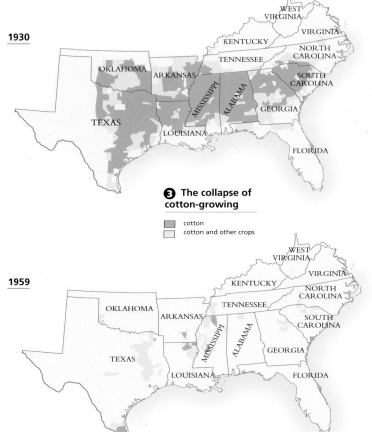

1930

❸ The collapse of cotton-growing

- cotton
- cotton and other crops

1959

KEY ELECTIONS 1948–96

In 1948 Democrat President Harry Truman won a shock victory over the Republican Thomas Dewey. However, the success of the pro-segregationist States Rights Party indicated that the Democrats might have problems maintaining the support of both blacks and Southerners, and in 1968 the Democrats lost every Southern state except Texas. Though Republicans held the Presidency throughout the 1980s, the elections of 1992 and 1996 proved that the Democrats could still win despite a largely Republican South.

The Chicago Daily Tribune was so confident of the outcome of the 1948 US Presidential elections that the paper was printed without confirmation of the results, leaving the victorious Democratic candidate Harry Truman to revel in the premature headline.

1948

1968

Alaska
Hawaii

1996

Alaska
Hawaii

❹ Presidential elections

States won by each party
- Republicans
- Democrats
- States Rights
- American Independent

US election results 1944–96

1944: Roosevelt (Democrat) elected for a fourth term but dies in April 1945
1948: Roosevelt's successor, Truman (Democrat) is surprise winner
1952: Eisenhower (Republican) wins election
1956: Eisenhower wins second term
1960: Kennedy (Democrat) elected President
1963: Assassination of Kennedy. Johnson becomes President. Reelected in 1964
1968: Nixon (Republican) elected. Reelected 1972
1974: Nixon resigns over Watergate scandal. Replaced by Gerald Ford
1976: Jimmy Carter (Democrat) elected
1980: Ronald Reagan (Republican) wins. Wins second term in 1984
1988: George Bush (Republican) wins
1992: Bill Clinton (Democrat) elected. Wins second term in 1996

1944   1952   1960   1968   1976   1984   1992

US intervention in Central America

Historically the US has acted to prevent instability and protect its business interests in Central America. During the Cold War, America's concern intensified, with the fear of Communist subversion in its own backyard. In 1954, US agents organized the downfall of a left-wing government in Guatemala. In 1962, a crisis over Soviet nuclear arms in Cuba *(see p.108)* almost caused nuclear war. During the 1980s, President Reagan acted against leftists in Grenada and Nicaragua. After the Cold War, the drugs trade presents a major reason for continued American involvement in the region.

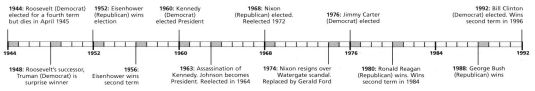

The Sandinista revolution of 1978 put an end to more than 40 years of military dictatorship in Nicaragua. The left-wing Sandinistas were distrusted by the US which sponsored Contra guerrillas based in Honduras *(left)* against the government.

In 1989, 23,000 US troops invaded Panama, arresting its ruler General Manuel Noriega *(above)* on drug trafficking charges. He was replaced by Guillermo Endara, a US-approved choice.

❺ US intervention in Central America and the Caribbean

- Cuban-sponsored guerilla activities 1959–68
- US intervention

UNITED STATES OF AMERICA

ATLANTIC OCEAN

US exploitation of cheap Mexican labour in free trade zone (see p.136)

Gulf of Mexico

Tropic of Cancer

MEXICO
1980s: Serious economic difficulties
1993–94: NAFTA creates free-trade community of US, Mexico, and Canada

BAHAMAS

CUBA
1961: Attempted invasion at Bay of Pigs by US-supported forces
1962: Cuban Missile Crisis
Apr–Sep 1980: Migration of thousands of Cubans to US
1990: Severe economic distress following withdrawal of Soviet aid

1991: Ongoing unrest; military coup ousts elected government

1978–90: Staging area for anti-Sandinista rebel army (Contras) organized and financed by US

BELIZE

1954: Military, with US backing topples democratic government pledged to land and social reforms
1961: Appearance of revolutionaries
1968–70: US ambassador and military advisors killed by rebels
1980s–90s: Ongoing guerrilla activity

GUATEMALA
HONDURAS
EL SALVADOR

NICARAGUA

Guantanamo Bay to US

JAMAICA

HAITI
1961: Assassination of President Trujillo
1965: US President Johnson intervenes with 22,000 troops

DOMINICAN REPUBLIC

PUERTO RICO to US

Caribbean Sea

1961: FSLN (Sandinista) rebels appear
1978: Sandinista revolution
1982–83: US finances guerrilla army fighting leftist Sandinista government
1990: Anti-Sandinista coalition wins election

1960s: The 'model' of the Alliance for Progress
1970: First revolutionaries appear
1991: Right-wing government and opposition leaders sign unbrokered peace treaty
1990s: Continued reliance on US aid; heavy influence of US ambassador

COSTA RICA
PANAMA

1959, 1964: Anti-US riots
1978: Panama Canal Treaties
Dec 1989: US invades Panama to capture General Noriega

Scale varies with perspective

5000 km (3110 miles)

5550 km (3450 miles)

PACIFIC OCEAN

ANTIGUA AND BARBUDA

ST. KITTS AND NEVIS

DOMINICA

ST. VINCENT AND THE GRENADINES   ST. LUCIA

Caracas

GRENADA
Oct 1983: Radical left-wing government overthrown by US intervention

BARBADOS

TRINIDAD AND TOBAGO

COLOMBIA
1980s/1990s: Flow of drugs to US causes serious crime

VENEZUELA

ECUADOR

GUYANA

SOUTH AMERICA
REGIONAL HISTORY

THE HISTORICAL LANDSCAPE

THE LAST CONTINENT – APART FROM ANTARCTICA – to be colonized by humans, (the first settlers arrived from North America no more than 20,000 years ago), South America remains a realm of harsh extremes of climate, environment, and human society. The cordillera spine of the Andes was the heartland of the first complex societies and civilizations. Early settlers spread through the fertile tracts of the Amazon Basin, but few ventured to the sterile salt pans of the Atacama Desert – one of the driest places on Earth – or Patagonia – one of the least hospitable. European contact in the 16th century brought, as elsewhere in the Americas, the decline of indigenous cultures, although here widespread intermarriage and the enforced importation of African slaves to work on plantations created an extraordinarily varied genetic, linguistic, and cultural pool. The continent struggled free of European colonialism in the 19th century only to be confronted by the challenge of economic, social, and political modernization, which was met with varying success. This process brought wealth for some, marginalization for many – especially in the continent's burgeoning but scattered centres of population – and a threat to the global ecosystem, as the resources of the Amazonian wilderness were increasingly placed under pressure.

The Andes were one of the sites of the earliest agricultural civilizations in South America, perhaps as much as 10,000 years ago. The mountains and temperate climate provided a wide range of habitats for wild plants. Tubers – such as potatoes and sweet potatoes – grew naturally and were simple to cultivate.

The Amazon rainforests now cover about 5,300,000 sq km of South America. At the height of the last Ice Age around 18,000 years ago, the cool arid climate, unsuitable for rainforest plants, had reduced to forest to only about 10% of its present area. Over the past 10,000 years, wetter climates have enabled the forest to grow in size.

The flat grassland plains of the pampas of southeastern South America were mainly desert during the era covered by the map (*opposite*). Higher levels of moisture have allowed grasslands to develop, but the area remains dry, and has always been a region of low human population.

Vegetation type

- ice cap and glacier
- tundra
- polar and alpine desert
- semi-desert or sparsely vegetated
- grassland
- forest or open woodland
- tropical rainforest
- temperate desert
- tropical desert
- coastline (present-day)
- coastline (18,000 years ago)

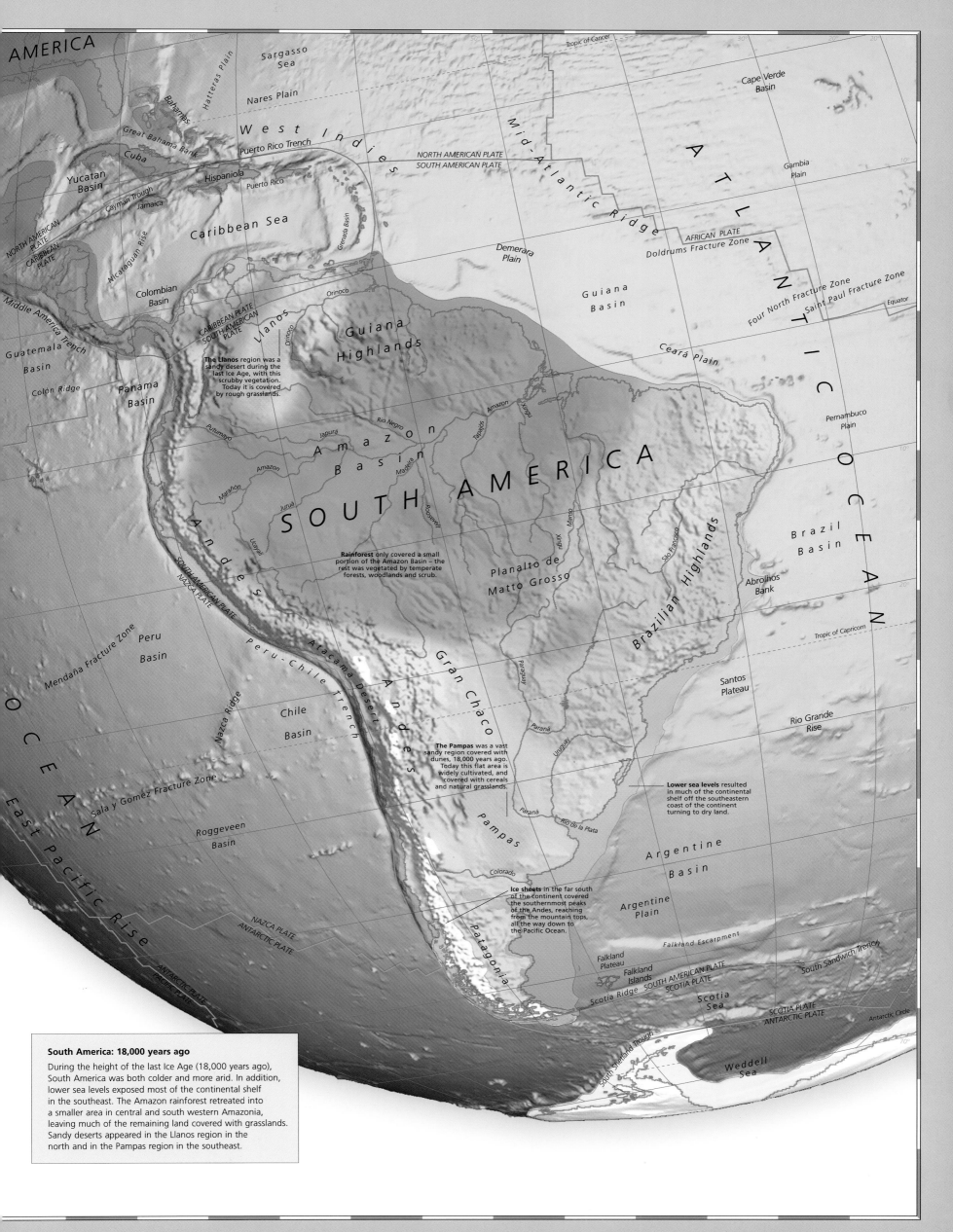

AMERICA

West Indies

Hatteras Plain
Nares Plain
Sargasso Sea
Bahamas
Great Bahama Bank
Cuba
Yucatan Basin
Hispaniola
Puerto Rico Trench
Puerto Rico
Cayman Trough
Jamaica
Caribbean Sea

Cape Verde Basin

Mid-Atlantic Ridge

ATLANTIC OCEAN

NORTH AMERICAN PLATE
SOUTH AMERICAN PLATE

AFRICAN PLATE
Doldrums Fracture Zone

Gambia Plain

NORTH AMERICAN PLATE
CARIBBEAN PLATE
Middle America Trench

Colombian Basin

Guatemala Basin

Colón Ridge

Panama Basin

CARIBBEAN PLATE
SOUTH AMERICAN PLATE

Llanos

Orinoco

Guiana Highlands

Demerara Plain

Guiana Basin

Four North Fracture Zone
Saint Paul Fracture Zone
Equator

Ceará Plain

The Llanos region was a sandy desert during the last Ice Age, with this scrubby vegetation. Today it is covered by rough grasslands.

Nicaraguan Rise

Putumayo
Japurá
Rio Negro
Amazon
Amazon Basin
Marañón
Juruá
Ucayali

Amazon
Madeira
Tapajós
Xingu
Roosevelt

SOUTH AMERICA

Pernambuco Plain

Brazil Basin

Abrolhos Bank

Rainforest only covered a small portion of the Amazon Basin – the rest was vegetated by temperate forests, woodlands and scrub.

São Francisco
Jaí
Manso
Planalto de Matto Grosso

Brazilian Highlands

SOUTH AMERICAN PLATE
NAZCA PLATE

Andes

Atacama Desert

Peru-Chile Trench

Mendaña Fracture Zone
Peru Basin

Nazca Ridge
Chile Basin

Tropic of Capricorn

Santos Plateau

Rio Grande Rise

Gran Chaco

Paraguay
Paraná

Sala y Gomez Fracture Zone

Roggeveen Basin

The Pampas was a vast sandy region covered with dunes, 18,000 years ago. Today this flat area is widely cultivated, and covered with cereals and natural grasslands.

Uruguay
Paraná
Rio de la Plata

Pampas

Lower sea levels resulted in much of the continental shelf off the southeastern coast of the continent turning to dry land.

Argentine Basin

NAZCA PLATE
ANTARCTIC PLATE

East Pacific Rise

Colorado

Ice sheets in the far south of the continent covered the southernmost peaks of the Andes, reaching from the mountain tops, all the way down to the Pacific Ocean.

Argentine Plain

Patagonia

Falkland Plateau
Falkland Islands

Falkland Escarpment

Scotia Ridge SOUTH AMERICAN PLATE
SCOTIA PLATE

South Sandwich Trench

SCOTIA PLATE
ANTARCTIC PLATE

Antarctic Circle

ANTARCTIC PLATE
PACIFIC PLATE

Scotia Sea

South Shetland Trough

Weddell Sea

South America: 18,000 years ago

During the height of the last Ice Age (18,000 years ago), South America was both colder and more arid. In addition, lower sea levels exposed most of the continental shelf in the southeast. The Amazon rainforest retreated into a smaller area in central and south western Amazonia, leaving much of the remaining land covered with grasslands. Sandy deserts appeared in the Llanos region in the north and in the Pampas region in the southeast.

SOUTH AMERICA
EXPLORATION AND MAPPING

The name America was coined to honour Amerigo Vespucci, an Italian explorer in the service of Portugal.

THOUGH THE INCAS left no maps, their Andean empire's extensive road system was testimony to their topographical skills. It was a long time before any Europeans had a similar understanding of the continent. When Columbus first sighted the South American coast in 1498, he realized he had found a continental landmass, but thought it was part of Asia. This was disproved by the voyages of Vespucci and others along the Atlantic coast, culminating in Ferdinand Magellan's reaching the Pacific in 1520. In the wake of Pizarro's conquest of Peru and theft of the Incas' gold, many explorers were fired by dreams of instant riches. The net products of most expeditions, however, were the alienation of native tribes and the spread of European killer diseases. From the mid-17th century to the late 18th century, when serious scientific surveys began, exploration was largely the preserve of intrepid missionaries, notably the Jesuits, and slave-raiders from Brazil.

European conquerors and explorers

Throughout the first two decades of the 16th century Portuguese and Spanish explorers of the Atlantic coast sailed into every wide estuary in the hope that it would prove to be a passage to the Indies. Magellan eventually demonstrated that such a route existed, but it proved impracticable for the purpose of trade with the East. As a result, the Atlantic coastal regions of the continent were soon well understood and mapped, further information coming from Portuguese traders who sailed there in search of brazil wood, a tree that produced a valuable red dye and gave its name to the region. In the Andes, Pizarro, Benalcázar, and their fellow *conquistadores* were able to follow the well-maintained roads of the Inca Empire, but in most other parts of the continent, expeditions were forced back by hostile indigenous peoples, trackless swamps and forests, or impassable rapids.

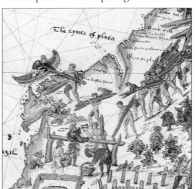

This detail from a map of South America produced by John Rotz in 1542 shows native Americans carrying logs of brazil wood for trade with Europeans.

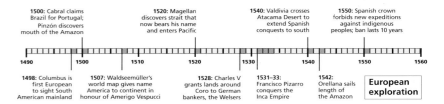

1500: Cabral claims Brazil for Portugal; Pinzón discovers mouth of the Amazon

1520: Magellan discovers strait that now bears his name and enters Pacific

1540: Valdivia crosses Atacama Desert to extend Spanish conquests to south

1550: Spanish crown forbids new expeditions against indigenous peoples; ban lasts 10 years

1498: Columbus is first European to sight South American mainland

1507: Waldseemüller's world map gives name America to continent in honour of Amerigo Vespucci

1528: Charles V grants lands around Coro to German bankers, the Welsers

1531–33: Francisco Pizarro conquers the Inca Empire

1542: Orellana sails length of the Amazon

European exploration

The Cantino planisphere, the earliest known map showing South America, was produced in Lisbon in 1502. It shows part of Brazil and the line agreed by the Treaty of Tordesillas in 1494, dividing the world between Portugal and Spain.

❶ **First European explorers of South America** ▶

Principal journeys

→ Spanish expedition

→ Portuguese expedition

→ German expedition

→ English expedition

→ Dutch expedition

Recife 1535   European settlement and date of foundation

Jesuit missions in the interior

Spanish Jesuits created frontier settlements – often of three or four thousand people – known as *reducciones*. These had their own churches, workshops, foundries, even armouries, and lands where the native Americans grew crops and raised herds of cattle. Money was not used, but the Jesuits traded with local Spanish settlers, who envied their success, especially among the Guaraní tribes. For the authorities, however, the *reducciones* formed a defence against Portuguese encroachment on Spanish lands; native Americans fought many battles with the slave-raiders from São Paulo known as Paulistas or *mamelucos*.

② **South America 1750** ▶

Areas colonized

- Spanish by 1650
- Spanish by 1750
- Portuguese by 1650
- Portuguese by 1750
- Dutch
- French

Missionary activity

- principal areas of Jesuit *reducciones*
- ✝ other major Jesuit missions
- ✝ major Franciscan missions
- *CHACO* *reduccion* with date
- *1732* of foundation
- 1630–32 active between these dates

Exploration of the interior

- → Jesuits
- → Franciscans
- → Paulista raids

The area covered by the detail from Father Fritz's map (*shown left*).

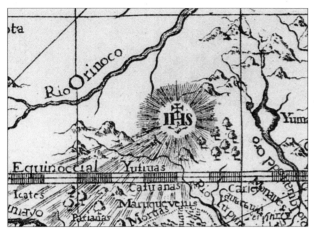

From the 17th century, most serious exploration and mapping of the interior of South America was the work of missionaries. This detail is from a map of the Amazon compiled by Samuel Fritz, a Bohemian-born Jesuit, and published in 1707. Note the Jesuits' IHS monogram above the Equator.

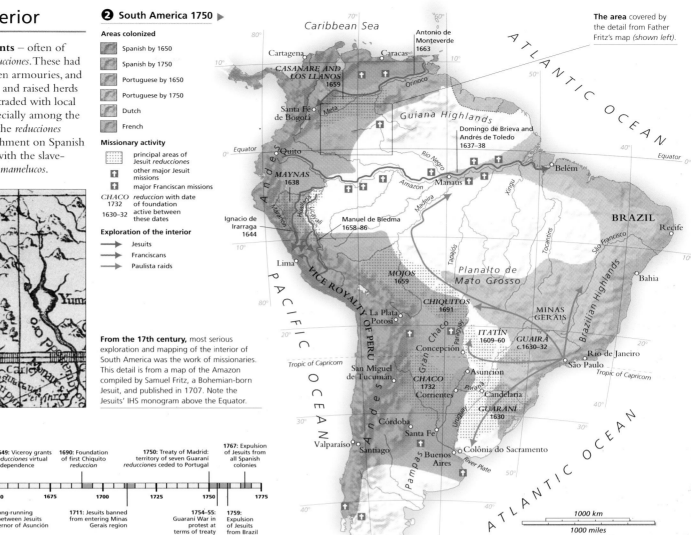

The Jesuits in South America

- **1550:** First Jesuits reach Brazil
- **1573:** Rules drawn up for planning Jesuit towns
- **1607:** Jesuits found province of Paraguay around Asunción
- **1631:** Father Ruiz de Montoya descends River Paraná with 12,000 Indians to escape slave-raiders
- **1641:** Indians and Jesuits defeat slave-raiders from São Paulo on River Uruguay
- **1640s:** Long-running quarrel between Jesuits and governor of Asunción
- **1649:** Viceroy grants *reducciones* virtual independence
- **1690:** Foundation of first Chiquito *reduccion*
- **1711:** Jesuits banned from entering Minas Gerais region
- **1750:** Treaty of Madrid: territory of seven Guaraní *reducciones* ceded to Portugal
- **1754–55:** Guaraní War in protest at terms of treaty
- **1759:** Expulsion of Jesuits from Brazil
- **1767:** Expulsion of Jesuits from all Spanish colonies

(timeline: 1550, 1575, 1600, 1625, 1650, 1675, 1700, 1725, 1750, 1775)

Later scientific exploration

Humboldt endured far greater hardship than this studio portrait suggests, as he travelled with French botanist, Aimé Bonpland, by canoe and on foot through the rainforests of the Orinoco.

For three centuries, the colonial authorities in South America did little to encourage scientific exploration. In the 19th century, however, scientists of all kinds began to explore the peaks of the Andes, the Amazon Basin, and even the wilds of Patagonia. The Prussian Alexander von Humboldt amassed unparalleled data on the geography, geology, meteorology, and natural history of South America. He mapped the course of the Casiquiare, a most unusual river in that it links the Amazon and Orinoco drainage basins. Of later travellers, the most famous was Charles Darwin, whose observations as a young naturalist aboard *HMS Beagle* in 1831–36 would inspire his theory of evolution expounded in *On the Origin of Species*. The French palaeontologist Alcide d'Orbigny, who spent eight years studying the continent's microfossils, published the first detailed physical map of South America in 1842.

③ **Scientific explorers**

Humboldt's journey
Aug 1799 ——— Mar 1803

Darwin's journey
Feb 1832 ——— Sep 1835

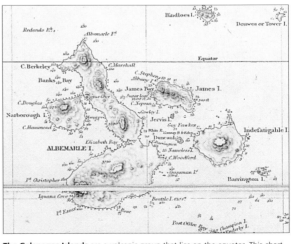

The Galapagos Islands are a volcanic group that lies on the equator. This chart was drawn by the officers of the *Beagle*, who were surveying the coast of South America for the British Navy. Darwin's interest was aroused by the peculiarities of the islands' fauna, such as the giant tortoises, which had evolved slightly different forms on each of the main islands, and the curious marine iguanas.

Large-billed seed-eating finch

Insectivorous warbler finch

The finches Darwin collected on the Galapagos Islands later provided powerful evidence for his theory of natural selection. Several closely related species had diverged from a common ancestor to occupy the various ecological niches on the islands.

Scientific exploration

- **1735:** Expedition to Quito led by French scientist La Condamine to test sphericity of the Earth
- **1783:** Spanish crown sponsors botanical expedition to South American colonies
- **1802:** Humboldt climbs to record height on the mountain of Chimborazo; correctly attributes altitude sickness to lack of oxygen
- **1826–34:** D'Orbigny studies continent's fossil-bearing strata
- **1832:** Darwin discovers fossils of giant mammals near Bahía Blanca, including *Megatherium*
- **1835:** Darwin encounters unique island fauna of the Galapagos Islands
- **1835–44:** Guiana region explored by Sir Robert Schomburgk, who fixes boundary of British colony
- **1859:** Naturalist Henry Bates returns to England with 8,000 insects new to science after 11 years in Amazon region
- **1872:** German Wilhelm Reiss scales Cotopaxi, which Humboldt had pronounced unclimbable

(timeline: 1725, 1750, 1775, 1800, 1825, 1850, 1875, 1900)

EARLY CULTURES OF SOUTH AMERICA

SOUTH AMERICA WAS COLONIZED by settlers from the north, possibly more than 20,000 years ago. Within 10,000 years, hunter-gatherers had reached its southern tip and, by 5000 BCE, were beginning to exploit local resources, such as maize, manioc, and potatoes. Successful agriculture led to growing populations and increasingly stratified societies. The distinctive temple mounds of Peru appeared by c.2500 BCE, and characteristic elements of South American religious iconography were disseminated all over Peru from the site of Chavín de Huantar, from c.1200 BCE. By 300 CE, Peru was dominated by two major civilizations: the Nazca, and the more expansionist Moche.

The Bahía people of coastal Ecuador made clay sculptures such as this figure holding a swaddled child.

The earliest settlements

The first South American settlers were hunter-gatherers, exploiting the big game which flourished following the last Ice Age. Spearheads and darts found at Fell's Cave indicate that this way of life had reached the far south of the continent by 10,000 BCE. In Chile, the site of Monte Verde (c.11,000 BCE) is a village of timber huts draped with animal hides. Finds of medicinal plants from the Andes, potato peelings, digging sticks, wooden bowls, and mortars, reveal an intimate knowledge of plant resources which supplemented a diet of small game and mastodon.

Monte Verde, the earliest known settlement in the southern half of the continent, is thought to have existed by at least 11,000 BCE. Stone tools found there include devices for chopping, scraping, and pounding (left).

Earliest settlements in South America

c.20,000 BCE: Linguistic and DNA evidence indicates first settlers arrived in South America

c.11,000 BCE: Evidence of settlement at Monte Verde in present-day Chile

c.2500 BCE: Masonry building and temple architecture at sites such as Aspero and Kotosh

c.1750 BCE: Massive ceremonial architecture at Sechin Alto

10,000 BCE: Evidence of hunter-gatherers at site of Fell's Cave, Patagonia

6000 BCE: Maize is cultivated in Ecuador

3000 BCE: Cotton cultivated in Central Andes. Large village settlements begin to appear

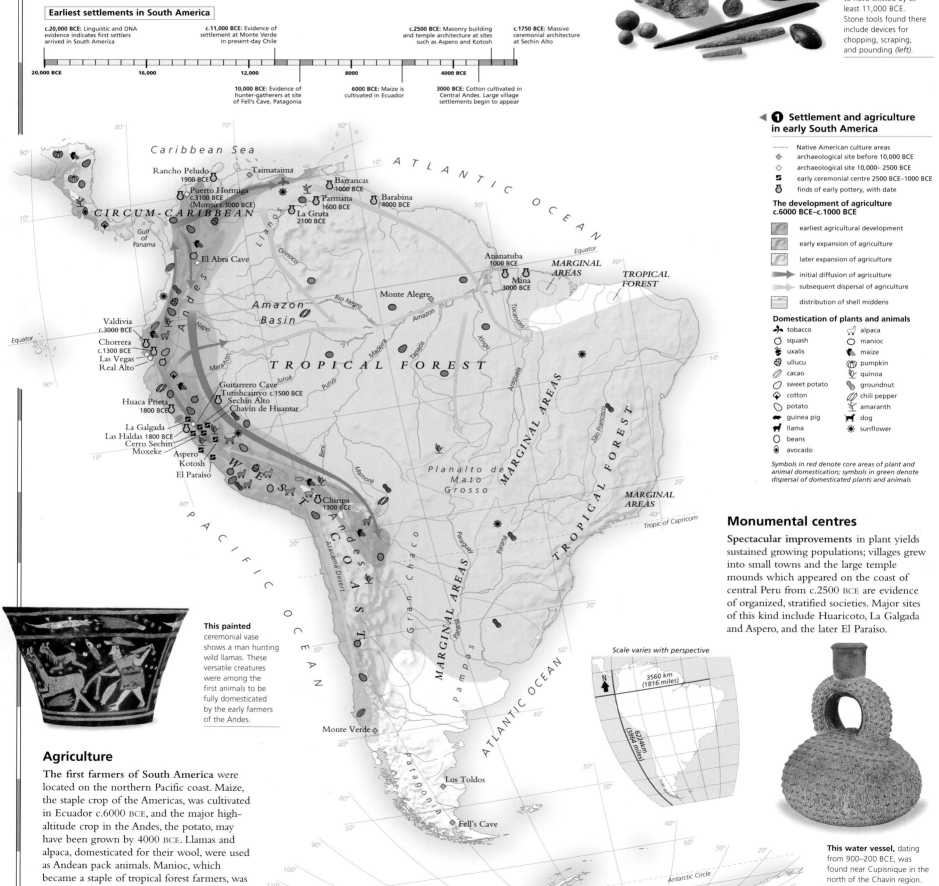

① Settlement and agriculture in early South America

This painted ceremonial vase shows a man hunting wild llamas. These versatile creatures were among the first animals to be fully domesticated by the early farmers of the Andes.

Monumental centres

Spectacular improvements in plant yields sustained growing populations; villages grew into small towns and the large temple mounds which appeared on the coast of central Peru from c.2500 BCE are evidence of organized, stratified societies. Major sites of this kind include Huaricoto, La Galgada and Aspero, and the later El Paraíso.

This water vessel, dating from 900–200 BCE, was found near Cupisnique in the north of the Chavín region.

Agriculture

The first farmers of South America were located on the northern Pacific coast. Maize, the staple crop of the Americas, was cultivated in Ecuador c.6000 BCE, and the major high-altitude crop in the Andes, the potato, may have been grown by 4000 BCE. Llamas and alpaca, domesticated for their wool, were used as Andean pack animals. Manioc, which became a staple of tropical forest farmers, was cultivated in the Amazon Basin by 3000 BCE.

The peoples of the Amazon Basin and the Atlantic coast

Rock shelters and flaked stone tools, dating to c.10,000 BCE provide the earliest evidence of settlement east of the Andes. The transition from hunting and gathering to agriculture – principally the cultivation of manioc – probably began c.3000 BCE. Large shell middens at the mouths of the Amazon and Orinoco rivers contain remains of pottery dating to c.5000 BCE – far earlier than the first pottery of Peru. When maize was introduced into the river flood plains in the 1st millennium BCE, populations expanded and hierarchical societies (chiefdoms) developed. Drainage earthworks on the Llanos de Mojos suggest that large populations were cooperating to farm the landscape.

◄ ② Early settlement of Amazonia and eastern South America

◇ early archaeological site 12,000–6000 BCE
⊻ early ceramic site 5000–1000 BCE
𝓅 early lithic site
⬛ earthworks and hydrological systems
⬮ shell midden

④ Coastal Peru c.600 BCE–600 CE

☐ Paracas cultural region c. 600–350 BCE
◇ major Paracas sites
☐ Ecuadorian cultural region c.500 BCE–500 CE
☐ Lima cultural region c.400 BCE–500 CE
☐ Nazca cultural region c.350 BCE–450 CE
☐ earliest Moche sites c.1 CE
☐ Moche cultural region c.1–600 CE
☐ Recuay cultural region c.500 CE
▽ irrigated river valley

The cultures of Peru 1300 BCE–600 CE

The most influential culture of the middle Andes was that of the Chavín which flourished at and around the major religious centre of Chavín de Huantar between 850 BCE and 200 BCE. The Chavín were distinguished by the sophistication of their architecture and sculptural style and by technological developments including the building of canals. As Chavín influence waned, from c.200 BCE, many distinctive regional cultures developed in the Andean highlands. Coastal Peru, however, was dominated by two major civilizations, Nazca in the south, and Moche in the north. As these cultures developed a strong identity, military rivalries intensified, paving the way for the appearance of other major states from 500 CE including Tiahuanaco and Huari.

Large cemeteries in the Paracas region contained thousands of mummified bodies wrapped in colourful wool. The motif of a large-eyed deity, the Occulate Being, on these textiles shows a strong affinity with the Chavín deity, known as the Smiling God.

Moche

Moche culture was centred on the capital of Moche, dominated by the famous Temple of the Sun, a massive structure of solid adobe, 40 m high. The Moche state was powerful, well-organized and expanded by military conquest. Mass labour was organized to participate in major public works and civil engineering projects and the construction of 'royal' tombs.

The stirrup-spout on this drinking vessel is a typical feature of Moche pottery, as is the marvellously realistic and sensitive modelling of the facial features.

Nazca

Based on the south coast of Peru, Nazca culture is famous for its superb and graphic pottery, textiles, and above all, the enigmatic 'Nazca lines', straight, geometric, or figurative designs etched onto the surface of the desert, possibly as offerings to the gods.

③ Chavín culture

☐ Chavín heartland
◇ early Chavín sites, 2000–850 BCE
◆ Chavín sites, 850–200 BCE
→ trade route

The Chavín

Chavín de Huantar (c.1200–200 BCE), with its large stone sculptures and grand temples, became a cult centre. Chavín motifs, in architecture, textiles, pottery, and goldwork, are found throughout Peru.

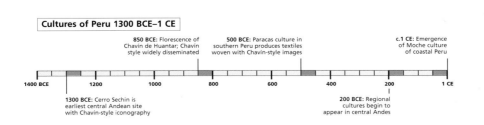

Cultures of Peru 1300 BCE–1 CE

850 BCE: Florescence of Chavín de Huantar; Chavín style widely disseminated

500 BCE: Paracas culture in southern Peru produces textiles woven with Chavín-style images

c.1 CE: Emergence of Moche culture of coastal Peru

1400 BCE   1200   1000   800   600   400   200   1 CE

1300 BCE: Cerro Sechin is earliest central Andean site with Chavín-style iconography

200 BCE: Regional cultures begin to appear in central Andes

This aerial view shows Nazca lines etched into the shape of a hummingbird. Some of these images can be over 100 m across.

THE EMPIRES OF SOUTH AMERICA

THE EMPIRES WHICH DOMINATED the Andes between 500 and 1450, Tiahuanaco, Huari, and Chimú, were important precursors of the Inca, laying down the religious and social foundations, and the authoritarian government which were to serve the Inca so well. The Inca Empire (1438–1532) was the greatest state in South America, exercising stringent control over its subjects, through taxation, forced labour, compulsory migration, and military service. With its unyielding hierarchy and ill-defined line of succession, the Empire was fatally weakened by a leadership crisis at the very point when Pizarro arrived in 1532, and was unable to prevent its own destruction at the hands of the Spanish *conquistadores*.

This gold knife in the form of a Chimú (or Sicán) sun god dates from c.1100 CE. The body is decorated with turquoises.

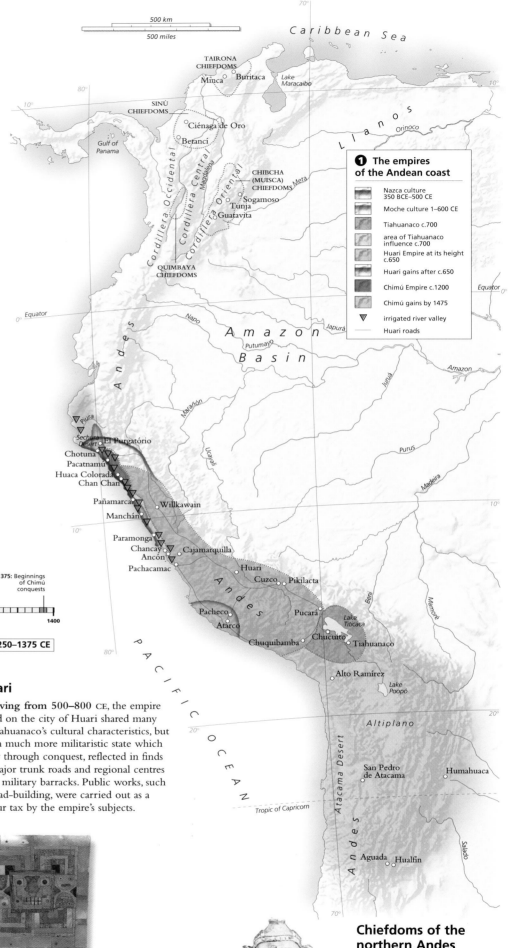

❶ The empires of the Andean coast

- Nazca culture 350 BCE–500 CE
- Moche culture 1–600 CE
- Tiahuanaco c.700
- area of Tiahuanaco influence c.700
- Huari Empire at its height c.650
- Huari gains after c.650
- Chimú Empire c.1200
- Chimú gains by 1475
- irrigated river valley
- Huari roads

Empires of the Andean coast 250–1375

The empires of Tiahuanaco and Huari, which together dominated the Andes from 500 CE, shared a similar art style, and probably the same religion. The city of Tiahuanaco, on the windswept Altiplano of modern Bolivia, was a major pilgrimage centre, and its cultural influence diffused throughout the south-central Andes from 500–1000. The contemporary Huari Empire, which controlled the coast around present-day Lima, was, by contrast, centralized and militaristic, expanding its influence through conquest. The Inca owed most to their direct predecessor, the Chimú Empire of the northern Andes, with its efficient administration, colonial expansionism, and stress on an effective communication system.

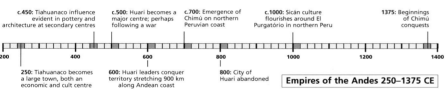

c.450: Tiahuanaco influence evident in pottery and architecture at secondary centres | c.500: Huari becomes a major centre; perhaps following a war | c.700: Emergence of Chimú on northern Peruvian coast | c.1000: Sicán culture flourishes around El Purgatório in northern Peru | 1375: Beginnings of Chimú conquests

250: Tiahuanaco becomes a large town, both an economic and cult centre | 600: Huari leaders conquer territory stretching 900 km along Andean coast | 800: City of Huari abandoned

Empires of the Andes 250–1375 CE

Tiahuanaco

By 500 CE the city of Tiahuanaco on Lake Titicaca's southeastern shore had become a major population centre, housing up to 40,000 people, and a focus of pilgrimage for the entire Andean region. It was dominated by palaces and a cult centre, consisting of temples, monumental gateways, and large monolithic sculptures. The city's iconography, with its symbolism of water, sun, and weather, spread throughout the south-central Andes.

Carved from a single slab of andesite, the Gateway of the Sun at Tiahuanaco is a representation of the cosmos, with the creator god at the centre of the frieze.

Huari

Thriving from 500–800 CE, the empire based on the city of Huari shared many of Tiahuanaco's cultural characteristics, but was a much more militaristic state which grew through conquest, reflected in finds of major trunk roads and regional centres with military barracks. Public works, such as road-building, were carried out as a labour tax by the empire's subjects.

Chimú

The Chimú Empire which ruled over the coast of northern Peru (c.700–1476) was centred on the capital of Chan Chan. A series of great royal compounds within the city served as both the palaces and mausolea of ten successive monarchs. The empire stretched for 1000 km along the Peruvian coast, administered by a series of regional centres.

The Chimú people were skilled metalworkers, producing a wide variety of ceremonial objects such as this gold dove with turquoise eyes.

The back of this Huari hand mirror contains a central face, with small heads at each side. The reflecting surface is of pyrite and the mosaic back of a variety of stones of contrasting texture and colour.

This small figure reflects the intricate casting and polishing typical of the goldsmiths of the Quimbaya chiefdoms. They also produced masks, spear tips, pendants, and helmets

Chiefdoms of the northern Andes

By the 15th century, many peoples of the northern Andes were organized into chiefdoms, based on large villages, supported by wetland farming, and capable of mobilizing sizeable armies. Their gold-working skills gave rise to myths of 'El Dorado' *(see p.149)*. Gold and copper resources were exploited by efficient mining operations – an indication of their impressive organizational ability.

The Inca Empire

The Inca emerged, in less than a century, as the preeminent state in South America; from 1470 they ruled vast territories from their capital, Cuzco. Their hierarchical society, ruled by the Sapa Inca (believed to be descended from the sun), depended on the mass organization of labour. Adult men were liable for forced labour, and worked in the fields, on public works (terracing, building, mining), and served in the army. An extensive road network, interspersed with way stations and regional centres, bound the empire together. Yet this complex bureaucracy had no form of writing, although arithmetic records were used for administration, tribute, and taxation.

The Inca *quipumayoc*, or grand treasurer, is shown holding a *quipu*, a device made of knotted strings, used to record administrative matters and sacred histories. Information was encoded in the colours of the strings and the style of the knots.

◄ **2** **South America c.1500**

- · · · · · · · · border of Inca Empire
- high civilization
- chiefdoms
- tropical forest farming villages
- other farming villages
- nomadic hunter-gatherers

Ona indigenous people

3 **The Inca Empire 1525**

Expansion of the Inca Empire
- by 1400
- in reign of Pachacutec 1438–71
- in reign of Tupac Yupanqui 1471–93
- in reign of Huayna Capac 1493–1525
- · · · · · · border of Inca Empire 1525
- —— Inca road

The Inca statuette of a dancing girl (right) dates from c.1438. Objects like this were produced in large numbers and in a remarkably uniform style.

The silver male figure (below) has long earlobes – an indication that he represents a person of elite status.

The peoples of South America c.1500

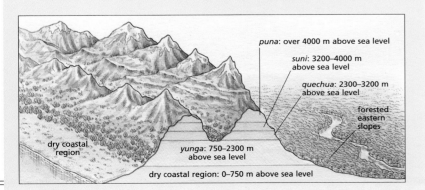

The golden raft, bearing a god-like figure surrounded by attendants is a detailed example of a *tunjo* or offering piece, produced by the Muisca (Chibcha) people of the northeastern Andes.

A great diversity of indigenous cultures existed in South America by the start of the 16th century, ranging from the high civilization of the Incas to the hunter-gatherers of Patagonia. Large populations lived along the Amazon, the upper river dominated by the Omagua people, its lower reaches controlled by the warlike Tapajosó. Many chiefdoms held sway over huge areas, some extracting forced labour from subject peoples, who were often engaged on extensive building projects. Ancestor cults, based on the mummified bodies of chiefs, were widespread.

This stylized carving in the shape of a tree is etched on a hillside in the coastal desert above present-day Paracas.

THE VERTICAL ECONOMY OF THE ANDES

The rugged terrain of the Andes provided a series of contiguous, but contrasting environments, fully exploited by the Incas and their predecessors. High, treeless, grassy plains (the *puna*) were used for grazing llamas. Below this, at heights up to 4000 m above sea level, lay the *suni*, where potatoes and tubers could be cultivated. Maize, squash, fruits, and cocoa grew in lower, frost-free valleys (the *quechua*), while the lower slopes of the mountains (the *yunga*) were planted with peppers, coca plants, and other fruits. Sources of shellfish and fish from the ocean were periodically disrupted by El Niño, an irregular climatic disturbance which warmed the ocean, leading to torrential rains and disastrous flooding.

- *puna*: over 4000 m above sea level
- *suni*: 3200–4000 m above sea level
- *quechua*: 2300–3200 m above sea level
- forested eastern slopes
- *yunga*: 750–2300 m above sea level
- dry coastal region
- dry coastal region: 0–750 m above sea level

The Inca Empire

1440s: Pachacutec Inca begins a series of conquests, from Lake Titicaca to Quito

1475: Chimú conquered by Inca

1525: Huayna Capac dies leaving two rival claimants to the throne; civil war ensues

1532: Francisco Pizarro defeats the Sapa Inca

1400 | 1425 | 1450 | 1475 | 1500 | 1525 | 1550

1438: Incas rise to power; attack Lake Titicaca basin, and establish upland empire

1500: Protracted military campaigns at northern and southern extremes of empire lead to establishment of second capital at Tomebamba

COLONIAL SOUTH AMERICA

Christianity in South America blended with local traditions to produce colourful spectacles such as this 18th-century Corpus Christi procession in Cuzco.

IN THEIR CONQUEST of South America the Spanish were so driven by the quest for gold and silver, that it took the *conquistadores* less than ten years to take over the rich, organized states of the Andes. The Portuguese were slower to settle Brazil, first trading with the Indians, then turning to sugar production. Wherever Europeans settled, the native population declined rapidly, mainly through lack of resistance to alien diseases. There were also periodic wars against the colonists. Large cattle stations that destroyed native arable smallholdings were a further factor in their decline. Emigration to South America from both Spain and Portugal was light; settlers mixed with the natives, creating a mixed-race *mestizo* population. To make up for shortages in labour, they imported African slaves. Catholic missionaries, notably the Jesuits, were active throughout the colonial era, often defending the rights of the Indians against the settlers. Both colonial empires collapsed in the 19th century, but the religion and languages of the conquerors survived.

The silver mine at Potosí was the prime source of revenue to the Spanish crown between 1550 and 1650. At first the native population supplied all the labour and technology. The silver was extracted using mercury, mined at Huancavelica.

The conquest of Peru

In 1531 Francisco Pizarro sailed from Panama to conquer Peru. By the time the expedition had penetrated inland to Cajamarca, where the reigning Inca, Atahualpa, and 40,000 men were camped, Pizarro had only 180 men. Yet he succeeded in capturing Atahualpa, whom he held for ransom. When this was paid, Atahualpa was executed, and the *conquistadores* moved on to capture the Inca capital, Cuzco. The Incas were in awe of the Spanish horses and guns, but this astonishing feat of conquest would have been impossible, had the Inca Empire not been weakened by a smallpox epidemic and civil war.

Atahualpa was given a summary trial by Pizarro and then garrotted, or – as this contemporary Inca illustration shows – beheaded.

1 Pizarro's conquest of the Inca Empire

→ 1524 expedition
→ 1526 expedition
→ 1531–33 expedition
····· extent of Inca Empire
1526 date of foundation

2 Spanish South America

- Spanish territory before 1650
- Spanish territory after 1650
- region disputed by Spain and Portugal up to 1777
- Jesuit mission states, with dates
- ·········· border with Brazil by Treaty of Madrid 1750
- – – – border with Brazil where modified by Treaty of San Ildefonso 1777
- ● Portuguese settlement
- ■ gold
- ■ silver
- ■ copper
- ● mercury
- ✂ drugs
- ✂ hides
- ✎ cocoa

Inca ornaments, such as this gold llama, are very rare, because most were melted down and shipped to Spain.

The founder of Spain's South American empire, Pizarro was an ageing soldier of fortune. Some of his own lieutenants rebelled against him and he was killed in a riot in Lima in 1541.

Spanish South America

Spain ruled her American colonies through two great viceroyalties, New Spain (centred on Mexico) and Peru. The viceroys' principal duty was to guarantee a steady flow of bullion for the Spanish Crown. When booty from the native empires was exhausted, the colonists turned to the region's mineral resources, using forced native labour (*mita*) to extract precious metals, in particular silver. Smaller administrative units called *audiencias* were presided over by a judge who enacted the complex laws devised in Spain for the running of the colonies. Attempts to expand the empire were thwarted in the south by the fierce Araucanian people, elsewhere by the inhospitable nature of the terrain.

Spanish South America 1500–1800

1533: Pizarro takes Inca capital, Cuzco
1535: City of Lima founded
1541: Pedro de Valdivia founds Santiago
1545: Discovery of silver at Potosí
1607: Jesuits found first mission villages on River Paraguay
1630s: Intense Jesuit missionary activity in Paraguay region
c.1680: Start of serious slump in economy of Spanish South America
1739: Viceroyalty of New Granada established to defend Caribbean coast
1750: Treaty of Madrid defines boundary between Spanish colonies and Brazil
1776: New viceroyalty of Río de la Plata centred on Buenos Aires
1777: Treaty of San Ildefonso

1500　1550　1600　1650　1700　1750　1800

Portuguese South America

Brazil was formally claimed by Portugal in 1500. There were no conspicuous mineral resources, so colonization depended on agriculture. In the 1530s, in an attempt to encourage settlement, João III made grants of land to 12 hereditary 'captains', each captaincy consisting of 50 leagues of coastline. Some failed completely and little of the coastal plain was settled before 1549 when a royal governor-general was sent to Bahia. The captaincy system continued, but the colonists' fortunes changed with the success of sugar. The native population living near the coast had been almost wiped out by disease and wars. The few that remained had no wish to labour on sugar plantations, so slaves were imported from Africa. In the 18th century, a gold boom opened up the Minas Gerais region, but apart from slave-raiders hunting for Indians and prospectors searching for gold and diamonds, penetration of the interior was limited.

Between 1550 and 1800, some 2.5 million African slaves were taken to Brazil, more than 70% of them to work for the sugar plantations and mills which were the backbone of the economy.

❸ Portuguese South America ▶

- Portuguese territory by 1600
- Portuguese territory by 1750
- Portuguese frontier territory
- region disputed by Spain and Portugal up to 1777
- **PARÁ 1616** captaincy and date of foundation
- □ capital city
- ▨ gold
- ◔ diamonds
- ✺ dyes
- ⚒ hides
- ⚓ sugar

Slaves were also employed at the gold and diamond mines of the interior. This early 19th-century print shows slaves washing diamond-bearing rock.

Brazil 1500–1800

1502: First expedition sent from Lisbon to exploit new-found coastline
1549: Direct royal rule imposed from new capital at Bahia
1580: Portugal and her empire come under rule of Spanish kings
1663: Brazil becomes viceroyalty
1674: Foundation of Manaus, 1,600 km from mouth of Amazon
1750: Portugal renounces claim to Colônia do Sacramento

1500 — 1525 — 1550 — 1575 — 1600 — 1625 — 1650 — 1675 — 1700 — 1725 — 1750 — 1775 — 1800

1532: First captaincies granted for purposes of settlement
1562–63: War and disease kill much of Indian population
1621: Formation of separate Estado do Maranhão with its own governor-general
1680s: Portuguese found Colônia do Sacramento
1695: Gold discovered in Minas Gerais region
1763: Rio de Janeiro becomes Brazilian capital

THE SEARCH FOR EL DORADO

From the 1530s until well into the 17th century, fantastic tales of the kingdom of El Dorado (the gilded man) inspired many foolhardy expeditions through the Andes, the Orinoco basin, and the Guiana Highlands. The English sea captain Walter Raleigh twice sailed to the Orinoco, but both his voyages ended in failure and on the second in 1617 his teenaged son was killed by the Spanish.

The legend of El Dorado took many forms. The most persistent was of a chieftain so rich that he was regularly painted in gold by his subjects.

Other colonial powers

For 150 years Portugal's hold on Brazil was far from secure. The French, who traded along the coast with the Indians, made several attempts to found colonies. In the first half of the 17th century, the defence of Portuguese colonies was neglected by the ruling Spanish kings. This allowed the Dutch to capture a long stretch of the northeast coast. They were finally expelled in 1654 and had to be content, like the English and French, with a small colony in the Guianas.

Dutch Brazil thrived under the governorship of Prince Maurits of Nassau (1636–44), when many new towns were built. The artist Franz Post painted idealized views of the colony during this period. This detail shows the slave quarters on a plantation.

▼ ❹ Brazil and the Guianas c.1640

- Portuguese possession and settlement
- Dutch possession and settlement
- French possession and settlement
- temporary French colonies in Brazil

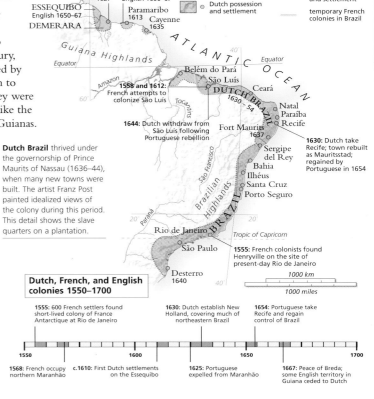

1558 and 1612: French attempts to colonize São Luís
1644: Dutch withdraw from São Luís following Portuguese rebellion
1630: Dutch take Recife; town rebuilt as Mauritsstad; regained by Portuguese in 1654
1555: French colonists found Henryville on the site of present-day Rio de Janeiro

Dutch, French, and English colonies 1550–1700

1555: 600 French settlers found short-lived colony of France Antarctique at Rio de Janeiro
1630: Dutch establish New Holland, covering much of northeastern Brazil
1654: Portuguese take Recife and regain control of Brazil

1550 — 1600 — 1650 — 1700

1568: French occupy northern Maranhão
c.1610: First Dutch settlements on the Essequibo
1625: Portuguese expelled from Maranhão
1667: Peace of Breda; some English territory in Guiana ceded to Dutch

THE AGE OF INDEPENDENCE

Pedro I became the emperor of an independent Brazil in 1822, when his father and the royal family returned from exile to Portugal.

AFTER THREE CENTURIES of rule by Spain, the colonial families of South America began to demand more autonomy. When Spain was invaded by Napoleon in 1808, it was cut off from its empire, and in 1810 several colonies established independent ruling juntas. The struggle for independence lasted until 1826, when the last Spanish troops departed. The heroic deeds of the Liberators, Simón Bolívar, José de San Martín, and others passed into legend, but the task of forming new republics proved harder. Liberals and Conservatives fought numerous civil wars and military dictators ran countries as their personal fiefs. The economies of the new states were dominated by foreign trading powers, especially Britain. Brazil gained its independence from Portugal more peacefully, a result of the royal family's flight to Brazil in 1807. The two states separated when they returned to Portugal in 1822.

The liberation of Spanish South America

The wars of liberation were fought between patriots and those who remained loyal to the Spanish crown. The longest struggle was that of Simón Bolívar in his native Venezuela and neighbouring Colombia. The first states to achieve independence were Paraguay and Argentina, from where in 1817 José de San Martín led an army over the Andes to help liberate Chile. Bolívar's campaigns regained momentum in 1818–22 in a triumphal progress from Venezuela to Ecuador. The armies of liberation from north and south then joined forces for the liberation of Peru and, in honour of Bolívar, Upper Peru was renamed Bolivia.

The llanero lancers from the plains of Venezuela, were praised by Bolívar as his 'cossacks'. They continually harrassed the army sent from Spain in 1815 to oppose the liberation movement.

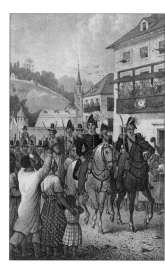

Bolívar enters Caracas in triumph in 1829 after putting down the uprising of his former lieutenant Antonio Páez. But it was Páez who became dictator of the new republic of Venezuela on Bolívar's death in 1830.

The break-up of Great Colombia

The personality of Simón Bolívar and the need for military unity in confronting the Spanish created the republic of Great Colombia. It proved an unwieldy state with a very remote capital at Bogotá. Commercial links and communications between the three former Spanish colonies of New Granada, Venezuela, and Quito (Ecuador) were very limited, and in 1830, the year of Bolívar's death, they became separate states under the leadership of generals Santander, Páez, and Flores respectively.

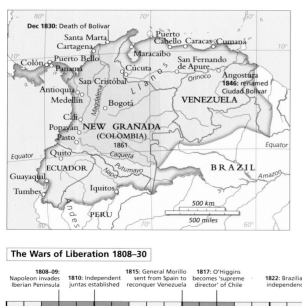

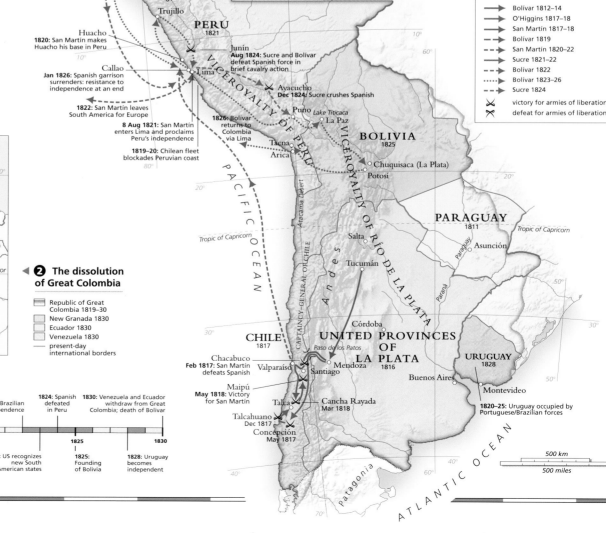

❸ Political and economic development in South America 1830–1930 ▶

approximate international borders 1830
international borders 1930
region temporarily independent

Major export products

- 🍌 bananas
- 🐂 beef
- ▨ cacao
- ☕ coffee
- ▥ copper
- ◇ cotton
- △ guano
- ✕ hides
- ▽ nitrates
- ⤧ rubber
- ▤ sugar
- ▥ silver
- ▥ tin
- ✽ tobacco
- ❃ wheat
- ▥ wool

---- major railways by 1910
⚑1853 date slavery abolished
✽ major port
⚔ major international and civil wars 1830–1930

Politics and economics in the 19th century

In the aftermath of liberation, many countries saw power seized by *caudillos*, military dictators such as Páez in Venezuela and Rosas in Argentina. When no strong leader took charge, all countries suffered from civil wars and there were frequent secessionist movements. Economies depended on raw materials for export: coffee and rubber from Brazil and salted and frozen meat from Argentina. Large profits were made by British and American firms which invested in mines and railways in Argentina and Chile. The abolition of slavery in Brazil in 1888 created a new demand for labour, which was met by immigrants from Europe. Many thousands of immigrants were also attracted to Argentina and Uruguay, as they too lay on the Atlantic seaboard. Often, however, immigrants moved on from there to other countries in search of work or land to farm. Argentina, the fastest growing economy, attracted large numbers of Italians.

Slavery was not abolished in Brazil until 1888. Slaves there worked on plantations, in skilled jobs, and as house servants. This painting shows a Brazilian planter with his slaves, two of whom are carrying his wife in a litter.

❹ The War of the Pacific

international borders in 1874
Chile before 1874
gained from Bolivia 1874
gained from Bolivia 1884
gained from Peru 1884
conquered by Chile 1884; awarded to Chile 1929
conquered by Chile 1884; awarded to Peru 1929
nitrate deposits
✕ Chilean victory

1881–1884: Lima and Callao occupied by Chilean forces

1880: Invasion of Arica and Tacna by General Baquedano and 12,000 men

1879: Sinking of Peruvian ironclad, the Huascar, gives Chile control of the sea

1880: Invasion of Arica and Tacna

1879: Invasion of Tarapacá

The War of the Pacific 1879–83

The war was fought over control of the Atacama Desert's rich deposits of nitrates, used in fertilizers and explosives. An Anglo-Chilean company was already working the deposits in the Bolivian part of the desert, when, in 1878, Bolivia demanded more tax. The company refused and Bolivia was backed by Peru. In 1879, Chile landed an army at Antofagasta and took the Bolivian coastline and the southern provinces of Peru. Fired up by their success, Chilean troops sailed to attack Lima and fighting continued in Peru till 1883. The peace treaty resulted in Bolivia's losing its access to the Pacific coast and a long-running border dispute between Chile and Peru, not resolved until 1929.

Juan Manuel de Rosas was the archetypal South American *caudillo*. He waged relentless war on the Patagonian Indians, and although only governor of Buenos Aires province, exercised control over the whole of Argentina.

Iquique was one of the railway terminals on the Pacific coast that owed its existence to nitrate deposits and British investment. It lay in the Tarapacá province, won by Chile from Peru in the War of the Pacific. Many saw the war as a cynical advancement of British business interests.

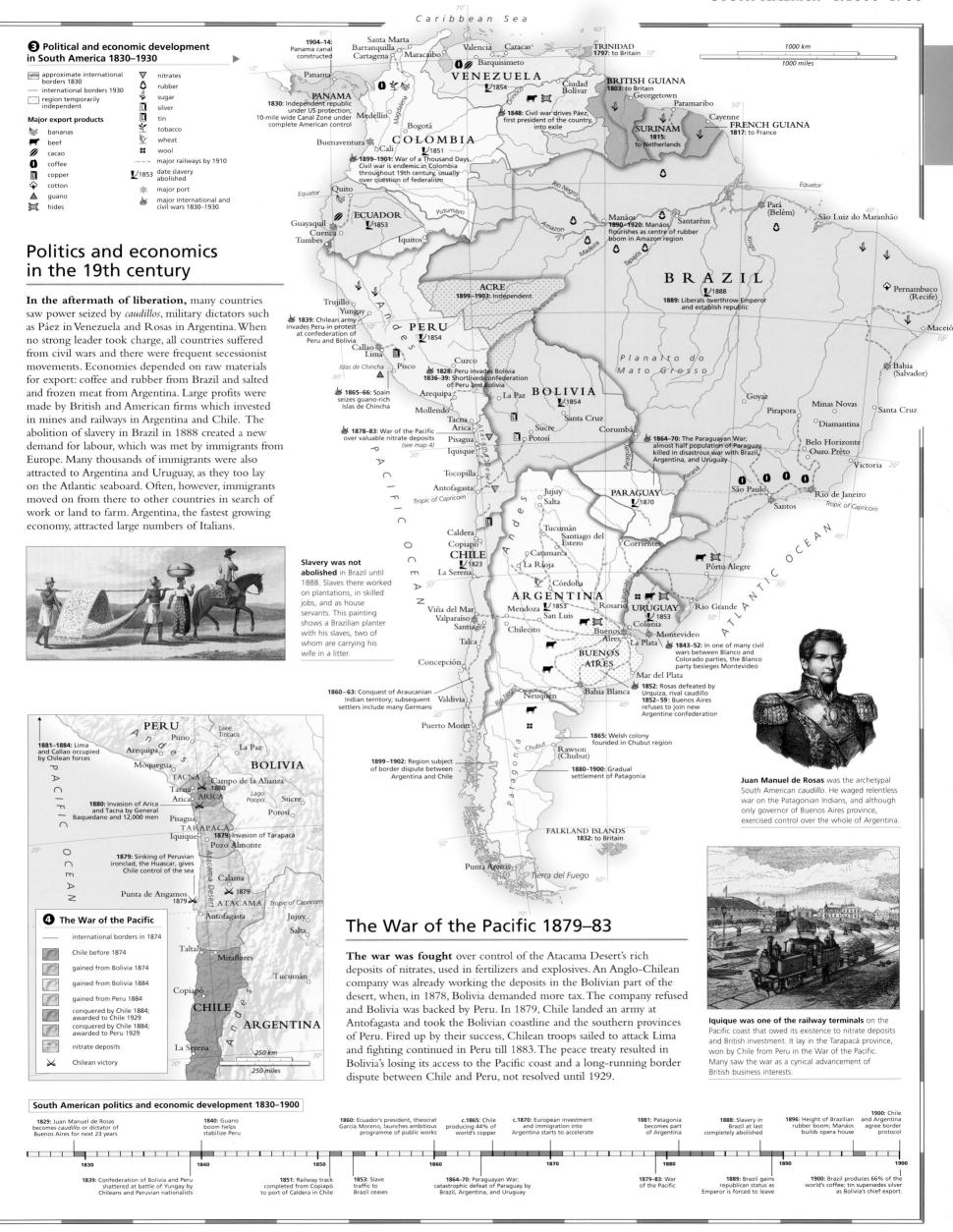

Map labels and annotations:

Caribbean Sea

1904–14: Panama canal constructed

TRINIDAD 1797: to Britain

BRITISH GUIANA 1803: to Britain

SURINAM 1815: to Netherlands

FRENCH GUIANA 1817: to France

PANAMA 1830: Independent republic under US protection; 10-mile wide Canal Zone under complete American control

1848: Civil war drives Páez, first president of the country, into exile

VENEZUELA

COLOMBIA
1899–1901: War of a Thousand Days. Civil war is endemic in Colombia throughout 19th century, usually over question of federalism

ECUADOR

1890–1920: Manáos flourishes as centre of rubber boom in Amazon region

BRAZIL
1889: Liberals overthrow Emperor and establish republic

ACRE 1899–1903: Independent

PERU
1839: Chilean army invades Peru in protest at confederation of Peru and Bolivia

1828: Peru invades Bolivia
1836–39: Shortlived confederation of Peru and Bolivia

1865–66: Spain seizes guano-rich Islas de Chincha

BOLIVIA

1878–83: War of the Pacific over valuable nitrate deposits (see map 4)

1864–70: The Paraguayan War; almost half population of Paraguay killed in disastrous war with Brazil, Argentina, and Uruguay

PARAGUAY

CHILE

ARGENTINA

URUGUAY

BUENOS AIRES

1843–52: In one of many civil wars between Blanco and Colorado parties, the Blanco party besieges Montevideo

1860–63: Conquest of Araucanian Indian territory; subsequent settlers include many Germans

1852: Rosas defeated by Urquiza, rival caudillo
1852–59: Buenos Aires refuses to join new Argentine confederation

1865: Welsh colony founded in Chubut region

1899–1902: Region subject of border dispute between Argentina and Chile

1880–1900: Gradual settlement of Patagonia

FALKLAND ISLANDS 1832: to Britain

PERU
BOLIVIA
TACNA
TARAPACÁ
ATACAMA
CHILE
ARGENTINA

1880: Campo de la Alianza
1879: Punta de Angamos

South American politics and economic development 1830–1900

1829: Juan Manuel de Rosas becomes *caudillo* or dictator of Buenos Aires for next 23 years

1840: Guano boom helps stabilize Peru

1860: Ecuador's president, theocrat García Moreno, launches ambitious programme of public works

c.1865: Chile producing 44% of world's copper

c.1870: European investment and immigration into Argentina starts to accelerate

1881: Patagonia becomes part of Argentina

1888: Slavery in Brazil at last completely abolished

1896: Height of Brazilian rubber boom; Manáos builds opera house

1900: Chile and Argentina agree border protocol

1839: Confederation of Bolivia and Peru shattered at battle of Yungay by Chileans and Peruvian nationalists

1851: Railway track completed from Copiapó to port of Caldera in Chile

1853: Slave traffic to Brazil ceases

1864–70: Paraguayan War; catastrophic defeat of Paraguay by Brazil, Argentina, and Uruguay

1879–83: War of the Pacific

1889: Brazil gains republican status as Emperor is forced to leave

1900: Brazil produces 66% of the world's coffee; tin supersedes silver as Bolivia's chief export

MODERN SOUTH AMERICA

Augusto Pinochet headed Chile's military government from 1974 to 1990.

POLITICAL AND ECONOMIC instability arose in South America as a result of the great depression of the 1930s. Various factors, including a sharp rise in population and rapid urbanization and industrialization, exerted great pressures on the weak democratic institutions of most nations. Opposition to the conservative status quo was pronounced among intellectuals, students, and trade unionists. In the late 1960s social conflicts and ideological battles shook governments. The crisis sent many countries towards repression and a new kind of conservative authoritarianism arose. In the 1980s, South American countries turned towards democracy and freer markets. Throughout the century, long-standing border disputes remained, but few flared up like the Chaco War of 1932–35.

South America: from instability to democracy

Founded in 1970, the Shining Path, the Peruvian revolutionary movement, asserts its authority in Ayacucho in 1989, by defiantly parading through the city's streets.

South America suffered the full force of the global recession of the 1930s. Populist governments shifted towards economic nationalism, energetically promoting industrial development. By the late 1950s economic and social progress had ushered in greater democracy. The impact of the Communist-inspired Cuban Revolution threatened the status quo. The US, fearing the spread of Communism, pledged $10 billion in aid, but massive population growth cancelled out the benefits of the grants. With increased conflict between leftist guerrillas and the ruling elite, military regimes, backed by the US, assumed power in order to contain social unrest. The tide of military rule receded in the early 1980s.

Political development from 1930

- **1932:** Chaco War begins between Bolivia and Paraguay
- **1937:** 'New State' in Brazil launched by Vargas
- **1946:** Peron comes to power in Argentina
- **1968:** Tupamaros urban guerilla group founded in Uruguay
- **1968:** Military junta take over Peru
- **1974:** Brutal dictatorship of Pinochet in Chile
- **1976:** 15,000 political subversives killed during 'Dirty War', by military and right-wing death squads in Argentina
- **1980s:** Many countries return to democracy
- **1982:** Argentina occupies South Georgia and Falkland Islands; surrenders to UK forces

(Timeline: 1930 1940 1950 1960 1970 1980)

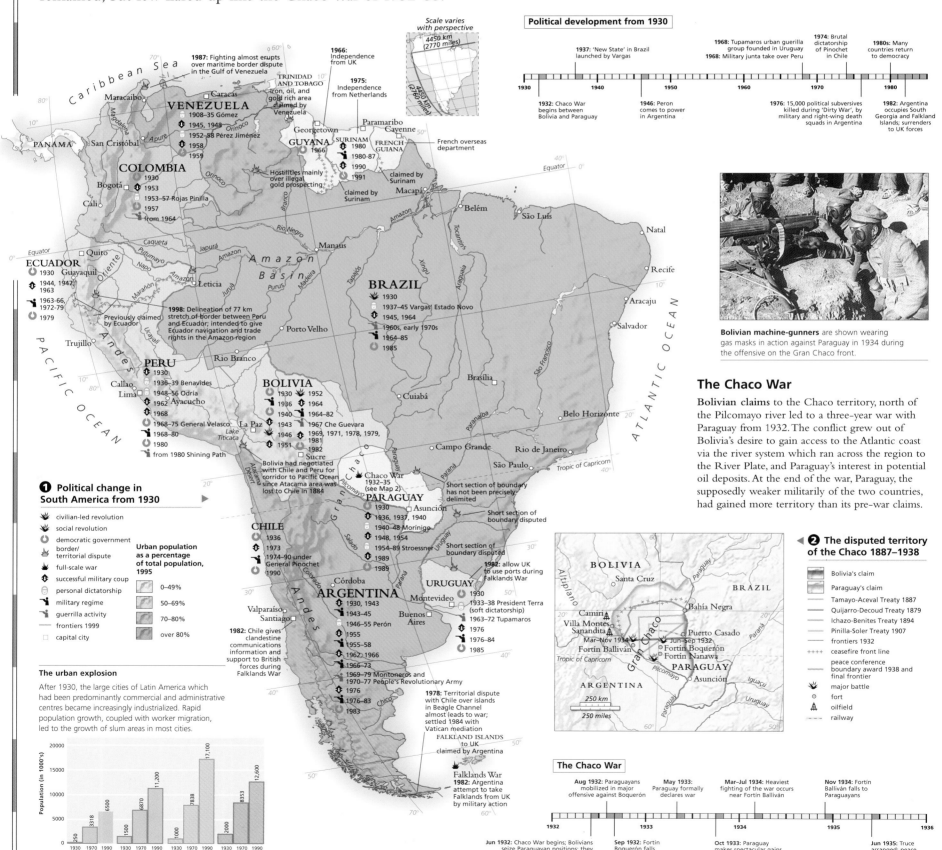

1987: Fighting almost erupts over maritime border dispute in the Gulf of Venezuela

1966: Independence from UK

1975: Independence from Netherlands

Scale varies with perspective

4450 km (2770 miles)

TRINIDAD AND TOBAGO Iron, oil, and gold rich area claimed by Venezuela

VENEZUELA
- 1908–35 Gómez
- 1945, 1948
- 1952–58 Pérez Jiménez
- 1958
- 1959

French overseas department

GUYANA 1966

SURINAM
- 1980
- 1980-87
- 1991

Hostilities mainly over illegal gold prospecting

claimed by Surinam

claimed by Surinam

COLOMBIA
- 1930
- 1953
- 1953–57 Rojas Pinilla
- 1957
- from 1964

1998: Delineation of 77 km stretch of border between Peru and Ecuador; intended to give Ecuador navigation and trade rights in the Amazon region

Previously claimed by Ecuador

ECUADOR
- 1930
- 1944, 1947, 1963
- 1963-66, 1972-79
- 1979

BRAZIL
- 1930
- 1937–45 Vargas' Estado Novo
- 1945, 1964
- 1960s, early 1970s
- 1964–85
- 1985

PERU
- 1930
- 1936–39 Benavides
- 1948–56 Odria
- 1962 Ayacucho
- 1968
- 1968–75 General Velasco
- 1968–80
- 1980
- from 1980 Shining Path

BOLIVIA
- 1930 1952
- 1936 1964
- 1940 1964–82
- 1943 1967 Che Guevara
- 1946 1969, 1971, 1978, 1979, 1981
- 1951 1982

Bolivia had negotiated with Chile and Peru for corridor to Pacific Ocean since Atacama area was lost to Chile in 1884

Chaco War 1932–35 (see Map 2)

Short section of boundary has not been precisely delimited

PARAGUAY
- 1936, 1937, 1940
- 1940–48 Morinigo
- 1948, 1954
- 1954–89 Stroessner
- 1989
- 1989

Short section of boundary disputed

Short section of boundary disputed

1982: allow UK to use ports during Falklands War

URUGUAY
- 1930
- 1933–38 President Terra (soft dictatorship)
- 1963–72 Tupamaros
- 1976
- 1976–84
- 1985

CHILE
- 1936
- 1973
- 1974–90 under General Pinochet
- 1990

1982: Chile gives clandestine communications information and support to British forces during Falklands War

ARGENTINA
- 1930, 1943
- 1943–45
- 1946–55 Perón
- 1955
- 1955–58
- 1962, 1966
- 1966–73
- 1969–79 Montoneros and 1970–77 People's Revolutionary Army
- 1976
- 1976–83
- 1983

1978: Territorial dispute with Chile over islands in Beagle Channel almost leads to war; settled 1984 with Vatican mediation

FALKLAND ISLANDS to UK claimed by Argentina

Falklands War **1982:** Argentina attempt to take Falklands from UK by military action

① Political change in South America from 1930

- civilian-led revolution
- social revolution
- democratic government
- border/territorial dispute
- full-scale war
- successful military coup
- personal dictatorship
- military regime
- guerrilla activity
- frontiers 1999
- capital city

Urban population as a percentage of total population, 1995
- 0–49%
- 50–69%
- 70–80%
- over 80%

The urban explosion

After 1930, the large cities of Latin America which had been predominantly commercial and administrative centres became increasingly industrialized. Rapid population growth, coupled with worker migration, led to the growth of slum areas in most cities.

(Bar chart: Population (in 1000's))

	1930	1970	1990
Lima	350	3318	6500
Rio de Janeiro	1900	6870	11,200
São Paulo	1000	7838	17,100
Buenos Aires	2000	8353	12,600

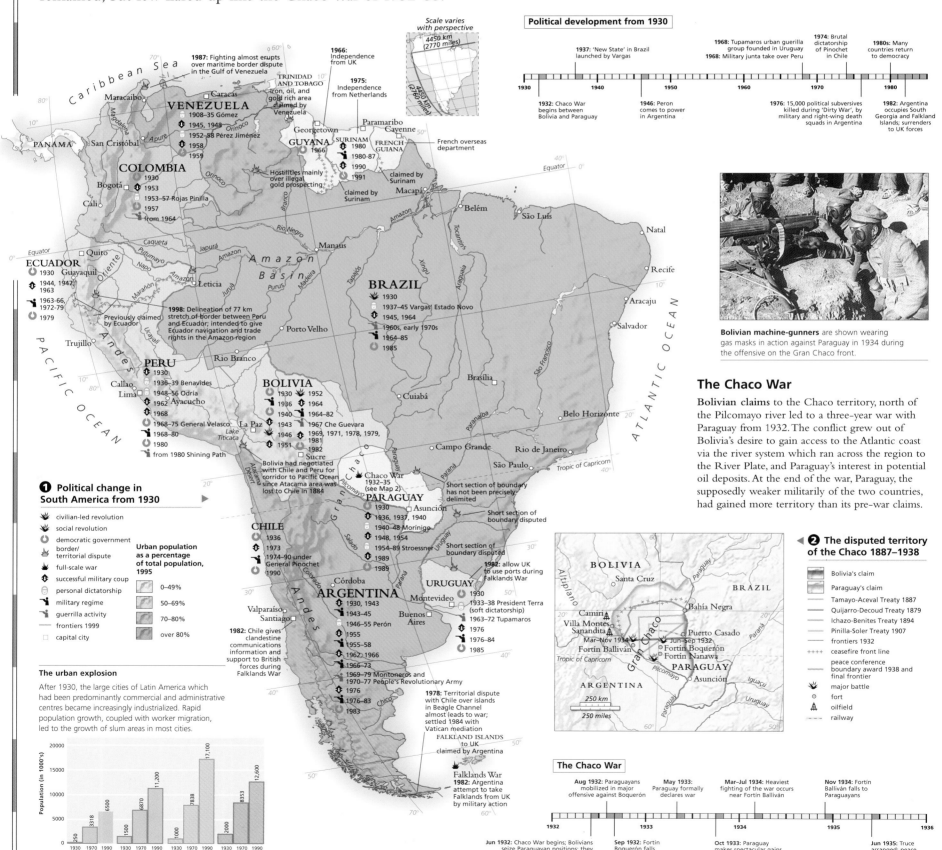

Bolivian machine-gunners are shown wearing gas masks in action against Paraguay in 1934 during the offensive on the Gran Chaco front.

The Chaco War

Bolivian claims to the Chaco territory, north of the Pilcomayo river led to a three-year war with Paraguay from 1932. The conflict grew out of Bolivia's desire to gain access to the Atlantic coast via the river system which ran across the region to the River Plate, and Paraguay's interest in potential oil deposits. At the end of the war, Paraguay, the supposedly weaker militarily of the two countries, had gained more territory than its pre-war claims.

② The disputed territory of the Chaco 1887–1938

- Bolivia's claim
- Paraguay's claim
- Tamayo-Aceval Treaty 1887
- Quijarro-Decoud Treaty 1879
- Ichazo-Benites Treaty 1894
- Pinilla-Soler Treaty 1907
- frontiers 1932
- +++ ceasefire front line
- peace conference boundary award 1938 and final frontier
- major battle
- fort
- oilfield
- railway

BOLIVIA — Santa Cruz
Altiplano
Camiri
Villa Montes
Sanandita
Mar–Nov 1934 Fortín Ballivián
Tropic of Capricorn
Gran Chaco
Jun–Sep 1932
Fortín Boquerón
Fortín Nanawa
BRAZIL
Bahía Negra
Puerto Casado
PARAGUAY
Asunción
ARGENTINA
250 km
250 miles

1982: Chile gives...

The Chaco War

- **Aug 1932:** Paraguayans mobilized in major offensive against Boquerón
- **May 1933:** Paraguay formally declares war
- **Mar–Jul 1934:** Heaviest fighting of the war occurs near Fortín Ballivián
- **Nov 1934:** Fortín Ballivián falls to Paraguayans

(Timeline: 1932 1933 1934 1935 1936)

- **Jun 1932:** Chaco War begins; Bolivians seize Paraguayan positions; they successfully attack Fortín Boquerón
- **Sep 1932:** Fortín Boquerón falls to Paraguay
- **Oct 1933:** Paraguay makes spectacular gains along the war front
- **Jun 1935:** Truce arranged; peace treaty signed in 1938

Economic development

After 1930, many South American nations adopted industrial development policies in an attempt to restructure economies which had relied upon the production of raw materials. Trade tariffs were imposed from the 1940s to accelerate industrialization whilst high inflation was tolerated in the hope of maintaining a strong demand for goods and services. Manufacturing industries became concentrated in a number of locations, yet income distribution remained unequal. More open economies from the 1980s attracted foreign and domestic investment. Economic reforms in the 1990s, which were aimed at defeating spiralling inflation, saw the privatization of many state-run enterprises.

❸ Industry and resources in modern South America ▶

Industry	Agricultural resources	Mineral resources
✈ aerospace	🐂 cattle	▯ bauxite (aluminium)
🚗 car/vehicle manufacture	🌿 cocoa	▯ copper
⚗ chemicals	🌽 corn (maize)	▯ diamonds
⚡ electronics	🌱 cotton	▯ gold
⚙ engineering	☕ coffee	▯ iron ore
Ⓢ finance	🐟 fishing	▯ lead
🍴 food processing (includes brewing, fish processing, meat processing, and sugar processing)	🍎 fruit	▯ manganese
	🌴 oil palms	▯ nickel
🛢 gas	🥜 peanuts	▯ silver
⚒ hi-tech industry	⚘ rubber	▯ tin
⚒ iron and steel	🐑 sheep	▯ coal field
⊙ metal refining	🦐 shellfish	▯ gasfield
⚱ narcotics	🌿 soya beans	▯ oilfield
⚓ oil	🌾 sugar cane	
⚕ pharmaceuticals	🍇 vineyards	**Gross national product per capita 1998**
🖨 printing and publishing	🌾 wheat	▱ less than $1000
⛴ shipbuilding		▱ $1000–$2500
🧵 textiles		▱ $2501–$4500
⚒ timber processing		▱ $4501–$7000
⚘ tobacco processing		▱ $7001–$10,000
▨ main industrial areas		

Development and deforestation in Amazonia

In the 1950s, the Brazilian government attempted to alleviate poverty amongst landless rural populations by granting resettlement plots along new roads in the Amazonian rainforest. From the 1960s, the government pursued vigorous economic policies which encouraged the development of the region. Subsidies and tax incentives made the clearing of Amazonia especially profitable for large land-holders involved in cattle ranching, and these farms were responsible for the destruction of 80% of the forest. By 1998, 12% of Brazil's rainforest had been cleared.

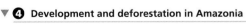

1964: Plans for highway network throughout Amazon Basin

1978: Trans-Amazon Highway completed, it extends 5000 km from Recife to Peruvian border

1981: United States provides $1.5 billion for conversion of forest land into pastures in Brazil

1953: SUDAM established to manage government granted settlement plots

1967: Daniel Ludwig sets up Jari Project in north Brazil; includes a wood-pulp plant and rice growing

1992: United Nations Conference on the Environment in Rio de Janeiro; Indians granted title to one million hectares in Amazonia

Economic development of the Brazilian rainforest from 1960

▼ ❹ Development and deforestation in Amazonia

Environmental issues
- ▨ tropical forests
- ▨ forest under medium / high threat
- ▨ deforested areas

Transportation network
- ┉ major Amazonian railway
- ── major Amazonian road

Mineral resources
- ▯ bauxite (aluminium)
- ▯ gold
- ▯ copper
- ▯ iron ore
- ▯ manganese
- ▯ nickel
- ▯ tin

Development programmes
- ── development area with type of development

Scientists believed that gas released during the burning of the Brazilian rainforest contributed to global warming. Burning resulted in the release of carbon dioxide which the destroyed forest could not absorb to produce free oxygen.

❺ The drugs trade ▶
- ▨ coca-growing areas
- ▨ poppy-growing areas
- ── provinces of Colombia
- ── border 1999

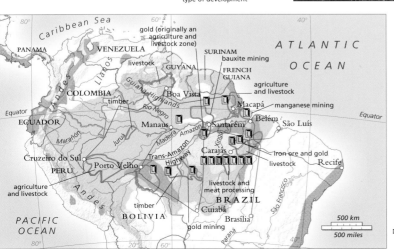

Semi-skilled assembly line work as in this car manufacturing plant in Argentina, was the main type of employment offered by foreign multi-national corporations to South American workers in the 1990s.

A child harvests the coca crop in Colombia, where the shrub thrives in the tropical climate. Coca has been traditionally chewed by the people of Andean South America to cope with altitude sickness.

The narcotics trade

From the 1970s, Latin American began to ship massive quantities of cocaine to its main overseas market, the United States. The Andean countries: Bolivia, Colombia, and Peru produced the coca leaf from which cocaine was derived, and the trade was organized and directed by the Medellín and Cali drugs cartels in Colombia. International intervention did little to depress the profits of drug barons, who later diversified into poppy growing in Colombia, for the production of heroin.

AFRICA
REGIONAL HISTORY

THE HISTORICAL LANDSCAPE

THE GEOGRAPHY AND CLIMATE OF AFRICA has, to possibly a greater extent than in any other continent, determined its role in world history. The earliest human remains have been found here, in the arid geological block faults of the Great Rift Valley and southern Africa. Although unaffected by the glaciation of the last Ice Age, attendant climatic changes witnessed a transformation of the Sahara from a desert during the Ice Age, into a belt of temperate grassland, inhabited by herds of game and groups of hunter-gatherers by 8000 years ago. By around 4000 BCE, the process of desiccation began which continues today, effectively isolating sub-Saharan Africa from the Mediterranean. Only the Nile valley provided a link, and here one of the world's oldest civilizations emerged. South of the Sahara, a wide range of isolated cultures developed, their nature determined largely by their environment, linked by rich non-literate oral traditions. The plateau nature of much of Africa, and the desert and jungle which dominate much of the landscape, meant that Africa was the last continent (excepting Antarctica) to be colonized by Europeans, and their brief and callous century of tenancy left a legacy of underdevelopment and political strife.

The Great Rift Valley was home to one of the earliest known human ancestors, *Australopithecus afarensis*, 3.8 million years ago. Modern humans (*Homo sapiens*) evolved here about 100,000 years ago, before migrating to Asia and Australasia, Europe, and finally the Americas.

The Sahara covers much of northern Africa, although sand dunes account for only a quarter of the desert's area. The rest is made up of barren, rock-strewn surfaces. Desert has existed in this part of Africa for almost five million years, and the harsh climate and inhospitable landscape have prevented the establishment of permanent settlements.

The River Nile winds its way across the hostile Sahara to the Mediterranean Sea, flanked by fertile floodplains. Humans have inhabited the Nile region since the early Stone Age, making use of the fertile soils that have built up as a result the annual flooding of the river.

Vegetation type

- semi-desert or sparsely vegetated
- grassland
- forest or open woodland
- tropical rainforest
- tropical desert (18,000 years ago)
- desert (8000 years ago)
- coastline (present-day)
- coastline (18,000 years ago)

EUROPE

ASIA

Mediterranean Sea

EURASIAN PLATE
AFRICAN PLATE

Atlas Mountains

Ionian Basin

ANATOLIAN PLATE
AFRICAN PLATE

Anatolia

Dead Sea

Tigris

Euphrates

IRANIAN PLATE
ARABIAN PLATE

Tropic of Cancer

Sea levels at the Strait of Gibraltar, between Africa and Europe, were lower, but the two continents were not joined. It is thought that seawater breached this narrow gap about 5.5 million years ago, flooding the deep basins of the Mediterranean.

Ahaggar

Sahara

DESERT MARGIN 8000 YEARS AGO

Lower sea levels meant that the Red Sea was narrower and shallower than it is today.

Arabian Peninsula

Red Sea

ARABIAN PLATE
AFRICAN PLATE

Owen Fracture Zone

Tibesti

The swampy inland delta of the Niger River is all that remains of this lake today.

MEGA CHAD
(8000 YEARS AGO)

Much of the Chad Basin was filled by the huge lake Mega Chad, as the climate warmed at the end of the last Ice Age. The deserts receded about 8000 years ago, allowing nomads and pastoralists to inhabit the Sahara.

Nile

Blue Nile

East Sheba Ridge

Alula-Fartak Trench

Socotra

ARAOUANE LAKE
(8000 YEARS AGO)

White Nile

Horn of Africa

Chain Ridge

Niger

Lake Chad

Ethiopian Highlands

Ogaden

Somali Basin

Lac de Kossou

Lake Volta

Ogoôue

Uele

Congo

White Nile

Lake Rudolf

Somali Plain

Equator

AFRICA

During the last Ice Age, the Congo Basin was not covered by dense rainforests as it is today. The colder, drier climate meant that most of the basin was covered by grassland and scrub.

Lomami

Lake Albert

Shebeli

INDIAN

Guinea Basin

Bioko

São Tomé

Congo Basin

Lake Victoria

OCEAN

Fracture Zone

Congo

Great Rift Valley

Lake Tanganyika

Great Rift Valley

Zanzibar

Amirante Trench

Chain Fracture Zone

Congo Canyon

Lake Rukwa

Lake Mweru

Comoro Islands

Angola Basin

Deserts extended from southern Africa, as far north as the Congo River.

Lake Nyasa

Comoro Basin

18,000 years ago Madagascar was covered with great temperate forests in place of the lush tropical forests that exist today.

SOUTH AMERICAN PLATE
AFRICAN PLATE

Cuando

Lake Cabora Bassa

Zambezi

Mascarene Plain

Walvis Ridge

Cubango

Sabi

Mozambique Plateau

Madagascar

Madagascar Basin

Mid-Atlantic Ridge

Kalahari Desert

LAKE MAKGADIKGADI

Rende

Limpopo

Tropic of Capricorn

ATLANTIC OCEAN

The area once covered by this vast lake is now occupied by the Okavango Delta.

Vaal

Orange River

Atlantis

Natal Basin

Madagascar Plateau

Orange River

Drakensberg

Natal Valley

Mozambique Plateau

Discovery II Fracture Zone

Southwest Indian Ridge

Indomed Fracture Zone

Cape Basin

Agulhas Plateau

Prince Edward Fracture

Du Toit Fracture Zone

Cape Rise

Agulhas Basin

AFRICAN PLATE
ANTARCTICA PLATE

Atlantic-Indian Ridge

Crozet Plateau

Africa: 18,000 years ago

Africa was both colder and drier during the Ice Age. These two factors produced a marked change in the vegetation of the continent. The Sahara expanded southwards, and rainforests shrank to a fraction of their present size, surviving in small strips next to rivers in the Congo Basin, and replaced for the most part by open grasslands and scrub. Deserts also spread in southwestern Africa, advancing northwards and inland from the dry coastal zone.

AFRICA

EXPLORATION AND MAPPING

To stake a territorial claim, Portuguese sailors would place a stone cross (*padrão*) on the African shore.

IN THE ABSENCE OF A WRITTEN historical record, little is known of early local knowledge of Africa south of the Sahara. Writing in the 5th century BCE, the Greek historian Herodotus reported an attempt by a Phoenician crew to circumnavigate the continent in 600 BCE. By 150 CE, the Greek geographer Ptolemy had mapped the area north of the line between Mombasa and the Canary Islands (*see p.44*). From 600 CE Arab merchants criss-crossed the Sahara establishing Muslim settlements. Several trading nations of Europe had secured coastal toeholds by 1600; however, by 1800, the African land mass remained relatively uncharted. The great 19th-century explorers of the interior meticulously recorded those features they encountered.

MEDIEVAL ACCOUNTS OF THE INTERIOR OF WEST AFRICA

Though the West Africans did not have maps, travellers in the region built up a considerable store of topographic information. It was this knowledge that Arabs and later the Portuguese tapped as their source for maps of the interior. Al-Idrisi, in 1154 reported a single river in West Africa. The Egyptian geographer al-'Umari had an account of a Nile of the Blacks which divided into two rivers, one flowing to the ocean, the other to the East African Nile via Lake Chad. Writing in 1456, a Portuguese squire called Diogo Gomes recounted the testimony of Buquer, an African merchant, who talked of a great river called Emin. The reports of Mandinka merchants in 1585 agreed with Buquer's account and gave additional detail.

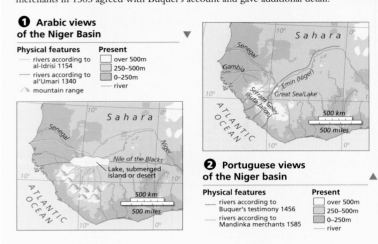

❶ Arabic views of the Niger Basin

Physical features	Present
rivers according to al-Idrisi 1154	over 500m
rivers according to al'Umari 1340	250–500m
mountain range	0–250m
	river

❷ Portuguese views of the Niger basin

Physical features	Present
rivers according to Buquer's testimony 1456	over 500m
rivers according to Mandinka merchants 1585	250–500m
	0–250m
	river

The caravel was a light sailing ship developed by the Portuguese for the exploration of coastal Africa. Its lateen sails allowed it to tack close to the wind.

❸ 14th- and 15th-century exploration

Moroccan
Ibn Battuta 1325–53

Chinese
Zheng He 1417–31

Portuguese
Gonçalo Cabral 1432
Gil Eanes 1433–35
Alfonso Baldaya 1436
Alvise Cadamosto 1455–56
Diogo Gomes 1458–60
Diogo Cão 1482
Diogo Cão 1485
Bartolomeu Dias 1487
Pero de Covilhã 1487–1520
Vasco da Gama 1497–99
Pedro Cabral 1500 (with Diogo Dias)
Pedro Cabral 1500
Diogo Dias 1500–01

area known to Greeks and Romans c.150
area known to Muslim traders c.1500
trade routes
† mariners' milestone (*padrão*)

1352: Ibn Battuta takes last journey crossing Sahara to West Africa

1434: Eanes is first European to successfully navigate the cape; area is subsequently explored by Portuguese for slaves

1325: Ibn Battuta begins travels by undertaking pilgrimage to Mecca

1327–30: Ibn Battuta visits Muslim settlements on east coast of Africa

1417–31: Zheng He undertakes three voyages which include journeys along the east coast of Africa

Jan 6–Feb 3 1488: Dias rounds the stormy cape by sailing away from land and then returning to a coastal route

By the mid-16th century, European navigators had considerable knowledge of the coasts of Madagascar and East Africa, as depicted in this Portuguese map of 1558.

Portuguese exploration

Systematic voyages of discovery were undertaken by the Portuguese along the western coast of Africa. These and later expeditions were made in the hope both of making contact with the gold-producing centres known to exist in West Africa, and of establishing a trade route to India around the tip of the continent. In consequence, the lower reaches of the rivers Gambia and Senegal were explored, contact was made with the Empire of Mali, and the Cape Verde Islands were discovered.

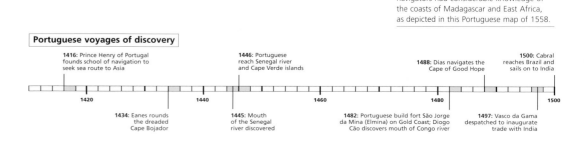

Portuguese voyages of discovery

1416: Prince Henry of Portugal founds school of navigation to seek sea route to Asia

1446: Portuguese reach Senegal river and Cape Verde islands

1488: Dias navigates the Cape of Good Hope

1500: Cabral reaches Brazil and sails on to India

1434: Eanes rounds the dreaded Cape Bojador

1445: Mouth of the Senegal river discovered

1482: Portuguese build fort São Jorge da Mina (Elmina) on Gold Coast; Diogo Cão discovers mouth of Congo river

1497: Vasco da Gama despatched to inaugurate trade with India

1420 1440 1460 1480 1500

Exploration of the African interior

The European exploration of the African interior is largely the story of the search for the sources of some of the world's greatest rivers. The Scottish explorer, James Bruce toured Ethiopia between 1768 and 1773, discovering the source of the Blue Nile in 1772. Systematic exploration may be said to have begun in 1778, under the auspices of the African Association, a group of English scientists and scholars. In 1795 the Association sponsored Mungo Park's first journey to West Africa; he investigated the Gambia river and reached the Niger, showing that it flowed eastward. British exploration intensified in the first half of the 19th century culminating in John Hanning Speke's triumphant discovery of the source of the Nile at Ripon Falls, Lake Victoria in 1862. In anticipation of the scramble for territorial control, a number of continental Europeans also embarked on investigative expeditions.

French explorer René Caillié made this sketch of Timbuktu in 1828, when he fulfilled his great ambition to visit the Saharan city. and secured a 10,000 francs prize for his efforts. The sum had been offered by the Société Géographique to the first European to return from the city.

The 19th century saw the systematic and scientific exploration of the African interior. As a result, cartographers were reluctant to represent uncertain data. Published in 1808, this map of Africa shows less information than its more speculative predecessors.

❹ 19th-century exploration ▶

British
- → James Bruce 1768–73
- → Mungo Park 1795–96
- ⇢ Mungo Park 1805–06
- → Hugh Clapperton, Dixon Denham, and Walter Oudney 1821–25
- → Hugh Clapperton and Richard Lander 1825–27
- → David Livingstone 1841–53
- ⇢ David Livingstone 1849
- ⇢ David Livingstone 1853–56
- ⋯ David Livingstone 1866–73
- → Samuel and Florence Baker 1861–65
- → Henry Stanley 1871–89
- ⋯ Mary Kingsley 1895

French
- → René Caillié 1827–28
- ⇢ Pierre Savorgnan de Brazza 1875–78
- ⋯ Jean-Baptiste Marchand 1897–98

German
- → Heinrich Barth 1850–55

Italian
- → Vittorio Bottego 1892–97

Portuguese
- → Alexandre Serpa Pinto 1877–79

Swedish
- → Charles Andersson 1853–59

1000 km
1000 miles

❺ Tracking the Nile
- → Richard Burton and John Speke 1856–59
- ⇢ John Speke 1858
- → John Speke and James Grant 1860–63
- → Samuel and Florence Baker 1863–65

300 km
300 miles

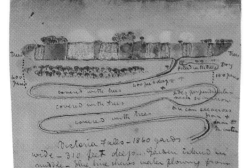

John Hanning Speke journeyed with Richard Burton in 1856–59. In 1862, James Grant and he came across the source of the Nile at Lake Victoria.

The source of the Nile

The quest for the source of the Nile captured the imagination of 19th-century Europe. The adventure stimulated intellectual debate and provoked fierce personal jealousies. After Speke had identified the source as Ripon Falls, Lake Victoria, he endured many attempts to discredit his discovery. The political and economic importance of the region made it the objective of rival imperialists.

Sir Henry Morton Stanley, the British-American journalist, was sent to Africa by the New York Herald in 1871 to find David Livingstone, of whom nothing had been heard for several months. In the 1880s he helped create Léopold's Congo Free State.

Livingstone carefully noted the dimensions of those physical features he encountered. He annotated this map of Victoria Falls with precise measurements and descriptive detail.

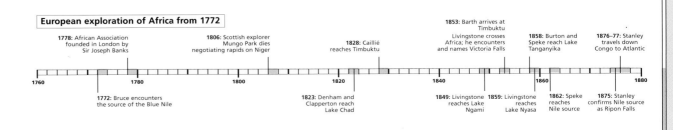

European exploration of Africa from 1772

- 1778: African Association founded in London by Sir Joseph Banks
- 1806: Scottish explorer Mungo Park dies negotiating rapids on Niger
- 1828: Caillié reaches Timbuktu
- 1853: Barth arrives at Timbuktu
- Livingstone crosses Africa; he encounters and names Victoria Falls
- 1858: Burton and Speke reach Lake Tanganyika
- 1876–77: Stanley travels down Congo to Atlantic

- 1772: Bruce encounters the source of the Blue Nile
- 1823: Denham and Clapperton reach Lake Chad
- 1849: Livingstone reaches Lake Ngami
- 1859: Livingstone reaches Lake Nyasa
- 1862: Speke reaches Nile source
- 1875: Stanley confirms Nile source as Ripon Falls

1760 1780 1800 1820 1840 1860 1880

157

THE EARLY HISTORY OF AFRICA

Hatshepsut *seized the throne in Egypt from her stepson and reigned from 1472 to 1458 BCE.*

THREE EVENTS contributed to the growth and spread of farming in Africa: the spread of cattle pastoralism in the Sahara, the domestication of indigenous crops further south, and the introduction of West Asian livestock and cereals to Egypt. Asian wheat and barley spread along the Mediterranean coast, down the Nile valley to the Sudan, and the Ethiopian Highlands. Drier conditions from 3000 BCE forced Saharan pastoralists to migrate to the Nile valley where from 5000 BCE, crops had thrived in fertile soil deposited by annual floods. Egypt thereafter emerged as a powerful state, organized conventionally into 30 'Dynasties', broken down into three 'Kingdoms' separated by two 'Intermediate Periods' of disunity and instability.

The development of agriculture

From 4000 BCE bulrush millet was cultivated alongside sorghum in southern Sudan.

Both the herding of wild cattle in the Sahara and the cultivation of indigenous plants further south began c.6000 BCE. From 5000 BCE, Asian wheat and barley were grown in Egypt. By 2000 BCE pastoralism was widespread north of the Equator. Farming and herding south of the Equator however, were impeded by dense forests and the presence of the parasitic tsetse fly. As a result pastoralism progressed only slowly down the east coast reaching southern Africa by 1000 CE.

Saharan rock art provide vivid pictures of what life was like in the region. This example from the Tassili n'Ajjer plateau, dates from c.6000 BCE. It depicts the hunting of giraffes, now only found south of the Sahara.

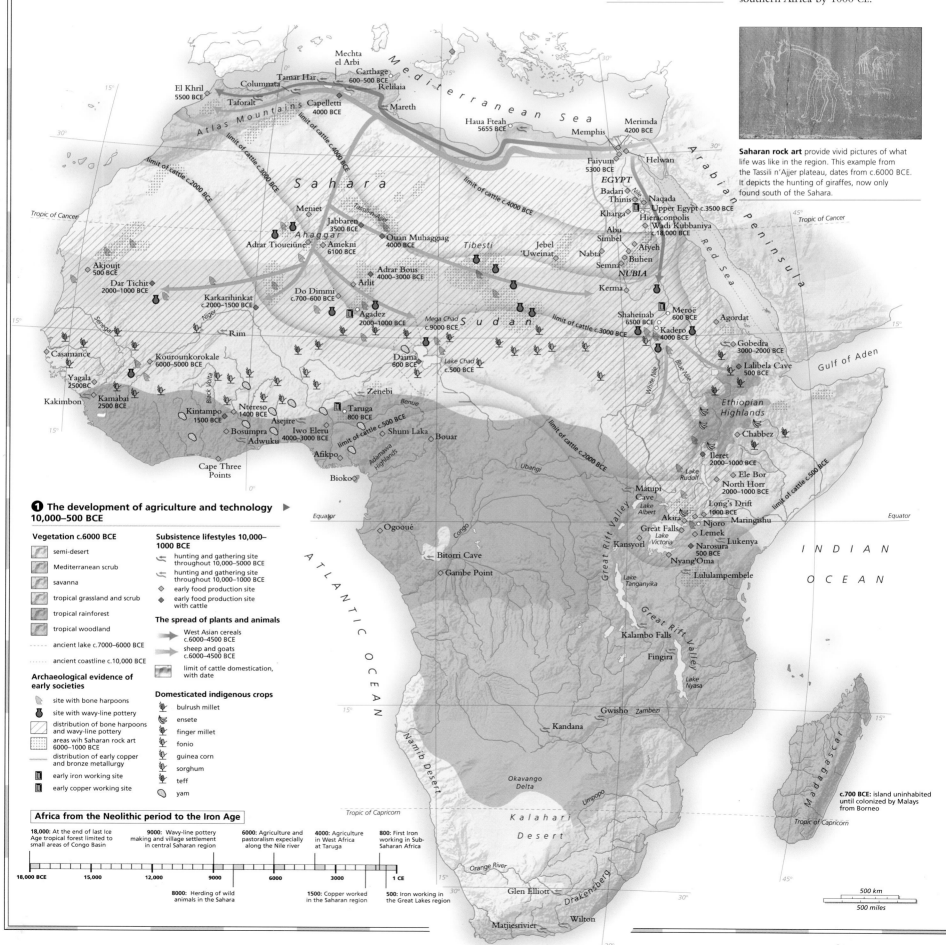

❶ The development of agriculture and technology 10,000–500 BCE ▶

Vegetation c.6000 BCE
- semi-desert
- Mediterranean scrub
- savanna
- tropical grassland and scrub
- tropical rainforest
- tropical woodland
- ---- ancient lake c.7000–6000 BCE
- ······ ancient coastline c.10,000 BCE

Archaeological evidence of early societies
- site with bone harpoons
- site with wavy-line pottery
- distribution of bone harpoons and wavy-line pottery
- areas wih Saharan rock art 6000–1000 BCE
- distribution of early copper and bronze metallurgy
- early iron working site
- early copper working site

Subsistence lifestyles 10,000–1000 BCE
- hunting and gathering site throughout 10,000–5000 BCE
- hunting and gathering site throughout 10,000–1000 BCE
- early food production site
- early food production site with cattle

The spread of plants and animals
- → West Asian cereals c.6000–4500 BCE
- → sheep and goats c.6000–4500 BCE
- limit of cattle domestication, with date

Domesticated indigenous crops
- bulrush millet
- ensete
- finger millet
- fonio
- guinea corn
- sorghum
- teff
- yam

Africa from the Neolithic period to the Iron Age

| 18,000: At the end of last Ice Age tropical forest limited to small areas of Congo Basin | 9000: Wavy-line pottery making and village settlement in central Saharan region | 6000: Agriculture and pastoralism especially along the Nile river | 4000: Agriculture in West Africa at Taruga | 800: First Iron working in Sub-Saharan Africa |

| 18,000 BCE | 15,000 | 12,000 | 9000 | 6000 | 3000 | 1 CE |

| 8000: Herding of wild animals in the Sahara | 1500: Copper worked in the Saharan region | 500: Iron working in the Great Lakes region |

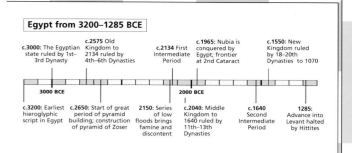

② Pre-dynastic Egypt c.5000–3000 BCE

- Confederacy of Thinis c.3500–3000 BCE
- Confederacy of Nubt c.3500–3000 BCE
- Confederacy of Nekhen c.3500–3000 BCE
- ◯ pre-dynastic kingdom of Hieraconpolis
- → military expansion of Hieraconpolis
- ○ early pre-dynastic site
- ▽ middle pre-dynastic site
- ▽ middle pre-dynastic Nubian site
- ◇ late pre-dynastic site
- □ late pre-dynastic Nubian site
- ⬡ oasis

Egypt from 3200–1285 BCE

c.3000: The Egyptian state ruled by 1st–3rd Dynasty
c.2575 Old Kingdom to 2134 ruled by 4th–6th Dynasties
c.2134 First Intermediate Period
c.1965: Nubia is conquered by Egypt; frontier at 2nd Cataract
c.1550: New Kingdom ruled by 18–20th Dynasties to 1070

3000 BCE — 2000 BCE

c.3200: Earliest hieroglyphic script in Egypt
c.2650: Start of great period of pyramid building; construction of pyramid of Zoser
2150: Series of low floods brings famine and discontent
c.2040: Middle Kingdom to 1640 ruled by 11th–13th Dynasties
c.1640 Second Intermediate Period
1285: Advance into Levant halted by Hittites

The growth of Egypt 3500–2134 BCE

From 5000 BCE settled communites of farmers in the Nile valley gradually coalesced into urban centres under local rulers who developed efficient administrations. Menes of the 1st Dynasty established the Egyptian state c.3000 BCE. From this time the use of hieroglyphic writing spread and Memphis was founded. With greater centralization of power the Old Kingdom emerged and the building of the great pyramids which served as royal burial places began. From 2400 BCE royal power began to decline and by 2034 BCE the Old Kingdom was divided between two rival dynasties in Upper and Lower Egypt. The 94 years of political instability which followed, became known as the First Intermediate Period.

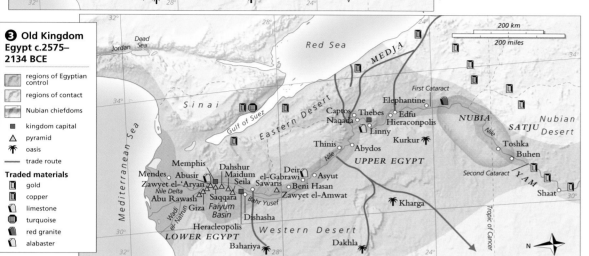

③ Old Kingdom Egypt c.2575–2134 BCE

- regions of Egyptian control
- regions of contact
- Nubian chiefdoms
- ■ kingdom capital
- △ pyramid
- ☥ oasis
- — trade route

Traded materials
- gold
- copper
- limestone
- turquoise
- red granite
- alabaster

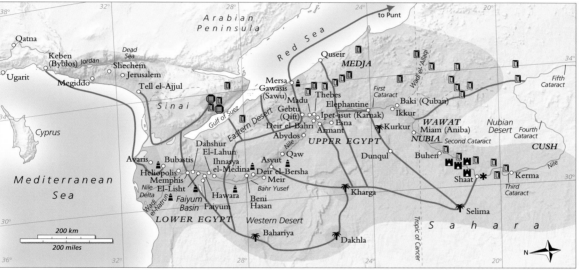

④ Middle Kingdom Egypt c.2040–1640 BCE ▶

- regions of Egyptian control
- regions of contact
- ✴ trading centre
- ⚔ Nubian fort
- Middle Kingdom temple
- ☥ oasis
- — trade route

Traded materials
- gold
- copper
- turquoise

The step-pyramid of Zoser dating from c.2700 BCE was the earliest pyramid built in Egypt. Its construction required the large-scale mobilization of thousands of workers

Hatshepsut's temple at Deir el-Bahri was built c.1473 BCE. A fine example of architecture from the 18th Dynasty, the building has a series of colonnades and courts on three levels.

Expansion and division in Egypt

The governors of Thebes emerged from the First Intermediate Period as rulers of Upper Egypt. They later successfully challenged Lower Egypt for control of the entire region, and the Middle Kingdom was established by c.2040 BCE. Its army and administration systematically enriched Egypt's economy by dominating, and eventually annexing, Wawat and northern Cush. The Second Intermediate saw Nubia lost from Egyptian control, and the division of the Nile Delta region into several kingdoms. From 1640 BCE much of Egypt was ruled by the Hyksos from the Levant. They were later expelled by Ahmose, king of Thebes, who became the first ruler of the New Kingdom. During the New Kingdom Egypt embarked on a policy of expansion both north and south which made it the major commercial power in the ancient world, however by 1000 BCE the New Kingdom was in decline.

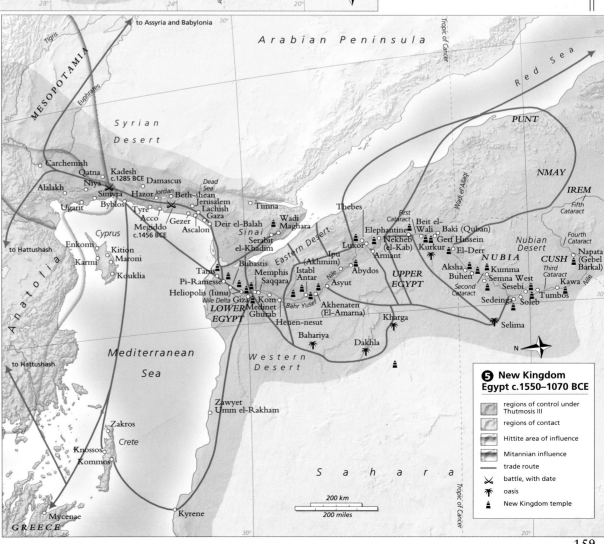

⑤ New Kingdom Egypt c.1550–1070 BCE

- regions of control under Thutmosis III
- regions of contact
- Hittite area of influence
- Mitannian influence
- — trade route
- ⚔ battle, with date
- ☥ oasis
- New Kingdom temple

159

THE SPREAD OF COMPLEX SOCIETIES

The Nok culture of West Africa was noted for its terracotta sculptures.

ALTHOUGH TRADE ROUTES connected sub-Saharan Africa to the Mediterranean civilizations of the north, the two regions developed very much in isolation. The southward migrations of Bantu-speakers from 2000 BCE, may have contributed to the diffusion of settled agriculture in sub-Saharan Africa. Sheep-herding and iron-working spread south at a later date. The Nok of West Africa were smelting iron by 600 BCE. In North Africa, the rich lands of the Mediterranean coast and Egypt attracted foreign invaders, including the Greeks and Romans. However, from 300 BCE, powerful native states also emerged in the region, notably Axum, which dominated the Red Sea, and the Berber states which competed with Rome for the lands of northwest Africa.

The Bantu influence

From their homeland in modern-day Nigeria on Africa's west coast, the Bantu-speaking peoples dispersed along eastern and western routes into the equatorial rainforests and then on to southern Africa during the 2nd millennium BCE. The migrating Bantu cleared forests and engaged in mixed farming. From the late 1st century BCE, their knowledge of iron-working gave them a distinct advantage over hunter-gatherers such as the Khoisan people. They established an economic basis for new societies which could sustain greater populations than those based on hunting and gathering. Thus the period from 500 BCE to 1000 CE saw the transfer of Bantu traditions to much of sub-Saharan Africa.

During the first millennium BCE the Bantu settled in villages on the edge of the rainforest in central Africa, engaging in mixed farming.

The spread of iron-working

The earliest evidence for iron-working south of the Sahara is found at the settlements of the Nok culture in West Africa, including Taruga and Samun Dukiya and dates from c.600 BCE. By 300 BCE, iron-working had spread as far south as the Congo river. From 1 CE, dates from sites on the sub-equatorial west coast correspond with those in East Africa. It is possible therefore, that iron smelting diffused southward along two separate routes: one along the eastern part of the continent and the other along the west. In addition to its use for tools such as hoes, axes, knives, and spears, iron was also a luxury trade item, and helped to sustain inter-community relations in the sub-Saharan region.

Paintings of chariots, are found along the great African overland trade routes. They may provide evidence for the transport of iron-working to sub-Saharan Africa.

The development of iron technology and social organization

c.600 BCE: First known iron-working in Nok region	**c.400 BCE:** Beginnings of iron-working in Ethiopian Highlands	**c. 200 BCE:** Earliest settlement in Jenne	**c.1 CE:** Sheep herded by Khoisans in southern Africa	**c.400 CE:** Jenne a substantial city with population of 12,000	**c.600 CE:** Cattle and iron-working widespread in southern Africa
600 BCE	400	200	1 CE	200	400	600 CE

c.300 BCE: Berber states begin to emerge in North Africa

c.300 CE: Bantu cereal cultivators in southeast Africa begin to herd cattle

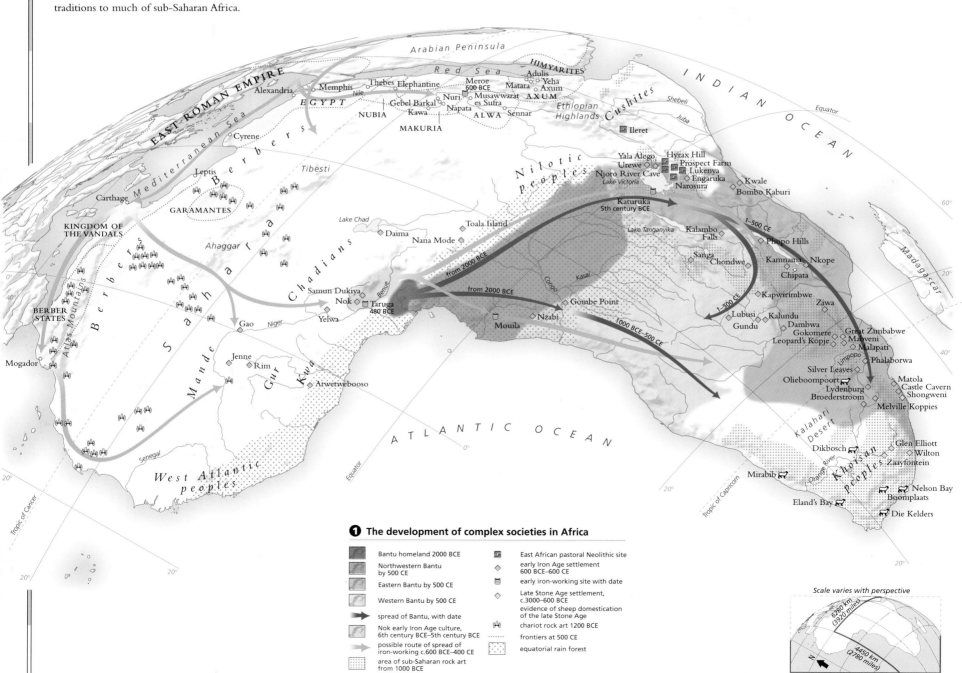

❶ The development of complex societies in Africa

- Bantu homeland 2000 BCE
- Northwestern Bantu by 500 CE
- Eastern Bantu by 500 CE
- Western Bantu by 500 CE
- → spread of Bantu, with date
- Nok early Iron Age culture, 6th century BCE–5th century BCE
- → possible route of spread of iron-working c.600 BCE–400 CE
- area of sub-Saharan rock art from 1000 BCE
- East African pastoral Neolithic site
- early Iron Age settlement 600 BCE–600 CE
- early iron-working site with date
- Late Stone Age settlement, c.3000–600 BCE
- evidence of sheep domestication of the late Stone Age
- chariot rock art 1200 BCE
- frontiers at 500 CE
- equatorial rain forest

Scale varies with perspective

Berber states in North Africa

From 300 BCE, the Berber inhabitants of North Africa, including the Mauri, Masaesyli, and Massyli, began to form states, building cities and developing administrative structures. In alliance with Rome the kingdoms were largely united to form Numidia by Masinissa of the Massyli in 201 BCE. Masinissa's grandson, Jugurtha later incited war with Rome and was defeated in 104 BCE. His territory was subsequently absorbed into the Roman Empire as a client state. In 33 BCE King Boccus II of the Mauri willed his kingdom to the empire thus completing the annexation of the region. The entire North African coast supplied Rome with agricultural products, primarily wheat and olives; cities on the coast, such as Carthage, were centres of exchange.

The Berber states issued their own coinage. This coin dating from the 2nd century BCE depicts Jugurtha, ruler of Numidia from 118 BCE until his defeat at the hands of the Romans in 104 BCE.

An enduring consequence of the Roman Empire was the spread of the Latin language and Roman architecture. As towns sprang up in North Africa, they acquired characteristic features of Roman cities and architecture such as this Roman amphitheatre at Thysdrus in present-day Tunisia. Built in 300 CE, the building could seat 50,000 people.

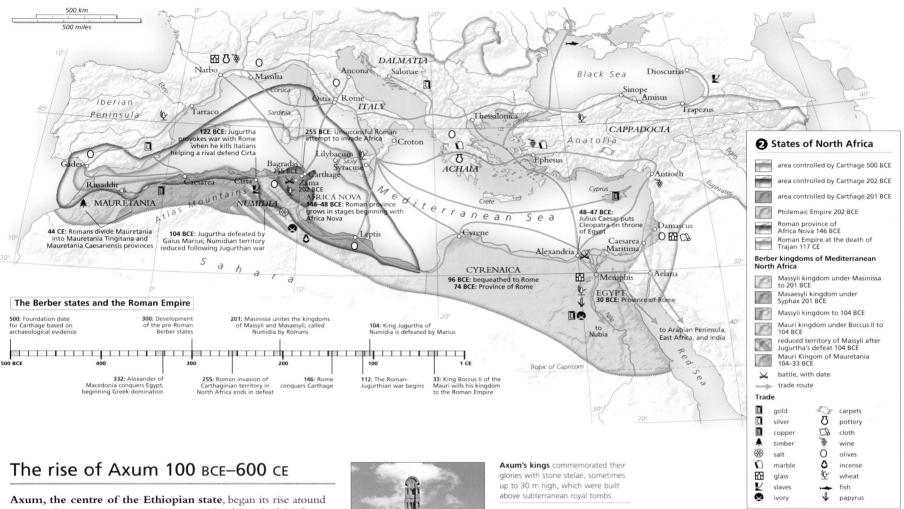

2 States of North Africa

- area controlled by Carthage 500 BCE
- area controlled by Carthage 202 BCE
- area controlled by Carthage 201 BCE
- Ptolemaic Empire 202 BCE
- Roman province of Africa Nova 146 BCE
- Roman Empire at the death of Trajan 117 CE

Berber kingdoms of Mediterranean North Africa
- Massyli kingdom under Masinissa to 201 BCE
- Masaesyli kingdom under Syphax 201 BCE
- Massyli kingdom to 104 BCE
- Mauri kingdom under Boccus II to 104 BCE
- reduced territory of Massyli after Jugurtha's defeat 104 BCE
- Mauri Kingom of Mauretania 104–33 BCE

⚔ battle, with date
→ trade route

Trade
gold			carpets
silver			pottery
copper			cloth
salt			wine
marble			olives
glass			incense
slaves			wheat
ivory			fish
			papyrus

The Berber states and the Roman Empire

500: Foundation date for Carthage based on archaeological evidence

300: Development of the pre-Roman Berber states

201: Masinissa unites the kingdoms of Massyli and Masaesyli, called Numidia by Romans

104: King Jugurtha of Numidia is defeated by Marius

| 500 BCE | 400 | 300 | 200 | 100 | 1 CE |

332: Alexander of Macedonia conquers Egypt, beginning Greek domination

255: Roman invasion of Carthaginian territory in North Africa ends in defeat

146: Rome conquers Carthage

112: The Roman-Jugurthian war begins

33: King Boccus II of the Mauri wills his kingdom to the Roman Empire

The rise of Axum 100 BCE–600 CE

Axum, the centre of the Ethiopian state, began its rise around 100 BCE, becoming a major trading power by the end of the first century CE. The kingdom grew wealthy through its control of the incense-trading port of Adulis on the Red Sea *(see p.225)*. Axum provided Egypt, India, Persia, and Arabia with tortoiseshell, ivory, and rhinoceros horn. The kingdom reached its peak during the reign of King Ezana who converted to Christianity c.350 CE. By 500 CE most of the country had adopted the new religion. In 525 CE Kaleb, one of Ezana's successors, conquered the southern part of the Arabian Peninsula, and Axum occupied this territory until 574 CE. With the spread of Islam, Axum lost its monopoly of the Red Sea to Muslim traders, and began to decline from around 600 CE.

Axum's kings commemorated their glories with stone stelae, sometimes up to 30 m high, which were built above subterranean royal tombs.

The rise and fall of kingdoms in northeast Africa

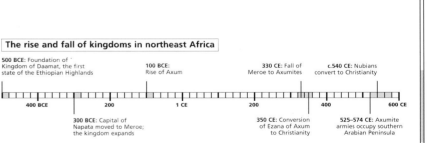

500 BCE: Foundation of Kingdom of Daamat, the first state of the Ethiopian Highlands

100 BCE: Rise of Axum

330 CE: Fall of Meroe to Axumites

c.540 CE: Nubians convert to Christianity

| 400 BCE | 200 | 1 CE | 200 | 400 | 600 CE |

300 BCE: Capital of Napata moved to Meroe; the kingdom expands

350 CE: Conversion of Ezana of Axum to Christianity

525–574 CE: Axumite armies occupy southern Arabian Peninsula

3 Northeast Africa 100 CE

- frankincense and myrrh
- gold
- ivory
- obsidian
- precious stones
- rhinoceros horn
- slaves
- tortoiseshell
- → trade route

4 Northeast Africa 350 CE

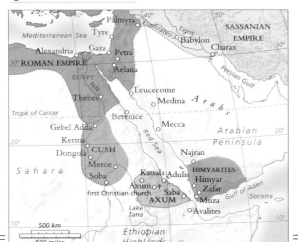

5 Northeast Africa 500 CE

† early Christian church 350 CE–600 CE

ISLAM AND NEW STATES IN AFRICA

Unearthed on the island of Pemba, these North African gold coins testify to Swahili trade with the Arab world.

FROM THE 10TH CENTURY, A SERIES of empires arose in the sub-Saharan savannah. They attracted Muslim Arab traders who travelled south in search of salt, gold, and slaves. Through frequent contact, Islam gradually infiltrated the region by means of peaceful conversion. When the Muslim Berber Almoravids captured the capital of Ghana in 1076, causing the collapse of the empire, their conquest did little to advance the spread of Islam. Christian Ethiopia also withstood Muslim advances. However, Ghana's successors, Mali and Songhay, owed much of their wealth and civilization to the advent and adoption of Islam, as did the Kanem-Bornu Empire around Lake Chad, and, after the 15th century, the Hausa city-states. From the late 10th century, Arab merchant colonies were established in the coastal towns of East Africa, stimulating African trade with Arabia and India, and accelerating the southward spread of Islam.

African trade and the spread of Islam

Built in the 14th century, the great mosque at Jenne in Mali was constructed with sun-dried mud bricks.

Islamic expansion out of Arabia began in earnest following the death of the Prophet Muhammad in 632. By 640 Egypt had fallen into the hands of Muslim soldiers and settlers. From the 8th century, traders and clerics were the agents of Islam, spreading the religion along the commercial arteries of the Sahara which extended into West Africa; and up the Nile. By the 13th century the Saifawa kings of Kanem had adopted the faith. Islam had also travelled down the east coast of Africa, taken by seafaring Arabs who set up coastal trading centres. Trade between Arabs and Bantus necessitated a new language, therefore Swahili became the *lingua franca* of the east coast.

Carved by West African craftsmen, this 16th-century ivory horn *(above)* was produced for the European market. This is confirmed by its Portuguese-style inscriptions.

Dating from the 16th century, this blue and white Ming dynasty bowl *(left)* was found on the east coast of Africa, and provides evidence of trade with China.

Islamic expansion in Africa from 600

632: Death of Muhammad
635–40: Conquest of Egypt by Arabs
c.800: Emergence of trading towns on East African coast.
909: Fatimid dynasty founded by Ubaydullah
1050: King of Takrur converts to Islam
1270: Beginning of Solomid dynasty in Ethiopia

| 600 | 700 | 800 | 900 | 1000 | 1100 | 1200 | 1300 |

625: First Islamic Arab invasion of Makuria
680: Arab armies reach Atlantic at Morocco
1076: King of Ghana converts to Islam

❶ African trade and the spread of Islam 500–1500 ▶

- ---- frontiers 1500
- → Muslim trade routes
- limit of Muslim influence by 900
- limit of Muslim influence by 1100
- limit of Muslim influence by 1300
- limit of Muslim influence by 1500
- limit of Muslim influence in Spain 1492
- Christians c.1100
- Christians c.1500
- ⊚ Portuguese possession in 1500

- copper
- gold
- dates
- fish
- flour
- ivory
- kola nuts
- leather
- porcelain
- perfume
- saffron
- salt
- silk
- slaves
- spice
- wax
- wool

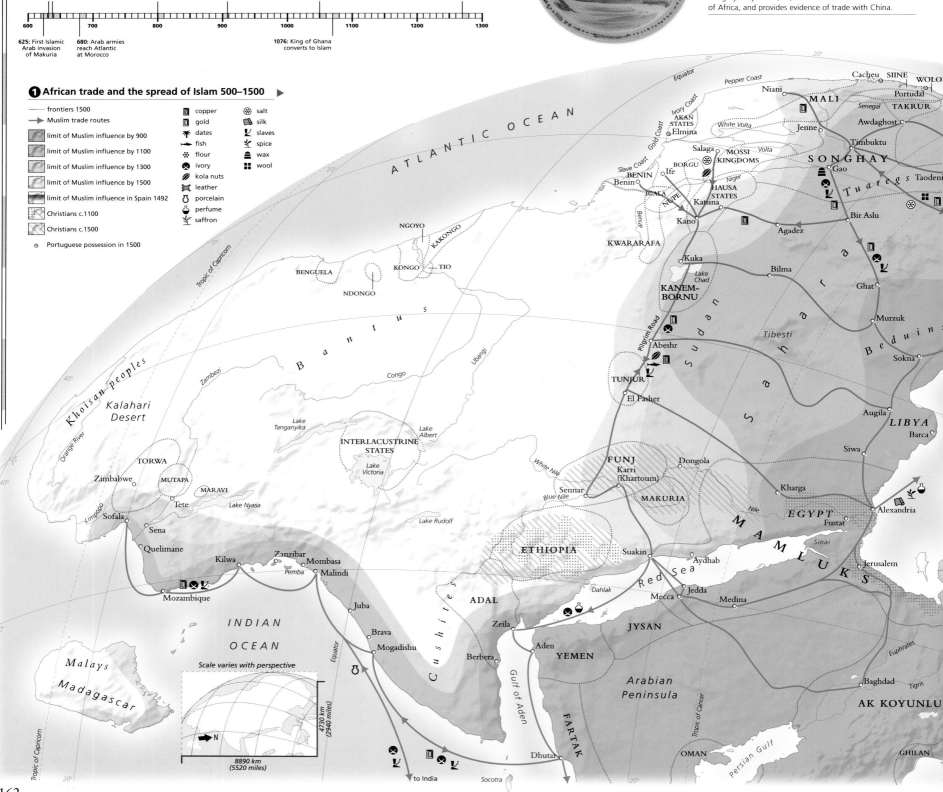

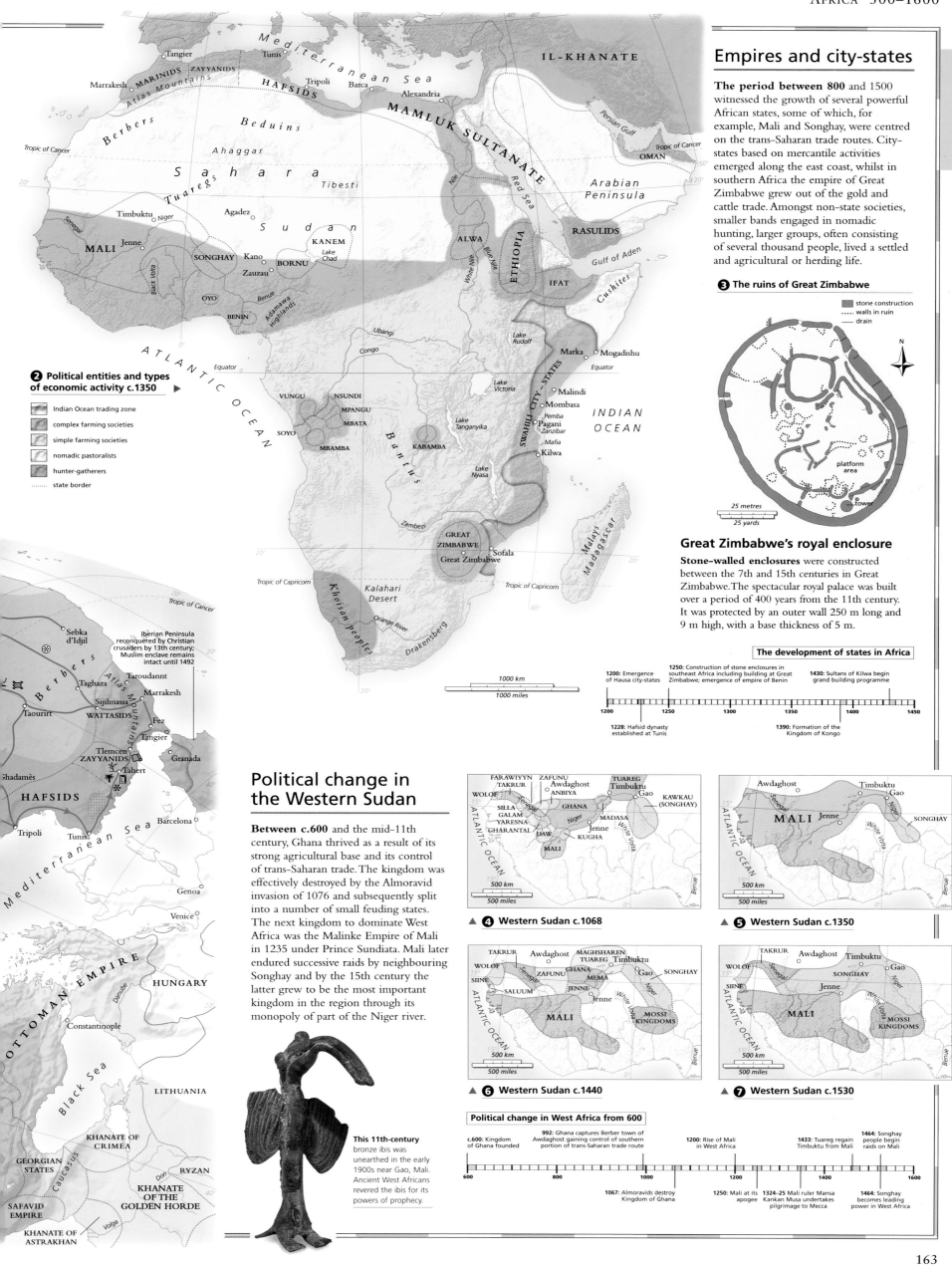

Empires and city-states

The period between 800 and 1500 witnessed the growth of several powerful African states, some of which, for example, Mali and Songhay, were centred on the trans-Saharan trade routes. City-states based on mercantile activities emerged along the east coast, whilst in southern Africa the empire of Great Zimbabwe grew out of the gold and cattle trade. Amongst non-state societies, smaller bands engaged in nomadic hunting, larger groups, often consisting of several thousand people, lived a settled and agricultural or herding life.

❸ The ruins of Great Zimbabwe

- ▓ stone construction
- ···· walls in ruin
- —— drain

platform area

tower

25 metres
25 yards

Great Zimbabwe's royal enclosure

Stone-walled enclosures were constructed between the 7th and 15th centuries in Great Zimbabwe. The spectacular royal palace was built over a period of 400 years from the 11th century. It was protected by an outer wall 250 m long and 9 m high, with a base thickness of 5 m.

❷ Political entities and types of economic activity c.1350 ▶

- Indian Ocean trading zone
- complex farming societies
- simple farming societies
- nomadic pastoralists
- hunter-gatherers
- ···· state border

The development of states in Africa

- 1200: Emergence of Hausa city-states
- 1250: Construction of stone enclosures in southeast Africa including building at Great Zimbabwe; emergence of empire of Benin
- 1430: Sultans of Kilwa begin grand building programme
- 1228: Hafsid dynasty established at Tunis
- 1390: Formation of the Kingdom of Kongo

| 1200 | 1250 | 1300 | 1350 | 1400 | 1450 |

Iberian Peninsula reconquered by Christian crusaders by 13th century; Muslim enclave remains intact until 1492

Political change in the Western Sudan

Between c.600 and the mid-11th century, Ghana thrived as a result of its strong agricultural base and its control of trans-Saharan trade. The kingdom was effectively destroyed by the Almoravid invasion of 1076 and subsequently split into a number of small feuding states. The next kingdom to dominate West Africa was the Malinke Empire of Mali in 1235 under Prince Sundiata. Mali later endured successive raids by neighbouring Songhay and by the 15th century the latter grew to be the most important kingdom in the region through its monopoly of part of the Niger river.

This 11th-century bronze ibis was unearthed in the early 1900s near Gao, Mali. Ancient West Africans revered the ibis for its powers of prophecy.

▲ **❹ Western Sudan c.1068**

▲ **❺ Western Sudan c.1350**

▲ **❻ Western Sudan c.1440**

▲ **❼ Western Sudan c.1530**

Political change in West Africa from 600

- c.600: Kingdom of Ghana founded
- 992: Ghana captures Berber town of Awdaghost gaining control of southern portion of trans-Saharan trade route
- 1200: Rise of Mali in West Africa
- 1433: Tuareg regain Timbuktu from Mali
- 1464: Songhay people begin raids on Mali
- 1067: Almoravids destroy Kingdom of Ghana
- 1250: Mali at its apogee
- 1324–25 Mali ruler Mansa Kankan Musa undertakes pilgrimage to Mecca
- 1464: Songhay becomes leading power in West Africa

| 600 | 800 | 1000 | 1200 | 1400 | 1600 |

EARLY MODERN AFRICA

Asante's well-armed warriors made it the most powerful state on the Gold Coast.

AFTER THE PORTUGUESE had led European expansion into Africa in the 15th century, a few colonies were established – in Angola, along the Zambezi valley, and in the region of the Cape of Good Hope – but for the most part, African rulers contained and controlled the activities of the newcomers. In parts of West Africa they allowed Europeans to establish coastal forts and trading posts. With this new presence came increased opportunities for external trade, principally in gold, ivory, and slaves. After 1700, however, the importance of all other goods was totally eclipsed by the value of the Atlantic slave trade.

The 16th century saw the Ottoman Empire advance across North Africa as far as the Atlas Mountains. To the south, the great empire of Songhay yielded to Moroccan invaders in 1591, though the cycle of empires continued in West Africa with Great Fulo. In the early 18th century powerful coastal kingdoms arose in Asante and Dahomey, while Rozwi replaced Mwenemutapa in southeast Africa.

Southern and East Africa

The Portuguese presence in the region was challenged in the 17th century by the Rozwi empire, which drove them from the highlands of Zimbabwe, while Omani fleets captured many of their coastal forts in East Africa. Portugal was left with the semi-independent *prazos* (estates) of the Zambezi valley and the coastal towns of Sofala, Mozambique, and Inhambane. In 1652 the Dutch East India Company founded its colony at Cape Town. Rapid expansion in the 18th century brought Dutch settlers into conflict with the many small states of the Nguni region.

Fort Jesus, built in 1593 to protect Portuguese trading interests in Mombasa, fell to the Omanis in 1698.

1652: Dutch establish colony at Cape of Good Hope

1696: Dombo Changamire expands Rozwi over Zimbabwe region

1729: Portuguese leave East Africa in wake of attacks from Oman

1779: Start of series of wars between Dutch settlers and Nguni

Southern and East Africa

1720–30: Dutch occupy Portuguese settlement at Delagoa Bay

1795: British capture Cape Town from the Dutch

① Southern and East Africa c.1700

- Portuguese possessions
- Dutch possessions
- ruined city

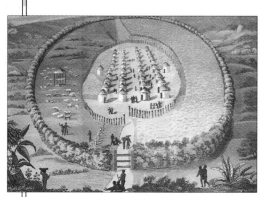

The Fulbe, who lived by raising cattle for their neighbours, were found throughout much of West Africa. This 1730 engraving shows a Fulbe town on the River Gambia with a plantation and a corral for livestock.

African political development

In the 17th century, much of sub-Saharan Africa consisted of many small, self-governing units, typically about 50 km across. In West Africa some 70% of the population probably lived in these 'mini-states'. Boundaries remained stable for long periods, the people choosing their leaders on the basis of heredity, election or other local customs. There were extensive empires, such as Songhay and Mali, but these lay in the sparsely populated region now known as the Sahel. These and the other larger states, which ruled the remainder of the population, usually grew by incorporating smaller units, although they continued to use the local polities to enforce the law and raise tribute. Taxation took the form of a head or house tax. There was no concept of land ownership; it could not be bought or sold. Land was regarded as belonging to whoever farmed it. Slave ownership, on the other hand, was an important measure of personal wealth.

The formidable Queen Njinga ruled the kingdom of Ndongo from 1624 to 1663. She fought the Portuguese to a standstill.

② States of West and Central Africa 1625

- Portuguese possessions
- Dutch settlement

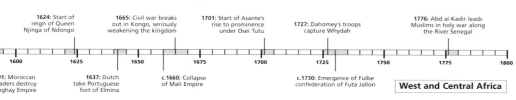

1624: Start of reign of Queen Njinga of Ndongo

1665: Civil war breaks out in Kongo, seriously weakening the kingdom

1701: Start of Asante's rise to prominence under Osei Tutu

1727: Dahomey's troops capture Whydah

1776: Abd al-Kadir leads Muslims in holy war along the River Senegal

1591: Moroccan invaders destroy Songhay Empire

1637: Dutch take Portuguese fort of Elmina

c.1660: Collapse of Mali Empire

c.1730: Emergence of Fulbe confederation of Futa Jallon

West and Central Africa

The struggle for the Horn of Africa

Ethiopia's domination of the region came to an end in the 16th century. The Christian empire's expansion into Muslim lands to the south had often involved forced conversion and the destruction of Islamic literature and places of worship. In 1529 a dynamic imam from Adal, Ahmad Grañ, proclaimed a holy war against Ethiopia, winning many striking victories. In 1540 the Ethiopians sought aid from Portugal and Grañ was killed in battle in 1543. This ultimately inconclusive war laid waste the region, which allowed the Oromo to invade from the south. Organized in many independent mobile bands, they took over both Christian and Muslim lands and founded new kingdoms of their own. Many Oromo embraced Islam and some fought as mercenaries in civil wars in Ethiopia. The fortunes of the Ethiopian empire revived somewhat in the Gondar period in the 17th century, but its lands were much reduced.

1529: Ahmad Grañ leads *jihad* against Ethiopia	**1540:** Portuguese come to the aid of Ethiopia	**1597:** Start of period of civil war	**1636:** King Fasiladas founds permanent capital at Gondar	**1682:** Accession of Iyasu I, last great king of Gondar period

The decline of Ethiopia

1543: Death of Ahmad Grañ, shot by a Portuguese musketeer — **1590:** Oromo bands begin occupation of southern Ethiopia — **1632:** End of civil wars. Jesuit missionaries expelled from Ethiopia

❸ Horn of Africa 1500–1700

Ethiopian King Fasiladas built the city of Gondar with this magnificent castle in 1636. Before his reign, the rulers of Ethiopia had never had a fixed residence, setting up a tented court for periods of six months to a year, then moving on to another part of the kingdom.

❹ The African slave trade c.1750

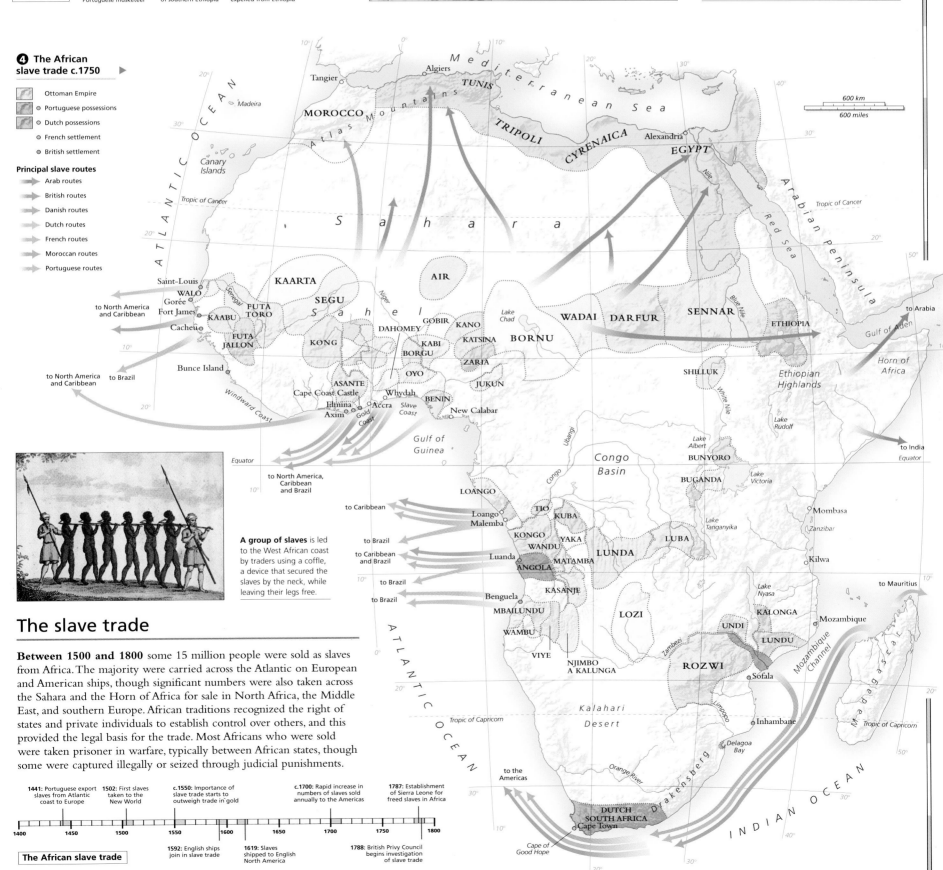

A group of slaves is led to the West African coast by traders using a coffle, a device that secured the slaves by the neck, while leaving their legs free.

The slave trade

Between 1500 and 1800 some 15 million people were sold as slaves from Africa. The majority were carried across the Atlantic on European and American ships, though significant numbers were also taken across the Sahara and the Horn of Africa for sale in North Africa, the Middle East, and southern Europe. African traditions recognized the right of states and private individuals to establish control over others, and this provided the legal basis for the trade. Most Africans who were sold were taken prisoner in warfare, typically between African states, though some were captured illegally or seized through judicial punishments.

The African slave trade

THE COLONIZATION OF AFRICA

Cecil Rhodes, the embodiment of colonialism, planned to extend British rule in Africa from Cairo to Cape Town.

THE 19TH CENTURY was a period of revolutionary change in Africa. The states of West Africa were convulsed by a series of reformist Islamic *jihads*, while in the south the rise of Zulu militarism had catastrophic consequences for neighbouring peoples. By the mid-19th century Africa was also undergoing a commercial revolution. Europeans could now offer high-quality machined goods in large quantities. As a result Africa was condemned to the role of producer of primary goods. By the end of the century, many African kingdoms and clan-based communities were being replaced by states organized along indigenous lines. However, this process was forestalled by the decision of the major European powers to carve up the continent between them.

Commerce in the 19th century

The Arab slave trader, Tibbu Tib organized his own state and security system in 1875 with the help of armed followers.

The development of new export goods in Europe had social implications for Africa. Reduced shipping costs brought about by the introduction of the steamship meant that European textile and metal goods arrived in force. The resultant decline in local industries was accompanied by a growth in the internal slave trade. The substantial carrying trade, especially the porterage trade of east and central Africa, was run by small-scale entrepreneurs. While such ventures did not bring large profit, those involved enjoyed new and elevated social positions. Often the carrying trade was organized from a particular region, giving it an ethnic character. Enterprising African traders took advantage of the expanding economy to gain political power, for example, the copper trader Msiri won himself a kingdom.

Commercial Africa from 1815

1816: Wool mills, flax mills, sugar refineries, indigo factories, and glassworks established in Egypt

c.1850: Atlantic slave trade, including clandestine operations, begins to die out

1875: Tibbu Tib establishes trading principality

1815 — 1825 — 1835 — 1845 — 1855 — 1865 — 1875

1830: 20,000 slaves exported from central African ports to Brazil

1866: Copper trader Msiri establishes trading principality

❶ Commercial and political Africa c.1830

- cloves
- cocoa
- coffee
- copper
- cotton
- diamonds
- gold
- gum arabic
- honey and wax
- ivory
- olives
- palm products
- peanuts
- rubber
- slaves/ migrant workers
- wheat
- wine
- → trade route

- British possession
- French possession
- Ottoman territory
- Portuguese possession
- Spanish possession
- commercial group

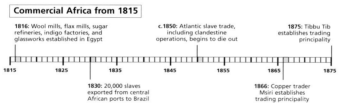

Zulu and Afrikaner expansion

Under the leadership of Shaka, the Zulu were organized into a highly militarized kingdom. They conquered neighbouring Nguni tribes and set off a series of wars which depopulated large parts of the southern interior, leaving it vulnerable to Afrikaner expansion. Afrikaners left Cape Colony between 1835 and the 1840s in search of pastureland, and to escape from unwelcome British rule. They successfully defeated powerful military kingdoms as they progressed northwards.

British reforms such as the abolition of slavery, caused the exodus of many Boers from Cape Colony. They undertook the 'Great Trek' in ox wagons.

❷ The Afrikaner treks and the Mfecane wars

- the nuclear Zulu chiefdom
- Shaka's Zulu kingdom 1817
- Sobhuza's Swazi kingdom 1820
- Moshoeshoe's Lesotho kingdom 1824
- Mzilikazi's Ndebele kingdom 1826
- Nguni victory
- British victory
- Boer victory
- → main Boer trek route 1836–54
- → Nguni migrations
- borders 1895

Shaka armed the Zulu with long-bladed, stabbing *assegais*, which forced them to fight at close quarters. Shield markings and headdress distinguished different regiments.

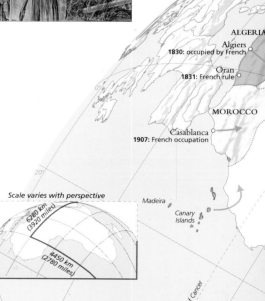

Zulu and Afrikaner expansion

1820: Nguni clans disperse to avoid Mfecane wars brought about by rise of Zulu Empire

1835: Zwangendaba crosses the Limpopo taking the Mfecane northward

1843: Short-lived Boer republic of Natal annexed by Britain

1852: Independence granted by British to Voortrekkers in Transvaal

1820 — 1830 — 1840 — 1850 — 1860

1816: Shaka becomes leader of the Zulu, a clan of the Nguni

1836: Start of the Great Trek

1854: Boers found the Orange Free State

Islamic wars in western Africa

1807: Hausa kings replaced by Fulani emirs

1820: Usuman dan Fodio establishes Sokoto Fulani Kingdom

1852: 'Umar Tal conquers the Senegal valley

1861: 'Umar Tal's forces conquer Segu

1800 1810 1820 1830 1840 1850 1860 1870

1804: *Jihad* of Usuman dan Fodio

1816: Inspired by Usuman dan Fodio, Amadu Lobbo launches *jihad* in Masina

1863: Timbuktu falls to 'Umar Tal; he founds Tukulor Empire

1864: 'Umar Tal is killed attemping to suppress Fulani rebellion

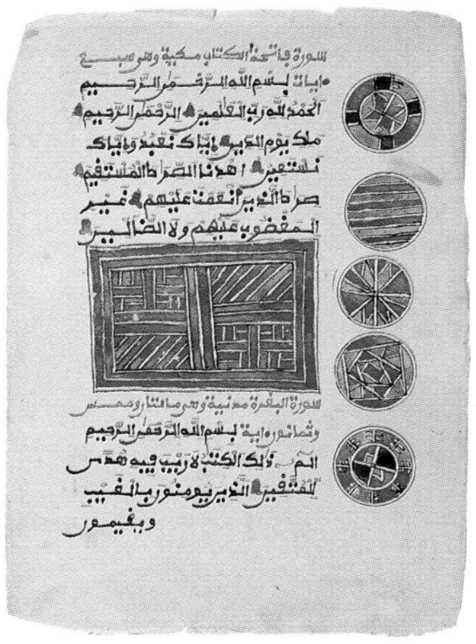

The text of this richly decorated 19th-century Koran is written in West African Sudani script. The large rectangular design marks the end of a chapter.

Islamic reform in West Africa

The *jihads* of West Africa were a source of major turmoil in the 19th century. The idea that reformers could overthrow governments they thought were unjust was deeply rooted in the region, and dated back to the 11th century Almoravid movement. Holy men challenged rulers, often because of their tyranny and corruption and demanded change. Social problems also promoted reform, for example, Fula herdsmen often backed reformers against those who taxed and mistreated them. In other cases, it was humble peasants or slaves who converted to Islam. Tukulor cleric Usuman dan Fodio's *jihad* in Hausaland in 1804, led to the establishment of the islamic Sokoto Fulani Kingdom in 1820. Fulani cleric, al–Hajj 'Umar Tal set about reforming the Segu region in 1851 and by 1863 had founded the Tukulor Empire.

❸ 19th-century West African *jihads*

- Sokoto Fulani Kingdom c.1820
- Tukulor Empire c.1864
- ⊙ British possession
- ⊙ French possession
- ⊙ Portuguese possesssion
- → *jihad* route of al–Hajj 'Umar Tal
- ⋯⋯ borders c.1850
- ✕ conflict

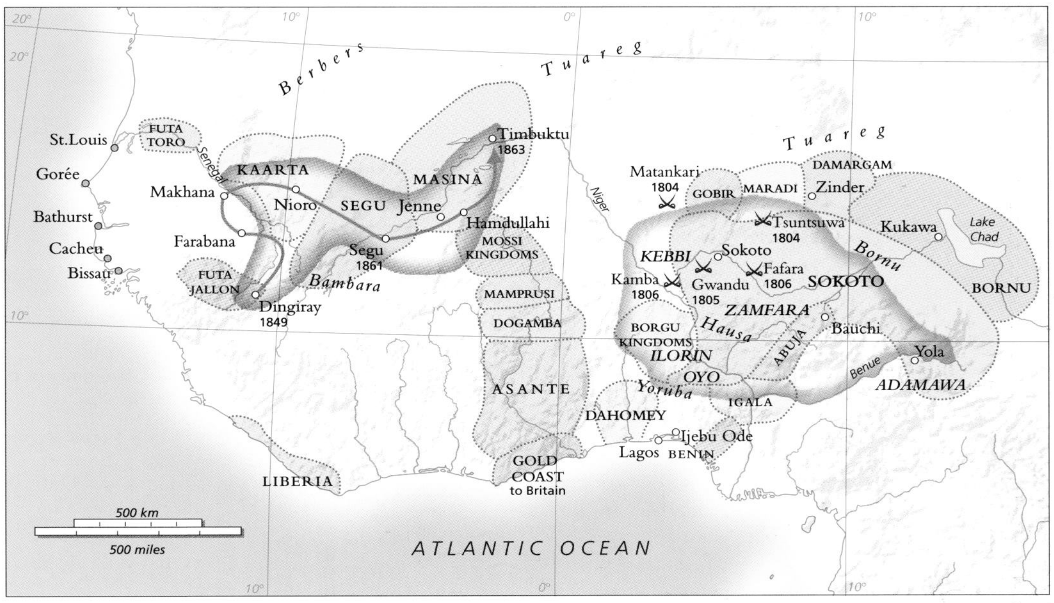

The conquest of the interior

The years after 1885 saw a race to complete the conquest of the African interior *(see p. 96)*. International rivalries between European powers, coupled with local merchant competition and the popularity of African conquest in the home arena ensured European governmental interest in the continent. In many cases, initial conquests were funded by commercial interests, such as Cecil Rhodes' De Beers Consolidated Mines company. Most of the fighting personnel were Africans, hired mercenaries, or militarily trained slaves. The use of commercial contacts with African traders and the exploitation of local rivalries were as effective as brute force and the Maxim gun.

The conquest of Africa from 1880

1883: France begins its conquest of Madagascar

1884: Berlin Conference on Africa; Samory Touré proclaims his Islamic theocracy

1894: Britain occupies Buganda

1896: France takes Madagascar

1900-01: Britain annexes Asante

1908: Belgium takes over Congo Free State

1880 1890 1900 1910

1882: Britain occupies Egypt; Congo Free State formed by King Leopold of Belgium

1889: Italy establishes its first colony in Eritrea

1892: France destroys the Tukulor Empire

1904: French create federation of French West Africa

❹ European penetration of Africa

Colonial territory c.1880
- Ottoman suzerainty
- British
- Portuguese
- French
- Spanish
- Boer Republics
- frontier of Christian missionary activities c.1880

European routes of expansion
- → Belgian
- → British
- → French
- → German
- → Italian
- → Portuguese
- → Spanish
- ⋯ main lines of missionary advance
- 1888 foundation date of colonial settlement

Colonial settlements
- ⊙ Belgian
- ⊙ Boer
- ⊙ British
- ⊙ French
- ⊙ German
- ⊙ Italian
- ⊙ Portuguese
- ○ other settlement

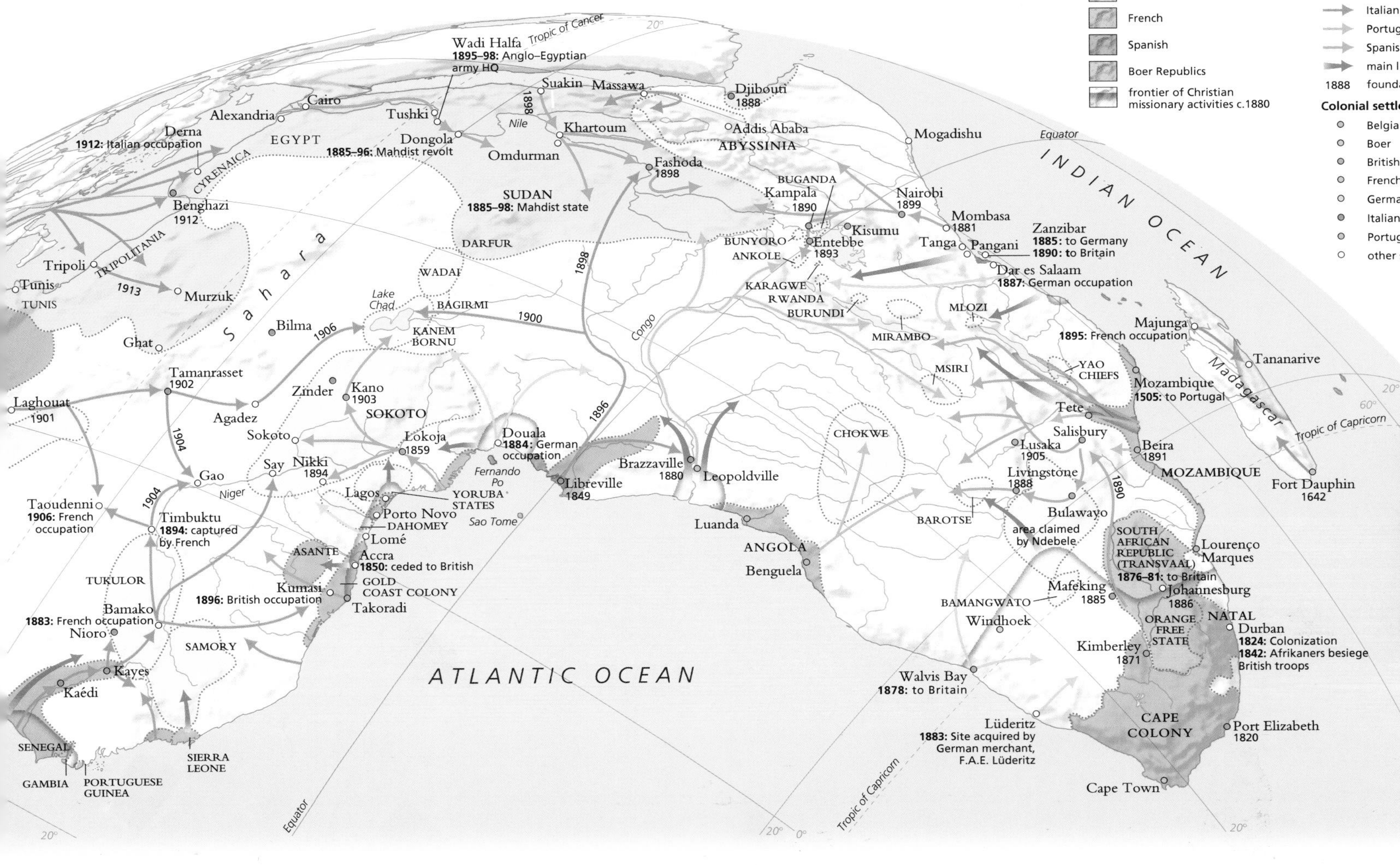

Armed and trained by France, these African soldiers, known as the Senegalese Rifles, helped France win territory in Africa.

POST-COLONIAL AFRICA

Julius Nyerere led the fight for independence in Tanganyika.

INDEPENDENT AFRICAN STATES, with few exceptions, were territorially identical to the European colonies they replaced. Most African countries gained independence between 1956 to 1968 and in many cases hasty attempts were made to set up European-style forms of government. However, often leaders became dictators, or the army seized power; many governments were corrupt and a number of countries were devastated by war. Moves were made towards multiparty democracy, most notably in South Africa where the system of apartheid was dismantled in 1990.

African independence

After the Second World War the colonial powers in Africa faced demands for self-determination and most countries gained independence around 1960. In the face of widespread opposition, Portugal clung on to its territories through the 1960s. This resulted in long and bloody wars in Angola, Guinea-Bissau, and Mozambique. There were also protracted struggles for majority rule in the former British colonies of Zimbabwe and South Africa. The presidential election victory of Nelson Mandela in 1994 marked the end of white minority rule in South Africa.

The national flag is raised in Ghana during an independence ceremony. The country was declared a republic on 1 July 1960 with Dr Kwame Nkrumah as the first president.

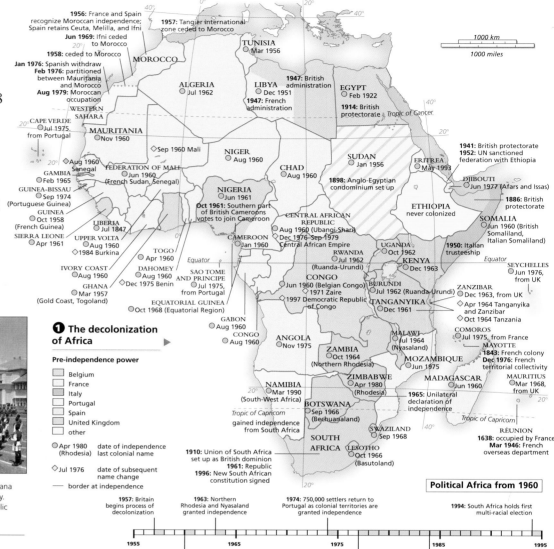

❶ The decolonization of Africa

Pre-independence power
- Belgium
- France
- Italy
- Portugal
- Spain
- United Kingdom
- other

◇ Apr 1980 (Rhodesia) date of independence / last colonial name
◇ Jul 1976 date of subsequent name change
— border at independence

Political Africa from 1960

1957: Britain begins process of decolonization
1963: Northern Rhodesia and Nyasaland granted independence
1974: 750,000 settlers return to Portugal as colonial territories are granted independence
1994: South Africa holds first multi-racial election

1955 — 1965 — 1975 — 1985 — 1995

1960: Belgium abandons the Congo; required to return to restore order weeks later
1977–88: Conflict between Somalia and Ethiopia over claims to Ogaden region
1984–85: Eritrean civil war causes widespread famine

The African economy

Industrial growth is government policy in a number of countries in Africa, and is seen as the way to progress economically. Countries with large manufacturing sectors include South Africa and oil-rich states such as Nigeria, Algeria, and Libya. Many other states rely on a single resource or cash crop for export income, leaving them vulnerable to market fluctuations.

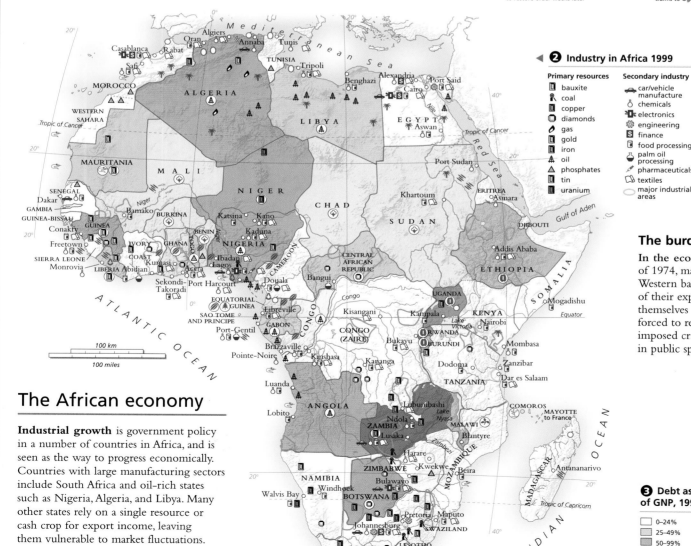

◀ ❷ Industry in Africa 1999

Primary resources
- bauxite
- coal
- copper
- diamonds
- gas
- gold
- iron
- oil
- phosphates
- tin
- uranium

Secondary industry
- car/vehicle manufacture
- chemicals
- electronics
- engineering
- finance
- food processing
- palm oil processing
- pharmaceuticals
- textiles
- major industrial areas

Major cash crops
- cocoa
- coffee
- cotton
- dates
- fruit
- olives
- rice
- rubber
- shellfish
- spices
- timber
- tobacco
- vineyards

Ecological tourism
- national parks

Percentages of total export earnings
40–59 60–80 more than 80
- agriculture and fishing
- crude oil and petroleum products
- metals and minerals
- ○ Main export product

The burden of debt

In the economic turmoil following the oil crisis of 1974, many African countries raised capital from Western banks to bridge the gap between the value of their exports and imports. In the 1980s they found themselves unable to service these loans, and were forced to reschedule their debts. The lenders then imposed crippling terms, including massive cuts in public spending.

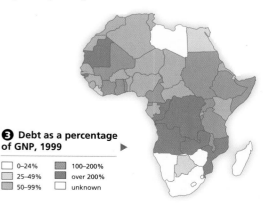

❸ Debt as a percentage of GNP, 1999 ▶
- 0–24%
- 25–49%
- 50–99%
- 100–200%
- over 200%
- unknown

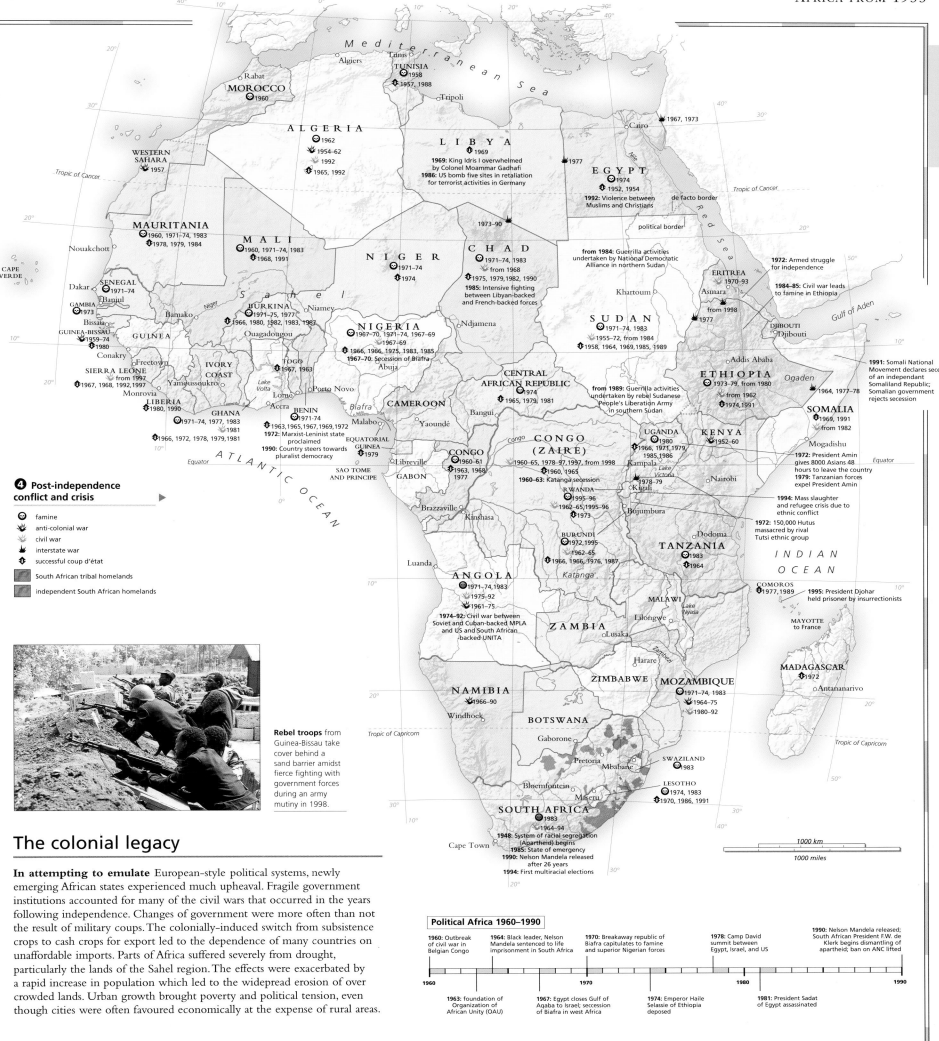

Mediterranean Sea

MOROCCO
☻ 1960
Rabat
Algiers
Tunis
TUNISIA
☻ 1958
☻ 1957, 1988
Tripoli

ALGERIA
☻ 1962
☣ 1954–62
☻ 1992
☻ 1965, 1992

WESTERN SAHARA
☣ 1957

LIBYA
☻ 1969
1969: King Idris I overwhelmed by Colonel Moammar Gadhafi
1986: US bomb five sites in retaliation for terrorist activities in Germany

☣ 1967, 1973
Cairo
EGYPT
☻ 1974
☻ 1952, 1954
1992: Violence between Muslims and Christians
de facto border
political border

☣ 1977

Tropic of Cancer

MAURITANIA
☻ 1960, 1971–74, 1983
☻ 1978, 1979, 1984
Nouakchott

CAPE VERDE

MALI
☻ 1960, 1971–74, 1983
☻ 1968, 1991

NIGER
☻ 1971–74
☻ 1974

CHAD
☻ 1971–74, 1983
☻ from 1968
1975, 1979, 1982, 1990
1985: Intensive fighting between Libyan-backed and French-backed forces

1973–90

from 1984: Guerrilla activities undertaken by National Democratic Alliance in northern Sudan

Khartoum

ERITREA
☻ 1970–93
Asmara
☣ from 1998
1972: Armed struggle for independence
1984–85: Civil war leads to famine in Ethiopia

Dakar
SENEGAL
☻ 1971–74
GAMBIA
☻ 1973
Banjul
Bissau
GUINEA-BISSAU
☣ 1959–74
☻ 1980

BURKINA
☻ 1971–75, 1977
☻ 1966, 1980, 1982, 1983, 1987
Bamako
Niamey
Ouagadougou

GUINEA
Conakry

NIGERIA
☻ 1967–70, 1971–74, 1967–69
1967–69
☻ 1966, 1966, 1975, 1983, 1985
1967–70: Secession of Biafra
Abuja
Ndjamena

SUDAN
☻ 1971–74, 1983
☻ 1955–72, from 1984
☻ 1958, 1964, 1969,1985, 1989

from 1989: Guerrilla activities undertaken by rebel Sudanese People's Liberation Army in southern Sudan

ETHIOPIA
☻ 1973–79, from 1980
☻ from 1962
☻ 1974,1991

Addis Ababa
Ogaden
☣ 1964, 1977–78

DJIBOUTI
Djibouti
Gulf of Aden

1991: Somali National Movement declares secession of an independant Somaliland Republic; Somalian government rejects secession

SIERRA LEONE
☻ from 1997
☻ 1967, 1968, 1992,1997
Freetown
Monrovia
Yamoussoukro

IVORY COAST

GHANA
☻ 1967, 1963
☻ 1971–74, 1977, 1983
☻ 1981
Accra
Lomé
Porto Novo
Lake Volta

TOGO
☻ 1967, 1963

BENIN
☻ 1971–74
☻ 1963,1965,1967,1969,1972
1972: Marxist-Leninist state proclaimed
1990: Country steers towards pluralist democracy

LIBERIA
☻ 1980, 1990
☻ 1966, 1972, 1978, 1979,1981

CENTRAL AFRICAN REPUBLIC
☻ 1974
☻ 1965, 1979, 1981
Bangui

CAMEROON
Yaoundé
Malabo
EQUATORIAL GUINEA
☻ 1979

KENYA
☣ 1952–60
Nairobi

UGANDA
☻ 1980
☻ 1966, 1971,1979, 1985,1986
Kampala
1972: President Amin gives 8000 Asians 48 hours to leave the country
1979: Tanzanian forces expel President Amin

SOMALIA
☻ 1969, 1991
☣ from 1982
Mogadishu
1972: President Amin gives 8000 Asians 48 hours to leave the country

ATLANTIC OCEAN
Equator

❹ Post-independence conflict and crisis ▶

☻ famine
☣ anti-colonial war
civil war
interstate war
☻ successful coup d'état
South African tribal homelands
independent South African homelands

CONGO
☻ 1960–61
☻ 1963, 1968
1977
Libreville
GABON
Brazzaville

CONGO (ZAIRE)
☻ 1960–65, 1978–97,1997, from 1998
☻ 1960, 1965
1960–63: Katanga secession

RWANDA
☻ 1995–96
☻ 1962–65,1995–96
☻ 1973
Kigali
Lake Victoria
Bujumbura

1994: Mass slaughter and refugee crisis due to ethnic conflict

1972: 150,000 Hutus massacred by rival Tutsi ethnic group

Kinshasa

BURUNDI
☻ 1972,1995
☻ 1962–65
☻ 1966, 1966, 1976, 1987

TANZANIA
☻ 1983
☻ 1964
Dodoma

INDIAN OCEAN

Luanda

ANGOLA
☻ 1971–74,1983
☣ 1975–92
☣ 1961–75
Katanga
1974–92: Civil war between Soviet and Cuban-backed MPLA and US and South African-backed UNITA

COMOROS
☻ 1977,1989
1995: President Djohar held prisoner by insurrectionists

MAYOTTE to France

ZAMBIA
Lusaka

MALAWI
Lilongwe
Lake Nyasa

MADAGASCAR
☻ 1972
Antananarivo

Harare

ZIMBABWE

MOZAMBIQUE
☻ 1971–74, 1983
☣ 1964–75
☣ 1980–92

NAMIBIA
☣ 1966–90
Windhoek

Tropic of Capricorn

BOTSWANA
Gaborone

SWAZILAND
☻ 1983

LESOTHO
☻ 1974, 1983
☻ 1970, 1986, 1991

Pretoria
Mbabane
Bloemfontein
Maseru

SOUTH AFRICA
☻ 1983
☣ 1964–94
1948: System of racial segregation (Apartheid) begins
1985: State of emergency
1990: Nelson Mandela released after 26 years
1994: First multiracial elections

Cape Town

1000 km
1000 miles

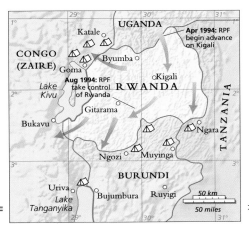

Rebel troops from Guinea-Bissau take cover behind a sand barrier amidst fierce fighting with government forces during an army mutiny in 1998.

The colonial legacy

In attempting to emulate European-style political systems, newly emerging African states experienced much upheaval. Fragile government institutions accounted for many of the civil wars that occurred in the years following independence. Changes of government were more often than not the result of military coups. The colonially-induced switch from subsistence crops to cash crops for export led to the dependence of many countries on unaffordable imports. Parts of Africa suffered severely from drought, particularly the lands of the Sahel region. The effects were exacerbated by a rapid increase in population which led to the widepread erosion of over crowded lands. Urban growth brought poverty and political tension, even though cities were often favoured economically at the expense of rural areas.

Political Africa 1960–1990

1960: Outbreak of civil war in Belgian Congo

1964: Black leader, Nelson Mandela sentenced to life imprisonment in South Africa

1970: Breakaway republic of Biafra capitulates to famine and superior Nigerian forces

1978: Camp David summit between Egypt, Israel, and US

1990: Nelson Mandela released; South African President F.W. de Klerk begins dismantling of apartheid; ban on ANC lifted

1960 — 1970 — 1980 — 1990

1963: foundation of Organization of African Unity (OAU)

1967: Egypt closes Gulf of Aqaba to Israel; secession of Biafra in west Africa

1974: Emperor Haile Selassie of Ethiopia deposed

1981: President Sadat of Egypt assassinated

The Rwandan crisis

Following a violent revolt in 1959 the Hutu ethnic group in Rwanda grasped political power from the Tutsi minority. An invasion from Uganda in 1990 by the Tutsi Rwandan Patriotic Front (RPF) was followed by an unsuccessful peace accord in 1992. A fragile peace was shattered by the death of President Hyabyarimana in 1994. Genocidal violence ensued and an estimated 500,000 Tutsi were massacred. Two million Hutus subsequently fled the country, seeking refuge in nearby states.

UGANDA
Katale
Byumba
Apr 1994: RPF begin advance on Kigali
CONGO (ZAIRE)
Goma
Lake Kivu
Aug 1994: RPF take control of Rwanda
RWANDA
Kigali
Gitarama
Bukavu
Ngara
TANZANIA
Ngozi
Muyinga
Ruyigi
BURUNDI
Uriva
Lake Tanganyika
Bujumbura

50 km
50 miles

◀ ❺ Crisis in Central Africa

advancing RPF (Tutsi) forces
migrating Hutu refugees
refugee camp

In 1994 over two million Rwandans, the majority of whom were Hutu, fled to refugee camps in neighbouring countries. Many were forced to live in unsanitary conditions and outbreaks of cholera in crowded camps killed thousands.

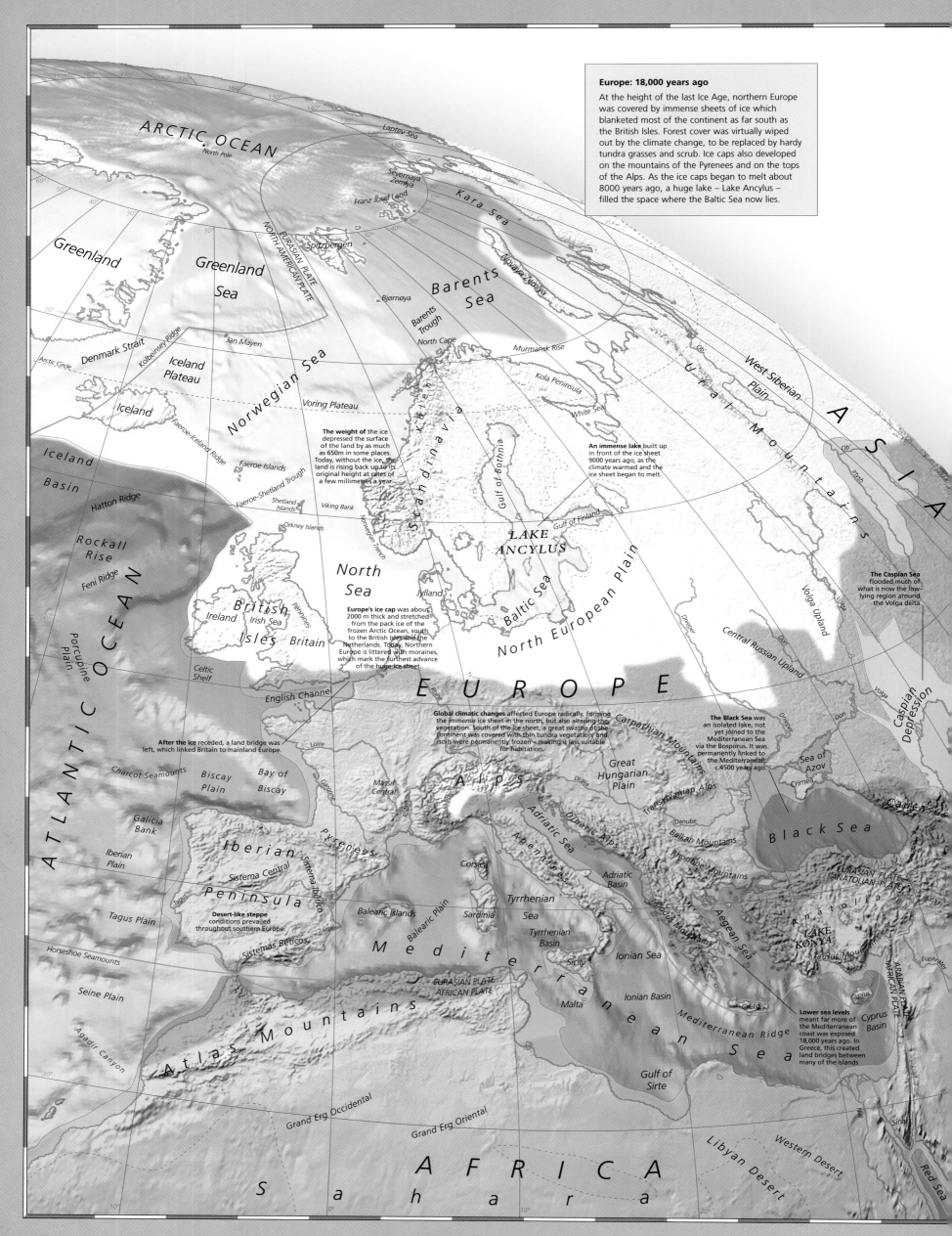

Europe: 18,000 years ago

At the height of the last Ice Age, northern Europe was covered by immense sheets of ice which blanketed most of the continent as far south as the British Isles. Forest cover was virtually wiped out by the climate change, to be replaced by hardy tundra grasses and scrub. Ice caps also developed on the mountains of the Pyrenees and on the tops of the Alps. As the ice caps began to melt about 8000 years ago, a huge lake – Lake Ancylus – filled the space where the Baltic Sea now lies.

ARCTIC OCEAN
North Pole

Greenland

Greenland Sea

Spitzbergen

EURASIAN PLATE
NORTH AMERICAN PLATE

Severnaya Zemlya

Franz Josef Land

Laptev Sea

Kara Sea

Bjørnøya

Barents Sea

Novaya Zemlya

West Siberian Plain

Ob'

Irtish

ASIA

Denmark Strait

Jan Mayen

Kolbeinsey Ridge

Arctic Circle

Iceland Plateau

Iceland

Faeroe-Iceland Ridge

Norwegian Sea

Voring Plateau

Barents Trough

North Cape

Murmansk Rise

Kola Peninsula

White Sea

Ural Mountains

Murmansk Rise

An immense lake built up in front of the ice sheet 9000 years ago, as the climate warmed and the ice sheet began to melt.

The Caspian Sea flooded much of what is now the low-lying region around the Volga delta.

Iceland Basin

Hatton Ridge

Faeroe Islands

Faeroe-Shetland Trough

Shetland Islands

Viking Bank

Scandinavia

Katten

Gulf of Bothnia

Gulf of Finland

The weight of the ice depressed the surface of the land by as much as 650m in some places. Today, without the ice, the land is rising back up to its original height at rates of a few millimetres a year.

Rockall Rise

Feni Ridge

Orkney Islands

Norwegian Trench

LAKE ANCYLUS

Volga Upland

Iceland

Porcupine Plain

North Sea

Jylland

Baltic Sea

North European Plain

Central Russian Upland

Don

Volga

Caspian Depression

British Isles

Ireland

Irish Sea

Pennines

Britain

Europe's ice cap was about 2000 m thick and stretched from the pack ice of the frozen Arctic Ocean, south to the British Isles and the Netherlands. Today, Northern Europe is littered with moraines, which mark the furthest advance of the huge ice sheet.

Celtic Shelf

ATLANTIC OCEAN

English Channel

EUROPE

Global climatic changes affected Europe radically, forming the immense ice sheet in the north, but also altering the vegetation. South of the ice sheet, a great swathe of the continent was covered with thin tundra vegetation and soils were permanently frozen – making it less suitable for habitation.

Carpathian Mountains

Dnieper

Dniester

Don

The Black Sea was an isolated lake, not yet joined to the Mediterranean Sea via the Bosporus. It was permanently linked to the Mediterranean c.4500 years ago.

Sea of Azov

Crimea

Caucasus

After the ice receded, a land bridge was left, which linked Britain to mainland Europe.

Charcot Seamounts

Biscay Plain

Bay of Biscay

Loire

Garonne

Massif Central

Alps

Drava

Great Hungarian Plain

Danube

Transylvanian Alps

Balkan Mountains

Rhodope Mountains

Black Sea

EURASIAN PLATE
ANATOLIAN PLATE

Galicia Bank

Iberian Plain

Pyrenees

Rhône

Adriatic Sea

Dinaric Alps

Apennines

Focus Mountains

Aegean Sea

Anatolia

LAKE KONYA

Tagus Plain

Iberian Peninsula

Sistema Central

Sistema Ibérico

Corsica

Balearic Plain

Sardinia

Adriatic Basin

Tyrrhenian Sea

EURASIAN PLATE
ARABIAN PLATE

Taurus Mountains

Euphrates

Horseshoe Seamounts

Balearic Islands

Tyrrhenian Basin

Desert-like steppe conditions prevailed throughout southern Europe.

Sistemas Béticos

Mediterranean Sea

Sicily

Ionian Sea

Malta

Ionian Basin

Mediterranean Ridge

Crete

Cyprus

Cyprus Basin

Seine Plain

Agadir Canyon

Atlas Mountains

EURASIAN PLATE
AFRICAN PLATE

Lower sea levels meant far more of the Mediterranean coast was exposed 18,000 years ago. In Greece, this created land bridges between many of the islands

Grand Erg Occidental

Grand Erg Oriental

Libyan Desert

Western Desert

Nile

Sinai

Red Sea

AFRICA

Sahara

Vegetation type

- ice cap and glacier
- polar or alpine desert
- tundra
- semi-desert or sparsely vegetated
- forest or open woodland
- temperate desert
- tropical desert
- desert
- coastline (present-day)
- coastline (18,000 years ago)

EUROPE
REGIONAL HISTORY

THE HISTORICAL LANDSCAPE

EUROPE, THE SECOND SMALLEST OF THE WORLD'S CONTINENTS, has a great diversity of topography, climate, and ecology, a rich pattern which contributed greatly to its inordinate influence on global history. Extensive oceanic and inland shorelines, abundantly fertile soils, and broadly temperate conditions provided innumerable heartlands for a wide array of cultures. Internecine rivalries created shifting patterns, themselves frequently overlaid by successive waves of migration and incursion. The shores of the Mediterranean provided a cradle for many powerful cultural groups, which formed myriad states and several empires until the 15th century, when the power base shifted to the emergent nations of the Atlantic coast. It was these aggressive, mercantile and pioneering maritime powers who vaulted Europe to a globally dominant position, through trade and colonialism, during the closing centuries of the 2nd millennium. As they collapsed, a seemingly ineradicable linguistic, economic, technological, and cultural imprint remained, which in the 20th century was widely adopted and adapted, creating an almost universal global culture.

During the Ice Age, the Alps were covered with extensive glacier systems that sculpted and carved the mountains into sharp pinnacles and peaks. The mountains provided a barrier between the cultures of the Mediterranean and those of Northern Europe.

The fertile plains of rivers such as the Danube provided the setting for early agricultural settlements, which spread north from the shores of the Aegean Sea from around 5000 BCE.

Europe's first cultures spread westward from Anatolia, reaching the fertile, often isolated coastal valleys around the Aegean between 7000 and 6000 BCE.

EUROPE

EXPLORATION AND MAPPING

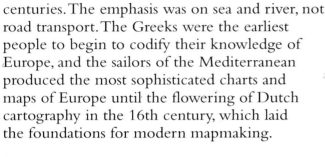

The theodolite was first used in the 17th century. This model, dating from 1765 could measure both altitude and azimuth.

EUROPEANS LEARNED TO KNOW their lands by practical experience and scientific study. Trade and the acquisition of new land provided an impetus for travel and exploration. Phoenician traders moving west in the 9th century BCE, and the Greeks from the 8th century BCE explored the Mediterranean. They were followed by the Romans, whose road system eventually covered much of southern and western Europe. Long-range travel was next developed by the wide-ranging Scandinavians of the 9th and 10th centuries. The emphasis was on sea and river, not road transport. The Greeks were the earliest people to begin to codify their knowledge of Europe, and the sailors of the Mediterranean produced the most sophisticated charts and maps of Europe until the flowering of Dutch cartography in the 16th century, which laid the foundations for modern mapmaking.

The Vikings in the North Atlantic

The extraordinary Viking voyages of the 9th and 10th centuries were primarily for booty – trade and the acquisition of new land came later. Sailing west from Norway into treacherous northern waters, the Vikings settled the Shetland islands and the Faeroes. Iceland was discovered in the mid-9th century, and despite the ice-logged winters, further travellers returned to colonize the island, founding settlements c.873, and establishing bases for voyages to Greenland and Labrador.

Viking ships were built with great care and attention to detail. The tiller (left) is carved in the shape of a snake, while the weather vane (below), made from polished bronze, is topped with a figure of a dog.

Mapping in the Classical era

This map reconstructs the Europe known to Pytheas. His journey was the first scientific exploration of northern Europe by Greeks. The map is based on Eratosthenes' three-continent (Europe, Africa, and Asia) world view. The Mediterranean familiar to the Greeks is accurately plotted; the northern topography is far more speculative.

The peoples of the Mediterranean made the earliest attempts at a survey of Europe. In 340 BCE, the Greek Pytheas travelled from Massalia to Britain, visiting the Orkneys and Shetlands; he later visited Norway and north Germany. The first attempts at scientific mapping were made in the Mediterranean: Eratosthenes successfully measured the diameter of the earth; Hipparchus suggested lines of latitude and longitude as reference points, and Ptolemy tried to show the surface of the earth using two conical projections, and provided points of reference for more than 8000 places.

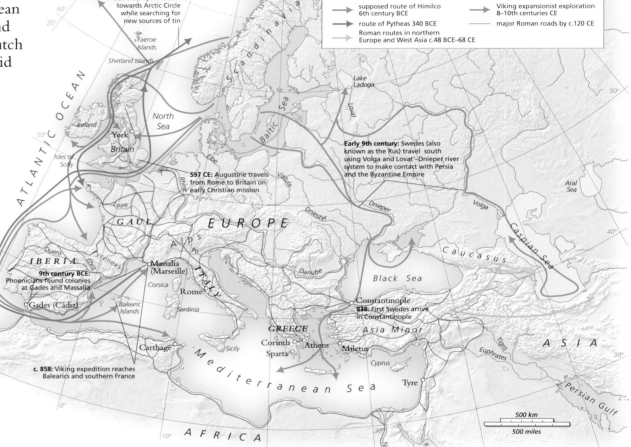

❶ Defining the boundaries of ancient Europe

→ supposed route of Himilco 6th century BCE
→ route of Pytheas 340 BCE
→ Roman routes in northern Europe and West Asia c.48 BCE–68 CE
→ Viking expansionist exploration 8–10th centuries CE
— major Roman roads by c.120 CE

320 BCE: Pytheas sails towards Arctic Circle while searching for new sources of tin

597 CE: Augustine travels from Rome to Britain on early Christian mission

9th century BCE: Phoenicians found colonies at Gades and Massalia

Early 9th century: Swedes (also known as the Rus) travel south using Volga and Lovat'–Dnieper river system to make contact with Persia and the Byzantine Empire

838: First Swedes arrive in Constantinople

c. 858: Viking expedition reaches Balearics and southern France

The Viking discovery of Iceland

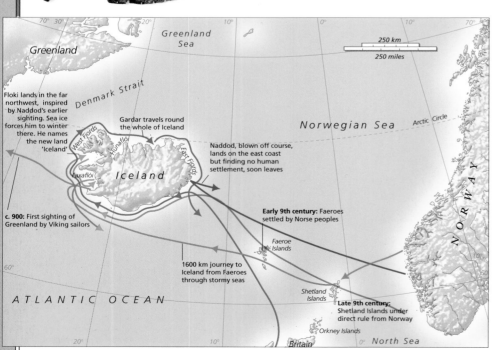

→ Gardar Svavarsson c. 860
→ Naddod c. 870
→ Floki Vilgerdarsson
→ other Viking explorers

Floki lands in the far northwest, inspired by Naddod's earlier sighting. Sea ice forces him to winter there. He names the new land 'Iceland'

Gardar travels round the whole of Iceland

Naddod, blown off course, lands on the east coast but finding no human settlement, soon leaves

c. 900: First sighting of Greenland by Viking sailors

Early 9th century: Faeroes settled by Norse peoples

1600 km journey to Iceland from Faeroes through stormy seas

Late 9th century: Shetland Islands under direct rule from Norway

The Peutinger Table, a strip map 7 m long and 32 cm wide, showed roads in the Roman Empire – such as the Via Appia – with little reference to the surrounding countryside. It was probably first drawn in the 3rd century CE and was a useful tool for actually planning journeys. Some 5000 places are recorded, mostly in Europe.

The Vikings in the North Atlantic

c.825: First settlement in the Faeroes
c.860: First trip round Iceland by Gardar Svavarsson
c.900: First sighting of Greenland by Viking seamen

750 — 800 — 850 — 900

795: First recorded Viking raid on isle of Iona
c.825: Irish monks probably first to discover Iceland
Late 860s: Brothers Ingolf and Hjerleif reconnoitre East Fjords
873: First permanent settlement started by Ingolf
Late 9th century: Shetlands come under direct Viking rule

Medieval mapping of Europe

Most of Europe was well known to travellers by the 11th century, but the accuracy with which it was mapped was extremely variable. The literate sailors of the Mediterranean were able to draw on the relatively sophisticated Portolan charts, which were made chiefly by Italian and Catalan navigators, but nothing comparable existed for the sailors of the north. Inland, largely imaginary wall maps represented Christian beliefs and the known world, with Jerusalem at the centre of the earth, Europe at left, and Africa on the right. A second type of map was based on accumulated knowledge, and gave a recognizable if distorted picture of Europe. Examples include Gough's map, and the maps of Matthew Paris (1200–1259 CE). From the 15th century, Ptolemy's map of Europe *(see p.44)* was once again available and it was added to, and corrected in the light of new knowledge and re-published in the *Tabulae Modernae*. In 1425, Clavus, a Dane who had visited Iceland and Southern Greenland, added these, plus Norway, to the Ptolemaic base map.

The Hereford wall map *(left)* is perhaps the best known of the 600 or so 'T-in-O maps' which are known to have survived. The T-shape of the Mediterranean Sea which divides the world into Europe, Africa and Asia is contained within a circle – the O.

Medieval mapping

- **1276:** Hereford wall map designed by Richard of Haldingham and Lafford
- **1321:** Pietro Vesconte's *Mappamundi* incorporates some features of portolan charts
- **1475:** Publication of Ptolemy's *Geography*
- **1485:** Bartolommeo dalli Sonetti's *Isolario* based on observation by navigators is published

1200 — 1300 — 1400 — 1500 — 1600

- **1276:** Publication of *Il Compasso da Navigare*, a collection of verbal descriptions of key routes
- **1472:** First publication of the *Etymologie* by Bishop Isodore of Seville, devisor of the concept of the T-in-O map in 7th century
- **16th century:** Latitude scales added to portolan charts
- **1539:** First printed portolan chart made in Venice by Giovanni Andrea di Vavasore

Portolan charts *(above)* were available to Mediterranean sailors from early Medieval times. They recorded the ports of the Mediterranean and Black Sea, giving landmarks, bearings, and distances, based on the Roman mile of 1000 paces.

The beginnings of modern cartography

In early modern Europe, increasing trade and a growing gentry class, interested in their surroundings, encouraged a new phase of map making. Overseas territories, and the possessions of the rich, were mapped using surveying instruments such as the theodolite. Dutch cartographers made some of the most important innovations. Gerardus Mercator was the first to break from the Ptolemaic model. Mercator's projection rejected Ptolemy's conical model to show bearings with a scale identical in all directions. This made it particularly useful for navigators, and it is still widely used today. Another Dutchman, Willebrord Snell (Snellius), was the first to use triangulation to survey a large area. After carefully measuring a base line, he then employed trigonometry to calculate the distances to far-off landmarks.

This map of Europe was produced by Mercator in 1554. It gives a detailed picture of settlement patterns, river networks, forest cover, and country boundaries, but some of the surrounding details, for example the proportions of Scandinavia, are far from accurate.

This detailed aerial view of Paris dates from 1576. It shows the original city wall, as well as building on the outskirts, agricultural areas – including windmills – and rough pasture on the edge of the city.

The Netherlands and the origins of modern cartography

- **1530:** Jacob van Deventer commissioned to survey and map five provinces and regions of the Netherlands
- **1569:** Mercator's new projection used for the first time in a world map
- **1606:** Mercator's *Atlas sive cosmographicae meditationes* is first use of term 'atlas' applied to book of maps

1530 — 1540 — 1550 — 1560 — 1570 — 1580 — 1590 — 1600 — 1610

- **1533:** Gemma Frisius publishes description of concise method of triangulation
- **1554:** Mercator publishes large wall map of Europe; establishes new standard of latitudinal accuracy
- **1570:** *Theatrum orbis terrarum* of Abraham Ortelius brings together elements of modern atlas for the first time
- **1606:** Later edition of Ortelius' *Atlas* contains superbly detailed mapping of northern Europe

Saxton's county map of England and Wales, published in 1579, shows the detail and accuracy which was being achieved by the 16th century. Other similar examples include Norden's county maps of 1593, and Ogilvie's road map published in *Britannia*.

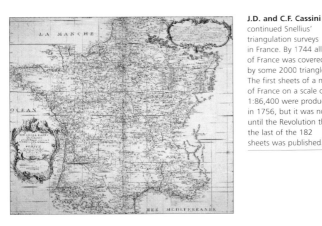

J.D. and C.F. Cassini continued Snellius' triangulation surveys in France. By 1744 all of France was covered by some 2000 triangles. The first sheets of a map of France on a scale of 1:86,400 were produced in 1756, but it was not until the Revolution that the last of the 182 sheets was published.

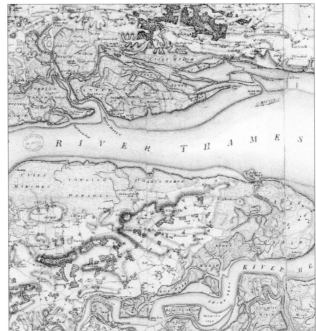

In England, fear of Napoleonic invasion and a need for detailed information about the land, led to a survey on a scale of two inches to the mile and publication on a scale of one inch to the mile. The first map of this series was sold as four sheets in 1801.

Surveyors from the Royal Engineers were responsible for making accurate maps of Britain and its Empire during the 19th century. Here they are shown undertaking a triangulation.

PREHISTORIC EUROPE

Mycenaean pottery, such as this goblet from Rhodes (c.1300 BCE), was traded throughout the eastern Mediterranean.

IN 7000 BCE, postglacial Europe, with its deciduous forests and increasingly temperate climate, was rich in natural resources and thinly populated by hunter-gatherers. By 1000 BCE, villages stretched from the Balkans to Scandinavia, and agriculture had reached even the marginal regions of the continent; there was a flourishing trans-continental traffic in salt, metals, and amber; and the first palace-based states had emerged on Crete and the Greek mainland. Although remains of settlements are rarely well preserved, a wide range of burials reveal, through grave goods as varied as woven textiles, ceramic vessels, and bronze axe-heads, an increasingly stratified society, in which individual possessions were a reflection of status.

The introduction of farming 7000–5000 BCE

The first potters of Central Europe used fired clay to make stylized human figures.

As agriculture spread from Anatolia into the Balkans and beyond, farming practices were adapted to more northerly latitudes, with an increased reliance on cattle and pigs and new, hardy strains of cereal. The mud-brick hill villages (tells) of the Middle East were replaced, in the thickly forested river valleys of Central Europe, by clusters of timber longhouses. The location of early farming communities can be charted by different pottery styles; incised Bandkeramik pottery is found from Hungary to the North Sea, while Cardial pottery, decorated with shell impressions, is found along the Mediterranean.

The spread of farming 7000–5000 BCE

c.7000: Farming spreads from Anatolia to southeastern Europe

c.6000: Farming starts to spread along the western coast of Mediterranean

c.5000: Agriculture well established in southern France and in the Netherlands

| 7000 BCE | 6500 | 6000 | 5500 | 5000 BCE |

c.6500: Rising postglacial sea levels separate British Isles from the rest of the European continent

c.6000: First farming villages appear in southern Italy and Sicily

c.5400: Farming communities using Bandkeramik pottery in Central Europe

Timber longhouses, such as this example from Bylany, in the Czech Republic, were built by the earliest farmers of Central Europe. The basic framework, made from plentiful timber supplies, was covered with wattle and daub. The buildings could be up to 45 m long, and housed one or more families, as well as livestock and stores of food.

❶ The introduction of farming 7000–5000 BCE ▶

- → spread of farming
- cultivated land by c.7000 BCE
- cultivated land by c.6000 BCE
- cultivated land by c.5000 BCE
- concentrations of Mesolithic settlements c.5000 BCE
- • early farming settlement
- Balkan painted ware site
- Bandkeramik pottery site
- Cardial and incised pottery site

Europe in the Copper Age 4500–2500 BCE

This was an era of technological innovation and contact between communities. Both horses and wheeled vehicles spread eastward from the steppes, reaching western Europe by c.2500 BCE, while the introduction of the scratch plough increased productivity. Copper technology, which evolved in eastern Europe c.5000 BCE, spread throughout Europe over the next millennium. Finds of high prestige metalwork in some individual burials indicate that society was becoming more hierarchical, while distinctive pottery styles, known as Beaker Ware and Corded Ware, became widespread in Central and western European burials, indicating the existence of a network of contact and exchange.

Marble figurines, made in the Cycladic Islands of Greece from c.2600 BCE, were placed in burials.

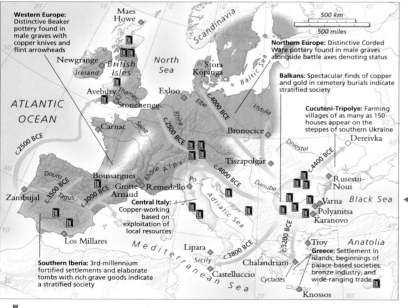

Western Europe: Distinctive Beaker pottery found in male graves with copper knives and flint arrowheads

Northern Europe: Distinctive Corded Ware pottery found in male graves alongside battle axes denoting status

Balkans: Spectacular finds of copper and gold in cemetery burials indicate stratified society

Cucuteni-Tripolye: Farming villages of as many as 150 houses appear on the steppes of southern Ukraine

Central Italy: Copper-working based on exploitation of local resources

Southern Iberia: 3rd-millennium fortified settlements and elaborate tombs with rich grave goods indicate a stratified society

❷ Europe in the Copper Age 4500–2500 BCE ◀

- early copper-working areas c.5000–4000 BCE
- copper resources
- → spread of copper-working, with date
- area of Corded Ware burials c.2900–2000 BCE
- area of Beaker burials c.2500–2000 BCE
- ◆ important archaeological site

Europe in the Copper Age 4500–2500 BCE

c.4000: Farming villages of the Cucuteni-Tripolye group appear in southern Ukraine

c.3500: Stone circles and alignments, henges, and menhirs appear throughout northwestern Europe.

c.3000: Copper-working begins in southern France

c.2500: Copper-working reaches British Isles. Bell beaker pottery found in individual burials in western Europe

| 4000 BCE | 3500 | 3000 | 2500 BCE |

c.4000: Copper mines being exploited in Bulgaria and Yugoslavia

c.3500: First wheeled vehicles in central Europe

c.2900: Appearance of Corded Ware pottery and stone battle-axes in burials in northern Europe

The stone alignments at Kermario in northwestern France date to c.3000 BCE. They were probably associated with processions and seasonal rituals.

Europe in the Bronze Age 2300–1500 BCE

The Bronze Age in Europe was a period of remarkable cultural and technological uniformity. Limited tin resources in western Europe, vital for bronze manufacture, were transported along long distance trade routes in exchange for other valued commodities – Baltic amber and salt. Access to these resources was a major factor in creating a distinct social elite, interred in large barrow burials, replete with a rich array of grave goods. By 1500 BCE, marginal land was being brought into cultivation to feed growing populations. These social and economic pressures led to increasing conflict, evident in the appearance of fortified settlements and the emergence of a warrior elite.

Many of the bronze artefacts made in Europe during the 2nd millennium BCE, such as this ritual bronze axe from Teteven in the Balkan Mountains, were status objects for the emerging warrior elite.

Scale varies with perspective

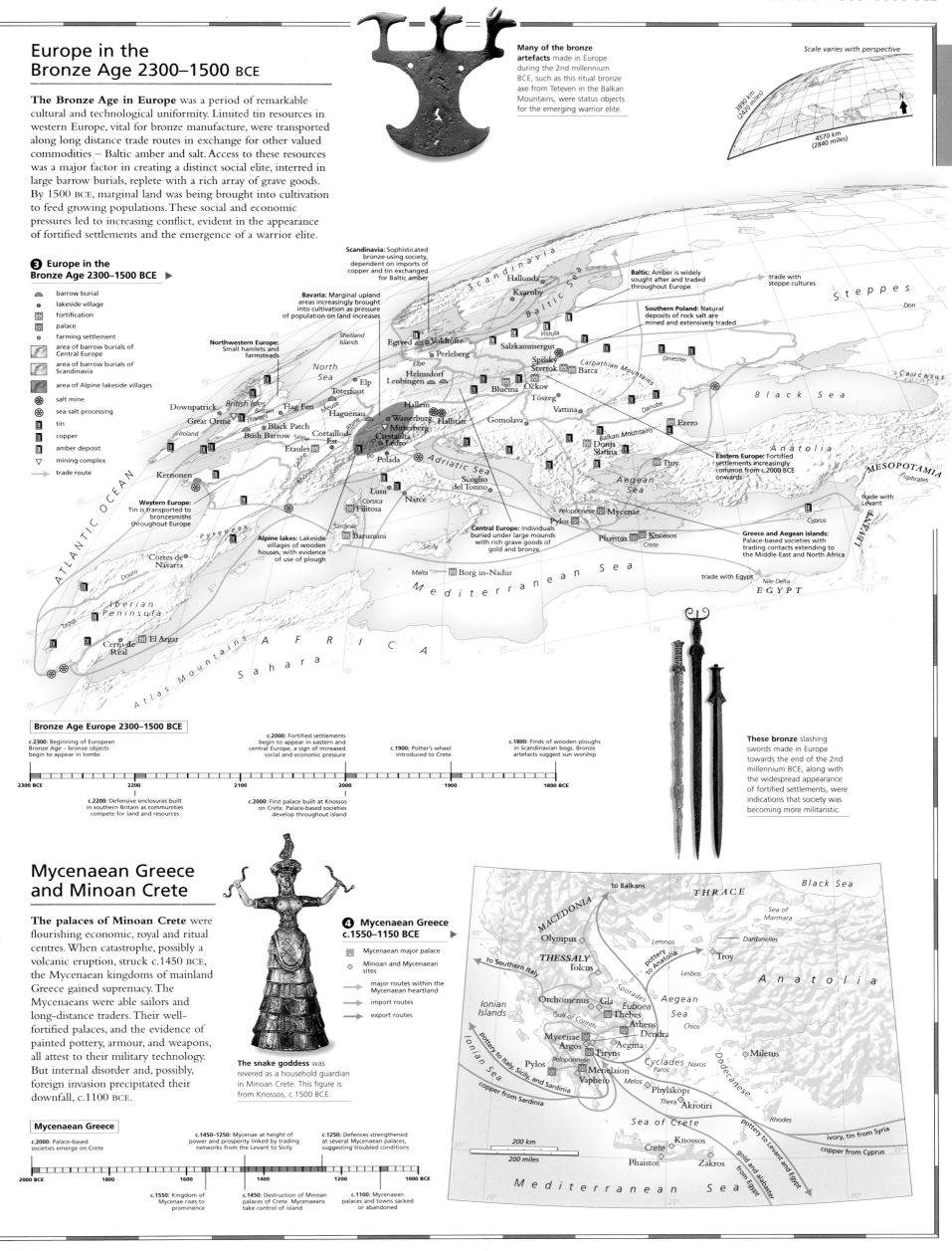

❸ Europe in the Bronze Age 2300–1500 BCE ▶

- barrow burial
- lakeside village
- fortification
- palace
- farming settlement
- area of barrow burials of Central Europe
- area of barrow burials of Scandinavia
- area of Alpine lakeside villages
- salt mine
- sea-salt processing
- tin
- copper
- amber deposit
- mining complex
- trade route

Scandinavia: Sophisticated bronze-using society, dependent on imports of copper and tin exchanged for Baltic amber

Baltic: Amber is widely sought after and traded throughout Europe

trade with steppe cultures

Bavaria: Marginal upland areas increasingly brought into cultivation as pressure of population on land increases

Southern Poland: Natural deposits of rock salt are mined and extensively traded

Northwestern Europe: Small hamlets and farmsteads

Eastern Europe: Fortified settlements increasingly common from c.2000 BCE onwards

Western Europe: Tin is transported to bronzesmiths throughout Europe

Alpine lakes: Lakeside villages of wooden houses, with evidence of use of plough

Central Europe: Individuals buried under large mounds with rich grave goods of gold and bronze

Greece and Aegean islands: Palace-based societies with trading contacts extending to the Middle East and North Africa

trade with Levant

trade with Egypt

These bronze slashing swords made in Europe towards the end of the 2nd millennium BCE, along with the widespread appearance of fortified settlements, were indications that society was becoming more militaristic.

Bronze Age Europe 2300–1500 BCE

c.2300: Beginning of European Bronze Age – bronze objects begin to appear in tombs

c.2200: Defensive enclosures built in southern Britain as communities compete for land and resources

c.2000: Fortified settlements begin to appear in eastern and central Europe, a sign of increased social and economic pressure

c.2000: First palace built at Knossos on Crete. Palace-based societies develop throughout island

c.1900: Potter's wheel introduced to Crete

c.1800: Finds of wooden ploughs in Scandinavian bogs. Bronze artefacts suggest sun worship

Mycenaean Greece and Minoan Crete

The palaces of Minoan Crete were flourishing economic, royal and ritual centres. When catastrophe, possibly a volcanic eruption, struck c.1450 BCE, the Mycenaean kingdoms of mainland Greece gained supremacy. The Mycenaeans were able sailors and long-distance traders. Their well-fortified palaces, and the evidence of painted pottery, armour, and weapons, all attest to their military technology. But internal disorder and, possibly, foreign invasion precipitated their downfall, c.1100 BCE.

The snake goddess was revered as a household guardian in Minoan Crete. This figure is from Knossos, c.1500 BCE.

❹ Mycenaean Greece c.1550–1150 BCE ▶

- Mycenaean major palace
- Minoan and Mycenaean sites
- major routes within the Mycenaean heartland
- import routes
- export routes

Mycenaean Greece

c.2000: Palace-based societies emerge on Crete

c.1550: Kingdom of Mycenae rises to prominence

c.1450–1250: Mycenae at height of power and prosperity linked by trading networks from the Levant to Sicily

c.1450: Destruction of Minoan palaces of Crete. Mycenaeans take control of island

c.1250: Defences strengthened at several Mycenaean palaces, suggesting troubled conditions

c.1100: Mycenaean palaces and towns sacked or abandoned

175

THE MEDITERRANEAN WORLD

This Phoenician carved ivory plaque was found at the Assyrian city of Nimrud.

BETWEEN 700 AND 300 BCE, the Mediterranean world shaped western civilization. The impact of Classical Greek ideas on art, architecture, literature, philosophy, science, and, through the revolutionary innovation of democratic government, on political institutions was profound and wide ranging. The conquests of Philip of Macedon and his son Alexander the Great *(see pp.40–41)* took the fundamental features of Greek culture as far as the borders of India. Of other major civilizations, the Etruscans were undoubtedly influenced by the Greeks, both in the layout of their grid-plan cities and in their lifesize terracotta statues. The Phoenicians, an energetic, maritime people based in city-states in the Levant, took their culture, through trade and colonization, to the western shores of the Mediterranean.

The colonization of the Mediterranean

This magnificent Attic red-figure vase, which illustrates the Homeric myth of Odysseus and the Sirens, dates from c.490 BCE.

Both the Phoenicians and the Greeks became colonists during the 1st millennium BCE. The limited fertile terrain of the Greek homelands could not support the growing population, and many Greek cities sent colonists to western Anatolia, the Black Sea shores, Sicily and southern Italy, and even southern France, where Massalia (Marseille) was founded. The city of Miletus alone was responsible for establishing over 80 colonies. The Phoenicians set out in search of metals, initially setting up a colony in Cyprus to mine copper, and eventually founding Gades (Cadiz) because of nearby silver deposits. Their greatest colony was Carthage, which became a major power in its own right.

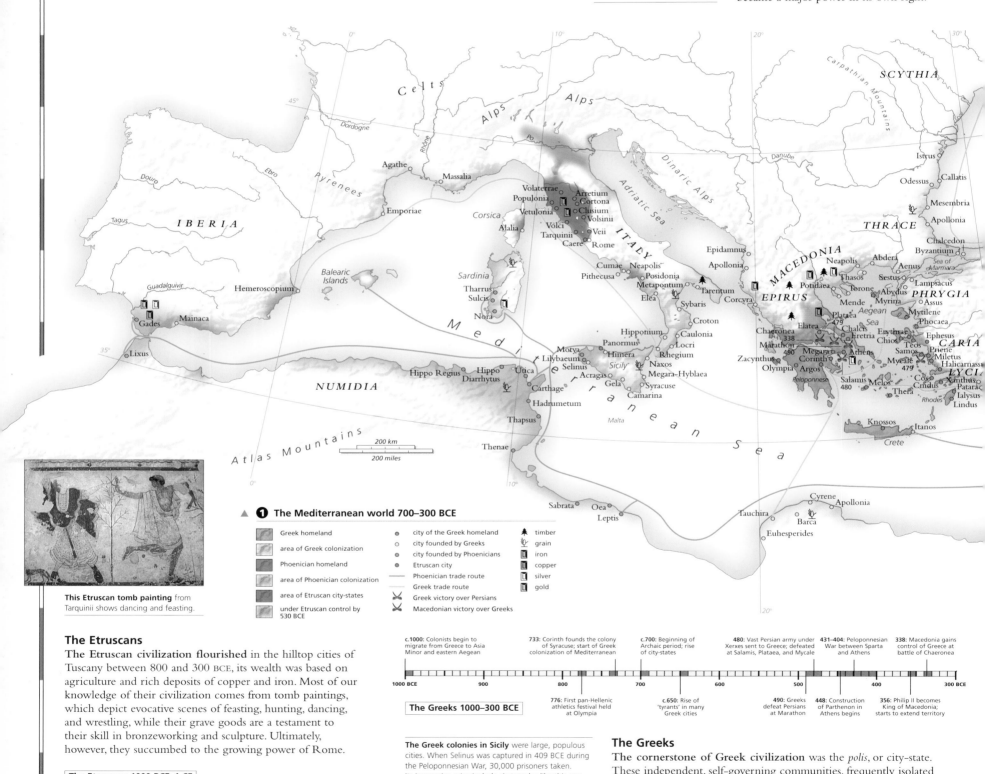

This Etruscan tomb painting from Tarquinii shows dancing and feasting.

▲ ❶ **The Mediterranean world 700–300 BCE**

Greek homeland	● city of the Greek homeland
area of Greek colonization	● city founded by Greeks
Phoenician homeland	● city founded by Phoenicians
area of Phoenician colonization	● Etruscan city
area of Etruscan city-states	— Phoenician trade route
under Etruscan control by 530 BCE	— Greek trade route

🌲 timber
🌾 grain
iron
copper
silver
gold

✕ Greek victory over Persians
✕ Macedonian victory over Greeks

The Etruscans

The Etruscan civilization flourished in the hilltop cities of Tuscany between 800 and 300 BCE, its wealth was based on agriculture and rich deposits of copper and iron. Most of our knowledge of their civilization comes from tomb paintings, which depict evocative scenes of feasting, hunting, dancing, and wrestling, while their grave goods are a testament to their skill in bronzeworking and sculpture. Ultimately, however, they succumbed to the growing power of Rome.

The Etruscans 1000 BCE–1 CE

c.1000: Earliest villages on Palatine and nearby hills of Rome
c.616: Etruscan king Tarquin I rules Rome
509: Romans expel Etruscan king Tarquin II
396: Etruscan city of Veii taken by Rome
c.100: Language and culture of Etruscans in terminal decline

1000 BCE   800   600   400   200   1 CE

c.800: Emergence of Etruscan city states
c.690: Etruscan script developed from Greek
c.530: Etruscan influence at its height; extends as far south as Neapolis
250: Whole Italian peninsula under control of Rome

c.1000: Colonists begin to migrate from Greece to Asia Minor and eastern Aegean
733: Corinth founds the colony of Syracuse; start of Greek colonization of Mediterranean
c.700: Beginning of Archaic period; rise of city-states
480: Vast Persian army under Xerxes sent to Greece; defeated at Salamis, Plataea, and Mycale
431–404: Peloponnesian War between Sparta and Athens
338: Macedonia gains control of Greece at battle of Chaeronea

1000 BCE   900   800   700   600   500   400   300 BCE

776: First pan-Hellenic athletics festival held at Olympia
c.650: Rise of 'tyrants' in many Greek cities
490: Greeks defeat Persians at Marathon
448: Construction of Parthenon in Athens begins
356: Philip II becomes King of Macedonia; starts to extend territory

The Greeks 1000–300 BCE

The Greek colonies in Sicily were large, populous cities. When Selinus was captured in 409 BCE during the Peloponnesian War, 30,000 prisoners taken. Its impressive ruins include six temples like this one, all dating from the 6th and 5th centuries BCE.

The Greeks

The cornerstone of Greek civilization was the *polis*, or city-state. These independent, self-governing communities, frequently isolated by Greece's rugged terrain, were based on walled cities, with outlying villages and farmland. Yet, despite the multiplicity of city-states, Greece was united by language, religion, and culture, reflected in harmonious architecture, sculpture, philosophy, and drama. Politically, the city-states swung between the extremes of oligarchy and democracy. While Athens was the birthplace of democracy, in Sparta a militaristic society was ruled by kings, supported by an underclass of serfs (*helots*).

The Phoenicians

A Semitic people, whose home cities lay along a narrow strip of the eastern Mediterranean coast, the Phoenicians were the foremost traders and craftsmen of the Mediterranean, renowned for their skill in ivory carving, metalworking and glass manufacture. Perhaps their greatest legacy was their alphabetic writing system, which formed the basis of both the Greek and Roman scripts. The city of Carthage, founded as a colony, became a great power in its own right, leading a confederation of Phoenician cities which controlled southern Iberia, the western Mediterranean islands, and North Africa.

The limestone bust of 'the Lady of Elche', from southern Iberia, shows the artistic influence of the Phoenician city of Carthage, which had close links with cities throughout the western Mediterranean.

The Phoenicians and the Carthaginians 1000–200 BCE

c. 1600: The Phoenicians begin to use the Canaanite script, the first alphabetic script

c. 1000: Phoenicians become main maritime power in Levant region

814: Traditional date for foundation of Carthage

264–241: First Punic War; Rome gains control of Carthaginian Sicily

1600 BCE   1400   1200   1000   800   600   400   200 BCE

c. 900: Phoenician ships sail westwards in search of metals, and found colonies near rich metal deposits

218–201: Second Punic War; Carthaginians invade Italy, but Rome eventually wins war to become regional superpower

The Athenian Empire

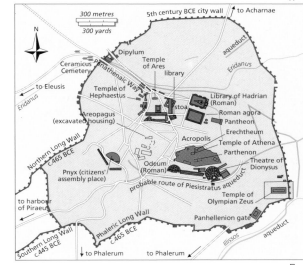

The city of Athens claimed a special affinity with its patroness Athene, goddess of wisdom, war, and arts and crafts.

The city-states of Greece were united in their bid to repulse the Persians, which culminated in famous victories at Marathon (490) and Salamis (480). In 478, Athens emerged as the leader of a loose maritime confederation of eastern Aegean states, based on the tiny island of Delos. Membership of the Delian League involved participating in a common military policy, and contributing to a common treasury. Athens came increasingly to dominate the League, transferring funds to the city in 454, and ruthlessly crushing any attempts at revolt. Greatly enriched by League funds, Athens now entered its greatest period of power and prosperity. The League had, in effect, become an Athenian empire, much resented in many Greek cities.

❷ The Athenian Empire 454–428 BCE

Areas paying tribute to Athens: (number of tribute-paying states in brackets)

- Islands (29)
- Thrace (62)
- Hellespont (45)
- Ionia (35)
- Caria (81)
- Athenian homeland
- non-tribute paying areas belonging to Delian League
- states with tribute assessment of over 5 silver talents per annum (454–428 BCE)
- states with tribute assessment of 1–5 silver talents per annum (454–428 BCE)
- overseas dependencies of Athens
- states in revolt against Athens

The Peloponnesian War

Athens' high-handed imperialism made war with Sparta inevitable, and a system of alliances embroiled much of Greece in the conflict. The Athenians withstood Sparta's attacks on Attica by withdrawing to the safety of the city, preferring to do battle at sea. A truce was reached in 421 BCE, but when Athens unwisely sent an expedition to attack Syracuse, the Spartans captured the Athenian navy, presaging the end of the conflict. Greece was plunged into disarray until it was forcibly united by Philip of Macedon in 338 BCE.

❸ The Peloponnesian War 431–404 BCE

- Athenian Empire
- Athenian ally
- Sparta and allied states
- neutral territory
- Athenian victory
- Spartan victory

The fiercely patriotic, militaristic culture of Sparta is embodied in this small bronze of a soldier.

Athenian expedition to Sicily in 415 ends in Spartan victory at Syracuse, 413

100 km
100 miles

416 BCE: taken by Athens

424 BCE: taken by Athens

❹ The city of Athens

- remains from 6th–5th century BCE
- remains from 4th century BCE–2nd century CE
- road
- aqueduct
- city wall

Athens

The mid-5th century was Athens' golden age. Governed by the eminent statesman, Pericles, and the home of such great intellectuals such as Plato, Sophocles, and Euripides, the city was dominated by the Parthenon temple, built of local marble by the sculptor Phidias, and approached by the monumental Propylea Gate. The Acropolis was the military and religious centre of the city, while commercial and municipal life dominated the agora, or town square.

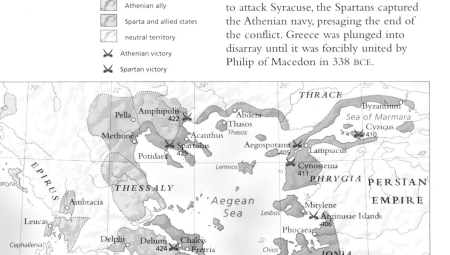

THE RISE OF ROME

ROME BEGAN THE 5TH CENTURY BCE as the most powerful city of the regional alliance known as the Latin League. By conquering the Etruscan city-state of Veii in 396 BCE, the Romans doubled their territory, and after the breakup of the Latin League in 338, they incorporated the whole Latin region. This gave them the manpower to defeat a coalition of Samnites, Etruscans, and Gauls in 295. When they faced the army of the Greek general Pyrrhus, they were able to sustain two crushing defeats before achieving victory in 275 BCE. With Italy now under its control, Rome turned its attention to foreign rivals. Following victory over Carthage in 202, it took less than a century to add North Africa, most of Iberia, southern Gaul, Macedon, Greece, and Asia Minor to its empire.

The legionaries of Rome's citizen army were unmatched in discipline and skill.

Rome and the Italian confederacy

From the 5th to the 3rd century BCE, the city of Rome extended its area of domination to create a confederacy that united all Italy. Some cities were simply annexed and their inhabitants enjoyed the status of full Roman citizens, while others were granted a halfway form of citizenship that did not include the right to vote or hold office in Rome. Other peoples were considered 'allies' and united to Rome by individual treaties. New towns known as 'Latin colonies' extended the Roman presence throughout Italy, while 'Roman colonies', where the inhabitants were full citizens, were established for defensive purposes, primarily along the Tyrrhenian coast. Beginning with the Via Appia in the 4th century BCE, the Romans built a road network that linked the whole peninsula.

Traditionally, this bronze bust of a stern Roman aristocrat has been identified as Lucius Junius Brutus, one of the founders of the Roman Republic in 509.

Rome and her Latin allies c.495 BCE

Rome was the most powerful of the Latin city-states when the Republic was established in 509, though it controlled just 800 sq km of territory.

The peoples of Italy in 500 BCE

Latin, the language Rome would spread throughout western Europe, was just one of many closely related Italic languages spoken by the tribes of central Italy. The most powerful peoples in the peninsula were the Greek colonists and the Etruscans, a sophisticated city-state people whose language suggests eastern Mediterranean origins. It had been the Etruscans' arrival in Rome in the 7th century BCE that transformed a cluster of small villages into a city.

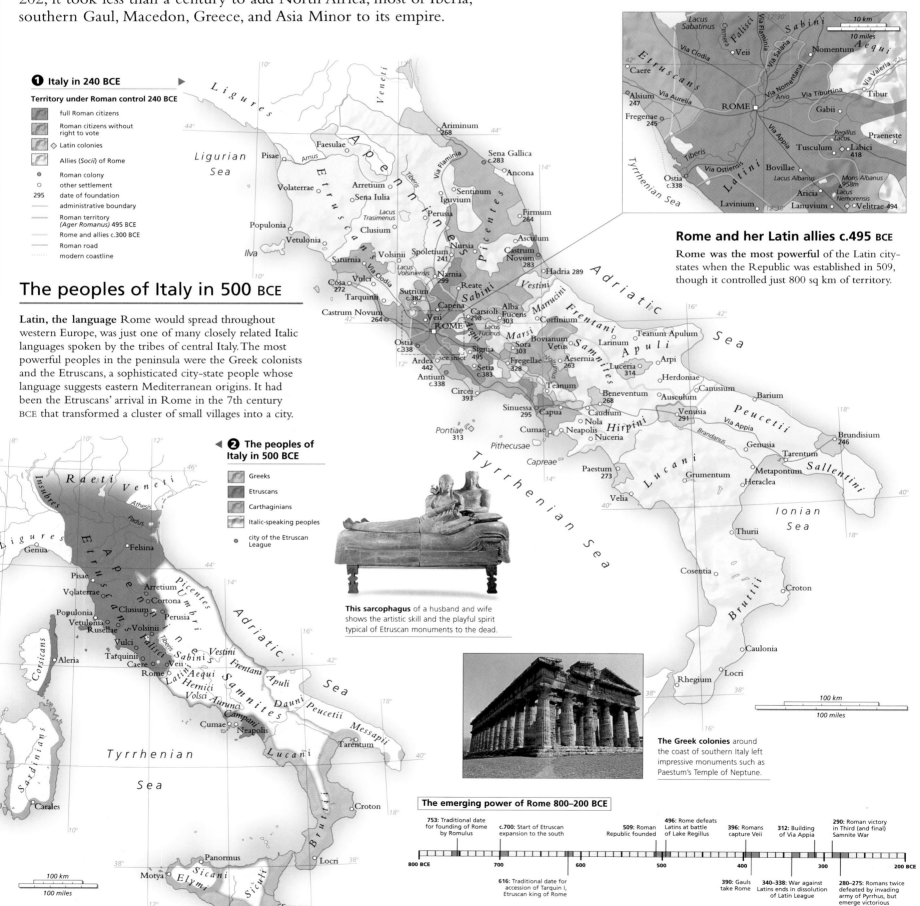

❶ Italy in 240 BCE

Territory under Roman control 240 BCE

- full Roman citizens
- Roman citizens without right to vote
- Latin colonies
- Allies (Soci) of Rome

- ● Roman colony
- ○ other settlement
- 295 date of foundation
- administrative boundary
- Roman territory (Ager Romanus) 495 BCE
- Rome and allies c.300 BCE
- Roman road
- modern coastline

❷ The peoples of Italy in 500 BCE

- Greeks
- Etruscans
- Carthaginians
- Italic-speaking peoples
- ● city of the Etruscan League

This sarcophagus of a husband and wife shows the artistic skill and the playful spirit typical of Etruscan monuments to the dead.

The Greek colonies around the coast of southern Italy left impressive monuments such as Paestum's Temple of Neptune.

The emerging power of Rome 800–200 BCE

753: Traditional date for founding of Rome by Romulus

c.700: Start of Etruscan expansion to the south

509: Roman Republic founded

496: Rome defeats Latins at battle of Lake Regillus

396: Romans capture Veii

312: Building of Via Appia

290: Roman victory in Third (and final) Samnite War

616: Traditional date for accession of Tarquin I, Etruscan king of Rome

390: Gauls take Rome

340–338: War against Latins ends in dissolution of Latin League

280–275: Romans twice defeated by invading army of Pyrrhus, but emerge victorious

800 BCE · 700 · 600 · 500 · 400 · 300 · 200 BCE

Rome and Carthage: the Punic Wars

Founded by Phoenicians (*Punici*) in 814 BCE, Carthage grew to be the pre-eminent naval power in the western Mediterranean. Rome came into conflict with the Carthaginians in 264, the start of a series of three wars. In the first, the Romans pushed their enemies out of Sicily. Then, in 218, Rome forced a second war by opposing Carthaginian actions in Iberia. Despite many defeats at the hands of Hannibal, the Romans won this war and stripped Carthage of its navy. The final war (149–146) ended in the destruction of Carthage and the enslavement of its people.

The Carthaginian general Hannibal *(left)* fought the Romans for 15 years in Italy. The smaller coin *(right)* shows an African elephant, used by the Carthaginians to strike terror into opposing armies.

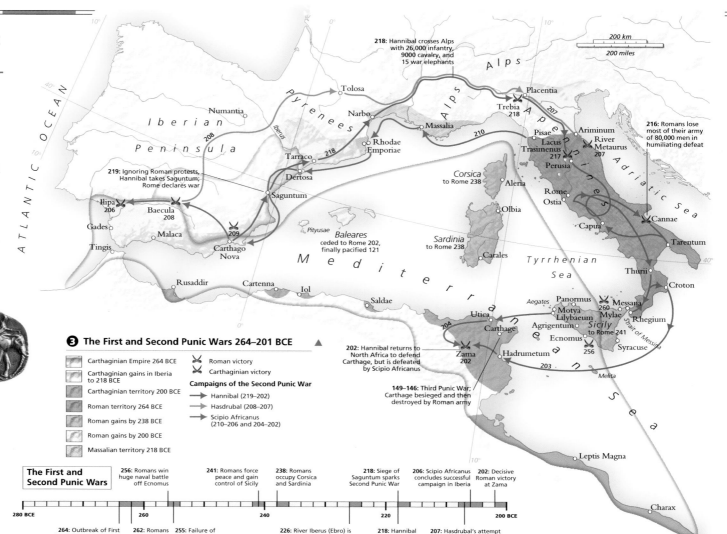

Map labels:
ATLANTIC OCEAN · Iberian Peninsula · Pyrenees · Alps · Apennines · Adriatic Sea · Tyrrhenian Sea · Mediterranean Sea

218: Hannibal crosses Alps with 26,000 infantry, 9000 cavalry, and 15 war elephants

216: Romans lose most of their army of 80,000 men in humiliating defeat

219: Ignoring Roman protests, Hannibal takes Saguntum; Rome declares war

202: Hannibal returns to North Africa to defend Carthage, but is defeated by Scipio Africanus

149–146: Third Punic War; Carthage besieged and then destroyed by Roman army

Numantia · Tolosa · Narbo · Placentia · Trebia 218 · Massalia · Rhodae · Emporiae · Ariminum · River Metaurus 207 · Tarraco 218 · Dertosa · Lacus Trasimenus 217 · Perusia · Rome · Ostia · Saguntum · Ilipa 206 · Baecula 208 · Gades · Malaca · Carthago Nova · Tingis · Rusaddir · Cartenna · Iol · Saldae · Utica · Carthage · Hadrumetum · Zama 202 · Leptis Magna · Charax · Pisae · Aleria · Olbia · Corsica *to Rome 238* · Sardinia *to Rome 238* · Carales · Capua · Cannae · Tarentum · Thurii · Croton · Rhegium · Messana 260 · Panormus · Motya · Lilybaeum · Agrigentum · Ecnomus 256 · Syracuse · Sicily *to Rome 241* · Aegates · Mylae · Pityusae · Baleares *ceded to Rome 202, finally pacified 121* · Melita

❸ The First and Second Punic Wars 264–201 BCE

- Carthaginian Empire 264 BCE
- Carthaginian gains in Iberia to 218 BCE
- Carthaginian territory 200 BCE
- Roman territory 264 BCE
- Roman gains by 238 BCE
- Roman gains by 200 BCE
- Massalian territory 218 BCE
- ✕ Roman victory
- ✕ Carthaginian victory

Campaigns of the Second Punic War
- → Hannibal (219–202)
- → Hasdrubal (208–207)
- → Scipio Africanus (210–206 and 204–202)

The First and Second Punic Wars *(timeline 280 BCE – 200 BCE)*

- 264: Outbreak of First Punic War over control of Strait of Messina
- 262: Romans capture Agrigentum
- 256: Romans win huge naval battle off Ecnomus
- 255: Failure of Roman invasion of North Africa
- 241: Romans force peace and gain control of Sicily
- 238: Romans occupy Corsica and Sardinia
- 226: River Iberus (Ebro) is agreed as limit of Carthage's expansion in Iberian Peninsula
- 218: Siege of Saguntum sparks Second Punic War
- 218: Hannibal crosses Alps
- 206: Scipio Africanus concludes successful campaign in Iberia
- 207: Hasdrubal's attempt to reinforce Hannibal in Italy ends in defeat
- 202: Decisive Roman victory at Zama

The subjugation of Greece by Rome

In 200 BCE the major powers of the Greek world were Macedon and the Seleucid Empire. Two Greek federations had also emerged: the Aetolian League and the Achaean League, which included Corinth, largest of the mainland Greek cities. Other city-states, such as Athens and Sparta, manoeuvred to maintain their independence, as did the Asian kingdom of Pergamum. Political tensions and appeals to Rome for help gave the Romans excuses for five major military interventions in the 2nd century. Macedon became a Roman province in 148; Greece succumbed in 146 after the Achaean War.

Map labels:
Black Sea · THRACE · Epidamnus · MACEDON · Apollonia · Pella · Thessalonica · Byzantium · Nicomedia · Cyzicus · Pydna 168 · Samothrace · Abydos · PERGAMUM · Lemnos · Mytilene · Pergamum · Corcyra · EPIRUS · Ambracia · Leucas · ACARNANIA · THESSALY · Cynoscephalae 197 · Thermopylae 191 · Delphi · EUBOEA · BOEOTIA · Chalcis · Magnesia 190 · Ephesus · SELEUCID EMPIRE · Lesbos · Chios · ELIS · Argos · Corinth · Athens · Zacynthus · Cephallenia · Messene · MESSENIA · Pylos · Sparta · LACONIA · Paros · Delos · Rhodes · RHODES · Aegean Sea · Sea of Crete · Crete · Mediterranean Sea · Ionian Sea

❹ Greece in 200 BCE

- Macedon
- ally of Macedon
- Aetolian League
- ally of Aetolian League
- Achaean League
- Seleucid Empire
- Ptolemaic Empire
- independent Greek states and cities
- Roman Empire
- ally of Rome
- ✕ Roman victory

This fine mosaic of a lion hunt decorated the royal palace in the Macedonian capital of Pella. Even before annexing Macedon and Greece, Rome eagerly embraced Hellenistic culture and customs.

Corinth was first an ally of Rome, then an enemy. It was razed to the ground in 146 by the Roman general Mummius. The ruins visible today *(left)* are of the later Roman city.

Rome's overseas provinces in 120 BCE

Following the defeat of Carthage in 202 BCE, Rome's empire expanded rapidly. Greece and the Greek states of Asia Minor were won through a combination of diplomacy and war, but long, costly campaigns were needed to subdue the tribes of the Iberian Peninsula. Carthage itself was added to the empire in 146. As the Romans extended their rule beyond Italy, they largely abandoned the principles of incorporation that they had applied in Italy and instead set up provinces. These were ruled by governors, who served short one- or two-year terms, maintained order, and oversaw the collection of taxes. Corruption and plundering by governors were common enough for a special permanent court to be set up to try such cases in 149.

Roman expansion 200–120 BCE *(timeline 200 BCE – 120 BCE)*

- 200–196: Second Macedonian War
- 192–189: War with Seleucid king Antiochus; Roman victories at Thermopylae and Magnesia
- 172–167: Third Macedonian War
- 168: Romans crush Macedonians at Pydna
- 148: Roman victory in Fourth Macedonian War
- 146: Roman armies destroy conquered cities of Corinth and Carthage
- 139: Defeat of Lusitani
- 133: Romans take Iberian city of Numantia
- 133: Rome bequeathed province of Asia by king of Pergamum

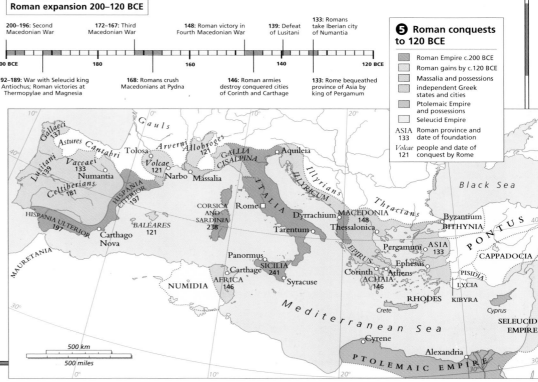

❺ Roman conquests to 120 BCE

- Roman Empire c.200 BCE
- Roman gains by c.120 BCE
- Massalia and possessions
- independent Greek states and cities
- Ptolemaic Empire and possessions
- Seleucid Empire
- ASIA 133 — Roman province and date of foundation
- *Volcae* 121 — people and date of conquest by Rome

Map labels:
Gauls · Gallaeci · Astures · Cantabri · Arverni · Allobroges 121 · Tolosa · Lusitani 138 · Vaccaei · Numantia 133 · Volcae 121 · GALLIA CISALPINA · Narbo · Massalia · Aquileia · Celtiberians 181 · HISPANIA CITERIOR 197 · HISPANIA ULTERIOR 197 · Rome · ITALIA · Illyrians · ILLYRICUM · Thracians · Byzantium · BITHYNIA · BALEARES 121 · CORSICA AND SARDINIA 238 · Tarentum · Dyrrachium · MACEDONIA 148 · Thessalonica · EPIRUS · PONTUS · Pergamum · ASIA 133 · CAPPADOCIA · Carthago Nova · Panormus · SICILIA 241 · Syracuse · Carthage · AFRICA 146 · NUMIDIA · MAURETANIA · Corinth · ACHAIA 146 · Athens · PISIDIA · LYCIA · Cyprus · RHODES · KIBYRA · Crete · Cyrene · Alexandria · PTOLEMAIC EMPIRE · SELEUCID EMPIRE · Mediterranean Sea · Black Sea

THE ROMAN EMPIRE

Constantine sealed the Empire's fate by moving the centre of power to the east.

REPUBLICAN ROME asserted military control over most of the Mediterranean, but a century of internal political conflict and civil war prevented the development of an orderly imperial system. The first emperor, Augustus (27 BCE–14 CE), ended this period of disorder with his defeat of Mark Antony in 31 BCE and established the Principate – the military and political system that defended and governed the empire until the reforms of Diocletian and Constantine at the end of the 3rd century. At the height of its power in the 2nd century Rome ruled over some 50 million people scattered in over 5000 administrative units. For the most part, subjects of the Empire accepted Roman rule, and, at least in the west, many adopted Roman culture and the Latin language. After 212 CE all free inhabitants of the Empire had the status of Roman citizens.

The Empire under Hadrian

The Empire reached its greatest extent early in the 2nd century under Trajan, who conquered Dacia, Arabia, Armenia, Assyria, and Mesopotamia. However, when Hadrian succeeded in 117 CE, he abandoned the last three provinces and adopted a defensive frontier strategy that would be followed by most of his successors. A professional army – under Hadrian it numbered just 300,000 – defended the frontiers and suppressed rebellions in trouble spots such as Britain and Judaea, while the navy kept the Mediterranean free of pirates. Fleets were also based on the Rhine and the Danube, which formed the northeastern frontier.

The Pont du Gard, part of the aqueduct that supplied Nemausus (Nîmes) in the south of France, is a fine example of the Romans' skill in civil engineering.

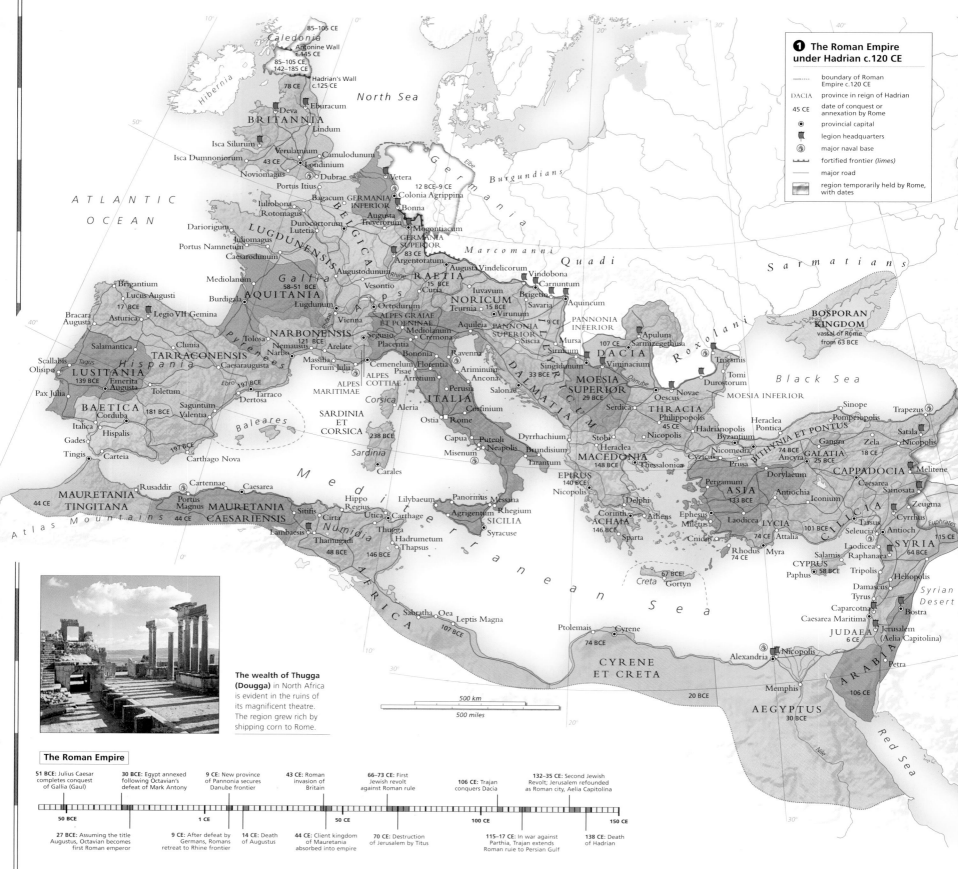

① The Roman Empire under Hadrian c.120 CE

- .... boundary of Roman Empire c.120 CE
- DACIA province in reign of Hadrian
- 45 CE date of conquest or annexation by Rome
- ⊙ provincial capital
- ■ legion headquarters
- ⚓ major naval base
- ⊥⊥⊥ fortified frontier (limes)
- ── major road
- region temporarily held by Rome, with dates

The wealth of Thugga (Dougga) in North Africa is evident in the ruins of its magnificent theatre. The region grew rich by shipping corn to Rome.

The Roman Empire

- **51 BCE:** Julius Caesar completes conquest of Gallia (Gaul)
- **30 BCE:** Egypt annexed following Octavian's defeat of Mark Antony
- **9 CE:** New province of Pannonia secures Danube frontier
- **43 CE:** Roman invasion of Britain
- **66–73 CE:** First Jewish revolt against Roman rule
- **106 CE:** Trajan conquers Dacia
- **132–35 CE:** Second Jewish Revolt; Jerusalem refounded as Roman city, Aelia Capitolina

| 50 BCE | 1 CE | | 50 CE | 100 CE | 150 CE |

- **27 BCE:** Assuming the title Augustus, Octavian becomes first Roman emperor
- **9 CE:** After defeat by Germans, Romans retreat to Rhine frontier
- **14 CE:** Death of Augustus
- **44 CE:** Client kingdom of Mauretania absorbed into empire
- **70 CE:** Destruction of Jerusalem by Titus
- **115–17 CE:** In war against Parthia, Trajan extends Roman rule to Persian Gulf
- **138 CE:** Death of Hadrian

The city of Rome

As the empire grew, so did Rome, reaching a population of about one million in the 2nd century CE. The city was sustained by food shipped up the Tiber from Ostia and aqueducts that delivered 400 litres of water per head per day. Many Romans did not work, but were eligible for the *annona*, a free handout of grain. Following the example of Augustus, every emperor aimed to leave his mark on the city by building magnificent forums, palaces, theatres, arenas, and temples.

The Colosseum, completed in 80 CE, vied with the Circus Maximus race track as Rome's most popular stadium. It regularly attracted a full house of 50,000 to its gladiatorial and wild animal combats.

Earthenware amphorae were used to transport and store wine, olive oil, and fish sauce.

❸ Supply routes to Rome

- —— major shipping route
- ▦ major grain-producing region
- 🍇 wine
- 🫒 olive oil
- 🏺 garum (fish sauce)
- 🍯 honey
- 👤 slaves
- 🐎 horses
- ✴ wool
- ✴ flax/linen
- ⊛ murex (purple dye)
- ▲ marble
- ♠ timber
- ▪ gold
- ▪ tin
- ▪ copper

❷ Imperial Rome c.300 CE

- temple
- stadium or theatre
- baths
- other important building
- built–up area within city wall
- city gate
- —— aqueduct
- ······ city wall in Republican era 4th century BCE
- —— wall of Aurelian 271

Supplying the city of Rome

Feeding the citizens of Rome required regular shipments of grain from Egypt and North Africa. These were landed at Ostia and Portus, a new port built by Trajan at the mouth of the Tiber, from where they were shipped on smaller galleys up river to the capital. Goods were carried by ship wherever possible, as this was much cheaper and faster than road transport. Rome imported food and raw materials from all over its empire. Marble for the pillars and statues that graced the city's temples and palaces often came from as far afield as Greece and Africa. Unusual imports included *garum*, a fermented fish sauce which the Romans used, rather like ketchup, to add flavour to a wide variety of dishes, and murex, a shellfish that produced the purple dye used for imperial togas. To give an idea of the volume of goods imported to the city, Mons Testaceus, a large hill, 50 m in height, was created in imperial times from the shards of broken amphorae from the rows of warehouses that lined the banks of the Tiber in the southwest of the city.

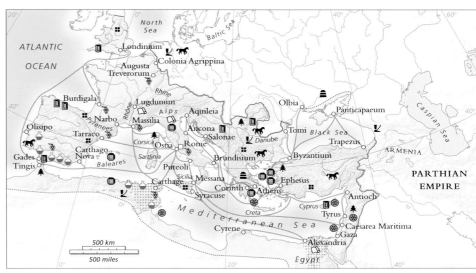

The Tetrarchy of Diocletian and the final division of the Empire

In the 3rd century CE, breakaway states, such as the Kingdom of Palmyra, threatened to destroy the Empire. To counter this, Diocletian (284–305) and Constantine (307–337) reorganized the structure of imperial administration. The existing provinces were divided into 100 smaller units, grouped in twelve larger regions called dioceses, each governed by a vicar. To share responsibility for defending the empire and to provide for an orderly succession, Diocletian established the joint rule of the Tetrarchy: two emperors with the title Augustus, one in the east, one in the west, each assisted by a junior emperor with the title of Caesar.

The later Roman Empire 250–400 CE

- c.250: Period of civil wars and runaway inflation
- 260: Gallic empire established by Postumus
- 270: Palmyra extends rule to Egypt
- 273: Empire reunited by Aurelian
- 293: Diocletian establishes Tetrarchy and twelve dioceses
- 305: Abdication of Diocletian
- 312: Battle of Milvian Bridge, just north of Rome; Constantine defeats rival Maxentius
- 324: Constantine sole ruler
- 337: Constantine's death leads to fresh struggles over succession
- 364: Rome loses war for control of Armenia to Sassanian Empire
- 395: Definitive division of empire into east and west on death of Theodosius

250 CE — 300 — 350 — 400 CE

❹ The Roman Empire 240–395 CE

Parts of Empire ruled by:
- Diocletian
- Maximian
- Galerius
- Constantius
- ----- boundary of Roman Empire 293 CE
- PONTUS diocese established by Diocletian 293 CE
- ○ principal residences of the tetrarchs
- Gallic Empire of Postumus 260–74 CE
- Kingdom of Palmyra 260–72 CE
- territory abandoned by Rome, with date
- —— division of Eastern and Western Empires 395 CE

The four tetrarchs ruled the Empire from 293 to 305. Similar forms of joint rule were tried during the 4th century until the Empire finally split in 395.

This gold coin shows the heads of Diocletian and Maximian, first co-rulers of the Roman Empire.

This floor mosaic of Orpheus decorated a villa in Daphne, a wealthy suburb of Antioch, capital of the province of Syria.

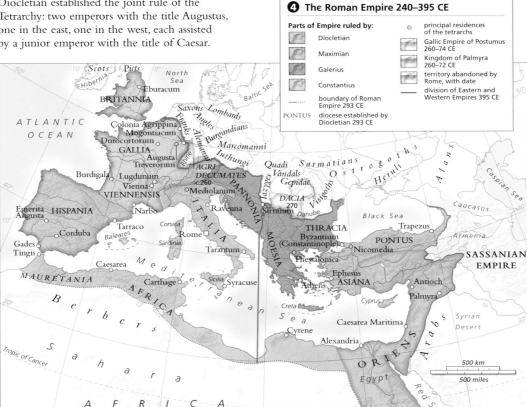

EUROPE AFTER THE FALL OF ROME

THE END OF THE WEST ROMAN EMPIRE in 476 did not signal an immediate descent into barbarism. The rulers of the new kingdoms maintained relations with the eastern emperor in Constantinople, and most pretended to govern on his behalf. In much of western Europe, Roman laws and institutions were retained and, sooner or later, the so-called 'barbarians' all converted to Christianity. The East Roman (Byzantine) Empire continued to exert influence in the west. In the 6th century, Justinian, the most powerful emperor of the period, won back much of the West Roman Empire. But, after failing to halt the Lombard invasion of Italy in 568, the Byzantines were unable to reassert their authority. The eventual successors to the Romans in the west were the Franks and the papacy.

This glass drinking horn would have been used at feasts of the Lombard rulers of Italy.

The kingdoms of the new order

The last Roman emperor of authority in the west was Theodosius. On his death in 395, the empire was divided definitively in two. The 5th century saw the transfer of power in western Europe from the emperors to Germanic immigrants, for the most part groups recruited by the Romans to help them defend their lands *(see pp. 52–53)*. Chief beneficiaries were the Goths. By 480 the Visigoths had established a large kingdom in Aquitaine and Iberia, with its capital at Toulouse. In 492 the Ostrogoths took Italy and the Dalmatian coast.

Christianity maintained a sense of continuity between the West Roman Empire and the kingdoms that replaced it. This late Roman sarcophagus is from Ravenna, capital of the Ostrogoths, successors to the Romans in Italy.

Classis was the port of Ravenna, capital of Ostrogothic and Byzantine Italy. This detail from a 6th-century mosaic shows the castle and ships riding at anchor in the harbour.

Europe in 500

The most powerful of the new kingdoms established in western Europe in 500 was that of Theodoric the Great, leader of the Ostrogoths. Though he ruled from Ravenna, the Senate still sat in Rome and relations between Romans and Goths were largely amicable. Royal marriages helped forge alliances with the Vandal and Visigothic kings in North Africa and Iberia. Theodoric hoped to create a power bloc to counter the might of the East Roman Empire, but after his death in 526 he was succeeded by his infant grandson, who died young, and the dynasty collapsed.

❶ The inheritors of the Roman Empire at 500

- Frankish expansion
- Ostrogothic expansion
- Byzantine reconquests
- Sassanian expansion

❷ The new kingdoms at 600

- Lombard Kingdom and duchies
- Kingdom of the Franks
- Frankish overlordship
- Visigothic conquests
- Lombard conquest of Liguria
- expansion of the Slavs (from 580s)

This Visigothic cross dates from the 6th century. Although Christian, the Visigoths were Arians (they denied the Trinity). This changed in 589, when King Reccared converted to the orthodox Catholicism of his Hispano-Roman subjects.

Europe in 600

The political map of Europe changed dramatically in the 6th century. In 600 the Visigoths still controlled the Iberian peninsula, but the Franks now ruled most of modern France. The East Roman Empire had reconquered North Africa, Italy, Illyria, and even part of southern Iberia. The destruction of the Roman heritage was far greater during the long war waged by the Byzantines against the Goths than during the previous century. Italy then fell prey to the Lombards (Langobardi), Germanic invaders from the northeast.

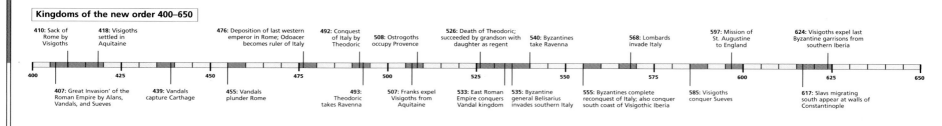

Kingdoms of the new order 400–650

- **410:** Sack of Rome by Visigoths
- **418:** Visigoths settled in Aquitaine
- **476:** Deposition of last western emperor in Rome; Odoacer becomes ruler of Italy
- **492:** Conquest of Italy by Theodoric
- **508:** Ostrogoths occupy Provence
- **526:** Death of Theodoric; succeeded by grandson with daughter as regent
- **540:** Byzantines take Ravenna
- **568:** Lombards invade Italy
- **597:** Mission of St. Augustine to England
- **624:** Visigoths expel last Byzantine garrisons from southern Iberia

- **407:** Great Invasion' of the Roman Empire by Alans, Vandals, and Sueves
- **439:** Vandals capture Carthage
- **455:** Vandals plunder Rome
- **493:** Theodoric takes Ravenna
- **507:** Franks expel Visigoths from Aquitaine
- **533:** East Roman Empire conquers Vandal kingdom
- **535:** Byzantine general Belisarius invades southern Italy
- **555:** Byzantines complete reconquest of Italy; also conquer south coast of Visigothic Iberia
- **585:** Visigoths conquer Sueves
- **617:** Slavs migrating south appear at walls of Constantinople

❸ Britain c.750 ▶

Anglo-Saxon
kingdoms
Mercia and
dependencies
Celtic kingdoms
Pictish kingdoms
⚔ battle
✝ important
monastery

**PICTISH
KINGDOMS**

⚔ Nechtansmere
685

Iona ✝
DALRIADA

✝ Lindisfarne
Melrose ✝ Bamburgh
Degsastan ✝ NORTHUMBRIA
603
✝ Hexham ✝ Jarrow
REGED ✝ Monkwearmouth

✝ Whitby

DEIRA
York
Winwaed 655
Humber

LINDSEY
⚔ Chester Lincoln
616 Nottingham Elmham
MERCIA
POWYS Lichfield ✝ Tamworth EAST
WELSH Worcester Oundle ANGLIA
PRINCIPALITIES Middle Angles Sutton Hoo
Cirencester Essex Colchester
DYFED London
Glastonbury KENT Canterbury
WESSEX Winchester
Dorchester SUSSEX
WEST WALES
(DUMNONIA) Exeter

Irish Sea
North Sea
English Channel

Excavation of a burial site at Sutton
Hoo unearthed the treasure of a 7th-
century Anglo-Saxon king or chieftain,
including this striking gilt bronze helmet.

100 km
100 miles

This gem-studded gold buckle is typical
of the jewellery worn by the Lombard
nobles who ruled Italy for two centuries.

Byzantine and Lombard Italy

After the expulsion of the Goths, control of Italy was contested by
the Byzantines and the Lombards, the latter gradually winning more and
more territory after their invasion of 568. Only rarely did the Lombard
kings, based at Pavia, exercise authority over the southern dukedoms of
Benevento and Spoleto. Similarly, representatives of Byzantium,
including the pope, often acted independently according to their own
interests. The Byzantines were ousted from Ravenna in 751, but
Lombard rule there lasted only until 756. At the pope's request, Pépin,
king of the Franks, invaded northern Italy and crushed the Lombards.

KINGDOM OF THE FRANKS
Alps
Following Lombard invasion of
Italy in 568, their former territories
are occupied by Avars and Slavs

NEUSTRIA AUSTRIA DUCHY
Monza OF
Turin Milan FRIULI Forum Julii
Pavia Verona (Cividale)
KINGDOM OF THE LOMBARDS Padua
Cremona
Genoa Parma Bologna
EMILIA Ravenna
Rimini
EXARCHATE OF
RAVENNA
Siena PENTAPOLIS
TUSCIA Perugia
Spoleto DUCHY OF
SPOLETO
Corsica
c.700: conquered
by Lombards Rome DUCHY OF
DUCHY BENEVENTO
OF
ROME Benevento
Monte Cassino Salerno APULIA Brindisi
Naples Amalfi
Sardinia

Adriatic Sea
Tyrrhenian Sea

❹ **The struggle for Italy 565–750**

East Roman Empire 565
Lombard territories 565
under Lombard rule 590
Lombard gains by 650
Lombard gains by 744
East Roman territory 744

External threats to Italy in the 7th century
➤ Franks
➤ Avars and Slavs

Sicily
Syracuse
Mediterranean Sea

100 km
100 miles

The struggle for Italy 550–750

568: Lombard invasion of Italy	**590–604:** Papacy of Gregory the Great, who negotiates with Lombards to save Rome	**653:** Conversion of Lombards to Christianity	**712:** Liutprand becomes Lombard king; tries to unite Italy	**751:** Lombards under Aistulf take Ravenna; end of Byzantine rule	**753–56:** Italy invaded by Pépin

550   600   650   700   750

554: Frankish invasion defeated; Italy under Byzantine control
643: Edict of Rothari: first book of Lombard law
663: Byzantine Emperor Constans II invades Italy and sacks Rome
773–74: Conquest of Lombards by Charlemagne; northern Italy comes under Frankish rule

Anglo-Saxon Britain 600–800

For the two centuries that followed the Roman withdrawal in 410, there are no
accounts of events in Britain. The Celtic Britons fought each other, as well as Scottish
invaders (from Ireland) and Angles, Saxons, and Jutes, who invaded across the North Sea
from Denmark and north Germany. Around 600, following St Augustine's mission from
Rome to convert the Anglo-Saxons, records appear of a number of kingdoms ruled by
Anglo-Saxon kings (though some of these have British names). The west, notably Wales
and West Wales (Dumnonia) remained in the hands of Celts. For most of the 7th century,
the most powerful kingdom was Northumbria, whose kings briefly controlled much of
Scotland. By 700, however, supremacy had passed to the midland kingdom of Mercia.

Early Anglo-Saxon kingdoms

597: St. Augustine begins conversion of Anglo-Saxon kings to Roman Christianity
655: Northumbrians defeat Mercians at Winwaed
663: Synod of Whitby. 'Roman' Christianity adopted instead of 'Celtic'
716: Ethelbald fights way to crown of Mercia; kingdom dominates all England south of Humber

600   650   700   750   800

603: Northumbrians defeat Scots at Degsastan
616: Northumbrians defeat Britons at Chester
679: Mercians conquer Lindsey from Northumbrians
685: Last great king of Northumbria killed by Picts at Nechtansmere
757: Accession of Offa, most powerful of Mercian Kings; treated as equal by Charlemagne

The early Frankish kingdoms 481–650

The only Germanic kingdom of any
permanence established in this period was
the Kingdom of the Franks, foundation of
modern France. The first Frankish dynasty,
the Merovingians, expanded from lands
around Tournai under Clovis, who pushed
southwest to the Loire, then defeated the
Visigoths in Aquitaine. Clovis's sons
destroyed the Burgundians and exercised
control over several Germanic tribes to
the east. When a powerful king such as
Clovis died, his territories were divided
between his heirs, provoking dynastic civil
wars. The three major Frankish kingdoms
were Neustria and Austrasia (together
referred to as Francia), and Burgundy.

Dagobert I's throne is a powerful emblem
of the continuity of the French kingdom,
which lasted till the Revolution in 1790.

The early Frankish kingdoms 481–650

c.481: Accession of Clovis I
c.497: Clovis converts to Christianity
558: Chlothar I sole king of the Franks
573: Beginning of major civil wars between the Franks
629: Chlothar II dies; succeeded by son, Dagobert I,
639: Death of Dagobert; kingdom divided between two sons

450   500   550   600   650

507: Clovis defeats Visigoths at Vouillé
511: Death of Clovis; his kingdom divided between four sons
561: Death of Chlothar I; kingdom divided between his four sons
613: Chlothar II king of all Gaul; civil wars end

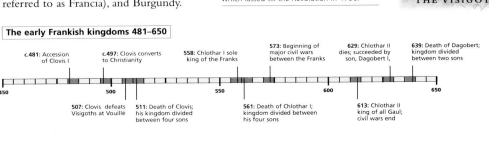

Frisians
Saxons Thuringians
Ripuarian Franks
Tournai Cologne
Salian Franks Meuse
c.486 Soissons Metz
Paris Rheims Alemanni
Bretons Orléans Strasbourg
Tours Loire
Vouillé KINGDOM OF
507 Bourges BURGUNDY Chalon
Poitiers Lyon
Clermont Vézeronce
AQUITAINE 526 KINGDOM OF THE
OSTROGOTHS
Bordeaux Garonne
Avignon
SEPTIMANIA Arles
Basques Marseille
KINGDOM OF
THE VISIGOTHS

200 km
200 miles

❺ **The Kingdom of the
Franks 486–537**

Frankish lands 486
conquered by Clovis by 507
conquered by 511
Kingdom of Franks at the death of Clovis 511
conquered by Clovis's sons 534
conquered by Clovis's sons 537
⚔ battle

Frisians
Saxons
Tournai Cologne Thuringians
AUSTRASIA
Meuse
Soissons Metz
Paris Rheims Strasbourg
Bretons Orléans Alemanni
Loire Bavarians
NEUSTRIA Bourges Chalon
Poitiers BURGUNDY RAETIA
Clermont Lyon
EAST ROMAN
EMPIRE
Bordeaux AUVERGNE
AQUITAINE Garonne Rhône
Toulouse SEPTIMANIA Arles PROVENCE
Basques Marseille
KINGDOM OF
THE VISIGOTHS

❻ **Division of the
Frankish kingdoms 561** ▶

Charibert
Sigebert
Guntram
Chilperic
territory of Frankish
overlordship
○ royal residence

200 km
200 miles

THE HOLY ROMAN EMPIRE

This bronze statue of Charlemagne is an idealized 9th-century portrait, created after the Emperor's death.

THE FRANKISH KINGS Pepin and Charlemagne crushed the Lombards in Italy, granted lands to the pope, and extended the frontiers of Christian Europe. The coronation of Charlemagne as Holy Roman Emperor in 800 was an ambitious attempt by the papacy to recreate the central authority of imperial Rome. Yet by 843, the empire was divided. In the 10th century, a smaller Holy Roman Empire was established under the Saxon Ottonian dynasty. Otto I, who, like Charlemagne, was crowned in Rome, helped convert the Bohemians, Danes, and Poles to Christianity and stopped the advancing Magyars. Meanwhile, Viking raiders terrorized much of western Europe and in Russia, Swedish Vikings helped establish the new state of Kievan Rus.

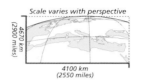

❶ The advance of Islam to 750

- Umayyad Caliphate in 750
- → Arab raid
- Byzantine Empire in 750

Scale varies with perspective

4670 km (2900 miles)

4100 km (2550 miles)

The advance of Islam

In the 7th century, Arab armies carried Islam across the Middle East and North Africa, then, in 711, to the Iberian Peninsula. The Byzantine Empire suffered severe losses and Constantinople had to withstand determined sieges in 674 and 717. In the west, an Islamic invasion of France was turned back in 732 at Poitiers by Charles Martel, the grandfather of Charlemagne. This stemmed the Muslim advance, but Arab raids on all the Christian states of the Mediterranean continued.

The empire of Charlemagne

Charlemagne was both a warrior and a reformer. By 800, he had established Christian hegemony over much of western Europe, his conquest and conversion of Saxony and defeat of the Avars taking the eastern borders of his empire to the Slav world. 'Marches', or buffer zones, protected the empire from the Slavs and from the Moorish Emirate of Cordova. The unity of western Christendom did not last: after the death of Louis the Pious in 840, the empire was divided between his three sons, and by 900 it had fragmented into smaller kingdoms. Local dukedoms and counties, the precursors of feudal domains, started to gain power at the expense of central authority.

Charlemagne's throne still stands in a vaulted chapel at Aachen (Aix-la-Chapelle), the most important of the emperor's many royal residences.

Pope Leo III crowned Charlemagne emperor in 800. This confirmed the Carolingians' right to their lands. When Charlemagne was born c.744, his father Pepin was not even king of the Franks, but mayor of the palace. He was elected king in 751.

❷ The empire of Charlemagne ▶

- Frankish kingdom in 751
- conquest of Pepin
- conquest of Charlemagne
- regions recognizing Charlemagne as overlord, at least nominally
- states of the Church, part of Charlemagne's empire
- marches
- Byzantine possessions

Major campaigns
- → in reign of Pepin 751–68
- → in reign of Charlemagne 768–814
- ■ royal palace

SAXONY 804 — division of Charlemagne's empire, with date of final conquest

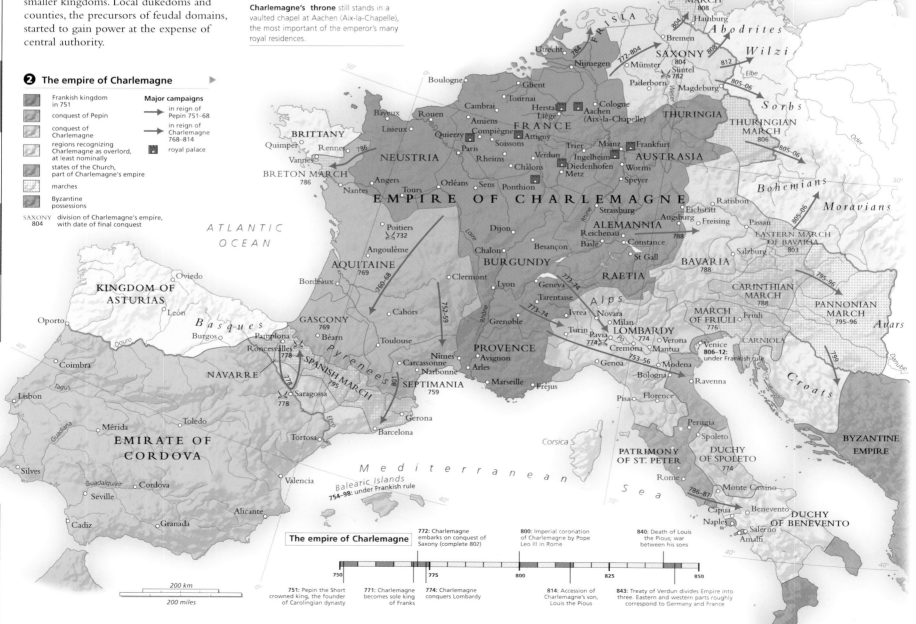

The empire of Charlemagne

- 772: Charlemagne embarks on conquest of Saxony (complete 802)
- 800: Imperial coronation of Charlemagne by Pope Leo III in Rome
- 840: Death of Louis the Pious; war between his sons

750 — 775 — 800 — 825 — 850

- 751: Pepin the Short crowned king, the founder of Carolingian dynasty
- 771: Charlemagne becomes sole king of Franks
- 774: Charlemagne conquers Lombardy
- 814: Accession of Charlemagne's son, Louis the Pious
- 843: Treaty of Verdun divides Empire into three. Eastern and western parts roughly correspond to Germany and France

Europe 800–1000

The fragmentation of the Carolingian Empire led, by 900, to its division into eastern and western parts. In 919, the East Frankish crown passed to Henry I of Saxony, who established the Ottonian dynasty, which was to dominate Europe for the next two centuries. The decisive Ottonian defeat of the Magyars earned the respect of rival noblemen, and Otto I's conquest of Italy, and coronation as Holy Roman Emperor (962), legitimized his rule. Otto's successors reinforced their power in Germany by constant movement around their empire. They controlled bishoprics and churches, encouraged learning and literature, and presided over the formation of Christian states in Poland, Hungary, and Bohemia.

Carvings of Viking ships appear on a picture stone in Gotland, dating from the 8th century, just before the raids began. This scene shows the spirits of dead heroes.

The Vikings of Scandinavia

The Vikings earned a fearsome reputation when they began their raids on Europe in the late 8th century. Their leaders were probably warlords who had been displaced by more powerful kings. They targeted the wealth of towns, monasteries, and churches in England, Ireland, and France. By the late 9th century, they ruled kingdoms in England and Ireland, and the Duchy of Normandy in France. Once settled, they adopted Christianity and established commercial towns. The Swedish Vikings raided and traded along the rivers of Russia, making contact with the Byzantine Empire and the Islamic world, a rich source of silver. They founded a merchant town at Novgorod and won control of Kiev, which became capital of the extensive state of Kievan Rus.

Otto II, who reigned from 973 to 983, receives homage from the subject nations of his empire. Portraits of Holy Roman Emperors emulated those of the Byzantine emperors, who were portrayed as God's representatives on earth.

❸ Europe c.800–1000 ▶

- —— frontiers c.1000
- Muslim lands
- Hungary
- Denmark
- Sweden
- Norway (under Danish rule)
- Byzantine Empire (under direct Byzantine rule)
- Byzantine dependencies (effectively independent)
- Holy Roman Empire

Viking settlement
- Danish
- Swedish
- Norwegian
- Danelaw 878–954

Expeditions and raids
- → Danish
- → Swedish
- → Norwegian
- ⇒ Magyar migration
- → Magyar raid
- → Muslim raid

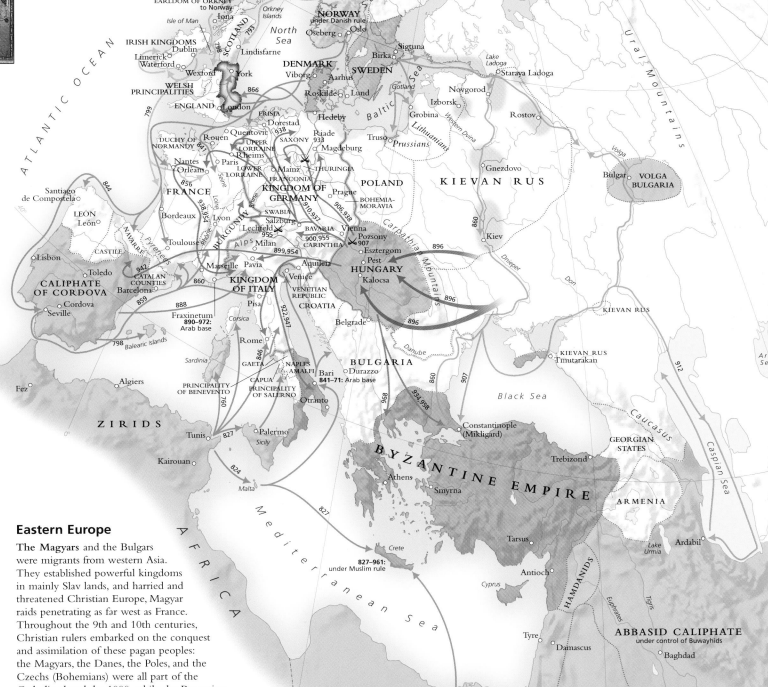

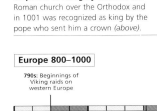

Stephen I of Hungary favoured the Roman church over the Orthodox and in 1001 was recognized as king by the pope who sent him a crown (above).

Eastern Europe

The Magyars and the Bulgars were migrants from western Asia. They established powerful kingdoms in mainly Slav lands, and harried and threatened Christian Europe, Magyar raids penetrating as far west as France. Throughout the 9th and 10th centuries, Christian rulers embarked on the conquest and assimilation of these pagan peoples: the Magyars, the Danes, the Poles, and the Czechs (Bohemians) were all part of the Catholic church by 1000, while the Byzantine Empire had crushed the Bulgars by 1018.

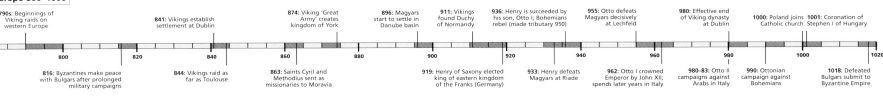

Europe 800–1000

- 790s: Beginnings of Viking raids on western Europe
- 816: Byzantines make peace with Bulgars after prolonged military campaigns
- 841: Vikings establish settlement at Dublin
- 844: Vikings raid as far as Toulouse
- 863: Saints Cyril and Methodius sent as missionaries to Moravia
- 874: Viking 'Great Army' creates kingdom of York
- 896: Magyars start to settle in Danube basin
- 911: Vikings found Duchy of Normandy
- 919: Henry of Saxony elected king of eastern kingdom of the Franks (Germany)
- 933: Henry defeats Magyars at Riade
- 936: Henry is succeeded by his son, Otto I; Bohemians rebel (made tributary 950)
- 955: Otto defeats Magyars decisively at Lechfeld
- 962: Otto I crowned Emperor by John XII; spends later years in Italy
- 980: Effective end of Viking dynasty at Dublin
- 980–83: Otto II campaigns against Arabs in Italy
- 990: Ottonian campaign against Bohemians
- 1000: Poland joins Catholic church
- 1001: Coronation of Stephen I of Hungary
- 1018: Defeated Bulgars submit to Byzantine Empire

780 · 800 · 820 · 840 · 860 · 880 · 900 · 920 · 940 · 960 · 980 · 1000 · 1020

EUROPE IN THE AGE OF THE CRUSADES

Emperor Frederick Barbarossa is shown in Crusader dress. He drowned in 1190 on his way to the Third Crusade.

FOLLOWING THE SUCCESS of the First Crusade *(see pp. 64–65)*, the spirit of the venture captured the imagination of Christian Europe. Expeditions to subdue the pagans of the Baltic and campaigns against the Muslims in Iberia were undertaken with papal blessing. Ideals of chivalry inspired the new religious orders of warrior clerics established to protect pilgrims to the Holy Land, such as the Templars and Hospitallers. These organizations became immensely wealthy with hundreds of priories and estates in Europe. At the same time, it was a period of great intellectual excitement. The rediscovery of Classical texts inspired an interest in philosophy; universities were founded and new religious orders gave renewed energy to the Catholic Church.

The crusading ideal in Europe

The Knights Templar were so well rewarded for their services in the Levant that they became a powerful political force throughout Europe.

The ideal of Holy War which inspired the Crusaders to fight in the Iberian Peninsula and the Holy Land was used to justify other wars, conflicts, and even racist atrocities. In 1096, German mobs attacked and massacred as 'unbelievers' the Jews in their own communities. Missionary efforts to convert the pagan peoples of Livonia, Lithuania, and Prussia became a crusade, preached by Pope Innocent III. One crusade was mounted against 'heretics' within Christian Europe – the Cathars (Albigensians) of southern France. In 1212 a French shepherd boy even set out to lead a children's crusade to Jerusalem. Most of his followers got no further than Genoa and Marseille.

The crusading ideal

1118: Founder of Knights Templar granted site close to Solomon's temple in Jerusalem
1126: Hospitallers of St. John adopt a military role
1208: Crusade against Cathars, or Albigensians, in southern France
1283: Conquest of Prussia completed by Teutonic Knights
1312: Order of Temple, accused of heresy and suppressed by Pope

| 1050 | 1100 | 1150 | 1200 | 1250 | 1300 | 1350 |

1096: Attacks on Jewish communities by Crusaders and their supporters
1197: Order of Teutonic Knights established in the Holy Land
1233: Inquisition established in Toulouse
1306–10: Hospitallers conquer Rhodes, which becomes their base

❶ The crusading ideal in Europe 1100–1300 ▶

- predominantly pagan lands c.1100
- Muslim lands c.1180
- main Cathar region
- Waldensian strongholds
- → direction of Reconquest in Spain

Crusades in the Baltic
- → Danish expeditions
- → Swedish expeditions
- → direction of advance of Sword Brothers
- → direction of advance of Teutonic Knights

Other crusades
- → Albigensian Crusade 1209–13
- → Children's Crusade 1212
- ✦ massacre of Jews 1096
- ⊕ major Templar house 1300
- ⊕ headquarters of crusading orders in Spain
- — frontiers 1180
- — Holy Roman Empire
- first state of Teutonic Knights 1211–15

The Norman conquest of England

The Duchy of Normandy was established in northern France by 911. In 1066, William, Duke of Normandy led an expedition to win the English throne from Harold, the last Anglo-Saxon king. Harold had seen off the threat of another claimant, Harald Hardrada of Norway, but, after a long march south, he was defeated by William at Hastings. Once England had been conquered, it was parcelled out in fiefs amongst William's Norman knights.

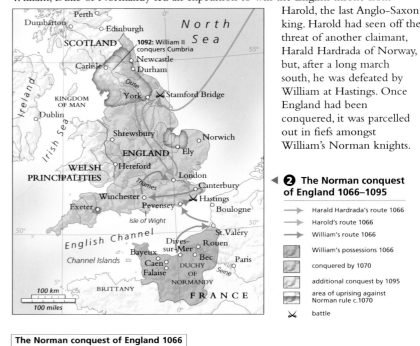

❷ The Norman conquest of England 1066–1095

- → Harald Hardrada's route 1066
- → Harold's route 1066
- → William's route 1066
- William's possessions 1066
- conquered by 1070
- additional conquest by 1095
- area of uprising against Norman rule c.1070
- ✗ battle

The Norman conquest of England 1066

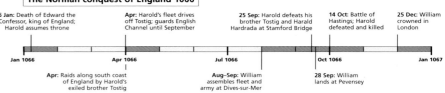

5 Jan: Death of Edward the Confessor, king of England; Harold assumes throne
Apr: Harold's fleet drives off Tostig; guards English Channel until September
25 Sep: Harold defeats his brother Tostig and Harald Hardrada at Stamford Bridge
14 Oct: Battle of Hastings; Harold defeated and killed
25 Dec: William crowned in London

| Jan 1066 | Apr 1066 | Jul 1066 | Oct 1066 | Jan 1067 |

Apr: Raids along south coast of England by Harold's exiled brother Tostig
Aug–Sep: William assembles fleet and army at Dives-sur-Mer
28 Sep: William lands at Pevensey

William's success depended on a large fleet to ship men and horses across the English Channel, but the Normans had long abandoned the seagoing life of their Viking forebears. Yet they managed to build a fleet, depicted here in a scene from the Bayeux Tapestry, large enough to transport an army of perhaps 7000 men to England.

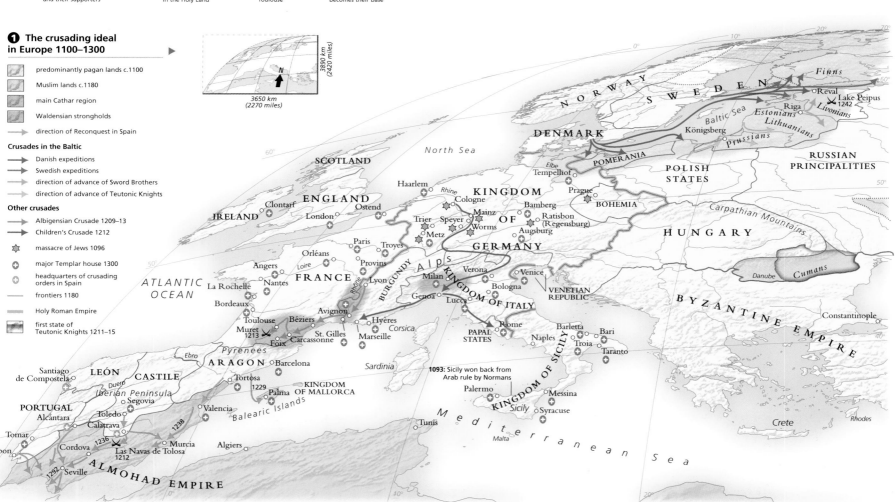

❸ The 12th-century renaissance in Europe ▶

- ▣ university with date of foundation
- ▣ other important theological school
- ▨ Muslim lands reconquered by Christians 1030–1200
- ▨ Muslim lands reconquered by Christians 1200–1300
- ◉ centre of contact with Arab scholarship
- † major Cistercian house with date of foundation
- ---- frontiers 1200
- ── Holy Roman Empire

Map labels:
NORWAY
SWEDEN
SCOTLAND
Alvastra 1143
† Newbattle 1140
† Melrose 1142
IRELAND
Mellifont 1142
North Sea
† Jervaulx 1150
† Rievaulx 1132
† Fountains 1132
† Kirkstall 1147
Denmark
WALES
ENGLAND
Oxford early 12th century
▣ Cambridge c.1209
London
Waverley 1128
▣ Canterbury
Rhine
Baltic Sea
Elbe
† Wagrowiec 1143
POLAND
RUSSIAN PRINCIPALITIES
Cologne
† Camp 1123
KINGDOM OF GERMANY
c.1200: University of Paris has colleges for students from all over western Europe
Bec
▣ Paris
▣ Rheims
Chartres
Angers
Orléans c.1236
▣ Prague 1348
Worms
† Jedrzejów 1149
Tours
Meung
Clairvaux 1115
Ebrach 1127
FRANCE
Pontigny 1114
Morimond 1115
Lützel
Eberbach 1135
La Ferté 1112
Cîteaux 1098
† Heiligenkreuz 1137
HUNGARY
† Czikador 1142
1308: University of Lisbon transferred to Coimbra
LEÓN
León
NAVARRE
▣ Cahors 1332
Grenoble 1339
Milan
Alps
Moreruela 1132
Pamplona
▣ Toulouse 1229
Avignon 1303
Piacenza 1248
Vicenza 1204
Padua (law) 1222
Venice
Coimbra Alcobaça 1148
PORTUGAL
▣ Salamanca 1218
Segovia
Narbonne
▣ Montpellier (medicine) 12th century
▣ Lérida 1300
Genoa
Bologna (law) 1088
Arezzo 1215
VENETIAN REPUBLIC
Lisbon 1290
CASTILE
ARAGON
Marseille
KINGDOM OF ITALY
Pisa
Siena 1246
Perugia 1308
Assisi
Tarazona
Toledo
Barcelona
Corsica
Rome c.1140 1245
PAPAL STATES
SERBIA
BULGARIA
Seville 1254
Cordova
Balearic Islands
Sardinia
Naples 1224
◉ Salerno (medicine) since 9th century
ALMOHAD EMPIRE
ATLANTIC OCEAN
Mediterranean Sea
Palermo
Sicily
KINGDOM OF SICILY
BYZANTINE EMPIRE
Danube
500 km
500 miles

The 12th-century renaissance

Christian idealism in this period was reflected in the growth of new monastic and teaching orders. The Cistercians, founded at Cîteaux in 1098, spread throughout Europe under the charismatic leadership of St. Bernard of Clairvaux. The early 13th century saw the even more rapid expansion of the orders founded by St. Francis of Assisi and St. Dominic. At the same time a renewed interest in scholarship led to the founding of new universities. The increased availability of the seminal texts of the ancient world, obtained through the medium of Arabic translations, was critically important for medieval scholars. By reconciling the science of Aristotle with Christian faith, St. Thomas Aquinas (d. 1274) gave Catholic theology an intellectual basis that lasted for centuries.

The Cistercians were founded in reaction to the idle life of monasteries financed by tithes. They worked their own land and were self-supporting, though they accepted gifts of marginal or recently conquered land. Their graceful architecture was plain and unadorned, as seen here in the refectory of Fountains Abbey in northern England.

The 12th-century renaissance

1126: Birth of Muslim philosopher, Averroes, in Cordova	**1158:** Frederick Barbarossa grants imperial protection to University of Bologna		**1249:** Foundation of Merton College, Oxford

1100 — 1150 — 1200 — 1250 — 1300

1098: Foundation of new monastery at Cîteaux	**1115:** Bernard founds Cistercian daughter house at Clairvaux	**1210:** St. Francis of Assisi gains papal recognition of his Order of friars dedicated to poverty	**1220:** First chapter of the Dominican order of Friars

The Angevin Empire

The laws of inheritance of feudal Europe enabled Henry II, Count of Anjou and King of England, to acquire lands that included England, Ireland, and most of western France. His marriage to Eleanor of Aquitaine meant that he ruled more of France than the French king, even though he was nominally the latter's vassal. He spent much of his reign defending his empire against Louis VII of France and the ambitions of his children. After his death in 1189, the Angevin empire soon disintegrated. In 1214, Philip II of France defeated Henry's son, John, ending English rule in Normandy. England, however, did keep western Aquitaine, and, in the 14th century, would renew its claims to France in the Hundred Years' War.

English possessions 1154–89

1152: Henry marries Eleanor of Aquitaine	**1154:** Succession of Henry II to English crown	**1173–74:** Henry quells French-backed rebellion by his sons	**1199:** Accession of John

1140 — 1160 — 1180 — 1200 — 1220

1151: Henry succeeds Geoffrey as Count of Anjou	**1189:** Succession of Richard the Lionheart	**1214:** Defeat of English and German allies at Bouvines

Henry II and Eleanor of Aquitaine had an intense, stormy relationship. She was imprisoned for intriguing against him on behalf of their eldest son Henry in 1173–74.

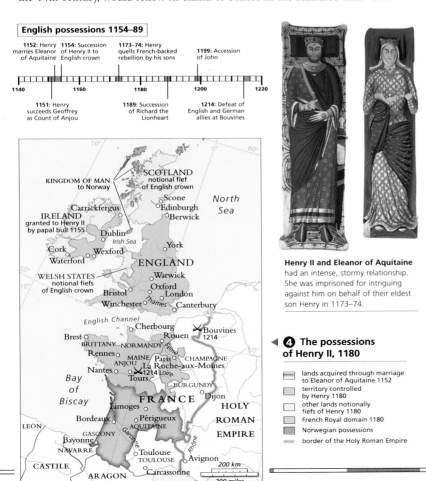

❹ The possessions of Henry II, 1180

- ▨ lands acquired through marriage to Eleanor of Aquitaine 1152
- ▨ territory controlled by Henry 1180
- ▨ other lands notionally fiefs of Henry 1180
- ▨ French Royal domain 1180
- ▨ Norwegian possessions
- ── border of the Holy Roman Empire

Map labels:
KINGDOM OF MAN to Norway
SCOTLAND notional fief of English crown
Scone
Edinburgh
Berwick
IRELAND granted to Henry II by papal bull 1155
Carrickfergus
Dublin
Irish Sea
North Sea
Cork
Waterford
Wexford
York
WELSH STATES notional fiefs of English crown
ENGLAND
Warwick
Bristol
Oxford
London
Winchester
Canterbury
English Channel
Cherbourg
Brest
BRITTANY
NORMANDY
Bouvines 1214
Rouen
Rennes
MAINE
ANJOU
Paris
CHAMPAGNE
La Roche-aux-Moines
Nantes
1214
Loire
Bay of Biscay
BURGUNDY
Dijon
LEÓN
Limoges
PÉRIGUEUX
AQUITAINE
HOLY ROMAN EMPIRE
Bordeaux
GASCONY
Garonne
Bayonne
NAVARRE
TOULOUSE
Toulouse
Avignon
Rhône
CASTILE
ARAGON
Carcassonne
FRANCE
200 km
200 miles

Venice and the Latin Empire

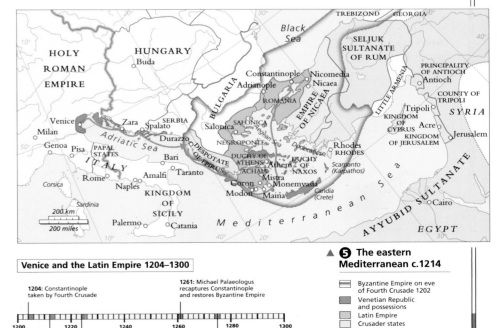

The Crusaders' motive for attacking Constantinople in 1203 was financial reward for restoring Alexius IV (son of deposed emperor Isaac Angelus) to the imperial throne. When the population rebelled and killed Alexius in 1204, the Crusaders took over the city for themselves.

As well as being the principal emporium for east-west trade, Venice also made money shipping Crusaders to the Levant. When the Fourth Crusade gathered in Venice in 1203, the leaders did not have enough money to pay. The Venetians diverted the fleet first to capture the Adriatic port of Zara, long coveted by Venice, then to Constantinople, where in 1204, the Crusaders sacked the city and installed their own emperor. The Empire was divided into Venetian colonies and Latin fiefs. There were now two empires in the east; the 'Latin' empire, ruled from Constantinople, and a rump Byzantine Empire, ruled from Nicaea.

Map labels (eastern Mediterranean):
HOLY ROMAN EMPIRE
HUNGARY
Buda
Black Sea
TREBIZOND
GEORGIA
SELJUK SULTANATE OF RUM
BULGARIA
SERBIA
Constantinople
Adrianople
Nicomedia
Nicaea
EMPIRE OF NICAEA
PRINCIPALITY OF ANTIOCH
Antioch
LITTLE ARMENIA
Venice
Milan
Genoa
Pisa
Zara
Spalato
Salonica
SALONICA
ROMANIA
COUNTY OF TRIPOLI
Tripoli
KINGDOM OF CYPRUS
Acre
SYRIA
Adriatic Sea
Durazzo
DESPOTATE OF EPIRUS
NEGROPONTE
Rhodes
RHODES
KINGDOM OF JERUSALEM
Jerusalem
PAPAL STATES
Bari
DUCHY OF ATHENS
Athens
DUCHY OF NAXOS
Scarpanto (Karpathos)
ITALY
Rome
Corsica
Amalfi
Taranto
ACHAIA
Mistra
Monemvasia
Coron
Modon
Maina
Candia (Crete)
Naples
KINGDOM OF SICILY
Sardinia
Palermo
Catania
Mediterranean Sea
AYYUBID SULTANATE
Cairo
EGYPT
200 km
200 miles

Venice and the Latin Empire 1204–1300

1204: Constantinople taken by Fourth Crusade		**1261:** Michael Palaeologus recaptures Constantinople and restores Byzantine Empire

1200 — 1220 — 1240 — 1260 — 1280 — 1300

1212: Venetians occupy Crete	**1224:** Latin kingdom of Salonica conquered by Despotate of Epirus	**1275:** Principality of Achaia inherited by Philip of Anjou; ruled from Naples

❺ The eastern Mediterranean c.1214

- ▨ Byzantine Empire on eve of Fourth Crusade 1202
- ▨ Venetian Republic and possessions
- ▨ Latin Empire
- ▨ Crusader states
- ▨ Byzantine states
- ▨ Muslim states
- → route of Fourth Crusade
- ── border of Holy Roman Empire

187

EUROPE IN CRISIS

THE CONSOLIDATION of nation states on the eastern and western edges of Europe was matched, in the 13th century, by the decline of the Holy Roman Empire, its power depleted by long struggles with the papacy and the Italian city-states. In the east, raids by Mongols destroyed Kiev in 1240, and Russia, subject to Mongol overlords, developed in isolation until the 15th century. In the northeast, German colonization brought political and economic change, with a new trading axis around the Baltic Sea. During the 14th century, however, social unrest swept through Europe, compounded by famines, economic decline, dynastic wars, and the Black Death of 1347 (see pp.72–73), which wiped out a third of Europe's population in just two years.

This silver pfennig shows the Emperor Frederick II, whose claim to rule Italy alienated the popes.

The Empire and the papacy

Under the Hohenstaufen dynasty, the aspirations of the Holy Roman Emperors to universal authority were blocked by the papacy in central Italy, and the city-based communes of northern Italy. Emperor Frederick II (1211–50) clashed with Rome at a time when popes exercised great political power. After his death, the papacy gave the Kingdom of Sicily to Charles of Anjou, and Frederick's heirs were eliminated. Confronted with the growing power of France and England, the Empire lost any pretence to political supremacy in Europe; in Germany, a mosaic of clerical states, principalities, and free cities continued to undermine imperial authority.

Under Innocent III (1198–1216) the medieval papacy was at the height of its spiritual authority and temporal power.

England, Scotland, and Wales

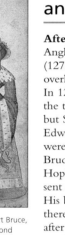

The Scottish king, Robert Bruce, pictured here with his second wife, was a noble of Norman descent like his English enemies.

After a century of peace along the Anglo-Scottish border, Edward I (1272–1307) set out to assert his overlordship over all the British Isles. In 1284 he annexed Wales, bestowing the title of Prince of Wales on his son, but Scotland proved more intractable; Edward's attempts to subdue the Scots were met with resistance led by Robert Bruce, the victor at Bannockburn (1314). Hoping to extend his domains, Bruce sent an expedition to Ireland in 1315. His brother Edward continued fighting there until his death in 1318. In 1328, after a devastating period of guerrilla warfare and border raiding, England acknowledged Scottish independence.

England, Scotland, and Wales 1284–1337

Timeline (above axis):
- **1284:** Edward I invades Wales
- **1305:** Execution of William Wallace, Scottish nationalist leader
- **1322:** Scottish barons assert independence in Declaration of Arbroath
- **1329:** Death of Robert Bruce
- **1337:** Start of Hundred Years' War; Scots ally with French against England

Scale: 1280 1290 1300 1310 1320 1330 1340 1350

Timeline (below axis):
- **1296:** Edward I invades Scotland
- **1314:** English defeated at Bannockburn
- **1318:** Edward Bruce killed in Ireland
- **1328:** Scottish independence confirmed by Treaty of Northampton

2 The British Isles 1200–1400

Legend:
- frontiers 1070
- to England 1092; to Scotland 1136
- southern limit of Scotland 1139–57
- to Scotland from Norway 1266
- northern limit of English control 1400
- Welsh Principalities, brought under English control gradually by 1247
- campaigns of Edward I, with dates
- Robert Bruce's campaign 1307–08
- region affected by Edward Bruce's invasions of Ireland 1315–18
- *MIDHE* Irish overkingdom c.1100
- Irish states brought under English control by Papal grant 1155; subdued gradually from 1169
- autonomous Irish chiefdoms 1300
- core area of Peasants' Revolt 1381

100 km / 100 miles

1 The Empire of Frederick II

Legend:
- frontier of Holy Roman Empire 1250
- Kingdom of Germany
- Kingdom of Italy
- under effective Hohenstaufen control 1250
- German lands largely under imperial or Hohenstaufen ownership
- Papal States 1178
- added by 1219
- added by 1278
- Venetian Republic and possessions
- member of Lombard League 1167
- frontiers 1250

200 km / 200 miles

The Hohenstaufens and the papacy

Timeline (above axis):
- **1167:** Lombard League formed to oppose Emperor Frederick I Barbarossa in northern Italy
- **1198:** Accession of Pope Innocent III
- **1211:** Frederick II becomes Emperor
- **1245:** Innocent IV excommunicates Frederick
- **1268:** Charles of Anjou defeats Conradin, Frederick's grandson, at Tagliacozzo
- **1282:** Sicilian Vespers; Charles of Anjou defeated by Aragonese

Scale: 1150 1170 1190 1210 1230 1250 1270 1290 1310

Timeline (below axis):
- **1194:** Emperor Henry VI crowned King of Sicily
- **1237:** Frederick II defeats Italian communes at Cortenuova
- **1250:** Death of Frederick
- **1305:** Pope Clement V takes up residency at Avignon, under French supervision

Eastward expansion in the Baltic

A German-led wave of migration, from 1100–1350, transformed eastern and Baltic Europe. As peasants moved east in search of land and resources, German language and law became predominant; New towns were bound together in the Hanseatic League, a trading association with links from Muscovy to London. Crusades in the east were spearheaded by the Knights of the Teutonic Order, who began to wage war on the pagans of Prussia and Lithuania in 1226. They also took over the Sword Brothers' lands in Livonia. The Livonians and Prussians were subdued, but Lithuania expanded to the southeast to become a powerful state. It was united with Poland in 1386.

Marienburg was the headquarters of the Teutonic Knights from 1309. Part abbey, part fortress, it was built of brick like many of the castles erected by the crusading order in Prussia and Livonia.

The Baltic 1200–1400

c.1200: Bishopric of Riga established

1226: Teutonic Knights invited to crusade in Prussia

1237: Start of Mongol invasion of Russia

1242: Russians defeat Teutonic Knights at Lake Peipus

1309: Teutonic Order's subjugation of Prussia complete

1342: Death of Gedymin, founder of Lithuania

1386: Poland and Lithuania joined through marriage alliance

▲ **3 The Baltic states 1100–1400**

- frontier of Kievan Rus c.1100
- Holy Roman Empire, 1100
- added to Holy Roman Empire by 1380
- Sweden
- added to Sweden by 1323
- main thrusts of Danish expansion
- under Danish control c.1225
- eastern frontier of ethnic German settlement 1100
- frontier of ethnic German settlement 1400
- possessions of the Hungarian Angevins
- ○ member of Hanseatic League (not all shown)
- ----- frontiers 1380

Central and southeastern Europe

After the setbacks of the early 13th century, when eastern Europe was devastated by Mongol invasions, the consolidation of powerful new states began. In Bohemia, the imperial ambitions of Ottakar II (1253–78) briefly expanded his domain from Silesia to the Adriatic, but he came into conflict with Bohemian and German princes, and the Habsburgs were able to seize power in Austria on his death. Powerful monarchies were established in Lithuania under Gedymin (c.1315–42), in Poland under Casimir the Great (1333–70), and in Hungary under Louis the Great (1342–82). Bohemia under the Luxembourg dynasty remained an influential state, especially when the king was elected as the Emperor Charles IV. In the Balkans, Stefan Dušan (1331–55) forged for himself a substantial Serbian Empire, but it fell to the Ottomans in 1389.

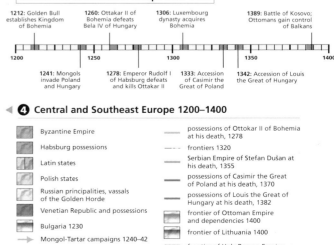

The Emperor Charles IV is shown with his Electors. His Golden Bull of 1356 set out clear rules for electing the emperor.

Central and southeastern Europe 1200–1400

1212: Golden Bull establishes Kingdom of Bohemia

1241: Mongols invade Poland and Hungary

1260: Ottakar II of Bohemia defeats Bela IV of Hungary

1278: Emperor Rudolf I of Habsburg defeats and kills Ottakar II

1306: Luxembourg dynasty acquires Bohemia

1333: Accession of Casimir the Great of Poland

1342: Accession of Louis the Great of Hungary

1389: Battle of Kosovo; Ottomans gain control of Balkans

◄ **4 Central and Southeast Europe 1200–1400**

- Byzantine Empire
- Habsburg possessions
- Latin states
- Polish states
- Russian principalities, vassals of the Golden Horde
- Venetian Republic and possessions
- Bulgaria 1230
- Mongol-Tartar campaigns 1240–42
- possessions of Ottokar II of Bohemia at his death, 1278
- ----- frontiers 1320
- Serbian Empire of Stefan Dušan at his death, 1355
- possessions of Casimir the Great of Poland at his death, 1370
- possessions of Louis the Great of Hungary at his death, 1382
- frontier of Ottoman Empire and dependencies 1400
- frontier of Lithuania 1400
- frontier of Holy Roman Empire

TRADE IN MEDIEVAL EUROPE

The seal of Lübeck shows a cog, the ship used for large cargoes in northern Europe.

THE EXPLOSION IN EUROPE'S POPULATION, which nearly doubled between the 10th and 14th centuries, was caused by greatly increased agricultural productivity, enhanced by technological innovations, in particular the use of the iron plough, and large land clearance projects, which brought marginal land, such as marshes and forests, under cultivation. This demographic surge inevitably led to increased trading activity; merchants traversed the continent, using the trans–Alpine passes which provided arterial routes between Italy and the north and, from c.1300, new maritime routes which opened up the North and Baltic Seas. Trade and commerce went hand in hand with urban development. Commercial wealth had a cultural impact; cities were enhanced with magnificent buildings and churches and, from c.1200, universities. As cities prospered, a new class, the bourgeoisie, emerged.

Medieval trade

From the 11th century the Alpine passes had linked the textile towns of Lombardy and manufacturing centres of the Po valley with northern Europe, rich in natural resources, such as timber, grain, wool, and metals. Merchants converged from all over Europe to trade at vast seasonal fairs. International bankers, such as the Florentine Peruzzi, facilitated payments and promoted business. Around 1300, the Genoese opened a new sea route to the North Sea, through the Strait of Gibraltar; Bruges, at the end of the route, became a major city. In the Mediterranean, Genoa competed with Venice for the carrying trade. Venice controlled the valuable eastern routes, profiting from trade in silks, sugar, spices, and gemstones from India and East Asia. In northern Germany, an association of trading cities centred on Lübeck, the Hanseatic League, promoted monopolies and sought exclusive trading rights with towns in England, Scandinavia, and Flanders.

Italian towns

Northern Italy was well-endowed with populous, wealthy cities, such as Milan and Florence. The Italian cities did not develop under the direct rule of kings, emperors, or the nobility, and took advantage of this to assert their municipal rights, evolving their own constitutions, codes of law, and military forces, the 'communal movement'.

The textile industry flourished in Flanders and northern Italy. The horizontal loom (above) was introduced to Europe in the 11th century.

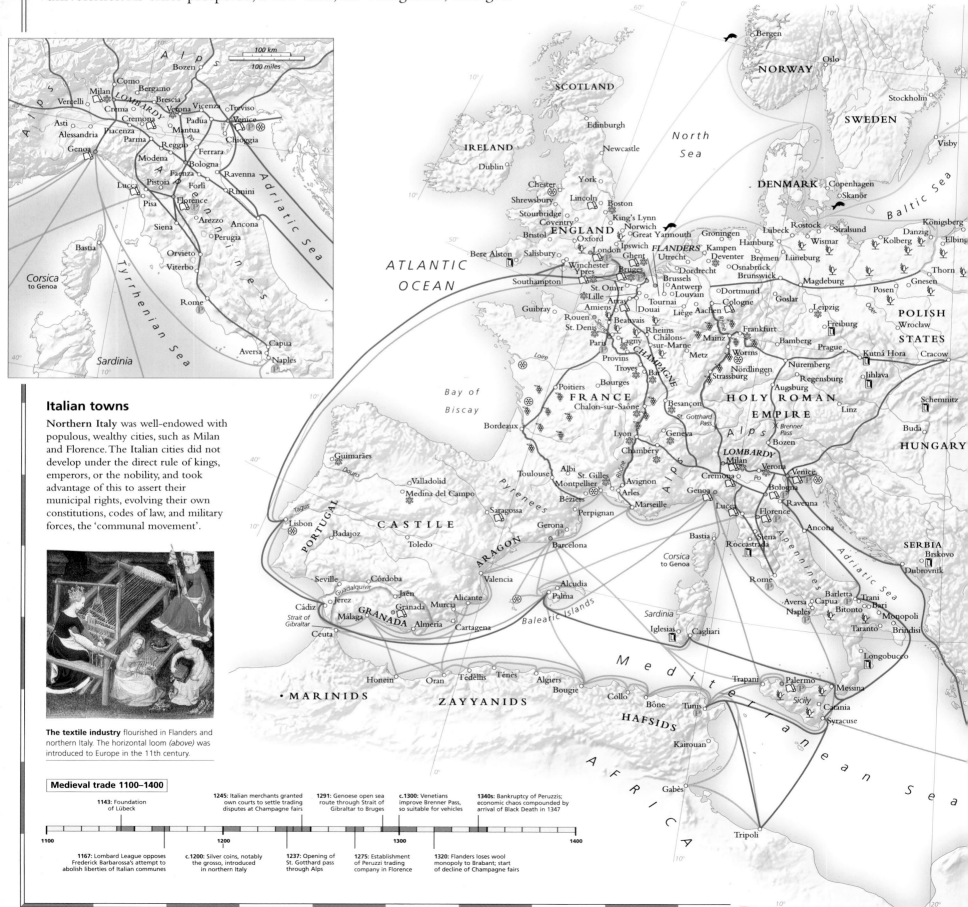

Medieval trade 1100–1400

1143: Foundation of Lübeck	**1245:** Italian merchants granted own courts to settle trading disputes at Champagne fairs	**1291:** Genoese open sea route through Strait of Gibraltar to Bruges	**c.1300:** Venetians improve Brenner Pass, so suitable for vehicles	**1340s:** Bankruptcy of Peruzzis; economic chaos compounded by arrival of Black Death in 1347
1167: Lombard League opposes Frederick Barbarossa's attempt to abolish liberties of Italian communes	**c.1200:** Silver coins, notably the grosso, introduced in northern Italy	**1237:** Opening of St. Gotthard pass through Alps	**1275:** Establishment of Peruzzi trading company in Florence	**1320:** Flanders loses wool monopoly to Brabant; start of decline of Champagne fairs

MONEY AND BANKING

Many gold and silver currencies circulated freely in Medieval Europe, irrespective of where they were minted, so money changing was inevitably an important profession. Travelling merchants left currency on deposit with money changers, in exchange for a receipt, the first stage in the evolution of banking. By the 14th century the use of the bill of exchange, where one person instructs another to pay a sum of money to a third party, was widespread. The organization of bills of exchange was lucrative, and banking families, such as the Peruzzi and Bardi of Florence, became rich and powerful.

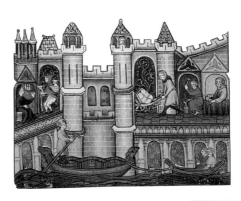

Venetian coinage included the silver grosso and the widely circulated gold ducat.

Medieval Italy gave the world the word 'bank' from the *banco* (counter) where bankers transacted their business, as shown in this 14th-century illustration.

Medieval cities

Many of the cities of Medieval Europe owed their development to trade and commerce. The cities of northern Italy emerged from the 10th century onwards, as entrepôts in the trade between Europe, Byzantium, and the Islamic world. In the 13th century, the demand for manufactured goods, such as glassware, textiles, and metalwork, led to the emergence of industrial centres, notably the Lombard textile towns and the wool centres of Flanders, such as Ghent, Bruges, and Ypres. By the mid-13th century, German expansion eastward had led to the growth of a thriving network of Baltic trading cities, including Lübeck, Hamburg, Danzig, and Riga.

The Seine was vital to the economy of Paris. Boats of all sizes delivered goods along the river and the fortified bridges carried a constant flow of traders.

Medieval Paris

From the 11th century, Paris benefited from the return of order and stability under the Capetian kings. Streets were paved, city walls enlarged and three 'divisions' of the city emerged; the merchants were based on the right bank of the Seine, the university (recognized in 1200) on the left bank, with civic and religious institutions on the Île de la Cité. In the 14th century, however, the city stagnated under the dual blows of the Black Death (*see pp.72–73*) and the Hundred Years' War; repeatedly fought over by the contending forces, it was beset by riots and civil disorder.

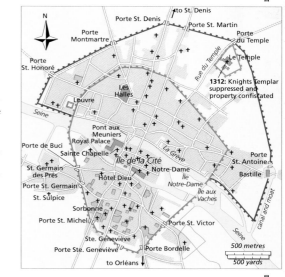

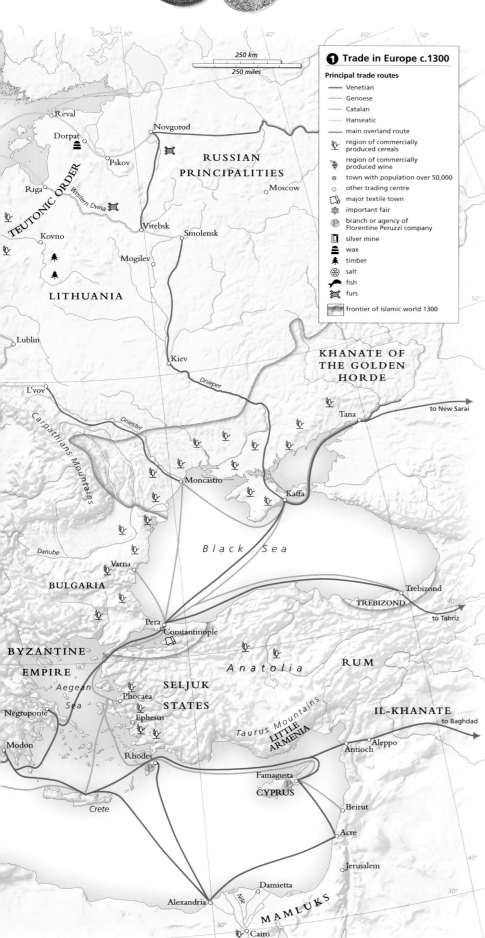

Medieval Venice

Venice was perceived as the symbolic centre of a liberal government and divinely ordered religious, civic, and commercial life. Its political focus was the Doge's Palace, residence of the elected Doge and centre of government. Since the city's wealth depended on maritime trade, the government maintained a vast shipyard – the Darsena – to build galleys for war and for merchant ventures.

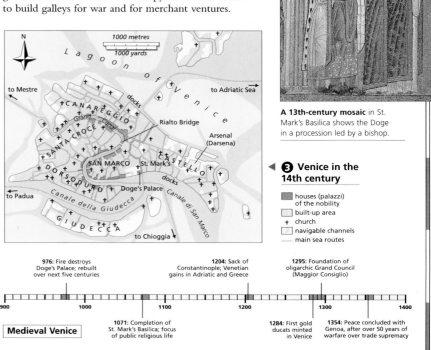

A 13th-century mosaic in St. Mark's Basilica shows the Doge in a procession led by a bishop.

THE EMERGENCE OF MODERN STATES

Joan of Arc (1412–31) led the French to a famous victory against the English at Orléans in 1429 during the Hundred Years' War.

THE MAP OF EUROPE was redrawn throughout the 15th century, as new nation states appeared. France emerged, bruised but victorious, from the Hundred Years' War, soon to become the model of a modern nation state. Newly-unified Spain vanquished the last Iberian outpost of Islam in 1492, emerging as a formidable power. The vast realm of Poland-Lithuania dominated Eastern Europe, while the Bohemians threw off imperial control. Feudal models of government were disappearing everywhere and monarchies increasingly relied on the endorsement of the 'estates', representative bodies of nobility, clergy, and the newly-emerging bourgeoisie. Commercial centres such as the Netherlands and Italy saw a flowering of humanist philosophy, science, literature, and art, known as the Renaissance.

The Hundred Years' War

Over a century of intermittent conflict between France and England (1337–1453) was precipitated by the English kings' possessions in France and their claims to the French throne. Six major royal expeditions to France, starting with Edward III's landing in Antwerp in 1338 and ending with the death of Henry V in 1422, were interspersed with skirmishes and provincial campaigns led by independent war parties. After many setbacks, the triumphs of Joan of Arc (1429–30) led to a resurgence of French confidence and ultimately to English defeat.

The skill of 10,000 English longbowmen proved the deciding factor against the French cavalry at the battle of Crécy in 1346.

▼ ❷ The Hundred Years' War after 1400

- → campaign of Henry V, 1415
- ⇢ campaign of Henry V, 1421–22
- ▨ held by England or Burgundy, 1429
- → campaign of Earl of Salisbury autumn 1428
- ▨ possessions of House of Burgundy 1429
- → campaign of Joan of Arc 1429
- ▨ under Burgundian control by 1453
- ▨ added to France 1477
- ▨ added to France 1481
- ▨ acquired or occupied by France temporarily, with dates
- — frontiers 1493

◀ ❶ The Hundred Years' War to 1400

- ▨ limit of lands held by England 1300
- ▨ held by England at outbreak of war 1338
- ▨ added at Treaty of Brétigny 1360
- ▨ under English influence at outbreak of war
- ⋯ remained under English control 1380
- → campaign of Edward III, 1339–40
- ⇢ campaign of Edward III, 1342
- ⇠ campaign of Edward III, 1346
- → campaign of Black Prince, 1355
- ⇢ campaign of Black Prince, 1356
- ⋯→ campaign of Edward III, 1359–60
- ▨ added to France gradually, 1301–16
- ▨ added to France 1349
- ▨ area of the *Jacquerie* 1358
- ▨ area affected by plundering of Great Companies 1360–66
- — frontiers 1380

1453: Calais is last English possession in France; held until 1558

May 1430: Joan of Arc captured by Burgundians

17 Jul 1429: Coronation of Charles VII

1422: Capture of Meaux secures northern France for Henry V

1428–29: Orléans besieged by English

French controlled area, 1429

The Hundred Years' War 1337–1453

1300	1350	1400	1450
1337: Philip VI of France confiscates Guyenne; Edward III claims kingdom of France	**1356:** English victory at Poitiers	**1360:** Treaty of Brétigny; peace lasts nine years, but bands of mercenaries, the Great Companies, ravage southeastern France	**1420:** Treaty of Troyes; Henry V marries Catherine of France	**1435:** Congress of Arras; Burgundy, an English ally, makes terms with France	**1450:** English lose Normandy
1346: English victory at Crécy	**1358:** Jacquerie: popular uprising against exploitation of countryside by soldiers	**1396:** 28-year truce agreed. Richard II marries Isabella of France	**1415:** Henry V invades France; English victory at Agincourt	**1429:** Joan of Arc relieves Orléans	**1453:** English lose Guyenne

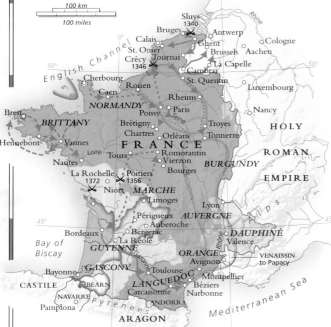

The *Reconquista*

The Christian reconquest of Moorish Spain began in earnest in the 11th century, led by the kingdoms of Navarre, Aragon, León-Castile, and Portugal. Despite strong Muslim counter-attacks, the Christians had reconquered all but the small kingdom of Granada by 1260. León-Castile now dominated Iberia, and Aragon acquired extensive possessions in the western Mediterranean. These kingdoms, united by the marriage of Ferdinand II of Aragon and Isabella of Castile, embarked on a final crusade, and Granada fell in 1492.

The Alhambra at Granada was built as a palace and fortress by the Moorish kings who ruled there until 1492. Following the expulsion of the Moors, much of the magnificent decoration was effaced or destroyed.

❸ The reconquest of Spain

- — limit of Umayyad Caliphate 732
- ▨ under Christian control by 1030
- → Almoravid campaigns 1080–1100
- ⊠ lands controlled by El Cid 1092
- ▨ under Christian control by 1100
- — frontier of Almoravid Empire 1115
- ▨ under Christian control by 1180
- — frontier of Almohad Empire 1180
- ▨ under Christian control by 1280
- ▨ under Christian control by 1492
- — frontiers 1493
- ⚔ Muslim victory with date
- ⚔ Christian victory with date
- → major campaigns of reconquest with date

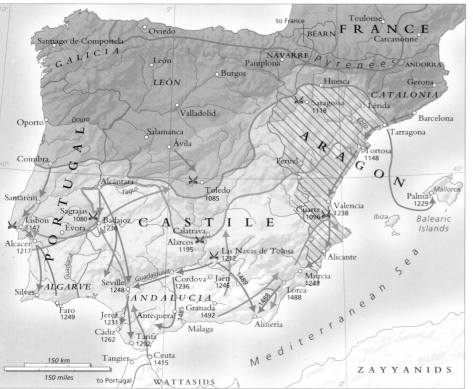

The *Reconquista*

1000	1100	1200	1300	1400	1500
	1085: Christian forces capture Toledo	**1094:** 'El Cid' takes Valencia	**1147:** Lisbon taken by Christians	**1248:** Seville falls to Christians	**1410:** Ferdinand, regent of Castile, takes Antequera; becomes king of Aragon	**1469:** Marriage of Ferdinand II and Isabella	**1492:** Capture of Granada
	1137: Union of Aragon and Catalonia	**1212:** Battle of Las Navas de Tolosa; defeat of Almohads	**1282:** Peter III of Aragon captures Sicily			**1479:** Union of Castile and Aragon

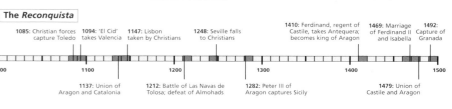

Central Europe in the 15th century

In Bohemia, the preachings of Jan Hus, which railed against the abuses of the clergy, were taken up by the Hussites, who called for a free Bohemia, and established a national Czech church. A new state in Bohemia was forged by Czech resistance to a series of bitter crusades launched by the Holy Roman Empire. The union of Poland and Lithuania in 1386 had created the largest realm in Christendom, its future secured by the defeat of the Teutonic Order in 1410. In the Holy Roman Empire, the Habsburgs sowed the seeds of future domination, acquiring, by treaty, marriage, and conquest, domains stretching from Austria and Styria to the Netherlands, and encompassing, from 1477, the lands of the Valois dukes of Burgundy.

The civil war initiated by the Hussites led to the deposing of Sigismund, king of Bohemia, who was forced to wage war on the Hussites on an almost annual basis until 1436. The picture *(left)* shows Hussite battle wagons drawn up in a defensive circle.

This coin was minted to honour Jan Hus, who was burnt at the stake for heresy in 1415.

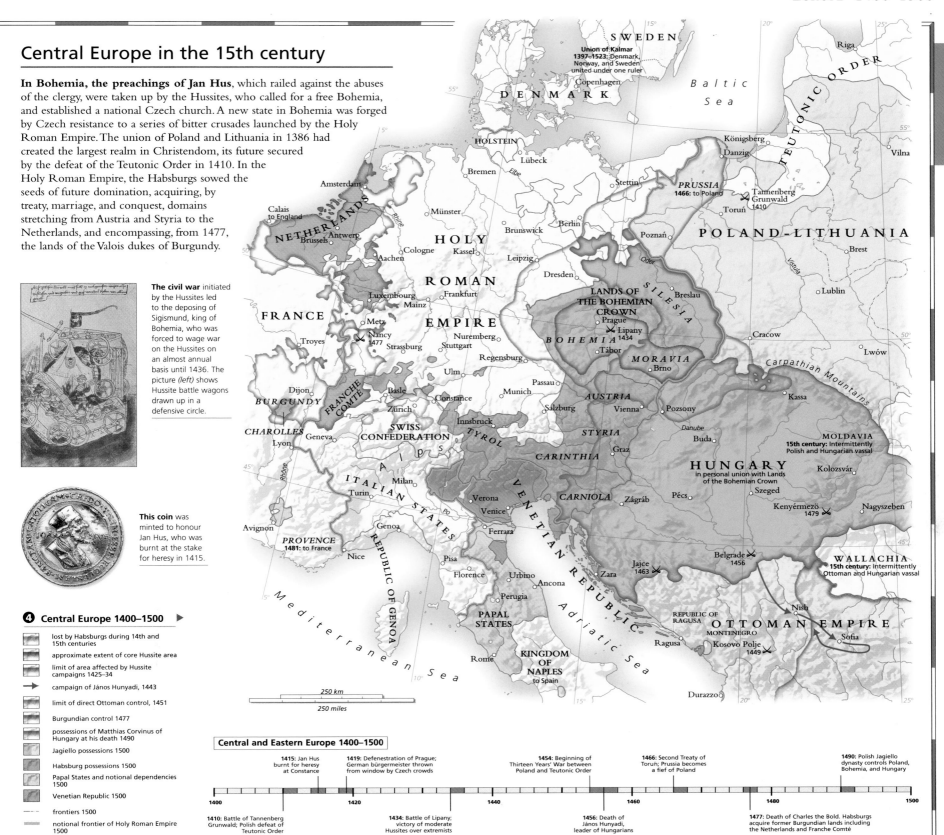

④ Central Europe 1400–1500 ▶

- lost by Habsburgs during 14th and 15th centuries
- approximate extent of core Hussite area
- limit of area affected by Hussite campaigns 1425–34
- → campaign of János Hunyadi, 1443
- limit of direct Ottoman control, 1451
- Burgundian control 1477
- possessions of Matthias Corvinus of Hungary at his death 1490
- Jagiello possessions 1500
- Habsburg possessions 1500
- Papal States and notional dependencies 1500
- Venetian Republic 1500
- ----- frontiers 1500
- notional frontier of Holy Roman Empire 1500

Central and Eastern Europe 1400–1500

1415: Jan Hus burnt for heresy at Constance	**1419:** Defenestration of Prague; German bürgermeister thrown from window by Czech crowds	**1454:** Beginning of Thirteen Years' War between Poland and Teutonic Order	**1466:** Second Treaty of Toruń; Prussia becomes a fief of Poland	**1490:** Polish Jagiello dynasty controls Poland, Bohemia, and Hungary
1400	1420	1440	1460	1480	1500
1410: Battle of Tannenberg Grunwald; Polish defeat of Teutonic Order	**1434:** Battle of Lipany; victory of moderate Hussites over extremists		**1456:** Death of János Hunyadi, leader of Hungarians	**1477:** Death of Charles the Bold. Habsburgs acquire former Burgundian lands including the Netherlands and Franche Comté	

The formation of Switzerland

The forest cantons of Switzerland were strategically placed to control vital Alpine passes, the route for pilgrims and merchants travelling between Italy and northern Europe. Increasingly, they resented attempts by their powerful neighbours to exert political control. In 1291, a union was formed by Uri, Schwyz, and Unterwalden, later joined by other cantons and cities, to defend a growing autonomy. The Swiss, in their conflicts with the Habsburgs and Burgundy, gained a formidable military reputation.

Victory in the Swabian War by 1499 brought *de facto* independence from the Empire. Membership of the Union continued to expand until the 16th century.

At the battle of Morgarten in 1315, a Swiss peasant army was able to defeat a Habsburg attack led by Leopold I of Austria and an army of knights.

The formation of Switzerland

1291: Union of Uri, Schwyz, and Unterwalden	**1332:** Luzern joins Union	**1476:** Battles of Grandson and Morat against Charles the Bold of Burgundy	**1499:** Swiss victory in Swabian War
1300	1400		1500
1315: Battle of Morgarten; defeat of Habsburgs	**1352:** Berne joins Union	**1386:** Habsburg emperor, Leopold III defeated and killed at Sempach	**1477:** Battle of Nancy; Charles the Bold killed

▲ ⑤ The growth of the Swiss Confederation

- first three cantons 1291
- added to Swiss Confederation by 1501
- added further by 1579
- frontier of Switzerland 1579
- ---- frontiers 1815

The growth of Hungary

Following the ravages of the Mongol campaigns of 1241, which reduced the population in some areas by up to 60%, a succession of Angevin and German princes were elected to the Hungarian throne. The growing threat from the Ottomans, who had taken Constantinople in 1453, precipitated a revolt led by János Hunyadi. In 1458 he secured the throne for his son, Matthias Corvinus (1458–90), who subsequently achieved many notable military successes against the Ottoman Turks.

Matthias Corvinus brought many of the ideas of the Renaissance to the business of government, simplifying the administration and laws. However, his subjects bore a heavy tax burden, partly to finance his huge standing army which was kept in readiness for campaigns against the Ottomans and other foreign adversaries.

THE AGE OF THE REFORMATION

Martin Luther's questioning of the doctrine and practice of Christianity led to the creation of the Protestant faith.

A SERIES OF PROFOUND CHANGES in theological doctrine and practice were to have violent political consequences in 16th-century Europe. The religious reformation, spearheaded by Martin Luther in 1517, divided much of the continent along religious lines, precipitating a series of wars which permanently sapped the strength of the Catholic Habsburg Empire. In northern Europe, new nations came to prominence; Sweden, Russia, and Denmark struggled for control of the Baltic, while in the Netherlands, a rising against the Catholic rule of Spain led to the independence of the Calvinist north. In the east, the expansion of the Ottoman Empire brought Christian Europe into conflict with Islam; the Turks exploited European disunity, penetrating as far as Vienna.

❶ The struggle for supremacy in Europe 1493–1551

- Habsburg possessions 1493
- added by 1551
- held temporarily, with details
- France 1493
- added by 1551, with date
- Bishoprics of Metz, Nancy, and Toul, to France 1552
- held temporarily 1499–1512
- held temporarily with date
- occupied by France 1536–39
- frontiers 1551
- frontier of Holy Roman Empire 1551

The Reformation

The spiritual complacency, material wealth, and abuses of power of the Roman Catholic church provoked a revolution in Christianity, inspired by the teachings of Martin Luther (1483–1546). His reformed theology, with its emphasis on study of the Bible, spread rapidly through northern Europe. Some opportunistic rulers, such as Henry VIII of England, embraced 'Protestant' forms of religion in order to seize church lands. By 1570, Protestantism prevailed over much of central and northern Europe. In 1547, the Catholic Church summoned the Council of Trent, which reaffirmed fundamental doctrine, but condemned the worst clerical abuses.

The Habsburg defeat of France at the battle of Pavia in 1525 is here commemorated in a contemporary tapestry. Even though Francis I of France was captured by the Spanish, the French finally abandoned their claim to Italy at the Treaty of Cateau-Cambrésis in 1559.

The Habsburgs and France

Charles V, Emperor from 1519–56, ruled Spain, Flanders, and much of Italy as well as the Habsburg lands of central Europe. He was opposed by the German princes, especially the Protestant ones, and Francis I and Henry II of France, who pursued the claims of their predecessors to Italy. Constant wars wasted many lives and much money, but gained nothing. In 1556, Charles V abdicated, dividing his empire between his brother and his son.

French-Habsburg rivalry 1515–59

1519: Charles V elected German Emperor
1525: Francis I captured at Pavia
1529: Francis I signs Treaty of Cambrai, abandoning his ambitions in Italy
1559: Henry II accepts Treaty of Cateau-Cambrésis; Habsburgs victorious

1510 — 1520 — 1530 — 1540 — 1550 — 1560

1515: Francis I invades nothern Italy; defeats Swiss at Marignano
1521: War between Francis I of France and Charles V
1543: Francis attacks Charles V in Netherlands and northern Spain
1552: Francis' successor, Henry II, forces Charles to abandon Siege of Metz (truce in 1556)

St. Ignatius Loyola founded the Society of Jesus in 1534 to champion the Catholic Counter-Reformation. Highly-educated and assertively evangelical, the Jesuits took Catholic teachings to territory throughout the rapidly expanding Spanish Empire.

The Reformation in Europe 1517–55

1529: At Diet of Speyer, Charles V attempts to reach compromise with Lutheran princes
1535: John Calvin formulates doctrine of predestination in Geneva
1545: Start of Council of Trent, which defines modern Catholicism

1510 — 1520 — 1530 — 1540 — 1550 — 1560

1517: Martin Luther posts 95 Theses condemning abuses of Catholic church at Wittenberg
1532: Henry VIII of England declares himself head of Church of England
1555: At Peace of Augsburg; Lutheran princes win right to choose their religion

❷ The religious map of Europe 1590 ▶

- almost exclusively Catholic, with just minimal Protestant presence in northern areas
- overwhelmingly Catholic, with appreciable Protestant minority
- Catholic majority, but with very strong Protestant minority
- exclusively or overwhelmingly Protestant, with only slight Catholic presence in places
- Protestant majority, with some Catholic presence
- mainly Catholic, with strong Greek Orthodox presence
- Greek Orthodox, with significant Muslim presence in some areas of the Balkans
- Muslim majority
- frontiers 1590
- frontier of Holy Roman Empire 1590

Calvinist locally dominant Protestant denomination

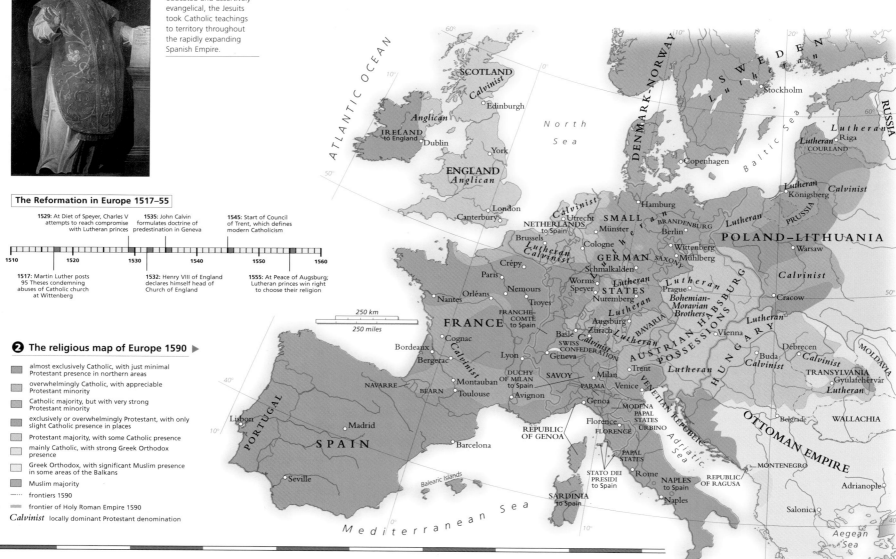

Conflict in the Baltic 1500–1595

The collapse of the Union of Kalmar, which bound Sweden, Denmark, and Norway together, in 1523, precipitated a century of warfare around the Baltic Sea, bringing the growing power of Sweden into conflict with Russia and Denmark, which controlled the narrow outlet to the North Sea, vital for Swedish trade interests. The Reformation had led to the collapse of crusading orders, such as the Teutonic Knights, opening up Livonia to the ambitions of Russia, Sweden, and Poland-Lithuania.

Ivan Vasilievich, Tsar of Russia from 1547 to 1584, was known as 'the Terrible' for his drastic reforming of the hereditary aristocracy. Although his wars with Sweden and Poland were largely unsuccessful, he was able to expand the Russian Empire to include non-Slav states.

❸ **The Baltic in the 16th century**

- area controlled by Teutonic Order 1450
- Poland-Lithuania and dependent territory 1558
- added to Poland by 1585, with date
- added to Sweden by 1583, with date
- to Sweden 1583–95
- Danish control 1558
- added to Denmark 1573
- possessions of Prince Magnus of Holstein 1564
- ▲▲ deepest advance of Russian forces into Livonia at various times during 1558–73
- to Russia 1563–70
- → campaigns of Polish King István Báthory 1579, 1580, 1581
- — frontier of Holy Roman Empire
- --- frontiers 1595

1561: Collapse of Teutonic Order in Livonia; region partitioned into Russian, Swedish, and Polish-Lithuanian spheres of interest

1567: Swedes take Oslo from Danes

1581: Swedes recapture Estonia

1582: Ivan IV forced to conclude peace with King István Báthory of Poland, after the latter's successful campaigns against Russia

1563: Denmark and Sweden go to war. Gothenburg (Sweden's sole outlet to North Sea) falls to Danes

1576: Ivan IV of Russia conquers most of Livonia, but his army is crushed by Polish-Swedish alliance at Wenden (1578)

1595: Treaty of Teusina: Russia renounces all claim to Estonia

| 1550 | 1560 | 1570 | 1580 | 1590 | 1600 |

Conflict in the Baltic 1500–1582

The expansion of Ottoman power

By 1500, the Ottomans controlled the lands to the south and west of the Black Sea. With the accession of Suleyman I – 'the Magnificent' – (1520–66), they turned their attention to Europe, increasing naval pressure on the eastern Mediterranean, and pushing northward into Moldavia, the Danube valley, and Hungary. In 1529, they were turned back after their unsuccessful siege of Vienna, but continued to maintain their pressure on the frontier of the Habsburg Empire, exploiting conflict in Europe by forming alliances with France against the Habsburgs, and gaining control of Transylvania in 1562.

This detail from an Italian manuscript records the victory of Habsburg forces over the Ottomans at the siege of Vienna in 1529. The illumination is one of a series entitled 'Triumphs of Charles V'.

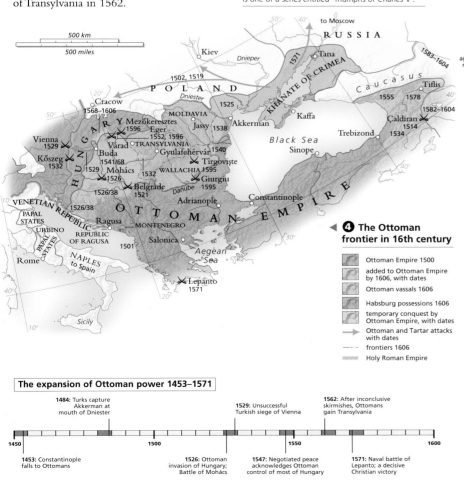

◄ ❹ **The Ottoman frontier in 16th century**

- Ottoman Empire 1500
- added to Ottoman Empire by 1606, with dates
- Ottoman vassals 1606
- Habsburg possessions 1606
- temporary conquest by Ottoman Empire, with dates
- → Ottoman and Tartar attacks with dates
- --- frontiers 1606
- — Holy Roman Empire

The expansion of Ottoman power 1453–1571

1484: Turks capture Akkerman at mouth of Dniester

1529: Unsuccessful Turkish siege of Vienna

1562: After inconclusive skirmishes, Ottomans gain Transylvania

| 1450 | 1500 | 1550 | 1600 |

1453: Constantinople falls to Ottomans

1526: Ottoman invasion of Hungary; Battle of Mohács

1547: Negotiated peace acknowledges Ottoman control of most of Hungary

1571: Naval battle of Lepanto; a decisive Christian victory

The Dutch Revolt

Philip II of Spain, a fierce champion of the Roman Catholic cause, was determined to suppress Calvinism in the Netherlands. He reacted harshly to demands by Dutch nobles for autonomy and religious freedom, and his reprisals, combined with onerous taxes, led to a general revolt under the leadership of William of Nassau, which the Spanish could not quell. In 1579, ten southern Catholic provinces were promised liberty; in reply, seven Calvinist northern provinces formed the Union of Utrecht. In a 1609 truce, their independence was conceded by Spain.

The Sea Beggars were Dutch rebels who took to the sea to combat the Spanish from foreign ports. In 1572, they mounted a successful attack on the fortress of Brill in southern Holland (above), encouraging Holland and Zeeland to join the revolt.

The Dutch Revolt 1565–1609

1568–72: Raids by Dutch 'Sea Beggars' on Spanish naval transports and bases

1574: Dutch capture Middelburg and force Spanish to retreat from siege of Leiden

1585: The Duke of Parma captures rebel town of Antwerp. English intervene on side of rebels

1600: Victory of United Provinces at Nieuwpoort

1609: 12-year truce negotiated with Spanish

| 1560 | 1570 | 1580 | 1590 | 1600 | 1610 |

1566: Riots in Netherlands against Philip II's unpopular religious and fiscal policies

1576: Unpaid Spanish army mutinies in Antwerp and sacks city

1579: Catholic nobility in the south sign Treaty of Arras with Philip II

1590: Dutch rebels make major gains in northeast

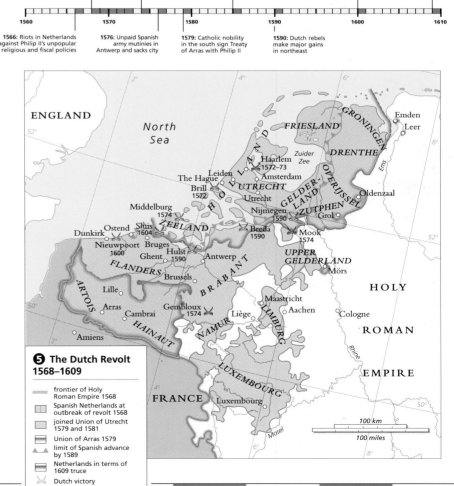

❺ **The Dutch Revolt 1568–1609**

- --- frontier of Holy Roman Empire 1568
- Spanish Netherlands at outbreak of revolt 1568
- joined Union of Utrecht 1579 and 1581
- Union of Arras 1579
- ▲▲ limit of Spanish advance by 1589
- Netherlands in terms of 1609 truce
- ✕ Dutch victory
- ✕ Spanish victory

EARLY MODERN EUROPE

Cardinal Richelieu, was Louis XIII's chief minister and the architect of royal absolutism in France.

IN THE 17TH CENTURY, following years of destructive warfare, the modern European state system began to evolve. States were ruled centrally by autocratic (or absolutist) monarchs and bounded by clear, militarily secure frontiers. The Thirty Years' War laid waste large parts of central Europe, causing a decline in population from some 21 million in 1618 to 13 million in 1648. Under Louis XIV, France was involved in four costly wars, but emerged as the leading nation in Europe, eclipsing Spain which entered a long period of decline. After a period of expansion under the Vasa kings, Sweden lost much of its Baltic empire by 1721. The Ottoman Turks struck once again at the heart of Europe, but were met by an increasingly powerful Austria, whose main rival in the region was Russia.

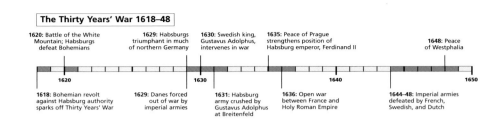

The Thirty Years' War 1618–48

| 1620: Battle of the White Mountain; Habsburgs defeat Bohemians | 1629: Habsburgs triumphant in much of northern Germany | 1630: Swedish king, Gustavus Adolphus, intervenes in war | 1635: Peace of Prague strengthens position of Habsburg emperor, Ferdinand II | 1648: Peace of Westphalia |

1618: Bohemian revolt against Habsburg authority sparks off Thirty Years' War — 1629: Danes forced out of war by imperial armies — 1631: Habsburg army crushed by Gustavus Adolphus at Breitenfeld — 1636: Open war between France and Holy Roman Empire — 1644–48: Imperial armies defeated by French, Swedish, and Dutch

The Thirty Years' War

The Thirty Years' War provoked great advances in methods of mass destruction, and involved an unprecedented number of soldiers, over a million of whom died before it ceased. Much of Germany was devastated, towns were sacked, and their inhabitants raped and murdered.

The Thirty Years' War saw Protestant-Catholic rivalry and German constitutional issues subsumed in a wider European struggle. Habsburg attempts to control Bohemia and crush Protestantism coincided with the breakdown of constitutional mechanisms for resolving conflict in the Holy Roman Empire. Spain intervened to secure supply lines to the Netherlands; Danish and Swedish involvement followed as they competed for control of the Baltic. Fear of imperial absolutism, prompted by Austrian Habsburg victories in 1621 and 1634–35, led France to intervene in 1635 in support of Sweden. Prolonged negotiations from 1643 culminated in the Treaty of Westphalia which fused attempts to secure peace in Europe with curbs on the emperor's authority in Germany.

❶ The Treaty of Westphalia, 1648

- Austrian Habsburg possessions
- Spanish Habsburg possessions
- Brandenburg possessions
- Danish possessions
- Swedish possessions
- Church lands
- ○ electorate
- boundary of Holy Roman Empire, 1648
- frontiers 1648
- ✗ major battle of Thirty Years' War

Political consolidation and resistance

European states were transformed in a process of internal political centralization and external consolidation. The legitimacy of these developments was often questioned, leading to civil wars and popular resistance. Foreign intervention turned local disputes into international conflicts, as in the Thirty Years' War. In western Europe, Spain's dominant position was broken by Portuguese and Dutch independence. The two rising powers in the region, France and England, developed in very different ways. In France, Louis XIV assumed absolute power, whereas in England, Charles I was arrested and executed for disregarding parliament, and although the English monarchy was restored, its powers were drastically curbed.

❷ Political consolidation and resistance in 17th-century Europe

- Austrian Habsburg possessions 1683
- Spanish Habsburg possessions 1683
- ⚔ civil war or widespread disturbance
- ⚑ local revolt or unrest
- ○ civic autonomy suppressed by territorial rulers
- frontiers 1683
- Holy Roman empire 1683

Expansionist tendencies
- → Sweden
- → Russia
- → England
- → Ottoman Empire
- → Austrian Habsburgs
- → France
- → United Provinces

The union of Spain and Portugal was ended in 1640 when the native House of Braganza led a nationalist revolt. The relief of the siege of the frontier town of Elvas during the War of Independence is depicted in a Portuguese tile painting *(above)*.

As one of the leading generals of the parliamentary army, Oliver Cromwell *(left)* played a decisive role in the English Civil War. After the execution of Charles I, he quelled the Royalists in Scotland and Ireland. Dissolving the 'Rump' Parliament, he became Lord Protector of the Commonwealth.

Civil wars and revolts 1625–65

| 1628–29: Siege of Protestant stronghold of La Rochelle | 1640: Portugal declares independence from Spain | 1649: Execution of Charles I of England | 1660: Restoration of English monarchy |

1640: Catalan Revolt

1640: Civil War breaks out in England — 1648–53: The Fronde: resistance to royal authority throughout France

❸ The Swedish Empire 1560–1721

- Sweden at the death of Gustavus Vasa 1560
- conquests by 1645
- conquests by 1658
- temporary Swedish acquisitions, with dates
- Russian gains from Sweden by treaty of Nystad, 1721
- → Swedish campaigns
- → Russians campaigns under Peter the Great
- trade routes
- frontiers, 1658

Habsburg–Ottoman conflict 1663–1718

In the mid-17th century, the Ottoman Empire resumed its expansion into southeastern Europe. Austrian attempts to challenge the Ottomans' control of Transylvania led to full-scale war in 1663. The Turkish advance on Vienna in 1664 was halted, but in 1683 the Turks besieged the city. The siege failed, and by 1687 the war had become a Habsburg war of conquest. The acquisition of Transylvania and Turkish Hungary transformed Austria into a great European power and loosened its traditional ties to the Holy Roman Empire.

In 1683 the Ottomans began their greatest onslaught on the Habsburg Empire by besieging Vienna with a huge army. Poland and the Papacy joined the German princes in an international relief effort which ended in Ottoman defeat.

Habsburg-Ottoman wars 1663–1718

- 1672: Greatest extent of Ottoman Empire
- 1699: Peace of Karlowitz confirms Austrian conquests
- 1716–18: Further Austrian victories, including capture of Belgrade
- 1664: Turkish advance on Vienna turned back at battle of St. Gotthard
- 1683: Siege of Vienna starts Great Turkish War

Sweden, Russia, and the Baltic

The 17th century witnessed the phenomenal growth of Sweden as an imperial power: by defeating regional rivals Denmark, Poland and Russia, it had, by 1648 established a Baltic empire, the high point of which was reached during the reign of Charles X (1654–60). Lacking indigenous resources, however, Sweden's strength rested on its control of strategic harbours and customs points along the Baltic shore. Defence of these positions forced Sweden into a series of costly wars from 1655. After the Great Northern War, much of the empire was lost to the rising powers of Russia, Prussia and Hanover.

Founded in 1703 by Peter the Great, St. Petersburg was modelled on European cities, its classical architecture and orderly street grid symbolizing the Tsar's westernizing policies.

The rise and fall of the Swedish Empire

- 1629: Sweden gains Livonia
- 1643: Sweden invades Denmark
- 1654: Start of reign of Charles X
- 1658: Peace of Roskilde; Denmark loses southern Sweden
- 1700: Great Northern War
- 1721: Peace of Nystad; Sweden cedes Ingria, Livonia, and Karelia to Russia
- 1632: Gustavus Adolphus dies at victorious battle of Lützen
- 1648: Substantial Swedish gains confirmed by Treaty of Westphalia
- 1675: Brandenburg defeats Sweden at Fehrbellin
- 1709: Charles XII's attempt to invade Russia halted at Poltava

❹ The Ottoman frontier 1683–1739

- Ottoman Empire 1683
- Habsburg possessions 1683
- Venetian Republic 1683
- Russia 1683
- Habsburg gains, with date
- temporary Habsburg gains, 1718–39
- aquired by Russia 1739
- Venetian gains 1699
- Habsburg-Ottoman frontier 1718
- ✕ Habsburg victory
- frontiers 1683
- Holy Roman Empire border

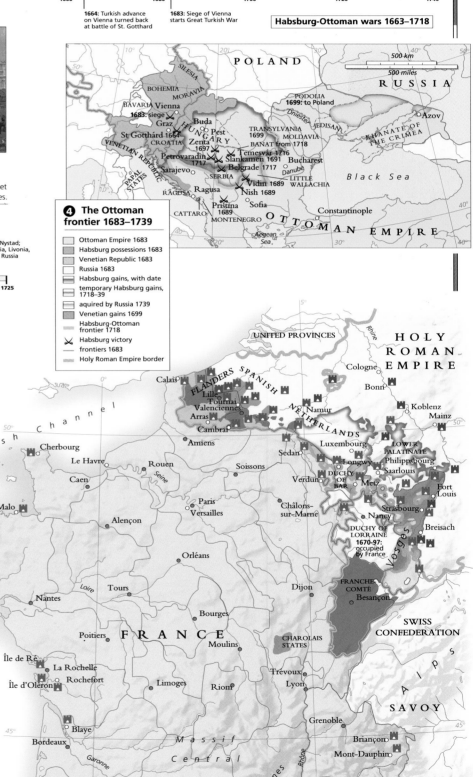

The French state under Louis XIV, 1660–1715

Under Louis XIV, France pursued an expansionist, anti-Spanish policy. The expense of maintaining a large army and building a ring of frontier fortresses was met by administrative reforms, and tax-collection in the provinces was overseen by royal officials *(intendants)*. In 1667–68 Louis' armies secured parts of the Spanish Netherlands. Although this provoked international opposition to French aggression, further gains were made in the Dutch War (1672–79). The occupation of various territories in 1679–84 (known as the *Réunions*) rationalized France's eastern frontier, but after defeat in the Nine Years' War (1688–97), most of these had to be given up. The War of the Spanish Succession (1701–14) brought France no further gains.

A ring of defensive fortresses was built by Vauban, a great military engineer, to secure French territory.

During his long reign, Louis XIV (left) established France as cultural and political leader of Europe.

The growth of France under Louis XIV

- 1667–68: France acquires parts of Flanders from Spain
- 1679–84: *Réunions*: annexation of territory west of the Rhine
- 1701–14: War of the Spanish Succession
- 1661: Louis XIV assumes personal rule
- 1672–79: Dutch War brings significant territorial gains
- 1688–97: Nine Years' War: Peace of Ryswick (Rijswijk) partially reverses the *Réunions*
- 1715: Death of Louis XIV

❺ France 1648–1715

- France 1648
- frontier of Holy Roman Empire 1648
- French frontier 1713/14
- administrative regions under Louis XIV *(intendances or généralités)*
- French gains confirmed 1659
- French gains confirmed 1661
- French gains confirmed 1668
- French gains confirmed 1678–79
- areas temporarily annexed under the *Réunions*, 1684–97
- further French gains by 1697
- ⌂ Vauban fortress
- ⌂ fortified town
- ⌂ barrier fortress
- ● administrative centre

THE AGE OF ENLIGHTENMENT

Catherine the Great ruled the Russian Empire as an enlightened despot from 1762 to 1796.

THE 18TH CENTURY was a period of relative stability, when well-established monarchies ruled most of Europe and almost all the land was controlled by the nobility or the state. The Russian Empire and Prussia became leading powers. The rest of Germany remained a jigsaw of small states, as did Italy, while Poland was swallowed up by its powerful neighbours. Improved methods of cultivation fed Europe's escalating populations; towns and cities increased in size and number; trade and industry expanded to reach global markets; philosophy, science, and the arts flourished. Intellectual curiosity encouraged the radical political theories of the 'Enlightenment', but alarmed reaction set in when the flag of liberty was raised in France in the last decade of the century. Though ultimately unsuccessful, the French Revolution would inspire many social and political reforms in the 19th century.

Cities and economic life 1700–1800

Despite the beginnings of industrialization in the 18th century, principally in textile production, in 1800 four out of five Europeans still depended on agriculture for their livelihood. The growing population – largely due to a fall in the death rate as a result of better health and hygiene – led to a rapid increase in the size of cities; in 1700 Europe had ten cities with over 100,000 inhabitants; by 1800 there were 17. At the same time, farmers adopted a more scientific approach to agriculture, introducing new, more productive crops and livestock. A general improvement in transport by sea, road, river, and canal greatly stimulated trade throughout Europe and, as colonialism developed, with the rest of the world.

Thomas Coke of Holkham, Norfolk was known as 'the father of experimental farms'. He pioneered new agricultural techniques and developed breeds of sheep, pigs, and cows that gave higher wool, meat, and milk yields.

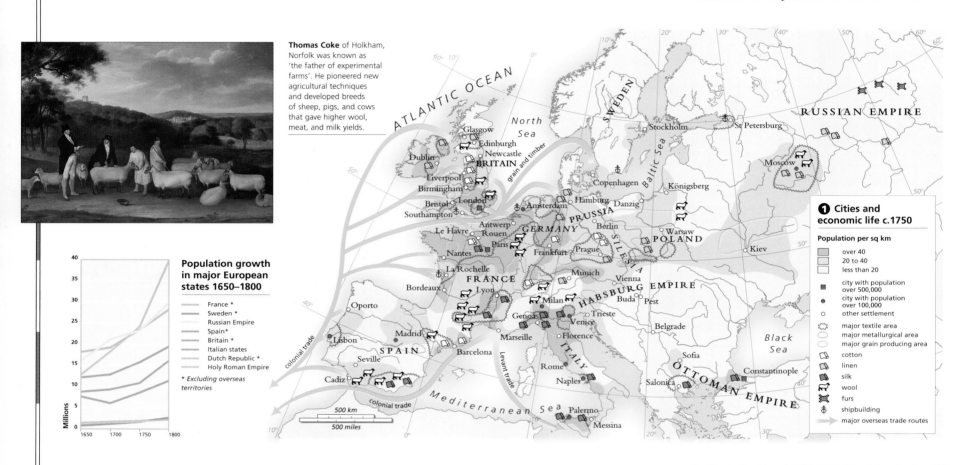

① Cities and economic life c.1750

Population per sq km
- over 40
- 20 to 40
- less than 20

- ■ city with population over 500,000
- ● city with population over 100,000
- ○ other settlement

- major textile area
- major metallurgical area
- major grain producing area

- cotton
- linen
- silk
- wool
- furs
- shipbuilding

➝ major overseas trade routes

Population growth in major European states 1650–1800

- France *
- Sweden *
- Russian Empire
- Spain *
- Britain *
- Italian states
- Dutch Republic *
- Holy Roman Empire

* Excluding overseas territories

The partitions of Poland

17th-century Poland was one of Europe's largest states, but suffered frequent territorial losses to its neighbours, especially Russia. The elective monarchy allowed foreign powers to interfere in Polish affairs, and in the late 18th century the Russians, the Habsburgs, and Prussia settled their differences at Poland's expense in three partitions which removed the country from the map.

◀ ② The partitions of Poland 1772–95

- frontier of Poland in 1699

Partition of Poland in 1772
- to Prussia
- to Russian Empire
- to Habsburg Empire

Partition of Poland in 1793
- to Prussia
- to Russian Empire

Partition of Poland in 1795
- to Prussia
- to Russian Empire
- to Habsburg Empire
- frontiers in 1795

The decline of Poland 1550–1795

1569: Poland united with Lithuania	1660: East Prussia gains independence from Poland	1697: Start of rule by Electors of Saxony	1772: First partition of Poland	1795: Third partition

1629: Sweden acquires Livonia	1667: Russia acquires East Ukraine	1764: Russia secures Polish crown for Stanislas Poniatowski	1793: Second partition

THE ENLIGHTENMENT

The 18th-century 'enlightened' writers, or *philosophes*, such as Voltaire and Diderot, appealed to human reason to challenge traditional assumptions about the Church, state, monarchy, education, and social institutions. 'Man is born free, but everywhere he is in chains', wrote Jean-Jacques Rousseau in his *Social Contract* (1762), in which he sought to show how a democratic society could work.

Voltaire (1694–1778) used poetry, drama, and satire to express his political views, including his opposition to the Catholic church. His radicalism often led to periods of exile from his native France.

Published in 28 volumes from 1751–72, the *Encyclopédie* spread the philosophic and scientific ideas of the Enlightenment. It gave a comprehensive account of contemporary institutions and technologies, while fine engravings illustrated the work of all kinds of craftsmen, such as the instrument makers above.

The rise of Brandenburg Prussia

After the Peace of Westphalia in 1648, Germany consisted of some 300 small principalities, some Catholic, some Protestant. By the end of the 17th century Brandenburg was the dominant Protestant state. Frederick William (the 'Great Elector'), gained full sovereignty in Prussia and created a powerful state with a huge standing army. With the accession of Frederick II (the 'Great') in 1740, expansion continued, including the acquisition of Silesia from the Habsburg Empire. With additional territory from the partitions of Poland, by the end of the century Prussia had become one of Europe's Great Powers.

❸ The rise of Brandenburg Prussia 1648–1795

- Brandenburg in 1648
- acquisitions 1648–1707
- area held 1713–42
- acquisitions 1715–20
- acquisitions by Frederick the Great 1740–86
- temporary acquisitions by Frederick the Great 1740–86
- acquisitions from Poland 1793
- acquisitions from Poland 1795
- Habsburg possessions in 1795
- frontier of Holy Roman Empire, 1789

200 km / 200 miles

These splendidly uniformed cavalry officers are representative of the highly-disciplined and efficient army which, by 1763, enabled Prussia to emerge as the dominant military force in 18th-century Europe.

The growth of Prussia in the 18th century

- **1713:** Accession of Frederick William I, King of Prussia
- **1713:** Treaty of Utrecht: Prussia gains Upper Gelderland and Neuchâtel
- **1715:** Prussia takes Stralsund in Great North War against Sweden
- **1720:** Treaty of Stockholm gives part of Western Pomerania to Prussia
- **1740:** Accession of Frederick II (the 'Great')
- **1740–48:** War of the Austrian Succession
- **1742:** Frederick completes rapid conquest of Silesia
- **1756–63:** Seven Years' War: Prussia faces coalition of Austria, Russia, and France
- **1760:** Austrian and Russian troops occupy Berlin, but Prussia survives
- **1763:** Treaty of Hubertusburg allows Prussia to keep Silesia
- **1772:** First partition of Poland; Prussian lands in the east now linked to Brandenburg
- **1786:** Death of Frederick the Great
- **1793:** Second partition of Poland
- **1795:** Third partition of Poland

1700 — 1740 — 1760 — 1780 — 1800

The French Revolution 1789–95

In May 1789, a political crisis forced Louis XVI to summon the Estates-General, a parliament of nobles, clergy, and commoners. The third estate (the commoners) demanded reform and declared itself a National Assembly. Noble and clerical privileges were abolished; provincial uprisings were directed against landowners, many of whom fled into exile. In 1792 the Revolution gathered momentum: Louis was imprisoned, the monarchy abolished, and France declared a republic. Mass conscription was introduced to meet the threat of invasion by Austria and Prussia and the king was executed. Power shifted to the radical Jacobins, who ruled by means of 'the Terror', executing all 'enemies of the people'. Many regions opposed these excesses, notably the Vendée in the west, but resistance was crushed. In 1794 the Jacobins shared the fate of their victims. France, however, had been saved from invasion and there followed a period of moderate rule – the Directory.

Although France's political crisis had begun a year earlier, the storming of the Bastille by a Paris mob on 14 July 1789 signalled the true start of the French Revolution. Chosen by the mob as a symbol of repression, the fall of the ancient prison demonstrated the power of the people to force change.

❹ The French Revolution 1789–95

- French territory 1789
- Vendée uprising 1793
- other areas of counter-revolutionary resistance 1792–99
- centre of revolution 1789
- centre of Federalist revolt 1793–94
- centre of execution
- **300** numbers executed by revolutionaries
- émigré centre

War of the First Coalition
- French victory
- French defeat
- offensives by French forces against Allies 1792–94
- offensives by Allies 1792–94
- territories annexed by France 1789–97

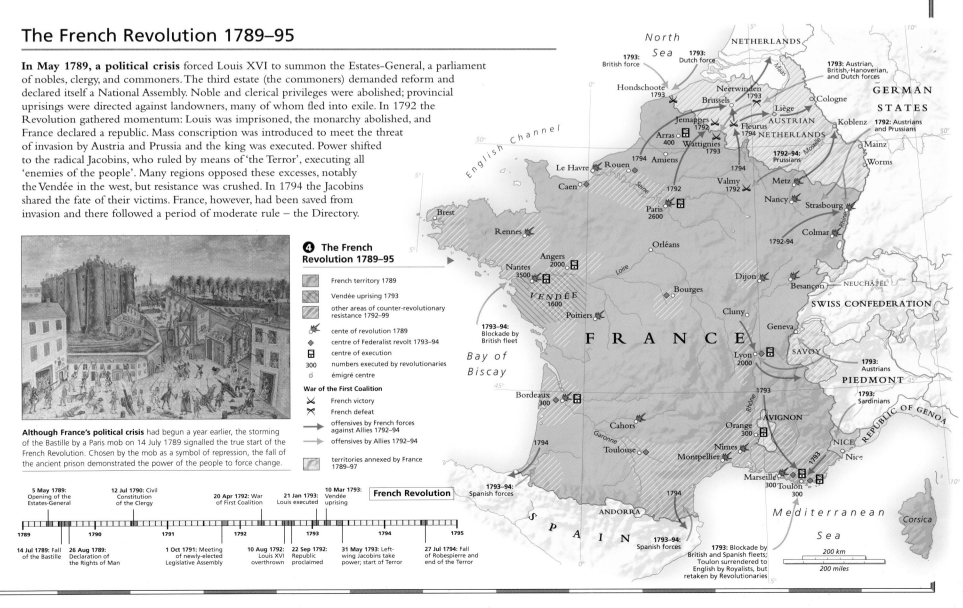

French Revolution

- **5 May 1789:** Opening of the Estates-General
- **14 Jul 1789:** Fall of the Bastille
- **26 Aug 1789:** Declaration of the Rights of Man
- **12 Jul 1790:** Civil Constitution of the Clergy
- **1 Oct 1791:** Meeting of newly-elected Legislative Assembly
- **20 Apr 1792:** War of First Coalition
- **10 Aug 1792:** Louis XVI overthrown
- **21 Jan 1793:** Louis executed
- **22 Sep 1792:** Republic proclaimed
- **10 Mar 1793:** Vendée uprising
- **31 May 1793:** Left-wing Jacobins take power; start of Terror
- **27 Jul 1794:** Fall of Robespierre and end of the Terror

1789 — 1790 — 1791 — 1792 — 1793 — 1794 — 1795

NAPOLEONIC EUROPE

THE BRILLIANT REVOLUTIONARY GENERAL, Napoleon Bonaparte, returned from his Egyptian campaign in 1799 to stage a *coup d'état* which made him ruler of France as First Consul. During the Consulate he began reforms of the administration, the legal system, the Church, and education. In 1804, just over ten years after revolutionaries had executed Louis XVI, Napoleon took the title of emperor and began to create a dynasty, members of his family being given the crowns of conquered states. His imperial ambitions were ultimately thwarted by Britain: its navy was used to blockade France and overrun French colonies, while a series of alliances completed an encirclement that contained and gradually reduced Napoleon's empire.

The Code Napoléon of 1804, the first modern law code, embraced many of the principles of the French Revolution.

The battle of Eylau in 1807 was fought in a blizzard, with the French heavily outnumbered and outgunned by the Russians. Though both sides claimed victory, the French lost more men. For the first time in his career, Napoleon had failed to win a major battle.

In this cartoon of 1812, Napoleon tries desperately to bridge the 2000 miles between Madrid and Moscow. The impossibility of personally masterminding both the Peninsular campaign in Spain and Portugal and the Russian campaign led to his downfall.

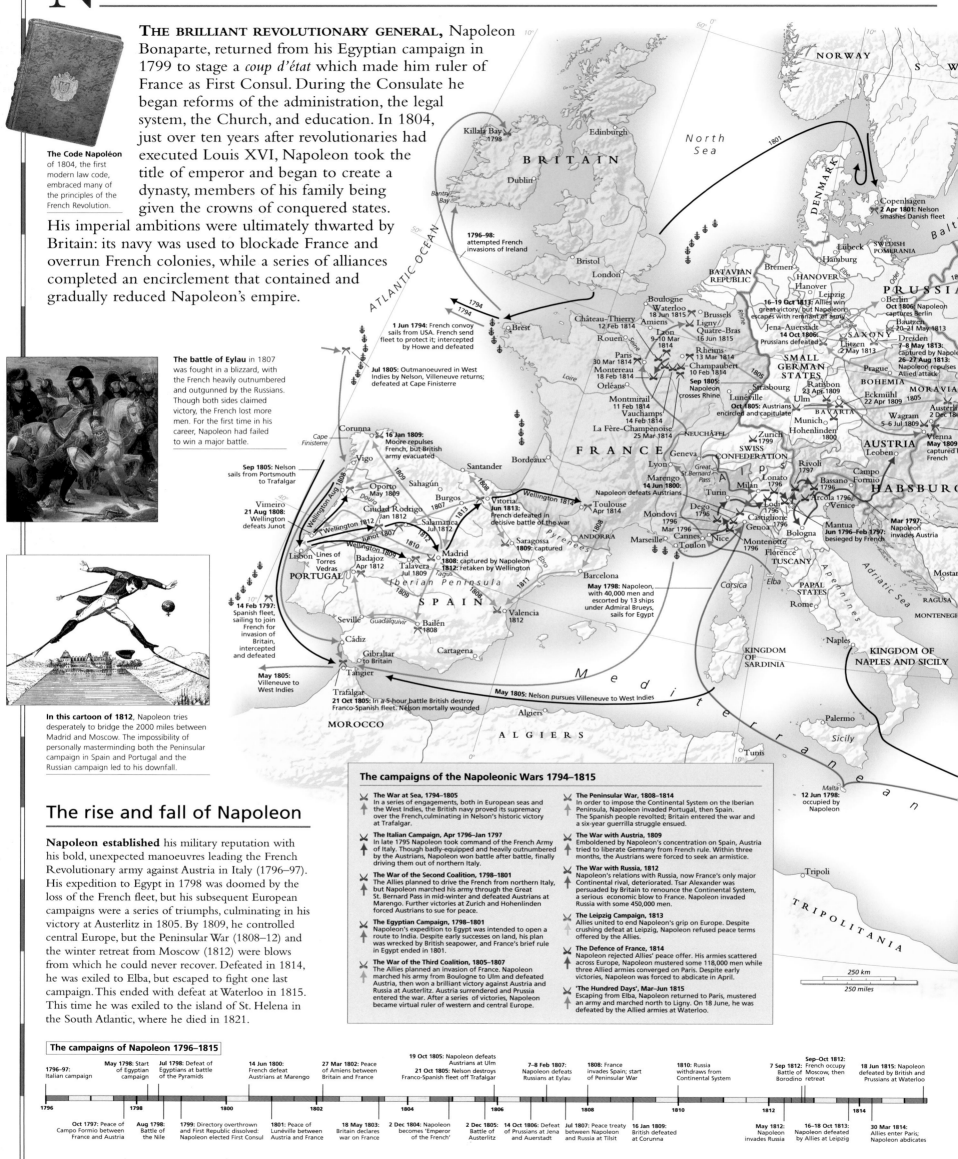

The rise and fall of Napoleon

Napoleon established his military reputation with his bold, unexpected manoeuvres leading the French Revolutionary army against Austria in Italy (1796–97). His expedition to Egypt in 1798 was doomed by the loss of the French fleet, but his subsequent European campaigns were a series of triumphs, culminating in his victory at Austerlitz in 1805. By 1809, he controlled central Europe, but the Peninsular War (1808–12) and the winter retreat from Moscow (1812) were blows from which he could never recover. Defeated in 1814, he was exiled to Elba, but escaped to fight one last campaign. This ended with defeat at Waterloo in 1815. This time he was exiled to the island of St. Helena in the South Atlantic, where he died in 1821.

The campaigns of the Napoleonic Wars 1794–1815

The War at Sea, 1794–1805
In a series of engagements, both in European seas and the West Indies, the British navy proved its supremacy over the French, culminating in Nelson's historic victory at Trafalgar.

The Italian Campaign, Apr 1796–Jan 1797
In late 1795 Napoleon took command of the French Army of Italy. Though badly-equipped and heavily outnumbered by the Austrians, Napoleon won battle after battle, finally driving them out of northern Italy.

The War of the Second Coalition, 1798–1801
The Allies planned to drive the French from northern Italy, but Napoleon marched his army through the Great St. Bernard Pass in mid-winter and defeated Austrians at Marengo. Further victories at Zurich and Hohenlinden forced Austrians to sue for peace.

The Egyptian Campaign, 1798–1801
Napoleon's expedition to Egypt was intended to open a route to India. Despite early successes on land, his plan was wrecked by British seapower, and France's brief rule in Egypt ended in 1801.

The War of the Third Coalition, 1805–1807
The Allies planned an invasion of France. Napoleon marched his army from Boulogne to Ulm and defeated Austria, then won a brilliant victory against Austria and Russia at Austerlitz. Austria surrendered and Prussia entered the war. After a series of victories, Napoleon became virtual ruler of western and central Europe.

The Peninsular War, 1808–1814
In order to impose the Continental System on the Iberian Peninsula, Napoleon invaded Portugal, then Spain. The Spanish people revolted; Britain entered the war and a six-year guerrilla struggle ensued.

The War with Austria, 1809
Emboldened by Napoleon's concentration on Spain, Austria tried to liberate Germany from French rule. Within three months, the Austrians were forced to seek an armistice.

The War with Russia, 1812
Napoleon's relations with Russia, now France's only major Continental rival, deteriorated. Tsar Alexander was persuaded by Britain to renounce the Continental System, a serious economic blow to France. Despite early victories, Napoleon invaded Russia with some 450,000 men.

The Leipzig Campaign, 1813
Allies united to end Napoleon's grip on Europe. Despite crushing defeat at Leipzig, Napoleon refused peace terms offered by the Allies.

The Defence of France, 1814
Napoleon rejected Allies' peace offer. His armies scattered across Europe, Napoleon mustered some 118,000 men while three Allied armies converged on Paris. Despite early victories, Napoleon was forced to abdicate in April.

'The Hundred Days', Mar–Jun 1815
Escaping from Elba, Napoleon returned to Paris, mustered an army and marched north to Ligny. On 18 June, he was defeated by the Allied armies at Waterloo.

The campaigns of Napoleon 1796–1815

1796–97: Italian campaign		
May 1798: Start of Egyptian campaign		
Jul 1798: Defeat of Egyptians at battle of the Pyramids		
14 Jun 1800: French defeat Austrians at Marengo		
27 Mar 1802: Peace of Amiens between Britain and France		
19 Oct 1805: Napoleon defeats Austrians at Ulm		
21 Oct 1805: Nelson destroys Franco-Spanish fleet off Trafalgar		
7–8 Feb 1807: Napoleon defeats Russians at Eylau		
1808: France invades Spain; start of Peninsular War		
1810: Russia withdraws from Continental System		
Sep–Oct 1812: French occupy Moscow, then retreat		
7 Sep 1812: Battle of Borodino		
18 Jun 1815: Napoleon defeated by British and Prussians at Waterloo		

Oct 1797: Peace of Campo Formio between France and Austria		
Aug 1798: Battle of the Nile		
1799: Directory overthrown and First Republic dissolved; Napoleon elected First Consul		
1801: Peace of Lunéville between Austria and France		
18 May 1803: Britain declares war on France		
2 Dec 1804: Napoleon becomes 'Emperor of the French'		
2 Dec 1805: Battle of Austerlitz		
14 Oct 1806: Defeat of Prussians at Jena and Auerstadt		
Jul 1807: Peace treaty between Russia and Napoleon at Tilsit		
16 Jan 1809: British defeated at Corunna		
May 1812: Napoleon invades Russia		
16–18 Oct 1813: Napoleon defeated by Allies at Leipzig		
30 Mar 1814: Allies enter Paris; Napoleon abdicates		

On 2 December 1804 Napoleon crowned himself 'Emperor of the French' in the Cathedral of Notre Dame, Paris, as recorded in this famous painting by Jacques-Louis David.

The Napoleonic Empire

Napoleon's empire grew in two stages. In the first (1800–07), his brilliant military victories established France as the dominant power in Europe. Lands that came under his rule before 1807 – France, the Low Countries, northern Italy, and western Germany – formed an 'inner empire'. Here, French institutions and the Napoleonic legal code took root, surviving the empire's fall in 1814–15. Those areas taken after 1807 – Spain, southern Italy, northern Germany, and Poland – felt the effects of Napoleonic rule less, and often fiercely rejected French influence.

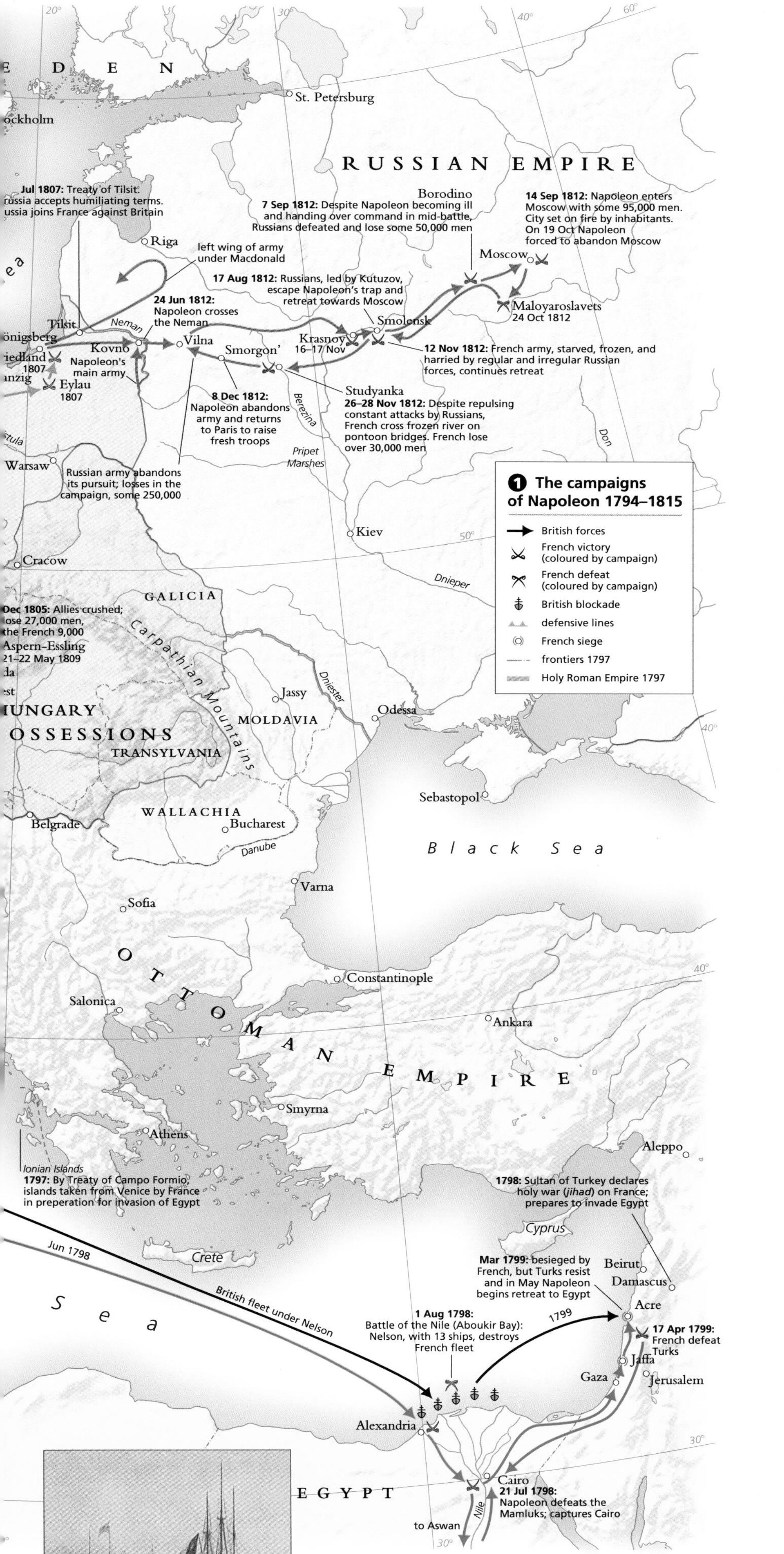
RUSSIAN EMPIRE
St. Petersburg
Jul 1807: Treaty of Tilsit: russia accepts humiliating terms. ussia joins France against Britain
7 Sep 1812: Despite Napoleon becoming ill and handing over command in mid-battle, Russians defeated and lose some 50,000 men
Borodino
14 Sep 1812: Napoleon enters Moscow with some 95,000 men. City set on fire by inhabitants. On 19 Oct Napoleon forced to abandon Moscow
Riga
left wing of army under Macdonald
Moscow
17 Aug 1812: Russians, led by Kutuzov, escape Napoleon's trap and retreat towards Moscow
Maloyaroslavets 24 Oct 1812
24 Jun 1812: Napoleon crosses the Neman
Smolensk
Krasnoy 16–17 Nov
12 Nov 1812: French army, starved, frozen, and harried by regular and irregular Russian forces, continues retreat
Tilsit
Kovno
Napoleon's main army
Eylau 1807
Vilna
Smorgon'
8 Dec 1812: Napoleon abandons army and returns to Paris to raise fresh troops
Studyanka
26–28 Nov 1812: Despite repulsing constant attacks by Russians, French cross frozen river on pontoon bridges. French lose over 30,000 men
Pripet Marshes
Warsaw
Russian army abandons its pursuit; losses in the campaign, some 250,000
Kiev
Cracow
GALICIA
Dec 1805: Allies crushed; lose 27,000 men, the French 9,000
Aspern–Essling 21–22 May 1809
Carpathian Mountains
Jassy
MOLDAVIA
Odessa
HUNGARY
TRANSYLVANIA
Sebastopol
WALLACHIA
Bucharest
Belgrade
Black Sea
Varna
Sofia
OTTOMAN EMPIRE
Constantinople
Salonica
Ankara
Smyrna
Athens
Ionian Islands
1797: By Treaty of Campo Formio, islands taken from Venice by France in preperation for invasion of Egypt
1798: Sultan of Turkey declares holy war (jihad) on France; prepares to invade Egypt
Aleppo
Cyprus
Crete
Jun 1798
British fleet under Nelson
Mar 1799: besieged by French, but Turks resist and in May Napoleon begins retreat to Egypt
Beirut
Damascus
1 Aug 1798: Battle of the Nile (Aboukir Bay): Nelson, with 13 ships, destroys French fleet
1799
Acre
17 Apr 1799: French defeat Turks
Jaffa
Jerusalem
Gaza
Alexandria
Cairo
21 Jul 1798: Napoleon defeats the Mamluks; captures Cairo
EGYPT
to Aswan
Nile
Sea
1 The campaigns of Napoleon 1794–1815
British forces
French victory (coloured by campaign)
French defeat (coloured by campaign)
British blockade
defensive lines
French siege
frontiers 1797
Holy Roman Empire 1797

Napoleon's invasion of Egypt in July 1798 was intended to secure an overland route to India, but the destruction of his fleet, by the British under Nelson at the battle of the Nile, left the French forces stranded.

500 km
500 miles
North Sea
NORWAY
SWEDEN
Stockholm
Edinburgh
Dublin
BRITAIN
Baltic Sea
Riga
DENMARK
Copenhagen
RUSSIAN EMPIRE
Tilsit
Hamburg
Lübeck
REPUBLIC OF DANZIG
Bristol
London
HOLLAND
Bremen
PRUSSIA
WESTPHALIA
BERG
Hanover
Berlin
GRAND DUCHY OF WARSAW
Warsaw
ATLANTIC OCEAN
Brussels
Rouen
CONFEDERATION OF THE RHINE
Paris
Frankfurt
Prague
Cracow
FRENCH EMPIRE
Zurich
Munich
AUSTRIAN EMPIRE
Vienna
Pest
Corunna
Geneva
HELVETIA
Bordeaux
Lyon
Buda
KINGDOM OF ITALY
Milan
Toulouse
GUASTALLA
Venice
ILLYRIAN PROVINCES
PORTUGAL
Lisbon
KINGDOM OF SPAIN
Madrid
Marseille
LUCCA
Bologna
Florence
Belgrade
Danube
CATALONIA
PIOMBINO
Barcelona
Corsica
Sofia
Cordova
Valencia
Rome
KINGDOM OF NAPLES
OTTOMAN EMPIRE
KINGDOM OF SARDINIA
Naples
Tangier
Gibraltar to Britain
Balearic Islands
Algiers
Corfu to France
Ionian Islands to Britain 1809
Palermo
KINGDOM OF SICILY
Athens
Tunis
Malta to Britain 1800
Crete
Mediterranean Sea

2 The Empire of Napoleon by 1812

- French territory ruled directly from Paris 1812
- dependent state 1812
- British or British occupied territory
- state ruled by Napoleon or member of his family at some time between 1805–12

Opposition to Napoleon

Between 1793 and 1815 France fought all the major European powers, either singly or in coalitions. After his defeat of the Third Coalition in 1807, Napoleon ruled virtually the entire continent. Only Britain opposed him. To cripple the British economically, Napoleon tried to prevent all trade between continental Europe and Britain, but this blockade, known as the Continental System, proved difficult to enforce. Russian withdrawal from the System provoked the fatal march on Moscow of 1812, which was to lead to his downfall.

In July 1807, Napoleon met King Frederick William III and Queen Marie Louise of Prussia, and Tsar Alexander I of Russia near Tilsit, Prussia, to discuss peace.

ATLANTIC OCEAN
North Sea
SWEDEN
Stockholm
BRITAIN
Copenhagen
Baltic Sea
Mar 1808: National revolt against French invasion supported by Britain, which sends armies under Moore and Wellington
London
Berlin
PRUSSIA
RUSSIAN EMPIRE
Warsaw
Brussels
SAXONY
Paris
Prague
FRANCE
Zurich
Vienna
AUSTRIAN EMPIRE
Geneva
PORTUGAL
Milan
Venice
Bucharest
Lisbon
Madrid
SPAIN
Marseille
Florence
Belgrade
Black Sea
Barcelona
Rome
Sofia
NAPLES
Naples
Constantinople
Ankara
Gibraltar to Britain
Mediterranean Sea
Palermo
Athens
OTTOMAN EMPIRE
500 km
500 miles

3 Alliances in opposition to France 1792–1815

Alliances against France in the Napoleonic Wars:

- wars of Second Coalition 1798–1800
- wars of Third Coalition 1805–07
- war with Austria 1809
- war with Russia 1812
- Wars of Liberation of France 1813–15

- France 1792
- annexed by France 1802
- satellites of France 1802
- Napoleon's Continental System
- Holy Roman Empire
- frontiers c.1802

THE GROWTH OF NATIONALISM

Otto von Bismarck, prime minister of Prussia 1862–1890, was chief architect of the unification of Germany.

TO RESTORE PEACE and stability after the turmoil of the Napoleonic Wars, the Congress of Vienna was convened in 1814. Attended by all the major European powers, but dominated by Austria, Britain, Russia, and Prussia, the Congress redrew the political map of Europe and restored many former ruling houses. The result was three decades of reactionary rule, during which nationalist and republican movements, inspired by the American and French models, challenged the status quo. In eastern Europe, Greece and the Balkan states took advantage of the weakness of the Ottoman Empire to gain independence. In the west, Italy and Germany finally achieved their dreams of unification. But traditional rivalry between royal houses was now replaced by rivalry between industrialized nation states – a rivalry which led, ultimately, to the First World War.

Europe under the Vienna system

The Congress of Vienna met to share out the spoils of victory over Napoleon, though painful compromise was required to achieve a workable balance of power in Europe. Political stability was re-established by restoring the hereditary monarchs overthrown by Napoleon. France, though deprived of all her conquests, once more had a Bourbon on the throne. But the restored monarchs ruled with too heavy a hand: liberal, republican, and nationalist revolts began to break out, reaching a crescendo in 1848 when the governments of France, Italy, and Austria were all shaken by insurrection.

The Congress of Vienna was attended by five monarchs and the heads of 216 princely families. It was dominated by the Austrian chancellor, Prince Metternich, seen here standing on the left at the signing of the final settlement.

Threats to the Vienna system 1814–50

1806: Abolition of Holy Roman Empire	**1814:** Napoleon abdicates; opening of Congress of Vienna	**1820–23:** Revolts in Spain, Portugal, Naples, Sicily, Piedmont, and the Balkans	**1830–31:** Belgian War of Independence	**1848:** Second Republic in France with Louis-Napoleon as president

| 1800 | 1810 | 1820 | 1830 | 1840 | 1850 |

1815: Napoleon escapes from exile, but is defeated at Waterloo; restoration of French monarchy	**1821:** Start of Greek War of Independence which lasts until 1833	**1830:** Revolution in Paris	**1833–39:** First Carlist War in Spain	**1848:** Revolutions throughout Europe

❶ Europe after the Congress of Vienna 1815–52

MAIN MAP ▶

- small German states
- areas in revolt against Louis-Napoleon in 1851
- German Confederation
- threat to Vienna System 1817–39
- revolution in 1848–49
- frontiers 1815

▼ **INSET: Belgian independence 1831–39**

- United Netherlands 1815–31
- boundary of German Confederation 1815
- boundary of German Confederation 1839
- boundary between French and Flemish speakers

400 km

400 miles

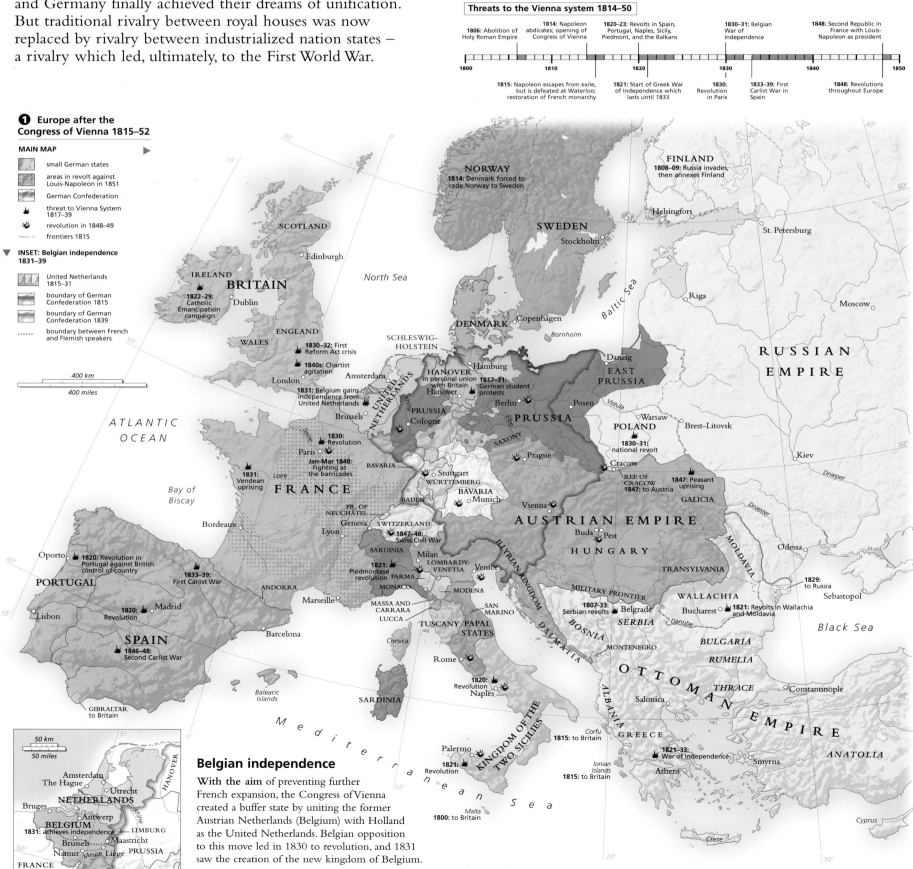

Belgian independence

With the aim of preventing further French expansion, the Congress of Vienna created a buffer state by uniting the former Austrian Netherlands (Belgium) with Holland as the United Netherlands. Belgian opposition to this move led in 1830 to revolution, and 1831 saw the creation of the new kingdom of Belgium.

The unification of Germany

In 1815 Germany's states were reduced to a Confederation of 39, under Austrian leadership. These states were further united in 1834 by the formation of a customs union (Zollverein). In 1866 Bismarck, prime minister of Prussia, proposed a German Confederation which would exclude Austria. When Austria refused, Bismarck – bent on German unification – declared war on Austria. Following Austria's defeat, Bismarck established the North German Confederation. The German Empire, including Bavaria and other south German states, was created after Prussia's victory in the Franco-Prussian War in 1870.

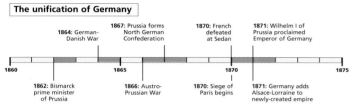

Spiked helmets such as this one worn by a dragoon officer became emblems of German militarism.

In 1870, alarmed at the intentions of Prussia, Napoleon III declared war, but the French were defeated. Here, Napoleon surrenders to the Prussian king, Wilhelm I.

② The unification of Germany

- boundary of German Confederation of 1815
- Prussia in 1815
- Prussian gains by 1866
- other states in North German Confederation 1867
- other German states 1866
- Austro-Hungarian Empire 1867
- frontiers in 1866
- → attack on Denmark by Austro-Prussian forces 1864
- ⇢ Prussian armies in war with Austria 1866
- → Prussian invasion of France in Franco-Prussian War 1870–71
- boundary of German Empire 1871

The unification of Germany

1864: German-Danish War	**1867:** Prussia forms North German Confederation	**1870:** French defeated at Sedan	**1871:** Wilhelm I of Prussia proclaimed Emperor of Germany

1860 — 1865 — 1870 — 1875

1862: Bismarck prime minister of Prussia
1866: Austro-Prussian War
1870: Siege of Paris begins
1871: Germany adds Alsace-Lorraine to newly-created empire

The unification of Italy

The restoration of the old order in 1815 provoked a movement to liberate and unite Italy. In 1859 Cavour, prime minister of Sardinia-Piedmont, enlisted the help of French emperor Napoleon III to drive the Austrians out of Lombardy. In 1860 Sicily and Naples were conquered by Garibaldi and his 1000 'Redshirts', then handed over to Victor Emmanuel II of Sardinia, who became king of a united Italy in 1861. Rome was finally added to the new kingdom in 1870.

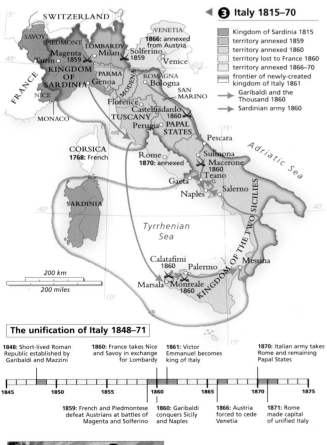

◀ ③ Italy 1815–70

- Kingdom of Sardinia 1815
- territory annexed 1859
- territory annexed 1860
- territory lost to France 1860
- territory annexed 1866–70
- frontier of newly-created kingdom of Italy 1861
- → Garibaldi and the Thousand 1860
- → Sardinian army 1860

The unification of Italy 1848–71

1848: Short-lived Roman Republic established by Garibaldi and Mazzini	**1860:** France takes Nice and Savoy in exchange for Lombardy	**1861:** Victor Emmanuel becomes king of Italy	**1870:** Italian army takes Rome and remaining Papal States

1845 — 1850 — 1855 — 1860 — 1865 — 1870 — 1875

1859: French and Piedmontese defeat Austrians at battles of Magenta and Solferino
1860: Garibaldi conquers Sicily and Naples
1866: Austria forced to cede Venetia
1871: Rome made capital of unified Italy

At the meeting in 1860 between Victor Emmanuel II and Garibaldi at Teano, Garibaldi – a lifelong Republican – effectively presented the king with half of Italy.

In this cartoon of 1908, Ottoman sultan, Abdul Hamid II, sulks as more Balkan territory is whipped from under his feet by Austria and Bulgaria.

Nationalism in the Balkans

Nationalism proved most volatile in the Balkans, where many subject peoples aspired to independence from the Ottomans. Initially only the Greeks were successful. Meanwhile Austria and Russia vied to replace the Turks as the dominant power in the region. Russian expansionism provoked the Crimean War in 1854, when Russia was defeated by Britain, France, Austria, and Turkey, and the Russo-Turkish War of 1877–78. At the Congress of Berlin in 1878, Turkey was forced to abandon all claims to Montenegro, Romania, and Serbia. In 1912, intent on seizing the Ottomans' last remaining European territories, Serbia, Bulgaria, and Greece were victorious in the First Balkan War. Resentment over the division of the spoils sparked a new war, from which Serbia emerged triumphant, but the precarious situation would be a major cause of the First World War.

④ The Balkans and the Black Sea to 1913

- international boundaries 1913
- Ottoman Empire 1913
- Russian Empire 1913
- Austro-Hungarian Empire 1913
- Italy and possessions 1913
- Serbia 1833
- Serbian gain 1878
- Serbian gain 1913
- Greece 1830
- Greek gain 1864
- Greek gain 1881
- Greek gain 1913
- Romania 1861
- Romanian gain 1878
- Romanian gain 1913
- Bulgaria 1878
- Bulgarian gain 1885
- Bulgarian gain 1913
- Montenegro 1878
- Montenegrin gain 1913
- Albania 1913
- → Russian forces in Crimean War
- → Allied forces in Crimean War
- → Russian forces in 1877–78
- ✕ significant Ottoman defeat

The Balkans and the Black Sea 1850–1913

1854–56: Crimean War	**1877–78:** Russia, Serbia, and Montenegro at war with Turkey	**1878:** Congress of Berlin alters terms of San Stefano treaty; Bulgaria becomes autonomous principality within Ottoman Empire	**1908:** Bulgaria declares full independence	**1913:** Treaty of London confirms independent Albania

1850 — 1860 — 1870 — 1880 — 1890 — 1900 — 1910 — 1920

1878: Treaty of San Stefano negotiated by Russia and Turkey
1885: Bulgaria granted Eastern Rumelia
1912: Serbia, Bulgaria, Greece and Montenegro form Balkan League; First Balkan War
1913: Second Balkan War

THE INDUSTRIAL REVOLUTION

Matthew Boulton's metal works in Birmingham developed the steam engine for industrial use.

IN THE LATTER HALF of the 18th century, rapid technological, social, and economic changes began to transform Britain from an agrarian into a largely urban, industrial society. This process, which became known as the Industrial Revolution, spread to Europe in the course of the 19th century. The population of the continent doubled in this period and was fed by a similar growth in agricultural production. Changes included the use of new power sources such as coal and steam; new building materials, chiefly iron and steel; and technical innovations and improved systems of transport. These developments led to large-scale production and the growth of the factory system.

The move to the towns

Industrial chimneys dominate the Manchester skyline in this 19th-century engraving. Industry in Britain concentrated in cities where rich coal and iron deposits were in close proximity.

Urban development was inextricably linked to the process of industrialization. The most marked 19th-century urban growth occurred in areas where labour-intensive, mechanized, and often factory-based industries were emerging. Rapid urbanization first occurred in Britain, where the urban population grew from 20% of the total population in 1800, to 41% in 1850. By the 1850s, many other European countries experienced urban growth at a rate comparable with that of Britain in the first half of the century.

The Industrial Revolution in Britain

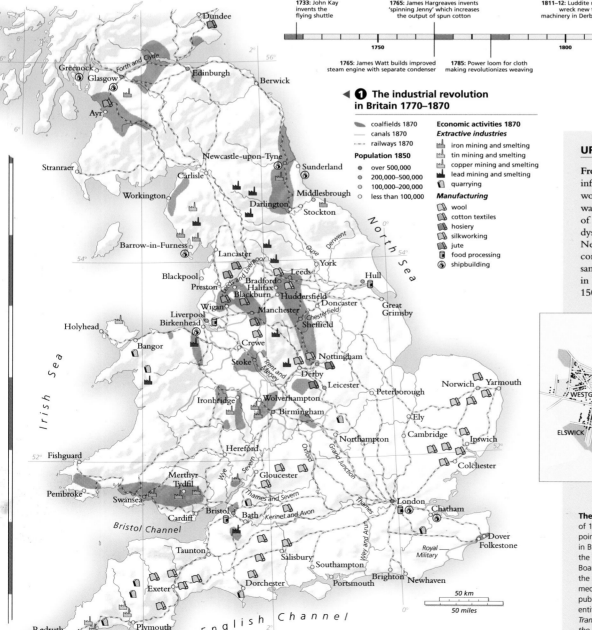

The replacement of water power with steam power greatly increased efficiency. Huge fly wheels could drive machinery, such as that used here to make cable, at greater speeds.

A combination of geographical, political, and social factors ensured that Britain became the first industrial nation. The country possessed a number of natural ports facing the Atlantic, an established shipping trade, and a network of internal navigable waterways. It was richly endowed with coal and iron ore and could draw on a large market both at home and overseas. British colonies supplied raw materials and custom and an expanding population ensured buoyant demand at home. The textile industry in Britain was the first to benefit from new technical innovations which brought about greater production efficiency and output.

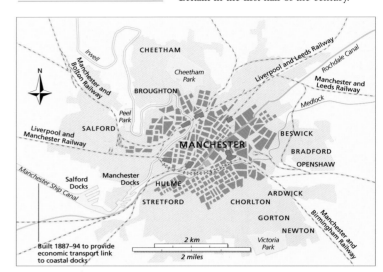

Built 1887–94 to provide economic transport link to coastal docks

2 km
2 miles

▲ 2 The growth of Manchester 1840–1900

- railway
- railway station
- Manchester South junction viaduct
- park
- built-up area 1840
- growth of city 1840–1900

The advance of British technology from 1733

1733: John Kay invents the flying shuttle

1765: James Hargreaves invents 'spinning jenny' which increases the output of spun cotton

1811–12: Luddite rioters wreck new textile machinery in Derbyshire

1837: First practical electric telegraph system produced by Cooke and Wheatstone

1838: Launch of I.K. Brunel's *Great Western* steamship

1842: Lord Shaftesbury's Mines Act; underground employment of women and children prohibited

1765: James Watt builds improved steam engine with separate condenser

1785: Power loom for cloth making revolutionizes weaving

1825: First passenger steam railway from Stockton to Darlington

1832: Outbreak of cholera kills 31,000 people in Britain

1840: Cheap postal system introduced; one penny per letter to anywhere in Britain

1750 1800 1850

◄ 1 The industrial revolution in Britain 1770–1870

- coalfields 1870
- canals 1870
- railways 1870

Population 1850
- ● over 500,000
- ● 200,000–500,000
- ○ 100,000–200,000
- ○ less than 100,000

Economic activities 1870
Extractive industries
- iron mining and smelting
- tin mining and smelting
- copper mining and smelting
- lead mining and smelting
- quarrying

Manufacturing
- wool
- cotton textiles
- hosiery
- silkworking
- jute
- food processing
- shipbuilding

URBANIZATION AND PUBLIC HEALTH

From the 1850s, industrial cities in Britain began to grow faster than the infrastructure needed to support the growing populations. Poorly built workers' tenement housing became severely over-crowded, and people drank water contaminated by sewage and industrial effluent. These poor standards of living resulted in the proliferation of diseases such as cholera, smallpox, dysentery, tuberculosis, and rickets. In 1854 and 1855, cholera broke out in Newcastle, where steep banks produced a concentration of settlement in the commercial areas along the river. Families lived five to a room, without sanitation or ready access to clean water, and of the 9453 houses in the city in 1854, 8032 were without toilets. During the cholera epidemic of 1853, 1500 of the 90,000 population died of the disease in a period of five weeks.

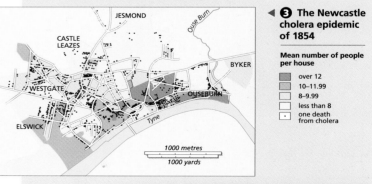

◄ 3 The Newcastle cholera epidemic of 1854

Mean number of people per house
- over 12
- 10–11.99
- 8–9.99
- less than 8
- one death from cholera

1000 metres
1000 yards

The Public Health Act of 1848 was a turning point for public health in Britain. It allowed for the formation of local Boards of Health and the appointment of medical officers. This public health poster entitled *Cholera Tramples the Victor and the Vanquish'd Both*, warned people that no class was immune from the disease.

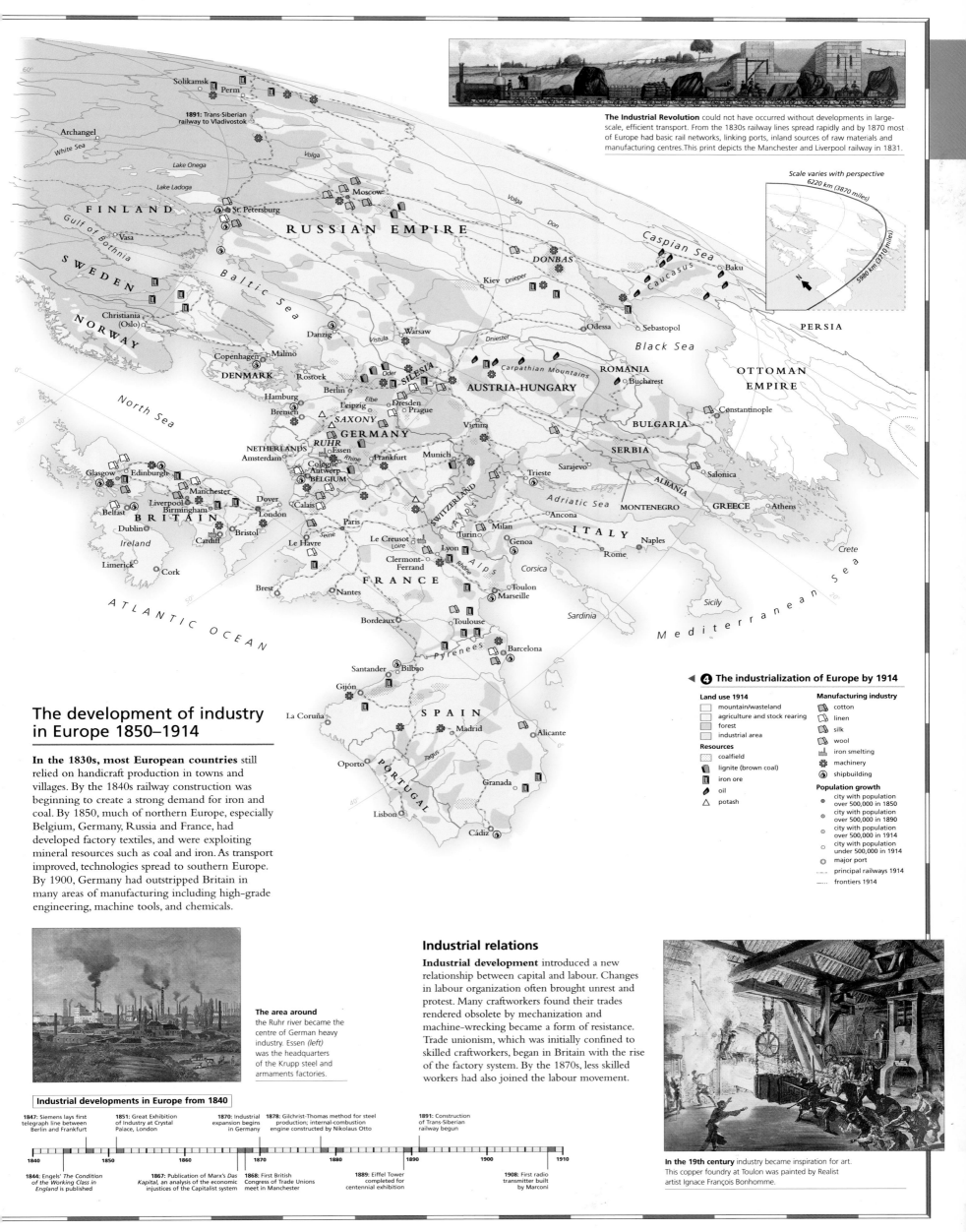

The Industrial Revolution could not have occurred without developments in large-scale, efficient transport. From the 1830s railway lines spread rapidly and by 1870 most of Europe had basic rail networks, linking ports, inland sources of raw materials and manufacturing centres. This print depicts the Manchester and Liverpool railway in 1831.

Scale varies with perspective
6220 km (3870 miles)
5980 km (3710 miles)

◀ 4 The industrialization of Europe by 1914

Land use 1914
- mountain/wasteland
- agriculture and stock rearing
- forest
- industrial area

Resources
- coalfield
- lignite (brown coal)
- iron ore
- oil
- potash

Manufacturing industry
- cotton
- linen
- silk
- wool
- iron smelting
- machinery
- shipbuilding

Population growth
- city with population over 500,000 in 1850
- city with population over 500,000 in 1890
- city with population over 500,000 in 1914
- city with population under 500,000 in 1914
- major port
- principal railways 1914
- frontiers 1914

The development of industry in Europe 1850–1914

In the 1830s, most European countries still relied on handicraft production in towns and villages. By the 1840s railway construction was beginning to create a strong demand for iron and coal. By 1850, much of northern Europe, especially Belgium, Germany, Russia and France, had developed factory textiles, and were exploiting mineral resources such as coal and iron. As transport improved, technologies spread to southern Europe. By 1900, Germany had outstripped Britain in many areas of manufacturing including high-grade engineering, machine tools, and chemicals.

The area around the Ruhr river became the centre of German heavy industry. Essen *(left)* was the headquarters of the Krupp steel and armaments factories.

Industrial relations

Industrial development introduced a new relationship between capital and labour. Changes in labour organization often brought unrest and protest. Many craftworkers found their trades rendered obsolete by mechanization and machine-wrecking became a form of resistance. Trade unionism, which was initially confined to skilled craftworkers, began in Britain with the rise of the factory system. By the 1870s, less skilled workers had also joined the labour movement.

Industrial developments in Europe from 1840

1847: Siemens lays first telegraph line between Berlin and Frankfurt

1851: Great Exhibition of Industry at Crystal Palace, London

1870: Industrial expansion begins in Germany

1878: Gilchrist-Thomas method for steel production; internal-combustion engine constructed by Nikolaus Otto

1891: Construction of Trans-Siberian railway begun

1840 1850 1860 1870 1880 1890 1900 1910

1844: Engels' *The Condition of the Working Class in England* is published

1867: Publication of Marx's *Das Kapital*, an analysis of the economic injustices of the Capitalist system

1868: First British Congress of Trade Unions meet in Manchester

1889: Eiffel Tower completed for centennial exhibition

1908: First radio transmitter built by Marconi

In the 19th century industry became inspiration for art. This copper foundry at Toulon was painted by Realist artist Ignace François Bonhomme.

THE FIRST WORLD WAR

THE FIRST WORLD WAR is one of history's watersheds. Austria–Hungary's attempt to assert its power developed into a protracted struggle that swept up most of Europe and the rest of the world in its train. The conflict mobilized 65 million troops, of whom nine million died and over one-third were wounded. Civilians also died – as a result of military action, starvation, and disease. The war was won by the Allied Powers, but at great cost. The German, Austro-Hungarian, Ottoman, and Russian empires were destroyed; European political and financial supremacy ended; and by 1918 the US had emerged as the greatest power in the world. The debt and disillusionment that followed paved the way for the revolutionary forces of the left and right that emerged in the 1930s in the wake of the Great Depression.

Dynamic recruiting posters appealed directly to the patriotism of Europe's young men.

The start of the First World War

The First World War began in Europe in August 1914. A decade of increasingly severe political crises, combined with military and naval arms races among Europe's major powers created an incendiary situation. The murder of Austrian Archduke Franz Ferdinand in Sarajevo, in June 1914 proved the catalyst. Serbia, Montenegro, Russia, France, Belgium, and Britain (the Allied Powers) found themselves opposed to Austria–Hungary, Germany, and Turkey (the Central Powers). The Central powers were joined by Bulgaria in 1915, while the Allied powers gathered Italy by 1915, Romania in 1916, and the US in 1917.

❶ The balance of power in Europe, 1879–1918

◇ Austro–German alliance 1879–1918
◇ Three Emperors' alliance 1881–87
◇ Austro–Serbian alliance 1881–95
◇ Triple alliance 1882–1915
◇ Austro–German–Romanian alliance 1883–1916
◆ Reinsurance treaty 1887–90
◆ Franco–Russian alliance 1894–1917
◇ Russo–Bulgarian military convention 1902–13

Alliances on the eve of the war
☐ Allied Powers 1914
☐ Central Powers 1914
☐ neutral states 1914

War on the Western Front

By November 1914 the war on the Western Front had become largely static. A German offensive against Paris via Belgium was rapidly met by French and British forces, who forced them back to Flanders. For three years, the British and French armies, and the Germans at Verdun, undertook a series of futile and exceptionally costly offensives in which gains were generally no more than a few kilometres. The front was marked by long lines of trenches, from which the two sides sought to defend their positions. It was impossible for them to achieve any measure of surprise, or, with no room for manoeuvre, to shift their position at all.

For several years, the war in Western Europe was fought along a barely shifting frontline, marked by a series of trenches. These British troops, from the Border Regiment, are squatting in 'funk holes' near Thiepval Wood, during the battle of the Somme in 1916.

Tanks were first used at the end of the 1916 battle of the Somme, and later during the Allied advance in the summer and autumn of 1918. Though they could cope with difficult terrain, the trench system provided considerable obstacles *(left)*.

Aircraft were used initially for reconnaissance and artillery spotting; later, in 1917–18 Germany and Britain used heavy bombers to destroy industrial and civilian targets.

The Western Front

Aug 1914: Battle of the Frontiers
Oct 1914: The 'race to the sea'
May 1916: Battle of Jutland in North Sea
Feb–Mar 1917: Germans withdraw to Hindenburg Line
Apr–May 1917: Allied offensives
Mar–Jul 1918: German offensives on Somme, Aisne, Noyon-Mondidier and Champagne-Marne lines

1915   1916   1917   1917   1919

Sep 1914: Battle of the Marne; first battle of the Aisne
Feb–Dec 1916: Battle of Verdun
Jul–Nov 1916: Battle of the Somme
Apr 1917: US declares war on Central powers
Aug–Nov 1917: Third battle of Ypres
Jul–Oct 1918: Counter-offensives by Allies
Nov 1918: Armistice ends war on Western Front

The German offensive leads to stalemate

Facing a war on two fronts against enemies with larger armies, Germany sought to defeat France before Russia could fully mobilize. They planned to outflank the main French defences by moving through Belgium and then through northern France to encircle France within six weeks. However, supply lines proved inadequate, and communications to, and between, the two main armies no better. The plan ignored British intervention, relying on the likelihood of French immobilization as the offensive progressed. French success at the battle of the Marne ended German hopes of a quick victory, and paved the way for the trench warfare that lasted until spring 1918.

❷ The Western Front 1914–16

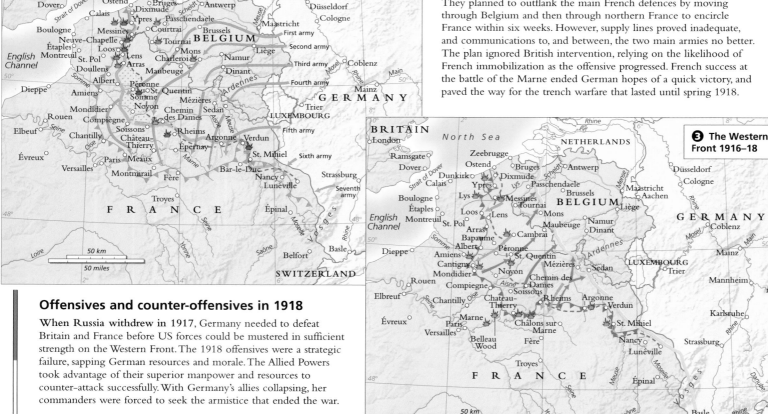

❸ The Western Front 1916–18

The Western Front 1914–1918
→ German invasion of France and Belgium, 1914
▲ furthest extent of German advance, 1914
→ German retreat
— line from end of 1914–Jul 1916
--- Hindenburg line
▫ gains by Allied powers 1916–17
⇒ Kaiserschlacht (the Kaiser's battles') 1918
▲ German offensive Mar–Jul 1918
⇒ Allied counter-attacks, 1918
— line at the Armistice 11 Nov 1918

Major battles
⚔ 1914
⚔ 1915
⚔ 1916
⚔ 1917
⚔ 1918

Offensives and counter-offensives in 1918

When Russia withdrew in 1917, Germany needed to defeat Britain and France before US forces could be mustered in sufficient strength on the Western Front. The 1918 offensives were a strategic failure, sapping German resources and morale. The Allied Powers took advantage of their superior manpower and resources to counter-attack successfully. With Germany's allies collapsing, her commanders were forced to seek the armistice that ended the war.

War on the Eastern Front

There was far more movement on the Eastern Front than in the West, partly because of the much greater distances involved. Though the Russian army was generally superior to Austria–Hungary militarily, they were invariably defeated by the force of German arms. By the end of 1915, Russia had lost most of Poland, with more than two million troops taken prisoner. Inadequate military supplies and poor leadership produced a consequently high casualty rate: war weariness and mutiny were key factors in bringing the Bolsheviks to power in 1917.

During the first German onslaught on the Eastern Front, casualty numbers were such that even churches were converted into makeshift field hospitals. The priest is giving a blessing to sick and injured troops.

The Eastern Front

| Sep–Oct 1914: German operations in southwestern Poland | Feb 1915: Second battle of Masurian Lakes | Jul–Sep 1915: Russian withdrawal | Aug–Sep 1916: Romanian offensive | Mar 1917: Russian Revolution | Jul 1917: Second Brusilov offensive | Dec 1917: Russian armistice |

1914   1915   1916   1917   1918

Aug 1914: Battle of Tannenberg
Sep 1914: First battle of Masurian Lakes
Nov 1914: Battle of Lodz
May 1915: German breakthrough at Gorlice-Tarnow
Jun–Aug 1916: Brusilov offensive by Russia
Sep–Dec 1916: Elimination of Romania
Jan 1918: Treaty of Brest-Litovsk allows Germany to occupy Ukraine and gain access to food supplies

④ The Eastern Front
- Russian advances, 1914
- front line in 1914–15 (limit of Russian advance)
- limit of Austro–German advances, 1915–16
- Brusilov offensives, 1916
- Armistice line Dec 1917
- German landings, 1917–18
- German offensives into Russia
- German penetration into Russia by Jun 1918
- Area occupied by Central Powers under Treaty of Brest-Litovsk

Major battles:
- 1914
- 1915
- 1916
- 1917

250 km / 250 miles

CASUALTIES OF WAR

The toll of military dead and wounded was appalling; of the millions mobilized on the Allied side, fewer than half escaped death or injury. The Central Powers' losses were even higher, particularly in Austria–Hungary. In total, nearly nine million men died in four years, with 23 million left physically or psychologically scarred. Civilians died too, from bombing raids, malnutrition, and disease.

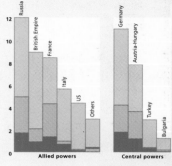

Military casualties (millions)
- troops mobilized
- troops killed
- troops wounded

Allied powers / Central powers

War in the Balkans

Serbia survived three invasion attempts in 1914, but succumbed in 1915 to an Austro-German offensive supported by Bulgaria, which checked an Anglo-French attempt to support the Serbian army from Salonica. In 1916, having successfully contained Allied forces at Salonica and invaded Romania, Bulgarian armies were joined by Austro-German forces that captured Bucharest in December. The Bulgarians were able to defeat several Allied offensives in front of Salonica until September 1918 when a major offensive broke the Bulgarian front and morale. Forced to sue for an armistice, the Bulgarians saw their capital occupied by British forces, while French and Serbian forces liberated Belgrade on 1 November.

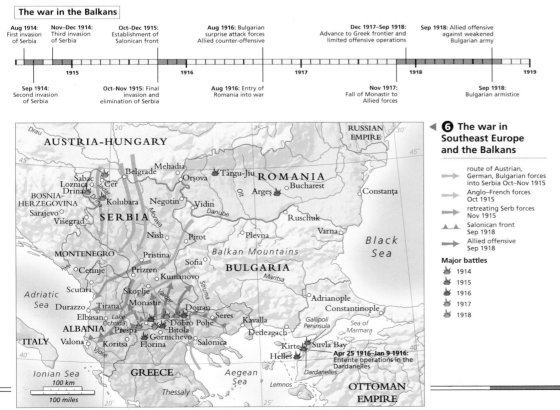

Lying in a key position at the head of the Gulf of Salonica, the port city of Salonica was a major focus for Allied operations in the Balkans during the First World War.

The war in the Balkans

Aug 1914: First invasion of Serbia
Nov–Dec 1914: Third invasion of Serbia
Oct–Dec 1915: Establishment of Salonican front
Aug 1916: Bulgarian surprise attack forces Allied counter-offensive
Dec 1917–Sep 1918: Advance to Greek frontier and limited offensive operations
Sep 1918: Allied offensive against weakened Bulgarian army

1915   1916   1917   1918   1919

Sep 1914: Second invasion of Serbia
Oct–Nov 1915: Final invasion and elimination of Serbia
Aug 1916: Entry of Romania into war
Nov 1917: Fall of Monastir to Allied forces
Sep 1918: Bulgarian armistice

⑥ The war in Southeast Europe and the Balkans
- route of Austrian, German, Bulgarian forces into Serbia Oct–Nov 1915
- Anglo–French forces Oct 1915
- retreating Serb forces Nov 1915
- Salonican front Sep 1918
- Allied offensive Sep 1918

Major battles
- 1914
- 1915
- 1916
- 1917
- 1918

100 km / 100 miles

The Italian Front

Italy entered the war in 1915 in an opportunistic arrangement engineered by its leaders with the Allies to secure territory at the expense of Austria–Hungary. Fighting on the Italian Front was some of the most bitter of the war, with much of the fighting occurring in a series of battles close to the river Isonzo. The great battle of Caporetto in 1917 almost led to Italian defeat. Italy was more successful in subsequent fighting, but the terrible disillusionment after the war over the price paid for Italy's gains contributed heavily to the rise to power of Benito Mussolini and the Fascists.

Italian civilians suffered great privations during the years of warfare in the north of the country. Here, women – wheeling handcarts – and children flee following the 6th battle of the Isonzo.

▲ ⑤ The Italian Front 1915–1918
- Italian offensives on the River Isonzo, 1915–17
- Austro–German campaigns, 1917
- front line in Sep 1917
- front line Dec 1917–Oct 1918
- Allied offensive, Oct 1918
- Armistice line 4 Nov 1918

Major battles
- 1915
- 1917
- 1918

Jun 1915–Sep 1917: 11 battles of the Isonzo

50 km / 50 miles

The war in Italy

Jun–Sep 1915: 1st and 2nd battle of the Isonzo
Mar 1916: 5th battle of the Isonzo
Aug–Sep 1916: 6th and 7th battles of the Isonzo
May–Jun 1917: 10th battle of the Isonzo
Oct–Nov 1917: Battle of Caporetto
Jun 1918: Battle of the Piave

1915   1916   1917   1918   1919

Oct–Nov 1915: 3rd and 4th battles of the Isonzo
May–Jun 1916: Asiago offensive by Austria
Oct–Nov 1916: 8th and 9th battles of the Isonzo
Aug–Sep 1917: 11th battle of the Isonzo
Nov 1918: Battle of Vittorio Veneto

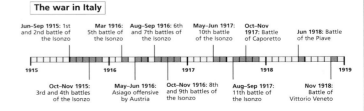

EUROPE BETWEEN THE WARS

Vladimir Illich Lenin was the architect of the Bolshevik revolution.

AS THE FIRST WORLD WAR drew to its close, the three great conservative empires of Europe – Russia, Austria–Hungary, and Germany – suffered cataclysmic change. Revolution in 1917 in Russia led to the seizure of power by Lenin and the Bolsheviks. After the end of the war, the victorious allies imposed peace treaties which dismembered Austria–Hungary and sliced territory from Germany – as well as imposing punitive financial penalties. New states sprang up right across Europe as nationalist aspirations coincided with the collapse of multi-national empires.

Europe after the First World War

Following the end of the First World War, Finland, Estonia, Latvia, and Lithuania gained independence from Russia; Czechoslovakia and Yugoslavia emerged from the wreckage of Austria–Hungary, while Poland re-appeared as an independent state for the first time since its partition in 1794. In western Europe too, long-frustrated national discontent finally brought about the establishment of an independent Irish Free State in 1921. The birth of new states and changes in regime did not happen easily, and Finland and the new Irish state were both engulfed by civil war.

The immense reparations imposed on Germany by the Treaty of Versailles proved an impossible burden to a nation already crippled by the costs of the war. Hyperinflation during the 1920s so devalued the national currency that it became totally worthless. These children are using Deutschmarks as building blocks.

The aftermath of the First World War

1919: Treaty of Versailles forces Germany to admit guilt for starting war and pay reparations to Allies	**1923:** Hyperinflation begins in Germany	**1924:** German reparations reduced by Dawes plan

1919	1921	1923	1925

| **1920:** League of Nations founded | **1921:** Birth of Irish Free State | **1923:** France occupies Ruhr region of Germany | **1925:** European boundaries stabilized by Treaty of Locarno |

❶ Europe after the First World War

European empires in 1914

— German Empire	— frontiers 1923
— Austro-Hungarian Empire	▢ new states
— Russian Empire	

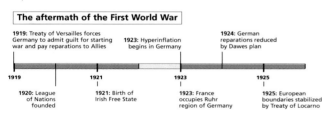

Revolution and civil war in Russia

In 1917, Russia's Tsarist regime, ravaged by war and a failing economy, collapsed. The provisional government which replaced it failed to improve the economy, and in October 1917, the socialist Bolsheviks seized key installations in Petrograd, and took control of a number of important towns. Civil war broke out as anti-Bolsheviks and pro-monarchists, aided by troops from other European nations (the Entente powers), tried to overthrow them. However the well-organized Bolsheviks (the 'Reds') held the heartland of Russia and by 1921 had defeated their weak, disunited opponents. Meanwhile, national groups on the periphery of Russia strove for independence. Finland, Estonia, Latvia, Lithuania, and Poland broke free and were able to remain so, but the independence of Armenia, Azerbaijan, and Georgia was short-lived. By 1924 the Bolsheviks were firmly in control and the Soviet Union came into being.

Scale varies with perspective

10,250 km (6370 miles)
6450 km (4010 miles)

The Russian Civil War

▢ Russian boundary after Treaty of Brest-Litovsk Mar 1918
→ Bolshevik forces
→ White Russian forces
→ Entente forces

▲ ❷ The Russian Revolution, the Russian Civil War, and the formation of the Soviet Union 1917–24

▢ the Russian Empire in 1914
▢ countries/republics which declared independence from Russia in 1917–18

The Bolshevik revolution
● towns where Bolsheviks gained control 1917
● towns where Bolsheviks gained control 1918

The formation of the Soviet Union

✦ republics temporarily independent from Russia 1917/18–21
▢ occupied by Japan 1918–22
▢ extent of Bolshevik territory in mid-1919
▢ Soviet Union by 1924
— frontiers 1924
--- Trans-Siberian railway

Revolution and civil war in Russia 1917–24

Mar 1917: Abdication of Tsar Nicholas II	**1918:** Start of civil war between Bolsheviks and White Russians **1918:** Treaty of Brest-Litovsk ends First World War in the east	**1920:** White Russia, Ukraine, and Caucasus Republics return to Russian control	**1922:** USSR (Union of Soviet Socialist Republics) is formed

1917	1919	1921	1923	1925

Nov 1917: Bolsheviks begin to take control of European Russia	**1920:** Start of peasant revolts throughout Russia	**1921:** Russian civil war ends with Bolshevik victory. New economic policy encourages peasants to produce more food while modernization is taking place	**1924:** Lenin dies and is succeeded by Josef Stalin

Economic crisis and political extremism

The US economic crisis of 1929 hit a Europe suffering from the aftermath of wartime dislocation. Industrial output and agricultural production fell sharply across the world, but the industrial nations were hardest hit. Farmers survived by retreating to subsistence production, but the collapse in industrial output brought unemployment on a massive scale. Without proper systems of social security to support the unemployed, poverty became widespread. The economic and social problems of the 1930s encouraged the growth of extreme political movements on both Left and Right, especially in Germany and Italy, where Fascism under Hitler and Mussolini became the defining political force.

In 1936 more than 200 men marched from Jarrow in northern England to London to draw attention to the plight of their town – formerly a centre for shipbuilding – where male unemployment had reached more than 70%.

❸ The Great Depression in Europe and the growth of political extremism

- ☐ Fascist regime
- ☐ Communist regime
- ☐ other dictatorship
- △ more than 20% unemployment by 1932
- ☆ right-wing activity
- ☆ strikes and riots during the 1930s
- 🏭 60% decrease in industrial output since 1929 (1932 figures as a percentage of 1929)

The Great Depression in Europe

1929: Wall Street crash precipitates worldwide depression | 1931: European central banks collapse leading to further economic downturn | 1933: Almost 25% of British workforce unemployed

1930: Almost 40% of German workforce unemployed

1925   1927   1929   1931   1933   1935

Revolution and nationalism in Europe

In March 1939 Nazi troops took control of the Czech lands and a puppet state was established in Slovakia. This photograph shows the entry of German troops into Prague, watched by wary Czech civilians.

On achieving power in 1933, Hitler began a campaign to restore Germany to its position as a great international power. In 1936, German troops marched back into the Rhineland. The response from the western powers was weak, and in March 1938, Nazi Germany annexed Austria in the *Anschluss*. At Munich six months later, Britain and France allowed Germany to annex the Czech Sudetenland, signalling the break-up of the Czechoslovak state. Fascist Italy aped Hitler, conquering Ethiopia in 1935–36 and occupying Albania in 1939. Finally, bolstered by the Nazi–Soviet Pact Hitler ignored British and French protests to invade Poland in September 1939.

❹ The Spanish Civil War 1936–39

Land held by Nationalist forces
- ☐ Jul 1936
- ☐ Oct 1937
- ☐ Jul 1938
- ☐ Feb 1939

Land held by Republican forces
- ☐ Feb 1939
- — temporary independence, with dates

❺ Territorial expansion in Central Europe 1936–39

Territory taken over by Germany
- ☐ 1936
- ☐ 1938
- ☐ 1939

Territory taken over by Italy
- ☐ 1939

Territory taken over by Hungary
- ☐ 1938
- ☐ 1939

- — frontiers 1936

The Spanish Civil War

The Spanish elections of 1936 brought in the left-wing Popular Front government, precipitating a military revolt by conservative groups. A brutal civil war followed, with the right-wing Nationalists, led by General Franco and supported by Germany and Italy, triumphant against Republican groups.

Many Spanish civilians were killed during the Civil War. This 1937 post card calls for aid for victims of air raids.

The growth of nationalism in Europe

1931: Republican success in Spanish elections leads to flight of king | 1934: Murder of Austrian Chancellor, Dollfuss by Nazi supporters | 1936: Germany reoccupies Rhineland | 1938: Break-up of Czechoslovakia | 1938: Germany occupies Austria (*Anschluss*) | 1939: Signing of Nazi-Soviet pact

1931   1933   1935   1937   1939

1933: Hitler becomes Chancellor of Germany | 1936: Start of Spanish Civil War | 1938: Munich Agreement allows Germany to occupy Czech Sudetenland | 1939: German invasion of Poland

THE SECOND WORLD WAR IN EUROPE

THE GREATEST WAR in Europe's history was initiated by a series of aggressive annexations and conquests by Hitler's Nazi Germany between 1939 and 1941. When the conflict ceased to be a series of campaigns and became a war, however, Germany was checked and then stripped of the initiative by an Allied force headed by two nations on the lateral extremes of Europe – Britain and the USSR – and from December 1941, a non-European nation, the US. Each of the latter proved more than Germany's equal in military and economic resources. The eventual Allied victory, following concerted assaults from the west, south, east, and the air, saved Europe from the scourge of Nazism but also completed Europe's devastation, bringing to an end 400 years of European global domination.

Women were encouraged to join the war effort both as civilians and in the armed forces.

Blitzkrieg in Europe 1939–42

Between 1939 and 1941, lightning campaigns on land and in the air enabled Nazi Germany to conquer many of its weaker neighbours. In temporary alliance with the USSR, Germany annihilated Poland in the autumn of 1939. Denmark, Norway, Belgium, France, and the Netherlands were overrun in April–June 1940. Yugoslavia and Greece were occupied in April–May 1941, Britain was isolated, and Bulgaria, Romania, and Hungary brought under Nazi domination. Although a large contingent of German forces was committed to support Italy in North Africa, in June 1941 Hitler ordered a surprise attack on the USSR, hoping to destroy it in a single campaign. The attempt ended in failure because of the distances involved and unexpected Soviet resistance. In mid-winter 1941, the Nazi invasion forces were halted outside Moscow.

Following the Blitz (September 1940–May 1941) London became the first city in history to undergo ballistic missile attack from V1 flying bombs and V2 rockets (1944–45).

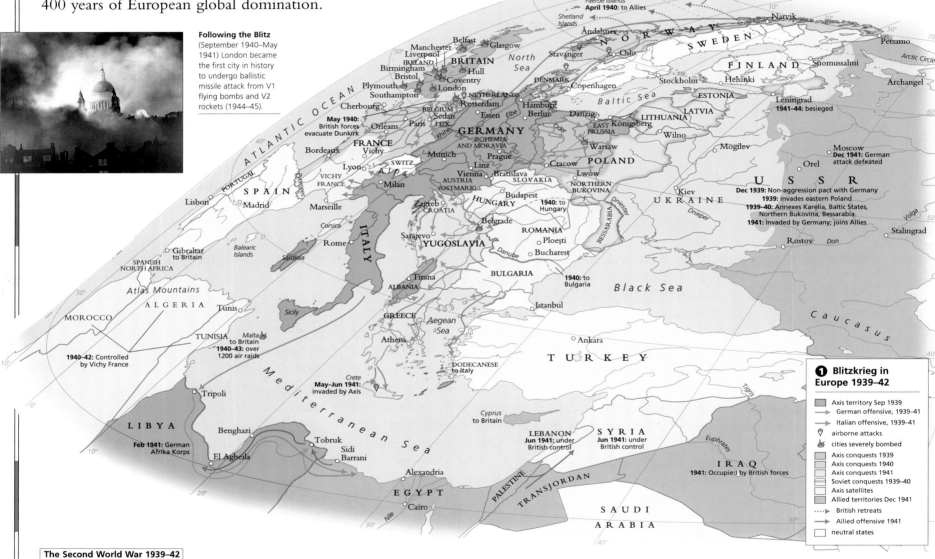

The Second World War 1939–42

Aug 1939: Germany and USSR sign non-aggression pact

Apr 1940: German invasion of Denmark and Norway

Jul–Oct 1940: Battle of Britain in skies over southern England

Apr 1941: German invasion of Yugoslavia and Greece

Dec 1941: Germany declares war on US

Sep 1942: Start of German siege of Stalingrad

Nov 1942: Germans occupy Vichy France

Sep 1939: Germany and USSR invade Poland; France and Britain declare war on Germany

May–Jun 1940: Germany invades France, Netherlands, and Belgium

Oct 1940: Italy invades Albania and Greece

Jun 1941: Operation Barbarossa: German invasion of USSR

Nov 1941: USSR counter-attacks against Germany

Oct–Nov 1942: UK defeats Germany at El Alamein

The battle of the Atlantic

The battle over the supply of Europe was fought in the Atlantic. British destruction or containment of German surface warship raiders, following the sinking of the *Bismarck* in May 1941 and the blockade of supplies to 'Fortress Europe', was followed by a German submarine (U-Boat) campaign against British shipping in western waters. Once the US entered the war in December 1941, U-boat attacks spread across the Atlantic. By summer 1943, US mass production of 'Liberty' merchantmen, the use of the convoy system, increasing air cover, and the Allied interception of German radio traffic critically inhibited the effectiveness of the U-Boat 'wolf-packs'.

This Enigma encoding machine is being used by German naval troops. By summer 1940, British counter-intelligence experts had managed to crack the Enigma code, enabling them to interpret German radio traffic, and disperse the intercepted messages (codenamed Ultra) throughout Allied High Command.

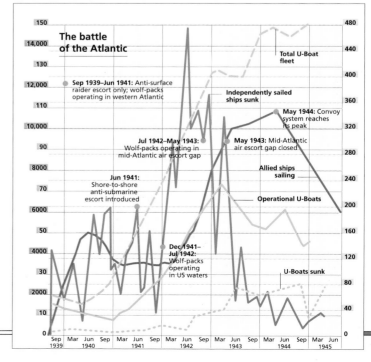

The battle of the Atlantic

Sep 1939–Jun 1941: Anti-surface raider escort only; wolf-packs operating in western Atlantic

Jun 1941: Shore-to-shore anti-submarine escort introduced

Dec 1941–Jul 1942: Wolf-packs operating in US waters

Jul 1942–May 1943: Wolf-packs operating in mid-Atlantic air escort gap

May 1943: Mid-Atlantic air escort gap closed

May 1944: Convoy system reaches its peak

Total U-Boat fleet

Independently sailed ships sunk

Allied ships sailing

Operational U-Boats

U-Boats sunk

❷ The Greater German Reich 1942

- Greater German Reich
- areas occupied by Germany and Finland
- Italy and areas occupied by Italy
- Axis satellites
- Allied territories
- neutral states

The Greater German Reich 1939–1943

The creation by the Nazis of a Greater German Reich encompassing their conquered and allied territories was based on five basic principles: pure 'Aryan' regions were annexed or occupied and integrated into Germany, under the aegis of the Gestapo secret police; non-incorporated areas were placed under military control; puppet and satellite states were strictly controlled and exploited by coercion; the conquered areas of the East were ravaged and cleared for German settlement; and underlying all these policies a principle of ethnic cleansing, targeting Jews, Gypsies, political dissidents, and 'social deviants', which began with imprisonment concentration camps or enslaved labour, but escalated by 1943 into a policy of systematic extermination.

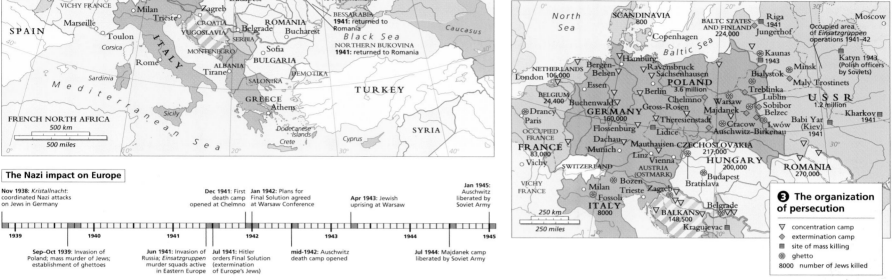

❸ The organization of persecution

- ▽ concentration camp
- ⊗ extermination camp
- ■ site of mass killing
- ⊛ ghetto
- 8000 number of Jews killed

The Nazi impact on Europe

Nov 1938: *Kristallnacht:* coordinated Nazi attacks on Jews in Germany

Dec 1941: First death camp opened at Chelmno

Jan 1942: Plans for Final Solution agreed at Warsaw Conference

Apr 1943: Jewish uprising at Warsaw

Jan 1945: Auschwitz liberated by Soviet Army

1939 1940 1941 1942 1943 1944 1945

Sep–Oct 1939: Invasion of Poland; mass murder of Jews; establishment of ghettoes

Jun 1941: Invasion of Russia; *Einsatzgruppen* murder squads active in Eastern Europe

Jul 1941: Hitler orders Final Solution (extermination of Europe's Jews)

mid-1942: Auschwitz death camp opened

Jul 1944: Majdanek camp liberated by Soviet Army

The Allied invasion of Europe 1943–45

A final German attempt to conquer the USSR brought their forces to Stalingrad by August 1942. The following winter saw their defeat there which, with Anglo-US victories in North Africa, brought the strategic initiative to the Allies. July 1943 witnessed Soviet victory at Kursk and Anglo-US landings in Sicily, initiating a Soviet onslaught in the east, and the collapse of Italy. A sustained Anglo-US bombing offensive (from January 1943) and landings in southern France and Normandy meant, by summer 1944, that Germany was in retreat on all fronts. With its infrastructure, industry, capital, and leadership effectively destroyed, by May 1945 Germany was powerless to stop Soviet and Anglo-US forces finally meeting on the Elbe, and enforcing an unconditional surrender.

The Second World War 1942–45

Jan 1943: Germans surrender at Stalingrad

Jun–Aug 1943: USSR defeats Germans in tank battle at Kursk

Jan 1944: End of 900-day siege of Leningrad

Jun 1944: D-Day: Allied forces land in Normandy

Oct–Nov 1944: Allies liberate Greece

Jan 1945: Soviet troops enter Budapest, Warsaw, and Auschwitz

May 1945: Germany surrenders

1943 1944 1945

Jul 1943: Allied forces land in Sicily

Sep–Oct 1943: Italian surrender to Allies; Germany occupies Rome and Milan. Italy declares war on Germany

Jul 1944: USSR enters Poland

Mar 1945: Allied forces cross Rhine

May 1945: Berlin surrenders to Soviet troops

The Allied invasion of northern Europe began with Operation Overlord, the largest combined operation and successful shore-to-shore invasion in history; eight seaborne and airborne divisions established a beachhead in Normandy, on D-Day (6 June 1944) supported by 6500 ships and 12,000 aircraft.

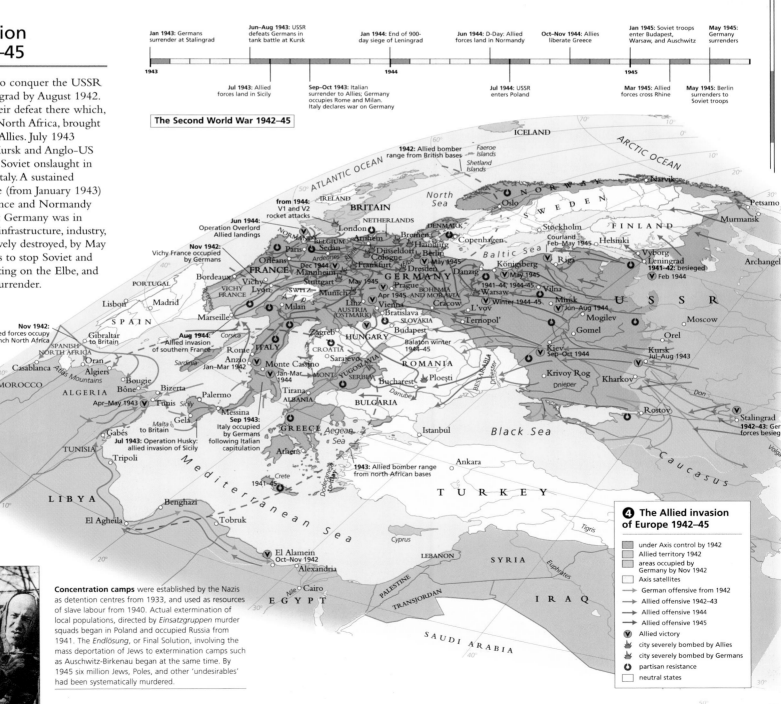

❹ The Allied invasion of Europe 1942–45

- under Axis control by 1942
- Allied territory 1942
- areas occupied by Germany by Nov 1942
- Axis satellites
- → German offensive from 1942
- → Allied offensive 1942–43
- → Allied offensive 1944
- → Allied offensive 1945
- ⊽ Allied victory
- ⚒ city severely bombed by Allies
- ⚒ city severely bombed by Germans
- ↻ partisan resistance
- neutral states

Concentration camps were established by the Nazis as detention centres from 1933, and used as resources of slave labour from 1940. Actual extermination of local populations, directed by *Einsatzgruppen* murder squads began in Poland and occupied Russia from 1941. The *Endlösung*, or Final Solution, involving the mass deportation of Jews to extermination camps such as Auschwitz-Birkenau began at the same time. By 1945 six million Jews, Poles, and other 'undesirables' had been systematically murdered.

THE DIVISION OF POSTWAR EUROPE

Joseph Stalin, leader of the Soviet Union 1929–53, headed a regime of terror and totalitarian rule.

AFTER THE SECOND WORLD WAR, Europe was divided into the capitalist West and Soviet-dominated Communist East. Germany, which by 1947 was partitioned along the same lines, played a pivotal role in the tensions between the two blocs. From 1945–52, millions of people were forcibly resettled while many others fled persecution. The US, fearing that Communism would be an attractive alternative to postwar poverty and dislocation, financed the 'Marshall Plan', an economic recovery programme for Europe. By 1948 a pro-Soviet bloc, bound by economic and military agreements, had been established in Eastern Europe. Attempts to challenge Soviet dominance in the Soviet bloc in the 1950s and 1960s were brutally suppressed.

The Allied occupation of postwar Germany

Following Germany's surrender in May 1945, the occupying powers, America, Britain, France and the USSR, divided Germany into four zones. Berlin, which lay within the Soviet zone, was similarly divided. In March 1948 the Western powers decided to unite their zones into a single economic unit. The USSR responded by launching a land blockade of Berlin in protest against the unification. The Western nations frustrated the blockade by airlifting essential supplies to their sectors of Berlin. The blockade was abandoned in 1949.

❶ The partition of Germany and Austria ▶

Occupation zones
- American
- British
- French
- Soviet
- Soviet allies
- ☐ checkpoint between East and West
- --- air corridor
- • four sector city

The occupation of Berlin

In accordance with agreements made at the Potsdam Conference in 1945, Berlin was partitioned in a similar way to Germany. Between 1949 and 1961, around 2.5 million East Germans fled from East to West Germany, including skilled workers and professionals. Their loss threatened to destroy the economic viability of the East German state. In response, East Germany built the Berlin Wall in 1961 to prevent migrations and possible economic catastrophe.

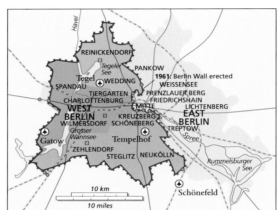

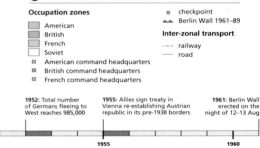

◀ ❷ The division of Berlin

Occupation zones
- American
- British
- French
- Soviet

- • checkpoint
- ⚏ Berlin Wall 1961–89

Inter-zonal transport
- --- railway
- — road

- ⬛ American command headquarters
- ⬛ British command headquarters
- ⬛ French command headquarters

With Soviet consent, the East German authorities constructed the Berlin Wall in 1961. For 28 years the wall served to segregate East Germans from West Germany becoming a potent symbol of the Cold War.

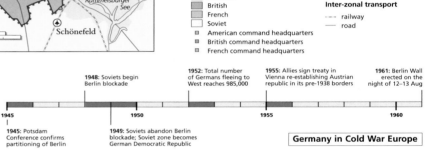

1948: Soviets begin Berlin blockade

1952: Total number of Germans fleeing to West reaches 985,000

1955: Allies sign treaty in Vienna re-establishing Austrian republic in its pre-1938 borders

1961: Berlin Wall erected on the night of 12–13 Aug

1945 — 1950 — 1955 — 1960

1945: Potsdam Conference confirms partitioning of Berlin

1949: Soviets abandon Berlin blockade; Soviet zone becomes German Democratic Republic

Germany in Cold War Europe

Refugees and resettlement 1945–52

The Second World War left millions of Europeans displaced. In an attempt to re-establish ethnic and linguistic uniformity within political boundaries, more than 31 million people were resettled between 1945 and 1952. Under the Potsdam agreement, Cossacks and Russian prisoners of war were forcibly repatriated, often to death or imprisonment. Millions of Germans fled Eastern Europe ahead of the Red Army. Mutual transfers of peoples were organized to coincide with shifts in boundaries, for example between Poland and the Baltic republics; and Hungary and Yugoslavia. Finns were displaced by the Soviet occupation of Karelia, and many Jewish Holocaust survivors fled to Palestine and the US.

These children were amongst millions forced to live in refugee camps while they waited to learn whether they could return to their former homes.

❸ Displaced peoples in East and Central Europe ▶

- ☐ USSR 1945
- ☐ Communist states by 1948
- --- pre-war boundary
- — post-war boundary
- — 'Iron Curtain' 1948

Movement of peoples 1945–52
- (300) number of refugees in thousands (with colour of peoples)
- ➤ Baltic peoples
- ➤ Czechs
- ➤ Finns
- ➤ Germans
- ➤ Greeks
- ➤ Hungarians
- ➤ Italians
- ➤ Poles
- ➤ Romanians
- ➤ Russians
- ➤ Russians forcibly repatriated
- ➤ Turks
- ★ Jewish emigration to Israel 1945–50 in thousands

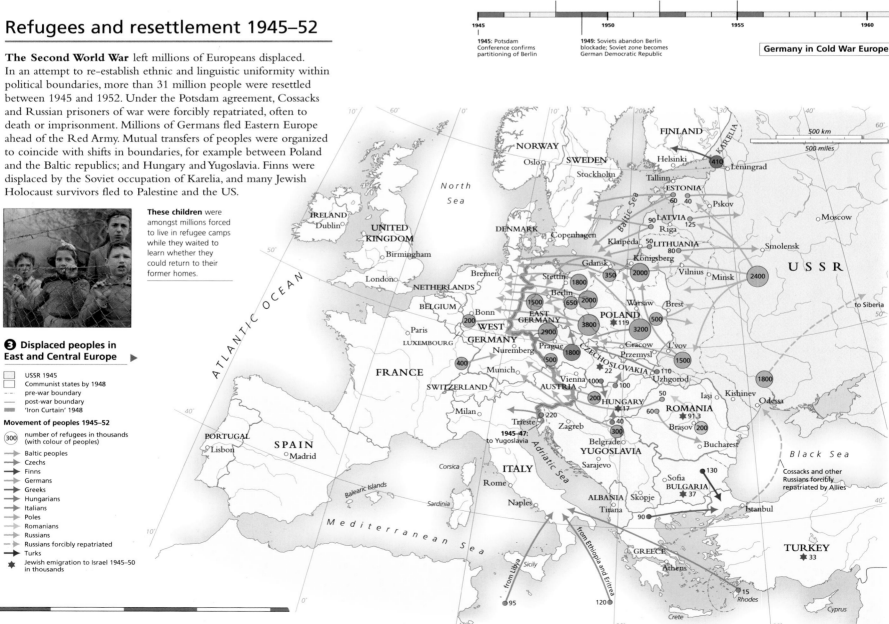

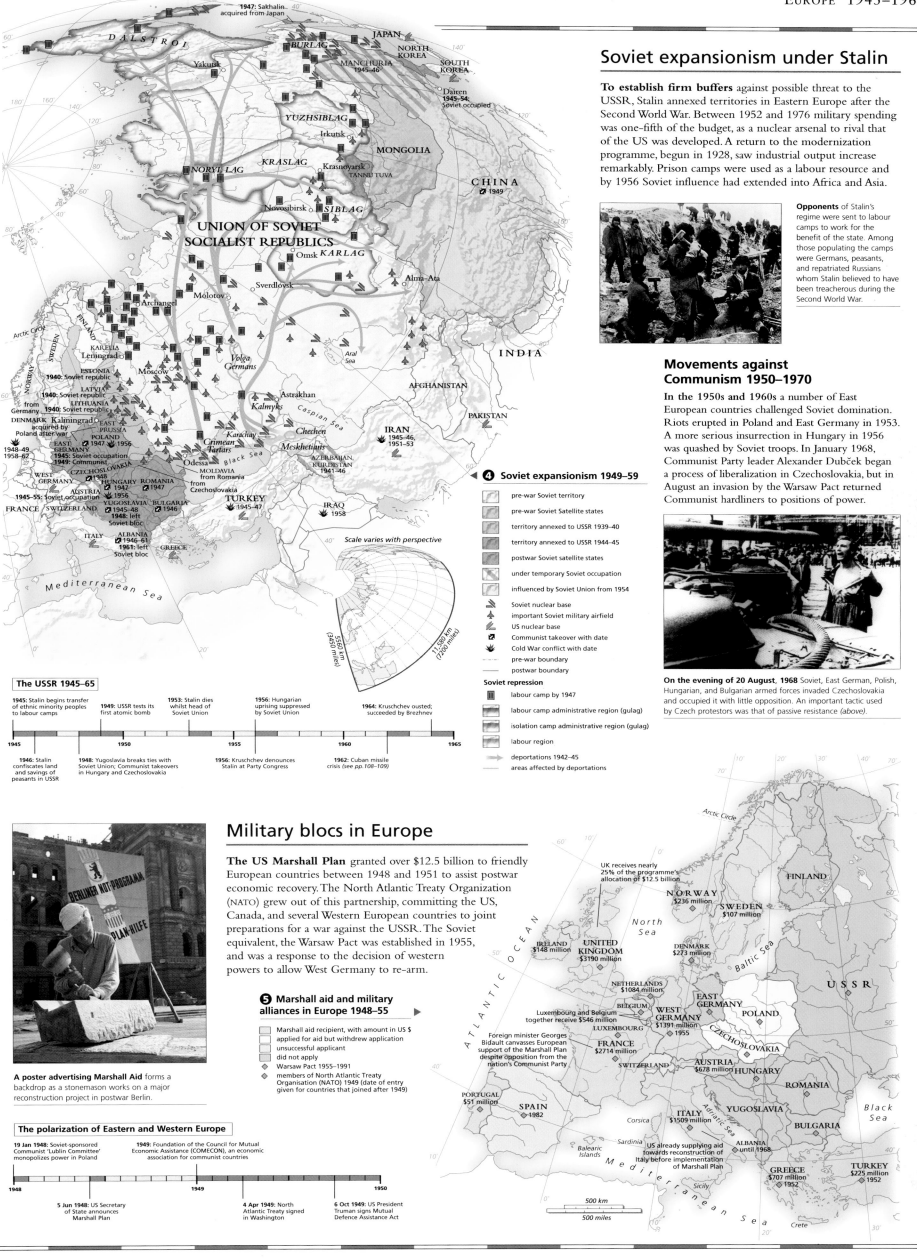

1947: Sakhalin acquired from Japan

BURLAG

JAPAN
NORTH KOREA
SOUTH KOREA

Yakutsk

MANCHURIA 1945–46

Dairen 1945–54: Soviet occupied

DALSTROI

YUZHSIBLAG

Irkutsk

MONGOLIA

NORYL LAG

KRASLAG

Krasnoyarsk

TANNU TUVA

CHINA ⚑ 1949

Novosibirsk

SIBLAG

UNION OF SOVIET SOCIALIST REPUBLICS

Omsk KARLAG

Sverdlovsk

Alma-Ata

INDIA

Archangel

Mólotov

Volga Germans

Aral Sea

AFGHANISTAN

FINLAND

SWEDEN

Leningrad

ESTONIA 1940: Soviet republic

Moscow

Astrakhan

Kalmyks

PAKISTAN

NORWAY

LATVIA 1940: Soviet republic from Germany

LITHUANIA 1940: Soviet republic

KARELIA

Karachay

Chechen

IRAN 1945–46, 1951–53

DENMARK acquired by Poland after war

Kaliningrad EAST PRUSSIA

Crimean Tartars

Meskhetians

Caspian Sea

IRAQ 1958

EAST GERMANY

POLAND 1947 1956

1948–49 1958–62

1945: Soviet occupation 1949: Communist

CZECHOSLOVAKIA 1948

Odessa

Black Sea

MOLDAVIA from Romania from Czechoslovakia

AZERBAIJAN, KURDISTAN 1941–46

WEST GERMANY

HUNGARY 1947

ROMANIA 1947

1945–55: Soviet occupation

AUSTRIA

1956

TURKEY 1945–47

FRANCE SWITZERLAND

YUGOSLAVIA 1945–48 1948: left Soviet bloc

BULGARIA 1946

ITALY

ALBANIA 1946–61 1961: left Soviet bloc

GREECE

Mediterranean Sea

Scale varies with perspective

5560 km (3450 miles)

11,580 km (7200 miles)

Soviet expansionism under Stalin

To establish firm buffers against possible threat to the USSR, Stalin annexed territories in Eastern Europe after the Second World War. Between 1952 and 1976 military spending was one-fifth of the budget, as a nuclear arsenal to rival that of the US was developed. A return to the modernization programme, begun in 1928, saw industrial output increase remarkably. Prison camps were used as a labour resource and by 1956 Soviet influence had extended into Africa and Asia.

Opponents of Stalin's regime were sent to labour camps to work for the benefit of the state. Among those populating the camps were Germans, peasants, and repatriated Russians whom Stalin believed to have been treacherous during the Second World War.

Movements against Communism 1950–1970

In the 1950s and 1960s a number of East European countries challenged Soviet domination. Riots erupted in Poland and East Germany in 1953. A more serious insurrection in Hungary in 1956 was quashed by Soviet troops. In January 1968, Communist Party leader Alexander Dubček began a process of liberalization in Czechoslovakia, but in August an invasion by the Warsaw Pact returned Communist hardliners to positions of power.

On the evening of 20 August, 1968 Soviet, East German, Polish, Hungarian, and Bulgarian armed forces invaded Czechoslovakia and occupied it with little opposition. An important tactic used by Czech protestors was that of passive resistance (above).

④ Soviet expansionism 1949–59

- pre-war Soviet territory
- pre-war Soviet Satellite states
- territory annexed to USSR 1939–40
- territory annexed to USSR 1944–45
- postwar Soviet satellite states
- under temporary Soviet occupation
- influenced by Soviet Union from 1954
- Soviet nuclear base
- important Soviet military airfield
- US nuclear base
- Communist takeover with date
- Cold War conflict with date
- pre-war boundary
- postwar boundary

Soviet repression
- labour camp by 1947
- labour camp administrative region (gulag)
- isolation camp administrative region (gulag)
- labour region
- deportations 1942–45
- areas affected by deportations

The USSR 1945–65

1945: Stalin begins transfer of ethnic minority peoples to labour camps

1946: Stalin confiscates land and savings of peasants in USSR

1948: Yugoslavia breaks ties with Soviet Union; Communist takeovers in Hungary and Czechoslovakia

1949: USSR tests its first atomic bomb

1953: Stalin dies whilst head of Soviet Union

1956: Kruschchev denounces Stalin at Party Congress

1956: Hungarian uprising suppressed by Soviet Union

1962: Cuban missile crisis (see pp.108–109)

1964: Kruschchev ousted; succeeded by Brezhnev

1945   1950   1955   1960   1965

Military blocs in Europe

The US Marshall Plan granted over $12.5 billion to friendly European countries between 1948 and 1951 to assist postwar economic recovery. The North Atlantic Treaty Organization (NATO) grew out of this partnership, committing the US, Canada, and several Western European countries to joint preparations for a war against the USSR. The Soviet equivalent, the Warsaw Pact was established in 1955, and was a response to the decision of western powers to allow West Germany to re-arm.

A poster advertising Marshall Aid forms a backdrop as a stonemason works on a major reconstruction project in postwar Berlin.

⑤ Marshall aid and military alliances in Europe 1948–55

- Marshall aid recipient, with amount in US $
- applied for aid but withdrew application
- unsuccessful applicant
- did not apply
- ◆ Warsaw Pact 1955–1991
- ◆ members of North Atlantic Treaty Organisation (NATO) 1949 (date of entry given for countries that joined after 1949)

The polarization of Eastern and Western Europe

19 Jan 1948: Soviet-sponsored Communist 'Lublin Committee' monopolizes power in Poland

5 Jun 1948: US Secretary of State announces Marshall Plan

1949: Foundation of the Council for Mutual Economic Assistance (COMECON), an economic association for communist countries

4 Apr 1949: North Atlantic Treaty signed in Washington

6 Oct 1949: US President Truman signs Mutual Defence Assistance Act

1948   1949   1950

UK receives nearly 25% of the programme's allocation of $12.5 billion

FINLAND

NORWAY $236 million

SWEDEN $107 million

North Sea

IRELAND $148 million

UNITED KINGDOM $3190 million

DENMARK $273 million

Baltic Sea

USSR

NETHERLANDS $1084 million

BELGIUM

EAST GERMANY

ATLANTIC OCEAN

Luxembourg and Belgium together receive $546 million

LUXEMBOURG

WEST GERMANY $1391 million 1955

POLAND

Foreign minister Georges Bidault canvasses European support of the Marshall Plan despite opposition from the nation's Communist Party

FRANCE $2714 million

CZECHOSLOVAKIA

SWITZERLAND

AUSTRIA $678 million

HUNGARY

ROMANIA

PORTUGAL $51 million

SPAIN 1982

Corsica

Sardinia

ITALY $1509 million

YUGOSLAVIA

Black Sea

BULGARIA

Balearic Islands

US already supplying aid towards reconstruction of Italy before implementation of Marshall Plan

ALBANIA until 1968

Sicily

GREECE $707 million 1952

TURKEY $225 million 1952

Mediterranean Sea

Crete

Arctic Circle

500 km

500 miles

MODERN EUROPE

BETWEEN 1948 AND 1989, the ideological divide between Communist Eastern Europe and the West stood firm. Divisions within Europe were compounded by economic growth in the West and stagnation and decline in the East. In November 1989, the fall of the Berlin Wall signalled the end of the Cold War, and a rise of nationalism in Eastern Europe brought about the collapse of Communism and the Soviet bloc. A range of newly-independent states were soon moving toward free elections, but political freedom had other, unforseen consequences. In 1991, historical ethnic tension fractured Yugoslavia. Conflict escalated into war in Bosnia in 1992, and bloody struggles in the Serbian province of Kosovo prompted NATO intervention in 1999.

In January 1999, the Euro was formally adopted as currency of the European Union.

① The growth of the European Union

members of European Coal and Steel Community (ECSC), European Atomic Energy Community (EAEC) and European Economic Community (EEC) 1957

EU original members 1957

EU members by 1973

EU members by 1986

EU members by 1995

applicants to EU (with date of application)

members of Council for Mutual Economic Assistance (COMECON) 1949

€ members of the European Monetary Union 1 Jan 1999

The European Union

The European Economic Community (EEC) was established in 1957, to guarantee the economic success of its members, and to develop a political union of states in an attempt to alleviate the risk of another war. The success of the liberalized trade policies sponsored by the EEC from the 1960s brought about efforts for further integration. In December 1991, the Maastricht Treaty created the European Union (EU) and committed the members to the introduction of a single currency. From an initial six members in 1957, by 1999, the EU had 15 member states.

The European Union headquarters have been based in Brussels since 1957.

The disintegration of the Communist bloc

By the 1970s it became clear that Communist economic policies were failing the nations of Eastern Europe. Economic instability throughout the 1970s and 1980s brought much of the Eastern bloc to the point of bankruptcy. The Soviet President, Gorbachev abandoned the satellite states in an effort to save the economy of the USSR. Beginning with protests in East Germany in 1989 which brought down the Communist government, nation after nation asserted their independence in a series of massive popular demonstrations which swiftly ended more than 50 years of Soviet control in Eastern Europe.

The decline of the Russian economy from 1990 forced many people to work within the 'informal economy' for income. This street hawker is selling toys from a makeshift stall.

② The collapse of Communism in Eastern Europe

Soviet Union to 1991

Soviet-dominated Eastern Europe to 1989

German Democratic Republic (GDR), united with Federal Republic of Germany 1990

Czechoslovakia to Dec 1992

Yugoslavia to 1991

other Communist state before 1991

1990 date of first free election

The rise of nationalism

The wave of nationalism which began in the German Democratic Republic was repeated throughout Eastern Europe. The reunification of Germany in 1990 was followed by the collapse of the USSR, and its division into 15 independent states. In 1993, Czechoslovakia split into two new republics: Slovakia and the Czech Republic. New governments were forced to implement strict economic measures to stem decline, and moderate socialism replaced Communism as the main political force in Eastern Europe.

In November 1989, these peaceful demonstrators in Prague united with other cities across Czechoslovakia in their protest against Communist rule to bring about the so-called 'Velvet Revolution'.

Conflict in Yugoslavia from 1991

Following the death of Communist premier Josip Broz (Tito) in 1980, the fragility of the multi-national Federal People's Republic of Yugoslavia quickly became apparent. The election of Serbian leader Slobodan Milošević in 1987 brought an upsurge of Serb nationalism which struck fear in the multi-ethnic republics. In June 1991, the provinces of Slovenia and Croatia declared their independence. Serbian forces attacked both republics in an effort to compel their return to the federation. In January 1992, Serbs in Bosnia and Herzegovina began the persecution of Bosnia's Muslims – a policy which became known as 'ethnic cleansing'. Bitter fighting between Serbs, Muslims, and Croats ensued, and foreign intervention was required to bring the war to an end in 1995. In 1998, further persecution of non-Serb peoples – this time the ethnic Albanians of Kosovo – provoked NATO military intervention.

Bosnian Muslim refugees take up temporary residence on a basketball court as they flee Serbian forces at the height of the 'ethnic cleansing' campaign in 1993.

3 Conflict in former Yugoslavia 1990–99

The ethnic composition of Yugoslavia, 1991
- Albanian
- Bulgarian
- Croat
- Hungarian
- Macedonian
- Muslim
- Romanian
- Serb and Montenegrin
- Slovene
- Yugoslav regions
- (Nov 1992) date of secession from Federal Republic of Yugoslavia

The Croatian conflict
- Serb advances by Dec 1991
- Serb controlled regions 1991–95/96
- Croat advances, autumn 1995

The Bosnian War
- secured by Yugoslav army and Bosnian Serb forces by Dec 1992
- area controlled by Bosnian Croat forces, Dec 1992
- attacking Serbs 1993
- attacking Bosnian Muslims 1993
- Autonomous Province of Western Bosnia Sep 1993–Aug 1994
- area remaining under control of breakaway Serbian forces, Oct 1995
- areas of combat between Croats and Bosnian Muslims
- Muslim secure zone

The Kosovan crisis
- Kosovo Liberation Army (KLA) stronghold
- Serb forces attacking KLA, 1999

The collapse of the Soviet Union

From 1985, Mikhail Gorbachev, leader of the Soviet Union, set about the political and economic reform of the Soviet system with his policy of *perestroika* (restructuring). The Supreme Soviet Council was replaced with a Congress of People's deputies in 1988 and a 450-strong parliament was elected in 1989. In 1990 nationalist unrest grew out of economic decline. An attempted coup by hard-line Communists in 1991, quashed by Russian president Boris Yeltsin, brought an end to Communist rule and accelerated the disbandment of the USSR. Fifteen Soviet republics declared their independence to found the Commonwealth of Independent States (CIS) in 1991, later known as the Russian Federation.

War and ethnic tension in Yugoslavia from 1974

1974: Revised Yugoslav constitution grants Kosovo autonomy

1989: Fearing secession attempt Milošević strips Kosovo of autonomy it has enjoyed since 1974; tension between Serbs and ethnic Albanians escalates

1992: All out war in Bosnia

1999: Peace talks collapse; NATO begins bombing campaign

1970 — 1980 — 1990 — 2000

1987: Slobodan Milošević rises to power in Yugoslavia

1991: Croatia, Slovenia, and Bosnia declare independence from Yugoslavia

1995: Peace agreement ends the Bosnian war

1998: Milošević sends troops into areas controlled by Kosovo Liberation Army (KLA)

Scale varies with perspective

5560 km (3450 miles)

12,320 km (7660 miles)

4 The disintegration of the Soviet Union
- territory controlled by USSR in 1945
- Russian federation from 1991
- autonomous regions
- major concentration of minority Russians
- Commonwealth of Independent States 1991
- interstate conflict
- civil war
- ethnic conflict (with date)
- AD autonomous district

The decline of Communism in Europe

1987: Washington arms control treaty decommissions one-fifth of Soviet arms

1988: Gorbachev initiates *perestroika* and *glasnost*

1990–91: Baltic republics declare independence; end of COMECON Jun 1991

1992: Civil war in Georgia, Bosnia-Herzegovina

1993: Czech Republic and Slovakia become separate states

1985 — 1995

1986: Gorbachev and US President Reagan meet at Reykjavik to discuss disarmament

1989: Nationalist protests across Eastern Europe signal rejection of Communism

1990: Reunification of Germany

1991: Unsuccessful coup attempt in USSR; disintegration of Soviet Union

1994: Russian troops march on Chechnya

1994: Chechen declaration of independence provokes war with Russia

1989–90: Uzbeks and Meskhetians

1989: Kazakhs and Lezgians

1990: Kirghiz and Uzbeks
1989: Kirghiz and Tajiks

1988: Armenians and Azerbaijanis

215

WEST ASIA
REGIONAL HISTORY

Vegetation type

ice cap and glacier

polar or alpine desert

tundra

semi-desert or sparsely vegetated

grassland

forest or open woodland

temperate desert

tropical desert

desert

coastline (present-day)

coastline (18,000 years ago)

THE HISTORICAL LANDSCAPE

A SEEMINGLY INHOSPITABLE REALM, arid, largely desert or mountainous plateau, West Asia lays claim to a panoply of grand names – the Garden of Eden, the Fertile Crescent, the Promised Land, the Cradle of Civilization, the Crossroads of History. Lying at the meeting point of the three Old World continents, Africa, Europe, and Asia, the region was blessed with the fertile soils, beneficent climate and diverse demography to earn these titles. As such it remained the pivotal point of Old World, or Afro-Eurasian, culture, communications, trade, and – inevitably – warfare, until relatively recent times. In addition, possibly as a consequence of this geographic primacy, the region was also the birthplace of Judaism, Christianity, and Islam, which became three of the most widely observed world religions. Despite the attentions of European colonial powers, West Asia has upheld its inherent qualities and traditions; rivalries and divisions persist alongside ways of life and artistic traditions now centuries old, a cultural longevity sustained by religion on the one hand and, in the 20th century, the region's control of the world's most valuable commodity – oil.

Most of West Asia is a combination of dry sandy deserts and mountainous plateaux that remain sparsely populated, or totally uninhabited even today.

The mountainous Iranian Plateau is cut off from the moist ocean air, and temperatures fluctuate greatly between night and day. Humans lived in the mountain fringes, but the plateau's interior remained empty of human settlement because of the cold, dry climate.

The banks of the Euphrates and Tigris rivers were where West Asia's first towns and cities were established. The fertile soils supported the world's first domesticated cereal crops from around 8000 BCE.

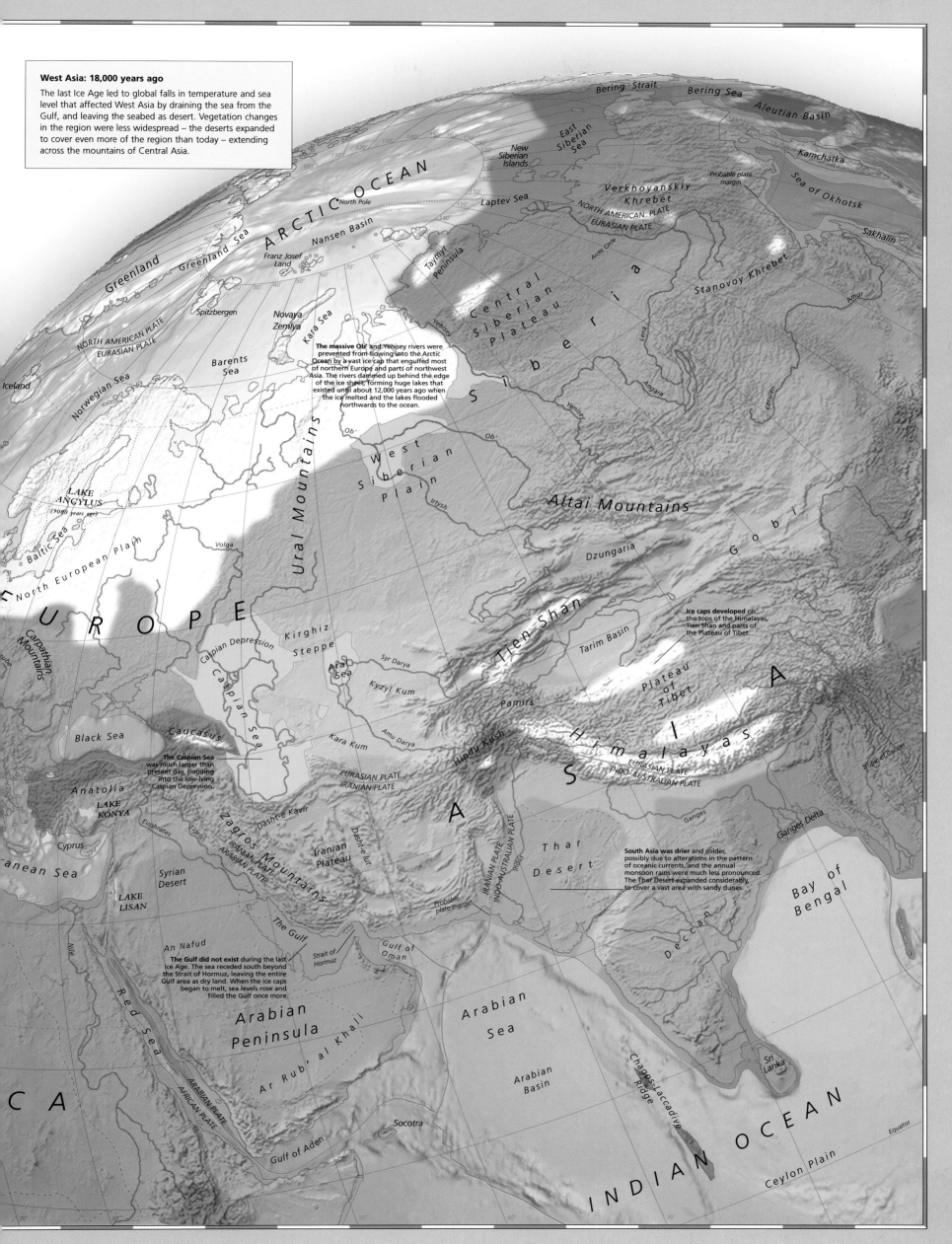

West Asia: 18,000 years ago

The last Ice Age led to global falls in temperature and sea level that affected West Asia by draining the sea from the Gulf, and leaving the seabed as desert. Vegetation changes in the region were less widespread – the deserts expanded to cover even more of the region than today – extending across the mountains of Central Asia.

The massive Ob' and Yenisey rivers were prevented from flowing into the Arctic Ocean by a vast ice cap that engulfed most of northern Europe and parts of northwest Asia. The rivers dammed up behind the edge of the ice sheet, forming huge lakes that existed until about 12,000 years ago when the ice melted and the lakes flooded northwards to the ocean.

Ice caps developed on the tops of the Himalayas, Tien Shan and parts of the Plateau of Tibet.

The Caspian Sea was much larger than present day, flooding into the low-lying Caspian Depression.

South Asia was drier and colder, possibly due to alterations in the pattern of oceanic currents, and the annual monsoon rains were much less pronounced. The Thar Desert expanded considerably, to cover a vast area with sandy dunes.

The Gulf did not exist during the last Ice Age. The sea receded south beyond the Strait of Hormuz, leaving the entire Gulf area as dry land. When the ice caps began to melt, sea levels rose and filled the Gulf once more.

ARCTIC OCEAN
Bering Strait
Bering Sea
Aleutian Basin
Kamchatka
Sea of Okhotsk
Greenland
Greenland Sea
North Pole
Nansen Basin
Laptev Sea
New Siberian Islands
East Siberian Sea
Verkhoyanskiy Khrebet
Probable plate margin
NORTH AMERICAN PLATE
EURASIAN PLATE
Sakhalin
Franz Josef Land
Taymyr Peninsula
Stanovoy Khrebet
Amur
Iceland
Spitzbergen
Novaya Zemlya
Kara Sea
Central Siberian Plateau
S i b e r i a
Norwegian Sea
NORTH AMERICAN PLATE
EURASIAN PLATE
Barents Sea
Yenisey
Ob'
Angara
Lena
Kerulen
LAKE ANCYLUS
(9000 years ago)
Baltic Sea
North European Plain
West Siberian Plain
Ob'
Irtysh
Altai Mountains
Yenisey
Gobi
E U R O P E
Ural Mountains
Volga
Dzungaria
Carpathian Mountains
Kirghiz Steppe
Caspian Depression
Aral Sea
Syr Darya
Tien Shan
Tarim Basin
Plateau of Tibet
A S I A
Black Sea
Caucasus
Caspian Sea
Kyzyl Kum
Kara Kum
Amu Darya
Pamirs
Himalayas
EURASIAN PLATE
INDO-AUSTRALIAN PLATE
Anatolia
LAKE KONYA
Hindu Kush
EURASIAN PLATE
IRANIAN PLATE
Dasht-e Kavir
Ganges
Tropic of Cancer
Cyprus
Euphrates
Tigris
Zagros Mountains
Iranian Plateau
Dasht-e Lut
IRANIAN PLATE
INDO-AUSTRALIAN PLATE
Thar Desert
Ganges Delta
...anean Sea
IRANIAN PLATE
ARABIAN PLATE
Syrian Desert
LAKE LISAN
Probable plate margin
Indus
Deccan
Bay of Bengal
An Nafud
The Gulf
Gulf of Oman
Nile
Red Sea
Arabian Peninsula
Strait of Hormuz
Arabian Sea
ARABIAN PLATE
AFRICAN PLATE
Ar Rub' al Khali
Arabian Basin
Sri Lanka
...CA
Gulf of Aden
Socotra
Chagos-Laccadive Ridge
INDIAN OCEAN
Ceylon Plain
Equator

217

WEST ASIA

EXPLORATION AND MAPPING

Invented by the Greeks, the astrolabe was developed by the Arabs into an indispensable tool of navigation.

SINCE THE EMERGENCE of city–states and trade, West Asia has formed the crossroads between Europe, Africa, and Asia. The Sumerians and Babylonians accumulated local geographical knowledge, but it was the Greeks, following the conquests of Alexander the Great, who began a systematic recording of the region's geography. The Romans built on the knowledge of the Greeks, as did the Arabs when, in the 7th century, Islam spread throughout West Asia. In the 13th century, when the Mongols controlled Central Asia, traffic between China and the West flourished, leaving the way open for the great journeys of Marco Polo and William of Rubruck. The region least well-known to outsiders, though its geography was well understood by its desert tribes, was Arabia, finally mapped in the 19th and 20th centuries.

The Graeco-Roman view

Many merchants from Greek colonies in Asia Minor traded eastwards to the Caspian Sea. Then, in the 4th century BCE, Alexander the Great led his army into West Asia, accompanied by a team of surveyors who recorded the route. Though none survive today, these records were a major source for subsequent geographers. Extending his quest for knowledge to the ocean, Alexander sent his admiral, Nearchus, to explore a route from the Indus to the Persian Gulf. The Greek merchant Hippalus was the first European sailor to recognize the regularity of the monsoon winds, harnessing them for his voyage to India. Arabia remained largely unknown, despite an exploratory expedition led by the Roman general Aelius Gallus.

This reconstructed map shows the world known to the Greeks in 5th century BCE. It is based on descriptions in the *History* of Herodotus, who travelled in Europe, Egypt, and West Asia, and gathered additional information from people he met en route.

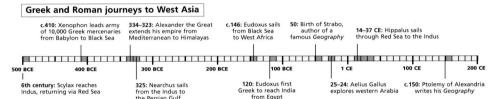

Greek and Roman journeys to West Asia

c.410: Xenophon leads army of 10,000 Greek mercenaries from Babylon to Black Sea
334–323: Alexander the Great extends his empire from Mediterranean to Himalayas
c.146: Eudoxus sails from Black Sea to West Africa
50: Birth of Strabo, author of a famous *Geography*
14–37 CE: Hippalus sails through Red Sea to the Indus

6th century: Scylax reaches Indus, returning via Red Sea
325: Nearchus sails from the Indus to the Persian Gulf
120: Eudoxus first Greek to reach India from Egypt
25–24: Aelius Gallus explores western Arabia
c.150: Ptolemy of Alexandria writes his *Geography*

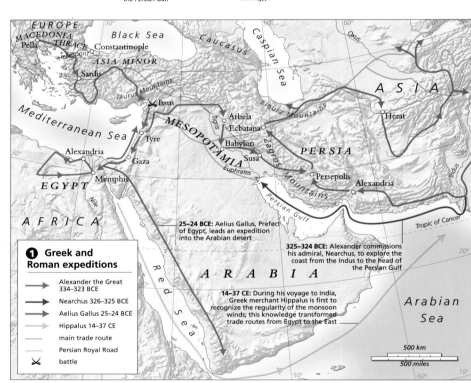

① **Greek and Roman expeditions**

→ Alexander the Great 334–323 BCE
→ Nearchus 326–325 BCE
→ Aelius Gallus 25–24 BCE
→ Hippalus 14–37 CE
— main trade route
— Persian Royal Road
⚔ battle

25–24 BCE: Aelius Gallus, Prefect of Egypt, leads an expedition into the Arabian desert

325–324 BCE: Alexander commissions his admiral, Nearchus, to explore the coast from the Indus to the head of the Persian Gulf

14–37 CE: During his voyage to India, Greek merchant Hippalus is first to recognize the regularity of the monsoon winds; this knowledge transformed trade routes from Egypt to the East

Islamic travellers

Within a century of the death of Muhammad in 632, the Muslim world stretched from the Iberian Peninsula to the borders of Tang China. Building on knowledge acquired by earlier civilizations, in particular the Greeks, and incorporating information gathered by merchants, sailors, and other travellers, Arab geographers were able to create maps of the vast Islamic realms. By the 12th century they had an excellent understanding of West Asia, Europe, and North Africa. In 1325 Ibn Battuta *(see p. 68)* began the first of the great journeys which were to take him to all corners of the Islamic world.

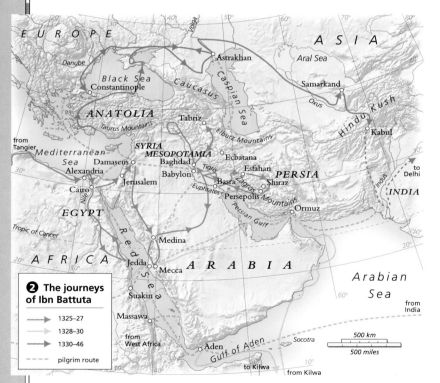

② **The journeys of Ibn Battuta**

→ 1325–27
→ 1328–30
→ 1330–46
--- pilgrim route

To a fanfare of trumpets, Muslims set out across the Arabian desert to make their annual pilgrimage to Mecca.

The Moroccan al-Idrisi was one of the most famous geographers of his day. The map shown here is a facsimile of the West Asian section of the beautiful world map he produced for Roger of Sicily c.1154. South is at the top, so the Mediterranean is on the right.

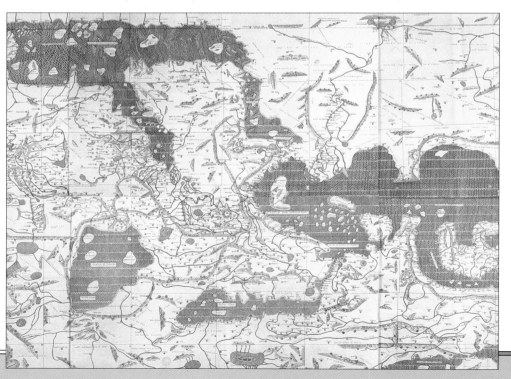

European pilgrims visit the Holy Sepulchre in Jerusalem in this illustration from an illuminated manuscript of the travels of Marco Polo.

Medieval and Renaissance travellers from Europe

In the late 13th century, in the lull following the first Mongol invasions, Europeans began to venture east across Asia. Both William of Rubruck's mission to the Mongol Khan for Louis IX of France and Marco Polo's epic journeys yielded a wealth of geographical information. But with the rise to power of the Ottoman Turks, Central Asia's trade routes were once more closed to Europeans. Later explorers, such as Sir Robert Sherley, focused their attention on Persia, sworn enemy of the Turks.

Juan de la Cosa's early 16th-century world map demonstrates how little Europeans of the period knew of West Asia to the east of the Holy Land. Inland from the coast of the Levant, the cartographer compensated for lack of detail with an attractive illustration of the Three Kings on their journey to Bethlehem.

❸ Medieval and Renaissance travellers

- William of Rubruck 1253–55
- possible route of Marco Polo 1271–95
- Anthony Jenkinson 1557–64
- John Newbery 1581–82
- Robert Sherley 1598–1600
- Thomas Herbert 1627–29

500 km
500 miles

European travellers in West Asia 1200–1700				
1200	1300	1400	1500	1600	1700

1253–55: William of Rubruck crosses Asia to Karakorum

1271–95: Marco Polo travels throughout Asia, returning by ship through Persian Gulf

1487–89: Portuguese Pero de Covilhã sails through Red Sea to India

1502: Italian Lodovico di Varthema visits Arabia disguised as an Arab

1557–64: Jenkinson travels through Russia to Caspian Sea

1581–82: Newbery visits Mesopotamia and Persia

1598: Anthony and Robert Sherley travel to Persia, where they meet Shah Abbas

1627: Herbert's travels in Persia

MAPS FOR PILGRIMS

The Holy Land has possibly been the subject of more maps than any other part of the world. To medieval Christians, the holy city of Jerusalem was the centre of their world, a concept depicted by many medieval maps which show a circular walled city, instead of a rectangular one, to symbolize the perfection of the Heavenly Jerusalem. Pilgrims and crusaders travelling to the Holy Land carried with them maps which were little more than illustrated itineraries of the towns they would pass through on their journey through Europe.

A 13th-century French map depicts the walled city of Jerusalem schematically, showing just the city's most important features, including the Holy Sepulchre and the Tower of David. Below, a crusader puts mounted Saracens to flight.

European travellers in Arabia

Although criss-crossed by Muslim pilgrim routes, maps of the interior of Arabia were rare until the 19th century. The region's hostile terrain and reputation for religious fanaticism remained considerable barriers to exploration by Europeans, despite the peninsula's wealth of valuable raw materials. Those that successfully penetrated Arabia did so armed with fluent Arabic and disguised as Muslims, particularly those who entered Islam's holy cities. The 19th century brought a rush of European explorers, especially the British, to Arabia. The last area to be explored was the Rub' al Khali (Empty Quarter), crossed first by Bertram Thomas in 1930–31 and explored more thoroughly by Wilfred Thesiger. The most detailed maps of the peninsula were made from the late 1920s following surveys by oil companies.

Europeans in the Arabian Peninsula 1800–1950					
1800	1850	1900	1950

1812: Burckhardt discovers Petra, ancient capital of Nabataea

1814: Burckhardt visits Mecca

1818: Sadleir makes first east–west crossing

1853: Richard Burton visits Mecca and Medina in Arab disguise

1862–63: Palgrave makes first west-east crossing through the Nafud

1864: Guarmani travels through northern Nejd

1876–78: Doughty's Arabian journeys

1879: Wilfrid Scawen Blunt and his wife, Anne, travel to Nejd to buy horses

1888: Publication of Doughty's classic Travels in Arabia Deserta

1930: Thomas first European to cross Empty Quarter

1932: Philby crosses Empty Quarter

1946–48: Thesiger's double crossing of Empty Quarter

In 1762 a Danish surveyor, Carsten Niebuhr, took part in the first scientific expedition to the Arabian Peninsula. A team of Scandinavian and German experts recorded the flora and fauna of the Yemen and studied its peoples. Most of the party died, but Niebuhr survived and published an account of the expedition, *Descriptions of Arabia*, with several detailed maps of the region.

Non-Muslims entered Islam's holy cities at their peril. Richard Burton, seen here convincingly disguised as a Muslim pilgrim, visited both Mecca and Medina.

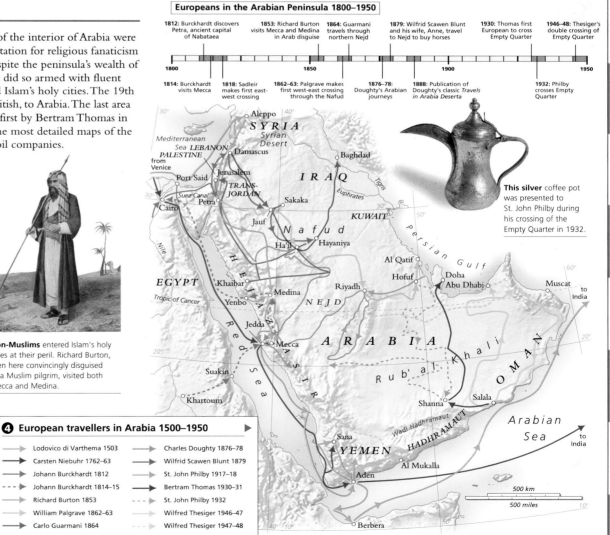

This silver coffee pot was presented to St. John Philby during his crossing of the Empty Quarter in 1932.

❹ European travellers in Arabia 1500–1950

- Lodovico di Varthema 1503
- Carsten Niebuhr 1762–63
- Johann Burckhardt 1812
- Johann Burckhardt 1814–15
- Richard Burton 1853
- William Palgrave 1862–63
- Carlo Guarmani 1864
- Charles Doughty 1876–78
- Wilfrid Scawen Blunt 1879
- St. John Philby 1917–18
- Bertram Thomas 1930–31
- St. John Philby 1932
- Wilfred Thesiger 1946–47
- Wilfred Thesiger 1947–48

500 km
500 miles

FROM VILLAGE TO EMPIRE

This inlaid chlorite vessel is decorated with a cat fighting a serpent Made in southern Persia, it was found at Nippur in Mesopotamia.

THE 'FERTILE CRESCENT' extends from the Persian Gulf along the flanks of the Zagros Mountains, swings west across northern Mesopotamia and down the Levant coast to Egypt. This region is traditionally seen as the cradle of civilization; here the first farming settlements were established, expanding into fortified walled towns. By 3500 BCE the first city-states, centres of production and trade *(see pp.24–25)*, had grown up in Mesopotamia. In 2300 BCE, a number of these were united by Sargon of Akkad to form the first empire. Other empires followed: the empire of Ur, the first Assyrian Empire, the first Babylonian Empire. In the 2nd millennium BCE, a new centre of power developed in Anatolia: the Hittite Empire, which battled with Egypt for control of the Levant.

The development of agriculture in the Fertile Crescent

Bounded by mountains to the north and east, and desert to the south, the Fertile Crescent is relatively well-watered. Wild grains, such as einkorn wheat and barley, grew on the moist mountain uplands, also home to the ancestors of domestic sheep and goats. By 10,000 BCE, this combination of resources enabled local groups to establish the first settled agricultural communities; cereals were cultivated and stored, and animals domesticated.

Larger settlements, such as Jericho (8000 BCE) in the Jordan valley and Çatal Hüyük (7000 BCE) in Anatolia, became regional centres, surrounded by cultivable land and showing evidence of crafts and long-distance trade.

A number of skulls, with features modelled in gypsum and cowrie shells for eyes, were found beneath the floors of houses at Jericho.

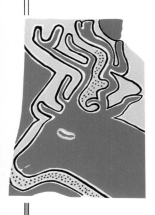

The wall of a shrine at Çatal Hüyük was decorated with this painting of a stag's head, seen here in an artist's reconstruction. One of the oldest towns in the world, Çatal Hüyük had tightly-packed houses built of mud bricks with flat roofs.

❶ Early farming in southwest Asia 8000–5000 BCE ▶

Vegetation
- floodplain
- Mediterranean forest
- forest
- steppe
- semi-desert
- desert
- more than 250 mm mean annual rainfall

Areas of domestication of principal staple crops
- barley
- einkorn wheat
- emmer wheat
- present-day coastline/river
- ○ site of major farming settlement

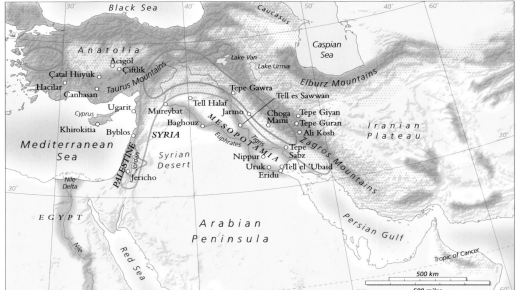

The first cities of West Asia

Farmers from northern and central Mesopotamia began to settle the alluvial plain of the Tigris and Euphrates around 6000 BCE. Irrigation enabled enough food to be produced to support large settled communities. In time, some settlements developed into cities. Each had at its heart a mud-brick temple raised on a high platform. These structures later became ziggurats like the one at Ur *(see pp.24–25)*, one of the great Sumerian cities of the 3rd millennium BCE. While sharing a common culture, each city remained an independent city-state.

After 3500: Development of first urban civilization at Sumer; rise of Uruk	3100: Cuneiform script emerges in Mesopotamia	2700: Gilgamesh rules Sumerian city of Uruk	2500: 'Royal Graves' of Ur

3500 BCE	3300	3100	2900	2700	2500 BCE

3250: Pictographic clay tablets used for temple accounts	3200: Evidence of use of wheeled transport in Sumer		The first cities

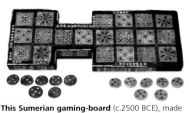

This Sumerian gaming-board (c.2500 BCE), made of wood and inlaid with shell, bone, and lapis lazuli, was found in the 'Royal Graves' at Ur. Players cast dice or threw sticks before moving their counters, which were kept in a drawer set into the board.

The growth of Uruk

From 4000 BCE, Uruk expanded into one of the leading Sumerian cities. Its closely-packed mud-brick houses were enclosed by a 9.5 km wall. Beyond the wall, crops such as barley, sesame, and onions grew in fields irrigated by a network of canals from the Euphrates. Two ceremonial complexes dominated the city; the Anu ziggurat, and the Sanctuary of Eanna. The latter contained a columned hall 30 m wide, the columns decorated with mosaics of coloured stone cones set in mud plaster. Many of the works of art found at Uruk, Ur, and other Sumerian cities used materials such as alabaster, gemstones, and lapis lazuli, from as far afield as Central Asia and the Indus Valley.

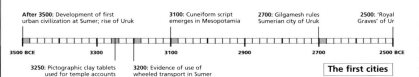

❷ The first cities c.4300–2300 BCE
- fertile area of early agriculture
- ⛨ ziggurat or temple
- ○ city or important site
- irrigation and ancient water course
- present-day coastline/river
- trade route

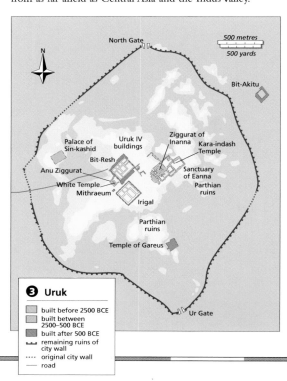

❸ Uruk
- built before 2500 BCE
- built between 2500–500 BCE
- built after 500 BCE
- remaining ruins of city wall
- original city wall
- road

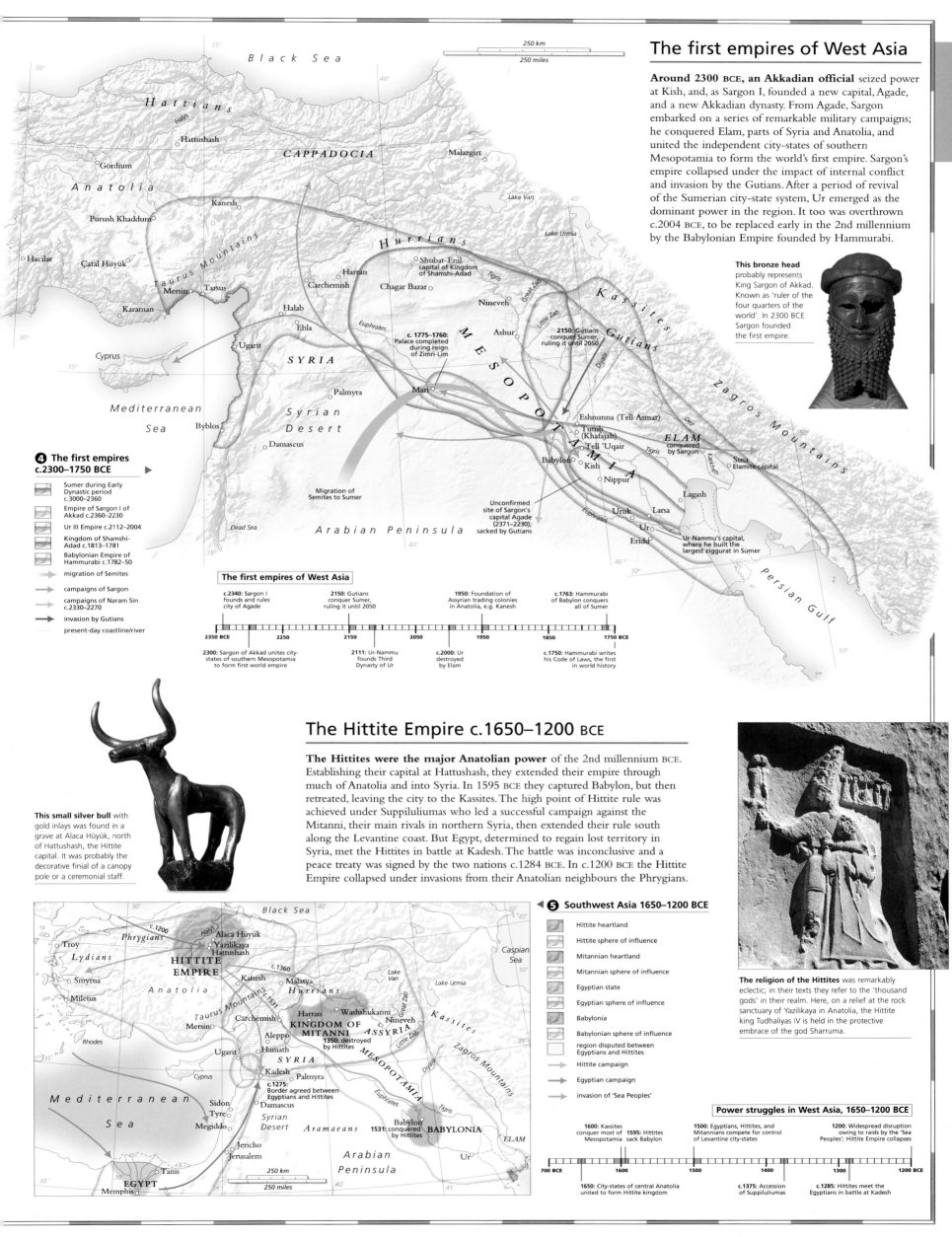

The first empires of West Asia

Around 2300 BCE, an Akkadian official seized power at Kish, and, as Sargon I, founded a new capital, Agade, and a new Akkadian dynasty. From Agade, Sargon embarked on a series of remarkable military campaigns; he conquered Elam, parts of Syria and Anatolia, and united the independent city-states of southern Mesopotamia to form the world's first empire. Sargon's empire collapsed under the impact of internal conflict and invasion by the Gutians. After a period of revival of the Sumerian city-state system, Ur emerged as the dominant power in the region. It too was overthrown c.2004 BCE, to be replaced early in the 2nd millennium by the Babylonian Empire founded by Hammurabi.

This bronze head probably represents King Sargon of Akkad. Known as 'ruler of the four quarters of the world'. In 2300 BCE Sargon founded the first empire.

The first empires c.2300–1750 BCE

- Sumer during Early Dynastic period c.3000–2360
- Empire of Sargon I of Akkad c.2360–2230
- Ur III Empire c.2112–2004
- Kingdom of Shamshi-Adad c.1813–1781
- Babylonian Empire of Hammurabi c.1782–50
- migration of Semites
- campaigns of Sargon
- campaigns of Naram Sin c.2330–2270
- invasion by Gutians
- present-day coastline/river

The first empires of West Asia

c.2340: Sargon I founds and rules city of Agade
2300: Sargon of Akkad unites city-states of southern Mesopotamia to form first world empire
2150: Gutians conquer Sumer, ruling it until 2050
2111: Ur-Nammu founds Third Dynasty of Ur
1950: Foundation of Assyrian trading colonies in Anatolia e.g. Kanesh
c.2000: Ur destroyed by Elam
c.1763: Hammurabi of Babylon conquers all of Sumer
c.1750: Hammurabi writes his Code of Laws, the first in world history

The Hittite Empire c.1650–1200 BCE

The Hittites were the major Anatolian power of the 2nd millennium BCE. Establishing their capital at Hattushash, they extended their empire through much of Anatolia and into Syria. In 1595 BCE they captured Babylon, but then retreated, leaving the city to the Kassites. The high point of Hittite rule was achieved under Suppiluliumas who led a successful campaign against the Mitanni, their main rivals in northern Syria, then extended their rule south along the Levantine coast. But Egypt, determined to regain lost territory in Syria, met the Hittites in battle at Kadesh. The battle was inconclusive and a peace treaty was signed by the two nations c.1284 BCE. In c.1200 BCE the Hittite Empire collapsed under invasions from their Anatolian neighbours the Phrygians.

This small silver bull with gold inlays was found in a grave at Alaca Hüyük, north of Hattushash, the Hittite capital. It was probably the decorative finial of a canopy pole or a ceremonial staff.

The religion of the Hittites was remarkably eclectic; in their texts they refer to the 'thousand gods' in their realm. Here, on a relief at the rock sanctuary of Yazilikaya in Anatolia, the Hittite king Tudhaliyas IV is held in the protective embrace of the god Sharruma.

Southwest Asia 1650–1200 BCE

- Hittite heartland
- Hittite sphere of influence
- Mitannian heartland
- Mitannian sphere of influence
- Egyptian state
- Egyptian sphere of influence
- Babylonia
- Babylonian sphere of influence
- region disputed between Egyptians and Hittites
- Hittite campaign
- Egyptian campaign
- invasion of 'Sea Peoples'

Power struggles in West Asia, 1650–1200 BCE

1600: Kassites conquer most of Mesopotamia
1595: Hittites sack Babylon
1650: City-states of central Anatolia united to form Hittite kingdom
1500: Egyptians, Hittites, and Mitannians compete for control of Levantine city-states
c.1375: Accession of Suppiluliumas
1200: Widespread disruption owing to raids by the 'Sea Peoples'; Hittite Empire collapses
c.1285: Hittites meet the Egyptians in battle at Kadesh

EARLY EMPIRES OF WEST ASIA

The Ishtar Gate, the entrance to the great city of Babylon, was built by King Nebuchadnezzar II.

THE FIRST MILLENNIUM BCE saw a succession of powerful empires in West Asia. The first, established in the 10th century, was the Assyrian Empire. The Assyrians built their empire on the prowess of their armies and their administrative efficiency. After their overthrow by a Babylonian-Mede coalition in 612 BCE, Babylon became the dominant regional power, until it was overthrown in turn by the Persians. Founded by Cyrus the Great, the Persian Empire expanded to become the largest the world had yet seen, stretching from the Aegean to the Indus. While its empires rose and fell, West Asia was responsible for an invention of lasting value to the whole world. From its early beginnings in Mesopotamia, writing was developed into an alphabet by the Phoenicians, who carried it into the Mediterranean world, where it was adopted by the Greeks.

THE HISTORY AND LEGENDS OF MESOPOTAMIA

Much modern knowledge of the early history of West Asia is based on the libraries of clay tablets found at the palaces of the great rulers of Mesopotamia. The Royal Library of the Assyrian king Ashurbanipal at Nineveh yielded a spectacular find of some 20,000 clay tablets dealing with almost every aspect of life. One of the great literary compositions is the story of Gilgamesh, a legendary Sumerian king, based on an epic that dates back to the early 2nd millennium BCE. There is also an account of the creation, and another of a great deluge that covers the face of the earth with water. There are clear similarities between the account of the flood and the Old Testament account of Noah's Flood in Genesis.

Gilgamesh was the legendary king of the Sumerian city-state of Uruk, and the hero of an epic in which he recounts his exploits during his search for immortality.

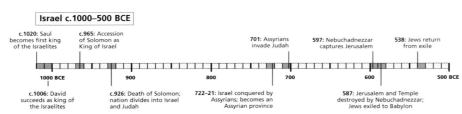

Israel c.1000–500 BCE

c.1020: Saul becomes first king of the Israelites
c.965: Accession of Solomon as King of Israel
701: Assyrians invade Judah
597: Nebuchadnezzar captures Jerusalem
538: Jews return from exile

c.1006: David succeeds as king of the Israelites
c.926: Death of Solomon; nation divides into Israel and Judah
722–21: Israel conquered by Assyrians; becomes an Assyrian province
587: Jerusalem and Temple destroyed by Nebuchadnezzar; Jews exiled to Babylon

Israel in the time of David

When David became as king of Israel c.1006 BCE, he moved the capital from Hebron to Jerusalem, establishing it as the political and religious centre of the Israelites. By defeating the Philistines, and extending Israelite rule in the region, David created a small empire. Under his successor, Solomon – builder of the Temple at Jerusalem – the nation prospered, but at his death in 926 BCE it divided into two kingdoms, Judah and Israel. In 721 BCE Israel was absorbed into the Assyrian Empire; Judah, having resisted repeated invasions, fell to Nebuchadnezzar of Babylon in 597 BCE. The city of Jerusalem was destroyed and the Jews forced into exile in Babylon for almost 50 years.

This ivory plaque was found at Megiddo, a small, but important palace/fortress in northern Israel. It shows that Egyptian influence was still strong in the Levant.

❶ Palestine at the time of David c.1006–966 BCE ▶

Judah and Israel
conquered kingdom
vassal
boundary of David's empire
boundary between kingdoms of Judah and Israel from 926

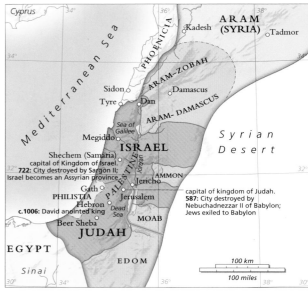

722: City destroyed by Sargon II; Israel becomes an Assyrian province.
587: City destroyed by Nebuchadnezzar II of Babylon; Jews exiled to Babylon

capital of kingdom of Judah.

The Assyrian and Babylonian empires

950: Assyrian Empire founded
880: Nimrud becomes capital of Assyria
722: Accession of Sargon II; Israel absorbed into Assyria
689: Babylon destroyed by Assyrian king Sennacherib
612: Assyrian Empire falls; destruction of Nineveh
539: Conquest of Babylonia by Persian king, Cyrus II

900: Establishment of Kingdom of Urartu, which lasts till its destruction by Assyrians in 714
744: Accession of Tiglath-Pileser III
705: Capital of Assyria moves to Nineveh
669: Assyrian king Esarhaddon conquers north Egypt
605: Nebuchadnezzar II succeeds to throne of Babylon

The Assyrian and Babylonian empires c.950–600 BCE

The first Assyrian Empire was established early in the 2nd millennium BCE, but collapsed under attacks from Babylon and the Mitanni. Under a series of powerful and ruthless kings it was revived, reaching its apogee during the reigns of Tiglath-Pileser III, Sargon II, and Ashurbanipal. Babylon was reconquered, the Kingdom of Urartu defeated, and the empire extended to the Mediterranean and, briefly, into northern Egypt. These conquests were achieved by a well-equipped, well-disciplined army that made skilful use of cavalry. But in the mid-7th century BCE, attacks by Medes and Scythians, combined with a revolt in Babylonia, sent the empire into a terminal decline. In 625 BCE the Chaldaeans took control of Babylon, and under Nebuchadnezzar II, the Babylonian Empire took over most of the former provinces of Assyria, including Syria and Palestine.

A relief from the Assyrian capital at Nineveh shows Assyrian soldiers using scaling ladders during King Ashurbanipal's siege of an Elamite city.

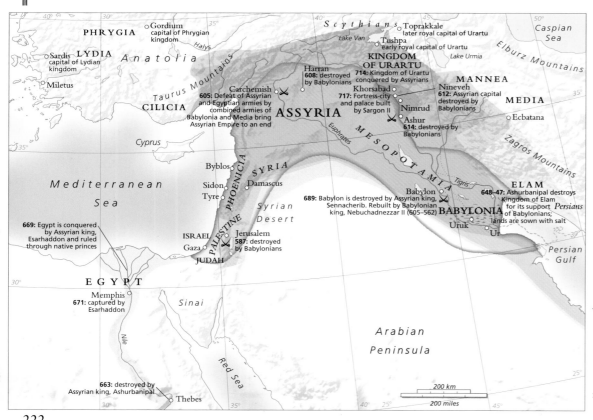

❷ The Assyrian and Babylonian Empires 950–539 BCE

under Ashur-dan II (934–912)
added by death of Shalmaneser III (858–824)
added by death of Sargon II (745–705)
added by death of Ashurbanipal (668–626)
New Babylonian Empire (625–539)
present-day coastline/river

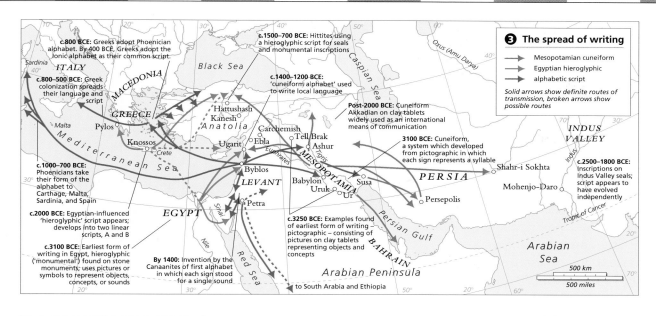

The spread of writing

❸ The spread of writing

→ Mesopotamian cuneiform
→ Egyptian hieroglyphic
→ alphabetic script

Solid arrows show definite routes of transmission, broken arrows show possible routes

c.800 BCE: Greeks adopt Phoenician alphabet. By 400 BCE, Greeks adopt the Ionic alphabet as their common script.

c.800–500 BCE: Greek colonization spreads their language and script

c.1000–700 BCE: Phoenicians take their form of the alphabet to Carthage, Malta, Sardinia, and Spain

c.2000 BCE: Egyptian-influenced 'hieroglyphic' script appears; develops into two linear scripts, A and B

c.3100 BCE: Earliest form of writing in Egypt, hieroglyphic ('monumental') found on stone monuments; uses pictures or symbols to represent objects, concepts, or sounds

c.1500–700 BCE: Hittites using a hieroglyphic script for seals and monumental inscriptions

c.1400–1200 BCE: 'cuneiform alphabet' used to write local language

Post-2000 BCE: Cuneiform Akkadian on clay tablets widely used as an international means of communication

3100 BCE: Cuneiform, a system which developed from pictographic in which each sign represents a syllable

c.3250 BCE: Examples found of earliest form of writing – pictographic – consisting of pictures on clay tablets representing objects and concepts

c.2500–1800 BCE: Inscriptions on Indus Valley seals; script appears to have evolved independently

By 1400: Invention by the Canaanites of first alphabet in which each sign stood for a single sound

to South Arabia and Ethiopia

The development of writing in West Asia

Pictographs, pictures which represented words, were the earliest form of writing, emerging in Mesopotamia in the 4th millennium BCE. In time, pictographs developed into the cuneiform script which was used to record several languages. The next step was taken by the Phoenicians: instead of using pictographs to represent words or ideas, they simplified writing into 22 different signs to represent the sounds of their speech. This alphabet is especially significant since it passed to the Greeks, then to the Romans, whose modified alphabet is still in use today.

The 7th-century BCE
tablet *(right)* is an Assyrian account of the legend of the flood. The cuneiform (from the Latin, *cuneus,* a wedge) characters are made up of wedge-shaped impressions in soft clay.

The language on the 5th-century BCE cylinder seal *(left)* is Aramaic, which used the Phoenician-Hebrew alphabet. Aramaic became the administrative language of the Persian Empire and was thus in use from Anatolia to the Indus.

The development of writing in West Asia

c.3250: First pictographic writing from Tell Brak, Mesopotamia

c.2500: Earliest syllabic script used in Sumerian literature

c.2000: Egyptian-influenced 'hieroglyphic' script in Crete; develops into two linear scripts, A and B

c.1000–700: Phoenicians take alphabet to Carthage, Malta, Sardinia, and Spain

3500 BCE — 3000 — 2500 — 2000 — 1500 — 1000 — 500 BCE

c.3100: Cuneiform writing emerges in Mesopotamia; hieroglyphic writing appears on Egyptian stone monuments

c.2500: Indus Valley civilization marks seals with inscriptions

c.1400: Development of first alphabets in Sinai and Levant

c.800: Greeks adopt Phoenician alphabet

The first Persian Empire

Babylonian rule in Mesopotamia was ended by Cyrus the Great. Uniting the Medes and Persians, he founded the Persian Empire, naming it the Achaemenid Empire after an ancestor. Once in power, Cyrus defeated the Lydians, then unseated Nabonidas, King of Babylon. A tolerant ruler and magnanimous victor, Cyrus released the Jews from captivity in Babylon and authorized the rebuilding of the Temple in Jerusalem. Under Darius I ('the Great') and Xerxes I, the empire was extended, organized into 20 provinces ruled by satraps (governors), and a major road network constructed. But both rulers failed in their attempts to conquer Greece. Weakened from without by raiding nomads, and from within by ambitious satraps, the empire was defeated at Issus in 333 by Alexander the Great.

The simple but imposing tomb
of Cyrus the Great at Pasargadae, where Cyrus built himself a permanent residence, commemorates his skill as an outstanding leader and founder of the Achaemenid Persian Empire.

The great palace in Persepolis was begun in 518 BCE by Darius, but built mainly under Xerxes I. The wide staircase leading to the audience hall, or *apadana,* was decorated with carved reliefs of subject peoples bearing tribute.

The first Persian Empire

547–46: Cyrus defeats Croesus, King of the Lydians

530: Cyrus killed in battle against the nomads of Central Asia

521: Darius the Great ruler of Persian Empire

500: Building of the Persian Royal Road

486: Xerxes I becomes ruler of Persian Empire

545 — 535 — 525 — 515 — 505 — 495 — 475 BCE

c.550: Persian Empire established by Cyrus the Great

539: Conquest of Babylon by Cyrus

525: Cambyses II conquers Egypt and advances to Nubia and Libya

513: Darius invades Scythia

490: Persian invasion force defeated by Athenians at Marathon

480: Xerxes brings huge army to Greece, but is defeated at Salamis

❹ The Achaemenid Empire c.550–331 BCE

- Persian homeland under Cyrus before 550 BCE
- Kingdom of Medes, annexed 550 BCE
- Kingdom of Lydians, annexed c.547 BCE
- Kingdom of Babylonians, annexed 539 BCE
- Kingdom of Egyptians, annexed 525 BCE
- annexed by Darius I and Xerxes I
- ········· Persian Empire at greatest extent
- —— Persian Royal Road
- LYDIA Persian administrative district (satrapy) ruled by governor
- → major campaigns of Cyrus and Darius I
- ✕ battle with date

Wars with Greece 490–479 BCE
- → Persian campaigns against Greece
- ✕ Greek victory
- ✕ Persian victory
- ✕ indecisive battle
- ········· present-day river/coastline

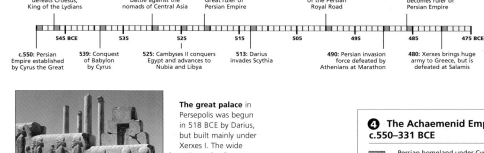

GREEK AND ROMAN EXPANSION

This opalescent vase of moulded glass was produced in Roman Syria in the 1st century CE.

ALEXANDER THE GREAT'S CONQUESTS (*see pp.40–41*) briefly united a vast tract of West Asia. Subsequently, empires competed and dynasties fell, but a widespread Hellenistic culture survived. In Persia and Mesopotamia, the Seleucids were ousted by the Parthians, who then clashed with an expansionist Rome. By 1 CE, Rome's empire formed a single vast trading area; its West Asian Greek-speaking provinces were the richest of all. A particularly valuable trade was in incense from southern Arabia. Unrest in the Roman Empire was often religious. Rome suppressed two Jewish revolts, provoking a diaspora, but it was a new offshoot of Judaism, Christianity, that spread most effectively through the region (*see pp.48–49*). In the east, c.226 CE, the Sassanians succeeded the Parthians, establishing a new capital at Ctesiphon.

Seleucus I took the largest portion of Alexander's empire. His dynasty lasted until 129 BCE, most of his lands falling to Rome and the Parthians.

Alexander's successors

The death of Alexander was followed by a long struggle for his empire between his generals. With the elimination of three principal contenders – Antigonus at the battle of Ipsus, Lysimachus at Corupedium, Cassander through disease – three great monarchies were established: Macedonia under the Antigonids; Egypt under the Ptolemies; Mesopotamia and Persia under Seleucus I. During the reign of Antiochus III, the greatest of the Seleucids, the Seleucid Empire was extended, but his invasion of Greece in 192 BCE led to conflict with Rome and he was forced to make peace. Thereafter the Seleucid Empire declined.

Alexander's successors in the 3rd century BCE

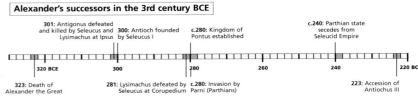

301: Antigonus defeated and killed by Seleucus and Lysimachus at Ipsus
300: Antioch founded by Seleucus I
c.280: Kingdom of Pontus established
c.240: Parthian state secedes from Seleucid Empire

| 320 BCE | 300 | 280 | 260 | 240 | 220 BCE |

323: Death of Alexander the Great
281: Lysimachus defeated by Seleucus at Corupedium
c.280: Invasion by Parni (Parthians)
223: Accession of Antiochus III

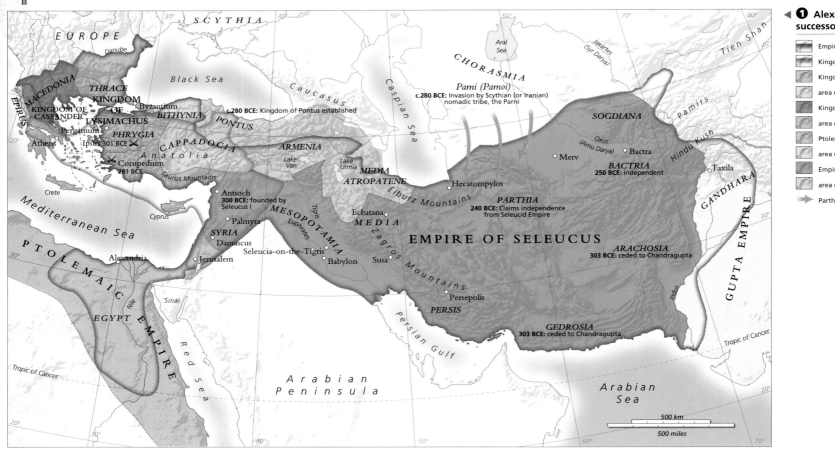

◀ ❶ Alexander's successors from 301 BCE

Empire of Alexander c.323 BCE
Kingdom of Antigonus 301 BCE
Kingdom of Lysimachus 301 BCE
area of influence of Lysimachus
Kingdom of Cassander 301 BCE
area of influence of Cassander
Ptolemaic Empire 301 BCE
area of Ptolemaic influence
Empire of Seleucus 301 BCE
area of Seleucid influence
Parthian invasion

Parthia and Rome

In about 240 BCE a Scythian people from the steppes of Turkmenistan broke away from Seleucid rule and established the Parthian state. A century later, under Mithridates I, they took Mesopotamia and founded a new capital at Ctesiphon. Roman expansion in the 1st century BCE brought conflict with Parthia; in 53 CE the Parthians defeated them at Carrhae. In the 2nd century CE, a weakened Parthia was invaded by Rome. Finally, 400 years of Parthian rule was ended by Ardashir, the first Sassanian ruler.

The Parthians were renowned for their heavily armoured cavalry and the skill of their mounted bowmen.

The Parthian Wars

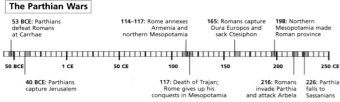

53 BCE: Parthians defeat Romans at Carrhae
114–117: Rome annexes Armenia and northern Mesopotamia
165: Romans capture Dura Europos and sack Ctesiphon
198: Northern Mesopotamia made Roman province

| 50 BCE | 1 CE | 50 CE | 100 | 150 | 200 | 250 CE |

40 BCE: Parthians capture Jerusalem
117: Death of Trajan; Rome gives up his conquests in Mesopotamia
216: Romans invade Parthia and attack Arbela
226: Parthia falls to Sassanians

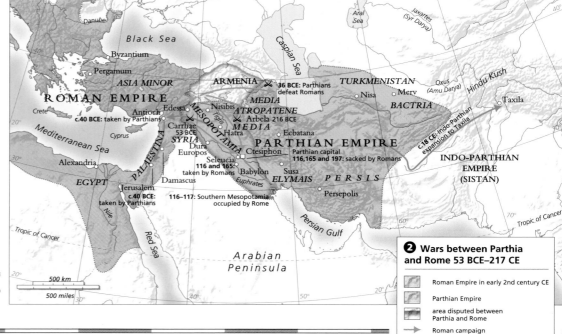

❷ Wars between Parthia and Rome 53 BCE–217 CE

Roman Empire in early 2nd century CE
Parthian Empire
area disputed between Parthia and Rome
Roman campaign
Parthian campaign

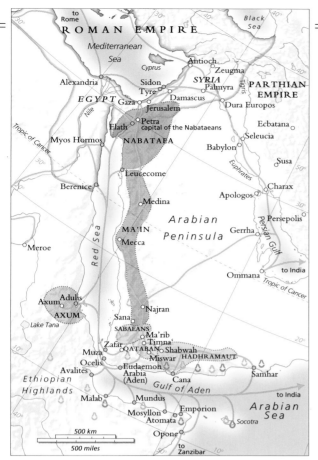

▲ 3 Red Sea trade in the 1st century CE

- limit of Roman Empire 117 CE
- myrrh
- frankincense
- major port
- trade route

Arabia's Red Sea trade

The aromatic gums, frankincense and myrrh, were prized commodities in the early civilizations of Egypt and West Asia. Both were widely used to make incense, perfumes, and cosmetics, while myrrh was also used for embalming. Mainly cultivated in southern Arabia, Ethiopia, and the island of Socotra, frankincense and myrrh were carried north by camel caravan to the cities of the eastern Mediterranean. Occupying a key point on this overland route, Petra, capital of the Nabataeans, became a wealthy city. As navigational skills improved and sailors learnt to harness the monsoon winds, frankincense and myrrh were increasingly transported by sea, thus benefiting those Arab states with major ports around the Gulf of Aden, such as Cana, Muza, and Eudaemon Arabia.

Incense consists of a mixture of gums and spices. The fragrant odour of burning incense was associated with religious rites and prayer throughout West Asia and the eastern Mediterranean, hence its great value. It was burnt on small stone altars, such as this example from southern Arabia.

Roman Palestine

In 63 BCE Judaea was conquered by Rome and it was in an atmosphere of anti-Roman protest by Jewish Zealots that Christianity developed in the 1st century CE. In 66 CE, discontent flared into open revolt, suppressed by a force of 60,000 men under Vespasian, and then by his son, Titus, who destroyed and looted the Jewish Temple in Jerusalem. Diehard Zealots took refuge on the rock fortress at Masada and, rather than submit to Rome, committed mass suicide. In 132 CE Bar Cochba led another revolt, which ended with the Roman destruction of Jerusalem.

After Christianity won acceptance under Constantine, many Roman artists turned from secular to sacred themes, such as the biblical scene depicted on this early Christian sarcophagus.

Rome and Palestine 63 BCE–135 CE

- **40 BCE:** Herod the Great becomes king of Judaea, which remains loyal client kingdom of Rome
- **4 BCE:** Generally accepted date of birth of Christ in Bethlehem
- **39–44:** Reign of Herod Agrippa I, Ethnarch of Judaea
- **67:** Vespasian invades Judaea; recovers Galilee
- **70:** Titus captures Jerusalem; Temple destroyed; province of Judaea established
- **132–35:** Second Jewish revolt, led by Bar Cochba
- **63 BCE:** Pompey brings Judaea under Roman control
- **4 BCE:** Death of Herod; kingdom divided between his three sons
- **6 CE:** Judaea placed under Roman military procurator
- **66:** Start of First Jewish Revolt
- **74:** Romans take Masada after lengthy siege
- **135:** Hadrian proceeds with building of Aelia Capitolina on ruins of Jerusalem

75 BCE — 45 — 1 CE — 45 — 75 — 105 — 135 CE

The Jewish diaspora 66–135 CE

The failed revolts of 66 and 132 CE precipitated a diaspora (Greek for 'dispersion') of Jews from Palestine. Vast numbers were sold into slavery, became refugees in Galilee or fled abroad, many to long-established centres in Babylonia and Mesopotamia. Jews were banished from Jerusalem, which was refounded as a Roman city (Aelia Capitolina). By the 2nd century CE Jews may have made up some 5–10% of the population of the Roman Empire; in some eastern cities, perhaps a quarter. Remaining loyal to their faith, the exiled Jews continued to regard Judaea as their homeland.

A detail from the triumphal arch of Titus shows the great candlestick (*menorah*) and other treasures being looted from the Temple at Jerusalem by Roman soldiers.

4 Jewish revolts 66–74 CE

- frontier of Roman Empire and client states 66 CE
- Kingdom of Herod 20 BCE
- Roman province of Judaea
- Kingdom of Agrippa II, 61 CE
- area of major revolt 66 CE
- area of revolt in 69 CE
- army of Vespasian 67–68 CE
- army of Titus 70 CE
- army of Bassus and Silva 71–74 CE
- siege
- Jewish victory

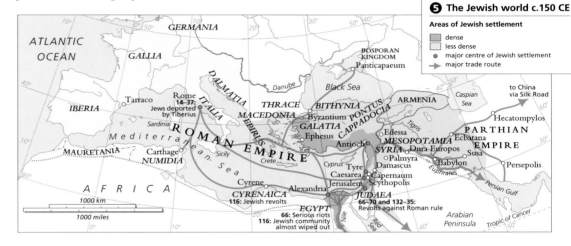

5 The Jewish world c.150 CE

Areas of Jewish settlement
- dense
- less dense
- major centre of Jewish settlement
- major trade route

Sassanian Persia

Ardashir I rebelled against the Parthian king, Artabanus V, c.226 CE, and founded the Sassanian Empire He kept Ctesiphon as his capital and reintroduced Zoroastrianism as the state religion. The empire reached its peak of prosperity under Khosrau I. In the 7th century, his son, Khosrau II, invaded the Byzantine Empire, but was met by a successful counter-offensive. The weakened empire then fell to the Muslim Arabs.

A cameo depicts the capture of the Emperor Valerian by Shapur I, following the great Persian victory against the Romans near Edessa in 259 CE.

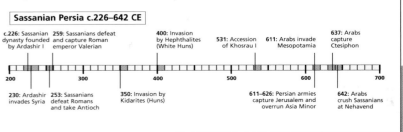

6 Sassanian Persia c.224–642

- Sassanian Empire at greatest extent
- East Roman Empire in 3rd century
- area disputed by Sassanians and East Roman Empire during 6th century
- Sassanian expedition
- Arab invasion
- Hunnish attack
- Sassanian victory over Romans
- Arab victory over Sassanians

Sassanian Persia c.226–642 CE

- **c.226:** Sassanian dynasty founded by Ardashir I
- **259:** Sassanians defeat and capture Roman emperor Valerian
- **400:** Invasion by Hephthalites (White Huns)
- **531:** Accession of Khosrau I
- **611:** Arabs invade Mesopotamia
- **637:** Arabs capture Ctesiphon
- **230:** Ardashir invades Syria
- **253:** Sassanians defeat Romans and take Antioch
- **350:** Invasion by Kidarites (Huns)
- **611–626:** Persian armies capture Jerusalem and overrun Asia Minor
- **642:** Arabs crush Sassanians at Nehavend

200 — 300 — 400 — 500 — 600 — 700

THE ADVENT OF ISLAM

This gold dinar shows Abd al-Malik, caliph from 685 to 705. He reorganized the army and the Islamic state.

IN 610, IN A CAVE south of Mecca, the Prophet Muhammad received the first of the messages from God which led him to found the Islamic faith. The clear, monotheistic message of Islam appealed to the Arabs, and within 30 years they had carried it to Persia and Palestine. The early Islamic empire was a single political entity, ruled by the caliph, or 'successor' of Muhammad (see pp.56–57). By 750 CE, Arab armies had carried Islam west to the Iberian Peninsula and east to Central Asia. The Abbasid Caliphate, with its capital usually at Baghdad, was founded in 750. It was an era of great prosperity, especially in the reign of Harun al-Rashid, but later caliphs lost all political power, ruling in name only over a steadily diminishing Caliphate.

Fine textiles decorated with the Cross and other Christian imagery were woven by Egypt's Copts under Byzantine and Islamic rule.

Religions in West Asia c.600

By 600 CE three major religions were firmly rooted in West Asia: Christianity, Judaism, and Zoroastrianism. Orthodox Christianity was the state religion of the Byzantine Empire; other Christian sects, such as the Nestorians, had strong followings in Mesopotamia and Persia. Jewish communities were scattered throughout the region. The most populous was probably in Babylonia, which was also the leading cultural centre of the Jewish world. The Sassanian rulers of Persia tolerated Christians and Jews, although Zoroastrianism was the state religion. The Islamic invasion led to the emigration of many Zoroastrians, mainly to India.

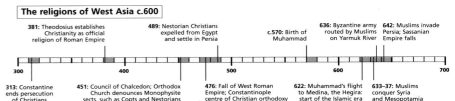

THE KORAN

A fragment from a copy of the Koran (c.900) shows the beauty of Arabic calligraphy, regarded as the supreme art in the Islamic world. It is written in Kufic script, with the vowels indicated in red.

The Koran (Qur'an) is the name given to the collected revelations transmitted to the Prophet Muhammad by the Archangel Gabriel, believed by Muslims to be the infallible word of Allah (God). Together, the revelations form the basis of Islam, the authority Muslims consult not only on questions of theological doctrine and ethics, but also on practical legal, political and social matters. The Koranic revelations were committed to memory by the first disciples of the Prophet, and in 651 CE the first authorized Arabic text was prepared. The Koran is about the length of the New Testament of the Bible, and is divided into 114 suras or chapters as revealed to the Prophet at Mecca or Medina.

The spread of Islam

In 622 Muhammad and his followers, faced with hostility in Mecca, fled to Medina. In 630 he returned to Mecca with an army and took the city, thenceforth the religious centre of Islam. At his death, he ruled almost half the Arabian Peninsula. His successors, who took the title 'caliph' (successor or deputy), continued to spread his message through conquest: Syria, Mesopotamia, Persia, and Egypt were overrun by armies fired by the spirit of jihad (holy war). In 661 control of the Caliphate was gained by the Umayyad dynasty, who set up a new political capital at Damascus and extended the empire west to the Atlantic and east to the Indus.

Pilgrims in the ritual costume of two pieces of white cloth gather around the Ka'ba in the Great Mosque at Mecca.

The Hegira (hijra)

Muhammad's flight from Mecca to Medina in 622 marks the start of the Islamic calendar. It was from Medina that Muhammad started to preach with success and spread the message of Islam. In recognition of this, the city's name was changed from Yathrib to Medina (the City), and it became the first political capital of the Islamic world. Mecca, however, had long been a holy city among the pagan tribes of the Arabian Peninsula and an important place of pilgrimage. Since it was also the birthplace of Muhammad and the site of his first revelations, it became the holiest city of Islam.

② The Hegira 622

— road
— route of Hegira

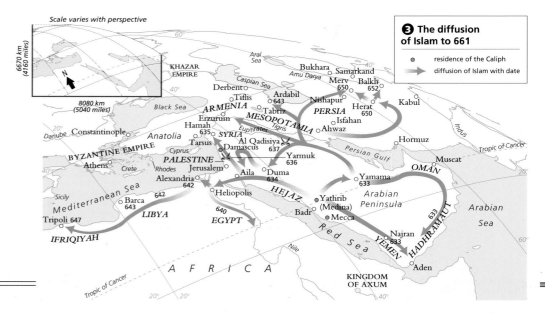

③ The diffusion of Islam to 661

○ residence of the Caliph
→ diffusion of Islam with date

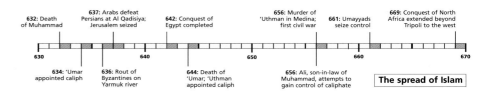

The spread of Islam

① The religions of West Asia c.600

☐ area converted to Christianity by 600
☐ area of Jewish settlement
☐ area predominantly Zoroastrian
— principal trade routes
→ dispersal of Jews to 500 CE

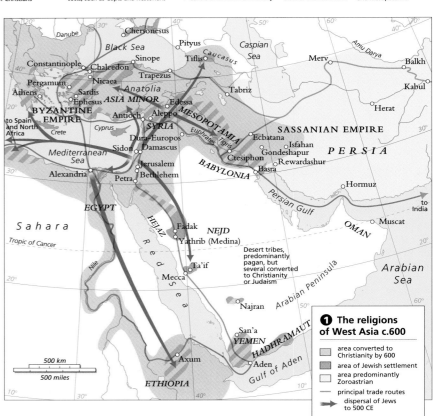

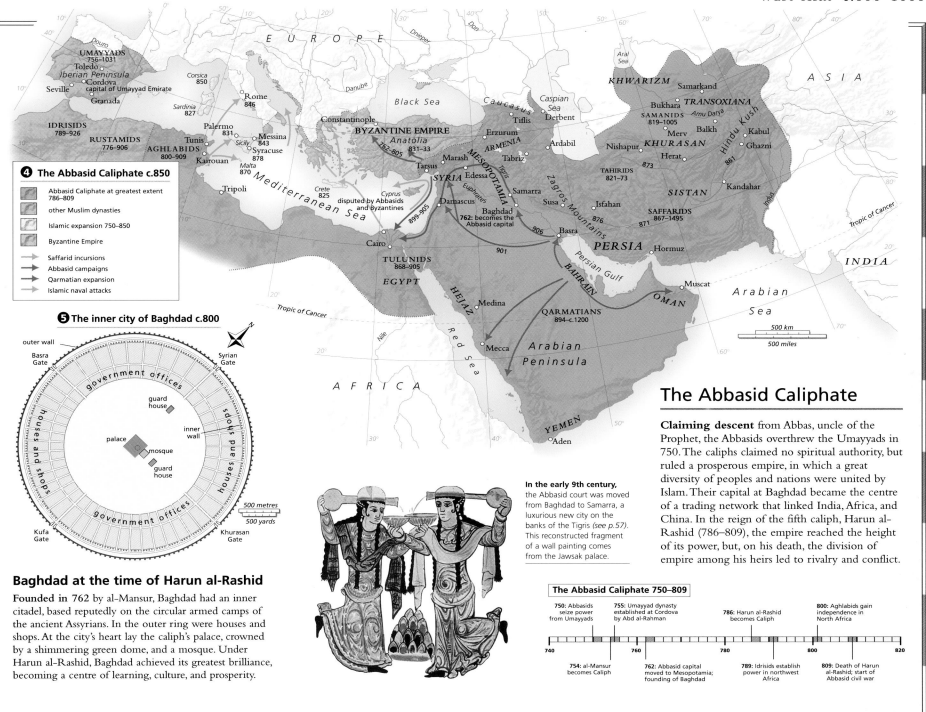

❹ The Abbasid Caliphate c.850

- Abbasid Caliphate at greatest extent 786–809
- other Muslim dynasties
- Islamic expansion 750–850
- Byzantine Empire
- → Saffarid incursions
- → Abbasid campaigns
- → Qarmatian expansion
- → Islamic naval attacks

❺ The inner city of Baghdad c.800

outer wall
Basra Gate
government offices
guard house
inner wall
palace
mosque
guard house
houses and shops
shops
government offices
Kufa Gate
Khurasan Gate
Syrian Gate

500 metres
500 yards

Baghdad at the time of Harun al-Rashid

Founded in 762 by al-Mansur, Baghdad had an inner citadel, based reputedly on the circular armed camps of the ancient Assyrians. In the outer ring were houses and shops. At the city's heart lay the caliph's palace, crowned by a shimmering green dome, and a mosque. Under Harun al-Rashid, Baghdad achieved its greatest brilliance, becoming a centre of learning, culture, and prosperity.

In the early 9th century, the Abbasid court was moved from Baghdad to Samarra, a luxurious new city on the banks of the Tigris *(see p.57)*. This reconstructed fragment of a wall painting comes from the Jawsak palace.

The Abbasid Caliphate

Claiming descent from Abbas, uncle of the Prophet, the Abbasids overthrew the Umayyads in 750. The caliphs claimed no spiritual authority, but ruled a prosperous empire, in which a great diversity of peoples and nations were united by Islam. Their capital at Baghdad became the centre of a trading network that linked India, Africa, and China. In the reign of the fifth caliph, Harun al-Rashid (786–809), the empire reached the height of its power, but, on his death, the division of empire among his heirs led to rivalry and conflict.

The Abbasid Caliphate 750–809

750: Abbasids seize power from Umayyads	755: Umayyad dynasty established at Cordova by Abd al-Rahman	786: Harun al-Rashid becomes Caliph	800: Aghlabids gain independence in North Africa

740 — 760 — 780 — 800 — 820

| 754: al-Mansur becomes Caliph | 762: Abbasid capital moved to Mesopotamia; founding of Baghdad | 789: Idrisids establish power in northwest Africa | 809: Death of Harun al-Rashid; start of Abbasid civil war |

The fragmentation of the Caliphate

Civil war on the death of Harun al-Rashid accelerated the Abbasids' loss of power, though they ruled in name until 1258. The lands of Islam, once ruled by a single caliph, fragmented into semi-autonomous dynasties. Among these were the Fatimids of Egypt, the Samanids of Transoxiana, and the Ghaznavids of Afghanistan, who played a major role in the introduction of Islam to India. In 946, a Persian dynasty, the Buwayhids, invaded and occupied Baghdad. They became protectors of the Caliphate, an event that inspired a revival of Persian national identity.

All mosques share certain features, modelled on Muhammad's house at Medina. These include the *kibla*, the wall facing Mecca, the *minbar*, or pulpit, and the minaret – the tower from which the faithful are called to prayer. The minaret shown here is from the 9th-century mosque of Ibn Tulun at Cairo.

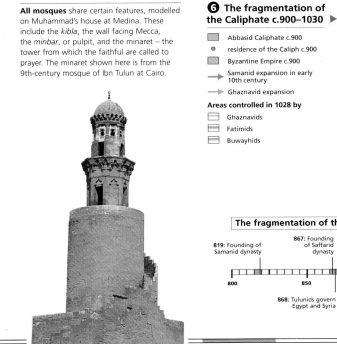

❻ The fragmentation of the Caliphate c.900–1030 ▶

- Abbasid Caliphate c.900
- residence of the Caliph c.900
- Byzantine Empire c.900
- → Samanid expansion in early 10th century
- → Ghaznavid expansion

Areas controlled in 1028 by
- Ghaznavids
- Fatimids
- Buwayhids

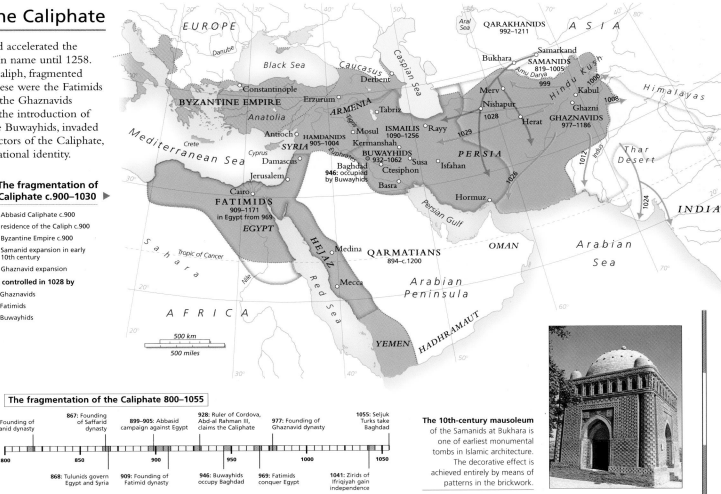

The fragmentation of the Caliphate 800–1055

819: Founding of Samanid dynasty	867: Founding of Saffarid dynasty	899–905: Abbasid campaign against Egypt	928: Ruler of Cordova, Abd-al Rahman III, claims the Caliphate	977: Founding of Ghaznavid dynasty	1055: Seljuk Turks take Baghdad

800 — 850 — 900 — 950 — 1000 — 1050

| 868: Tulunids govern Egypt and Syria | 909: Founding of Fatimid dynasty | 946: Buwayhids occupy Baghdad | 969: Fatimids conquer Egypt | 1041: Zirids of Ifriqiyah gain independence |

The 10th-century mausoleum of the Samanids at Bukhara is one of earliest monumental tombs in Islamic architecture. The decorative effect is achieved entirely by means of patterns in the brickwork.

TURKISH AND MONGOL INVADERS

The Islamic warrior was armed with a long curved sword, often of highly-tempered steel and finely engraved.

IN THE 11TH CENTURY West Asia was invaded by the Seljuk Turks, nomads from Central Asia. Reuniting the central Abbasid lands, they emerged as the dominant power in Mesopotamia, Persia, and Anatolia. Their crushing victory at Manzikert in 1071 drove the Byzantines out of Asia Minor and provoked the Crusades. The Crusaders set out to regain the lands lost to Islam, but their capture of Jerusalem in 1099 was countered a century later by Saladin, who also became ruler of Egypt. In the mid-13th century, a new threat was presented by the Mongols, who conquered much of the region, but were halted by the Mamluks, who now ruled Egypt. In the late 14th century, Timur, the last Mongol conqueror, launched a series of campaigns which took him from Ankara to Delhi.

The Seljuk Turks and the Byzantines

The Seljuks were great builders. Their architectural forms and intricate abstract designs had a lasting influence on Islamic art. This glazed tilework in Isfahan's Friday Mosque dates from the late 11th century.

In about 1040, a group of Turkish tribes swept out of the lands north of the Oxus. The Seljuks were the dominant clan. By 1055 they reached Baghdad, where they ruled in the name of the Abbasid caliph. Recent converts to Sunni Islam, the Seljuks planned to subdue all Shi'ites and infidels. Conquering Armenia, they then struck at the Byzantines in Asia Minor, defeating them at Manzikert in 1071. The seizure of Syria and much of Palestine from the Fatimids followed. After a period of civil war, the Seljuk Empire was split in two by the establishment in Anatolia of the independent Sultanate of Rum, with its capital at Konya. The Seljuks' control over their empire waned and they were crushed by the Mongols at Köse Dagh in 1243.

Saladin and the Ayyubid Sultanate

Saladin was a Kurdish general in the army of Nur al-Din, Zangid ruler of Mosul, who fought successfully against the Crusaders (see pp.64–65) and his Muslim neighbours. Ousting the Fatimids from Egypt, he united Egypt and Syria under his rule. Hostilities with the Crusader states led in 1187 to Saladin's annihilation of Christian forces at Hattin and the capture of Jerusalem and Acre. This provoked the Third Crusade, in which the Crusaders recaptured most of the coastal plain of Palestine. The dynasty founded by Saladin, the Ayyubids, dominated the region until it fell to the Mamluks in 1250.

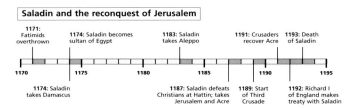

Saladin and the reconquest of Jerusalem

- 1171: Fatimids overthrown
- 1174: Saladin becomes sultan of Egypt
- 1174: Saladin takes Damascus
- 1183: Saladin takes Aleppo
- 1187: Saladin defeats Christians at Hattin; takes Jerusalem and Acre
- 1189: Start of Third Crusade
- 1191: Crusaders recover Acre
- 1192: Richard I of England makes treaty with Saladin
- 1193: Death of Saladin

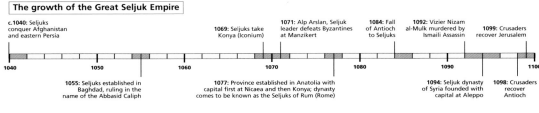

The growth of the Great Seljuk Empire

- c.1040: Seljuks conquer Afghanistan and eastern Persia
- 1055: Seljuks established in Baghdad, ruling in the name of the Abbasid Caliph
- 1069: Seljuks take Konya (Iconium)
- 1071: Alp Arslan, Seljuk leader defeats Byzantines at Manzikert
- 1077: Province established in Anatolia with capital first at Nicaea and then Konya; dynasty comes to be known as the Seljuks of Rum (Rome)
- 1084: Fall of Antioch to Seljuks
- 1092: Vizier Nizam al-Mulk murdered by Ismaili Assassin
- 1094: Seljuk dynasty of Syria founded with capital at Aleppo
- 1098: Crusaders recover Antioch
- 1099: Crusaders recover Jerusalem

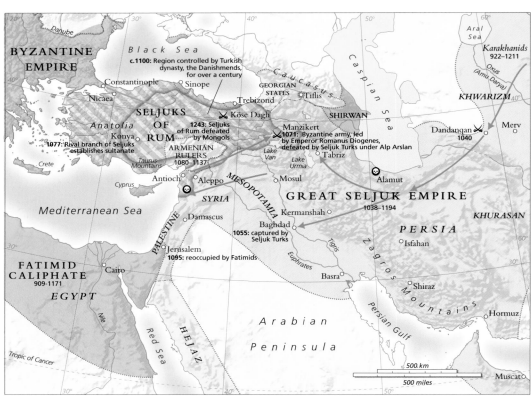

① The Seljuk Turks and the Byzantine Empire from c.1025

- Byzantine frontier in Asia c.1025
- Byzantine Empire 1095
- Seljuk Empire c.1095
- Seljuk tributary states
- Byzantine territory overrun by Seljuks by 1095
- eastern frontier of area recovered by the Byzantine Empire by 1180
- other Muslim dynasty
- route of Seljuk invasion from Asia c.1038
- route of Byzantine army
- ⊛ stronghold of the sect of the Assassins

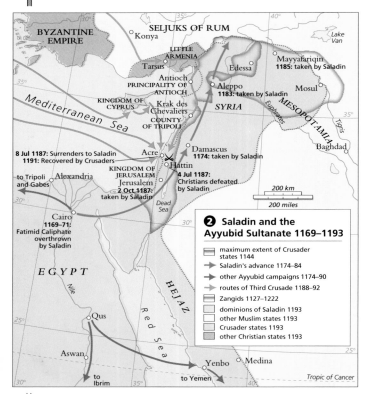

② Saladin and the Ayyubid Sultanate 1169–1193

- maximum extent of Crusader states 1144
- Saladin's advance 1174–84
- other Ayyubid campaigns 1174–90
- routes of Third Crusade 1188–92
- Zangids 1127–1222
- dominions of Saladin 1193
- other Muslim states 1193
- Crusader states 1193
- other Christian states 1193

In this Persian illustration, Timur leads his army through the Hindu Kush in 1398, before falling upon the cities of the Punjab and sacking Delhi. This, like most of his conquests, was carried out in the name of Islam.

At the head of an army from Egypt, the Muslim leader Saladin (1138–1193) drove the Crusaders out of most of Palestine and Syria and recaptured Jerusalem, restoring the Dome of the Rock, one of Islam's oldest surviving shrines, to Muslim worship. Though a formidable leader, Saladin was recognized, even by the Crusaders, as a chivalrous opponent.

Mamluks and Mongols

The Mamluks, who seized power in Egypt in 1250, were chiefly Circassians from the Caucasus, captured in childhood and trained as slave bodyguards. Once in power, they extended their rule into Syria, and built up a trading network in Africa and the Indian Ocean. Within five years of the Mamluks' rise to power, the Mongol Hülegü (*see pp.68–69*) led a powerful army into West Asia. After destroying Alamut, the stronghold of the Assassins (an Ismaili Shi'ite sect), Hülegü sacked Baghdad. The Mongol threat was averted by the death of the Mongol khan, Möngke which required Hülegü to withdraw his main army. Seizing their advantage, in 1260 the Mamluks marched north in the defence of Islam, and crushed the Mongol army at Ain Jalut.

The Mamluk warrior was superbly trained, studying both the theory and practice of combat in military manuals, such as this one which shows four cavalrymen exercising around a pool.

The Mongols and Mamluks in West Asia

- **1250:** Mamluks seize power from Ayyubids
- **1251:** Mamluks defeat Syrians at al-'Abbasa
- **1256:** Hülegü crosses Oxus (Amu Darya)
- **1256–57:** Assassins' stronghold at Alamut falls to Hülegü
- **1258:** Hülegü sacks Baghdad; last Abbasid caliph executed
- **1259:** Great Khan Möngke dies
- **1260:** Mamluks defeat Mongols at Ain Jalut; take Aleppo and Damascus
- **1265:** Death of Hülegü
- **1268:** Mamluks capture Antioch from Crusaders

❸ The rise of the Mamluks and the Il-Khanate 1250–1300

- boundary of Ayyubid Sultanate c.1247
- Mamluk territory in 1250
- annexed by Mamluks 1253
- annexed by Mamluks 1260
- Christian territory in the Levant conquered by Mamluks 1263–1291
- Christian territory after 1291
- Il-Khanate and vassals c.1259
- route of Mongol invasion under Hülegü
- sacked by Mongols

The Il-Khanate c.1260–1353

The first Il-Khan, Hülegü, entered a period of conflict with Berke, Khan of the Golden Horde. Berke, who had converted to Islam and allied himself with the Mamluks, resented Hülegü's new empire. By 1262 the situation had stabilized, and Hülegü settled on the well-watered plains of Azerbaijan and built a capital at Maragheh, from where he ruled the lands he had gained in Persia, Mesopotamia, Asia Minor, and the Caucasus. The Mongol dynasty established by Hülegü – the Il-Khanate – ruled Persia until 1353.

In 1258 the Mongols under Hülegü sacked the great city of Baghdad, the very heart of Arab civilization, and reputedly murdered 800,000 of its inhabitants. The last Abbasid caliph was captured, rolled in a carpet, and then trampled to death by galloping horses.

The dominions of Timur

Claiming descent from Genghis Khan, Timur the Lame became master of Transoxiana in 1369. Making Samarkand his capital, he embarked on a series of campaigns against Persia, the Golden Horde, the Sultanate of Delhi, the Mamluks, and the Ottomans. At Ankara in 1402, he defeated and captured the Ottoman Sultan Bayezid. In 35 years Timur created a vast empire; plans for invading China ceased with his death. Though his conquests struck fear into Muslim Asia, Timur's empire proved short-lived.

Timur is buried beneath a slab of jade in the Gur-i Mir, Samarkand.

The campaigns of Timur 1379–1405

- **1379:** Timur marches on Urgench
- **1380:** Timur launches series of attacks on Persia
- **1384:** Herat rebels; Timur suppresses ruling dynasty
- **1387:** Isfahan rebels; in reprisal, Timur kills 70,000, building towers with their skulls
- **1388–91:** War against Mongol Khanate of the Golden Horde
- **1392–94:** Further campaigns in Persia
- **1393:** Capture of Baghdad
- **1395:** Sack of New Sarai, capital of Golden Horde
- **1398:** Invasion of India; sack of Delhi
- **1400:** Sack of Aleppo and Damascus
- **1401:** Sack of Baghdad
- **1402:** Defeat of Ottomans at Ankara
- **1405:** Death of Timur

❹ The dominions of Timur

- Empire of Timur
- Ottoman Empire
- Mamluk Sultanate

Campaigns of Timur: 1379–1405
- against Khwarizm and Persia 1379–88
- against Golden Horde 1388–91 and 1395
- against Sultanate of Delhi 1398–99
- against Mamluk Sultanate and Baghdad 1399–1401
- against Ottomans 1402
- planned invasion of China 1404–05
- city sacked by Timur

THE OTTOMAN EMPIRE

The conquests of Osman I (1299–1326) formed the nucleus of the Ottoman Empire.

THE OTTOMAN EMPIRE was one of the great world powers of the early modern age. At its height, the empire stretched from the Indian Ocean to Algiers, Hungary, and the Crimea. Constantinople, captured from the Byzantines in 1453 was a key centre of power that had resisted non-Christian attack for 1000 years. Turkish expansion in the Balkans led to shifts in religious, ethnic, linguistic, and economic frontiers, which still have serious consequences in the modern world. The conquest of Egypt and Syria established a powerful presence in Africa and West Asia, although, in the east, the Ottomans faced powerful opposition from Safavid Persia, which flourished in the 16th and 17th centuries.

The rise of the Ottomans

The Ottoman state started as a small frontier principality dedicated to raids on Christian Byzantium. In the 14th century, led by a succession of warrior sultans, Osman I, Orkhan, and Murad I, the Ottomans began a series of rapid conquests. Sultans often waged war to obtain more land and money to reward their loyal troops. In an attempt to halt their progress, the threatened Christian states of the Balkans amassed an army, but were defeated at Kosovo in 1389. Sultan Bayezid I exploited this victory by annexing Bulgaria and invading Hungary, but expansion eastwards was temporarily halted by Timur in 1402. Constantinople was finally taken by Mehmed II (the 'Conqueror') in 1453.

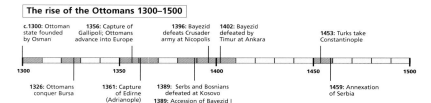

The rise of the Ottomans 1300–1500

c.1300: Ottoman state founded by Osman | 1356: Capture of Gallipoli; Ottomans advance into Europe | 1396: Bayezid defeats Crusader army at Nicopolis | 1402: Bayezid defeated by Timur at Ankara | 1453: Turks take Constantinople

1326: Ottomans conquer Bursa | 1361: Capture of Edirne (Adrianople) | 1389: Serbs and Bosnians defeated at Kosovo 1389: Accession of Bayezid I | 1459: Annexation of Serbia

The Ottomans' rise to become a world power was based on their highly-trained army, seen here besieging Belgrade in 1456. The most feared troops were the janissaries, drawn from young slaves given in tribute and trained from childhood.

① Rise of the Ottoman Empire c.1300–1500

- nucleus of Ottoman Empire c.1300
- conquests of Osman I, c.1300–26
- conquests of Orkhan, 1326–62
- conquests of Murad I, 1362–89
- conquests of Bayezid I, 1389–1402
- Ottoman eastern frontier following Timur's invasion 1402
- Ottoman territory by 1451
- further Ottoman conquest by 1481
- vassal of Ottoman Empire by 1481
- under Venetian control c.1450
- Holy Roman Empire c.1480
- frontiers in 1481
- ⚔ battle, with date
- ⊙ siege, with date

1517: Selim I orders construction of Ottoman fleet at Suez; Portuguese attack on Jedda repulsed | 1538: Ottomans subjugate Yemen and Aden and take occupy port of Basra on Persian Gulf | 1546: Ottomans retake Basra after revolt | 1551–52: Ottomans fail to oust Portuguese from Hormuz

1516–17: Ottomans conquer Syria, Egypt, the Hejaz, and Yemen | 1525: Ottomans again defeat Portuguese fleet in Red Sea | 1538: Failure of Ottoman blockade of Portuguese at Diu

Ottoman attempts to control trade in the Indian Ocean

Trade in the Indian Ocean

With their conquest in the early 16th century of Egypt, Mesopotamia, the Hejaz, and Yemen, the Ottomans gained control of trade through the Persian Gulf and the Red Sea. Ships carrying goods such as spices from India and the Moluccas, and slaves from East Africa, docked at Aden and Jedda; from there they were transported overland to the markets of Cairo, Aleppo, Damascus, and north into Anatolia. Responding to persistent threats to their trade from the Portuguese, the Ottomans assembled fleets at Suez and Basra and made several attempts to oust the Portuguese from the region, but without lasting success.

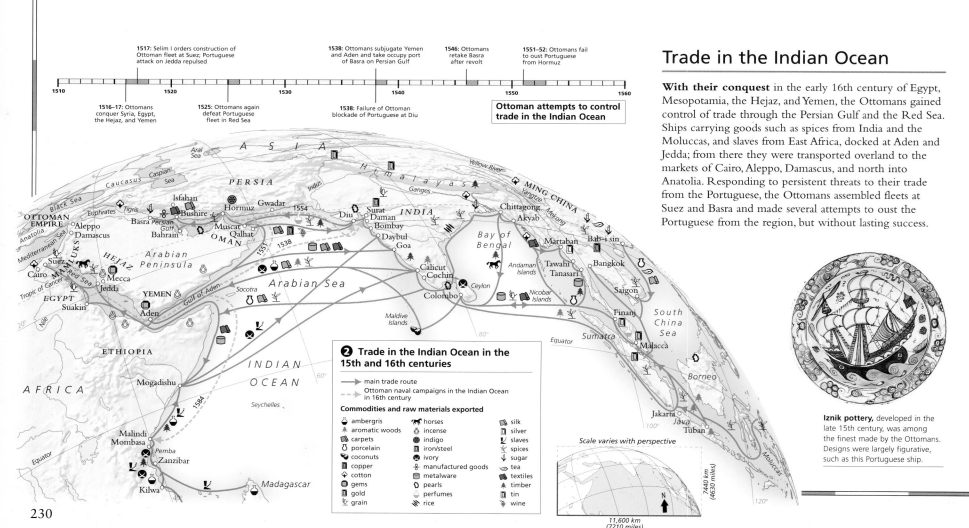

② Trade in the Indian Ocean in the 15th and 16th centuries

- main trade route
- Ottoman naval campaigns in the Indian Ocean in 16th century

Commodities and raw materials exported

ambergris	horses	silk
aromatic woods	incense	silver
carpets	indigo	slaves
porcelain	iron/steel	spices
coconuts	ivory	sugar
copper	manufactured goods	tea
cotton	metalware	textiles
gems	pearls	timber
gold	perfumes	tin
grain	rice	wine

Scale varies with perspective

7440 km (4630 miles)

11,600 km (7210 miles)

Iznik pottery, developed in the late 15th century, was among the finest made by the Ottomans. Designs were largely figurative, such as this Portuguese ship.

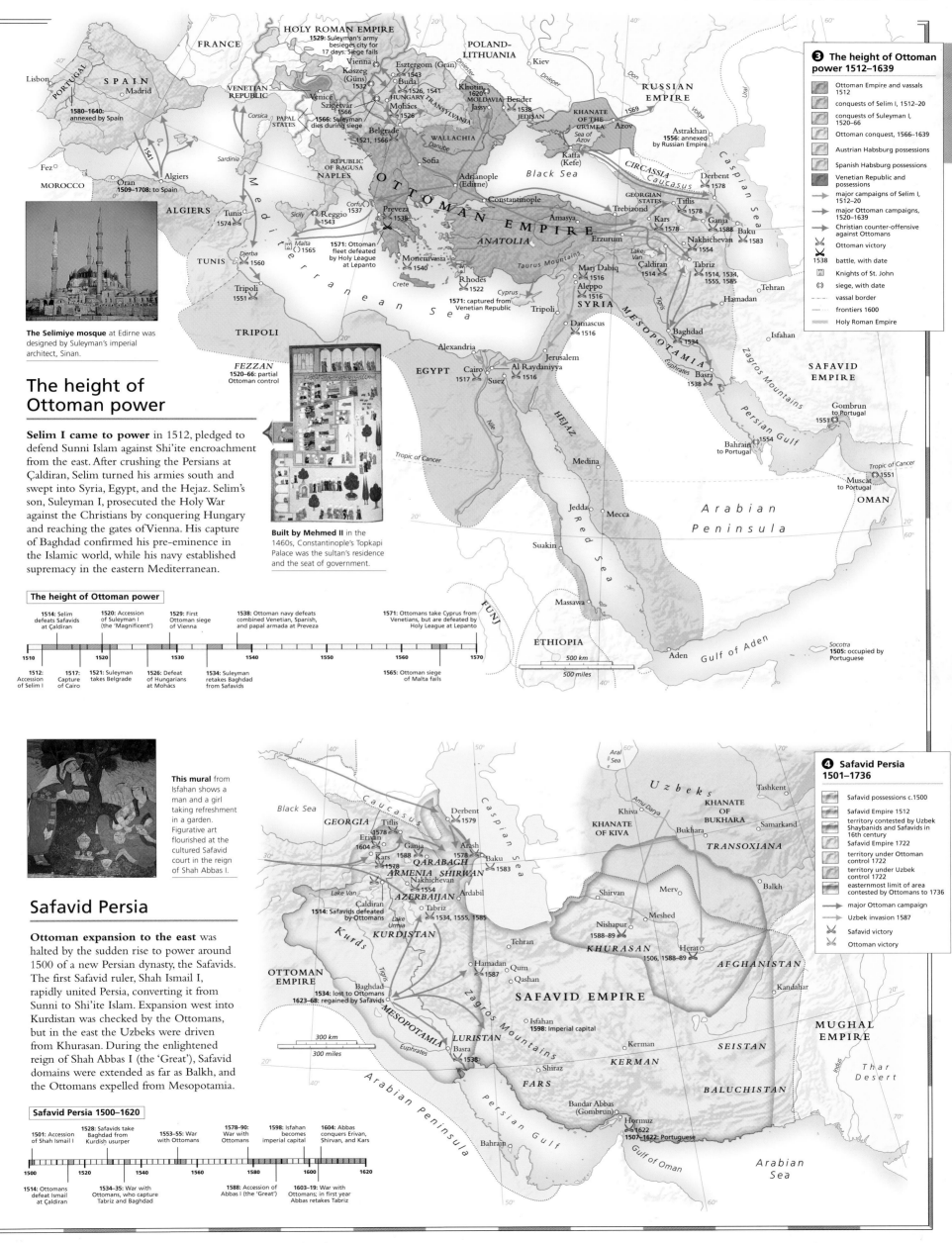

The height of Ottoman power

Selim I came to power in 1512, pledged to defend Sunni Islam against Shi'ite encroachment from the east. After crushing the Persians at Çaldiran, Selim turned his armies south and swept into Syria, Egypt, and the Hejaz. Selim's son, Suleyman I, prosecuted the Holy War against the Christians by conquering Hungary and reaching the gates of Vienna. His capture of Baghdad confirmed his pre-eminence in the Islamic world, while his navy established supremacy in the eastern Mediterranean.

The Selimiye mosque at Edirne was designed by Suleyman's imperial architect, Sinan.

Built by Mehmed II in the 1460s, Constantinople's Topkapi Palace was the sultan's residence and the seat of government.

3 The height of Ottoman power 1512–1639

- Ottoman Empire and vassals 1512
- conquests of Selim I, 1512–20
- conquests of Suleyman I, 1520–66
- Ottoman conquest, 1566–1639
- Austrian Habsburg possessions
- Spanish Habsburg possessions
- Venetian Republic and possessions
- major campaigns of Selim I, 1512–20
- major Ottoman campaigns, 1520–1639
- Christian counter-offensive against Ottomans
- Ottoman victory
- 1538 battle, with date
- Knights of St. John
- siege, with date
- vassal border
- frontiers 1600
- Holy Roman Empire

The height of Ottoman power

1510	1520	1530	1540	1550	1560	1570

1514: Selim defeats Safavids at Çaldiran
1520: Accession of Suleyman I (the 'Magnificent')
1529: First Ottoman siege of Vienna
1538: Ottoman navy defeats combined Venetian, Spanish, and papal armada at Preveza
1571: Ottomans take Cyprus from Venetians, but are defeated by Holy League at Lepanto

1512: Accession of Selim I
1517: Capture of Cairo
1521: Suleyman takes Belgrade
1526: Defeat of Hungarians at Mohács
1534: Suleyman retakes Baghdad from Safavids
1565: Ottoman siege of Malta fails

Safavid Persia

Ottoman expansion to the east was halted by the sudden rise to power around 1500 of a new Persian dynasty, the Safavids. The first Safavid ruler, Shah Ismail I, rapidly united Persia, converting it from Sunni to Shi'ite Islam. Expansion west into Kurdistan was checked by the Ottomans, but in the east the Uzbeks were driven from Khurasan. During the enlightened reign of Shah Abbas I (the 'Great'), Safavid domains were extended as far as Balkh, and the Ottomans expelled from Mesopotamia.

This mural from Isfahan shows a man and a girl taking refreshment in a garden. Figurative art flourished at the cultured Safavid court in the reign of Shah Abbas I.

4 Safavid Persia 1501–1736

- Safavid possessions c.1500
- Safavid Empire 1512
- territory contested by Uzbek Shaybanids and Safavids in 16th century
- Safavid Empire 1722
- territory under Ottoman control 1722
- territory under Uzbek control 1722
- easternmost limit of area contested by Ottomans to 1736
- major Ottoman campaign
- Uzbek invasion 1587
- Safavid victory
- Ottoman victory

Safavid Persia 1500–1620

1500	1520	1540	1560	1580	1600	1620

1501: Accession of Shah Ismail I
1528: Safavids take Baghdad from Kurdish usurper
1553–55: War with Ottomans
1578–90: War with Ottomans
1598: Isfahan becomes imperial capital
1604: Abbas conquers Erivan, Shirvan, and Kars

1514: Ottomans defeat Ismail at Çaldiran
1534–35: War with Ottomans, who capture Tabriz and Baghdad
1588: Accession of Abbas I (the 'Great')
1603–19: War with Ottomans; in first year Abbas retakes Tabriz

THE DECLINE OF THE OTTOMANS

Abdul Hamid II failed to modernize his empire and was deposed by the Young Turks in 1908.

AT THE HEIGHT OF ITS POWER, in the 16th century, the Ottoman Empire stretched from the gates of Vienna to the Indian Ocean, and from the Crimea to Algiers. By the end of the 18th century the empire was shrinking, its power eroded by a loss of internal authority and by the ambitions of the major European powers. Attempts to westernize and strengthen the Empire foundered, and when the Turks entered the First World War *(see pp.206–207)*, on the side of the Central Powers, they had lost all their territories in Africa, and most of them in Europe. Defeat in the war brought the empire to an end: British and French mandates were imposed in Mesopotamia and the Levant, and Saudi Arabia became independent. The Turks, however, established a new national identity for themselves by driving the Greeks from Anatolia and creating the modern republic of Turkey in 1923.

The empire in decline 1800–1913

By 1900 Turkey was attracting European tourists, seen here against the backdrop of Constantinople's domes and minarets. Many Turks now wore Western dress and had adopted Western habits.

Under pressure from the West, attempts were made to modernize the empire, notably in the period 1839–76. In 1908 a movement for more liberal government, led by the Young Turks, succeeded in deposing the sultan, Abdul Hamid II. The Ottomans' hold over the Balkans was broken by Greece gaining independence in 1830, followed by Serbia, Montenegro, and Romania in 1878, while Russia challenged Turkish control of the Black Sea. In Africa, the French seized Algeria and Tunisia, Britain occupied Egypt, and the Italians conquered Libya.

❶ The Ottoman Empire 1800–1913 ▶

- area lost by 1832
- area autonomous or under only nominal control by 1833
- area lost by 1882
- autonomous 1878; lost 1908
- area lost by 1913
- Ottoman Empire 1913

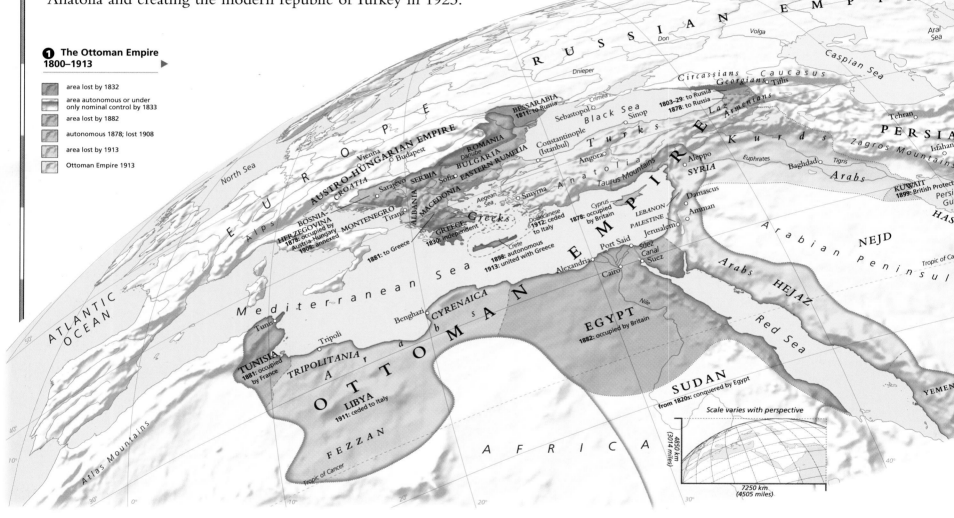

Scale varies with perspective

4850 km (3014 miles)

7250 km (4505 miles)

The Ottoman Empire 1815–1913

1830: Algiers occupied by France

1840: Empire under threat from Egypt; saved by British and Austrian intervention

1854–56: Crimean War; French and British come to aid of Turks against Russia

1878: Cyprus occupied by British

1881: Tunisia occupied by French

1908: Bosnia-Herzegovina annexed by Austro-Hungarian Empire

1912–13: Balkan Wars

1815 1825 1835 1845 1855 1865 1875 1885 1895 1905 1915

1821–30: Greek War of Independence

1839–61: Sultan Abdul Majid I makes series of liberal *Tanzimat* decrees

1853: Russians defeat Turkish navy at Sinop

1878: Independence of Serbia, Montenegro, and Romania recognized at Berlin Congress

1882: Egypt occupied by British

1908: Bulgaria declares independence

1911: Libya occupied by Italy

Emir Faisal, seen here with his bodyguard, united the Arabs and in 1916, together with Colonel T. E. Lawrence, led a successful revolt against the Turks. After the war Faisal became king of Iraq under the British mandate.

EGYPT AND THE SUEZ CANAL

An early sign of Ottoman decline was Muhammad Ali's establishment of a virtually independent Egypt after 1805. He and his successors encouraged European investment and in 1859 Egypt became the site of one of the century's greatest feats of engineering. The brainchild of a French diplomat, Ferdinand de Lesseps, who supervised its construction, the 170-km Suez Canal linked the Mediterranean to the Red Sea. Cutting the sea journey from Britain to India by 9,700 km, the canal opened in 1869 and became one of the world's most heavily used waterways. In 1875 Britain paid the bankrupt Khedive of Egypt four million pounds for a controlling interest in the canal, thus securing a lifeline to its empire in the east.

On the day after the opening ceremony in Port Said, 68 ships, headed by the *Aigle* with Empress Eugénie of France on board, sailed the length of the Suez Canal. This painting is from Eugénie's souvenir album of the event.

The First World War

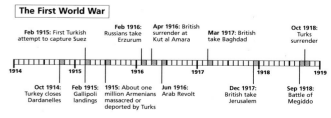

Feb 1915: First Turkish attempt to capture Suez

Feb 1916: Russians take Erzurum

Apr 1916: British surrender at Kut al Amara

Mar 1917: British take Baghdad

Oct 1918: Turks surrender

1914 1915 1916 1917 1918 1919

Oct 1914: Turkey closes Dardanelles

Feb 1915: Gallipoli landings

1915: About one million Armenians massacred or deported by Turks

Jun 1916: Arab Revolt

Dec 1917: British take Jerusalem

Sep 1918: Battle of Megiddo

The partition of the Ottoman Empire 1918–23

Following the Turkish surrender in 1918, Syria became a French mandate while Palestine, Iraq, and Transjordan became British mandates. By the Treaty of Sèvres (1920), Turkey was forced to give up all her non-Turkish lands; eastern Thrace and Smyrna were given to Greece. The Turkish sultan accepted the Treaty's conditions, but the Allies had underestimated the fervour of the Turkish Nationalists; led by Kemal Pasha, they launched an attack on the Greek invaders, driving them out of Anatolia. The present frontiers of Turkey were recognized by the Treaty of Lausanne in 1923. In the same year the last Ottoman sultan, Mehmed VI, was overthrown and Turkey became a republic.

In an attempt to cover the retreat of their own troops, a Greek cavalry detachment charges a Turkish force near Smyrna in 1922. Under the inspired leadership of Mustafa Kemal Pasha, Turkish Nationalists fought a fierce three-year campaign, eventually regaining eastern Thrace and Smyrna.

③ Southwest Asia after the First World War

☐ British mandate	☐ area annexed by Turkey 1921
☐ French mandate	☐ area restored to Turkey by
☐ Turkey after Treaty	Treaty of Lausanne (1923)
of Sèvres (1920)	— international border 1926

Postwar Turkey

- **May 1919:** Greek forces land at Smyrna
- **Aug 1919:** Kemal Pasha breaks away from authority of Istanbul government
- **Aug 1920:** Treaty of Sèvres
- **Dec 1920:** Armenia cedes half her territory to Turkey
- **1921:** Turkish Nationalist government established in Ankara
- **Sep 1922:** Turks recapture Smyrna
- **Jul 1923:** Treaty of Lausanne recognizes Turkish sovereignty over Smyrna and eastern Thrace
- **Oct 1923:** Turkish Republic proclaimed with Kemal Pasha as first president

② The First World War in Southwest Asia

☐ Ottoman Empire 1914	▲▲▲ Russian/Turkish front 1917	--→ Allied forces under Col T.E. Lawrence
☐ British Empire 1914	▲▲▲ Turkish lines at surrender, 1918	→ French forces
☐ Russian Empire 1914	→ Turkish forces	→ Russian forces
☐ area of Arab revolt (1916–18)	→ Allied forces	— railway line

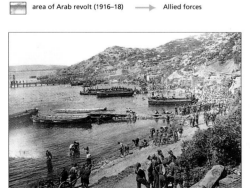

British and Australian troops (left) land on the Gallipoli peninsula. They abandoned the offensive in January 1916, having lost over 250,000 men.

French General d'Esperey lands in Istanbul in 1919 to be greeted by British General Wilson (below). Behind Wilson stands Kemal Pasha (later known as Atatürk), who was to lead Turkey in its struggle to become a modern state.

The First World War 1914–18

The Turks began the war well, pinning down an Allied force on the Gallipoli peninsula for nine months and halting the British in Mesopotamia. But they twice failed to take Suez and in 1916 their Third Army was virtually destroyed by the Russians at Erzurum. The end came in 1918 when British forces, supported by Arab irregulars, drove north in a two-pronged attack, capturing Baghdad and Jerusalem, and eventually reaching Damascus.

The emergence of Saudi Arabia 1800–1932

The modern Saudi state has its origins in the 18th century when the Wahhabis – an orthodox sect attempting to preserve the 'purity of Islam' – united the previously divided Arab tribes. Led by the Saud family, the Wahhabis raided into Mesopotamia, the Hejaz, and Syria, capturing Mecca in 1806. But in a series of campaigns (1812–18), the Wahhabis were crushed by armies from Egypt and Ottoman forces from the north. In 1902, Abd al-Aziz Ibn Saud led a Saudi resurgence. The Saud family gradually consolidated its power within the peninsula and, in 1932, the kingdom of Saudi Arabia was proclaimed.

Abd al-Aziz Ibn Saud regained his family's homelands around Riyadh, then founded a kingdom that he ruled until his death in 1953.

The Arabian Peninsula 1750–1950

- **c.1750:** Emergence of Wahhabi movement
- **1806:** Wahhabis take Mecca
- **1812:** Egyptian forces retake Mecca and Medina
- **1818:** Wahhabi resistance crushed by Egyptian forces
- **1843:** Fortunes of Saud family restored by Faisal
- **c.1880:** Birth of Abd al-Aziz Ibn Saud in Kuwait
- **1887:** Riyadh taken by Rashidis, who dominate Nejd
- **1902:** Ibn Saud reclaims his patrimony by capturing Riyadh
- **1926:** Ibn Saud crowns himself King of the Hejaz and Sultan of Nejd
- **1932:** Kingdom of Saudi Arabia proclaimed
- **1938:** First oil exported from Saudi

④ The formation of Saudi Arabia

▼ MAIN MAP: 1912–1932	INSET: 1800–1812 ▶
☐ Ottoman Empire c.1912	☐ Ottoman Empire c.1800
☐ Saudi territory c.1912	☐ Wahhabi territory c.1800
☐ Saudi gains 1913	→ Wahhabi expansion in early 19th century
☐ Saudi gains 1920	1805 date captured by Wahhabis
☐ Saudi gains 1921–22	
☐ Saudi gains 1924–25	

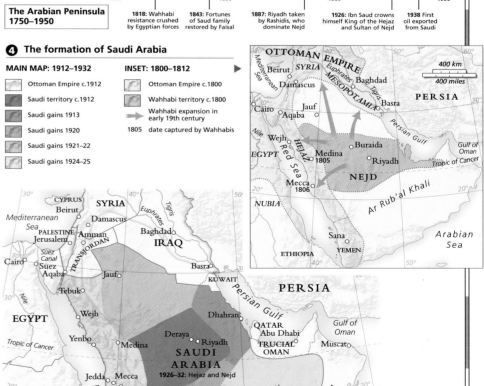

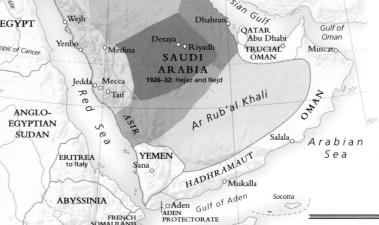

MODERN WEST ASIA

Yasser Arafat, the chairman of the PLO since 1969, led the fight for recognition of Palestinian rights.

THE HISTORY OF WEST ASIA after the Second World War was dominated by two factors: oil, and the creation of the state of Israel. The discovery of huge reserves of oil throughout the Gulf region had an enormous impact on the economies and political status of all the states concerned. The UN decision of 1947 to partition Palestine into two states to form a Jewish homeland sparked off the Arab–Israeli conflicts, which continue to this day. Israel has been recognized by the PLO and by its neighbours Egypt and Jordan, but not by states such as Syria and Iraq, while southern Lebanon remains a battleground between Israel and Arab guerrilla forces. A further threat to the region's stability is the resurgence of Islam: fundamentalist principles inspire many groups opposed to Israel and to the influence of the US and the West.

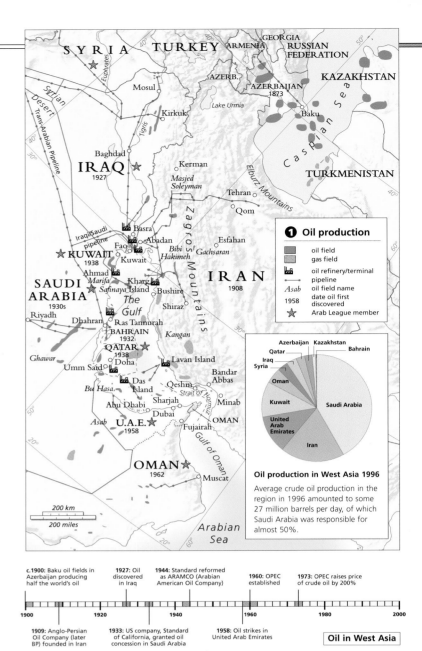

① Oil production

- oil field
- gas field
- oil refinery/terminal
- pipeline
- *Asab* oil field name
- 1958 date oil field first discovered
- ☆ Arab League member

Oil production in West Asia 1996

Average crude oil production in the region in 1996 amounted to some 27 million barrels per day, of which Saudi Arabia was responsible for almost 50%.

Oil production in the Gulf

The Gulf remains the world's most valuable and heavily exploited region of oil and natural gas production. As producers of 35% of the world's oil requirements by 1993, the Gulf states were able to exert powerful influence on the world's economies; increases in the price of crude oil, such as that imposed by OPEC (the Organization of Petroleum Exporting Countries) in 1973–74, had worldwide repercussions and regional conflicts that disrupt oil supplies were a cause for worldwide concern. In the 1990s, new oilfields in the Caspian Sea region north of the Gulf attracted substantial foreign investment.

The kingdom of Saudi Arabia contains an estimated 25.9% of the world's known oil reserves, 3.7% of its gas reserves, and is the world's leading oil exporter.

c.1900: Baku oil fields in Azerbaijan producing half the world's oil	1927: Oil discovered in Iraq	1944: Standard reformed as ARAMCO (Arabian American Oil Company)	1960: OPEC established	1973: OPEC raises price of crude oil by 200%	

1900	1920	1940	1960	1980	2000

1909: Anglo-Persian Oil Company (later BP) founded in Iran	1933: US company, Standard of California, granted oil concession in Saudi Arabia	1958: Oil strikes in United Arab Emirates	**Oil in West Asia**

Arab-Israeli wars

The state of Israel was established in May 1948. The next day five Arab armies invaded; Israel survived, but its refusal to acknowledge Palestinian claims, and the refusal of Arab states to recognize Israel, led to a succession of wars in which the Arabs were defeated and Israel occupied more territories. Disputes over these territories, and the Palestinian problem, continue to destabilize the region, despite an Egyptian–Israeli peace treaty in 1979. In 1993 Israel and the PLO signed an agreement in Oslo. Israel promised to give up land for peace, but putting this into practice is a long and difficult task.

② The Palestinian problem 1947–82

MAIN MAP: Arab-Israeli Wars
- Israel in 1949
- occupied by Israel after 1967 war
- occupied by Israel after 1973 war
- occupied by Israel after 1967 war reoccupied by Egypt after 1973 war
- demilitarized zone held by UN after Israel-Syria agreement, 1974, and 2nd Sinai agreement, 1975
- route of Israel's invasion of Lebanon 1982
- ⌂ Palestinian refugee camps 1982
- disputed border

INSET: UN Partition plan 1947
- border of British mandate 1923
- proposed Arab State
- proposed Jewish State
- proposed international zone

Israeli trucks transport Egyptian prisoners from the battlefield in the Six Day War of 1967. In one of modern history's most efficient military operations, Israel defeated the combined forces of Egypt, Jordan, and Syria in six days. Launching a lightning air strike, Israel destroyed the Arab air forces, while its tanks swept into Sinai.

Arab-Israeli Wars

1956: Suez crisis; Israel, France, and Britain invade Egypt	1967: Six Day War; Israel takes Sinai, Gaza, Golan Heights, West Bank, and Jerusalem	1979: Egypt and Israel sign peace treaty based on Camp David accords	

1940	1950	1960	1970	1980	1990

1947: UN partition of Palestine	1948: Invading Arab armies repulsed; some 725,000 Arabs flee Palestine	1973: Yom Kippur War	1982: Israel invades Lebanon

Jewish and Palestinian Migrations

Jewish immigration to Palestine from Europe increased sharply in the 1930s and 1940s as a result of persecution and the Holocaust. While the Jews accepted the UN partition plan, the Arabs declined it; in the subsequent civil war and Israel's 1948–49 war against the invading Arab states, tens of thousands of Palestinians fled their homes and became refugees (*left*). Since 1948 Israel has absorbed even greater numbers of immigrants (*below*).

③ Migration 1947–96

▲ SMALL MAP:
Palestinian emigration
→ 1947–48

▼ LARGE MAP:
Jewish migration to Israel
→ 1948–71
→ 1972–96

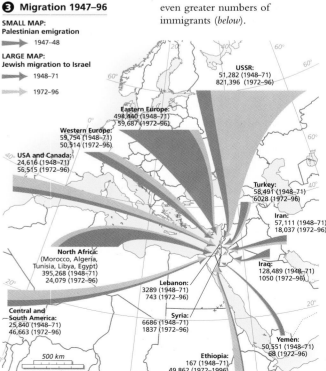

USSR:
51,282 (1948–71)
821,396 (1972–96)

Eastern Europe:
498,440 (1948–71)
59,687 (1972–96)

Western Europe:
59,754 (1948–71)
50,514 (1972–96)

USA and Canada:
24,616 (1948–71)
56,515 (1972–96)

North Africa:
(Morocco, Algeria, Tunisia, Libya, Egypt)
395,268 (1948–71)
24,079 (1972–96)

Central and South America:
25,840 (1948–71)
46,663 (1972–96)

Turkey:
58,491 (1948–71)
6028 (1972–96)

Iran:
57,111 (1948–71)
18,037 (1972–96)

Iraq:
128,489 (1948–71)
1050 (1972–96)

Lebanon:
3289 (1948–71)
743 (1972–96)

Syria:
6686 (1948–71)
1837 (1972–96)

Yemen:
50,551 (1948–71)
68 (1972–96)

Ethiopia:
167 (1948–71)
49,862 (1972–1996)

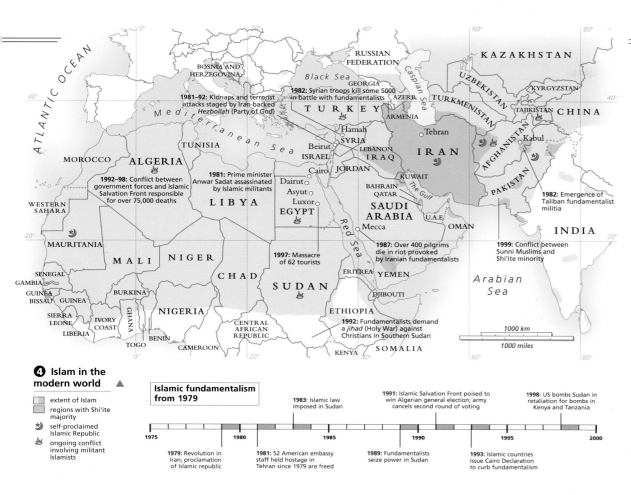

Islamic fundamentalism

The current resurgence of Islam was inspired by Ayatollah Khomeini, ruler of the new Islamic Republic of Iran, who proclaimed a form of government in which the state is a religious institution and is ruled accordingly. Islamic fundamentalist movements seek to preserve the basic elements ('fundamentals') of the Sharia or Islamic law, and to oppose liberalism. The numerous manifestations of this resurgence – especially in the Sudan, Egypt, Algeria, and Afghanistan – have caused concern in the West and the former Soviet Union that Islamic fundamentalism might threaten the world's economic and political status quo.

Amid scenes of uncontrollable grief, Ayatollah Khomeini, Iran's leader and symbol of the Iranian revolution, is escorted to his grave by mourners in June 1989.

❹ Islam in the modern world ▲

☐ extent of Islam
☐ regions with Shi'ite majority
☪ self-proclaimed Islamic Republic
⚔ ongoing conflict involving militant Islamists

Islamic fundamentalism from 1979

1983: Islamic law imposed in Sudan

1991: Islamic Salvation Front poised to win Algerian general election; army cancels second round of voting

1998: US bombs Sudan in retaliation for bombs in Kenya and Tanzania

1975 — 1980 — 1985 — 1990 — 1995 — 2000

1979: Revolution in Iran; proclamation of Islamic republic

1981: 52 American embassy staff held hostage in Tehran since 1979 are freed

1989: Fundamentalists seize power in Sudan

1993: Islamic countries issue Cairo Declaration to curb fundamentalism

Conflict in the Gulf

The resurgence of Shi'ite Islam in Iran, and a dispute over territory, led Saddam Hussein, ruler of predominantly Sunni Iraq, to invade his neighbour in 1980. The bloody, but inconclusive Iran-Iraq War lasted until 1988 when the UN brokered a cease-fire, making it the 20th century's longest conventional war. In 1990, with the intention of gaining control of Kuwait's oil reserves to rebuild his war machine, Saddam invaded Kuwait. The UN condemned the move, demanding Iraq's withdrawal. Iraq failed to comply and in January 1991 a US-led coalition of 29 states launched air and ground attacks. Kuwait was liberated and the defeated Iraqis subjected to harsh economic sanctions, but continued US-Iraqi hostility could plunge the region into another war.

Thousands of huge posters depicting Saddam Hussein in a war-like posture have been erected throughout Iraq. Behind the gun-toting president, his victorious armies can be seen in action.

The plight of the Kurds

Kurdish territories overlap large areas of Turkey, Iran, and Iraq. As a result of Kurdish insurgents allying with Iran during the Iran-Iraq War, in 1988 Saddam Hussein unleashed a campaign of vengeance against them involving the use of chemical weapons. Following Iraq's defeat in the Gulf War, a Kurdish rebellion erupted in northern Iraq which was brutally suppressed by Saddam. Over one million Kurds fled into Turkey and Iran. In May 1992 the Kurds elected their own government and became a semi-independent political entity.

Kurdish refugees flee across the mountains to Turkey in 1991 in the wake of Saddam Hussein's chemical attacks on their communities in northern Iraq.

Oil pollution

The Gulf wars left a terrible legacy of oil pollution. As Iraq's forces withdrew from Kuwait in 1991, they set on fire almost all of the country's 950 oil wells. The subsequent conflagration left a dense pall of black smoke over the entire region and an oil-slick covering huge areas of the Gulf. Many of the blazing wells continued to burn for months.

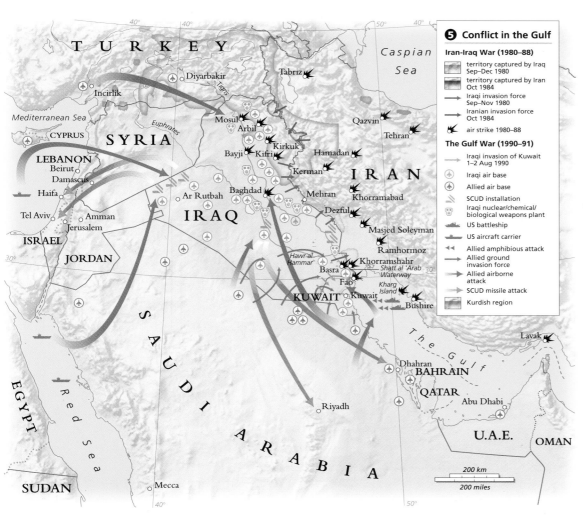

❺ Conflict in the Gulf

Iran-Iraq War (1980–88)
☐ territory captured by Iraq Sep–Dec 1980
☐ territory captured by Iran Oct 1984
→ Iraqi invasion force Sep–Nov 1980
→ Iranian invasion force Oct 1984
✈ air strike 1980–88

The Gulf War (1990–91)
→ Iraqi invasion of Kuwait 1–2 Aug 1990
⊕ Iraqi air base
⊕ Allied air base
⚡ SCUD installation
⚛ Iraqi nuclear/chemical/biological weapons plant
⚓ US battleship
⚓ US aircraft carrier
◄◄ Allied amphibious attack
→ Allied ground invasion force
→ Allied airborne attack
→ SCUD missile attack
☐ Kurdish region

Pictures of seabirds like this cormorant, helpless in the face of the tide of oil released into the Gulf, became powerful emblems of the ecological damage caused by the Gulf War.

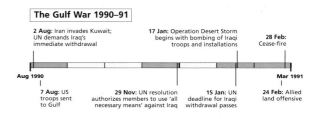

The Gulf War 1990–91

2 Aug: Iraq invades Kuwait; UN demands Iraq's immediate withdrawal

17 Jan: Operation Desert Storm begins with bombing of Iraqi troops and installations

28 Feb: Cease-fire

Aug 1990 — Mar 1991

7 Aug: US troops sent to Gulf

29 Nov: UN resolution authorizes members to use 'all necessary means' against Iraq

15 Jan: UN deadline for Iraqi withdrawal passes

24 Feb: Allied land offensive

SOUTH AND SOUTHEAST ASIA

REGIONAL HISTORY

Vegetation type

ice cap and glacier

polar or alpine desert

tundra

semi-desert or sparsely vegetated

grassland

forest or open woodland

tropical rainforest

temperate desert

tropical desert

desert

coastline (present-day)

coastline (18,000 years ago)

THE HISTORICAL LANDSCAPE

LYING LARGELY BETWEEN THE TROPICS, this region enjoys a complex geography incorporating the world's greatest mountains, some of the world's largest river systems and tropical rainforests, and the globe's most extensive archipelago. During the last Ice Age, lower sea levels rendered the shallow seas surrounding Southeast Asia into dry land, allowing humans to migrate from the Asian mainland, through the islands of Southeast Asia. The Indian subcontinent was home to some of the world's earliest civilizations, founded on the banks of the Indus and Ganges rivers. Historically, the sheer size of the Indian subcontinent and variety of its peoples have attracted and resisted political unity in equal parts, and Hinduism, Buddhism, and Islam have provided the inspiration for remarkable eras of cultural, economic, and political efflorescence. The region is well-endowed with valuable natural resources and has attracted and fostered trade since the earliest times. Only in the recent centuries of colonial rivalry, have concerns about self-determination been overtaken by the need to meet the demands of soaring population growth.

The Mekong is one of many great rivers which radiate south and east from the Plateau of Tibet. The fluvial soils that accumulate around the lower reaches of these rivers are exceptionally fertile, and have long been utilized by humans for agriculture – especially the cultivation of rice.

The Himalayas have always provided a barrier to human migration between South and East Asia. The first settlers entered southern Asia by passes that still provide the only means of traversing the mountains.

The Indus river flows from the Himalayas, through mountain meadows and down across fertile plains to the sea. The Indus valley civilizations were the most sophisticated early societies in southern Asia.

The Thar Desert in western India is a small remnant of the larger Great Indian Sand Desert, that covered much of western India at the end of the last Ice Age.

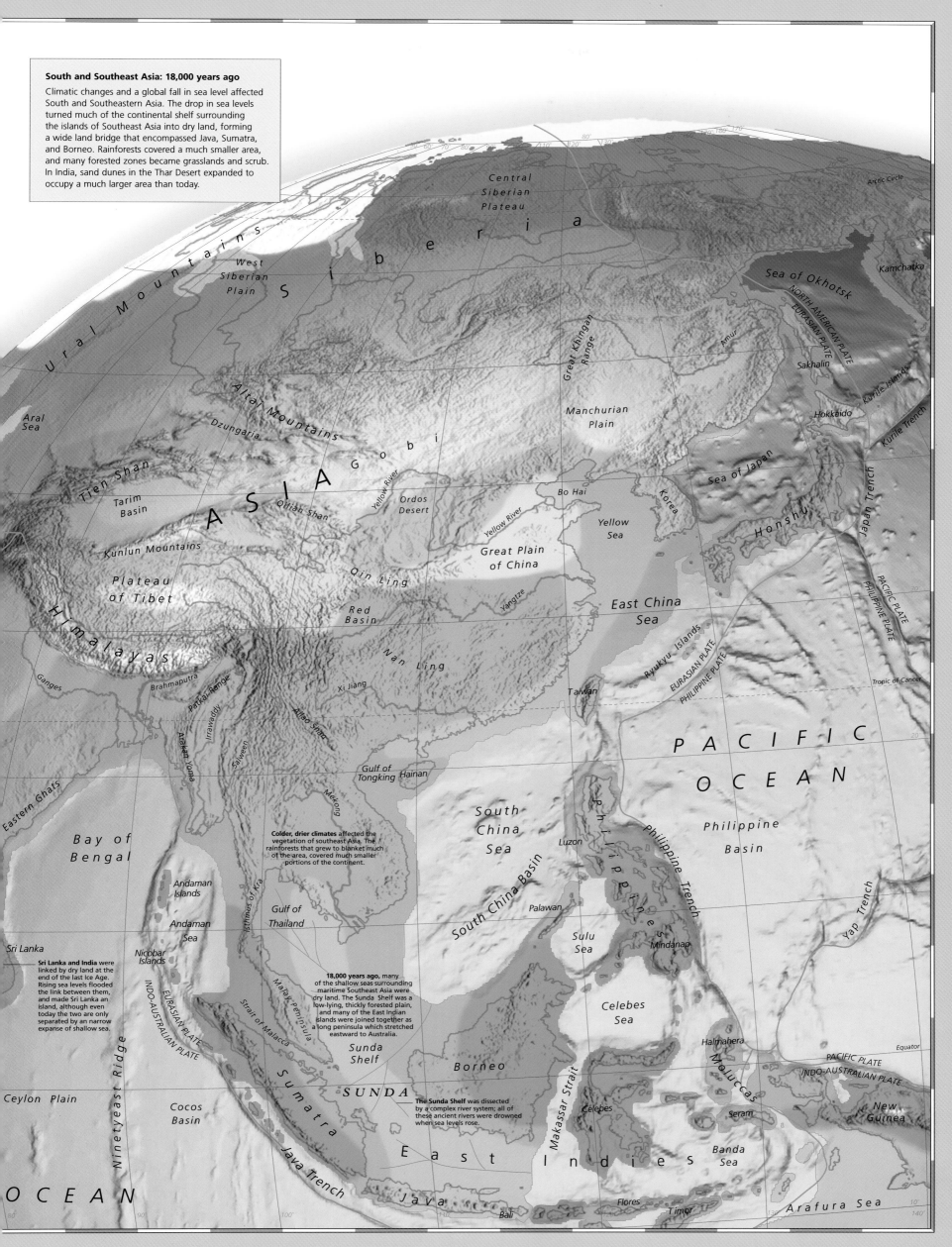

Central
Siberian
Plateau

Arctic Circle

S i b e r i a

West
Siberian
Plain

Ural Mountains

Sea of Okhotsk

Kamchatka

NORTH AMERICAN PLATE
EURASIAN PLATE

Altai Mountains

Great Khingan Range

Amur

Sakhalin

Kurile Islands

Hokkaido

Kurile Trench

Aral
Sea

Dzungaria

G o b i

Manchurian
Plain

Sea of Japan

Honshu

Japan Trench

Tien Shan

Tarim
Basin

A S I A

Qilian Shan

Yellow River

Ordos
Desert

Bo Hai

Korea

Yellow
Sea

PACIFIC PLATE

Kunlun Mountains

Yellow River

Great Plain
of China

East China
Sea

PHILIPPINE PLATE

Plateau
of Tibet

Qin Ling

Yangtze

Tropic of Cancer

Himalayas

Red
Basin

Ryukyu Islands

EURASIAN PLATE
PHILIPPINE PLATE

Ganges

Brahmaputra

Nan Ling

Taiwan

Patkai Range

Xi Jiang

P A C I F I C

Irrawaddy

Ailao Shan

Eastern Ghats

Salween

Arakan Yoma

Gulf of
Tongking

Hainan

O C E A N

Bay of
Bengal

Colder, drier climates affected the vegetation of southeast Asia. The rainforests that grew to blanket much of the area, covered much smaller portions of the continent.

South
China
Sea

Philippine
Basin

Andaman
Islands

Luzon

Andaman
Sea

Sri Lanka

Sri Lanka and India were linked by dry land at the end of the last Ice Age. Rising sea levels flooded the link between them, and made Sri Lanka an island, although even today the two are only separated by an narrow expanse of shallow sea.

Nicobar
Islands

Isthmus of Kra

Gulf of
Thailand

South China Basin

Palawan

Sulu
Sea

Mindanao

Yap Trench

Philippine Trench

EURASIAN PLATE
INDO-AUSTRALIAN PLATE

Nineteast Ridge

Ceylon Plain

Cocos
Basin

Malay Peninsula

Strait of Malacca

18,000 years ago, many of the shallow seas surrounding maritime Southeast Asia were dry land. The Sunda Shelf was a low-lying, thickly forested plain, and many of the East Indian islands were joined together as a long peninsula which stretched eastward to Australia.

Sunda
Shelf

Borneo

Celebes
Sea

Halmahera

Equator

PACIFIC PLATE
INDO-AUSTRALIAN PLATE

New
Guinea

Sumatra

S U N D A

The Sunda Shelf was dissected by a complex river system; all of these ancient rivers were drowned when sea levels rose.

Makassar Strait

Celebes

Seram

Moluccas

Banda
Sea

O C E A N

Java Trench

Java

E a s t   I n d i e s

Bali

Flores

Timor

Arafura Sea

SOUTH AND SOUTHEAST ASIA

EXPLORATION AND MAPPING

THE RELIGIONS OF SOUTH ASIA all have a long tradition of cosmography, though surviving maps are of relatively recent date. While some early maps may have related to secular themes, most would have been associated with religion and the place of humankind in a greater universe, reflecting the sacred geography of the Hindu, Jain, and Buddhist traditions. Despite the sophistication of Indian science and the great distances travelled by Indian – especially Buddhist – missionaries and merchants, there is little evidence of conventional geographical mapping until well after the establishment of Islam in the region. Following the establishment of the Portuguese in western India after 1498, European colonists, with competing territorial claims, spurred on the Western mapping of South and Southeast Asia. Commercial, economic, and military motives, combined with a zeal for knowledge, led to the British Survey of India from 1767, an epic project to map and define their eastern empire.

This 18th-century Hindu globe shows the heavens (in the top half) and the earthly realm (below).

The cosmographic tradition

A Jain diagram of the universe shows Mount Meru surrounded by concentric circles representing different continents and oceans.

The cosmographic conceptions of Hinduism, Buddhism, and Jainism, which attempted to locate the sacred places of this world in an imagined universe, were remarkably complex. Within each of them, Jambudvipa – the world inhabited by humans – formed only a very small part. In all cultures of Asia there is a strong belief that the fortunes of humans are affected by extra-terrestrial forces whose influence can be foretold, in part, through astrology, with which astronomy was closely associated. Thus, mapping the heavens (on an astrolabe or other astronomical instruments) was a much more important concern than the geographic mapping of topography.

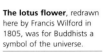

The lotus flower, redrawn here by Francis Wilford in 1805, was for Buddhists a symbol of the universe.

Indigenous mapping of South and Southeast Asia

Scarcely any surviving indigenous maps of the region are earlier than the 16th century. Maps were drawn for a variety of reasons: to provide information for the military; to illustrate itineraries or journeys; to legitimize territorial possessions. Maritime navigation charts from Gujarat date to the 17th century. Yet few surviving maps are strictly geographical, and virtually none are drawn to a fixed scale. Cosmographic views were sometimes combined with geographical knowledge of the known world.

The astronomical observatory at Jaipur was one of five built by the Rajput king Sawai Jai Singh between 1722 and 1739. It contained remarkably accurate masonry instruments.

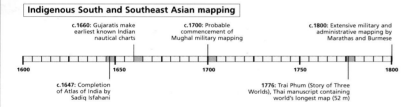

Indigenous South and Southeast Asian mapping

c.1660: Gujaratis make earliest known Indian nautical charts

c.1700: Probable commencement of Mughal military mapping

c.1800: Extensive military and administrative mapping by Marathas and Burmese

1600 — 1650 — 1700 — 1750 — 1800

c.1647: Completion of Atlas of India by Sadiq Isfahani

1776: Trai Phum (Story of Three Worlds), Thai manuscript containing world's longest map (52 m)

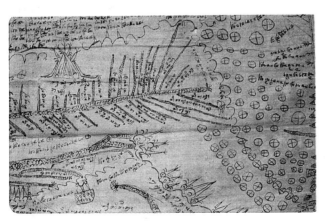

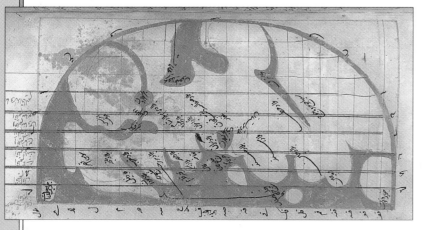

The sacred map of the Sundanese chiefdom of Timbanganten in western Java *(left)* was drawn in the late 16th century. It is still venerated by local villagers for its protective powers against the volcano clearly depicted on the left of the map.

The Mughal Emperor Jahangir is shown embracing Shah Abbas of Persia on a geographic globe, based on an Elizabethan model brought to the court by the first English ambassador in 1615 *(right)*.

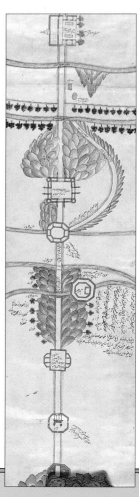

An encyclopedic work in Persian by Sadiq Isfahani of Jaunpur in northern India was finished in 1647. The section on travel contains a map *(left)* of the 'inhabited quarter' (Africa and Eurasia), drawn in the traditional style of Islamic cosmography.

The detail *(right)* is from a Mughal map showing the route from Delhi to Kandahar by means of a system of straight lines and nodal points.

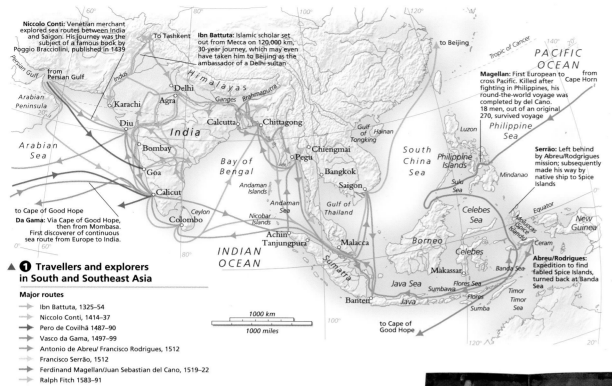

Niccolo Conti: Venetian merchant explored sea routes between India and Saigon. His journey was the subject of a famous book by Poggio Bracciolini, published in 1439

To Tashkent

Ibn Battuta: Islamic scholar set out from Mecca on 120,000 km, 30-year journey, which may even have taken him to Beijing as the ambassador of a Delhi sultan

to Beijing

Magellan: First European to cross Pacific. Killed after fighting in Philippines, his round-the-world voyage was completed by del Cano. 18 men, out of an original 270, survived voyage

from Cape Horn

from Persian Gulf

Da Gama: Via Cape of Good Hope, then from Mombasa. First discoverer of continuous sea route from Europe to India.

Serrão: Left behind by Abreu/Rodrigues mission; subsequently made his way by native ship to Spice Islands

Abreu/Rodrigues: Expedition to find fabled Spice Islands, turned back at Banda Sea

to Cape of Good Hope

1000 km
1000 miles

▲ **❶ Travellers and explorers in South and Southeast Asia**

Major routes

→ Ibn Battuta, 1325–54
→ Niccolo Conti, 1414–37
→ Pero de Covilhã 1487–90
→ Vasco da Gama, 1497–99
→ Antonio de Abreu/ Francisco Rodrigues, 1512
→ Francisco Serrão, 1512
→ Ferdinand Magellan/Juan Sebastian del Cano, 1519–22
→ Ralph Fitch 1583–91
→ Jean Baptiste Tavernier 1639–67 (five visits)

Travellers in South and Southeast Asia

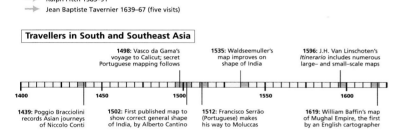

1498: Vasco da Gama's voyage to Calicut; secret Portuguese mapping follows

1535: Waldseemuller's map improves on shape of India

1596: J.H. Van Linschoten's *Itinerario* includes numerous large– and small-scale maps

1400 | 1450 | 1500 | 1550 | 1600

1439: Poggio Bracciolini records Asian journeys of Niccolo Conti

1502: First published map to show correct general shape of India, by Alberto Cantino

1512: Francisco Serrão (Portuguese) makes his way to Moluccas

1619: William Baffin's map of Mughal Empire, the first by an English cartographer

Travellers in South and Southeast Asia

The most celebrated medieval traveller in the region was Ibn Battuta of Tangier in the 14th century, even if his claim to have journeyed as far China may not be true. A century later Vasco da Gama was piloted across the Indian Ocean by a Gujarati Muslim. A yet more southerly route opened up the richest prize of Southeast Asia – the fabled Spice Islands, subject of a Portuguese monopoly from 1512. In the 1590s the Dutch began to probe the southern Indian Ocean, using Mauritius as a staging post.

This map of India and Ceylon dating from 1596 appears in Jan Huygen van Linschoten's *Itinerario*, a work instrumental in encouraging Dutch and English trade with India.

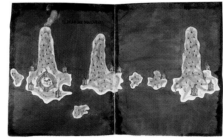

A Portuguese map of the Moluccas (1646) shows major settlements, volcanoes, and types of vegetation on the islands (*left*).

This 17th-century French map shows the Kingdom of Siam, the Malay Peninsula, Sumatra, and Java, including political boundaries and areas of influence (*right*).

The Survey of India

Although European mapping of India began in the wake of Vasco da Gama's 1498 landfall, it was not until after James Rennell's 1767 appointment as the first Surveyor General of the newly acquired province of Bengal that the British began to survey and map the country systematically. Initially, maps were based on observation, reports, and intelligence. From the late 18th century, British Army officers, such as Colin Mackenzie and William Lambton, began formal trigonometrical surveys. Sir George Everest, Lambton's successor, planned a vast network of triangulations, operated by a huge staff. He was careful to placate local princes, who feared that land surveys would infringe on their already eroded sovereignty.

James Rennell, surveyor of Bengal and Bihar, published this map in 1782, four years after his return to England. The cartouche depicts Britannia receiving the sacred scriptures of India from a Brahmin.

George Everest planned his trigonometrical triangulations on a grid overlying the entire subcontinent. His predecessor, William Lambton laid down the central north-south axis.

The Indian Atlas of J. & C. Walker was commissioned by the East India Company in 1823. It was produced at a scale of four miles to one inch.

The Survey of India

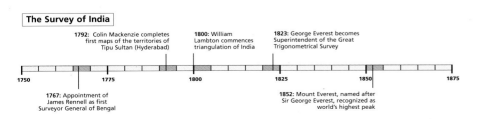

1792: Colin Mackenzie completes first maps of the territories of Tipu Sultan (Hyderabad)

1800: William Lambton commences triangulation of India

1823: George Everest becomes Superintendent of the Great Trigonometrical Survey

1750 | 1775 | 1800 | 1825 | 1850 | 1875

1767: Appointment of James Rennell as first Surveyor General of Bengal

1852: Mount Everest, named after Sir George Everest, recognized as world's highest peak

The scientific exploration of Southeast Asia

In 1854, the British naturalist Alfred Wallace set out for Singapore, and spent the next eight years travelling around the islands of the East Indies and New Guinea. He observed and collected a vast number of animal species, many previously unknown to western science. Most importantly, he observed a dramatic change in fauna at the centre of the region; the eastern species are distinctly Australian, the western, Asian. He argued that the eastern part of the archipelago was therefore once part of a Pacific continent. The boundary between the two faunal regions came to be called the Wallace Line.

Alfred Wallace's account of his Southeast Asian travels, published in 1869, contains many fine illustrations of the species encountered on his journey such as this black cockatoo from the Aru Islands.

MAP of AMBOYNA. with parts of BOURU and CERAM. and Mr Wallace's routes

The series of maps published in Alfred Wallace's account of his journey to Southeast Asia show, in great detail, the terrain which he explored. This map, of Ceram in the Moluccas, shows the region where he encountered and carefully observed many different types of birds of paradise, and first began to devise his theories about species evolution.

▼ **❷ The scientific journeys of Alfred Wallace in Southeast Asia**

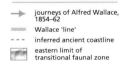

→ journeys of Alfred Wallace, 1854–62
--- Wallace 'line'
----- inferred ancient coastline
▭ eastern limit of transitional faunal zone

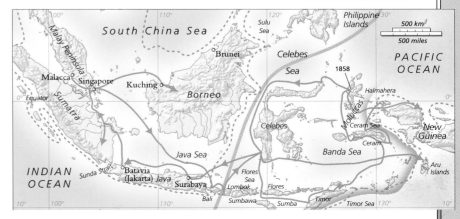

500 km
500 miles

EARLY CIVILIZATIONS OF SOUTH ASIA

This perforated pot from Mohenjo-Daro was used for carrying perfume.

COPPER AND BRONZE technology, reaching South and Southeast Asia during the 5th to 3rd millennia BCE, may have encouraged the development of urban civilizations in the Indus valley in the mid-3rd millennium BCE. The cities of the Indus established trading links which extended to Mesopotamia. The cities' demise c.1500 BCE may have been caused by Sanskrit-speaking Aryan invaders, whose influence spread across India over the next thousand years. In the 5th century BCE, the region of Magadha gained ascendancy over the small states of the Ganges plain. Chandragupta Maurya established a vigorous new dynasty with its capital at Pataliputra in 321 BCE, which reached its apogee in the following century in the reign of Ashoka. In Southeast Asia, Sanskrit inscriptions from c.400 BCE are evidence of early Indian influence in the region.

The development of Harappan culture

This bust of a bearded man from Mohenjo-Daro c.2100 BCE, possibly represents a priest-king.

Harappan culture arose from agricultural and pastoral cultures in the hills of nearby Baluchistan during the late 4th millennium BCE and expanded from its core area on the Indus valley as far east as the Ganges river and south to present-day Maharashtra. Indus civilization is marked by regularly laid-out cities, built of baked brick, and dominated by imposing citadels, which contained religious, ceremonial and administrative buildings. Many of the streets of the residential areas had brick-roofed drains with regular inspection holes. Weights, measures, and bricks were all standardized, indicating a high level of cultural uniformity. The demise of Indus civilization may have been caused by invasion or by environmental change which disrupted the delicate balance between the cities and their agricultural base.

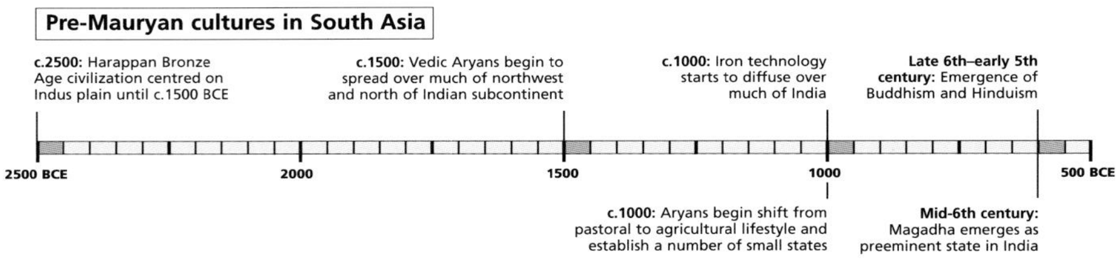

Pre-Mauryan cultures in South Asia

- **c.2500:** Harappan Bronze Age civilization centred on Indus plain until c.1500 BCE
- **c.1500:** Vedic Aryans begin to spread over much of northwest and north of Indian subcontinent
- **c.1000:** Iron technology starts to diffuse over much of India
- **Late 6th-early 5th century:** Emergence of Buddhism and Hinduism
- **c.1000:** Aryans begin shift from pastoral to agricultural lifestyle and establish a number of small states
- **Mid-6th century:** Magadha emerges as preeminent state in India

(Timeline: 2500 BCE — 2000 — 1500 — 1000 — 500 BCE)

① The citadel at Mohenjo-Daro

college
stupa
great bath
granary

200 metres
200 yards

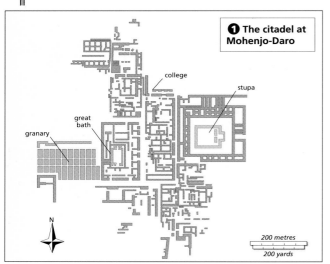

Bronze tools and weapons from Mohenjo-Daro reveal the city's high level of technological sophistication.

Mohenjo-Daro

This ancient city, along with Harappa, was one of the two greatest urban centres of Harappan civilization. With an area of 60 hectares, the city's population may have been as high as 50,000. The houses of the lower town were divided into nine blocks by regular streets. The city was a major centre of both trade and manufacture.

Stylish Harappan bronzes include this elegant dancer.

② The development of Harappan culture, late 4th–early 2nd millennium BCE ►

Baluchistan hill cultures
- hill cultures of Baluchistan, late 4th–late 3rd millennium BCE
- ◆ major site
- ◇ other site (selected)

Harappan cultures
- area of early Harappan culture, mid- to late 3rd millennium BCE
- limit of mature Harappan culture, to mid-2nd millennium BCE
- ◆ major site
- ◇ other site
- major clusters of urban sites
- ◇ other important contemporary site

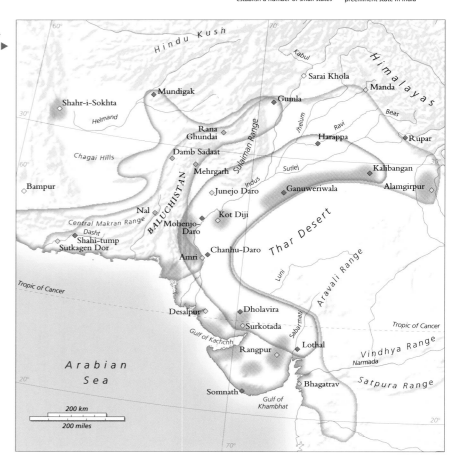

Map labels: Hindu Kush, Himalayas, Kabul, Sarai Khola, Manda, Mundigak, Gumla, Shahr-i-Sokhta, Helmand, Beas, Rana Ghundai, Damb Sadaat, Harappa, Ravi, Chagai Hills, Mehrgarh, Sutlej, Kalibangan, Bampur, Junejo Daro, Ganuweriwala, Alamgirpur, Nal, Kot Diji, Mohenjo-Daro, Thar Desert, Central Makran Range, Dasht, Shahi-tump, Sutkagen Dor, Amri, Chanhu-Daro, Luni, Aravali Range, Tropic of Cancer, Desalpur, Dholavira, Surkotada, Gulf of Kachchh, Sabarmati, Rangpur, Lothal, Vindhya Range, Arabian Sea, Narmada, Satpura Range, Somnath, Bhagatrav, Gulf of Khambhat

200 km
200 miles

The Bronze Age in Southeast Asia to 1000 BCE

Archaeologists have unearthed numerous and diverse bronzes from Southeast Asia, some possibly dating as far back as 2000 BCE. However, the associated level of civilization prior to the diffusion of Indian and Chinese influences is only vaguely understood. Certainly, the presence of bronze artefacts in some of the burials of the period, notably at Non Nok Tha and Ban Chiang in Thailand, indicates that society was becoming increasingly stratified. Sophisticated techniques, such as lost-wax casting and closed moulds, were used, and earthenware crucibles found near the burials suggest that the craftsmanship was local.

This pottery urn mounted on four supporting legs was made in Thailand c.3000–2000 BCE.

Bronze Dong Son drums, such as this one from Vietnam, c.500 BCE have been found throughout the region.

③ Bronze Age Southeast Asia from c.1500 BCE
- ◇ major Bronze Age site
- ○ find of Dong Son-type drum

Map labels: Salween, Red River, Dong Son, Irrawaddy, Mekong, PACIFIC OCEAN, Ban Chiang, Non Nok Tha, Luzon, Sai Yok, Ban Kao, Nong Chae Sao, South China Sea, Philippine Islands, Andaman Sea, Palawan, Buang Bep, Sulu Sea, Mindanao, Gua Bintong, Bukit Tengku Lembu, Gua Cha, Gua Musang, Gua Kechil, Celebes Sea, Jenderam Hilir, Dengkil, Sumatra, Borneo, Celebes, Molucca Sea, Moluccas, New Guinea, Ceram, INDIAN OCEAN, Java Sea, Java, Banda Sea, Kai Islands, Gilimanuk, Timor, Equator

500 km
500 miles

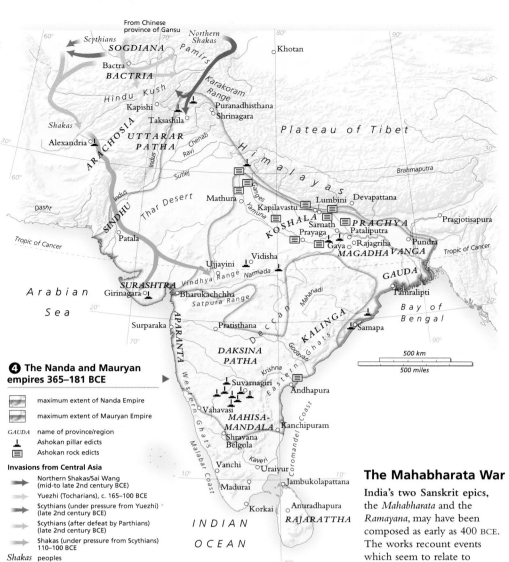

④ The Nanda and Mauryan empires 365–181 BCE

- maximum extent of Nanda Empire
- maximum extent of Mauryan Empire
- *GAUDA* name of province/region
- ⚲ Ashokan pillar edicts
- ▣ Ashokan rock edicts

Invasions from Central Asia
- → Northern Shakas/Sai Wang (mid-to late 2nd century BCE)
- → Yuezhi (Tocharians), c. 165–100 BCE
- → Scythians (under pressure from Yuezhi) (late 2nd century BCE)
- → Scythians (after defeat by Parthians) (late 2nd century BCE)
- → Shakas (under pressure from Scythians) 110–100 BCE
- *Shakas* peoples

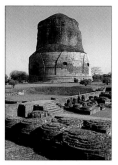

The Nanda and Mauryan empires c.365–181 BCE

A Buddhist stupa still stands at Sarnath, a Mauryan city on the northern Ganges plain.

By c.600 BCE, the Ganges plain was dominated by 16 distinct political units which, over the next century, all came under the control of the state of Magadha. By the time of the Nanda dynasty (c.365–321 BCE) the extent of the Magadhan Empire was already substantial. The succeeding Mauryan Empire (321–181 BCE), however, was the first to achieve pan-Indian status and its political and cultural influence extended well beyond the subcontinent. When the Mauryan leader Ashoka converted to Buddhism (c.260 BCE), he foreswore war. Following the decline of the empire, northwest India suffered a series of invasions by peoples from northeast Asia, propelled into migration by the expansion of Han China.

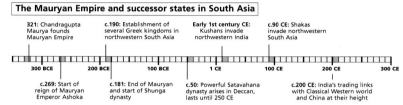

The Mauryan Empire and successor states in South Asia

321: Chandragupta Maurya founds Mauryan Empire	**c.190:** Establishment of several Greek kingdoms in northwestern South Asia	**Early 1st century CE:** Kushans invade northwestern India	**c.90 CE:** Shakas invade northwestern South Asia		

| 300 BCE | 200 BCE | 100 BCE | 1 CE | 100 CE | 200 CE | 300 CE |

| **c.269:** Start of reign of Mauryan Emperor Ashoka | **c.181:** End of Mauryan and start of Shunga dynasty | **c.50:** Powerful Satavahana dynasty arises in Deccan, lasts until 250 CE | **c.200 CE:** India's trading links with Classical Western world and China at their height |

The Mahabharata War

India's two Sanskrit epics, the *Mahabharata* and the *Ramayana*, may have been composed as early as 400 BCE. The works recount events which seem to relate to a great war fought in northwestern India several centuries earlier. The later magnification of this conflict into a pan-Indian struggle is probably the result of post-Mauryan mythology. The peoples identified in this map are among those who came within the ambit of expanding Mauryan power.

The central narrative of the *Mahabharata* tells the story of the struggle for supremacy between two groups of cousins – the Kauravas and the Pandavas. This manuscript illustration shows a chariot battle between the two forces.

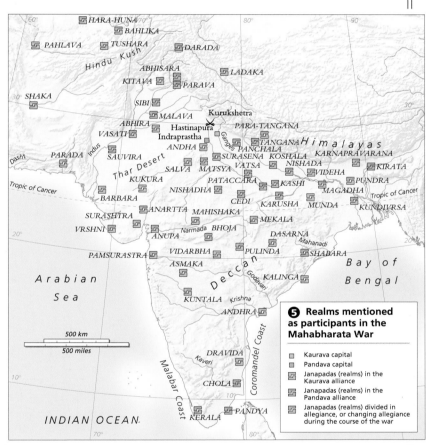

⑤ Realms mentioned as participants in the Mahabharata War

- ▣ Kaurava capital
- ▣ Pandava capital
- ▣ Janapadas (realms) in the Kaurava alliance
- ▣ Janapadas (realms) in the Pandava alliance
- ▣ Janapadas (realms) divided in allegiance, or changing allegiance during the course of the war

⑥ Areas influenced by India in Southeast Asia to 650 CE

- areas influenced by India
- ● major city of Indianized state
- *TUN-SUN* ancient Indianized state

Indian influence in Southeast Asia to 650 CE

To ancient Indians Southeast Asia was known as *Suvarnadvipa*, the continent of gold. The number of Indians who traded and migrated there was not great, but their influence was profound. Brahmin, the high-caste priests of Hindu India, acted as ritual specialists, while other advisers attended numerous royal courts. Although indigenous cultures revered Indian traditions, art, and music, they also marked Hinduism and Buddhism with a distinctive local character.

A bronze statue of the Hindu deity, Vishnu from Thailand (7th century CE) reflects the impact of Indian civilization on Southeast Asia.

Early Southeast Asian civilizations

111: Chinese Han Empire conquers and incorporates northern Vietnam	**1st century CE:** Buddhism starts to spread to many coastal localities of mainland Southeast Asia	**c.192:** Establishment of Lin-yi/Champa, longest-lived Hinduized state of Southeast Asia	**6th century:** Rise of Indianized Mon state of Dvaravati in what is now Thailand	

| 300 BCE | 150 | 1 CE | 150 | 300 | 450 | 600 CE |

| **257:** State of Au Lac established in Red River basin; succeeded by Nam Viet in 207 | **1st century CE:** Funan, precursor of Cambodia, arises as first Hinduized state of Southeast Asia | **c.550:** Khmer state of Chenla overthrows its former suzerain, Funan |

THE RELIGIONS OF SOUTHERN ASIA

This relief of the Buddha is in the Gandhara style, inspired by Graeco-Roman sculpture.

THE HISTORY OF SOUTH AND SOUTHEAST ASIA is inextricably linked to the diffusion and development of religions, and the interaction between different systems of belief. Indeed, the identity of most of the region's populations has long been defined by religion. India was the cultural birthplace of both Hinduism and Buddhism, as well as other, less widespread, faiths, such as Jainism and Sikhism. Buddhism once enjoyed substantial political patronage from Indian rulers, but ultimately failed to become established among the masses. The resurgence of Hinduism in the course of the 1st millennium CE and the spread of Islam in the 8th–13th centuries also contributed to the demise of Buddhism in the land of its birth. Many imported faiths, including Buddhism, Hinduism, Islam, and, most recently, Christianity, have planted roots in the receptive soil of various parts of Southeast Asia.

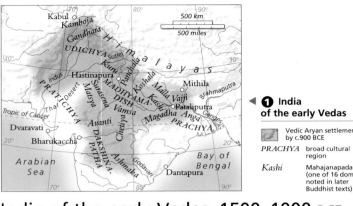

① India of the early Vedas

Vedic Aryan settlement by c.900 BCE

PRACHYA broad cultural region

Kashi Mahajanapada (one of 16 domains noted in later Buddhist texts)

India of the early Vedas, 1500–1000 BCE

The *Rig Veda* (completed c.900 BCE) is the great literary monument left by the early Aryan settlers of northern India. This collection of sacred hymns traces the development of religious ideas as they were passed down orally from generation to generation. They depict the Aryans as chariot-driving warriors, formerly nomadic pastoralists, gradually adapting to a settled way of life. Later Buddhist texts abound in geographic references and mention the 16 great domains of north and central India – the *Mahajanapadas*.

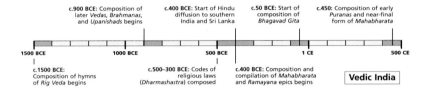

c.900 BCE: Composition of later *Vedas, Brahmanas,* and *Upanishads* begins	**c.400 BCE:** Start of Hindu diffusion to southern India and Sri Lanka	**c.50 BCE:** Start of composition of *Bhagavad Gita*	**c.450:** Composition of early *Puranas* and near-final form of *Mahabharata*	

1500 BCE — 1000 BCE — 500 BCE — 1 CE — 500 CE

c.1500 BCE: Composition of hymns of *Rig Veda* begins — **c.500–300 BCE:** Codes of religious laws (*Dharmashastra*) composed — **c.400 BCE:** Composition and compilation of *Mahabharata* and *Ramayana* epics begins — **Vedic India**

India of the Puranas

During the 1st millennium BCE, as the Aryan tribes coalesced into small kingdoms and republics, their religion became more comparable to the current form of Hinduism. As non-Aryan peoples were conquered and absorbed, a caste-based social order dominated by a Brahman priesthood, who oversaw increasingly elaborate rituals, and by a warrior caste (*Kshatriyas*) emerged. At first conquered peoples formed the lower strata of society. The expansion of Hindu culture can be traced through sacred texts; the collection of encyclopedic works – known as the *Puranas* – are rich in geographic content. They divide India up into a series of states or realms known as *janapadas*.

This bronze figure of Shiva, dating from the 11th century CE, depicts him as Lord of the Dance. He is surrounded by a circle of fire, which symbolizes both death and rebirth.

The hearth of Buddhism and Jainism

Buddhism and Jainism arose in the Gangetic Plain during the 6th century BCE, partly in reaction to the ritual excesses and social inequalities within Brahmanism. Both faiths stress *ahisma* (non-violence), non-attachment to worldly possessions, and religious meditation. Both diffused widely and enjoyed the patronage of numerous political rulers prior to the advent of Islam in northern India, although the number of followers, especially of Jainism, may not have been great.

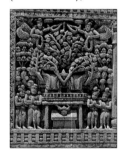

India's largest collection of Buddhist monuments is found at Sanchi in central India. They were built from the 3rd century BCE to the 11th century CE.

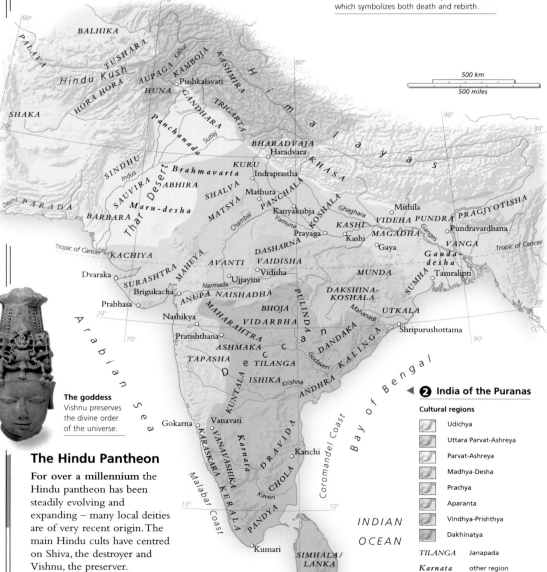

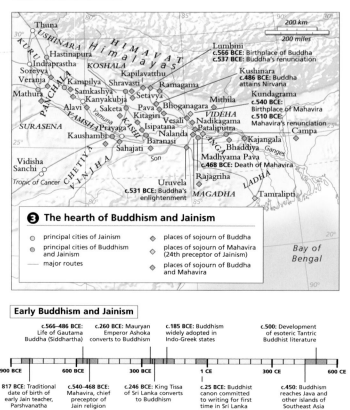

③ The hearth of Buddhism and Jainism

- ○ principal cities of Jainism
- ○ principal cities of Buddhism and Jainism
- — major routes
- ◆ places of sojourn of Buddha
- ◇ places of sojourn of Mahavira (24th preceptor of Jainism)
- ◆ places of sojourn of Buddha and Mahavira

c.566 BCE: Birthplace of Buddha
c.537 BCE: Buddha's renunciation
c.486 BCE: Buddha attains Nirvana
c.540 BCE: Birthplace of Mahavira
c.510 BCE: Mahavira's renunciation
c.468 BCE: Death of Mahavira
c.531 BCE: Buddha's enlightenment

② India of the Puranas

Cultural regions
- Udichya
- Uttara Parvat-Ashreya
- Parvat-Ashreya
- Madhya-Desha
- Prachya
- Aparanta
- Vindhya-Prishthya
- Dakhinatya

TILANGA Janapada
Karnata other region

The goddess Vishnu preserves the divine order of the universe.

The Hindu Pantheon

For over a millennium the Hindu pantheon has been steadily evolving and expanding – many local deities are of very recent origin. The main Hindu cults have centred on Shiva, the destroyer and Vishnu, the preserver.

Early Buddhism and Jainism

c.566–486 BCE: Life of Gautama Buddha (Siddhartha)	**c.260 BCE:** Mauryan Emperor Ashoka converts to Buddhism	**c.185 BCE:** Buddhism widely adopted in Indo-Greek states	**c.500:** Development of esoteric Tantric Buddhist literature

900 BCE — 600 BCE — 300 BCE — 1 CE — 300 CE — 600 CE

817 BCE: Traditional date of birth of early Jain teacher, Parshvanatha — **c.540–468 BCE:** Mahavira, chief preceptor of Jain religion — **c.246 BCE:** King Tissa of Sri Lanka converts to Buddhism — **c.25 BCE:** Buddhist canon committed to writing for first time in Sri Lanka — **c.450:** Buddhism reaches Java and other islands of Southeast Asia

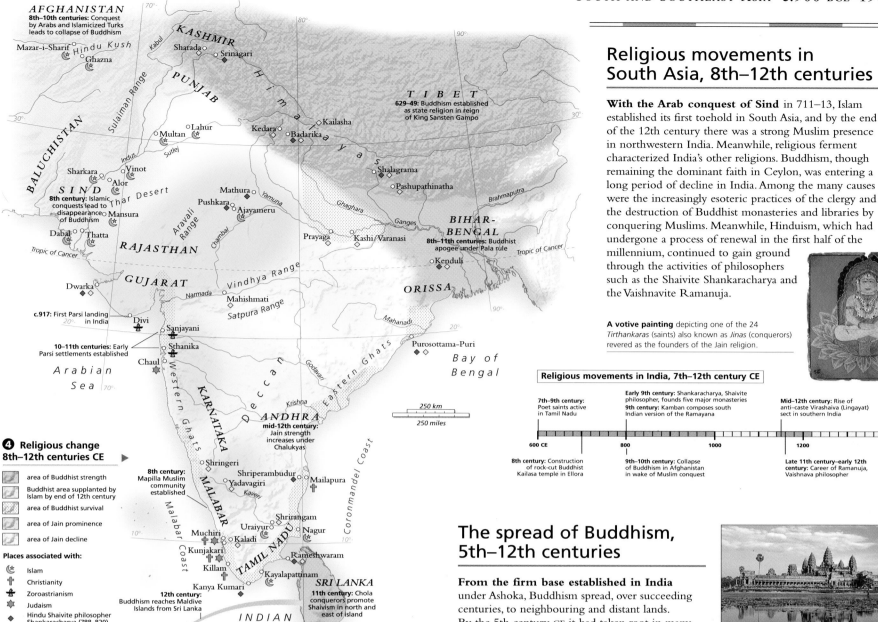

AFGHANISTAN
8th–10th centuries: Conquest by Arabs and Islamicized Turks leads to collapse of Buddhism

629–49: Buddhism established as state religion in reign of King Sansten Gampo

BIHAR-BENGAL
8th–11th centuries: Buddhist apogee under Pala rule

SIND
8th century: Islamic conquests lead to disappearance of Buddhism

c.917: First Parsi landing in India

10th–11th centuries: Early Parsi settlements established

ANDHRA
mid-12th century: Jain strength increases under Chalukyas

8th century: Mapilla Muslim community established

12th century: Buddhism reaches Maldive Islands from Sri Lanka

SRI LANKA
11th century: Chola conquerors promote Shaivism in north and east of island

④ Religious change 8th–12th centuries CE ▶

- area of Buddhist strength
- Buddhist area supplanted by Islam by end of 12th century
- area of Buddhist survival
- area of Jain prominence
- area of Jain decline

Places associated with:
- ☾ Islam
- ✝ Christianity
- ⚹ Zoroastrianism
- ✡ Judaism
- ◆ Hindu Shaivite philosopher Shankaracharya (788–820)
- ◇ Hindu Vaishnava philosopher Ramanuja (11th century)

Religious movements in South Asia, 8th–12th centuries

With the Arab conquest of Sind in 711–13, Islam established its first toehold in South Asia, and by the end of the 12th century there was a strong Muslim presence in northwestern India. Meanwhile, religious ferment characterized India's other religions. Buddhism, though remaining the dominant faith in Ceylon, was entering a long period of decline in India. Among the many causes were the increasingly esoteric practices of the clergy and the destruction of Buddhist monasteries and libraries by conquering Muslims. Meanwhile, Hinduism, which had undergone a process of renewal in the first half of the millennium, continued to gain ground through the activities of philosophers such as the Shaivite Shankaracharya and the Vaishnavite Ramanuja.

A votive painting depicting one of the 24 *Tirthankaras* (saints) also known as *Jinas* (conquerors) revered as the founders of the Jain religion.

Religious movements in India, 7th–12th century CE

7th–9th century: Poet saints active in Tamil Nadu

Early 9th century: Shankaracharya, Shaivite philosopher, founds five major monasteries

9th century: Kamban composes south Indian version of the Ramayana

Mid–12th century: Rise of anti-caste Virashaiva (Lingayat) sect in southern India

8th century: Construction of rock-cut Buddhist Kailasa temple in Ellora

9th–10th century: Collapse of Buddhism in Afghanistan in wake of Muslim conquest

Late 11th century–early 12th century: Career of Ramanuja, Vaishnava philosopher

The spread of Buddhism, 5th–12th centuries

From the firm base established in India under Ashoka, Buddhism spread, over succeeding centuries, to neighbouring and distant lands. By the 5th century CE it had taken root in many parts of Southeast Asia, frequently in conjunction with Hinduism and sponsored by increasingly Indianized states. The Mahayana and Theravada schools were both initially well represented; new contacts coming from Ceylon in the 12th century led to the increasing dominance of the latter.

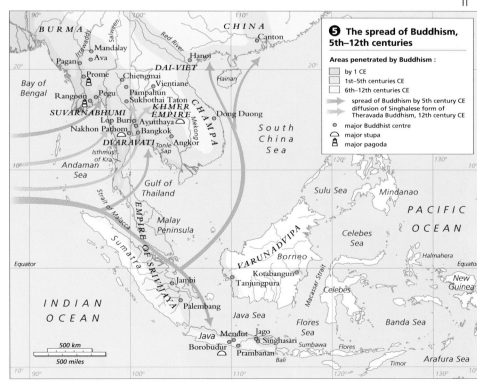

The great temple complex of Angkor Wat in Cambodia was built by the Khmer ruler, Suryavarman II (1113–50) as a monument to his own divinity as the embodiment of Lord Vishnu.

⑤ The spread of Buddhism, 5th–12th centuries

Areas penetrated by Buddhism:
- by 1 CE
- 1st–5th centuries CE
- 6th–12th centuries CE
- → spread of Buddhism by 5th century CE
- → diffusion of Singhalese form of Theravada Buddhism, 12th century CE
- ◦ major Buddhist centre
- 🛕 major stupa
- 🛕 major pagoda

The spread of Islam in Southeast Asia

Indian Muslim traders settled in the mercantile centres of Southeast Asia as early as the 10th century, but it was only after the conversion to Islam of the ruler of the powerful Sumatran state of Achin that the mainly peaceful process of Islamization began in earnest. In rapid succession, the princes of other small trading states also embraced the new faith. From their coastal capitals, Islam gradually penetrated inland, a process still underway in parts of present-day Indonesia.

A Dutch engraving of 1596 shows an envoy from Mecca meeting the governor of Bantam in west Java, an example of the East Indies' strong links with the Muslim world.

The diffusion of Islam in South and Southeast Asia

711–12: Arab conquest of Sind introduces Islam to South Asia

c.1000: Mahmud of Ghazna conquers northwest India

1295: Conversion of Sultan of Achin to Islam, which spreads over much of the East Indies

c.750: Muslim merchants establish Islam in Kerala, southwest India

c.1200: Muslim Sufi saint, Mu'in al-Din Chishti, founds first Sufi order in subcontinent

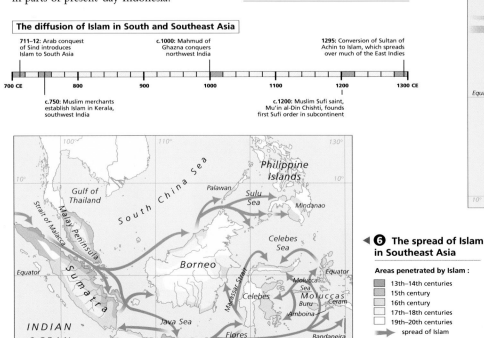

⑥ The spread of Islam in Southeast Asia

Areas penetrated by Islam:
- 13th–14th centuries
- 15th century
- 16th century
- 17th–18th centuries
- 19th–20th centuries
- → spread of Islam

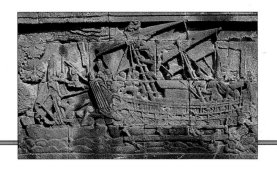

The Buddhist stupa at Borobudur, Java, symbolizes via its structure, the Buddhist transition from reality at its base – for example in this panel showing sailing vessels – to the achievement of spiritual enlightenment at the summit.

STATES AND EMPIRES 300–1525

Bajang Ratu was the capital of the Majapahit kingdom in central Java.

SOUTH ASIA WAS ruled by a great diversity of regional powers for much of this period. However, in the 4th century CE, the Gupta dynasty succeeded in uniting much of the Indian subcontinent. The next 200 years are often described as a 'golden age' of Indian civilization. It was not until the 13th century that so much of India again came under the control of a single state, the Delhi Sultanate. The Turkish dynasties that ruled the Sultanate were unable to maintain effective control over so vast an area, and its power declined in the 14th century. Southeast Asia also witnessed the rise and fall of numerous states. Kambujadesha, with its magnificent capital at Angkor, dominated the mainland, while the two greatest states of the Indonesian archipelago were Srivijaya and, later, Majapahit.

Medieval states 550–1206

This rock carving depicts a scene from the epic poem *Mahabharata*.

The multiplicity of regional powers that dominated India during this period all developed distinctive cultural styles, whose legacy survives in architecture, literature, and tradition. Some of them achieved, for brief periods, quasi-imperial status. The struggle for control of the Ganges plain was dominated by three major states: the Gurjara-Pratiharas, the Palas, and the Rashtrakutas. In the south, two major powers emerged; the Chalukyas in the west, and the Tamil Cholas in the east. Under Rajaraja (985–1014), the Cholas conquered much of southern India and Ceylon, their rule extending to the Malay Peninsula.

Medieval states

320: Chandra Gupta I founds Gupta Empire; India's 'golden age'	**c.495:** Huna invasions weaken Guptas in northern India	**c.880:** Gurjara-Pratiharas rule over virtually the whole of northern India	**c.1025:** Apogee of Tamil Chola dynasty

300 | 500 | 700 | 900 | 1100

c.540: King Harsha restores mighty Hindu state in Kanyakubja, northern India	**c.750:** Apogee of Pala dynasty, the last major Buddhist state in South Asia	**c.825:** Rashtrakuta dynasty rules over south India and Sri Lanka	

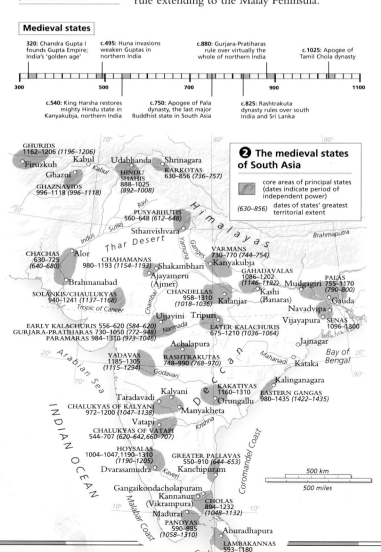

❷ The medieval states of South Asia

▨	core area of principal states (dates indicate period of independent power)
(630–856)	dates of states' greatest territorial extent

The imperial Guptas c.300–550

This wall painting, depicting a scene from the life of the Buddha, is from the spectacular cave sanctuaries at Ajanta, central India.

The authority of the Guptas extended over many conquered states whose rulers remained on their thrones in a tributary relationship to the Gupta sovereign. They held sway over other regional powers by virtue of diplomacy and marital alliances. Peace, prosperity, scholarly debate, and religious tolerance all encouraged a florescence of Indian art – in particular, in sculpture, painting, poetry, and drama. But Gupta rule was shattered by the invasion of Hunas (Hephthalites), nomads from Central Asia, in the 6th century.

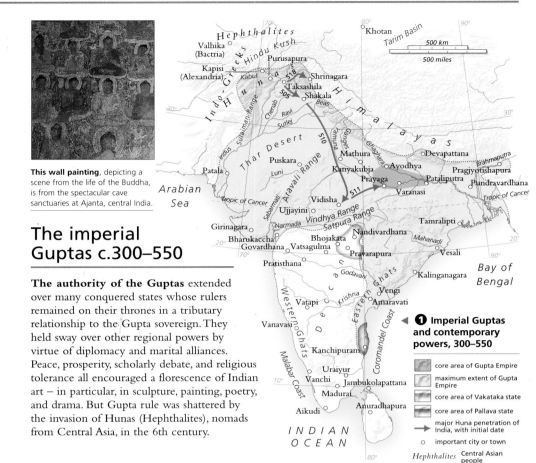

❶ Imperial Guptas and contemporary powers, 300–550

▨	core area of Gupta Empire
	maximum extent of Gupta Empire
	core area of Vakataka state
	core area of Pallava state
→	major Huna penetration of India, with initial date
○	important city or town
Hephthalites	Central Asian people

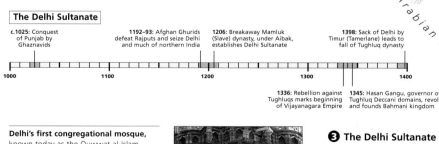

The Brihadeshwana temple at Thanjavur (Tanjore) is one of several fine Dravidian temples in the city, dating from the 11th century when it was the capital of the Chola kingdom.

The Delhi Sultanate 1206–1526

The invasion of Mahmud of Ghazna in the 11th century, highlighted India's political and military vulnerability, and subsequent invasions by Turkish peoples from Central Asia led to the establishment of the Mamluk dynasty of the Delhi Sultanate in 1206. The territory controlled by the five successive dynasties that ruled the Sultanate fluctuated greatly, reaching its greatest extent under the Tughluqs. Administrative inefficiency and an ill-advised attempt to move the capital south to Daulatabad hastened the Sultanate's decline and much of India fragmented once again into warring kingdoms.

The Delhi Sultanate

c.1025: Conquest of Punjab by Ghaznavids	**1192–93:** Afghan Ghurids defeat Rajputs and seize Delhi and much of northern India	**1206:** Breakaway Mamluk (Slave) dynasty, under Aibak, establishes Delhi Sultanate	**1398:** Sack of Delhi by Timur (Tamerlane) leads to fall of Tughluq dynasty

1000 | 1100 | 1200 | 1300 | 1400

1336: Rebellion against Tughluqs marks beginning of Vijayanagara Empire	**1345:** Hasan Gangu, governor of Tughluq Deccani domains, revolts and founds Bahmani kingdom

Delhi's first congregational mosque, known today as the Quwwat al-Islam mosque was built by Qutb ud-Din Aibak, after the capture of Delhi in 1192.

The ornate sandstone pillar of Delhi's Qutb Minar, built c.1200, is adorned with Arabic calligraphy.

❸ The Delhi Sultanate

▨	area of Sultanate at accession of Jalal ud-din Khalji, 1290
	additional territory at some time under direct Khalji administration
	limit of nominal Khalji vassals
→	possible route of Khalji raids against Mongols
	extent of Sultanate at accession of Ghiyas ud-din Tughluq, 1320
	maximum extent of Sultanate under direct Tughluq administration
	limit of nominal Tughluq vassals
Ahoms	peoples and dynasties
SIND	cultural region

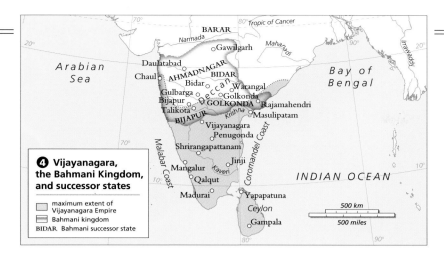

④ Vijayanagara, the Bahmani Kingdom, and successor states

- maximum extent of Vijayanagara Empire
- Bahmani kingdom
- **BIDAR** Bahmani successor state

500 km
500 miles

The Vijayanagara Empire 1335–1570

The decline of the Delhi Sultanate led to the breakaway of the Muslim-controlled areas of the Deccan and the creation, in 1347, of the Bahmani Kingdom. To the south, in the Krishna valley, the powerful new Hindu kingdom of Vijayanagara was firmly established by 1345. Its splendid capital, Vijayanagara (modern Hampi), was a magnificent temple city, with massive fortifications and a royal palace. Vijayanagara successfully withstood repeated attempts by the Bahmani Kingdom to expand southward. The Bahmani Kingdom divided into five sultanates in 1518, and Vijayanagara finally succumbed in 1570, after a disastrous defeat at Talikota in 1564.

The royal capital of Vijayanagara ('city of victory'), founded in the mid-14th century, was destroyed by invaders from the Deccani sultanates in 1565.

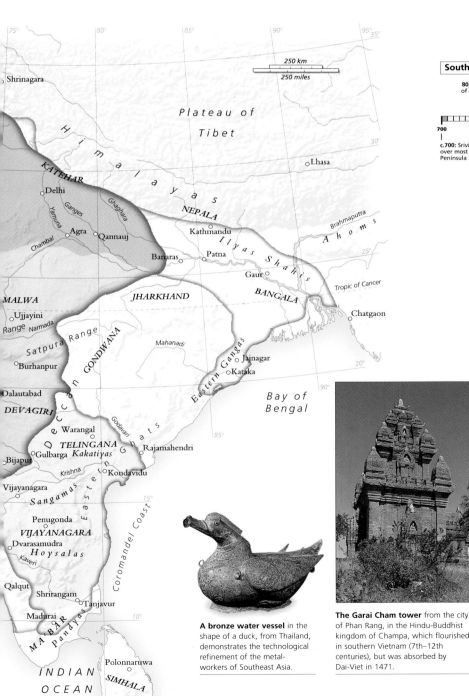

250 km
250 miles

A bronze water vessel in the shape of a duck, from Thailand, demonstrates the technological refinement of the metal-workers of Southeast Asia.

The Garai Cham tower from the city of Phan Rang, in the Hindu-Buddhist kingdom of Champa, which flourished in southern Vietnam (7th–12th centuries), but was absorbed by Dai-Viet in 1471.

Major states of Southeast Asia 650–1250

The major states of mainland Southeast Asia, although extensive, were loosely controlled and included substantial tribal populations. Their civilizations were clearly Indianized, but this influence generally diminished with distance from their core regions. The Khmer state of Kambujadesha, with its impressive capital at Angkor, dominated the mainland. In the East Indies, the leading states were bound together largely by commercial ties. The maritime empire of Srivijaya, with its capital at Palembang in Sumatra, controlled international trade through the straits of Malacca and Sunda.

This carved relief from the 13th-century temple complex at Angkor Thom, part of the Khmer capital of Angkor, shows mounted soldiers accompanying a war elephant being transported in a cart pulled by asses.

⑤ Southeast Asia, 650–1250

- core area of Pagan
- outermost limit of Pagan
- core area of Dai-Viet
- outermost limit of Dai-Viet
- core area of Champa
- outermost limit of Champa
- core area of Kambujadesha
- outermost limit of Kambujadesha
- core area of Srivijaya
- outermost limit of Srivijaya
- core area of Kadiri
- outermost limit of Kadiri

650–1320 period of state's duration
(740–1025) period of state's apogee

500 km
500 miles

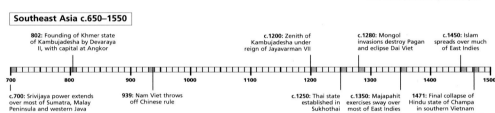

Southeast Asia c.650–1550

802: Founding of Khmer state of Kambujadesha by Devaraya II, with capital at Angkor

c.1200: Zenith of Kambujadesha under reign of Jayavarman VII

c.1280: Mongol invasions destroy Pagan and eclipse Dai Viet

c.1450: Islam spreads over much of East Indies

| 700 | 800 | 900 | 1000 | 1100 | 1200 | 1300 | 1400 | 1500 |

c.700: Srivijaya power extends over most of Sumatra, Malay Peninsula and western Java

939: Nam Viet throws off Chinese rule

c.1250: Thai state established in Sukhothai

c.1350: Majapahit exercises sway over most of East Indies

1471: Final collapse of Hindu state of Champa in southern Vietnam

Major states of Southeast Asia 1250–1550

During this period there was a marked increase in the number of medium-sized contenders for power throughout the region. The decline of Kambujadesha was matched by the rise of several ethnically Thai states and the destruction of the long-lived state of Champa by the sinicized kingdom of Dai-Viet. In the East Indies, dominance passed from Srivijaya to Majapahit which, in the 14th century, established the most extensive commercial empire that the area was to see in pre-colonial times.

▼ ⑥ Southeast Asia, 1250–1550

Outer limits of areas at some time subject to the following major states:

- Toungoo
- Ava
- Pegu
- Sukhothai
- Ayuthia
- Kambuja
- Champa
- Dai-Viet
- Singhasari
- Melaka
- Majapahit
- **BALI** other states

500 km
500 miles

MUGHALS, MARATHAS, EUROPEANS

Shah Jahan (1627–58) was one of the greatest of the Mughal emperors.

THE CONQUEST OF NORTHERN INDIA in 1526 by the Muslim Mughal chief, Babur, was to usher in a new era, marked by orderly government, economic prosperity, and great achievements in the arts, notably architecture, miniature painting, and literature. When, after the stern rule of Aurangzeb, the empire fell into disarray, the Hindu Marathas expanded rapidly from their Deccan base and dominated Indian affairs until their defeat by the British early in the 19th century. Vasco da Gama's voyage to India in 1498 opened up new trade routes, enabling European powers to establish commercial toeholds; spices, textiles, and jewels were soon being exported to western markets.

The Mughals, 1526–1857

This miniature shows Shah Jahan with his four sons. His third son, Aurangzeb, deposed him in 1658.

In 1526 the Mughals, led by Babur, a descendant of Timur *(see p.229)*, swept across much of northern India. His successor, Humayun, expelled by the governor of Bihar in 1539, returned in 1555 to establish a long-lived dynasty and an expansionist empire. The reign of Akbar (1556–1605) was a time of cultural florescence and religious tolerance. Later in the 17th century, Aurangzeb's long and harsh rule led to revolt. Many provinces seceded, and the rise of the Maratha confederacy from 1646 eventually reduced the Mughals to puppet rulers.

The tomb of Sheikh Salim lies in the Great Mosque at Fatehpur Sikri. Construction of the spectacular red limestone city began in the 1570s in the reign of Akbar.

Emperor Shah Jahan built the Taj Mahal c.1654 as a mausoleum for his beloved wife, Mumtaz. This exquisite structure of white marble is one of the masterpieces of Mughal architecture.

The Mughal Empire

1526: Babur conquers Delhi and founds Mughal Empire
1658–1707: Empire reaches maximum extent during reign of Aurangzeb
1739: Sack of Delhi by Persians and Afghans under Nadir Shah
1803: British occupy Delhi

| 1500 | 1600 | 1700 | 1800 | 1900 |

1556–1605: Reign of Akbar marked by territorial expansion and cordial Hindu-Muslim relations
1724: Independent rule over Deccan by Nizam of Hyderabad hastens disintegration of empire
1788: Mughal emperors become puppets of Marathas
1857: Last Mughal Emperor, the puppet Bahadur Shah II, dethroned and exiled by British

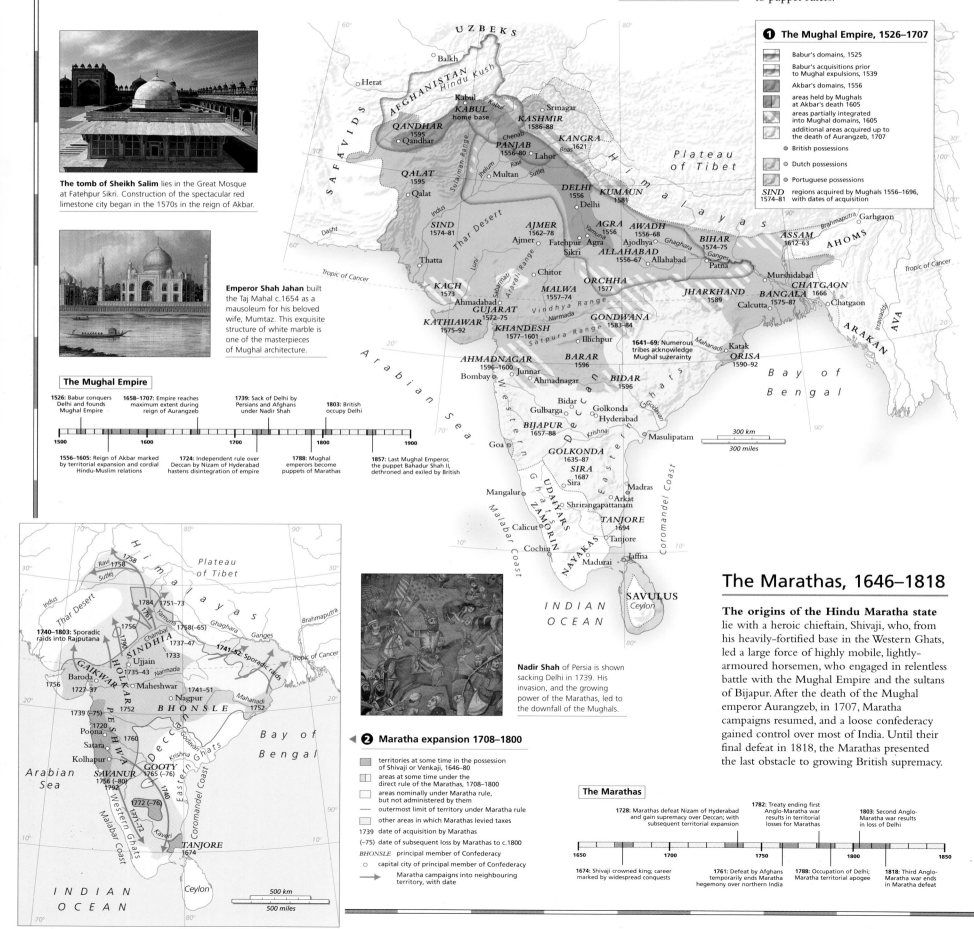

Nadir Shah of Persia is shown sacking Delhi in 1739. His invasion, and the growing power of the Marathas, led to the downfall of the Mughals.

❶ The Mughal Empire, 1526–1707

- Babur's domains, 1525
- Babur's acquisitions prior to Mughal expulsions, 1539
- Akbar's domains, 1556
- areas held by Mughals at Akbar's death 1605
- areas partially integrated into Mughal domains, 1605
- additional areas acquired up to the death of Aurangzeb, 1707
- British possessions
- Dutch possessions
- Portuguese possessions

SIND 1574–81 regions acquired by Mughals 1556–1696, with dates of acquisition

❷ Maratha expansion 1708–1800

- territories at some time in the possession of Shivaji or Venkaji, 1646–80
- areas at some time under the direct rule of the Marathas, 1708–1800
- areas nominally under Maratha rule, but not administered by them
- — outermost limit of territory under Maratha rule
- other areas in which Marathas levied taxes

1739 date of acquisition by Marathas
(–75) date of subsequent loss by Marathas to c.1800
BHONSLE principal member of Confederacy
○ capital city of principal member of Confederacy
→ Maratha campaigns into neighbouring territory, with date

The Marathas, 1646–1818

The origins of the Hindu Maratha state lie with a heroic chieftain, Shivaji, who, from his heavily-fortified base in the Western Ghats, led a large force of highly mobile, lightly-armoured horsemen, who engaged in relentless battle with the Mughal Empire and the sultans of Bijapur. After the death of the Mughal emperor Aurangzeb, in 1707, Maratha campaigns resumed, and a loose confederacy gained control over most of India. Until their final defeat in 1818, the Marathas presented the last obstacle to growing British supremacy.

The Marathas

1728: Marathas defeat Nizam of Hyderabad and gain supremacy over Deccan; with subsequent territorial expansion
1782: Treaty ending first Anglo-Maratha war results in territorial losses for Marathas
1803: Second Anglo-Maratha war results in loss of Delhi

| 1650 | 1700 | 1750 | 1800 | 1850 |

1674: Shivaji crowned king; career marked by widespread conquests
1761: Defeat by Afghans temporarily ends Maratha hegemony over northern India
1788: Occupation of Delhi; Maratha territorial apogee
1818: Third Anglo-Maratha war ends in Maratha defeat

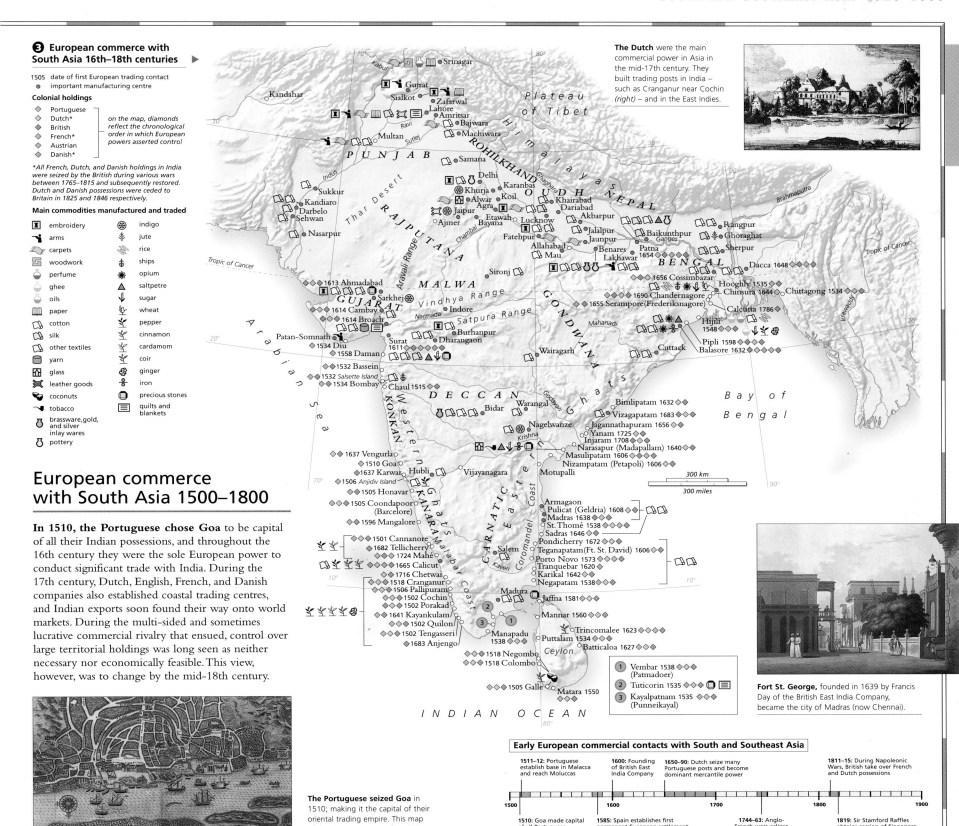

❸ European commerce with South Asia 16th–18th centuries ▶

1505 date of first European trading contact
● important manufacturing centre

Colonial holdings

◇ Portuguese
◇ Dutch*
◇ British
◇ French*
◇ Austrian
◇ Danish*

on the map, diamonds reflect the chronological order in which European powers asserted control

*All French, Dutch, and Danish holdings in India were seized by the British during various wars between 1765–1815 and subsequently restored. Dutch and Danish possessions were ceded to Britain in 1825 and 1846 respectively.

Main commodities manufactured and traded

▥ embroidery	✿ indigo
⚔ arms	✦ jute
carpets	rice
woodwork	⚓ ships
perfume	✹ opium
ghee	△ saltpetre
oils	sugar
paper	wheat
cotton	✿ pepper
silk	cinnamon
other textiles	cardamom
yarn	coir
glass	ginger
leather goods	● iron
coconuts	precious stones
tobacco	quilts and blankets
brassware, gold, and silver inlay wares	
pottery	

The Dutch were the main commercial power in Asia in the mid-17th century. They built trading posts in India – such as Cranganur near Cochin (right) – and in the East Indies.

European commerce with South Asia 1500–1800

In 1510, the Portuguese chose Goa to be capital of all their Indian possessions, and throughout the 16th century they were the sole European power to conduct significant trade with India. During the 17th century, Dutch, English, French, and Danish companies also established coastal trading centres, and Indian exports soon found their way onto world markets. During the multi-sided and sometimes lucrative commercial rivalry that ensued, control over large territorial holdings was long seen as neither necessary nor economically feasible. This view, however, was to change by the mid-18th century.

The Portuguese seized Goa in 1510; making it the capital of their oriental trading empire. This map of the city was engraved c.1600.

Fort St. George, founded in 1639 by Francis Day of the British East India Company, became the city of Madras (now Chennai).

| ① Vembar 1538 ◇◇◇ (Patmadoer) |
| ② Tuticorin 1535 ◇◇◇ ▣ ▤ |
| ③ Kayalpatnam 1535 ◇◇◇ (Punneikayal) |

Early European commercial contacts with South and Southeast Asia

1511–12: Portuguese establish base in Malacca and reach Moluccas

1600: Founding of British East India Company

1650–90: Dutch seize many Portuguese posts and become dominant mercantile power

1811–15: During Napoleonic Wars, British take over French and Dutch possessions

1500 — 1600 — 1700 — 1800 — 1900

1510: Goa made capital of all Portuguese possessions in Asia

1585: Spain establishes first permanent European settlement at Cebu, in Philippines

1744–63: Anglo-French wars eclipse French power in Asia

1819: Sir Stamford Raffles obtains cession of Singapore for British East India Company

European and Southeast Asian contacts 1500–1800

The commercial penetration of Southeast Asia by Europeans began shortly after the Portuguese arrival in India. The Spanish established links with the Philippines after Magellan's discovery of the islands in 1521 during the first circumnavigation of the globe. Dutch and British trade in the region did not begin until the 17th century. As in India, the European powers established 'factories', often fortified, at many points along the coast. They cooperated with local magnates, both indigenous and Chinese, who had already carved out trading domains.

The Moluccan island of Ambon (right) was reached by the Portuguese in 1512. They were ousted by the Dutch in 1605. This 17th-century engraving shows Dutch East India Company ships sailing near the island.

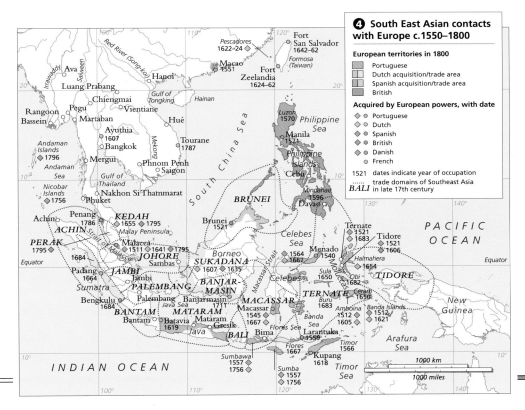

❹ South East Asian contacts with Europe c.1550–1800

European territories in 1800

◻ Portuguese
◻ Dutch acquisition/trade area
◻ Spanish acquisition/trade area
◻ British

Acquired by European powers, with date

◇ Portuguese
◇ Dutch
◇ Spanish
◇ British
◇ Danish
◇ French

1521 dates indicate year of occupation
— trade domains of Southeast Asia
BALI in late 17th century

THE AGE OF COLONIAL EXPANSION

Sir Stamford Raffles re-founded the port city of Singapore in 1819.

BETWEEN 1765 AND 1914 the European powers completed their conquest and annexation of most of South and Southeast Asia. Nepal and Afghanistan were greatly reduced in size and made protectorates of Britain, while Siam, though shorn of most of its outer territories, maintained its independence, acting as a buffer between the British and the French. There were many reasons for European conquest, including commercial disputes, the desire to control resources, diplomatic entanglements, and strategic considerations. All were the inevitable result of interaction between nations with vastly differing military and naval resources in an age of imperial expansion.

Major indigenous powers confronting British and French colonizers

1749: Mysore starts to become major power in southern India
1754: Powerful Burmese dynasty established on capture of Ava by Alaungpaya
1802: With French aid, Nguyen Anh unites and becomes emperor of Vietnam
1857–59: Revolt ('Mutiny') attempts to oust British from India

c.1720: Marathas start to expand over most of India
1757: Expansion of Gurkha (Nepali) domains over much of Himalayas
1782: Siam reaches territorial apogee under Rama I
1785: Burmese invasion of Siam and counter-invasion by Siam of Burma
1839–42: Afghans under Dost Mohammed defeat British in First Afghan War

(timeline: 1700 1750 1800 1850 1900)

Warren Hastings, the first British governor-general of India (1774–85), is shown here dining with Indian princes. He was forced to confront both the Marathas and Mysore, during the first phase of British expansion in India.

Indigenous powers and colonization

Even after the collapse of the Mughal Empire in 1761, significant states stood in the path of Western colonial expansion in both India and Southeast Asia. In India, the foremost power was the Maratha Confederacy, while in Southeast Asia, Burma, Siam, and Vietnam expanded in size and strength. At the dawn of the 19th century no large states remained over most of the East Indies, but Dutch commercial dominance was not yet reflected in territorial holdings.

British control in South Asia 1757–1914

Britain's imperial ventures in India began with the commercial activities of the East India Company. In 1757, the victory of Robert Clive at Plassey over a French and Mughal force and the acquisition of the right to collect taxes in Bengal began an era of territorial expansion which ended with British claims to the Northeast Frontier Agency in 1914. With a pivotal role in the British Empire, India became enmeshed in European rivalries; from 1848, colonial acquisitions along the periphery of the subcontinent had greater strategic than economic impact.

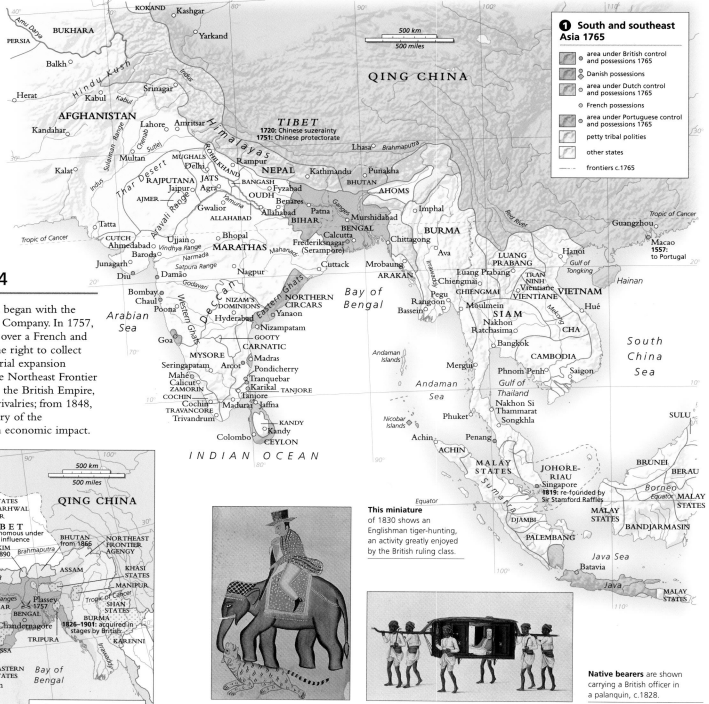

① South and southeast Asia 1765

- area under British control and possessions 1765
- Danish possessions
- area under Dutch control and possessions 1765
- French possessions
- area under Portuguese control and possessions 1765
- petty tribal polities
- other states
- frontiers c.1765

TIBET 1760: Chinese suzerainty 1751: Chinese protectorate

This miniature of 1830 shows an Englishman tiger-hunting, an activity greatly enjoyed by the British ruling class.

1819: re-founded by Sir Stamford Raffles

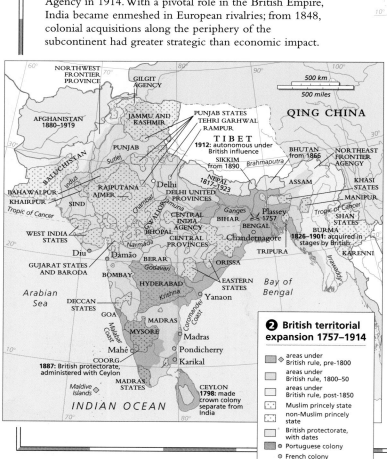

② British territorial expansion 1757–1914

- areas under British rule, pre-1800
- areas under British rule, 1800–50
- areas under British rule, post-1850
- Muslim princely state
- non-Muslim princely state
- British protectorate, with dates
- Portuguese colony
- French colony

1912: autonomous under British influence
SIKKIM from 1890
NEPAL 1817, 1923
BHUTAN from 1866
NORTHEAST FRONTIER AGENCY
AFGHANISTAN 1880–1919
BALUCHISTAN
BAHAWALPUR
KHAIRPUR
Plassey 1757
Chandernagore
BURMA 1826–1901: acquired in stages by British
1887: British protectorate, administered with Ceylon
1798: made crown colony separate from India

Native bearers are shown carrying a British officer in a palanquin, c.1828.

Territorial expansion of British in South Asia and Burma

1757: Battle of Plassey; British victory over combined French and Mughal force
1803: Second Anglo-Maratha war leads to British acquisition of Delhi
1815: Victory in Anglo-Gurkha war extends British possessions into the Himalayas
1849: British annex Punjab after two Sikh wars
1885: Third Anglo-Burmese War; British annex Upper Burma

1799: British-led coalition defeats and partitions Mysore; British obtain the Carnatic coast
1815: British annex Ceylonese kingdom of Kandy
1826: First Anglo-Burmese War; British acquire coastal areas
1852: Second Anglo-Burmese War; British occupy Lower Burma

(timeline: 1750 1770 1790 1810 1830 1850 1870 1890)

The Revolt of 1857–59

Much more than a mutiny, the revolt of 1857–59 involved not merely the defection of large sections of the British Indian army, but also a series of peasant insurrections, led either by local rulers or *zamindars* (great landlords), aimed at throwing off the imperial yoke. The revolt failed because of its lack of a coordinated command structure and British superiority in military intelligence, organization, and logistics.

British troops are shown rushing to quell the revolt at Umballa in 1859. The reforms made after the Revolt helped secure the British presence in India for another 90 years.

❸ The Revolt of 1857–59 ▶

- princely states in rebellion
- states in which princes were loyal to British, but troops were in rebellion
- neutral princely states
- states actively aiding British
- British India
- areas in which British administration was disputed
- ⚫ post at which Indian Sepoy troops mutinied
- site of major revolt, 29 Mar 1857–31 Aug 1858
- site of significant British victory, 16 Aug 1857–21 May 1859

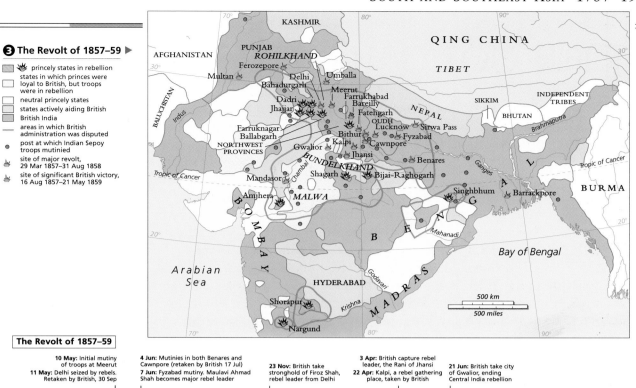

The Revolt of 1857–59

10 May: Initial mutiny of troops at Meerut
11 May: Delhi seized by rebels. Retaken by British, 30 Sep

29 Mar 1857: Mutiny of Mangal Pande, a sepoy from Oudh, initiates revolt
30 May: First battle of Revolt at Hindan River
30 May: Lucknow mutiny

4 Jun: Mutinies in both Benares and Cawnpore (retaken by British 17 Jul)
7 Jun: Fyzabad mutiny. Maulavi Ahmad Shah becomes major rebel leader

18 Jun: Fatehgarh mutiny. Re-occupied by British, Jan 1858
27 Jun: Massacre of British evacuees at Cawnpore

16 Aug: British capture place of exile of Maratha rebel leader, Nana Sahib
17 Aug: 8th Madras Native Regiment disbanded after refusing to go north

23 Nov: British take stronghold of Firoz Shah, rebel leader from Delhi

22 Mar 1858: British retake Lucknow after 20-day siege

3 Apr: British capture rebel leader, the Rani of Jhansi
22 Apr: Kalpi, a rebel gathering place, taken by British

6 May: British take Bareilly, capital of Rohilkhand leader

21 Jun: British take city of Gwalior, ending Central India rebellion

31 Aug: Disarmed troops revolt at Multan

1857   1858   1859

The economy of India and Ceylon by 1857

India became an essential part of a global economic network created by Britain during the 18th and 19th centuries. In some cases, British imports wiped out Indian industry – India was obliged to import woven cotton from Lancashire by 1853. India was an overwhelmingly peasant society in 1857, but railways, canals, plantations, mines, small-scale factories, and the growth of busy port cities and administrative centres were transforming its economic landscape.

❹ The economy of India and Ceylon, 1857 ▶

Agriculture
- mainly peasant agriculture
- scattered cultivation, hunting and gathering, and limited pastoralism
- predominantly pastoralism, with scattered pockets of agriculture
- forested areas

Industry
- coal-mining areas
- sites of extraction of other minerals

Manufacturing centres
- metalworking
- arms
- ship building
- textiles
- glazed pottery, tiles, and ceramics
- woodworking and furniture making
- jewellery
- ivory carving

Transport
- important road
- railway
- railway under construction

Population
- ⚫ city with population of over 500,000
- ⦿ city with population of 100,000–500,000
- ◉ city with population of 50,000–100,000
- ○ important city with population of less than 50,000

Prinicipal types of agricultural produce
areca	pepper
cacao	potato
cinnamon	rape
coconuts	salt
coffee	sandalwood
cotton	sesame
dates	spices
fruits	sugar
indigo	sunflower
jute	tea
mustard	teak
opium	tobacco
palm sugar	

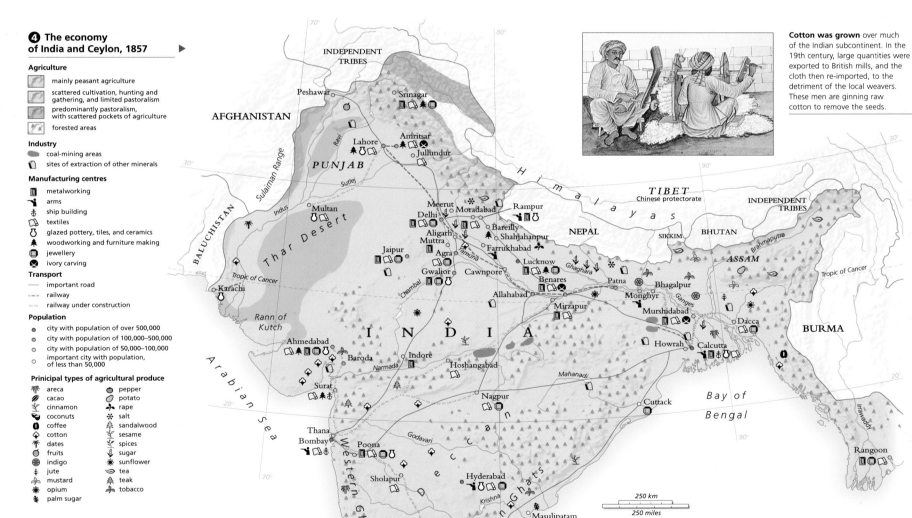

Cotton was grown over much of the Indian subcontinent. In the 19th century, large quantities were exported to British mills, and the cloth then re-imported, to the detriment of the local weavers. These men are ginning raw cotton to remove the seeds.

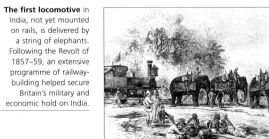

The first locomotive in India, not yet mounted on rails, is delivered by a string of elephants. Following the Revolt of 1857–59, an extensive programme of railway-building helped secure Britain's military and economic hold on India.

THE COLONIAL APOGEE AND DEMISE

M.K. Gandhi (1869–1948), was the hero of India's independence movement.

TWO NEW COLONIAL POWERS, the US and Japan, entered Southeast Asia at the beginning of the 20th century. The Philippines were annexed by the US following the Spanish–American War of 1898; the Japanese took over the German Pacific island colonies north of the equator in 1919 and acquired virtually the whole of Southeast Asia by force in the Second World War. Though the early 20th century can be seen as the apogee of colonialism in the region, especially in British India, there was already strong opposition to foreign rule. The Indian National Congress, founded in 1885, initially sought reforms, but by the 1930s demanded complete independence. In the Philippines, a revolutionary independence movement was well established when the Americans took over. But whereas India's freedom struggle was, on the whole, peaceful, the struggle in most of Southeast Asia was bloody, nowhere more so than in Vietnam.

The partition and reunification of Bengal 1905–12

Lord Curzon's 1905 partition of India's most populous province, Bengal, was fiercely opposed on many grounds by both Hindus and Muslims. Some upper-class Hindus, for example, feared that the creation of East Bengal and Assam, a Muslim-majority province, would restrict their access to government employment. The Muslim League, formed in 1906, urged that legislation should provide for separate electorates for Muslim minorities, to guarantee their representation in Hindu-majority areas. In 1912, the Bengali-speaking areas of the old province were reunited.

▼ **2** The partition and reunification of Bengal, 1905–12

- — national border
- — provincial boundary
- ⋯⋯ provincial boundary prior to 1905
- — line of 1905 partition
- ▦ Muslim majority area
- ▨ British districts
- ☐ native states and protectorates
- ☐ frontier area

The independence struggle 1879–1947

Indian nationalist movements took many forms in the course of the long struggle for independence. The Indian National Congress, originally an organization of the Western-educated elite, became a mass, popular movement after the return to India in 1915 of the charismatic Mohandas K. Gandhi. By the 1930s, cautious calls for self-rule had become unequivocal demands for independence.

British officers serving in India led lives of conspicuous ease, their lifestyles supported by domestic staff, as this photograph of a servant giving a pedicure shows.

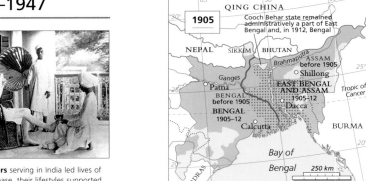

The freedom movement in India

1885: Founding of the Indian National Congress
1920: Start of civil disobedience campaigns by M. K. Gandhi in support of independence struggle
1939: Congress ministries resign because India given no voice in respect to participation in World War II
1945: India becomes UN charter member
1947: New independent dominions of India and Pakistan are born

1906: Foundation of Muslim League
1918: Indian contribution to World War I earns it membership in League of Nations
1937: Burma is separated from India and made crown colony
1948: Burma and Ceylon become independent; former withdraws from Commonwealth

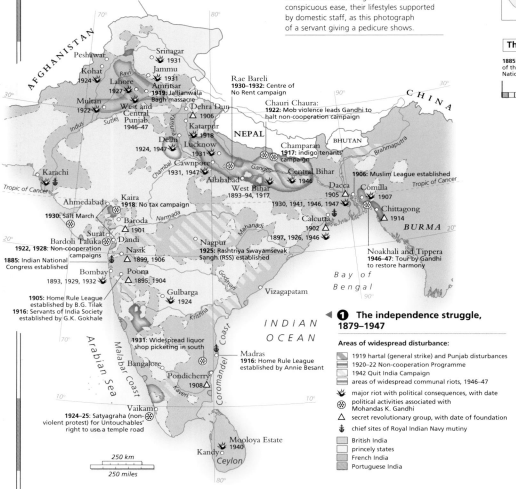

◀ **1** The independence struggle, 1879–1947

Areas of widespread disturbance:
- ▨ 1919 hartal (general strike) and Punjab disturbances
- ▤ 1920–22 Non-cooperation Programme
- ▦ 1942 Quit India Campaign
- ▧ areas of widespread communal riots, 1946–47
- ♨ major riot with political consequences, with date
- ⊛ political activities associated with Mohandas K. Gandhi
- △ secret revolutionary group, with date of foundation
- ⚓ chief sites of Royal Indian Navy mutiny
- ☐ British India
- ☐ princely states
- ☐ French India
- ☐ Portuguese India

The Second World War in South and Southeast Asia

The Japanese swiftly overran Southeast Asia, occupying the whole region by March 1942. The Allied counter-offensive comprised US advances across the western Pacific from 1943, and the advance of British and Indian troops through Burma from 1944. But Japanese occupation had unleashed a tide of nationalism which was to have a grave impact on the postwar maintenance of the status quo, leading to the creation of new nations and the end of the European empires.

These Japanese prisoners of war were taken after the capture of Guadalcanal in 1942 – a key campaign in the US amphibious offensive.

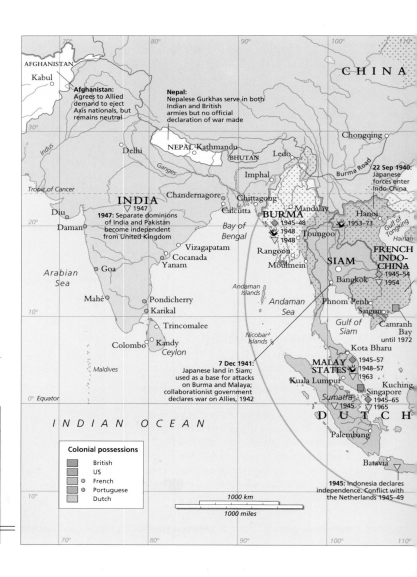

Colonial possessions
- ☐ British
- ☐ US
- ☐ French
- ☐ Portuguese
- ☐ Dutch

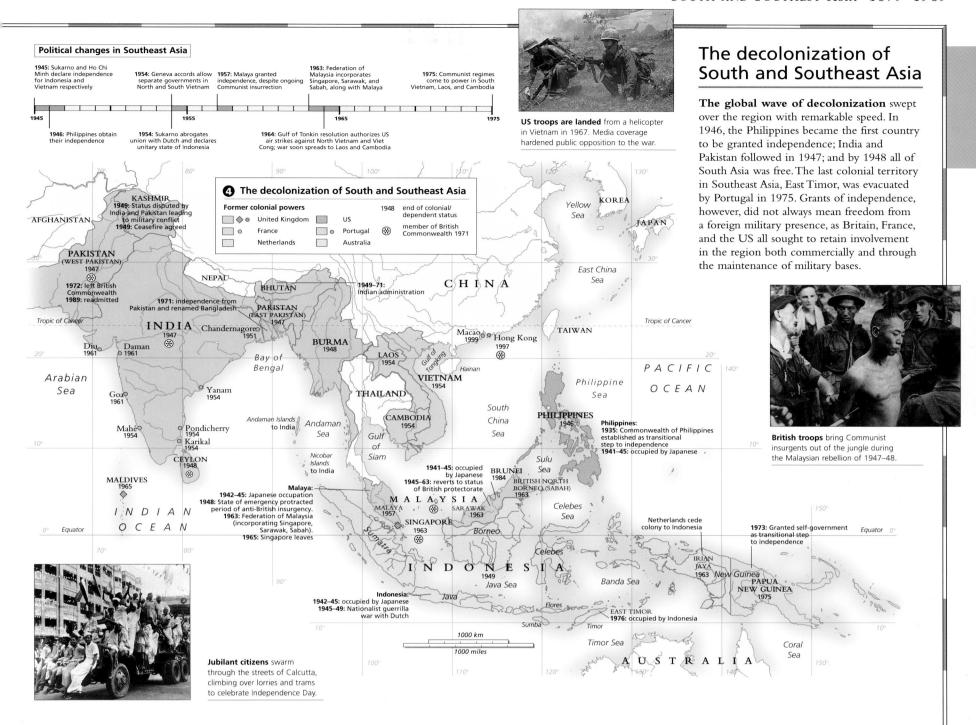

Political changes in Southeast Asia

1945: Sukarno and Ho Chi Minh declare independence for Indonesia and Vietnam respectively

1954: Geneva accords allow separate governments in North and South Vietnam

1957: Malaya granted independence, despite ongoing Communist insurrection

1963: Federation of Malaysia incorporates Singapore, Sarawak, and Sabah, along with Malaya

1975: Communist regimes come to power in South Vietnam, Laos, and Cambodia

1946: Philippines obtain their independence

1954: Sukarno abrogates union with Dutch and declares unitary state of Indonesia

1964: Gulf of Tonkin resolution authorizes US air strikes against North Vietnam and Viet Cong; war soon spreads to Laos and Cambodia

US troops are landed from a helicopter in Vietnam in 1967. Media coverage hardened public opposition to the war.

④ The decolonization of South and Southeast Asia

Former colonial powers

United Kingdom		US	
France		Portugal	
Netherlands		Australia	

1948 end of colonial/dependent status

member of British Commonwealth 1971

The decolonization of South and Southeast Asia

The global wave of decolonization swept over the region with remarkable speed. In 1946, the Philippines became the first country to be granted independence; India and Pakistan followed in 1947; and by 1948 all of South Asia was free. The last colonial territory in Southeast Asia, East Timor, was evacuated by Portugal in 1975. Grants of independence, however, did not always mean freedom from a foreign military presence, as Britain, France, and the US all sought to retain involvement in the region both commercially and through the maintenance of military bases.

British troops bring Communist insurgents out of the jungle during the Malaysian rebellion of 1947–48.

KASHMIR
1949: Status disputed by India and Pakistan leading to military conflict
1949: Ceasefire agreed

PAKISTAN (WEST PAKISTAN) 1947
1972: left British Commonwealth
1989: readmitted

1971: independence from Pakistan and renamed Bangladesh

PAKISTAN (EAST PAKISTAN) 1947

1949–71: Indian administration

INDIA 1947
Chandernagore 1951
Diu 1961
Daman 1961
Goa 1961
Yanam 1954
Mahé 1954
Pondicherry 1954
Karikal 1954
CEYLON 1948
MALDIVES 1965

NEPAL
BHUTAN
BURMA 1948
LAOS 1954
VIETNAM 1954
THAILAND
CAMBODIA 1954

Macao 1999
Hong Kong 1997

PHILIPPINES 1946
Philippines:
1935: Commonwealth of Philippines established as transitional step to independence
1941–45: occupied by Japanese

1941–45: occupied by Japanese
1945–63: reverts to status of British protectorate

BRUNEI 1984
BRITISH NORTH BORNEO (SABAH) 1963

Malaya:
1942–45: Japanese occupation
1948: State of emergency protracted period of anti-British insurgency.
1963: Federation of Malaysia (incorporating Singapore, Sarawak, Sabah).
1965: Singapore leaves

MALAYSIA
MALAYA 1957
SARAWAK 1963
SINGAPORE 1963

INDONESIA 1949

Indonesia:
1942–45: occupied by Japanese
1945–49: Nationalist guerrilla war with Dutch

Netherlands cede colony to Indonesia

IRIAN JAYA 1963
New Guinea
PAPUA NEW GUINEA 1975

1973: Granted self-government as transitional step to independence

EAST TIMOR
1976: occupied by Indonesia

1000 km
1000 miles

Jubilant citizens swarm through the streets of Calcutta, climbing over lorries and trams to celebrate Independence Day.

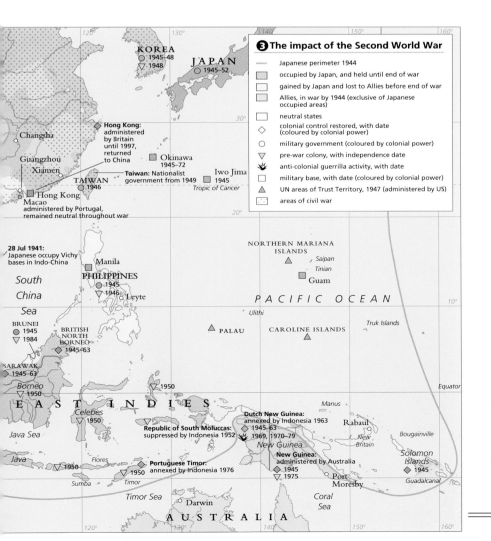

The impact of the Cold War 1946–89

The Vietnam War, the most violent and protracted conflict in Southeast Asia in the 20th century was, in many ways, a proxy struggle for the US, China, and the USSR within the global context of the Cold War. Although Vietnam's independence was proclaimed at the end of the Second World War, it took three decades of bloody struggle – affecting both Vietnam and the neighbouring states of Laos and Cambodia – before the French, and then the Americans who replaced them, were evicted from French Indochina.

❸ The impact of the Second World War

	Japanese perimeter 1944
	occupied by Japan, and held until end of war
	gained by Japan and lost to Allies before end of war
	Allies, in war by 1944 (exclusive of Japanese occupied areas)
	neutral states
◇	colonial control restored, with date (coloured by colonial power)
○	military government (coloured by colonial power)
▽	pre-war colony, with independence date
⚓	anti-colonial guerrilla activity, with date
□	military base, with date (coloured by colonial power)
△	UN areas of Trust Territory, 1947 (administered by US)
	areas of civil war

KOREA 1945–48, 1948
JAPAN 1945–52
Changsha
Changzhou
Guangzhou
Xiamen
Hong Kong: administered by Britain until 1997, returned to China
Okinawa 1945–72
Taiwan: Nationalist government from 1949
Iwo Jima 1945
TAIWAN 1946
Hong Kong
Macao administered by Portugal, remained neutral throughout war

28 Jul 1941: Japanese occupy Vichy bases in Indo-China

Manila
PHILIPPINES 1945, 1946
Leyte
NORTHERN MARIANA ISLANDS
Saipan
Tinian
Guam

BRUNEI 1945, 1984
BRITISH NORTH BORNEO 1945–63
SARAWAK 1945–63
Borneo 1950

Ulithi
PALAU
CAROLINE ISLANDS
Truk Islands

EAST INDIES
Celebes 1950
Republic of South Moluccas: suppressed by Indonesia 1952
Java 1950
Sumatra
Timor
Dutch New Guinea: annexed by Indonesia 1963 1945–63, 1969, 1970–79
Portuguese Timor: annexed by Indonesia 1976

Manus
Rabaul
New Guinea
New Britain
New Guinea: administered by Australia 1945, 1975
Bougainville
Port Moresby
Solomon Islands 1945
Guadalcanal

Darwin
AUSTRALIA

❺ The Vietnam War

The First Vietnam War, 1946–54

⚔ major battle
🏯 French border posts, captured by Viet Minh 1951

The Second Vietnam War, 1964–75

Major battles with US involvement:
⚔ 1965–66
⚔ 1967–69
▭ western limit of Pathet Lao areas, 1967
⚜ Tet offensive 1968
⚜ Viet Cong Eastertide offensive, 1972
⚜ Final offensive, 1974–75

Communist supply lines
→ Ho Chi Minh trail
→ Sihanouk trail

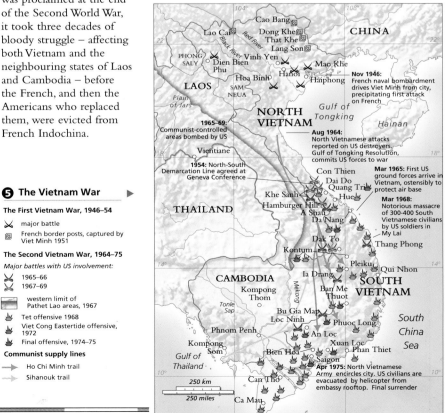

Nov 1946: French naval bombardment drives Viet Minh from city, precipitating first attack on French

CHINA
Cao Bang
Dong Khe
That Khe
Lang Son
Lao Cai
Vinh Yen
Mao Khe
PHONG SALY
Dien Bien Phu
Hoa Binh
Hanoi
Haiphong

LAOS
SAM NEUA
Plain of Jars
NORTH VIETNAM
Gulf of Tongking
Hainan

1965–69: Communist-controlled areas bombed by US

Vientiane

Aug 1964: North Vietnamese attacks reported on US destroyers, Gulf of Tongking Resolution, commits US forces to war

1954: North-South Demarcation Line agreed at Geneva Conference

Con Thien
Dai Do
Quang Tri
Khe Sanh
Hamburger Hill
A Shau
Hue
Da Nang

Mar 1965: First US ground forces arrive in Vietnam, ostensibly to protect air base

Mar 1968: Notorious massacre of 300-400 South Vietnamese civilians by US soldiers in My Lai

THAILAND

Dak To
Kontum
Ia Drang
Pleiku
Qui Nhon

Thang Phong

CAMBODIA
Kompong Thom
Tonle Sap
Phnom Penh
Kompong Som
Mekong
Bu Gia Map
Loc Ninh
Ban Me Thuot
An Loc
Xuan Loc
Bien Hoa
Phan Thiet

SOUTH VIETNAM
Phuoc Long

Gulf of Thailand
Saigon
Can Tho
Ca Mau

South China Sea

Apr 1975: North Vietnamese Army encircles city. US civilians are evacuated by helicopter from embassy rooftop. Final surrender

250 km
250 miles

MODERN SOUTH AND SOUTHEAST ASIA

Jawaharlal Nehru, his daughter Indira Gandhi, and grandson Rajiv Gandhi *(above)* all served as Indian prime ministers.

IN MOST OF THE COUNTRIES of the region, securing independence failed to usher in an era of political peace and stability. The ethnic, religious, and linguistic heterogeneity of their populations quickly led to demands for readjustment of the political map and, in many instances, to secessionist movements and wars for independence. Notwithstanding all these internal and external stresses, most of the countries in South and Southeast Asia took great strides on the path of economic, social, and cultural development under a variety of political systems and economic philosophies. Life expectancy, levels of literacy, and per capita material consumption, especially for the growing middle and upper classes, were far higher than they were during the colonial era and the economic infrastructure greatly expanded, with the development of a varied commercial base.

Territorial changes since 1947

In 1984 the Indian army attacked Sikh militants who were occupying the Golden Temple of Amritsar, the Sikhs' holiest shrine.

The urgent task of integrating more than 600 largely autonomous princely states into the new Indian union was accomplished by 1950. But demands for more linguistically homogeneous states soon surfaced. The partition of the multi-lingual state of Madras in 1954 was the first in a long series of changes, including the creation of a number of tribal states, that have altered India's political map.

South Asia from 1948

In creating Pakistan, the 1947 partition of India established a political entity which could not withstand the many subsequent stresses between its two distant wings. In 1971 Pakistan was split between its eastern and western halves, and the new state of Bangladesh was formed. There were also a series of international disputes over areas whose borders were not adequately defined during the colonial era or, in the still-unresolved case of Kashmir, over an area whose future was left undecided when the British left India.

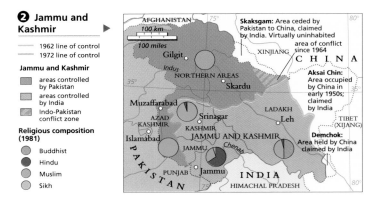

❷ Jammu and Kashmir

— 1962 line of control
— 1972 line of control

Jammu and Kashmir
- areas controlled by Pakistan
- areas controlled by India
- Indo-Pakistan conflict zone

Religious composition (1981)
- Buddhist
- Hindu
- Muslim
- Sikh

Skaksgam: Area ceded by Pakistan to China, claimed by India. Virtually uninhabited area of conflict since 1964

Aksai Chin: Area occupied by China in early 1950s; claimed by India

Demchok: Area held by China claimed by India

Conflict over Jammu and Kashmir

India and Pakistan have contested possession of the Muslim–majority state of Kashmir since 1947, when the Hindu maharajah acceded to India, and fought wars over the territory in 1947–48 and 1965. Since 1989, there has been an independence movement in the Indian–held portion of the state, although India insists this is the handiwork of terrorists aided by Pakistan.

Territorial conflicts in South Asia

1947: Start of Indo-Pakistani War fought over Jammu and Kashmir; UN ceasefire line agreed in 1949

1962: India set back in brief Sino-Indian border war after years of intermittent clashes

1971: Successful rebellion leads to creation of Bangladesh. Third Indo-Pakistani war as India intervenes in Bangladesh freedom struggle

1950 | 1960 | 1970 | 1980 | 1990

1955: Afghan government supports movement for separation of Pakhtunistan from Pakistan

1965: Second inconclusive Indo–Pakistani war over Jammu and Kashmir

1989: Start of violent insurrection against Indian rule in Jammu and Kashmir

The birth of Bangladesh

The two sectors of Pakistan had little in common apart from their Muslim faith, and the stresses on federalism and parliamentary democracy in the union caused its rupture. The Bangladeshi independence struggle was led by the Awami League, with active military support from India.

❸ The birth of Bangladesh

- ▽ site of violent clash between Bengalis and Pakistan army, 1–2 May 1971
- △ site of Pakistan army 'crackdown' 25–26 Mar 1971
- ◇ site of major act of sabotage by Mukti Bahini guerrillas (Bengal Liberation Army)
- ▢ area of marked guerrilla activity
- ▣ site of Indo-Pakistani border incident
- → refugees fleeing Bangladesh (with number of refugees)

Map labels:

NORTHWEST FRONTIER PROVINCE
1947: became part of Pakistan

1969: Tribal areas absorbed into Pakistan

NORTHERN AREAS

Nominally independent, but recognized only by Pakistan

1963: Area ceded to China by Pakistan but claimed by India

Aksai Chin: early 1950s: occupied by China **1962:** Ceasefire line following Sino-Indian conflict

AZAD KASHMIR

AFGHANISTAN
1979–89: occupied by Soviet Union **from 1992:** Civil war

Pakhtunistan:
1948–63: Area of ethnic Pathans; claims to independence supported by Afghanistan

Kabul
Peshawar
Islamabad
Srinagar

Centrally administered tribal areas

1971: Ceasefire line agreed after third Indo-Pakistani War

JAMMU AND KASHMIR (1949)
Princely state partitioned into two parts. Northwest area controlled by Pakistan; remainder constituted as Indian state

HIMACHAL PRADESH (1971)
Former princely states reconstituted as fully-fledged state

TIBET
1949: Chinese proclaim 'liberation' of Tibet **1950:** Chinese invasion of eastern Tibet

CHINA

1961: Minor adjustments of Sino-Nepali border based on treaty

ARUNACHAL PRADESH (1987)
formerly Northeast Frontier Agency. Most of this state claimed by China, but all is integrated within India; **1962:** fought over by India and China **1972:** Union territory

Quetta
PAKISTAN

(EAST) PUNJAB (1947)
Former province divided between India and Pakistan **1966:** Indian portion partitioned

Amritsar
Lahore
Simla
Chandigarh

HARYANA (1966)
created on partition of Punjab

1950: made Indian protectorate **1974:** associate state **1975:** annexed as a state

BHUTAN
1949: Indian protectorate **1971:** Sovereignty broadened on admission to UN

WEST PAKISTAN
1956: Declared single province **1971:** dissolved

(WEST) PUNJAB
1947: formed from former Punjab province of India

DELHI
1956: Union territory
New Delhi
1995: National capital territory

NEPAL
Kathmandu

SIKKIM (1975)
Gangtok

Itanagar

ASSAM (1950)
Dispur
Shillong

NAGALAND (1961)
Kohima

BALUCHISTAN
1952: Baluchistan States Union formed; **1970:** reconstituted as separate province

Lucknow

UTTAR PRADESH (1947)
before 1950: called United Provinces

MEGHALAYA (1972)

MANIPUR (1972)
Imphal

Gwadar:
1958: ceded by Oman to Pakistan

SIND
1947: Became part of Pakistan

Karachi

RAJASTHAN (1949)
Jaipur

Patna

BIHAR (1948)

TRIPURA (1972)
Agartala

Aizawl

MIZORAM (1986)

Rann of Kutch:
1968: Minor border adjustments based on tribunal award of 1968

Gandhinagar

GUJARAT (1960)
created on division of Bombay

Bhopal

MADHYA PRADESH (1948)
1948: formed incorporating Madhya Bharat, a union of 20 princely states **1956:** incorporated former state of Bhopal

Dhaka

WEST BENGAL (1947)
Calcutta

1951: ceded to India

BANGLADESH
Former East Pakistan
Mar 1971: Declared independence from Pakistan
Dec 1971: Independence secured following civil war and Indian military intervention

BURMA

Junagadh:
Aug 1947: Decision to accede to Pakistan; taken over by India in Nov

Diu
1961: became Union territory with Goa

Daman
1961: became Union territory with Goa

DADRA AND NAGAR HAVELI
1961: Union territory

MAHARASHTRA (1960)
created on division of Bombay

ORISSA (1948)

Bhubaneswar

Bay of Bengal

Bombay (Mumbai)

BOMBAY
1956: incorporated part of former state of Hyderabad **1960:** divided into Gujarat and Maharashtra

Godavari

Hyderabad

❶ The formation of contemporary South Asia, 1947–99 ▶

Boundaries in 1975

— agreed or *de facto* international boundaries, demarcated
--- extent of international territorial claim
····· line of control in Kashmir
— state or province after 1975

Territories

- Union territories created after 1956, now fully-fledged states
- East and West Pakistan 1967
- Area disputed between India and Pakistan
- former protectorate
- former French colonial possessions
- former Portuguese colonial possessions
- contemporary Indian state, with date of formation
- ▢ national capital
- ○ state capital
- (1947) achievement of statehood

GOA (1987)
1961: annexed by India
Panaji

ANDHRA PRADESH (1953)
1953: separation from Madras **1956:** incorporated part of former state of Hyderabad

Krishna

Yanam
1955: ceded to India

Arabian Sea

KARNATAKA (1947)
1947–73: called Mysore **1953:** boundaries altered **1956:** part of former state of Hyderabad was incorporated

Bangalore

Coromandel Coast

Mahe
1955: ceded to India

Malabar Coast

TAMIL NADU (1947)
1947: called Madras

Madras (Chennai)

Pondicherry
1955: ceded to India

Karikal
1955: ceded to India

KERALA (1956)
1949: Travancore and Cochin state formed **1956:** incorporated former state of Travancore and Cochin

Palk Strait:
Indo-Sri Lankan accord on division of water and islands

Trivandrum

INDIAN OCEAN

SRI LANKA (CEYLON)
1947: dominion status
1948: full independence

Colombo

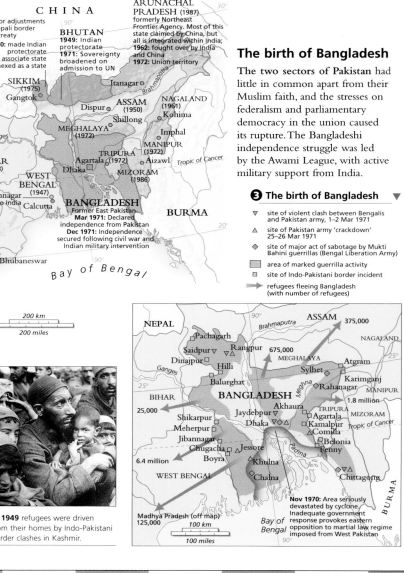

NEPAL
Pachagarh
Saidpur ▽ △ Rangpur
Dinajpur ▽ Hilli
Balurghat
Shikarpur ▽
Meherpur ▽
Jibannagar
Chugacha
Boyra
Khulna
Chalna
6.4 million
WEST BENGAL
BIHAR
25,000
Jaydebpur ▽
Dhaka ▽ △ △
675,000
Sylhet △
Karimganj
Rahanagar
ASSAM **375,000**
Brahmaputra
NAGALAND
MEGHALAYA
Atgram
Akhaura △
Jaydebpur ▽
Agartala △
Kamalpur
Comilla
Belonia
Feny
TRIPURA
MIZORAM
MANIPUR **1.8 million**
Tropic of Cancer
Madhya Pradesh (off map) 125,000
Bay of Bengal
BURMA
Chittagong

Nov 1970: Area seriously devastated by cyclone. Inadequate government response provokes eastern opposition to martial law regime imposed from West Pakistan

In 1949 refugees were driven from their homes by Indo-Pakistani border clashes in Kashmir.

Secessionist movements and regional cooperation

The post-independence era in South and Southeast Asia has been characterized by a multitude of internal movements among sub-national groups who have called for greater recognition, autonomy, and even independence. These have been treated with varying degrees of tolerance by the national governments. At the same time, the nations of South and Southeast Asia have embarked upon endeavours to bring about greater supranational and extra-regional cooperation. The latter efforts have been, in varying degrees, military, political, and economic in nature.

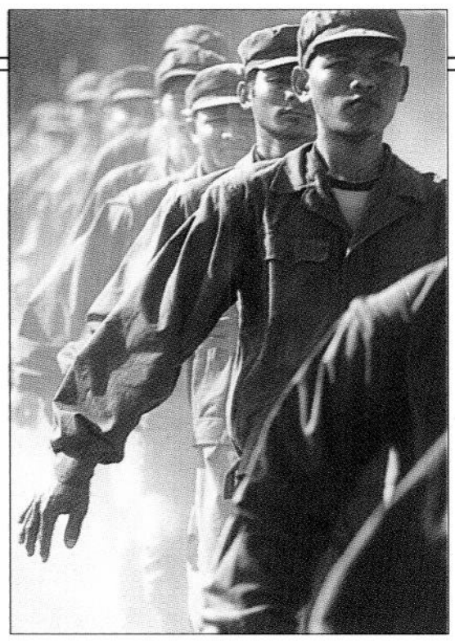

The Communist Khmer Rouge operated from a rural power base.

Cambodia

From 1975, the Communist Khmer Rouge conducted a social programme in Cambodia which led to the deaths of over a million people, and the forced 're-education' of millions more. The Vietnamese invaded in 1979 and withdrew in 1989. In 1993, the Khmer Rouge refused to take part in UN-sponsored elections.

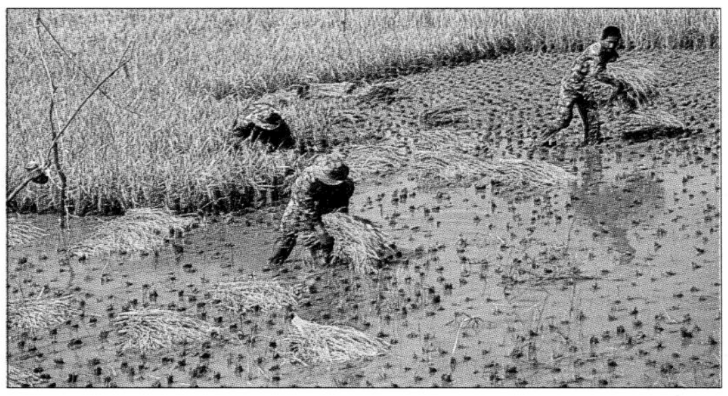

Indonesian army troops are seen looting rice in from paddy fields in East Timor, where repression of pro-secessionists has been particularly brutal.

East Timor

Originally a Portuguese colony, East Timor was invaded by Indonesia in 1975. The secessionist FRETILIN (East Timor Revolutionary Liberation Front) continues to resist Indonesian occupation. East Timor's incorporation as a province of Indonesia is not recognized by the UN.

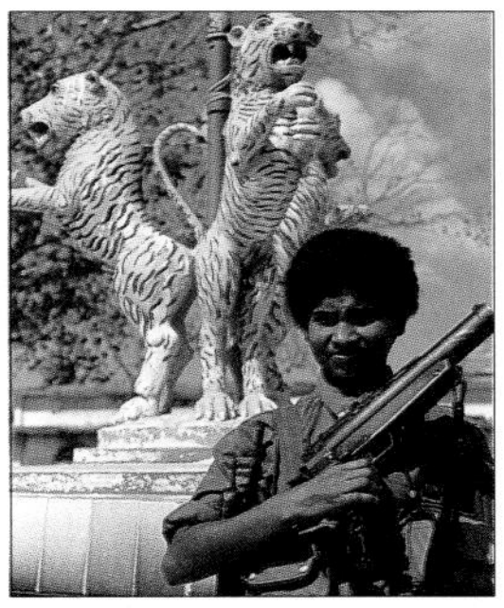

The Tamil Tigers have been fighting for Tamil independence from the rest of Sri Lanka since the early 1980s. They remain the most feared militant group.

Sri Lanka

Since Sri Lanka gained independence in 1948, relations have deteriorated between the Sinhalese-speaking, mainly Buddhist, majority and the mainly Hindu Tamils, the island's principal minority. A bloody secessionist war began in 1984.

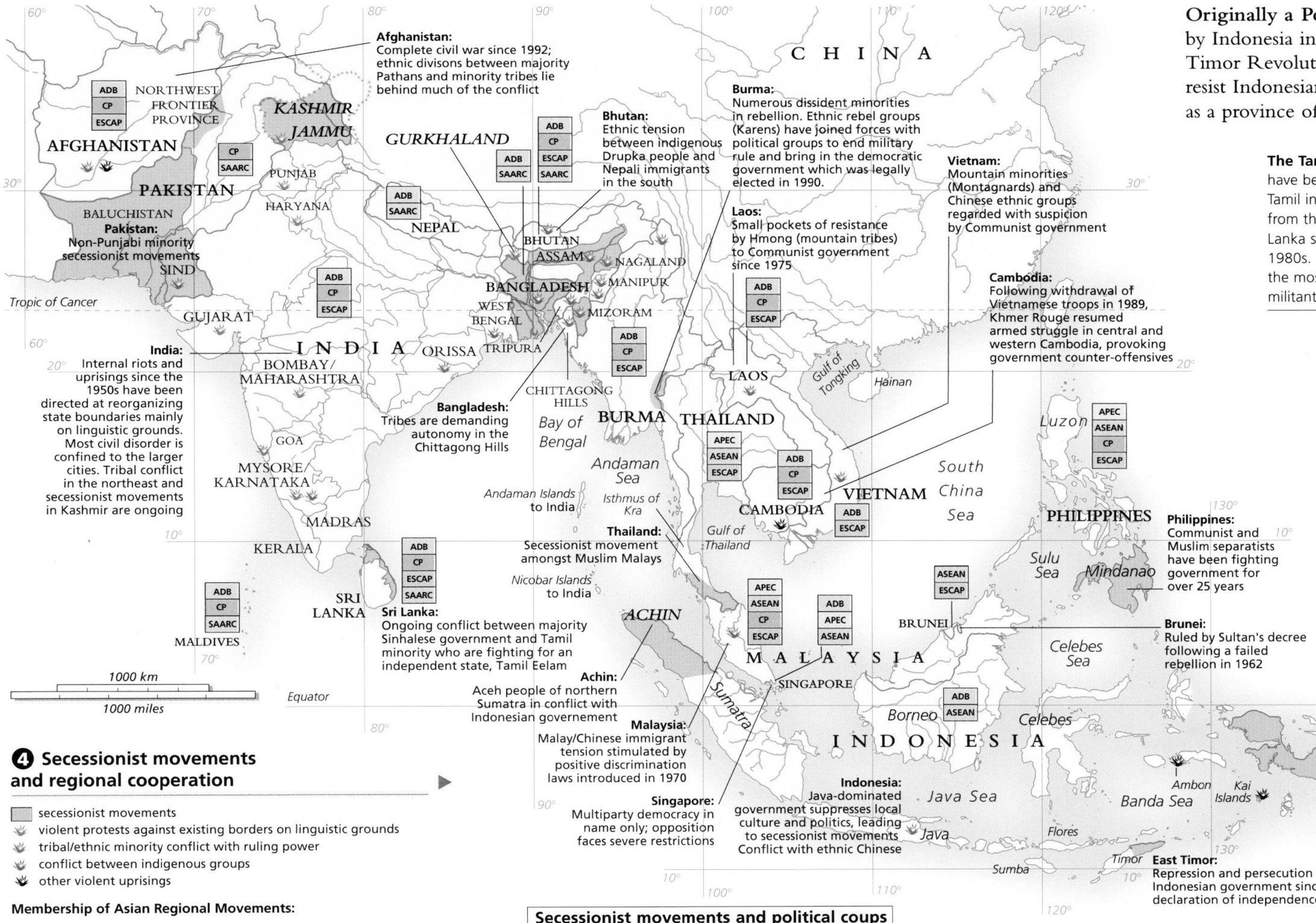

Afghanistan: Complete civil war since 1992; ethnic divisons between majority Pathans and minority tribes lie behind much of the conflict
Burma: Numerous dissident minorities in rebellion. Ethnic rebel groups (Karens) have joined forces with political groups to end military rule and bring in the democratic government which was legally elected in 1990.
Bhutan: Ethnic tension between indigenous Drupka people and Nepali immigrants in the south
Vietnam: Mountain minorities (Montagnards) and Chinese ethnic groups regarded with suspicion by Communist government
Laos: Small pockets of resistance by Hmong (mountain tribes) to Communist government since 1975
Cambodia: Following withdrawal of Vietnamese troops in 1989, Khmer Rouge resumed armed struggle in central and western Cambodia, provoking government counter-offensives
Pakistan: Non-Punjabi minority secessionist movements
India: Internal riots and uprisings since the 1950s have been directed at reorganizing state boundaries mainly on linguistic grounds. Most civil disorder is confined to the larger cities. Tribal conflict in the northeast and secessionist movements in Kashmir are ongoing
Bangladesh: Tribes are demanding autonomy in the Chittagong Hills
Thailand: Secessionist movement amongst Muslim Malays
Sri Lanka: Ongoing conflict between majority Sinhalese government and Tamil minority who are fighting for an independent state, Tamil Eelam
Achin: Aceh people of northern Sumatra in conflict with Indonesian governement
Malaysia: Malay/Chinese immigrant tension stimulated by positive discrimination laws introduced in 1970
Singapore: Multiparty democracy in name only; opposition faces severe restrictions
Indonesia: Java-dominated government suppresses local culture and politics, leading to secessionist movements Conflict with ethnic Chinese
Philippines: Communist and Muslim separatists have been fighting government for over 25 years
Brunei: Ruled by Sultan's decree following a failed rebellion in 1962
Irian Jaya: Free Papua movement seeking autonomy from Indonesia. Outbreaks of violence in 1977, 1978 and 1981
East Timor: Repression and persecution by Indonesian government since declaration of independence in 1985
CHINA
AFGHANISTAN
NORTHWEST FRONTIER PROVINCE
KASHMIR JAMMU
GURKHALAND
PAKISTAN
PUNJAB
HARYANA
BALUCHISTAN
NEPAL
BHUTAN
ASSAM
NAGALAND
MANIPUR
BANGLADESH
WEST BENGAL
MIZORAM
TRIPURA
SIND
GUJARAT
INDIA
ORISSA
BOMBAY/ MAHARASHTRA
CHITTAGONG HILLS
GOA
MYSORE/ KARNATAKA
MADRAS
KERALA
SRI LANKA
MALDIVES
BURMA
THAILAND
LAOS
VIETNAM
CAMBODIA
PHILIPPINES
BRUNEI
MALAYSIA
SINGAPORE
INDONESIA
ACHIN
IRIAN JAYA
Bay of Bengal
Andaman Sea
Andaman Islands to India
Nicobar Islands to India
Isthmus of Kra
Gulf of Thailand
Gulf of Tongking
Hainan
South China Sea
Luzon
Mindanao
Sulu Sea
Celebes Sea
Borneo
Celebes
Sumatra
Java Sea
Java
Flores
Sumba
Timor
Banda Sea
Ambon
Kai Islands
New Guinea
Tropic of Cancer
Equator
1000 km
1000 miles

4 Secessionist movements and regional cooperation

- secessionist movements
- violent protests against existing borders on linguistic grounds
- tribal/ethnic minority conflict with ruling power
- conflict between indigenous groups
- other violent uprisings

Membership of Asian Regional Movements:

ADB	Asian Development Bank, est. 1966
APEC	Asia-Pacific Economic Cooperation, est. 1989
ASEAN	Association for Southeast Asian Nations, est. 1967
CP	Colombo Plan, est. 1951
ESCAP	Economic and Social Commission for Asia and Pacific, est. 1947
SAARC	South Asian Association for Regional Cooperation, est. 1985

Secessionist movements and political coups

- 1955: Naga uprising in northeastern India, the first of numerous tribal insurrections
- 1958: Abortive secessionist uprisings in Baluchistan, Pakistan
- 1962: Military take over rule of Burma
- 1965: Failed Marxist coup and military counter-coup in Indonesia ends Sukarno regime
- 1972: Ferdinand Marcos declares martial law in Philippines
- 1975: Khmer Rouge take over Cambodia; impose regime of extreme terror
- 1979: Deposition of monarchy in Afghanistan; Soviet invasion and civil war
- 1981: Start of Sikh struggle for independent state of Khalistan in Indian Punjab
- 1982: Start of struggle in Sri Lanka for independent state of Tamil Eelam

The urbanization of South and Southeast Asia

The development of South and Southeast Asia is reflected dramatically in its burgeoning cities, some of which, notably Bombay (Mumbai), are among the largest in the world. Of the roughly 1.8 billion people now inhabiting the region about 500 million live in urban areas. However, growing populations, the majority still dependent on agriculture and living in densely settled areas such as the great river valleys of the Ganges, Indus, and Mekong, place an increasing burden on fragile ecosystems, with potentially disastrous consequences for the environment.

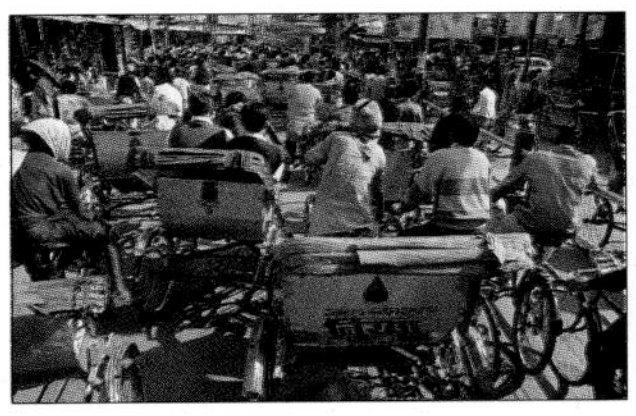

Poverty drives many of India's rural poor to the increasingly overcrowded cities.

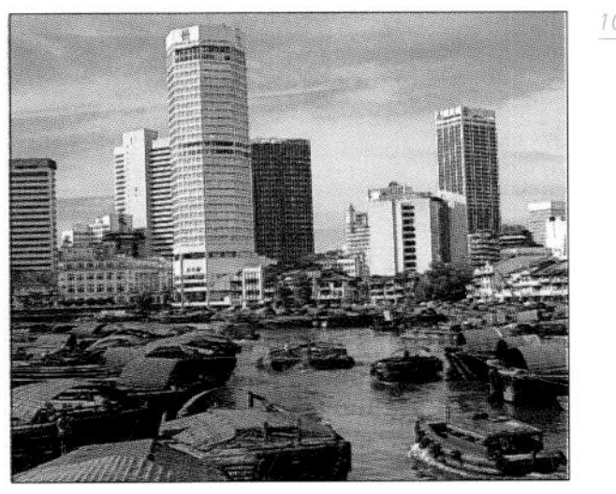

The modern financial centre of Singapore towers over the harbour, a reminder of the island state's origins as a strategic trading settlement.

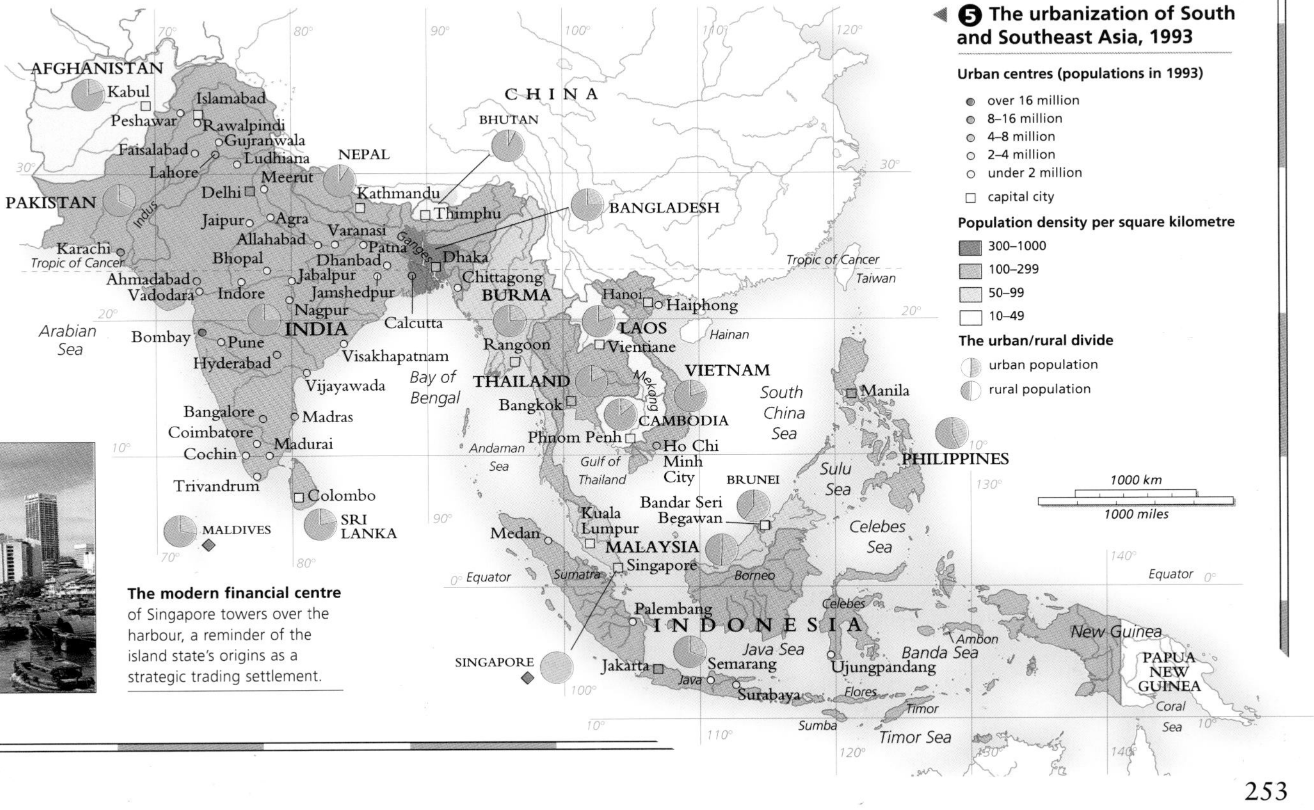

AFGHANISTAN
Kabul
Peshawar
Islamabad
Rawalpindi
Gujranwala
Faisalabad
Ludhiana
Lahore
Meerut
Delhi
PAKISTAN
Indus
Jaipur
Agra
Allahabad
Varanasi
Patna
Karachi
Bhopal
Dhanbad
Ahmadabad
Jabalpur
Vadodara
Indore
Jamshedpur
Nagpur
INDIA
Calcutta
Bombay
Pune
Hyderabad
Visakhapatnam
Vijayawada
Bangalore
Madras
Coimbatore
Madurai
Cochin
Trivandrum
Colombo
SRI LANKA
MALDIVES
NEPAL
Kathmandu
BHUTAN
Thimphu
CHINA
BANGLADESH
Dhaka
Ganges
Chittagong
BURMA
Rangoon
THAILAND
Bangkok
Hanoi
Haiphong
LAOS
Vientiane
VIETNAM
Mekong
CAMBODIA
Phnom Penh
Ho Chi Minh City
BRUNEI
Bandar Seri Begawan
Kuala Lumpur
MALAYSIA
Medan
Singapore
SINGAPORE
Palembang
INDONESIA
Jakarta
Semarang
Surabaya
Ujungpandang
Manila
PHILIPPINES
PAPUA NEW GUINEA
Arabian Sea
Bay of Bengal
Andaman Sea
Gulf of Thailand
South China Sea
Sulu Sea
Celebes Sea
Java Sea
Banda Sea
Timor Sea
Coral Sea
Hainan
Taiwan
Sumatra
Borneo
Celebes
Java
Flores
Sumba
Timor
Ambon
New Guinea
Tropic of Cancer
Equator
1000 km
1000 miles

5 The urbanization of South and Southeast Asia, 1993

Urban centres (populations in 1993)

- over 16 million
- 8–16 million
- 4–8 million
- 2–4 million
- under 2 million
- capital city

Population density per square kilometre

- 300–1000
- 100–299
- 50–99
- 10–49

The urban/rural divide

- urban population
- rural population

NORTH AND EAST ASIA
REGIONAL HISTORY

THE HISTORICAL LANDSCAPE

THE FRAGMENTED GEOGRAPHY of this, the world's largest uninterrupted land mass, has produced a wide variety of historical scenarios. The mountainous massifs at its heart – the Plateau of Tibet, the Altai, Tien Shan, and Pamir ranges – enclose the arid Takla Makan, Gobi, and Ordos deserts, which together comprise a hostile and sparsely inhabited realm. Stretching in a wide arc around this region are the massive steppes, long home to pastoral nomads whose turbulent history was punctuated by sorties against their sedentary neighbours and, occasionally, violent irruptions which impelled their skilled and fast-moving horsemen across Eurasia. Broad rivers flow north across Siberia to the Arctic, and west to inland deltas and landlocked seas such as the Aral and Caspian. To the east, the fertile floodplains of the Yellow River and the Yangtze were the focus of the world's oldest surviving civilization, that of China, an enormous demographic and cultural fulcrum which dominates East Asia, and whose influence has been cast far across the peninsulas and archipelagos of the Pacific Rim.

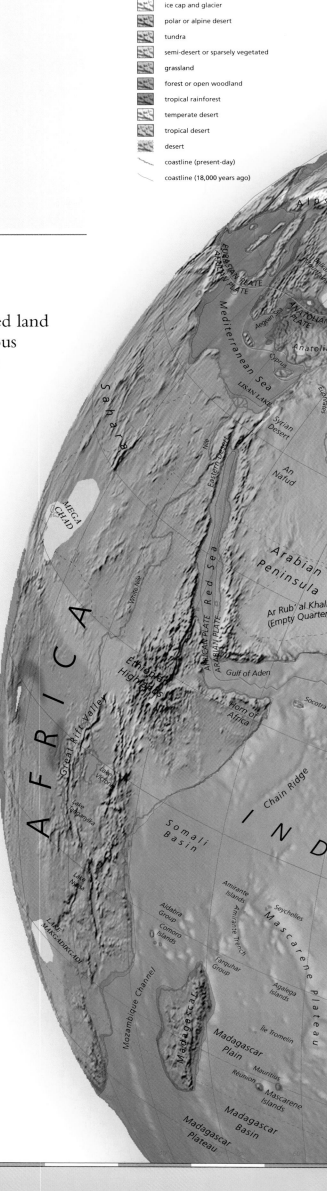

Vegetation type

ice cap and glacier
polar or alpine desert
tundra
semi-desert or sparsely vegetated
grassland
forest or open woodland
tropical rainforest
temperate desert
tropical desert
desert
coastline (present-day)
coastline (18,000 years ago)

Japan was settled by hunter-gatherers by about 30,000 years ago. At the the time of the last Ice Age, most of the Japanese islands were densely forested with settlement only in the coastal regions.

The Yellow River flows down to the plains of eastern China across a plateau of fertile *loess* – fine silty soils created by the erosion of glacial material. The river cuts down through the soft sediments, washing them downstream and depositing them on the Great Plain of China, resulting in exceptionally fertile soils, suitable for a wide range of crops.

Siberia was a cold, frozen region at the time of the last Ice Age, sparsely inhabited by hunter-gatherers. Unlike northern Europe and North America, Siberia was not covered by an ice cap because of the lack of moisture across the region. The extreme cold preserved the remains of creatures such as mammoths, along with evidence of the shelters built by the people who hunted them.

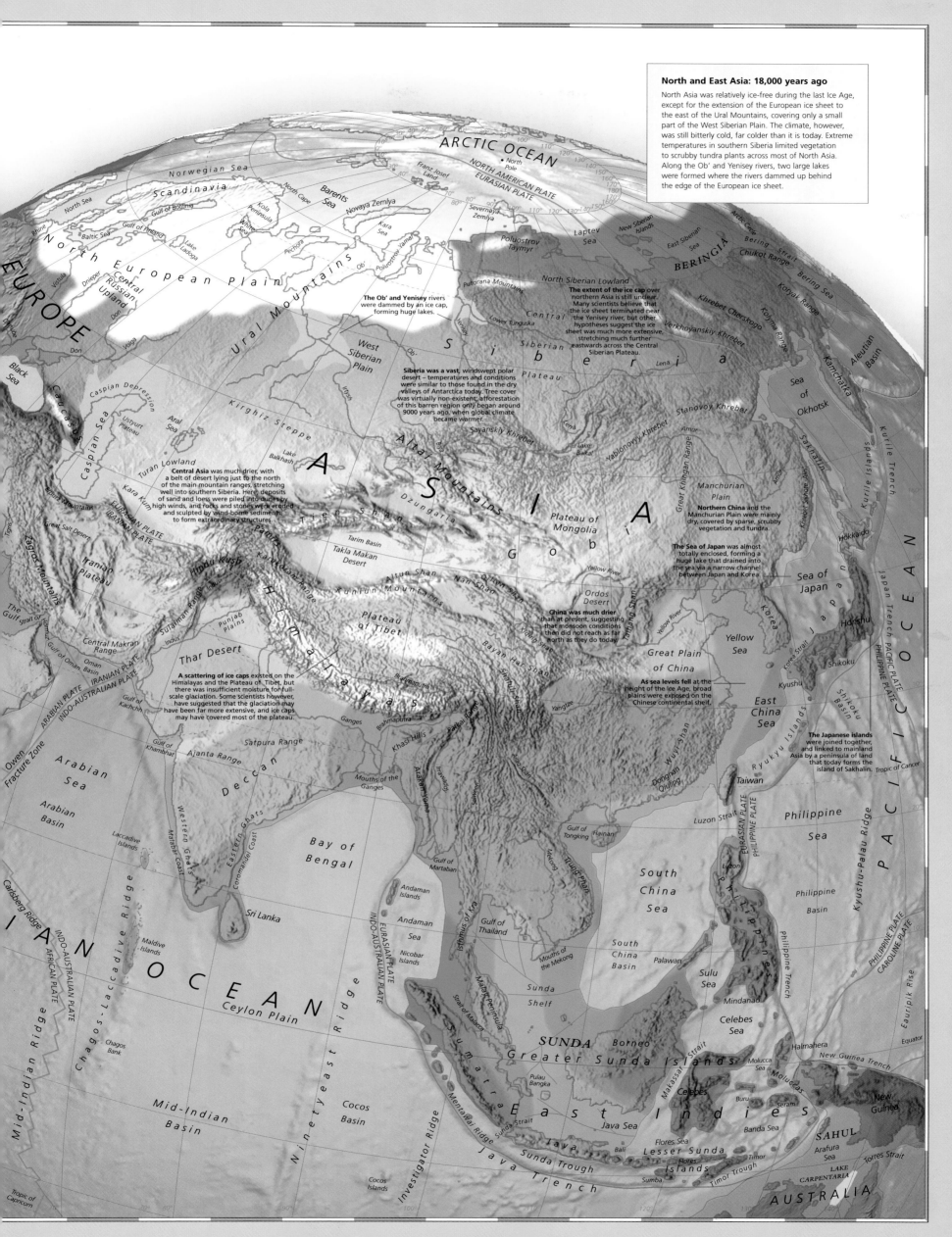

North Pole

NORTH AMERICAN PLATE
EURASIAN PLATE

North and East Asia: 18,000 years ago

North Asia was relatively ice-free during the last Ice Age, except for the extension of the European ice sheet to the east of the Ural Mountains, covering only a small part of the West Siberian Plain. The climate, however, was still bitterly cold, far colder than it is today. Extreme temperatures in southern Siberia limited vegetation to scrubby tundra plants across most of North Asia. Along the Ob' and Yenisey rivers, two large lakes were formed where the rivers dammed up behind the edge of the European ice sheet.

Norwegian Sea

Scandinavia

North Sea
North Cape
Barents Sea
Novaya Zemlya
Franz Josef Land
Severnaya Zemlya

Rhine
Gulf of Bothnia
Kola Peninsula
White Sea
Poluostrov Yamal
Laptev Sea
New Siberian Islands
East Siberian Sea
Arctic Circle
BERINGIA
Bering Strait
Chukot Range
Koryak Range
Bering Sea

Baltic Sea
Lake Ladoga
Pechora
Poluostrov Taymyr

North European Plain
Central Russian Upland
Ob'
Putorana Mountains
North Siberian Lowland
Khrebet Cherskogo
Kolyma Range
Verkhoyanskiy Khrebet

EUROPE

Vistula
Dnieper
Don
Volga
Ural Mountains
West Siberian Plain
Lower Tunguska
Central Siberian Plateau
Lena
Stanovoy Khrebet
Sea of Okhotsk
Kamchatka
Aleutian Basin

The Ob' and Yenisey rivers were dammed by an ice cap, forming huge lakes.

The extent of the ice cap over northern Asia is still unclear. Many scientists believe that the ice sheet terminated near the Yenisey river, but other hypotheses suggest the ice sheet was much more extensive, stretching much further eastwards across the Central Siberian Plateau.

Black Sea
Caucasus
Caspian Depression
Aral Sea
Kirghiz Steppe
Irtysh
Yenisey
Sayanskiy Khrebet
Lena
Lake Baikal
Yablonovyy Khrebet
Amur
Great Khingan Range
Khrebet Sikhote Alin
Sakhalin
Kurile Islands

Caspian Sea
Ustyurt Plateau
Lake Balkhash
Altai Mountains
ASIA
Manchurian Plain
Amur

Siberia was a vast, windswept polar desert – temperatures and conditions were similar to those found in the dry valleys of Antarctica today. Tree cover was virtually non-existent; afforestation of this barren region only began around 9000 years ago, when global climate became warmer.

Turan Lowland
Kara Kum
Dzungaria
Plateau of Mongolia
Gobi

Central Asia was much drier, with a belt of desert lying just to the north of the main mountain ranges, stretching well into southern Siberia. Here, deposits of sand and loess were piled into dunes by high winds, and rocks and stones were eroded and sculpted by wind-borne sediments, to form extraordinary structures.

Elburz Mountains
Zagros Mountains
Tigris
Great Salt Desert
Iranian Plateau
EURASIAN PLATE
IRANIAN PLATE
Pamir
Tien Shan
Karakoram Range
Hindu Kush
Tarim Basin
Takla Makan Desert
Altun Shan
Kunlun Mountains
Nan Shan
Qilian Shan
Ordos Desert
Yellow River
Tarbagatai Shan
Sea of Japan
Korea
Japan
Honshu

Northern China and the Manchurian Plain were mainly dry, covered by sparse, scrubby vegetation and tundra.

The Sea of Japan was almost totally enclosed, forming a huge lake that drained into the sea via a narrow channel between Japan and Korea.

The Gulf
Strait of Hormuz
Central Makran Range
Oman Basin
Sulaiman Range
Indus
Punjab Plains
Plateau of Tibet
Bayan Har Shan
Xiao Shan
Yellow River
Yangtze

China was much drier than at present, suggesting that monsoon conditions then did not reach as far north as they do today.

ARABIAN PLATE
INDO-AUSTRALIAN PLATE
IRANIAN PLATE
Gulf of Kachchh
Thar Desert
Himalayas
Ganges
Brahmaputra
Khasi Hills
Great Plain of China
Wuyi Shan
Yellow Sea
East China Sea
Kyushu
Shikoku
Ryukyu Islands
Taiwan
PACIFIC OCEAN
Japan Trench
PHILIPPINE PLATE

A scattering of ice caps existed on the Himalayas and the Plateau of Tibet, but there was insufficient moisture for full-scale glaciation. Some scientists however, have suggested that the glaciation may have been far more extensive, and ice caps may have covered most of the plateau.

As sea levels fell at the height of the Ice Age, broad plains were exposed on the Chinese continental shelf.

The Japanese islands were joined together, and linked to mainland Asia by a peninsula of land that today forms the island of Sakhalin.
Tropic of Cancer

Owen Fracture Zone
Arabian Sea
Arabian Basin
Deccan
Satpura Range
Ajanta Range
Western Ghats
Eastern Ghats
Mouths of the Ganges
Arakan Yoma
Irrawaddy
Salween
Mekong
Gulf of Tongking
Hainan
Luzon Strait
Luzon
EURASIAN PLATE
PHILIPPINE PLATE
Philippine Sea
Kyushu-Palau Ridge
PHILIPPINE PLATE
CAROLINE PLATE

Laccadive Islands
Maldive Islands
Malabar Coast
Coromandel Coast
Sri Lanka
Bay of Bengal
Andaman Islands
Andaman Sea
Nicobar Islands
Isthmus of Kra
Gulf of Thailand
Mouths of the Mekong
South China Sea
Palawan
South China Basin
Sulu Sea
Mindanao
Philippine Basin
Philippine Trench
philippine plate

INDIAN OCEAN
Carlsberg Ridge
Mid-Indian Ridge
Chagos-Laccadive Ridge
Ceylon Plain
Ninetyeast Ridge
Malay Peninsula
Strait of Malacca
Sunda Shelf
SUNDA
Borneo
Celebes Sea
Celebes
Makassar Strait
Molucca Sea
Halmahera
New Guinea Trench
Eauripik Rise
Equator

INDO-AUSTRALIAN AFRICAN PLATE
Chagos Bank
Maldive Islands
Investigator Ridge
Mentawai Ridge
Sumatra
Sunda Strait
Java Sea
Greater Sunda Islands
Pulau Bangka
Java
Bali
Flores Sea
Banda Sea
Buru
Seram
Moluccas
New Guinea

Mid-Indian Basin
Cocos Basin
Cocos Islands
Java Trench
Sunda Trough
East Indies
Lesser Sunda Islands
Flores
Sumba
Timor
Timor Trough
Arafura Sea
SAHUL
LAKE CARPENTARIA
Torres Strait

Tropic of Capricorn

AUSTRALIA

NORTH AND EAST ASIA

EXPLORATION AND MAPPING

This 3rd-century Chinese view of the world placed the imperial capital at the centre of a grid, with outlying areas organized in a regular, diminishing hierarchy.

THE GROWTH OF KNOWLEDGE of Central Asia was very gradual. Mountain barriers, extensive deserts, and climatic extremes hemmed in and defined the cultures of the region. The rulers of both China and India rarely looked beyond their frontiers, while remote states such as Tibet and Japan actively shunned external contact. In the Classical and Medieval eras perilous trade routes provided limited passage for missionaries and entrepreneurs, supplanted in the 16th century by the growth of maritime trade and European colonialists. In the 19th-century imperial European powers vied for control of Asia's land and wealth, a struggle echoed today as rich mineral resources attract increasing attention.

The early mapping of Japan

Following the introduction of Chinese administrative ideas during the 7th century CE, the southern Japanese islands were divided into 68 provinces. The limited size of the state made it possible to conduct surveys of land and population in order to raise taxes; the first maps were of individual estates, but with the creation of centralized government in 710, the Buddhist priest Gyogi began to draw up national diagrams featuring the provinces. Gyogi-style maps typically show south at the top, and often include fantastical lands.

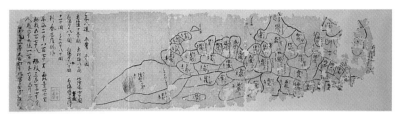

A Gyogi-style map of Honshu from 1305, orientated with south at the top, naming and listing the 68 Japanese provinces.

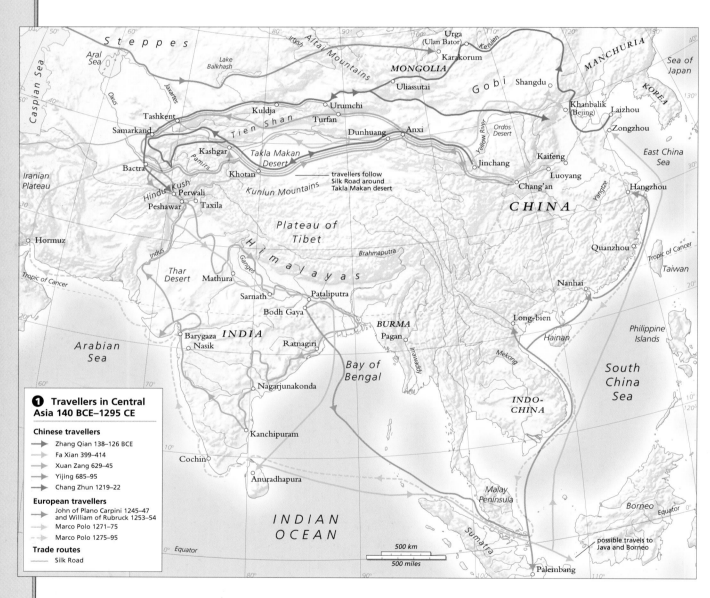

❶ Travellers in Central Asia 140 BCE–1295 CE

Chinese travellers
- Zhang Qian 138–126 BCE
- Fa Xian 399–414
- Xuan Zang 629–45
- Yijing 685–95
- Chang Zhun 1219–22

European travellers
- John of Plano Carpini 1245–47 and William of Rubruck 1253–54
- Marco Polo 1271–75
- Marco Polo 1275–95

Trade routes
- Silk Road

Mapping was an essential tool in administering the vast Chinese empire. Here a cartographer presents a Tang emperor with a map of his domains.

The conquest of Central Asia by the Mongols in the 13th century re-opened the Silk Road for trans-Asian trade. This Persian painting shows some Chinese merchant traders.

Travellers in Central Asia

The first recorded travellers in Central Asia were diplomatic missions, such as Zang Qian, or Chinese Buddhist priests on pilgrimage to India, such as Fa Xian and Xuan Zang. Over 1000 years later the 'Mongol Peace' encouraged further missions (Chang Zhun), while the secure trading routes drew Christian missionaries and traders such as Marco Polo to the east. Their extensive accounts contributed greatly to knowledge of the region.

A 17th-century European copy of a Chinese map by Zhu Siben, a leading 14th-century Chinese cartographer. It is notable for the details of coastline and drainage – knowledge of river systems was regarded as a vital means of controlling China; the use of a grid to establish a projection was a Chinese invention.

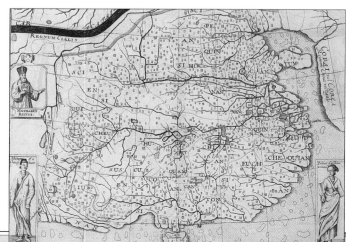

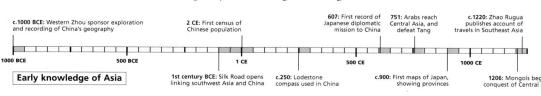

c.1000 BCE: Western Zhou sponsor exploration and recording of China's geography

2 CE: First census of Chinese population

607: First record of Japanese diplomatic mission to China

751: Arabs reach Central Asia, and defeat Tang

c.1220: Zhao Rugua publishes account of travels in Southeast Asia

| 1000 BCE | 500 BCE | 1 CE | 500 CE | 1000 CE |

Early knowledge of Asia

1st century BCE: Silk Road opens linking southwest Asia and China

c.250: Lodestone compass used in China

c.900: First maps of Japan, showing provinces

1206: Mongols begin conquest of Central Asia

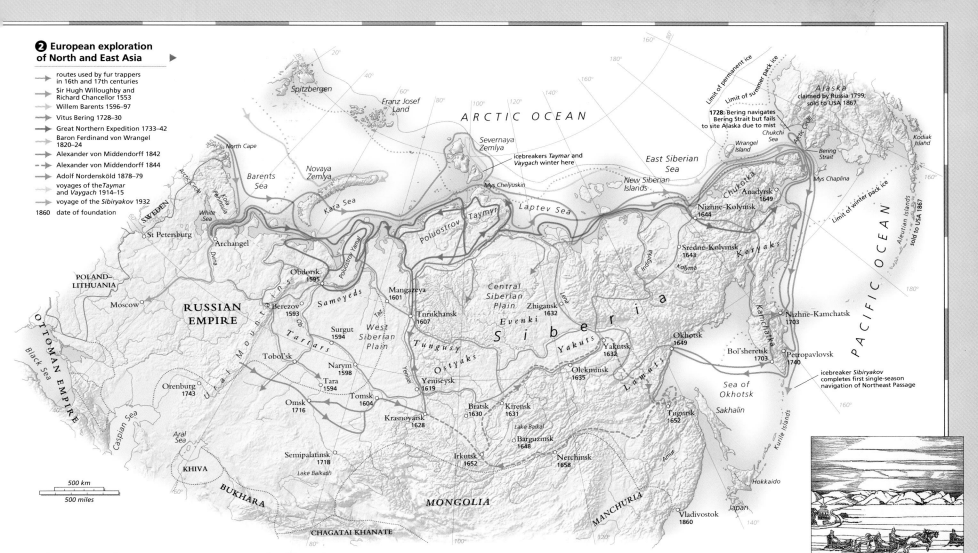

❷ European exploration of North and East Asia ▶

→ routes used by fur trappers in 16th and 17th centuries
→ Sir Hugh Willoughby and Richard Chancellor 1553
→ Willem Barents 1596–97
→ Vitus Bering 1728–30
→ Great Northern Expedition 1733–42
→ Baron Ferdinand von Wrangel 1820–24
→ Alexander von Middendorff 1842
--→ Alexander von Middendorff 1844
→ Adolf Nordensköld 1878–79
→ voyages of the *Taymar* and *Vaygach* 1914–15
→ voyage of the *Sibiryakov* 1932
1860 date of foundation

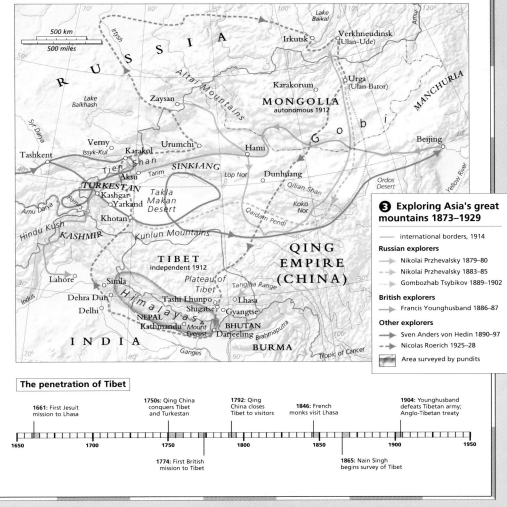

The Northeast Passage and Siberia

The repeated failure to find a Northeast passage to Asia, and the abundance of furs and minerals beyond the Urals, led to a sudden and rapid expansion of the Russian Empire across Siberia. Military forays such as the great Northern Expedition followed fur traders' routes, subdued local tribes, and paved the way for colonists. Between the 1580s and 1650 Russians gained the largest land empire yet seen, crossed the Bering Strait and claimed Alaska. Only in the 20th century did icebreakers open the maritime route across the Arctic Ocean.

The conquest of Siberia 1580–1932

1581–82: Yermak begins Russian conquest of Siberia
1649: Russians reach Pacific coast
1733–42: Great Northern Expedition under Bering surveys northern coasts of Siberia
1914–15: First icebreakers complete navigation of Northeast Passage from east

1550 — 1650 — 1750 — 1850 — 1950

1689: Treaty of Nerchinsk agrees Russian and Chinese spheres of influence in east Asia
1728: Vitus Bering navigates Bering Strait
1878–79: Nordensköld completes first navigation of Northeast Passage from west
1932: First single-season traverse of Northeast Passage by icebreaker *Sibiryakov*

Russian traders and colonists in Siberia frequently travelled by sleigh, following the frozen courses of the vast river systems, which in summer they traversed by boat portage.

On the roof of the world

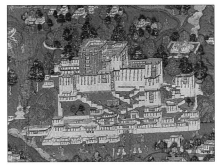

Nominally under Chinese control during the 19th century, in effect Tibet remained independent, closed to the outside world. This 18th-century Tibetan painting maps the splendour of the Dalai Lama's Potala palace in Lhasa.

Both Russia and Britain regarded accurate mapping (*below*) as essential to imperial control. The maps of Nepal and Tibet produced covertly by native 'pundits', provided essential intelligence for Anglo-Indian imperialists.

As the imperial world map was filled in during the 19th century, so the most remote regions of Central Asia began to be explored and claimed. Jesuit missionaries and diplomatic missions (frequently backed by force) had limited success in penetrating the fastnesses of Tibet. In India, the British recruited local guides as secret agents (pundits) to conduct clandestine surveys. Only during the last century did scientists (often Russian) such as Przhevalsky and Roerich explore the plateaus and mountains in any detail.

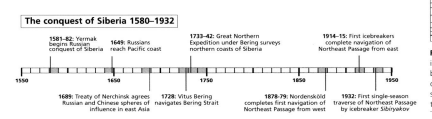

❸ Exploring Asia's great mountains 1873–1929

— international borders, 1914
Russian explorers
→ Nikolai Przhevalsky 1879–80
--→ Nikolai Przhevalsky 1883–85
····→ Gombozhab Tsybikov 1889–1902
British explorers
→ Francis Younghusband 1886–87
Other explorers
→ Sven Anders von Hedin 1890–97
→ Nicolas Roerich 1925–28
▨ Area surveyed by pundits

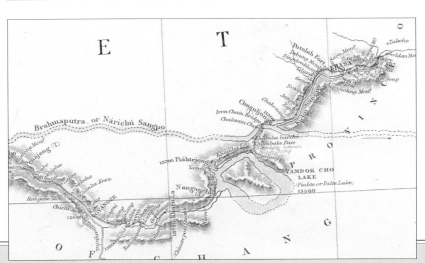

The penetration of Tibet

1661: First Jesuit mission to Lhasa
1750s: Qing China conquers Tibet and Turkestan
1792: Qing China closes Tibet to visitors
1846: French monks visit Lhasa
1904: Younghusband defeats Tibetan army; Anglo-Tibetan treaty

1650 — 1700 — 1750 — 1800 — 1850 — 1900 — 1950

1774: First British mission to Tibet
1865: Nain Singh begins survey of Tibet

257

THE FIRST EAST ASIAN CIVILIZATIONS

Some of the earliest Chinese script is preserved on oracle bones from the Shang period c.1400 BCE.

THE EMERGENCE OF ORGANIZED CULTURES in East Asia took a variety of forms. The fertile soils of the Yellow River basin, and the Yangtze valley provided the potential for the development of the first agricultural communities in the region 8000 years ago. Pottery working with kilns and bronze technology developed, accompanied by the first Chinese states and empires; the region remains to this day the heartland of China's culture and population. In Japan, the abundance of natural resources, especially fish and seafood, meant that hunter-gathering persisted, alongside features normally associated with sedentary agriculture – the world's earliest pottery is found here. Across the steppe grasslands of Central Asia, dominated by seasonal migration in search of pasture, communities developed a mobile culture now revealed through elaborate burials and decorated grave goods.

The agricultural revolution in Central and East Asia from c.10,000 BCE

The hardy yak provided abundant meat, furs for clothing and tents, and dairy products for the nomadic pastoralists of Central Asia.

A wide range of crops and plants was domesticated across East Asia from c.10,000 BCE. The pig was the most widely domesticated animal, and varieties of cattle such as oxen, yak, and banteng supported migratory herders. It was the domestication of staple crops such as millet and rice that provided the basis for population growth and, later, the first Chinese cities and states. Rice was cultivated in the Yangtze valley around 6000 BCE, reaching Korea some 4000 years later and Japan in the 1st millennium BCE. In the Yellow River valley of northern China, millet was domesticated.

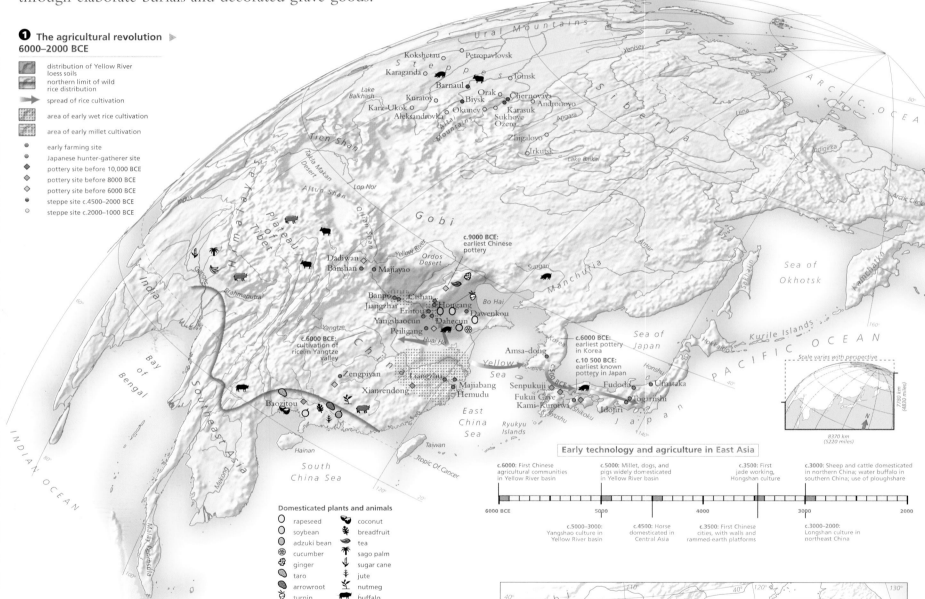

① The agricultural revolution 6000–2000 BCE

- distribution of Yellow River loess soils
- northern limit of wild rice distribution
- → spread of rice cultivation
- area of early wet rice cultivation
- area of early millet cultivation
- ● early farming site
- ▲ Japanese hunter-gatherer site
- ◆ pottery site before 10,000 BCE
- ◇ pottery site before 8000 BCE
- ◇ pottery site before 6000 BCE
- ● steppe c.4500–2000 BCE
- ○ steppe site c.2000–1000 BCE

Early technology and agriculture in East Asia

c.6000: First Chinese agricultural communities in Yellow River basin	c.5000: Millet, dogs, and pigs widely domesticated in Yellow River basin	c.3500: First jade working, Hongshan culture	c.3000: Sheep and cattle domesticated in northern China; water buffalo in southern China; use of ploughshare
c.5000–3000: Yangshao culture in Yellow River basin	c.4500: Horse domesticated in Central Asia	c.3500: First Chinese cities, with walls and rammed-earth platforms	c.3000–2000: Longshan culture in northeast China

Domesticated plants and animals

- rapeseed
- soybean
- adzuki bean
- cucumber
- ginger
- taro
- arrowroot
- turnip
- lemon
- peach
- grapefruit
- banana
- coconut
- breadfruit
- tea
- sago palm
- sugar cane
- jute
- nutmeg
- buffalo
- banteng
- yak
- pig

Neolithic China c.4000–2000 BCE

The geometric decoration of Yangshao pottery probably had a ritualistic significance.

The early agricultural communities in the Yellow River basin developed common cultural characteristics known to us through settlement patterns, burial practices and pottery. The Yangshao was the first identifiable culture, producing distinctive decorated pottery vessels. By about 3000 BCE this was replaced by the more prosperous and sophisticated Longshan culture, which spread throughout the basin and the coastal plain. Technological advances occurred in pottery, copper-working was introduced, the ploughshare was in use, and by 2700 BCE silk weaving had begun.

② Neolithic China

- area of Yangshao culture
- area of Longshan culture by c.2500 BCE
- ● major neolithic site
- ◇ site with pottery kilns from c.4000 BCE

Shang China 1800–1027 BCE

In about 1800 BCE, the nucleus of the first Chinese state emerged in the Yellow River valley of northern China. The Shang state was feudal, with its core territory under the direct control of the kings, but outlying areas less securely attached. The Shang kings used ancestor worship and divination to confirm their dynastic status. Their successive capitals were mainly ritual centres with palace complexes and elaborate royal burial places. The Shang were skilled in writing, and were exponents of martial conquest, divination, and human sacrifice. Bronze-working (often for military purposes), stone carving, and pottery making, were harnessed to religion and the state.

Although the Shang used bronze widely for everyday objects and armaments, they produced sophisticated vessels – often in the shape of animals – for specific ritualistic and sacrificial functions.

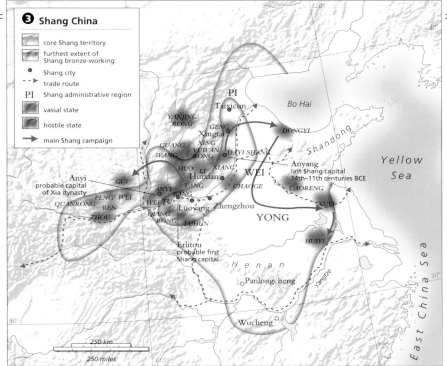

Shang China

c.2000: Xia dynasty, probable forerunners of the Shang, established
c.1800: Beginnings of Shang state
1400: Anyang becomes Shang capital
1027: Western Zhou dynasty supplants Shang

2000 BCE   1800   1600   1400   1200   1000 BCE

c.1700: First bronze vessels cast
c.1400: Earliest evidence of Chinese writing on oracle bones
c.1200: Wheeled chariots spread to China from Central Asia

Shang China

Zhou China 1027–403 BCE

The 11th century BCE saw political control wrested from the Shang by the Zhou (Chou), based west of the Shang capital. Under the Western Zhou greater political unity developed, the royal family assigning territories to their vassals to create a proto-feudal state. Human sacrifice declined, defensive walls began to be built and the first literary records of Chinese history emerged. Constant rivalry and dissent gradually eroded centralized power, and from 770 BCE a new capital was established at Luoyang under the Eastern Zhou. A looser political federation came about, bound together by the need for defence against hostile neighbours, and by common cultural values reflected in the use of coinage, in richly decorated tombs, and in the writings of Confucius.

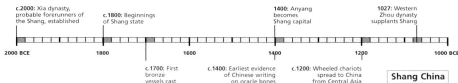

The first Chinese coins came into use around 500 BCE, and were normally cast in bronze in the form of tools.

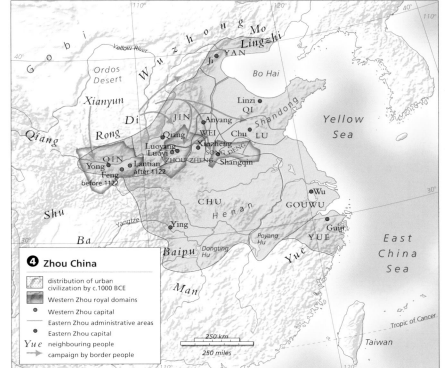

Zhou China

1027: Shang dynasty overthrown by Western Zhou
770: Eastern Zhou establish new capital at Luoyang; beginning of Springs and Autumns period
520: Death of Lao-tzu, founder of Taoism
479: Death of Confucius
403: Beginning of Warring States period

1100 BCE   900   700   500   300 BCE

722–481: 'Annals' period; China in loose confederation under nominal control of Eastern Zhou
c.500: Introduction of first Chinese coinage
458–424: Qin domain partitioned

Qin China 221–206 BCE

The Zhou confederation eventually collapsed into bitter civil war. The Warring States period (403–221 BCE) was gradually brought to an end by the Qin dynasty, who created by alliance, diplomacy, and conquest, the first unified Chinese empire. A series of ruthless campaigns by Shi Huangdi (the First Emperor) extended Qin domains far to the north and to the south beyond the Yangtze valley to the borders of modern Vietnam; in their wake, a process of centralization and standardization was introduced to minimize regional differences and tribal dissent. The area of the Chinese state was effectively tripled in 16 years, while the constant threat to the northern borders by nomadic steppe peoples such as the Xiongnu led to the construction of the first Great Wall.

247: King Zheng (later Shi Huangdi) becomes ruler of Qin domain
230: Campaigns of Shi Huangdi begin
221: Qin Empire established, organized into 36 commanderies
214: Slave labour used to link ramparts to form Great Wall
210: Death of Shi Huangdi, entombed with vast terracotta army

250 BCE   240   230   220   210   200 BCE

Qin China

221–207: General disarmament, standardization of weights, measures, and axle widths to facilitate commerce
213: Proscription of non-scientific books; standardization and simplification of Chinese script
206: Beginning of Han dynasty

Thousands of life-size terracotta soldiers and horses were buried near Shi Huangdi's tomb outside Xianyang, a testament to his military might and concern for his destiny in the afterlife.

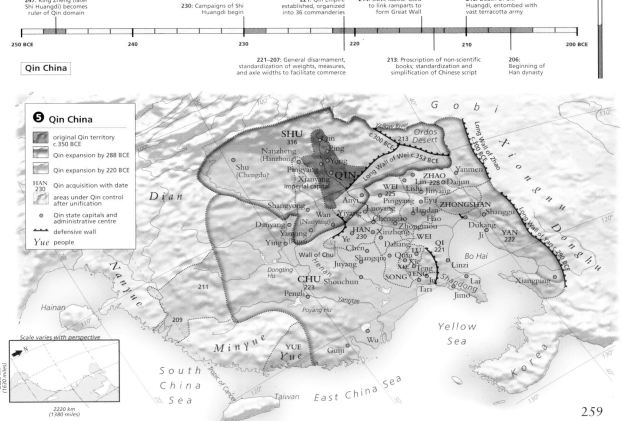

Scale varies with perspective

2620 km (1630 miles)

2220 km (1380 miles)

THE HAN AND THE GREAT MIGRATIONS

A ceremonial bronze bridle from the Han period reflects the importance of their cavalry skills.

THE UNIFICATION OF CHINA under an authoritarian, centralized regime by the Qin in 221 BCE paved the way for the Han, who assumed control in 206 BCE. The Han consolidated Chinese control of the south, pushing indigenous populations into more marginal areas, as well as expanding far into Central Asia along the Silk Road. In doing so, the Han established a domain by far the greatest the world had ever seen, and provided a template for Chinese territorial aspirations for the next two millennia. Largely self-sufficient, the Han nevertheless benefited from trans-Asian trade *(see pp. 44–45)*, but were constantly troubled by the steppe peoples, especially the Xiongnu, mounted pastoralists who harassed their northern borders.

Han China 206 BCE–220 CE

Tomb pottery from the Han period often celebrates daily life, as in this model of a farm building, complete with sheep and ass.

The Han, who ruled China for over 400 years (apart from a brief interregnum under Wang Mang from 9–25 CE), established China as the most dominant cultural, political, and economic force in Asia. They constructed a new Great Wall to protect their northern borders, and established military garrisons from Korea in the east to Champa (Vietnam) in the south and Ferghana in the west to protect their expanding empire. Trade – along the great trans-Eurasian land routes and by sea – flourished; Buddhism entered China during this period (although the Han bureaucracy was structured on Confucian principles); and by 2 CE the first imperial census revealed a Chinese population of over 57 million, living mainly in the river valleys of the north.

The Han dynasty

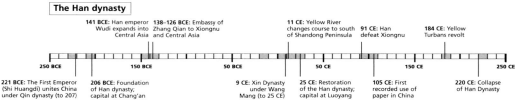

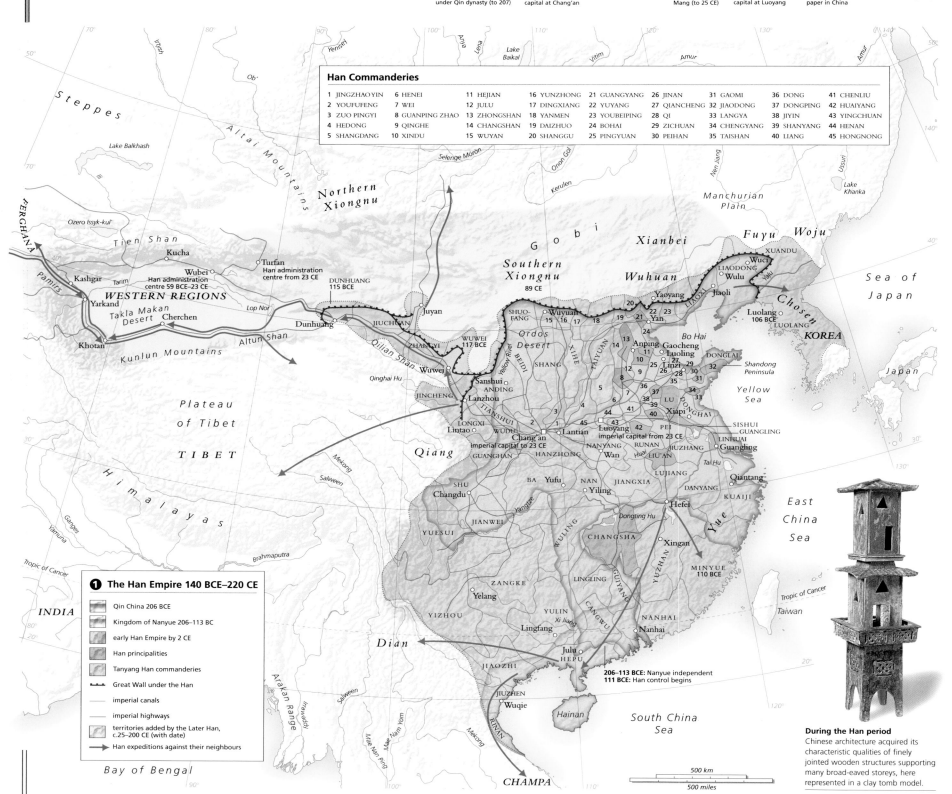

Han Commanderies

1 JINGZHAOYIN	6 HENEI	11 HEJIAN	16 YUNZHONG	21 GUANGYANG	26 JINAN	31 GAOMI	36 DONG	41 CHENLIU
2 YOUFUFENG	7 WEI	12 JULU	17 DINGXIANG	22 YUYANG	27 QIANCHENG	32 JIAODONG	37 DONGPING	42 HUAIYANG
3 ZUO PINGYI	8 GUANPING ZHAO	13 ZHONGSHAN	18 YANMEN	23 YOUBEIPING	28 QI	33 LANGYA	38 JIYIN	43 YINGCHUAN
4 HEDONG	9 QINGHE	14 CHANGSHAN	19 DAIZHUO	24 BOHAI	29 ZICHUAN	34 CHENGYANG	39 SHANYANG	44 HENAN
5 SHANGDANG	10 XINDU	15 WUYAN	20 SHANGGU	25 PINGYUAN	30 PEIHAN	35 TAISHAN	40 LIANG	45 HONGNONG

1 The Han Empire 140 BCE–220 CE

Qin China 206 BCE
Kingdom of Nanyue 206–113 BC
early Han Empire by 2 CE
Han principalities
Tanyang Han commanderies
Great Wall under the Han
imperial canals
imperial highways
territories added by the Later Han, c.25–200 CE (with date)
Han expeditions against their neighbours

During the Han period Chinese architecture acquired its characteristic qualities of finely jointed wooden structures supporting many broad-eaved storeys, here represented in a clay tomb model.

② The Three Kingdoms c.250 CE ▲

⑤ China c.560 CE ▲

The fragmentation of China 220–589 CE

The threat posed by the steppe warriors' extraordinary horsemanship is illustrated in this relief tile from Sichuan. The mounted archer is performing a 'Parthian' shot at full gallop, in full control of both his weapon and his speeding horse.

A series of revolts, the inability to collect taxes from northern vassals, and an increasing reliance on mercenaries recruited from steppe tribes, led to the collapse of the Han dynasty and a prolonged period of turmoil in China. The north fell prey to a succession of non-Chinese peoples, the most notable being the Turkic Toba (or Northern) Wei, while the Chinese aristocracy withdrew to the south. During this period the collapse of Chinese institutions saw a decline in respect for Confucian values and the growth of Taoist cults and Buddhism.

The fragmentation of China

③ The later Sixteen Kingdoms period c.400 CE ▲

④ The Toba Wei c.440–500 CE ▲

Imperial Toba Wei pastures   Toba Wei conquests c.500 BCE

The steppe kingdoms of Central Asia

The collapse of Han China was only one product of the emergence of organized, militaristic confederations among the steppe peoples of northern and Central Asia. Between the 3rd and 6th centuries, jostling for territory and opportunistic campaigns against the more sedentary states to their south – the most serious being those of the Xiongnu – caused a domino pattern of migratory movements south and west, the effects of this irruption being felt across all Eurasia.

The Xiongnu owed much of their military success to their understanding of cavalry tactics. In addition to the fast, lightly armoured skirmishers associated with steppe peoples, they maintained a heavy cavalry (left) capable of breaking through massed infantry.

▼ **⑥ The steppe kingdoms of Central Asia**

- area occupied by nomadic agriculturalists
- Xiongnu homeland
- Han Empire at greatest extent c.200 CE
- Gupta Empire at greatest extent c.400 CE
- Sassanian Persia c.250 CE
- Kushan Empire c.275 CE
- Toba Wei c.500 CE
- Eastern Turks c.600 CE
- Western Turks c.600 CE
- — Silk Road

Major movements of steppe peoples:
- 1st–3rd century CE
- 300–350
- 350–500
- after 500

This iron Bactrian plaque plated in sheet gold with turquoise gems, and depicting a horseman, is typical of the intricate but very portable art of the steppe peoples.

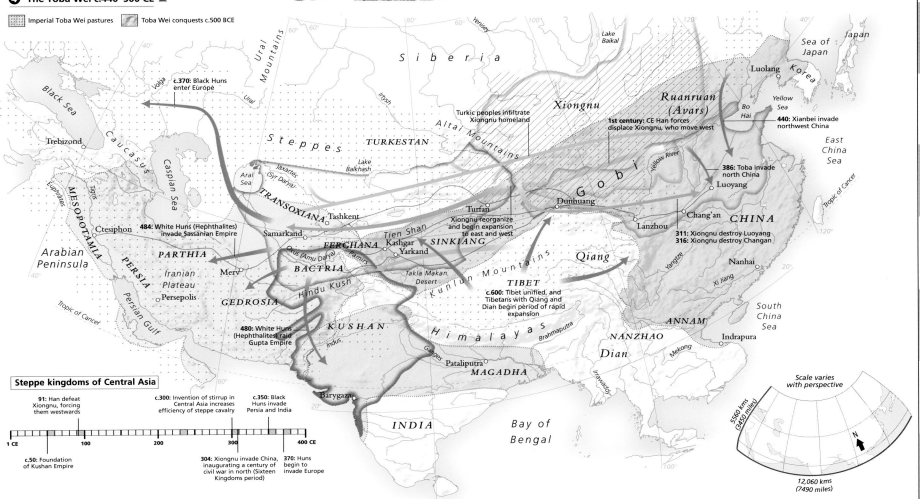

Steppe kingdoms of Central Asia

EARLY MEDIEVAL EAST ASIA

THE TANG BROUGHT CHINA under a unified administration in 618, and rapidly extended its domains far into Central Asia, briefly achieving by 742 a territorial extent and era of stable growth comparable to that of their Han forebears. The influence of Chinese culture also spread during this period, which in turn saw the establishment of similarly organized states around their frontiers on all sides. Chinese forces were defeated in 751 by Arab armies on the Talas River, which inaugurated a process of Islamicization in Central Asia and loosened Tang control in the region. But China's greatest threats continued to lie to the north, where coalitions of steppe peoples began to establish expansionist regimes, eager to control the Chinese heartland.

This porcelain incense burner in the shape of a duck dates from the Song period. Song pottery was widely traded.

Tang China

Tang China was unified under a centralized government, political and commercial integration established by a network of highways and canals, centred on the capital Chang'an. The Yangtze valley became an increasingly important economic region, while commerce focused on the coastal plain. The stability and prosperity of Tang China attracted both emulation and envy among its neighbours. But the Tang dynasty was fatally weakened by peasant revolts from the 870s and the empire eventually fragmented into local regimes which vied for power for over a century.

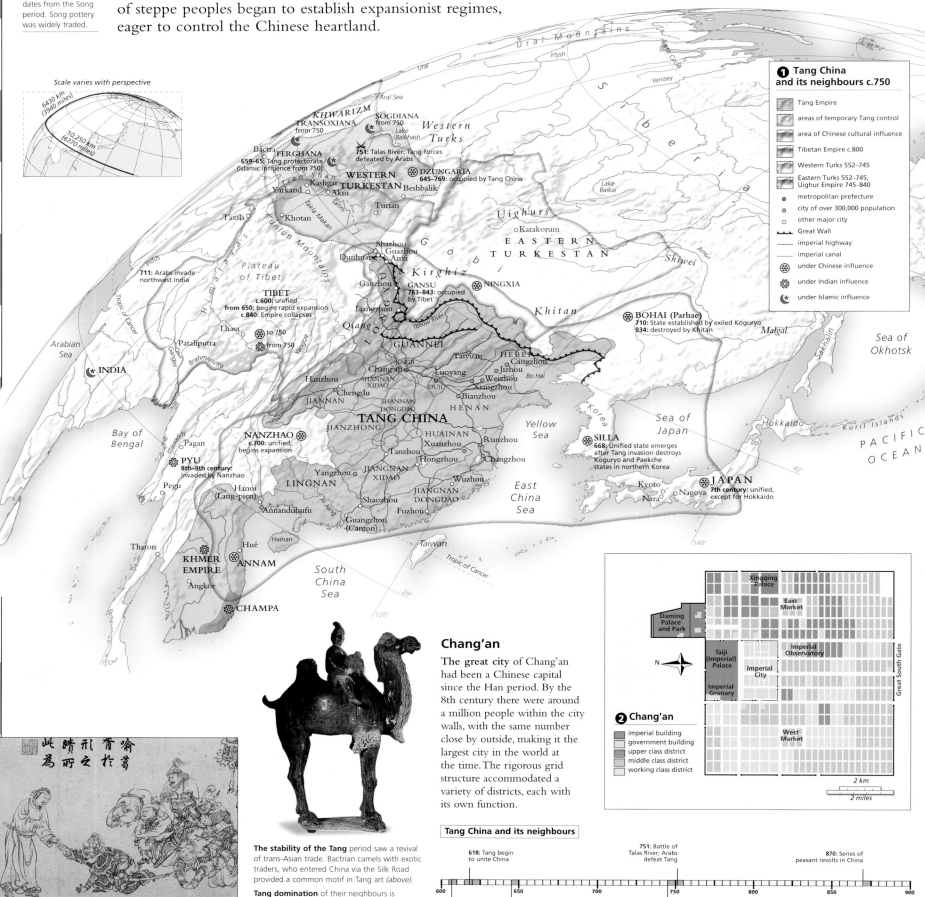

Scale varies with perspective

① Tang China and its neighbours c.750

- Tang Empire
- areas of temporary Tang control
- area of Chinese cultural influence
- Tibetan Empire c.800
- Western Turks 552–745
- Eastern Turks 552–745, Uighur Empire 745–840
- ● metropolitan prefecture
- ◉ city of over 300,000 population
- ○ other major city
- ▬ Great Wall
- imperial highway
- imperial canal
- ✹ under Chinese influence
- ✿ under Indian influence
- ☾ under Islamic influence

659–65: Tang protectorate (Islamic influence from 750)

711: Arabs invade northwest India

751: Talas River: Tang forces defeated by Arabs

645–769: occupied by Tang China

TIBET c.600: unified from 650: begins rapid expansion c.840: Empire collapses

763–843: occupied by Tibet

BOHAI (Parhae) 710: State established by exiled Koguryo 934: destroyed by Khitan

NANZHAO c.700: unified; begins expansion

PYU 8th–9th century: invaded by Nanzhao

SILLA 668: Unified state emerges after Tang invasion destroys Koguryo and Paekche states in northern Korea

JAPAN 7th century: unified, except for Hokkaido

Chang'an

The great city of Chang'an had been a Chinese capital since the Han period. By the 8th century there were around a million people within the city walls, with the same number close by outside, making it the largest city in the world at the time. The rigorous grid structure accommodated a variety of districts, each with its own function.

② Chang'an

- imperial building
- government building
- upper class district
- middle class district
- working class district

The stability of the Tang period saw a revival of trans-Asian trade. Bactrian camels with exotic traders, who entered China via the Silk Road, provided a common motif in Tang art (above).

Tang domination of their neighbours is recorded here as caricatured Uighurs pay homage to an unarmed Tang general (left).

Tang China and its neighbours

600	650	700	750	800	850	900

618: Tang begin to unite China

751: Battle of Talas River; Arabs defeat Tang

870: Series of peasant revolts in China

607: Tibet unified (to 842)

645: Introduction of Chinese institutions to Japan

745: Foundation of Uighur Empire (to 840)

Song China

The anarchy which followed the fragmentation of the Tang Empire was followed by the period known as the Five Dynasties and Ten Kingdoms, when China was broken up into as many as ten states. The Song arose in northern China in 960, expanding to form a Chinese empire by 979, although they lost control of the north to the Khitans, who established the Liao Empire in Manchuria, balanced to the west by another steppe empire, the Tangut Xixia Empire. The Jurchen, vassals of the Liao, established the Jin state, which seized the Song capital of Kaifeng, restricting Song rule to the south. The Song period was nevertheless one of great prosperity.

⑤ The Southern Song 1127–1234

☐ capital city
☐ Song empire
☐ other states/empires

③ The Five Dynasties 881–979 ▲

☐ Chinese states
☐ states occupied by non-Chinese peoples

The growth in trade under the Tang and Song brought a need for currency. The mercantile practice of issuing paper receipts in place of weighty bullion transactions was adopted by the government in the 1120s, resulting in the world's first paper money; this printed banknote dates from 1287.

④ Song China 960–1127 ▲

— imperial canal
— imperial highway
☐ national capital
● provincial capital

Fine porcelain and stoneware was produced in a range of regional centres in Song China, where mass production techniques developed to meet international demands.

POPULATION CHANGE IN CHINA

A shift in Chinese population distribution had occurred by the Song period; the Yellow River remained heavily populated, while the area south of Yangtze basin became agricultural.

⑥ Chinese population

☐ high density
☐
☐
☐ low density

742

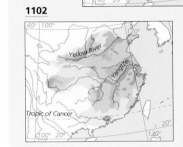

1102

916: Foundation of Khitan Empire

947: Khitans invade northern China, establishing Liao Dynasty at Beijing

1035: Foundation of Xixia Empire

1126: Jin take control of northern China

907: Beginning of Five Dynasties and Ten Kingdoms period (to 960)

939: Annam independent

974: Song dynasty unites China

| Song China |

The Yuan (Mongol) invasion

The Mongol conquest of Jin in 1234 occasioned enormous violence and destruction. But the Mongols rapidly adopted Chinese customs and institutions *(see pp.68–69)*, and the eventual conquest of the Song south in 1278 was less brutal. Subsequent campaigns brought outlying areas under temporary Mongol control, and expanded Chinese administration far to the southwest, but the Mongols only exercised temporary control over Tibet and Southeast Asia.

⑦ The Mongol (Yuan) period c.1300

☐ southern extent of Mongol conquest to 1279
☐ Mongol conquest 1280–1368
☐ imperial capital
● provincial capital
GANSU Yuan province
☐ area of loose or temporary Mongol control

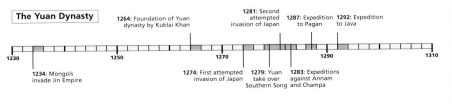

This illustration from an early military manual shows a portable scaling ladder, used in siege warfare. Other innovations of this period included the catapult.

The Japanese defeat of Kublai's armies in 1274 (30,000 troops) and 1281 (140,000 troops), the largest amphibious invasion forces of pre-modern times, were recorded in an illustrated scroll in the 1290s *(left)*.

| The Yuan Dynasty |

1264: Foundation of Yuan dynasty by Kublai Khan

1281: Second attempted invasion of Japan

1287: Expedition to Pagan

1292: Expedition to Java

1234: Mongols invade Jin Empire

1274: First attempted invasion of Japan

1279: Yuan take over Southern Song

1283: Expeditions against Annam and Champa

THE FIRST STATES IN JAPAN AND KOREA

Dotaku ceremonial bells, c.100 BCE, are typical of early Japanese bronze casting.

DURING THE FIRST CENTURIES CE a group of powerful states developed to the east of China. Yamato, centred on what was to became the traditional heartland of Japan, grew to dominate the southern Japanese islands, while Korea saw the development of three states, Paekche, Silla, and Koguryo. Both areas came under the influence of Buddhism and of Chinese culture and politics during the 5th and 6th centuries. The various states of Korea would continue to be regarded by the Chinese as vassals, but Japan affirmed its independent status, maintaining an imperial court, albeit dominated by a succession of warrior lords.

State formation in Japan and Korea

Japanese *haniwa* warrior figures, placed on tombs, reflect the martial qualities of Japan in the 5th and 6th centuries CE.

The basis for state formation in East Asia was the agricultural surplus provided by the spread of rice cultivation, associated with Yayoi culture in Japan. In southeast Japan, the Yamato state began to expand from about 500 CE, and in doing so provoked neighbouring cultures such as Kibi and Izumo, to become more politically organized in defense of their territory. In Korea, partly occupied by Han China in the 1st century BCE, the states of Koguryo, Paekche, and Silla emerged, Silla growing to dominate the peninsula by the end of the 7th century. Yamato came under increasing Chinese influence and the introduction of Buddhism in the mid-6th century began a transformation of Japanese society.

▲ **①** **State formation in Korea and Japan 100 BCE–650 CE**

	spread of Yayoi culture to 100 BCE	SILLA early states emerging c.100–650 CE
	100 BCE–100 CE	⟶ expansion of Yamato state
	after 100 CE	⟶ expansion of Silla state
	Han Empire c.108 BCE	⊙ state capital

The first states

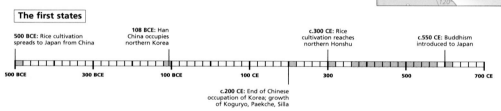

500 BCE: Rice cultivation spreads to Japan from China

108 BCE: Han China occupies northern Korea

c.300 CE: Rice cultivation reaches northern Honshu

c.550 CE: Buddhism introduced to Japan

c.200 CE: End of Chinese occupation of Korea; growth of Koguryo, Paekche, Silla

500 BCE   300 BCE   100 BCE   100 CE   300   500   700 CE

◄ **②** **The first empires c.300–900 CE**

YANGJU administrative divisions of Silla

	extent of Paekche to 660
	furthest southern extent of Chinese (Han and Wei) control in Korea
	extent of Silla power 670–935
	extent of Nara state by 600
	trade route

Phases of Japanese settlement and expansion

	by mid-8th century
	by late 8th century
	by early 9th century
	by mid-9th century

This Shinto shrine at Hakata in Kyushu is typical of traditional Japanese religion. Shinto observes the *kami*, the combined forces of nature and ancestral spirits. Shrines are often located on rocks, islands, and waterfalls, and include a *torii* or sacred gateway, significant features being linked by a straw rope, replaced each year.

The first empires c.600–900 CE

Early imperial ambitions from about 500 CE focused on the Korean peninsula. The Japanese Yamato state had exercised some influence in the south, and formed an alliance with Paekche against Silla. Tang China, which regarded all these states as effectively vassals, provided Silla with forces to overwhelm Paekche and the northern mountain state of Koguryo in the 660s. Thereafter, Japan withdrew and began to establish formal diplomatic relations with China, while the defeated Koguryo retreated north to establish an empire in Manchuria – Pohai which was similarly based on the Chinese model.

The struggle for Korea

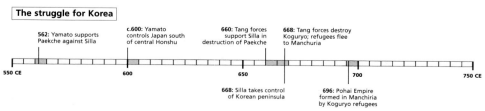

562: Yamato supports Paekche against Silla

c.600: Yamato controls Japan south of central Honshu

660: Tang forces support Silla in destruction of Paekche

668: Tang forces destroy Koguryo; refugees flee to Manchuria

550 CE   600   650   700   750 CE

668: Silla takes control of Korean peninsula

696: Pohai Empire formed in Manchuria by Koguryo refugees

The Taika Reform and the Ritsuryo state

From the 6th century, the increasing influence of Chinese institutions and of Buddhism began to transform Japan from a clan-based society into an imperial state. Under Prince Shotoku a new imperial structure was introduced (based on Chinese criminal (*ritsu*) and civil (*ryu*) law). Provinces were linked by highways and there was a centralized tax system. New capitals were built at Fujiwara then Heijo-kyo, and Buddhism formalized as a state religion alongside traditional Shinto. By the 10th century the provincial governors, tasked with quelling regional rebellion, were also involved in internecine warfare, conflict which also drew in other groups such as the substantial armies of warrior priests maintained by Buddhist temples.

❸ Japan under the Nara Ritsuryo state ▶

- district boundaries after Taika Reform (646)
- ○ provincial centre
- highway
- seaway
- ▲ sacred Buddhist mountain

This gilded bronze Buddha dates from the 8th century. Buddhism, introduced to Japan during the 6th century, had a profound impact on all aspects of Japanese live.

The rise of the warrior lords

- **645:** Taika Reform under Prince Shotoku
- **794–1185 CE:** Heian Period; transition from Chinese influence to warrior lords
- **c.1160:** Taira clan gain political control
- **710–784:** Nara Period. Establishment of new capital, imperial court, and Japanese Buddhism
- **858–1160:** Ascendancy of the Fujiwara clan
- **1051–1087:** Minamoto clan gain control of north and east Honshu

❹ The rise of Taira and the Bushi ▼

Bushido warrior clans
- Taira
- Minamoto
- Fujiwara
- Buddhist temple army
- → Minamoto campaigns to suppress the north 1051–62, 1083–87
- Taira fiefdoms c.1150
- daimyo boundary

❺ The age of the Shoguns ▶

- daimyo boundaries

Areas of control in early 1180s
- Taira
- Northern Fujiwara
- Minamoto Yoritomo
- Minamoto Yoshinaka
- area of Yoritomo control 1190
- Later Paekche 892–930
- → Mongol invasion 1274
- → Mongol invasion 1281
- → Minamoto campaigns
- Noriyori Minamoto generals
- ⚔ battle, with date

SONG CHINA

LIAO — early 10th century: Khitan peoples establish state in Manchuria

fortified barrier wall to keep Liao at bay

KORYO from 935: under Gaoli Dynasty 1196–1392: accepting Jin, Yuan (Mongol), and Ming overlordships

1281: Mongols fight sea battles in Hakata Bay. Invasion again fails as fleets devastated overnight by typhoon. Japanese attribute good fortune to 'divine winds' (*kamikaze*)

1274: Mongols land at Hakata Bay. They return to ships after battle but fleet is dispersed by gales

1185: Taira leaders killed

Scale varies with perspective

Minamoto Yoritomo, founder of the Kamakura Shogunate, an outstanding general who wrested power from the Taira, is here represented in stylized form as an enlightened administrator and politician.

The Kamakura Shoguns 1160–1333

The ascendency of the Taira clan in Japan proved short-lived. They had gained effective power in the imperial court by destroying the Hogen (1156) and Heiji (1159) uprisings, and went on to defeat a revolt led by Minamoto Yoritomo in 1180. But he regrouped and marched on the capital. In a series of campaigns led by generals from his family, Yoritomo crushed the Taira clan, and the child emperor. Yoritomo founded the Kamakura Shogunate (1185–1333), which was charged by the imperial government to oversee the military affairs of the state. Noted for administrative wisdom and justice, the state was able, under the Minamoto successors, the Hojo, to repel Mongol invasion attempts in 1274 and 1281.

The samurai military elite observed the cult of the warrior (*bushido*), and were noted for their military, administrative, and literary skills. Eventually, they were allowed to wear two finely wrought steel swords (*daisho*), while commoners were forbidden to wear any.

The Kamakura Shogunate

- **1185:** Start of Kamakura Shogunate
- **1189:** Yoritomo destroys Fujiwara rising in northern Honshu
- **1274:** First Mongol invasion defeated
- **1180–1185:** Campaigns of Minamoto Yoritomo
- **1185:** Taira clan eliminated
- **1219:** Minamoto line ends; Hajo clan act as regents for Fujiwara shogun
- **1281:** Second Mongol invasion defeated
- **1333:** End of Kamakura Shogunate

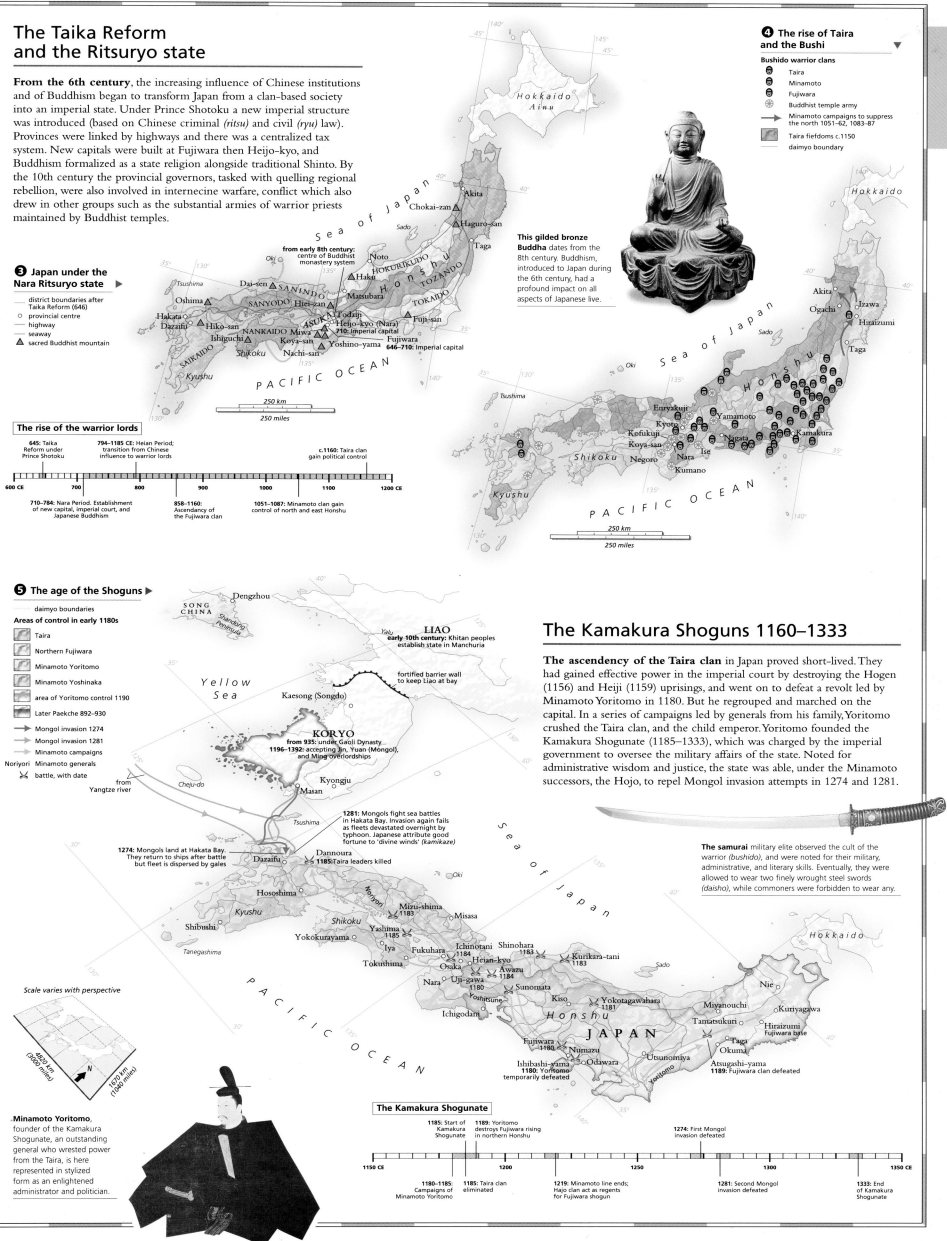

EAST ASIA AND THE MING

Zhu Yuanzhang, founder of the Ming Dynasty, ousted the Mongols to become emperor.

WITH THE ESTABLISHMENT of the Ming by Zhu Yuanzhang in 1368, China came under the unified control of a native dynasty for the first time in over 400 years. After an initial phase of expansionism and international diplomacy, most notably the missions of the great admiral Zheng He, the haughty and aristocratic Ming rulers became passive, inward-looking, and dominated by eunuch bureaucrats. Nevertheless, Ming China prospered greatly from the creation (largely by Europeans) of a global trading network, and the population boomed to some 150 million by 1600. Ming consolidation was emulated by their neighbours, with the growth of wealthy trading states across Central Asia, and the reunification of Japan under the Ashikaga Shogunate and their successors.

China under the Ming dynasty

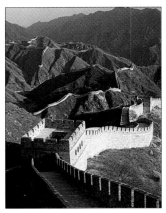

The Great Wall had its origins in the Qin dynasty (221 BCE) but it was the Ming who, after ejecting the Mongol (Yuan) dynasty, rebuilt it and extended it in its current form.

The Ming arose from the increasing chaos which attended the decline of the Mongol Yuan dynasty. One rebel leader, Zhu Yuanzhang (or Taizu) eventually overcame his rivals and established a capital at Nanjing in 1356, and within 12 years had ousted the remaining Mongols. An initially aggressive foreign policy led to the reincorporation of the southwest and campaigns in Annam and Mongolia, but by the mid-15th century the empire became increasingly defensive and factionalized. However, the Chinese infrastructure grew under imperial patronage, and the impact of trade led to the growth of great industrial centres – including Yangzhou and Nanjing – at the mouth of the Yangtze, linked to Beijing by the Grand Canal. The unwieldy Ming bureaucracy was to prove incapable of responding swiftly to change.

Under Taizu's son, Chengzu, Ming expansionism reached its apogee with the voyages of Zheng He to Southeast Asia and the Indian Ocean. Conceived on a grand scale (the fourth voyage, 1413–15, involved over 60 large vessels and 28,000 men), these missions were designed to exact tribute to the Ming court. This silk painting records a giraffe brought back from Africa on the seventh voyage (1431–33).

Revolts under the Ming

The ineffective government of the Ming was beset by internal dissent, often arising from crop failures and floods, exacerbated by resistance to taxation and the pressures of rapid urban growth and inflation. Rebellions in the 1440s led to over a million deaths, but two major revolts in the 1640s directly challenged Ming authority. When Li Zicheng's rebel forces took Beijing in 1644, the last Ming emperor committed suicide.

② Revolts under the Ming

- Ming China
- widespread agrarian unrest 1626–41
- area controlled by Zhang Xianzhong 1641–44
- area controlled by Zhang Xianzhong 1644–47
- area controlled by Li Zicheng 1641–45
- urban riots

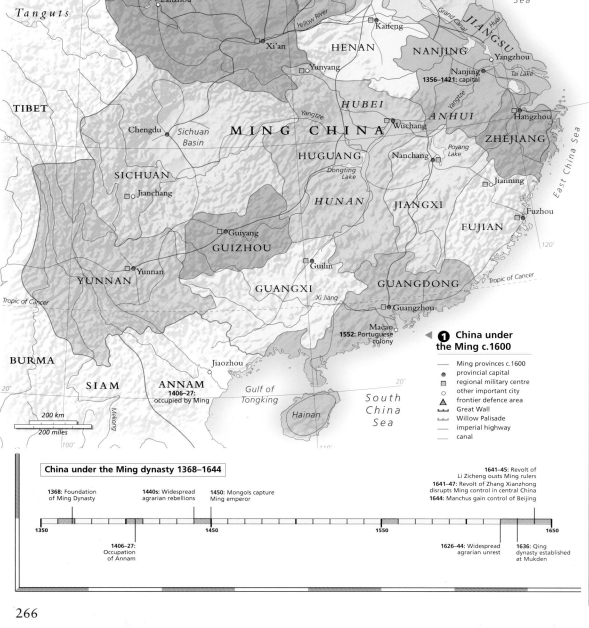

① China under the Ming c.1600

- Ming provinces c.1600
- ● provincial capital
- ■ regional military centre
- ○ other important city
- △ frontier defence area
- Great Wall
- Willow Palisade
- imperial highway
- canal

China under the Ming dynasty 1368–1644

- **1368:** Foundation of Ming Dynasty
- **1440s:** Widespread agrarian rebellions
- **1450:** Mongols capture Ming emperor
- **1406–27:** Occupation of Annam
- **1626–44:** Widespread agrarian unrest
- **1636:** Qing dynasty established at Mukden
- **1641–45:** Revolt of Li Zicheng ousts Ming rulers
- **1641–47:** Revolt of Zhang Xianzhong disrupts Ming control in central China
- **1644:** Manchus gain control of Beijing

1350 — 1450 — 1550 — 1650

The states of Central Asia

By the mid-16th century, a range of largely Islamic states had evolved across Central Asia, thriving on control of the revitalized east–west trade that had emerged under the so-called 'Mongol Peace'. Some of these were devolved successor states to the brief era of Mongol dominance but others, such as the Uzbek Empire, were of Turkic origin. Although rulers constantly vied for territorial control, the region enjoyed an era of cultural wealth and continuity, thriving on the periphery of, and exchange between, older and more stable civilizations.

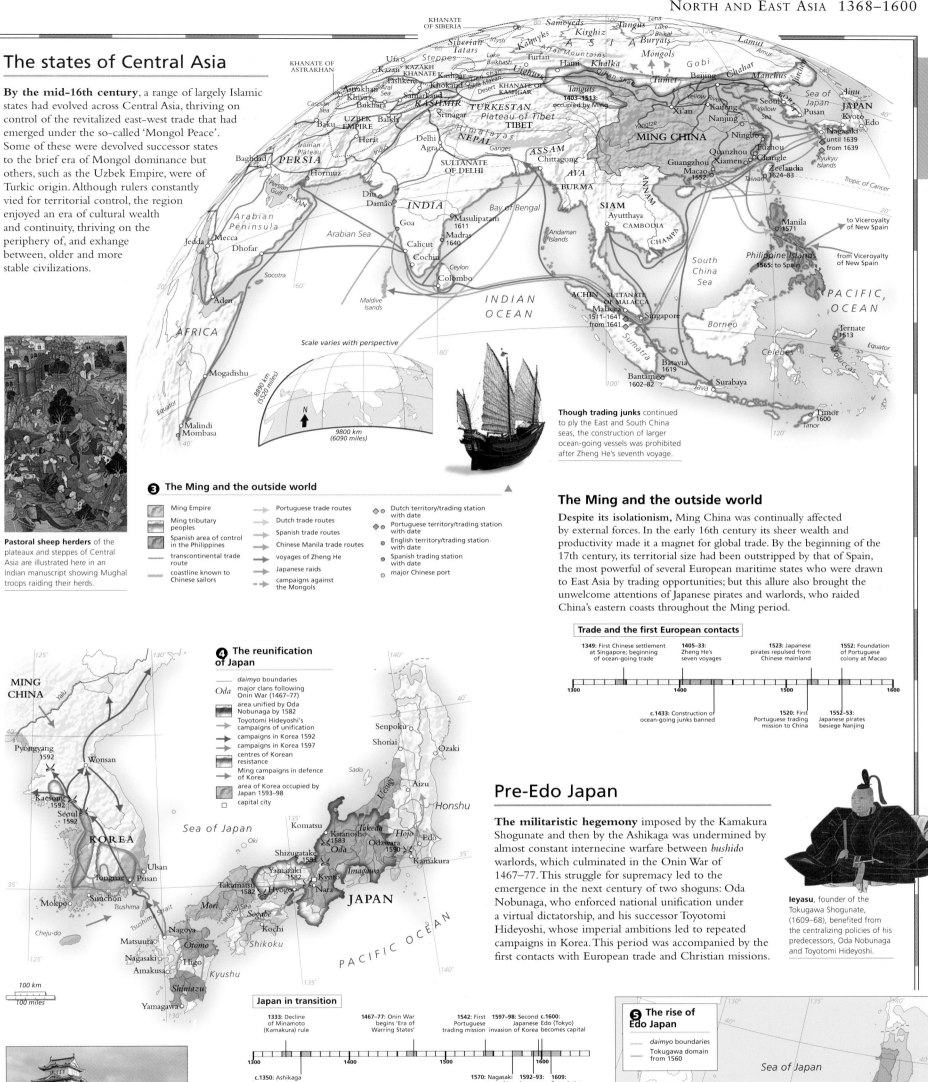

Pastoral sheep herders of the plateaux and steppes of Central Asia are illustrated here in an Indian manuscript showing Mughal troops raiding their herds.

Though **trading junks** continued to ply the East and South China seas, the construction of larger ocean-going vessels was prohibited after Zheng He's seventh voyage.

Scale varies with perspective

8890 km (5520 miles)

9800 km (6090 miles)

N

❸ The Ming and the outside world

Ming Empire	Portuguese trade routes	Dutch territory/trading station with date
Ming tributary peoples	Dutch trade routes	Portuguese territory/trading station with date
Spanish area of control in the Philippines	Spanish trade routes	English territory/trading station with date
transcontinental trade route	Chinese Manila trade routes	Spanish trading station with date
coastline known to Chinese sailors	voyages of Zheng He	major Chinese port
	Japanese raids	
	campaigns against the Mongols	

The Ming and the outside world

Despite its isolationism, Ming China was continually affected by external forces. In the early 16th century its sheer wealth and productivity made it a magnet for global trade. By the beginning of the 17th century, its territorial size had been outstripped by that of Spain, the most powerful of several European maritime states who were drawn to East Asia by trading opportunities; but this allure also brought the unwelcome attentions of Japanese pirates and warlords, who raided China's eastern coasts throughout the Ming period.

Trade and the first European contacts

1349: First Chinese settlement at Singapore; beginning of ocean-going trade
1405–33: Zheng He's seven voyages
1523: Japanese pirates repulsed from Chinese mainland
1552: Foundation of Portuguese colony at Macao

c.1433: Construction of ocean-going junks banned
1520: First Portuguese trading mission to China
1552–53: Japanese pirates besiege Nanjing

1300 — 1400 — 1500 — 1600

❹ The reunification of Japan

	daimyo boundaries
Oda	major clans following Onin War (1467–77)
	area unified by Oda Nobunaga by 1582
	Toyotomi Hideyoshi's campaigns of unification
	campaigns in Korea 1592
	campaigns in Korea 1597
	centres of Korean resistance
	Ming campaigns in defence of Korea
	area of Korea occupied by Japan 1593–98
▢	capital city

Pre-Edo Japan

The militaristic hegemony imposed by the Kamakura Shogunate and then by the Ashikaga was undermined by almost constant internecine warfare between *bushido* warlords, which culminated in the Onin War of 1467–77. This struggle for supremacy led to the emergence in the next century of two shoguns: Oda Nobunaga, who enforced national unification under a virtual dictatorship, and his successor Toyotomi Hideyoshi, whose imperial ambitions led to repeated campaigns in Korea. This period was accompanied by the first contacts with European trade and Christian missions.

Ieyasu, founder of the Tokugawa Shogunate, (1609–68), benefited from the centralizing policies of his predecessors, Oda Nobunaga and Toyotomi Hideyoshi.

Himeji castle, Hyogo, was one of over 200 heavily fortified castles built between 1570 and 1630 to enforce imperial authority, and designed in response to the challenge of gunpowder.

Japan in transition

1333: Decline of Minamoto (Kamakura) rule
1467–77: Onin War begins 'Era of Warring States'
1542: First Portuguese trading mission
1597–98: Second Japanese invasion of Korea
c.1600: Edo (Tokyo) becomes capital

c.1350: Ashikaga shoguns dominant
1570: Nagasaki opened to foreign trade
1592–93: Japanese campaigns in Korea
1609: Foundation of Tokugawa Shogunate

1300 — 1400 — 1500 — 1600

The Edo period

The death of Hideyoshi in 1598 ignited a brief power struggle which was settled at the battle of Sekigahara (1600) by the victory of Tokugawa Ieyasu. Under the Tokugawa the imperial capital was established at Edo (Tokyo), European missions were violently suppressed, and Japan entered a 250-year period of isolationism.

❺ The rise of Edo Japan

	daimyo boundaries
	Tokugawa domain from 1560

1638: Uprising of Christian converts suppressed
1641: Dutch traders confined to Deshima island
1570: Opened to European trade
1542: First Portuguese trade mission
1600: Capital
1651,1652: abortive coups
1675: destroyed by fire
1641: Dutch trading post

THE ERA OF THE QING EMPIRE

Qing China produced porcelain, jade, intaglio, carpets, and silk goods specifically for Western markets.

THE MANCHUS had already built a state along Chinese lines in southern Manchuria, based at Mukden, and were poised to take advantage of the Ming collapse in 1644. They swiftly suppressed the rebels and by the end of the 17th century had reduced Ming resistance in the south. The 18th century was a stable period of expansion and prosperity, as the Manchu, or Qing dynasty, adopted Chinese ways. Successive campaigns established an enormous empire and an array of tributary states, while regional uprisings were ruthlessly crushed. But by the 19th century the pressures of European imperial expansion and internal dissent on an unprecedented scale brought regression, isolationism, resistance to reform, and political decay.

China under the Qing

The military expansion of the Qing Empire continued throughout the 17th and 18th centuries, provoked in part by the threat of Russian, British, and French moves into Asia. Only part of the vast Qing realms were directly governed by the Manchus or settled by the Chinese, but were secured through military garrisons. The cost of this expansion was huge, and was funded by trade, largely paid for in bullion. In the 19th century, as the Qing economy faltered under pressure from European manipulation, so did the Manchu ability to administer their domains.

The Manchu rulers of the Qing Dynasty rapidly adopted the courtly manners, customs, and aristocratic aloofness of their Ming forebears. Here Kangxi (r.1662–1722) is portrayed in formal imperial splendour.

The expansion of Qing China

1636: Manchus establish Qing imperial rule at Mukden
1644: Qing forces enter Beijing
1683: Conquest of Taiwan
1689: Treaty of Nerchinsk; acquisition of Amur and Ussuri regions from Russia
1696–97: Suppression of Mongolia
1720: Formal control of Xinjiang established
1751: Invasion of Tibet
1758–59: Campaigns against Kalmyks
1765–69: Attempted invasion of Burma; establishment of suzerainty
1788: Attempted invasion of Annam
1792: Invasion of Nepal

1600 — 1700 — 1800

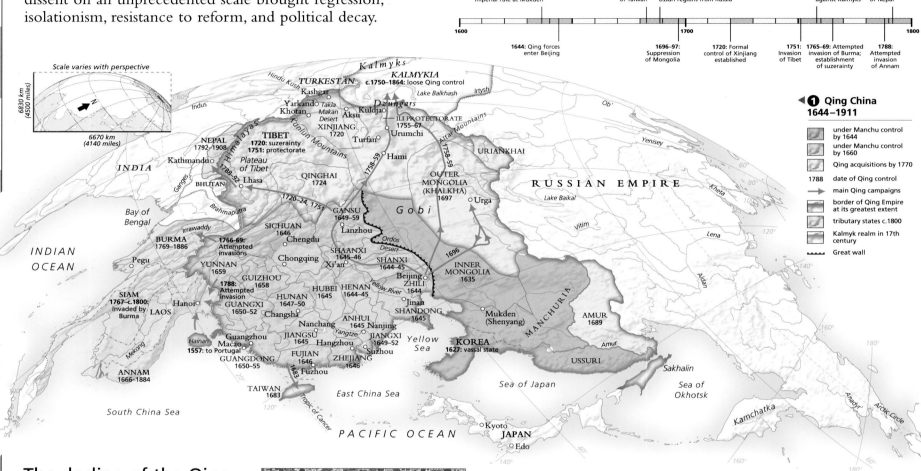

① Qing China 1644–1911

- under Manchu control by 1644
- under Manchu control by 1660
- Qing acquisitions by 1770
- 1788 date of Qing control
- main Qing campaigns
- border of Qing Empire at its greatest extent
- tributary states c.1800
- Kalmyk realm in 17th century
- Great wall

The decline of the Qing

The Manchus successfully suppressed a major rebellion by Ming supporters in southern China, largely by reduction and coercion, early in their reign. Subsequent revolts took a variety of forms: tribal uprisings, Muslim *jihads,* and millenarian sects. In most instances these were provoked by population pressures and economic distress. The great Taiping and Nian peasant rebellions in the mid-19th century left some 25 million dead and although they vitally threatened Qing stability they were ultimately unsuccessful. The former, led by a Christian visionary, invoked tacit support among the hawkish European powers. In contrast, the populist Boxer rebellion was explicitly anti-European and enjoyed covert support from the Qing rulers.

The Taiping rebellion began in southern China in 1850; by 1853 the rebel armies had moved north to establish a base at Nanjing *(above).* From here they courted foreign powers based at Shanghai, to threaten the Qing in Beijing.

Revolts against the Qing

1674: Start of pro-Ming revolts in southern China; finally suppressed 1683
1850: Start of Taiping rebellion; widespread uprising in southern China; ends 1863
1853: Nian peasant rebellion around Kaifeng; ends 1868
1855: Jihad of Yunnan Muslims; ends 1873
1863: Start of Northwest uprising; largest Muslim jihad; ends 1873
1900–01: Boxer rebellion; popular anti-Western rebellion

1700 — 1800 — 1900

② Revolts under the Qing Empire

- area of Three Feudatories and other pro-Ming rebellions, 1674–83
- Qing Empire
- tribal risings
- Muslim revolts
- area of Northwestern Muslim rising 1863–73
- sectarian uprising
- area controlled by Taiping rebels 1853–63
- Taiping rebellion
- area of Nian rebellion 1853–68
- Nian rebellion
- area of Boxer uprising 1900–01
- Guizhou Muslim uprising 1854–72
- frontier of Qing Empire 1850

Russian expansion in North Asia 1600–1914

The Russian march across Siberia, in the wake of fur trappers, involved physical hardship but provoked little resistance from native peoples. The expansion to the south and east was more hard fought, against the Kazakhs and Turkic peoples of Central Asia, but western military techniques prevailed. Further east, the conquest of the Amur and Ussuri regions from Qing China gave Russia access to the Pacific. With the abolition of serfdom in 1861, a wave of Russian migrants swept east. Russian progress resulted in an Anglo-Japanese alliance (1902), and was only finally halted by the Russo-Japanese War of 1904–05 *(see page 270)*.

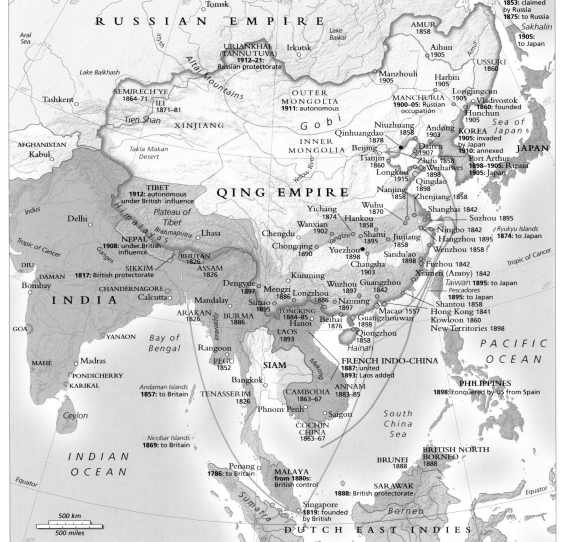

The Trans-Siberian Railway, covering 7360 km between Moscow and Vladivostok, was designed to bind Russia's Asian provinces together and to reinforce its presence in the Pacific.

The growth of Russia in Asia

1697: Start of conquest of Kamchatka; completed in 1732 it gives Russian control of Siberia

1858–60: Russia regains control of Amur-Ussuri region
1860: Foundation of Vladivostok

1868–70: Suppression of Muslim states of Bukhara and Samarkand

1900–05: Occupation of Manchuria

1689: Treaty of Nerchinsk settles territorial dispute with Qing China

1730–34: Suppression of Khazaks

1864: Establishment of control in Kalmykia (Semipalatinsk)

1891: Construction of Trans-Siberian Railway started; completed 1917

1904–05: Russo-Japanese war halts Russian expansion

③ Russian expansion in Asia 1600–1914

- Russian Empire c.1600
- acquisitions 1600–1725
- acquisitions 1726–1855
- acquisitions 1856–76
- acquisitions 1877–1914
- temporary acquisition, with dates
- Russian sphere of influence, 1914
- **1788** date of foundation or acquisition
- Trans-Siberian Railway, built 1891–1917
- borders 1914

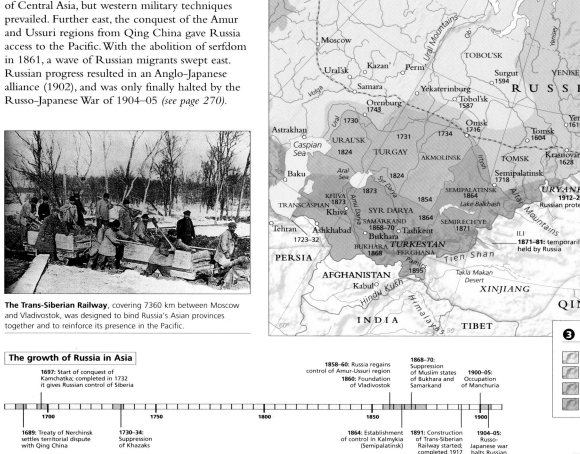

Foreign imperialism in East Asia

The rapidly expanded Qing economy of the 18th century made it prey to foreign ambitions. The dynasty's failure to halt the highly profitable illegal British trade in opium in 1839–42 revealed its weaknesses. Hong Kong was the first of many territorial and trading concessions which gave not only the Europeans but the Russians and Japanese valuable toeholds in the Middle Kingdom. Qing complacency, resistance to modernization, and their inability to counter growing internal dissent played into their adversaries' hands. By the end of the 19th century, despite belated attempts to reform, the Qing were a power in name only.

Foreign incursions into China

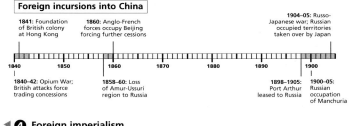

1841: Foundation of British colony at Hong Kong

1860: Anglo-French forces occupy Beijing forcing further cessions

1904–05: Russo-Japanese war; Russian occupied territories taken over by Japan

1840–42: Opium War; British attacks force trading concessions

1858–60: Loss of Amur-Ussuri region to Russia

1898–1905: Port Arthur leased to Russia

1900–05: Russian occupation of Manchuria

④ Foreign imperialism in East Asia, 1840–1910

Area of control
- Russian
- Japanese
- French
- British
- Dutch
- American
- Portuguese
- **1893** date of acquisition by foreign power

Area of influence
- Russian
- Japanese
- French
- British
- German

Leased territory
- Japanese
- French
- British
- Portuguese
- German

Treaty ports
- Japanese
- French
- British
- American
- open port

Qing Empire at its greatest extent c.1850

Foreign attacks on China
- British (Opium War 1840–42)
- Anglo-French campaigns 1858–60
- French 1883–85

Western warehouses and shipping dominated the Guangzhou waterfront from the 1830s onward.

THE MODERNIZATION OF EAST ASIA

BOTH JAPAN AND CHINA entered the 19th century under feudal, courtly, isolationist, and reactionary regimes which had held power since the 17th century. By 1900 their development stood in stark contrast. Japan under the Tokugawa Shogunate was a prosperous, sophisticated society, socially developed, universally literate, and ready for modernization. When this came – through international trade pressure – Japan adopted the role of a progressive industrialized state, keen to dominate East Asian affairs. It was aided by the Qing dynasty's rejection of external pressures and internal demands for reform in China. The end of the Qing dynasty coincided with Japanese territorial aspirations, widespread factionalism among reforming groups in China itself, and the rise of Communism in its largest neighbour, Russia.

Jiang Jieshi (Chiang Kai-shek) assumed control of the Chinese Nationalist Party in 1925.

Japanese modernization 1868–1919

When US Commodore Perry's fleet entered Tokyo Bay in 1853 to demand international trading rights with Japan, the 200-year policy of isolationism under the Tokugawa Shogunate (Bakufu) effectively ended. Reformist forces based in the south conducted a campaign (the Boshin War 1868–69) which restored the Meiji ('enlightened rule') emperor, and inaugurated political, social, and economic reform. The nation was divided into prefectures, and a centralized bureaucracy introduced a new constitution, the construction of a railway system, and the creation of modern industries, such as shipbuilding.

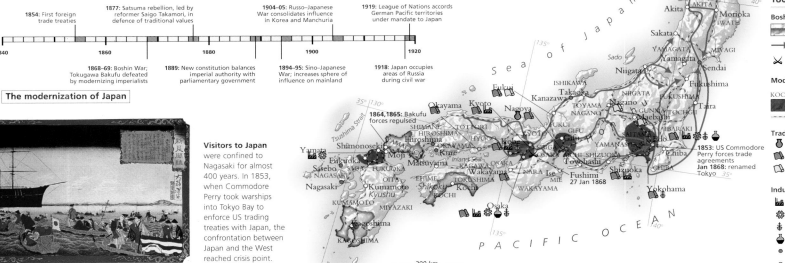

The modernization of Japan

1854: First foreign trade treaties
1868–69: Boshin War; Tokugawa Bakufu defeated by modernizing imperialists
1877: Satsuma rebellion, led by reformer Saigo Takamori, in defence of traditional values
1889: New constitution balances imperial authority with parliamentary government
1904–05: Russo–Japanese War consolidates influence in Korea and Manchuria
1894–95: Sino–Japanese War; increases sphere of influence on mainland
1919: League of Nations accords German Pacific territories under mandate to Japan
1918: Japan occupies areas of Russia during civil war

1840 1860 1880 1900 1920

① Japanese modernization 1868–1918

Boshin War 1868–69
- imperial (anti-Bakufu) alliance
- route of imperial army
- battle, with date

Modernization under the Meiji
- KOCHI prefectures established 1871
- main industrial areas by 1918
- railways built 1868–1918

Traditional industries
- ceramics
- textiles
- silk

Industries developed after 1868
- manufacturing
- machine-building
- shipbuilding
- chemicals
- city of over 500,000 in 1918
- city of over 100,000 in 1918
- other major city

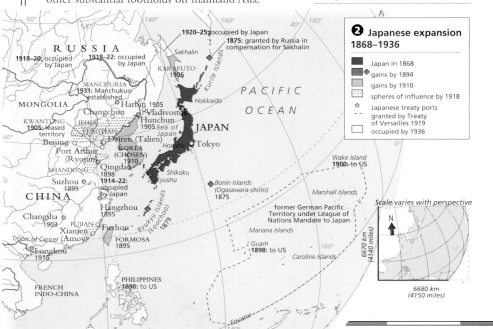

Visitors to Japan were confined to Nagasaki for almost 400 years. In 1853, when Commodore Perry took warships into Tokyo Bay to enforce US trading treaties with Japan, the confrontation between Japan and the West reached crisis point.

Japanese expansion 1868–1936

The entry of Japan onto the world's stage in 1868 was accompanied by an active policy of territorial expansion to support its rapidly expanding economy. Supported by the US (its principal trading partner by 1918), Japan claimed neighbouring islands and gained territory as a result of wars against China (1894–95) and Russia (1904–05) – leading to the annexation of Formosa and Korea. Japan's firm commitment to the Allies during the First World War (1914–18) gave her lands in the Pacific, and she rapidly gained other substantial footholds on mainland Asia.

After the Meiji revolution Japanese transport modernized rapidly; steamships, railways, and automobiles were introduced.

③ The Sino-Japanese War 1894–95

- area of Tonghak rebellion
- Japanese advance
- Japanese victory
- area leased to Japan 1895

The Sino-Japanese War 1894–95

Upon the outbreak of a populist, quasi-religious nationalist rebellion, the Tonghak Revolt (1894), the Korean court appealed to both Qing China and Japan for support. The Japanese forces compromised the Korean royal family, and open conflict with China erupted; the modern equipment and tactics employed by the Japanese forced Qing forces back to the Liaodong Peninsula, which with Taiwan was ceded to the victors, and Korea entered the Japanese sphere of influence.

The Russo-Japanese War 1904–05

Territorial rivalry and mutual animosity between Russia and Japan, already overheated by Russia's adventurist occupation of Manchuria in 1897, came to a head when Japanese vessels bombarded Russian ships at Port Arthur in 1904. The Japanese moved rapidly to secure a series of successes in southern Manchuria, exploiting their effective control of Korea, and victory was sealed when the Russian Baltic Fleet was savaged by Japanese ships in the Tsushima Strait (1905).

④ The Russo-Japanese War 1904–05
- Qing China
- to Russia 1897, to Japan 1905
- area leased to Japan 1895
- Japanese advances 1904–05
- route of Russian Baltic fleet
- Japanese victory, with date

② Japanese expansion 1868–1936
- Japan in 1868
- gains by 1894
- gains by 1910
- spheres of influence by 1918
- Japanese treaty ports granted by Treaty of Versailles 1919
- occupied by 1936

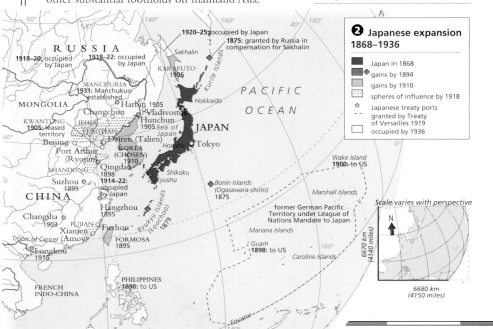

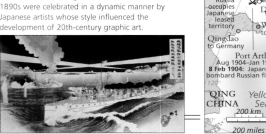

National victories against China and Russia in the 1890s were celebrated in a dynamic manner by Japanese artists whose style influenced the development of 20th-century graphic art.

Scale varies with perspective

6670 km (4140 miles)

6680 km (4150 miles)

The Chinese Revolution of 1911

After a century of almost continual internal dissent, and some ten attempted revolutions since 1890, the Qing dynasty finally recognized the need for reform in 1911. An almost spontaneous eruption of revolt across China (orchestrated by telegraph) led within five months to the abdication of the boy emperor in favour of a reformist Qing general, Yuan Shikai. Meanwhile, the leader of the Nationalist uprising, Sun Zhongshan, proclaimed a republican constitution in Nanjing. The fragile situation, with Yuan rapidly adopting dictatorial measures, began to collapse into bitter regional strife.

The Dowager Empress Cixi, was photographed in regal splendour as the Qing dynasty drew to its close. Her regency between 1861 and 1908 represented the last bastion of Qing conservatism in the face of reform and modernization.

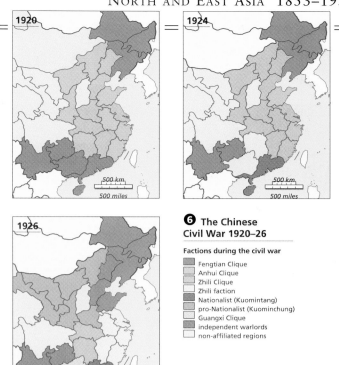

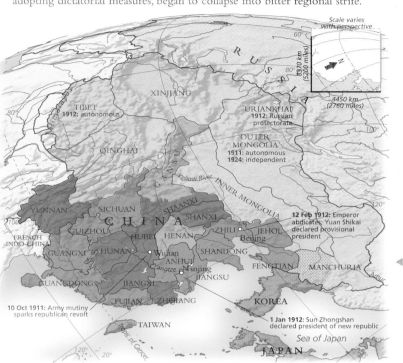

⑤ The Chinese Revolution 1911
- joined revolt Oct 1911
- joined revolt Nov 1911
- joined revolt after Nov 1911
- rest of Qing Empire
- occupied by Japan

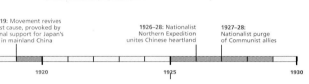

10 Oct 1911: Mutiny by reformist army officers sparks nationwide revolt

1913: Parliamentary elections; Nationalists win over 50% of seats. Yuan refuses to endorse constitution

4 May 1919: Movement revives Nationalist cause, provoked by international support for Japan's claims in mainland China

1926–28: Nationalist Northern Expedition unites Chinese heartland

1927–28: Nationalist purge of Communist allies

Jan 1912: Sun Zhongshan declares republican constitution in Nanjing
Feb 1912: Abdication of last Qing emperor; Yuan Shikai assumes power as president
1915: Yuan announces plans to become emperor
1925: Sun Zhongshan dies, succeeded by Jiang Jieshi

Revolution in China 1911–28

The Chinese Civil War 1920–26

⑥ The Chinese Civil War 1920–26

Factions during the civil war
- Fengtian Clique
- Anhui Clique
- Zhili Clique
- Zhili faction
- Nationalist (Kuomintang)
- pro-Nationalist (Kuominchung)
- Guangxi Clique
- independent warlords
- non-affiliated regions

Following the death of Yuan Shikai in 1916, the Chinese republic faltered. The nation fragmented further into regional power groups, often dominated by local warlords. Over the next 12 years a constantly shifting pattern of factionalism and alliance dominated the map of China. The 4 May Movement of 1919 in Shanghai provoked an upsurge of nationalist fervour, in the wake of which the Chinese Communist Party was formed (1921); Sun Zhongshan's Nationalists (Kuomintang) formed an alliance with the Communists, and began a campaign of unification which culminated in the Northern Expedition of 1926–28. This was led by Sun's successor, Moscow-trained Jiang Jieshi (Chiang Kai-shek), who then inaugurated a bloody purge of the Communists.

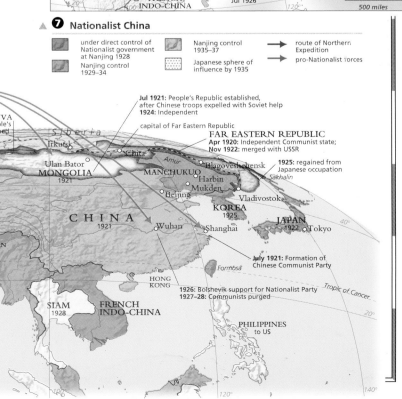

⑦ Nationalist China
- under direct control of Nationalist government at Nanjing 1928
- Nanjing control 1929–34
- Nanjing control 1935–37
- Japanese sphere of influence by 1935
- route of Northern Expedition
- pro-Nationalist forces

The Red Flag over Asia

Bolshevik 'Agitation-Instruction' trains decorated with revolutionary themes travelled to every corner of the USSR to spread the gospel of Communism.

In the wake of the Civil War (1918–21), the Russian Bolsheviks moved swiftly to consolidate their control of Asian areas of Russia. They harnessed technology and modernism with propaganda techniques to achieve the socialist revolution. Communist republics had been set up in the Far East, at Tannu-Tuva, and in Central Asia. These were gradually coerced into merging with the Soviet Union, while military support was provided to oust Chinese troops from Mongolia. The active export of Bolshevik Communism (Comintern) continued in various forms, notably in China and India.

The spread of Communism in Asia

1917: Bolshevik revolution in Russia
4 May 1919: Movement in China, resurgence of Nationalism
1921: Chinese Communist Party founded
1925: Asiatic borders of USSR consolidated
1927–28: Chinese Nationalists purge Communists

1918–22: Civil war and foreign intervention in Russia
1919: Third International (Comintern); Bolsheviks commit to international revolution
1924: Death of Lenin
1926: Jiang Jieshi leads Nationalist campaign to unify China

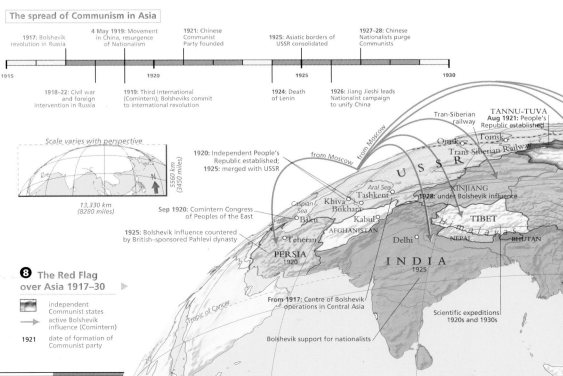

⑧ The Red Flag over Asia 1917–30
- independent Communist states
- active Bolshevik influence (Comintern)
- 1921 date of formation of Communist party

THE WAR IN THE PACIFIC

FOLLOWING THE FIRST WORLD WAR, Japan was accorded an extended sphere of territorial control in the Pacific. The Chinese civil war enabled Japan to extend its territorial ambitions on the East Asian mainland, culminating in outright warfare in China by 1937. But international sanctions, designed to limit Japan's aspirations resulted, by 1940, in a political stand-off. Next year, Japan went to war, calculating its chances on the basis of its rapid industrial development, the colonial powers' involvement in Hitler's war in Europe, and the bounty which would accrue from the establishment of an anti-Western 'Greater East Asia Co-Prosperity Sphere'. By June 1942 Japan was trying to maintain a front line over 35,000 km in extent – inevitably, it proved indefensible.

Japanese expansionism in Manchuria and Jehol accelerated in 1937 with a full-scale invasion of China.

The Japanese offensive 1941–42

Almost simultaneous pre-emptive strikes in December 1941 against the US naval base at Pearl Harbor, Hawaii, the US-controlled Philippines, the Dutch East Indies, and the British Malayan states created, at a stroke, for a brief

historical moment, the largest contiguous empire the world has ever seen. Campaigns in New Guinea, the Solomons, and Burma extended it even further. The combination of surprise (Japan attacked before declaring war), detailed strategic planning, the use of innovative aggressive methods (amphibious landings, aircraft carriers, tactical bombing, jungle tactics), and a disregard for the 'acceptable' rules of warfare proved initially irresistible.

The Japanese army's comprehensive training in military techniques such as jungle warfare and amphibious assaults proved an essential element in their initial successes in China and tropical Southeast Asia.

The surprise Japanese bombing raid on the US naval base at Pearl Harbor on 7 December 1941 was designed, at least temporarily, to destroy US sea power in the Pacific. Only 18 of the 94 warships at anchor were actually put out of action, but as a result, the US was drawn into war against Japan and its Axis allies.

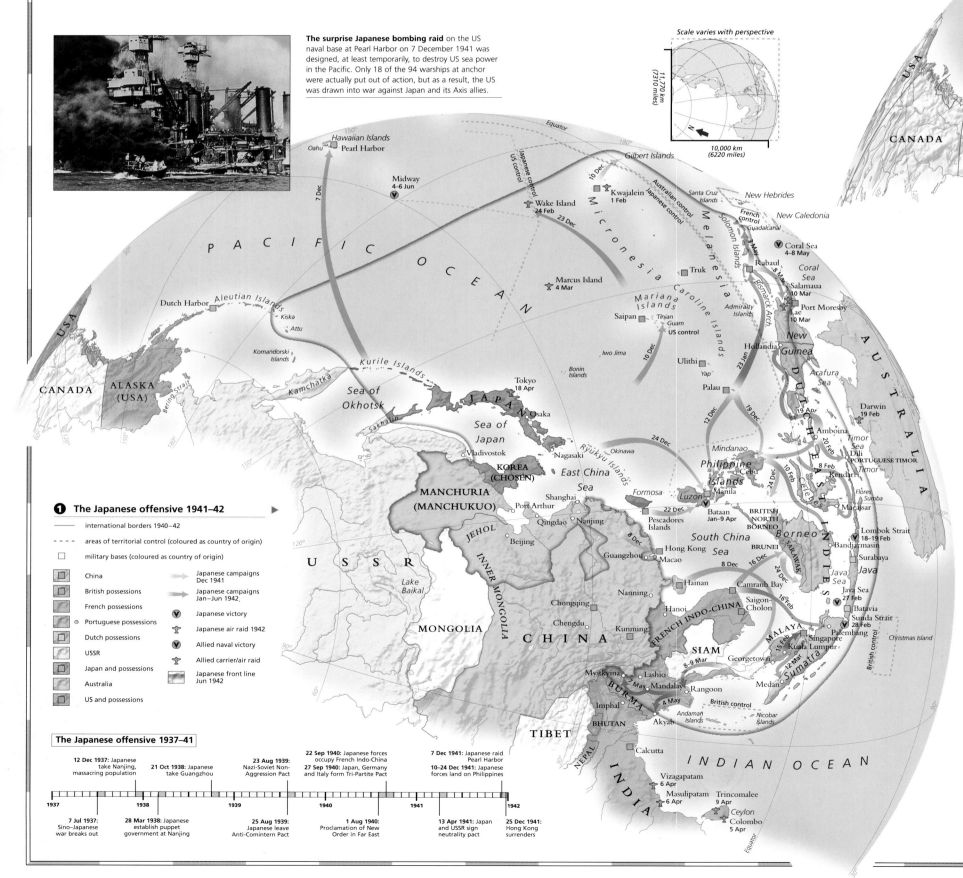

① The Japanese offensive 1941–42

— international borders 1940–42

- - - areas of territorial control (coloured as country of origin)

☐ military bases (coloured as country of origin)

☐ China
☐ British possessions
☐ French possessions
☐ Portuguese possessions
☐ Dutch possessions
☐ USSR
☐ Japan and possessions
☐ Australia
☐ US and possessions

→ Japanese campaigns Dec 1941
→ Japanese campaigns Jan–Jun 1942
Ⓥ Japanese victory
☆ Japanese air raid 1942
⚓ Allied naval victory
Ⓐ Allied carrier/air raid
▨ Japanese front line Jun 1942

Scale varies with perspective

11,770 km (7310 miles)

10,000 km (6220 miles)

The Japanese offensive 1937–41

1937	1938	1939	1940	1941	1942

12 Dec 1937: Japanese take Nanjing, massacring population

21 Oct 1938: Japanese take Guangzhou

23 Aug 1939: Nazi-Soviet Non-Aggression Pact

22 Sep 1940: Japanese forces occupy French Indo-China
27 Sep 1940: Japan, Germany and Italy form Tri-Partite Pact

7 Dec 1941: Japanese raid Pearl Harbor
10–24 Dec 1941: Japanese forces land on Philippines

7 Jul 1937: Sino-Japanese war breaks out

28 Mar 1938: Japanese establish puppet government at Nanjing

25 Aug 1939: Japanese leave Anti-Comintern Pact

1 Aug 1940: Proclamation of New Order in Far East

13 Apr 1941: Japan and USSR sign neutrality pact

25 Dec 1941: Hong Kong surrenders

The Allied counter-offensive 1942–45

In mid-1942 the Allied defeat of naval forces in the Coral Sea and at Midway halted the Japanese advance. Over the next year, bitter campaigns on and around Guadalcanal in the Solomons proved a turning point. American industrial mobilization on a massive scale fed a selective island-hopping campaign designed to disrupt the internal communications of the Japanese empire and to bring air power within striking distance of the Japanese home islands. Japanese resistance was so fierce that it took the US explosion of two newly-developed atomic bombs over Japan, which was followed by a Soviet land campaign in Manchuria, to force a surrender.

The war in the Pacific 1942–45

6 May 1942: US forces on Philippines surrender
4 Jun 1942: Japanese defeated at Midway
Aug 1943: Allied victory in New Guinea
Oct 1944: Battle of Leyte Gulf, US begin reconquest of Philippines
Jun 1945: Allied forces secure Okinawa
8 Aug 1945: USSR declares war on Japan

1942 · 1943 · 1944 · 1945 · 1946

9 Mar 1942: Dutch East Indies capitulate
4–8 May 1942: Japanese repulsed at Coral Sea
Feb 1943: Japanese evacuate Guadalcanal after six months of US offensive
19–20 Jun 1944: Japanese defeat at Philippine Sea
6 Aug 1945: Atom bomb dropped on Hiroshima
2 Sep 1945: Japanese surrender

The US refinement of amphibious operations, landing large forces supported by naval bombardment and carrier-borne air power, was a key element in their reconquest of the Pacific.

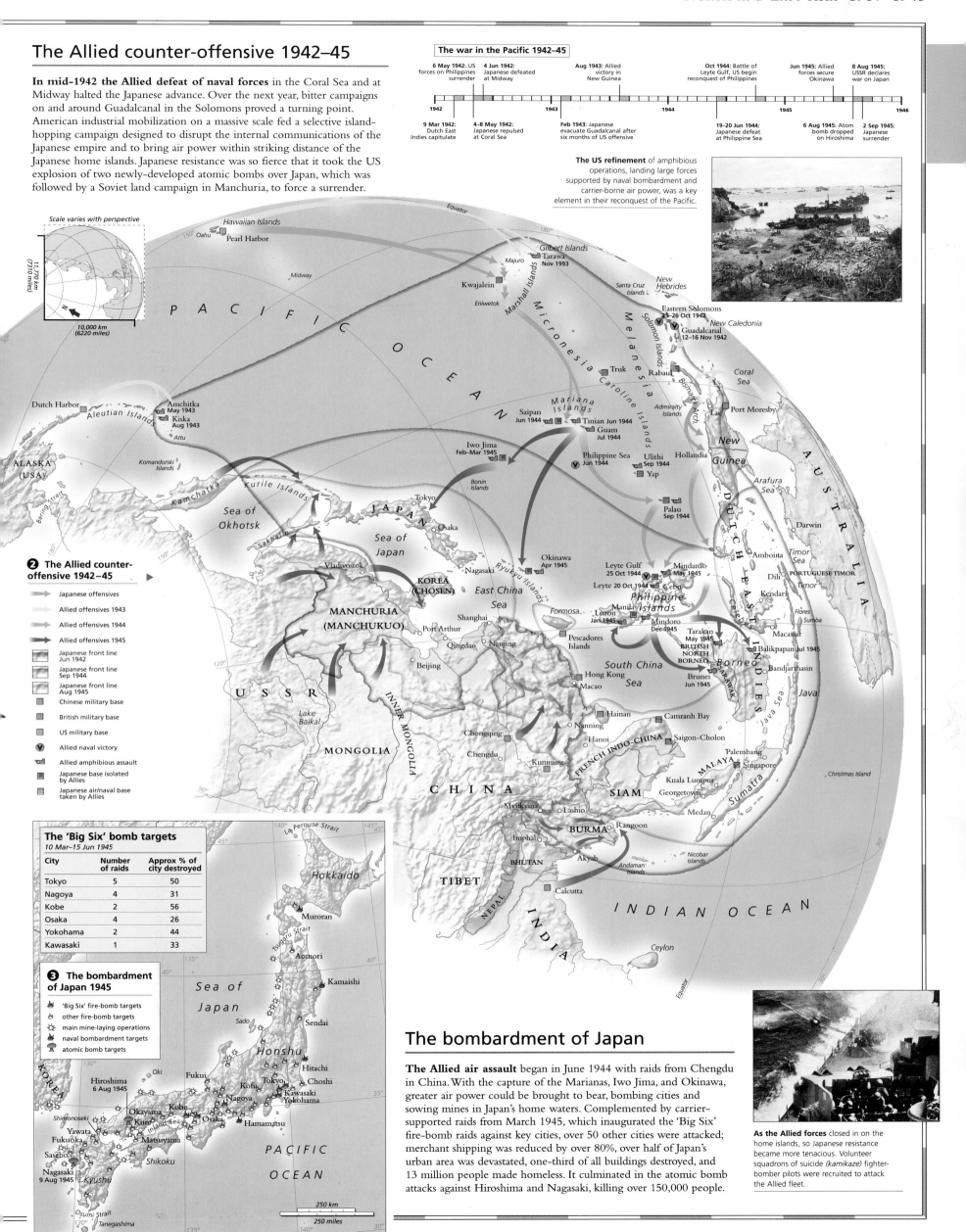

❷ The Allied counter-offensive 1942–45

- → Japanese offensives
- → Allied offensives 1943
- → Allied offensives 1944
- → Allied offensives 1945
- Japanese front line Jun 1942
- Japanese front line Sep 1944
- Japanese front line Aug 1945
- ■ Chinese military base
- ■ British military base
- ■ US military base
- Ⓥ Allied naval victory
- Allied amphibious assault
- Japanese base isolated by Allies
- Japanese air/naval base taken by Allies

The 'Big Six' bomb targets
10 Mar–15 Jun 1945

City	Number of raids	Approx % of city destroyed
Tokyo	5	50
Nagoya	4	31
Kobe	2	56
Osaka	4	26
Yokohama	2	44
Kawasaki	1	33

❸ The bombardment of Japan 1945

- 'Big Six' fire-bomb targets
- other fire-bomb targets
- main mine-laying operations
- naval bombardment targets
- atomic bomb targets

The bombardment of Japan

The Allied air assault began in June 1944 with raids from Chengdu in China. With the capture of the Marianas, Iwo Jima, and Okinawa, greater air power could be brought to bear, bombing cities and sowing mines in Japan's home waters. Complemented by carrier-supported raids from March 1945, which inaugurated the 'Big Six' fire-bomb raids against key cities, over 50 other cities were attacked; merchant shipping was reduced by over 80%, over half of Japan's urban area was devastated, one-third of all buildings destroyed, and 13 million people made homeless. It culminated in the atomic bomb attacks against Hiroshima and Nagasaki, killing over 150,000 people.

As the Allied forces closed in on the home islands, so Japanese resistance became more tenacious. Volunteer squadrons of suicide (*kamikaze*) fighter-bomber pilots were recruited to attack the Allied fleet.

COMMUNISM AND CAPITALISM

A high-speed train passing Mount Fuji exemplifies Japan's rapid development as one of the world's leading economies

THE HISTORY OF EAST ASIA from 1945 was dominated by the contrasting ideologies of Communism and capitalism. In China, where the population increased by one-third to 880 million between 1950 and 1970, Mao Zedong and his successors sought a social revolution through centralization, collectivization, and the ruthless elimination of dissent. Japan, rebuilt and supported by its Western conquerors, enjoyed an unprecedented economic boom. Spurred by the Japanese example, and supported by the US in an attempt to contain the spread of Communism, this success spread around the Pacific Rim. In Central Asia, the collapse of the Soviet Union in 1990 saw Islam revitalized, accompanied by a resurgence of traditional ethnic rivalries.

Mao Zedong's vision of a Communist revolution in China was underpinned by the mobilization of the masses down to a family level, spread by his writings, mass education, and by propaganda (above).

The Communist revolution in China 1927–49

Following the schism with the Nationalists in 1927, the Communists withdrew to isolated mountain bases. In 1934, Mao Zedong led the Communists north (the Long March) to Yenan. During the war against Japan, Communist guerrilla groups operated extensively within occupied territory, and organized popular resistance, while the Nationalists withdrew to Chongqing in the remote southwest. Upon the Japanese surrender, Soviet forces occupied Manchuria, giving the Communists a further advantage, and they rapidly gained control of the cultural and industrial heartland of the northeast. By 1948 open warfare had broken out, but with the collapse of their forces north of the Yangtze, the Nationalists withdrew to Taiwan. The People's Republic of China was established in 1949.

China under the Communists

The victorious Chinese Communists were confronted by the immediate need to implement socialist reforms, to create a centralized, Party-led, political and economic infrastructure, and to modernize industry, after almost 40 years of turmoil. Mao Zedong used propaganda and coercion to mobilize the peasants through collectivization of agriculture and mass labour projects. Energy-producing programmes increased coal and oil output, and hydro-electric and nuclear plants were constructed. The Great Leap Forward attempted to divert labour from agriculture towards industry, but resulted in famine and 30 million deaths. Ideological purges continued, notably during the Cultural Revolution (1966). After Mao's death in 1976, China began tentative liberalization although this faltered with the massacre of pro-democracy protestors in 1989.

The Great Leap Forward (1957–58) redirected peasant labour to massive public works projects, to transform China from an agricultural to an industrial economy. The nation's agricultural capacity was drastically reduced, causing widespread famine in the 1960s.

① The Communist Revolution in China

- Communist centres 1934
- Long March Oct 1934–Oct 1935
- area under Japanese control 1944
- area under Communist (PLA) control 1946
- area under Communist (PLA) control by mid-1949
- area of Communist guerrilla operations 1944–49
- battle
- principal Communist campaigns
- city with date of Communist control

China under Communist rule

1950–56: Land reform and collectivization of agriculture; millions of landowners executed	**1959:** Start of Three Hard Years; widespread famine	**1968:** Red Guards disbanded	**1978:** Beginnings of economic liberalization under Deng Xiaoping	**1989:** Suppression of pro-democracy movement

1950 — 1960 — 1970 — 1980 — 1990

1957–59: Great Leap Forward; attempt to increase productivity and boost industry
1966: Cultural Revolution; massive purge, formation of revolutionary Red Guard
1976: Death of Mao Zedong

② Chinese economic development from 1950

- boundary of Autonomous Regions

Percentage population growth 1950–90
- over 100%
- 75–100%
- 55–75%
- less than 55%

Economic development under Mao Zedong
- oilfield
- coalfield
- nuclear plant
- industrial centre

Economic development since 1980
- Special Economic Zone
- open port
- average income more than 80% of national average, 1990s
- average income less than 80% of national average, 1990s

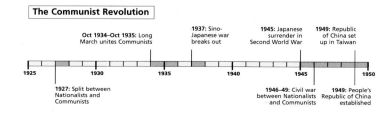

The Long March of 1934–35 strategically relocated and united the forces of the Communist party. The 8000 or so survivors of the campaign later became the core of the Party, although it was only following a bitter power struggle that Mao Zedong, seen here addressing his troops, became supreme leader.

The Communist Revolution

Oct 1934–Oct 1935: Long March unites Communists	**1937:** Sino-Japanese war breaks out	**1945:** Japanese surrender in Second World War	**1949:** Republic of China set up in Taiwan	

1925 — 1930 — 1935 — 1940 — 1945 — 1950

1927: Split between Nationalists and Communists
1946–49: Civil war between Nationalists and Communists
1949: People's Republic of China established

Chinese expansionism from 1949

The cooling of relations between the West and the Communist bloc was further chilled by China's involvement in the Korean War, its covert support for Communist guerrillas elsewhere, and by its ideological split with the Soviet Union in 1960, sparked off by the Amur-Ussuri border dispute. Chinese isolationism was balanced by an aggressive internal and foreign policy. Tibet was invaded and occupied, and the divine ruler, the Dalai Lama, exiled in 1959. It was formally absorbed as an Autonomous Region of China in 1965. Border disputes brought a brief war with India in 1962, and a temporary invasion of North Vietnam in 1979. Irredentist Taiwan remained a thorn in China's side, while the need to control potential oil and gas deposits saw China defending remote claims in the South China Sea.

The invasion of Tibet in 1950 was the most significant incident of Chinese expansionism since the Communist Revolution. Traditional ways of life and beliefs were suppressed and, following a revolt in 1959, Tibet's spiritual and political leader, the Dalai Lama, was forced into exile.

❸ Chinese expansion from 1949

- ☐ Chinese provinces
- ☐ Autonomous Regions (Zizhiqu)
- territorial/border dispute
- → Chinese invasion
- ★ Chinese support for Communist insurgents
- Soviet support for Communists after 1960
- 🏛 suppression of anti-Communist movements

The expansion of China, 1950–1980

- **1950:** Chinese invasion of Tibet
- **1950:** Chinese troops invade Korea
- **1959:** Tibetan rebellion crushed, religious institutions banned
- **1960:** Amur-Ussuri border dispute; ideological split with USSR
- **1962:** Sino-Indian war over border claim at Arunachal Pradesh; rectification of border claims with Pakistan, Nepal, and Burma
- **1971:** China admitted to United Nations; Taiwan expelled
- **1979:** US severs relations with Taiwan in return for detente with China
- **1979:** Invasion of North Vietnam

(1950 1955 1960 1965 1970 1975 1980)

The 'Tiger' economies from 1960

During the US occupation of Japan (1945–52) a new conservative pro-capitalist constitution was created, along with the conditions for rapid economic growth. As a standing army was banned, greater investment could be made in industry. Japan's phenomenal growth focused on shipbuilding, electronic goods, cameras, and cars. By the 1970s Japan, the world's third largest industrial nation, had launched a global outward investment programme. The Japanese example encouraged the development of a string of economic successes around the Pacific Rim over the next 20 years.

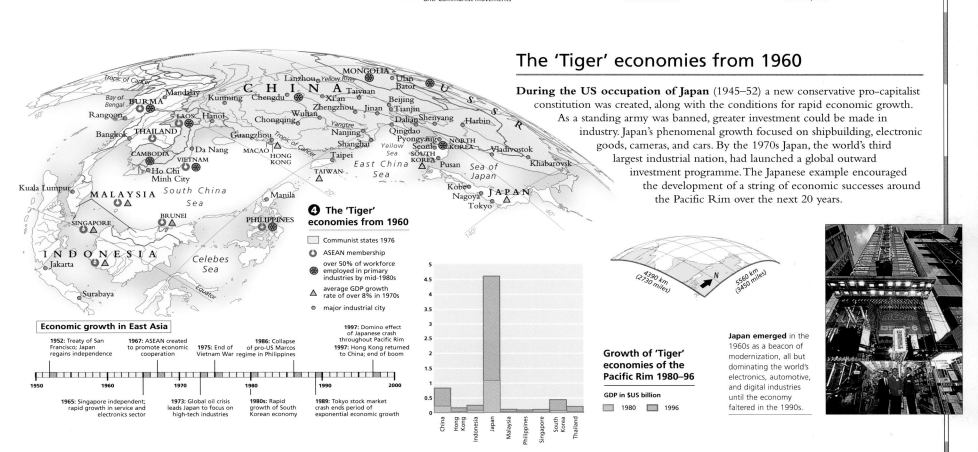

❹ The 'Tiger' economies from 1960

- ☐ Communist states 1976
- ⬡ ASEAN membership
- ⬤ over 50% of workforce employed in primary industries by mid-1980s
- △ average GDP growth rate of over 8% in 1970s
- ⊙ major industrial city

Growth of 'Tiger' economies of the Pacific Rim 1980–96

GDP in $US billion
- ☐ 1980
- ☐ 1996

(Chart categories: China, Hong Kong, Indonesia, Japan, Malaysia, Philippines, Singapore, South Korea, Thailand)

Economic growth in East Asia

- **1952:** Treaty of San Francisco; Japan regains independence
- **1965:** Singapore independent; rapid growth in service and electronics sector
- **1967:** ASEAN created to promote economic cooperation
- **1973:** Global oil crisis leads Japan to focus on high-tech industries
- **1975:** End of Vietnam War
- **1980s:** Rapid growth of South Korean economy
- **1986:** Collapse of pro-US Marcos regime in Philippines
- **1989:** Tokyo stock market crash ends period of exponential economic growth
- **1997:** Domino effect of Japanese crash throughout Pacific Rim
- **1997:** Hong Kong returned to China; end of boom

(1950 1960 1970 1980 1990 2000)

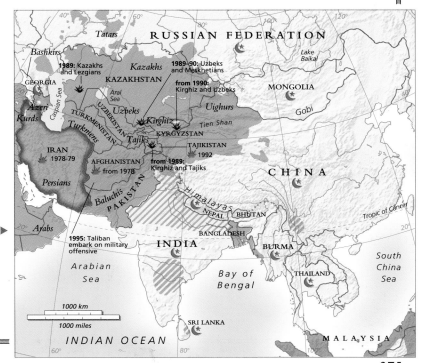

Japan emerged in the 1960s as a beacon of modernization, all but dominating the world's electronics, automotive, and digital industries until the economy faltered in the 1990s.

Islam and nationalism in Central Asia

The Islamic states of Central Asia inherited widespread environmental damage, especially in Kazakhstan, where the Soviet nuclear testing and space centre at Baykonur (above) was based.

Islam in Central Asia survived suppression and political change, to re-emerge as a vital force in the region's politics. Signalled by the *mujahedin* rebellion in Afghanistan (from 1973), and the establishment of an Islamic Republic in Iran in 1979, the revival progressed with the *mujahedin* defeat of a Soviet invasion (1979–89), and the collapse of the USSR in 1990. Ethnic rivalry flared up across the new republics, with persistent tensions between Shia and Sunni Muslims, notably in the 1995 military offensive in Afghanistan by the mainly Sunni Taliban.

❺ Islam and nationalism in Asia

- ☐ predominantly Muslim populations
- Muslim minorities
- ☐ Shia majority
- ⚔ ethnic conflict
- Islamic revolution/civil war

North and Central Asia since 1970

- **1973:** Mujahedin rebellion in Afghanistan
- **1979:** Islamic revolution in Iran
- **1979:** Soviet invasion of Afghanistan
- **1989:** Soviet troops withdraw from Afghanistan
- **1990–91:** Collapse of USSR; creation of Central Asian republics
- **1995:** Taliban militia reignites Afghan civil war

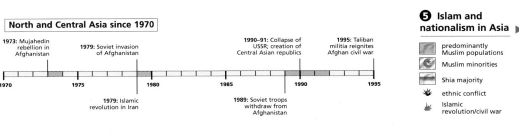

(1970 1975 1980 1985 1990 1995)

AUSTRALASIA AND OCEANIA

REGIONAL HISTORY

THE HISTORICAL LANDSCAPE

THE INSULAR CONTINENT OF AUSTRALIA and the myriad island groups of Melanesia, Micronesia, and Polynesia, strewn across the Pacific Ocean, share the most unlikely chapter in world history. Australia and New Guinea were first colonized some 60,000 years ago by migrants crossing the Southeast Asian landbridge, who completed their journey by boat – the world's first navigators. As sea levels rose after the last Ice Age, they became divided and isolated, maintaining simple, sustainable lifestyles in remote communities until European contact in the 18th century when their vulnerability was fatally exposed. The settlement of the Pacific islands, beginning some 30,000 years ago, again depended on navigational skills, and developed from about 1500 BCE into a process of active colonization. By 1000 CE, Polynesians were the most widely distributed ethnic group on the face of the earth, with settlements from New Zealand to Hawaii. The region was the penultimate target of European imperialists, leaving only the barren tracts of the Arctic ice cap and continental Antarctica as the final, ephemeral prizes in Europe's race for global domination – a race of heroic futility played out across the opening years of the 20th century.

Initially settlements were concentrated around the coasts; then, as the population grew, people moved inland to colonize the flat glacial plains of the interior.

Australia's deserts were more extensive during the last Ice Age. As the land bridge between Australia and New Guinea was flooded, settlers retreated south into the desert margins of Australia.

Most Pacific islands are volcanic, formed by eruptions on the sea floor which accumulate a cone of volcanic material, eventually rising above the ocean surface. As the volcano becomes extinct, coral reefs grow around the island's fringes. Humans first sailed to the Pacific islands from New Guinea and the Solomon Islands, reaching Fiji by 1500 BCE.

Vegetation type

 ice cap and glacier

 tundra

 semi desert or sparsely vegetated

 grassland

 forest or open woodland

tropical rainforest

tropical desert

desert

 coastline (present-day)

coastline (18,000 years ago)

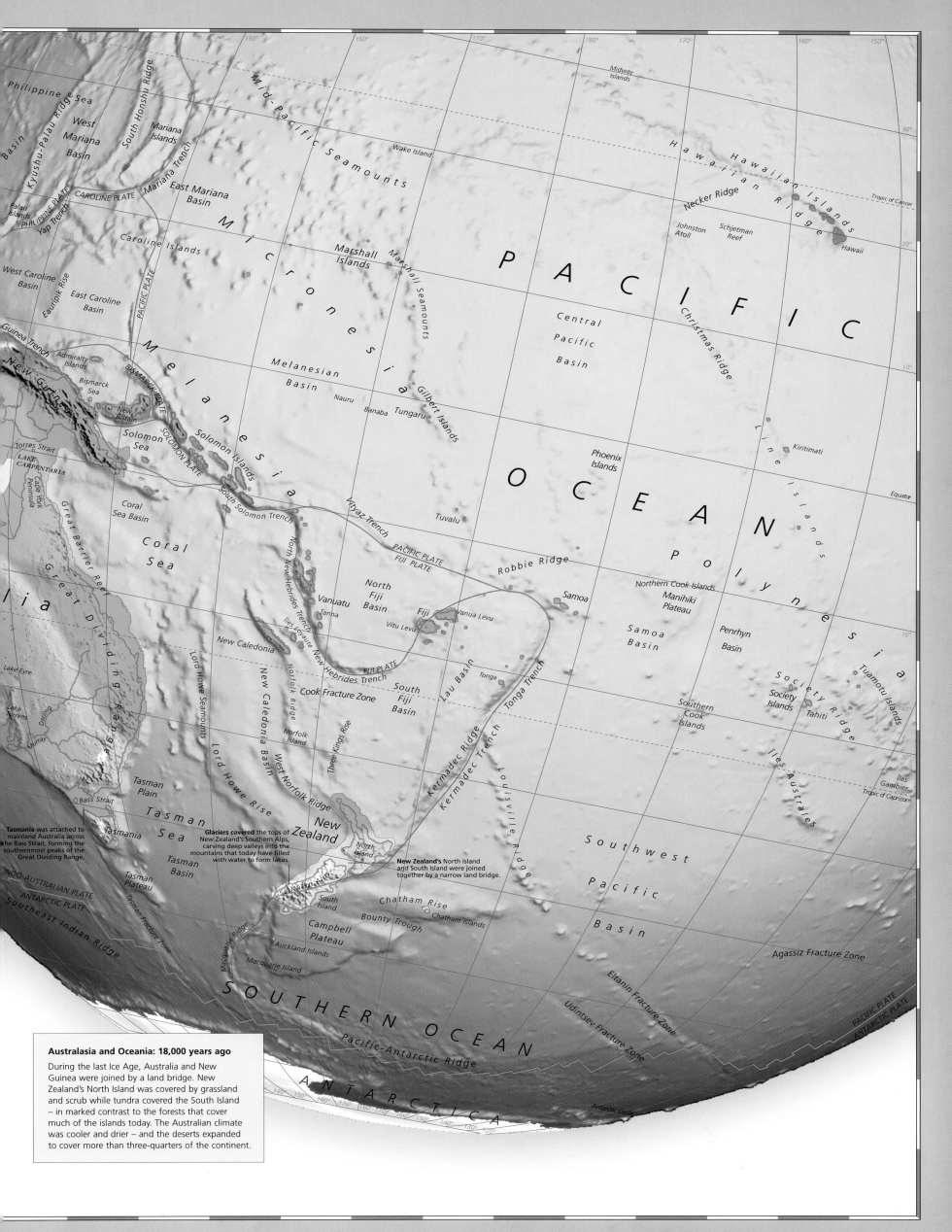

PACIFIC OCEAN

SOUTHERN OCEAN

ANTARCTICA

Australasia and Oceania: 18,000 years ago

During the last Ice Age, Australia and New Guinea were joined by a land bridge. New Zealand's North Island was covered by grassland and scrub while tundra covered the South Island – in marked contrast to the forests that cover much of the islands today. The Australian climate was cooler and drier – and the deserts expanded to cover more than three-quarters of the continent.

Tasmania was attached to mainland Australia across the Bass Strait, forming the southernmost peaks of the Great Dividing Range.

Glaciers covered the tops of New Zealand's Southern Alps, carving deep valleys into the mountains that today have filled with water to form lakes.

New Zealand's North Island and South Island were joined together by a narrow land bridge.

AUSTRALASIA AND OCEANIA
EXPLORATION AND MAPPING

Abel Tasman reached Tasmania and New Zealand in 1642 in his search for a great southern continent.

ALMOST ALL THE PACIFIC ISLANDS had been discovered and, when habitable, settled by Polynesian voyagers, some 500 years before European explorers ventured into the ocean. After Magellan's pioneering crossing of 1521, it took three centuries to chart the whole Pacific. The continent of Australia presented even greater problems. Ever since Classical times, European world maps had included a vast southern continent, *Terra Australis Incognita*. It was not until James Cook's voyages in the 18th century that the true extent of Australia was established. New Guinea's mountainous interior was not explored by Europeans until the 20th century.

STICK CHARTS OF THE MARSHALL ISLANDS

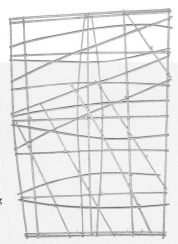

The Melanesian and Polynesian peoples who have been sailing the Pacific for four millennia have built up a vast store of knowledge of its islands, winds, and currents. The inhabitants of the Marshall Islands make charts of sticks and shells. Some are actual maps of surrounding islands and are carried aboard their canoes. Others are teaching aids. The *mattang*, for example, is not a map as such; it demonstrates the way islands affect patterns in the ocean's swell, an invaluable means of detecting the presence of low-lying atolls.

This typical *mattang* chart is made of the midribs of coconut fronds. Shells mark the location of islands and the sticks show variations in ocean swell.

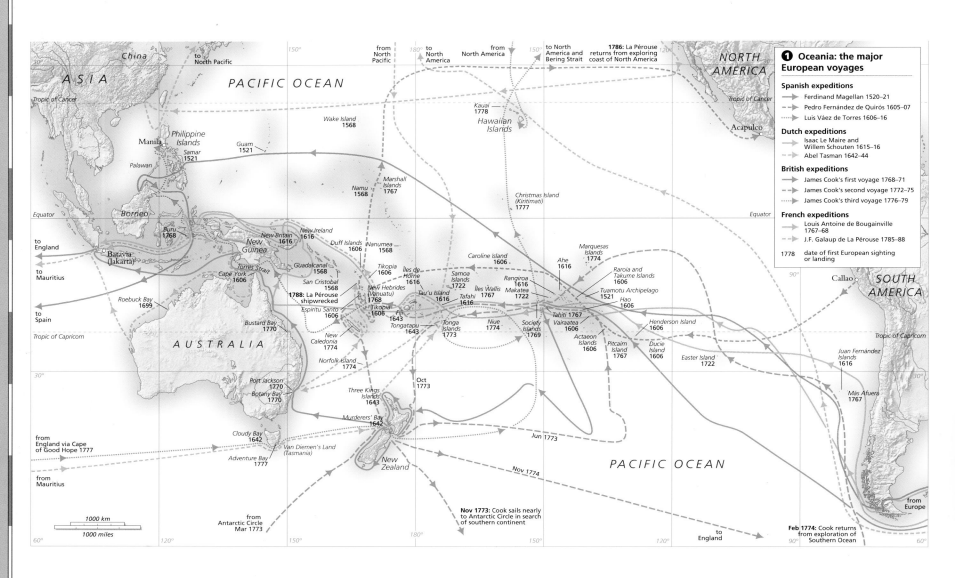

❶ Oceania: the major European voyages

Spanish expeditions
- Ferdinand Magellan 1520–21
- Pedro Fernández de Quirós 1605–07
- Luis Váez de Torres 1606–16

Dutch expeditions
- Isaac Le Maire and Willem Schouten 1615–16
- Abel Tasman 1642–44

British expeditions
- James Cook's first voyage 1768–71
- James Cook's second voyage 1772–75
- James Cook's third voyage 1776–79

French expeditions
- Louis Antoine de Bougainville 1767–68
- J.F. Galaup de La Pérouse 1785–88

1778 date of first European sighting or landing

European voyages of discovery

In the 16th century the Spanish sailed into the Pacific out of curiosity and greed, seeking routes to the riches of China and the 'Spice Islands'. At first they did not intrude too greatly on the life of the islands, using them as stopovers to pick up food and water. In Australasia the Dutch led the way, but, seeing no potential profit in Australia or New Zealand, left them alone. Things changed in the 18th century when the French and the British were competing for domination of the globe. The three voyages of Captain James Cook transformed Europe's understanding of Oceania and it was in part the popularity of accounts of Cook's voyages that spurred European and American exploitation and colonization of the region in the 19th century.

Dutch mariners provided the data for this 1593 map. It gives a reasonably accurate picture of the Solomon Islands and part of the north coast of New Guinea, but the shape and extent of Australia are still a mystery. Here, it is at least divided from New Guinea by a strait – many later maps show the two islands attached.

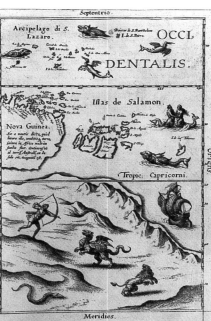

The *Resolution*, James Cook's ship on his epic second voyage of 1772–75, was originally built to carry coal.

European exploration of the Pacific

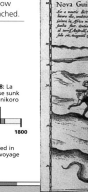

1520: Magellan enters the Pacific

1606: Torres sails through strait that now bears his name and proves New Guinea is an island

1642: Tasman, searching for a southern continent, finds Tasmania and New Zealand

1699: Dampier surveys west coast of Australia, but is unimpressed

1768: Cook's first voyage

1788: La Pérouse sunk off Vanikoro

| 1500 | 1550 | 1600 | 1650 | 1700 | 1750 | 1800 |

1526: Jorge de Meneses first European to sight New Guinea

1567–69: Alvaro de Mendaña explores Solomon Islands

1688: William Dampier first Englishman to visit Australia

1721–22: Jacob Roggeveen visits many Polynesian islands

1779: Cook killed in Hawaii on third voyage

Burke and Wills set off in 1860 to cross Australia from south to north in a fanfare of publicity. Their confidence was misplaced; Aboriginals they encountered helped them find food and water, but eventually they died of hunger.

❷ Exploration in Australia and New Guinea 1798–1928 ▶

- George Bass and Matthew Flinders 1798–99
- Matthew Flinders 1802–03
- Charles Sturt 1828–46
- Thomas Mitchell 1836–46
- Edward Eyre 1839–41
- Ludwig Leichhardt 1844–45
- Edmund Kennedy 1848
- Robert Burke and William Wills 1860–61
- John Stuart 1861–62
- Peter Warburton 1872–73
- John Forrest 1874
- Ernest Giles 1875–76
- Luigi Maria d'Albertis 1876
- Alexander Forrest 1879
- Charles Karius 1927–28

Exploring Australia and New Guinea

1802–03: Flinders circumnavigates Australia	1829–30: Sturt's journeys pave way for founding of colony of South Australia in 1836	1875: D'Albertis makes first of three trips up Fly River	1927–28: Karius expedition crosses New Guinea from south to north	

1800 — 1825 — 1850 — 1875 — 1900 — 1925 — 1950

1813: Route found across Blue Mountains

1841: Eyre is first European to cross Nullarbor Plain

1879: Forrest explores from Port Hedland across Kimberley Plateau

Australia and New Guinea: explorers of the interior

Australia never aroused the curiosity of the Dutch who knew only the hostile west coast. The British, who settled in the more temperate southeast, were gradually drawn to the interior, first by the lure of gold and the search for grazing land, later by curiosity about the vast deserts of the interior. Expeditions such as those of Burke and Leichhardt used imported camels. New Guinea was even more unwelcoming to intruders with its mountains and dense rainforest. Most 19th-century explorers of the island followed the courses of rivers, while parts of the highlands remained inaccessible until the age of the aeroplane.

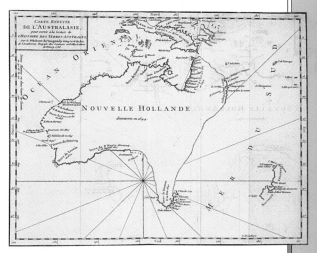

James Cook took a copy of this French map of 1756 with him on his voyage of 1768–71. The west coast of Australia is well charted because Dutch ships bound for the East Indies were often blown ashore there. The east was unexplored until Cook himself charted it and the fact that Tasmania was an island was established by Flinders and Bass in 1798–99.

Sealers, whalers, and traders

The first outsiders to have a significant impact in the Pacific were American sealers in the late 18th century. Traders soon followed to supply their sailing ships, establishing stations throughout the Pacific. By the 1820s, with Atlantic whale stocks depleted, whalers were also starting to arrive in large numbers, with calamitous results: introduced diseases caused the destruction of entire island societies. In the 1860s came a further threat – 'blackbirders', slave raiders operating initially out of Peru, later carrying off the young males of many islands to work in the canefields of Queensland, Australia.

Sperm whales were the chief quarry of Pacific whalers, due to the growing market for their oil, used in industrialized Europe and the US for lubricating machinery.

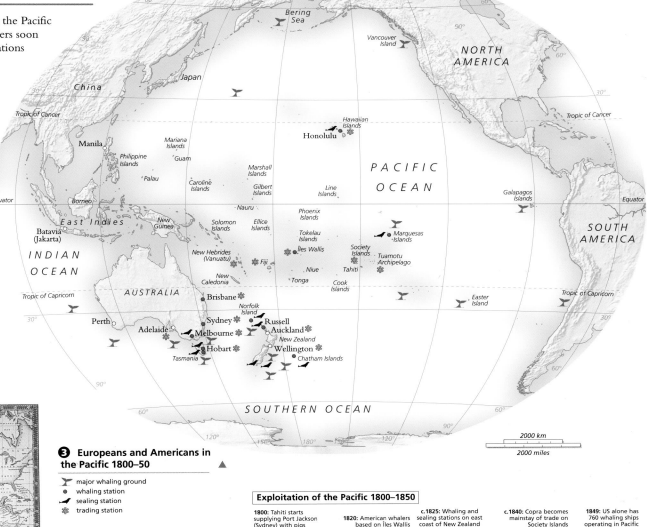

❸ Europeans and Americans in the Pacific 1800–50 ▲

- ⌄ major whaling ground
- ● whaling station
- ⚓ sealing station
- ✿ trading station

Knowledge of the Pacific expanded rapidly with the arrival of American and European whaling ships in the 19th century. By 1837, when this map was published, the picture was almost complete.

Exploitation of the Pacific 1800–1850

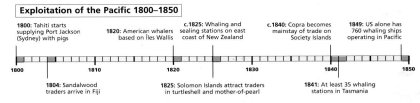

1800: Tahiti starts supplying Port Jackson (Sydney) with pigs	1820: American whalers based on Îles Wallis	c.1825: Whaling and sealing stations on east coast of New Zealand	c.1840: Copra becomes mainstay of trade on Society Islands	1849: US alone has 760 whaling ships operating in Pacific

1800 — 1810 — 1820 — 1830 — 1840 — 1850

1804: Sandalwood traders arrive in Fiji

1825: Solomon Islands attract traders in turtleshell and mother-of-pearl

1841: At least 35 whaling stations in Tasmania

PREHISTORIC OCEANIA

This fine carving from Rurutu in the Austral Islands shows the local god A'a.

DURING THE ICE AGES, Australia, New Guinea, and Tasmania were linked by land bridges to form the continent of Sahul. The first people to inhabit the region were Australoids, ancestors of today's Papuans and Australia's Aborigines, who may have reached Sahul as early as 60,000 years ago. The next significant wave of immigrants did not come until 6000 BCE, when Austronesian people fanned out through the Philippines and the East Indies. They mixed with the resident Australoids to produce the heterogeneous population of Melanesia. Around 1500 BCE the Austronesians, the greatest seafarers of prehistory, reached Fiji, and soon after that Samoa, starting point for later Polynesian expansion to the eastern Pacific and the eventual settlement of islands as far apart as Hawaii and New Zealand.

The spirit figure in this rock painting in Kakadu National Park is Barrginj, wife of Lightning Man.

The settlement of Australia, Tasmania, and New Guinea

No one knows exactly when or by what route the first settlers reached Australia and New Guinea. What is certain is that they would have had to cross a stretch of open sea. In the case of Australia, this was probably from the island of Timor, 70 km from the mainland when sea level was at its lowest. Although Australia enjoyed a better climate with higher rainfall than today, settlement would have been largely near the coast. Valuable archaeological evidence was lost when sea levels rose again at the end of the last Ice Age. At this point the Tasmanians, who may have been an early wave of immigrants, were cut off from the mainland.

❶ The settlement of Australia, Tasmania, and New Guinea

Archaeological sites with approximate date of earliest human presence

◇ pre 20,000 BCE
◆ post 20,000 BCE

→ probable migration routes
→ possible migration routes
--- maximum extent of Sahul landmass c.16,000 BCE
--- maximum extent of Sunda landmass c.16,000 BCE

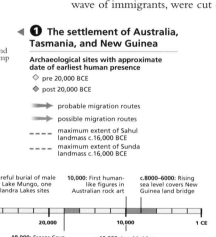

Map labels:
PACIFIC OCEAN
Sunda
New Guinea — Huon Peninsula 38,000 BCE
Klowa 8300 BCE
Yuku 8000 BCE
Matenkupkum 31,000 BCE
New Ireland
New Britain — Buka 24,000 BCE — Bougainville
Kafiavana 9000 BCE
Nawamoyn and Malangangerr 21,000 BCE
Kosipe 26,000 BCE
Misisil 10,000 BCE
Solomon Islands
Early Man Shelter 11,000 BCE
Timor
Minwun 16,000 BCE
8000–6000 BCE: New Guinea land bridge lost
Colless Creek 16,000 BCE
Sahul
Walkunder Arch 17,500 BCE
Coral Sea
Mount Newman 18,000 BCE
Puntutjarba 8000 BCE
Talgai 14,000 BCE
Kenniff Cave 17,000 BCE
Upper Swan 37,000 BCE
Allen's Cave 23,000 BCE
Menindee Lake 24,000 BCE
Willandra Lakes 33,000 BCE
Bass Point 15,000 BCE
Kings Table 20,000 BCE
Mammoth Cave 35,000 BCE
Roonka 16,000 BCE
Keilor 43,000 BCE
Clogg's Cave 15,000 BCE
Cohuna and Kow Swamp 60,000 BCE
Kalgan Hall 17,000 BCE
Cave Bay Cave 21,000 BCE
10,000–8000 BCE: Tasmanian land bridge lost
Fraser Cave 18,000 BCE

500 km / 500 miles

The settlement of Australia and New Guinea

| 60,000: Possible date of partial male skeleton found at Kow Swamp on Murray River | 40,000: Australoids start voyaging out towards Solomon Islands | 30,000: Careful burial of male body near Lake Mungo, one of the Willandra Lakes sites | 10,000: First human-like figures in Australian rock art | c.8000–6000: Rising sea level covers New Guinea land bridge |

| 60,000 BCE | 50,000 | 40,000 | 30,000 | 20,000 | 10,000 | 1 CE |

| 38,000: Campfire site on New Guinea's Huon Peninsula | 18,000: Fraser Cave on southern tip of Tasmania occupied | c.10,000: Land bridge connecting Australia and Tasmania starts to disappear |

Within their home range, most Aborigines led a largely nomadic life, following the food supply according to the seasons. The men were armed with spears for hunting, as in this rock painting; the women carried digging sticks and baskets.

Prehistoric agricultural development on New Guinea

The Australoids of Sahul were hunter-gatherers. However, as early as 10,000 BCE, New Guineans began clearing dense forests, placing them among the world's first crop gardeners. Remains of pigs and dogs dating from 4000–3000 BCE suggest these were brought to New Guinea by Austronesian immigrants, who also introduced techniques of taro cultivation and swamp drainage and management. These soon spread from coastal regions to the Western Highlands. The inhabitants of the Eastern Highlands, however, grew a different staple rootcrop, *Pueraria lobata*, while continuing to hunt and gather.

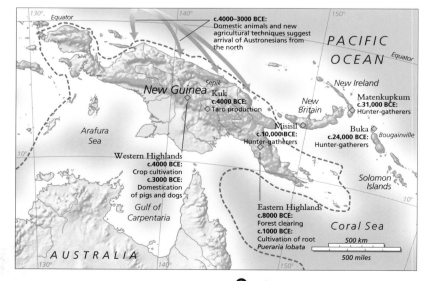

Map labels:
Equator
c.4000–3000 BCE: Domestic animals and new agricultural techniques suggest arrival of Austronesians from the north
PACIFIC OCEAN
New Guinea
Sepik
Kuk c.4000 BCE: Taro production
New Ireland
New Britain
Matenkupkum c.31,000 BCE: Hunter-gatherers
Misisil c.10,000 BCE: Hunter-gatherers
Buka c.24,000 BCE: Hunter-gatherers
Bougainville
Arafura Sea
Western Highlands c.4000 BCE: Crop cultivation c.3000 BCE: Domestication of pigs and dogs
Gulf of Carpentaria
Eastern Highlands c.8000 BCE: Forest clearing c.1000 BCE: Cultivation of root Pueraria lobata
Solomon Islands
Coral Sea
AUSTRALIA
500 km / 500 miles

❷ Prehistoric New Guinea

→ possible routes of Austronesians
--- maximum extent of Sahul landmass c.16,000 BCE
◇ archaeological site

Horticulture in New Guinea has changed little over 10,000 years. Yams, introduced from Asia by Austronesian peoples in about 4000 BCE, became a staple throughout the Pacific.

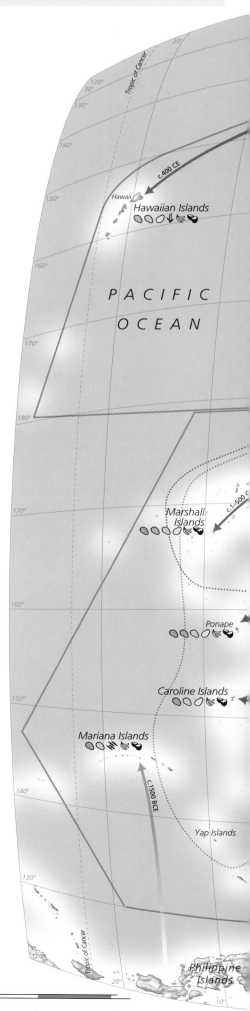

Map labels (right map):
Tropic of Cancer
Hawaii — Hawaiian Islands — c.400 CE
PACIFIC OCEAN
c.1500
Marshall Islands
Ponape
Caroline Islands
Mariana Islands
c.1500 BCE
Yap Islands
Tropic of Cancer
Philippine Islands

The peopling of the Pacific

Settlement of the Pacific was accomplished in two epic series of migrations. From about 2000 BCE Austronesian peoples settled Melanesia, sailing from the Philippines, the Bismarck Archipelago, the Solomons, and ultimately Fiji. Their spread can be charted by their distinctive Lapita pottery. The Fiji-Tonga-Samoa crescent was the cradle of a new, equally dynamic culture: the Polynesians. A major migration, probably from Samoa, to the Marquesas, was the springboard that launched the Polynesians to the remaining far-flung islands of the Pacific, from New Zealand in the south to Hawaii in the north and Rapa Nui (Easter Island) in the east.

Prehistoric migrations in the Pacific

c.6000: Migrations from Southeast Asia give rise to Austronesian culture	c.4000: Austronesians reach southwestern Pacific islands	2000: Austronesians settle New Caledonia	c.1000: Emergence of archaic Polynesian society in Fiji, Tonga, and Samoa	1000 CE: Almost all Pacific islands inhabited

6000 BCE   5000 BCE   4000 BCE   3000 BCE   2000 BCE   1000 BCE   1 CE   1000 CE

1600: Earliest datable Lapita pottery from Bismarck Archipelago

c.200: Migration of Samoans to the Marquesas

c.300 CE: Rapa Nui (Easter Island) settled

Many deities with a clear common ancestry appear in slightly different forms throughout Polynesia. This wooden carving of the war-god Ku was made in Hawaii in the early 19th century.

The boats used by the Polynesians for their great migrations were double-hulled canoes like this modern reconstruction. As well as staple crops, they took with them pigs, chickens, and dogs.

This ornate carved head of a Maori war canoe was recorded by a 19th-century illustrator. In cool, temperate New Zealand, the Maori way of life was very different from that of societies on smaller, warmer islands to the north, but in their arts and beliefs the Maori still display many aspects of their Polynesian roots.

Scale varies with perspective

11,580 km (7200 miles)

N

8890 km (5520 miles)

Rapa Nui (Easter Island)

Rapa Nui's history reflects its geographical isolation. Settled around 300 CE, it once supported a population of perhaps 7000. The society that erected the famous giant statues started to collapse around 1680. The once palm-covered island was by then denuded of trees. With no wood for boats and therefore no fish, islanders fought for control of the scarce food resources: chickens, bananas, sweet potatoes, and yams. Another catastrophe came in 1862 when some 1300 islanders, one third of the population, were carried off by Peruvian slavers.

Rapa Nui's statues were made to stand on stone platforms, altars sacred to the island's various clans. Many had topknots of red tufa. These examples were left near the quarry, when the society collapsed in the 17th century.

❹ Rapa Nui (Easter Island) ▼

- ▢ main area of statues
- ◇ restored statue site
- ● ceremonial centre
- ○ settlement
- ▣ quarry for red topknots
- ▢ quarry for statues
- △ mountain

❸ Austronesian and Polynesian migrations

- → migration between 2000 BCE and 1000 BCE
- → migration between 1000 BCE and 1 CE
- → migration between 1 CE and 500 CE
- → migration between 500 CE and 1000 CE
- → back migration c.500 CE
- ▢ Melanesia
- ▢ Micronesia
- ▢ Polynesia
- ◇ Lapita pottery site
- ◆ source of obsidian

Crops cultivated
- ‥‥ area of cultivated breadfruit
- ‥‥ area of cultivated taro
- atoll taro
- taro
- cassava
- yams
- sweet potato
- rice
- sugar cane
- bananas
- coconuts
- roots of native fern and cabbage tree

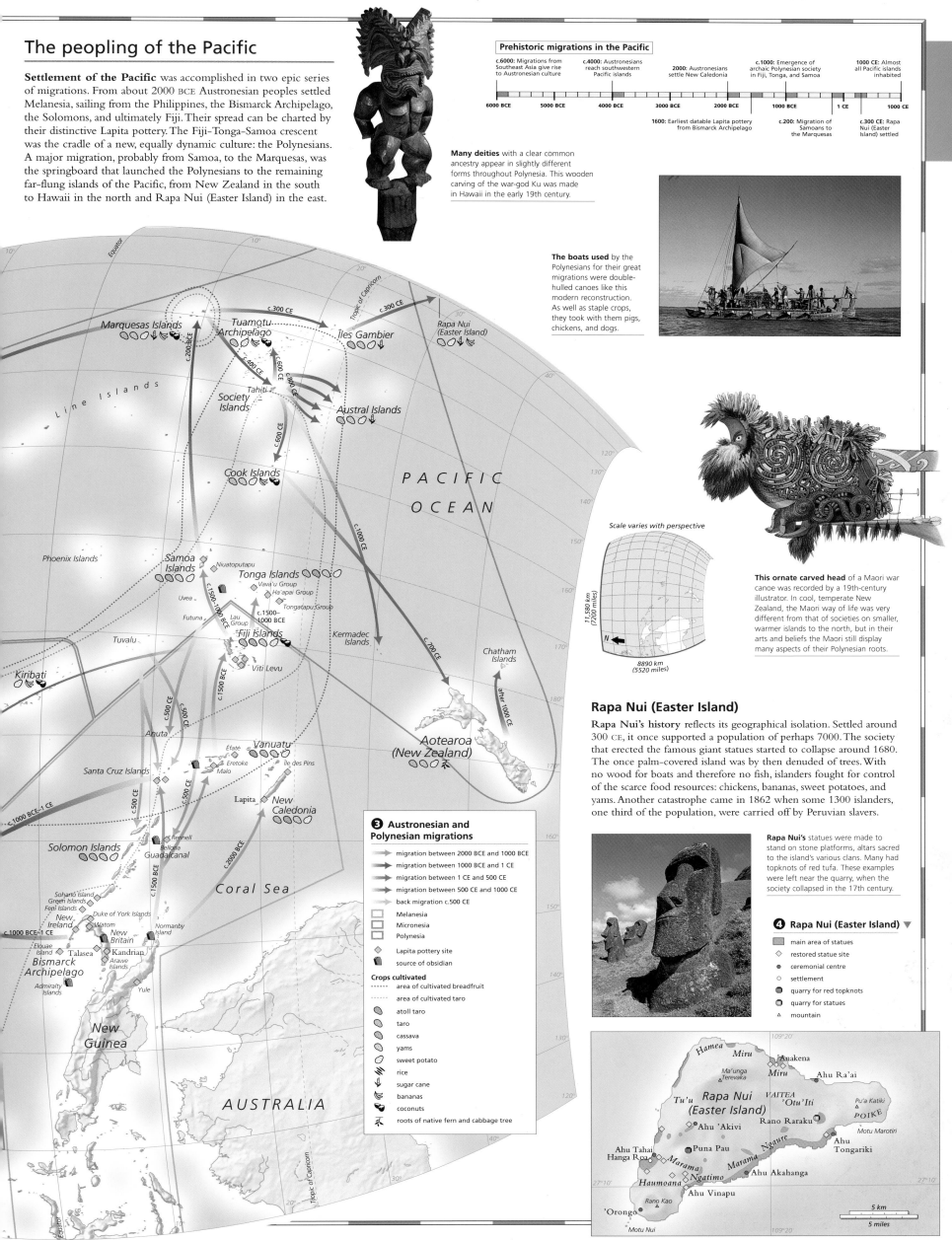

PACIFIC OCEAN

Marquesas Islands · Tuamotu Archipelago · Îles Gambier · Rapa Nui (Easter Island) · Society Islands · Tahiti · Austral Islands · Cook Islands · Line Islands · Phoenix Islands · Samoa Islands · Niuatoputapu · Tonga Islands · Vava'u Group · Ha'apai Group · Uvea · Tongatapu Group · Futuna · Lau Group · Fiji Islands · Viti Levu · Kermadec Islands · Chatham Islands · Tuvalu · Kiribati · Anuta · Aotearoa (New Zealand) · Vanuatu · Éfaté · Eretoke · Malo · Île des Pins · Santa Cruz Islands · Lapita · New Caledonia · Rennell · Bellona · Guadalcanal · Coral Sea · Solomon Islands · Sohano Island · Green Islands · Feni Islands · New Ireland · Watom · Duke of York Islands · Normanby Island · Elouae Island · Talasea · Kandrian · Arawe Islands · Bismarck Archipelago · Admiralty Islands · Yule · New Britain · New Guinea · AUSTRALIA · Equator · Tropic of Capricorn

Hamea · Miru · 'Anakena · Ma'unga Terevaka · Miru · Ahu Ra'ai · Tu'u · Rapa Nui (Easter Island) · VAITEA · 'Otu'Iti · Pu'a Katiki · POIKE · Ahu 'Akivi · Rano Raraku · Motu Marotiri · Ahu Tahai · Hanga Roa · Puna Pau · Marama · Ngaure · Ahu Tongariki · Haumoana · Ngatimo · Marama · Ahu Akahanga · Ahu Vinapu · Rano Kao · 'Orongo · Motu Nui

5 km / 5 miles

THE COLONIZATION OF AUSTRALASIA

Australian convicts working in road gangs wore distinctive dress and were chained.

THE BRITISH COLONIES in Australia and New Zealand rank with the US as the most successful transplantations of European culture to another continent. Neither colony had auspicious beginnings: Australia was where Britain transported its unwanted criminals; New Zealand was a convenient base for sealers and whalers in search of quick profits. In time, both started to attract emigrants from Europe in their tens of thousands. As in the US, the colonists simply drove out the native peoples by any means available. The Aborigines of Australia and the Maori of New Zealand were treated as obstacles to the progress of settlers who wanted to raise familiar European crops and livestock on their lands. In Tasmania, settlers wiped out the entire population in the space of 70 years.

THE FIRST FLEET AND BOTANY BAY

In January 1788, to the astonishment of the local Aborigines, a fleet of 11 British ships sailed into Botany Bay. On board were 778 convicts and their jailers. After his visit in 1770, Captain Cook had described Botany Bay as well-watered and fertile, but this proved untrue and the convicts were moved to Port Jackson, a natural harbour to the north. The penal settlement at Port Jackson grew to become Australia's largest city – Sydney. However, it was the name Botany Bay that stuck in the British imagination as the time-honoured destination for transported convicts.

A detachment of ships from the First Fleet sails to join the others anchored in Botany Bay.

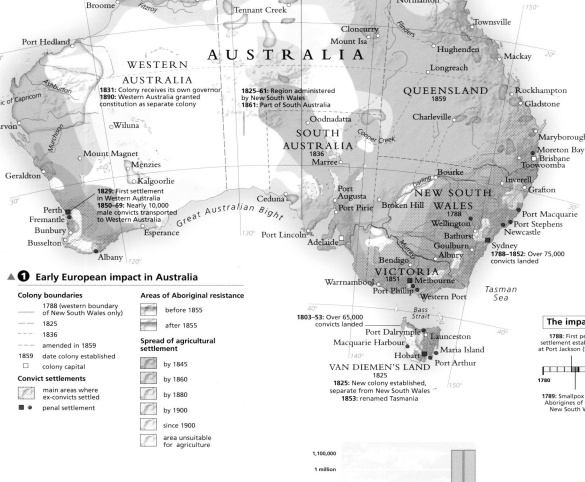

① Early European impact in Australia

Colony boundaries
— 1788 (western boundary of New South Wales only)
- - - 1825
···· 1836
—·· amended in 1859
1859 date colony established
□ colony capital

Convict settlements
▨ main areas where ex-convicts settled
■ penal settlement

Areas of Aboriginal resistance
▨ before 1855
▨ after 1855

Spread of agricultural settlement
▨ by 1845
▨ by 1860
▨ by 1880
▨ by 1900
▨ since 1900
▨ area unsuitable for agriculture

European impact in Australia

Britain's decision to colonize New South Wales was in part a result of the loss of its North American colonies, where convicted criminals had been transported in the past. The impact of the first convict settlement at Port Jackson (Sydney) indicated the course Australia's history would take. Aborigines living nearby were nearly wiped out by introduced disease, then driven off by force of arms. Further penal colonies were established, the most notorious being on Tasmania (Van Diemen's Land), where convicts were first landed in 1803. In 1821 over half the island's population consisted of convicts. Free immigrants came to New South Wales as early as 1793 and free colonies were established in Western Australia in 1829 and South Australia in 1836. The former suffered from a labour shortage, so convicts were shipped there in the 1850s. As the immigrant population grew, both with freed convicts and new settlers, pressure for new land for grazing resulted in frequent clashes between drovers and Aborigines.

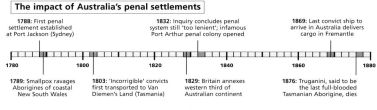

The impact of Australia's penal settlements

1788: First penal settlement established at Port Jackson (Sydney)	1832: Inquiry concludes penal system still 'too lenient'; infamous Port Arthur penal colony opened	1869: Last convict ship to arrive in Australia delivers cargo in Fremantle
1780 　 **1800** 　 **1820** 　 **1840** 　 **1860** 　 **1880**		
1789: Smallpox ravages Aborigines of coastal New South Wales	1803: 'Incorrigible' convicts first transported to Van Diemen's Land (Tasmania) / 1829: Britain annexes western third of Australian continent	1876: Truganini, said to be the last full-blooded Tasmanian Aborigine, dies

The lure of gold

The event that accelerated the growth of the Australian colonies was the discovery of gold in New South Wales and Victoria in 1851. The richest finds were at Bendigo and Ballarat, and in the 1850s more than 1000 tonnes of gold were dug up in Victoria. In a gold rush to rival that of California in 1849, the population of Australia trebled in less than a decade. A later gold rush occurred in the 1890s when gold was discovered at Kalgoorlie in the remote deserts of Western Australia.

Gold rushes in Australia 1851–1900

1851: First gold strike at Bathurst, New South Wales	1861: At Lambing Flat, white miners burn camps of 3000 Chinese miners	c.1890: Gold discovered at Kalgoorlie, Western Australia
1850 　 **1860** 　 **1870** 　 **1880** 　 **1890** 　 **1900**		
1854–55: Eureka uprising by Ballarat miners; police kill 45. In following year New South Wales and Victoria granted parliaments		1890: Western Australia last state to be granted self-government

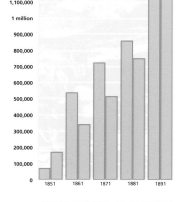

Population growth in Victoria and New South Wales 1851–91

▨ Victoria
▨ New South Wales

Miners pump water for gold-panning on a claim near Bathurst. Many who arrived in Australia in the 1850s were experienced prospectors from the California gold rush.

② Australian goldfields 1850–90

Discovery of goldfields
▨ 1850–60　■ 1860–70　■ 1870–90

Federation Australia

The Commonwealth of Australia was established in 1901 after referendums in the six states had voted for a federation. Throughout the 20th century, traditional agriculture and stock-rearing met problems through lack of water, and disasters such as a plague of introduced rabbits. After the Second World War, however, the country enjoyed a period of prosperity with the discovery of valuable mineral reserves and immigration was encouraged. In the late 1980s the Aboriginal population found a new political consciousness and began to lodge claims to traditional tribal lands.

Aboriginal protesters at the Australian bicentennial celebrations of 1988 display the Aboriginal flag to draw attention to two centuries of neglect and marginalization.

Federation Australia 1901–99

1901: Australia becomes self-governing federation within British Empire

1930s: Australia hit hard by global depression

1948: White immigration, especially from UK, becomes post-war policy

1975: Restrictions imposed on immigration

1988: Bicentennial celebrations occasion Aboriginal protests

1900 — 1920 — 1940 — 1960 — 1980 — 2000

1914–18: Over 60,000 Australian troops lose lives in First World War

1942: Australia under threat of invasion as Japanese bomb Darwin

1972: Labour government of Gough Whitlam challenges paternalistic attitude of UK to Australia

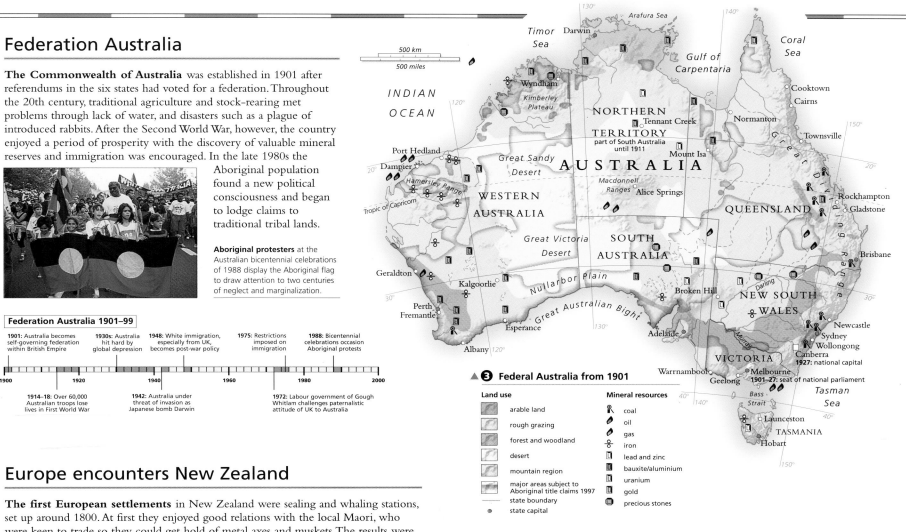

▲ ❸ Federal Australia from 1901

Land use
- arable land
- rough grazing
- forest and woodland
- desert
- mountain region
- major areas subject to Aboriginal title claims 1997
- —— state boundary
- • state capital

Mineral resources
- coal
- oil
- gas
- iron
- lead and zinc
- bauxite/aluminium
- uranium
- gold
- precious stones

Europe encounters New Zealand

The first European settlements in New Zealand were sealing and whaling stations, set up around 1800. At first they enjoyed good relations with the local Maori, who were keen to trade so they could get hold of metal axes and muskets. The results were disastrous: inter-tribal warfare took on a totally new character, tribes with muskets being able to massacre those without, and migrations spread the conflict throughout both islands. It was against this background that the New Zealand Company was set up to encourage British immigrants with assisted passages.

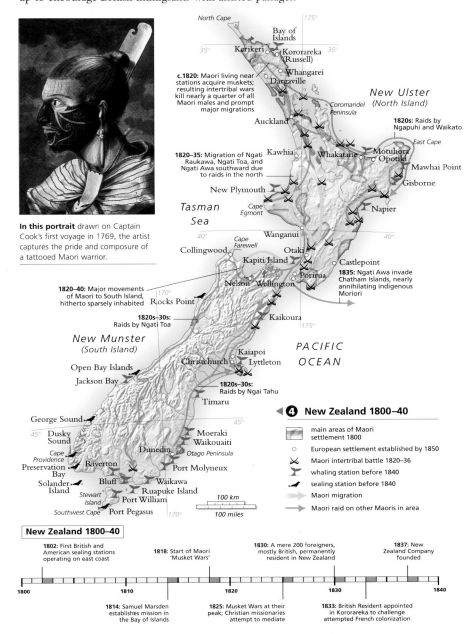

In this portrait drawn on Captain Cook's first voyage in 1769, the artist captures the pride and composure of a tattooed Maori warrior.

c.1820: Maori living near stations acquire muskets; resulting intertribal wars kill nearly a quarter of all Maori males and prompt major migrations

1820s: Raids by Ngapuhi and Waikato

1820–35: Migration of Ngati Raukawa, Ngati Toa, and Ngati Awa southward due to raids in the north

1835: Ngati Awa invade Chatham Islands, nearly annihilating indigenous Moriori

1820–40: Major movements of Maori to South Island, hitherto sparsely inhabited

1820s–30s: Raids by Ngati Toa

1820s–30s: Raids by Ngai Tahu

◀ ❹ New Zealand 1800–40

- main areas of Maori settlement 1800
- ○ European settlement established by 1850
- ✕ Maori intertribal battle 1820–36
- whaling station before 1840
- sealing station before 1840
- → Maori migration
- ⟶ Maori raid on other Maoris in area

New Zealand 1800–40

1802: First British and American sealing stations operating on east coast

1818: Start of Maori 'Musket Wars'

1830: A mere 200 foreigners, mostly British, permanently resident in New Zealand

1837: New Zealand Company founded

1800 — 1810 — 1820 — 1830 — 1840

1814: Samuel Marsden establishes mission in the Bay of Islands

1825: Musket Wars at their peak; Christian missionaries attempt to mediate

1833: British Resident appointed in Kororareka to challenge attempted French colonization

---

New Zealand becomes British

The Treaty of Waitangi, signed in 1840 by over 500 Maori chiefs, gave sovereignty over New Zealand to Britain, while guaranteeing Maori ownership of the land. In practice, the Crown – and later private individuals – purchased the land for trifling sums. In response to this, the Maori fought long, bloody wars against the intruders. Unlike Australia's Aborigines, who used hit-and-run tactics, the Maori waged sustained battles from fortified stockades and earthworks. After their defeat, they were reduced to marginal existence. Only in the 1990s did the Maori, some 15% of the population, start to receive substantial compensation for the wrongs of Waitangi.

New Zealand 1840–70

1840: Treaty of Waitangi

1845–46: Northern War, started by Ngapuhi chiefs deprived of trade when capital moved from Russell to Auckland

1860: Settler population over 100,000; Europeans outnumber Maori

1861: Gold discovered in Otago province

1870: Maori resistance effectively crushed

1840 — 1850 — 1860 — 1870

1841: New Zealand becomes a separate Crown Colony

1852: Constitution Act divides New Zealand into six provinces

1858: King Movement demands Maori state and opposes further land sales

1862: Second Maori War

c.1865: Some 14,000 British troops deployed in New Zealand

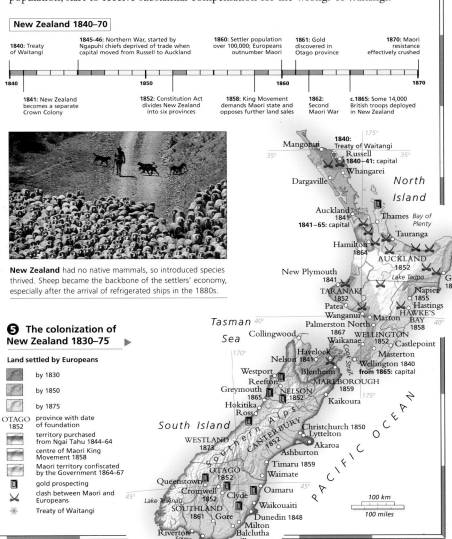

New Zealand had no native mammals, so introduced species thrived. Sheep became the backbone of the settlers' economy, especially after the arrival of refrigerated ships in the 1880s.

❺ The colonization of New Zealand 1830–75 ▶

Land settled by Europeans
- by 1830
- by 1850
- by 1875
- OTAGO 1852 province with date of foundation
- territory purchased from Ngai Tahu 1844–64
- centre of Maori King Movement 1858
- Maori territory confiscated by the Government 1864–67
- gold prospecting
- ✕ clash between Maori and Europeans
- ✳ Treaty of Waitangi

1840: Treaty of Waitangi

1840–41: capital

1841–65: capital

from 1865: capital

THE COLONIZATION OF THE PACIFIC

A Hawaiian surfer typifies the modern image of the Pacific as a vast playground for leisure pursuits.

THE 19TH CENTURY WITNESSED the near annihilation of many Pacific island societies. Firearms made intertribal warfare more lethal, but many more deaths were caused by alien diseases, especially measles and influenza. Killings by colonial powers as they asserted their authority, and 'blackbirding' (slave-raiding for labourers in the sugar-cane fields of Queensland and elsewhere) also contributed to the rapid depopulation of the islands. Many demoralized communities experienced an alarming fall in birth rate. However, subsequent repopulation by immigrant Europeans, Indians, Chinese, Japanese, North and South Americans rebuilt many island societies with new forms of trade, culture, and administration. European and American governments put in place political structures that, over time, enabled remnant Pacific peoples to survive as a host of new nations, territories and federations. Many of these now seek a wider forum. In the 1990s governments started to make calls for a 'United States of the Pacific'.

MISSIONARIES IN THE SOUTH SEAS

Throughout most of the Pacific, a region that had hitherto known only nature and ancestor worship, ancient values and practices were swept away by the arrival of Christianity. In the 17th century the Spanish founded missions in Micronesia, but by the mid-19th century Roman Catholic, Anglican, and Wesleyan missions were operating across Polynesia. Often the islanders' first contact with European customs, the missions paved the way for the wholesale Europeanization of Pacific cultures. Today a conservative, communal Christianity is the dominant feature of many Pacific island communities.

The high priest of Tahitian ruler Pomare II kneels before representatives of the London Missionary Society. The conversion of Pomare, who took control of Tahiti in 1815, was seen as a triumph for the society.

Imperialism in the Pacific

The expense of administering far-flung islands in the Pacific did not always appeal to the great 19th-century colonial powers. As a rule, they preferred to promise friendly rulers the status of protectorate. Towards the end of the century, however, colonial rivalry, especially between the French, Germans, and British led to the formal annexation of many territories. In larger territories, such as Fiji and Hawaii, where there was the possibility of establishing plantations, annexation was followed by the importation of large numbers of migrant workers.

❶ Imperialism in the Pacific ▶

Period of first European contact
- 16th century
- 17th century
- 18th century

European and US trading posts
- ✳ by 1700
- ✳ by 1850

Protectorates and colonies
- ○ protectorate with date established
- ◇ colony with date established
- ◇ Australian
- ◉ ◆ British
- ◇ Chilean
- ◇ Dutch
- ◉ ◇ French
- ◉ ◇ German
- ◇ Japanese
- ◆ NZ
- ◇ Spanish
- ◉ ◇ US
- ▬ Australian mandate 1920
- ▬ frontiers 1900

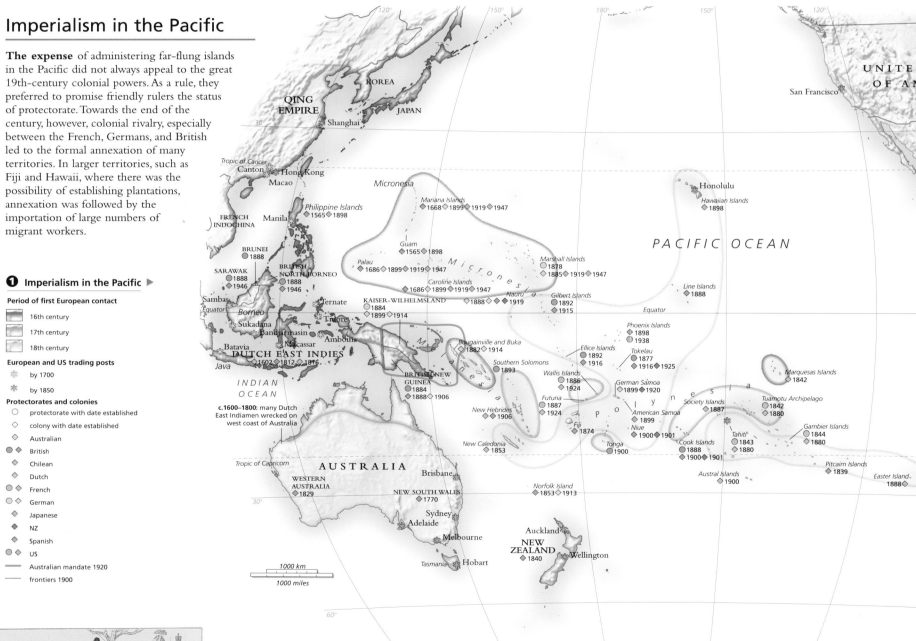

This pictorial proclamation, issued in Australia in 1829, aimed to show the fairness of British justice. If an Aborigine killed a European, he would be hanged; if a European killed an Aborigine, he would suffer the same fate. In practice, this ideal was very rarely implemented in any of the European colonies in the Pacific.

The colonization of the Pacific

1780 — 1788: The 'First Fleet' of convict settlers lands in New South Wales — 1800 — 1820 — 1840: Start of influx of British settlers into New Zealand — c.1850: Migrant workers begin arriving in Hawaii from China, Japan, the Philippines — 1864: First French convict settlers in New Caledonia — 1865–66: 1000 Chinese brought to Tahiti to work cotton plantation — 1860 — 1874: Indian sugar-cane workers arrive in Fiji — c.1870: Germans start to buy up large tracts of Western Samoa — 1880 — 1888: Chile starts colonization of Easter Island — 1898: US annexes Hawaii and seizes Guam from Spain — 1900

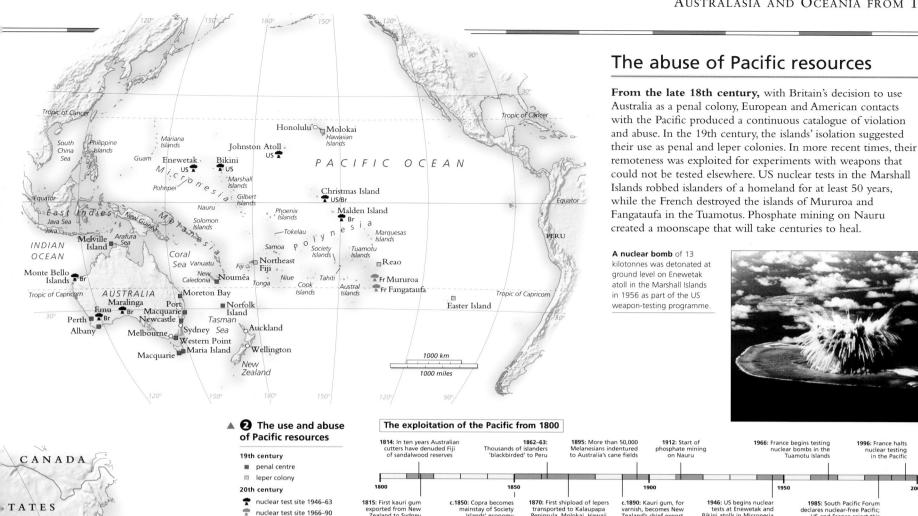

The abuse of Pacific resources

From the late 18th century, with Britain's decision to use Australia as a penal colony, European and American contacts with the Pacific produced a continuous catalogue of violation and abuse. In the 19th century, the islands' isolation suggested their use as penal and leper colonies. In more recent times, their remoteness was exploited for experiments with weapons that could not be tested elsewhere. US nuclear tests in the Marshall Islands robbed islanders of a homeland for at least 50 years, while the French destroyed the islands of Mururoa and Fangataufa in the Tuamotus. Phosphate mining on Nauru created a moonscape that will take centuries to heal.

A nuclear bomb of 13 kilotonnes was detonated at ground level on Enewetak atoll in the Marshall Islands in 1956 as part of the US weapon-testing programme.

▲ ② **The use and abuse of Pacific resources**

19th century
- ■ penal centre
- ▫ leper colony

20th century
- nuclear test site 1946–63
- nuclear test site 1966–90

The exploitation of the Pacific from 1800

1814: In ten years Australian cutters have denuded Fiji of sandalwood reserves

1862–63: Thousands of islanders 'blackbirded' to Peru

1895: More than 50,000 Melanesians indentured to Australia's cane fields

1912: Start of phosphate mining on Nauru

1966: France begins testing nuclear bombs in the Tuamotu Islands

1996: France halts nuclear testing in the Pacific

1815: First kauri gum exported from New Zealand to Sydney

c.1850: Copra becomes mainstay of Society Islands' economy

1870: First shipload of lepers transported to Kalaupapa Peninsula, Molokai, Hawaii

c.1890: Kauri gum, for varnish, becomes New Zealand's chief export

1946: US begins nuclear tests at Enewetak and Bikini atolls in Micronesia

1985: South Pacific Forum declares nuclear-free Pacific; US and France reject this

Decolonization and nationhood

Australia achieved nationhood on 1 January 1901, New Zealand six years later. However, in both countries the native peoples had been dispossessed by colonists. It was many years before colonized Pacific peoples were deemed to have reached political majority. The Second World War loosened colonial ties and encouraged a sense of national identity. In 1962 Western Samoa became the first indigenous Pacific state to achieve full nationhood. Within 18 years, eight others had followed. Today, a wide variety of political systems and free associations with former colonial powers coexist – from Tonga's independent monarchy to Hawaii's US statehood.

Western Samoa became fully independent from New Zealand in 1962. The capital Apia, with its post office and town clock, still has the look of a colonial town. Ties with New Zealand remain strong: the rising population and a shortage of jobs compel many islanders to migrate there in search of work.

1945: War in Pacific ends

1951: ANZUS security pact between Australia, New Zealand, and US

1971: First South Pacific Forum, annual meeting of heads of government

1987: Two military-led coups disrupt Fijian democracy

1998: End of bloody civil war in Bougainville

1962: Western Samoa gains independence

1983: Federated States of Micronesia and Marshall Islands enter free association with US

1997: First settlements in New Zealand's review of 1840 Treaty of Waitangi

The Pacific from 1945

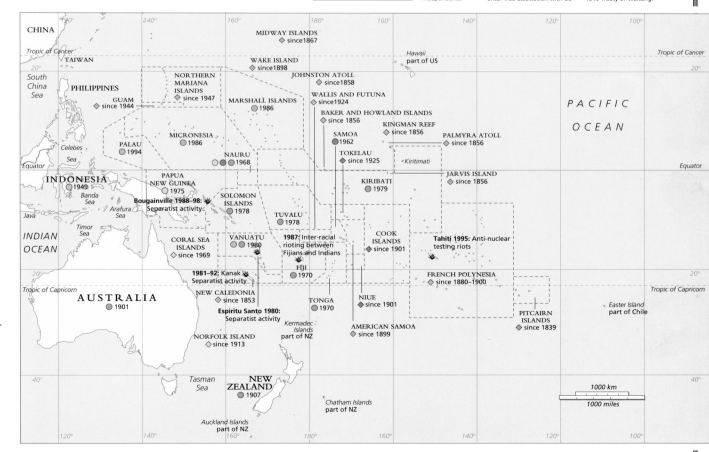

③ Decolonization and nationhood ▶

- ○ independent from (with date)
- ◇ dependency of
- ○◇ Australia
- ○◇ France
- ○ Netherlands
- ●○ New Zealand
- ○◇ UK
- ○◇ US
- ☩ conflict since 1980

THE ARCTIC AND ANTARCTICA
EXPLORATION AND MAPPING

The Norwegian
Roald Amundsen led expeditions to the Arctic and Antarctica.

THE FROZEN LIMITS OF THE GLOBE – the Arctic an icy ocean, the Antarctic an ice-capped mountainous continent – were not fully explored until the 20th century. Their hostile environment still provides a challenge for explorers. Viking sailors travelled to Iceland and Greenland in the 9th and 10th centuries, establishing settlements on both islands. Not until the 16th century were serious attempts made to forge a passage around the Arctic Ocean. Despite the efforts of those who braved the turbulent southern waters in search of a new continent, the Antarctic remained mysterious until the 20th century, when it was confirmed that it was indeed a continent rather than an ice mass linking a series of islands. Further knowledge of both the Arctic and the Antarctic was gained by air exploration and of the Arctic by the use of submarines.

The search for northern routes to Asia

Aiming to circumvent Iberian control of the central Atlantic, Dutch and British sailors sought northern routes to Asia and the Pacific during the 16th century. Early attempts to find a northeast route were sponsored by the Muscovy Company, and Richard Chancellor was able to set up a trading partnership with Russia. Willem Barents, experienced in Arctic conditions, reached Novaya Zemlya in 1596. Martin Frobisher's 1576 journey was the first to attempt a western passage. In 1585–87, John Davis travelled between Greenland and Baffin Island, reaching 72°N. Henry Hudson bore west, to enter the vast bay that bears his name in 1610, and William Baffin, piloting Hudson's ship, *Discovery*, traced the northern reaches of Baffin Bay, although all attempts to find a viable northern passage to the Pacific were unsuccessful until the 19th century.

② **Charting the Arctic coast and the race to the North Pole** ▶

The western Arctic
→ James Clark Ross (British) 1829–33
→ John Franklin (British) 1845–47
→ Roald Amundsen (Norwegian) 1903–06
→ Vilhjalmur Stefansson (Canadian) 1913–18

The eastern Arctic
→ Edward Parry (British) 1827
→ Nils Nordenskjöld (Swedish) 1878–79
→ Fridtjof Nansen (Norwegian) 1893–96

Exploring the North Pole
→ Robert Peary (American) 1909
→ Richard Evelyn Byrd (American) 1926
→ Umberto Nobile (Italian) 1926

Russian icebreakers
--- voyages of the *Taymyr* and *Vaygach* 1914–15
···· voyage of the *Sibiryakov* 1932

① **The search for new routes to Asia: explorers of the far north 1550–1820**

Northeast passage
→ Sir Hugh Willoughby and Richard Chancellor (English) 1553–54
→ Willem Barents (Dutch) 1556

Northwest passage
→ Martin Frobisher (English) 1576
→ John Davis (English) 1585–87
→ Henry Hudson (English) 1610–11
→ William Baffin (English) 1616
→ Alexander Mackenzie (British) 1789
→ John Franklin (British) 1819
→ Vitus Bering (Russian) 1728–30

500 km
500 miles

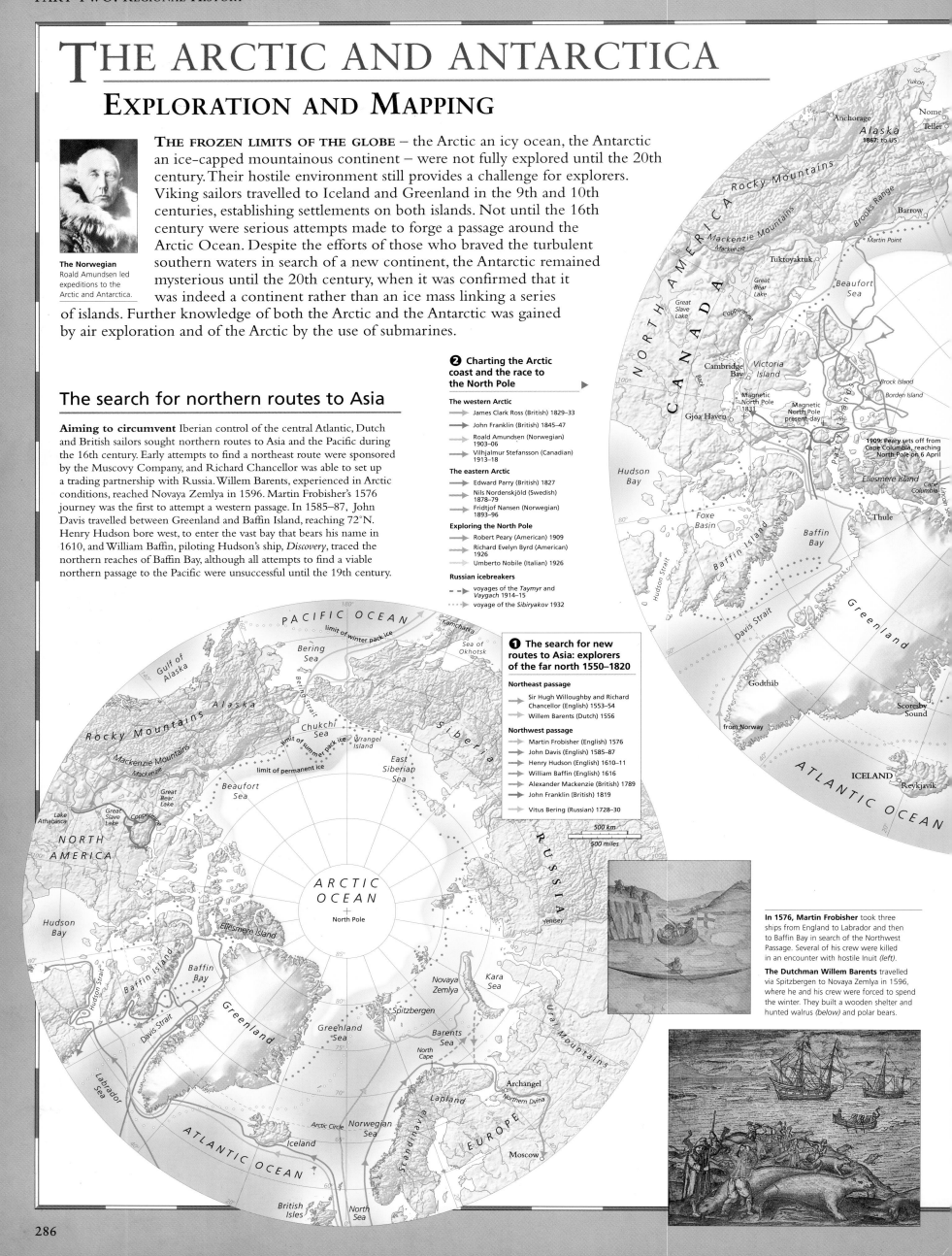

1909: Peary sets off from Cape Columbia, reaching North Pole on 6 April

1867: to US

In 1576, Martin Frobisher took three ships from England to Labrador and then to Baffin Bay in search of the Northwest Passage. Several of his crew were killed in an encounter with hostile Inuit *(left)*.

The Dutchman Willem Barents travelled via Spitzbergen to Novaya Zemlya in 1596, where he and his crew were forced to spend the winter. They built a wooden shelter and hunted walrus *(below)* and polar bears.

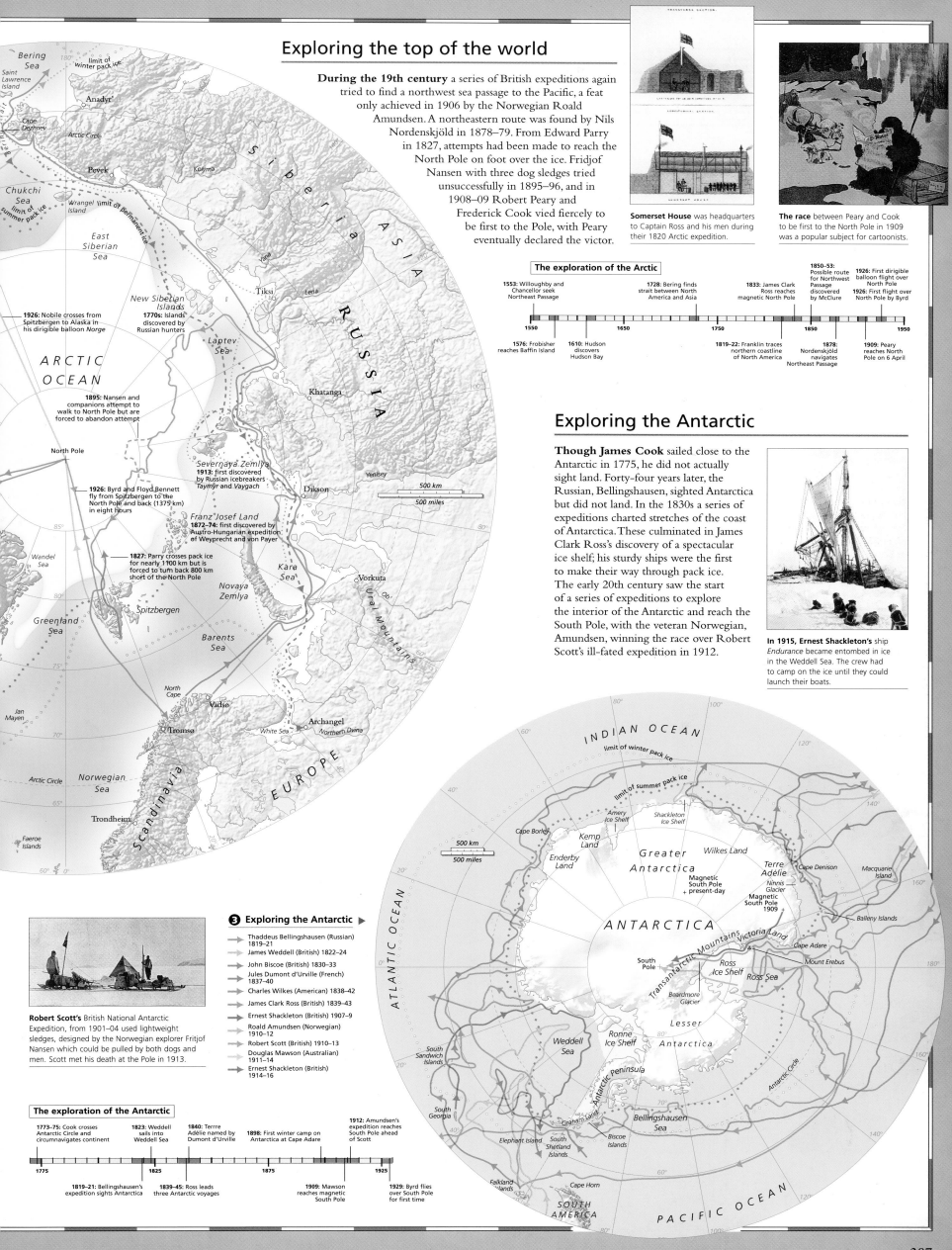

Exploring the top of the world

During the 19th century a series of British expeditions again tried to find a northwest sea passage to the Pacific, a feat only achieved in 1906 by the Norwegian Roald Amundsen. A northeastern route was found by Nils Nordenskjöld in 1878–79. From Edward Parry in 1827, attempts had been made to reach the North Pole on foot over the ice. Fridjof Nansen with three dog sledges tried unsuccessfully in 1895–96, and in 1908–09 Robert Peary and Frederick Cook vied fiercely to be first to the Pole, with Peary eventually declared the victor.

Somerset House was headquarters to Captain Ross and his men during their 1820 Arctic expedition.

The race between Peary and Cook to be first to the North Pole in 1909 was a popular subject for cartoonists.

The exploration of the Arctic

1553: Willoughby and Chancellor seek Northeast Passage

1728: Bering finds strait between North America and Asia

1833: James Clark Ross reaches magnetic North Pole

1850–53: Possible route for Northwest Passage discovered by McClure

1926: First dirigible balloon flight over North Pole

1926: First flight over North Pole by Byrd

1576: Frobisher reaches Baffin Island

1610: Hudson discovers Hudson Bay

1819–22: Franklin traces northern coastline of North America

1878: Nordenskjöld navigates Northeast Passage

1909: Peary reaches North Pole on 6 April

1926: Nobile crosses from Spitzbergen to Alaska in his dirigible balloon *Norge*

1770s: Islands discovered by Russian hunters

1895: Nansen and companions attempt to walk to North Pole but are forced to abandon attempt

1926: Byrd and Floyd Bennett fly from Spitzbergen to the North Pole and back (1375 km) in eight hours

1913: first discovered by Russian icebreakers *Taymyr* and *Vaygach*

1872–74: first discovered by Austro-Hungarian expedition of Weyprecht and von Payer

1827: Parry crosses pack ice for nearly 1100 km but is forced to turn back 800 km short of the North Pole

Exploring the Antarctic

Though James Cook sailed close to the Antarctic in 1775, he did not actually sight land. Forty-four years later, the Russian, Bellingshausen, sighted Antarctica but did not land. In the 1830s a series of expeditions charted stretches of the coast of Antarctica. These culminated in James Clark Ross's discovery of a spectacular ice shelf; his sturdy ships were the first to make their way through pack ice. The early 20th century saw the start of a series of expeditions to explore the interior of the Antarctic and reach the South Pole, with the veteran Norwegian, Amundsen, winning the race over Robert Scott's ill-fated expedition in 1912.

In 1915, Ernest Shackleton's ship *Endurance* became entombed in ice in the Weddell Sea. The crew had to camp on the ice until they could launch their boats.

Robert Scott's British National Antarctic Expedition, from 1901–04 used lightweight sledges, designed by the Norwegian explorer Fritjof Nansen which could be pulled by both dogs and men. Scott met his death at the Pole in 1913.

❸ Exploring the Antarctic

Thaddeus Bellingshausen (Russian) 1819–21
James Weddell (British) 1822–24
John Biscoe (British) 1830–33
Jules Dumont d'Urville (French) 1837–40
Charles Wilkes (American) 1838–42
James Clark Ross (British) 1839–43
Ernest Shackleton (British) 1907–9
Roald Amundsen (Norwegian) 1910–12
Robert Scott (British) 1910–13
Douglas Mawson (Australian) 1911–14
Ernest Shackleton (British) 1914–16

The exploration of the Antarctic

1773–75: Cook crosses Antarctic Circle and circumnavigates continent

1823: Weddell sails into Weddell Sea

1840: Terrre Adélie named by Dumont d'Urville

1898: First winter camp on Antarctica at Cape Adare

1912: Amundsen's expedition reaches South Pole ahead of Scott

1819–21: Bellingshausen's expedition sights Antarctica

1839–45: Ross leads three Antarctic voyages

1909: Mawson reaches magnetic South Pole

1929: Byrd flies over South Pole for first time

KEY TO MAP FEATURES

PHYSICAL FEATURES

—— coastline	········ ancient river course	▨ perennial lake	▨ ice cap / sheet	▵ elevation above sea level (mountain height)
········ ancient coastline	—— canal	▨ seasonal lake	▨ ice shelf	▲ volcano
—— major river	—— aqueduct	▨ perennial salt lake	▨ glacier	✕ pass
—— minor river	⊸ dam	▨ ancient lake	• • • summer pack ice limit	
----- major seasonal river	○ spring / well / waterhole / oasis	▨ marsh / salt marsh	◦ ◦ ◦ winter pack ice limit	

GRATICULE FEATURES

—— Equator	
—— lines of latitude / longitude	
----- tropics / polar circles	
45° degrees of longitude / latitude	

BORDERS

—— international border	----- maritime border
·········· undefined border	—— internal border
----- vassal state border	
·········· disputed border	

COMMUNICATIONS

—— major road	
—— minor road	
------ major railway	
━━━ railway under construction	

SETTLEMENT / POSSESSION

○ settlement symbol	
◇ colonial possession	

TYPOGRAPHIC KEY

REGIONS

state / political region...**LAOS**

administrative region within a state.... HENAN

cultural / undefined region / group...............*FERGHANA*

SETTLEMENTS

settlement / symbol location / definition...........Farnham

PHYSICAL FEATURES

continent / ocean.............*AFRICA*

INDIAN OCEAN

landscape features........*Mekong*

Lake Rudolf

Tien Shan

Sahara

MISCELLANEOUS

tropics / polar circles.................... *Antarctic Circle*

people / cultural group.. *Samoyeds*

annotation.....................**1914**: British protectorate

POLITICAL COLOUR GUIDE

◇ ○ China	◇ ○ Italy	◇ ○ Spain (Aragon)	◆ ○ New Zealand
◇ ○ Persia / Iran	◇ ○ Ottoman / Turkey	◇ ○ Portugal	◇ ○ Australia
◆ ○ Rome	◆ ○ England / Britain / UK	◇ ○ Netherlands	◇ ○ Belgium
◇ ○ Japan	◇ ○ France	◇ ○ Germany	◇ other state / cultural region
◆ ○ Norway	◇ ○ Denmark	◇ ○ Russia	
◇ ○ USA	◇ ○ Spain (Castile)	◇ ○ India	

(NB. the colours which identify political regions have, as far as possible, been used consistently throughout the atlas. Any variations are clearly identified in the individual map keys)

RELIGION COLOUR GUIDE

- Buddhism
- Islam
- Hinduism
- Confucianism / Taoism
- Christianity
- Roman Catholic
- Judaism
- other religion

GUIDE TO MAP INTERPRETATION

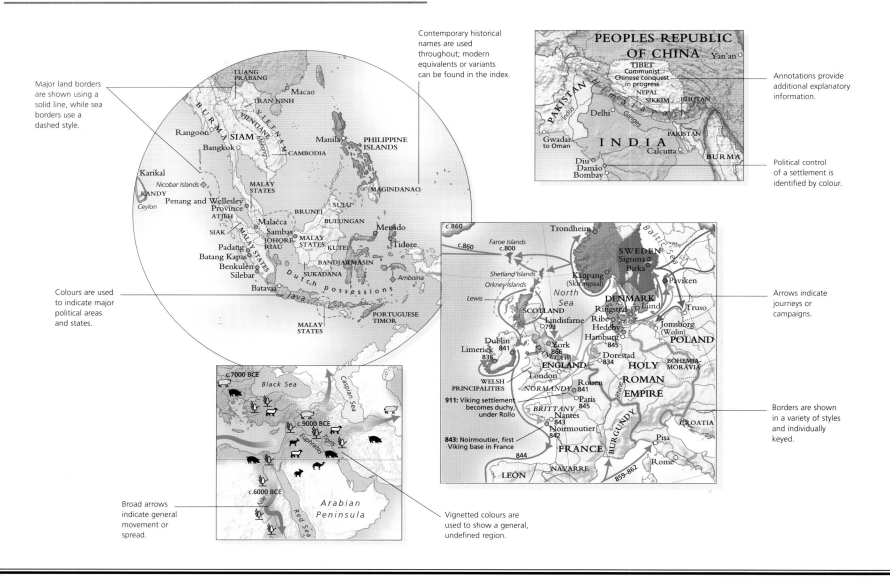

Major land borders are shown using a solid line, while sea borders use a dashed style.

Contemporary historical names are used throughout; modern equivalents or variants can be found in the index.

Annotations provide additional explanatory information.

Political control of a settlement is identified by colour.

Colours are used to indicate major political areas and states.

Arrows indicate journeys or campaigns.

Borders are shown in a variety of styles and individually keyed.

Broad arrows indicate general movement or spread.

Vignetted colours are used to show a general, undefined region.

SUBJECT INDEX AND GLOSSARY

In addition to acting as a page reference guide to the people, events and themes referred to in the Atlas, the Subject Index and Glossary is intended to provide supplementary information and explanation of those features which appear in the Atlas.

Page references are indicated using the following symbols:

- ✣ text reference ● timeline reference
- ◆ map reference, indicating page number and map number;
- ❑ picture/caption reference.

Dates in the Atlas are expressed in the following way:

BP Before Present. Generally used for dates more than 10,000 years ago.

BCE Before Common Era (indicating number of years before the supposed year of Christ's birth).

CE Common Era (indicating number of years since the supposed year of Christ's birth).

A

Abbas I (*aka* Abbas the Great) (c.1571–1629) Safavid shah of Persia (r.1588–1629). Crushed the Uzbek rebellions, and recovered Persian territories from the Ottomans, expelling them from Mesopotamia. In 1598 he established the Persian capital at Isfahan. ✣79, ✣219●, ✣231, ✣231●, ❑238
Abbasid Caliphate (c.750–1258). The second great Islamic dynasty, replacing the Umayyads in 750 CE. The Abbasid capital from 762 was Baghdad, from where they exercised control over the Islamic world until the 10th century. The last Abbasid Caliph was killed by the Mongols in 1258. ✣56, ✣227, ◆57 (2), ◆58–9, ◆227 (4)
  dynasty founded (750) ✣59, ✣61
  fragmentation (800–1055) ✣227, ◆227 (6)
  overthrown by Mongols (1258) ✣67●
  rulers of Baghdad ✣228
Abd al-Qadir (1830s). Algerian resistance leader ✣90, ✣91●
Abd al-Rahman ibn Umar al-Sufi 10th-century astronomer ✣59
Ahmad Khan *see* Ahmad Shah Abdali
Ahmad Shah Abdali (*var.* Ahmad Khan) (1724–73)
  founds Afghanistan (1747) ✣87●
Abdul Hamid II (1842–1918) Ottoman sultan (r.1876–1909). An autocratic ruler, noted for suppression of revolts in the Balkans, which led to wars with Russia (1877–78), and for the Armenian massacres (1894–96). His failure to modernize his empire led to his deposition in 1909, following a revolt by the Young Turks. ❑232
Abdul Majid I (1823–61) Ottoman sultan (r.1839–61). Urged by Western Powers, Abdul Majid I issued a series of liberal decrees, known as the Tanzimat (1839–61) to reform the judiciary and administration of the Ottoman Empire. ✣232●
ABM *see* Anti-Ballistic Missile
Aborigines Native people of Australia, who probably first settled the continent c.60,000 years ago. From c.8000 BCE, when the land bridge to New Guinea was severed by rising sea levels, they lived in more or less complete isolation until the 18th century CE. In the north, there was occasional contact with sailors from the islands of the Torres Strait and Indonesia. ◆280 (1), ✣282
  armed for hunting ❑280
  bicentennial celebrations ❑283
  British justice ❑284
  civilization destroyed ✣91
  dreamtime ✣280
  resistance to colonization ◆282 (1)
  rock carving ❑15
  spirit figure rock painting ❑280
Abreu, António de 16th-century Portuguese explorer. Embarked on a voyage to India in 1508. He set out for the Spice Islands in 1511, exploring Amboina, Sumatra, Java and parts of New Guinea. He was appointed governor of Malacca in 1526. ◆239 (1)
Abydos Royal tombs ✣25
Abyssinia (*var.* Ethiopia). Italian defeat at ⚔ of Adowa (1896) ✣95●
Academy Award first Oscar ceremony (1929) ✣35●
Acadia Founded (1604–08) ✣82●
Achaean League Confederation of Greek city-states of the northern Peloponnese, dating back to the 4th-century BCE. The league's traditional enemy was Sparta. It was after the league attacked Sparta in 150 BCE, that the Romans destroyed Corinth, the leading city of the league, and made Achaea a Roman province. ✣179
Achaemenes *see* Achaemenid Empire
Achaemenid Empire (c.550–330 BCE). Greek name for the Persian royal dynasty named after Achaemenes (Hakhamani), an ancestor of Cyrus II 'the Great'. From c.550 BCE, Cyrus presided over the expansion of the Persian empire, conquering Lydia, Phrygia, Ionia, and Babylonia. The empire lasted until 330 BCE, when Darius III was killed after his defeat by Alexander at ⚔ Gaugamela. ✣35, ◆34–5, ✣39●, ✣223, ✣223●, ◆223 (4)
Achin (*var.* Atjeh). The Indonesian island of Sumatra became, from the 7th century CE, the centre of a powerful Hindu kingdom, established by Indian emigrants. In the 13th century CE, Arabs invaded the Sumatran kingdom of Achin, which converted to Islam. At the end of 16th century, the Dutch attempted to gain supremacy in Achin, a struggle which was to last for the next three centuries. ◆245 (1) (2) ◆248 (1)
Acolhua, Aztec civilization ✣125
Acre Crusader loss (1291) ✣64●, ✣65, ◆64–5 (1) (2)
Acropolis Ancient Greek fortified hilltop citadel, the best-known being that of Athens, rebuilt by Pericles after the Persian invasion in the second half of the 5th century BCE. It comprised a complex of buildings including the national treasury and many shrines, mostly devoted to Athene, the city's patron goddess. ✣177
Act of Supremacy (1534). Parliamentary Act which recognized King Henry VIII, and every British sovereigns thereafter, as supreme head of the Church of England. ✣78●
Adelaide Founded 1835–36 ✣91, ◆279 (2)
Adena culture (c.500–100 BCE). A series of North American communities, based around what is now southern Ohio, formed the Adena culture. Principally hunter-gatherers, they built circular houses with conical roofs constructed of willow and bark, used stone tools and produced simple pottery. Finds of copper and shell ornaments indicate long-distance trade.
  BCE culture ✣30●, ✣34, ◆36 (1), ✣38●, ✣42●
  moundbuilders ◆121 (4)
Adowa ⚔ of Italian invasion of Abyssinia (1896). Serious Italian defeat put an end to Italian colonial ambitions in Ethiopia. A settlement after the battle acknowledged the full sovereignty and independence of Ethiopia, but preserved Italian rights to Eritrea. ✣95, ✣97
Adrianopolis ⚔ (378). Visigothic victory over Romans. ◆52–3 (1)
Aegospotami ⚔ of Peloponnesian Wars (405 BCE). Spartan victory over Athens. ◆177 (3)
Aelfred *see* Alfred the Great
Aelius Gallus Roman general of the 1st century BCE, who led his troops on an exploratory expedition into Arabia. ◆218 (1)
Aetolian League Federal state of Aetolia, in ancient Greece, which by c.340 BCE became a leading military power. Having successfully resisted invasions by Macedonia in 322 BCE and 314–311 BCE, the league rapidly grew in strength expanding into Delphi and allying with Boeotia c.300 BCE. ✣179
Afghanistan
  British protectorate ◆248 (2)
  founded (1747) ✣87●
  emergence of Taliban ◆235 (4)
  Mahmud of Ghazni's kingdom ✣59, ✣63, ◆227 (6)
  Marathas defeated at Panipat (1761) ✣87
  Persian subjugation (1722–36) ✣87●
  Second Afghan War (1878–79) ✣95●
  Soviet invasion (1979–89) ✣111●, ✣138
Africa Nova Roman province (146 BCE) ◆161 (2)
Africa 154–169
  BCE ✣14, 15●, ✣16, ✣19, ✣30, ✣34
  (c.1300) ◆68 (2)
  diaspora ✣112
  exploration and mapping
    14th–15th century ◆156 (3)
    Niger Basin ◆156 (1) (2)
    African interior (19th century) ◆157 (4)
    Boer (Afrikaner) treks ✣90, ◆166 (2)
  history
    colonization ✣39●, ✣42, ✣62, ✣66–7, ✣95 ✣169, ◆166–67 (1) (2) (4)
    complex societies ✣160–1, ◆160 (1)
    early history ✣158–9
    early modern ✣164–5
    historical landscape ✣154–5, ❑154, ◆154–5
    Islam and new states ✣162–3, ✣163●
    Muslim empire (1863) ✣95●
    post-colonial ✣168–9
    Roman province ✣43●, ✣46
  home affairs
    agriculture ✣82
    conflict and crisis ✣169, ◆169 (4)
    independence ✣107, ✣168, ◆168 (1)
    tribal conflict ✣90
    Zulu War (1879) ✣95
  innovations
    Nok sculpture (BCE) ❑38
  Northeast Africa
    rise and fall of kingdoms ◆161 (4) (5)
    trade ◆161 (3)
    political development ✣164, ✣166, ◆166 (1) ✣168●, ✣169●,
  religion
    Donatist schism (311) ✣50●
    Roman Christian rebellion (400) ✣50●
  struggle for the Horn (1500–1700) ◆165 (3)
  trade and industry
    economy in 1999 ✣168, ◆168 (2) (3)
    Arab coastal settlements ✣58
    commerce (19th century) ✣166, ◆166 (1)
    Eurasian and African ◆44–5
    gold ✣66, ✣70
    Indian Ocean network (13th century) ◆66
    iron-working ✣38
    links with Morocco ✣78
    links with Portugal ✣78, ✣79●
  and the spread of Islam ◆162 (1)
  see also Boers; individual countries; slavery; trans-Saharan trade
African Association Club formed in London in 1788 'for promoting the discovery of the interior parts of Africa'. ✣157●
African National Congress (ANC). Organization founded in S Africa in 1912 to promote equality for Africans. It was banned by the South African government in 1961, and although its leaders were jailed or forced into exile, became the focus for resistance to the apartheid regime. The ANC signed an agreement with the ruling Nationalists in 1990 and came to power under Nelson Mandela at the election of 1994. ✣169
Afrikaner South African of European descent whose first language is Afrikaans, a development of Dutch. *See* Boers
Aghlabids (*var.* Banu Al-aghlab). Arab Muslim dynasty that ruled Ifriqiyah in present-day Tunisia and eastern Algeria from 800 to 909 CE. The Aghlabids were nominally subject to the Abbasid caliphs of Baghdad but were in fact independent. ◆227 (4)
  dynasty founded (800) ✣58●
  expelled by Fatimids (909) ✣58●
Agincourt ⚔ of Hundred Years' War (1415). French defeat by English. ✣75●
agriculture
  advent and spread of ✣20–1, ◆18–19, ◆21 (2), ◆22–3, ✣34
  African ◆158 (1), ◆166 (1)
  Andean ✣147, ❑147
  Australian (1845–1900) ◆22 (1)
  development of technology ◆158 (1)
  diffusion of staple crops ✣73, ◆73 (3)
  domestication ✣21, ✣21●
  early settlements ✣120, ◆121 (1), ❑171
  E Asian revolution (6000–2000 BCE) ◆258 (1)
  Europe ✣62, ✣198, ◆198 (1)
  grindstones ✣16
  Maya civilization ✣50
  mechanized ✣90
  Pacific ✣281 (3)
  prehistoric New Guinea ✣280, ❑280, ◆280 (2)
  source of Egypt's wealth (BCE) ❑27
  S America ◆144 (1), ◆153 (3)
  See also farming; irrigation
Ahmad ibn Fadi Allan Al-'umari *see* al 'Umari
Ahuitzotl Aztec ruler (1486–1502) ◆124 (1)
Ahura Mazda Zoroastrian god ❑36
Ai Khanoum Hellenistic city. ✣21
  Silver disc ❑21
Ain Jalut ⚔ of Mongol invasions (1260). Mongol defeat ✣67●, ✣69, ✣229
Aistulf (d.756) Lombard king, who captured Ravenna from the Byzantines and threatened to take Rome. The pope summoned the Frankish King Pepin to defeat him. 183●
Ajanta Buddhist centre ❑43
Akbar (*aka* Akbar the Great) (1542–1605) Mughal emperor (r.1556–1605). Became emperor at the age of 14. For the first seven years of his reign, Akbar was engaged in permanent conflict, which left him the undisputed ruler of an empire which stretched from Bengal to Sind, and Kashmir to the Godavari river. He evolved a standardized tax system, incorporated the rulers of conquered territory into his own army, and introduced a policy of marriage alliances between the Mughal nobles and the Rajput princely families. He was tolerant towards the Hindu religion, and encouraged a great florescence in the arts, particularly in miniature painting and architecture, which was remarkable for its synthesis of western and Islamic styles. ✣79●, ✣246, ❑246, ◆78–9, ◆246 (1)
Akhenaton (*var.* Ikhnaton, Amenhotep, Amenophis IV) 18th Dynasty pharaoh of Egypt (r.1353–1336 BCE). A religious and cultural revolutionary who replaced the existing Egyptian pantheon with a monotheistic cult of the solar disc – Aten. He changed his name to reflect his beliefs, replaced the capital at Thebes with his own, El-Amarna (*var.* Akhetaten), and persecuted the older gods, expunging Amon's name from monuments across the country. A significant change in artistic style is representative of his rule, with both royals and commoners portrayed in a naturalistic rather than a formalized way. His unpopular religious reforms, and this artistic tradition, were reversed by Tutankhamun.
  Egyptian pharaoh ✣26, ✣27●, ❑28
  founds the city of El-Amarna ✣29, ✣29 (5)
  Great Palace fragment ❑29
Akkad *see* Sargon I of Akkad
Al-Azhar University established (970s) ✣58●
Al-Hajj Umar Ibn Said Tal *see* 'Umar Tal, Al-Hajj
Al-Idrisi *see* Idrisi
Al-Istakhri 10th-century Islamic geographer. ❑55
Al-Mu'tasim (794–842) Abbasid caliph (r.833–842). A son of Harun al-Rashid, al-Mu'tasim moved the Abbasid capital from Baghdad to Samarra. He waged war successfully against the Byzantines in Asia Minor and employed large numbers of Turkish slave soldiers, who subsequently became a powerful force in the Caliphate. (c.836) ✣59●
al-Rashid, Harun (*var.* Harun Ar-rashid, Ibn Muhammad al-Mahdi, Ibn al-mansur al-'Abbasi) (766/763–809). The fifth caliph of the Abbasid dynasty (786–809), who ruled Islam at the zenith of its empire. ✣58●, ✣227, ✣227●, ❑56, ❑227, ◆58–9
al 'Umari (*var.* Shihab Ad-din, Ahmad Ibn Fadl Allah Al-'umari) (1301–1349). Scholar and writer descended from 'Umar, the second Islamic caliph. His works on the administration of the Mamluk dominions of Egypt and Syria became standard sources for Mamluk history. ✣156
Alamo, The ⚔ of Texas Revolution (1836). Mexican victory. ◆129 (2)
Alans People who migrated to Europe from the steppes near the Caspian Sea. They joined the Vandals and Sueves in the Great Migration of 406 from Germany to the Iberian Peninsula. They briefly established a kingdom there, but were ousted by the Visigoths.
  migrations and invasions (300–500 CE) ✣50●, ✣182●, ◆52–3 (1)
Alaric (c.370–410). Chief of the Visigoths from 395 and leader of the army that sacked Rome in 410, an event that came to symbolize the fall of the Western Roman Empire. ✣50●, ✣53
Alaska
  Bering's first reconnaissance (1728) ✣86●
  discovery of gold (1880) ✣93
  Eskimos' Thule culture (c.900) ✣58●
  Russian expeditions ✣257, ◆119 (3) ✣128, ◆128–9(2)
Alaska Purchase (*aka* Seward's Folly). In 1867, US Secretary of State William H. Seward organized the purchase of Alaska from Russia for $7,200,000. ✣128–9
Alaung Phra *see* Alaungpaya
Alaungpaya (*var.* Alaung Phra, Alompra, Aungzeya) (1714–1760). King (r.1752–60) who unified Burma, and founded the Alaungpaya dynasty which held power in Burma until the British annexed the northern part of the region in 1886.
  founds Rangoon (1755) ✣87●
Albanel, Father Charles (1616–96). French Jesuit, who travelled in E Canada, reaching Hudson Bay and travelling along the Saguenay River, in search of fur-trading routes. ◆119 (2)
Albert, Prince of Saxe-Coburg-Gotha *see* Victoria
Albertis, Luigi Maria d' (1841–1901) Italian explorer of New Guinea. ◆279 (2)
Albigensians (*aka* Cathars). Heretical sect which flourished in southern France in the 12th century. It had little to do with Christianity; its most extreme followers believed in the evil of matter and aspired to reach the state of the 'perfect', those who had forsaken the material world. The Albigensian Crusade (1210–26) not only stamped out the heretics but also placed Toulouse and much of southern France under the control of the French crown.
  Albigensian Crusade ✣186●, ◆186 (1)
Aleut
  Arctic nomadic hunters ✣123
  sites ◆123 (3)
Alexander I (1777–1825) Tsar of Russia (r.1801–25). The early years of his reign were marked by attempts to reform Russia, but he failed to abolish serfdom. Initially a member of the coalition against Napoleon, but defeats at Austerlitz and Friedland led to Alexander concluding the Treaty of Tilsit (1807) with France. When Napoleon's invasion of Russia (1812) broke the treaty, Russia joined the Allied pursuit of the French to Paris. ❑201
Alexander III (*aka* Alexander the Great) (356–323 BCE) Greek emperor (r.336–323 BCE). Son of Philip II of Macedon, Alexander led one of the most rapid and dramatic military expansions in history, extended Hellenistic culture and conquest as far as India, founding cities and vassal-states throughout West Africa. ❑40
  conquests ✣38, ✣40, ✣223
  empire ◆38–9, ◆40–1 (1)
  expeditions ◆218 (1)
  legacy ✣41, ✣41l
  oracle worship ✣37
  Pompeii mosaic ❑39
  sarcophagus ❑40
  successors ✣224, ✣224●, ◆224 (1)
  death ✣38l, ✣39
Alexandria City founded by and named after Alexander the Great, on the delta of the River Nile. From the 3rd century BCE, for over a thousand years, the city of Alexandria became the commercial, cultural and scientific hub of all Eurasia, boasting the world's greatest library, and generating important schools of literature, poetry, drama, medicine, philosophy and cosmology.
  founded (332 BCE) ✣39●, ✣40●
  Christian centre (100 CE) ✣47●
  Classical scholarship ✣55
  Muslims at prayer ❑113
Alexius IV (d.1204) Byzantine emperor (r.1203–1204). He ascended the throne with the help of the Fourth Crusade but was deposed a year later by a national revolt. ✣187
Alfonso VI (*aka* Alfonso the Brave, *Sp.* Alfonso El Bravo) (1040–1109). King of León (r.1065–70) and king of reunited Castile and León (1072–1109), who by 1077 had proclaimed himself 'emperor of all Spain'. His oppression of his Muslim vassals led to the invasion of Spain by an Almoravid army from North Africa in 1086.
  takes Toledo (1085) ✣64●
Alfred the Great (*var.* Aelfred) King of Wessex (r.871–899). Ruler of a Saxon kingdom in SW England. He prevented England from falling to the Danes and promoted learning and literacy. Compilation of the Anglo-Saxon Chronicle began during his reign, c. 890.
  reconquers London (885) ✣58●
Algeria
  French invasion (1830) ✣90, ✣232
  industrial growth ✣168, ◆168 (2)
  Islamic fundamentalism ✣235●
  uprising against France (1954) ✣107●
Algonquin N American sub-Arctic nomadic hunters ✣123
  war with Iroquois (1609) ✣126●
Alhambra Moorish palace in Granada, S Spain ❑192
Allegheny River Survey (1729) ✣119●
Allies (*aka* Allied Powers). General term applied to the victorious Great Powers at the end of WW I (after the US joined the Entente Powers – Britain, France, Russia – in 1917). More generally used to describe the alliance ranged against the Axis powers during WW II headed by Britain, France, Poland, and the USSR and US (from 1941). ✣◆104–5●, ◆✣206–211●
Allied Powers *see* Allies
Allouez, Father Claude (1622–89). French Jesuit missionary who explored the Great Lakes region of N America as well as the St. Lawrence River, setting up missions in present-day Wisconsin.
  expedition (1665–67) ◆119 (2)
Almagro, Diego de (1475–1538) Spanish *conquistador*. Companion of Pizarro in the conquest of Peru in 1532. In 1535 he set off southward in an attempt to conquer Chile. He later quarrelled with Pizarro and civil war broke out between their followers. ◆142 (1)
Almohad dynasty (1130–1269). Muslim dynasty. Founded by a revival Muslim revival movement, the Almohads eventually commanded North Africa as far east as Tripoli, as well as controlling most of the Iberian peninsula. ◆186 (1), 192●, ◆192 (3)
  defeated by Marinids (1269) ✣67●
  empire collapses (1228) ✣67●
  in Morocco and Spain (1147) ✣63●
  takeover of Almoravids (1128) ✣63●
Almoravid Empire Confederation of Berbers whose religious zeal and military enterprise built an empire in NW Africa and Muslim Iberia in the 11th and 12th centuries. ◆192 (3)
  12th century ✣62–3
  invasion of Ghana ✣163
  in N Africa and Iberia (c.1050) ✣63
  reconquest of Spain ✣192, ✣192●, ◆192 (3)
  takeover by Almohads (1128) ✣63●
Alodia Coptic Christianity ✣58
Alompra *see* Alaungpaya
alphabet *see* writing

Key to index: ✣ text ● timeline ❑ picture ◆ map *var.* variant name *aka* also known as *f/n* full name *prev.* previously known as r. ruled ⚔ battle WW I First World War WW II Second World War

SUBJECT INDEX AND GLOSSARY: **Atlantic Ocean – Benin**

use of air cover and the convoy system. ✤210●, ✤211 (2)
Atlantic Ocean
coastal expeditions ✤118
convoy system (1564) ✤81●
shipping routes (1870–1910) ◆92 (1)
Atlas Contractus (Visscher) ❑119
Atlas Major (Blaeu) ✤83
Atlas (Ortelius) ✤173●
Atlas sive cosmographicae meditationes (Mercator) ✤173●
Aton *see* Aten
Atsugashi-yama ⚔ (1189). Defeat of Fujiwari clan. ◆265 (5)
Attalid Dynasty (282–133 BCE). Line of rulers, founded by Philetaerus, of a kingdom of Pergamum, in northwest Asia Minor, in the 3rd and 2nd centuries BCE. ✤40
Attila the Hun (c.400–453). Ruler of the Huns from c.445. Attila devastated much of the East Roman Empire and forced the emperor to pay tribute and grant his people lands in the Balkans. In 451 he invaded Gaul, but was defeated by a Roman and Gothic army at the battle of the Catalaunian Fields. After one more raid – into northern Italy in 452, when the Huns destroyed Aquileia – he died and his empire rapidly disintegrated.
✤50●, ✤53, ◆50–1.
See also Huns.
Augusta ⚔ of American Revolutionary War, 29 Jan 1779, British victory. ◆127 (3)
Augustine of Hippo, St. (354–430). Christian bishop and theologian, author of *The City of God*. ◆52 (1)
Augustine, St. (St. Augustine of Canterbury) (d.604). Christian missionary, who travelled to Britain in 597. His mission led to the conversion of many of the southern Anglo-Saxon kingdoms of Britain.
Papal missionary (597) ✤54●, ✤183●
Augustus Caesar (*var.* Octavian) (63 BCE–14 CE) First Roman emperor (27 BCE–14 CE). Octavian was the great nephew and adopted heir of Julius Caesar. On Caesar's death, he gradually won control of the Roman Empire, completing the task with his defeat of Mark Antony and Cleopatra. The Roman senate then granted him the title Augustus and guaranteed his authority for life. ✤42, ✤46●, ✤180
Aungzeya *see* Alaungpaya
Aurangzeb (1618–1707) Mughal emperor (r.1658–1707). The first Mughal emperor to conquer the sultans of the Delhi Sultanate and to extend his authority to the extreme south, Aurangzeb fought hard to maintain Mughal supremacy in the face of opposition from the Maratha Confederacy. His long reign was harsh and repressive, leading ultimately to the revolt and secession of many provinces. ✤83●, ✤87●, ❑246
Aurelius, Marcus *see* Marcus Aurelius
Aurignacian tool technology Technology which evolved in the Middle East about 45,000 years ago. Small flint tools were set into wooden or bone handles and spread rapidly throughout S Europe. ✤15●
Austerlitz ⚔ of Napoleonic Wars (1805). Russian/Austrian defeat by French forces. The victory that gave Napoleon virtual control of mainland Europe.
✤90●, ◆200–1 (1)
Australia 276–285
colonization
✤282–3
Botany Bay settled (1788) ✤87●
British (1829) ✤91
Federation (from 1901) ✤99●, ✤283, ✤283●, ◆281 (3)
Pacific imperialism ◆284 (1)
Pacific nationhood ✤285, ◆285 (3)
desert landscape ❑276
exploration and mapping ✤279, ❑279, ◆279 (2)
foreign affairs
possessions
1925 ◆98–9
1950 ◆102–3
1975 ◆106–7
home affairs
British justice ❑284
dingo introduced (c.2500 BCE) ✤27●
early European impact ◆282 (1)
gold fields ✤282, ❑282, ◆292 (2)
mineral finds (late 19th century) ◆93 (2)
penal settlements ✤91, ✤282●, ✤285, ❑282, ◆282 (1)
population growth (1851–91) ❑282
settlement ✤280, ✤280●, ◆280 (1)
whaling ✤279●
rock engravings ✤17, ◆17 (5)
rock painting ❑280
WW II, mobilization and casualty figures ✤105
Australoids People who colonized Australia and New Guinea some 60,000 years ago: the ancestors of the Australian Aboriginals and the Papuans. ✤280
Australopithecines (meaning 'southern ape'). The genus of ape-like, bipedal hominids which evolved in eastern Africa over 4 million years ago. Several species of *A. Australopithecus* have been identified, based on variations in skulls and teeth. It is still uncertain whether these early hominids are the precursors of fully modern humans, or represent a separate evolutionary line. ✤12
Australopithecus afarensis Present from c.4 to 3.2 million years ago, *A. afarensis* is represented by the virtually complete 3.4-million year-old skeleton of an adult female, known as 'Lucy' found in the Hadar region of Ethiopia. *A. Afarensis*, with its ape-like body and small brain, is seen as crossing the line from ape to human. ✤12
Australopithecus africanus (c.3 to 2 million years ago). Found in cave sites of southern Africa, *A. Africanus* is distinguished by higher, rounder braincase than *A. Afarensis*, more powerful teeth and long powerful arms. ✤12
Australopithecus anamensis Represented by 4.2-million-year-old fossils found near the shores of Lake Rudolf in Kenya. The oldest known member of the Australopithecine genus. ✤12
Australopithecus boisei (c.2.7 to 1.7 million years ago). A robust species found in eastern Africa, distinguished by a powerful upper body, long upper jaw and the largest molars of any hominid. ✤12
Australopithecus genus ✤12, ◆12 (1), ✤154,
Australopithecus robustus (c.2 to 1 million years ago). Found in southern Africa, and distinguished by heavy jaws, a brow ridge , a bony crest along the top of the skull, and a larger brain capacity than any other Australopithecine. ✤12
Austria 188–9, 193–203, 207–214
alliances opposing France (1792–1815) ✤201, ◆201 (3)
consolidation and resistance (17th century)
✤196, ✤196●, ◆196 (2)
Empire, 1850 ◆90–1
European power ✤197
Habsburg possessions
1200–1400 ◆189 (4)
1400 ◆70–1
1500 ◆74–5, ◆193 (4)
1600 ◆78–9
1700 ◆82–3
1795 ◆199 (3)
Habsburg territories 1800 ◆86–7
Napoleonic Wars (1805) ✤90●
partition ✤212, ◆212 (1)
rise of Brandenburg Prussia ✤199, ◆199 (3)
Treaty of Westphalia, ◆196 (1)
unification of Germany ✤203, ◆203 (2)
See also Habsburg Empire
Austria-Hungary
dual monarchy (1867) ✤94●
First World War *see* Wars, First World
rivalry with Germany ✤98
Austrian Succession, War of the (1740–48) On the succession of Maria Theresa to the Austrian throne, Frederick II of Prussia seized Silesia. France allied with Prussia, while Britain formed an alliance with Austria. In Italy, Austria confronted a Bourbon alliance of France and Spain. The war involved conflict in Silesia, Austria, the Austrian Netherlands, southern Germany, Italy, India and North America. At the end of the war Prussia's seizure of Silesia was recognized. ✤199●
Austronesians People who spread southeast from Asia through Indonesia c.6000 BCE, reaching New Guinea and the Bismarck Archipelago, from where they set out into the Pacific on voyages of colonization. The Austronesian language group includes most of the languages of Indonesia, all the Polynesian languages, and the language of Madagascar.
migrations ◆282 (3)
settlement of Pacific ✤281
automobiles *see* transport
Avar Empire *see* Avars
Avars Steppe nomads who migrated westwards in the 6th century. In the 7th century they settled on the Danube Plain where they ruled the local Slavic population. Their empire was totally crushed by Charlemagne in 796. ✤54● ◆54–5, ✤184, ◆184 (1)
See also Ruanruan
Averroes (b.1126) Muslim philosopher. ✤187●
Avidius Cassius Gaius (d.175 CE). Roman military commander. The son of one of Hadrian's civil servants, Avidius Cassius directed Rome's wars with the Parthians (161–65), and became commander of all the military forces in the eastern provinces. He usurped the throne for three months in 175 on hearing a false rumour of Marcus Aurelius' death, but was assassinated by one of his soldiers before Aurelius could arrive to confront him. ✤47
Avignon Papal residence (1309) ✤70●
Avila, Pedro Arias *see* Davila, Pedrarias
Axayacatl Aztec ruler (1469–81) ◆124 (1)
Axis (*var.* Axis Powers). General term for Germany, Japan and Italy during WW II. Originating with the Pact of Steel (*var.* Axis Pact) between Germany and Italy (May 1939), consolidated by Tripartite Pact between Germany, Italy and Japan (Sep 1940) assuring mutual military, political and economic assistance in the event of war spreading beyond Europe.
◆104–105, ◆210–211
Sep 1939–Dec 1941 ◆104 (1)
Dec 1941–Jul 1943 ◆104 (2)
Jul 1943–Aug 1945 ◆104 (3)
global warfare ◆104 (4)
WW II nationalist states ✤104
Axis Powers *see* Axis
Axum ◆161 (3) (4) (5)
converts to Christianity (c.330) ✤50●
incense trade ✤46
kingdom emerges (c.50) ✤47●
major trading power ✤161
Meroë kingdom invasion (c.350) ✤50●
Roman-Indian trading link ✤50
stone stelae ❑161
Ayacucho ⚔ of wars of S American liberation (Dec 1824). Victory by Sucre liberated upper Peru (Bolivia). ◆150 (1)
Ayuthia *see* Ayutthaya
Ayutthaya (*var.* Ayuthia). Capital of Siam founded c.1350. ✤71●
Ayyubid dynasty (1171–1250). Sunni Muslim dynasty founded by Saladin. The Ayyubids ruled most of the Middle East and Egypt until 1250, when they were defeated by the Mamluks.
founded (1174) ✤63●
Aztec Empire (mid-14th century–1521). Dominant state in Mexico before the Spanish conquest of the 16th century. Centred on the valley of Mexico, the empire grew to include most of central and southern Mexico and was the focus of a sophisticated civilization.
✤66, ✤74, ✤78, ✤124, ◆76 (2), , ◆124 (1) (2) (3), ◆125 (4) (5)
conquered by Hernán Cortés (1519–22)
✤78, ✤81●, ✤125, ◆125 (5)
cosmology ❑124
entry into valley of Mexico ✤122●
expansion ◆124 (1)
human sacrifice ❑74
rise and fall ✤124●
rulers ✤74●, ✤78●, ✤124
triple alliance (1434) ✤74●

B

Babur (*var.* Babar, Baber) (1483–1530) Founder of the Mughal dynasty (r.1526–30). At the battle of Panipat (1525) Babur confronted the forces of the Afghan Lodi sultans, and occupied Delhi and Agra. By 1530 his empire stretched from the Oxus to the frontier of Bengal and from the Himalayas to Gwalior.
✤79, ✤246, ✤246●, ◆246 (1)
Babylonian Empires (c.1795–1538 BCE) (612–539 BCE). Ancient empires of southern Mesopotamia. The first Babylonian empire was created by Hammurabi (c.1795–1750 BCE), with Babylon on the Euphrates as its capital. Following a Hittite attack in c.1595, the Empire was ruled by the Kassites for 400 years. The second empire was established following the overthrow of Assyria in 612 BCE. Under its greatest ruler, Nebuchadnezzar II (605–562 BCE) it extended into Mesopotamia, Egypt and Palestine. It was brought to an end by the Persian conquest of 539–538 BCE.
astronomy ❑31, ✤39
city-state ✤27
conquest of Egypt (BCE) ✤34
Empire (612–539 BCE) ✤34–5, ✤222, ◆222 (2)
mapping ❑34
rebuilt by Nebuchadnezzar II (604 BCE) ✤35●
Bacon's Rebellion (1676). N America. Attempt by Nathaniel Bacon, a Virginia planter, to expand into Indian territory. It was denounced by Governor William Berkeley as a rebellion, and Bacon, in response, turned his forces against Berkeley and for a while had control over most of Virginia. ✤126, ◆126 (1)
Bactria
classical world trade ◆44–5
coin showing King Demetrios ❑41
invaded by Kushans ✤47
plaque ❑261
secession ✤43
Baecula ⚔ of Punic Wars (208 BCE). Roman victory over Carthage. ◆179 (3)
Baffin, William (1584–1622) English navigator who searched for a Northwest Passage to Asia. He discovered Baffin Bay and used the position of the moon to determine longitude at sea. ✤239●, ◆286 (1)
Baghdad
Abbasid capital ✤59●, ✤227, ❑227, ◆227 (5)
arts and learning centre (786) ✤59●
Black Death (1347) ✤71●
captured by Buwayhids (945) ✤59●
Egypt's independence (969) ✤58
sacked by Mongols (1258) ✤67, ✤69●, ✤229, ❑229
sacked by Timur (1393) ✤71●
slave trade (9th–10th century) ✤85
Turkish control (936) ✤59●
Bahamas Columbus lands (1492) ✤80●, ✤118●, ✤125●
Bahia (*var.* Salvador). Capital of Brazil (1549–1763).
clay sculpture ❑145
royal rule imposed (1549) ✤149●
Bahmani Kingdom (1347–1583). The earliest Muslim dynasty in the Deccan, founded by Alauddin in 1347, with its capital at Gulbarga. The Bahmani kingdom disintegrated into five independent Deccani kingdoms towards the end of the 14th century. ✤245, ◆74–5, ◆245 (4)
Bahram V (d.439) Sassanian king (421–439) ❑51
Bajazet *see* Bayazid
Baker, Samuel (1821–93). English explorer who, with John Hanning Speke, helped to locate the source of the Nile (1861–65). ◆157 (4)
Baku Azerbaijan, oil production (c.1900) ✤234●
Balaton ⚔ of WW II (Mar 1945). Battle in NE Hungary in which a Soviet counter-offensive destroyed German military strength in SE Europe. ◆211 (4)
Balboa Núñez de, Vasco (c.1475–1519). Spanish conquistador and explorer. On an expedition across the Isthmus of Panama in 1513, he and his men were the first Spaniards to sight the Pacific Ocean. ✤125
Baldaya, Alfonso 15th-century Portuguese navigator, who explored the coast of West Africa on behalf of Prince Henry of Portugal (Henry the Navigator). ◆156 (3)
Baldwin I (*var.* Baldwin of Boulogne, *Fre.* Baudouin) (1058–1118). One of the leaders of the First Crusade, Baldwin captured Edessa in 1098, making the County of Edessa the first Crusader state. He was chosen to be King of Jerusalem and crowned in 1100. ◆64–5 (2)
Baldwin of Boulogne *see* Baldwin I
Balfour Declaration (1917). Contained in a letter from Britain's Foreign Secretary, Arthur Balfour, to Lord Rothschild, a prominent Zionist, the declaration stated the British government's support for the establishment of a national home for the Jewish people in Palestine. ✤99●
Bali Conquered by Majapahit (1343) ✤71●
Balkan Wars (1912–1913). Two short wars fought for possession of the Ottoman Empire's European territories. In the first, Montenegro, Bulgaria, Greece and Serbia attacked and defeated Turkey, which was forced to surrender most of her territories in Europe on condition that a new state of Albania was created. The second war was precipitated by disputes among the victors over the division of Macedonia. Romania joined Greece and Serbia against Bulgaria, which was heavily defeated and lost territory to all its enemies. ✤202●, ◆202 (5)
Balkans
bronze ritual axe ❑175
cartoon of Ottoman sultan (1908) ❑203
Crimean War (1854) ✤94
and WW I (1914) ✤98●
First World War *see* Wars, First World
invaded by Bulgars (680) ✤54●
nationalism ✤203, ◆203 (4)
Ottoman control ✤189●
religious map of Europe (1590) ◆194 (2)
separatism ✤112
slave trade (9th–10th century) ✤85
Wars against Ottomans (1912–13) ✤99●
Baltic states
conflict ✤195, ✤195●, ✤197, ◆195 (3), ◆197 (3)
Crusades ◆186 (1)
eastward expansion ✤189
states (1100–1400) ✤189●, ◆189 (3)
Bandkeramik pottery Pottery decorated with incised linear decorations by the earliest farming cultures of C Europe (c.5000 BCE), who are named after their pottery style.
✤20●, ✤174●
Bangladesh (*prev.* East Pakistan) founded (1971) ✤107●, ✤252, ◆252 (3)
banking *see* coins; economy
Banks, Sir Joseph (1743–1820). British explorer and naturalist. He was a long-time president of the Royal Society and was notable for his promotion of science.
African Association (1778) ✤157●
Bannockburn ⚔ (1314). Victory by Scots, led by Robert Bruce over English forces. ◆188 (2)
Banpo
China, BCE farming village ✤19
wattle-and-daub house ❑21
Banshan culture (*var.* Panshan). Chinese Neolithic culture named after the site of Ban-shan in Gansu province, and known for its distinctive painted pottery, mostly large urns, produced between c.2500–2000 BCE. ✤23●
banteng Wild ox of SE Asia. ◆20 (1), ✤258
Bantu Linguistic group occupying much of the southern part of the African continent. From their homeland in present-day Nigeria, the Bantu migrated southward along eastern and western routes during the 2nd millennium BCE. They had reached present-day Zimbabwe by the 8th century CE.
at war with Boers (1779–80) ✤87●
colonize Africa (c.500 BCE) ✤39●, ✤42, ✤160, ◆160 (1)
farming village ❑160
Banu Al-aghlab *see* Aghlabids
Barbarossa Code name for the German invasion of the USSR during WW II (summer–autumn 1941). ✤104●, ✤210●, ◆210 (1)
Barents, Willem (c.1550–97). Dutch navigator who searched for a Northeast Passage to Asia. He discovered Bear Island and Spitzbergen and travelled beyond Novaya Zemlya, where he and his crew were the first recorded Europeans to winter in the Arctic.
search for Northeast passage (1556) ❑286, ◆257 (2), ◆286 (1)
barley Early domestication ✤19
barrow (*var.* tumulus, cairn). Neolithic and Bronze Age burial traditions included raising an earth mound over single or communal graves (where made of stone, known as a cairn) a practice characteristic of European and central and south Asian communities of the 3rd and 2nd millennia BCE. Barrows marked either inhumation or cremation burials, and sometimes also covered burial structures of wood, stone or megalithic chambers. They vary in shape, but are most commonly round or elongated ovals. ✤175, ◆175 (3)
Barth, Heinrich (1821–65) German geographer and explorer of Africa. He travelled the Mediterranean coastal areas that are now part of Tunisia and Libya (1845–47) and published his observations in 1849. ◆157 (4)
Basil II (958–1025) Byzantine emperor. Sole ruler of the empire (976–1025). He extended Byzantine rule to the Balkans, Georgia, Armenia and Mesopotamia. His 15-year war with Bulgaria culminated in victory and earned him the nickname 'Bulgar Slayer'.
✤58●, ✤63●
Bass, George (1771–1803). English surgeon and sailor who surveyed coastal Australia. ◆279 (2)
Bataan ⚔ of WW II in the Pacific (Jan–Apr 1941). Japanese victory over Allied forces. ◆272 (1)
Batavia (*mod.* Jakarta). Administrative and commercial centre of Dutch East Indies.
◆247 (4)
founded (1619) ✤83
trading centre ✤83
Bates, Henry (1825–92). English naturalist and scientific explorer, who spent 11 years in S America. On his travels in Brazil, he studied forms of mimicry, in which a defenseless organism bears a close resemblance to a noxious and conspicuous one. This form is called Batesian, in honour of its discoverer. ✤143●
Baton Rouge ⚔ of American Revolutionary War (21 Sep 1779). Victory by Spanish forces led to Spain controlling the area for the next 20 years. ◆127 (3)
Batts, Thomas (d.1698) Explorer of N America. Searched for South Sea with Robert Fallam, in 1671, reaching the edge of the Mississippi watershed. ◆119 (2)
Batu (d.1255). Mongol leader, a grandson of Genghis Khan, who led the invasion of Europe (1236–42).
campaigns in Europe ✤69●, ◆68–9 (1)
Bayeux Tapestry ❑186 *See also* William I
Bayezid I (*var.* Bayezit, Bajazet) (c.1360–1403) Ottoman Sultan (r.1389–1403). Known as 'the Thunderbolt', he conquered much of Anatolia and the Balkans, besieged Constantinople and invaded Hungary. He was defeated by Timur at the ⚔ of Ankara (1402). ✤230●
Bayezit *see* Bayezid
Bayinnaung (d.1581) Ruler of the Toungoo Kingdom in Burma (r.1551–81). Captured the Siamese capital of Ayutthaya, subdued the Shan states, and ruled over the whole of Burma, except Arakan. His constant warfare, however, reduced his own province to desolation and his son, Nandabayin, completed the ruin of the Toungoo kingdom. ✤79●
Baykonur Soviet space centre ❑275
Beaker culture Neolithic culture which may have originated in the lower Rhine region, and spread through western Europe around 2600–2200 BCE. It is named for its distinctive geometrically decorated pottery; one variety, so called Bell Beaker pottery, being shaped like an inverted bell. These pots are often found deposited with weapons as grave goods, and are seen as signalling a move away from earlier traditions of communal burial towards ostentatious statements of individual status and wealth. The burials of this period are frequently single graves covered with an earthen mound or barrow. ✤174
beans Early domestication ✤18, ◆120 (1), ◆144 (1)
Becan Maya fortified site (c.250 BCE) 121●
Beck, Harry Designer of London Underground map ❑102
Behaim, Martin Geographer.
Martin Behaim's globe (1490–92) ✤75, ❑75, ◆76 (8)
Beijing (*var.* Peking)
captured by Manchu army ✤83
courtyards of the Forbidden City ❑75
founded by Kublai Khan (1266) ✤68●
occupation ✤95●
Song capital (1005) ✤63●
Tiananmen Square demonstration (1989) ✤111●
See also Khanbaliq
Belgium
devolution ✤112
expansion in Africa ✤96, ✤167●, ◆96 (1), ◆167 (4), ◆168 (1)
independence ✤90●, ✤202, ◆202 (1)
possessions
1925 ◆98–9
1975 ◆106–7
World Wars *see* Wars, First World; Second World
Bell, Alexander Graham (1847–1922) US inventor. Patented his design for the telephone in 1876. Later invented the photophone and the gramophone and founded the journal *Science* in 1883. He later concentrated on aeronautical design. ✤92●, ✤95, ✤135
Bell beaker *see* Beaker culture
Belle Isle, Strait of explored by Cartier (1532) ✤80
Bellingshausen, Thaddeus (*var.* Faddey Faddeyvich Bellinsgauzen) (1778–1852) Russian naval officer. Made circumnavigation of Antarctica 1820–21 and is credited with the first sighting of the continent. He discovered Peter I and Alexander I islands. ◆287 (3)
Bemis Heights ⚔ of American Revolutionary War (7 Oct 1777). British victories. ◆127 (3)
Benalcázar, Sebastián (c.1495–1551) Spanish *conquistador*. A member of Francisco Pizarro's expedition to Peru, he conquered the northern Inca capital of Quito in 1533. ◆142 (1)
Benedict, St. (c.480–c.547) Italian founder of Western monasticism. Established the monastery on Monte Cassino near Naples, Italy. The Benedictine Rule served as the basis of Christian monastic organization.
regulates monasteries (529) ✤49●
Bengal
partition and reunification ✤99●, ✤250, ◆250 (2)
survey of India ❑239
under British control (1765) ❑87
Benin State established (c.1500) ✤79●, ✤163●
bronze statue ❑75
sculpture of horse ❑78

SUBJECT INDEX AND GLOSSARY: **Cúcuta – Edward I**

Cúcuta ⚔ of wars of S American independence in Colombia (Feb 1813). ◆150 (1)
Cucuteni-Tripolye Villages (c.4000 BCE) ✤174
cults
bull ❑37
Chavin (850 BCE) ✤30
origins of religion ✤37
Cultural Revolution (*aka* 'Great Proletarian Cultural Revolution). Movement to reaffirm core ideological values of Chinese Communism launched by Mao Zedong in 1966. It was fervently implemented by student groups organized into the Red Guard,. They revived extreme collectivism and attacked revisionists, intellectuals and any suspected of ideological weakness. This resulted in thousands of executions, and the purge of many of Mao's original coterie. After losing control of the movement, Mao disbanded the Red Guard in 1968, but depradations continued under, initially, the military control of Lin Biao, and then under the 'Gang of Four' (led by Mao's wife, Jiang Qing) until Mao's death in 1976. ✤274–5●
culture, US popular
baseball star 'Babe' Ruth ❑135
growth of US popular culture ✤135, ✤135●
movie-going (1929–45) ❑135
radio sets in the US (1921–35) ❑135
sale of records (US 1921–25) ❑135
Walt Disney's Mickey Mouse ❑135
Cumberland Gap Strategic route through the Cumberland Mountains close to the borders of Virginia, Kentucky and Tennessee in the eastern US. Daniel Boone's Wilderness Road ran through the Gap, which had been named in 1750 by Thomas Walker.
Daniel Boone and settlers ❑119
explored by John Finley (1752) ✤119●
cuneiform Form of writing developed by the Sumerians and used in southwest Asia for over 3000 years from the end of the 4th millennium BCE. It originally used pictographs which became stylized to represent words, syllables and phonetic elements. The earliest cuneiform was written from top to bottom.
✤25, ❑25, ✤32●, ◆32 (1), ✤220●, ✤224●,
Cush, Nubian kingdom (BCE) ✤30, ✤31●, ✤34, ◆159 (4) (5), ◆161 (3) (4)
Cuzco
captured by Pizarro (1533) ✤78●, ✤148, ◆148 (1)
Corpus Christi procession ❑148
Inca settlement (c.1200) ✤62●
Cybele BCE cult ❑37 (3)
Cyclades Marble figurine (c.2600 BCE) ❑174
Cynoscephalae ⚔ (197 BCE). Roman victory over Greece. ◆179 (4)
Cyprus Occupied by British (1878) ✤232●
Cyril, St. (826–69) Christian missionary, originally called Constantine, who, with his brother Methodius (825–884), took the Orthodox faith from Constantinople to the Slavs of Moravia. Cyril invented an alphabet, based on Greek characters, to translate the Bible into Slavonic languages. A later version of the alphabet, called Cyrillic, is used in modern Russian and Bulgarian.
185●
Cyrus II (*aka* Cyrus the Great) (c.580/590 BCE–529 BCE). Cyrus created the Persian Achaemenid Empire, named after his ancestor Achaemenes, by defeating the Medes, Lydians and Babylonians. His empire extended from the Mediterranean to the Hindu Kush, and he was known for his enlightened and tolerant policies of religious conciliation. ✤35, ✤223, ✤223●, ❑223, ◆223 (4)
Czechoslovakia State of central Europe established (1918) following WW I, comprising ethnic former regions of Austria-Hungary (Bohemia, Moravia, Slovakia, Trans-Carpathia); occupied and partitioned by Germany during WW II, entering the Eastern Bloc following Soviet liberation; liberalism suppressed (1968); dissolved into separate states of Czech Republic and Slovakia (1993) following 'Velvet Revolution' and free elections (1990).
end of Communism (1989) ✤110●, ◆214 (2)
home affairs
Communist takeover (1948) ✤102●, ✤213
invaded by Germany (1938) ✤102●, ✤209, ❑209, ◆209 (5)
national church established ✤193
'Prague Spring' (1968) ✤106●
Soviets crush reforms (1968) ✤108●, ❑213
Soviet-sponsored regime (1948) ✤108●
See also Wars, First World; Second World

D

D-Day *see* Normandy Landings
Dagobert I (r.623–638). Merovingian king of the Franks, who briefly reunited the Frankish Empire and made Paris his capital. ✤183●, ❑183
Dahomey
captures Whydah (1727) ✤164●
conquered by French (1893) ✤95●
defeated by Oyo (1747) ✤87●
slave trade ✤82
Dai-Viet Northern Vietnam won independence from China, which had dominated it for ten centuries, in 946. The newly independent kingdom was re-named Dai-Viet ('Greater Viet') in 1009. Dai-Viet repelled a Chinese invasion in 1076. When the Ming invaded in 1406, their oppressive rule led to a Vietnamese national resistance movement, and the Chinese armies were routed in 1426. Vietnamese independence was recognized in 1427, and a new capital was established at Hanoi. ◆245 (1) (2)
Daimler, Gottlieb Wilhelm (1834–1900). Developed early automobile. 92●
Daimyo (10th–19th centuries CE). Medieval Japanese provincial feudal lordships. ◆265 (4) (5)
Dakota Gold find (1876–78) ✤93●
Dakota *see* Sioux
Dalai Lama (*var.* Tenzin Gyatso) (1935–). Spiritual and titular leader of Tibet, regarded as reincarnation of Compassionate Buddha. Designated 14th Dalai Lama in 1937, installed in 1940 but ruled under regency until 1950, and negotiated autonomy agreement after Communist Chinese invasion of Tibet (1950). Following suppression of Tibetan uprising (1959) has ruled in exile.
Nobel Peace Prize 1989. ❑275
Damascus
Crusade siege abandoned (1148) ✤64●
Islamic centre (661) ✤55●
Dampier, William (c.1651–1715) English adventurer and explorer. Dampier gained notoriety as a buccaneer, raiding Spanish colonies in the Caribbean and S America. The first Englishman to land in Australia in 1688, he was later sent by the Admiralty on an official voyage of exploration around Australia and New Guinea (1699–1701). ✤278●
Darius I (*aka* Darius the Great) (550–486 BCE). King of Persia (522–486 BCE). Noted for his administrative reforms and religious toleration. Darius's military conquests consolidated the frontiers of the Achaemenid Empire, and his division of land into administrative provinces, or satrapies, outlasted the empire itself. His famed building projects included a renowned road system and a palace at Persepolis. ✤35, ✤39, ◆40 (1), ✤223●, ◆223 (4)
Darius III (*var.* Codomannus) (381–331 BCE) Persian king (r.336–331 BCE). Distant relative of Artaxerxes III who successfully fought against the Cadusians and ascended to the Persian throne in 336 BCE. He was defeated by Alexander at the battles of Issus and Gaugamela (331 BCE), and was subsequently murdered by the Bactrian satrap Bessus.
Persian Emperor ✤39
at the battle of Issus ❑40
Darwin, Charles Robert (1809–82). The first scientist to put forward the theory of evolution through natural selection following observations made in the Galapagos Islands. ✤143, ✤143●, ◆143 (3)
David (r.c.1000–966 BCE). The second king of Israel, David was the first of the dynasty that ruled Judaea and Israel together, uniting the Jewish tribes into a settled nation. He moved the capital from Hebron to Jerusalem (Zion, the 'City of David'), where he brought the Ark of the Covenant, said to contain the Ten Commandments. David defeated the Philistines when he slew their giant warrior Goliath. ✤31, ✤37
Davila, Pedrarias (*var.* Pedro Arias Avila) (c.1440–1531). Spanish soldier and colonial administrator who led the first Spanish expedition to found permanent colonies in the New World.
colonizing expedition (1514–19) ✤125, ◆125 (4)
Davis, John (c.1550–1605). English navigator. Explored Davis Strait, Baffin Island and the Cumberland Sound in search of Northwest Passage to India between 1585 and 1587. In 1591 he travelled as far south as the Falkland Islands. He also published works on navigation and developed navigational instruments including the double quadrant. ◆118 (1), ◆286 (1)
Dawes Plan The report which outlined German reparations as compensation for WW I. Starting at 1,000,000,000 gold marks in 1924, payments were to rise to 2,500,000,000 by 1928, but no total amount was fixed. An initial loan of 800,000,000 marks was given to Germany. ✤208●
Dawson's City Gold rush settlement ✤93
DDR *see* East Germany
De Beers Consolidated Mines ✤167
Deccan First cities (c.200) ✤47●
Declaration of Independence Document drawn up by the Congressional representatives of the original 13 states of the US, declaring independence from Britain. It was signed on 4 Jul 1776. ✤127●
Deerfield European and native conflict (1676) ✤126
Delagoa Bay Dutch occupy Portuguese settlement (1720–30) ✤164●
Del Cano, Juan Sebastián (c.1476–1526). Basque navigator who sailed with Magellan. Captain of the one ship that completed the circumnavigation of the world on Magellan's voyage of 1519–21. After Magellan was killed in the Philippine Islands in 1521, Del Cano sailed the *Victoria* back to Spain with a valuable cargo of cloves from the East Indies, so becoming the first man to complete the circumnavigation of the globe. ✤80–1 (1)
Delhi ◆244 (3)
British occupation ✤246●
Ibn Battuta serves as judge (1334–41) ✤68●
mausoleum of ibn Tughluq (1321) ❑71
Qutb Minar minaret ❑67
Quwwat-al-Islam mosque (1199) ✤67
route map to Kandahar ❑238
Delhi Sultanate (1206 to 1398) Turkish-Afghan dynasty, based at Delhi. Its control over northern India fluctuated along with its various rulers' fortunes; in 1294, under Alauddin Khalji, conquering armies invaded Gujarat, Rajputana and the southernmost tip of the subcontinent. Under the Sultanate, Muslims were appointed to high office, and Hindus became vassals. ✤67, ✤71, ✤79, ✤244, ◆244 (3)
Delian League Confederacy of ancient Greek states under the leadership of Athens, with headquarters at Delos, founded in 478 BCE during the Graeco-Persian wars. ✤177, ◆177 (2)
Delphi Site of Pythian Games ❑38
democracy From the Greek, meaning rule by the people, although in the Greek city-states suffrage was far from universal. The ideal of democracy was revived in Europe the 18th century, notably in the French Revolution. Since then, in most of the world's states, the granting of the vote to all members of society has led to the widely accepted modern ideal of democratic government ✤90
Democratic Party Major US political party. Originally founded by Thomas Jefferson as the Democratic Republican party, the modern name was first used c.1828. Until the 1930s, support for the Democrats was drawn mainly from the southern US, but the New Deal policies of Franklin D. Roosevelt in the 1930s, and the passage of social reform and civil rights legislation in the 1960s has drawn a wider base of support. ✤139, ◆135 (5), ◆139 (4)
Denham, Dixon (1786–1828). English soldier who became one of the early explorers of western Africa. He accompanied Walter Oudney and Hugh Clapperton on an expedition across the Sahara to the Lake Chad basin (1921–1926). ◆157 (4)
Denmark
800–1000 ◆185 (3)
Baltic conflict (16th century) ✤195, ✤195●, ◆195 (3)
Baltic states (1100–1400) ◆189 (3)
Danes besiege Paris (896) ✤58●
foreign affairs
accession of Canute (1016) ✤62●
end of rule in England (1042) ✤60●
possessions
1000 ◆58–9
1600 ◆78–9
1700 ◆82–3
1800 ◆86–7
1900 ◆94–5
1925 ◆98–9
1950 ◆102–3
1975 ◆106–7
WW II, mobilization and casualty figures ✤105
Treaty of Westphalia, ◆196 (1)
Union of Kalmar (1397) ✤70●
Desert Storm (1991) Allied campaign against Iraqi forces which ended Gulf War.
✤235●, ◆235 (5)
See also Gulf War
Detroit Race riots (1940s) ✤137●, ◆137 (6)
Deventer, Jacob van 16th-century Dutch cartographer. ✤173●
Diamond Sutra, the Earliest documented printed work. ❑59
diamonds
commercial Africa (19th century) ❑95, ◆166 (1)
finds ✤148, ◆93 (2)
Dias, Bartolomeu (1450–1500). Portuguese navigator and explorer who led the first European expedition round the Cape of Good Hope in 1488, opening the sea route to Asia via the Atlantic and Indian oceans.
exploration of Africa (1487) ✤76, ◆156 (3)
Dias, Diogo Portuguese navigator, a member of Cabral's expedition to India in 1500. On the outward journey he became separated from the main fleet and discovered Madagascar.
✤156●, ◆156 (3)
diaspora General term for migration or wide dispersion of a people. ✤47●, ✤48●, ✤225, ◆225 (5)
See also Jewish Diaspora.
Diaz de Solis, Juan (c.1470–1516). Spanish explorer of the Atlantic coast of S America. He sailed with Vicente Yáñez Pinzón and Amerigo Vespucci. He was killed by indigenous people while exploring the Plate river in search of a route to the Pacific. ✤125 (4)
Diaz, Porfirio (1830–1915). Mexican statesman and soldier. A hero of the war of the Reform (1857–60) and the French intervention (1861–67). Became president in 1876, after rebelling against the fourth re-election of Benito Juárez. Elected again in 1884, he ruled uninterrupted until he was deposed in 1911 at the start of the Mexican Revolution. ✤133
Diderot, Denis (1713–84) French philosopher and writer. Chief editor of the *Encyclopédie* (1751–72) which attempted to encompass the full breadth of Enlightenment thought. ✤198
Dien Bien Phu ⚔ (3 Feb–7 May 1954). Attempting to regain control in Vietnam, the French were surrounded by Viet-Minh. Subsequently they withdrew from Vietnam. ◆151 (5)
Difaqane *see* Mfecane
Dilmun (Bahrain), trading links (BCE) ✤24–5
Diocletian (245–316) Roman emperor (r.284–305). Responsible for reorganizing the administration of the Roman Empire, dividing it into four regions to be ruled by two senior and two junior emperors. His reign also saw widespread persecution of Christians.
✤50, ✤180, ❑181
persecution of Christians (304 CE) ✤48●
Tetrarchy ✤181, ◆181 (4)
Directoire *see* Directory
Directory (*var. Fr.* Directoire). Name given to the revolutionary executive power in France between Nov 1795 and Nov 1799. It came to an end when Napoleon staged a *coup d'état* and made himself First Consul. ✤199, ✤200●
diseases
cholera (1832) ✤204●, ◆204 (3)
diphtheria ✤81
European colonial settlement ✤126, ✤282●
influenza ✤81, ✤284
measles ✤81, ✤126, ✤284
origin and movement ◆81 (2)
smallpox ✤81
Spanish colonization ✤125, ✤142, ✤148
syphilis, 16th-century death toll ✤81
tuberculosis ✤102
whooping cough ✤81
Disney, Walter Elias (Walt) (1901–69). US animator and film producer. Set up a studio producing animated cartoons in the 1920s. Creator of Mickey Mouse, and producer of some of the most technically advanced animated films, his company grew to become a huge entertainment empire. ❑135
Diu
Portuguese colony in India.
Portuguese victory over Ottoman fleet (1507) ✤79●, ◆247 (3)
Djet, King Egyptian ivory label ❑24
Djoser *see* Zoser
Doge Title of the elected ruler of Venice, from the Latin *dux*, from c.697 to the end of the Venetian Republic in 1797. ✤191, ◆191 (3), ❑191
dolmens *see* chamber tombs
Domesday Book *see* William I
Dominic, St. (c.1170–1221) Spanish founder of the Dominicans, the Order of Friars Preachers. He was canonized in 1234. ✤187, ✤187●
Dominican Republic US invasion ✤133●
Domino effect (*aka* Domino theory). Theory that, in the event of a Communist victory in the Vietnam War (1954–75), the adjacent states of SE Asia would fall successively under Communist control. ✤251
Domino theory *see* Domino effect
Dong Son Prehistoric Indo-Chinese culture named after the northern Vietnamese village where many remains have been found. The Dong Son used iron and built stone monuments, but are best known for their highly skilled bronze-working, especially the ritual kettle drums found at the site. ✤240, ◆240 (3), ❑240
Dorylaeum ⚔ of crusades (1147). Turkish victory over emperor Conrad. ✤64●, ◆64 (1)
Dougga *see* Thugga
Doughty, Charles Montagu (1843–1926). British explorer, writer and poet. From 1876–78 he travelled from Damascus to Mecca, recording his journey in his acclaimed *Travels in Arabia Deserta*, published in 1888. ◆219 (4)
Dr Strangelove (film 1964) ✤108●
Drake, Francis (c.1540–1596) English privateer. Regarded in Spain as a dangerous pirate, Drake made a career of attacking Spanish ships and ports in search of bullion. He played an important role in the defeat of the Spanish Armada in 1588. His greatest feat of navigation was his round-the world voyage of 1577–80 in the *Golden Hind*. ✤80, ✤85
N American expedition (1579) ◆118 (1)
privateer route (16th century) ◆85 (2)
Dred Scott decision (6 Mar 1857). Landmark decision about the spread of slavery in the US. Scott, a slave who had been taken by his master into the West argued that he should be free as slavery was not legal in the new territory. The Supreme Court ruled that Congress had no power to exclude slavery from the territories, thus making slavery legal in all US territories. ✤130, ◆130 (4)
Dubček, Alexander (1921–92). First secretary of the Communist Party of Czechoslovakia (5 Jan 1968–17 Apr 1969) whose liberal reforms led to the Soviet invasion and occupation of Czechoslovakia in Aug 1968. ✤213
Dublin Viking settlement ✤185●
Dumont d'Urville, Jules Sébastien-César (1790–1842). French naval officer. Acted as naturalist on a series of expeditions to the Pacific in 1826–29. In 1837–40 he travelled to Antarctica where he discovered Terre Adélie and Joinville Island. ✤286–287
Dunhuang Chinese Buddha ❑59
Dušan, Stefan (c.1308–55). Ruler of Serbia. Through his successful campaigns in the Balkans, Stefan carved out a large Serbian Empire. ✤189, ◆189 (4)
Dust Bowl Name given to the prairie states of the US (Oklahoma, Kansas etc.) which suffered from serious soil erosion during the 1930s following a prolonged period of drought. Thousands of farmers were forced to abandon their ruined land. ✤134, ✤134
Dutch East India Company (*var.* United East India Company; *Dut.* Vereenigde Oost-Indische Compagnie). Company founded by the Dutch in 1602 to protect their trade in the Indian Ocean and to assist in their war of independence from Spain. It was dissolved in 1799.
17th-century official cartographers ✤83
founds Cape Town colony (1652) ✤164
Java headquarters ✤83, ❑243
Moluccas spice trade ✤83
trade monopoly abolished (1834) ✤91●
Dutch East Indies General historic term for Dutch colonial holdings in SE Asia, 17th–20th centuries. ✤80, 86, 90, 94, ◆97 (3), ◆247 (4), ◆251 (4)
decolonization ◆97 (3)
Japanese colonizing occupations ◆250–51 (3)
dyke Chinese timber and brushwood ❑83
Dzungaria Invaded by China (1751) ✤87● *See also* Xiankiang

E

Eanes, Gil 15th-century Portuguese explorer credited with rounding Cape Bojador, Africa, in 1434.
exploration of Africa (1433–35) ✤156●, ◆156 (3)
earth Babylonian depiction ❑34
Jain depiction of universe ❑238
East, the *see* Communist Bloc
East Africa
Arab coastal trading (c.900) ✤61
inter-ethnic warfare ✤111
Portuguese map (1558) ❑156
Portuguese possessions ✤78, ✤82, ◆164 (1)
East Asia General geographic term for traditional regions of China, Mongolia, Manchuria, Korea and the Japanese archipelago.
BCE ✤15, ✤15●, ✤19, ✤31●, ✤35, ✤39
agrarian unrest (1850) ✤95
agricultural revolution (BCE) ◆258 (1)
c.1500 ✤77, ◆77 (4)
Communism and capitalism ✤274–5
early medieval (618–c.1300) ✤262–3
economic growth ✤275●
era of the Qing Empire ✤268, ◆268 (1) (2)
first civilizations ✤258–9
first states in Japan and Korea ✤264–5
foreign imperialism ✤269, ◆269 (4)
the Han and the great migrations ✤260–1
historical landscape ✤254–5, ◆254–5
internal rebellion (8th century) ✤59
Ming dynasty ✤266–7
modernization of the East ✤270–1
Russian expansion ✤269, ◆269 (3)
See also individual countries
East Germany (*var.* German Democratic Republic, DDR). Communist state formed (1949) by Soviet Union following post-war occupation of Germany, dissolved upon German reunification (1990). ✤212–3●, ◆212–3 (1) (3) (4) (5), ✤214●, ◆214 (1) (2)
East Indies General geographic term for the archipelagos of Maritime SE Asia.
Arab trading ✤61, ◆61 (3)
colonization and trade with Europeans ◆247 (4)
decolonization ✤97●, ◆97 (3), ◆247 (5)
development of states and empires ✤245●, ◆245 (5) (6)
Dutch surrender to Japan (1942) ✤104●
establishment of Islam ✤61, ◆243 (6)
East Pakistan *see* Bangladesh.
East Timor
independence (1975) ✤251, ◆251 (4)
occupied by Indonesia (1975) ✤111●
troops looting rice ❑253
Easter Island *see* Rapa Nui
Eastern Bloc *see* Communist Bloc
Eastern Front The eastern theatre of war during WW I, including eastern Germany, Austria-Hungary, Poland, Romania and Russia. ✤207●, ◆207 (4)
Eastern Han *see* Han dynasty.
Eastern Zhou *see* Zhou dynasty.
East, the *see* Communist Bloc
EC *see* European Union.
economy
BCE tax levy ✤35
18th-century Europe ✤198–9, ◆198 (1)
19th-century growth of USA ✤94
inventions and the economic revolution (1835–95) ✤92●
medieval Europe ✤191, ❑191
plantation ✤82, ❑84, ❑90, ❑149
and political entities ◆163 (2)
S American ✤152, ◆152 (3)
'Tiger' economies from 1960 ◆275 (4)
world market domination ✤90, ✤112
See also Industrial Revolution; trade
ECSC *see* European Coal and Steel Community
Ecuador
BCE ✤42●
cultural region ◆145 (4)
achieves independence ✤150, ◆150 (1)
decolonization ◆153 (4)
Edessa
Crusader state ✤63, ✤65
falls to Muslims (1144) ✤63●
political and economic development ◆151 (3)
Valerian defeated (260) ✤51●
Edo Imperial capital of Tokugawa Japan ✤267
Edward I (1239–1307) King of England (r.1272–1307). Eldest son of Henry III. He supported Simon de Montfort in the Barons' War (1264–67), later joining his father

Key to index: ✤ text ● timeline ❑ picture ◆ map *var.* variant name *aka* also known as *f/n* full name *prev.* previously known as r. ruled ⚔ battle WW I First World War WW II Second World War

Key to index: ✣ text   ❑ picture   *var.* variant name   *f/n* full name   *r.* ruled   WW I First World War
● timeline   ◆ map   *aka* also known as   *prev.* previously known as   ⚔ battle   WW II Second World War

SUBJECT INDEX AND GLOSSARY: **Jiang Jieshi – Korea**

mass extermination under the Nazis ✤102●, ◆211, ◆211 (3)
migration (1880–1914) ✤101, ✤101●, ◆101 (2)
migration to Israel ◆234 (3)
settlement in New York ❑100
Jiang Jieshi (*var.* Chiang Kai-shek) (1887–1975). Chinese general and political leader. Leader of the Kuomintang from 1926, president of the republic 1928–31. Opposed the Chinese Communist Party until defeated in 1949 when he withdrew to Taiwan. ✤103●, ❑270–1
Jiang Qing *see* Cultural Revolution
jihad Holy war ✤56, ✤167, ◆235 (4)
Jin dynasty Chinese dynasty of the Sixteen Kingdoms period. ◆261 (3)
dynasty unifies China (280) ✤51●
Eastern dynasty moves to Nanjing ✤51
Jin dynasty (*var.* Chin dynasty) (r.1115–1234). Dynasty of northern China.
founded by the Jurchen ✤263
alliance with Song China ✤63 (c.1206) ◆68–9 (1)
capital city ✤69
conquered by Mongols ✤263, ◆263 (7)
first Mongol invasion (1211) ✤69●
Jin Empire *see* Jin dynasty
Jinghis Khan *see* Genghis Khan
Joan of Arc (*var. Fr.* Jeanne d'Arc, *aka* the Maid of Orleans, *Fr.* La Pucelle) (c.1412–31). French national heroine. Claiming to hear voices urging her to rid France of English domination, she led an army which raised the siege of Orleans (1429), enabling the dauphin to be crowned Charles VII at Rheims. Captured and sold to the English, she was convicted of heresy and burnt at the stake. She was canonized in 1920. ❑192
campaigns ◆192 (2)
saves Orléans (1429) ✤75●, ✤192, ✤192●
João III (1502–57) King of Portugal (r.1521–57). His kingdom suffered, both socially and economically, because of his subservience to the clerical party. He tried to stimulate the colonization of the new Portuguese territory in Brazil by granting captaincies. ✤148
João V (1689–1750) King of Portugal (1707–50). A supporter of the Triple Alliance (between Britain, Austria, and the Netherlands, he embarked on a series of unsuccessful campaigns in Castile during the War of the Spanish Succession. Though his treasury benefited from the recent discovery of gold in Brazil, João V was entirely under the influence of the clergy and the administration suffered from his neglect. ❑88
John (1167–1216) King of England (r.1199–1216). His reign saw the renewal of war with Philip II Augustus of France, to whom he had lost several continental possessions. Tensions between John and Pope Innocent III led to the imposition of an interdict over England in 1208 and the king's excommunication in 1212. He was also forced to grant the Magna Carta at Runnymede. ✤66●
Johnson, Lyndon Baines (1908–73) 36th President of the US (Democrat, 1963–68). Became President following the assassination of John F. Kennedy in 1963. His administration passed the Civil Rights Act (1964), the Voting Rights Act (1965) aimed at improving the position of African Americans, and introduced a series of economic and social reforms under the slogan the 'Great Society', but his personal standing was severely weakened by public protests against the escalation of the Vietnam War.
Democrat President ✤139
Civil Rights legislation ✤139
Jolliet, Father Louis (1645–1700). Explorer of N America. Born in Canada, Jolliet discovered the source of the Mississippi River with Jacques Marquette. In 1672–73 they travelled along the river to within 640 km of the Gulf of Mexico. ◆119 (2)
Jolson, Al (*prev.* Asa Yoelson) (1886–1950) Russian-born American actor and singer. He toured with various stage and minstrel shows, making his Broadway debut in 1911. In 1928, he made screen history when he starred in the first full-length 'talkie', *The Jazz Singer*. In 1928, his first big record hit 'Sonny boy/there's a rainbow round my shoulder' sold over three million copies. ✤135●
Jomon culture Hunters, fishers and gatherers who lived in Japan from c.7500 to 250 BCE. They fully exploited an abundance of fish, animal and plant resources and, in the densely populated east, lived in permanent villages, but there is no evidence of plant cultivation. Jomon pottery dates back to c.10,000 BCE, the earliest known anywhere in the world. The culture is named from the cord-decorated pottery found at the Omori shell mounds near Tokyo. ✤19
Jordan Six Day War (1967) ✤107●
Juan Carlos I (1938–) King of Spain (r.1978–). The grandson of Alfonso XIII (who abdicated in 1931), he was named successor to the dictator, General Franco in 1969, and proclaimed king in 1975. Juan Carlos presided over a rapid, and peaceful, transition to democracy; by 1978 Spain was declared a parliamentary monarchy. In 1981 King Juan Carlos foiled a Francoist military coup by taking preventative action and winning pledges of loyalty from military commanders. ✤110●
Juan-juan *see* Ruanruan
Juárez, Benito (Pablo) (1806–72) Mexican statesman (r.1861–72). As part of the Liberal government which replaced the Conservative Santa Anna, Juárez helped pass the anti-clerical and liberal constitution of 1857. In 1861 he assumed the role of president of Mexico, a post he held until his death. A French invasion under Maximilian forced him to retreat to the north, but after the French were defeated in 1867 he was able to restore Republican rule. ◆128–129 (2), ✤129
Judaism Religion of the Jewish people, developed among the ancient Hebrews and characterized by a belief in one God, its ethical system and its ritual practices, based on the Pentateuch as interpreted by the rabbis of the Talmudic period in the first five centuries CE and their successors up to the present day.
candelabra ❑37
origins ✤36–7
spread of (600 BCE) ◆48 (1)
Jugurtha (160–104 BCE) King of Numidia (r.118–105 BCE). Struggled to free his N African kingdom from Roman rule. ✤43●
Julio-Claudian dynasty The four successors of the Roman Emperor Augustus (r.31 BCE–14 CE), all indirectly descended from Julius Caesar. The Emperor Augustus, who had extended the frontiers of the empire and introduced stable and efficient government, was succeeded by Tiberius (14–37 CE), the most able of the dynasty. Caligula (37–41 CE), was famous for his excesses and capricious behaviour. He was succeeded by Claudius (41–54 CE), who devoted himself to public works and administrative reforms, although he never gained the respect of his subjects. The tyrannical Nero (54–68) was notorious for his ruthless murders, and the revenge he took on the Christians for the great fire of Rome (64 CE) which, it was rumoured, he had started himself. ✤46●
Juneau, Joe 19th-century French explorer of Alaska. Founded town of Juneau.
finds gold in Alaska (1880) ✤93, ◆93 (3)
Jupiter (*var. Gr.* Zeus). Most powerful god in the Greco-Roman pantheon. ✤37
Jurchen People originating in the mountains of eastern Manchuria, Central Asia. Established the Jin state and seized northern China 1126, restricting Song rule to the south of China. ✤263, ◆263 (5)
See also Jin dynasty
Justinian I (483–565) Byzantine Emperor. Born in what is now Yugoslavia, he was adopted by his uncle Justin I, who ascended the throne in 518, and succeeded him in 527. He is famous for his reforms of the Roman law codes and imperial constitutions, and the publication of the Codex Justinianus (534). His programme of costly public works included the building of the church of Santa Sophia in Constantinople. He engaged in major campaigns against the Vandals in Spain and North Africa and the Goths in Italy, but his victories proved fragile. ❑54
Jutes Germanic people who, with the Angles and Saxons, invaded Britain in the 5th century CE. ✤183, ◆52–3 (1)
Jutland Naval ⚔ of WW I (31 May 1916) between the British and German fleets in the North Sea. Though the result was inconclusive, the Allies thereafter retained control of the North Sea. ✤206●

K

K'ang-hsi *see* Kangxi
Kabul, captured by Taliban (1996) ✤111●
Kadesh ⚔ between the Egyptians and Hittites (c.1285 BCE). First recorded battle in world history. ✤27●, ✤221, ◆221 (5)
Kadphises I (*var.* Kujula Kadphises, Chiu-Chiu-Chueh) Kushan ruler who achieved political unity of the Yuezhi tribes in the 1st century CE, and ruled over northern India, Afghanistan and parts of central Asia. ✤47
Kaifeng
captured by Mongols (1233) ✤67●, ◆68–9 (1)
scroll depicting 12th-century street life ❑63
Song capital ✤263, ◆263 (7)
Kairouan Great Mosque ❑56
Kalahari Desert, environmental survival strategies (BCE) 16
Kalewa ⚔ of WW II (May 1942). Marked furthest point of Japanese advance in Burma. ◆104 (2)
Kalhotia Mesolithic painting ❑14
Kali Important goddess in Hinduism, associated with death, disease and destruction. ❑48
Kalidasa 4th-century Indian poet and playwright. ✤51●
Kalmar, Union of (Jun 1397). Scandinavian union that brought the kingdoms of Norway, Sweden, and Denmark together under a single monarch until 1523. ✤70●, ✤195, ◆70–1, ◆74–5, ◆195 (3)
Kalmyks Buddhist Mongolian people of Central Asia who came under pressure from Qing China 1758–59. ✤268●, ◆268 (2)
Kamakura Shogunate (1185–1333) Military rulers of Japan. ✤71, ✤265, ✤265●
Kambujadesha The Khmer state of Kambujadesha, founded by Devaraya II in 802, controlled most of SE Asia for the next four centuries from the magnificent city of Angkor in southern Cambodia. Although Hinduism was the state religion, it combined many elements of Buddhism, as can be seen in the magnificent monumental architecture of Angkor, which reached its zenith under the rule of Jayavarman VII (c.1200). ✤245●, ◆245 (5)
Kamehameha I (1782–1819). The king of one of the four kingdoms of Hawaii who, with superior vessels and firearms, as well as foreign aid, succeeded in conquering all the islands, with the exception of Kauai and Niihau, by 1795. He reorganized government, encouraged industry, while withstanding foreign cultural influence and adhering to traditional Hawaiian religious practices (abolished after his death by his favourite queen, Kaahumanu). ✤91●
kami The combined forces of nature and ancestral spirits, central to Shinto religious observance. ❑264
kamikaze Japanese term for 'divine wind', a typhoon which halted second Mongol invasion attempt (1281); adopted as name by Japanese suicide fighter-bomber squadrons during final campaigns of WW II. ✤273, ❑273
Kaminaljuyú (*fl.* 500 BCE) Central American civilization ✤121
Kanab Desert US Geological Survey sketch (1880) ❑119
Kandahar *see* Gandhara
Kanem-Bornu W African kingdom ✤58
See also Bornu
Kangxi (*var.* K'ang-hsi) (1654–1722) Emperor of the Manchu (Qing) dynasty of China (r.1661–1722). ✤83●, ❑268
Kanishka (*var.* Kaniska) (r.c.78–96 CE). Ruler of the Kushan, or Kushana, Empire of south central Asia whose adoption of (Mahayana) Buddhism was instrumental in the spread of the faith to Central Asia and along the Silk Road to China. ✤47●, ✤48
Kansas Nebraska Act (1854). The third of the critical decisions regarding the extension of slavery in the US, the Kansas-Nebraska Act applied the principle of popular sovereignty to the territorial organization of Kansas and Nebraska. The passage of the act led to the formation of the Republican Party to oppose the expansion of slavery into new territories. ✤130, ◆130 (3)
Kao Tsu *see* Gao Zhu
Kara Khitai Muslim empire in central Asia which rose to prominence in the 12th century. In 1141 the Kara Khitai defeated the Seljuk Turks at Samarkand. ◆68–9 (1)
Karakorum ◆68–9 (1) (2)
Mongol capital built (1235) ✤68●
slave trade centre (13th century) ✤85
Karius, Charles 20th-century British explorer of New Guinea (1927–28). ◆279 (2)
Karlowitz, Peace of (*var.* Carlowitz) (1699). Peace settlement that ended hostilities (1683–99) between the Ottoman Empire and the Holy League (Austria, Poland, Venice, and Russia) which significantly diminished Turkish influence in east-central Europe, making Austria the dominant power there. ✤197●, ◆197 (4)
Kashmir
Indian-Pakistan war (1965) 107●
and Jammu ✤252, ◆252 (2)
refugees ❑252
Kassapa (447–495). Ruler of Sigiriya in Sri Lanka, who usurped power and believed he was a god-king.
god-king of Sigiriya ✤51●
palace, two heavenly maidens (5th century) ❑51
Katanga Secedes from Congo (1960) ✤107●
Kay, John Inventor of flying shuttle (1733) ✤204●
Kazakhs People of Central Asia. Traditionally pastoral nomads; incorporated into the Russian Empire in the mid-19th century, now mainly settled in Kazakhstan. ◆89 (2), ◆267 (3)
Kebana Neanderthal burial site ❑12
Kemal Pasha, Mustafa *see* Atatürk
Kennedy, Edmund (1818–48). Born in the Channel Islands, he migrated to New South Wales in 1840. Trained as a surveyor, he joined Sir Thomas Mitchell's expedition into central Queensland in 1847. In 1848 he led an expedition up the eastern coast of Queensland to Cape York. During the course of the arduous journey all his party perished – Kennedy was speared by Aborigines while within sight of his supply ship. ◆279 (2)
Kennedy, John Fitzgerald (1917–1963) 35th President of the US (Democrat, 1960–63). Following service in US navy during WW II, became the youngest elected US president at the age of 43. He aimed to introduce legislation for the improvement of civil rights and for the extension of funding for healthcare and education. Foreign policy issues included the unsuccessful invasion of the Bay of Pigs in Cuba, the division of Europe, the Cuban Missile Crisis which brought the world to the brink of nuclear war, and the continuing involvement of the US in Vietnam. He was assassinated in Dallas, Texas on 22 Nov 1963. ✤139●, ❑108
Kennesaw Mountain ⚔ of American Civil War (27 Jun 1864). Confederate victory. ◆131 (7)
Kent King converted to Christianity (597) ✤54●
Kenya 167–169
British penetration in 19th century ◆167 (3)
independence ◆168 (1)
terrorist bombing (1998) ✤235●
Kermario Stone alignments (c.3000 BCE). ❑174
Khanbaliq (*var.* Beijing, Cambaluc). founded by Kublai Khan (1266) ✤68●
Italian map (15th century) ❑69
Khedive of Egypt The title, granted by the Sultan of Turkey in 1867, to his viceroy in Egypt, Ismail. 'Khedive' is a Persian word meaning prince, or sovereign. The title was abandoned in 1914 when the title 'Sultan' was adopted. ✤232
Khitans (*var.* Liao) (907–1125). People of Mongolia who established the Liao Empire in Manchuria in the 10th century. ✤263, ◆263 (3) (4)
Khmer Rouge A Marxist party in Cambodia, led by Pol Pot, organized to oppose the right-wing government of Lon Nol, 1970–75. They overthrew the government in 1975 and instituted a reign of terror which led to the death of over two million Cambodians. They were overthrown in 1979 following a Vietnamese invasion. ✤253●, ◆253 (4), ❑253
Khmer state
✤245, ✤245●, ◆245 (5)
temple carvings ❑63
See also Kambujadesha
Khomeini, Ayatollah Ruhollah (1900–1989). Iranian religious and political leader. A Shi'ite Muslim whose bitter opposition to the pro-Western regime of Muhammad Reza Shah Pahlavi led to his exile from Iran in 1964. Following a popular revolution and the overthrow of the Shah's government in 1979, he returned to Iran and was proclaimed religious leader of the Islamic Revolution. Islamic law was once more imposed, and a return to strict fundamentalist Islamic tradition enforced. ❑235
Khosrau I (*var.* Khosrow I, *aka* Khosrau the Just) (r.531–579). Sassanian Persian Shah who quelled the Mazdakite rebellion and successfully resisted the Byzantines. ✤55, ✤225
Khosrau II (*var.* Khosrow II, *aka* Khosrau the Victorious) (r.591–628). Persian Shah at the apogee of the Sassanian era. In 601 he attacked Byzantium, capturing Antioch, Jerusalem and Alexandria. ✤225
Khrushchev, Nikita Sergeyevich (1894–1971) Soviet statesman and successor to Stalin. First Secretary of the Communist Party (1953–64). Deposed in a coup and replaced by Leonid Brezhnev. ❑108
Khufu (c.2575–2465 BCE) Egyptian pharaoh of the 4th dynasty who initiated the building of the largest pyramid at Giza: 147 m high, consisting of c.2.3 million blocks, each weighing c.2.5 tonnes. ✤23●
Khwarizm Empire (*aka* Empire of the Khwarizm Shah, Uzbek Empire) State of Turkic origin, broadly corresponding with ancient Chorasmia, N Persia, based around Samarkand from the 12th century. Overrun by Mongols, then forming part of Khanate of the Golden Horde, and subsequently conquered by Timur (1378), the state fragmented into a number of Muslim khanates based around Bukhara and Samarkand which were finally absorbed into the Russian Empire during the 19th century.
(1219) ◆66–7
(c.1206–19) ◆68–9 (1)
invaded by Mongols (1219) ✤67●, ✤69●
Kibi Ancient people of southern Honshu, Japan. ✤264
Kiev ⚔ of WW II (Sep–Nov 1943) Soviet forces defeat of German counter-offensive in Ukraine. ◆105 (3), ◆211 (4)
Kiev
captured by Vikings ✤185
Russian capital ✤58●
Kievan Rus State established in 840 by Vikings from Sweden who were trading along the rivers between the Baltic and the Black seas. Kiev became a flourishing capital; through trading links with Byzantium the Christian faith became established there at the end of the 10th century. Repeated sackings by nomads from the east reduced Kiev to a number of independent and warring principalities from the middle of the 11th century. ✤185, ◆185 (3), ◆189 (3)
possessions ◆58–9
founded by Varangians ✤60
Kilwa
building programme ✤163●
coastal trading colony (c.800) ✤58
Kimberley South Africa, gold finds (1867) ✤93●
King, Clarence (1842–1901). American explorer and geologist. In 1867, as director in charge of the United States Geological Exploration of the Fortieth Parallel he began extensive ten-year survey of a 160–km-wide strip of land running from Cheyenne, Wyoming to the eastern Sierra Nevada. ◆119 (3)
King, Martin Luther (1929–1968) US civil rights leader. A baptist minister in Alabama, Martin Luther King founded the Southern Christian Leadership Conference in 1957 to organize activities for the promotion of black civil rights throughout the US. He advocated a policy of non-violence and passive resistance, an effective strategy which undoubtedly helped the passage of the Civil Rights Act of 1964 and the Voting Rights Act of 1965. He was awarded the Kennedy Peace Prize and the Nobel Prize. In 1969 he was assassinated in Memphis, Tennessee. The third Monday in January is now celebrated as Martin Luther King Day in the US.
assassination (1968) ✤137●
heads protest movement (1957) ✤137●
portrait ❑136
Washington march (1963) ✤137●
King Movement A Maori movement of the late 1850s that opposed land sales to European settlers and demanded a Maori state. It was led by chief 'King' Te Wherowhero. ✤283●
King Philip's War (1675–76) Conflict between English colonists and Indians in New England following the rapid expansion of European settlement into Indian territory from 1640 onwards. The conflict involved most of the tribes of New England including the Wapanoag and the Narragansett, and may have led to the loss of perhaps 600 settlers and 3000 Indians, who thereafter fled north and west. ✤126, ◆126 (1)
King's Mountain ⚔ of American Revolutionary War, 7 Oct 1780, American victory. ◆127 (3)
Kingsley, Mary (1862–1900). English traveller who journeyed through western and equatorial Africa and became the first European to enter parts of present-day Gabon. ◆157 (4)
Kisesse Decorated caves (29,000 BP) ✤17●
Klerk, F.W. de (*f/n* Frederik Willem de Klerk) (1936–). Politician who as president of South Africa (1989–94), brought the apartheid system of racial segregation to an end. Both he and Nelson Mandela jointly received the Nobel Peace Prize in 1993, in recognition of their efforts to establish non-racial democracy in South Africa.
begins dismantling of apartheid (1990) ✤169●
Klondike Gold rush ✤93, ◆93 (3)
Knights Hospitallers (*var.* Knights of St. John). Military/religious order established at Jerusalem in the early 12th century following the success of the First Crusade. Its purpose was to care for pilgrims to the Holy Land, but the Knights also played an important role in the defence of the Crusader states. In 1310, the Hospitallers took Rhodes, which remained their base until 1522, when it was taken by the Ottomans. They were then granted the island of Malta by Charles V. ✤186, ◆189 (3)
conquer Rhodes (1306–10) ✤186●
fall of Rhodes to Ottomans ◆231 (3)
military order (c.1130) ✤64●, ✤186●
Knights of St. John *see* Knights Hospitallers
Knights Templar Military/religious order founded c.1118 to protect pilgrim routes to Jerusalem. In the 12th and 13th centuries, knights of the order fought in all the major campaigns against Islam. They acquired estates all over Christian Europe, but their wealth and influence made them enemies. In 1307, Philip IV of France had the order accused of heresy and other crimes and it was suppressed in 1312.
Order founded (c.118) ✤64●, ✤186●
European political force ❑186
Order suppressed (1312) ✤70●
Templar houses, ◆186 (1)
Knossos Bronze Age city on Crete, a focus of the Minoan civilization, and known for the artistic and architectural brilliance of its palace, built c.2000 BCE, which dominated the city's mansions, houses and paved roads. Knossos flourished for some 1500 years, despite its palace being destroyed several times (once by the erupton of Thera), and invasion by the Mycenaeans c.1450. It was finally destroyed by the Romans 68–67 BCE. *See* Minoan civilization.
Knut *see* Canute
Koguryo North Korean ruling clan destroyed by the Tang in 668. *See also* Korea.
controls Korea (c.220) ✤47●
establishes Pohai empire ✤264
Kök Türk (Blue Turk) Empire (551–72). ◆54–5
Konbaung dynasty Founded (1752) in Burma. ✤87●
Kongo
Kingdom formed (c.1390) ✤71●, ✤163●
outbreak of civil war (1665) ✤164●
Portuguese attempt colonization ✤82
Kongzi *see* Confucius
Königsberg ⚔ of WW II (Feb–Apr 1945) Prolonged siege of German forces by Soviet troops. ✤105, ◆211 (4)
Koran (*var.* Qu'ran). The holy book of Islam. ✤226, ❑56, ❑67, ❑167
See also Islam.
Korea Peninsula of E Asia, frequently under Chinese and Japanese influence and control; early states included Koguryo (c.150–668 CE), Paekche (c.250–663 CE) and Silla (from 313 CE). Silla Period (676–935). Koryo Period (936–1392). I (or Li) dynasty, capital at Kyongsang, ruled often as Ming or Qing vassals (1392–1910). Annexed to Japan 1910–1945. Partitioned into independent states of N and S Korea (1948).
agriculture (BCE) ✤23●, ✤31, ✤258
dynasties
Buddhist ✤59
Yi (1392) ✤71●
home affairs
annexed by Japan (1910) ✤99●
BCE subsistence ✤19●
controlled by native states (c.200) ✤47●
first empires ◆264 (2)
Koryo kingdom founded (935) ✤59●
peninsula united by Silla ✤55●
Silla's struggle for power ✤264●
state formation (100 BCE–650 CE) ✤264, ◆264 (1) (2) (3) (4)
innovations
bronze technology ✤31
earliest pottery ◆258 (1)
iron-working introduced (400 BCE) ✤39●

SUBJECT INDEX AND GLOSSARY: **Luoyang – Melanesia**

project, which had led to the destruction of large tracts of tropical rain forest. ✤153●
Luoyang
conquered by Qin (256 BCE) ✤39
northern Wei capital (c.490) ✤51●
Luther, Martin (1483–1546). German scholar and priest whose questioning of certain church practices led to the Protestant Reformation. He first clashed with the Catholic authorities in 1517 after his *95 Theses* attacking the sale of indulgences denied that the pope and clergy could forgive sins. He inspired a movement that revolutionized religious thought, incidentally provoking much social and political upheaval in northern Europe.
✤78●, ✤194, ✤194●
Luxembourg dynasty The counts of Luxembourg were a powerful dynasty in the late Middle Ages. They were also kings of Bohemia and four of their number were elected emperor, the most famous being Charles IV.
possessions ✤70–1, ✤189, ◆189 (4), ◆194 (2)
creation of modern duchy , ✤202, ◆202 (1 inset)
Luxor *see* Thebes ❑29
Lyasu I Ethiopian king ✤165●
Lydia
(BCE) ✤35, ✤223, ◆34–5, ◆223 (4)
issues first coins (BCE) ✤35
Lysimachus (*var. Gre.* Lysimachos) (360–281 BCE) General of Alexander the Great. Following Alexander's death in 323, Lysimachus became ruler of Thrace. He extended his territories in the wars between Alexander's successors, but was killed in battle against Seleucus, with whom he had formerly been allied. ✤224●, ◆224 (1)

M

Maastricht Treaty (*var.* European Union Treaty) (Dec 1991). International agreement between the states of the European Community (EC) in Maastricht, Netherlands which established the European Union (EU), with Union citizenship for every person holding the nationality of a member state. It provided for the establishment of a central banking system and the implementation of a common foreign and security policy. ✤214
Macao Portuguese colony in China.
16th-century voyages by Portuguese ✤80
returned to China (1999) ◆111
Macedonia
Antigonid dynasty ✤41, ✤224, ✤224●, ◆224 (1)
(BCE) ◆34–5, ◆38–9
Byzantine rulers (867–1081) ✤59
growth of power ✤40●
Machu Picchu Inca sacred shrine ❑74
MacKenzie, Colin (c.1753–1821) Officer in the British East India Company's army, whose accurate mapping led to his appointment as Surveyor-general of India in 1819. ✤239, ✤239●, ❑239
Mackenzie, Sir Alexander (c.1755–1820) Explorer and fur-trader. In 1789, on behalf of the Northwestern Company, he ventured to Great Slave Lake and down what was to become the Mackenzie River to the Arctic Ocean. His next expedition, starting from Lake Athabasca in 1792, eventually reached the Pacific Ocean, making him the first white man to cross N America north of Mexico. ◆286 (1)
MAD *see* Mutually Assured Destruction
Madaba 6th-century mosaic ❑51
Madagascar
Arab trading settlements ✤58, ✤61, ◆61 (3)
colonized by Malays ✤61
French conquest (1883–96) ✤167●, ◆167
Portuguese map (1558) ❑156
Madero, Francisco Indalecio (1873–1913) Mexican revolutionary and statesman. In 1908, Madero launched a presidential campaign against the dictator, Porfirio Díaz. Imprisoned by Díaz, he then fled to the US and launched a military campaign, capturing Ciudad Juárez, which he made his capital in May 1911. He made moderate reforms as President, but was increasingly beset by revolts demanding land reform. He was murdered in Feb 1913 following a military coup by Victoriano Huerta, assisted by the US ambassador. ✤133, ◆133 (3)
Mafia (*aka* Cosa Nostra). International criminal organization, originally based in Sicily and dating from the 13th century. In the US, the Mafia became one of the major forces in the development of organized crime, especially during the Prohibition era. ✤113, ◆113 (4)
Magadha One of the 16 mahajanapadas (great realms) which dominated the Ganges plain from c.600 BCE. Gradually all the other kingdoms were absorbed into Magadha, with its capital at Pataliputra (Patna), which dominated the lucrative Ganges trade routes. Magadha became the nucleus of the first Indian empire, the Mauryan Empire when its throne was seized by Chandragupta Maurya in 327 BCE. Magadha was the scene of many of the incidents in the life of Gautama Buddha. Later the centre of the Gupta dynasty. ✤36, ✤39, ✤241, ◆241 (4)
Magellan, Ferdinand (c.1480–1521). Portuguese navigator, who undertook his most famous voyage in the service of the Spanish crown. In 1519 he sailed with five ships to discover a westward route to the Indies. This he achieved, sailing through the Strait of Magellan, then crossing the Pacific to the Philippines. There, Magellan was killed after intervening in a local war. One of his ships, captained by Sebastián del Cano, made the journey back to Spain, thus completing the first circumnavigation of the globe.
16th-century Portuguese navigator ✤78, ◆239 (1)
global circumnavigation ✤76, ❑80
Oceania voyages ◆278 (1)
reaches the Pacific (1520) ✤142
Magnesia, ⚔ (190 BCE). Roman victory over Seleucid king Antiochus III. ◆179 (4)
Magyars People of the steppes, the ancestors of today's Hungarians, who migrated into present-day Hungary in the late 9th century. Their raids at first struck fear into western European states, but following their defeat by Otto I at Lechfeld in 955, the Magyars started to lead a more settled existence and in the 11th century Hungary became a Christian kingdom.
defeated by Otto I ✤58, ✤58●
raids (c.800–1000) ◆185 (3)
settle in Danube basin ✤185●
Mahabharata Sanskrit epic which, along with the *Ramayana*, was composed c.450 BCE. It tells the story of an epic struggle for supremacy between two groups of cousins, the Kauravas and the Pandavas. The battle was fought in northwestern India, and is probably an account of Mauryan expansion.
✤241, ❑241, ❑244, ◆241 (5)
Mahavira (c.540–468 BCE) Brought up as a pious Jain near Patna, Mahavira became a monk, who instructed 11 disciples, and became the foremost preceptor of the Jain religion.
✤242●, ◆242 (3)
Mahayana Buddhism (*aka* Greater Vehicle). Interpretation of Buddhism developed from 1st century CE which spread from NW India into China, Korea, Japan and Tibet; focusing on the concept of the Bodhisattva, who would postpone entry into *nirvana* until all others are similarly enlightened, Mahayana regards the historical Buddha as a temporary manifestation of the eternal and innate nature of the Buddha. *See also* Buddhism.
Mahmud of Ghazni (*var.* Muhammad of Ghazni) (r.971–1030). Ruler of an empire, consisting of Afghanistan, northeastern Persia, and northwest India (r.998–1030). Mahmud was the son of a Turkish ruler of Khurasan, a vassal of the Samanids. His reign was notable for the frequent raids he made on northern India. The Ghaznavid dynasty continued to rule until the late 12th century when they were overthrown by the Ghurids. ✤59●, ✤63, ◆227 (6)
Mainz First use of movable metal type ✤74
Majapahit Empire Javanese empire from the late 13th to the 16th century. Although Majapahit probably exercised direct rule only over Java and nearby small islands, in its heyday in the 14th century, its powerful fleets controlled trade over a far wider area, including the Moluccan Spice Islands.
✤71●, ✤245●, ❑244, ◆245 (6)
Majuba Hill ⚔ (190 BCE). Roman victory over Greece.
◆96 (2), ◆161 (5)◆166 (2)
Makuria
Arab invasion ✤162●
Coptic Christianity ✤58
Malacca
founded (c.1400) ✤75●
captured by Dutch (1641) ✤83●
captured by Portuguese (1510) ✤79●, ◆247 (4)
converts to Islam (1445) ✤75●
trading centre ✤75
Malay Peninsula
Chola conquests ✤59
rubber plantations ❑97
Malaya (now Malaysia)
Independence (1957) ✤251, ◆251 (4)
rebellion (1947–48) ❑251
seized by Japan (1942) ✤103●
Mali Empire West African state at its most powerful in the 13th and 14th centuries. The empire was founded by Sundiata c.1235, though a small state had existed there for some two centuries before. ◆162 (1)–(7)
founded ✤67●, ✤163●
collapses (c.1660) ✤164●
conquered by Songhay (1546) ✤79●
conquered by Sunni Ali ✤75
control of caravan trade ✤70, ✤163
Ibn Battuta's visit (1352) ✤71●
Jenne mosque ❑162
Mansa Musa 14th-century ruler ❑71
usurps Kingdom of Ghana (13th century) ✤66
Malinke West African people, the most influential of the Mali Empire, famous as travelling merchants. ✤163
Mamluks (*var.* Mamelukes). Slave soldiers in many medieval Islamic states, frequently of Turkish origin, noted for their skill and bravery. Mamluks often rose to occupy positions of great power. In Egypt they ruled the country from 1250 until 1517, when it was conquered by the Ottomans.
and Mongols in W Asia ✤67●, ✤69, ✤229, ✤229●, ◆229 (3)
conquered by Ottomans (1517) ✤79●
superbly trained warriors ❑229
takeover of Egypt (1250) ✤67●
Manassas *see* Bull Run
Manaus Founded (1674) ✤149●
Manchester
expansion in 19th century ◆204 (2)
market for finished cloth ✤93
Manchuria
army topples Ming dynasty (1644) ✤83
invasion of Burma (1765–69) ✤87●
Mekong Delta settlement (1679) ✤83●
rulers of the Qing dynasty ✤268
occupied by Japan (1918–20) ✤99●
Song–Jin alliance ✤63
trade
BCE jade imports ✤19●
bronze technology ✤31
Manchu dynasty *see* Qing dynasty
Manda Coastal trading colony (c.800) ✤58
Mandela, Nelson (*f/n* Nelson Rolihlahla Mandela) (1918–). South African Black nationalist and statesman, who was imprisoned for 28 years (1962–90) but was subsequently elected to the presidency in 1994.
imprisoned (1964–90) ✤107●, ✤111, ✤169●
portrait ❑111
wins presidency (1994) ✤111●, ✤168
Mandinka Merchants' topographic reports ✤156
Manichaeism Dualist religion founded in Persia in the 3rd century CE by Mani, who tried to integrate the messages of Zoroaster, Jesus and Buddha into one universal creed. Often regarded as a Christian heresy. ◆49 (4)
Manila galleon Every year, from the late16th century, the Spanish sent a galleon laden with silver from Acapulco to Manila in the Philippines to pay for silk and other luxury goods from China. The galleon returned to Mexico, laden with silks and oriental luxury goods that were then shipped on to Spain. ✤81, ◆81 (3)
Mansa Musa Ruler of Mali Empire (r.c.1312–1337). Under Mansa Musa, the Mali Empire reached the height of its power, largely through its control of the West African gold trade. He demonstrated his country's great wealth on his pilgrimage to Mecca in 1324.
pilgrimage to Mecca (1324) ✤70
ruler of Mali (14th century) ❑71
Mansurah ⚔ of the Crusades (1250). Defeat of the crusader army of Louis IX as it advanced into Egypt. ✤64●, ◆65 (3)
Mansvelt, Edward 17th-century Dutch sailor, who raided Spanish colonies in the Caribbean. ◆85 (2)
Mansurah ⚔ (1250). Louis IX of France defeated and captured by Egyptian army. ◆65 (3)
Manuv *see* Dharma Shastras
Manzikert ⚔ of 1071. Decisive victory of the Seljuk Turks over the Byzantines which resulted in the collapse of Byzantine power in Asia Minor. ✤228●, ◆228 (1)
Mao Tse-tung *see* Mao Zedong
Mao Zedong (*var.* Mao Tse-tung) (1893–1976). Chinese Communist leader and first Chairman of the People's Republic of China (1949).
Chinese Communists win civil war (1949) ✤103●, ✤274, ◆274 (1)
'Great Leap Forward' begins (1958) ✤107●, ✤274, ❑274
imposes Cultural Revolution (1966–70) ✤107●
'Little Red Book' ✤107
portrait ❑107
Maori Indigenous people of New Zealand of Polynesian origin. They reached New Zealand (Aotearoa) c.700 BCE, making it one of the last Pacific island groups to be colonized. ✤283
carved canoe head ❑281
resistance to colonization ✤283●
Maori 'Musket Wars' ✤283 (4) (5)
migration ◆283 (4)
mappamundi ✤173●, ❑66
maquilladora Name given to foreign-owned (often US) assembly plants in Mexico which are used for the import and assembly of duty-free items. ◆136 (1)
Maranhão
established as separate colony from Brazil (1621) ✤149●, ◆149 (3)
occupied by France (1568) ✤149●
Portuguese expelled by Dutch (1625) ✤149●
Maratha Confederacy Hindu state, based in the rock forts of the Western Ghats, the Maratha Confederacy was founded by Sivaji. Although the Mughal emperor Aurangzeb checked the advance of the Marathas during his lifetime, after his death in 1707 the Confederacy gained control over much of India. In 1761 the Marathas confronted invading Afghans and were routed at ⚔ Panipat. Yet the Marathas continued to present a formidable military obstacle to the growing power of the British. The three Anglo-Maratha wars, which took place from 1775–1818 ultimately led to Maratha defeat.
✤87●, ✤246, ✤246●, ◆246 (2)
Marathon ⚔ (490 BCE). Athenian defeat of Persians. ◆223 (4)
Marchand, Jean-Baptiste (1863–1934). French soldier and explorer who in 1898 occupied Fashoda in the Sudan. ◆157 (4)
Marconi, Guglielmo Marchese (1874–1937) Italian physicist and inventor of wireless telegraphy (1895). ✤92●
Marcos, Ferdinand (1917–89). US-sponsored President of the Philippines (r.1965–86), accused of repression, fraud and corruption. Died in exile in Hawaii following electoral defeat. ✤252●
Marcus Antonius *see* Mark Antony
Marcus Ulpius Traianus *see* Trajan
Mari Ancient Mari was the most important city on the middle Euphrates in the 3rd and 2nd millennia BCE, until its destruction by the Babylonians in 1759 BCE. Its importance as the centre of a vast trading network covering northwest Mesopotamia is evidenced by around 20,000 cuneiform tablets which were found there. ✤27
Mariana Islands ⚔ of WW II (Jun–Aug 1944). Scene of a series of major US amphibious assaults during the'island-hopping' campaign in central Pacific.
◆105 (3), ◆272 (1), ✤273, ◆273 (2)
Marie Antoinette (1755–93) Queen of France. The daughter of Maria Theresa of Austria, she married the future Louis XVI of France in 1770. As an Austrian, she was never popular with the French. Her reputation sank even lower with the Revolution and she was tried and executed in 1793. ✤86
Marienburg Teutonic Knights headquarters ❑189
Marignano ⚔ (1515). Swiss defeated by Francis I of France. ◆194 (1)
Marin, Luis 16th-century Spanish colonizer of Mexico. ✤125
Marinids Berber dynasty that ruled Morocco from the 13th to the 15th century.
defeat Almohads (1269) ✤67●
take Tunis (1347) ✤71●
Marius, Gaius (157–86 BCE). Roman general and politician, who married into the aristocracy and achieved high position due to his military talents, including his role in suppressing the rebellious Numidian king, Jugurtha. Ruthlessly ambitious, he held an unprecedented seven consulships, and reformed the army by recruiting men of no property to create a professional fighting force, with the legions divided for the first time into cohorts and centuries. ✤43●
Mark Antony (*var.* Marcus Antonius) (83 BCE–30 BCE). A relative and staunch supporter of Julius Caesar. After Caesar's death in 44 BCE, he almost assumed absolute power in Rome, laying the foundations of future power struggles with Caesar's heir Octavian. While reorganizing the government of the eastern provinces he met Cleopatra, by whom he had several children. When he started giving large areas of Rome's eastern territories to his children, declaring Cleopatra's son by Julius Caesar heir in Octavian's place, Octavian rallied Rome against him. Antony was defeated at Actium in 31 BCE, and committed suicide soon after. ✤180
Market Garden, Operation *see* Arnhem
Marne ⚔ of WW I (Sep 1914). Saw the Allied halting of the German advance on Paris. ◆206 (2)
Marne ⚔ of WW I (Jul 1918). Ended the German offensive on the Western Front. ◆206 (3)
Marquesas Islands Settled by Polynesians ✤60
Marquette, Father Jacques (1637–75) French Jesuit missionary, who accompanied Louis Jolliet down the Mississippi River in 1673, coming to within 640 km of its mouth. ◆119 (2)
Marshall Plan (*aka* European Recovery Program) (Apr 1948–Dec 1951). US-sponsored programme designed to rehabilitate the economies of 17 European nations in order to create stable conditions in which democratic institutions could survive.
✤102●, ✤108●, ✤138, ✤213, ❑213, ◆213 (5)
Martínez de Irala, Domingo (c.1512–56) Commander of the precarious Spanish colony at Asunción in the 1540s and 1550s. He explored the Gran Chaco region and discovered a route across the continent to Peru. ◆142 (1)
Masada Mass suicide of Zealots ✤225
Masaeyli kingdom N African Berber tribal group.
Masina Amadu Lobbo's *jihad* (1816) ✤167●
Masinissa (c.240–148 BCE). Masaeyli ruler of the N African kingdom of Numidia who assisted Rome conquer Carthaginian territory. ✤161●, ◆161 (2)
Massachusetts Bay English colony founded (1630) ✤82●
Massalia (*var. Lat.* Massilia, *mod.* Marseille). Greek colony in the south of France that was a significant political and economic power in the 3rd and 2nd centuries BCE. Gradually absorbed by Rome. ✤34●, ◆38–9
possessions in 3rd century BCE ◆179 (3)
possessions in 120 BCE ◆179 (4)
mastodon relative of the elephant, hunted to extinction c.10,000 years ago. ✤18
Mataram Sultanate of Java
expansion in 17th century ✤83●, ◆245 (5), ◆247 (4)
mathematics
Babylonian text ❑33
16th-century revival of Chinese ✤80
calculating device ❑147
Egyptian counting stick ❑33
evolution of numerical systems ✤33, ◆33 (2)
Maya civilization ✤54
Rhind mathematical papyrus ❑33
Matthias Corvinus *see* Matthias I Hunyadi
Matthias I Hunyadi (*aka* Matthias Corvinus) (1443–90) King of Hungary (r.1458–90). During his reign, Hungary was almost continually at war against Bohemia and the Turks. In 1477 his armies invaded Austria, besieging and capturing Vienna. Patron of learning and science and founder of the Corvina Library at Buda. ❑193, ◆193 (4)
Mauretania
Christian converts (c.150 CE) ✤47●
Roman control ✤46
Mauri Berber inhabitants of the Roman province of Mauretania. ◆161 (2)
Maurits of Nassau (1604–79). Sent by his cousin, the stadholder, Frederick Henry, to govern the colony in Brazil which the Dutch had taken from the Portuguese. After his successful governorship (1836–44) he returned to Europe and fought in wars against Britain and France. ✤149
Mauryan dynasty (321–180 BCE). Ancient Indian dynasty and the first to establish control over all India. Founded by Chandragupta Maurya in 321 BCE and extended by his son Bindusara and his grandson Ashoka. The dynasty's power declined under Ashoka's successors and finally ended in c.180 BCE. ✤43, ✤241, ✤241●, ◆38–9, ◆241 (4)
Mauryan Empire *see* Mauryan dynasty.
Mawson, Sir Douglas (1882–1958) Australian explorer and geologist. Accompanied Shackleton to the Antarctic in 1907–09 and reached the Magnetic S Pole. Led the Australasian Antarctic Expedition 1911–14, and a joint British, Australasian and New Zealand Antarctic expedition in 1929–31. ◆287 (3)
Maya People of Central American and the dominant culture of Central America, between 250 and 900 CE, in present-day southern Mexico, Guatemala, northern Belize and western Honduras. The Maya are famed for their skills in astronomy, including developing solar and sacred calendars, hieroglyphic writing and ceremonial architecture. An elite of priests and nobles ruled the agricultural population from political centres, characterized by plazas and vast palaces and pyramid temples.
(200–790 CE) ◆122 (2)
Arch of Labna ❑122
calendar ✤54
Classic Age (c.300–600) ✤50, ✤54●
collapse in southern lowlands (850) ✤58●
controlled by Aztecs (1519) ✤124
early Central America ◆121 (2)
El Mirador complex (1 CE) ✤46●
Mayapán founded (1283) ✤66●
in post-Classic period ◆124 (1)
state religion ◆36 (1)
Temple of the Jaguars ❑58
vase ❑50
Meadowcroft Rock Shelter (15,000 BCE) ✤14●, ✤120●, ◆120 (1)
Mecca Capital of the Hejaz region of western Saudi Arabia. The birthplace of the Prophet Muhammad, it is Islam's holiest city and the centre of pilgrimage. *See also* Haj.
annual Muslim pilgrimage ❑218
captured by Wahhabis (1806) ✤233
Ibn Battuta's first pilgrimage (1325) ✤68●
Islamic religious centre ✤226, ✤56, ❑226, ◆226 (2) (3)
pilgrimage by Mansa Musa (1324) ✤70
Medes Ancient people who lived to the south-west of the Caspian Sea. They were at their peak during the 7th century BCE when, alongside the Babylonians, they conquered the Assyrians and extended their power westwards to central Anatolia and eastwards through most of Persia. Their empire was overwhelmed by the Persians in the mid-6th century BCE. ✤31, ◆34–35
Medina Muhammad's capital (622) ✤55●, ✤56, ✤226
Mediterranean
700–300 BCE ◆176–7, ◆177 (1)
colonization ✤176
religions (BCE) ◆37 (3)
megaliths (*var.* cromlechs, *Gr.* mega lithas: large stones). – European prehistoric structures, often tombs, were constructed of massive, roughly dressed stone slabs and were built across Europe during the Neolithic period, from c.5000 BCE. They are comparable, although unrelated, to megalithic monuments found in S India, Tibet, and SE Asia. ◆22
Mehmet Ali *see* Muhammad Ali
Megiddo ⚔ of WWI (18–23 Sep 1918). Final battle of the Palestine campaign fought by British and Commonwealth troops against Turkey. A British and Commonwealth victory, it also marked the last use of massed cavalry in warfare.
✤232●, ◆233 (2)
Mehmet II 'the Conqueror' (1432–1481) Ottoman Sultan (r.1451–81) who in 1453 captured Constantinople (Istanbul) and pursued the rapid expansion of the empire into Greece, the Balkans, and Hungary.
fall of Constantinople (1453) ✤75, ✤230
Topkapi palace ❑231
Mehmet VI (1861–1926) Ottoman Sultan (r.1918–22). His failure to suppress the Turkish Nationalists, led by Mustafa Kemal (Atatürk), resulted in the abolition of the sultanate, and his subsequent exile. ✤233
Mehrgarh Early pottery discovered ✤19, ✤20●, ✤23●
Meiji Japanese term meaning 'enlightened rule'. The restoration of the Meiji emperor in 1868 ended Japan's two centuries of isolationism under the Tokugawa Shogunate and initiated a period of political and economic reform.
modernization of Japan ◆270 (1)
Melanesia One of three broad geographical divisions of the Pacific, the others being Micronesia and Polynesia. Melanesia includes New Guinea, New Caledonia, the Solomons and Vanuatu. ✤276

SUBJECT INDEX AND GLOSSARY: **Melbourne – Muhammad**

Melbourne Founded (1835–36) ✤91
Memphis ⚔ of American Civil War (5 Jun 1862). Union victory. ◆131 (6)
Memphis (Egypt)
founded (3100 BCE) ✤23●
BCE invasions ✤34, ✤35●
Mena *see* Narmer
Mencius (*var.* Meng-tzu) (c.371–c.289 BCE) Chinese philosopher who continued the teachings of Confucius. Developed a school to promote Confucian ideas, and from the age of 40 travelled China for 20 years searching for a ruler to implement Confucian morals and ideals. Believed that man was by nature good, but required the proper conditions for moral growth. ✤37
Mendaña, Álvaro de (c.1542–95) Spanish explorer of the Pacific. On Mendaña's first Pacific voyage in 1568, he discovered the Solomon Islands. He was attempting to return there and establish a colony in 1595, but he could not find the islands. He died on Santa Cruz Island. ✤278●
Mendoza, Hurtado de 16th-century Spanish explorer of Lower California. ✤125, ◆125 (4)
Menéndez de Avilés, Pedro 16th-century Spanish *conquistador* and explorer of N America. Founded San Agustín in Florida (1565). ✤125, ◆125 (4)
Menes *see* Narmer
Meneses, Jorge de 16th-century Portuguese traveller in the East Indies. Sighted New Guinea (1526) ✤278●
Meng-tzu *see* Mencius
Meni *see* Narmer
Mercator, Gerardus (*prev.* Gerhard Kremer) (1512–94) Flemish cartographer. Originator of the Mercator projection and publisher of the first book to use the world 'Atlas' to describe a set of maps. ✤79, ✤173, ✤173●, ❑173
Meroë
BCE–CE capital of Egypt ✤34–5, ✤42
Cushite temple relic ❑35
invaded by Axumites (c.350) ✤50●
Merovingians (c.448–751) The first dynasty of Frankish kings of Gaul, named after Merovech, grandfather of Clovis I. ✤183, ◆183 (5) (6)
Mesa Verde cliff dwellings (c.1100) ✤62●, ✤123●
Mesolithic Literally the 'middle stone age', this is a term applied to the transitional period between the Palaeolithic (old stone age) and Neolithic (new stone age) in western Europe. The Mesolithic covers around five millennia from the end of the last Ice Age, c.10,000 BCE and the adoption of farming, c.5000 years ago. The Mesolithic is a transitional period, when Ice Age hunters gradually adapted to climatic changes and new environments and resources. It is characterized in the archaeological record by chipped stone tools, in particular microliths, very small stone tools intended for mounting on a shaft. These, as well as tools made of bone, antler and wood, were used by hunter-gatherer communities, roughly contemporary with Neolithic farming groups further east. ✤14, ❑14, ✤18●
Mesopotamia The area between the Tigris and Euphrates, literally 'land between the rivers'. Lower Mesopotamia covered Baghdad to the Persian Gulf, and was home to the world's first urban civilizations in the 4th millennium BCE. Upper Mesopotamia extended from Baghdad north-west to the foothills of eastern Anatolia. ◆222 (1)
BCE ✤19, ✤35, ✤43, ◆36 (1)
city-states ✤27
history and legends ✤222, ❑222
Ottoman and Safavid clashes ✤79
pictograph writing (c.3250) ✤23
Seleucid Empire ✤41, ✤224, ◆38–9, ◆224 (1)
trading links ✤25
urban expansion and revolution (BCE) ✤23, ✤24●, ✤28, ◆28 (1)
metallurgy The range of techniques associated with metal-working: extracting metals from their ores, converting them into useful forms such as alloys, and fabricating objects.
BCE use ✤18–19, ✤23●, ✤30–1, ✤34, ✤174–5
development ✤26●
Eurasian and African tin trade (c.1 CE) ◆44–5
gold rushes ✤90●, ✤93
See also bronze; copper; gold; silver
Metaurus River ⚔ of Punic Wars (207 BCE). Roman victory. ◆179 (3)
Metternich, Clemens Fürst von (1773–1859) Austrian statesman. In 1809 he became Austrian foreign minister and was instrumental in the fall of Napoleon. He was the architect of the 'Vienna system' in 1814–15, and the major force in European politics from 1814 until he was forced from office by the Viennese revolution of 1848. ❑202
Mexican Civil War (1858–67). Broke out between conservatives and liberals in 1858. The liberal leader Benito Juárez became president. His defeat of the conservative forces in 1860 was dependent on loans from western powers. France, Spain and Britain invaded Mexico to enforce loan repayments; in 1863 a French army occupied Mexico city. The French appointed Archduke Maximilian of Austria as Mexican emperor. He was ousted in 1867 by Juárez' forces, and Juárez was re-elected as president (1867–72). ✤94●, ◆128–9●
Mexican Revolution (1910–20). Beginning in 1910 with a revolt against the incumbent dictator Porfirio Diáz, and the entrenched interests of landowners and industrialists, the Mexican Revolution drew in a range of different factions in a protracted struggle which eventually led to the creation of Mexico as a constitutional republic. ✤133, ◆133 (3)
See also Victoriano Huerta, Francisco Madero, Pancho Villa, Emiliano Zapata
Mexican-American War (*var. Sp.* Guerra de 1847, Guerra de Estados Unidos) (Apr 1846–Feb 1848). The result of the US annexation of Texas in 1845 and a subsequent dispute over the territorial extent of Texas. A series of battles on land and sea resulted in US victory, and the military phase of the war ended with the fall of Mexico City. Via the Treaty of Guadalupe Hidalgo, the US gained the territory that would become the states of New Mexico, Utah, Nevada, Arizona, California, Texas, and western Colorado for $15,000,000. ✤129●, ◆128–9 (2)
Mexico ◆118–129, ✤133 (3), ◆136–139
church of St. Francis at Tlaxcala ❑125
cultures
Aztec ✤66
Aztec rule in the Valley ◆124 (2)
major civilizations ◆122 (1)
Mexica ✤66
Olmec (1200 BCE) ✤30
Toltec ✤58, ◆122 (1)
foreign affairs
Texan rebellion (1836) ✤90●
US war (1846–48) ✤90●, ✤128, ✤129●, ◆128–9 (2)
home affairs
centre of Spanish Empire in N America (1521) ✤81
city-states ✤66, ✤122
Civil War (1858) ✤94●, ✤129●
Cortés' invasion and conquest (1519–21) ◆125 (5)
Federalist (Centralist wars ✤129●
gains independence (1821) ✤90●
regional inequality ✤136
revolution (1910) ✤98●, ✤128, ✤129●, ✤132–3, ❑133, ◆133 (3)
Spanish colonization ✤125●
pottery dog ❑122
Mfecane (*var.* Difaqane, 'the Crushing'). A series of Zulu and other Nguni wars and forced migrations in southern Africa during the first half of the 19th century which were set in motion by the rise of the Zulu military kingdom under Shaka. ✤166●, ◆166 (2)
Michael Palaeologus (c.1277–1320). Byzantine co-emperor with his father, Andronicus II, from 1295, who failed to stem the decline of the empire, despite his efforts in fighting the Turks and in resisting the invasions of Catalan mercenaries. ✤187●
Mickey Mouse First appearance (1928) ❑135
microliths Tool technology which developed in Africa c.30,000 years ago, and some time after the peak of the last Ice Age, c.16,000 years ago, in Europe. Small (microlithic) flints were mounted in a range of bone or wooden hafts, to make 'composite' tools, which could be used to exploit the much wider range of food resources becoming available as the last Ice Age ended. ✤16●
Micronesia Region of the western Pacific, dotted with tiny archipelagos, including the Marianas and the Marshall Islands. The peoples of Micronesia are of more mixed ancestry than those of Polynesia to the east, having had more frequent contact with mainland E Asia. ✤276, ◆281 (3)
microscopes *see* optical instruments
Middendorff, Alexander von 19th-century Russian explorer of Siberia. ◆257 (2)
Middleburg ⚔ of Dutch Revolt (1574). Dutch victory over Spain. ◆195 (5)
Middle East
Arab-Israeli wars ✤234●, ◆234 (2) (3)
peace process begins (1977) ✤111●
spread of Communism (1958) ✤138●
territorial crisis ✤98
See also individual countries, West Asia
Middle Kingdom Division of ancient Egyptian history, c.2050–1750 BCE, which saw some expansion into Palestine, and fortification of the Nubian frontier. ✤27●, ✤159●, ◆159 (4)
Midway Naval ⚔ of WW II (Jun 1942). Defeat of Japanese by US forces in mid-Pacific Ocean, marking turning point in Pacific War. ✤103●, ◆104 (2), ◆272 (1)
migration
aims ✤52
of peoples (300–500 CE) ✤92–3●, ◆92–3 (1) (2) (3)
19th century ✤100
depictions
Chinese construction workers ❑101
hardship and overcrowding on ships ❑100
settlers populate western USA ❑94
to the US ❑100
US Indians 'Trail of Tears' ✤129, ❑129
from Ireland (1845) ✤90●
German-led ✤189
global ✤100–1
indentured labour ✤101, ✤151, ◆101 (3)
inheritors of western Europe (526 CE) ✤53, ◆53 (2)
and invasions ✤52–3
Jewish (1880–1914) ✤101, ✤101●, ◆101 (2)
Jewish and Palestinian (1947–96) ◆234 (3)
Magyar ◆185 (3)
mass ✤90
Polynesian ✤60, ◆60 (2)
steppe kingdoms of Central Asia ✤261, ◆261 (6)
to the New World ✤100●
in the USA ✤134–5, ✤134●, ◆134 (3)
world (c.1860–1920) ◆100 (1)
Milan, Edict of (313 CE). Proclamation that permanently established religious toleration for Christianity within the Roman Empire. It was the outcome of a political agreement concluded in Milan between the Roman emperors Constantine I and Licinius in Feb 313 CE. ✤48●
Milne Bay ⚔ of WW II (Aug 1942). Defeat of Japanese landing force in southeastern New Guinea. ✤104, ◆104 (2)
Milošević, Slobodan (1941–). Politician and administrator who, as leader of the League of Communists of Serbia (from 1987) and president (1989–97), pursued Serb nationalist policies that led to the breakup of Yugoslavia. ✤215
Milvian Bridge ⚔ (312). Constantine defeated his rival Maxentius just north of Rome to become master of the western half of the Roman Empire. He attributed his victory to a vision of the cross of Christ he had seen on the eve of the battle. ✤181●
Min *see* Narmer
Minamoto Yoritomo (1147–99). Founder of the Kamakura Shogunate in Japan, who crushed the Taira clan. ✤63●, ❑265
Minas Gerais The rich gold-mining area of Brazil, which helped prop up the Portuguese economy in the 18th century. Gold was first discovered there in 1695.
gold discovered (1695) ✤149●
Jesuits banned from region (1711) ✤143●, ◆143 (3), ✤149 (3)
minerals
deposits in Africa ◆96 (2)
early Central American resources ◆121 (2)
late 19th-century finds ◆93 (2) (3)
S American resources ◆153 (3)
Mines Act (1842) Act passed by British parliament, forbidding employment of women and children underground. ✤204●
Ming dynasty (1368–1644) Ruling dynasty of China.
rulers of China ✤266–7, ✤70–1, ◆78–9, ◆266–7 (1)
bowl (16th century) ❑162
campaign against Mongols ✤75●, ✤266
guardian of the spirit world ❑71 and the outside world ✤267●, ◆267 (3)
restores Chinese values ✤71
revolts ✤22, ◆266 (2)
self-sufficiency policy ✤75●
toppled by Manchus (1644) ✤83
Zhu Yuanzhang founder of dynasty ✤71, ✤266
Ming Empire *see* Ming dynasty
Minoan civilization Named after the legendary King Minos of Crete, the Minoans were the first great European civilization, c.2000 BCE, whose main cities were Knossos and Phaestus. They had strong trade links with Egypt, and flourished due to their control of sea routes c.2200–1450 BCE. Evidence from their complex palaces attests their high standards of art, metal-working and jewellery-making. Early Minoan pictorial writing has been found, dating to around 1880 BCE, which was superseded by the still undeciphered Linear A and then early Greek writing known as Linear B.
civilization (2000 BCE) ✤27●, ✤175●, ◆175 (4)
frescoes of bull-leaping game ❑27
palace built (2000 BCE) ✤27●
snake goddess (c.1500 BCE) ❑175
Minos The first king of Crete, according to legend, the son of Zeus and Europa, and husband of Pasiphae. Knossos was said to have been his capital from where he ruled a powerful seafaring empire. The ancient civilization of Crete, Minoan civilization, is named after him. His palace at Knossos was built c.2000 BCE.
bull cult ✤37
Minsk ⚔ of WW II (Jun–Aug 1943). Encirclement of German forces by Soviets in Belorussia. ◆211 (3) (4)
MIRV *see* Multiple Independently Targeted Warhead Re-entry Vehicle.
Mississippian culture (c.800–1500 CE). Based in the river valleys of the present-day states of Mississippi, Alabama, Georgia, Arkansas, Missouri, Kentucky, Illinois, Indiana, and Ohio, with scattered populations in Wisconsin and Minnesota and on the Great Plains. A settled agricultural culture, they are distinctive for the oval earthworks which dominated most settlements. ✤66●, ✤123 (5)
first towns (c.750) ✤58●
missionary expeditions ✤119●
true towns (c.1050) ✤62●
Mississippi River
earth mounds ✤66, ✤74
explored by Jolliet and Marquette (1673) ✤119●
explored by La Salle (1682) ✤119●
Missouri Compromise (1820). The measure which allowed for the admission of Missouri as the 24th US state in 1821. James Tallmadge's attempt to add an anti-slavery amendment legislation for the admission of new states to the US led to a major debate over the right of the government to restrict slavery in new states. The issue remained unresolved in Dec 1819 when the northern state of Maine applied for statehood. The Senate passed a bill allowing Maine to enter the Union as a free state and Missouri to be admitted with no restriction on slavery. A further amendment was then added that allowed Missouri to become a slave state but banned slavery in the rest of the Louisiana Purchase north of latitude 36°30'. ✤130, ◆130 (1)
Mitanni Indo-Persian people whose empire in northern Mesopotamia flourished between c.1500–1360 BCE. Their capital, Wahshukanni, was probably in the Khabur River region, and at their height they ruled over lands from the Zagros Mountains west to the Mediterranean.
conflict with Egyptians and Hittites (1250 BCE) ✤27●, ◆26–7
Mitchell, Thomas (1792–1855) Scottish-born soldier and explorer. Surveyor-General of New South Wales from 1827, he led several important expeditions into the Australian interior. ◆279 (2)
Mithraism Worship of Mithras, an ancient Indian and Persian god of justice and law. Spread as a mystery cult in the Roman Empire, with Mithras as a divine saviour. Ousted by Christianity in the 4th century CE.
BCE cult ❑37 (3)
portrayal of Mithras ❑48
spread of (600 BCE) ✤48, ◆48 (1)
Mithras *see* Mithraism
Mithradates II (d.88 BCE). After recovering the eastern provinces that had been overrun during his father's reign, Mithridates was one of the most successful Parthian kings, concluding the first treaty between Parthia and Rome in 92 BCE. ◆42–3
Mobile (⚔ of Mobile Bay). ⚔ of American Civil War (5 Aug 1864). Union victory. ◆131 (7)
Mobuto, Sese Seko Koko Ngbendu wa za Banga (Joseph-Désiré) (1930–97). President of Zaire. Mobutu staged a coup to become president in 1965 and held on to power for over 30 years despite the flagrant corruption of his regime. He finally lost control Zaire, while in Europe for medical treatment in 1997 and never returned.
overthrown (1997) ✤111
portrait ❑107
moccasin BCE antelope hide ❑18
Moche culture (*var.* Mohica). The earliest major civilization on the north coast of Peru, based in the ancient city of Moche around 200 BCE–550 CE. It is best known for the twin brick pyramids of the Sun and Moon, Huaca del Sol and Huaca de la Luna, which were richly decorated with multi-coloured murals. The Moche people also carried out extensive irrigation, fortified their ceremonial centres, and produced cast, alloyed and gilded metalwork. ✤42●, ✤145, ◆145 (4), ◆146 (1)
fanged deity pot ❑46
stirrup-spouted vessel ❑54, ❑145
Mogollon Native American culture of the US Southwest.
✤58, ◆123 (4)
defensive pueblos (1050) ✤123●
Mimbres pottery ❑123
Mogul dynasty *see* Mughal dynasty
Mohács ⚔ of (1526). Ottomans crush Hungarian army. ✤79●, ◆195 (2)
Mohammed *see* Muhammed
Mohenjo-Daro ✤23, ❑240, ◆240 (1)
Mohica *see* Moche culture
Moluccas (Spice Islands) ✤79, ✤80, ❑239, ❑247
money *see* coins; economy
Möngke (d.1259) Mongol leader, a grandson of Genghis Khan, elected Great Khan in 1251. Möngke's rule saw the start of the so-called 'Mongol Peace', when travel and trade across Central Asia flourished. ✤68
See also Mongols.
Mongols Pastoralist, nomadic people of Central Asia. Their conquests from the 13th century onwards were the last assault by nomadic armies inflicted upon the settled peoples of western Asia. ◆68–9 (1) (2)
age of the Mongols ✤68–9
campaigns ✤69, ✤75●, ◆68–9 (1), ◆189 (4), ◆263 (7), ◆265 (5)
capital of Karakorum founded (1235) ✤68●
cavalryman ❑69
Chinese rebellions (1335) ✤71●
conquests
13th century ✤69●
Central Asia (1206) ✤256●
Chinese (1449) ✤75●
Kaifeng captured (1233) ✤67●
Khwarizm Empire (1219) ✤67●
northern China (1211) ✤67●
Russian ✤66●, ✤69, ✤75, ✤189●
sacking of Baghdad (1258) ✤67, ✤69●, ✤229, ❑229
Song resistance crushed (1279) ✤69●
converts to Islam ✤67
defeats
Ain Jalut (1260) ✤67●, ✤69●
Annam and Pagan forays ✤67
invasions of Japan (1274, 1281) ✤67●, ✤69●
Java (1293) ✤67
Mamluk ✤67●, ✤69, ✤229, ✤229●, ◆229 (3)
periods of peace ✤68, ✤68●, ✤267
Yuan period (c.1300) ✤263, ◆263 (7)
Monmouth Court House ⚔ of American Revolutionary War (28 Jun 1778). Inconclusive result. ◆127 (3)
monotheism ✤37, ◆36 (1)
monsoon Wind system involving seasonal reversal of prevailing wind direction. Occurs mainly in the Indian Ocean, the western Pacific, and off the W African coast. The term also applies to the rainy seasons of much of southern and eastern Asia, and of E and W Africa.
Montagnais Native American peoples of northeastern N America. ✤119, ◆126 (1)
Montcalm, Louis Joseph, Marquis de (1712–59). Commander of the French troops in Canada in the Seven Years' War. He was mortally wounded defending Quebec. ✤127, ◆127 (2)
Monte Albán
influential Mexican city ❑122, ◆122 (1)
Los Danzantes ❑34
Zapotec culture ✤38●, ✤121
Monte Cassino *see* Cassino
Monte Verde
early settlements ✤144●, ◆144 (1)
environmental survival strategies (BCE) ✤14● 16
stone tools ❑144
Montejos, the 16th-century Spanish explorers of N America (1527, 1545). ✤125, ◆125 (4)
Montenegro ✤203, ◆203 (4), ◆232 (1), ✤232
See also Balkans, nationalism
Montezuma II *see* Moteuczoma Xocoyotl
Montgomery, Alabama Boycott against segregation (1955) ✤137●, ◆137 (2)
Montmirail ⚔ of Napoleon's defence of France (11 Feb 1814). French victory. ◆200 (1)
Montoya, Father Ruiz de 17th-century Jesuit missionary in South America. ✤143●
Montreal
captured by British (1760) ✤127●, ◆127 (2)
European and native conflict (1689) ✤126
French settlement map (1642) ❑126
Morgan, Sir Henry (c.1635–88) Welsh buccaneer who operated in the West Indies, preying primarily on Spanish ships and territories including Panama, which he captured in 1671. Though arrested and transported to London to placate the Spanish, he returned to the West Indies and became a wealthy planter. ❑85, ◆85 (2)
Morgarten ⚔ (1315). Austrian Habsburg forces defeated by Swiss peasant army. ◆193 (5)
Morocco 165–169
Almohad sect established (1147) ✤63●
Almohads defeated by Marinids (1269) ✤67●
Ceuta captured by Portuguese (1415) ✤75●
French occupation ◆167 (4)
independence ◆168 (1)
Muhammad III becomes Sultan (1757) ✤87●
Portuguese invasion crushed (1578) ✤79●
Songhay Empire captured (1591) ✤79●
Morse Code Code consisting of dots and dashes devised for use with the electric telegraph he had designed by American painter and inventor Samuel Morse (1791–1872). ✤98
mosaics
Aztec serpant pendant ❑124
castle, ships and harbour of Ravenna (6th century) ❑182
Darius III at ⚔ Issus ❑40
floor mosaic of Orpheus ❑181
Macedonian lion hunt ❑179
map of Jerusalem ❑51
Roman ❑47
The Nile in flood ❑47
Vandal landowner ❑52
Moscow ⚔ of WW II (Dec 1941). Soviet forces halted German advance during *Operation Barbarossa*. ◆210 (1)
Moscow Napoleon's retreat (1812) ✤90●
Moshoeshoe Lesotho kingdom (1824) ◆166 (2)
Moslem *see* Muslim
Moteuczoma I Aztec ruler (1440–68) ✤74●, ◆124 (1)
Moteuczoma Xocoyotl (*aka* Montezuma II) (1466–1520) 9th emperor of the Aztec Empire (1502–20). During the Spanish conquest of Mexico by Hernán Cortés and his conquistadors, he was deposed as ruler and imprisoned.
Aztec ruler (1502) ✤78●, ✤124, ◆124 (1)
last Aztec emperor ✤78●
moundbuilders *see* earthworks
Moundville Mississippian cultural site ✤123, ◆123 (5)
Mount Olympus, cult centre ✤37
Mozambique independence (1975) ✤107●, ✤111●, ✤168, ◆168 (1)
post-independence ◆169 (4)
MPLA *see* People's Movement for the Liberation of Angola
MRV *see* Multiple Re-entry Vehicle
Msiri 19th-century trader who settled with his Nyamwezi followers in southern Katanga, central Africa in 1856. Msiri dominated the region by about 1870. ✤166
Mughal dynasty (*var.* Mogul dynasty) (1526–1857). The victory of Babur, an Afghan Muslim, at Panipat in 1525, was the beginning of the Mughal Empire, which was to dominate India until 1739. The empire reached its peak during the reign of Akbar, when it extended from Bengal to Sind and Gujarat, and from Kashmir to the Godavari river. From the 1670s, confrontation with the Marathas, a new Hindu power, depleted the power of the Mughals and decline soon set in. In 1739 Nadir Shah of Persia swept into India, and sacked Delhi, and from this point the Mughals were merely puppet emperors. ✤79, ✤246, ✤246●, ◆78–9, ◆246 (1)
Persian incursions ✤87
powers declines (1707) ✤87
route map ❑238
troops raiding sheep herds ❑267
Mughal Empire *see* Mughal dynasty.
Muhammad (*var.* Mohammed) (c.570–632). Founder of Islamic religion, born in Mecca (Saudi Arabia). In 610 a vision of the Angel Gabriel revealed messages

Key to index: ✤ text ● timeline ❑ picture ◆ map *var.* variant name *aka* also known as *f/n* full name *prev.* previously known as r. ruled ⚔ battle WW I First World War WW II Second World War

SUBJECT INDEX AND GLOSSARY: **Muhammad III – Newton, Sir Isaac**

from God. These messages, written down as the Koran (meaning 'Reading' or 'Recitation'), are revered as the Holy Book of Islam. In 622 Muhammad and his followers were forced to move to Medina, a migration (*Hegira*) which marks the beginning of the Islamic calendar. As a religious leader (Umma), he conquered Mecca in 630, destroyed the pagan idols and unified much of Arabia. His legacy passed to his father-in-law, Abu Bakr, the first caliph. ✤55, ✤56, ✤66, ✤61●, ✤218, ✤226
Hegira ◆226 (2)

Muhammad III Sultan of Morocco (r.1757–90), who introduced administrative reforms and reopened trade with Europe after a long embargo. ✤87●

Muhammad al Ghur *see* Muhammad of Ghur

Muhammad Ali (c.1769–1849) (*var.* Mehmet Ali, Mohammed Ali). Viceroy of Egypt (1805–48), who made Egypt the leading power in the eastern Mediterranean. An Albanian military officer, he went to Egypt (1801) in command of an Ottoman army sent to face Napoleon. After many successful military campaigns, he turned against the Ottomans, defeating them in Asia Minor (1839), but European intervention prevented the overthrow of the sultan. ✤232
possessions 1840 ◆90–1
Viceroy of Egypt (1804) ✤90

Muhammad Ibn Adullah *see* Ibn Battuta

Muhammad of Ghazni *see* Mahmud of Ghazni

Muhammad of Ghur (*var.* Ghiyas al-Din) (d.1202) (r.1173–1202). Leader of an Afghan army, in 1191 he defeated the Rajput clans of northern India, and in 1206 his general, Qutb al-Din Aybak, established the first Turko-Afghan dynasty in Delhi, ruling it as sultan.
defeats Rajput clans (1191) ✤63●
Ghurid dynasty ◆244 (2)

Muisca (*var.* Chibcha). Native people of the highlands around Bogotá. It was in Muisca lands that the legend of El Dorado caught the imagination of Spanish *conquistadores*. ❑147

Mujahedin (*var.* Mujahideen). Islamic nationalist forces during Afghan civil war (from 1973) who spearheaded resistance to Soviet invasion (1979–89) with Pakistani backing, forming a government (1983), but opposed by Taliban from 1995. ◆235 (4)

Mujahideen *see* Mujahedin

Multiple Re-entry Vehicle (MRV) ICBM developed by US in the early 1960s that could deliver a 'footprint' of warheads in a selected area, greatly increasing US nuclear potential during the Cold War. ✤109

Multiple Independently Targeted Warhead Re-entry Vehicle (MIRV) ICBM developed by US in late 1960s, that could select several targets, greatly escalating US nuclear potential during the Cold War. ✤109

Mumbai *see* Bombay

mummification Preservation of human and animal bodies by embalming and wrapping in lengths of cloth, after removal of the internal organs. Mummification is associated with belief in life after death, and was practised by the ancient Egyptians amongst others.
ancestor cults ✤147
Chimú funerary mask ❑66
Egyptian ❑31
goddess Anubis ❑37
Paracas region ❑145
Roman mummy case ❑47

Mungo, Lake Site of first known cremation (26,000 BP) ✤16●

Murad I (c.1326–89) Third Ottoman Sultan, who pursued the expansion of the empire in the Balkans, annexing Bulgaria and much of Serbia. He was killed at the battle of Kosovo Polje. ✤230, ◆230 (1)

Muret ⚔ of Albigensian Crusade (1213). Peter II of Aragon killed by crusading army. ◆186 (2)

Murfreesboro (⚔ of Stones River). ⚔ of American Civil War (31 Dec 1862–2 Jan 1863). Union victory. ◆131 (6)

Muscovy State created by the Grand Princes of Moscow in the 13th century. Though isolated, Muscovy became increasingly powerful through the annexation of Novgorod and the proclamation of independence from the Mongols in 1480. By 1556 Muscovy had annexed the Khanate of Astrakhan, controlling the Volga down to the Caspian Sea. In 1571 Moscow was sacked by Crimean Tatars.
14th century ◆70–1
throws off Mongol yoke (1480) ✤75●

Muscovy Company Formed in 1555 by the navigator and explorer Sebastian Cabot and various London merchants in order to trade with Russia, the company was granted a monopoly of Anglo-Russian trade.
sponsors of Arctic exploration ✤286

Musket Wars A series of conflicts between Maori tribes in the 1820s, sparked by the introduction of European firearms into New Zealand. ✤283, ◆283 (4)

Muslim (*var.* Moslem, Mussulman) Of or pertaining to the Islamic faith. *See* Islam.

Muslim League Formed in 1906, as a result of the conflicts created within Bengal by Lord Curzon's 1905 partition of the province. The League's original aim was to promote separate electorates for Muslim minorities within Hindu majority areas, but by the 1940s it had started to demand a separate Muslim state. It was pressure from the League that led to the creation of Pakistan in 1947. ✤250●

Mussolini, Benito Amilcare Andrea (1883–1945) Italian dictator (1925–43). Expelled from the socialist party for pressing for support of the Allies during WW I; after the war Mussolini founded the *Fasci di Combattimento* (Fascist movement). Aided by Blackshirt supporters, he attacked Communism, and in 1922 marched on Rome. He was appointed Prime Minister by King Victor Emmanuel III, and by 1925 had declared himself *Il Duce* (the leader) and swiftly established a totalitarian regime within Italy. In 1935 he invaded Ethiopia as part of a plan to form an Italian empire, and by 1936 had formed the Rome-Berlin axis with Hitler, declaring war on the Allies in 1940. Dependence on Hitler broke support for Mussolini and he was deposed and executed in 1945. ✤207, ✤209, ◆209 (3)

Mutapa Empire (var. Muwenutapa). Kingdom of southern Africa that flourished between the 15th and 18th centuries. ✤164
absorbs Great Zimbabwe (c.1450) ✤75●

Mustafa Kemal Pasha *see* Atatürk

Mutually Assured Destruction (MAD). Term coined by US Secretary of State John Foster Dulles (1953–59) to describe Cold War intercontinental arms stalemate between US and Soviet Union. ✤108●

Mwenemutapa *see* Mutapa Empire

Mycale (*var.* Gre. Mykale) ⚔ (479 BCE) Defeat of the Persian navy by the Greeks off the coast of Asia Minor. ✤39, ◆176 (1)

Mycenaean Greece Named after its capital Mycenae, Bronze Age Greek culture which dominated mainland Greece between 1580–1120 BCE. The Mycenaeans appear to have conquered Knossos in Crete around 1450 BCE, and they traded widely in Asia Minor, Cyprus and Syria. Their sacking of Troy c.1200 BCE was later mythologized in Homer's *Iliad*. Archaeological evidence points to great wealth and skill, with palaces at Mycenae, Tiryns and Pylos at the centre of a system of government by a distinct warrior class overseeing a redistributive economy. The final destruction or abandonment of these palaces is now thought to be due to internal unrest rather than external conquest. 175●, ◆175 (4)
bronze dagger blade ❑26
civilization (1250 BCE) ◆26–7
dominant power on Greek mainland (1550 BCE) ✤27●
mythology ✤37
pot ❑31
ritual sprinkler ❑37

Mysore Conquered by Britain (1799) ✤87●

mythology Origins of religion ✤36–7

Mzilikazi Ndebele kingdom (1826) ◆166 (2)

N

Naddod 9th-century Viking explorer who visited Iceland (c.870). ◆172 (2)

Nadir Shah (1688–1747). A bandit chieftain of Turkish origin, in 1736 he seized the Safavid throne of Persia, immediately embarking on campaigns against neighbouring states. In 1739 he attacked Delhi, capital of Mughul India, slaughtered its citizens and stole the Koh-i-noor diamond. Cruel and ruthless, he was eventually assassinated by his own troops. ✤87, ✤246, ✤246●, ❑246

NAFTA *see* North American Free Trade Agreement

Nagasaki Atom bombs dropped (1945) ✤103●, ✤105●, ✤273●, ◆273 (3)

Nain Singh 19th-century Indian surveyor, who made an epic journey in disguise through Tibet on behalf of the Survey of India. ✤257●, ◆257 (3)

Nanda Empire ✤241, ◆241 (4)

Nanjing
centre of Jin dynasty ✤51
rebellion (1853) ✤95●
Treaty (1842) ✤91●

Nanjing, Treaty of *see* Opium War.

Nansen, Fridjof (1861–1930). Norwegian scientist, explorer and statesman. Crossed Greenland icecap in 1888 on foot. In his specially-designed ship, the *Fram*, he explored the Arctic from 1893–96, stopping to take part in a bid for the North Pole. In 1918 he became a commissioner to the League of Nations and was awarded the Nobel Peace Prize in 1923 for his work in assisting famine-struck regions of the Soviet Union. ◆286–7 (2)

Nantes, Edict of (1598). Order signed by Henry IV of France granting Huguenots the right to practise their own religion. It was revoked in 1685 by Louis XIV, and as a result many non-Catholics fled the country. ✤78●

Napoleon I, Bonaparte (1769–1821) French military and political leader, and Emperor of France (1804–1815). Following successful Italian campaign (1796–7) and invasion of Egypt (1798), he assumed power as First Consul in 1799. A brilliant general, he defeated every European coalition which fought against him. Decline set in with failure of Peninsular War in Spain and disastrous invasion of Russia (1812). Defeated at Leipzig (1813) by a new European alliance, he went into exile but escaped and ruled as emperor during the Hundred Days. Finally defeated at Waterloo (1815) and exiled to St. Helena. As an administrator, his achievements were of lasting significance and include the *Code Napoléon*, which remains the basis for French law. ◆200–1 (1) (2)
abdicates (1814) ✤202●
aftermath of wars ✤90
campaigns ◆200–1, ✤200●, ❑200, ◆200–1 (1)
Code Napoléon ❑200
coup brings power in France ✤86●
defeated at Waterloo (1815) ✤200, ✤202●
Emperor of France ❑201
French Empire 1812 ◆90–1, ◆201 (2)
occupies Egypt (1798) ✤87●, ✤200, ❑201
opposition alliances ✤201, ◆201 (3)
retreats from Moscow (1812) ✤90●, ✤200
rise and fall ✤200
Tilsit peace talks ❑201

Napoleon III (*var.* Charles Louis Napoléon Bonaparte) (1808–1873). Nephew of Napoleon I, Emperor of the French (1852–71). Involved France in the Crimean War (1853–6) and allowed Bismarck to provoke him into the Franco-Prussian War (1870–1), which ended in France's defeat and Napoleon's exile to Britain. *See also* Crimean War, Franco-Prussian War.
elected emperor Napoleon III (1852)
president of Second Republic (1848) ✤202●
revolts against his rule ◆202 (1)
surrenders to Wilhelm I ❑203

Naqa Cushite temple relic ❑35

Naqada Founded (c.3300) ✤24●

Nara period (710–784). Period of Japanese history that began with the establishment of a capital at Heijo-kyo (to the west of the modern city of Nara). ✤55●, ✤265●, ✤265, ◆265 (3)

Narbo (Narbonne), Visigothic state (414) ✤53●

Narmer, King (*var.* Menes, Mena, Meni, Min). The first pharaoh of the New Kingdom in Egypt (the height of his rule was c.2925 BCE), Narmer unified the formerly discrete fortified towns of Upper and Lower Egypt into a powerful state, and is credited with founding the capital at Memphis near Cairo. According to the 3rd century BCE historian Manetho, Narmer ruled for 62 years and was killed by a hippo. ✤22

Narváez, Panfilo de (c.1478–1528) Spanish *conquistador*. Took part in conquest of Cuba and Cortés's conquest of Mexico. Commissioned to conquer Florida in 1526. The journey took ten months and decimated the crew, and Narváez himself who died on the Texas coast, although survivors of the party did go on to complete the map of the northern Gulf coast. ✤125, ◆118 (1), ◆125 (4)

NASA *see* National Aeronautics and Space Administration

Nashville ⚔ of American Civil War (15–16 Dec 1864). Union victory. ◆131 (7)

Nassau, William I, Prince of Orange (*aka* William of Nassau,1533–84) Dutch statesman who martialled resistance to Spanish Catholic rule in the Netherlands.
Dutch revolt (1568–1609) ✤195, ✤195●, ◆195 (5)

Natal ◆96 (2), ◆166 (2)
annexed by Britain ✤91●
annexed by Britain (1843) ✤166●

National Aeronautics and Space Administration (NASA)
space programme (1969) ✤106●

National Front for the Liberation of Angola (FNLA). Political party of Angola. ◆109 (5)

National Recovery Administration (NRA). US government agency set up as part of Roosevelt's New Deal programme. The National Industrial Recovery Act authorized the introduction of industry-wide codes to reduce unfair trade practices and cut down unemployment, establish minimum wages and maximum hours, and guarantee right of collective bargaining. The NRA ended when it was invalidated by the Supreme Court in 1935, but many of its provisions were included in subsequent legislation. ❑134

nationalism
European growth ✤202–3, ✤214
movements ✤90, ✤94, ✤99
Serb ✤215

NATO *see* North Atlantic Treaty Organization

Natufian peoples Levantine people, named after the site of Wadi en-Natuf in Israel. From c.13,000 BCE, Natufian peoples intensively harvested wild cereals, using grindstones to crush the grains. They were the precursors of the first farmers. ✤15●

navigation
Arab traders in the Indian Ocean ◆61 (3)
harnessing winds ✤61, ✤75, ✤78, ✤218
instruments
astrolabe ❑77, ❑218
Chinese magnetized needle (13th century) ❑67
Harrison's chronometer ❑86
lodestone compass used in China (c.250) ✤256●
measuring longitude ✤86
Magellan's global circumnavigation ❑80
mapping
latitude scales (16th century) ✤173●
medieval ◆173
Portolan charts ✤70, ✤173, ❑173
stick chart ❑278
Northeast Passage ◆257 (2)
Polynesian ✤55, ✤60
technology
global (c.1500) ◆76–7 (1)
and mariners ✤77
satellite imagery ❑106
trading network ✤78

Nazca culture Coastal culture of southern Peru which flourished between c.200 BCE and 500 CE. The Nazca are noted for their ceramic human and animal figures but are best known for the 'Nazca lines' large abstract designs and animal shapes which they laid out on a huge scale by clearing and aligning stones, and which are best seen from the air. ✤38●, ❑42, ◆145 (4), ◆146 (1)
desert figures (c.450) ✤51●, ❑145
empire ◆146 (1)
pottery figure ❑42

Nazi Party (*var.* National-Sozialistische Deutsche Arbeiterpartei) *see* Nazism

Nazi-Soviet Non-Aggression Pact Treaty signed Aug 1939 arranging for division of Poland. Paved way for outbreak of WW II in Europe. ✤209●

Nazism Political creed developed by Adolf Hitler in the 1920s and implemented by his National Socialist (Nazi) party after Hitler became Chancellor of Germany in 1933. Based on extreme nationalism, anti-Communism and racism (especially anti-semitism), Nazi policies of social and economic mobilization led to the dramatic recovery of Germany in the 1930s, but also led the nation into a programme of territorial aggression which plunged Europe into WW II. ✤209●, ◆209 (3)
Nationalist Socialist ✤102, ✤104
concentration camps ✤138, ❑211
impact on Europe ✤211●
Yalta 'Big Three' conference (1945) ❑105

Ndebele African Kingdom (1826) ◆166 (2)

Ndongo Portuguese seize territory (1663) ✤82

Neanderthals (c.120,000 to 35,000 years ago). Human ancestors. Named after the Neander Valley in Germany, where the first skull cap of their type was recognized, the Neanderthals lived in Europe and the Middle East. Distinguished by their strong, heavy skeleton, projecting face, broad nose and large teeth, their brain capacity was at least the size of modern humans. They were accomplished tool-makers, and were the first type of human known to bury their dead. They demonstrated, in their cultural behaviour and social organization, many of the characteristics of modern humans. ✤12, ❑12, ✤15●, ◆13 (2)

Nearchus (d.312 BCE) Admiral of Alexander the Great's fleet. In 325 BCE he was instructed to sail west along the coast from the mouth of the Indus to the mouth of the Euphrates. His voyage opened a coastal trading route to India for Greek merchants. ◆218 (1)

Nebuchadnezzar II (c.630–562 BCE). Babylon's most famous king and founder of the new Babylonian empire, (r.605–562 BCE) during which time the Babylonian civilization reached its peak. Nebuchadnezzar instituted many major building projects including the Hanging Gardens, one of the Seven Wonders of the ancient world. He led his father's army to victory over the Egyptians at Carchemish, and famously exiled the Jews after capturing Jerusalem in 586 BCE.
✤35●, ✤222, ❑222

Needham, James (d.1673) 17th-century explorer of N America. Gained experience of the frontier with Henry Woodward and then accompanied Gabriel Arthur on the journey to find a route to the 'South Sea'. ◆119 (2)

Nehru, Jawaharlal (1889–1964) First prime minister of independent India (r.1947–64). He joined the nationalist movement in 1920, and was President of the Indian National Congress Party 1920–30, 1936–7, 1946, 1951–4. ❑252

Neilson hot blast process (1824) ❑90

Nekhen Confederacy (BCE) ◆159 (2)

Nelson, Horatio, Viscount (1758–1805) British admiral. On the outbreak of war with France in 1793, he achieved a series of brilliant and decisive victories at the Nile (1798) and at Copenhagen (1801). His defeat of a united Spanish and French fleet at Trafalgar (1805) saved Britain from the threat of invasion by Napoleon. He was mortally wounded in the battle.
◆200 (1), , ✤200●

Nemausus (*var.* Nîmes), Pont du Gard ❑180

Neo-Assyrian Empire *see* Assyrian Empire

Neolithic The last period of the Stone Age, encompassing the period in human history when crops and animals were domesticated, pottery was manufactured, and efficient stone tools were made by grinding and polishing.
Africa ◆160 (1)
China ◆258 (2)

Nepal Mapping and exploration ◆257 (3)

Nerchinsk, Treaty of (1689). Peace agreement between Russia and China, in which Russia withdrew from the area north of the Amur river. First treaty between China and a European power.
✤83, ✤275●

Nero (37–68 CE) Roman Emperor. The last of the family of Augustus Caesar to rule Rome (r.54–68). Palace intrigues and murders (including that of his mother) gave Nero's reign a notoriety unmatched by that of any previous emperor. He committed suicide as provincial governors joined in revolt against him. ✤48●

Nestorian Church Followers of Nestorius, whose Christian teachings, condemned by the councils of Ephesus (431) and Chalcedon (451), emphasized the independence of the divine and human natures of Christ. Represented today by the Syrian Orthodox Church.
✤226, ✤226●, ◆49 (4)

Netherlands
foreign affairs
voyages of expansion (1492–1597) ◆80–1 (1)
possessions
1600 ◆78–9
1700 ◆164 (1)
Africa
Angola captured (1641) ✤83●
British seize Cape colony (1795) ✤87●
Cape of Good Hope colony established (1652) ✤83●
Orange River settled (1720) ✤87●
S and E Africa (c.1700) ◆164 (1)
W and Cemtral Africa (1625) ◆164 (2)
America
colonization and settlement of N America ✤126, ◆126 (1)
New Amsterdam colony seized (1664) ✤82●
S American exploration ◆142–3 (1) (2)
trading posts in north ✤82
Asia
Indonesia gains independence (1949) ✤103●
Malacca captured (1641) ✤83●
rebellion against Dutch rule (1926–27) ✤103●
Southeast trading ✤83●, ❑247
Brazil, colonization (1630–54) ✤82●, ✤149, ◆149 (4)
Guiana, colony (c.1640) ✤149, ◆149 (4)
Pacific imperialism ◆284 (1)
home affairs
Dutch revolt (1568–1609) ✤195, ✤195●, ◆195 (5)
population growth (1650–1800) ❑198
possessions ◆78–9
Second World War *see* Wars

Netjerykhet *see* Zoser

New Amsterdam
colonized ◆126 (1)
Dutch colony in America ✤82●
seized by English; renamed New York (1664) ✤82●

New Caledonia Settled by French (1864) ✤284●, ◆284 (1), ◆285 (2)

New Deal *see* Roosevelt, Franklin

New England Settlement begins (1620) ✤126●, ◆126 (1)

New Granada
Viceroyalty established (1739) ✤148●
independence secured ✤90●

New Guinea
BCE drainage and cultivation ✤19●
Dutch annex west (1825) ✤91
exploration and mapping ◆279, ◆279 (2)
prehistoric agricultural development ✤280, ❑280, ◆280 (2)
seized by Japan (1942) ✤103●
settlement ✤280, ✤280●, ◆280 (1)

New Haven European and native conflict (1637) ✤126, ◆126 (1)

New Holland Established by Dutch (1630) ✤149●

New Kingdom (c.1550–1050 BCE). Period of ancient Egyptian history marked by strong central government control in ancient Egypt, and one which saw the height of Egyptian power. Punctuated by the El-Amarna period of Akhenaten. ✤26●, ◆26, ✤159●

New Spain (*var. Sp.* Virreinato de Nueva España). Spanish Viceroyalty established in 1535 to govern Spain's conquered lands north of the Isthmus of Panama and regions in present-day Lower California. ◆126 (1), ◆148 (2)

New State (*var. Port.* Estado Novo). Dictatorship (1937–45) of President Getúlio Vargas of Brazil, initiated by a new constitution issued in Nov 1937. Vargas himself wrote it with the assistance of his minister of justice, Francisco Campos. ✤82●, ◆152 (1)

New York
English colony (1664) ✤82●
See also New Amsterdam

New Zealand
Captain Cook's map ❑87
colonization
British ✤91, ✤283, ✤284●, ◆283 (5)
European (1800–40) ✤283, ◆283 (4)
Pacific decolonization and nationhood ✤285, ◆285 (3)
Pacific imperialism ◆284 (1)
Polynesian ✤55●, ✤60
Maori carved canoe head ❑281
possessions
1925 ◆98–9
1975 ◆106–7
Second World War, mobilization and casualty figures ✤105
trade and industry
refrigerated shipping ✤92●, ✤283
sheep farming ❑283
whaling ✤279●, ◆283 (4)

Newbery, John 16th-century English explorer and merchant. Travelling to Hormuz in 1581–83 to survey its commercial prospects, he became the first Englishman to sail down the Euphrates and visit Hormuz, Shiraz and Isfahan. He returned overland through Persia to Constantinople. ◆219 (3)

Newfoundland Reached by Vikings (c.1000 CE) ✤60

Newton, Sir Isaac (1642–1727). English mathematician and physicist. His work on calculus, the laws of motion, gravity, and light made him the most celebrated scientist of his age. ❑83

Key to index:

❖ text	❏ picture	var. variant name	f/n full name	r. ruled	WW I First World War
● timeline	◆ map	aka also known as	prev. previously known as	⚔ battle	WW II Second World War

SUBJECT INDEX AND GLOSSARY: Pachacuti Inca – Pike, Lt. Zebulon Montgomery

P

Pachacuti Inca (*var.* Pachacutec). The ruler in whose reign (1438–71) the Inca Empire expanded from its heartlands around Cuzco to dominate the Andean region as far north as Quito. ✤74●, ◆147 (3)
Pacific Ocean
colonization
(19th century)
✤284–5, ✤284●
c.1500 ✤27, ◆26–7
decolonization and nationhood ✤285, ◆285 (3)
imperialism ◆284 (1)
Japan takes German colonies (1914) ✤99
Japanese naval power limited (1922) ✤99●
missionaries in the South Seas ✤284, ❑284
Polynesian ✤55
reached by Russians (1649) ✤257●
use and abuse of resources ◆185 (2)
migrations
Austonesian and Polynesian ✤281, ◆280–1 (3)
importation of migrant workers ✤284
prehistoric ✤281●
Panama Canal opened (1914) ✤98●
trade
European and American ✤279, ◆279 (3)
exploitation ✤279●, ✤285, ◆285●
playground for wealthy tourists ❑284
volcanic landscape ❑276
War (1879–93) ✤94●
Pacific Rim Geopolitical term for those countries of E Asia, Australasia and the Americas with Pacific shorelines, used in relation to trans-Pacific trade agreements and associated with the region's economic boom during the 1980s and 1990s. ◆275 (4)
See also Tiger Economies.
Pacific War (1937–45). General term for the war in the eastern theatre of operations during WW II. ✤272–273●, ◆272–273, ❑272–273
Pacific, War of the (1879–83). War between Chile, Peru, and Bolivia, fought over the valuable nitrate deposits in the Atacama Desert. Chile made substantial territorial gains from both Bolivia and Peru; Bolivia lost its access to the Pacific coast for ever. ✤151, ◆151 (4)
padrão Mariner's milestone placed by Portuguese navigators along the coast of Africa during the 14th–15th centuries. ❑156
Paekche Ancient kingdom of the Korean Peninsula. *See also* Korea. ✤264
Páez, Jose Antonio (1790–1873) Venezuelan revolutionary who fought against the Spanish with Simón Bolivar, and Venezuela's first president. In 1829 he led the movement to separate Venezuela from Gran Colombia and controlled the new country from his election as president in 1831 until 1846 when he was forced into exile. Returned as dictator 1861–63 and died in exile in New York. ❑150
Pagan (c.1050–1287) Burmese empire. The capital was at the predominantly Buddhist temple-city of Pagan (founded 847) on the banks of the Irrawaddy River. The empire was sacked by Mongol invaders in the 1287. ✤63, ✤245, ◆245 (5)
first Burmese state (1044) ✤63●
Mongol raids (13th century) ✤67
Pakistan 252–3
conflict zones ◆252 (2)
divided (1971) ✤107●
Independence (1947) ✤103●, ✤252, ✤251, ◆251 (4)
Islamic Republic (1956) ✤107●
See also India
Palaeolithic Period of human history from c.850,000 BCE (Lower Palaeolithic), when the first hominids reached Europe from Africa, to the Middle Palaeolithic (c.200,000 BCE), and ending with the Upper Palaeolithic (c.35,000–10,000 BCE). The Upper Palaeolithic in Europe is associated with evidence of complex social structures, organized settlements, technological innovation and the florescence of rock art and carving. ✤17, ◆17 (2), ❑17
Palas Late 8th-century Indian dynasty which maintained power in NE India, with strong Buddhist ties with Tibet. ✤59, ◆244 (2)
Palenque, Maya city built (c.300) ✤50●
Pale of Settlement (*var. Rus.* Cherta Osedlosti) Area within the Russian Empire where Jews were permitted to live. Arose following the partitions of Poland in the late 18th century. Between 1783 and 1794, Catherine the Great issued a series of decrees restricting the rights of Jews to operate commercially within the newly-annexed areas. By the 19th century, the Pale included Russian Poland, Lithuania, Belorussia, most of Ukraine, the Crimea and Bessarabia, and with few exceptions, Jews were increasingly restricted to this area with further restriction occurring towards the end of the 19th century, when a census revealed a population of nearly 5 million Jews within the Pale, with about 200,000 elsewhere in Russia. ✤101●, ◆101 (2)
Palestine
at the time of David (c.1006–966 BCE) ✤222, ◆222 (1)
Balfour Declaration (1917) ✤99●
British mandate ✤233
conquered by Rome (63 BCE) ✤225, ✤225●
emigration (1947–48) ◆234 (3)
immigration (c.1930–40s) ✤103●, ✤234
Jewish diaspora (66–135 CE) ✤48●, ✤225, ◆225 (5)
Jewish revolts ✤225, ◆225 (4)
Jewish settlement (c.1200 BCE) ✤31
united with Syria (c.1100 BCE) ✤31
See also Holy Land, Israel
Palestine Liberation Organizaton (PLO). Organization led by Yasser Arafat to restore the Palestinian people to their homeland. In 1974 it was recognized by the Arab nations as the 'sole legitimate representative of the Palestinian people'. In 1993 the PLO signed an agreement with Israel formally recognizing the state of Palestine and Israel. chairman Yasser Arafat ❑234
Israel agreement extends self-rule (1995) ✤11●
Palestinian problem (1947–82) ◆234 (2)
signs Oslo Accord with Israel (1993) ✤234
West Bank self-rule extended (1995) ✤111●
See also Arafat, Yasser
Palgrave, William Gifford (1826–88) British Jesuit explorer. Working as a spy for Napoleon III of France, he was the first European to make the west-east crossing of the Arabian Peninsula in 1862–63. ◆219 (4)
Palliser, Lt. John 19th-century Irish explorer of Canada, who conducted a major survey of the prairies and the Rocky Mountains in the 1850s. ◆119 (3)
Panama Canal Shipping canal across the Isthmus of Panama (64.85 km wide), linking the Atlantic and Pacific Oceans. In 1903 a strip of territory was granted to the US by Panama; construction of the canal began early in 1904. It was opened to traffic on 15 Aug, 1914. Further work to deepen and widen the canal was begun in 1959.
opened (1914), ◆96 (1) ✤98●
Zone ceded to US (1903) ✤98●, ✤133●, ◆133 (4)
Panaramittee, rock engravings (petroglyphs) ❑17
Panda Zulu king (r.1840–72). ❑91
Panipat ⚔ of (20 Apr 1526). A victory by the Mughal leader, Babur, who confronted the forces of the Afghan Lodi Sultanate. Babur's use of artillery was decisive, the Sultan was routed, and control of the entire Ganges valley passed to the Mughals. ✤87
Pannonia Roman province including territory now mostly in Hungary and Yugoslavia. ✤53, ◆180 (1), ◆184 (2)
Pantheon Temple to all the gods built in Rome c.27 BCE, well preserved to the present day. ❑43
Paoli ⚔ of American Revolutionary War (20 Sep 1777). British victory. ◆127 (3)
Papacy *see* Catholicism
Papal States (*var.* Patrimony of St. Peter). ◆188 (1), ◆193 (4)
paper
Chinese writing material ❑46
invention (105 CE) ✤46
money introduced by Chinese ✤59●, ✤263
papyrus ❑30
printed banknotes (c.1287) ❑263
Paracas culture Centred on a barren Peruvian peninsula, and renowned for its ornate prehistoric pottery and colourful textiles. Many artefacts have been found in mummified burials dating from about 600–100 BCE. ✤34●, ✤38●, ✤145, ❑147, ◆145 (4)
Paraguay
mission founded by Jesuits (1607) ✤143●, ✤148●
Chaco War (1932–35) ✤102●, ◆152 (2)
defeats Bolivia in Chaco War (1932–35) ✤102●
freed from Spanish control ✤150, ◆150 (1)
Paraguayan War (1864–70) Boundary disputes led Paraguay to go to war with Brazil in 1864, resulting in an invasion of Paraguay by an alliance of Argentina, Brazil and Uruguay early in 1865. An intense five-year struggle followed, involving every able-bodied citizen and only ending with the complete defeat of the Paraguayan forces. The total population of 1,337,439 was reduced to less than 250,000. ✤94●
Parhae *see* Pohai Empire
Paris, Matthew (c.1200–1259) Benedictine monk and chronicler. Produced the *Chronica Majora*, generally acknowledged to be the finest chronicle of the 13th century. ✤173
Paris
besieged by Danes ✤58●
entered by German troops (1940) ✤104●
liberated by Allies (1944) ✤105●
medieval (c.1400) ✤191, ✤191●, ◆191 (2)
medieval map (1576) ❑173
sacked by Vikings (845 CE) ✤60●
siege (1870) ✤203●
trade along the Seine ❑191
Park, Mungo (1771–1806) Scottish explorer and author of *Travels in the Interior of Africa*. He worked as chief medical officer with East India Company before carrying out two explorations of the Niger River system.
exploration of African interior (1795–96, 1805–06) ◆157 (4)
sponsored by African Associaton ✤157
Parry, Sir William Edward (1790–1855) British navigator and explorer. Travelled to Arctic on behalf of Royal Navy to protect whales from over-hunting. Led four expeditions to the Arctic between 1818 and 1827, navigating more than half of the Northeast Passage, and attempting to reach the N Pole on foot from Spitzbergen. ◆286–7 (2)
Parthenon The greatest temple of Athens, situated on the summit of the Acropolis, replacing an earlier Temple of Athena destroyed by the Persians in 480 BCE. Constructed during the rule of Pericles, it is built entirely from marble and decorated with a remarkable frieze, part of which is to be found in the British Museum in London (the Elgin Marbles). It was finally completed in 432 BCE. ✤177
Parthians Scythian people from Central Asia who in c.240 BCE rebelled against Seleucid rule, formed their own state, and came to dominate Asia Minor and Persia from about 140 BCE. In 53 BCE they defeated the Romans at the battle of Carrhae, and in 40 BCE they captured Jerusalem. The Parthians were attacked by the Romans in 216 CE, and finally crushed by the Sassanians in 224 CE.
Empire ✤43●, ✤45, ✤47
drinking cup ❑43
skilled mounted bowmen ❑224
wars with Rome ✤224, ◆224 (2)
pastoralism The practice of herding animals, such as cattle, sheep, camels, which is common in climates which are too dry, mountainous or cold for agriculture. Pastoralists tend to be nomadic to varying degrees, and as a result may be important long-distance traders.
Patayán (Hakataya) culture of southwestern N America. ◆123 (4)
Patna ⚔ (1759). Challenge by Mughal crown prince repulsed by British army under Clive. ◆88 (1)
Paul, St. Jewish convert to Christianity who became the leading missionary and theologian of the early Church, undertaking great journeys to Greece and Asia Minor. Probably martyred in Rome between 62 and 68 CE.
journeys ✤48●, ◆48 (1)
martyrdom (64 CE) ✤48●
Paulistas In the 17th and 18th centuries, lawless bands of adventurers from São Paulo, who went on raids into the jungles of Brazil in search of Indians to enslave. In the 17th century they came into conflict with the Jesuits of Paraguay. ✤143
See also São Paulo.
Pazyryk Burial site (BCE) ✤39●
Pearl Harbor (1941) Japanese air attack on the US naval base in Hawaii which led to US entry into WW II. ✤102●, ✤104●, ◆104 (4)✤134●, ✤138, ✤272, ❑272, ◆272 (1)
Peary, Robert Edwin (1856–1920) US explorer of the Arctic. Reputedly the first man to reach the N Pole (6 Apr 1909). ❑286, ◆286–7 (2)
Peasants' Revolt (1381). Uprising in England led by Wat Tyler to protest against the Poll Tax. ✤70●
Pedro I, Emperor of Brazil (also Pedro IV, King of Portugal) (1798–1834) (r.1822–31 in Brazil). When Brazil and Portugal split in 1822, Pedro, son of King João VI, remained in Brazil as its first emperor. His father returned to Portugal, but died in 1826. This made Pedro king of Portugal, but he abdicated in favour of his daughter, Maria. In 1831 Pedro had to return to Portugal to fight his brother Miguel, who was trying to usurp the throne. ❑150, ◆150 (1)
Peipus, Lake ⚔ (1142). Russians defeat of Teutonic Knights. ◆186 (1)
Peking *see* Beijing
Peloponnesian Wars (431–404 BCE). Series of land and sea battles between Athens and Sparta. Caused by the threat of Athenian imperialism, the conflict only ended when the Persians intervened on the Spartans' side, leading to the dismantling of the Athenian Empire. ✤177, ◆177 (3)
penicillin ✤102
Peninsular War (1808–14). Campaign during the Napoleon Wars fought out in the Iberian Peninsula between France and an alliance of Britain, Spain and Portugal. Napoleon's invasion of Portugal (1807) and installation of his brother Joseph on the Spanish throne, sparked off a long guerrilla struggle. The initial British intervention ended in retreat. When Napoleon withdrew French troops to Russia, the future Duke of Wellington, Arthur Wellesley, invaded Spain from Portugal, winning a decisive battle at Vitoria in 1813.
✤200●, ◆200 (1)
People's Movement for the Liberation of Angola (MPLA). Political party of Angola founded in 1956 and backed during the civil war (1975–91) by Cuba and the Soviet Union. ✤109, ◆109 (5)
Pepin (*var.* Pepin the Short, *var. Fre.* Pépin le Bref) (c.714–68). Frankish king. Mayor of the Palace of the last Merovingian king of the Franks, Childeric III. He forced Childeric to abdicate and was crowned in his place. In 753 he won Ravenna from the Lombards for the Papacy.
campaigns (751–68) ◆184 (1) (2)
founder of Carolingian dynasty ✤184●
Pequot War (1637) Indian uprising against European encroachment in New England (N America). ✤126●, ◆126 (1)
Pergamum (*var. Gr.* Pergamon).
Asian kingdom ✤41, ✤179, ◆179 (4)
capital of the Attalid dynasty ✤40
statue of 'The Dying Gaul' ❑40
Pericles (c.495–429 BCE) Athenian general who became the uncrowned king of Athens' Golden Age (r.443–429). A political radical, he was responsible for establishing full democracy in Athens, and his opposition to Sparta was instrumental in provoking the Peloponnesian Wars. ✤38●
Periplus of the Erythraean Sea Greek trading manual of the 1st century CE. ✤45
Perón, Eva Wife of Juan Perón. ❑102
Perón, Juan (1895–1974) (*f/n* Juan Domingo Perón). Army colonel who became president of Argentina (1946–55, 1973–74), founder and leader of the Peronist movement. ✤102●
Pérouse, Jean François Galaup de la (1741–88) French explorer of the Pacific. His voyage of 1785–88 was financed by King Louis XVI. It was the most far-ranging voyage to the Pacific yet attempted, although it failed in its prime aim: to find the Northwest Passage. La Pérouse and his two ships were last seen by members of the First Fleet at Botany Bay in Mar 1788. It was later established that they sank off Vanikoro in the Santa Cruz Islands. ◆278 (1) (2)
Perry, Commodore Matthew (1794–1858) US naval commander. Led the expedition to Japan 1853–54 which forced Japan to end its isolation of two centuries and open trade and diplomatic relations with the world. ✤270, ❑270, ◆270 (1)
Perryville ⚔ of American Civil War (8 Oct 1862). Union victory. ◆131 (6)
Persepolis Capital of Achaemenid Persia, founded by Darius I c.151 BCE.
palace decoration (BCE) ❑35, ❑223
Persia 223–235
dynasties
Achaemenid ✤223●, ◆223 (4)
Parthian ✤43●, ✤45, ✤47
Safavid (1501–1736) ✤79, ✤231, ◆231 (4)
Sassanian ✤44●, ✤47, ✤51, ✤55, ✤225, ✤225●, ◆225 (6)
Seleucid ✤41, ✤224, ◆38–9, ◆224 (1)
foreign affairs
clashes with Ottomans ✤79, ✤231
conquest of Egypt (BCE) ✤34
on death of Nadir Shah (1747) ◆86–7
Hephthalite incursions ✤51
possessions ◆86–7
subjugation of Afghans (1722–36) ✤87●
home affairs
BCE empire ✤39, ✤223, ✤223●, ◆34–5, ◆223 (4)
conquered by Alexander the Great ✤38
overrun by Arabians (656) ✤55●
state religion (BCE) ◆36 (1)
innovations
decorated tile (13th century) ❑67
wind power ✤63
See also Achaemenid Empire, Parthian Empire, Safavid Empire, Sassanian Empire, Seleucid Empire, Iran
Persian Gulf, BCE farm settlements ✤19
Persian Royal Road *see* Royal Road
Perth Founded ✤91
Peru 142–3, 148, 150–3
cultures
✤30, ✤38●, ✤42, ✤46, ✤145, ✤145●, ◆145 (4)
early farming ✤26●
liberated by San Martín ✤90, ✤150, ◆150 (1)
metal-working ✤26●
Pizarro's conquest ✤148, ◆148 (1)
revolts against Spanish ✤86
revolutionary movement ❑152
slave trade ✤279, ✤281
Spanish Viceroyalty (16th century) ✤81, ✤148
War of Pacific (1879–83) ✤94●, ✤151, ◆151 (4)
Peruzzi Powerful banking family of Florence with branches across Europe from c.1275. The Peruzzi went bankrupt in the 1340s after Edward III of England had defaulted on repayment of large loans. ✤190–1, ◆190–1 (1)
Peshawar Kushan capital ✤47
Peter the Great (Peter I) (1672–1725) Tsar of Russia. He succeeded to the throne in 1682, taking full control in 1689. Following an extensive tour of Europe (1697–8), he set about the westernization of Russia. He fought major wars with the Ottoman Empire, Persia and Sweden, defeating the latter in the Great Northern War (1700–1721) which gained for Russia the Baltic coast where Peter founded his new capital, St. Petersburg.
founds St Petersburg (1703) ✤86●
Tsar of Russia, accession (1682) ✤82●
See also Great Northern War
Petra Capital of the Nabataeans from 4th century BCE–2nd century CE, it derived its prosperity from its position on the caravan trade route from southern Arabia, especially during the height of the frankincense trade. Petra was annexed by the Romans in 106 CE. The remains of the city include temples and tombs carved into the pink rock of the surrounding hills.
annexed by Rome (106) ✤47
discovered by Burckhardt (1812) ✤219●
rock-cut tombs ❑47
petroglyph Prehistoric rock carving, often taken to be some of the earliest examples of writing. ❑17, ✤118
Petrograd *see* Leningrad
Peul *see* Fulbe
Peutinger Table Copy (1265) of a Roman map showing road systems and routes within the Roman Empire. The map drastically reduces north-south distances, concentrating instead on routes from west to east. ❑172
Pharaonic Egypt During the New Kingdom from c.1500 BCE onwards Egypt was ruled by the Pharaohs or god-kings, who wielded immense religious, military and civil power and were believed to the sons of the god Osiris ruling on earth. They were the mediators between their mortal subjects and the gods and under their rule Egypt's power and territory greatly increased. The term was only used by the Egyptians themselves from 950 BCE onwards.
✤22●, ✤159● ◆159 (2)–(5)
Phidias (*var.* Pheidias) (c.490–430 BCE). Greece's greatest sculptor, was commissioned by Pericles to carry out Athens' major works and ultimately became superintendent of public works. His legacy includes the Parthenon, where he carried out the gold and ivory work. When accused of stealing the gold from his statue of Zeus at Olympia, Phidias fled from Athens. ✤177
Philby, Harry St. John (1885–1960) English explorer and Arabist. In 1932 he crossed the Rub' al Khali, or 'Empty Quarter', of Arabia. *See also* Rub' al Khali. ❑219, ◆219 (4)
Philip II of France (*var.* Augustus, Philip Augustus, *Fr.* Philippe Auguste) (1165– 1223). The first great Capetian king of medieval France (r.1179–1223), who gradually re-claimed French territories held by the kings of England and also extended the royal sphere into Flanders and Languedoc. He was a major figure in the Third Crusade to the Holy Land in 1191.
◆64–5 (2), ✤187
Philip II (c.382–336 BCE) King of Macedon. Rose to the Macedonian throne in 359 BCE and proceeded to recruit a formidable army. After the battle of Chaeronea (338 BCE), he assumed control of the Greek forces and planned an expedition to reverse the expansion of the Persian Empire, but was murdered in Aegeae before he could fulfil it. Father of Alexander the Great. ✤38●
Philip II (1527–98) King of Spain (r.1556–98), and king of Portugal as Philip I (r.1580–98) who championed the Roman Catholic Counter-Reformation. His reign saw the apogee of the Spanish Empire, though he failed to suppress the revolt of the Netherlands which began in 1566, and lost the Armada in the attempted invasion of England in 1588.
Dutch revolt (1568–1609) ✤195, ✤195●, ◆195 (5)
empire ✤81, ◆81 (3)
portrait ❑81
seizes Portuguese crown (1580) ✤78●
Philippines
colonized by Spain (16th century) ✤78, ✤79●, ✤81
gain independence (1946) ✤103●, ✤251
seized by Japan (1942) ✤103●
Spanish-American War (1898) ✤94●, ✤133, ◆133 (4)
Philistines An ancient people of the southeast coastal Mediterranean; originally a seafaring people who settled in south Palestine in the 12th century BCE. They gained powerful control of land and sea routes and were long-standing enemies of the Israelites until their defeat by King David. ✤31
Phoenicians Decendents of the Canaanites, the Phoenicians dominated the coastal strip of the eastern Mediterranean in the 2nd millennium BCE. They made this area their base for expansion across the whole of the Mediterranean, establishing trading posts in the western Mediterranean and N Africa. The Phoenicians are noted for developing one of the first alphabets, which consisted purely of consonants.
✤30–1, ✤176–7, ✤177●
carved ivory plaque ❑177
Mediterranean world (700–300 BCE) ◆176 (1)
state religion (BCE) ◆36 (1)
phosphate mining On Nauru ✤285, ◆285 (2)
Phrygians Originating in Europe around 1200 BCE, the Phrygians occupied the central plateau and western edge of Asia Minor, reaching their widest extent at the start of the 1st millennium BCE. Their power declined in the 6th century BCE with the occupation by the Lydians. ✤31, ◆221 (5)
Piankhi (r.c.741–715 BCE) King of ancient Nubia (Cush). Subdued Upper Egypt c.721 BCE and defeated Tefnakhte of Lower Egypt, but returned to Nubian capital at Napata c.718 BCE. ✤34
pictograph (*var.* pictogram). The earliest forms of writing were based on these stylized outline representations of objects. The earliest examples come from c.3000 BCE Egypt, but they occur across the world; because they represent objects rather than linguistic elements, pictograms cross conventional language boundaries. ✤32●, ◆32 (1), ✤223
See also hieroglyphics
Picts Group of tribes who occupied N Scotland in early Christian times, known for their fierce raiding. Connections between the kings of the Picts and the Scots of SW Scotland grew closer in the 9th century, leading to the creation of the medieval kingdom of Scotland. ◆52–3 (1)
Pike, Lt. Zebulon Montgomery (1779–1813) US soldier and explorer. In 1805–06, he led an expedition in search of the source of the Mississippi. In 1806–07, he travelled up the Arkansas River to the Colorado Mountains where he attempted to climb Pike's Peak. His party was captured by the Spanish, but later released. ◆119 (3)

Key to index: ✤ text ❑ picture var. variant name f/n full name r. ruled WW I First World War
● timeline ◆ map aka also known as prev. previously known as ⚔ battle WW II Second World War

SUBJECT INDEX AND GLOSSARY: **rainforest – Russia**

US network ✤94–5, ✤132, ❑92, ❑128, ❑129, ◆128 (2), ◆132 (1)
rainforest
Amazon ❑140
Brazilian Yanomami tribe ❑110
development of Brazilian ✤153●, ◆153 (4)
equitorial ◆160 (1)
Maya cities ✤50
Rajaraja the Great (r.985–1014). Chola king who extended Chola control into the eastern Deccan, Ceylon and the Malay Peninsula. By the time he died, he was the paramount ruler of southern India. ✤244, ◆244 (2)
Rajendra I (r.1014–44). King of the Chola dynasty of southern India. Under his rule the Chola navy took control of the eastern sea route between Arabia and China. He ruled from the city of Tanjore.
Chola ruler (1014) ✤63●
conquers Ceylon (1018) ✤63●
Rajput clans People of Rajputana, N India. Defeated in 1191 by the Afghan leader Muhammad of Ghur. ✤63●, ◆244 (3)
Raleigh, Sir Walter (c.1554–1618). English adventurer. He found favour under Elizabeth I and named the colony he founded at Roanoke Island in 1584 Virginia after the 'virgin queen'. Fell out of favour with Elizabeth and under James I was imprisoned. Released in 1616 to undertake a voyage to Guiana in search of El Dorado. This ended in disaster and Raleigh was executed on his return to England. ✤149
Ramayana Classical Sanskrit epic of India relating the adventures of Rama, probably composed in the 3rd century BCE. Based on numerous legends, the epic was revised and set down in its best known form by the poet Tulsi Das (1532–1623). ✤241, ◆36 (2)
Rameses III (*var.* Ramesses) (r.c.1184–53 BCE) Second king of the 20th dynasty of Egypt. Went to war with the Philistines and the 'Sea Peoples'. ✤31●
Ramesses *see* Rameses III
Rangoon Founded (1755) ✤87●
Rapa Nui (*var.* Easter Island)
colonized by Chile ✤284●
settled by Polynesians ✤55●, ✤60, ✤281, ◆281 (4)
temple platforms ✤60●, ❑281
Rashtrakutas A powerful kingdom established in 753 CE in the northern Deccan. At its peak, Rashtrakuta control extended from southern Gujarat to Tanjore. ✤244●, ◆244 (2)
Ravenna Capital of Italy under the Ostrogoths and Byzantines.
captured by Lombards (752) ✤58●
captured by Ostrogoths (492) ✤53, ✤182
detail from mosaic (6th century) ❑182
sarcophagus ❑182
Raymond of Toulouse Crusade route (1096–99) ◆64–5 (2)
Reagan, Ronald Wilson (1911–). 40th president of the United States (Republican, 1981–89). A former movie actor, as president of the Screen Actors' Guild, Reagan cooperated with efforts to combat alleged Communist influences in the American film industry. He was governor of California from 1967–74. In 1980 he won the Presidential elections in a landslide victory. During his tenure he greatly increased military spending while reducing taxes and cutting back on general government expenditure. He introduced the controversial SDI (Strategic Defense Initiative) and signed the INF treaty with the Soviet Union which limited intermediate range missiles. His administration was damaged by revelations that profits from arms deals with Iran had been used to support the Contra rebels against the Sandinista government of Nicaragua. ✤139, ✤139●
Recife Taken by Portuguese (1654) ✤149●
Reconquest of Spain (*var. Sp.* Reconquista). The reconquest of Muslim Spain by the Christian states, from the 11th to the 15th century. ✤192, ✤192●, ◆186 (1), ◆192 (3)
Reconquista *see* Reconquest of Spain
Reconstruction (1865–77). Period following the US Civil War in which the southern states were controlled by a Federal government and social legislation, including the granting of new rights to Blacks was introduced. The return of a new Republican government returned power to white leaders who reintroduced segregation in the South. ✤132
Recuay Cultural region ◆145 (4)
Red River Indian War (1874–75). Major uprising by members of the Arapaho, Cheyenne, Comanche, Kiowa and Kataka tribes from reservations in Oklahoma and Texas against white settlers in the area. US forces led by General William Sherman were forced to fight 14 battles against the Indians in the Red River Valley, before their eventual surrender. ✤128–9●, ✤128–9
Red Scare Name given to the fear of Communist subversion in the US which arose in the late 1940s, leading to the setting up of schemes such as the Federal Employee Loyalty Program, and Senator Joseph McCarthy's list of government employees whom he claimed had Soviet sympathies. The scare led to a significant degree of persecution of those suspected of Communist sympathies, and many people – especially in the government, schools, universities, and the mass media – found themselves unable to work because of their suspected beliefs. ✤135●
Red Sea trade (1st century CE) ✤225, ◆225 (3)
reducciones Jesuit frontier settlements in Spanish S America ✤143, ◆143 (2)
Reformation Religious revolution of the 16th century which took place in the Roman Catholic church, led by Martin Luther and John Calvin. The Reformation had long-term political, economic, and social effects, and laid the groundwork for the foundation of Protestantism. ✤194–5, ✤195●
refrigeration First commercial units (1856) ✤92●
refugees and resettlement ✤212, ◆212 (3)
Reiss, Wilhelm 19th-century German explorer of S America, who scaled the volcano Cotopaxi in 1872. ✤143●
religion
Buddhism (to 400 CE) ◆49 (3)
characteristics ◆36 (1)
development of organized ✤36–7
global ◆48–9
Mediterranean cults ◆37 (3)
Mithraism, Judaism, and Christianity (to 600 BCE) ◆48 (1)
old world ✤49, ◆49 (4)
South Asian ◆36 (2)
state ◆36 (1)
Taoism and Confucianism ◆37 (4)
Remojadas Early Mexican civilization (c.600–900 CE) ◆122 (1)
Renaissance (*var.* Renascence, c.1300–1550). Period of cultural, economic and political efflorescence in medieval Europe, characterized by the rediscovery of classical Greek and Roman culture, which found expression, initially in Italy, in the growth of Humanist studies and writing, and in a revitalization of architecture, painting, sculpture and the arts in general.
comes into being ✤75
in Europe (12th century) ✤187, ✤187●, ◆187 (3)
travellers in W Asia ◆219 (3)
Renascence *see* Renaissance
Rennell, James (1742–1830). British naval officer who became the Surveyor-General of Bengal in 1764. He was responsible for the first consistent mapping of the Indian subcontinent, the Survey of India. ✤239●, ❑239
Republican Party One of the two major political parties of the US. Formed in 1854 to support anti-slavery policies prior to the Civil War, Abraham Lincoln was its first president. Today, it favours limited government and interventionist foreign policy and is generally considered to be more right-wing than the Democratic Party. ✤130–1, ◆135 (5), ◆139 (4)
Réunions Lands occupied by France during the reign of Louis XIV following the decisions of a special court convened for the purpose, the Chambre des Réunions. Important annexations included Luxembourg (1679) and Strasbourg (1684). Most of the territories had to be returned by the Treaty of Ryswijk (1697). ✤197●, ◆197 (5)
revolts
against rule of Louis-Napoleon ✤202, ✤202●
Boxer rebellion (1898) ✤95, ◆97, ❑97, ◆268 (2)
Dutch (1568–1609) ✤195, ✤195●, ◆195 (5)
English Peasants' (1381) ✤70●, ◆188 (2)
European students (1968) ✤106●
following Black Death ✤70
fragmentation of China (220–589) ✤261
Hungarian Hunyadi ✤193●
Indian Mutiny ✤95●, ✤249, ✤249●, ◆249 (3)
movements against colonial rule (1880–1920) ✤97, ◆97 (4)
Taiping rebellion (1850–64) ✤95●, ❑268
Warsaw Pact crushes Hungarian (1956) ✤106●
Yellow Turbans (147 CE) ✤47●
revolutions
American (1775) ✤86, ✤126–7, ◆127 (3)
Chinese (1911) ✤271, ◆271 (5)
Cuban ✤152
economic ✤92–3
era of revolution 1768–1868 ✤89, ✤89●, ◆88–9 (2)
in Europe ✤90●, ✤202●, ✤209
factors leading to industrial ✤86
French ✤82, ✤86, ✤90, ✤199, ❑199, ◆199 (4)
impact of industrial ✤92, ◆92 (1)
inventions and world economy (1835–95) ✤92●
Liberty on the Barricades (painting) ❑89
political crackdowns ✤100●
Russian (1905, 1917) ✤98●, ✤99●, ✤208, ◆208 (2)
See also industrial revolution
Rhodes, Cecil (1853–1902). Financier, statesman, and empire builder of British South Africa. He was prime minister of Cape Colony (1890–96) and founder of the diamond mining company De Beers Consolidated Mines Limited (1888).
De Beers Consolidated Mines ✤167
Hospitallers headquarters (1310) ✤64●
portrait ❑166
Rhodesia ◆168 (1)
Northern Rhodesia granted independence (1963) ✤168●
See also Zimbabwe
Ri dynasty *see* Yi dynasty
Ricci, Matteo (1552–1610) Italian Jesuit missionary and cartographer. Joined Jesuit mission in Macao in 1582, and then established mission on Chinese territory, eventually settling in Beijing in 1601. His maps and other data, gave the Western world unprecedented access to information about China. ✤80
Richard I of England (*aka* Richard the Lion-Heart, Lion-Hearted, *Fr.* Richard Coeur de Lion) (1157–1199). Duke of Aquitaine from 1168 and of Poitiers from 1172 and king of England, Duke of Normandy, and Count of Anjou (r.1189–99). His prowess in the Third Crusade (1189–92) made him a popular king in his own time.
Crusade route (1189–92) ◆64–5 (2)
jousts with Saladin ❑64
succession (1189) ✤187●
Richard II (1367–1400) King of England (r.1377–99). Son of Edward the Black Prince. Deposed in 1399 by his cousin, Henry of Lancaster, later crowned Henry IV. He died in prison, possibly murdered. ✤192●
Richelieu, Cardinal Chief minister of Louis XIII with whom he collaborated to make France a leading European power. ❑196
Riel Rebellions (1869) (1885). Rebellions by the Metis (mixed blood descendants of Cree Indians and French fur traders) and their Indian allies against incursions of European settlers into their lands. ✤129 (2)
Rig Veda Completed c.900 BCE, this is the great literary monument of Aryan settlers of the Punjab. A collection of sacred hymns, it traces the religious development of Aryan India and depicts the Aryan settlers as chariot-driving warriors who gradually adapt to a more sedentary life. It is rich in geographical references. ✤36, ✤242, 242●, ◆242 (1)
Rio de Janeiro
Brazilian capital (1763) ✤149●
Carnival dancers ❑112
France Antarctique colony (1555) ✤149●
Río de la Plata Viceroyalty established (1776) ✤148●
Ripon Falls Source of Nile ✤157
roads
maps ❑99
Ogilvie's maps ✤173
Peutinger Table ❑172
Roman (by c.120 CE) ◆172 (1)
Robert I 'the Bruce' (1274–1329) King of Scotland (r.1306–29). Crowned in 1306 in defiance of King Edward I of England. Decisively defeated the English at the battle of Bannockburn (1314). English acknowledgement of Scottish independence and Robert's right to the throne came in 1328.
victor at Bannockburn ✤188●, ❑188, ◆188 (2)
Robert of Normandy (c.1054–1134) Duke of Normandy (r.1087–1106). Eldest son of King William I of England. Inherited Normandy upon the death of his father, whilst his brother William inherited the throne of England. Took part in the First Crusade (1096–1100).
Crusade route (1096–99) ◆64–5 (2)
Robespierre, Maximilien François Marie-Isidore de (1758–94). French revolutionary and Jacobin leader, who played a key role in the overthrow of the moderate Girondins. A member of the Committee for Public Safety which instituted the Reign of Terror (1793–4). Overthrown by the Convention, he was tried and guillotined. ✤199●
See also French Revolution, Jacobins, Terror, Reign of
rock art The oldest known art form, dating back to c.30,000 BCE in Western Europe, usually depicting hunting scenes, and found in caves or, commonly in African examples, rock shelters and exposed rock faces. The images are either painted or etched into the rock surface, and are not purely decorative: some occur in recesses so difficult to access that they are thought to have played a part in ritual activities. Rock art is more abundant in the Saharan region than anywhere else in the world. ✤17●, ◆17 (3) (5)
Roerich, Nicolas (1874–1947) Russian traveller and painter in Central Asia. ◆257 (3)
Roger II of Sicily (1095–1154) (r.1101–54) First Norman king of Sicily whose court at Palermo was one of the most magnificent in Europe, a meeting place for Christian and Arab scholars. Commissioned the *Book of Roger*, a medieval book of maps. ✤62, ✤218
Roggeveen, Jacob (1659–1729). Dutch explorer. His voyage across the Pacific in 1722 established the first European contact with a number of islands, including Rapa Nui (Easter Island) and Samoa. ✤278●
Roman Catholicism *see* Catholicism
Roman Empire The largest empire ever established in Europe, stretching from northern Britain to Egypt. From its apogee in the 2nd century CE, the empire became increasingly difficult to govern and in 395, it was divided into two. The Western Empire fell in 476, but the East Roman (or Byzantine) Empire, with its capital at Constantinople, survived until 1453. ✤42–3, ◆46–7, ◆50–1, ◆52–3, ◆54–5
51 BCE to 138 CE ✤180●
c.117 CE at the death of Trajan ◆161 (2)
c.120 CE under Hadrian ◆180 (1)
240–395 CE ✤181, ◆181 (4)
250–400 CE ✤180●
476 CE end of the Empire ✤182
Attila the Hun defeated (451) ✤50●
and Carthage: the Punic Wars ✤42, ✤179, ◆179 (3)
conflict with Sassanian ✤50
conquests (to 120 BCE) ✤179, ◆179 (5)
depictions
exotic animal combat ❑44
maritime trade ❑44
mummy case ❑47
The Nile in Flood mosaic ✤47
Europe after the fall ✤182, ◆182 (1)
expansion programme ✤42, ✤179●, ✤224–5, ◆224 (2)
exploration and mapping ✤42, ✤47, ◆218 (1)
Africa (c.150) ✤156 (3)
boundaries of ancient Europe ◆172 (1)
Hadrian's defensive strategy ✤180
Italian confederacy (264 BCE) ✤38●
mythological pantheon ✤37
overseas provinces (120 BCE) ✤179
Palatine Hill village (BCE) ✤31●
subjugation of Greece ✤179, ◆179 (4)
territory (240 BCE) ◆178 (1)
Tetrarchy of Diocletian ✤50, ✤181, ❑181, ◆181 (4)
trade, classical world ◆44–5
Western Empire collapses (476) ✤50●
See also Rome
Romania
end of Communism (1989) ✤110●
granted independence ✤232
See also Balkans, nationalism; Wars, First World; Second World
Rome Rome began as a small city-state which, through military might combined with skilful use of threats and alliances, conquered first the Italian Peninsula, then, by the 1st century BCE, the entire Mediterranean world. The city of Rome's importance declined from the 4th century CE. From the 7th century, it regained prestige as the seat of the pope and headquarters of the Roman Catholic Church. It was ruled by the Papacy until it became the capital of the newly-united kingdom of Italy in 1871.
earthenware amphora ❑181
Imperial Rome (c.300 CE) ✤181, ◆181 (2)
legionary ❑178
politics
capital of united Italy (1871) ✤94●
and the Italian Confederacy ✤178
and Latin allies (c.495 BCE) ✤178
ruins of Colosseum ❑181
sacked by Vandals (455) ✤52●
sacked by Visigoths (410) ✤53●, ✤182●
saved from Huns ✤53
saved from Lombards ✤183●
supply routes ✤181, ◆181 (3)
See also Roman Empire.
Rome, Treaty of *see* European Union
Romulus Augustus Roman Emperor, deposed (476) ✤50●
Roosevelt, Franklin Delano (*aka* FDR) (1882–1945) 32nd President of the US (Democrat, 1932–45). Roosevelt became president in 1932, on the cusp of the worst years of the Great Depression. He immediately launched a series of reforms collectively known as the 'New Deal' to combat the depression; these included the abandonment of the gold standard and agricultural price support, as well as programmes such as the Works Progress Administration, aimed at providing work for the unemployed and the creation of a Social Security Act. His 'common touch' and immense personal popularity saw him elected for an unprecedented four terms. Though initially opposed to involvement in conflict in Europe, by the outbreak of WW II, he broke with neutrality to support the Allied position, bringing the US fully into the war following the bombing of Pearl Harbor in Dec 1941.
American President (1932–45) ✤134, ✤139
New Deal
✤102, ✤134, ✤134●, ✤135
FDR effect ✤135
NRA recovery programme ❑134
WPA (Works Progress Administration) ❑134
portrait ❑135
Second World War
Casablanca conference (1943) ✤104●
Tehran conference ✤105●
Yalta 'Big Three' conference (1945) ❑105
Roosevelt, Theodore (Teddy) (1858–1919) 26th President of the US. Republican. (1901–09). After commanding the 'Roughriders' in the Spanish-American War (1898), Roosevelt returned as Governor of New York from 1898–1900, and was subsequently elected Vice-President. He became president following the assassination of William McKinley. He initiated the building of the Panama Canal, strengthened the US navy, and won the Nobel Peace Prize in 1906 for his part in ending the Russo-Japanese war. He formed a 'progressive' movement in the Republican party but was defeated on the Progressive ticket in the elections of 1910.
US President 1901–09 ✤132
era of economic boom ❑132
Rosas, Juan Manuel de (1793–1877) Argentinian dictator. Although his official title was only Governor of Buenos Aires province, Rosas was the effective ruler of Argentina from 1829–52. He owed his position to his loyal force of gauchos, and his wars of conquest against the Patagonian Indians. ❑151
Rosebloom, Johannes 17th-century explorer in N America. Employed by Governor Thomas Dongan to discover new routes for the fur trade. Reached Michilimackinac between Lakes Huron and Michigan in 1685 after travelling for three months. ◆119 (2)
Rosenberg, Ethel and Julius (1915–53), (1918–53). American Communists and part of a transatlantic spy ring. Convicted of passing on atomic secrets to the Soviet Union and executed. They were the first US citizens to be executed for espionage. ❑108
Rosetta stone Basalt slab inscribed by priests of Ptolemy V of Egypt in hieroglyphic, demotic and Greek. Found near the city of Rosetta in Egypt in 1799 and taken by the British in 1801; now in the British Museum in London. Served as the key to understanding Egyptian hieroglyphic. ❑42
Ross, Sir James Clark (1800–62) British naval officer and explorer of the Poles. Accompanied both Edward Parry and his uncle John Ross on expeditions in the Arctic. In 1839–43 he led the navy's first major Antarctic expedition. He discovered the Ross Sea, the Ross Ice Shelf, Ross Island and Victoria Land.
Antarctic exploration (1839–43) ◆287 (3)
Arctic explorer (1829–33) ❑287, ◆286–7 (2)
Rotz, John Early map of S America (1542) ❑142
Rousseau, Jean Jacques (1712–78) French philosopher and writer. Believed in the original goodness of human nature and that it was society that created inequality and misery. His most famous work, *Du Contrat Social* (1762), profoundly influenced French revolutionary thought. ✤198
Royal Road Road constructed under the Persian Achaemenid Empire in the 6th century BCE from Susa, the ancient capital of Persia, to Sardis, on the Aegean Sea.
construction ✤35, ✤223●, ◆223 (4)
Rozwi Empire Empire of southern Africa (c.1684–early 19th-century)
challenges Portuguese (17th century) ✤164
replaces Mwenemutapa ✤164
Ruanruan (*var.* Juan-juan, Avars). Nomadic steppe peoples whose expulsion from Mongolia by the Blue (Celestial) Turks in the 4th century CE impelled them westwards, entering Europe in the mid-6th century. *See also* Avars. ✤261●, ◆261 (4)
Rub' al Khali (*var.* the 'Empty Quarter'). Area of waterless desert covering some 777,000 sq km (3,000,000 sq miles) of the southern Arabian Peninsula.
19th- and 20th-century explorers ✤219●
Rudolf I (1218–91) Count of Habsburg and Holy Roman Emperor. The first Habsburg to be elected Emperor, Rudolf secured Austria as the centre of the Habsburg domains through his defeat of Ottokar II of Bohemia in 1278. ✤189●
Rukh (1377–1447). Mongol shah, son of Timur ✤75
Rum Seljuk Sultanate in Anatolia in the 12th and 13th centuries, with its capital at Konya (Iconium). Its name is derived from Rome, because its lands had been captured from the Byzantine (East Roman) Empire. ◆65 (1) (2), ✤228
Rurik the Viking (r.c.862–79). Semi-legendary Swedish ruler of the merchant town of Novgorod, seen as the founder of the Russian state (named after 'Rus', the Finnish word for Swede). ✤60●
Russia State originating in rise of Muscovy in 16th century under Ivan IV, who defeated the Tatars and united neighbouring principalities, proclaiming himself Tsar. Consolidated power in eastern Europe and expanded beyond Urals in 17th century (notably under Peter the Great), to dominate northern and central Asia by 18th century. Tsarist rule toppled by Bolshevik (Communist) revolution in 1917. 194–215, 257–273
See also USSR
foreign affairs
Alaskan expeditions (1816–65) ◆119 (3)
Balkan nationalism ✤203, ◆203 (4)
Baltic states, conflict ✤195, ✤195●, ✤197, ◆195 (3), ◆197 (3)
Bering Strait-Alaska exploration (16th–17th century) ✤257
claim on N America (1821) ◆128 (2)
conquers and annexes Crimea (1783) ✤86●
Crimean War (1854) ✤94, ✤203
Empire *see below*
First World War *see* Wars, First World
France, opposition alliances (1792–1815) ✤90●, ✤201, ◆201 (3)
neutrality pact with Japan (1939) ✤103●
Second World War see Wars, Second World
Treaty of Nerchinsk with China (1689) ✤83●, ✤257●
Turkey and the Black Sea ✤203, ✤232, ◆203 (4)
withdraws from Amur basin (1689) ✤83●
Golden Horde vassals (1200–1400) ◆189 (4)
home affairs
Bolshevik Revolution (1917) ✤98●
Mongol conquest begins (1237) ✤66●
Mongol raids (1222) ✤68
population growth (1650–1800) ❑198
revolutions (1905, 1917) ✤98●, ✤99●, ✤208, ◆208 (2)
serfdom abolished (1861) ✤94●, ✤269
trade and industry, Japanese commercial talks (1804) ✤91●
Russian Empire ✤195, ✤208
1800 ◆86–7
1850 ◆90–1
1900 ◆94–5
expansion ✤78, ✤82, ✤257, ✤269, ✤269●, ◆269 (3)
European, consolidation and resistance (17th century) ✤196, ✤196●, ◆196 (2)

Key to index: ✛ text ❑ picture var. variant name f/n full name r. ruled WW I First World War
● timeline ◆ map aka also known as prev. previously known as ✕ battle WW II Second World War

Key to index: ✦ text ❑ picture var. variant name f/n full name r. ruled WW I First World War
● timeline ◆ map aka also known as prev. previously known as ⚔ battle WW II Second World War

316

W

INDEX–GAZETTEER

Glossary of Abbreviations

This glossary provides a comprehensive guide to the abbreviations used in this Atlas, in the Subject Index and Glossary and in the Index-Gazetteer.

A
abbrev. abbreviated
Afr. Afrikaans
aka also known as
Alb. Albanian
Amh. Amharic
anc. ancient
approx. approximately
Ar. Arabic
Arm. Armenian
ASEAN Association of South East Asian Nations
ASSR Autonomous Soviet Socialist Republic
Aust. Australian
Az. Azerbaijani
Azerb. Azerbaijan

B
Basq. Basque
BCE before Common Era
Bel. Belorussian
Ben. Bengali
Ber. Berber
B-H Bosnia-Herzegovina
Bibl. Biblical
bn billion (one thousand million)
BP British Petroleum
Bret. Breton
Brit. British
Bul. Bulgarian
Bur. Burmese

C
C central
C. Cape
Cam. Cambodian
Cant. Cantonese
CAR Central African Republic
Cast. Castilian
Cat. Catalan
Chin. Chinese
CIS Commonwealth of Independent States
Cro. Croat
Cz. Czech
Czech Rep. Czech Republic

D
Dan. Danish
Div. Divehi
Dom. Rep. Dominican Republic
Dut. Dutch

E
E east
EC see EU
EEC see EU
ECU European Currency Unit
EMS European Monetary System
Eng. English
est estimated
Est. Estonian
EU European Union (previously European Community [EC], European Economic Community [EEC])

F
Faer. Faeroese
Fij. Fijian
Fin. Finnish
fl. floruit
Fln. full name
Fr. French
Fris. Frisian
ft foot/feet
FYROM Former Yugoslav Republic of Macedonia

G
Gael. Gaelic
Gal. Galician
GDP Gross Domestic Product (the total value of goods and services produced by a country excluding income from foreign countries)
Geor. Georgian
Ger. German
Gk Greek
GNP Gross National Product (the total value of goods and services produced by a country.)

H
Heb. Hebrew
HEP hydro-electric power
Hind. Hindi
hist. historical
Hung. Hungarian

I
I. Island
Icel. Icelandic
In. Inuit (Eskimo)
Ind. Indonesian
Intl International
Ir. Irish
Is Islands
It. Italian

J
Jap. Japanese

K
Kaz. Kazakh
Kir. Kirghiz
km kilometre(s)
km² square kilometre (singular)
Kor. Korean
Kurd. Kurdish

L
L. Lake
Lao. Laotian
Lapp. Lappish
Lat. Latin
Latv. Latvian
Liech. Liechtenstein
Lith. Lithuanian
Lux. Luxembourg

M
m million/metre(s)
Mac. Macedonian
Maced. Macedonia
Mal. Malay
Malg. Malagasy
Malt. Maltese
mi. mile(s)
mod. modern
Mong. Mongolian
Mt. Mountain
Mts Mountains

N
N north
NAFTA North American Free Trade Agreement
Nep. Nepali
Neth. Netherlands
Nic. Nicaraguan
Nor. Norwegian
NZ New Zealand

O
off. officially/ official name

P
Pash. Pashtu
PNG Papua New Guinea
Pol. Polish
Poly. Polynesian
Port. Portuguese
prev. previously known as

R
r. ruled
Rep. Republic
Res. Reservoir
Rmsch Romansch
Rom. Romanian
Rus. Russian
Russ. Fed. Russian Federation

S
S south
SCr. Serbo-Croatian
Sinh. Sinhala
Slvk. Slovak
Slvn. Slovene
Som. Somali
Sp. Spanish
St., St Saint
Strs Straits
Swa. Swahili
Swe. Swedish
Switz. Switzerland

T
Taj. Tajik
Th. Thai
Thai. Thailand
Tib. Tibetan
Turk. Turkish
Turkm. Turkmenistan

U
UAE United Arab Emirates
Uigh. Uighur
UK United Kingdom
Ukr. Ukrainian
UN United Nations
Urd. Urdu
US/USA United States of America
USSR Union of Soviet Socialist Republics
Uzb. Uzbek

V
var. variant
Vtn. Vietnamese

W
W west
Wel. Welsh
WWI First World War
WWII Second World War

Y
Yugo. Yugoslavia

This index lists all the place names and features shown on the maps in this Atlas.

Place name spelling

The policy followed throughout the Atlas is to use the contemporary historical name or spelling appropriate for the period or theme of the map. English conventional names, where they exist, have been used for international features e.g. oceans and country names.

All European language spellings use full diacritics, but no diacritics have been used for transliterated spellings (e.g. from Chinese or Cyrillic).

In translating Chinese names, the Pinyin system has been used throughout the Atlas, although alternative spelling systems have been cross referred.

In spelling pre-Columbian Central and South American names, the later addition of Spanish accents has been avoided.

The index also contains commonly-found alternative names and variant spellings, which are fully cross-referenced.

Index structure

All main entry names are those of settlements unless otherwise indicated by the use of italicized definitions.

In order to avoid unnecessary repetition, the names of frequently recurring states on the World Era Overview maps have been omitted. Those places which *only* appear on the World Era overview Maps have been included.

A

Aachen *anc.* Aquae Grani, Aquisgranum; *Dut.* Aken, *Fr.* Aix-la-Chapelle Central Europe (Germany) early modern states *193* (4) economy *190* (1) Franks *184* (2) medieval states *188* (1), (2) Reformation *195* (5) WWI *206* (3)
Aarhus *var.* Århus Scandinavia (Denmark) medieval states *185* (3)
Abadan *oil terminal* Southwest Asia (Iran) economy *234* (1)
Abai *see* Blue Nile
Abaj Takalik Central America (Mexico) first civilizations *121* (2)
Abancay South America (Peru) Incas *147* (3)
Abariringa *see* Canton Island
Abay Wenz *see* Blue Nile
Abbasid Caliphate *state* Southwest Asia early Islam *57* (2) medieval states *185* (3) Mongols *68–69* (1)
Abbeville France medieval states *192* (2)
Abdera Greece ancient Greece *177* (3) first civilizations *177* (1)
Abdera *settlement/state* Greece ancient Greece *177* (2)
Abéché *see* Abeshr
Abenaki *people* North America colonization *126* (1)
Abensberg *battle* Central Europe (Germany) Napoleon *200–201* (1)
Aberbrothock *see* Arbroath
Aberdeen *anc.* Devana British Isles (United Kingdom) medieval states *188* (2)
Abergwaun *see* Fishguard
Abertawe *see* Swansea
Aberteifi *see* Cardigan
Aberystwyth British Isles (Wales) medieval states *188* (2)
Abeshr *mod.* Abéché Central Africa (Chad) Islam *163* (1)
Abhiras *dynasty* South Asia first empires *241* (5) world religions *242* (2)
Abhisara *state* South Asia first empires *241* (5)
Abidjan West Africa (Ivory Coast) economy *168* (2)
Abina South Asia (India) medieval voyages *61* (3)
Abitibi *people* North America cultural groups *123* (3)
Abkhazia *region* Southwest Asia Soviet Union *214–215* (4)
Åbo Scandinavia (Finland) early modern states *195* (3) medieval states *189* (3)
Åbo *see* Surabaya
Abodrites *people* Central Europe Franks *184* (2)
Aboriginal Hunter-Gatherers of Australia *people* Australia the world in 2500 BCE *22–23* *see also* Australian Aborigines
Abu Dhabi *var.* Abū Ẓabī; *Ar.* Abū Ẓaby Southwest Asia (United Arab Emirates) 20th-century politics *233* (4) economy *234* (1) exploration *219* (4)
Abu Dulaf *congregational mosque* Southwest Asia (Iraq) early Islam *57* (3)
Abu Hurayrah *see* Abu Hureyra
Abu Hureyra *var.* Abu Hurayrah Southwest Asia (Syria) the world in 5000 BCE *18–19*
Abuja *state* West Africa the world in 1850 *90–91*
Abu Rawash Egypt ancient Egypt *159* (3)
Abu Salabikh Southwest Asia (Iraq) first cities *220* (2)
Abu Simbel *early food production site* Egypt early agriculture *158* (1)
Abusir Egypt ancient Egypt *159* (2), (3)
Abū Ẓabī *see* Abu Dhabi
Abū Ẓaby *see* Abu Dhabi
Abydos *var.* Abydus Egypt ancient Egypt *159* (2), (3), (4), (5) first cities *28–29* (1) first civilizations *24* (2)
Abydos *var.* Abydus *settlement/state* Southwest Asia (Turkey) ancient Greece *177* (2) first civilizations *177* (1)
Abydus *see* Abydos
Abyssinia *mod.* Ethiopia *state* East Africa 20th-century politics *233* (4) European imperialism *96* (1), *97* (4) trade *165* (3), *167* (1) WWII *104* (2) *see also* Ethiopia
Acachinamco Central America (Mexico) Aztecs *124* (3)
Acadia *mod.* Nova Scotia *region* North America the world in 1700 *82–83* *see also* Nova Scotia
Acalbixca Central America (Mexico) Aztecs *124* (2)
Acanceh Central America (Mexico) first civilizations *123* (2)
Acanthus *settlement/state* Greece ancient Greece *177* (2), (3)
Acapulco *var.* Acapulco de Juárez Central America (Mexico) European expansion *80–81* (1), *81* (3), *84–85* (1) exploration *143* (3) first civilizations *122* (1) US economy *136* (2)
Acapulco de Juárez *see* Acapulco
Acarí South America (Peru) Incas *147* (3)
Acarnania *state* Greece ancient Greece *179* (4)
Acatitla Central America (Mexico) Aztecs *124* (3)
Acatlan Central America (Mexico) first civilizations *122* (1)
Acayocan Central America (Mexico) Aztecs *124* (3)
Accho *see* Acco, Acre
Acco *mod.* 'Akko; *Bibl.* Accho, Ptolemaïs; *Eng.* Acre, *Fr.* Saint-Jean-d'Acre Southwest Asia (Israel) ancient Egypt *159* (5) *see also* Acre
Accra *var.* Fort James West Africa (Ghana) colonization *167* (4) economy *168* (2) empire and revolution *88* (1) slave trade *165* (4) trade *164* (2)
Acemhüyük Southwest Asia (Turkey) first cities *28–29* (1)
Achaea *see* Achaia
Achaean League *var.* Principality of Achaia *state* Greece the world in 250 BCE *38–39* *see also* Achaia
Achaia *var.* Achaea Greece ancient Greece *177* (3)
Achaia, Principality of *see* Achaean League
Achalapura South Asia (India) early medieval states *244* (2)
Acheh *see* Achin
Achin *var.* Acheh, Atchin, Atjeh; *mod.* Aceh Maritime Southeast Asia (Indonesia) colonialism *247* (4) early medieval states *245* (6) Soviet Union *214–215* (4)
Achin *mod.* Aceh; *prev.* Acheh, Atjeh *region/state* Maritime Southeast Asia colonialism *247* (4) early medieval states *245* (6) European imperialism *97* (3) post-war politics *253* (4) trade *267* (3)
Acigöl Southwest Asia (Turkey) early agriculture *220* (1)
Acolapissa *people* North America colonization *126* (1)
Acolhuacan *state* Central America Aztecs *124* (1)
Acolman Central America (Mexico) Aztecs *124* (2)
Acoma *people* North America colonization *126* (1)
Açores *see* Azores
Açores, Arquipélago dos *see* Azores
Açores, Ilhas dos *see* Azores
Acragas Italy first civilizations *177* (1)
Acre *mod.* 'Akko; *prev.* Acco; *Bibl.* Accho, Ptolemaïs; *Fr.* Saint-Jean-d'Acre Southwest Asia (Israel) crusades *228* (2), *65* (3) economy *190* (1) exploration *219* (3) medieval states *187* (5) Mongols *229* (3), *68* (2) Napoleon *200–201* (1) *see also* Acco
Acre *state* South America empire and revolution *151* (3)
Acropolis *temple* Greece ancient Greece *177* (4)
Acrothooi *state* Greece ancient Greece *177* (2)
Actaeon Islands *island group* Pacific Ocean exploration *278* (1)
Actium *Gk.* Aktion Greece the world in 1 CE *42–43*
Acton *battle* North America (USA) the growth of the US *129* (2)
Adab Southwest Asia (Iraq) first cities *220* (2) first civilizations *24* (3)
Adal *state* East Africa Islam *163* (1) trade *165* (3)
Adalia *mod.* Antalya; *prev.* Attalia; *anc.* Attaleia Southwest Asia (Turkey) 20th-century politics *233* (3) crusades *65* (3), *64–65* (2) *see also* Attalia
Adamawa *region* West Africa Islam *167* (3)
Adamawa Highlands *Mountain range* West Africa economy *163* (2)
Adamello *mountain* Italy WWI *207* (5)
Adamstown Pacific Ocean (Pitcairn Islands) decolonization *285* (3)
'Adan *see* Aden, Eudaemon Arabia
Adana *var.* Seyhan Southwest Asia (Turkey) 20th-century politics *233* (3) early Islam *56–57* (1) Ottomans *230* (1)
Adare, Cape *headland* Antarctica Antarctic Exploration *287* (3)
Ad Dawḩah *see* Doha
Addis Ababa *Amh.* Ādīs Ābeba East Africa (Ethiopia) colonization *167* (4) economy *168* (2)
Adelaide Australia colonization *282* (1), (2), *283* (3), *284–285* (1) exploration *279* (2), (3) imperial global economy *92* (1) prehistoric culture *17* (5)
Adélie, Terre *physical region* Antarctica Antarctic Exploration *287* (3)
Adelong *goldfield* Australia colonization *282* (2)
Aden *var.* Eudaemon Arabia; *Ar.* 'Adan, *Chin.* A-tan Southwest Asia (Yemen) ancient trade *44–45* (1) biological diffusion *72–73* (1) early Islam *56–57* (1), *57* (2) European expansion *84–85* (1) exploration *156* (3), *219* (4) imperial global economy *92* (1) Islam *163* (1), *226* (2), *227* (4) medieval voyages *61* (3) Mongols *68* (2) Ottomans *231* (3) trade *230* (2), *267* (3) 20th-century politics *233* (4) *see also* Eudaemon Arabia
Adena North America (USA) first religions *36* (1)
Adena *burial mound* North America (USA) first civilizations *121* (4)
Adena/Hopewell Culture *people* North America the world in 250 BCE *38–39* the world in 1 CE *42–43*
Adena Park *burial mound* North America (USA) first civilizations *121* (4)
Aden, Gulf of *var.* Badyarada 'Adméd *gulf* Southwest Asia early agriculture *158* (1) early cultures *161* (3), (4), (5) early trade *225* (3) economy *163* (2), (3) exploration *218* (2) Islam *163* (1) Ottomans *231* (3) slave trade *165* (4) Timur *229* (4) trade *165* (3), *230* (2) 20th-century politics *233* (4)
Aden Protectorate *colonial possession/state* Southwest Asia 20th-century politics *233* (4) Cold War *109* (1) WWII *104* (1)
Adige *Ger.* Etsch *river* Italy WWI *207* (5)
Ādīs Ābeba *see* Addis Ababa
Admiralty Island *island* North America exploration *278* (1)
Admiralty Islands *island group* Pacific Ocean early cultures *280–281* (3) medieval voyages *60* (2) WWII *272* (1), *273* (2)
Adobe Walls *battle* North America (USA) the growth of the US *129* (2)
Adrar Bous West Africa (Niger) early agriculture *158* (1)
Adrar Tioueïne North Africa (Algeria) early agriculture *158* (1)
Adria *see* Hadria
Adrianople *mod.* Edirne; *anc.* Adrianopolis, Hadrianopolis *Christian archbishopric/settlement* Southwest Asia (Turkey) crusades *64–65* (2) medieval states *187* (5), *189* (4) Ottomans *195* (4), *230* (1), *231* (3) Reformation *194* (2) world religions *48* (1) WWI *207* (6) *see also* Adrianopolis, Edirne, Hadrianopolis
Adrianopolis *Eng.* Adrianople, *Turk.* Edirne Southwest Asia (Turkey) ancient Rome *182* (1) *see also* Adrianople, Edirne
Adrianopolis *battle* Southwest Asia (Turkey) great migrations *52–53* (1)
Adriatic Sea *sea* Southeast Europe ancient Rome *179* (3) Bronze Age *175* (3) Copper Age *174* (2) early agriculture *174* (1) early modern states *193* (4) early states *178* (1), (2) economy *190* (1) empire and revolution *202* (3) first civilizations *177* (1) inter-war *209* (3), (5) medieval states *183* (4), *187* (5), *188* (1), *189* (4) Ottomans *230* (1) post-war economy *213* (5), *214* (2), *215* (3) post-war politics *212* (3) Reformation *194* (2) WWI *207* (5), (6)
Adulis *settlement/state* East Africa (Eritrea) ancient trade *44* (2), *44–45* (1) early cultures *160* (1), *161* (3), (4), (5) early trade *225* (3)
Adventure Bay *bay* Australia exploration *278* (1)
Adwuku West Africa (Ghana) early agriculture *158* (1)
Adygeya *region* Eastern Europe Soviet Union *214–215* (4)
Aegae Greece Hellenistic world *40–41* (1)
Aegates *mod.* Isole Egadi *island group* Italy ancient Rome *179* (3)
Aegean Sea *Gk.* Aigaíon Pélagos, Aigaío Pélagos, *Turk.* Ege Denizi *sea* Greece ancient Greece *177* (2), (3), *179* (4) Bronze Age *175* (3) early agriculture *174* (1) economy *190* (1) first civilizations *175* (4), *177* (1) medieval states *187* (5), *189* (4) Ottomans *197* (4), *230* (1) Reformation *194* (2) WWI *207* (6) WWII *210* (1), *211* (4) 20th-century politics *233* (3)
Aegina *var.* Aíyina, Egina *settlement/state* Greece ancient Greece *177* (2) first civilizations *175* (4)
Aegospotami *battle* Southwest Asia (Turkey) ancient Greece *177* (3)
Aegyptus *province* North Africa ancient Rome *180–181* (1) ancient trade *44* (2)
Aelana Southwest Asia (Jordan) early cultures *161* (2), (3), (4), (5)
Aelaniticus, Sinus *see* Aqaba, Gulf of
Aelia Capitolina *see* Jerusalem
Aemona *see* Ljubljana
Aenea Greece ancient Greece *177* (2)
Aenus Greece first civilizations *177* (1)
Aenus *state* Greece ancient Greece *177* (2)
Aequi *people* Italy early states *178* (1), (2)
Aesernia *mod.* Isernia Italy early states *178* (1)
Aethiopia *region* East Africa ancient trade *44* (2)
Aetolia *region* Greece Hellenistic world *40–41* (1)
Afalou Bou Rhummel North Africa (Algeria) the world in 10,000 BCE *14–15*
Afars and Issas, French Territory of the *mod.* Djibouti; *prev.* French Somaliland *state* East Africa the world in 1975 *106–107* *see also* Djibouti, French Somaliland
Afghanistan *region/state* Central Asia Cold War *109* (1) colonialism *248* (1), (2), *269* (3), (4) Communism *271* (8) decolonization *250* (1), *251* (4) economy *249* (4) empire and revolution *249* (3) historical geography *275* (5) Islam *227* (4) medieval Persia *231* (4) Ottomans *232–233* (1) post-war economy *253* (5) post-war politics *252* (1), *253* (4) Soviet Union *208* (2), *213* (4) the world in 1950 *102–103* the modern world *113* (3), (4) US superpower *138* (1) world religions *226* (1), *243* (4) WWII *251* (3) 20th century *234* (2)
Afikpo *early food production site* West Africa (Nigeria) early agriculture *158* (1)
Africa *continent* *154-169* **Africa, Exarchate of** *state* North Africa medieval states *183* (4)
Africa, Horn of *physical region* East Africa European expansion *84–85* (1) slave trade *165* (4) trade *165* (3)
Africa Nova *province* North Africa early cultures *161* (2)
Afuddo *mod.* Nimule East Africa (Sudan) exploration *157* (4), (5)
Afyeh *early food production site* Egypt early agriculture *158* (1)
Agadès *see* Agadez
Agadez *prev.* Agadès West Africa (Niger) colonization *167* (4) early agriculture *158* (1) economy *163* (2) exploration *157* (4) Islam *163* (1)
Agadir North Africa (Morocco) exploration *157* (4)
Agana Pacific Ocean (Guam) decolonization *285* (3)
Agartala South Asia (India) post-war politics *252* (1), (3)
Agatha *see* Agathe
Agathe *var.* Agatha; *mod.* Agde France first civilizations *177* (1)
Agde *see* Agathe
Agendicum *see* Sens
Aggassiz, Lake *lake* North America the world in 10,000 BCE *14–15*
Aghlabids *dynasty* North Africa early Islam *57* (2) Islam *227* (4)
Agincourt *battle* France medieval states *192* (2)
Aginsky Buryat Ad *autonomous region* Siberia (Russian Federation) Soviet Union *214–215* (4)
Agordat *early food site* East Africa (Eritrea) early agriculture *158* (1)
Agra South Asia (India) colonialism *248* (1) early medieval states *244–245* (3) economy *249* (4) Mughal Empire *246* (1) post-war economy *253* (5) trade *267* (3)
Agra *state* South Asia Mughal Empire *246* (1)
Agra and Oudh, United Provinces of *see* Uttar Pradesh
Agram *see* Zagreb, Zágráb
Agri Decumates *region* Central Europe ancient Rome *181* (4)
Agrigento *see* Agrigentum
Agrigentum *mod.* Agrigento Italy ancient Rome *179* (3), *180–181* (1) first religions *37* (3)
Aguada South America (Colombia) early cultures *146* (1)
Aguascalientes Central America (Mexico) Mexican Revolution *133* (3)
Agulhas, Cape *Afr.* Kaap Agulhas *headland* South Africa European imperialism *96* (2)
Agulhas, Kaap *see* Agulhas, Cape
Ahaggar *mountain range* North Africa ancient trade *44–45* (1) early cultures *160* (1) economy *163* (2) first humans *13* (2) historical geography *154–155* (1)
Ahe *island* Pacific Ocean exploration *278* (1)
Ahicchatra *religious site* South Asia (India) first religions *36* (2)
Ah Kin Chel *state* Central America Aztecs *124* (1)
Ahmad *oil terminal* Southwest Asia (Kuwait) economy *234* (1)
Ahmadābād *see* Ahmadabad
Ahmadnagar *var.* Ahmednagar South Asia (India) Mughal Empire *246* (1)
Ahmadnagar *state* South Asia early medieval states *245* (4) Mughal Empire *246* (1)
Ahmedabad *var.* Ahmadābād South Asia (India) colonialism *247* (3), *248* (1) decolonization *250* (1) economy *249* (4) imperial global economy *93* (5) post-war economy *253* (5)
Ahmednagar *see* Ahmadnagar
Ahoms *dynasty* South Asia early medieval states *244–245* (3) Mughal Empire *246* (1)
Ahtena *people* North America cultural groups *123* (3)
Ahteut North America (USA) cultural groups *123* (3)
Ahu Akahanga *archaeological site* Pacific Ocean (Eastern Island) early cultures *281* (4)
Ahu 'Akivi *archaeological site* Pacific Ocean (Eastern Island) early cultures *281* (4)
Ahuehuetlan Central America (Mexico) Aztecs *124* (3)
Ahuilizapan Central America (Mexico) colonization *125* (5)
Ahu Ra'ai *archaeological site* Pacific Ocean (Eastern Island) early cultures *281* (4)
Ahu Tongariki *archaeological site* Pacific Ocean (Eastern Island) early cultures *281* (4)
Ahu Vinapu *archaeological site* South America (Chile) early cultures *281* (4)
Aichi *var.* Aiti *prefecture* Japan economy *270* (1)
Aigaíon Pélagos *see* Aegean Sea
Aigaío Pélagos *see* Aegean Sea
Aigues-Mortes France crusades *64–65* (2)
Aigun *see* Aihun
Aihun *var.* Aigun East Asia (China) colonialism *269* (4)
Ai Khanoum *see* Alexandria ad Oxum
Aikudi South Asia (India) early medieval states *244* (1)
Aila *var.* Elath; *mod.* Eilat, Elat Southwest Asia (Israel) medieval voyages *61* (3) *see also* Eilat, Elath
Ailah Southwest Asia (Israel) crusades *65* (3)
Ain Jalut *battle* Southwest Asia (Israel) Mongols *229* (3), *68–69* (1)
Ainu *people* Japan early modern states *265* (5) medieval states *262–263* (1), (2), *265* (3) trade *267* (3)
Air *state* West Africa slave trade *165* (4)
Airgialla *state* British Isles medieval states *188* (2)
Ais *people* North America colonization *125* (4), *126* (1)
Aisne *river* France WWI *206* (2), (3)
Aiti *see* Aichi
Aix-en-Provence France early modern states *197* (5)
Aix-la-Chapelle *see* Aachen
Aíyina *see* Aegina
Aizawl South Asia (India) post-war politics *252* (1)
Aizu Japan early modern states *267* (4)
Ajanta *Buddhist centre/settlement* South Asia (India) first religions *36* (2) world religions *49* (3)
Ajayameru *var.* Ajmer, Ajmere South Asia (India) early medieval states *244* (2) world religions *243* (4) *see also* Ajmer
Ajdabiya North Africa (Libya) early Islam *56–57* (1)
Ajman Southwest Asia (United Arab Emirates) first civilizations *24* (3)
Ajmer *var.* Ajayameru, Ajmere South Asia (India) colonialism *247* (3) Mughal Empire *246* (1) *see also* Ajayameru
Ajmer *var.* Ajmere *state* South Asia colonialism *248* (2) Mughal Empire *246* (1)
Ajmere *see* Ajmer, Ajayameru
Ajnadain Southwest Asia (Israel) Islam *226* (2)
Ajnadain *battle* Southwest Asia (Israel) early Islam *56–57* (1)
Ajodhya South Asia (India) Mughal Empire *246* (1)
Akaba *see* Aelana, Aqaba
Akamagaseki *see* Shimonoseki
Akan States *state* West Africa Islam *163* (1) trade *164* (2)
Akaroa New Zealand colonization *283* (5)
Akbarpur South Asia (India) colonialism *247* (3)
Aken *see* Aachen
Akermanceaster *see* Bath
Akhaura South Asia (Bangladesh) post-war politics *252* (3)
Akhenaten Egypt ancient Egypt *159* (5)
Akhetaten *var.* Tell el-Amarna Egypt ancient Egypt *159* (5)
Akhisar *see* Thyatira
Akhmim *var.* Ipu Egypt ancient Egypt *159* (5)
Akira *early food production site* East Africa (Kenya) early agriculture *158* (1)
Akita Japan economy *270* (1) medieval states *264* (2), *265* (3), (4)
Akita *prefecture* Japan economy *270* (1)
Akjoujt *prev.* Fort-Repoux West Africa (Mauritania) early agriculture *158* (1)
Akkad Southwest Asia (Iraq) the world in 1250 BCE *26–27*
Akkad *state* Southwest Asia first civilizations *221* (4)
Akkerman Eastern Europe (Ukraine) Ottomans *195* (4)
'Akko *see* Acco, Acre

INDEX-GAZETTEER: Ak Koyunlu – Aquincum

Ak Koyunlu var. Akkoyunlu, Aq Qoyunlu state Southwest Asia Islam 163 (1)
Akmola Central Asia (Kazakhstan) Soviet Union 214–215 (4)
Akmolinsk region Central Asia/Siberia colonialism 269 (3)
Akron North America (USA) US politics 135 (6)
Akrotiri Southwest Asia (Cyprus) first civilizations 175 (4)
Aksai Chin Chin. Aksayqin region South Asia post-war economy 275 (3) post-war politics 252 (1), (2)
Aksayqin see Aksai Chin
Aksha Egypt ancient Egypt 159 (5)
Aksu var. Aqsu East Asia (China) ancient trade 44–45 (1) early modern states 268 (1) empire and revolution 268 (2) medieval states 262–263 (1) world religions 49 (3)
Aksum see Axum
Aktion see Actium
Akwamu state West Africa the world in 1700 82–83
Akwe Shavante people South America early cultures 147 (2)
Akyab Mainland Southeast Asia (Burma) trade 230 (2) WWII 272 (1), 273 (2)
Ala Italy WWI 207 (5)
Alabama state North America imperial global economy 93 (5) the growth of the US 129 (1) US Civil War 130 (2), (3), (4), (5), 131 (6), (7) US economy 134 (2), 139 (3) US society 137 (6) US superpower 139 (5)
Alabama people North America colonization 125 (4), 126 (1)
Alabama river North America US Civil War 131 (6)
Al-'Abbasa Egypt Mongols 229 (3)
Al 'Abbasa Egypt Mongols 229 (3)
Al Abyaḍ, Al Baḥr see White Nile
al Abyaḍ, An Nil see White Nile
Alaca Hüyük Southwest Asia (Turkey) first cities 28–29 (1) first civilizations 221 (5)
Alacant see Alicante
Alaka people South America early cultures 145 (2)
Alalakh Greece ancient Egypt 159 (5)
Alalia mod. Aleria France first civilizations 177 (1) see also Aleria
Alamanni see Alemanni
Al 'Amārah see Amara
Alamgirpur archaeological site South Asia (India) first cities 240 (2)
Alamo, The battle North America (USA) the growth of the US 129 (2)
Alamut assassins site/settlement Southwest Asia (Iran) Mongols 229 (3), 68–69 (1) Seljuks 228 (1)
Alans people Eastern Europe ancient Rome 181 (4) great migrations 52–53 , (1) Mongols 68–69 (1)
Al 'Arabīyah as Su'ūdīyah see Saudi Arabia
Alarcos Iberian Peninsula (Spain) Islam 192 (3)
Al 'Aṣab see Asab
Alasca, Golfo de see Alaska, Gulf of
Alashiya see Cyprus
Alaska prev. Russian America colonial possession/state North America Cold War 109 (1) colonialism 269 (3) Communism 273 (3) empire and revolution 88–89 (2) exploration 257 (2) imperial global economy 93 (3) the growth of the US 129 (2), 132 (1) US economy 136 (2) WWII 104 (1), 273 (2)
Alaska, Gulf of var. Golfo de Alasca gulf North America cultural groups 123 (3) exploration 118 (1), 119 (2), (3), 286 (1) the growth of the US 129 (2)
Alaska Range mountain range North America the growth of the US 129 (2)
Alavi South Asia (India) world religions 242 (3)
al Azraq, An Nil see Blue Nile
Albacete Iberian Peninsula (Spain) inter-war 209 (4)
Alba Fucens Italy early states 178 (1)
Al Baḥrayn see Bahrain
Albania Alb. Shqipëria state Southeast Europe Cold War 108 (3), 109 (1) early 20th century 206 (1) economy 205 (4) inter-war 209 (3), (5) Ottomans 202 (4), 230 (1) post-war economy 213 (5), 214 (1), (2), 215 (3) post-war politics 212 (3) Soviet Union 213 (4) the modern world 112 (2), 113 (3), (4) WWI 208 (1) WWII 104 (1), 211 (2), (4)
Albanians people Southeast Europe the modern world 112 (2)
Albanus, Lacus lake Italy early states 178 (1)
Albanus, Mons mountain Italy early states 178 (1)
Albany penal colony/settlement Australia colonization 282 (1), 283 (3) environmentalism 285 (2) exploration 279 (2)
Albany North America (USA) colonization 126 (1) empire and revolution 127 (2), (3) exploration 119 (2) the growth of the US 129 (2), 132 (1) US politics 135 (6) US society 137 (6)
Alba Regia see Székesfehérvár
Al Başrah see Basra
Albert France WWI 206 (2), (3)
Alberta province North America the growth of the US 129 (2), 132 (1) US economy 136 (2)
Albert Edward Nyanza see Edward, Lake
Albert, Lake var. Albert Nyanza, Lac Mobutu Sese Seko lake East Africa early agriculture 158 (1) exploration 157 (4), (5) historical geography 154–155 (1) Islam 163 (1) slave trade 165 (4)
Albert Nyanza see Albert, Lake
Albi anc. Albiga France economy 190 (1)
Albiga see Albi
Albigensian crusade France crusades 186 (1)
Albion region British Isles ancient trade 44 (2)
Albis see Elbe
Alborz, Reshteh-ye Kūhhā-ye see Elburz Mountains
Albreda West Africa (Gambia) the world in 1700 82–83
Albreda island West Africa empire and revolution 88 (1)
Albury Australia colonization 282 (1)
Alcacer Iberian Peninsula (Portugal) Islam 192 (3)
Alcántara Iberian Peninsula (Spain) crusades 186 (1) Islam 192 (3)
Alcobaça cistercian house Iberian peninsula (Spain) medieval states 187 (3)
Alcudia Iberian Peninsula (Spain) economy 190 (1)
Aldan river Eastern Europe early modern states 268 (1) Soviet Union 214–215 (4)
al Dar al Baida see Rabat
Aleksandrovka archaeological site Siberia (Russian Federation) early agriculture 258 (1)
Alemanni var. Alamanni people Central Europe ancient Rome 181 (4), 182 (1) Franks 183 (5), (6) great migrations 53 (2) medieval states 182 (2)
Alemannia region Central Europe Franks 184 (2)
Alençon France early modern states 197 (5)
Alep see Aleppo
Aleppo var. Yamkhad; anc. Beroea; Ar. Ḥalab, Fr. Alep Southwest Asia (Syria) ancient Persia 223 (4) biological diffusion 72–73 (1) crusades 228 (2), 65 (1), (3) economy 190 (1) exploration 219 (3) first cities 28–29 (1) first civilizations 221 (4), (5) Islam 184 (1) Mongols 229 (3), 68–69 (1) Napoleon 200–201 (1) Ottomans 230 (1), 231 (3), 232–233 (1) Seljuks 228 (1) Timur 229 (4) trade 230 (2) world religions 226 (1) WWI 233 (2) 20th-century politics 233 (3)
Aleria France ancient Rome 179 (3), 180–181 (1) early states 178 (2)
Alessandria Fr. Alexandrie Italy economy 190 (1), 190–191 medieval states 188 (1)
Aleut people North America cultural groups 123 (3)
Aleutian Islands island group North America cultural groups 123 (3) exploration 257 (2) the growth of the US 129 (2) US superpower 138 (1) WWII 272 (1), 273 (2)
Alexander, Empire of state Southwest Asia Hellenistic world 224 (1)
Alexandretta Turk. İskenderun Southwest Asia (Turkey) crusades 65 (3) WWI 233 (2)
Alexandria North America (USA) empire and revolution 127 (2)
Alexandria Ar. Al Iskandarīyah Egypt ancient Persia 225 (6) ancient Rome 179 (5), 180–181 (1), 181 (3), (4), 182 (1), 224 (2), 225 (5) ancient trade 44 (2), 44–45 (1) biological diffusion 72–73 (1) colonization 167 (4) crusades 228 (2), 65 (3) early cultures 160 (1), 161 (2), (3) early Islam 57 (2) early trade 225 (3) economy 163 (2), 190 (1) exploration 156 (3), 157 (4), 218 (1), (2) first cities 240 (2) first empires 241 (4) Hellenistic world 224 (1), 41 (2) Islam 163 (1), 226 (2), 227 (4), (5) medieval states 185 (3) Mongols 229 (3) Napoleon 200–201 (1) Ottomans 232–233 (1) slave trade 165 (4) world religions 226 (1), 49 (4) WWI 233 (2) WWII 210 (1), 211 (4) 20th-century politics 233 (3)
Alexandria battle Egypt early Islam 56–57 (1) Islam 226 (2)
Alexandria ad Caucasum var. Kapisa; mod. Begram Central Asia (Afghanistan) Hellenistic world 41 (2) see also Kapisa
Alexandria ad Oxum var. Ai Khanoum Central Asia (Afghanistan) Hellenistic world 40–41 (1)
Alexandria Arachoton Central Asia (Afghanistan) Hellenistic world 40–41 (1)
Alexandria Areion var. Aria; mod. Herat Central Asia (Afghanistan) ancient trade 44–45 (1) exploration 218 (1), 219 (3) Hellenistic world 40–41 (1), 41 (2) see also Herat
Alexandria Eschate var. Kokand Central Asia (Uzbekistan) Hellenistic world 40–41 (1)
Alexandria Margiana mod. Merv Central Asia (Turkmenistan) Hellenistic world 41 (2)
Alexandrie see Alessandria
Alexandroupolis see Dedeagach
Al Fāshir see El Fasher
Al Faw var. Fao Southwest Asia (Iraq) economy 234 (1) see also Fao
Al Fujayrah see Fujairah
Al Furāt see Euphrates
Al Fustat Egypt early Islam 56–57 (1)
Algarve region Iberian Peninsula (Portugal) Islam 192 (3)
Alger see Algiers
Algeria prev. Algiers; anc. Icosium colonial possession/state North Africa early Islam 57 (2) economy 168 (2), (3) European imperialism 96 (1), 97 (4) inter-war 209 (4) Islam 235 (4) the modern world 112 (1), 113 (3), (4) WWII 104 (1), 211 (4) Cold War 109 (1) colonization 167 (4) decolonization 168 (1) early 20th century 206 (1) see also Algiers
al Gharbīyah, Aş Şaḥrā' see Western Desert
Algiers var. Al Jazair; Fr. Alger North Africa (Algeria) biological diffusion 72–73 (1) colonization 167 (4) crusades 186 (1) economy 168 (2), 190 (1) European expansion 84–85 (1) exploration 157 (4) Islam 184 (1) medieval states 185 (3) Napoleon 200–201 (1), 201 (2) Ottomans 231 (3), 232–233 (1) slave trade 165 (4) US superpower 138 (1) WWII 211 (4)
Algiers mod. Algeria; anc. Icosium state North Africa Napoleon 200–201 (1) slave trade 165 (4) trade 167 (1) see also Algeria
Algoa Bay bay South America exploration 156 (3)
Algonquin people North America colonization 126 (1) cultural groups 123 (3)
Al Hadhar see Hatra
Al Ḥaḍr see Hatra
Al-Hajj Umar Ahmadu Sefu state West Africa colonization 167 (4)
Al Hamad see Syrian Desert
Al Ḥijāz see Hejaz
Al Hira Southwest Asia (Iraq) early Islam 56–57 (1)
Al Hufūf see Hasa
Alicante Lat. Lucentum; Cat. Alacant Iberian Peninsula (Spain) economy 190 (1), 205 (4) Franks 184 (2) inter-war 209 (4) Islam 192 (3)
Alice Boër archaeological site South America (Brazil) early cultures 145 (2)
Alice Springs Australia colonization 283 (3) decolonization 285 (3) exploration 279 (2)
Alids dynasty Southwest Asia Islam 227 (4)
Aligarh South Asia (India) economy 249 (4)
Ali Kosh Southwest Asia (Iraq) early agriculture 220 (1)
Al Iskandarīyah see Alexandria
al-Istabulat cantonment Southwest Asia (Iraq) early Islam 56–57 (1)
Al Jawf see Jauf
Al Jīzah see Giza
Al Kūfah see Kufa
Al-Kuwait see Kuwait
Al Kuwayt see Kuwait
Allada state West Africa the world in 1700 82–83
Allahabad South Asia (India) colonialism 247 (3), 248 (1) decolonization 250 (1) economy 249 (4) Mughal Empire 246 (1) post-war economy 253 (5)
Allahabad state South Asia Mughal Empire 246 (1)
'Allaqi, Wadi el- river Egypt ancient Egypt 159 (4)
Allen's Cave Australia exploration 280 (1)
Allia Bay archaeological site East Africa (Kenya) first humans 12 (1)
al Lībīyah, Aş Şaḥrā' see Libyan Desert
Allobroges people France ancient Rome 179 (5)
Al Lubnān see Lebanon
Alma battle Eastern Europe (Ukraine) Ottomans 202 (4)
Alma-Ata Eastern Europe (Russian Federation) Soviet Union 213 (4)
Al Madain Southwest Asia (Iraq) early Islam 56–57 (1)
Al Madīnah see Medina
Al Mahdīyah see Mahdia
Almalyk var. Almalyq East Asia (China) biological diffusion 72–73 (1) Mongols 68–69 (1)
Al Mamlakah see Morocco
Al Manāmah see Manama
Al-Mariyya see Almeria
al-Masharrahet hunting palace Southwest Asia (Iraq) early Islam 57 (3)
Almaty Central Asia (Kazakhstan) Soviet Union 214–215 (4)
Al Mawşil see Mosul
al Mayyit, Al Baḥr see Dead Sea
Almeria anc. Unci; Lat. Portus Magnus; Ar. Al-Mariyya Iberian Peninsula (Spain) economy 190 (1) inter-war 209 (4) Islam 192 (3)
Almohad Empire state North Africa crusades 64–65 (2), 186 (1)
Almohads dynasty North Africa crusades 186 (1) early Islam 57 (2)
Almoravid Empire state Iberian Peninsula/North Africa crusades 64–65 (2) early Islam 57 (2)
Al Mukalla Southwest Asia (Yemen) exploration 219 (4)
Al Mukallā see Al Mukalla
Alodia state East Africa the world in 750 CE 54–55 the world in 1000 58–59
Alofi Pacific Ocean (Niue) decolonization 285 (3)
Alor South Asia (Pakistan) early medieval states 244 (2) world religions 243 (4)
Alpes Cottiae province France ancient Rome 180–181 (1)
Alpes Graiae et Poeninae var. Alpes Penninae province France ancient Rome 180–181 (1)
Alpes Maritimae province France ancient Rome 180–181 (1)
Alpes Penninae see Alpes Graiae et Poeninae
Alpi see Alps
Alpi Giulie see Julian Alps
Alps Fr. Alpes, Ger. Alpen, It. Alpi mountain range Central Europe ancient Rome 179 (3), 180–181 (1), 181 (3) biological diffusion 72–73 (1) Bronze Age 175 (3) Copper Age 174 (2) crusades 186 (1), 64–65 (2) early agriculture 174 (1) early Islam 56–57 (1), 57 (2) early modern states 193 (4), (5) economy 190 (1) European expansion 84–85 (1) exploration 172 (1) first religions 37 (3) Franks 183 (5), (6), 184 (2) great migrations 52–53 (1) medieval states 185 (3), 192 (1), (2) Napoleon 200–201 (1) Ottomans 232–233 (1) prehistoric culture 17 (3), (4) world religions 48 (1), 49 (4) WWI 207 (5) WWII 210 (1), 211 (4)
Al Qadisiya Southwest Asia (Iraq) ancient Persia 225 (6)
Al Qadisiya battle Southwest Asia (Iraq) Islam 226 (2)
Al Qāhirah see Cairo, Fustat
Al Qatif Southwest Asia (Saudi Arabia) exploration 219 (4)
Al Qayrawān see Kairouan
Al Quds see Jerusalem
Al Quds ash Sharif see Jerusalem
Al Raydaniyya Egypt Ottomans 231 (3)
Alsace-Lorraine region France empire and revolution 202 (1i), (2) WWI 208 (1)
Alsium Italy early states 178 (1)
Alt see Olt
Altai region Siberia Soviet Union 214–215 (4)
Altai see Altai Mountains
Altaic Peoples people East Asia the world in 750 BCE 30–31
Al Ṭa'if see Taif
Altai Mountains var. Altai; Chin. Altay Shan, Rus. Altay mountain range East Asia/Siberia ancient trade 44–45 (1) biological diffusion 72–73 (1) colonialism 269 (3), (4) early agriculture 258 (1) exploration 256 (1), 257 (3) first humans 13 (2) first states 260 (1) Hellenistic world 40 (1) medieval states 261 (6) Mongols 68–69 (1) trade 267 (3) world religions 49 (3), (4)
Altamira Central America (Mexico) first civilizations 121 (2)
Altamira archaeological site/settlement Iberian Peninsula (Spain) prehistoric culture 17 (3)
Altar de Sacrificios Central America (Mexico) first civilizations 121 (2)
Altar, Desierto de see Sonoran Desert
Altay see Altai Mountains
Altay Shan see Altai Mountains
Altepetlac Central America (Mexico) Aztecs 124 (3)
Altiplano physical region South America early cultures 145 (2), (4) politics 152 (2)
Alto Paraná see Paraná
Alto Ramirez South America (Chile) early cultures 146 (1)
Alto Salaverry early ceremonial centre South America (Peru) early cultures 144 (1)
Altun Shan mountain range East Asia early agriculture 258 (1) first states 260 (1)
Altxerri archaeological site Iberian Peninsula (Spain) prehistoric culture 17 (3)
Al Urdunn see Jordan
Alvastra major cistercian house Scandinavia (Sweden) medieval states 187 (3)
Alwa state East Africa early cultures 160 (1), 161 (5) economy 163 (2)
Al Wajh see Wejh
Alwar South Asia (India) colonialism 247 (3)
Amadzimba Southern Africa (South Africa) the world in 5000 BCE 18–19
Amakusa Japan early modern states 267 (4)
Amalfi colonial possession/settlement Italy Franks 184 (2) medieval states 182 (2), 183 (4), 185 (3), 187 (5), 188 (1)
Amantlan Central America (Mexico) Aztecs 124 (3)
Amara var. Al 'Amārah Southwest Asia (Iraq) WWI 233 (2)
Amaravati Buddhist centre/settlement South Asia (India) early medieval states 244 (1) world religions 49 (3)
Amasia mod. Amasya Christian archbishopric Southwest Asia (Turkey) world religions 48 (1) see also Amasya
Amasya anc. Amasia Southwest Asia (Turkey) Ottomans 231 (3) see also Amasia
Amathus Southwest Asia (Cyprus) first civilizations 177 (1)
Amazon Port/Sp. Amazonas river South America colonization 148 (2), 149 (3), (4) early agriculture 20–21 (2) early cultures 144 (1), 145 (2), 146 (1), 147 (2) economy 153 (3) empire and revolution 150 (1), (2), 151 (3), 88 (1), 88–89 (2) environment 153 (4) European expansion 84–85 (1) exploration 142 (1), 143 (2), (3) global immigration 100 (1) global knowledge 76–77 imperial global economy 92 (1) Incas 147 (3), 148 (1) narcotics 153 (5) prehistoric culture 16 (1) the world in 1300 66–67 the modern world 110–111
Amazonas see Amazon
Amazon Basin basin South America colonization 149 (3) early agriculture 20–21 (2) early cultures 145 (4), 147 (2) environment 153 (4) Incas 148 (1)
Ambala see Umballa
Ambato South America (Ecuador) Incas 147 (3)
Ambianum see Amiens
Amboina prev. Ambon, Amboyna Maritime Southeast Asia (Indonesia) colonization 284–285 (1) empire and revolution 88 (1) WWII 272 (1), 273 (2)
Amboina var. Ambon; mod. Pulau Ambon island Maritime Southeast Asia colonialism 247 (4) Islam 243 (6) post-war politics 253 (4)
Ambon see Amboina
Ambon, Pulau see Amboina
Amboyna see Amboina
Ambracia Greece ancient Greece 177 (3), 179 (4)
Ameca Central America (Mexico) first civilizations 122 (1)
Amekni West Africa (Algeria) early agriculture 158 (1)
Amequemecan Central America (Mexico) colonization 125 (5)
America see United States of America
American Samoa colonial possession Pacific Ocean colonization 284–285 (1) decolonization 285 (3) environmentalism 285 (2) exploration 279 (3) the growth of the US 133 (4) US superpower 138 (1) WWII 273 (2)
American Virgin Islands var. Virgin Islands of the United States; prev. Danish West Indies colonial possession West Indies Cold War 108 (2)
Amery Ice Shelf ice feature Antarctica Antarctic Exploration 287 (3)
Amida mod. Diyarbakir Christian archbishopric Southwest Asia (Turkey) world religions 48 (1) see also Diyarbakir
Amiens anc. Ambianum, Samarobriva France early modern states 197 (5) economy 190 (1) Franks 184 (2) Reformation 195 (5) WWI 206 (2), (3)
Amirante Islands var. Amirantes Group island group Indian Ocean the world in 1850 90–91 the world in 1900 94–95 the world in 1925 98–99
Amirantes Group see Amirante Islands
Amisus mod. Samsun Christian archbishopric/settlement Southwest Asia (Turkey) early cultures 161 (2) Hellenistic world 40–41 (1) world religions 48 (1)
Amjhera state South Asia empire and revolution 249 (3)
Amman var. 'Ammān; anc. Philadelphia, Bibl. Rabbah Ammon, Rabbath Ammon Southwest Asia (Jordan) early Islam 56–57 (1) Ottomans 232–233 (1) WWI 233 (2) 20th century 234 (2) 20th-century politics 233 (3), (4), 235 (5)
Ammon state Southwest Asia first civilizations 222 (1)
Amnok-kang see Yalu
Amol var. Amul Southwest Asia (Iran) Hellenistic world 40–41 (1) Mongols 68–69 (1)
Amoy see Xiamen
Amphipolis battle/settlement/state Greece ancient Greece 177 (2), (3)
Ampurias see Emporiae
Amri archaeological site South Asia (Pakistan) first cities 240 (2)
Amritsar South Asia (India) colonialism 247 (3), 248 (1) decolonization 250 (1) economy 249 (4) post-war politics 252 (1)
Amsa-dong archaeological site East Asia (South Korea) early agriculture 258 (1)
Amsterdam Low Countries (Netherlands) Cold War 108 (3) early modern states 193 (4) economy 198 (1), 205 (4) empire and revolution 202 (1), (1i), (2) European expansion 84–85 (1) global immigration 100 (1) Reformation 195 (5), 196 (1)
Amud archaeological site Southwest Asia (Israel) first humans 13 (2)
Amu Darya anc. Oxus; Rus. Amudar'ya, Taj. Dar"yoi Amu, Turkm. Amyderya, Uzb. Amudaryo river Central Asia ancient trade 44–45 (1) colonialism 248 (1), 269 (3) early Islam 56–57 (1), 57 (2) exploration 257 (3) first civilizations 24 (2), 25 (3) first humans 13 (2) Islam 226 (2), 227 (4), (5) medieval Persia 231 (4) Mongols 68 (2), 68–69 (1) Ottomans 232–233 (1) world religions 226 (1) see also Oxus
Amudaryo see Amu Darya
Amu, Dar"yoi see Amu Darya
Amur region/state Siberia colonialism 269 (3), (4) early modern states 268 (1)
Amur Chin. Heilong Jiang river Siberia/East Asia ancient trade 44–45 (1) biological diffusion 72–73 (1) Chinese revolution 271 (5) colonialism 269 (3), (4) Communism 271 (8) early agriculture 20–21 (2), 258 (1) early modern states 265 (5) empire and revolution 268 (2) exploration 256 (1), 257 (2), (3) first states 260 (1) imperialism 270 (2) medieval states 261 (6), 262–263 (1), 263 (6), 264 (1), (2) Mongols 68–69 (1) post-war economy 275 (3) post-war politics 274 (2) Soviet Union 214–215 (4) trade 267 (3) world religions 49 (4)
Amyderya see Amu Darya
Ana Southwest Asia (Iraq) early Islam 56–57 (1)
Anadolu see Anatolia
Anadyr' Siberia (Russian Federation) exploration 287 (2)
Anadyr' see Anadyrsk
Anadyrsk var. Novomarinsk; mod. Anadyr' Siberia (Russian Federation) exploration 257 (2)
Anadyrskiy Khrebet see Chukot Range
Anahilapataka South Asia (India) the world in 750 CE 54–55
Anakena South America (Chile) early cultures 281 (4)
Ananatuba archaeological site South America (Brazil) early cultures 144 (1), 145 (2)
Anartta state South Asia first empires 241 (5)
Anasazi Culture state North America the world in 1200 62–63
Anatolia physical region Southwest Asia biological diffusion 72–73 (1) Bronze Age 175 (3) crusades 64–65 (2) early agriculture 174 (1) early cultures 161 (2) early Islam 56–57 (1), 57 (2) economy 190 (1) exploration 218 (2), 219 (3) first cities 220 (2) first civilizations 175 (4), (5), 222 (2) first humans 13 (2) first religions 37 (3) global knowledge 76–77 (1) Hellenistic world 224 (1) historical geography 154–155 (1) Islam 227 (4) Mongols 68 (2), 68–69 (1) Ottomans 202 (4), 230 (1) Seljuks 228 (1) trade 230 (2) 20th-century politics 233 (3)
Anazarbus Christian archbishopric Southwest Asia (Turkey) world religions 48 (1)
Anbiya state West Africa trade 163 (4)
An Canul state Central America Aztecs 124 (1)
Anchorage North America (USA) exploration 287 (2)
Ancón archaeological site/settlement South America (Peru) early cultures 145 (3), 146 (1)
Ancona Italy ancient Rome 180–181 (1), 181 (3) early cultures 161 (2) early modern states 193 (4) early states 178 (1) economy 190 (1), 205 (4) medieval states 188 (1)
Ancud see San Carlos de Ancud
Ancylus, Lake lake Scandinavia historical geography 170–171 (1)
Ancyra mod. Ankara, Eng. Angora Southwest Asia (Turkey) ancient Rome 180–181 (1) Hellenistic world 40–41 (1) world religions 48 (1) see also Angora, Ankara
Andahuaylas South America (Peru) Incas 147 (3)
Åndalsnes Scandinavia (Norway) WWII 210 (1)
Andalucia region Iberian Peninsula (Spain) Islam 192 (3)
Andaman Islands island group South Asia ancient trade 44–45 (1) biological diffusion 72–73 (1) colonialism 248 (1), (2), 269 (4) decolonization 251 (4) European imperialism 97 (3) exploration 239 (1) historical geography 236–237 (1) medieval voyages 61 (3) post-war politics 253 (4) trade 230 (2), 267 (3) WWII 251 (3), 272 (1)
Andaman Sea sea Indian Ocean Bronze Age 240 (3) colonialism 247 (4), 248 (1), (2) decolonization 251 (4) early medieval states 245 (5), (6) European imperialism 97 (3) exploration 239 (1) medieval voyages 61 (3) Mongols 68–69 (1) post-war economy 253 (5) post-war politics 253 (4) world religions 243 (5) WWII 251 (3)
Andean Chiefdoms state South America the world in 500 CE 50–51 the world in 750 CE 54–55 the world in 1300 66–67
Anderson burial mound North America (USA) first civilizations 121 (4)
Andes mountain range South America colonization 148 (2) early agriculture 20–21 (2) early cultures 144 (1), 145 (2), (3), (4), 146 (1), 147 (2) empire and revolution 150 (1), (2), 151 (3) environment 153 (4) European expansion 84–85 (1) exploration 142 (1), 143 (2), (3) global knowledge 76–77 (1) imperial global economy 92 (1) Incas 147 (3), 148 (1) narcotics 153 (5) politics 151 (4) prehistoric culture 16 (1)
Andha state South Asia first empires 241 (5)
Andhapura South Asia (India) first empires 241 (4)
Andhra region/state South Asia first empires 241 (5) medieval states 261 (6) world religions 242 (2), 243 (4), 49 (3)
Andhra Pradesh region South Asia post-war politics 252 (1)
Anding province East Asia first states 260 (1)
Andong var. Antung; mod. Dandong; Jap. Antō East Asia (South Korea) colonialism 269 (4) Sino-Japanese War 270 (3) the growth of the US 133 (4) see also Dandong
Andorra Cat. Valls d'Andorra, Fr. Vallée d'Andorre state Iberian Peninsula empire and revolution 199 (4), 202 (1) Islam 192 (3) medieval states 192 (1), (2) Napoleon 200–201 (1) the modern world 112 (2)
Andravida Greece medieval states 189 (4)
Andronovo archaeological site/settlement Siberia (Russian Federation) early agriculture 258 (1)
Andros Greece ancient Greece 177 (3)
Andros island/state Greece ancient Greece 177 (2) Ottomans 230 (1)
Androsovo see Andrusovo
Andrusovo mod. Androsovo Eastern Europe (Russian Federation) empire and revolution 198 (2)
Anga region/state South Asia ancient India 242 (1) first religions 36 (2) world religions 242 (3)
Angara river Eastern Europe early agriculture 258 (1) first states 260 (1)
Angel North America (USA) cultural groups 122 (5)
Angers anc. Juliomagus settlement/university France crusades 186 (1) empire and revolution 199 (4) Franks 184 (2) medieval states 187 (3) see also Juliomagus
Angevin Empire state British Isles/France the World in 1300 66–67 (1)
Angkor Mainland Southeast Asia (Cambodia) biological diffusion 72–73 (1) early medieval states 245 (6) medieval states 262–263 (1) Mongols 68 (2) world religions 243 (5), 49 (4)
Angkor Borei see Naravaranagara
Angles people Central Europe ancient Rome 181 (4) great migrations 53 (2)
Angles-sur-l'Anglin archaeological site France prehistoric culture 17 (3), (4)
Anglia see England
Anglo-Egyptian Sudan mod. Sudan state East Africa 20th-century politics 233 (4) European imperialism 96 (1), 97 (4) WWII 104 (1) see also Sudan
Anglo-Saxon Kingdoms state British Isles medieval states 182 (2)
Angola prev. People's Republic of Angola, Portuguese West Africa state Southern Africa Cold War 109 (1), (5) decolonization 168 (1) economy 168 (2), (3) European expansion 84–85 (1) European imperialism 96 (1), 97 (4) slave trade 165 (4) the modern world 112 (1), 113 (4) trade 164 (2), 167 (1)
Angora mod. Ankara; anc. Ancyra Southwest Asia (Turkey) 20th-century politics 233 (3) Ottomans 232–233 (1) WWI 233 (2) see also Ancyra, Ankara
Ango-Saxons people British Isles ancient Rome 182 (1) medieval states 182 (2)
Angostura mod. Ciudad Bolívar South America (Venezuela) empire and revolution 150 (1), (2) exploration 143 (3) see also Ciudad Bolívar
Angoulême anc. Iculisma France Franks 184 (2)
Anguilla colonial possession West Indies Cold War 108 (2)
An-hsi see Anxi
Anhui var. Anhwei, Wan province East Asia Chinese revolution 271 (5) early modern states 268 (1) empire and revolution 268 (2) post-war politics 271 (7), 274 (2)
Anhui Clique movement East Asia Chinese Civil War 271 (6)
Anhwei see Anhui
Aniba var. Miam Egypt ancient Egypt 159 (4)
Anio river Italy early states 178 (1)
Anjengo South Asia (India) colonialism 247 (3)
Anjidiv Island South Asia (India) colonialism 247 (3)
Anjou France medieval states 187 (4)
Anjou region France medieval states 187 (4)
Anju East Asia (North Korea) Sino-Japanese War 270 (3)
Ankara prev. Angora, anc. Ancyra Southwest Asia (Turkey) early Islam 56–57 (1) first civilizations 221 (4) Napoleon 200–201 (1), 201 (3) Ottomans 230 (1) Timur 229 (4) WWI 233 (2) WWII 210 (1), 211 (4) Cold War 108 (3) see also Angora, Ancyra
Ankole state East Africa colonization 167 (4)
An Loc battle Mainland Southeast Asia (Vietnam) post-war politics 251 (5)
Annaba prev. Bône North Africa (Algeria) economy 168 (2) see also Bône
Annam mod. Trung Phân state Mainland Southeast Asia biological diffusion 72–73 (1) colonialism 269 (4) early modern states 266 (1), (2), 268 (1) European expansion 80–81 (1) European imperialism 97 (3), (4) medieval states 262–263 (1), 263 (3), (6) Mongols 68–69 (1) trade 267 (3)
Annanduhufu East Asia (China) medieval states 262–263 (1)
Annapolis North America (USA) the growth of the US 129 (2)
Anniston North America (USA) US society 137 (6)
Annomadu West Africa (Ghana) empire and revolution 88 (1)
Anping East Asia (China) first states 260 (1)
Anshan Southwest Asia (Iran) first cities 28–29 (1) first civilizations 24 (2), 25 (3)
Antakya see Antioch
Antalya see Adalia, Attalia
Antananarivo Madagascar economy 168 (2) politics 169 (4)
Antandros see Antandrus
Antandrus var. Antandros state Greece ancient Greece 177 (2)
Antarctica continent 286-287
Antarctic Peninsula coastal feature Antarctica Antarctic exploration 287 (3)
Antequera see Oaxaca
Antietam North America (USA) US Civil War 131 (6)
Antigua island West Indies empire and revolution 88 (1) WWII 104 (2)
Antigua river South America colonization 125 (5)
Antigua and Barbuda state West Indies the modern world 112 (1) US economy 136 (2) US politics 139 (4)
Antioch mod. Antakya; anc. Antiochia Southwest Asia (Turkey) ancient Persia 225 (6) ancient Rome 180–181 (1), 181 (3), (4), 182 (1), 224 (2), 225 (5) ancient trade 44–45 (1) crusades 228 (2), 65 (3) early cultures 161 (2) early trade 225 (3) economy 190 (1) first religions 37 (3) Hellenistic world 224 (1), 41 (2) Islam 184 (1), 226 (2), 227 (5) medieval states 185 (3), 187 (5) Mongols 229 (3), 68 (2) Seljuks 228 (1) world religions 226 (1)
Antiochia var. Antiochia Pisidiae, Eng. Antioch in Pisidia Southwest Asia (Turkey) ancient Rome 180–181 (1)
Antiochia Pisidiae see Antiochia
Antioch in Pisidia see Antiochia
Antioch, Principality of state Southwest Asia crusades 228 (2), 65 (3) medieval states 187 (5)
Antioquia South America (Colombia) empire and revolution 150 (2)
Antissa state Greece ancient Greece 177 (2)
Antium mod. Anzio Italy early states 178 (1) see Anzio
Antō see Andong, Dandong
Antofagasta South America (Chile) empire and revolution 151 (3) environment 153 (4) politics 151 (4)
Antonine Wall Lat. Vallum Antonini wall British Isles ancient Rome 180–181 (1)
Antoniniana, Aqua aqueduct Italy ancient Rome 181 (2)
Antoninianae, Thermae see Caracalla, Baths of
Antonini, Vallum see Antonine Wall
Antonio Plaza archaeological site Central America (Mexico) first civilizations 121 (3)
An tSionainn see Shannon
Antung see Andong, Dandong
Antwerp Fr. Anvers Low Countries (Belgium) early modern states 193 (4) economy 190 (1), 205 (4) empire and revolution 202 (1i) global immigration 100 (1) medieval states 188 (1), (2) Reformation 195 (5) WWI 206 (2), (3)
Anupa region/state South Asia first empires 241 (5) world religions 242 (2)
Anuradhapura South Asia (Sri Lanka) early medieval states 244 (1), (2) exploration 256 (1) first empires 241 (4) world religions 49 (3)
Anuta var. Cherry Island island Pacific Ocean early cultures 280–281 (3) medieval voyages 60 (2)
Anu Ziggurat building Southwest Asia (Iraq) first cities 220 (3)
Anvers see Antwerp
Anxi var. An-hsi East Asia (China) ancient trade 44–45 (1) biological diffusion 72–73 (1) exploration 256 (1) medieval states 262–263 (1)
Anyang archaeological site/settlement East Asia (China) early agriculture 258 (2) early systems 32 (1), 33 (2), (3) first cities 259 (3), (4), 28–29 (1)
Anyi East Asia (China) first cities 259 (3), (5) first religions 37 (4)
Anyi vassal state East Asia first cities 259 (3)
Anzio battle/settlement Italy WWII 105 (3), 211 (4)
Aomen see Macao
Aomori Japan Communism 273 (3) economy 270 (1)
Aomori prefecture Japan economy 270 (1)
Aoos see Vjosë
Aornos battle Central Asia (Tajikistan) Hellenistic world 40–41 (1)
Aotearoa mod. New Zealand state New Zealand early cultures 280–281 (3) medieval voyages 60 (2)
Ao Thai see Siam, Gulf of; Thailand, Gulf of
Apache people North America colonization 126 (1)
Apalachee people North America colonization 125 (4), 126 (1)
Apamea Southwest Asia (Turkey) Hellenistic world 40–41 (1), 41 (2) world religions 48 (1)
Aparanta region South Asia first empires 241 (4)
Aparanta/Pascad-Desa region South Asia early religions 48 (2)
Apatzingan Central America (Mexico) first civilizations 122 (1)
Apennines mountain range Central Europe ancient Rome 179 (3) early states 178 (1), (2) economy 190 (1) medieval states 183 (4) Napoleon 200–201 (1)
Aphrodisias Southwest Asia (Turkey) Hellenistic world 40–41 (1)
Aphytis settlement/state Greece ancient Greece 177 (2)
Apia Pacific Ocean (Samoa) decolonization 285 (3)
Apollo religious site Southwest Asia (Turkey) first religions 37 (3)
Apollo II Cave archaeological site Southern Africa (Namibia) prehistoric culture 17 (2)
Apollonia mod. Sozopol; prev. Sizebolu Southeast Europe (Bulgaria) ancient Greece 179 (4) first civilizations 177 (1) Hellenistic world 40–41 (1)
Apollonis Southwest Asia (Turkey) Hellenistic world 41 (2)
Apologos Southwest Asia (Kuwait) early trade 225 (3)
Appalachian Mountains mountain range North America colonization 126 (1) cultural groups 122 (5) early agriculture 120 (1), 20–21 (2) exploration 118 (1), 119 (2), (3) first civilizations 121 (4) the growth of the US 129 (2)
Appia, Aqua aqueduct Italy ancient Rome 181 (2)
Appian Way see Via Appia
Appia, Via Eng. Appian Way road Italy ancient Rome 181 (2) early states 178 (1)
Appomattox North America (USA) US Civil War 131 (7)
Apuli people Italy early states 178 (1), (2)
Apulia region Italy medieval states 183 (4)
Apulum prev. Bălgrad, Karlsburg, Károly-Fehérvár; Ger. Karlsburg, Weissenburg Hung. Gyulafehérvár, Rom. Alba Iulia Southeast Europe (Romania) ancient Rome 180–181 (1) world religions 48 (1) see also Gyulafehérvár
Apure river South America empire and revolution 150 (1) exploration 143 (3) politics 152 (1)
Aqaba var. Akaba, 'Aqabah; anc. Aelana, Elath Southwest Asia (Jordan) 20th century 234 (2) 20th-century politics 233 (4) WWI 233 (2)
Aqaba, Gulf of var. Gulf of Elat; anc. Sinus Aelaniticus; Ar. Khalīj al 'Aqabah gulf Southwest Asia crusades 65 (3) 20th century 234 (2)
'Aqabah, Khalīj al see Aqaba, Gulf of
Aq Qoyunlu see Ak Koyunlu
Aqsu see Aksu
Aqua Antoniniana aqueduct Italy ancient Rome 181 (2)
Aqua Appia aqueduct Italy ancient Rome 180–181 (1)
Aqua Claudia aqueduct Italy ancient Rome 181 (2)
Aquae Calidae see Bath
Aquae Grani see Aachen
Aquae Solis see Bath
Aqua Marcia aqueduct Italy ancient Rome 181 (2)
Aqua Traiana aqueduct Italy ancient Rome 181 (2)
Aqua Virgo aqueduct Italy ancient Rome 181 (2)
Aquila Italy medieval states 189 (4)
Aquileia Italy ancient Rome 179 (5), 180–181 (1), 181 (3) ancient trade 44–45 (1) great migrations 52–53 (1) medieval states 182 (2), 185 (3) world religions 48 (1)
Aquiles Serdán Central America (Mexico) first civilizations 121 (2)
Aquincum mod. Budapest legion headquarters Central Europe (Hungary)

INDEX-GAZETTEER: Aquisgranum – Bactria

ancient Rome 180–181 (1) see also Buda, Budapest
Aquisgranum see Aachen
Aquitaine mod. Guyenne; anc. Aquitania region France Franks 183 (6), 184 (2) medieval states 187 (4) see also Aquitania, Guyenne
Aquitania province France ancient Rome 180–181 (1)
Arabia region Southwest Asia ancient Persia 223 (4) ancient Rome 180–181 (1) ancient trade 44 (2) crusades 65 (1) exploration 156 (3), 157 (4), 218 (1), (2), 219 (3), (4), 239 (1) Islam 226 (2), 227 (4), (5) medieval voyages 61 (3) Mongols 68 (2) the modern world 113 (4) world religions 226 (1)
Arabian Desert var. Aş Şaḩrā' ash Sharqīyah; Eng. Eastern Desert desert Egypt ancient Egypt 159 (2), (3), (5) early agriculture 220 (1) early trade 225 (3) first cities 220 (2) first civilizations 221 (4) see also Eastern Desert
Arabian Peninsula physical region Southwest Asia ancient Egypt 159 (5) ancient Persia 223 (4) biological diffusion 72–73 (1) early agriculture 20–21 (2) early cultures 160 (1), 161 (3) early Islam 57 (2) early systems 223 (3) economy 163 (2) first civilizations 222 (2) Hellenistic world 41 (2) imperial global economy 92 (1) Islam 163 (1) medieval Persia 231 (4) medieval states 261 (6) Ottomans 231 (3), 232–233 (1) prehistoric culture 16 (1) slave trade 165 (4) trade 165 (3), 230 (2), 267 (3) world religions 49 (4) WWI 233 (2)
Arabian Sea var. Sinus Arabicus sea Indian Ocean ancient Persia 225 (6) ancient trade 44–45 (1) biological diffusion 72–73 (1) colonialism 247 (3), 248 (1), (2) decolonization 251 (4) early agriculture 20–21 (2) early Islam 57 (2) early medieval states 244 (1), 244–245 (3) early religions 48 (2) early trade 225 (3) economy 249 (4) empire and revolution 249 (3), 88–89 (2) exploration 156 (3), 218 (1), (2), 219 (4), 239 (1) first cities 28–29 (1) first civilizations 24 (2), 25 (3) first religions 36 (2) Hellenistic world 224 (1) historical geography 236–237 (1), 275 (5) Islam 227 (4) Marathas 246 (2) medieval states 261 (6) medieval voyages 61 (3) Mongols 229 (3), 68–69 (1) post-war economy 253 (5) post-war politics 252 (1) Timur 229 (4) trade 230 (2) world religions 243 (4), 49 (3) WWII 251 (3) see also Arabicus, Sinus
Arabicus, Sinus sea Indian Ocean ancient trade 44 (2)
'Arab, Khalīj al see Persian Gulf
Arabs people North Africa ancient Rome 181 (4), 182 (1) ancient trade 44–45 (1) historical geography 275 (5) medieval states 182 (2) Ottomans 232–233 (1)
Aracaju South America (Brazil) politics 152 (1)
Arachosia region South Asia ancient Persia 223 (4) first empires 241 (4) Hellenistic world 224 (1)
Aradus Fr. Rouad; Bibl. Arvad; later Arwad Southwest Asia (Lebanon) first civilizations 177 (1) Hellenistic world 40–41 (1)
Arafura Sea Ind. Laut Arafuru sea Southeast Asia Bronze Age 240 (3) colonization 282 (1), 283 (3) European imperialism 97 (3) exploration 279 (2) Islam 243 (6) world religions 243 (5) WWII 272 (1), 273 (2)
Arafuru, Laut see Arafura Sea
Arago archaeological site Iberian Peninsula (France) first humans 13 (2)
Aragon Sp. Aragón state Iberian Peninsula crusades 186 (1), 64–65 (2) early modern states 194 (1) Islam 192 (3) medieval states 187 (3), (4), 192 (1), (2) Reformation 196 (2)
Araguaia var. Araguaya, Rio Araguaia river South America colonization 149 (3) early cultures 144 (1), 145 (2) environment 153 (4)
Araguaia, Rio see Araguaia
Araguaya see Araguaia
Arakan prev. Candra state Mainland Southeast Asia colonialism 269 (4) early medieval states 245 (6) Mughal Empire 246 (1) see also Candra
Araks var. Aras Nehri river Southwest Asia first civilizations 24 (2), 25 (3)
Aral Sea Kaz. Aral Tengizi, Rus. Aral'skoye More, Uzb. Orol Dengizi inland sea Central Asia ancient Persia 225 (6) ancient trade 44–45 (1) colonialism 269 (3) Communism 271 (8) early Islam 56–57 (1), 57 (2) exploration 172 (1), 218 (2), 219 (3), 256 (1) first humans 13 (2) global knowledge 76–77 (1) Hellenistic world 224 (1) historical geography 275 (5) Islam 226 (2), 227 (4) medieval states 261 (6), 262–263 (1) Mongols 68 (2), 68–69 (1) Ottomans 232–233 (1) Seljuks 228 (1) Soviet Union 208 (2), 213 (4) Timur 229 (4) trade 230 (2), 267 (3) world religions 226 (1), 49 (3), (4)
Aral'skoye More see Aral Sea
Aral Tengizi see Aral Sea
Araluen goldfield Australia colonization 282 (2)
Aram var. Syria state Southwest Asia first civilizations 222 (1) see also Syria
Aramaeans people Southwest Asia first civilizations 221 (5)
Aram-Damascus state Southwest Asia first civilizations 222 (1)
Aramis hominid site Central Africa (Chad) first humans 12 (1)
Aram-Zobah state Southwest Asia first civilizations 222 (1)
Araouane Lake lake West Africa historical geography 154–155 (1)
Ara Pacis building Italy ancient Rome 181 (2)
Arapaho people North America colonization 126 (1)
Araquinoid people South America the world in 500 CE 50–51 the world in 1000 58–59 the world in 1300 66–67
Ararat goldfield Australia colonization 282 (2)
Arash battle Southwest Asia (Azerbaijan) medieval Persia 231 (4)
Aras Nehri see Araks
Araucanians people South America early cultures 147 (2)
Arausio mod. Orange church council France world religions 48 (1) see also Orange
Aravaipa Apache people North America colonization 125 (4)
Aravali Range mountain range South Asia colonialism 247 (3), 248 (1) early medieval states 244 (1), 244–245 (3) first cities 240 (2) Mughal Empire 246 (1) world religions 243 (4)
Arawak people West Indies colonization 125 (4)
Arawe Islands island group New Guinea early cultures 280–281 (3) medieval voyages 60 (2)
Araxes river Southwest Asia Hellenistic world 40–41 (1)
Arbela var. Erbil, Irbil; mod. Arbīl; Kurd. Hawlēr Christian archbishopric/settlement Southwest Asia (Iraq) exploration 218 (1) Hellenistic world 40–41 (1) world religions 48 (1) see also Arbil
Arbela battle Southwest Asia (Turkey) ancient Rome 224 (2)
Arbil Southwest Asia (Iraq) 20th-century politics 235 (5)
Arbroath anc. Aberbrothock British Isles (United Kingdom) medieval states 188 (2)
Archangel Rus. Arkhangel'sk Eastern Europe (Russian Federation) economy 205 (4) European expansion 80–81 (1) exploration 257 (2), 286 (1), 287 (2) Soviet Union 208 (2), 213 (4) WWII 210 (1), 211 (4) see also Arkhangel'sk
Arcola battle Italy Napoleon 200–201 (1)
Arcot South Asia (India) colonialism 248 (1)
Arctic region North America early agriculture 120 (1) exploration 286–287
Arctic hunter-gatherers people Eastern Europe/Siberia/North America the world in 1250 BCE 26–27
Arctic Ocean ocean biological diffusion 73 (2) cultural groups 123 (3) early agriculture 120 (1) empire and revolution 88 (1), 88–89 (2) European expansion 80–81 (1), 81 (2) exploration 257 (2), 286 (1), 287 (2) first humans 13 (2) global immigration 100 (1) medieval states 185 (3), 262–263 (1) Soviet Union 208 (2), 213 (4) the growth of the US 129 (2), 132 (1), 133 (4) US superpower 138 (1) WWII 104 (1), (2), 105 (3), 211 (4) Cold War 109 (1) colonialism 269 (3)
Arcy-sur-Cure archaeological site France prehistoric culture 17 (3)
Ardabil Southwest Asia (Iran) early Islam 56–57 (1) Islam 226 (2), 227 (4) medieval Persia 231 (4) medieval states 185 (3)
Ardea Italy early states 178 (1)
Ardeal see Transylvania
Ardennes battle Low Countries (Belgium) WWII 105 (3)
Ardennes physical region Low Countries (Belgium) WWI 206 (2), (3) WWII 211 (4)
Ardwick British Isles economy 204 (2)
Arelas see Arelate, Arles
Arelate mod. Arles Christian archbishopric/settlement France ancient Rome 180–181 (1) world religions 48 (1) see also Arles
Arene Candide Italy early agriculture 174 (1)
Areopagus building Greece ancient Greece 177 (4)
Arequipa South America (Peru) colonization 148 (2) empire and revolution 151 (3) environment 153 (4) politics 151 (4)
Ares, Temple of temple Greece ancient Greece 177 (4)
Arezzo anc. Arretium settlement/university Italy economy 190 (1) medieval states 187 (3) see also Arretium
Argentina prev. Argentine Confederation state South America empire and revolution 151 (3) environment 153 (4) global immigration 100 (1), 101 (2) imperial global economy 92 (1) narcotics 153 (5) politics 151 (4), 152 (1), (2) the growth of the US 133 (4) the modern world 112 (1), 113 (4) US superpower 138 (1) WWII 105 (3) Cold War 109 (1) economy 153 (3) see also Argentine Confederation
Argentine Confederation mod. Argentina state South America the world in 1850 90–91 see also Argentina
Argentoratum mod. Strasbourg legion headquarters/mithraic site France ancient Rome 180–181 (1) world religions 48 (1) see alsoStrasbourg, Strassburg
Argeş battle Southeast Europe (Romania) WWI 207 (6)
Argesh Southeast Europe (Romania) Ottomans 230 (1)
Argilus state Greece ancient Greece 177 (2)
Arginusae Insulae see Arginusae Islands
Arginusae Islands Lat. Arginusae Insulae battle Greece ancient Greece 177 (3)
Argissa Greece early agriculture 174 (1)
Argonne France WWI 206 (2), (3)
Argos Greece ancient Greece 177 (3), 179 (4) first civilizations 175 (4), 177 (1)
Arguin West Africa (Mauritania) European expansion 84–85 (1)
Arguin Island island West Indies the world in 1500 74–75 the world in 1600 78–79 the world in 1700 82–83 the world in 1800 86–87 the world in 1850 90–91
Århus see Aarhus
Aria province/region Central Asia ancient Persia 223 (4) ancient trade 44 (2) Hellenistic world 40–41 (1)
Aria see Alexandria Areion, Herat
Arica prev. San Marcos de Arica South America (Chile) colonization 148 (2) empire and revolution 150 (1), 151 (3) environment 153 (4) European expansion 81 (3) politics 151 (4)
Arica battle South America (Chile) politics 151 (4)
Aricara battle North America (USA) the growth of the US 129 (2)
Aricia Italy early states 178 (1)
Arīḥā see Jericho
Arikara people North America colonization 126 (1)
Ariminum mod. Rimini Italy ancient Rome 179 (3), 180–181 (1) early states 178 (1), (2) world religions 48 (1) see also Rimini
Arisbe settlement/state Southwest Asia (Turkey) ancient Greece 177 (2)
Aristé people South America the world in 1300 66–67
Arizona region/state North America Mexican Revolution 133 (3) the growth of the US 129 (1) US economy 134 (2)
Arizpe fort Central America (Mexico) colonization 125 (4)
Arkansas region North America imperial global economy 93 (5) the growth of the US 129 (1) US Civil War 130 (2), 130 (3), (4), (5), 131 (6), (7) US economy 134 (2), 139 (3) US society 137 (6) US superpower 139 (5)
Arkansas river North America colonization 125 (4), 126 (1) cultural groups 122 (5) exploration 118 (1), 119 (2) first civilizations 121 (4) the growth of the US 129 (2) US Civil War 131 (6)
Arkat mod. Arcot South Asia (India) Mughal Empire 246 (1) see also Arcot
Arkhangel'sk Eng. Archangel Eastern Europe (Russian Federation) Cold War 108 (3) Soviet Union 214–215 (4) see also Archangel
Arles var. Arles-sur-Rhône; anc. Arelas, Arelate France economy 190 (1) Franks 183 (5), (6), 184 (2) medieval states 188 (1) see also Arelate
Arles, Kingdom of state Central Europe/France medieval states 188 (1)
Arles-sur-Rhône see Arelate, Arles
Arlit West Africa (Niger) early agriculture 158 (1)
Armagaon South Asia (India) colonialism 247 (3)
Armagnac region France medieval states 192 (2)
Armant anc. Hermonthis Egypt ancient Egypt 159 (2), (4), (5)
Armenia prev. Armenian Soviet Socialist Republic; anc. Urartu; Arm. Hayastan region/state Southwest Asia ancient Persia 223 (4), 225 (6) ancient Rome 180–181 (1), 181 (3), (4), 224 (2), 225 (5) ancient trade 44 (2), 44–45 (1) crusades 65 (3) early Islam 56–57 (1) economy 234 (1) Hellenistic world 224 (1) Islam 226 (2), 227 (4), (5), 235 (4) medieval Persia 231 (4) medieval states 185 (3), 187 (5) Ottomans 232–233 (1) post-war economy 214 (2) Soviet Union 208 (2), 214–215 (4) world religions 226 (1) WWI 233 (2) 20th-century politics 233 (3) see also Armenian Soviet Socialist republic, Urartu
Armenian Rulers state Southwest Asia Seljuks 228 (1)
Armenians people Southwest Asia Ottomans 232–233 (1)
Armenian Soviet Socialist Republic state Southwest Asia 20th-century politics 233 (3)
Armstrong region North America first civilizations 121 (4)
Arnhem Low Countries (Netherlands) WWII 211 (4)
Arno see Arnus
Arnus mod. Arno river Italy early states 178 (1)
Aromata East Africa (Somalia) ancient trade 44–45 (1)
Arpi Italy early states 178 (1)
Arras anc. Nemetocenna France early modern states 197 (5) economy 190 (1) empire and revolution 199 (4) medieval states 192 (2) Reformation 195 (5) WWI 206 (2), (3)
Arretium mod. Arezzo Italy ancient Rome 180–181 (1) early states 178 (1), (2) first civilizations 177 (1) see also Arezzo
Arriaca see Guadalajara
Ar Riyāḑ see Riyadh
Arroyo Sonso archaeological site Central America (Mexico) first civilizations 121 (3)
Ar Rub 'al Khali Eng. Empty Quarter, Great Sandy Desert desert southwest Asia exploration 219 (4) historical geography 170–171 (1) 20th-century politics 233 (4)
Ar Rutbah var. Rutba Southwest Asia (Iraq) 20th-century politics 235 (5)
Arsenal var. Darsena building Italy economy 191 (3)
Arsur battle Southwest Asia (Israel) crusades 65 (3)
Arta anc. Ambracia Greece medieval states 189 (4) see also Ambracia
Artacoana Central Asia (Afghanistan) Hellenistic world 40–41 (1)
Artashat Christian patriarchate Southwest Asia (Armenia) world religions 48 (1)
Artemita Southwest Asia (Iraq) Hellenistic world 41 (2)
Artois region France medieval states 192 (2) Reformation 195 (5)
Arua people South America the world in 1400 70–71
Aruaki people South America early cultures 147 (2)
Aruba island West Indies the world in 1800 86–87 the world in 1850 90–91 the modern world 110–111
Aru Islands island Maritime Southeast Asia exploration 239 (2)
Arumvale Australia the World in 10,000 BCE 14–15
Arunachal Pradesh prev. North East Frontier Agency region South Asia post-war economy 275 (3) post-war politics 252 (1)
Arvac people South America the world in 1500 74–75 the world in 1600 78–79 the world in 1700 82–83
Arvad see Aradus
Arvand Rūd see Shatt al 'Arab Waterway
Arverni people France ancient Rome 179 (5)
Arwad see Aradus
Aryan people South Asia ancient India 242 (1)
Asab Ar. Al 'Aşab oil field Southwest Asia economy 234 (1)
Asabon Southwest Asia (Oman) ancient trade 44–45 (1)
Asahikawa Japan economy 270 (1)
Asaku Japan medieval states 264 (1)
Asante var. Ashanti state West Africa colonization 167 (4) slave trade 165 (4) trade 167 (1)
Ascalon mod. Ashqelon Southwest Asia (Israel) ancient Egypt 159 (5) crusades 64–65 (2), 65 (3)
Ascension island Atlantic Ocean exploration 156 (3)
Ascensión Central America (Mexico) Mexican Revolution 133 (3)
Ascension Island see Pohnpei, Ponape
Ascoli Satriano see Asculum
Asculum mod. Ascoli Satriano Italy early states 178 (1)
Asejire West Africa (Nigeria) early agriculture 158 (1)
Ashanti see Asante
A Shau battle Mainland Southeast Asia (Vietnam) post-war politics 251 (5)
Ashburton New Zealand colonization 283 (5)
Ashburton River river Australia prehistoric culture 17 (5) colonization 282 (1) exploration 279 (2)
Ashgabat prev. Poltoratsk, earlier Ashkhabad Central Asia (Turkmenistan) Soviet Union 214–215 (4) see also shkhabad
Ashkhabad mod. Ashgabat; prev. Poltoratsk Central Asia (Turkmenistan) colonialism 269 (3) see also Ashgabat
Ashmaka region South Asia ancient India 242 (1) world religions 242 (2)
Ashmore and Cartier Islands colonial possession Indian Ocean global immigration 100 (1)
Ashqelon see Ascalon
Ash Shām see Damascus
Ash Shāriqah see Sharjah
ash Sharqīyah, Aş Şaḩrā' see Arabian Desert, Eastern Desert
Ashur Southwest Asia (Iraq) early systems 223 (3) first cities 220 (2) first civilizations 221 (4), 222 (2), 25 (3)
Asia continent 216-255 ancient trade 44–45 (1) biological diffusion 73 (3) crusades 65 (1) early agriculture 20–21 (2) early Islam 56–57 (1), 57 (2) early systems 32 (1), 33 (2), (3) empire and revolution 88 (1) European expansion 80–81 (1), 81 (2), (3) European imperialism 96 (1) exploration 156 (3), 172 (1), (2), 219 (3), 287 (2) first humans 13 (2) first religions 36 (1) global immigration 100 (1), 101 (3) historical geography 154–155 (1) imperial global economy 93 (2) Ottomans 232–233 (1) trade 230 (2), 267 (3) world religions 49 (4)
Asia province Southwest Asia ancient Rome 179 (5), 180–181 (1)
Asiago Italy WWI 207 (5)
Asia Minor region Southwest Asia ancient Rome 224 (2) ancient trade 44–45 (1) biological diffusion 72–73 (1) crusades 65 (1) early systems 223 (3) exploration 172 (1) Islam 226 (2), 227 (5) Ottomans 231 (3) world religions 226 (1), 49 (4)
Asiana province Southwest Asia ancient Rome 181 (4)
Asir state Southwest Asia the world in 1925 98–99
Asir Ar. 'Asīr mountain range Southwest Asia 20th-century politics 233 (4) exploration 219 (4)
Asmaka region/state South Asia first empires 241 (5) first religions 36 (2)
Asmara East Africa (Eritrea) economy 168 (2) politics 169 (4)
Aspadana see Isfahan
Aspern-Essling battle Central Europe (Germany) Napoleon 200–201 (1)
Aspero early ceremonial centre/settlement South America (Peru) early cultures 144 (1)
Asphaltites, Lacus see Dead Sea
Aspinwall see Colón
Assam region/state South Asia colonialism 248 (2), 269 (4) decolonization 250 (2) early modern states 266 (1) economy 249 (4) Mughal Empire 246 (1) post-war politics 252 (1), (3), 253 (4)
Assamese States state South Asia the world in 1500 74–75 the world in 1600 78–79
Assassins people Southwest Asia crusades 65 (3)
Assiniboin people North America colonization 126 (1)
Assinie West Africa (Ivory Coast) the world in 1700 82–83
Assiout see Asyut
Assisi Italy medieval states 187 (3)
Assiut see Asyut
Asslou see Bir Aslu
Assos settlement/state Southwest Asia (Turkey) ancient Greece 177 (2)
Assouan see Aswān, Qus, Syene
Assuan see Aswān, Qus, Syene
Assus Southwest Asia (Turkey) first civilizations 177 (1)
As Suways see Suez
Assyria province Southwest Asia ancient Persia 223 (4)
Asta Colonia see Asti
Astacus settlement/state Southwest Asia (Turkey) ancient Greece 177 (2)
Astana Buddhist centre East Asia (China) world religions 49 (3)
Asta Pompeia see Asti
Asti anc. Asta Colonia, Asta Pompeia, Hasta Colonia, Hasta Pompeia Italy economy 190 (1), 190–191
Astrakhan Eastern Europe (Russian Federation) colonialism 269 (3) exploration 219 (3) Ottomans 231 (3) Soviet Union 208 (2), 213 (4) Timur 229 (4) trade 267 (3)
Astrakhan, Khanate of state Central Asia/Eastern Europe Islam 163 (1) trade 267 (3)
Astures people Iberian Peninsula ancient Rome 179 (5)
Asturias state Iberian Peninsula Franks 184 (2) Islam 184 (1)
Asturias see Oviedo
Asturica Iberian Peninsula (Spain) ancient Rome 180–181 (1)
Astypalaea settlement/state Greece ancient Greece 177 (2)
Asuka Japan medieval states 264 (2)
Asuka region Japan medieval states 265 (3)
Asunción South America (Paraguay) colonization 148 (2) empire and revolution 150 (1) environment 153 (4) exploration 143 (2) politics 152 (1), (2)
Asuncion Mita Central America (Mexico) first civilizations 123 (2)
Asuristan state Southwest Asia ancient Persia 225 (6)
Aswān var. Assouan, Assuan, Qus; anc. Syene Egypt crusades 228 (2) early Islam 56–57 (1) economy 168 (2) Mongols 229 (3) see also Qus, Syene
Asyut var. Assiout, Assiut, Sauty, Siut; anc. Lycopolis Egypt ancient Egypt 159 (3), (4), (5) exploration 157 (5) first cities 28–29 (1) Islam 235 (4) see also Sauty
Atacama region/state South America politics 151 (4) the world in 250 BCE 38–39
Atacama people South America early cultures 147 (2)
Atacama Desert Eng. Desierto de Atacama desert South America early cultures 144 (1), 145 (2) empire and revolution 150 (1), 151 (3) Incas 147 (3) politics 151 (4)
Atacama, Desierto de see Atacama Desert
Atacama, San Pedro de South America (Chile) early cultures 146 (1)
Atakapa people Central America colonization 125 (4), 126 (1)
A-tan see Aden, Eudaemon Arabia
Atapuerca archaeological site Iberian Peninsula (Spain) first humans 13 (2)
Atarco South America (Peru) early cultures 146 (1)
Atazta Central America (Mexico) first civilizations 122 (1)
Atbara var. 'Aţbārah East Africa (Sudan) exploration 157 (5)
Atbara var. Nahr 'Aţbārah river East Africa exploration 157 (5)
'Aţbārah see Atbara
'Aţbārah, Nahr see Atbara
Atchin see Aceh, Achin
Aten Temple var. Aton building Egypt first cities 29 (5)
Atepehuacan Central America (Mexico) Aztecs 124 (3)
Atepetla Central America (Mexico) Aztecs 124 (3)
Atgram South Asia (Bangladesh) post-war politics 252 (3)
Athabasca var. Athabaska river North America the growth of the US 129 (2)
Athabasca, Lake lake North America colonization 126 (1) early agriculture 120 (1) exploration 119 (3), 286 (1) the growth of the US 129 (2)
Athabaska see Athabasca
Athenae see Athens
Athena, Temple of temple Greece ancient Greece 177 (4)
Athens prev. Athinai, anc. Athenae; Gk. Athina Greece ancient Greece 177 (3), 179 (4) ancient Persia 223 (4) ancient Rome 179 (5), 180–181 (1), 181 (3), (4), 182 (1) biological diffusion 72–73 (1) Cold War 108 (3) early systems 32 (1), 33 (2), (3) economy 205 (4) empire and revolution 202 (1) exploration 172 (1) first cities 28–29 (1) first civilizations 175 (4), 177 (1) first religions 36 (1) great migrations 52–53 (1) Hellenistic world 224 (1) inter-war 209 (3) Islam 226 (2) medieval states 182 (2), 185 (3), 187 (5), 189 (4) Napoleon 200–201 (1), 201 (2), (3) Ottomans 202 (4), 230 (1) post-war politics 212 (3) world religions 48 (1) WWII 210 (1), 211 (2), (4)
Athens state Greece medieval states 187 (5), 189 (4)
Athesis river Italy early states 178 (2)
Athina see Athens
Athinai see Athens
Athr Southwest Asia (Saudi Arabia) early Islam 56–57 (1) medieval voyages 61 (3)
Athribis Egypt first cities 28–29 (1)
Atico South America (Peru) Incas 147 (3)
Atitlan, Lago de lake Central America first civilizations 123 (2)
Atjeh see Achin
Atlacomulco Central America (Mexico) first civilizations 122 (1)
Atlacuihuayan Central America (Mexico) Aztecs 124 (2), (3)
Atlan state Central America Aztecs 124 (1)
Atlanta North America (USA) the growth of the US 129 (2), 132 (1) US Civil War 130 (5), 131 (7) US economy 134 (1) US politics 135 (6) US society 137 (6)
Atlanta battle North America (USA) US Civil War 131 (7)
Atlantic and Pacific Railroad railway North America the growth of the US 129 (2)
Atlantic Ocean Port. Oceano Atlântico ocean ancient trade 44–45 (1) biological diffusion 72–73 (1), 73 (2), (3) colonization 125 (4), 126 (1), 148 (2), 149 (3), (4) empire and revolution 127 (2), (3), 150 (1), 151 (3), 202 (1), 88–89 (2) environment 153 (4) European expansion 80–81 (1), 81 (2), (3), 84–85 (1), 85 (2) European imperialism 96 (1), (2), 97 (4) exploration 118 (1), 119 (2), (3), 142 (1), 143 (2), (3), 156 (1), (2), (3), 172 (1), (2), 286 (1), 287 (2) global immigration 100 (1), 101 (2), (3) global knowledge 76 (1), (2), 76–77 (1), 77 (5) great migrations 52–53 (1), 53 (2) imperial global economy 92 (1), 93 (2) inter-war 209 (3) medieval voyages 60–61 (1) politics 152 (1) post-war economy 213 (5) post-war politics 212 (3) slave trade 165 (4) the growth of the US 129 (2), 132 (1), 133 (4) the world in 1300 66–67 trade 163 (4), (5), (6), (7), 164 (2), 167 (1) US Civil War 131 (6), (7) US economy 138 (2) US superpower 138 (1) WWI 208 (1) WWII 104 (1), (2), 105 (3), (4), 210 (1), 211 (2), (4) see also Occidental, Oceanus
Atlapulco Central America (Mexico) Aztecs 124 (2)
Atlas Mountains mountain range North Africa ancient Rome 180–181 (1) ancient trade 44–45 (1) biological diffusion 72–73 (1) Bronze Age 175 (3) crusades 64–65 (2) early agriculture 174 (1) early cultures 160 (1), 161 (2) early Islam 56–57 (1), 57 (2) economy 163 (2) global knowledge 76–77 (1) Islam 163 (1) medieval states 182 (2) Ottomans 232–233 (1) slave trade 165 (4) WWII 210 (1), 211 (4)
Atlatonco Central America (Mexico) Aztecs 124 (2)
Atlazolpa Central America (Mexico) Aztecs 124 (3)
Atlixio Central America (Mexico) colonization 125 (5)
Atomata major port/settlement East Africa (Somalia) early trade 225 (3)
Aton see Aten Temple
Atontonilco state Central America Aztecs 124 (1)
Atoyac Central America (Mexico) Aztecs 124 (3)
Atoyac river North America colonization 125 (5)
Atsugashi-yama battle Japan early modern states 265 (5)
Attaleia see Adalia, Attalia
Attalia later Adalia; mod. Antalya; anc. Attaleia Southwest Asia (Turkey) ancient Rome 180–181 (1) Hellenistic world 41 (2) see also Adalia
Attica region Greece ancient Greece 177 (2)
Attigny France Franks 184 (2)
Attikamek people North America colonization 126 (1)
Attu island North America WWII 272 (1), 273 (2)
Atwetwebooso archaeological site West Africa (Ghana) early cultures 160 (1)
Atzacualco Central America (Mexico) Aztecs 124 (3)
Atzalan North America (USA) cultural groups 122 (5)
Atzcapotzalco see Azcapotzalco
Auberoche France medieval states 192 (1)
Auch France early modern states 197 (5)
Auckland New Zealand colonization 283 (4), (5), 284–285 (1) decolonization 285 (3) environmentalism 285 (2) exploration 279 (3)
Auckland region New Zealand colonization 283 (5)
Auckland Islands island group New Zealand decolonization 285 (3) exploration 276–277 (1)
Auerstedt see Jena Auerstädt
Augila var. Awjilah North Africa (Libya) Islam 163 (1)
Augsbourg see Augsburg
Augsburg anc. Augusta Vindelicorum; Fr. Augsbourg Central Europe (Germany) biological diffusion 72–73 (1) crusades 186 (1) economy 190 (1) Franks 184 (2) medieval states 188 (1) Reformation 194 (2) see also Augusta Vindelicorum
Augusta North America (USA) empire and revolution 127 (3) the growth of the US 129 (2) US Civil War 131 (7)
Augusta battle North America (USA) empire and revolution 127 (3)
Augusta see London, Londinium
Augusta Suessionum see Soissons
Augusta Taurinorum mod. Torino; Eng. Turin Italy great migrations 52–53 (1)
Augusta Treverorum mod. Trier, Eng. Treves, Fr. Trèves Central Europe (Germany) ancient Rome 180–181 (1), 181 (3), (4) ancient trade 44 (2), 44–45 (1) great migrations 52–53 (1) world religions 48 (1) see also Trier
Augusta Vangionum see Worms
Augusta Vindelicorum mod. Augsburg Central Europe (Germany) ancient Rome 180–181 (1) see also Augsburg
Augustobona Tricassium see Troyes
Augustodunum mod. Autun France ancient Rome 180–181 (1)
Augustodurum see Bayeux
Augustoritum Lemovicensium see Limoges
Augustus, Mausoleum of building Italy ancient Rome 181 (2)
Aupaga region South Asia world religions 242 (2)
Auraitis cultural region Southwest Asia ancient Rome 225 (4)
Aurelianum see Orléans
Aurelia, Via road Italy ancient Rome 181 (2) early states 178 (1)
Aurunci people Italy early states 178 (2)
Auschwitz-Birkenau concentration camp Central Europe WWII 211 (3)
Ausculum Italy early states 178 (1)
Aussa state East Africa the world in 1600 78–79
Austerlitz Central Europe (Austria) Napoleon 200-201 the world in 1850 90–91
Austin North America (USA) the growth of the US 129 (2), 132 (1)
Australia prev. Australian Colonies, New Holland state Australia early agriculture 20–21 (2) early cultures 280–281 (3) environmentalism 285 (2) European expansion 80–81 (1) exploration 276–277 (1), 279 (2), (3) first humans 13 (2) global immigration 100 (1), 101 (3) historical geography 254–255 (1) imperial global economy 92 (1), 93 (2) medieval voyages 60 (2) the growth of the US 133 (4) US economy 138 (2) US superpower 138 (1) WWII 104 (1), 105 (4), 251 (3), 272 (1), 273 (2) Cold War 109 (1) colonization 282 (1) decolonization 251 (4), 285 (3) see also Australian Colonies
Australian Aborigines people Australia the world in 750 BCE 30–31 passim
Australian Colonies mod. Australia; prev. New Holland colonial possession Australia the world in 1850 90–91 the world in 1900 94–95 see also Australia
Austral Islands island group Pacific Ocean colonization 284–285 (1) early cultures 280–281 (3) environmentalism 285 (2) exploration 279 (3) medieval voyages 60 (2)
Australia region Central Europe Franks 183 (6), 184 (2)
Austria Ger. Österreich region/state Central Europe early modern states 193 (4), (5), 194 (1) empire and revolution 198 (2), 199 (3), 202 (1) inter-war 209 (3), (5) medieval states 183 (4), 188 (1), 189 (4) Napoleon 200–201 (1) post-war economy 213 (5), 214 (1), (2), 215 (3) post-war politics 212 (1), (3) Reformation 196 (1), (2) Soviet Union 213 (4) the modern world 112 (2), 113 (3) WWI 208 (1) WWII 210 (1), 211 (2), (3), (4) Cold War 108 (3), 109 (1)
Austria-Hungary state Central Europe economy 205 (4) global immigration 100 (1) imperial global economy 92 (1) WWI 207 (6)
Austrian Empire state Central Europe/Eastern Europe empire and revolution 202 (1) Napoleon 201 (2) Ottomans 232–233 (1)
Austrian Habsburg Possessions state Central Europe Reformation 194 (2)
Austrian Netherlands vassal state Low Countries empire and revolution 199 (3), (4)
Austro-Hungarian Empire state Central Europe empire and revolution 202 (3) Ottomans 202 (4) WWI 207 (4), (5) early 20th century 206 (1)
Autun see Augustodunum
Auvergne region France Franks 183 (6) medieval states 192 (1)
Ava Mainland Southeast Asia (Burma) colonialism 247 (4), 248 (1) early medieval states 245 (6) world religions 243 (5)
Ava region/state Mainland Southeast Asia Mughal Empire 246 (1) trade 267 (3)
Avalites East Africa (Djibouti) ancient trade 44–45 (1) early cultures 161 (3), (4), (5) early trade 225 (3)
Avanti South Asia (India) early religions 48 (2)
Avanti region/state South Asia ancient India 242 (1) early religions 48 (2) first religions 36 (2) world religions 242 (2)
Avar Empire state Central Europe early Islam 56–57 (1) medieval states 182 (2)
Avaricum see Bourges
Avaris Egypt ancient Egypt 159 (4)
Avars people Eastern Europe Franks 184 (2) medieval states 182 (2)
Avarua Pacific Ocean (Cook Islands) decolonization 285 (3)
Avebury archaeological site British Isles (United Kingdom) Copper Age 174 (2)
Avenio see Avignon
Aventine Hill Lat. Mons Aventinus hill Italy ancient Rome 181 (2)
Aventinus, Mons see Aventine Hill
Aversa Italy economy 190 (1)
Avignon anc. Avenio settlement/university France crusades 186 (1) early modern states 193 (4), 197 (5) economy 190 (1) Franks 183 (5), 184 (2) medieval states 187 (3), (4), 88 (1), (2) Reformation 194 (2)
Avignon anc. Avenio state France empire and revolution 199 (4)
Awadh state South Asia Mughal Empire 246 (1)
Awazu battle Japan early modern states 265 (5)
Awdaghost West Africa (Mauritania) Islam 163 (1) trade 163 (4), (5), (6), (7)
Awjilah see Augila
Axim West Africa (Ghana) exploration 156 (3) slave trade 165 (4) trade 164 (2)
Axiós see Vardar
Axocopan state Central America Aztecs 124 (1)
Axotla Central America (Mexico) Aztecs 124 (3)
Axum East Africa (Ethiopia) ancient trade 44–45 (1) early cultures 160 (1), 161 (3), (4), (5) early trade 225 (3) world religions 49 (4)
Axum state East Africa ancient trade 44–45 (1) early cultures 160 (1), 161 (3), (4), (5) Islam 226 (2) world religions 226 (1), 49 (4)
Ayacucho South America (Peru) Incas 148 (1) narcotics 153 (5)
Ayacucho battle South America (Peru) empire and revolution 150 (1), 88–89 (2)
Ayacucho Valley South America (Peru) the world in 5000 BCE 18–19
Ayas see Laias
Ayaviri South America (Peru) Incas 147 (3)
Aydhab Egypt biological diffusion 72–73 (1) Islam 163 (1)
Ayeyarwady see Irrawaddy
Ayodhya South Asia (India) early medieval states 244 (1) world religions 48 (2)
Ayodhya state South Asia first religions 36 (2) Mughal Empire 246 (1)
Ayotzinco Central America (Mexico) colonization 125 (5)
Ayr British Isles (United Kingdom) economy 204 (1)
Ayuthia see Ayutthaya
Ayutla Central America (Mexico) Aztecs 124 (1)
Ayutthaya var. Ayuthia, Phra Nakhon Si Ayutthaya settlement/temple Mainland Southeast Asia (Thailand) early medieval states 245 (6) Marathas 246 (2) trade 267 (3) world religions 243 (5)
Ayyubid Sultanate state Egypt/North Africa/Southwest Asia crusades 65 (3) medieval states 187 (5) Mongols 68–69 (1)
Azad Kashmir region South Asia post-war politics 252 (1), (2)
Azak see Azov
Azărbaycan see Azerbaijan
Azcapotzalco var. Atzcapotzalco Central America (Mexico) Aztecs 124 (2), (3) first civilizations 122 (1)
Azerbaijan Az. Azărbaycan region Central Asia economy 234 (1) Islam 227 (4) medieval Persia 231 (4) post-war economy 214 (2) Soviet Union 208 (2), 214 (4) the modern world 113 (3) WWI 233 (2)
Azerbaijani Republic see Azerbaijan
Azeri people Southwest Asia Islam 275 (5)
Azimabad see Patna
Azores Port. Açores, Ilhas dos Açores, Arquipélago dos Açores island group Atlantic Ocean Cold War 109 (1) European expansion 80–81 (1) US superpower 138 (1) WWII 104 (2)
Azov Turk. Azak Eastern Europe (Ukraine) Ottomans 197 (4), 231 (3)
Azov, Sea of sea Eastern Europe Ottomans 202 (4), 230 (1), 231 (3) WWI 207 (4)
Azraq, Bahr El see Blue Nile
Aztec Empire state Central America the world in 1500 74–75 , 76 (2), 124-125
Aztecs people Central America colonization 126 (1)
'Azza see Gaza
Az Zāb al Kabīr see Great Zab
Aẓ Ẓahran see Dhahran

B

Ba var. Pa province/region East Asia first religions 37 (4) first states 260 (1)
Ba people East Asia first cities 259 (4)
Ba see Pegu
Baalbek var. Ba'labakk; anc. Heliopolis Lebanon Southwest Asia (Lebanon) crusades 65 (3) first religions 37 (3) see also Heliopolis
Bab-i Sin East Asia (China) trade 230 (2)
Babi Yar massacre Eastern Europe WWII 211 (3)
Babylon Southwest Asia (Iraq) ancient Persia 223 (4), 225 (6) ancient Rome 224 (2), 225 (5) ancient trade 44 (2), 44–45 (1) early cultures 161 (3), (4), (5) early medieval states 244 (1) early systems 223 (3) exploration 218 (1), (2) first civilizations 221 (4), (5), 222 (2) Hellenistic world 40–41 (1), 41 (2)
Babylonia province Southwest Asia ancient Persia 223 (4) first civilizations 221 (5), 222 (2) Hellenistic world 40–41 (1), 41 (2)
Bachiniva Central America (Mexico) Mexican Revolution 133 (3)
Back river North America exploration 287 (2)
Bactra var. Valhika, Zariaspa; mod. Balkh Buddhist centre/settlement Central Asia (Afghanistan) ancient Persia 223 (4) ancient trade 44 (2), 44–45 (1) exploration 256 (1) first empires 241 (4) Hellenistic world 224 (1) medieval states 262–263 (1) world religions 49 (3), (4) see also Balkh, Valhika
Bactria region/state Central Asia ancient Persia 223 (4), 225 (6) ancient Rome 224 (2) ancient trade 44 (2), 44–45 (1) first empires 241 (4) Hellenistic world 224 (1)

INDEX-GAZETTEER: Celebes Sea – Cold Harbor

trade *267* (3) world religions *243* (5), *49* (4) WWII *251* (3), *272* (1), *273* (2)
Celebes Sea *Ind.* Laut Sulawesi *sea* Maritime Southeast Asia Bronze Age *240* (3) colonialism *247* (4) decolonization *251* (4) early medieval states *245* (6) European imperialism *97* (3) exploration *239* (1), (2) Islam *243* (6) post-war economy *253* (5) post-war politics *253* (4) world religions *243* (5)
Celenderis Southwest Asia (Turkey) first civilizations *177* (1)
Celestial Empire *see* China, Han Empire
Celtiberi *see* Celtiberians
Celtiberians *Lat.* Celtiberi *people* Iberian Peninsula ancient Rome *179* (5)
Celtic peoples *people* British Isles/France/Germany the world in 250 BCE *38–39* the world in 500CE *50–51*
Celts *people* Western Europe ancient trade *44–45* (1) early systems *33* (3) first civilizations *177* (1) great migrations *53* (2) the world in 500 BCE *34–35*
Cemenelum *see* Cemenelum
Cemenelum *var.* Cemenelum Italy ancient Rome *180–181* (1)
Cempoala Central America (Mexico) first civilizations *122* (1)
Cempohuallan Central America (Mexico) colonization *125* (5)
Central African Empire *see* Central African Republic
Central African Republic *abbrev.* CAR; *prev.* Central African Empire, Ubangi-Shari, Oubangui-Chari *state* Central Africa Cold War *109* (1) decolonization *168* (1) economy *168* (2), (3) Islam *235* (4) the modern world *112* (1), *113* (3) *see also* Ubangi-Shari
Central America *region* Central America first religions *36* (1) US economy *138* (2)
Central America, United Provinces of *state* Central America empire and revolution *88–89* (2)
Central Asia *region* Asia biological diffusion *73* (2)
Central Bihar *region* South Asia decolonization *250* (1)
Central India Agency *state* South Asia colonialism *248* (2)
Central Makran Range *mountain range* South Asia first cities *240* (2)
Central Overland Route *wagon train route* North America the growth of the US *129* (2)
Central Pacific Railroad *railway* North America global immigration *100* (1) the growth of the US *129* (2)
Central Provinces *state* South Asia colonialism *248* (2)
Central Siberian Plain *plain* Siberia exploration *257* (2)
Central Western Queensland *archaeological site* Australia prehistoric culture *17* (5)
Cephalonia *island* Greece ancient Greece *177* (3), *179* (4) Ottomans *230* (1)
Cer *battle* Southeast Europe (Yugoslavia) WWI *207* (6)
Ceram *var.* Serang, Pulau Seram, Seram *island* Maritime Southeast Asia colonialism *247* (4) early medieval states *245* (6) exploration *239* (1), (2) Islam *243* (6)
Ceramicus Cemetery *Gr.* Kerameikos Cemetery *cemetery* Greece ancient Greece *177* (4)
Ceram Sea *var.* Seram Sea; *Ind.* Laut Seram *sea* Maritime Southeast Asia early medieval states *245* (6) exploration *239* (2)
Ceras *state* South Asia Mongols *68–69* (1)
Cerdaña *see* Cerdagne
Ceres Sea *sea* Indian Ocean Islam *243* (6)
Ceribon *see* Cheribon
Cerignola *battle* Italy early modern states *194* (1)
Cerrillos South America (Peru) early cultures *145* (4)
Cerro Iberian Peninsula (Spain) Bronze Age *175* (3)
Cerro de la Bomba Central America (Mexico) first civilizations *121* (2)
Cerro de las Mesas *region/settlement* Central America first civilizations *121* (2), *122* (1)
Cerro Gordo Central America (Mexico) the growth of the US *129* (2)
Cerros Central America (Mexico) first civilizations *123* (2)
Cerro Sechin *early ceremonial centre* South America (Peru) early cultures *144* (1), *145* (3)
Cerro Vicús South America (Peru) early cultures *145* (4)
Cerveteri *see* Caere
Cēsis *see* Wenden
Česká Republika *see* Czech Republic
Cetinje Southeast Europe (Yugoslavia) WWI *207* (6)
Ceuta *var.* Sebta North Africa (Spain/Morocco) biological diffusion *72–73* (1) economy *190* (1) Islam *192* (3)
Cévennes *mountain range* France early modern states *197* (5)
Ceylon *var.* Saylan, Sarandib; *mod.* Sri Lanka; *Chin.* Hsi-lan; *anc.* Taprobane, Simhala, Sinhala, Lambakannas, Lanka *region/state/island* South Asia biological diffusion *72–73* (1) colonialism *247* (3), *248* (1), (2) decolonization *250* (1), *251* (4) economy *249* (4) European expansion *84–85* (1) exploration *239* (1) global immigration *100* (1) Marathas *246* (2) Mongols *68* (2) Mughal Empire *246* (1) trade *230* (2), *267* (3) WWII *251* (3), *272* (1), *273* (2) *see also* Lambakannas, Lanka, Simhala, Sri Lanka, Taprobana
Ceyre to the Caribs *see* Marie Galante
Chacabuco *battle* South America (Chile) empire and revolution *150* (1), *88–89* (2)
Chacalapan *see* Chicolapan
Chachalacas Central America (Mexico) first civilizations *122* (1)
Chachas *state* South Asia early medieval states *244* (2)
Chaco *region* South America colonization *148* (2) exploration *143* (2)
Chaco Canyon *archaeological site/settlement* North America (USA) cultural groups *123* (4)
Chad *Fr.* Tchad *state* Central Africa decolonization *168* (1) economy *168* (2), (3) Islam *235* (4) the modern world *112* (1), *113* (3), (4)
Chadians *people* Central Africa/West Africa ancient trade *44–45* (1) early cultures *160* (1)
Chad, Lake *Fr.* Lac Tchad *lake* Central Africa ancient trade *44–45* (1) early cultures *160* (1) economy *163* (2)
European imperialism *96* (1) exploration *157* (4) first humans *12* (1), *13* (2) historical geography *154–155* (1) Islam *163* (1), *167* (3) slave trade *165* (4)
Chagai Hills *mountain range* South Asia first cities *240* (2)
Chagar Bazar Southwest Asia (Syria) first civilizations *221* (4)
Chagatai Khanate *var.* Khanate of Kashgar, Chagatayids *state/region* Central Asia/East Asia biological diffusion *72–73* (1) Mongols *229* (3), *68* (2) Timur *229* (4)
Chagatais *people* South Asia early medieval states *244–245* (3)
Chagatayids *see* Chagatai Khanate
Chagos Archipelago *var.* Chagos Islands; *mod.* British Indian Ocean Territory *island group* Indian Ocean the world in 1850 *90–91* the world in 1900 *94–95* the world in 1925 *98–99* the world in 1950 *102–103* *see also* British Indian Ocean Territory
Chagos Islands *see* British Indian Ocean Territory, Chagos Archipelago
Chahamanas *state* South Asia early medieval states *244* (2)
Chahar *region* East Asia post-war politics *271* (7)
Chahar *people* East Asia trade *267* (3)
Chakan *state* Central America Aztecs *124* (1)
Chakchiuma *people* Central America colonization *125* (4)
Chalandriani *archaeological site* Greece Copper Age *174* (2)
Chalcatzinco Central America (Mexico) first civilizations *121* (2), *122* (1)
Chalcedon Southwest Asia (Turkey) first civilizations *177* (1) world religions *226* (1)
Chalcedon *state* Greece ancient Greece *177* (2)
Chalchuapa Central America (El Salvador) first civilizations *121* (2)
Chalcis Southwest Asia (Syria) ancient Rome *225* (4)
Chalcis *mod.* Chalkida; *var.* Halkida; *prev.* Khalkis *settlement/state* Greece ancient Greece *177* (2), (3), *179* (4) first civilizations *177* (1)
Chalco Central America (Mexico) Aztecs *124* (2)
Chalco *state* Central America Aztecs *124* (1)
Chalco, Lake *lake* Central America Aztecs *124* (2)
Chaldiran *see* Çaldiran
Chalkida *see* Chalcis
Chalma Central America (Mexico) Aztecs *124* (3)
Chalna *var.* Pankhali South Asia (Bangladesh) post-war politics *252* (3)
Chalon France Franks *183* (5), (6), *184* (2)
Châlons France Franks *184* (2)
Châlons-sur-Marne France early modern states *197* (5) economy *190* (1) WWI *206* (3)
Chalon-sur-Saône *anc.* Cabillonum France economy *190* (1)
Chaluka North America (USA) cultural groups *123* (3)
Chalukyas *people/state* South Asia world religions *243* (4)
Chama Central America (Mexico) first civilizations *123* (2)
Chambal *river* South Asia colonialism *247* (3), *248* (2) decolonization *250* (1) early medieval states *244* (2), *244–245* (3) economy *249* (4) Marathas *246* (2) post-war politics *252* (1) world religions *242* (2), *243* (4)
Chambéry *anc.* Camberia France economy *190* (1)
Champa South Asia (India) early religions *48* (2)
Champa *region/state* Mainland Southeast Asia ancient India *241* (6) biological diffusion *72–73* (1) early medieval states *245* (5) first states *260* (1) medieval states *261* (6), *262–263* (1), *263* (6) Mongols *68–69* (1) trade *67* (3) world religions *243* (5), *49* (4)
Champagne *region* France economy *190* (1) medieval states *187* (4)
Champaran *region* South Asia decolonization *250* (1)
Champaubert *battle* France Napoleon *200–201* (1)
Champlain, Lake *lake* North America colonization *126* (1) empire and revolution *127* (2) exploration *119* (2)
Champutun *state* Central America Aztecs *124* (1)
Chams *people* Mainland Southeast Asia ancient trade *44–45* (1)
Chanca *people* South America early cultures *147* (2)
Chancay South America (Peru) early cultures *146* (1)
Chance North America (USA) cultural groups *122* (5)
Chancellorsville North America (USA) US Civil War *131* (6)
Chan Chan South America (Peru) early cultures *146* (1) Incas *147* (3)
Chandannagar *prev.* Chandernagore South Asia (India) post-war politics *252* (1) *see also* Chandernagore
Chandellas *state* South Asia early medieval states *244* (2)
Chandernagore *colonial possession/settlement* South Asia colonialism *247* (3), *248* (2), *269* (4) decolonization *251* (4) empire and revolution *88* (1) WWII *251* (3)
Chandigarh South Asia (India) post-war politics *252* (1)
Chandra *state* Mainland Southeast Asia ancient India *241* (6)
Chandragupta, Empire of *state* South Asia Hellenistic world *224* (1)
Chang'an *var.* Ch'ang-an East Asia (China) ancient trade *44–45* (1) exploration *256* (1) first religions *37* (4) first states *260* (1), *261* (2), (3) medieval states *261* (5), (6), *262–263* (1) world religions *49* (3), (4) *see also* Xi'an
Changbai East Asia (China) Cold War *109* (4)
Changchou *see* Changzhou
Changchun *var.* Ch'ang-ch'un; *prev.* Hsinking East Asia (China) imperialism *270* (2) Russo-Japanese War *270* (4)
Changchun *battle* East Asia (China) economy *274* (1) post-war politics *274* (2)
Changde East Asia (China) medieval states *263* (6)
Chang Jiang *see* Yangtze
Changle East Asia (China) trade *267* (3)
Changsha *var.* Ch'angsha, Ch'ang-sha East Asia (China) biological diffusion *72–73* (1) colonialism *269* (4) early modern states *268* (1) economy *274* (1) imperialism *270* (2) post-war politics *271* (7), *274* (2) world religions *49* (3) WWII *251* (3)
Changsha *province* East Asia first states *260* (1)
Changwu *archaeological site* East Asia (China) first humans *13* (2)
Changyang *archaeological site* East Asia (China) first humans *13* (2)
Changzhou *var.* Changchou East Asia (China) medieval states *262–263* (1)
Chanhu-Daro *archaeological site/settlement* South Asia (Pakistan) first cities *240* (2) first civilizations *24* (2)
Channel Islands *Fr.* Îles Normandes *island group* English Channel medieval states *186* (2)
Chantilly France WWI *206* (2), (3)
Chao *see* Zhao
Ch'ao-an *see* Chaozhou
Chaochow *see* Chaozhou
Chaoge *vassal state* East Asia first cities *259* (3)
Chaozhou *var.* Ch'ao-an; *prev.* Chaochow East Asia (China) medieval states *263* (5)
Chaplina, Mys *Eng.* Cape Chaplino *headland* Siberia exploration *257* (2)
Chaplino, Cape *see* Chaplina, Mys
Chapultepec Central America (Mexico) Aztecs *124* (2), (3) colonization *125* (5) first civilizations *122* (1)
Charax Southwest Asia (Iraq) ancient trade *44–45* (1) early cultures *161* (3), (4), (5) early trade *225* (3) Hellenistic world *41* (2)
Charay North Africa (Libya) ancient Rome *179* (3)
Charcas, Presidencia of *region* South America colonization *148* (2)
Charlemagne, Empire of *state* France Franks *184* (2)
Charleroi Low Countries (Belgium) WWI *206* (2), (3)
Charleston North America (USA) colonization *126* (1) empire and revolution *127* (3) European expansion *84–85* (1) imperial global economy *93* (5) the growth of the US *129* (2), *132* (1) US Civil War *130* (5), *131* (6), (7) US society *137* (6)
Charleston *battle* North America (USA) empire and revolution *127* (3)
Charleville Australia colonization *282* (1)
Charlotte North America (USA) empire and revolution *127* (3)
Charlottenburg Central Europe (Germany) post-war politics *212* (2)
Charlottesville North America (USA) empire and revolution *127* (3)
Charlottetown North America (Canada) the growth of the US *129* (2), *132* (1)
Charolais States *state* France early modern states *197* (5)
Charolles *state* France early modern states *194* (1)
Charsadda South Asia (Pakistan) first religions *36* (2) Hellenistic world *41* (2)
Chartres France medieval states *187* (3)
Chasniki Eastern Europe (Belorussia) early modern states *195* (3)
Château-Thierry France WWI *206* (2), (3)
Château-Thierry *battle* France Napoleon *200–201* (1)
Chatgaon *mod.* Chittagong; *var.* Ch'attag'am South Asia (Bangladesh) early medieval states *244–245* (3) Mughal Empire *246* (1) *see also* Chittagong
Chatgaon *state* South Asia Mughal Empire *246* (1)
Chatham British Isles (United Kingdom) economy *204* (1)
Chatham Islands *island group* Pacific Ocean decolonization *285* (3) early cultures *280–281* (3) medieval voyages *60* (2)
Chatot *people* Central America colonization *125* (4)
Chāttagām *see* Chatgaon, Chittagong
Chattahoochee *river* North America cultural groups *122* (5) US Civil War *131* (6)
Chattanooga North America (USA) US Civil War *131* (6), (7)
Chaul South Asia (India) colonialism *247* (3) early medieval states *245* (4) world religions *243* (4)
Chaulukyas *dynasty* South Asia Mongols *68–69* (1)
Chauri Chaura South Asia (India) decolonization *250* (1)
Chauvet *archaeological site* France prehistoric culture *17* (2)
Chavin *state* South America first religions *36* (1)
Chavín de Huantar *early ceremonial centre* South America (Peru) early cultures *144* (1), *145* (3), (4) first religions *36* (1)
Chawasha *people* Central America colonization *125* (4)
Cheb *see* Eger
Chechen *people* Southwest Asia Soviet Union *213* (4)
Che-chiang *see* Zhejiang
Chechnya *region* Eastern Europe Soviet Union *214–215* (4)
Chedi *var.* Cedi *region/state* South Asia first empires *241* (5) first religions *36* (2)
Cheetham British Isles (United Kingdom) economy *204* (2)
Chefoo *see* Zhifu
Cheju-do *prev.* Quelpart; *Jap.* Saishū *island* East Asia Cold War *109* (4) early modern states *265* (5), *267* (4) medieval states *264* (1), (2) *see also* Quelpart
Chekiang *see* Zhejiang
Chełmno *concentration camp* Central Europe WWII *211* (3)
Chełmno *see* Kulm
Chelyabinsk Eastern Europe (Russian Federation) Soviet Union *214–215* (4)
Chelyuskin, Cape *see* Chelyuskin, Mys
Chelyuskin, Mys *Eng.* Cape Chelyuskin *headland* Siberia exploration *257* (2)
Chemin des Dames France WWI *206* (2), (3)
Chemulpo *see* Inchon
Chen East Asia (China) first cities *259* (5) first religions *37* (4)
Chen *state* East Asia medieval states *261* (5)
Chenab *river* South Asia colonialism *248* (1) early medieval states *244* (1) first cities *240* (2) Mughal Empire *246* (1) post-war politics *252* (2)
Ch'eng-chou, Chengchow *see* Zhengzhou
Chengdu *var.* Chengtu, Ch'eng-tu; *prev.* Shu East Asia (China) ancient trade *44–45* (1) biological diffusion *72–73* (1) colonialism *269* (4) early modern states *266* (1), (2), *268* (1) first states *260* (1), *261* (3) Islam *275* (4) medieval states *262–263* (1), *263* (3), (4), (5), (6) Mongols *68–69* (1) post-war economy *275* (3) post-war politics *274* (2) world religions *49* (3) WWII *272* (1), *273* (2)
Chenggao East Asia (China) first cities *259* (5)
Chenghsien *see* Zhengzhou
Chengtian *rebellion* East Asia early modern states *266* (2)
Ch'eng-tu, Chengtu *see* Chengdu
Chengziya *archaeological site/settlement* East Asia (China) early agriculture *258* (2)
Chenkiang *see* Zhenjiang
Chenla *mod.* Cambodia; *prev.* Funan, *later* Khmer, Kambujadesha *state* Mainland Southeast Asia ancient India *241* (6) world religions *49* (4) *see also* Cambodia, Funan, Kambujadesha, Khmer
Chenla and Empire of Funan *see* Chenla
Chennai *see* Madras
Cheraw North America (USA) empire and revolution *127* (3)
Cheraw *people* North America colonization *125* (4)
Cherbourg *anc.* Carusbur France early modern states *197* (5) medieval states *187* (4), *192* (1), (2) WWII *210* (1)
Cherchell *see* Caesarea, Iol
Cherchen *Chin.* Qiemo East Asia (China) biological diffusion *72–73* (1) first states *260* (1)
Cheribon *mod.* Ceribon; *Dut.* Tjeribon *state* Maritime Southeast Asia the world in 1600 *78–79*
Cherkess *see* Circassians
Chernigov *Ukr.* Chernihiv Eastern Europe (Ukraine) Mongols *68–69* (1)
Chernihiv *see* Chernigov
Chernobyl Eastern Europe (Ukraine) Soviet Union *214–215* (4)
Chernomen *var.* Maritsa *battle* Greece medieval states *189* (4)
Cherno More *see* Black Sea
Chernovaya *archaeological site/settlement* Siberia (Russian Federation) early agriculture *258* (1)
Chernoye More *see* Black Sea
Cherokee *people* North America colonization *125* (4), *126* (1)
Cherry Island *see* Anuta
Cherry Valley North America (USA) empire and revolution *127* (3)
Chersonesus *state* Greece ancient Greece *177* (2)
Chesapeake Bay *inlet* North America empire and revolution *127* (2), (3)
Cheshire *region* British Isles imperial global economy *93* (4)
Chesowanja *archaeological site* East Africa (Kenya) first humans *12* (1)
Chester *hist.* Legaceaster, *Lat.* Deva, Devana Castra; *Wel.* Caerleon British Isles (United Kingdom) economy *190* (1) medieval states *183* (3), *188* (2) *see also* Deva
Chester *battle* British Isles (United Kingdom) medieval states *183* (3)
Chesterfield *canal* British Isles economy *204* (1)
Chetiya *region* South Asia ancient India *242* (1) world religions *242* (3)
Chetwai South Asia (India) colonialism *247* (3)
Chevdar Southeast Europe (Bulgaria) early agriculture *174* (1)
Cheyenne North America (USA) the growth of the US *129* (2)
Cheyenne *people* North America colonization *126* (1)
Ch'i *see* Qi, Qi Empire
Chiaha *people* North America colonization *125* (4)
Chiang-hsi *see* Jiangxi
Chiang-ling *see* Jiangling
Chiang Mai *see* Chiengmai
Chiangnan Hsitao *see* Jiangnan Xidao
Chiang-su *see* Jiangsu
Chian-ning *see* Nanjing
Chiapa de Corzo Central America (Mexico) first civilizations *121* (2), *122* (1), *123* (2)
Chiapas *state* Central America Mexican Revolution *133* (3) the growth of the US *129* (2)
Chiauhtla Central America (Mexico) Aztecs *124* (2)
Chiba *var.* Tiba *prefecture* Japan economy *270* (1)
Chibcha *people/state* South America early cultures *147* (2)
Chibcha (Muisca) Chiefdoms *state* South America early cultures *146* (1)
Chicago North America (USA) exploration *119* (3) imperial global economy *92* (1) the growth of the US *129* (2), *132* (1) the modern world *113* (4) US Civil War *130* (5) US economy *134* (1), (3), *136* (2) US politics *135* (6)
Chicama *archaeological site* South America (Peru) early cultures *145* (3)
Chichén Itzá Central America (Mexico) Aztecs *124* (1) first civilizations *123* (2) first religions *36* (1)
Chichou *see* Jizhou
Chickamauga North America (USA) US Civil War *131* (7)
Chickamauga *var.* Chickamauga Creek *battle* North America (USA) US Civil War *131* (7)
Chickasaw *people* North America colonization *125* (4), *126* (1)
Chiclayo South America (Peru) environment *153* (4) narcotics *153* (5)
Chicolapan *var.* Chacalapan Central America (Mexico) Aztecs *124* (2)
Chiconautla Central America (Mexico) Aztecs *124* (2)
Chien-Chung *see* Jianzhong
Chiengmai *var.* Chiangmai, Kiangmai; *mod.* Chiang Mai Mainland Southeast Asia (Thailand) colonialism *247* (4), *248* (1) exploration *239* (1) world religions *243* (5)
Chiengmai *var.* Chiangmai, Kiangmai; *mod.* Chiang Mai *state* Mainland Southeast Asia the world in 1300 *66–67* the world in 1400 *70–71* the world in 1500 *74–75* the world in 1700 *82–83*
Chien-k'ang *see* Jiankang
Chiennan *see* Jiannan
Chien-yeh *see* Jianye, Nanjing
Chihli *see* Zhili
Chihuahua Central America (Mexico) Mexican Revolution *133* (3)
Chihuahua *state* Central America Mexican Revolution *133* (3) the growth of the US *129* (2)
Chihuahua *battle* Central America (Mexico) the growth of the US *129* (2)
Chihuahua Desert *desert* North America/Central America cultural groups *123* (4)
Chikinchel *state* Central America Aztecs *124* (1)
Chilca South America (Peru) the world in 2500 BCE *22–23*
Chilcotin *people* North America cultural groups *123* (3)
Children's Crusade *crusade* Central Europe crusades *186* (1)
Chile *state* South America economy *153* (3) empire and revolution *150* (1), *151* (3), *88–89* (2) environment *153* (4) global immigration *100* (1), *101* (2) imperial global economy *92* (1) narcotics *153* (5) politics *151* (4), *152* (1) the growth of the US *133* (4) the modern world *112* (1), *113* (4) US superpower *138* (1) WWII *105* (3) Cold War *109* (1)
Chile, Captaincy-General and Presidencia of *region* South America colonization *148* (2)
Chilecito South America (Argentina) empire and revolution *151* (3) Incas *147* (3)
Chi-lin *see* Jilin, Kirin
Chillon *river* South America early cultures *145* (3)
Chiloé, Isla de *var.* Isla Grande de Chiloé *island* South America European expansion *80–81* (1) exploration *143* (3)
Chimalhuacan Central America (Mexico) Aztecs *124* (2)
Chimbote South America (Peru) environment *153* (4)
Chimú *people/state* South America early cultures *147* (2)
Chin *state* East Asia medieval states *263* (3)
China *var.* People's Republic of China; *prev.* Cathay, Sinae, Qing Empire *region/state* East Asia ancient trade *44–45* (1) biological diffusion *72–73* (1) Chinese revolution *271* (5) early medieval states *245* (5) early systems *32* (1), *33* (2), (3) economy *274* (1) empire and revolution *88* (1) European expansion *84–85* (1) exploration *257* (3) first humans *13* (2) first religions *36* (1), *37* (4) global immigration *100* (1), *101* (2), (3) global knowledge *77* (6) imperial global economy *92* (1) imperialism *270* (2) Islam *235* (4) medieval states *261* (6), *264* (2) medieval voyages *61* (3) Mongols *68* (2) post-war economy *253* (5), *275* (3) post-war politics *251* (5), *252* (1), *253* (4), *274* (2) Soviet Union *208* (2), *213* (4) the growth of the US *133* (4) the modern world *113* (3), (4) world religions *243* (5), *49* (3), (4) WWII *104* (2), *105* (4), *251* (3), *272* (1), *273* (2) Cold War *109* (1), (4) colonization *284–285* (1) Communism *271* (8) decolonization *250* (1), *251* (4), *285* (3) *see also* Cathay, Qing Empire, Sinae
Chi-nan *see* Jinan
China, People's Republic of *see* China
China, Republic of *var.* Formosa, Formo'sa; *mod.* Taiwan *state* East Asia the world in 1950 *102–103* *see also* Taiwan
Chincha, Islas de *island group* South America empire and revolution *151* (3)
Chin-ch'ang *see* Jinchang
Chin-ch'uan *see* Jinchuan
Chindaka-Nagas *dynasty* South Asia Mongols *68–69* (1)
Chingchi *see* Jingji
Ch'ing Hai *see* Qinghai, Hu
Chinghai *see* Qinghai
Ching-nan *state* East Asia medieval states *263* (3)
Ch'ing-tao *see* Qingdao, Tsingtao
Chinkiang *see* Zhenjiang
Chinkultic Central America (Mexico) first civilizations *123* (2)
Chinmen Tao *see* Quemoy
Chinnereth *see* Galilee, Sea of
Chinon France medieval states *192* (2)
Chinsura *prev.* Chunchura South Asia (India) colonialism *247* (3)
Chin-t'ien *see* Jintian
Chinwangtao *see* Qinhuangdao
Chioggia *anc.* Fossa Claudia Italy economy *190* (1)
Chios *var.* Hios, Khios; *It.* Scio, *Turk.* Sakiz-Adasi *settlement/island* Greece ancient Greece *177* (2), (3), *179* (4) first civilizations *175* (4), *177* (1)
Chipata Southern Africa (Malawi) early cultures *160* (1)
Chipewyan *people* North America colonization *126* (1) cultural groups *123* (3)
Chippewa, Lake *lake* North America the world in 10,000 BCE *14–15*
Chiquihuitillo Central America (Mexico) first civilizations *122* (1)
Chiquito *people* South America early cultures *147* (2)
Chiquitos *region* South America colonization *148* (2) exploration *143* (2)
Chiquitoy South America (Peru) Incas *147* (3)
Chirand South Asia (India) the world in 2500 BCE *22–23*
Chire *see* Shire
Chiricahua Apache *people* North America colonization *125* (4)
Chiripa *archaeological site* South America (Bolivia) early cultures *144* (1)
Chishima-rettō *see* Kurile Islands
Chisholm Trail *wagon train route* North America the growth of the US *129* (2)
Chita Siberia (Russian Federation) colonialism *269* (3) Communism *271* (8) Soviet Union *208* (2)
Chitambo East Africa (Zambia) exploration *157* (4)
Chitato Southern Africa (Angola) Cold War *109* (5)
Chitimacha *people* Central America/North America colonization *125* (4), *126* (1)
Chitor South Asia (India) early medieval states *244–245* (3) Mughal Empire *246* (1)
Chittagong *prev.* Chatgaon; *Ben.* Chāttagām South Asia (Bangladesh) biological diffusion *72–73* (1) colonialism *247* (3), *248* (1) decolonization *250* (1) exploration *239* (1) post-war economy *253* (5) post-war politics *252* (3) trade *230* (2), *267* (3) WWII *251* (3) *see also* Chatgaon
Chittagong Hills *region* South Asia post-war politics *253* (4)
Chiusi *see* Clusium
Chkalov *see* Orenburg
Chocola Central America (Mexico) first civilizations *123* (2)
Choctaw *people* North America colonization *125* (4), *126* (1)
Chocuan *state* Central America Aztecs *124* (1)
Choga Mami Southwest Asia (Iraq) early agriculture *220* (1)
Choga Mish Southwest Asia (Iran) first cities *220* (2)
Chogwe East Africa (Tanzania) exploration *157* (4)
Chokai-zan *mountain* Japan medieval states *265* (3)
Chokwe *var.* Cokwe *people/state* Central Africa/Southern Africa colonization *167* (4) trade *167* (1)
Cholas *region/state* South Asia ancient trade *44–45* (1) early medieval states *244* (2) Mongols *68–69* (1) world religions *242* (2)
Cholm *see* Kholm
Chololan Central America (Mexico) colonization *125* (5)
Cholula Central America (Mexico) first civilizations *122* (1)
Chondwe *archaeological site* Southern Africa (Zambia) early cultures *160* (1)
Chongjin East Asia (North Korea) Cold War *109* (4)
Chongoyapa *archaeological site* South America (Peru) early cultures *145* (3)
Chongqing *var.* Ch'ung-ch'ing, Chungking, Pahsien, Yuzhou East Asia (China) biological diffusion *72–73* (1) colonialism *269* (4) early modern states *266* (2), *268* (1) economy *274* (1) Islam *275* (4) medieval states *263* (6) post-war politics *271* (7), *274* (2) WWII *251* (3), *272* (1), *273* (2)
Chonju *region* East Asia medieval states *264* (2)
Chonos Archipelago *island group* South America exploration *143* (3)
Chopani-Mando South Asia (India) the world in 5000 BCE *18–19*
Chorasmia *province* Central Asia ancient Persia *223* (4)
Chorlton British Isles (United Kingdom) economy *204* (2)
Chorne More *see* Black Sea
Chorrera *archaeological site/settlement* South America (Ecuador) early cultures *144* (1)
Chosan East Asia (North Korea) Cold War *109* (4)
Chōsen *see* Choson, Korea, Koryo, Silla
Chōsen-kaikyō *see* Korea Strait
Choshi *Jap.* Chōshi *bomb target* Japan Communism *273* (3)
Choson *var.* Chosen; *later* Silla; *mod.* Korea; Koryo *state* East Asia the world in 250 BCE *38–39* *see also* Korea, Silla, Koryo
Chotuna South America (Peru) early cultures *146* (1)
Christchurch New Zealand colonization *283* (4), (5) decolonization *285* (3)
Christiania *var.* Kristiania, *mod.* Oslo Scandinavia (Norway) early modern states *197* (3) economy *205* (4) *see also* Oslo
Christmas Island *colonial possession/state* Indian Ocean the world in 1975 *106–107* the modern world *110–111*
Christmas Island *mod.* Kiritimati *island/nuclear test* Pacific Ocean environmentalism *285* (2) WWII *272* (1), *273* (2) *see also* Kiritimati
Chryse Chersonesus *region* Greece ancient trade *44* (2)
Chu *region/state* East Asia first cities *259* (4), (5) first religions *37* (4) medieval states *263* (3)
Chubut *river* South America empire and revolution *151* (3) environment *153* (4)
Chubut *see* Rawson
Chucalissa North America (USA) cultural groups *122* (5)
Chucuito South America (Peru) early cultures *146* (1) Incas *147* (3)
Chudskoye Ozero *see* Peipus, Lake
Chu-fu *see* Zhufu
Chugacha South Asia (Bangladesh) post-war politics *252* (3)
Chukchi *people* Siberia the world in 1700 *82–83* the world in 1800 *86–87*
Chukchi Sea *sea* Arctic Ocean exploration *257* (2), *286* (1), *287* (2)
Chukotka *region* Siberia exploration *257* (2)
Chukumuk Central America (Mexico) first civilizations *123* (2)
Chu-lu *see* Zhulu
Chunchura *see* Chinsura
Ch'ung-ch'ing, Chungking *see* Chongqing
Chung nan Shan *see* Zhongnan Shan
Chung t'iao Shan *see* Zhongtiao Shan
Chupicuaro Central America (Mexico) first civilizations *121* (2)
Chuquiabo South America (Bolivia) Incas *147* (3)
Chuquibamba South America (Peru) early cultures *146* (1)
Chuquicamata South America (Chile) environment *153* (4)
Chuquisaca *var.* La Plata; *mod.* Sucre South America (Bolivia) empire and revolution *150* (1) *see also* Sucre
Chur *anc.* Curia, Curia Rhaetorum; *Fr.* Coire, *It.* Coira, *Rmsch.* Cuera, Quera Central Europe (Switzerland) early modern states *193* (5) *see also* Curia
Churchill River *river* North America colonization *126* (1) the growth of the US *129* (2)
Chustenahlah *battle* North America (USA) the growth of the US *129* (2)
Chuuk *var.* Hogoley Islands; *prev.* Truk Islands *island group* Pacific Ocean environmentalism *285* (2) *see also* Truk
Chu, Wall of *wall* East Asia (China) first cities *259* (5)
Ciboney *people* West Indies colonization *125* (4)
Ciénaga de Oro South America (Colombia) early cultures *146* (1)
Çiftlik Southwest Asia (Turkey) early agriculture *174* (1)
Cihuatlan *state* Central America Aztecs *124* (1)
Cilicia *region* Southwest Asia ancient Rome *180–181* (1) crusades *65* (3) first civilizations *222* (2) Hellenistic world *40–41* (1)
Cimmerians *people* Southwest Asia the world in 750 BCE *30–31*
Cina Selatan, Laut *see* South China Sea
Cincinnati North America (USA) the growth of the US *129* (2), *132* (1) US Civil War *131* (6), (7) US economy *134* (1), (3) US politics *135* (6)
Cipangu *var.* Japan *island group* Japan global knowledge *76* (9) *see also* Japan
Circassia *region* Eastern Europe Ottomans *231* (3)
Circassians *var.* Cherkess *people* Eastern Europe Mongols *68–69* (1) Ottomans *232–233* (1)
Circei *mod.* San Felice Circco Italy early states *178* (1)
Circeo *archaeological site* Italy first humans *13* (2)
Circum-Caribbean *region/physical region* West Indies early agriculture *120* (1) early cultures *144* (1)
Circus Maximus *building* Italy ancient Rome *181* (2)
Cirencester *anc.* Corinium, Corinium Dobunorum British Isles (United Kingdom) medieval states *183* (3)
Cirta North Africa (Algeria) ancient Rome *180–181* (1) early cultures *161* (2)
Cisalpine Republic *state* Italy the world in 1800 *86–87*
Cishan *archaeological site/settlement* East Asia early agriculture *258* (1), (2)
Cîteaux *major cistercian house/settlement* France medieval states *187* (3), *188* (1)
Citlaltepec Central America (Mexico) Aztecs *124* (2)
Ciudad Bolívar *prev.* Angostura South America (Venezuela) empire and revolution *151* (3) *see also* Angostura
Ciudad del Este *prev.* Presidente Stroessner, Puerto Presidente Stroessner South America (Paraguay) environment *153* (4)
Ciudad de México *see* Mexico, Mexico City, Tenochtitlan
Ciudad de Panamá *see* Panamá, Panamá City
Ciudad Guayana South America (Venezuela) environment *153* (4)
Ciudad Juárez Central America (Mexico) Mexican Revolution *133* (3)
Ciudad Madero Central America (Mexico) Mexican Revolution *133* (3)
Ciudad Real South America (Paraguay) colonization *148* (2)
Ciudad Rodrigo *battle* Iberian Peninsula (Spain) Napoleon *200–201* (1)
Ciudad Trujillo *see* Santo Domingo
Cividale Italy WWI *207* (5)
Civitas Nemetum *see* Speyer
Clairvaux *major cistercian house* France medieval states *187* (3)
Clasons Point North America (USA) cultural groups *122* (5)
Claudia, Aqua *aqueduct* Italy ancient Rome *181* (2)
Claudius, Temple of *building* Italy ancient Rome *181* (2)
Clausentum *see* Southampton
Clazomenae *settlement/state* Southwest Asia (Turkey) ancient Greece *177* (2) first civilizations *177* (1)
Clearwater *battle* North America (USA) the growth of the US *129* (2)
Clemsons Island North America (USA) cultural groups *122* (5)
Cleonae *state* Greece ancient Greece *177* (2)
Clermont France crusades *64–65* (2) Franks *183* (5), (6), *184* (2)
Clermont-Ferrand France economy *205* (4)
Cleveland North America (USA) the growth of the US *129* (2), *132* (1) US economy *134* (1), (3)
Cleves *Ger.* Kleve *region* Central Europe empire and revolution *199* (3)
Clipperton Island *colonial possession/state/island* Pacific Ocean the world in 1950 *102–103* the world in 1975 *106–107* the modern world *110–111*
Clodia, Via *road* Italy early states *178* (1)
Clodia, Via *road* Italy early states *178* (1)
Clogg's Cave Australia exploration *280* (1)
Cloncurry Australia colonization *282* (1)
Clontarf British Isles (Ireland) crusades *186* (1)
Cloudy Bay *bay* New Zealand exploration *278* (1)
Clovis North America (USA) the world in 10,000 BCE *14–15*
Clunes *goldfield* Australia colonization *282* (2)
Clunia Iberian Peninsula (Spain) ancient Rome *180–181* (1)
Cluny France empire and revolution *199* (4)
Clusium *mod.* Chiusi Italy early states *178* (1), (2) first civilizations *177* (1)
Clyde New Zealand colonization *283* (5)
Cnidus Southwest Asia (Turkey) ancient Greece *177* (3) ancient Rome *180–181* (1) first civilizations *177* (1) Hellenistic world *40–41* (1), *41* (2)
Cnidus *state* Greece ancient Greece *177* (2)
Cnossus *see* Knossos
Coahuila *state* Central America Mexican Revolution *133* (3) the growth of the US *129* (2)
Coahuiltec *people* Central America/North America colonization *125* (4), *126* (1)
Coast Mountains *Fr.* Chaîne Côtière *mountain range* North America the growth of the US *129* (2)
Coatepec Central America (Mexico) Aztecs *124* (2)
Coatlayauhcan Central America (Mexico) Aztecs *124* (3)
Coatlinchan Central America (Mexico) Aztecs *124* (2)
Coatzacoalcos *river* Central America first civilizations *121* (3)
Coba Central America (Mexico) first civilizations *123* (2)
Cobar *goldfield* Australia colonization *282* (2)
Coblenz Central Europe (Germany) WWI *206* (2), (3)
Cocanada South Asia (India) WWII *251* (3)
Cochabamba *prev.* Oropeza South America (Bolivia) Incas *147* (3) narcotics *153* (5)
Cochimi *people* Central America colonization *125* (4)
Cochin *var.* Kochi; *early Chin.* Ko-chih South Asia (India) colonialism *247* (3), *248* (1) Mughal Empire *246* (1) post-war economy *253* (5) trade *230* (2), *267* (3)
Cochin China *colonial possession/state* Mainland Southeast Asia colonialism *269* (4) European imperialism *97* (3)
Cochinos, Bahía de *see* Pigs, Bay of
Coco *people* Central America colonization *125* (4)
Cocopa *people* Central America colonization *125* (4), *126* (1)
Cocos Islands *colonial possession/island group* Indian Ocean the world in 1900 *94–95* the world in 1925 *98–99* the world in 1975 *106–107* the modern world *110–111*
Cod, Cape *headland* North America empire and revolution *127* (2)
Cognac *anc.* Compniacum France Reformation *194* (2)
Cohuna and Kow Swamp Australia exploration *280* (1)
Coimbatore South Asia (India) post-war economy *253* (5)
Coimbra *anc.* Conimbria, Conimbriga *settlement* Iberian Peninsula (Portugal) Franks *184* (2) Islam *192* (3) medieval states *187* (3)
Coira *see* Chur, Curia
Coire *see* Chur, Curia
Coixtlahuacan *state* Central America Aztecs *124* (1)
Cokwe *see* Chokwe
Cola *state* South Asia first empires *241* (5)
Colas *see* Cholas
Colchester *hist.* Colneceaste; *anc.* Camulodunum British Isles (United Kingdom) economy *204* (1) medieval states *183* (3)
Colchi South Asia (India) ancient trade *44–45* (1)
Colchis *region* Eastern Europe Hellenistic world *40–41* (1)
Cold Harbor *battle* North America (USA) US Civil War *131* (7)

INDEX-GAZETTEER: Dapenkeng – Éfaté

medieval states 189 (3), (4) Napoleon 200–201 (1) WWI 207 (4) WWII 210 (1), 211 (4)
Dapenkeng *archaeological site* East Asia early agriculture 258 (1)
Darada *state* South Asia first empires 241 (5)
Daradus *river* West Africa (Senegal) ancient trade 44 (2)
Dara-i-Kur Central Asia (Uzbekistan) the world in 2500 BCE 22–23
Darbelo South Asia (Pakistan) colonialism 247 (3)
Dardanelles *var.* Hellespont; *Turk.* Çanakkale Boğazı *sea waterway* Southwest Asia (Greece) first civilizations 175 (4) WWI 207 (6), 233 (2)
Dar-el-Beida *see* Casablanca
Dar es Salaam East Africa (Tanzania) colonization 167 (4) economy 168 (2) exploration 156 (3), 157 (4), (5)
Dar es-Soltan *archaeological site* North Africa (Morocco) first humans 13 (2)
Darfur *state* East Africa colonization 167 (4) slave trade 165 (4) trade 167 (1)
Dargaville New Zealand colonization 283 (4), (5)
Dariabad South Asia (India) colonialism 247 (3)
Darién, Golfo del *see* Darien, Gulf of
Darien, Gulf of *Sp.* Golfo del Darién *gulf* South America colonization 148 (2) Incas 148 (1)
Darien, Isthmus of *see* Panama, Isthmus of
Dariorigum France ancient Rome 180–181 (1)
Dar'īyah *see* Deraya
Darjeeling South Asia (India) exploration 257 (3)
Darling *river* Australia colonization 282 (1), (2), 283 (3) early agriculture 20–21 (2) exploration 279 (2) prehistoric culture 17 (5)
Darlington British Isles (United Kingdom) economy 204 (1)
Darsena *see* Arsenal
Dar Tichit West Africa (Mauritania) early agriculture 158 (1)
Darwin *prev.* Palmerston, Port Darwin Australia colonization 282 (1), 283 (3), 284–285 environmentalism 285 (2) exploration 279 (2) prehistoric culture 17 (5) WWII 251 (3), 272 (1)
Dās *island* Southwest Asia economy 234 (1)
Dasapura South Asia (India) early religions 48 (2)
Dasharna *region/state* South Asia first empires 241 (5) world religions 242 (2)
Dashhowuz *see* Dashkhovuz
Dashiqiao *var.* Tashihkiao East Asia (China) Russo-Japanese War 270 (4)
Dashkhovuz *prev.* Tashauz; *Turkm.* Dashhowuz Central Asia (Turkmenistan) Soviet Union 214–215 (4)
Dasht *river* South Asia first cities 240 (2) first civilizations 24 (2), 25 (3) first empires 241 (4), (5) Mughal Empire 246 (1) world religions 242 (2)
Dating East Asia (China) medieval states 263 (5)
Datong East Asia (China) medieval states 263 (4)
Datong East Asia (China) early modern states 266 (1) medieval states 263 (5) world religions 49 (3)
Daugava *see* Western Dvina
Daugavpils *see* Dünaburg
Daulatabad South Asia (India) early medieval states 245 (4)
Dauni *people* Italy early states 178 (2)
Dauphiné *region* France medieval states 192 (1), (2)
Davao *off.* Davao City Philippines colonialism 247 (4)
Davao City *see* Davao
Davis Strait *sea waterway* North America exploration 286 (1), 287 (2) the growth of the US 129 (2)
Daw *state* West Africa trade 163 (4)
Dawaro *state* East Africa the world in 1200 62–63 the world in 1300 66–67
Dawenkou *archaeological site* East Asia early agriculture 258 (1), (2)
Dawson *see* Dawson City
Dawson City *mod.* Dawson North America (Canada) imperial global economy 93 (3)
Dawston *see* Degsastan
Daybul *var.* Daibol South Asia (India) medieval voyages 61 (3) trade 230 (2)
Daybul *see* Daibul
Dayi Shang *vassal state* East Asia first cities 259 (3)
Dayton North America (USA) US politics 135 (6)
Da Yunhe *see* Grand Canal
Dazaifu Japan early modern states 265 (5) medieval states 264 (2), 265 (3)
Dazhangheguo *state* East Asia medieval states 263 (3)
DDR *see* German Democratic Republic
Dead Sea *var.* Bahret Lut, Lacus Asphaltites; *Ar.* Al Baḩr al Mayyit, Baḩrat Lūt, *Heb.* Yam HaMelaḩ *salt lake* Southwest Asia 20th century 234 (2) 20th-century politics 233 (3) ancient Rome 225 (4) crusades 65 (3) first civilizations 221 (4), 222 (1)
De Blicquy North America (Canada) cultural groups 123 (3)
Debrecen *prev.* Debreczen; *Ger.* Debreczin, *Rom.* Debreţin Central Europe (Hungary) Reformation 194 (2)
Debreczen, Debreczin *see* Debrecen
Debreţin *see* Debrecen
Decapolis *state* Southwest Asia ancient Rome 225 (4)
Deccan *plateau/region* South Asia colonialism 247 (3), 248 (1) early medieval states 244 (1), (2), 244–245 (3) economy 249 (4) first empires 241 (4), (5) first religions 36 (2) imperial global economy 93 (5) Marathas 246 (2) Mughal Empire 246 (1) post-war politics 252 (1) world religions 242 (2), 243 (4)
Deccan States *state* South Asia colonialism 248 (2)
Dedeagach *mod.* Alexandroupolis Greece WWI 207 (6)
Dego *battle* Italy Napoleon 200–201 (1)
Degsastan *var.* Dawston *battle* British Isles (United Kingdom) medieval states 183 (3)
Dehli *see* Delhi, Indraprastha
Dehra Dun South Asia (India) decolonization 250 (1) exploration 257 (3)
Deira *region* British Isles medieval states 183 (3)
Deir el-Bahri Egypt ancient Egypt 159 (4)
Deir el-Balah Southwest Asia (Israel) ancient Egypt 159 (5)
Deir el-Bersha Egypt ancient Egypt 159 (4)
Deir el-Gabrawi Egypt ancient Egypt 159 (3)
Delagoa Bay *var.* Baía de Lourenço Marques *bay* Southern Africa slave trade 165 (4)
Delaware *state* North America empire and revolution 127 (2), (3) the growth of the US 129 (1) US Civil War 130 (2), (3), (4), (5), 131 (6), (7) US economy 134 (2)
Delaware *people* North America colonization 126 (1)
Delgado, Cape *headland* Southern Africa exploration 156 (3)
Delhi *var.* Dehli, *Hind.* Dilli; *prev.* Indraprastha; *hist.* Shahjahanabad South Asia (India) biological diffusion 72–73 (1) colonialism 247 (3), 248 (1), 269 (4) Communism 271 (8) decolonization 250 (1) early medieval states 244–245 (3) economy 249 (4) empire and revolution 249 (3) exploration 239 (1), 257 (3) global immigration 101 (3) imperial global economy 92 (1), 93 (5) Mongols 68 (2) Mughal Empire 246 (1) post-war economy 253 (5) Timur 229 (4) trade 267 (3) US superpower 138 (1) WWII 251 (3) *see also* Indraprastha
Delhi *region* South Asia post-war politics 252 (1)
Delhi, Sultanate of *state* South Asia Mongols 68–69 (1) Mughal Empire 246 (1) Timur 229 (4)
Delhi United Provinces *state* South Asia colonialism 248 (2)
Delium *battle* Greece ancient Greece 177 (3)
Delos Greece ancient Greece 179 (4)
Delphi *religious site/settlement* Greece ancient Greece 177 (3), 179 (4) ancient Rome 180–181 (1) first religions 36 (1), 37 (3)
Demchok *var.* Dêmqog *region* South Asia post-war politics 252 (1)
Demerara *colonial possession* South America colonization 149 (4)
Demetrias Greece Hellenistic world 41 (2)
Demnat North Africa (Morocco) exploration 157 (4)
Demotika *state* Southeast Europe WWII 211 (2)
Dêmqog *see* Demchok
Dendra Greece first civilizations 175 (4)
Deng *state* East Asia first cities 259 (4)
Dengchong East Asia (China) medieval states 263 (6)
Dengkil *archaeological site* Mainland Southeast Asia (Malaysia) Bronze Age 240 (3)
Dengyue *var.* Tengchung East Asia (China) colonialism 269 (4)
Dengzhou *var.* Teng-chou East Asia (China) early modern states 265 (5), 266 (1) medieval states 264 (2) Mongols 68–69 (1)
Denison, Cape *headland* Antarctica Antarctic Exploration 287 (3)
Denjong *see* Sikkim
Denkyera *state* West Africa the world in 1700 82–83
Denmark *anc.* Hafnia; *Dan.* Danmark; *state* Scandinavia crusades 186 (1), 64–65 (2) early modern states 193 (4), 197 (3) economy 190 (1), 205 (4) empire and revolution 199 (3), 202 (1), (2) European expansion 84–85 (1) inter-war 209 (3), (5) medieval states 185 (3), 188 (1), 189 (3), (4) medieval voyages 60–61 (1) Mongols 68–69 (1) Napoleon 200–201 (1), 201 (2) post-war economy 213 (5), 214 (1), (2) post-war politics 212 (1), (3) Reformation 196 (1) Soviet Union 213 (4) the modern world 112 (2) US superpower 138 (1) WWII 210 (1), 211 (2), (4) Cold War 108 (3), 109 (1) early 20th century 206 (1)
Denmark-Norway *state* Scandinavia early modern states 195 (3) Reformation 194 (2)
Denmark Strait *var.* Danmarksstraedet *sea waterway* Atlantic Ocean exploration 172 (2)
Denver North America (USA) the growth of the US 129 (2), 132 (1) US economy 134 (1), 136 (2) US politics 135 (6)
Depford Culture *people* North America the world in 250 BCE 38–39
Deraya *Ar.* Dar'īyah Southwest Asia (Saudi Arabia) 20th-century politics 233 (4)
Derbend *see* Derbent
Derbent Eastern Europe (Russian Federation) Islam 226 (2), 227 (4), (5) medieval Persia 231 (4) Mongols 229 (3), 68–69 (1) Ottomans 231 (3) Timur 229 (4)
Derby British Isles (United Kingdom) economy 204 (1)
Derbyshire *region* British Isles imperial global economy 93 (4)
Dereivka *archaeological site* Eastern Europe (Ukraine) Copper Age 174 (2)
Derna North Africa (Libya) colonization 167 (4)
Dertosa *mod.* Tortosa Iberian Peninsula (Spain) ancient Rome 179 (3), 180–181 (1) *see also* Tortosa
Derwent *river* British Isles economy 204 (1)
Desalpur *archaeological site* South Asia (India) first cities 240 (2)
Deseado *river* South America colonization 148 (2)
Desert Gatherers *people* North America the world in 250 CE 46–47 *passim.*
Des Moines North America (USA) the growth of the US 129 (2)
Desmumu *state* British Isles medieval states 188 (2)
Desna *river* Eastern Europe WWI 207 (4)
Desterro *mod.* Florianópolis South America (Brazil) colonization 149 (3), (4)
Detroit *prev.* Fort Pontchartrain North America (USA) colonization 126 (1) the growth of the US 129 (2), 132 (1) US economy 134 (1), (3) US politics 135 (6)
Deutschland *see* Germany
Deutsch-Südwestafrika *see* Southwest Africa, German Southwest Africa
Deva *var.* Legaceaster, Devana Castra; *mod.* Chester; *Wel.* Caerleon; *legion headquarters/mithraic site* British Isles (United Kingdom) ancient Rome 180–181 (1) world religions 48 (1) *see also* Chester
Devagiri South Asia (India) early religions 48 (2)
Devagiri *region* South Asia early medieval states 244–245 (3)
Devana *see* Aberdeen
Devana Castra *see* Chester, Deva
Devapattana South Asia (Nepal) early medieval states 244 (1) first empires 241 (4)
Deventer Low Countries (Netherlands) economy 190 (1)
Devils Lake *burial mound* North America (USA) first civilizations 121 (4)
Dez *river* Southwest Asia first cities 220 (2) first civilizations 221 (4)
Dezful Southwest Asia (Iran) 20th-century politics 235 (5)
Dezhnev, Cape *headland* Siberia exploration 287 (2)
Dhahran *Ar.* Az̧ Z̧ahran Southwest Asia (Saudi Arabia) 20th-century politics 233 (4), 235 (5) economy 234 (1) US superpower 138 (1)
Dhaka *prev.* Dacca South Asia (Bangladesh) post-war economy 253 (5) post-war politics 252 (1), (3) *see also* Dacca
Dhanbad South Asia (India) post-war economy 253 (5)
Dharangaon South Asia (India) colonialism 247 (3)
Dharwar South Asia (India) economy 249 (4)
Dhlo Dhlo Southern Africa (Zimbabwe) trade 164 (1)
Dhodhekánisos *see* Dodecanese
Dhofar Southwest Asia (Yemen) trade 267 (3)
Dholavira *archaeological site* South Asia (Pakistan) first cities 240 (2)
Dhualdadr *see* Dulkadir
Dhu Qar Southwest Asia (Iraq) ancient Persia 225 (6)
Di *people* East Asia first cities 259 (4) first states 261 (2)
Diamantina South America (Brazil) colonization 149 (3) empire and revolution 151 (3)
Dian *people/state* East Asia/Mainland Southeast Asia first cities 259 (5) first states 260 (1) medieval states 261 (6)
Dias Point *see* Volta, Cape da
Dibio *see* Dijon
Dickson North America (USA) cultural groups 122 (5)
Dicle *see* Tigris
Didyma *religious site* Southwest Asia (Turkey) first religions 37 (3)
Diedenhofen *var.* Thionville France Franks 184 (2)
Diegueño *people* North America colonization 125 (4)
Die Kelders *archaeological site* Southern Africa (South Africa) early cultures 160 (1) first humans 13 (2)
Dien Bien Phu *battle* Mainland Southeast Asia (Vietnam) post-war politics 251 (5)
Dieppe France WWI 206 (2), (3)
Dieu, Hôtel *building* France economy 191 (2)
Dihang *see* Brahmaputra
Dijlah *see* Tigris
Dijon *anc.* Dibio France early modern states 193 (4), 197 (5) empire and revolution 199 (4) Franks 184 (2) medieval states 187 (4), 192 (2)
Dikbosch *archaeological site* Southern Africa (South Africa) early cultures 160 (1)
Dikson Siberia (Russian Federation) exploration 287 (2)
Dikwa West Africa (Nigeria) exploration 157 (4)
Dili *var.* Dilli, Dilly Maritime Southeast Asia (Indonesia) WWII 272 (1), 273 (2)
Dilli, Dilly *see* Dili
Dilli *see* Delhi, Indraprastha
Dilmun Arabian Peninsula first civilizations 24 (2), 25 (3)
Dimashq *see* Damascus
Dinajpur South Asia (Bangladesh) post-war politics 252 (3)
Dinant Low Countries (Belgium) WWI 206 (2), (3)
Dingcun *archaeological site* East Asia (China) first humans 13 (2)
Dingiray West Africa (Guinea) Islam 167 (3)
Dingliao *military base /rebellion* East Asia early modern states 266 (1), (2)
Diocaesarea *Christian archbishopric* Southwest Asia (Syria) world religions 48 (1)
Diocletian, Baths of *Lat.* Thermae Diocletiani *building* (Italy) ancient Rome 181 (2)
Diocletiani, Thermae *see* Diocletian, Baths of
Dion *state* Greece ancient Greece 177 (2)
Dionysus, Theatre of *building* Greece ancient Greece 177 (4)
Dioscurias Southwest Asia (Georgia) early cultures 161 (2) first civilizations 177 (1)
Diospolis Magna *see* Thebes
Dipylon *see* Dipylum
Dipylum *var.* Dipylon *building* Greece ancient Greece 177 (4)
Dire Dawa *archaeological site* East Africa (Ethiopia) first humans 13 (2)
Dishasha Egypt ancient Egypt 159 (3)
Dispur South Asia (India) post-war politics 252 (1)
Diu South Asia (India) colonialism 247 (3), 248 (1), 269 (4) decolonization 251 (4) empire and revolution 88–89 (2) exploration 239 (1) post-war politics 252 (1) trade 230 (2), 67 (3) WWII 251 (3)
Divi *mod.* Diu South Asia (India) world religions 243 (4) *see also* Diu
Divodurum Mediomatricum *see* Metz
Divostin Southeast Europe (Yugoslavia) early agriculture 174 (1)
Dixmude Low Countries (Belgium) WWI 206 (2), (3)
Diyala *var.* Rudkhaneh-ye Sīrvān, Sirwan, Diyālá, Nahr *river* Southwest Asia first cities 220 (2) first civilizations 221 (4), (5)
Diyarbakir Southwest Asia (Turkey) 20th-century politics 235 (5)
Djailolo *see* Halmahera
Djakarta *see* Batavia, Jakarta
Djambi *see* Jambi
Djawa *see* Java
Djenné *see* Jenne
Djerba *island* North Africa Ottomans 231 (3)
Djibouti East Africa (Djibouti) colonization 167 (4) European imperialism 96 (1)
Djibouti *var.* Jibuti; *prev.* French Somaliland, French Territory of the Afars and Issas; *Fr.* Côte Française des Somlis *state* East Africa decolonization 168 (1) economy 168 (2) Islam 235 (4) the modern world 112 (1), 113 (3) *see also* French Somaliland, French Territory of the Afars and Issas
Dnepr *see* Dnieper
Dnepropetrovsk *see* Dnipropetrovs'k, Yekaterinoslav
Dnestr *see* Dniester
Dnieper *Bel.* Dnyapro, *Rus.* Dnepr, *Ukr.* Dnipro *river* Eastern Europe ancient trade 44–45 (1) biological diffusion 72–73 (1) crusades 64–65 (2) early Islam 56–57 (1) economy 190 (1) empire and revolution 198 (2), 202 (1) exploration 172 (1) first humans 13 (2) Islam 227 (4) medieval states 185 (3) medieval voyages 60–61 (1) Mongols 68–69 (1) Napoleon 200–201 (1) Ottomans 202 (4), 230 (1), 231 (3), 232–233 (1) prehistoric culture 17 (4) Timur 229 (4) WWI 207 (4) WWII 210 (1), 211 (4)
Dniester *anc.* Tyras; *Rom.* Nistru, *Rus.* Dnestr, *Ukr.* Dnister *river* Eastern Europe Bronze Age 175 (3) Copper Age 174 (2) crusades 64–65 (2) early agriculture 174 (1) economy 190 (1), 205 (4) empire and revolution 198 (2), 202 (1) exploration 172 (1) great migrations 52–53 (1), 53 (2) medieval states 189 (4) Mongols 68–69 (1) Napoleon 200–201 (1) Ottomans 197 (4), 230 (1), 231 (3) WWI 207 (4) WWII 210 (1), 211 (4)
Dnipro *see* Dnieper
Dnipropetrovs'k *var.* Yekaterinoslav; *Rus.* Dnepropetrovsk Eastern Europe (Ukraine) Soviet Union 214–215 (4) *see also* Yekaterinoslav
Dnister *see* Dniester
Dnyapro *see* Dnieper
Doboj Southeast Europe (Bosnia and Herzegovina) post-war economy 215 (3)
Dobro Polje *battle* Southeast Europe (FYR Macedonia) WWI 207 (6)
Dobruja *region/vassal state* Southeast Europe Ottomans 202 (4), 230 (1)
Dodecanese *var.* Dodecanese Islands, Nóties Sporádes; *prev.* Dhodhekánisos *state/island group* Greece ancient Greece 177 (2), (3) first civilizations 175 (4) medieval states 187 (5) Ottomans 202 (4), 232–233 (1) WWI 210 (1), 233 (2) WWII 211 (2), (4) 20th-century politics 233 (3)
Dodecanese Islands *see* Dodecanese
Do Dimmi West Africa (Niger) early agriculture 158 (1)
Dodoma East Africa (Tanzania) economy 168 (2) exploration 157 (5)
Dodona *religious site* Greece first religions 37 (3)
Doge's Palace *building* Italy economy 191 (3)
Dogrib *people* North America cultural groups 123 (3)
Doha Southwest Asia (Qatar) economy 234 (1) exploration 219 (4)
Dojran *battle* Southeast Europe (FYR Macedonia) WWI 207 (6)
Dolní Věstonice *archaeological site/settlement* Central Europe (Poland) prehistoric culture 17 (4)
Dolomites *var.* Dolomiti; It. Dolomitiche, Alpi *mountain range* Italy WWI 207 (5)
Dolomiti, Dolomitiche, Alpi *see* Dolomites
Dominica *colonial possession/state/island* West Indies empire and revolution 150 (1) European expansion 85 (2) the growth of the US 129 (2) the modern world 112 (1) US economy 136 (2) US politics 139 (4)
Dominican Republic *state* West Indies Cold War 108 (2), 109 (1) the growth of the US 129 (2), 133 (4) the world in 1850 90–91 the world in 1900 94–95 the world in 1925 98–99 the world in 1950 102–103 the world in 1975 106–107 the modern world 110–111 , 112 (1), 113 (4) US economy 136 (2) US politics 139 (4) US superpower 138 (1) WWII 104 (1)
Domitian, Stadium of *building* Italy ancient Rome 181 (2)
Domrémy France medieval states 192 (2)
Don *anc.* Tanais *river* Eastern Europe ancient trade 44–45 (1) biological diffusion 72–73 (1) Bronze Age 175 (3) early agriculture 174 (1) early Islam 56–57 (1) economy 205 (4) first humans 13 (2) great migrations 52–53 (1) Islam 163 (1), 227 (4) medieval states 185 (3) Mongols 68–69 (1) Napoleon 200–201 (1) Ottomans 230 (1), 231 (3), 232–233 (1) prehistoric culture 17 (4) Timur 229 (4) WWI 207 (4) WWII 210 (1), 211 (4)
Donau *see* Danube
Donbas *region* Eastern Europe economy 205 (4)
Doncaster *anc.* Danum British Isles (United Kingdom) economy 204 (1)
Don Cossacks *people* Eastern Europe/Siberia Reformation 196 (2)
Donets *river* Eastern Europe WWI 207 (4)
Donets'k Eastern Europe (Ukraine) Soviet Union 214–215 (4)
Dong Ap Bia *see* Hamburger Hill
Dong Dau Mainland Southeast Asia (Vietnam) the world in 2500 BCE 22–23
Dong Duong Mainland Southeast Asia (Vietnam) world religions 243 (5), 49 (4)
Dong Hai *see* East China Sea
Donghu *state* East Asia first cities 259 (5)
Dong Khe *fort* Mainland Southeast Asia post-war politics 251 (5)
Dongola *var.* Donqola, Dunqulah East Africa (Sudan) ancient trade 44–45 (1) colonization 167 (4) early cultures 161 (3), (4), (5) Islam 163 (1)
Dong Son *archaeological site/settlement* Mainland Southeast Asia (Thailand) Bronze Age 240 (3)
Dongting Hu *lake* East Asia early modern states 266 (1) first cities 259 (4), (5) first states 260 (1)
Dongyi *state* East Asia first cities 259 (3)
Donja Slatina *fort* Southeast Europe (Yugoslavia) Bronze Age 175 (3)
Donqola *see* Dongola
Doornik *see* Tournai
Dorchester *anc.* Durnovaria British Isles (United Kingdom) economy 204 (1) medieval states 183 (3)
Dordogne *river* France first civilizations 177 (1)
Dordrecht *var.* Dordt, Dort Low Countries (Netherlands) economy 190 (1)
Dordt *see* Dordrecht
Dorestad Low Countries (Netherlands) medieval states 185 (3) medieval voyages 60–61 (1)
Dori West Africa (Burkina) exploration 157 (4)
Dornach *battle* Central Europe (Switzerland) early modern states 193 (5)
Dorpat Eastern Europe (Estonia) early modern states 195 (3) economy 190 (1) medieval states 189 (3)
Dorsoduro Italy economy 191 (3)
Dort *see* Dordrecht
Dortmund Central Europe (Germany) economy 190 (1) medieval states 188 (1)
Dorylaeum Southwest Asia (Turkey) ancient Rome 180–181 (1)
Dorylaeum *battle* Southwest Asia (Turkey) crusades 64–65 (2)
Dospad Dagh *see* Rhodope Mountains
Douai *anc.* Duacum; *prev.* Douay France economy 190 (1)
Douala *var.* Duala Central Africa (Cameroon) colonization 167 (4) economy 168 (2)
Douanas *river* Mainland Southeast Asia ancient trade 44 (2)
Douay *see* Douai
Doullens France WWI 206 (2)
Douro *Sp.* Duero *river* Iberian Peninsula Bronze Age 175 (3) Copper Age 174 (2) crusades 64–65 (2) early agriculture 174 (1) economy 190 (1) first civilizations 177 (1) great migrations 52–53 (1), 53 (2) *see also* Duero
Dove Creek *battle* North America (USA) the growth of the US 129 (2)
Dover British Isles (United Kingdom) economy 204 (1), 205 (4) WWI 206 (2), (3)
Dover North America (USA) the growth of the US 129 (2)
Dover, Strait of *var.* Straits of Dover; *Fr.* Pas de Calais *sea waterway* Western Europe WWI 206 (2), (3)
Dover, Straits of *see* Dover, Strait of
Downpatrick *Ir.* Dún Pádraig British Isles (United Kingdom) Bronze Age 175 (3)
Drač *see* Durazzo
Draç *see* Durazzo
Drakensberg *physical region* Southern Africa economy 163 (2) first humans 12 (1) slave trade 165 (4) trade 164 (1)
Drancy *ghetto* France WWII 211 (3)
Drangiana *region* Central Asia Hellenistic world 40–41 (1)
Drapsaca Central Asia (Afghanistan) Hellenistic world 40–41 (1)
Drau *var.* Drava; *Eng.* Drave, *Hung.* Dráva *river* Southeast Europe WWI 207 (5), (6) *see also* Drava
Drava *var.* Drau; *Eng.* Drave, *Hung.* Dráva *river* Southeast Europe post-war economy 215 (3) *see also* Drau
Dráva, Drave *see* Drau, Drava
Dravida *region/state* South Asia early religions 48 (2) first empires 241 (5) world religions 242 (2)
Drenthe *province* Low Countries Reformation 195 (5)
Drepanum *see* Trapani
Dresden Central Europe (Germany) early modern states 193 (4) economy 205 (4) empire and revolution 199 (3) post-war politics 212 (1) Reformation 196 (1) WWII 211 (4)
Dresden *battle* Central Europe (Germany) Napoleon 200–201 (1)
Drina *river* Southeast Europe exploration 257 (2) post-war economy 215 (3) WWI 207 (6)
Drontheim *see* Trondheim
Druk-yul *see* Bhutan
Dry Creek *archaeological site* North America the world in 10,000 BCE 14–15
Duacum *see* Douai
Duala *see* Douala
Dubai *Ar.* Dubayy Southwest Asia (United Arab Emirates) economy 234 (1)
Dubayy *see* Dubai
Dublin British Isles (Ireland) biological diffusion 72–73 (1) economy 190 (1), 205 (4) empire and revolution 202 (1) inter-war 209 (3) medieval states 185 (3), 186 (2), 187 (4), 188 (2) medieval voyages 60–61 (1) Napoleon 200–201 (1), 201 (2) post-war politics 212 (3) Reformation 194 (2) WWII 211 (2)
Dubrae *var.* Dubris; *mod.* Dover *archaeological site* British Isles (United Kingdom) ancient Rome 180–181 (1) *see also* Dover
Dubris *see* Dover, Dubrae
Dubrovnik *It.* Ragusa Southeast Europe (Croatia) post-war economy 215 (3) *see also* Ragusa
Ducie Island *island* Pacific Ocean exploration 278 (1)
Duero *Port.* Douro *river* Iberian Peninsula crusades 186 (1) early Islam 56–57 (1) exploration 172 (1) Franks 184 (2) inter-war 209 (4) Islam 192 (3) Napoleon 200–201 (1) prehistoric culture 17 (3) *see also* Douro
Duff Islands *island group* Pacific Ocean exploration 278 (1)
Dufile East Africa (Uganda) exploration 157 (4)
Duinekerke *see* Dunkirk
Duji *var.* Tuchi *province* East Asia medieval states 262–263 (1)
Dukang East Asia (China) first cities 259 (5)
Duke of York Island *island* Pacific Ocean medieval voyages 60 (2)
Duke of York Islands *island group* Pacific Ocean early cultures 280–281 (3)
Dulkadir *var.* Dhualdadr *state* Southwest Asia the world in 1400 70–71 the world in 1500 74–75
Dumbarton British Isles (United Kingdom) medieval states 186 (2)
Dumyât *see* Damietta
Duna *see* Danube
Düna *see* Western Dvina
Dünaburg Eastern Europe (Latvia) early modern states 195 (3) medieval states 189 (3)
Dunaj *see* Danube, Vienna
Dunărea, Dunav *see* Danube
Dundee British Isles (United Kingdom) economy 204 (1)
Dunedin *settlement/whaling station* New Zealand colonization 283 (4), (5)
Dunholme *see* Durham
Dunhuang *settlement* East Asia (China) ancient trade 44–45 (1) exploration 256 (1), 257 (3) first states 260 (1), 261 (3) medieval states 261 (6), 262–263 (1), 263 (6) world religions 49 (3), (4)
Dunhuang *province* East Asia first states 260 (1)
Dunkerque *see* Dunkirk
Dunkirk *prev.* Dunquerque; *Flem.* Duinekerke, *Fr.* Dunkerque, France Reformation 195 (5) WWI 206 (3)
Dún Pádraig *see* Downpatrick
Dunquerque *see* Dunkirk
Dunqul Egypt ancient Egypt 159 (4)
Dunqulah *see* Dongola
Du Page County *region* North America
Dura Europos *settlement* Southwest Asia (Iraq) ancient Persia 225 (6) ancient Rome 180–181 (1), 224 (2), 225 (5) early trade 225 (3) Hellenistic world 41 (2) world religions 226 (1)
Durango Central America (Mexico) colonization 125 (4) Mexican Revolution 133 (3)
Durango *state* Central America Mexican Revolution 133 (3) the growth of the US 129 (2)
Durazzo *anc.* Dyrrachium; *mod.* Durrës, Dursi; *SCr.* Drač, *Turk.* Draç Southeast Europe (Albania) crusades 64–65 (2) early modern states 193 (4) medieval states 185 (3), 187 (5), 188 (1), 189 (4) Ottomans 230 (1) WWI 207 (6) *see also* Dyrrachium
Durban *var.* Port Natal Southern Africa (South Africa) colonization 166 (2), 167 (4) economy 168 (2) European imperialism 96 (2)
Durham *prev.* Dunholme British Isles (United Kingdom) medieval states 186 (2)
Dürnkrut *battle* Central Europe (Austria) medieval states 189 (4)
Durnovaria *see* Dorchester
Durocortorum France ancient Rome 180–181 (1), 181 (4)
Durostorum *var.* Silistria; *mod.* Silistra, *legion headquarters* Southeast Europe (Bulgaria) ancient Rome 180–181 (1) *see also* Silistria
Durovernum *see* Canterbury
Durrës *see* Durazzo
Durrës *see* Dyrrachium
Dursi *see* Durazzo
Dushanbe *var.* Dyushambe; *prev.* Stalinabad, *Taj.* Stalinobod Central Asia (Tajikistan) Soviet Union 214–215 (4)
Dusky Sound *sealing station* New Zealand colonization 283 (4)
Düsseldorf Central Europe (Germany) WWI 206 (2), (3) WWII 211 (4)
Dust Bowl *drought* North America US economy 134 (3)
Dutch Brazil *colonial possession* South America colonization 149 (4)
Dutch East Indies *mod.* Indonesia; *prev.* Netherlands East Indies *colonial possession* Maritime Southeast Asia colonialism 269 (4) colonization 284–285 (1) European imperialism 97 (3), (4) exploration 279 (3) empire and revolution 88–89 (2) global immigration 100 (1) the growth of the US 133 (4) WWII 104 (1), 251 (3), 272 (1), 273 (2) *see also* Indonesia
Dutch Guiana *var.* Netherlands Guiana; *mod.* Surinam, Suriname *colonial possession/state* South America Cold War 109 (1) WWII 104 (1) *see also* Surinam
Dutch Harbor *military base* North America (USA) WWII 104 (2), 272 (1), 273 (2)
Dutch Netherlands *rebellion* Low Countries empire and revolution 88–89 (2)
Dutch New Guinea *colonial possession/state* New Guinea Cold War 109 (1) European imperialism 97 (3)
Dutch Republic *see* Batavian Republic, Netherlands, United Provinces
Dutch South Africa *colonial possession* Southern Africa slave trade 165 (4) trade 164 (1)
Dutch West Indies *see* Netherlands Antilles
Dvaraka South Asia (India) world religions 242 (2)
Dvarasamudra South Asia (India) early medieval states 244 (2), 244–245 (3)
Dvaravati South Asia (India) ancient India 242 (1) early religions 48 (2)
Dvaravati *region/state* South Asia ancient India 241 (6) early medieval states 245 (5) world religions 243 (5), 49 (4)
Dvin *Christian archbishopric* Southwest Asia (Armenia) world religions 48 (1)
Dvina *river* Eastern Europe early modern states 197 (3) WWI 207 (4)
Dvinsk Eastern Europe (Latvia) WWI 207 (4)
Dvinsk *see* Dünaburg
Dwarka South Asia (India) early medieval states 244–245 (3) world religions 243 (4)
Dyfed *region* British Isles medieval states 183 (3)
Dyrrhachium *mod.* Durrës; *It.* Durazzo, *SCr.* Drač, *Turk.* Draç Southeast Europe (Albania) ancient Rome 179 (5), 180–181 (1) *see also* Durazzo
Dyushambe *see* Dushanbe
Dza Chu *see* Mekong
Dzhruchula *archaeological site* Eastern Europe (Russian Federation) first humans 13 (2)
Dzibilchaltún Central America (Mexico) first civilizations 121 (2)
Dzungaria *region* Central Asia ancient trade 44–45 (1) medieval states 262–263 (1)
Dzungars *people/rebellion* Central Asia early modern states 268 (1) empire and revolution 268 (2)
Dzungars, Khanate of the *state* East Asia
Dzvina *see* Western Dvina

E

Eagle Pass North America (USA) Mexican Revolution 133 (3)
Eagle Rock North America (USA) US economy 135 (4)
Eanna *building* Southwest Asia (Iraq) first cities 220 (3)
Early Kalachuris *dynasty* South Asia early medieval states 244 (2)
Early Man Shelter Australia exploration 280 (1)
Early Mississippian Culture *people* North America the world in 1000 58–59
East Anglia *state* British Isles medieval states 183 (3)
East Antarctica *see* Greater Antarctica
East Asia *region* East Asia biological diffusion 73 (2)
East Bengal and Assam *region* South Asia decolonization 250 (2)
East Berlin Central Europe (Germany) post-war politics 212 (2)
East Cape *headland* Australia colonization 283 (4)
East China Sea *Chin.* Dong Hai *sea* East Asia ancient trade 44–45 (1) biological diffusion 72–73 (1) decolonization 251 (4) early agriculture 20–21 (2), 258 (1), (2) early modern states 266 (1) economy 274 (1) first cities 259 (3), (4), (5) first states 260 (1) Islam 275 (4) medieval states 262–263 (1), 263 (6) Mongols 68 (2), 68–69 (1) post-war politics 271 (7) world religions 49 (3) WWII 272 (1), 273 (2)
Easter Island *var.* Isla de Pascua, Rapa Nui *island* Pacific Ocean colonization 284–285 (1) decolonization 285 (3) environmentalism 285 (3) exploration 278 (1), 279 (3) *see also* Rapa Nui
Eastern Chalukyas *dynasty* South Asia the world in 1000 58–59
Eastern Desert *var.* Aş Şaḩrā' ash Sharqīyah; *Eng.* Arabian Desert *desert* Egypt ancient Egypt 159 (5) *see also* Arabian Desert
Eastern Europe *region* Eastern Europe US economy 138 (2)
Eastern Gangas *dynasty* South Asia early medieval states 244 (2), 244–245 (3) Mongols 68–69 (1)
Eastern Ghats *mountain range* South Asia early medieval states 244 (1), 244–245 (3) economy 249 (4) first empires 241 (4) first religions 36 (2) Mughal Empire 246 (1) colonialism 247 (3), 248 (1)
Eastern Jin *state* East Asia first states 261 (3)
Eastern March *region* Eastern Europe Franks 184 (2)
Eastern Pomerania *region* Central Europe empire and revolution 199 (3)
Eastern Rumelia *region* Southeast Europe Ottomans 202 (4), 232–233 (1)
Eastern Sierra Madre *see* Sierra Madre Oriental
Eastern Solomons *battle* Pacific Ocean (Solomon Islands) WWII 273 (2)
Eastern States *state* South Asia colonialism 248 (2)
Eastern Thrace *region* Southwest Asia 20th-century politics 233 (3)
Eastern Turkestan *state* East Asia medieval states 262–263 (1)
Eastern Woodland Culture *people* North America the world in 500 CE 50–51 the world in 750 CE 54–55
East Fjords *fjords Atlantic Ocean* (Iceland) exploration 172 (2)
East Florida *colonial possession* North America empire and revolution 127 (3)
East Friesland *see* East Frisia
East Frisia *var.* East Friesland *region* Central Europe empire and revolution 199 (3)
East Germany *state* Central Europe Cold War 109 (1) post-war economy 213 (5) post-war politics 212 (3) Soviet Union 213 (4)
East Greenland Inuit *people* North America cultural groups 123 (3)
East Indies *island group* Maritime Southeast Asia ancient trade 44–45 (1) global knowledge 76–77 (1) medieval voyages 61 (3)
East Java Kingdom *state* Maritime Southeast Asia the world in 1000 58–59
East London *prev.* Emonti; *Afr.* Oos-Londen, Port Rex Southern Africa (South Africa) economy 168 (2) European imperialism 96 (2)
Eastmain North America (Canada) colonization 126 (1)
East Pakistan *mod.* Bangladesh *state* South Asia Cold War 109 (1) decolonization 251 (4) *see also* Bangladesh
East Prussia *region* Central Europe empire and revolution 198 (2), 199 (3), 202 (2) inter-war 209 (3), (5) Soviet Union 213 (4) WWI 207 (4), 208 (1) WWII 210 (1)
East River *river* North America the growth of the US 132 (2)
East Roman Empire *var.* Byzantine Empire *state* Southeast Europe/Southwest Asia ancient Rome 182 (1) early cultures 160 (1), 161 (5) Franks 183 (6) medieval states 182 (2), 183 (4) *see also* Byzantine Empire
East Siberian Sea *sea* Arctic Ocean exploration 257 (2), 286 (1), 287 (2)
East Timor *region* Maritime Southeast Asia decolonization 251 (4)
East Ukraine *region* Eastern Europe empire and revolution 198 (2)
Ebbou *archaeological site* France prehistoric culture 17 (3)
Eberbach *major cistercian house* Central Europe medieval states 187 (3)
Ebla Southwest Asia (Syria) early systems 223 (3) first civilizations 221 (4), 24 (2)
Eblana *see* Dublin
Ebora *see* Évora
Eboracum *see* Eburacum, York
Ebrach *major cistercian house* Central Europe medieval states 187 (3)
Ebro *Lat.* Iberus *river* Iberian Peninsula ancient Rome 180–181 (1) crusades 186 (1) early cultures 161 (2) early Islam 56–57 (1) exploration 172 (1) first civilizations 177 (1) Franks 184 (2) inter-war 209 (4) Islam 192 (3) medieval states 182 (2) Napoleon 200–201 (1) prehistoric culture 17 (3) *see also* Iberus
Eburacum *var.* Eboracum; *mod.* York *legion headquarters/mithraic site/settlement* British Isles (United Kingdom) ancient Rome 180–181 (1), 181 (4) world religions 48 (1) *see also* York
Ebusus *see* Ibiza
Ecab *state* Central America Aztecs 124 (1)
Ecatepe Central America (Mexico) Aztecs 124 (2)
Ecbatana *mod.* Hamadan Southwest Asia (Iran) ancient Persia 223 (4), 225 (6) ancient Rome 224 (2), 225 (5) ancient trade 44–45 (1) early trade 225 (3) exploration 218 (1) first civilizations 222 (2) Hellenistic world 224 (1) world religions 226 (1) *see also* Hamadan
Echunga *goldfield* Australia colonization 282 (2)
Eckmühl Central Europe (Germany) Napoleon 200–201 (1)
Ecuador *state* South America economy 153 (3) empire and revolution 150 (2), 151 (3) environment 153 (4) imperial global economy 92 (1) politics 152 (1) the growth of the US 133 (4) the modern world 112 (1), 113 (4) US superpower 138 (1) WWII 105 (3) Cold War 109 (1)
Edendale North America (USA) US economy 135 (4)
Edessa *mod.* Şanliurfa, Urfa *Christian archbishopric/settlement* Southwest Asia (Turkey) ancient Rome 224 (2), 225 (5) crusades 228 (2), 65 (3) Hellenistic world 41 (2) Islam 227 (4) world religions 226 (1)ancient Persia 225 (6) crusades 64–65 (2)
Edessa, County of *state* Southwest Asia Crusades 65 (3)
Edfu *var.* Idfu Egypt ancient Egypt 159 (3) first cities 28–29 (1) first civilizations 24 (2)
Edinburgh British Isles (United Kingdom) biological diffusion 72–73 (1) economy 190 (1), 205 (4) empire and revolution 202 (1) medieval states 186 (2), 187 (4), 188 (1) Napoleon 200–201 (1), 201 (2) Reformation 194 (2)
Edirne Greece Ottomans 202 (4)
Edmonton North America (Canada) the growth of the US 129 (2), 132 (1) US economy 136 (2) US superpower 138 (1)
Edo *mod.* Tokyo, Tōkyō (Japan) early modern states 267 (4), 268 (1) economy 270 (1) trade 267 (3) *see also* Tokyo
Edom *state* Southwest Asia first civilizations 222 (1)
Edward, Lake *var.* Albert Edward Nyanza, Edward Nyanza, Lac Idi Amin, Lake Rutanzige *lake* East Africa exploration 157 (4) first humans 12 (1)
Edward Nyanza *see* Edward, Lake
Edward VII Land *physical region* Antarctica Antarctic Exploration 287 (3)
Edzna Central America (Mexico) first civilizations 123 (2)
Eems *see* Ems
Eesti *see* Estonia
Éfaté *settlement/island* Pacific Ocean (Vanuatu) early cultures 280–281 (3) environmentalism 285 (2) medieval voyages 60 (2)

F

G

H

I

INDEX-GAZETTEER: **Mississippi – Nassau**

Mississippi *state* North America imperial global economy 93 (5) the growth of the US 129 (1) US Civil War 130 (2), (3), (4), (5), 131 (6), (7) US economy 134 (2), 139 (3) US society 137 (6) US superpower 139 (5)
Mississippi *river* North America colonization 125 (4), 126 (1) cultural groups 122 (5) early agriculture 120 (1), 20–21 (2) empire and revolution 127 (3), 88 (1) European expansion 84–85 (1) exploration 118 (1), 119 (2), (3) first civilizations 121 (4) first religions 36 (1) imperial global economy 92 (1) prehistoric culture 16 (1) the growth of the US 129 (2), 132 (1) US Civil War 130 (5), 131 (6), (7)
Mississippian Cultures *people* North America the world in 1200 62–63 the world in 1300 66–67 the world in 1400 70–71 the world in 1500 74–75
Missoula, Lake *lake* North America the world in 10,000 BCE 14–15
Missouri *state* North America the growth of the US 129 (1) US Civil War 130 (2), (3), (4), (5), 131 (6), (7) US economy 134 (2)
Missouri *people* North America colonization 126 (1)
Missouri *river* North America colonization 126 (1) cultural groups 122 (5) early agriculture 120 (1), 20–21 (2) exploration 118 (1), 119 (2), (3) first civilizations 121 (4) first religions 36 (1) the growth of the US 129 (2) US Civil War 130 (5)
Mistra Greece medieval states 187 (5), 189 (4)
Miswar Southwest Asia (Yemen) early trade 225 (3)
Mitanni, Kingdom of *state* Southwest Asia first civilizations 221 (5)
Mitau *Latv.* Jelgava; *Rus.* Mitava Eastern Europe (Latvia) early modern states 195 (3) *see also* Mitava
Mitava *Latv.* Jelgava; *Rus.* Mitau Eastern Europe (Latvia) WWI 207 (4) *see also* Mitau
Mithila South Asia (India) ancient India 242 (1) world religions 242 (3)
Mithraeum *building* Southwest Asia (Iraq) first cities 220 (3)
Mitla Central America (Mexico) first civilizations 122 (1)
Mitrovica *var.* Kosovska Mitrovica Southeast Europe (Yugoslavia) post-war economy 215 (3)
Mits'iwa *see* Massawa
Mitte Central Europe (Germany) post-war politics 212 (2)
Mitte *region* Eastern Europe WWII 211 (2)
Mitterberg *mine* Central Europe Bronze Age 175 (3)
Mittimatalik North America (Canada) cultural groups 123 (3)
Mitylene
Miwa *mountain* Japan medieval states 265 (3)
Mixcoac Central America (Mexico) Aztecs 124 (2), (3)
Mixco Viejo Central America (Guatemala) Aztecs 124 (1)
Mixincan Central America (Mexico) Aztecs 124 (3)
Mixquic Central America (Mexico) Aztecs 124 (2)
Mixtlan Central America (Mexico) Aztecs 124 (1)
Miyagi *prefecture* Japan economy 270 (1)
Miyanouchi Japan early modern states 265 (5)
Miyazaki *prefecture* Japan economy 270 (1)
Mizda North Africa (Libya) exploration 157 (4)
Mizoram *region* South Asia post-war politics 252 (1), (3), 253 (4)
Mizquic Central America (Mexico) colonization 125 (5)
Mizu-shima *battle* Japan early modern states 265 (5)
Mladec *archaeological site* Central Europe (Czech Republic) the world in 10,000 BCE 14–15
Mlozi *state* East Africa colonization 167 (4)
Mo *people* East Asia first cities 259 (4)
Moab *state* Southwest Asia first civilizations 222 (1)
Mobile North America (USA) Cold War 108 (2) European expansion 84–85 (1) the growth of the US 129 (2) US Civil War 131 (7) US society 137 (6)
Mobile *battle* North America (USA) US Civil War 131 (7)
Mobile *people* Central America colonization 125 (4)
Mobutu Sese Seko, Lac *see* Albert, Lake
Moçambique *see* Mozambique, Portuguese East Africa
Moçâmedes *see* Mossamedes, Namibe
Moccassin Bluff North America (USA) cultural groups 122 (5)
Moche South America (Peru) early cultures 145 (4)
Moche *region/state* South America early cultures 145 (4)
Moche *river* South America early cultures 145 (3), (4)
Moche/Chan Chan *state* South America the world in 1000 58–59
Moctezuma *river* Central America first civilizations 121 (2)
Modder River *Afr.* Modderrivier *battle* Southern Africa (South Africa) European imperialism 96 (2)
Modderrivier *see* Modder River
Modena *anc.* Mutina Italy economy 190 (1) Franks 184 (2) medieval states 188 (1) *see also* Mutina
Modena *state* Italy empire and revolution 202 (1), (3) Reformation 194 (2), 196 (1), (2)
Modon Greece economy 190 (1) medieval states 187 (5)
Moeraki *whaling station* New Zealand colonization 283 (4)
Moero, Lac *see* Mweru, Lake
Moers *see* Mörs
Moesia *province/region* Southeast Europe ancient Rome 180–181 (1), 181 (4) ancient trade 44 (2) world religions 48 (1)
Moesia Inferior *province* Southeast Europe ancient Rome 180–181 (1)
Moesia Superior *province* Southeast Europe ancient Rome 180–181 (1)
Mogadishu early *Chin.* Mo-ku-ta-shu, *Som.* Muqdisho East Africa (Somalia) biological diffusion 72–73 (1) colonization 167 (4) economy 163 (2) European expansion 80–81 (1) exploration 156 (3) global immigration 100 (1) Islam 163 (1) medieval voyages 61 (3) Mongols 68 (2) trade 165 (3), 230 (2), 267 (3)
Mogador *mod.* Essaouira North Africa (Morocco) early cultures 160 (1) exploration 157 (4)
Mogilev Eastern Europe (Belorussia) economy 190 (1) Soviet Union 208 (2) WWI 207 (4) WWII 210 (1), 211 (4)
Mogollon *archaeological site* North America (USA) cultural groups 123 (4)
Mogollon Culture *region/state* North America/Central America cultural groups 123 (4)
Mogontiacum *mod.* Mainz *settlement* Central Europe (Germany) ancient Rome 180–181 (1), 181 (4) great migrations 52–53 (1) *see also* Mainz
Mogul Empire *see* Mughal Empire
Mohács Central Europe (Hungary) Ottomans 231 (3)
Mohács *battle* Southeast Europe Ottomans 195 (4)
Mohammerah *see* Khorramshahr
Mohelnice Central Europe (Czech Republic) early agriculture 174 (1)
Mohenjo-Daro *archaeological site/settlement* South Asia (Pakistan) early systems 223 (3) first cities 240 (2) first civilizations 24 (2), 25 (3)
Mohican *see* Mahican
Mojave *people* North America colonization 125 (4), 126 (1)
Mojave Desert *desert* North America cultural groups 123 (4)
Moji Japan economy 270 (1)
Mojos *people* South America colonization 148 (2) exploration 143 (2)
Mokpo *Jap.* Moppo East Asia (South Korea) Cold War 109 (4) early modern states 267 (4) Russo-Japanese War 270 (4)
Moktama *see* Martaban
Mo-ku-ta-shu *see* Mogadishu
Moldavia *var.* Moldova *region/state* Southeast Europe early modern states 193 (4) empire and revolution 198 (2), 202 (1) medieval states 189 (3), (4) Napoleon 200–201 (1) Ottomans 195 (4), 231 (3) post-war economy 214 (1), (2) Reformation 194 (2) Soviet Union 213 (4) the modern world 112 (2) WWI 207 (4)
Moldova *see* Moldavia
Mollendo South America (Peru) empire and revolution 151 (3)
Mologa *river* Eastern Europe Mongols 68–69 (1)
Molokai *leper colony* Pacific Ocean environmentalism 285 (2)
Molopo *river* Southern Africa European imperialism 96 (2)
Molotov Eastern Europe (Russian Federation) Soviet Union 213 (4)
Moluccas *prev.* Spice Islands; *Dut.* Molukken, *Eng.* Moluccas *island group* Maritime Southeast Asia ancient trade 44–45 (1) biological diffusion 72–73 (1) Bronze Age 240 (3) European expansion 80–81 (1), 81 (3) exploration 239 (1), (2) Islam 243 (6) trade 230 (2), 267 (3)
Molucca Sea *Ind.* Laut Maluku *sea* Maritime Southeast Asia Bronze Age 240 (3) early medieval states 245 (6) Islam 243 (6)
Molukken *see* Moluccas
Mombasa East Africa (Kenya) colonization 167 (4) economy 163 (2) European expansion 81 (3), 84–85 (1) European imperialism 96 (1) exploration 156 (3), 157 (4), (5) global immigration 100 (1) Islam 163 (1) Mongols 68 (2) slave trade 165 (4) trade 164 (1), 230 (2), 267 (3)
Mon *state* Mainland Southeast Asia world religions 49 (4)
Monacan *people* North America colonization 125 (4), 126 (1)
Monaco *var.* Monaco-Ville; *anc.* Monoecus *state* France empire and revolution 202 (1), (3) the modern world 112 (2), 113 (4)
Monaco *see* Munich
Monaco-Ville *see* Monaco
Mon and Malay States *state* Mainland Southeast Asia the world in 250 CE 46–47 the world in 500 CE 50–51
Monastir *var.* Bitolj; *mod.* Bitola *fort/settlement* Southeast Europe (FYR Macedonia) early Islam 56–57 (1) WWI 207 (6) *see also* Bitola, Bitolj
Moncastro Eastern Europe (Ukraine) economy 190 (1) medieval states 189 (4)
Mondidier France WWI 206 (2), (3)
Mondovi *battle* Italy Napoleon 200–201 (1)
Monemvasia Greece medieval states 187 (5) Ottomans 230 (1), 231 (3)
Monfalcone Italy WWI 207 (5)
Monghyr *var.* Munger South Asia (India) economy 249 (4)
Mongol Empire *state* East Asia medieval states 263 (5)
Mongolia *prev.* Outer Mongolia; *Mong.* Mongol Uls *region/state* East Asia biological diffusion 72–73 (1) Chinese revolution 271 (5) colonialism 269 (4) early modern states 266 (2) economy 274 (1) exploration 257 (3) historical geography 275 (5) Islam 275 (4) medieval states 261 (6) post-war economy 275 (3) post-war politics 271 (7), 274 (2) Soviet Union 208 (2), 213 (4) the modern world 113 (3), (4) world religions 49 (4) WWII 104 (1), (2), 272 (1), 273 (2) Cold War 109 (1) Communism 271 (8) *see also* Oirats, Khanate of the, Outer Mongolia
Mongolia, Plateau of *plateau* East Asia Mongols 68–69 (1)
Mongols *people* East Asia/Siberia early modern states 266 (1) Mongols 68–69 (1) trade 267 (3)
Mongol Uls *see* Mongolia, Oirats, Khanate of the, Outer Mongolia
Monkchester *see* Newcastle-upon-Tyne
Mon-Khmer Peoples *people* Mainland Southeast Asia ancient trade 44–45 (1)
Monkwearmouth *religious building* British Isles (United Kingdom) medieval states 183 (3)
Monmouth North America (USA) empire and revolution 127 (3)
Monmouth Court House *battle* North America (USA) empire and revolution 127 (3)
Monoecus *see* Monaco
Monopoli Italy economy 190 (1)
Monrovia West Africa (Liberia) economy 168 (2) US superpower 138 (1)
Mons Low Countries (Belgium) WWI 206 (2), (3)
Montagnais *people* North America colonization 126 (1) cultural groups 123 (3)
Montana *state* North America the growth of the US 129 (1) US economy 134 (2)
Montauban France early modern states 197 (5) Reformation 194 (2)
Mont-Dauphin France early modern states 197 (5)
Monte Alban *region* Central America first civilizations 122 (1)
Monte Albán Central America (Mexico) Aztecs 124 (1) first civilizations 121 (2), 122 (1) first religions 36 (1)
Monte Alegre *archaeological site* South America (Brazil) early cultures 144 (1)
Monte Alto Central America (Mexico) first civilizations 123 (2)
Monte Bello Islands *nuclear test* Australia environmentalism 285 (2)
Monte Cassino Italy Franks 184 (2) medieval states 183 (4) WWII 211 (4)
Montecristi West Indies (Dominican Republic) European expansion 85 (2)
Monteleone di Calabria *see* Hipponium
Montenegro *SCr.* Crna Gora *state/vassal state* Southeast Europe early modern states 193 (4) economy 205 (4) Napoleon 200–201 (1), 201 (2) Ottomans 195 (4), 232–233 (1) Reformation 194 (2) WWI 207 (6) WWII 211 (2), (4) early 20th century 206 (1)
Montenegro-Serbia *region* Southeast Europe post-war economy 215 (3)
Montenotte *battle* Italy Napoleon 200–201 (1)
Montereau *battle* France Napoleon 200–201 (1)
Monterey North America (USA) the growth of the US 129 (2)
Monterey *see* Monterrey
Monterrey *var.* Monterey Central America (Mexico) exploration 119 (2), (3) Mexican Revolution 133 (3) the growth of the US 129 (2) US economy 136 (2) Cold War 108 (2)
Montespan *archaeological site* France prehistoric culture 17 (3)
Monte Verde *archaeological site/settlement* South America (Chile) early cultures 144 (1)
Montevideo South America (Uruguay) colonization 148 (2) empire and revolution 150 (1), 151 (3) environment 153 (4) exploration 143 (3) global immigration 100 (1) imperial global economy 92 (1) politics 152 (1)
Montezuma Castle *archaeological site* North America (USA) cultural groups 123 (4)
Montferrat *state* Italy Reformation 196 (1)
Montgaudier *archaeological site* France prehistoric culture 17 (3)
Montgomery British Isles (United Kingdom) medieval states 188 (2)
Montgomery North America (USA) the growth of the US 129 (2), 132 (1) US Civil War 131 (7) US society 137 (6)
Montmaurin *archaeological site* France first humans 13 (2)
Montmirail France WWI 206 (2), (3) *battle* 200–201 (1)
Montpelier North America (USA) the growth of the US 129 (2)
Montpellier *settlement/university* France early modern states 197 (5) economy 190 (1) empire and revolution 199 (4) medieval states 187 (3), 192 (1)
Montreal *var.* Hochelaga; *Fr.* Montréal North America (Canada) colonization 126 (1) empire and revolution 127 (2), (3), 88 (1) European expansion 84–85 (1) exploration 119 (2), (3) imperial global economy 92 (1) the growth of the US 129 (2), 132 (1) US economy 136 (2) *see also* Hochelaga
Montréal *fort* Southwest Asia (Jordan) crusades 65 (3)
Montreuil France WWI 206 (2)
Montserrat *var.* Emerald Isle *colonial possession* West Indies the world in 1975 106–107 the modern world 110–111
Monza Italy medieval states 183 (4)
Mook *battle* Low Countries (Netherlands) Reformation 195 (5)
Mooloya Estate *rebellion* South Asia (Sri Lanka) decolonization 250 (1)
Moose Factory North America (Canada) colonization 126 (1)
Mootwingee *archaeological site* Australia prehistoric culture 17 (5)
Moppo *see* Mokpo
Moquegua South America (Peru) politics 151 (4)
Moradabad South Asia (India) economy 249 (4)
Morat *Ger.* Murten *battle* Central Europe (Switzerland) early modern states 193 (5)
Morava *var.* Glavn'a Morava, March, Velika Morava; *Ger.* Grosse Moravavar *river* Central Europe WWI 207 (6) *see also* Velika Morava
Moravia *region/state* Central Europe early modern states 193 (4) empire and revolution 199 (3) medieval states 189 (4) Napoleon 200–201 (1) Ottomans 197 (4)
Moravians *people* Central Europe Franks 184 (2)
Mordovia *region* Eastern Europe Soviet Union 214–215 (4)
Morea *vassal state* Greece Ottomans 230 (1)
Morelos *state* Central America Mexican Revolution 133 (3)
Moreruela *major cistercian house* Iberian Peninsula medieval states 187 (3)
Moreton Bay *bay* Australia exploration 279 (2)
Moreton Bay *penal centre* Australia colonization 282 (1) environmentalism 285 (2)
Morgan Hill North America (USA)
Morgarten *battle* Central Europe (Switzerland) early modern states 193 (5)
Mori *region* Japan early modern states 267 (4)
Morimond *major cistercian house* France medieval states 187 (3)
Morioka Japan economy 270 (1)
Mormon Trail *wagon train route* North America (USA) the growth of the US 129 (2)
Morocco *Ar.* Al Mamlakah, *Fr.* Maroc, *Sp.* Marruecos *region/state* North Africa colonization 167 (4) decolonization 168 (1)early Islam 57 (2) economy 168 (2), (3) European expansion 84–85 (1) European imperialism 96 (1), 97 (4) global immigration 101 (2) Islam 235 (4) Napoleon 200–201 (1) Ottomans 231 (3) slave trade 165 (4) the modern world 112 (1), 113 (3), (4) trade 164 (2), 167 (1) WWII 104 (1), 211 (4) early 20th century 206 (1) Cold War 109 (1)
Mörs *var.* Moers Central Europe (Germany) Reformation 195 (5)
Mörs *region* Central Europe empire and revolution 199 (3)
Moscow *Rus.* Moskva Eastern Europe (Russian Federation) biological diffusion 72–73 (1) colonialism 269 (3) economy 190 (1), 205 (4) empire and revolution 202 (1) exploration 257 (2), 286 (1) global immigration 100 (1), 101 (2) imperial global economy 92 (1) Mongols 68 (2), 68–69 (1) Napoleon 200–201 (1) post-war politics 212 (3) Reformation 196 (2) Soviet Union 208 (2), 213 (4) Timur 229 (4) WWII 104 (2), 210 (1), 211 (2), (3), (4) Cold War 108 (3)
Mosega *battle* Southern Africa (South Africa) colonization 166 (2)
Mosel *Fr.* Moselle *river* France Reformation 195 (5) *see also* Moselle
Moselle *Ger.* Mosel *river* France empire and revolution 199 (4), 202 (2) WWI 206 (2), (3) *see also* Mosel
Moskva *see* Moscow
Mosquito Coast *colonial possession/state* Central America colonization 126 (1) empire and revolution 88 (1)
Mosquito Protectorate *state* Central America the world in 1850 90–91
Mossamedes *var.* Namibe; *mod.* Moçâmedes Southern Africa (Angola) exploration 157 (4) *see also* Namibe
Mossel Bay *bay* Southern Africa exploration 156 (3)
Mossi *state* West Africa Islam 163 (1) trade 163 (4), (6), (7), 164 (2)
Mostagedda Egypt ancient Egypt 159 (2)
Mostar Southeast Europe (Bosnia and Herzegovina) Napoleon 200–201 (1) Ottomans 230 (1) post-war economy 215 (3)
Mosul *Ar.* Al Mawşil Southwest Asia (Iraq) 20th-century politics 233 (3), 235 (5) crusades 228 (2) early Islam 56–57 (1), 57 (2), (3) economy 234 (1) exploration 219 (3) Islam 227 (5) Mongols 229 (3) Seljuks 228 (1) Timur 229 (4) WWI 233 (2)
Mosyllon East Africa (Somalia) early trade 225 (3)
Motagua *river* Central America first civilizations 123 (2)
Motecuzoma Central America (Mexico) Aztecs 124 (3)
Motuhora *whaling station* New Zealand colonization 283 (4)
Motul *var.* Motul de Felipe Carrillo Puerto Central America (Mexico) first civilizations 122 (1)
Motul de Felipe Carrillo Puerto *see* Motul
Motu Marotiri *island* Pacific Ocean early cultures 281 (4)
Motu Nui *island* Pacific Ocean early cultures 281 (4)
Motupalli South Asia (India) colonialism 247 (3)
Motya Italy ancient Rome 179 (3) early states 178 (2) first civilizations 177 (1)
Mouhoun *see* Black Volta
Mouila *archaeological site* Central Africa (Gabon) early cultures 160 (1)
Moukden *see* Mukden, Shenyang
Moulins France early modern states 197 (5)
Moulmein *var.* Maulmain, Mawlamyine Mainland Southeast Asia (Burma) WWII 251 (3)
Mound Bottom North America (USA) cultural groups 122 (5)
Mound Building Villages *region* North America the world in 500 BCE 34–35
Mound City *burial mound* North America (USA) first civilizations 121 (4)
Mounds State Park *burial mound* North America (USA) first civilizations 121 (4)
Moundville North America (USA) cultural groups 122 (5)
Moun Hou *see* Black Volta
Mount Acay South America (Argentina) Incas 147 (3)
Mountain *people* North America cultural groups 123 (3)
Mountain View North America (USA)
Mount Burr Australia the world in 5000 BCE 18–19
Mount Cameron West *archaeological site* Australia prehistoric culture 17 (5)
Mount Isa Australia colonization 282 (1), 283 (3)
Mount Lyell *goldfield* Australia colonization 282 (2)
Mount Magnet Australia colonization 282 (1)
Mount Newham Australia exploration 280 (1)
Mount Olympus *religious site* Greece first religions 36 (1), 37 (3)
Mount Royal North America (USA) cultural groups 122 (5)
Mourzouk *see* Murzuk
Moxeke *early ceremonial centre* South America (Peru) early cultures 144 (1), 145 (3)
Moyen-Congo *see* Congo
Mozambique *Port.* Moçambique Southern Africa (Mozambique) colonization 167 (4) European expansion 81 (3), 84–85 (1) exploration 156 (3) Islam 163 (1) slave trade 165 (4) trade 164 (1)
Mozambique *prev.* Portuguese East Africa, Moçambique *state* Southern Africa decolonization 168 (1) economy 168 (2), (3) European expansion 84–85 (1) European imperialism 96 (1), (2) the modern world 112 (1), 113 (3) trade 167 (1) Cold War 109 (1) *see also* Portuguese East Africa
Mozambique, Canal de *see* Mozambique Channel
Mozambique Channel *Fr.* Canal de Mozambique, *Mal.* Lakandranon' i Mozambika *sea waterway* Indian Ocean first humans 12 (1), 13 (2) slave trade 165 (4)
Mpangu *state* Central Africa economy 163 (2)
Mpondo *see* Pondo
Mrohaung *var.* Myohaung Mainland Southeast Asia (Burma) colonialism 248 (1) early medieval states 245 (6)
Msalala East Africa (Tanzania) exploration 157 (5)
Msiri *state* Central Africa colonization 167 (4)
Msiri *people* Central Africa trade 167 (1)
Msiris Southern Africa (Congo (Zaire)) exploration 157 (4)
Mtamvuna *var.* Orange River, Oranjerivier *river* Southern Africa colonization 166 (2) *see also* Orange River
Mtkvari *see* Kura
Mtskheta Southwest Asia (Georgia) world religions 48 (1)
Mubi West Africa (Nigeria) exploration 157 (4)
Muchiri South Asia (India) world religions 243 (4)
Mudgagiri South Asia (India) early medieval states 244 (2)
Muenchen *see* Munich
Muenster *see* Münster
Mughal Empire *var.* Mogul Empire *state* South Asia medieval Persia 231 (4)
Mughals *state* South Asia colonialism 248 (1)
Mugharet el-'Aliya *archaeological site* North Africa (Morocco) first humans 13 (2)
Mugi East Africa (Sundan) exploration 157 (5)
Muhammerah *see* Khorramshahr
Muhi *battle* Central Europe (Hungary) medieval states 189 (4)
Mühlberg Central Europe (Germany) Reformation 194 (2)
Mühlhausen *var.* Mühlhausen in Thüringen Central Europe (Germany) medieval states 189 (3)
Mühlhausen in Thüringen *see* Mühlhausen
Muju *region* East Asia medieval states 264 (2)
Mukalla *Ar.* Al Mukallā Southwest Asia (Yemen) 20th-century politics 233 (4)
Mukden *prev.* Fengtien; *Chin.* Shenyang, Shen-yang, *Eng.* Moukden East Asia (China) early modern states 266 (1) post-war politics 271 (7) Russo-Japanese War 270 (4) Sino-Japanese War 270 (3) Communism 271 (8) *see also* Shenyang
Mülhausen *see* Mulhouse
Mulhouse *Ger.* Mülhausen Central Europe (France) early modern states 193 (5)
Multan South Asia (Pakistan) biological diffusion 72–73 (1) colonialism 247 (3), 248 (1) decolonization 250 (1) early Islam 56–57 (1), 57 (2) early medieval states 244–245 (3) economy 249 (4) empire and revolution 249 (3) imperial global economy 93 (5) Mongols 68 (2), 68–69 (1) Mughal Empire 246 (1) world religions 243 (4), 49 (3)
Multan *region/state* South Asia early medieval states 244–245 (3)
Mumbai *see* Bombay
Mumhain *region* British Isles medieval states 188 (2)
München *see* Munich
Munda *region/state* South Asia first empires 241 (5) world religions 242 (2)
Mundigak *archaeological site/settlement* Central Asia (Afghanistan) first cities 240 (2) first civilizations 24 (2), 25 (3)
Mundus East Africa (Somalia) early cultures 161 (3), (5) early trade 225 (3)
Munger *see* Monghyr
Mu Nggava *see* Rennell
Munich *Ger.* München, Muenchen; *It.* Monaco Central Europe (Germany) early modern states 193 (4) economy 205 (4) empire and revolution 202 (1), (2) inter-war 209 (5) Napoleon 200–201 (1), 201 (2) post-war politics 212 (1), (3) Reformation 196 (1) WWII 210 (1), 211 (2), (3), (4)
Munster *region* British Isles medieval states 186 (2)
Münster *var.* Muenster, Münster in Westfalen *rebellion/settlement* Central Europe (Germany) early modern states 193 (4) Franks 184 (2) medieval states 189 (3) Reformation 194 (2)
Münster in Westfalen *see* Münster
Muqdisho *see* Mogadishu
Murchison River *river* Australia colonization 282 (1) exploration 279 (2) prehistoric culture 17 (5)
Murcia Iberian Peninsula (Spain) economy 190 (1) Islam 192 (3)
Murderer's Bay *bay* Australia exploration 278 (1)
Muret *battle* France crusades 186 (1)
Mureybat Southwest Asia (Turkey) early agriculture 220 (1)
Murfreesboro North America (USA) US Civil War 131 (6)
Mūrītānīyah *see* Mauritania
Murmansk Eastern Europe (Russian Federation) early modern states 197 (3) WWII 211 (4)
Muroran *bomb target* Japan WWII 273 (3)
Murray River *river* Australia colonization 282 (1), (2), 283 (3) exploration 279 (2) prehistoric culture 17 (5)
Murrumbidgee Australia exploration 279 (2)
Mursa Southeast Europe (Croatia) ancient Rome 180–181 (1)
Murshidabad South Asia (India) colonialism 248 (1) economy 249 (4) Mughal Empire 246 (1)
Murten *see* Morat
Murzuch *see* Murzuk
Murzuk *var.* Marzūq, Mourzoule; *Ar.* Murzuq, *It.* Murzuch North Africa (Libya) ancient trade 44–45 (1) colonization 167 (4) exploration 157 (4) Islam 163 (1)
Murzuq *see* Murzuk
Musang Cave Philippines the world in 5000 BCE 18–19
Musawwarat es Sufra East Africa (Sudan) early cultures 160 (1)
Musay'īd *see* Umm Saīd
Muscat *var.* Maskat, Mascat; *Ar.* Masqaţ Southwest Asia (Oman) biological diffusion 72–73 (1) early Islam 56–57 (1), 57 (2) economy 234 (1) European expansion 81 (3), 84–85 (1) exploration 219 (4) Islam 226 (2), 227 (4) medieval voyages 61 (3) Seljuks 228 (1) trade 230 (2) world religions 226 (1) 20th-century politics 233 (4)
Muscat and Oman *see* Oman
Muscoda Mounds *burial mound* North America (USA) first civilizations 121 (4)
Muscovy *region/state* Eastern Europe biological diffusion 72–73 (1)
Muskogean *see* Tallahassee
Mutapa *state* Southern Africa Islam 163 (1)
Mutina *mod.* Modena *mithraic site* Italy world religions 48 (1) *see also* Modena
Muttra *var.* Mathura, Mathuru South Asia (India) economy 249 (4) *see also* Mathura
Mu Us Shamo *see* Ordos Desert
Muza Southwest Asia (Yemen) ancient trade 44 (2) early cultures 161 (3), (4), (5) early trade 225 (3)
Muzaffarabad South Asia (Pakistan) post-war politics 252 (2)
Muziris South Asia (India) ancient trade 44–45 (1)
Muzumbo a Kalunga *state* Southern Africa trade 164 (2)
Mwanza East Africa (Tanzania) exploration 157 (5)
Myanmar *see* Burma
Mycale *battle* Southwest Asia (Turkey) ancient Persia 223 (4)
Mycenae Greece Bronze Age 175 (3) first cities 28–29 (1) first civilizations 175 (4)
Myitkyina Mainland Southeast Asia (Burma) WWII 272 (1), 273 (2)
Mylae Italy ancient Rome 179 (3)
Myohanug
Myongju *region* East Asia medieval states 264 (2)
Myos Hormus *var.* Myus Hormus Egypt ancient trade 44–45 (1) early cultures 161 (3), (5) early trade 225 (3)
Myra *Christian archbishopric/settlement* Southwest Asia (Turkey) ancient Rome 180–181 (1) world religions 48 (1)
Myrina Greece first civilizations 177 (1)
Mysia *region* Southwest Asia first religions 37 (3) Hellenistic world 40–41 (1)
Mysore South Asia (India) economy 249 (4) imperial global economy 93 (5)
Mysore *region/state* South Asia colonialism 248 (1), (2) post-war politics 253 (4)
Mytilene Greece ancient Greece 179 (4)
Mytilene *state* Greece ancient Greece 177 (2)
Myus Hormus *see* Myos Hormos
Mzimvubu *river* Southern Africa colonization 166 (2)

N

Nabataea *province/state* Southwest Asia early cultures 161 (3), (5)
Nabataeans *people* Southwest Asia ancient Rome 225 (4)
Nabesna *people* North America cultural groups 123 (3)
Nabta Egypt the world in 5000 BCE 18–19
Nabta Playa Egypt early agriculture 158 (1)
Nachi-san *mountain* Japan medieval states 265 (3)
Nadikagama South Asia (India) world religions 242 (3)
Nad-i-Ali Central Asia (Afghanistan) Hellenistic world 40–41 (1)
Nafplio *see* Nauplia
Naga ed-Der Egypt ancient Egypt 159 (2)
Naga Hills *mountain range* South Asia economy 249 (4)
Nagaland *region* South Asia post-war politics 252 (1), 253 (4)
Nagano *prefecture* Japan economy 270 (1)
Nagappattinam *var.* Negapatam *Buddhist centre* South Asia (India) world religions 49 (3) *see also* Negapatam
Nagara Sridharmaraj *see* Nakhon Si Thammarat
Nagarjunakonda *settlement* South Asia (India) exploration 256 (1) world religions 49 (3)
Nagasaki Japan biological diffusion 72–73 (1) WWII 273 (3) early modern states 267 (4), (5) economy 270 (1) European expansion 80–81 (1) trade 267 (3) WWII 272 (1), 273 (2)
Nagasaki *prefecture* Japan economy 270 (1)
Nagata Japan medieval states 265 (4)
Nagelwanze South Asia (India) colonialism 247 (3)
Nagidus Southwest Asia (Turkey) first civilizations 177 (1) Hellenistic world 40–41 (1)
Nagorno-Karabakh *region* Eastern Europe Soviet Union 214–215 (4)
Nagoya Japan early modern states 267 (4) economy 270 (1) Islam 275 (4) medieval states 262–263 (1) WWII 273 (3)
Nagpur South Asia (India) colonialism 248 (1) decolonization 250 (1) economy 249 (4) Marathas 246 (2) post-war economy 253 (5)
Nagur South Asia (India) world religions 243 (4)
Nagysalló *battle* Central Europe (Hungary) empire and revolution 88–89 (2)
Nagyszeben *mod.* Sibiu Southeast Europe (Romania) early modern states 193 (4)
Nahr *see* Diyala
Naimans *people* East Asia/Siberia Mongols 68–69 (1)
Na'in *see* Nayin
Nairobi East Africa (Kenya) colonization 167 (4) economy 168 (2)
Naishadha *region* South Asia world religions 242 (2)
Naissus *see* Niš, Nish
Najd *see* Nejd
Najima *see* Fukuoka
Najran Southwest Asia (Saudi Arabia) early cultures 161 (3), (4), (5) early Islam 56–57 (1) early trade 225 (3) Islam 226 (2) world religions 226 (1)
Nakambé *see* White Volta
Nakhichevan Southwest Asia (Azerbaijan) medieval Persia 231 (4) Ottomans 231 (3)
Nakhon Pathom *settlement/temple* Mainland Southeast Asia (Thailand) early medieval states 245 (5) world religions 243 (5)
Nakhon Ratchasima *var.* Khorat, Korat Mainland Southeast Asia (Thailand) colonialism 247 (4), 248 (1)
Nakhon Si Thammarat *var.* Nagara Sridharmaraj, Nakhon Sithamnaraj Mainland Southeast Asia (Thailand) colonialism 248 (2)
Nakhon Sithamnaraj *see* Nakhon Si Thammarat
Naknek North America (USA) cultural groups 123 (3)
Nakum Central America (Mexico) first civilizations 123 (2)
Nal *archaeological site* South Asia (Pakistan) first cities 240 (2)
Nalanda South Asia (India) ancient trade 44–45 (1) first religions 36 (2) world religions 242 (3)
Nama *people* Southern Africa trade 164 (1)
Namen *see* Namur
Namibe *Port.* Moçâmedes, Mossamedes Southern Africa (Angola) Cold War 109 (5) *see also* Mossamedes
Namibia *prev.* German Southwest Africa, Southwest Africa *state* Southern Africa decolonization 168 (1) economy 168 (2), (3) the modern world 112 (1), 113 (4) *see also* German Southwest Africa, Southwest Africa
Namiquipa Central America (Mexico) Mexican Revolution 133 (3)
Namnetes *see* Nantes
Nam Tun East Asia (China) the world in 5000 BCE 18–19
Namu *island* Pacific Ocean exploration 278 (1)
Namur *Dut.* Namen Low Countries (Belgium) early modern states 197 (5) WWI 206 (2), (3)
Namur *province* Low Countries Reformation 195 (5)
Nan *province* East Asia first states 260 (1)
Nanagunas *river* South Asia ancient trade 44 (2)
Nana Mode *archaeological site* Central Africa (Central African Republic) early cultures 160 (1)
Nanchang *var.* Nan-ch'ang, Nanch'ang-hsien *rebellion/settlement* East Asia (China) biological diffusion 72–73 (1) early modern states 266 (1), (2), 268 (1) economy 274 (1) post-war politics 271 (7)
Nanch'ang-hsien *see* Nanchang
Nanchao *see* Nanzhao, Yunnan
Nan-chao *see* Nanzhao, Yunnan
Nan-ching *see* Jianye, Nanjing
Nancy France empire and revolution 199 (4) medieval states 192 (1), (2) WWI 206 (2), (3) *battle* early modern states 193 (4), 197 (5)
Nandivardhana South Asia (India) early medieval states 244 (1)
Nan Hai *see* South China Sea
Nanhai *var.* Canton, Guangzhou East Asia (China) ancient trade 44–45 (1) exploration 256 (1) first states 260 (1) medieval states 261 (6) *see also* Canton, Guangzhou
Nanhai *province* East Asia first states 260 (1)
Nan-han *state* East Asia medieval states 263 (3)
Nanjing *var.* Nan-ching, Nanking; *prev.* Chianning, Chian-ning, Kiang-ning East Asia (China) colonialism 269 (4) early modern states 266 (1) economy 274 (1) empire and revolution 268 (2) first religions 37 (4) Islam 275 (4) medieval states 263 (5) Mongols 68–69 (1) post-war politics 271 (7), 274 (2) trade 267 (3) WWII 272 (1), 273 (2) Chinese revolution 271 (5)
Nanjing *province* East Asia early modern states 266 (1), (2)
Nankaido *region* Japan medieval states 265 (3)
Nanking *see* Jianye, Nanjing
Nanning *var.* Nan-ning; *prev.* Yung-ning East Asia (China) biological diffusion 72–73 (1) colonialism 269 (4) WWII 272 (1), 273 (2)
Nansei-shotō *see* Ryukyu Islands
Nan Shan *mod.* Qilian Shan *mountain range* East Asia exploration 257 (3) *see also* Qilian Shan
Nansha Qundao *see* Spratly Islands
Nantes *anc.* Condivincum, Namnetes; *Bret.* Naoned France crusades 186 (1) early modern states 197 (5) economy 205 (4) empire and revolution 199 (4) Franks 184 (2) medieval states 185 (3), 187 (4), 192 (1), (2) medieval voyages 60–61 (1) Reformation 194 (2)
Nantong East Asia (China) post-war politics 274 (2)
Nanyang *Buddhist centre* East Asia (China) world religions 49 (3)
Nanyue *state* East Asia first cities 259 (5)
Nanzhao *var.* Nan-chao; *mod.* Yunnan *region/state* East Asia early medieval states 245 (5) medieval states 262–263 (1) Mongols 68–69 (1) world religions 49 (3), (4) *see also* Yunnan
Nanzheng *var.* Hanzhong, Han-Chung East Asia (China) first cities 259 (5) *see also* Hanzhong
Naoned *see* Nantes
Napata *var.* Gebel Barkal East Africa (Sudan) ancient Egypt 159 (5) early cultures 160 (1) *see also* Gebel Barkal
Napier *settlement/whaling station* New Zealand colonization 283 (4), (5)
Naples *anc.* Neapolis; *It.* Napoli, *Ger.* Neapel *settlement/university* Italy biological diffusion 72–73 (1) crusades 186 (1) early modern states 194 (1) economy 190 (1), 205 (4) empire and revolution 202 (1), (3) Franks 184 (2) global immigration 100 (1) medieval states 182 (2), 183 (4), 187 (3), (5), 188 (1), 189 (4) Napoleon 200–201 (1), 201 (2), (3) Ottomans 230 (1) post-war politics 212 (3) Reformation 194 (2) the modern world 113 (4) *see also* Neapolis
Naples *colonial possession/state* Italy early modern states 193 (4), 194 (1) medieval states 185 (3), 189 (4) Napoleon 201 (2) Ottomans 195 (4), 230 (1), 231 (3) Reformation 194 (2), 196 (1), (2)
Napo *river* South America early cultures 144 (1), 145 (4), 146 (1) empire and revolution 150 (2) exploration 142 (1) Incas 147 (3) politics 152 (1)
Napochi *people* North America colonization 125 (4)
Napoli *see* Naples, Neapolis
Naqa East Africa (Sudan) the world in 500 BCE 34–35
Naqada Egypt ancient Egypt 159 (2), (3) first civilizations 24 (2)
Nara Japan early modern states 265 (5), 267 (4) medieval states 262–263 (1), 264 (2), 265 (4) world religions 49 (4)
Nara *prefecture* Japan economy 270 (1)
Naranjo Central America (Mexico) first civilizations 123 (2)
Narasapur *var.* Madapallam South Asia (India) colonialism 247 (3)
Naravaranagara *mod.* Angkor Borei Mainland Southeast Asia ancient India 241 (6)
Narbo *mod.* Narbonne *settlement* France ancient Rome 179 (3), 180–181 (1), 181 (3), (4) early cultures 161 (2) great migrations 52–53 (1) world religions 48 (1) *see also* Narbonne
Narbonensis *province* France ancient Rome 180–181 (1)
Narbonne *anc.* Narbo *settlement* France Franks 184 (2) Islam 184 (1) medieval states 182 (2), 187 (3), 192 (1) *see also* Narbo
Narbonne *battle* France early Islam 56–57 (1)
Narce Italy Bronze Age 175 (3)
Narev *Pol.* Narew *river* Central Europe WWI 207 (4)
Narew *see* Narev
Nargund *state* South Asia empire and revolution 249 (3)
Nariokotome *archaeological site* East Africa (Kenya) first humans 13 (2)
Narmada *archaeological site* South Asia (India) first humans 13 (2)
Narmada *river* South Asia colonialism 247 (3), 248 (1), (2) decolonization 250 (1) early medieval states 244 (1), (2), 244–245 (3), 245 (4) economy 249 (4) first cities 240 (2) first empires 241 (4), (5) first religions 36 (2) Marathas 246 (2) Mughal Empire 246 (1) post-war politics 252 (1) world religions 242 (2), 243 (4)
Narni *see* Narnia
Narnia *mod.* Narni Italy early states 178 (1)
Narosura *archaeological site/settlement* East Africa (Kenya) early agriculture 158 (1) early cultures 160 (1)
Narraganset *people* North America colonization 126 (1)
Narva Eastern Europe (Estonia) early modern states 195 (3)
Narvik Scandinavia (Norway) WWII 104 (2), 210 (1), 211 (4)
Narym Eastern Europe (Russian Federation) exploration 257 (2)
Nasarpur South Asia (Pakistan) colonialism 247 (3)
Nashikya South Asia (India) world religions 242 (2)
Nashville *battle/settlement* North America (USA) the growth of the US 129 (2), 132 (1) US Civil War 131 (6), (7) US society 137 (6)
Nasik South Asia (India) decolonization 250 (1) exploration 256 (1)
Naskapi *people* North America cultural groups 123 (3)
Nassau West Indies (Bahamas) Cold War 108 (2)

INDEX-GAZETTEER: **Possession Island – Rio**

Possession Island *island* Pacific Ocean exploration *278* (1)
Potano *people* North America colonization *126* (1)
Potchefstroom Southern Africa (South Africa) colonization *166* (2)
Potidaea *var.* Potidea *settlement/state* Greece ancient Greece *177* (2), (3) first civilizations *177* (1)
Potidea *see* Potidaea
Potomac *river* North America colonization *126* (1) empire and revolution *127* (3)
Potosí South America (Bolivia) colonization *148* (2) empire and revolution *150* (1), *151* (3) exploration *143* (2) politics *151* (4)
Potrero Nuevo *archaeological site* Central America (Mexico) first civilizations *121* (3)
Potsdam Central Europe (Germany) empire and revolution *199* (3)
Poverty Point Central America (Mexico) the world in 1250 BCE *26–27*
Powder River *battle* North America (USA) the growth of the US *129* (2)
Powhatan *people* North America colonization *126* (1)
Powys *region* British Isles medieval states *183* (3)
Poyang Hu *lake* East Asia early modern states *266* (1)
Poygars *see* Polygar Kingdoms
Poznań *Ger.* Posen, Posnania Central Europe (Poland) early modern states *193* (4) medieval states *188* (1), *189* (3), (4) *see also* Posen
Pozo Almonte South America (Chile) politics *151* (4)
Pozsony *mod.* Bratislava; *Ger.* Pressburg Central Europe (Slovakia) early modern states *193* (4) medieval states *188* (1), *189* (4) *see also* Bratislava
Pozsony *battle* Southeast Europe medieval states *185* (3)
Prabang *see* Lan Chang
Prabhasa South Asia (India) world religions *242* (2)
Prachya *region* South Asia ancient India *242* (1) first empires *241* (4)
Pracya/Purva-Desa *region* South Asia early religions *48* (2)
Praeneste Italy early states *178* (1)
Praenestina, Via *road* Italy ancient Rome *181* (2)
Prag *see* Prague
Praga *see* Prague
Pragjyotisapura South Asia (India) early medieval states *244* (1) first empires *241* (4)
Pragjyotisha *region* South Asia world religions *242* (2)
Prague *Cz.* Praha, *Ger.* Prag, *Pol.* Praga Central Europe (Czech Republic) crusades *186* (1) early modern states *193* (4) economy *190* (1), *205* (4) empire and revolution *199* (3), *202* (1), (2) inter-war *209* (5) medieval states *185* (3), *188* (1), *189* (3), (4) Napoleon *200–201* (1), *201* (2), (3) post-war politics *212* (3) Reformation *194* (2), *196* (1) WWII *105* (3), *210* (1), *211* (4) Cold War *109* (1)
Prague, Defenestration of *riot* Central Europe Reformation *196* (2)
Praha *see* Prague
Prambanan Maritime Southeast Asia (Indonesia) world religions *243* (5)
Prasodes Mare *sea* Indian Ocean ancient trade *44* (2)
Prasum Promontorium *headland* East Africa ancient trade *44* (2)
Prathet Thai *see* Siam, Thailand
Pratichya *region* South Asia ancient India *242* (1)
Pratisthana South Asia (India) early medieval states *244* (1) first empires *241* (4) world religions *242* (2)
Pravarapura South Asia (India) early medieval states *244* (1)
Prayaga South Asia (India) early medieval states *244* (1) early religions *48* (2) first empires *241* (4) first religions *36* (2) world religions *242* (2), (3), *243* (4)
Predmosti Central Europe (Slovakia) the world in 10,000 BCE *14–15*
Prenzlauer Berg Central Europe (Germany) post-war politics *212* (2)
Preservation Bay *sealing station* New Zealand colonization *283* (4)
Presidente Stroessner *see* Ciudad del Este
Presidi, Stato Dei *state* Italy Reformation *194* (2)
Prespa *battle* Southeast Europe (Serbia) WWI *207* (6)
Prespa, Limni *see* Prespa
Prespës, Liqeni i *see* Prespa, Lake
Pressburg *see* Bratislava, Pozsony
Preston British Isles (United Kingdom) economy *204* (1) imperial global economy *93* (4)
Pretoria *var.* Epitoli, Tshwane Southern Africa (South Africa) colonization *166* (2) economy *168* (2) European imperialism *96* (2)
Preussen *see* Prussia
Preveza Greece Ottomans *231* (3)
Priene Southwest Asia (Turkey) first civilizations *177* (1) Hellenistic world *40–41* (1)
Primorskiy Kray *see* Maritime Territory
Prince-Edouard, Île-du *see* Prince Edward Island
Prince Edward Island *Fr.* Île-du Prince-Edouard; *prev.* Ile St Jean, *Eng.* Isle St John *province* North America the growth of the US *129* (2), *132* (1) US economy *136* (2)
Prince of Wales Island *island* North America imperial global economy *93* (3)
Prince's Island *see* Principe
Princeton *battle* North America (USA) empire and revolution *127* (3), *88–89* (2)
Principe *var.* Principe Island, *Eng.* Prince's Island *island* West Africa exploration *156* (3)
Principe Island *see* Principe
Pripet *Bel.* Prypyats', *Ukr.* Pryp"yat' *river* Eastern Europe WWI *207* (4)
Pripet Marshes *wetland* Eastern Europe early agriculture *174* (1) Napoleon *200–201* (1) WWI *207* (4)
Pristina *settlement/battle* Southeast Europe (Yugoslavia) Ottomans *197* (4) post-war economy *215* (3) WWI *207* (6)
Prizren *Alb.* Prizreni Southeast Europe (Yugoslavia) post-war economy *215* (3) WWI *207* (6)
Prizreni *see* Prizren
Progreso Central America (Mexico) Mexican Revolution *133* (3)
Prome Mainland Southeast Asia (Burma) world religions *243* (5), *49* (4)
Prospect Farm *archaeological site* East Africa (Kenya) early cultures *160* (1)
Provence *region* France early modern states *193* (4) Franks *183* (6), *184* (2) medieval states *192* (2)
Providence North America (USA) empire and revolution *127* (3) the growth of the US *129* (2), *132* (1)
Providence, Cape *headland* New Zealand colonization *283* (4)
Provins France crusades *186* (1) economy *190* (1)
Prusa *later* Brusa, Brussa; *mod.* Bursa Southwest Asia (Turkey) ancient Rome *180–181* (1) *see also* Brusa, Bursa
Prussia *state* Central Europe/Eastern Europe early modern states *195* (3) empire and revolution *198* (2), *202* (1), (2) Napoleon *200–201* (1), *201* (2) Reformation *194* (2), *196* (1), (2)
Prussians *people* Central Europe crusades *186* (1), *64–65* (2) medieval states *185* (3)
Prut *see* Pruth
Pruth *var.* Prut *river* Eastern Europe WWI *207* (4)
Pryp"yat' *see* Pripet
Prypyats' *see* Pripet
Przemyśl Central Europe (Poland) post-war politics *212* (3) WWI *207* (4)
Przheval'sk *see* Karakol
Pskov *Ger.* Pleskau; *Latv.* Pleskava Eastern Europe (Russian Federation) early modern states *195* (3) economy *190* (1) medieval states *189* (3) post-war politics *212* (3) Soviet Union *208* (2) WWI *207* (4)
Pskov *Ger.* Pleskau; *Latv.* Pleskava *state* Eastern Europe medieval states *189* (3)
Ptolemaic Empire *state* Egypt/Southwest Asia ancient Rome *179* (5) Hellenistic world *224* (1)
Ptolemais Southwest Asia (Syria) ancient Rome *225* (4)
Ptolemais North Africa (Libya) ancient Rome *180–181* (1)
Ptolemaïs *var.* Acco, Acre Southwest Asia (Israel) world religions *48* (1)
Ptolemaïs *see* Acco, Acre
Ptuj *see* Poetovio
Pucará South America (Peru) early cultures *146* (1)
Pucará de Andalgalá South America (Argentina) Incas *147* (3)
Pu-chou *see* Puzhou
Puduchcheri *see* Pondicherry
Puebla *var.* Puebla de Zaragoza Central America (Mexico) colonization *125* (4) Mexican Revolution *133* (3)
Puebla *state* Central America Mexican Revolution *133* (3) the growth of the US *129* (2)
Puebla de Zaragoza *see* Puebla
Pueblo Grande *archaeological site* North America (USA) cultural groups *123* (4)
Pueblos *region* North America the world in 750 CE *54–55*
Puelche *people* South America early cultures *147* (2)
Puerto Bello *var.* Porto Bello; *mod.* Portobelo Central America (Panama) empire and revolution *150* (2) *see also* Portobelo
Puerto Cabello South America (Venezuela) empire and revolution *150* (1), (2)
Puerto Casado *fort* South America (Paraguay) politics *152* (2)
Puerto Deseado *see* Port Desire
Puerto Hormiga *archaeological site* South America (Colombia) early cultures *144* (1)
Puerto Montt South America (Chile) empire and revolution *151* (3)
Puerto Plata West Indies (Dominican Republic) European expansion *85* (2)
Puerto Presidente Stroessner *see* Ciudad del Este
Puerto Príncipe *mod.* Camagüey West Indies (Cuba) European expansion *85* (2)
Puerto Rico *colonial possession/island* West Indies colonization *125* (4), *126* (1) empire and revolution *150* (1) European expansion *85* (2) global immigration *100* (1) historical geography *140–141* (1) the growth of the US *133* (4) the modern world *113* (4) US politics *139* (4) Cold War *108* (2), *109* (1)
Puerto San Julián *var.* San Julián South America (Argentina) European expansion *80–81* (1)
Pukapuka *island* Pacific Ocean exploration *278* (1)
Puket *see* Phuket
Pulicat *var.* Pālghāt, Geldria South Asia (India) colonialism *247* (3)
Pulinda *region/state* South Asia first empires *241* (5) world religions *242* (2)
Pumpo South America (Peru) Incas *147* (3)
Punakha South Asia (Bhutan) colonialism *248* (1)
Puna Pau *archaeological site* Pacific Ocean early cultures *281* (4)
Pundra South Asia (Bangladesh) first empires *241* (4)
Pundra *region/state* South Asia (Bangladesh) early religions *48* (2) first empires *241* (5) world religions *242* (2)
Pundravardhana South Asia (Bangladesh) early medieval states *244* (1) world religions *242* (2)
Pune *prev.* Poona South Asia (India) post-war economy *253* (5) *see also* Poona
Punjab *region/state* South Asia colonialism *247* (3), *248* (2) economy *249* (4) empire and revolution *249* (3) post-war politics *252* (1), *253* (4) world religions *243* (4)
Punjab, (East) *region* South Asia post-war politics *252* (1)
Punjab, (West) *region* South Asia post-war politics *252* (1)
Punjab States *state* South Asia colonialism *248* (2)
Punkuri *archaeological site* South America (Peru) early cultures *145* (3)
Punneikayal *see* Kayalapattinam
Puno South America (Peru) empire and revolution *150* (1) politics *151* (4)
Punta Arenas *prev.* Magallanes South America (Chile) empire and revolution *151* (3) environment *153* (4)
Punta de Angamos *battle* South America (Chile) politics *151* (4)
Puntutjarpa Australia exploration *280* (1)
Pura *mod.* Iranshahr Southwest Asia (Iran) Hellenistic world *40–41* (1)
Puranadhisthana *var.* Shrinagara South Asia (India) first empires *241* (4)
Puri South Asia (India) biological diffusion *72–73* (1)
Puritjarra Australia the world in 10,000 BCE *14–15*
Purosottama-Puri South Asia (India) world religions *243* (4)
Purus *Sp.* Río Purús *river* South America colonization *149* (3) early cultures *144* (1), *145* (2), (4), *146* (1) environment *153* (4)
Purusapura *mod.* Peshwar South Asia (Pakistan) Hellenistic world *224* (1)
Purush Khaddum Southwest Asia (Turkey) first civilizations *221* (4)
Purús, Río *see* Purus
Pusan *var.* Busan; *Jap.* Fusan East Asia (South Korea) early modern states *267* (4) Islam *275* (4) Russo-Japanese War *270* (4) Sino-Japanese War *270* (3) trade *267* (3) Cold War *109* (4)
Pushkar *see* Puskara
Pushkari *archaeological site* Eastern Europe (Russian Federation) the world in 10,000 BCE *14–15*
Pusilha Central America (Mexico) first civilizations *123* (2)
Puskalavati South Asia (Pakistan) world religions *242* (2)
Puskara *mod.* Pushkar South Asia (India) early medieval states *244* (1) world religions *243* (4)
Pusyabhutis *state* South Asia early medieval states *244* (2)
Putan Maya *state* Central America Aztecs *124* (1)
Puteoli Italy ancient Rome *180–181* (1), *181* (3)
Puttalam South Asia (Sri Lanka) colonialism *247* (3)
Putumayo *region* South America narcotics *153* (5)
Putumayo *var.* Rio Içá *river* South America colonization *148* (2) early cultures *145* (4), *146* (1) empire and revolution *150* (2), *151* (3) environment *153* (4) Incas *148* (1)
Puyang East Asia (China) first religions *37* (4)
Puye *archaeological site* North America (USA) cultural groups *123* (4)
Puyo East Asia (Korea) medieval states *264* (1), (2)
Puzhou *var.* Pu-chou East Asia (China) Mongols *68–69* (1)
Pydna *battle* Greece ancient Greece *179* (4)
Pygela *state* Greece ancient Greece *177* (2)
Pylos Greece ancient Greece *177* (3), *179* (4) Bronze Age *175* (3) early systems *223* (3) first cities *28–29* (1) first civilizations *175* (4)
Pyongyang *prev.* Luolang; *var.* P'yŏngyang-si, P'yŏngyang East Asia (North Korea) Cold War *109* (4) early modern states *267* (4) Islam *275* (4) Sino-Japanese War *270* (3) world religions *49* (3) *see also* Luolang
P'yŏngyang-si *see* Luolang, Pyongyang
Pyramid Lake *battle* North America (USA) the growth of the US *129* (2)
Pyrenaei Montes *see* Pyrenees
Pyrenees *Fr.* Pyrénées, *Sp.* Pirineos; *anc.* Pyrenaei Montes *mountain range* France/Iberian Peninsula ancient Rome *179* (3), *180–181* (1), *181* (3) Bronze Age *175* (3) crusades *186* (1), *64–65* (2) early agriculture *174* (1) early Islam *56–57* (1), *57* (2) early modern states *197* (5) economy *190* (1), *205* (4) exploration *172* (1) first religions *37* (3) Franks *183* (5), (6), *184* (2) great migrations *52–53* (1) historical geography *170–171* (1) Islam *192* (3) medieval states *185* (3), *192* (1), (2) Napoleon *200–201* (1) prehistoric culture *17* (3), (4) world religions *48* (1) WWII *210* (1), *211* (4)
Pyrrha *state* Greece ancient Greece *177* (2)
Pyu *region/state* Mainland Southeast Asia medieval states *262–263* (1) the world in 750 CE *54–55* world religions *49* (3), (4)

Q

Qābis *see* Gabès
Qadesh Southwest Asia (Lebanon) first cities *28–29* (1)
Qadisiya *battle* Southwest Asia (Iraq) early Islam *56–57* (1)
Qafzeh *archaeological site* Southwest Asia (Israel) first humans *13* (2)
Qaidam Pendi *see* Tsaidam Basin
Qalat *mod.* Kalat South Asia (Pakistan) Mughal Empire *246* (1) *see also* Kalat
Qalat *state* South Asia Mughal Empire *246* (1)
Qalhat *see* Kalhat
Qalqut *var.* Kalikod; *mod.* Calicut, Kozhikode South Asia (India) early medieval states *244–245* (3) *see also* Calicut, Kalikod
Qānāq *see* Thule
Qandahar *mod.* Kandahar South Asia (Pakistan) early medieval states *244–245* (3) Mughal Empire *246* (1) *see also* Kandahar
Qandahar *state* South Asia Mughal Empire *246* (1)
Qandahār *see* Kandahar, Qandahar
Qannauj South Asia (India) early medieval states *244–245* (3)
Qaqortoq *see* Julianehaab
Qarabagh *mod.* Karabakh *region* Southwest Asia medieval Persia *231* (4)
Qaraghandy *see* Karaganda
Qarakhanids *var.* Karakhanids *state* Central Asia early Islam *57* (2) *see also* Karakhanids
Qarmatians *dynasty* Southwest Asia early Islam *57* (2) Islam *227* (4), (5)
Qarmatis *dynasty* South Asia the world in 1000 *58–59*
Qars *see* Kars
Qatar *colonial possession/state* Southwest Asia economy *234* (1) Islam *235* (4) the modern world *113* (3) US economy *138* (2) 20th-century politics *233* (4), *235* (5) Cold War *109* (1)
Qatna Southwest Asia (Syria) ancient Egypt *159* (4), (5)
Qaw Egypt ancient Egypt *159* (2)
Qaw el-Kebir Egypt ancient Egypt *159* (4)
Qazaqstan *see* Kazakhstan
Qazris *see* Cáceres
Qazvin *var.* Kazvin Southwest Asia (Iran) early Islam *56–57* (1) Mongols *229* (3), *68–69* (1) 20th-century politics *235* (5) *see also* Kazvin
Qeshm Southwest Asia (Iran) economy *234* (1)
Qeshm *var.* Jazīreh-ye Qeshm, Qeshm Island *island* Southwest Asia economy *234* (1)
Qeshm Island *see* Qeshm
Qeshm, Jazireh-ye *see* Qeshm
Qi *var.* Ch'i *region/state* East Asia first cities *259* (4), (5) first religions *37* (4)
Qian East Asia (China) medieval states *263* (6)
Qiang East Asia (China) first cities *259* (4)
Qiang *state* East Asia first cities *259* (3)
Qiang *people* East Asia first cities *259* (4) first states *260* (1), *261* (2) medieval states *261* (4), (6), *262–263* (1)
Qiantang East Asia (China) first states *260* (1)
Qiemo *see* Cherchen
Qi Empire *var.* Ch'i *state* East Asia the world in 500 CE *50–51* *see also* China
Qift Egypt ancient Egypt *159* (4)
Qilian Shan *mountain range* East Asia early agriculture *258* (1) early modern states *266* (1) first cities *259* (5) first religions *37* (4) first states *260* (1) trade *267* (3)
Qin *state* East Asia first cities *259* (4), (5) first religions *37* (4)
Qin Empire *state* East Asia the world in 250 BCE *38–39* *see also* China
Qing *see* Qinghai
Qingdao *var.* Ching-Tao, Ch'ing-tao, Tsingtao, Tsintao; *Ger.* Tsingtau East Asia (China) economy *274* (1) imperialism *270* (2) Islam *275* (4) post-war politics *274* (2) Russo-Japanese War *270* (4)
Qingdao *var.* Tsingtao *colonial possession* East Asia colonialism *269* (4)
Qing Empire *mod.* China *state* East Asia colonialism *248* (1), (2), *269* (3), (4) decolonization *250* (2) economy *249* (4) empire and revolution *249* (3), *88–89* (2) European imperialism *97* (3), (4) Russo-Japanese War *270* (4) Sino-Japanese War *270* (3) *see also* China
Qinghai *var.* Chinghai, Qing, Tsinghai *province/state* East Asia Chinese revolution *271* (5) early modern states *266* (1), (2), *268* (1) empire and revolution *268* (2) post-war economy *275* (3) post-war politics *271* (7), *274* (2)
Qinghai Hu *var.* Ch'ing Hai, Tsing Hai, *Mong.* Koko Nor *lake* East Asia early modern states *266* (1) first states *260* (1)
Qingjiang East Asia (China) medieval states *263* (6)
Qingliangang *archaeological site* East Asia (China) early agriculture *258* (2)
Qingtang Xiang *state* East Asia medieval states *263* (3)
Qingyang *rebellion* East Asia early modern states *266* (2)
Qingzhou *prev.* Yidu *rebellion/settlement* East Asia (China) early modern states *266* (2) medieval states *263* (4)
Qinhuangdao *var.* Chinwangtao East Asia (China) colonialism *269* (4) post-war politics *274* (2)
Qiong *see* Hainan
Qiongzhou *var.* Kiungchow East Asia (China) colonialism *269* (4)
Qita Ghazzah *see* Gaza Strip
Qizhou *military base* East Asia early modern states *266* (1)
Qom *var.* Kum, Qum Southwest Asia (Iran) economy *234* (1) *see also* Qum
Qomul *see* Hami
Quadi *people* Eastern Europe ancient Rome *180–181* (1), *181* (4)
Quang Tri *battle* Mainland Southeast Asia (Vietnam) post-war politics *251* (5)
Quanrong *state* East Asia first cities *259* (3)
Quanzhou East Asia (China) ancient trade *44–45* (1) medieval states *263* (5) Mongols *68* (2), *68–69* (1) trade *267* (3)
Quapaw *people* North America colonization *126* (1)
Quarai *archaeological site* North America (USA) cultural groups *123* (4)
Quban Egypt ancient Egypt *159* (4), (5)
Quebec *var.* Québec North America (Canada) colonization *126* (1) empire and revolution *127* (2), (3) empire and revolution *88* (1)European expansion *84–85* (1) exploration *118* (1), *119* (2), (3) global immigration *100* (1), *101* (3) the growth of the US *129* (2), *132* (1) the world in 1800 *86–87* US economy *136* (2)
Quebec *colonial possession/province* North America empire and revolution *127* (3) the growth of the US *129* (2), *132* (1) US economy *136* (2)
Queen Elizabeth Islands *see* Parry Islands
Queensland *region* Australia colonization *282* (1), (2), *283* (3)
Queenstown New Zealand colonization *283* (5)
Quelimane *var.* Kilimane, Kilmain, Quilimane Southern Africa (Mozambique) exploration *157* (4) Islam *163* (1) trade *164* (1)
Quelpart *Jap.* Saishū; *Kor.* Cheju-do *island* East Asia Sino-Japanese War *270* (3) *see also* Cheju-do
Quemoy *var.* Chinmen Tao, Jinmen Dao *island* East Asia Cold War *109* (1) post-war economy *275* (3)
Quentovic France medieval states *185* (3)
Que Que *see* Kwekwe
Quera *see* Chur, Curia
Querero South America the world in 10,000 BCE *14–15*
Queres *people* North America colonization *126* (1)
Querétaro *state* Central America Mexican Revolution *133* (3) the growth of the US *129* (2)
Quetta South Asia (Pakistan) Hellenistic world *40–41* (1) post-war politics *252* (1)
Quetzaltepec Central America (Mexico) Aztecs *124* (1)
Qufu East Asia (China) first cities *259* (5) first religions *37* (4)
Quiahuac Central America (Mexico) Aztecs *124* (3)
Quiahuitztlan Central America (Mexico) colonization *125* (5)
Quiauhteopan *state* Central America Aztecs *124* (1)
Quiberon Bay *battle* France empire and revolution *88* (1)
Quierzy France Franks *184* (2)
Quilimane *see* Quelimane
Quilon *var.* Kolam, Kollam South Asia (India) biological diffusion *72–73* (1) colonialism *247* (3)
Quimbaya *state* South America the world in 1200 *62–63*
Quimbaya Chiefdoms *state* South America early cultures *146* (1)
Quimper *anc.* Quimper Corentin France Franks *184* (2)
Quimper Corentin *see* Quimper
Qui Nhon *battle* Mainland Southeast Asia (Vietnam) post-war politics *251* (5)
Quintana Roo *state* Central America Mexican Revolution *133* (3)
Quirigua Central America (Guatemala) first civilizations *121* (2), *123* (2)
Quirinal Hill *Lat.* Collis Quirinalis *hill* Italy ancient Rome *181* (2)
Quirinalis Collis *see* Quirinal Hill
Quito South America (Ecuador) colonization *148* (2) empire and revolution *150* (1), (2), *151* (3) environment *153* (4) exploration *142* (1), *143* (2), (3) Incas *147* (3), *148* (1) politics *152* (1)
Quito, Presidencia of *region* South America colonization *148* (2)
Qujialing *archaeological site* East Asia (China) early agriculture *258* (2)
Qum *mod.* Qom Southwest Asia (Iran) medieval Persia *231* (4) Mongols *229* (3), *68–69* (1) *see also* Qom
Qumis Southwest Asia (Iran) early Islam *56–57* (1)
Quonset North America (USA) WWII *104* (2)
Qūqon *see* Kokand
Qurein *see* Kuwait
Qus *var.* Assouan, Assuan, Aswân; *anc.* Syene Egypt crusades *228* (2) *see also* Aswân, Syene

R

Rabat *var.* al Dar al Baida North Africa (Morocco) early Islam *56–57* (1) economy *168* (2)
Rabaul *military base/settlement* New Guinea (Papua New Guinea) WWII *104* (2), *251* (3), *272* (1), *273* (2)
Rabbah Ammon *see* Amman
Rabbath Ammon *see* Amman
Rabeh *people* Central Africa trade *167* (1)
Racibórz *see* Ratibor
Radom Central Europe (Poland) empire and revolution *198* (2)
Rae Bareli *region* South Asia decolonization *250* (1)
Raeti *people* Italy early states *178* (2)
Raetia *var.* Rhaetia *province* Central Europe ancient Rome *180–181* (1) Franks *184* (2) *see also* Rhaetia
Rafa *see* Rafah
Rafah *var.* Rafa, Rafaḥ; *Heb.* Rafiaḥ, Raphiah Southwest Asia (Gaza Strip) 20th century *234* (2)
Rafiah *see* Rafah
Ragusa *mod.* Dubrovnik Southeast Europe (Croatia) early modern states *193* (4) economy *190* (1) medieval states *188* (1), *189* (4) Ottomans *195* (4) Reformation *196* (2) *see also* Dubrovnik
Ragusa *state* Southeast Europe early modern states *193* (4), *194* (1) Ottomans *195* (4), *230* (1), *231* (3) Reformation *194* (2)
Rahanagar South Asia (Bangladesh) post-war politics *252* (3)
Rahovec *see* Orahovac
Rai *see* Rayy
Rajagriha South Asia (India) first empires *241* (4) first religions *36* (2) world religions *242* (3)
Rajamahendri South Asia (India) early medieval states *244–245* (3), *245* (4)
Rajarattha *region* South Asia first empires *241* (4)
Rajasthan *region/state* South Asia post-war politics *252* (1) world religions *243* (4)
Rajgir *religious site* South Asia (India) first religions *36* (2)
Rajputana *region/state* South Asia colonialism *247* (3), *248* (1), (2)
Rajputs *people* South Asia early medieval states *244–245* (3)
Rajput States *state* South Asia the world in 1500 *74–75*
Rakka *see* Raqqa
Rakvere *see* Wesenberg
Raleigh North America (USA) the growth of the US *129* (2), *132* (1) US Civil War *131* (7) US society *137* (6)
Ramagama South Asia (India) world religions *242* (3)
Ramazan *state* Southwest Asia the world in 1400 *70–71* the world in 1500 *74–75*
Rameshwaram South Asia (India) world religions *243* (4)
Ramhormoz Southwest Asia (Iran) 20th-century politics *235* (5)
Rampur South Asia (India) colonialism *248* (1) economy *249* (4)
Rampur *state* South Asia colonialism *248* (2)
Ramsay's Mill North America (USA) empire and revolution *127* (3)
Ramsgate British Isles (United Kingdom) WWI *206* (2), (3)
Rana Ghundai *archaeological site* South Asia (India) first cities *240* (2)
Ranas Central America (Mexico) first civilizations *122* (1)
Ranchillos South America (Argentina) Incas *147* (3)
Rancho la Chua North America (USA) colonization *125* (4)
Rancho Peludo *archaeological site* South America (Venezuela) early cultures *144* (1), *145* (2)
Rangiroa *island* Pacific Ocean exploration *278* (1)
Rangoon *var.* Yangon; *anc.* Dagon Mainland Southeast Asia (Burma) colonialism *247* (4), *248* (1), *269* (4) economy *249* (4) European expansion *84–85* (1) European imperialism *97* (3) Islam *275* (4) post-war economy *253* (5) US superpower *138* (1) world religions *243* (5) WWII *251* (3), *272* (1), *273* (2)
Rangpur *archaeological site/settlement* South Asia (Bangladesh) colonialism *247* (3) first cities *240* (2) post-war politics *252* (3)
Rano Kao *see* Rano Kau
Rano Kau *var.* Rano Kao *volcano* Pacific Ocean early cultures *281* (4)
Rano Raraku *archaeological site* South America (Chile) early cultures *281* (4)
Rapa Nui *var.* Isla de Pascua, Easter Island *island* Pacific Ocean early cultures *280–281* (3), *281* (4) medieval voyages *60* (2) *see also* Easter Island
Raphiah *see* Rafah
Raqqa *var.* Rakka Southwest Asia (Syria) early Islam *56–57* (1)
Raroia *island* Pacific Ocean exploration *278* (1)
Ra's al Junayz Southwest Asia (Oman) first civilizations *25* (3)
Ras al Khaimah *Ar.* Ra's al Khaymah Southwest Asia (United Arab Emirates) economy *234* (1)
Ra's al Khaymah *see* Ras al Khaimah
Ras Dashen *mountain* East Africa (Ethiopia) exploration *157* (5)
Rashtrakutas *dynasty* South Asia early medieval states *244* (2) the world in 750 CE *54–55*
Ra's Shamrah *see* Ugarit
Ras Tannura *oil terminal* Southwest Asia (Saudi Arabia) economy *234* (1)
Rasulids *dynasty* Southwest Asia economy *163* (2)
Ratiaria *Christian archbishopric* Southeast Europe (Bulgaria) world religions *48* (1)
Ratibor *mod.* Racibórz Central Europe (Poland) medieval states *189* (3)
Ratisbon *anc.* Castra Regina, Reginum; *hist.* Ratisbona; *Fr.* Ratisbonne, *Ger.* Regensburg *massacre/settlement* Central Europe (Germany) crusades *186* (1) early modern states *193* (4) Franks *184* (2) medieval states *188* (1), *189* (3), (4) Napoleon *200–201* (1) *see also* Castra Regina, Regensburg
Ratisbona *see* Castra Regina, Ratisbon, Regensburg
Ratisbonne *see* Castra Regina, Ratisbon, Regensburg
Ratnagiri South Asia (India) exploration *256* (1)
Ratomagus *see* Rotomagus
Raukawa *see* Cook Strait
Ravenna Italy ancient Rome *180–181* (1), *181* (4), *182* (1) economy *190* (1) Franks *184* (2) great migrations *52–53* (1) medieval states *182* (2), *183* (4) Ottomans *230* (1) world religions *48* (1) early modern states *194* (1)
Ravenna, Exarchate of *state* Italy medieval states *183* (4)
Ravensberg *region* Central Europe empire and revolution *199* (3)
Ravensbrück *concentration camp* Central Europe WWII *211* (3)
Ravi *river* South Asia colonialism *247* (3) early medieval states *244* (1), (2), *244–245* (3) economy *249* (4) Marathas *246* (2) Mughal Empire *246* (1)
Rawak *Buddhist centre* East Asia (China) world religions *49* (3)
Rawalpindi South Asia (Pakistan) post-war economy *253* (5)
Rawson South America (Argentina) empire and revolution *151* (3)
Ray *see* Rayy
Rayigama South Asia (Sri Lanka) early medieval states *244–245* (3)
Raysut Southwest Asia (Oman) early Islam *56–57* (1) medieval voyages *61* (3)
Rayy *var.* Rai, Ray, Rey; *anc.* Rhagae Southwest Asia (Iran) biological diffusion *72–73* (1) Islam *227* (5) Mongols *229* (3), *68–69* (1)
Real Alto *archaeological site/settlement* South America (Ecuador) early cultures *144* (1)
Reao *leper colony* Pacific Ocean environmentalism *285* (2)
Reate Italy early states *178* (1)
Recife *var.* Pernambuco; *Dut.* Mauritsstad South America (Brazil) colonization *149* (3), (4) economy *153* (3) environment *153* (4) exploration *142* (1), *143* (2) politics *152* (1) *see also* Pernambuco
Recuay South America (Peru) early cultures *145* (4)
Recuay *region* South America early cultures *145* (4)
Reddis *dynasty* South Asia the world in 1400 *70–71*
Red River *river* North America colonization *125* (4) cultural groups *122* (5) early agriculture *120* (1) exploration *118* (1), *119* (2) first civilizations *121* (4) the growth of the US *129* (2) US Civil War *131* (6), (7)
Red River *var.* Yuan, *Chin.* Yuan Jiang, *Vtn.* Sông Hông Hà *river* East Asia ancient India *241* (6) Bronze Age *240* (3) colonialism *247* (4), *248* (1) early medieval states *245* (5), (6) post-war politics *251* (5) world religions *243* (5)
Redruth British Isles (United Kingdom) economy *204* (1)
Red Sea *anc.* Sinus Arabicus *sea* Africa/Asia ancient Egypt *159* (2), (3), (4), (5) ancient Persia *223* (4) ancient Rome *180–181* (1), *181* (4), *224* (2), *225* (5) ancient trade *44–45* (1) biological diffusion *72–73* (1) crusades *65* (3) early agriculture *158* (1) early cultures *160* (1), *161* (2), (3), (4), (5) early Islam *56–57* (1), *57* (2) early systems *223* (3) early trade *225* (3) economy *163* (2), (3) exploration *156* (3), *157* (5), *172* (1), (2), *219* (3), (4) first cities *220* (2), *28–29* (1) first civilizations *222* (2) first humans *12* (1), *13* (2) first religions *37* (3) Hellenistic world *224* (1), *41* (2) Islam *163* (1), *226* (2), (3), *227* (4) medieval states *261* (6) medieval voyages *61* (3) Mongols *229* (3) Ottomans *231* (3), *232–233* (1) Seljuks *228* (1) slave trade *165* (4) Timur *229* (4) trade *165* (3), *167* (1), *230* (2) world religions *226* (1), *49* (4) WWI *233* (2) 20th century *234* (2) 20th-century politics *233* (4)
Redstone Fort North America (USA) empire and revolution *127* (3)
Reefton *see* Reef Town
Reef Town *mod.* Reefton New Zealand colonization *283* (5)
Reged *region* British Isles medieval states *183* (3)
Regensburg *anc.* Castra Regina, Reginum; *Eng.* Ratisbon; *hist.* Ratisbona; *Fr.* Ratisbonne Central Europe (Germany) economy *64–65* (2), *65* (1) economy *190* (1) *see also* Castra Regina, Ratisbon
Reggio *var.* Reggio di Calabria; *anc* Rhegium Italy economy *190* (1) medieval states *188* (1) Ottomans *231* (3) *see also* Rhegium
Regillus Lacus *lake* Italy early states *178* (1)
Regina North America (Canada) the growth of the US *129* (2)
Reginum *see* Castra Regina, Ratisbon, Regensburg
Reichenau Central Europe (Poland) Franks *184* (2)
Reichskommissariat-Ostland *region* Eastern Europe WWII *211* (2)
Reichskommissariat-Ukraine *region* Eastern Europe WWII *211* (2)
Reims *see* Durocortorum, Rheims
Reindeer Lake *lake* North America the growth of the US *129* (2)
Reine-Charlotte, Îles de la *see* Queen Charlotte Islands
Reine-Élisabeth, Îles de la *see* Queen Elizabeth Islands
Reinickendorf Central Europe (Germany) post-war politics *212* (2)
Reka *see* Rijeka
Reka Ili *see* Ili
Remedello *archaeological site* Italy Copper Age *174* (2)
Remedios *military base* West Indies (Cuba) Cold War *108* (2)
Remi *see* Rheims
Remojadas Central America (Mexico) first civilizations *121* (2), *122* (1)
Remojadas *region* Central America first civilizations *122* (1)
Ren *state* East Asia first cities *259* (3)
Rennell *var.* Mu Nggava *island* Pacific Ocean early cultures *280–281* (3) medieval voyages *60* (2)
Renner *burial mound* North America (USA) first civilizations *121* (4)
Rennes *anc.* Condate; *Bret.* Roazon France empire and revolution *199* (4) Franks *184* (2) medieval states *187* (4)
Resolute North America (Canada) cultural groups *123* (3)
Réunion *prev.* Bourbon *colonial possession/island/state* Indian Ocean European expansion *84–85* (1) European imperialism *96* (1) global immigration *101* (3) *see also* Bourbon
Reval *var.* Revel; *mod.* Tallinn; *Rus.* Tallin Eastern Europe (Estonia) crusades *186* (1) early modern states *195* (3) economy *190* (1) medieval states *189* (3) *see also* Revel, Tallin
Revel Eastern Europe (Estonia) early modern states *197* (3) Soviet Union *208* (2)
Revillagigedo Islands *see* Revillagigedo, Islas
Revillagigedo, Islas *Eng.* Revillagigedo Islands *island group* North America the modern world *110–111*
Rewardashur *Christian archbishopric* Southwest Asia (Iran) world religions *48* (1)
Rey *see* Rayy
Reykjavik Europe (Iceland) exploration *287* (2) medieval voyages *60–61* (1) WWII *104* (2)
Reżā'īyeh, Daryācheh-ye *see* Urmia, Lake
Rha *river* Eastern Europe ancient trade *44* (2)
Rhaetia *var.* Raetia *province/region* Central Europe Franks *183* (6) world religions *48* (1) *see also* Raetia
Rhagae Southwest Asia (Iran) Hellenistic world *40–41* (1)
Rhapta East Africa (Ethiopia) ancient trade *44* (2)
Rhegium *var.* Reggio; *mod.* Reggio di Calabria Italy ancient Rome *179* (3), *180–181* (1) early states *178* (1) first civilizations *177* (1) *see also* Reggio
Rheims *academic centre/settlement* France ancient Rome *182* (1) economy *190* (1) Franks *183* (5), (6), *184* (2) medieval states *185* (3), *188* (1), (2) Napoleon *200–201* (1) WWI *206* (2), (3)
Rhein *see* Rhine
Rhenus *see* Rhine
Rhin *see* Rhine
Rhine *Dut.* Rijn, *Fr.* Rhin, *Ger.* Rhein; *Lat.* Rhenus *river* Central Europe, Low Countries ancient Rome *180–181* (1), *181* (3), (4) ancient trade *44–45* (1) biological diffusion *72–73* (1) Bronze Age *175* (3) Copper Age *174* (2) crusades *186* (1), *64–65* (2) early agriculture *174* (1), *20–21* (2) early Islam *56–57* (1) early modern states *193* (4), (5) economy *190* (1) empire and revolution *199* (3), (4), *202* (1), (1), (2) exploration *172* (1) first humans *13* (2) Franks *183* (5), (6), *184* (2) great migrations *52–53* (1), *53* (2) medieval states *182* (2), *185* (3), *188* (1), (2) Napoleon *200–201* (1), *201* (2) prehistoric culture *16* (1) Reformation *195* (5), *196* (1) world religions *48* (1) WWI *206* (2), (3) WWII *210* (1), *211* (4)
Rhine, Confederation of the *state* Central Europe Napoleon *201* (2)
Rhodanus *see* Rhône
Rhode Iberian Peninsula (Spain) ancient Rome *179* (3)
Rhode Island *colonial possession/state* North America empire and revolution *127* (2), (3) the growth of the US *129* (1) US Civil War *130* (2), (5) US economy *134* (2)
Rhodes Greece (Rhodes) ancient Greece *177* (3), *179* (4) early Islam *56–57* (1) economy *190* (1) Hellenistic world *40–41* (1) medieval states *187* (5) Ottomans *230* (1) world religions *48* (1) Islam *226* (2)s
Rhodes *var.* Ródhos; *Gr.* Ródos; *Lat.* Rhodus, *It.* Rodi *state/island* Greece ancient Greece *177* (2), (3), *179* (4) ancient Persia *223* (4) ancient Rome *179* (5) crusades *64–65* (2) first civilizations *175* (4), *177* (1), *221* (5) Islam *226* (2) medieval states *187* (5) Ottomans *230* (1) post-war politics *212* (3)
Rhodesia *mod.* Zimbabwe; *prev.* Southern Rhodesia *state* Southern Africa the world in 1975 *106–107* *see also* Southern Rhodesia, Zimbabwe
Rhodos *see* Rhodes
Rhodus Greece ancient Rome *180–181* (1)
Rhône *Lat.* Rhodanus *river* France ancient Rome *180–181* (1), *181* (3) ancient trade *44–45* (1) biological diffusion *72–73* (1) Bronze Age *175* (3) Copper Age *174* (2) crusades *186* (1), *64–65* (2) early agriculture *174* (1) early Islam *56–57* (1) early modern states *193* (4) economy *190* (1), *205* (4) first civilizations *177* (1) Franks *183* (5), (6), *184* (2) great migrations *52–53* (1), *53* (2) medieval states *185* (3), *187* (4), *188* (1) prehistoric culture *17* (3) world religions *48* (1)
Rialto Bridge *bridge* Italy economy *191* (3)
Ribe Scandinavia (Denmark) medieval voyages *60–61* (1)
Ribeira Grande *var.* Concelho de Ribeira Grande *island* Atlantic Ocean the world in 1500 *74–75*
Richmond North America (USA) colonization *126* (1) empire and revolution *127* (3) European expansion *84–85* (1) the growth of the US *129* (2), *132* (1) US Civil War *130* (5), *131* (6), (7) US society *137* (6)
Rievaulx *major cistercian house* British Isles (United Kingdom) medieval states *187* (3)
Rift Valley *see* Great Rift Valley
Riga *Latv.* Rīga *settlement* Eastern Europe (Latvia) biological diffusion *72–73* (1) crusades *186* (1) early modern states *193* (4), *195* (3) economy *190* (1) empire and revolution *198* (2), *202* (1) medieval states *189* (3) Napoleon *200–201* (1), *201* (2) post-war politics *212* (3) Reformation *194* (2) Soviet Union *214–215* (4) WWI *207* (4) WWII *211* (2), (3), (4) Cold War *108* (3)
Rigaer Bucht *see* Riga, Gulf of
Riga, Gulf of *Est.* Liivi Laht, *Ger.* Rigaer Bucht, *Latv.* Rīgas Jūras Līcis, *Rus.* Rizhskiy Zaliv; *prev. Est.* Riia Laht *gulf* Eastern Europe WWI *207* (4)
Rīgas Jūras Līcis *see* Riga, Gulf of
Riia Laht *see* Riga, Gulf of
Rijeka *anc.* Tarsatica; *Ger.* Sankt Veit am Flaum; *It.* Fiume; *Slvn.* Reka Southeast Europe (Croatia) post-war economy *215* (3)
Rijn *see* Rhine
Rijssel *see* Lille
Rim *archaeological site/settlement* West Africa (Burkina) early agriculture *158* (1) early cultures *160* (1)
Rimini *anc.* Ariminum Italy economy *190* (1) medieval states *183* (4), *188* (1) *see also* Ariminum
Rinaldone Italy the world in 2500 BCE *22–23*
Rinan *province* Mainland Southeast Asia first states *260* (1)
Ringsted Scandinavia (Sweden) medieval voyages *60–61* (1)
Rio *see* Rio de Janeiro

S

Sunomata *battle* Japan early modern states *265* (5)
Süntel *battle* Central Europe (Germany) Franks *184* (2)
Suomenlahti *see* Finland, Gulf of
Suomen Tasavalta *see* Finland
Suomi *see* Finland
Suomussalmi Scandinavia (Finland) WWII *210* (1)
Supara South Asia (India) medieval voyages *61* (3)
Superior, Lake *lake* North America colonization *126* (1) cultural groups *123* (3) early agriculture *120* (1) exploration *118* (1), *119* (2), (3) first civilizations *121* (4) the growth of the US *129* (2), *132* (1) US Civil War *131* (6)
Suqutra *see* Socotra
Sūr *see* Syria
Surabaja *see* Surabaya
Surabaya *prev.* Soerabaja, Surabaja *military base/settlement* Maritime Southeast Asia (Indonesia) exploration *239* (2) Islam *275* (4) post-war economy *253* (5) trade *267* (3) WWII *272* (1)
Surasena *region/state* South Asia ancient India *242* (1) first empires *241* (5) first religions *36* (2) world religions *242* (3)
Surashtra *region/state* South Asia first empires *241* (4), (5) world religions *242* (2)
Surat South Asia (India) colonialism *247* (3) decolonization *250* (1) early medieval states *244–245* (3) economy *249* (4) empire and revolution *88* (1) trade *230* (2)
Surgut Eastern Europe (Russian Federation) colonialism *269* (3) exploration *257* (2)
Surinam *var.* Suriname; *prev.* Dutch Guiana, Netherlands Guiana *state* South America colonization *149* (4) economy *153* (3) empire and revolution *150* (1), *151* (3) environment *153* (4) global immigration *101* (3) politics *152* (1) the modern world *112* (1), *113* (3) *see also* Dutch Guiana
Suriname *see* Dutch Guiana, Surinam
Sūrīya *see* Syria
Surkotada *archaeological site* South Asia (India) first cities *240* (2)
Surparaka South Asia (India) early religions *48* (2) first empires *241* (4)
Surt *see* Sirt
Susa *mod.* Shūsh; *Bibl.* Shushan Southwest Asia (Iran) ancient Persia *223* (4), *225* (6) ancient Rome *224* (2), *225* (5) early Islam *56–57* (1) early systems *223* (3) early trade *225* (3) exploration *218* (1) first cities *220* (2), *28–29* (1) first civilizations *221* (4), *24* (2), *25* (3) Hellenistic world *224* (1) Islam *227* (4), (5)
Susia Central Asia (Turkmenistan) Hellenistic world *40–41* (1)
Susiana *province/region* Southwest Asia ancient Persia *223* (4) Hellenistic world *40–41* (1)
Susquehanna *var.* Conestoga *people* North America colonization *126* (1)
Susquehanna *river* North America empire and revolution *127* (3)
Sussex *state* British Isles medieval states *183* (3)
Sutkagen Dor *archaeological site* South Asia (Pakistan) first cities *240* (2)
Sutlej *river* South Asia ancient India *242* (1) colonialism *247* (3), *248* (1), (2) decolonization *250* (1) early medieval states *244* (1), (2), *244–245* (3) economy *249* (4) Marathas *246* (2) Mughal Empire *246* (1) world religions *242* (2), *243* (4)
Sutrium Italy early states *178* (1)
Sutton Hoo British Isles (United Kingdom) medieval states *183* (3)
Suva (Fiji) decolonization *285* (3) WWII *104* (2)
Suvarnagiri South Asia (India) first empires *241* (4)
Suvla Bay *battle* Southwest Asia (Turkey) WWI *207* (6)
Suways, Khalīj as *see* Suez, Gulf of
Suways, Qanāt as *see* Suez Canal
Suzdal Eastern Europe (Russian Federation) Mongols *68–69* (1)
Suzhou *var.* Soochow, Su-chou, Suchow; *prev.* Wuhsien East Asia (China) colonialism *269* (4) early modern states *266* (1) imperialism *270* (2) medieval states *263* (6)
Svalbard *var.* Spitsbergen, Spitzbergen *colonial possession/island group* Arctic Ocean exploration *286* (1), *287* (2) *see also* Spitsbergen
Sverdlovsk Eastern Europe (Russian Federation) Soviet Union *213* (4)
Sverige *see* Sweden
Svizhden *state* Eastern Europe medieval states *189* (4)
Svizzera *see* Helvetia, Helvetian Republic, Swiss Confederation, Switzerland
Svobodnyy Eastern Europe (Russian Federation) Soviet Union *214–215* (4)
Swabia *region* Central Europe crusades *64–65* (2) medieval states *185* (3), *188* (1)
Swahili City-States *region/state* East Africa/Southern Africa economy *163* (2)
Swanscombe *archaeological site* British Isles (United Kingdom) first humans *13* (2)
Swansea *Wel.* Abertawe British Isles (United Kingdom) economy *204* (1)
Swartkrans *archaeological site* Southern Africa (South Africa) first humans *12* (1)
Swatow *see* Shantou
Swazi *people* Southern Africa the world in 1850 *90–91*
Swazi *see* Swaziland
Swaziland *prev.* Swazi *state* Southern Africa decolonization *168* (1) economy *168* (2), (3) European imperialism *96* (1) trade *167* (1)
Sweden *Swe.* Sverige *state* Scandinavia colonialism *269* (3) crusades *186* (1), *64–65* (2) early 20th century *206* (1) early modern states *193* (4), *195* (3) economy *190* (1), *205* (4) empire and revolution *198* (2), *199* (3), *202* (1), (2) imperial global economy *92* (1) inter-war *209* (3), (5) medieval states *185* (3) medieval voyages *60–61* (1) Mongols *68–69* (1) Napoleon *200–201* (1), *201* (2) post-war economy *213* (5), *214* (1), (2) post-war politics *212* (3) Reformation *194* (2), *196* (1), (2) Soviet Union *208* (2), *213* (4) the modern world *112* (2) WWI *207* (4), *208* (1) WWII *104* (1), *211* (2), (4) Cold War *108* (3)
Swedes *people* Scandinavia medieval states *185* (3) the modern world *112* (2)
Swedish Pomerania *colonial possession* Central Europe empire and revolution *199* (3) Napoleon *200–201* (1)
Swiss Confederation *var.* Switzerland; *Fr.* La Suisse, *Ger.* Schweiz, *It.* Svizzera; *prev.* Helvetia, Helvetian Republic; *anc.* Helvetia *state* Central Europe early modern states *193* (4), *197* (5) empire and revolution *199* (3), (4) Napoleon *200–201* (1) Reformation *194* (2), *196* (1), (2) *see also* Helvetia, Helvetian Republic, Switzerland
Switzerland *var.* Swiss Confederation, *Fr.* La Suisse, *Ger.* Schweiz, *It.* Svizzera; *prev.* Helvetia, Helvetian Republic; *state* Central Europe early 20th century *206* (1) economy *205* (4) empire and revolution *202* (1), (2), (3) inter-war *209* (3), (5) post-war economy *213* (5), *214* (1), (2) post-war politics *212* (1), (3) Soviet Union *213* (4) the modern world *112* (2), *113* (3), (4) WWI *206* (2), (3), *207* (5), *208* (1) WWII *104* (1), *211* (2), (3), (4) Cold War *108* (3) *see also* Helvetia, Helvetian Republic, Swiss Confederation
Sword Brothers *crusade* Eastern Europe crusades *186* (1)
Syagrius, Kingdom of *state* France Franks *183* (5)
Sybaris Italy first civilizations *177* (1)
Sycaminum *see* Haifa
Sydney *settlement* Australia colonization *282* (1), (2), *283* (3), *284–285* (1) decolonization *285* (3) environmentalism *285* (2) exploration *279* (2), (3) global immigration *100* (1) imperial global economy *92* (1) prehistoric culture *17* (5)
Syedpur *see* Saidpur
Syene *var.* Assouan, Assuan, Qus; *Ar.* Aswân Egypt Hellenistic world *40–41* (1) *see also* Aswân, Qus
Sylhet South Asia (Bangladesh) post-war politics *252* (3)
Synnada Southwest Asia (Turkey) world religions *48* (1)
Syracusa, Syracusae *see* Syracuse
Syracuse *mod.* Siracusa; *Lat.* Syracusae; *It.* Syracusa *settlement* Italy ancient Rome *179* (3), (5), *180–181* (1), *181* (3), (4) crusades *186* (1) early cultures *161* (2) early states *178* (2) economy *190* (1) first civilizations *177* (1) first religions *37* (3) Islam *184* (1), *227* (4) medieval states *183* (4)
Syr Darya *region* Central Asia colonialism *269* (3)
Syr Darya *var.* Sai Hun, Sir Darya, Syrdarya, *Kaz.* Syrdariya, *Rus.* Syrdar'ya, *Uzb.* Sirdaryo *river* Central Asia ancient trade *44–45* (1) biological diffusion *72–73* (1) colonialism *269* (3) early Islam *56–57* (1) exploration *257* (3) first humans *13* (2) Mongols *68–69* (1) the world in 1500 *74–75* *see also* Jaxartes
Syrdar'ya *see* Jaxartes, Syr Darya
Syria *var.* Siria, Syrie, Sūrīya *region/state* Southwest Asia ancient Persia *225* (6) ancient Rome *180–181* (1), *224* (2), *225* (4), (5) ancient trade *44–45* (1) crusades *65* (3), *228* (2) early cultures *161* (3), (5) early Islam *56–57* (1), *57* (2) early trade *225* (3) economy *234* (1) exploration *218* (2), *219* (4) first religions *37* (3) Hellenistic world *224* (1), *41* (2) Islam *226* (2), *227* (4), (5), *235* (4) medieval states *187* (5) Mongols *229* (3) Napoleon *200–201* (1) Ottomans *231* (3), *232–233* (1) Seljuks *228* (1) Soviet Union *208* (2), *214–215* (4) the modern world *113* (3) US economy *138* (2) world religions *226* (1), *49* (4) WWI *233* (2) WWII *104* (1), (2), *210* (1), *211* (2), (4) 20th century *234* (2) 20th-century politics *233* (3), (4), *235* (5) Cold War *109* (1) *see also* Aram
Syrian Desert *Ar.* Al Hamad, Bādiyat ash Shām *desert* Southwest Asia ancient Persia *223* (4) ancient Rome *180–181* (1), *181* (4) early agriculture *220* (1) economy *234* (1) exploration *219* (4) first cities *220* (2), *28–29* (1) first civilizations *221* (4), *222* (1), (2), *25* (3) Hellenistic world *40–41* (1)
Syrie *see* Syria
Szabadka *see* Subotica
Száva *see* Sava
Szczecin *see* Stettin
Szechuan, Szechwan *see* Sichuan
Szeged *Ger.* Szegedin, *Rom.* Seghedin Central Europe (Hungary) early modern states *193* (4) medieval states *189* (4)
Szegedin *see* Szeged
Székesfehérvár *anc.* Alba Regia; *Ger.* Stuhlweissenberg Central Europe (Hungary) medieval states *188* (1)
Szemao *see* Simao
Szigetvár Central Europe (Hungary) Ottomans *231* (3)
Szisszek *see* Sisak
Szlovákia *see* Slovakia

T

Tabaristan *state* Central Asia early Islam *56–57* (1)
Tabariya, Bahr, Tabariya, Bahrat *see* Galilee, Sea of
Tabasco *state* Central America Mexican Revolution *133* (3) the growth of the US *129* (2)
Tabon Cave Philippines (Philippines) the world in 10,000 BCE *14–15*
Tábor Central Europe (Czech Republic) early modern states *193* (4)
Tabora *var.* Unyanyembe, Kazeh East Africa (Tanzania) exploration *157* (4), (5)
Tabriz Southwest Asia (Iran) biological diffusion *72–73* (1) exploration *218* (2), *219* (3) Islam *226* (2), *227* (4), (5) medieval Persia *231* (4) Mongols *68* (2), *68–69* (1) Ottomans *231* (3) Seljuks *228* (1) Soviet Union *208* (2) Timur *229* (4) world religions *226* (1) WWI *233* (2) 20th-century politics *233* (3), *235* (5)
Tabuk Philippines (Philippines) early Islam *56–57* (1)
Tabun *archaeological site* Southwest Asia (Israel) first humans *13* (2)
Tacna South America (Peru) empire and revolution *150* (1), *151* (3) politics *151* (4)
Tacna *region* South America politics *151* (4)
Tacuba Central America (Mexico) Aztecs *124* (2) colonization *125* (5)
Tacubaya Central America (Mexico) Aztecs *124* (2)
Tadmor Southwest Asia (Syria) first civilizations *222* (1)
Tadmor, Tadmur *see* Palmyra
Tadzhikistan *see* Tajikistan
Taegu East Asia (South Korea) Cold War *109* (4)
Taehan-haehyŏp *see* Korea Strait
Taehan Min'guk *see* South Korea
Taejon *Jap.* Taiden East Asia (South Korea) Cold War *109* (4)
Taensa *people* Central America colonization *125* (4)
Tafahi *island* Pacific Ocean exploration *278* (1)
Taforalt *archaeological site* North Africa (Algeria) first humans *13* (2)
Taga Japan early modern states *265* (5) medieval states *264* (2), *265* (3), (4)
Taghaza West Africa (Mauritania) exploration *156* (3) Islam *163* (1)
Tagish *people* North America cultural groups *123* (3)
Tagliacozzo *battle* Italy medieval states *188* (1)
Tagliamento *river* Italy WWI *207* (5)
Tagus *Port.* Rio Tejo, *Sp.* Río Tajo *river* Iberian Peninsula ancient Rome *180–181* (1) Bronze Age *175* (3) Copper Age *174* (2) crusades *64–65* (2) early agriculture *174* (1) economy *190* (1), *205* (4) first civilizations *177* (1) Franks *184* (2) great migrations *52–53* (1), *53* (2) inter-war *209* (4) Islam *192* (3) Napoleon *200–201* (1), *201* (2) prehistoric culture *17* (3)
Tahert North Africa (Algeria) early Islam *56–57* (1) Islam *163* (1)
Tahirids *dynasty* Central Asia Islam *227* (4)
Tahiti *island* Pacific Ocean colonization *284–285* (1) early cultures *280–281* (3) environmentalism *285* (2) exploration *278* (1), *279* (3) medieval voyages *60* (2)
Tahltan *people* North America cultural groups *123* (3)
Ta'if *Ar.* Al Ţa'if Southwest Asia (Saudi Arabia) early Islam *56–57* (1) Islam *226* (3) world religions *226* (1) 20th-century politics *233* (4)
Tai Hu *lake* East Asia early modern states *266* (1) first states *260* (1)
Taiji *var.* Imperial Palace *palace* East Asia (China) medieval states *262* (2)
Taimataima *archaeological site/settlement* South America (Venezuela) early cultures *144* (1)
Taimyr Peninsula *see* Taymyr, Poluostrov
Taipei East Asia (Taiwan) Islam *275* (4)
Taiping *military campaign* East Asia empire and revolution *88–89* (2)
Taira Japan economy *270* (1)
Tairona *state* South America the world in 1200 *62–63*
Tairona Chiefdoms *state* South America early cultures *146* (1)
Tai Shan *var.* T'ai Shan *mountain* East Asia first religions *37* (4)
Taiwan *prev.* China, Republic of *island/state* East Asia ancient trade *44–45* (1) colonialism *269* (4) decolonization *251* (4), *285* (3) early agriculture *258* (1) early modern states *266* (2), *268* (1) economy *274* (1) empire and revolution *268* (2) European imperialism *97* (3) first cities *259* (4), (5) first religions *37* (4) first states *260* (1), *261* (2), (3) historical geography *236–237* (1) imperialism *270* (2) Islam *275* (4) medieval states *261* (4), (5), *262–263* (1), *263* (3), (4), (5), (6) Mongols *68–69* (1) post-war economy *253* (5), *275* (3) post-war politics *271* (7) the growth of the US *133* (4) the modern world *113* (4) WWII *251* (3) Chinese revolution *271* (5) Cold War *109* (1) *see also* China, Republic of
Taiwanese *rebellion* East Asia empire and revolution *268* (2)
Taixicun East Asia (China) first cities *259* (3)
Taiyuan *prev.* T'ai-yuan, T'ai-yüan, Yangku East Asia (China) biological diffusion *72–73* (1) early modern states *266* (1) economy *274* (1) Islam *275* (4) medieval states *262–263* (1), *263* (4), (5) post-war politics *271* (7), *274* (2)
Tajikistan *Rus.* Tadzhikistan, *Taj.* Tojikiston *state* Central Asia Islam *235* (4) post-war economy *275* (3) Soviet Union *214–215* (4) the modern world *113* (3)
Tajiks *people* Central Asia historical geography *275* (5)
Tajo, Río *see* Tagus
Takamatsu *battle* Japan early modern states *267* (4)
Takaoka Japan economy *270* (1)
Takapoto *island* Pacific Ocean exploration *278* (1)
Takaroa *island* Pacific Ocean exploration *278* (1)
Takeda *region* Japan early modern states *267* (4)
Takedda West Africa (Mali/Niger) exploration *156* (3)
Ta Kieu Mainland Southeast Asia (Vietnam) ancient India *241* (6)
Takkola Mainland Southeast Asia (Thailand) ancient India *241* (6)
Takla Makan Desert *Chin.* Taklimakan Shamo *desert* East Asia ancient trade *44–45* (1) biological diffusion *72–73* (1) colonialism *269* (4) early agriculture *258* (1) empire and revolution *268* (2) exploration *256* (1), *257* (3) first cities *259* (5) first states *260* (1) medieval states *261* (6), *262–263* (1), *263* (6) Mongols *68–69* (1) trade *267* (3) world religions *49* (3), (4)
Taklimakan Shamo *see* Takla Makan Desert
Takoradi West Africa (Ghana) colonization *167* (4)
Takrur *var.* Toucouleur *state* West Africa Islam *163* (1) trade *163* (4), (6), (7)
Taksashila *var.* Taxila South Asia (Pakistan) early medieval states *244* (1) first empires *241* (4) *see also* Taxila
Takume *island* Pacific Ocean exploration *278* (1)
Takushan *see* Dagushan
Talasea *island* Pacific Ocean early cultures *280–281* (3) medieval voyages *60* (2)
Talas River *battle* Central Asia (Kazakhstan) early Islam *56–57* (1) Islam *226* (2)
Talavera *var.* Talavera de la Reina Iberian Peninsula (Spain) Napoleon *200–201* (1)
Talavera de la Reina *see* Talavera
Talca South America (Chile) empire and revolution *150* (1), *151* (3) environment *153* (4) Incas *147* (3)
Talcahuano *battle* South America (Chile) empire and revolution *150* (1)
Talgai Australia exploration *280* (1)
Ta-lien *see* Dairen, Dalian
Tal-i Ghazir Southwest Asia (Iran) first cities *220* (2)
Tal-i Iblis Southwest Asia (Iran) first civilizations *24* (2)
Tal-i Malyan Southwest Asia (Iran) first cities *220* (2)
Tallahassee *prev.* Muskogean North America (USA) the growth of the US *129* (2) US Civil War *131* (6), (7) US society *137* (6)
Tallasahatchee *battle* North America (USA) the growth of the US *129* (2)
Tallin *see* Reval, Revel, Tallinn
Tallinn *prev.* Revel; *Ger.* Reval, *Rus.* Tallin Eastern Europe (Estonia) post-war politics *212* (3) Soviet Union *214–215* (4) *see also* Reval, Revel
Tall-i Qaleh Southwest Asia (Iran) first civilizations *25* (3)
Taltal South America (Chile) politics *151* (4)
Tamanrasset *var.* Tamenghest North Africa (Algeria) colonization *167* (4)
Tamar *see* Palmyra, Tadmor
Tamar Hat *archaeological site* North Africa (Algeria) prehistoric culture *17* (2)
Tamathli *people* North America colonization *125* (4)
Tamatsukuri Japan early modern states *265* (5)
Tamaulepec *people* Central America colonization *125* (4)
Tamaulipas *state* Central America Mexican Revolution *133* (3) the growth of the US *129* (2)
Tamazultec *people* Central America colonization *125* (4)
Tambo Colorado South America (Peru) Incas *147* (3)
Tambora *island* Maritime Southeast Asia European expansion *84–85* (1)
Tambov Eastern Europe (Russian Federation) Soviet Union *208* (2)
Tambo Viejo South America (Peru) early cultures *145* (4)
Tambralinga Mainland Southeast Asia (Thailand) ancient India *241* (6) early medieval states *245* (5)
Tambralinga *region* Mainland Southeast Asia early medieval states *245* (5)
Tame South America (Colombia) empire and revolution *150* (1)
Tamenghest *see* Tamanrasset
Tamil Nadu *region/state* South Asia post-war politics *252* (1) world religions *243* (4)
Tamils *people* South Asia the world in 250 CE *46–47*
Ta-ming *see* Daming
Tamluk *religious site/settlement* South Asia (India) ancient trade *44–45* (1) first religions *36* (2)
Tammaulipeco *people* Central America colonization *126* (1)
Tampa North America (USA) Cold War *108* (2)
Tampico Central America (Mexico) colonization *125* (4), *126* (1) exploration *118* (1) Mexican Revolution *133* (3) the growth of the US *129* (2) Cold War *108* (2)
Tamralipti South Asia early medieval states *244* (1) early religions *48* (2) first empires *241* (4) world religions *242* (2), (3)
Tamuin Central America (Mexico) first civilizations *122* (1)
Tamworth British Isles (United Kingdom) medieval states *183* (3)
Tana Eastern Europe (Russian Federation) economy *190* (1) Ottomans *195* (4)
T'ana Hāyk' *see* Tana, Lake
Tanais *see* Don
Tana, Lake *var.* T'ana Hāyk' *lake* East Africa early cultures *161* (3), (4), (5) early trade *225* (3) exploration *157* (5) first humans *12* (1), *13* (2) trade *165* (3)
Tanana *people* North America cultural groups *123* (3)
Tanana *river* North America imperial global economy *93* (3)
Tanasari Mainland Southeast Asia (Burma) trade *230* (2)
Tancah Central America (Mexico) first civilizations *123* (2)
Tanchon East Asia (North Korea) Cold War *109* (4)
Tanchou *see* Tanzhou
Tanegashima *island* Japan early modern states *265* (5) Communism *273* (3)
Tang *vassal state* East Asia first cities *259* (3)
Tangana *state* South Asia first empires *241* (5)
Tanganhuato Central America (Mexico) first civilizations *122* (1)
Tanganyika *mod.* Tanzania; *prev.* German East Africa *colonial possession* East Africa WWII *104* (1) Cold War *109* (1) *see also* German East Africa, Tanzania
Tanganyika, Lake *lake* East Africa early agriculture *158* (1) early cultures *160* (1) economy *163* (2) European imperialism *96* (1) exploration *156* (3), *157* (4), (5) first humans *12* (1), *13* (2) Islam *163* (1) slave trade *165* (4)
Tang Empire *state* East Asia medieval states *262–263* (1) world religions *49* (4)
Tanger, Tánger, Tangerk *see* Tangier, Tingis
Tanggula Shan *see* Tanglha Range
Tangier *var.* Tangiers; *anc.* Tingis; *Fr./Ger.* Tangerk, *Sp.* Tánger North Africa (Morocco) early Islam *57* (2) economy *163* (2) European imperialism *96* (1) exploration *156* (3), *157* (4) inter-war *209* (4) Islam *163* (1), *192* (3) Mongols *68* (2) Napoleon *200–201* (1), *201* (2) slave trade *165* (4) *see also* Tingis
Tangiers *see* Tangier, Tingis
Tangjin *battle* East Asia (South Korea) Sino-Japanese War *270* (3)
Tanglha Range *Chin.* Tanggula Shan *mountain range* East Asia exploration *257* (3)
Tang Protectorate *see* Ferghana
Tanguts *people* East Asia early modern states *266* (1) medieval states *263* (3) trade *267* (3)
Tangxiang *state* East Asia medieval states *263* (3)
Tanis *var.* Avaris Egypt ancient Egypt *159* (5) first civilizations *221* (5) *see also* Avaris
Tanjavur South Asia (India) early medieval states *244–245* (3)
Tanjore *var.* Thanjāvūr South Asia (India) colonialism *248* (1) economy *249* (4) Mughal Empire *246* (1)
Tanjore *region/state* South Asia colonialism *248* (1) Marathas *246* (2) Mughal Empire *246* (1)
Tanjungpura Maritime Southeast Asia (Indonesia) early medieval states *245* (6) exploration *239* (1) world religions *243* (5)
Tanna *island* Pacific Ocean exploration *278* (1)
Tannenberg *var.* Grunwald *battle* Central Europe (Poland) early modern states *193* (4) WWI *207* (4)
Tannu Tuva *region/state* Siberia colonialism *269* (3) Communism *271* (8) Soviet Union *208* (2), *213* (4) WWII *104* (1)
Tan-Tan *state* Maritime Southeast Asia ancient India *241* (6)
Tan-tung *see* Andong, Dandong
Tanzania *prev.* German East Africa, Tanganyika and Zanzibar, *state* East Africa decolonization *168* (1) economy *168* (2), (3) the modern world *112* (1), *113* (3), (4) *see also* German East Africa, Tanganyika, Zanzibar
Tanzhou *var.* Tanchou East Asia (China) medieval states *262–263* (1), *263* (3), (4)
Taodeni *Fr.* Taoudenni, Taoudenit West Africa (Mali) Islam *163* (1)
Taos North America (USA) colonization *126* (1) exploration *119* (3)
Taos *people* North America colonization *126* (1)
Taoudenit *see* Taodeni, Taoudenni
Taoudenni *var.* Taoudenit, Taodeni West Africa (Mali) colonization *167* (4) *see also* Taodeni
Taourirt North Africa (Morocco) Islam *163* (1)
Tapajó *people* South America early cultures *147* (2)
Tapajós *state* South America the world in 1500 *74–75*
Tapajós *var.* Tapajóz *river* South America colonization *149* (3) early cultures *144* (1), *145* (2) empire and revolution *151* (3) environment *153* (4) exploration *142* (1), *143* (2)
Tapajoso *var.* Santarém *region* South America early cultures *145* (2)
Tapajóz *see* Tapajós
Tapasha *region* South Asia world religions *242* (2)
Taprobane *var.* Sarandib, Saylan, Sri Lanka *island* South Asia ancient trade *44* (2) world religions *49* (3) *see also* Ceylon, Lambakannas, Lanka, Simhala, Sri Lanka
Taquira Tradition *people* South America the world in 1000 *58–59*
Tara Eastern Europe (Russian Federation) exploration *257* (2)
Tarābulus *see* Tripoli, Tripolis
Ţarābulus al Gharb *see* Oea, Tripoli
Ţarābulus ash Shām *see* Tripoli, Tripolis
Taradavadi South Asia (India) early medieval states *244* (2)
Tarahumara *people* Central America colonization *125* (4)
Tarakan *military campaign* Maritime Southeast Asia WWII *273* (2)
Taranaki *region* New Zealand colonization *283* (5)
Tarangambādi *see* Tranquebar
Taranto *var.* Tarantum, Tarentum Italy crusades *186* (1), *64–65* (2) economy *190* (1) medieval states *187* (5) *see also* Tarantum, Tarentum
Tarantum *var.* Tarentum; *mod.* Taranto Italy ancient Rome *180–181* (1), *181* (4) *see also* Taranto, Tarentum
Tarapacá *region* South America politics *151* (4)
Tarawa *military campaign* Gilbert Islands WWII *273* (2)
Tarazona Iberian Peninsula (Spain) medieval states *187* (3)
Tardanizats *battle* France Reformation *196* (2)
Tarentaise France Franks *184* (2)
Tarentum *var.* Tarantum; *mod.* Taranto Italy ancient Rome *179* (3), (5) early states *178* (1), (2) first civilizations *177* (1) *see also* Taranto, Tarantum
Târgovişte *see* Tûrgovişte
Târgu-Jiu *battle* Southeast Europe (Romania) WWI *207* (6)
Târguşor *prev.* Tîrguşor, Têrguşor Southeast Europe (Romania) world religions *48* (1) *see also* Tîrguşor
Tarī East Asia (China) first cities *259* (5)
Tarifa Iberian Peninsula (Spain) Islam *192* (3)
Tarija South America (Bolivia) narcotics *153* (5)
Tarim *river* East Asia exploration *257* (3) first states *260* (1) medieval states *262–263* (1) Mongols *68–69* (1)
Tarka Southern Africa (South Africa) colonization *166* (2)
Tarkhan Egypt ancient Egypt *159* (2)
Tarma South America (Peru) Incas *147* (3)
Tarnow Central Europe (Poland) WWI *207* (4)
Taroudant *var.* Taroudant North Africa (Morocco) Islam *163* (1)
Taroudant *see* Taroudannt
Tarquinia *see* Tarquinii
Tarquinii *mod.* Tarquinia; *hist.* Corneto Italy early states *178* (1), (2) first civilizations *177* (1)
Tarraco *mod.* Tarragona *settlement* Iberian Peninsula (Spain) ancient Rome *179* (3), *180–181* (1), *181* (3), (4), *225* (5) early cultures *161* (2) great migrations *52–53* (1) world religions *48* (1) *see also* Tarragona
Tarraconensis *province* Iberian peninsula ancient Rome *180–181* (1)
Tarragona Iberian Peninsula (Spain) ancient Rome *182* (1) inter-war *209* (4) Islam *192* (3) medieval states *182* (2)
Tarsatica *see* Rijeka
Tarsus *settlement* Southwest Asia (Turkey) ancient Rome *180–181* (1) crusades *228* (2), *65* (3) early Islam *56–57* (1) first civilizations *221* (4), *24* (2) Hellenistic world *40–41* (1) Islam *226* (2), *227* (4) medieval states *185* (3) Mongols *229* (3) world religions *48* (1)
Tartars *see* Tatars
Tartu *see* Dorpat
Taruga *archaeological site/settlement* West Africa (Nigeria) ancient trade *44–45* (1) early agriculture *158* (1) early cultures *160* (1)
Taruma *state* Maritime Southeast Asia ancient India *241* (6)
Tarut Southwest Asia (Saudi Arabia) first civilizations *24* (3)
Tarvisium *see* Treviso
Tarxien (Malta) the world in 2500 BCE *22–23*
Tases *state* Central America Aztecs *124* (1)
Tashauz *see* Dashkhovuz
Tashi Chho Dzong *see* Thimphu
Tashihkiao *see* Dashiqiao
Tashi Lhunpo East Asia (China) exploration *257* (3)
Tashkent *Uzb.* Toshkent Central Asia (Uzbekistan) biological diffusion *72–73* (1) colonialism *269* (3), (4) Communism *271* (8) exploration *256* (1), *257* (3) global immigration *100* (1) Hellenistic world *40–41* (1) medieval Persia *231* (4) medieval states *261* (6) Mongols *68–69* (1) Ottomans *232–233* (1) Soviet Union *208* (2), *214–215* (4) trade *267* (3)
Tasmania *prev.* Van Diemen's Land *region/island* Australia colonization *282* (1), (2), *283* (3) early cultures *280–281* (3) exploration *276–277* (1), *279* (2), (3) medieval voyages *60* (2)
Tasman Sea *sea* Pacific Ocean colonization *282* (1), *283* (4), (5) early cultures *280–281* (3) environmentalism *285* (2)
exploration *279* (2) medieval voyages *60* (2) prehistoric culture *17* (5)
Tatars *var.* Tartars *people* East Asia/Siberia historical geography *275* (5) Mongols *68–69* (1)
Tatarstan *state* Eastern Europe Soviet Union *214–215* (4)
Tatta South Asia (Pakistan) colonialism *248* (1)
Tatta *see* Thatta
Ta-t'ung, Tatung *see* Datong
Tauchira North Africa (Libya) first civilizations *177* (1)
Taung *archaeological site* Southern Africa (South Africa) first humans *12* (1)
Taunton British Isles (United Kingdom) economy *204* (1)
Taunum Central Europe (Germany) world religions *48* (1)
Taupo, Lake *lake* New Zealand colonization *283* (5)
Tauranga New Zealand colonization *283* (5)
Tauroggen *region* Eastern Europe empire and revolution *199* (3)
Taurus Mountains *var.* Toros Dağları *mountain range* Southwest Asia ancient Persia *223* (4), *225* (6) crusades *64–65* (2) early agriculture *220* (1) exploration *218* (1), (2), *219* (3) first cities *220* (2), *28–29* (1) first civilizations *221* (4), (5), *222* (2) Hellenistic world *224* (1) Ottomans *231* (3), *232–233* (1) Seljuks *228* (1) WWI *233* (2)
Tau'u Island *island* Pacific Ocean exploration *278* (1)
Tavascan *see* Michoacan
Tawahi Mainland Southeast Asia (Burma) trade *230* (2)
Tawakoni *people* North America colonization *125* (4)
Taxila *Buddhist centre/religious site/settlement* South Asia (India) ancient Persia *225* (6) ancient Rome *224* (2) ancient trade *44* (2), *44–45* (1) exploration *256* (1) first religions *36* (2) Hellenistic world *224* (1), *41* (2) medieval states *262–263* (1) world religions *49* (3), (4)
Taxla Central America (Mexico) first civilizations *121* (2)
Tayasal Central America (Guatemala) Aztecs *124* (1)
Taylor's Battle *battle* North America (USA) the growth of the US *129* (2)
Taymyr, Poluostrov *Eng.* Taimyr Peninsula *headland* Siberia exploration *257* (2)
Tayspun *see* Ctesiphon
Taz *river* Eastern Europe exploration *257* (2)
Tazoult *see* Lambaesis
Tazumal Central America (Mexico) first civilizations *123* (2)
T'bilisi *Eng.* Tiflis Southwest Asia (Georgia) Soviet Union *214–215* (4) *see also* Tiflis
Tchad *see* Chad
Tchefuncte Culture *people* North America the world in 250 BCE *38–39*
Tchongking *see* Chongqing
Te Anau, Lake *lake* New Zealand colonization *283* (5)
Teano *see* Teanum
Teanum *var.* Teanum Sidicinum; *mod.* Teano Italy early states *178* (1)
Teanum Apulum Italy early states *178* (1)
Teanum Sidicinum *see* Teanum
Tebuk Southwest Asia (Saudi Arabia) 20th-century politics *233* (4)
Tecama Central America (Mexico) Aztecs *124* (2)
Tecklenburg *region* Central Europe empire and revolution *199* (3)
Tecoac Central America (Mexico) colonization *125* (5)
Tédellis North Africa (Algeria) economy *190* (1)
Tegasta *fort* North America (USA) colonization *125* (4)
Tegel *airport* Central Europe (Germany) post-war politics *212* (2)
Tegeler See *lake* Central Europe post-war politics *212* (2)
Tegucigalpa Central America (Honduras) the growth of the US *129* (2)
Teheran *see* Tehran
Tehran *var.* Teheran; Pers. Tehrān Southwest Asia (Iran) colonialism *269* (3) economy *234* (1) Islam *235* (4) medieval Persia *231* (4) Ottomans *231* (3), *232–233* (1) 20th-century politics *235* (5) Communism *271* (8)
Tehri Garhwal *state* South Asia colonialism *248* (2)
Tehuacán Central America (Mexico) first civilizations *122* (1) Mexican Revolution *133* (3)
Tehuacán Valley *valley* Central America early agriculture *20* (1)
Tehuantepec *var.* Santo Domingo Tehuantepec Central America (Mexico) first civilizations *122* (1) Mexican Revolution *133* (3)
Tehuantepec, Golfo de *see* Tehuantepec, Gulf of
Tehuantepec, Gulf of *var.* Tehuantepec, Golfo de *gulf* Central America Aztecs *124* (1) Mexican Revolution *133* (3)
Tehuantepec, Isthmus of *var.* Istmo de Tehuantepec *coastal feature* Central America Aztecs *124* (1)
Tehuantepec, Istmo de *see* Tehuantepec, Isthmus of
Tehuelche *people* South America early cultures *147* (2)
Tejo, Rio *see* Tagus
Teke *state* Central Africa the world in 1700 *82–83* the world in 1800 *86–87* the world in 1850 *90–91*
Tekesta *people* North America colonization *125* (4), *126* (1)
Telanaipura *see* Jambi
Tel Aviv Southwest Asia (Israel) 20th-century politics *235* (5)
Tel Aviv-Yafo Southwest Asia (Israel) 20th century *234* (2)
Telingana *region/state* South Asia early medieval states *244–245* (3)
Tell Agrab *var.* Tell Ajrab *settlement/temple* Southwest Asia (Iraq) first cities *220* (2) first civilizations *24* (2), *25* (3)
Tell 'Asmar, Tell Asmar *see* Eshnunna
Tell Aswad Southwest Asia (Iraq) first cities *220* (2)
Tell Brak Southwest Asia (Syria) early systems *223* (3), *32* (1) first cities *28–29* (1) first civilizations *24* (2)
Tell el-Ajjul Southwest Asia (Israel) ancient Egypt *159* (4)
Tell el-Amarna *see* Akhetaten
Tell el 'Ubaid Southwest Asia (Iraq) early agriculture *220* (1) first cities *220* (2)
Teller North America (USA) exploration *287* (2)
Tell es Sawwan Southwest Asia (Iraq) early agriculture *220* (1)
Tell Halaf Southwest Asia (Syria) early agriculture *220* (1)
Tell Ibrahim Awad Egypt ancient Egypt *159* (2)
Tellicherry *var.* Thalassery South Asia (India) colonialism *247* (3)
Telloh Southwest Asia (Iraq) first cities *220* (2)
Tell Sleimeh Southwest Asia (Iran) first civilizations *24* (3)
Tell 'Uqair *settlement/temple* Southwest Asia (Iraq) first cities *220* (2) first civilizations *221* (4)
Teloapan Central America (Mexico) Aztecs *124* (1)
Teloloapan Central America (Mexico) first civilizations *122* (1)
Telo Martius *see* Toulon
Telugucodas *state* South Asia Mongols *68–69* (1)
Temazcalpan Central America (Mexico) Aztecs *124* (2)
Temesvár *battle* Southeast Europe (Romania) Ottomans *197* (4)
Tempelhof Central Europe (Germany) crusades *186* (1)
Tempelhof *airport* Central Europe (Germany) post-war politics *212* (2)
Tenango Central America (Mexico) first civilizations *122* (1)
Tenanitla Central America (Mexico) Aztecs *124* (3)
Tenasserim *state/colonial possession* Mainland Southeast Asia colonialism *269* (4) European imperialism *97* (3)
Tenayuca Central America (Mexico) Aztecs *124* (3)
Tenayucan Central America (Mexico) Aztecs *124* (2)
Tenerife *battle* South America (Colombia) empire and revolution *150* (1)
Ténès North Africa (Algeria) economy *190* (1)
Teng East Asia (China) first cities *259* (5)
Teng *state* East Asia first cities *259* (5)
Tenganapatam *var.* Ft. St. David South Asia (India) colonialism *247* (3)
Tengasseri South Asia (India) colonialism *247* (3)
Teng-chou *see* Dengzhou
Tengchung *see* Dengyue
Tennant Creek Australia colonization *282* (1), *283* (3) exploration *279* (2)
Tennessee *state* North America the growth of the US *129* (1) US Civil War *130* (2), (3), (4), (5), *131* (6), (7) US economy *134* (2), *139* (3) US society *137* (6) US superpower *139* (5)
Tennessee *river* North America cultural groups *122* (5) first civilizations *121* (4) the growth of the US *129* (2) US Civil War *131* (6)
Tenochtitlan *mod.* Ciudad de Mexico, México, Mexico City *archaeological site/settlement* Central America (Mexico) Aztecs *124* (1), (2), (3) colonization *125* (5) exploration *118* (1) first civilizations *121* (3) *see also* México, Mexico City
Tenos *mod.* Tínos *island* Greece Ottomans *230* (1)
Teodomiro *state* Iberian Peninsula the world in 750 CE *54–55*
Teos *settlement/state* Greece ancient Greece *177* (2) first civilizations *177* (1)
Teotihuacan Central America (Mexico) Aztecs *124* (2) first civilizations *122* (1)
Teotihuacan *region* Central America first civilizations *122* (1)
Teotitlán Central America (Mexico) first civilizations *122* (1)
Teotitlan del Cassino *state* Central America Aztecs *124* (1)
Tepahue *people* Central America colonization *125* (4)
Tepeacac Central America (Mexico) first civilizations *122* (1)
Tepeacac *state* Central America Aztecs *124* (1)
Tepecano *people* Central America colonization *125* (4)
Tepecuacuilco *state* Central America Aztecs *124* (1)
Tepe Gawra *settlement/temple* Southwest Asia (Iraq) early agriculture *220* (1) first cities *220* (2)
Tepe Giyan Southwest Asia (Iran) early agriculture *220* (1) first civilizations *24* (2)
Tepe Guran Southwest Asia (Iran) early agriculture *220* (1)
Tepe Hissar Southwest Asia (Iran) first civilizations *24* (3)
Tepehuan *people* Central America colonization *125* (4), *126* (1)
Tepe Sabz Southwest Asia (Iraq) early agriculture *220* (1)
Tepetlacalco Central America (Mexico) Aztecs *124* (3)
Tepetlaztinco Central America (Mexico) Aztecs *124* (3)
Tepetzinco Central America (Mexico) Aztecs *124* (3)
Tepexic Central America (Mexico) first civilizations *122* (1)
Tepexpan Central America (Mexico) Aztecs *124* (2)
Tepeyacac Central America (Mexico) Aztecs *124* (2), (3) colonization *125* (5)
Tepe Yahya Southwest Asia (Iran) first civilizations *24* (3)
Tepic Central America (Mexico) Mexican Revolution *133* (3)
Tepoatlan Central America (Mexico) first civilizations *122* (1)
Tepotzotlan Central America (Mexico) Aztecs *124* (2)
Tequexquinahuac Central America (Mexico) Aztecs *124* (3)
Tequisistlan Central America (Mexico) Aztecs *124* (2)
Terevaka, Cerro *mountain* Pacific Ocean early cultures *281* (4)
Târguşor *see* Târguşor, Tîrguşor
Ternate Maritime Southeast Asia (Indonesia) colonialism *247* (4) colonization *284–285* (1) trade *267* (3)
Ternate *island* Maritime Southeast Asia colonialism *247* (4) early medieval states *245* (6) exploration *239* (2) Islam *243* (6) world religions *243* (5)
Ternopol' Eastern Europe (Ukraine) WWII *211* (4)
Terranova di Sicilia *see* Gela
Terranova Pausania *see* Olbia
Terre-Neuve *see* Newfoundland
Terror, Mount *mountain* Antarctica Antarctic Exploration *287* (3)
Teruel *anc.* Turba Iberian Peninsula (Spain) inter-war *209* (4) Islam *192* (3)
Tešetice-Kyjovice Central Europe (Czech Republic) early agriculture *174* (1)
Teshik Tash *archaeological site* Central Asia (Uzbekistan) first humans *13* (2)
Tete Southern Africa (Mozambique) colonization *167* (4) exploration *157* (4) Islam *163* (1) trade *164* (1)
Tetecpilco Central America (Mexico) Aztecs *124* (3)
Tetelco Central America (Mexico) Aztecs *124* (2)
Teton *people* North America colonization *126* (1)
Tetzcoco Central America (Mexico) colonization *125* (5)
Teul *people* Central America colonization *125* (4)

INDEX-GAZETTEER: **Teurnia – Tucson**

Teurnia Central Europe (Austria) ancient Rome *180–181* (1)
Teutonic Knights *crusade/state* Eastern Europe crusades 186 (1) Mongols *68–69* (1)
Teutonic Order *var.* Knights of the Cross *state* Eastern Europe early modern states 193 (4) economy 190 (1) medieval states 188 (1), 189 (3), (4)
Teutonic Peoples *people* Central Europe/Eastern Europe/Scandinavia the world in 250 CE *46–47*
Tevere *see* Tiber, Tiberis
Tewa *people* North America colonization 125 (4)
Texas *region/state* North America imperial global economy 93 (5) Mexican Revolution 133 (3) the growth of the US 129 (1) US Civil War *130* (2), (3), (4), (5), 131 (6), (7) US economy 134 (2), 139 (3) US superpower 139 (5)
Texcoco Central America (Mexico) Aztecs 124 (1), (2)
Texcoco, Lake *lake* Central America Aztecs 124 (1), (2), (3) colonization 125 (5) first civilizations 122 (1)
Texcotzinco Central America (Mexico) Aztecs 124 (2)
Tezampa Central America (Mexico) Aztecs 124 (2)
Tezoyuca Central America (Mexico) Aztecs 124 (2)
Thaba Bosiu Southern Africa (South Africa) colonization 166 (2)
Thaba Nchu Southern Africa (South Africa) colonization 166 (2)
Thailand *prev.* Siam; *Thai* Prathet Thai *state* Mainland Southeast Asia Bronze Age 240 (3) decolonization 251 (4) historical geography 275 (5) Islam 275 (4) post-war economy 253 (5), 275 (3) post-war politics 251 (5), 253 (4) the modern world 113 (3), (4) US superpower 138 (1) WWII 104 (1), (2) Cold War 109 (1) *see also* Siam
Thailand, Gulf of *var.* Gulf of Siam, *Thai* Ao Thai, *Vtn.* Vinh Thai Lan *gulf* Mainland Southeast Asia ancient India 241 (6) colonialism 247 (4), 248 (1) early medieval states 245 (5), (6) exploration 239 (1) Islam 243 (6) post-war economy 253 (5) post-war politics 253 (4) world religions 243 (5) *see also* Siam, Gulf of
Thais *people* Mainland Southeast Asia the world in 750 CE *54–55* the world in 1000 *58–59* the world in 1200 *62–63*
Thalassery *see* Tellicherry
Thalcozauhtitlan *state* Central America Aztecs 124 (1)
Thalner South Asia (China) early medieval states *244–245* (3)
Thames New Zealand colonization 283 (5)
Thames *river* British Isles Bronze Age 175 (3) Copper Age 174 (2) early agriculture 174 (1) economy 204 (1) great migrations *52–53* (1) medieval states 186 (2), 187 (4), 188 (2)
Thames and Severn *canal* British Isles economy 204 (1)
Tham Khuyen *archaeological site* Mainland Southeast Asia (Vietnam) first humans 13 (2)
Thamugadi North Africa (Algeria) ancient Rome *180–181* (1)
Thana *mod.* Thāne South Asia (India) economy 249 (4)
Thāne *see* Thana
Thang Long *see* Hanoi
Thang Phong *battle* Mainland Southeast Asia (Vietnam) post-war politics 251 (5)
Thanh Hoa Mainland Southeast Asia (Vietnam) early medieval states 245 (6) Mongols *68–69* (1)
Thanjārur *see* Tanjore
Thanjāvūr *see* Tanjore
Thanlwin *see* Salween
Thapsacus Southwest Asia (Syria) Hellenistic world *40–41* (1)
Thapsus North Africa (Tunisia) ancient Rome *180–181* (1) first civilizations 177 (1)
Thara Southwest Asia (Iran) medieval voyages 61 (3)
Thar Desert *var.* Great Indian Desert, Indian Desert *desert* South Asia ancient India 242 (1) ancient trade *44–45* (1) biological diffusion *72–73* (1) colonialism 247 (3), 248 (1) early Islam *56–57* (1) early medieval states 244 (1), (2), *244–245* (3) early religions 48 (2) economy 249 (4) first cities 240 (2) first empires 241 (5) first humans 13 (2) first religions 36 (2) Marathas 246 (2) medieval Persia 231 (4) Mughal Empire 246 (1) post-war politics 252 (1) world religions 242 (2), 243 (4), 49 (3)
Tharrus Italy first civilizations 177 (1)
Thasos Greece ancient Greece 177 (3) first civilizations 177 (1)
Thasos *state/island* Greece ancient Greece 177 (2), (3)
That Khe *fort* Mainland Southeast Asia post-war politics 251 (5)
Thaton Mainland Southeast Asia (Burma) ancient trade *44–45* (1) medieval states *262–263* (1)
Thaton *state* Mainland Southeast Asia the world in 750 CE *54–55* the world in 1000 *58–59*
Thatta *var.* Tatta South Asia (Pakistan) early medieval states *244–245* (3) Mughal Empire 246 (1) world religions 243 (4)
Thebae *see* Thebes
Thebes Egypt ancient Egypt 159 (3) ancient Persia 223 (4) early cultures 160 (1), 161 (3), (4), (5) Hellenistic world *40–41* (1)
Thebes *settlement* Greece ancient Greece 177 (3) first cities *28–29* (1) first civilizations 175 (4), 222 (2) first religions 37 (3) Hellenistic world *40–41* (1)
The Hague Low Countries (Netherlands) empire and revolution 202 (1i), (2) inter-war 209 (5) Reformation 195 (5)
The Illinois Post North America (USA) colonization 126 (1)
Theiss *see* Tisza
Thenae North Africa (Tunisia) first civilizations 177 (1)
Theodosia *var.* Caffa, Kefe; *mod.* Feodosiya; *It.* Kaffa Eastern Europe (Ukraine) first civilizations 177 (1) Hellenistic world *40–41* (1) *see also* Kaffa
Theodosiopolis *see* Erzurum
Thera Greece first civilizations 177 (1)
Thera *var.* Santorini *island* Greece first civilizations 175 (4)
Theresienstadt *concentration camp* Central Europe WWII 211 (3)
Thermopylae Greece great migrations *52–53* (1) ancient Greece 179 (4) ancient Persia 223 (4)
Thessalonica *mod.* Thessaloníki; *Eng.* Salonica, Salonika, *SCr.* Solun, *Turk.* Selânik Greece ancient Greece 179 (4) ancient Rome 179 (5), *180–181* (1), *181* (4), 182 (1) crusades *64–65* (2) early cultures 161 (2) Hellenistic world 41 (2) world religions 48 (1) *see also* Salonica
Thessaloníki *see* Salonica, Thessalonica
Thessaly *region* Greece ancient Greece 177 (3), 179 (4) first civilizations 175 (4) first religions 37 (3) Ottomans 202 (4) WWI 207 (6)
The States *see* United States of America
The Wilderness *battle* North America (USA) US Civil War 131 (7)
Thimbu *see* Thimphu
Thimphu *var.* Thimbu; *prev.* Tashi Chho Dzong South Asia (Bhutan) post-war economy 253 (5)
Thionville *see* Diedenhofen
Third Cataract *waterfall* Egypt ancient Egypt 159 (4), (5)
Thirteen Colonies *colonial possession* North America empire and revolution 127 (3)
Thiruvanathapuram *see* Trivandrum
Thiva *see* Thebes
Thomas Quarry *archaeological site* North Africa (Morocco) first humans 13 (2)
Thon Buri Mainland Southeast Asia (Thailand) biological diffusion *72–73* (1)
Thorn *Pol.* Toruń Central Europe (Poland) economy 190 (1) medieval states 188 (1) WWI 207 (4) *see also* Toruń
Thornton Island *see* Caroline Island
Thospitis *see* Van, Lake
Thovela *state* Southern Africa the world in 1700 *82–83*
Thrace *anc.* Thracia *region* Greece/ Southeast Europe ancient Greece 177 (2), 179 (4) ancient Persia 223 (4) ancient Rome 225 (5) ancient trade *44–45* (1) exploration 218 (1) first civilizations 175 (4), 177 (1) first religions 37 (3) Hellenistic world 224 (1) Ottomans 202 (4), 230 (1) world religions 48 (1) *see also* Thracia
Thracia *var.* Thrace *province* Southeast Europe ancient Rome *180–181* (1), *181* (4) *see also* Thrace
Thracians *people* Southeast Europe ancient Rome 179 (5)
Three Kings Islands *island group* Pacific Ocean exploration 278 (1)
Thugga North Africa (Tunisia) ancient Rome *180–181* (1)
Thule *var.* Qânâq North America (Greenland) cultural groups 123 (3) exploration 287 (2) the growth of the US 129 (2)
Thule *island* Atlantic Ocean ancient trade 44 (2)
Thuna South Asia (India) world religions 242 (3)
Thurii Italy ancient Rome 179 (3) early states 178 (1)
Thüringen *see* Thuringia
Thuringia *Fr.* Thuringe; *Ger.*Thüringen *region/state* Central Europe empire and revolution 202 (2) Franks 184 (2) medieval states 185 (3), 188 (1)
Thuringian March *region* Central Europe Franks 184 (2)
Thuringians *people* Central Europe ancient Rome 182 (1) Franks 183 (5), (6) great migrations 53 (2) medieval states 182 (2)
Thyatira *mod.* Akhisar *seven churches of asia* Southwest Asia world religions 48 (1)
Thyssus *state* Greece ancient Greece 177 (2)
Tiahuanaco South America (Bolivia) early cultures 146 (1) Incas 147 (3)
Tiahuanaco *state* South America the world in 250 BCE *38–39* the world in 1 CE *42–43* the world in 1000 *58–59* the world in 1200 *62–63*
Tianjin *var.* Tientsin East Asia (China) colonialism 269 (4) empire and revolution 268 (2) Islam 275 (4) post-war politics 274 (2)
Tianjin *province* East Asia post-war politics 274 (2)
Tianjin *battle* East Asia (China) economy 274 (1)
Tianlin *prev.* Leli East Asia (China) medieval states 263 (6)
Tian Shan *see* Tien Shan
Tianshui *province* East Asia first states 260 (1)
Tianshui *var.* T'ien-shui *Buddhist centre/sacred mountain* East Asia (China) world religions 49 (3)
Tiayo Central America (Mexico) first civilizations 122 (1)
Tiba *see* Chiba
Tibbu Tib *people* East Africa/Central Africa trade 167 (1)
Tiber *river* Italy medieval states 183 (4)
Tiberias Southwest Asia (Israel) ancient Rome 225 (4)
Tiberias, Lake *lake* Southwest Asia crusades 65 (3)
Tiberis *mod.* Tevere; *Eng.* Tiber *river* Italy ancient Rome 181 (2) early states 178 (1), (2) *see also* Tevere, Tiber
Tibesti *var.* Tibesti Massif, *Ar.* Tībistī *mountain range* North Africa ancient trade *44–45* (1) early cultures 160 (1) economy 163 (2) first humans 13 (2) Islam 163 (1)
Tibesti Massif *see* Tibesti
Tibet *var.* Hsi-tsang; *anc.* Xizang; *Chin. prev.* T'u-fan, Bhota *province/region/state* East Asia colonialism 248 (1), (2), 269 (3), (4) early modern states 266 (1), (2), 268 (1) empire and revolution 249 (3), 268 (2) exploration 257 (3) first states 260 (1) medieval states 261 (6), *262–263* (1), 263 (3), (4), (5), (6) Mongols 68 (2), *68–69* (1) post-war economy 275 (3) post-war politics 252 (1), (2), 271 (7), 274 (2) trade 267 (3) world religions 243 (4), 49 (3), (4) WWII 272 (1), 273 (2) Chinese revolution 271 (5) Cold War 109 (1) Communism 271 (8)
Tibetans *people* East Asia ancient trade *44–45* (1) empire and revolution 268 (2) medieval states 263 (3)
Tibet, Plateau of *var.* Xizang Gaoyuan, Qingzang Gaoyuan *plateau* East Asia ancient trade *44–45* (1) biological diffusion *72–73* (1) colonialism 247 (3) early agriculture 258 (1) early religions 48 (2) exploration 256 (1), 257 (3) first humans 13 (2) first religions 37 (4) first states 260 (1) global knowledge *76–77* (1) Marathas 246 (2) medieval states *262–263* (1), 263 (3), (4), (5), (6) Mughal Empire 246 (1) trade 267 (3) world religions 49 (3), (4)
Tībistī *see* Tibesti
Tibur Italy early states 178 (1)
Tiburón, Cabo *headland* South America European expansion *80–81* (1)
Tiburtina vetus, Via *road* Italy ancient Rome 181 (2)
Tiburtina, Via *road* Italy ancient Rome 181 (2) early states 178 (1)
Tichitt West Africa (Mauritania) the world in 2500 BCE *22–23*
Ticoman Central America (Mexico) Aztecs 124 (3)
Tidore *var.* Soasiu Maritime Southeast Asia (Indonesia) colonialism 247 (4) colonization *284–285* (1)
Tidore *region* Maritime Southeast Asia colonialism 247 (4) early medieval states 245 (6)
Tien Shan *Chin.* Tian Shan, *Rus.* Tyan'-Shan'; *var.* T'ien Shan *mountain range* East Asia ancient trade *44–45* (1) biological diffusion *72–73* (1) colonialism 269 (4) early agriculture 258 (1) empire and revolution 268 (2) exploration 256 (1), 257 (3) first cities 259 (5) first humans 13 (2) first states 260 (1) historical geography 275 (5) medieval states 261 (6), *262–263* (1) Mongols *68–69* (1) trade 267 (3) world religions 49 (3)
T'ien-shui *see* Tianshui
Tientsin *see* Tianjin
Tieoman Central America (Mexico) Aztecs 124 (3)
Tiergarten Central Europe (Germany) post-war politics 212 (2)
Tierra del Fuego *island* South America empire and revolution 151 (3) exploration 142 (1)
Tieum Southwest Asia (Turkey) first civilizations 177 (1)
Tiflis *var.* T'bilisi Southwest Asia (Georgia) early Islam *56–57* (1), 57 (2) Islam 226 (2), 227 (4) medieval Persia 231 (4) Mongols *68–69* (1) Ottomans 195 (4), 231 (3), *232–233* (1) Seljuks 228 (1) Timur 229 (4) world religions 226 (1) *see also* T'bilisi
Tighina *see* Bender
Tigris *Ar.* Dijlah, *Turk.* Dicle *river* Southwest Asia ancient Persia 223 (4), 225 (6) ancient Rome *180–181* (1), 224 (2), 225 (5) ancient trade *44–45* (1) biological diffusion *72–73* (1), 73 (3) crusades 228 (2) early agriculture 174 (1), *20–21* (2), 220 (1) early cultures 161 (3), (4), (5) early Islam *56–57* (1), 57 (2), (3) early systems 223 (3) early trade 225 (3) economy 234 (1) exploration 172 (1), 219 (3), (4) first cities 220 (2), *28–29* (1) first civilizations 221 (4), (5), 222 (2), 25 (3) first religions 36 (1) great migrations *52–53* (1) Hellenistic world 224 (1), 41 (2) Islam 163 (1), 226 (2), 227 (4), (5) medieval Persia 231 (4) medieval states 185 (3) Mongols 229 (3), *68–69* (1) Ottomans 230 (1), 231 (3), *232–233* (1) Seljuks 228 (1) Timur 229 (4) trade 230 (2) world religions 226 (1), 49 (4) WWI 233 (2) 20th-century politics 233 (3), (4), 235 (5)
Ti-hua, Tihwa *see* Urumchi, Ürümqi
Tikal Central America (Guatemala) early systems 32 (1), 33 (2), (3) first civilizations 121 (2)
Tikopia *island* Pacific Ocean exploration 278 (1)
Tiksi Siberia (Russian Federation) exploration 287 (2)
Tilanga *region* South Asia world religions 242 (2)
Tilantango Central America (Mexico) first civilizations 122 (1)
Tilcara South America (Argentina) Incas 147 (3)
Tilimsen *see* Tlemcen
Tilio Martius *see* Toulon
Tilsit Eastern Europe (Russian Federation) Napoleon *200–201* (1), 201 (2)
Timaru *settlement/whaling station* New Zealand colonization 283 (4), (5)
Timbuktu *Fr.* Tombouctou West Africa (Mali) ancient trade *44–45* (1) biological diffusion *72–73* (1) colonization 167 (4) crusades 65 (1) economy 163 (2) European expansion *84–85* (1) exploration 156 (3), 157 (4) Islam 163 (1), 167 (3) Mongols 68 (2) trade 163 (5)
Timna' Southwest Asia (Yemen) ancient Egypt 159 (5) early cultures 161 (3), (5) early trade 225 (3)
Timor *island* Maritime Southeast Asia (Indonesia) colonialism 247 (4) decolonization 251 (4) early medieval states 245 (6) European expansion 81 (3), *84–85* (1) European imperialism 97 (3) exploration 239 (1), (2) Islam 243 (6) post-war economy 253 (5) post-war politics 253 (4) trade 267 (3) world religions 243 (5) WWII 251 (3), 272 (1), 273 (2)
Timor Sea *sea* Maritime Southeast Asia Bronze Age 240 (3) colonialism 247 (4) decolonization 251 (4) early medieval states 245 (6) exploration 239 (1), (2) WWII 272 (1), 273 (2)
Timucua *people* North America colonization 125 (4)
Timur, Empire of *state* Southeast Asia Timur 229 (4)
Timurids *state* South Asia/Southwest Asia the world in 1500 *74–75*
Tingis *mod.* Tanger; *var.* Tangiers; *Eng.* Tangier, *Fr./Ger.* Tangerk, *Sp.* Tanger North Africa (Morocco) ancient Rome 179 (3), *180–181* (1), 181 (3), (4) ancient trade *44–45* (1) *see also* Tangier
Tingo Maria South America (Peru) narcotics 153 (5)
Tingzhou East Asia (China) medieval states 263 (6)
Tinian *island* Pacific Ocean exploration 278 (1) WWII 251 (3), 272 (1)
Tinos *see* Tenos
Tin Tellust West Africa (Niger) exploration 157 (4)
Tio *state* Central Africa Islam 163 (1) slave trade 165 (4) trade 167 (1)
Tipecanoe *battle* North America (USA) the growth of the US 129 (2)
Tirana Southeast Europe (Albania) Cold War 108 (3) Ottomans *232–233* (1) post-war politics 212 (3) WWI 207 (6) WWII 210 (1), 211 (2), (4)
Tirangole East Africa (Sudan) exploration 157 (4)
Tirgușor *var.* Târgușor, Têrgușor Southeast Europe (Romania) world religions 226 (1) *see also* Târgușor,
Tirnovo *mod.* Veliko Tŭrnovo Southeast Europe (Bulgaria) medieval states 189 (4)
Tiruchchirappalli *see* Trichinopoly
Tiryns *palace/settlement* Greece first cities *28–29* (1) first civilizations 175 (4)
Tisza *Ger.* Theiss *river* Southeast Europe Mongols *68–69* (1) post-war economy 215 (3)
Tiszapolgár *archaeological site* Central Europe (Hungary) Copper Age 174 (2)
Titicaca, Lake *lake* South America colonization 148 (2) early cultures 145 (2), (4), 146 (1), 147 (2) empire and revolution 150 (1) environment 153 (4) Incas 147 (3), 148 (1) narcotics 153 (5) politics 151 (4), 152 (1)
Titograd *see* Podgorica
Tiwa *people* North America colonization 125 (4)
Tizapan Central America (Mexico) Aztecs 124 (2)
Tizapantzinco Central America (Mexico) colonization 125 (5)
Tizayucan Central America (Mexico) Aztecs 124 (2)
Tjeribon *see* Cheribon
Tlaceteco Central America (Mexico) Aztecs 124 (3)
Tlacho *state* Central America Aztecs 124 (1)
Tlachquiaucho *state* Central America Aztecs 124 (1)
Tlacopan Central America (Mexico) Aztecs 124 (1), (2), (3) colonization 125 (5)
Tlacopaque Central America (Mexico) Aztecs 124 (3)
Tlacoquemecan Central America (Mexico) Aztecs 124 (3)
Tlalnepantla Central America (Mexico) Aztecs 124 (2), (3)
Tlaloc, Cerro *mountain range* Central America Aztecs 124 (2)
Tlalpan Central America (Mexico) Aztecs 124 (2)
Tlaltenango Central America (Mexico) Aztecs 124 (3)
Tlapacoya Central America (Mexico) Aztecs 124 (2) first civilizations 121 (2)
Tlapacoyan *state* Central America Aztecs 124 (1)
Tlapan *state* Central America Aztecs 124 (1)
Tlatayan Central America (Mexico) first civilizations 122 (1)
Tlateloco Central America (Mexico) Aztecs 124 (2), (3)
Tlatilco Central America (Mexico) first civilizations 121 (2)
Tlatlauhquitepec *state* Central America Aztecs 124 (1)
Tlaxcala Central America (Mexico) Aztecs 124 (1)
Tlaxcala *state* Central America Mexican Revolution 133 (3) the growth of the US 129 (2)
Tlaxcalan Central America (Mexico) colonization 125 (5)
Tlaxcalan *state* Central America Aztecs 124 (1)
Tlaxcalan *people* Central America colonization 125 (4)
Tlaxialtemalco Central America (Mexico) Aztecs 124 (2)
Tlemcen *var.* Tilimsen, Tlemsen North Africa (Algeria) Islam 163 (1)
Tlemsen *see* Tlemcen
Tliltuacan Central America (Mexico) Aztecs 124 (3)
Tlingit *region* North America the world in 1700 *82–83* the world in 1800 *86–87*
Tmutarakan Eastern Europe (Russian Federation) medieval states 185 (3)
Toala Island *archaeological site* Central Africa (Chad) early cultures 160 (1)
Toba *var.* Northern Wei; *Chin.* T'o-pa *state* East Asia medieval states 261 (4) the world in 500 CE *50–51*
Tobago *island* West Indies empire and revolution 88 (1) European expansion *84–85* (1)
Tobol'sk *var.* Tobolsk Siberia (Russian Federation) colonialism 269 (3) exploration 257 (2) Soviet Union 208 (2)
Tobol'sk *region* Eastern Europe colonialism 269 (3)
Toboso *people* Central America colonization 125 (4), 126 (1)
Tobruk North Africa (Libya) WWII 210 (1), 211 (4)
Tocabaga *fort* North America (USA) colonization 125 (4)
Tocantins *river* South America colonization 149 (3), (4) early cultures 144 (1), 145 (2) environment 153 (4) exploration 142 (1), 143 (2) politics 152 (1)
Tochari *var.* Tocharians *people* East Asia the world in 500 BCE *34–35* ancient trade *44–45* (1)
Tocharian Principalities *state* Central Asia the world in 1 CE *42–43*
Tochigi *var.* Totigi *prefecture* Japan economy 270 (1)
Tochpan *state* Central America Aztecs 124 (1)
Tochtepec *state* Central America Aztecs 124 (1)
Tocobaga *jesuit mission* North America (USA) colonization 125 (4)
Tocopilla South America (Chile) empire and revolution 151 (3)
Tocuyanoid *region* South America early cultures 145 (2)
Todaiji Japan medieval states 265 (3)
Todmorden British Isles (United Kingdom) imperial global economy 93 (4)
Toeban *see* Tuban
Togariishi *archaeological site* Japan early agriculture 258 (1)
Togiak North America (USA) cultural groups 123 (3)
Togo *prev.* French Togoland, Togoland *colonial possession/state* West Africa decolonization 168 (1) economy 168 (2) European imperialism 96 (1) Islam 235 (4) the modern world 112 (1), 113 (3) WWII 104 (1)
Togoland *see* Togo
Tohome *people* Central America colonization 125 (4)
Tojikiston *see* Tajikistan
Tokaido *region* Japan medieval states 265 (3)
Tokelau *island group/state* Pacific Ocean colonization *284–285* (1) decolonization 285 (3) environmentalism 285 (2) exploration 279 (3) the modern world *110–111*
Tokio *see* Edo, Tokyo
Tokushima Japan early modern states 265 (5)
Tokushima *var.* Tokusima *prefecture* Japan economy 270 (1)
Tokyo *Jap.* Tōkyō; *prev.* Edo Japan Communism 271 (8), 273 (3) imperial global economy 92 (1) imperialism 270 (2) Islam 275 (4) WWII 272 (1), 273 (2) *see also* Edo
Tolan Central America (Mexico) Aztecs 124 (3)
Toledo *anc.* Toletum *settlement* Iberian Peninsula (Spain) ancient Rome 182 (1) crusades 186 (1), *64–65* (2), 65 (1) early Islam *56–57* (1) economy 190 (1) Franks 184 (2) inter-war 209 (3), (4) Islam 192 (3), 226 (2), 227 (4) medieval states 182 (2), 185 (3) *see also* Toletum
Toletum *mod.* Toledo *Christian archbishopric/settlement* Iberian peninsula (Spain) ancient Rome *180–181* (1) great migrations *52–53* (1) world religions 48 (1) *see also* Toledo
Toliman Central America (Mexico) first civilizations 122 (1)
Tollantzinco Central America (Mexico) first civilizations 122 (1)
Tolmezzo Italy WWI 207 (5)
Tolosa *mod.* Toulouse France ancient Rome 179 (3), (5), *180–181* (1) ancient trade 44 (2) great migrations *52–53* (1) *see also* Toulouse
Toltec Empire *state* Central America the world in 1000 *58–59*
Tomar Iberian Peninsula (Portugal) crusades 186 (1)
Tombouctou *see* Timbuktu
Tomebamba South America (Ecuador) Incas 147 (3)
Tomi *mod.* Constanța Southeast Europe (Romania) ancient Rome *180–181* (1), 181 (3) *see also* Constanța
Tomóchic Central America (Mexico) Mexican Revolution 133 (3)
Tomsk *region/archaeological site/settlement* Siberia (Russian Federation) colonialism 269 (3), (4) Communism 271 (8) early agriculture 258 (1) exploration 257 (2) Soviet Union 208 (2), *214–215* (4)
Tonala Central America (Mexico) first civilizations 122 (1), 123 (2)
Tonga *var.* Friendly Islands *colonial possession/island group/state* Pacific Ocean colonization *284–285* (1) decolonization 285 (3) early cultures *280–281* (3) environmentalism 285 (2) exploration *276–277* (1), 279 (3) medieval voyages 60 (2)
Tongatapu *island* Pacific Ocean exploration 278 (1)
Tongatapu Group *island group* Pacific Ocean early cultures *280–281* (3) medieval voyages 60 (2)
Tongchuan East Asia (China) medieval states 263 (4)
Tonggou *mod.* Ji'an East Asia (China) medieval states 264 (1) *see also* Ji'an
Tongguan *var.* T'ung-kuan East Asia Mongols *68–69* (1)
Tonghua East Asia (China) Cold War 109 (4)
Tongking *var.* Tonking *state* Mainland Southeast Asia colonialism 269 (4) European imperialism 97 (3)
Tongking, Gulf of *gulf* Mainland Southeast Asia colonialism 247 (4), 248 (1) decolonization 251 (4) early medieval states 245 (5), (6) early modern states 266 (1) exploration 239 (1) medieval voyages 61 (3) post-war politics 251 (5), 253 (4) WWII 251 (3)
Tongnae East Asia (South Korea) early modern states 267 (4)
Tongzi *archaeological site* East Asia (China) first humans 13 (2)
Tonkawa *people* North America colonization 125 (4), 126 (1)
Tonking *see* Tongking
Tonle Sap *Eng.* Great Lake *lake* Mainland Southeast Asia post-war politics 251 (5) world religions 243 (5)
Tonto *archaeological site* North America (USA) cultural groups 123 (4)
Toolesboro Mounds *burial mound* North America (USA) first civilizations 121 (4)
Toowoomba Australia colonization 282 (1)
T'o-pa *see* Toba
Topeka North America (USA) the growth of the US 129 (2)
Topoc Maze *archaeological site* North America (USA) cultural groups 123 (4)
Toprakkale Southwest Asia (Turkey) first civilizations 222 (2)
Torgut *people* East Asia early modern states 266 (1)
Torino *see* Augusta, Taurinorum, Turin
Tornacum *see* Tournai
Tornaval South America (Peru) early cultures 145 (4)
Toro Egypt exploration 156 (3)
Toro *state* East Africa the world in 1700 *82–83* the world in 1800 *86–87* the world in 1850 *90–91*
Torone Greece first civilizations 177 (1)
Torone *state* Greece ancient Greece 177 (2)
Toronto North America (Canada) the growth of the US 129 (2), 132 (1) US economy 136 (2)
Toropets Eastern Europe (Russian Federation) early modern states 195 (3)
Toros Dağları *see* Taurus Mountains
Torrance North America (USA)
Torreón Central America (Mexico) Mexican Revolution 133 (3)
Torres Strait *sea waterway* Australia exploration *276–277* (1), 279 (2)
Tortoise Islands *see* Galapagos Islands
Tortosa *anc.* Dertosa Iberian Peninsula (Spain) crusades 186 (1) Franks 184 (2) Islam 192 (3) *see also* Dertosa
Tortuga *var.*Tortuga Island; *mod.* Île de la Tortue *island* West Indies empire and revolution 89 (3) European expansion 85 (2)
Toruń *Ger.* Thorn Central Europe (Poland) early modern states 193 (4) medieval states 189 (3) *see also* Thorn
Torwa *state* Southern Africa Islam 163 (1)
Torzhok *var.* Toržok Eastern Europe (Russian Federation) Mongols *68–69* (1)
Toržok *see* Torzhok
Toscana *see* Tuscany
Toshkent *see* Tashkent
Tószeg Southeast Europe (Yugoslavia) Bronze Age 175 (3)
Toterfout *burial mound* Low Countries (Netherlands) Bronze Age 175 (3)
Totigi *see* Tochigi
Totopec *state* Central America Aztecs 124 (1)
Tottori *prefecture* Japan economy 270 (1)
Touggourt *see* Tuggurt
Toulon *anc.* Telo Martius, Tilio Martius France early modern states 197 (5) economy 205 (4) empire and revolution 199 (4) European expansion *84–85* (1) Napoleon *200–201* (1) WWII 211 (2)
Toulouse *anc.* Tolosa *settlement* France ancient Rome 182 (1) crusades 186 (1), *64–65* (2) early modern states 197 (5) economy 190 (1), 205 (4) empire and revolution 199 (4) Franks 183 (5), (6), 184 (2) inter-war 209 (3) Islam 184 (1), 192 (3), 226 (2) medieval states 182 (2), 185 (3), (4), 192 (1), (2) Napoleon *200–201* (1), 201 (2) prehistoric culture 17 (3) Reformation 194 (2) *see also* Tolosa
Toulouse *region* France crusades *64–65* (2) medieval states 187 (4)
Toulouse *battle* France early Islam *56–57* (1)
Toungoo Mainland Southeast Asia (Burma) early medieval states 245 (6) WWII 251 (3)
Toungoo *state* Mainland Southeast Asia the world in 1400 *70–71* the world in 1500 *74–75*
Tournai *var.* Tournay; *anc.* Tornacum; *Dut.* Doornik Low Countries (Belgium) early modern states 197 (5) economy 190 (1) Franks 183 (5), (6), 184 (2) WWI 206 (2), (3)
Tournay *see* Tournai
Tours *anc.* Caesarodunum, Turoni *settlement* France early modern states 197 (5) Franks 183 (5), 184 (2) medieval states 187 (3), 192 (1), (2) *see also* Caesarodunum, Turoni
Towa *var.* Jemex *people* North America colonization 125 (4)
Town Creek North America (USA) cultural groups 122 (5)
Townsville Australia colonization 282 (1), 283 (3)
Towosahgy North America (USA) cultural groups 122 (5)
Toyama *prefecture* Japan economy 270 (1)
Toyohashi *var.* Toyohasi Japan economy 270 (1)
Toyohasi *see* Toyohashi
Tozando *region* Japan medieval states 265 (3)
Trâblous *see* Tripoli, Tripolis
Trabzon *see* Trapezus, Trebizond
Trachonitis *state* Southwest Asia ancient Rome 225 (4)
Trafalgar *battle* Iberian Peninsula (Spain) Napoleon *200–201* (1)
Traiana, Aqua *aqueduct* Italy ancient Rome 181 (2)
Traiani, Thermae *see* Trajan, Baths of
Traiectum ad Mosam, Traiectum Tungorum *see* Maastricht
Trajan, Baths of *Lat.* Thermae Traiani *building* Italy ancient Rome 181 (2)
Trajan, Temple of *building* Italy ancient Rome 181 (2)
Trajectum ad Rhenum *see* Utrecht
Trang Mainland Southeast Asia (Thailand) ancient trade *44–45* (1)
Trani *anc.* Turenum Italy economy 190 (1)
Tran Ninh *state* Mainland Southeast Asia the world in 1600 *78–79* the world in 1700 *82–83* the world in 1800 *86–87*
Tranquebar *mod.* Tarangambādi South Asia (India) colonialism 247 (3)
Trans-Amazon Highway *road* South America economy 153 (3)
Transantarctic Mountains *mountain range* Antarctica Antarctic Exploration 287 (3)
Transbaikal *region* Siberia colonialism 269 (3)
Transcaspian *region* Central Asia colonialism 269 (3)
Trans-Gangem *region* South Asia ancient trade 44 (2)
Transilvania *see* Transylvania
Transjordan *mod.* Jordan *region/state* Southwest Asia exploration 219 (4) WWII 104 (1), 211 (4) 20th century 234 (2) 20th-century politics 233 (3), (4) *see also* Jordan
Transnistria *state* Eastern Europe WWII 211 (2)
Transoxiana *region/state* Central Asia ancient trade *44–45* (1) early Islam *56–57* (1), 57 (2) Islam 227 (4) medieval Persia 231 (4) medieval states 261 (6), *262–263* (1) Timur 229 (4) world religions 49 (3)
Trans-Siberian Railway *railway* Siberia global immigration 100 (1)
Transvaal *state* Southern Africa European imperialism 96 (2)
Transylvania *Eng.* Ardeal, Transilvania, *Ger.* Siebenbürgen, *Hung.* Erdély *region/state* Southeast Europe medieval states 189 (4) Napoleon *200–201* (1) Ottomans 195 (4), 230 (1) Reformation 194 (2) WWI 208 (1)
Trapani *anc.* Drepanum Italy economy 190 (1)
Trapezus *Eng.* Trebizond, *Turk.* Trabzon *archaeological site/settlement* Southwest Asia (Turkey) ancient Rome *180–181* (1), 181 (3), (4) ancient trade *44–45* (1) early cultures 161 (2) first civilizations 177 (1) Hellenistic world *40–41* (1) world religions 226 (1) *see also* Trebizond
Trasimene, Lake *see* Trasimenus, Lacus
Trasimeno, Lago *see* Trasimenus, Lacus
Trasimenus, Lacus *Eng.* Lake Trasimene, Lago Trasimeno *battle* Italy ancient Rome 179 (3)
Trau *see* Trogir
Travancore *state* South Asia colonialism 248 (1)
Trebia *battle* Italy ancient Rome 179 (3)
Trebinje Southeast Europe (Bosnia and Herzegovina) post-war economy 215 (3)
Trebizond *anc.* Trapezus; *Turk.* Trabzon Southwest Asia (Turkey) biological diffusion *72–73* (1) crusades *64–65* (2) early Islam *56–57* (1) exploration 219 (3) medieval states 185 (3), 261 (6) Ottomans 195 (4), 230 (1) Seljuks 228 (1) WWI 233 (2) 20th-century politics 233 (3) *see also* Trapezus
Trebizond, Empire of *state* Southwest Asia economy 190 (1) Mongols 229 (3), *68–69* (1) Timur 229 (4)
Treblinka *concentration camp* Central Europe (Poland) WWII 211 (3)
Trempealeau *burial mound* North America (USA) first civilizations 121 (4)
Tremper *burial mound* North America (USA) first civilizations 121 (4)
Trent *It.* Trento Italy WWI 207 (5)
Trent and Mersey *canal* British Isles economy 204 (1)
Trento *see* Trent
Trenton North America (USA) empire and revolution 127 (3) the growth of the US 129 (2)
Trenton *battle* North America (USA) empire and revolution 127 (3), *88–89* (2)
Treptow Central Europe (Germany) post-war politics 212 (2)
Tres Zapotes Central America (Mexico) first civilizations 121 (2), (3), 122 (1)
Treves *see* Augusta Taurinorum, Augusta Treverorum, Trier
Treviso *anc.* Tarvisium Italy economy 190 (1) WWI 207 (5)
Trévoux France early modern states 197 (5)
Trichinopoly *mod.* Tiruchchirappalli South Asia (India) economy 249 (4)
Trier *anc.* Augusta Taurinorum, Augusta Treverorum; *Eng.* Treves, *Fr.* Trèves *massacre/settlement* Central Europe (Germany) ancient Rome 182 (1) crusades 186 (1) Franks 184 (2) medieval states 182 (2), 188 (1) WWI 206 (2), (3)
Trieste *Slvn.* Trst Italy economy 205 (4) medieval states 189 (4) post-war politics 212 (3) WWI 207 (5) WWII 211 (2), (3)
Trieste, Free Territory of *state* Italy the world in 1950 *102–103*
Trigarta *region* South Asia world religions 242 (2)
Trinacria *see* Sicily
Trincomalee *var.* Trinkomali *air raid/settlement* South Asia (Sri Lanka) colonialism 247 (3) WWII 251 (3), 272 (1)
Trindade *island* Atlantic Ocean the modern world *110–111*
Trinidad *colonial possession/island* West Indies colonization 125 (4) empire and revolution 150 (2) European expansion 85 (2) global immigration 101 (3)
Trinidad and Tobago *colonial possession/state* West Indies Cold War 108 (2) environment 153 (4) politics 152 (1) the modern world 112 (1) US economy 136 (2) US politics 139 (4) US superpower 138 (1)
Trinil *archaeological site* Maritime Southeast Asia (Indonesia) first humans 13 (2)
Trinkomali *see* Trincomalee
Tripoli *var.* Tarābulus, Ṭarābulus ash Shām, Trâblous; *anc.* Tripolis Southwest Asia (Lebanon) crusades 65 (3) medieval states 187 (5) 20th-century politics 233 (3) *see also* Tripolis
Tripoli *var.* Ṭarābulus al Gharb, Oea; *Ar.* Ṭarābulus North Africa (Libya) biological diffusion 72 (1) colonization 166 (4) early Islam 56 (1) economy 162 (2), 168 (2), 190 (1) European Expansion 84 (1) exploration 156 (4) Islam 162 (1), 226 (2), (4) Napoleon 200 (1) Ottomans 230 (1), 232 (1) US superpower 138 (1) WWII 210 (1) *see also* Oea
Tripoli *region/state* North Africa early Islam *56–57* (1) slave trade 165 (4) trade 167 (1)
Tripoli *var.* County of Tripoli, Kingdom of Tripoli *state* Southwest Asia crusades 228 (2), 65 (3) medieval states 187 (5)
Tripolis Southwest Asia (Lebanon) ancient Rome *180–181* (1)
Tripolitania *region/state* North Africa colonization 167 (4) first civilizations 177 (1) Ottomans *232–233* (1)
Tripura *var.* Hill Tippera *region/state* South Asia colonialism 248 (2) post-war politics 252 (1), 253 (4)
Tripuri South Asia (India) early medieval states 244 (2)
Tristan da Cunha *colonial possession/island* Atlantic Ocean the modern world *110–111*
Trivandrum *var.* Thiruvanathapuram South Asia (India) colonialism 248 (1) economy 249 (4) post-war economy 253 (5) post-war politics 252 (1)
Troesmis *archaeological site/legion headquarters* Southeast Europe (Romania) ancient Rome *180–181* (1)
Trogir *It.* Trau Southeast Europe (Croatia) medieval states 189 (4)
Troia Italy crusades 186 (1)
Tromelin, Île *island* Indian Ocean the modern world *110–111*
Tromsø Scandinavia (Norway) exploration 287 (2)
Trondheim *prev.* Nidaros, Trondhjem; *Ger.* Drontheim Scandinavia (Norway) early modern states 197 (3) exploration 287 (2) medieval states 185 (3) medieval voyages *60–61* (1) WWII 104 (2)
Trondheim *region* Scandinavia early modern states 197 (3)
Trondhjem *see* Trondheim
Troy *archaeological site/religious site/settlement* Southwest Asia (Turkey) Bronze Age 175 (3) Copper Age 174 (2) first cities 220 (2) first civilizations 175 (4), 221 (5) first religions 37 (3)
Troyes *anc.* Augustobona Tricassium France crusades 186 (1) early modern states 193 (4) economy 190 (1) medieval states 188 (1), (2) Reformation 194 (2) WWI 206 (2), (3)
Trst *see* Trieste
Trucial Coast *see* Trucial Oman, United Arab Emirates
Trucial Oman *mod.* United Arab Emirates; *prev.* Trucial Coast; *later* Trucial States *colonial possession/state* Southwest Asia 20th-century politics 233 (4) *see also* United Arab Emirates
Trucial States *see* Trucial Oman, United Arab Emirates
Truckee *battle* North America (USA) the growth of the US 129 (2)
Trujillo South America (Venezuela) empire and revolution 150 (1)
Trujillo South America (Peru) colonization 126 (1), 148 (2) empire and revolution 150 (1), 151 (3) exploration 143 (3) politics 152 (1)
Truk *island group* Pacific Ocean WWII 104 (2), 251 (3), 272 (1), 273 (2)
Trundholm Scandinavia (Denmark) the world in 1250 BCE *26–27*
Trung Phân *see* Annam
Truso Central Europe (Poland) medieval states 185 (3) medieval voyages *60–61* (1)
Tsaidam Basin *Chin.* Qaidam Pendi *basin* East Asia exploration 257 (3)
Tsangchou *see* Cangzhou
Tsangpo *see* Brahmaputra
Tsarigrad *see* Byzantium, Constantinople, Istanbul
Tsaritsyn *mod.* Volgograd; *prev.* Stalingrad *see* Stalingrad, Volograd Eastern Europe (Russian Federation) Soviet Union 208 (2)
Tsetsaut *people* North America cultural groups 123 (3)
Tshwane *see* Pretoria
Tsinan *see* Jinan
Tsing Hai, Tsinghai *see* Koko Nor, Qinghai Hu
Tsingtao, Tsingtau, Tsintao *see* Qingdao
Tsou *see* Zou
Tsugaru-kaikyō *see* Tsugaru Strait
Tsugaru Strait *Jap.* Tsugaru-kaikyō *sea waterway* Japan Communism 273 (3)
Tsushima *battle* Japan Russo-Japanese War 270 (4)
Tsushima *var.* Tsushima-tō, Tusima *island group* Japan Cold War 109 (4) early modern states 265 (5), 267 (4) medieval states 264 (1), (2), 265 (3), (4)
Tsushima-kaikyō *see* Tsushima Strait
Tsushima Strait *var.* Tsushima-kaikyō *sea waterway* Japan early modern states 267 (4) economy 270 (1) Sino-Japanese War 270 (3)
Tsushima-tō *see* Tsushima
Tu *state* East Asia first cities 259 (3)
Tuadmumu *state* British Isles medieval states 188 (2)
Tuamotu, Archipel des, Tuamotu, Îles *see* Tuamotu Islands
Tuamotu Islands *Fr.* Îles Tuamotu; *var.* Archipel des Tuamotu, Dangerous Archipelago *island group* Pacific Ocean colonization *284–285* (1) early cultures *280–281* (3) exploration 279 (3) medieval voyages 60 (2)
Tuareg *state* West Africa trade 163 (4)
Tuaregs *people* North Africa/West Africa economy 163 (2) Islam 163 (1)
Tuban *prev.* Toeban Maritime Southeast Asia (Indonesia) trade 230 (2)
Tubar *people* Central America colonization 126 (1)
Tubuai, Îles, Tubuai Islands *see* Australes, Îles
Tuchi *see* Duji
Tucson North America (USA) the growth of the US 129 (2), 132 (1)

U

V

INDEX-GAZETTEER: Vientiane – Xiuhtetelco

Vientiane Mainland Southeast Asia (Laos) colonialism 247 (4), 248 (1) post-war economy 253 (5) post-war politics 251 (5) world religions 243 (5)
Vientiane state Mainland Southeast Asia the world in 1800 86–87
Vierzon France medieval states 192 (1)
Vietnam state Mainland Southeast Asia (Vietnam) Bronze Age 240 (3) colonialism 248 (1) decolonization 251 (4) economy 274 (1) Islam 275 (4) post-war economy 253 (5) post-war politics 251 (5), 253 (4), 274 (2) the modern world 113 (4) US superpower 138 (1) Cold War 109 (1)
Vigo Iberian Peninsula (Spain) Napoleon 200–201 (1)
Viipuri see Viborg, Vyborg
Vijaya mod. Binh Đinh Mainland Southeast Asia (Vietnam) ancient India 241 (6) early medieval states 245 (5), (6)
Vijayanagar state South Asia the world in 1400 70–71 the world in 1500 74–75
Vijayanagara region/settlement South Asia colonialism 247 (3) early medieval states 244–245 (3), 245 (4)
Vijayans dynasty South Asia the world in 1 CE 42–43
Vijayapura South Asia (India) early medieval states 244 (2)
Vijayapura state Maritime Southeast Asia ancient India 241 (6)
Vijayawada prev. Bezwada South Asia (India) post-war economy 253 (5)
Vijosa, Vijosë see Vjosë
Vikings people Scandinavia medieval states 185 (3)
Vila Artur de Paiva see Cubango
Vila Bela var. Mato Grosso South America (Brazil) colonization 149 (3)
Vila da Ponte see Cubango
Vila do Zumbo see Zumbo
Világos mod. Şiria battle Central Europe (Hungary) empire and revolution 88–89 (2)
Vila Henrique de Carvalho see Saurimo
Vila Marechal Carmona see Uíge
Vila Serpa Pinto see Menongue
Vilcas South America (Peru) Incas 147 (3)
Vilcas Huamán South America (Peru) Incas 148 (1)
Viljandi see Fellin
Villa Alta var. S.I. Villa Alta Central America (Mexico) first civilizations 122 (1)
Villach Central Europe (Austria) WWI 207 (5)
Villa Concepción see Concepción
Villa da Barra see Manáos, Manaus
Villa de la Veracruz Central America (Mexico) colonization 125 (5)
Villa do Forte de Assumpeão see Ceará, Fortaleza
Villahermosa see San Juan Bautista
Villa Montes South America (Bolivia) politics 152 (2)
Villa San Luis Central America (Mexico) colonization 125 (4)
Villefranche-de-Conflent France early modern states 197 (5)
Vilna mod. Vilnius; Ger. Wilna, Pol. Wilno Eastern Europe (Lithuania) early modern states 193 (4), 195 (3) empire and revolution 198 (2) medieval states 189 (3), (4) Napoleon 200–201 (1) WWI 207 (4) see also Wilno
Vilnius prev. Vilna; Ger. Wilna, Pol. Wilno Eastern Europe (Lithuania) post-war politics 212 (3) Soviet Union 214–215 (4) see also Vilna, Wilno
Vilno see Vilna
Vimeiro Iberian Peninsula (Portugal) Napoleon 200–201 (1)
Viminacium legion headquarters Southeast Europe (Yugoslavia) ancient Rome 180–181 (1)
Viminal Hill Lat. Collis Viminalis hill Italy ancient Rome 181 (2)
Viminalis Collis see Viminal Hill
Viña del Mar South America (Chile) empire and revolution 151 (3)
Vinča Southeast Europe (Yugoslavia) early agriculture 174 (1)
Vincennes fort North America (USA) empire and revolution 127 (3)
Vindava Ger. Windau, Lat. Ventspils Eastern Europe (Latvia) WWI 207 (4) see also Windau
Vindhya Mountains see Vindhya Range
Vindhya-Prstha region South Asia early religions 48 (2)
Vindhya Range var. Vindhya Mountains mountain range South Asia colonialism 247 (3), 248 (1) early medieval states 244 (1), 244–245 (3) first empires 241 (4) Mughal Empire 246 (1) world religions 243 (4)
Vindobona mod. Wien; anc. Vindobona; Eng. Vienna, Hung. Bécs, Slvk. Videň, Slvn. Dunaj legion headquarters Central Europe (Austria) ancient Rome 180–181 (1) see also Vienna
Vine Mound burial mound North America (USA) first civilizations 121 (4)
Vinh Thai Lan see Siam, Gulf of; Thailand, Gulf of
Vinh Yen battle Mainland Southeast Asia (Vietnam) post-war politics 251 (5)
Vinjha region South Asia world religions 242 (3)
Vinland region North America medieval voyages 60–61 (1)
Vinot South Asia (Pakistan) world religions 243 (4)
Virginia colonial possession/state North America empire and revolution 127 (2), (3) the growth of the US 129 (1) US Civil War 130 (2), (3), (4), (5), 131 (6), (7) US economy 134 (2), 139 (3) US society 137 (6) US superpower 139 (5)
Virginia Capes battle North America (USA) empire and revolution 127 (3)
Virgin Islands state/island group West Indies Cold War 108 (2) empire and revolution 88 (1) the growth of the US 133 (4)
Virgin Islands of the United States see American Virgin Islands
Virgo, Aqua aqueduct Italy ancient Rome 181 (2)
Virú river South America early cultures 145 (3)
Virunum Central Europe (Austria) ancient Rome 180–181 (1)
Visakhapatnam South Asia (India) post-war economy 253 (5)
Visby Ger. Wisby Scandinavia (Sweden) economy 190 (1) see also Wisby
Višegrad Southeast Europe (Bosnia and Herzegovina) WWI 207 (6)
Visigoths people Southeast Europe/Southwest Asia ancient Rome 181 (4) great migrations 52–53 (1)
Visigoths, Kingdom of the state France/Iberian Peninsula ancient Rome 182 (1) early Islam 56–57 (1) Franks 183 (5), (6) great migrations 52–53 (1), 53 (2) medieval states 182 (2)
Vistula Pol. Wisła, Ger. Weichsel river Central Europe Bronze Age 175 (3) Copper Age 174 (2) crusades 64–65 (2) early agriculture 174 (1) early modern states 193 (4) economy 205 (4) empire and revolution 198 (2), 199 (3), 202 (2) exploration 172 (1) great migrations 52–53 (1) medieval states 189 (3), (4) Mongols 68–69 (1) Napoleon 200–201 (1), 201 (2), (3) prehistoric culture 17 (4) WWI 207 (4)
Vitcos South America (Peru) Incas 147 (3)
Vitebsk var. Vitsyebsk Eastern Europe (Belorussia) early modern states 195 (3) economy 190 (1) Soviet Union 208 (2)
Viterbo anc. Vicus Elbii Italy economy 190 (1) medieval states 188 (1)
Vitez Southeast Europe (Bosnia and Herzegovina) post-war economy 215 (3)
Viti Levu island Pacific Ocean early cultures 280–281 (3) environmentalism 285 (2) medieval voyages 60 (2) US superpower 138 (1)
Vitim river Eastern Europe early modern states 268 (1) first states 260 (1)
Vitoria Iberian Peninsula (Spain) Napoleon 200–201 (1)
Vitória prev. Victoria South America (Brazil) colonization 149 (3) see also Victoria
Vitsyebsk see Vitebsk
Vittorio Veneto Italy WWI 207 (5)
Viye state Southern Africa slave trade 165 (4) trade 167 (1)
Vizagapatam air raid/settlement South Asia (India) colonialism 247 (3) decolonization 250 (1) WWII 251 (3), 272 (1)
Vizcaíno, Desierto de desert Central America cultural groups 123 (4)
Vjosë var. Vijosa; Vijosë, Gk. Aóos river Southeast Europe WWI 207 (6)
Vladimir var. Volodymyr-Volyns'kyy; Pol. Włodzimierz Eastern Europe (Russian Federation) medieval states 189 (4) Mongols 68–69 (1) see also Włodzimierz
Vladimir state Eastern Europe medieval states 189 (4)
Vladimir-Galich see Galicia-Volhynia
Vladivostok Siberia (Russian Federation) colonialism 269 (3), (4) Communism 271 (8) exploration 257 (2) global immigration 100 (1) imperialism 270 (2) Islam 275 (4) Russo-Japanese War 270 (4) Soviet Union 208 (2), 214–215 (4) Cold War 109 (4)
Vlonë, Vlora, Vlorë see Valona
Vogelherd archaeological site Central Europe (Germany) prehistoric culture 17 (2)
Vojvodina Ger. Wojwodina province Southeast Europe post-war economy 215 (3)
Volaterrae Italy early states 178 (1), (2) first civilizations 177 (1)
Volcae people France ancient Rome 179 (5)
Volcano Islands Jap. Kazan-rettō island group Pacific Ocean US superpower 138 (1) WWII 273 (2)
Volci var. Vulci Italy first civilizations 177 (1) see also Vulci
Voldtofte Scandinavia (Denmark) Bronze Age 175 (3)
Volga river Eastern Europe ancient trade 44–45 (1) biological diffusion 72–73 (1) early agriculture 20–21 (2) early Islam 56–57 (1) early modern states 197 (3) economy 205 (4) empire and revolution 202 (1) exploration 172 (1), 218 (2), 219 (3) first humans 13 (2) global immigration 100 (1) great migrations 52–53 (1), 53 (2) Islam 163 (1) medieval states 185 (3), 261 (6) medieval voyages 60–61 (1) Mongols 68–69 (1) Ottomans 231 (3), 232–233 (1) prehistoric culture 16 (1), 17 (4) Soviet Union 208 (2) Timur 229 (4) WWII 210 (1), 211 (4)
Volga Bulgaria state Eastern Europe medieval states 185 (3)
Volga Bulgars var. Bulgars, White Bulgars people Eastern Europe Mongols 68–69 (1)
Volga Germans people Eastern Europe Soviet Union 213 (4)
Volgograd prev. Stalingrad, Tsaritsyn Eastern Europe (Russian Federation) Soviet Union 214–215 (4) see also Stalingrad, Tsaritsyn
Vol'mar see Wolmar
Volodymyr-Volyns'kyy see Vladimir, Włodzimierz
Vologda mod. Kirov Eastern Europe (Russian Federation) Soviet Union 208 (2)
Volsci people Italy early states 178 (2)
Volsiniensis, Lacus lake Italy early states 178 (1)
Volsinii Italy early states 178 (1), (2) first civilizations 177 (1)
Volta river West Africa Islam 163 (1)
Volta Blanche see White Volta
Volta, Cape da var. Dias Point headland West Africa exploration 156 (3)
Volta, Lake reservoir West Africa economy 168 (2), (3)
Volta Noire see Black Volta
Volterra see Volaterrae
Volturno see Volturnus
Volturnus mod. Volturno river Italy early states 178 (1)
Volubilis mithraic site North Africa (Morocco) world religions 48 (1)
Vorkuta Eastern Europe (Russian Federation) exploration 287 (2)
Voronezh Eastern Europe (Russian Federation) Soviet Union 208 (2), 214–215 (4)
Vorskla river Eastern Europe WWI 207 (4)
Vosges mountain range France early modern states 197 (5) WWI 206 (2), (3)
Vouillé battle France Franks 183 (5)
Vrijji see Vrjji
Vrjji var. Vrijji region South Asia first religions 36 (2)
Vrshni state South Asia first empires 241 (5)
Vryburg Southern Africa (South Africa) European imperialism 96 (2)
Vukovar Hung. Vukovár Southeast Europe (Croatia) post-war economy 215 (3)
Vulci Italy early states 178 (1), (2)
Vungu state Central Africa economy 163 (2)
Vyadhapura Mainland Southeast Asia (Cambodia) ancient India 241 (6) medieval states 261 (6)
Vyatka mod. Kirov Eastern Europe (Russian Federation) Soviet Union 208 (2)
Vyborg Eastern Europe (Russian Federation) early modern states 195 (3) WWI 207 (4) WWII 211 (4)

W

Waalo state West Africa trade 167 (1)
Wabash river North America US Civil War 131 (6), (7)
Waccamaw people North America colonization 125 (4)
Wadai var. Ouadaï, Ouaddaï state Central Africa colonization 167 (4) slave trade 165 (4) trade 167 (1)
Wad Al-Hajarah see Guadalajara
Wadan West Africa (Mauritania) biological diffusion 72–73 (1)
Wadi Halfa var. Wādī Ḥalfā' Egypt colonization 167 (4)
Wadi Maghara Southwest Asia (Saudi Arabia) ancient Egypt 159 (5)
Wagadugu state West Africa trade 167 (1)
Wagram Central Europe (Czech Republic) Napoleon 200–201 (1)
Wągrowiec major cistercian house Central Europe medieval states 187 (3)
Wahabites Rising rebellion Southwest Asia empire and revolution 88–89 (2)
Wahgi Valley New Guinea (Papua New Guinea) early cultures 280 (2)
Wahhabi Expansion historical period 20th-century politics 233 (4)
Wahhabi Territory region Southwest Asia 20th-century politics 233 (4)
Wahran see Oran
Waicuri people Central America colonization 125 (4)
Waikanae New Zealand colonization 283 (5)
Waikawa whaling station New Zealand colonization 283 (4)
Waikouaiti settlement/whaling station New Zealand colonization 283 (4), (5)
Waimate New Zealand colonization 283 (5)
Wairagarh South Asia (India) colonialism 247 (3)
Wakayama Japan economy 270 (1)
Wakayama off. Wakayama-ken prefecture Japan economy 270 (1)
Wake Island colonial possession/ island Pacific Ocean exploration 276–277 (1) imperialism 270 (2) the growth of the US 133 (4) US superpower 138 (1) WWII 272 (1) Cold War 109 (1)
Walachei, Walachia see Wallachia
Walata West Africa (Mauritania) exploration 156 (3)
Waldensians people Italy crusades 186 (1)
Wales Wel. Cymru state British Isles empire and revolution 202 (1) medieval states 188 (2) the modern world 112 (2)
Walhalla goldfield Australia colonization 282 (2)
Walkunder Arch Australia exploration 280 (1)
Wallachia var. Walachia; Ger. Walachei, Rom. Valachia, Turk. Eflâk region Southeast Europe early modern states 193 (4) empire and revolution 202 (1) medieval states 189 (4) Napoleon 200–201 (1), 201 (2) Ottomans 195 (4), 230 (1), 231 (3) Reformation 194 (2)
Walla Walla battle North America (USA) the growth of the US 129 (2)
Wallis and Futuna colonial possession/island group Pacific Ocean decolonization 285 (3) environmentalism 285 (2)
Wallis, Îles var. Wallis Islands island group Pacific Ocean colonization 284–285 (1) exploration 278 (1), 279 (3)
Walnut Canyon archaeological site North America (USA) cultural groups 123 (4)
Walo state West Africa slave trade 165 (4)
Walvisbaai see Walvis Bay
Walvis Bay Afr. Walvisbaai Southern Africa (Namibia) colonization 167 (4) economy 168 (2) European imperialism 96 (1), (2)
Walvis Bay Afr. Walvisbaai state Southern Africa the world in 1900 94–95 the world in 1925 98–99
Walvis Bay bay Southern Africa exploration 156 (3)
Wambu state Southern Africa slave trade 165 (4) trade 167 (1)
Wan var. Nanyang East Asia (China) first cities 259 (5) first states 260 (1) see also Nanyang
Wan see Anhui
Wandel Sea sea Arctic Ocean exploration 287 (2)
Wandiwash battle South Asia (India) empire and revolution 88 (1)
Wandu state Southern Africa slave trade 165 (4)
Wang vassal state East Asia first cities 259 (3)
Wanganui New Zealand colonization 283 (4), (5)
Wangchenggang archaeological site East Asia early agriculture 258 (1)
Wanhsien see Wanxian
Wankarani state South America the world in 500 BCE 34–35
Wanxian var. Wanhsien East Asia (China) colonialism 269 (4)
Warangal South Asia (India) colonialism 247 (3) early medieval states 244–245 (3), 245 (4)
Warash Southwest Asia (Turkey) early Islam 56–57 (1)
Warka Southwest Asia (Iraq) the world in 5000 BCE 18–19
Warmia Ger. Ermeland region Central Europe early modern states 195 (3)
Warrnambool Australia colonization 282 (1), 283 (3)
Warsaw Central Europe (Poland) economy 205 (4) empire and revolution 198 (2), 199 (3), 202 (1), (1i) global immigration 101 (2) medieval states 189 (3), (4) Napoleon 200–201 (1), 201 (2), (3) post-war politics 212 (3) prehistoric culture 17 (4) Reformation 194 (2) Soviet Union 208 (2) WWI 207 (4) WWII 210 (1), 211 (2), (3), (4) Cold War 108 (3)
Warsaw, Grand Duchy of state Central Europe Napoleon 201 (2)
Warschau, Warszawa see Warsaw
Warwick British Isles (United Kingdom) medieval states 187 (4)
Washington var. Washington Territory state/settlement/settlement/settlement/settlement/road/region North America empire and revolution 127 (3) the growth of the US 129 (1), (2), 132 (1) US Civil War 130 (4), (5), 131 (6), (7) US economy 134 (1), (2), (3), 135 (4), 136 (2) Cold War 108 (2)
Washington DC North America (USA) Cold War 108 (2) the growth of the US 132 (1) the modern world 113 (4) US economy 134 (1), (3), 136 (2)
Washita battle North America (USA) the growth of the US 129 (2)
Washshukanni Southwest Asia (Iraq) first civilizations 221 (5)
Wasserburg mod. Wasserburg am Inn Central Europe (Germany) Bronze Age 175 (3)
Wasserburg am Inn see Wasserburg
Wateree people North America colonization 125 (4)
Waterford Ir. Port Láirge British Isles (Ireland) medieval states 185 (3), 187 (4)
Waterloo battle France Napoleon 200–201 (1)
Watom island Pacific Ocean early cultures 280–281 (3) medieval voyages 60 (2)
Wattasids dynasty North Africa Islam 163 (1), 192 (3)
Wattignies battle France empire and revolution 199 (4)
Waverley major cistercian house British Isles (United Kingdom) medieval states 187 (3)
Wawat state Egypt ancient Egypt 159 (4)
Wearmouth see Sunderland
Weddell Sea sea Antarctica Antarctic Exploration 287 (3)
Wedding Central Europe (Germany) post-war politics 212 (2)
Weeden Island settlement/state North America (USA) cultural groups 122 (5)
Weeden Island Culture state North America the world in 500 CE 50–51
Weenen Southern Africa (South Africa) colonization 166 (2)
Wei province/state East Asia first cities 259 (3), (4), (5) first states 261 (2), (3)
Weichou see Weizhou
Weichsel see Vistula
Weihaiwei East Asia (China) Russo-Japanese War 270 (4)
Weihaiwei battle East Asia (China) Sino-Japanese War 270 (3)
Weihaiwei colonial possession East Asia (China) colonialism 269 (4)
Wei, Long Wall of wall East Asia (China) first cities 259 (5)
Weissenburg see Apulum, Gyulafehérvár
Weissensee Central Europe (Germany) post-war politics 212 (2)
Weissenstein Est. Paide Scandinavia (Sweden) early modern states 195 (3)
Weizhou var. Weichou East Asia (China) medieval states 262–263 (1)
Wejh Ar. Al Wajh Southwest Asia (Saudi Arabia) 20th-century politics 233 (4)
Welle see Uele
Wellington New Zealand colonization 283 (4), (5), 284–285 (1) decolonization 285 (3) environmentalism 285 (2) exploration 279 (3)
Wellington region New Zealand colonization 283 (5)
Wellington penal colony Australia colonization 282 (1)
Welsh Principalities state British Isles crusades 64–65 (2) medieval states 183 (3), 186 (2)
Welsh States state British Isles medieval states 187 (4)
Wen-chou, Wenchow see Wenzhou
Wenden mod. Cēsis; Latv. Cesis Eastern Europe (Latvia) early modern states 195 (3) medieval states 189 (3)
Wends people Central Europe crusades 64–65 (2)
Wenzhou var. Wen-chou, Wenchow East Asia (China) colonialism 269 (4) medieval states 263 (5) post-war politics 274 (2)
Wesenberg Est. Rakvere Eastern Europe (Estonia) early modern states 195 (3)
Weser river Central Europe empire and revolution 199 (3) Franks 184 (2)
Wessex state British Isles medieval states 183 (3)
West Alaskan Inuit people North America cultural groups 123 (3)
West and Central Punjab region South Asia decolonization 250 (1)
West Antarctica see Lesser Antarctica
West Asia region Asia biological diffusion 73 (2)
West Atlantic Peoples people West Africa early cultures 160 (1)
West Bank region Southwest Asia 20th century 234 (2)
West Bengal region South Asia post-war politics 252 (1), (3), 253 (4)
West Berlin Central Europe (Germany) post-war politics 212 (2)
West Bihar region South Asia decolonization 250 (1)
West Coast physical region South America early cultures 144 (1)
West Coast see Westland
West Dawson North America (Canada) imperial global economy 93 (3)
Westeregeln Central Europe (Germany) early agriculture 174 (1)
Western Australia region Australia colonization 282 (1), (2)
Western Bug see Bug
Western Christendom region Western Europe global knowledge 77 (5)
Western Cree people North America cultural groups 123 (3)
Western Desert var. Aṣ Ṣaḥrā' al Gharbīyah, Sahara el Gharbîya desert North Africa ancient Egypt 159 (2), (3), (5)
Western Dvina Bel. Dzvina, Ger. Düna, Latv. Daugava, Rus. Zapadnaya Dvina river Eastern Europe economy 190 (1) medieval states 185 (3) Timur 229 (4)
Western Europe region Europe US economy 138 (1)
Western Ghats mountain range South Asia colonialism 247 (3), 248 (1) early medieval states 244 (1), 244–245 (3) economy 249 (4) first empires 241 (4) first religions 36 (2) Mughal Empire 246 (1)
Western Liang state East Asia first states 261 (3)
Western Pomerania region Central Europe empire and revolution 199 (3)
Western Port penal centre Australia colonization 282 (1) environmentalism 285 (2)
Western Regions region Central Asia first states 260 (1)
Western Sahara region/state North Africa decolonization 168 (1) economy 168 (2), (3) Islam 235 (4) the modern world 113 (3)
Western Samoa var. Sāmoa-i-Sisifo; prev. German Samoa; mod. Samoa state Pacific Ocean decolonization 285 (3) environmentalism 285 (2) see also German Samoa, Samoa
Western Shoshoni people North America colonization 126 (1)
Western Sierra Madre see Madre Occidental, Sierra
Western Tarahumara people North America colonization 126 (1)
Western Turkestan region Central Asia medieval states 262–263 (1)
Western Turks people Central Asia medieval states 261 (4), (5), 262–263 (1)
Western Ukrainian Republic see West Ukraine
West Fjords fjords Iceland exploration 172 (2)
West Florida colonial possession North America empire and revolution 127 (3)
West Galicia region Central Europe empire and revolution 198 (2)
Westgate British Isles (United Kingdom) economy 204 (3)
West Germany state Central Europe Cold War 108 (3), 109 (1) post-war economy 213 (5), 214 (1) post-war politics 212 (3) Soviet Union 213 (4) US superpower 138 (1)
West Greenland Inuit people North America cultural groups 123 (3)
West India States state South Asia colonialism 248 (2)
West Indies island group North America colonization 126 (1) early agriculture 20–21 (2)
West Irian see Dutch New Guinea, Irian Jaya, Netherlands New Guinea
Westland mod. West Coast region New Zealand colonization 283 (5)
West Malaysia see Malaya
West New Guinea see Dutch New Guinea, Irian Jaya, Netherlands New Guinea
West Pakistan state South Asia decolonization 251 (4) post-war politics 252 (1)
Westphalia region Central Europe empire and revolution 202 (2)
West Point North America (USA) empire and revolution 127 (3)
West Pomerania region Central Europe early modern states 197 (3)
Westport New Zealand colonization 283 (5)
West Prussia region Central Europe empire and revolution 198 (2), 199 (3), 202 (2) WWI 207 (4)
West River burial mound North America (USA) first civilizations 121 (4)
West River see Xi Jiang
West Roman Empire state Europe/Africa great migrations 52–53 (1)
West Siberian Plain plain Siberia exploration 257 (2)
West Turkana archaeological site East Africa (Kenya) first humans 12 (1)
West Ukraine var. Western Ukrainian Republic region Eastern Europe empire and revolution 198 (2)
West Virginia state North America the growth of the US 129 (1) US Civil War 130 (5), 131 (6), (7) US economy 134 (2), 139 (3) US superpower 139 (5)
West Wales var. Wessex state British Isles medieval states 183 (3) see also Wessex
Wexford Ir. Loch Garman British Isles (Ireland) medieval states 185 (3), 187 (4)
Wey and Arun canal British Isles economy 204 (1)
Whakatane New Zealand colonization 283 (4)
Whales, Bay of bay Antarctica Antarctic Exploration 287 (3)
Whangarei New Zealand colonization 283 (4), (5)
Whitby religious building British Isles (United Kingdom) medieval states 183 (3)
Whitebird Creek battle North America (USA) the growth of the US 129 (2)
White Bulgars see Volga Bulgars
Whitehorse North America (Canada) the growth of the US 129 (2) US superpower 138 (1)
White Huns see Ephthalites; Hephthalites, Empire of the
White Lotus rebellion East Asia empire and revolution 268 (2)
White Mountain battle Central Europe (Czech Republic) Reformation 196 (1)
White Nile Ar. Al Baḥr al Abyaḍ, An Nīl al Abyaḍ, Bahr el Jebel river East Africa early agriculture 158 (1) economy 163 (2) exploration 157 (5) Islam 163 (1) slave trade 165 (4) trade 165 (3)
White Plains battle North America (USA) empire and revolution 127 (3)
White Russia state Eastern Europe Soviet Union 208 (2)
White Sea Rus. Beloye More sea Arctic Ocean exploration 257 (2) historical geography 170–171 (1)
Whitestone Hill battle North America (USA) the growth of the US 129 (2)
White Temple temple Southwest Asia (Iraq) first cities 220 (3)
White Volta var. Nakambé, Fr. Volta Blanche river West Africa Islam 163 (1) trade 163 (4), (5), (6), (7), 164 (2)
Whittier North America (USA)
Whydah mod. Ouidah; Eng. Wida West Africa empire and revolution 88 (1) slave trade 165 (4) see also Ouidah
Wichita people North America colonization 125 (4), 126 (1)
Wichita Village battle North America (USA) the growth of the US 129 (2)
Wida see Ouidah, Whydah
Wien see Vienna, Vindobona
Wigan British Isles (United Kingdom) economy 204 (1)
Wight, Isle of island British Isles medieval states 186 (2)
Wigorna Ceaster see Worcester
Wila state Southern Africa trade 164 (2)
Wilkes-Barre North America (USA) empire and revolution 127 (3)
Wilkes Land physical region Antarctica Antarctic Exploration 287 (3)
Willandra Lakes Australia exploration 280 (1)
Will County region North America
Willendorf archaeological site Central Europe (Switzerland) prehistoric culture 17 (4)
Williamsburg North America (USA) empire and revolution 127 (2), (3)
Willkawain South America (Peru) early cultures 146 (1)
Wilmersdorf Central Europe (Germany) post-war politics 212 (2)
Wilmington North America (USA) empire and revolution 127 (2), (3) US Civil War 131 (6), (7)
Wilna see Vilna, Vilnius, Wilno
Wilno Eastern Europe (Lithuania) WWII 210 (1), 211 (4)
Wilson Butte Cave North America (USA) the world in 10,000 BCE 14–15
Wilson's Creek battle North America (USA) US Civil War 131 (6)
Wilson's Promontory Australia the world in 5000 BCE 18–19
Wilton archaeological site/settlement Southern Africa (South Africa) early agriculture 158 (1) early cultures 160 (1)
Wiluna Australia colonization 282 (1)
Wilzi people Central Europe Franks 184 (2)
Winburg Southern Africa (South Africa) colonization 166 (2)
Winburg-Potchefstroom, Republic of state Southern Africa the world in 1850 90–91
Winchester hist. Wintanceaster; Lat. Venta Belgarum British Isles (United Kingdom) economy 190 (1) medieval states 183 (3), 186 (2), 187 (4)
Windau var. Vindava, mod. Ventspils; Eastern Europe (Latvia) medieval states 189 (3) see also Vindava
Windhoek Ger. Windhuk Southern Africa (Namibia) colonization 167 (4) economy 168 (2) European imperialism 96 (2)
Windhuk see Windhoek
Windward Coast physical region West Africa slave trade 165 (4)
Windward Islands colonial possession/state West Indies the world in 1900 94–95 the world in 1925 98–99 the world in 1950 102–103
Winneba West Africa (Ghana) empire and revolution 88 (1)
Winnebago people North America colonization 126 (1)
Winnipeg North America (Canada) the growth of the US 129 (2), 132 (1) US economy 136 (2)
Winnipeg, Lake lake North America colonization 126 (1) cultural groups 123 (3) exploration 118 (1), 119 (2), (3) the growth of the US 129 (2)
Wintanceaster see Winchester
Winterville North America (USA) cultural groups 122 (5)
Winwaed battle British Isles (United Kingdom) medieval states 183 (3)
Wisby mod. Visby Scandinavia (Sweden) medieval states 189 (3) see also Visby
Wisconsin state North America the growth of the US 129 (1) US Civil War 130 (2), (3), (4), (5) US economy 134 (2)
Wisła see Vistula
Wismar Central Europe (Germany) economy 190 (1) medieval states 189 (3)
Wismar region Central Europe early modern states 197 (3)
Wittenberg Central Europe (Germany) Reformation 194 (2)
Wittstock battle Central Europe (Germany) Reformation 196 (1)
Włodzimierz var. Volodymyr-Volyns'kyy; Rus. Vladimir Eastern Europe (Russian Federation) medieval states 189 (3) see also Vladimir
Woccon people North America colonization 125 (4)
Woju people East Asia first states 260 (1)
Wojwodina see Vojvodina
Wollongong Australia colonization 283 (3)
Wolmar Latv. Valmiera; Rus. Vol'mar Eastern Europe (Latvia) early modern states 195 (3)
Wolof state West Africa Islam 163 (1) trade 163 (4), (6), (7)
Wolverhampton British Isles (United Kingdom) economy 204 (1)
Wonju Jap. Genshū East Asia (South Korea) Cold War 109 (4)
Wonsan East Asia (North Korea) early modern states 267 (4) Russo-Japanese War 270 (4) Sino-Japanese War 270 (3) Cold War 109 (4)
Wood Lake battle North America (USA) the growth of the US 129 (2)
Woodland Culture people North America/South America the world in 1000 58–59 the world in 1200 62–63 the world in 1300 66–67 the world in 1400 70–71 the world in 1500 74–75 the world in 1700 82–83
Worcester anc. Wigorna Ceaster British Isles (United Kingdom) medieval states 183 (3)
Workington British Isles (United Kingdom) economy 204 (1)
Wormatia see Worms
Worms anc. Augusta Vangionum, Borbetomagus, Wormatia settlement Central Europe (Germany) ancient Rome 182 (1) crusades 186 (1) economy 190 (1) Franks 184 (2) medieval states 182 (2), 187 (3) Reformation 194 (2) see also Borbetomagus
Wounded Knee battle North America (USA) the growth of the US 129 (2)
Wrangel Island island Arctic Ocean colonialism 269 (3) exploration 257 (2)
Wrangell see Fort Wrangell
Wrocław Ger. Breslau Central Europe (Poland) economy 190 (1) medieval states 188 (1) see also Breslau
Wu East Asia (China) first cities 259 (4), (5) first religions 37 (4)
Wu region/state East Asia first religions 37 (4) first states 261 (2) medieval states 263 (3)
Wubei East Asia (China) first states 260 (1)
Wuchang var. Wu-ch'ang settlement East Asia (China) biological diffusion 72–73 (1) early modern states 266 (1), (2) medieval states 263 (6) world religions 49 (3)
Wuchang see Hankou, Wuhan
Wucheng East Asia (China) first cities 259 (3)
Wu-chou, Wuchow see Wuzhou
Wuci East Asia (China) first states 260 (1)
Wudahai East Asia (China) Mongols 68–69 (1)
Wudang Shan var. Wu Tang Shan mountain East Asia first religions 37 (4)
Wudu province East Asia first states 260 (1)
Wuhan var. Hankou, Han-kou, Han-k'ou, Hanyang, Wuchang, Wu-han; prev. Hankow East Asia (China) Chinese revolution 271 (5) Communism 271 (8) economy 274 (1) Islam 275 (4) post-war economy 275 (3) post-war politics 271 (7), 274 (2) see also Hankou
Wuhsien see Suzhou
Wu-hsing see Wuxing
Wuhu var. Wu-na-mu East Asia (China) colonialism 269 (4)
Wuhuan people East Asia first states 260 (1), 261 (2)
Wuling province East Asia first states 260 (1)
Wulu East Asia (China) first states 260 (1)
Wu-lu-k'o-mu-shi, Wu-lu-mu-ch'i see Urumchi, Ürümqi
Wu-na-mu see Wuhu
Wupatki archaeological site North America (USA) cultural groups 123 (4)
Wuqie Mainland Southeast Asia (Vietnam) first states 260 (1)
Württemberg state Central Europe early modern states 193 (5) empire and revolution 202 (1), (2)
Wusuli Jiang, Wusuri see Ussuri
Wu Tang Shan see Wudang Shan
Wuwei Buddhist centre/settlement East Asia (China) ancient trade 44–45 (1) first states 260 (1), 261 (3) world religions 49 (3)
Wuwei province East Asia first states 260 (1)
Wuxing var. Wu-hsing Buddhist centre East Asia (China) world religions 49 (3)
Wuyi Buddhist centre East Asia (China) world religions 49 (3)
Wuyi Shan mountain range East Asia historical geography 254–255 (1)
Wuyne state East Asia medieval states 263 (3)
Wuyuan East Asia (China) first states 260 (1)
Würzburg Central Europe (Germany) medieval states 189 (3)
Wuzhong people East Asia first cities 259 (4)
Wuzhou var. Wu-chou, Wuchow East Asia (China) colonialism 269 (4) medieval states 262–263 (1)
Wye Wel. Gwy river British Isles economy 204 (1)
Wyndham Australia colonization 282 (1), 283 (3)
Wyoming state North America the growth of the US 129 (1) US economy 134 (2)
Wyoming battle North America (USA) empire and revolution 127 (3)

X

Xacalta Central America (Mexico) first civilizations 122 (1)
Xalpan Central America (Mexico) Aztecs 124 (3)
Xaltenco Central America (Mexico) Aztecs 124 (3)
Xaltocan Central America (Mexico) Aztecs 124 (2) colonization 125 (5)
Xaltocan, Lake lake Central America Aztecs 124 (2) colonization 125 (5)
Xam Nua see Sam Neua
Xanthus Southwest Asia (Turkey) first civilizations 177 (1) Hellenistic world 40–41 (1)
Xäzär Dänizi see Caspian Sea
Xeloc Central America (Mexico) Aztecs 124 (2)
Xhosa people Southern Africa the world in 1800 86–87
Xia state East Asia first states 261 (3)
Xiaguan see Dali
Xiamen var. Hsia-men; prev. Amoy East Asia (China) colonialism 269 (4) economy 274 (1) empire and revolution 88–89 (2) imperialism 270 (2) post-war politics 274 (2) trade 267 (3) WWII 251 (3)
Xi'an var. Changan, Ch'ang-an, Hsi-an, Sian, Signan, Siking, Singan, Xian East Asia biological diffusion 72–73 (1) early agriculture 258 (2) early modern states 266 (1), (2), 268 (1) economy 274 (1) Islam 275 (4) Mongols 68–69 (1) post-war economy 275 (3) post-war politics 271 (7), 274 (2) trade 267 (3) see also Chang'an
Xianbei people East Asia first states 260 (1), 261 (2) medieval states 261 (6)
Xianbi var. Hsien-pi, Sienpi, Tungus people East Asia the world in 250 CE 46–47
Xiang vassal state East Asia first cities 259 (3)
Xianggang see Hong Kong
Xiangping East Asia (China) first cities 259 (5)
Xiangyang var. Hsiang-yang settlement East Asia (China) early modern states 266 (2) medieval states 263 (4), (5) Mongols 68–69 (1) world religions 49 (3)
Xiangzhou var. Hsiangchou East Asia (China) medieval states 262–263 (1)
Xianrendong archaeological site East Asia early agriculture 258 (1)
Xianyang East Asia (China) first cities 259 (5)
Xianyun people East Asia first cities 259 (4)
Xiapi East Asia (China) first states 260 (1)
Xico Central America (Mexico) Aztecs 124 (2) first civilizations 122 (1)
Xicochimalco Central America (Mexico) colonization 125 (5)
Xie East Asia (China) first cities 259 (5) first religions 37 (4)
Xie state East Asia first cities 259 (5)
Xigazê see Shigatse
Xiiqtepec state Central America Aztecs 124 (1)
Xi Jiang var. Hsi Chiang, Eng. West River river East Asia early modern states 266 (1), (2) first cities 28–29 (1) first religions 37 (4) first states 260 (1) medieval states 261 (6), 262–263 (1), 263 (4), (6) Mongols 68–69 (1) post-war politics 274 (2)
Xi Jiang Delta region East Asia first cities 28–29 (1)
Xin see Sin Kiang, Turkestan, Xinjiang
Xing vassal state East Asia first cities 259 (3)
Xingan East Asia (China) first states 260 (1)
Xingqing Palace palace East Asia (China) medieval states 262 (2)
Xingkai Hu see Khanka, Lake
Xingqingfu East Asia (China) medieval states 263 (4), (5)
Xingtai East Asia (China) first cities 259 (3)
Xingu river South America colonization 149 (3) early cultures 144 (1), 145 (2) economy 153 (3) empire and revolution 151 (3) environment 153 (4) exploration 142 (1), 143 (2)
Xingyuan East Asia (China) medieval states 263 (4)
Xingzhong East Asia (China) medieval states 263 (5)
Xining East Asia (China) economy 274 (1)
Xinje state Southern Africa trade 164 (2)
Xinjiang var. Sinkiang, Sinkiang Uighur Autonomous Region, Xin, Turkestan province/state East Asia ancient trade 44–45 (1) colonialism 269 (3), (4) Communism 271 (8) early modern states 268 (1) empire and revolution 268 (2) exploration 257 (3) medieval states 261 (6) post-war economy 275 (3) post-war politics 252 (2)
Xinjiang see Sinkiang, Turkestan
Xinye var. Hsin-yeh Buddhist centre East Asia (China) world religions 49 (3)
Xinzheng East Asia (China) first cities 259 (4), (5) first religions 37 (4)
Xiong'er Jiang river East Asia first cities 29 (4)
Xiongnu var. Hsiung-nu, Huns people East Asia ancient trade 44–45 (1) first cities 259 (5) first states 260 (1), 261 (2) medieval states 261 (6)
Xiongnu, Empire of the var. Hsiung-nu, Hun tribal confederacy state East Asia the world in 250 BCE 38–39
Xi Shan mountain East Asia first religions 37 (4)
Xiuhquilpan Central America (Mexico) first civilizations 122 (1)
Xiuhtetelco Central America (Mexico) first civilizations 122 (1)

BIBLIOGRAPHY

World history

Atlases:

Atlante Storico De Agostini Novara, 1995

Atlante Storico del Cristianesimo Andrea Dué, Juan Maria Laboa, Milan, 1997

Atlas Historico Universal y de Espagna Santillana Madrid, 1995

Atlas of Ancient Archaeology Jacquetta Hawkes (ed.), London, 1974

Atlas of Atlases: The Map Makers Vision of the World Phillip Allen, New York, 1992

Atlas of Disease Distributions: Analytical Approaches to Epidemiological Data Andrew D. Cliff and Peter Haggett, Oxford, 1988

Atlas of Food Crops J. Bertin (et al.), Paris, 1971

Atlas of Islamic History H.W. Hazard, Princeton, 1952

Atlas of Jewish History Dan Cohen-Sherbok, London and New York, 1996

Atlas of Modern Jewish History (revised from the Hebrew edn.) Evyatar Friesel, Oxford, New York,1990

Atlas of the Christian Church Henry Chadwick and G.R. Evans (eds.), Oxford, 1987

Atlas of the Jewish World Nicholas de Lange, Oxford, 1995

Atlas zur Geschichte V.E.B. Hermann Haack, GDR, 1988

Atlas zur Kirchengeschichte H. Jedin, K.S. Latourette, J. Martin, Freiburg, 1970

Cambridge Illustrated Atlas: Warfare, Renaissance to Revolution 1492–1792 Jeremy Black,Cambridge, 1996

Cambridge Illustrated Atlas: Warfare, The Middle Ages 768–1487 Nicholas Hooper and Matthew Bennett, Cambridge, 1996

Cassell Atlas of World History John Haywood, Brian Catchpole, Simon Hall, Edward Barratt, Oxford, 1997

Chambers Atlas of World History, Edinburgh, 1975

Collins Atlas of Twentieth Century World History Michael Dockrill, 1991

Grand Atlas Historique Georges Duby, Paris,1996

Grosser Atlas zur Weltgeschichte, Braunschweig, 1997

Grosser Historischer Weltatlas (3 vols.) Bayerischer Schulbuch-Verlag, Munich, 1981

Hammond Atlas of World History, Maplewood, New Jersey, 1997

Historical Atlas of Islam William C. Brice (ed.), Leiden, 1981

Historical Atlas of the Muslim Peoples R. Roolvink, London, 1957

Historical Atlas of World Mythology Vol. I: The Way of the Animal Powers J. Campbell, New York, 1984

Historical Atlas of World Mythology Vol. II: The Way of the Seeded Earth, Part I: The Sacrifice Joseph Campbell, New York, 1988

Historical Atlas of the World's Religions, Isma'il Ragi al Faruqi, New York, 1974

New Cambridge Modern History Atlas, H.C. Darby, Harold Fullard (eds.), 1970

Past Worlds: The Times Atlas of Archaeology C. Scarre (ed.) London, 1988

Philip's Atlas of Exploration, London, 1996

Putzger Historische Weltatlas, Berlin, 1997

Rand McNally Atlas of World History 1993 (published in England as **Philip's Atlas of World History**, London, 1992)

Review and Atlas of Palaeovegetation: Preliminary Land Ecosystem Maps of the World Since the last Glacial Maximum J.M. Adams and H. Faure (eds.), Quaternary Environments Network, www.soton.ac.uk/~tjms/adams4.html

Soguatlas, Stockholm, 1992

Társadalom – És Művelődéstörténeti Atlasz Budapest, 1991

The World...its History in Maps W.H. McNeill, M.R. Buske, A.W. Roehm, Chicago, 1969

Times Atlas of Exploration Felipe Fernandez-Armesto (ed.), London, 1991

Times Atlas of the 20th Century Richard Overy (ed.), London, 1996

Times Atlas of the Second World War J. Keegan (ed.), London, 1989

Times Atlas of World History Geoffrey Barraclough (ed.), London, 1993

Times Concise Atlas of World History Geoffrey Barraclough (ed.), London, 1994

Tortenelmi Vilagatlasz, Budapest, 1991

WDTV Atlas zur Weltgeschichte (2 vols.) H. Kinder & W. Hilgemann, Stuttgart, 1964 (Published in English as **The Penguin Atlas of World History** London, 1974 and 1978)

WWF Atlas of the Environment Geoffrey Lean and Don Hinrichsen, Oxford, 1992

West Point Atlas of American Wars: Volume II, 1900-1953 Vincent J. Esposito (chief ed.), New York, 1959

West Point Military History Series: Atlas for the Arab-Israeli War and the Korean War Thomas E. Greiss (series ed.), Wayne, New Jersey,1986

West Point Military History Series: Atlas for the Great War Thomas E. Greiss (series ed.), Wayne New Jersey, 1986

West Point Military History Series: Atlas for the Second World War (vols. I–III) Thomas E. Greiss (series ed.), Wayne, New Jersey,1985

Other works:

A History of Discovery and Exploration: The Search Begins London,1973

A History of Islamic Societies I.M. Lapidus, Cambridge, 1988

A History of World Societies John P. McKay, Bennett D. Hill, John Buckler, Boston, 1997

A Study of History Arnold Toynbee, Oxford, 1972

Asia Before Europe: Economy and Civilization of the Indian Ocean from the Rise of Islam to 1750 K.N. Chauduri, Cambridge, 1991

Before European Hegemony: The World System AD 1250-1350 J.L. Abu-Lughod, Oxford, 1991

Claudius Ptolemy: The Geography Translated and edited by Edward Luther Stevenson, London, 1991

Columbia Lippincott Gazetteer of the World Saul B. Cohen (ed.), New York, 1999

Cross-cultural Trade in World History P.D. Curtin, Cambridge, 1984

Encyclopedia of World History, revised edn. W.L. Langer (ed.), London, 1987

Heck's Pictorial Archive of Military Science, Geography and History J.G. Heck, New York, 1994

Into the Unknown National Geographic Society: Washington, 1987

Maps and History J. Black, New Haven, 1997

Maps and Politics J. Black, London,1997

Maps from the Age of Discovery, Columbus to Mercator Kenneth Nebenzahl, London, 1990

Navies and Nations: Warships, Navies and State Building in Europe and America 1500-1860 J. Glete, Stockholm, 1993

Peoples and Places of the Past National Geographic Society: Washington, 1983

Plagues and Peoples W.H. McNeill, New York, 1992

Portugaliae Monumenta Cartographica Lisbon, 1960

The Atlantic Slave Trade P.D. Curtin, Madison, 1972

The Atlantic Slave Trade: Effects on Economy, Society and Population in Africa, America and Europe J.E. Inikori, S.L. Engerman, Durham, NC 1992

The Discoverers: An Encyclopedia of Explorers and Exploration Helen Delpar (ed.), New York, 1980

The Distribution of Wild Wheats and Barleys J.R. Harlan, D. Zohary, Science, 1966

The Earth and its Peoples: a Global History Richard W. Bulliet, Pamela Kyle, Crossley, Daniel R. Headrick, Steven W. Hirsch, Lyman L. Johnson, David Northrup, Boston, New York, 1997

The Evolution of International Business G. Jones, London, 1996

The First Imperial Age: European Overseas Expansion c. 1400–1715 G.V. Scammel London, 1992

The Geography behind History W.G. East, London, 1965

The History of Cartography (various vols.) J.B. Harley, D. Woodward, Chicago, 1987–

The Hutchinson History of the World, revised edn. J.M. Roberts, London, 1987

The Mapmaker's Art: A History of Cartography John Goss, London, 1993

The Osprey Companion to Military History Robert Cowley and Geoffrey Parker, London, 1996

The Oxford History of the British Empire II, the Eighteenth Century P.J. Marshall (ed.), Oxford, 1998

The Oxford History of the British Empire: The Origins of Empire Nicholas Canny (ed.), Oxford, 1998

The Oxford Illustrated History of Modern War C. Townshend (ed.), Oxford, 1999

The Plants and Animals that Nourish Man J.R. Harlan, Scientific American, 1976

The Revolutionary Age 1760–1791 H. Quebec Neaty, London, 1966

The Rise of Christianity: A Sociologist Reconsiders History R. Stark, Princeton, 1996

The Rise of the West: A History of the Human Community W.H, McNeill, Chicago, 1991

The Rise of Western Christendom: Triumph and Diversity 200–1000 P. Brown, Oxford, 1996

The Story of Archaeology Paul G. Bahn (ed.), London, 1996

The Wealth and Property of Nations D. Landes, London, 1998

The World since 1500: A Global History, 6th edn L.S. Stavrianos, Englewood Cliffs NJ, 1991

The World to 1500: A Global History, 5th edn L.S. Stavrianos, Englewood Cliffs NJ, 1991

The World: an Illustrated History Geoffrey Parker (ed.), London, 1986

The World's Religions Ninian Smart, Cambridge, 1992

War and the World: Military Power and the Fate of Continents 1450–2000 J Black, New York, 1998

War in the Early Modern World 1450–1815 J. Black (ed.), London, 1999

Why Wars Happen J. Black, London, 1998

North America

Atlases:

Atlas of Ancient America Michael Coe, Dean Snow, Elizabeth Benson, Oxford and New York, 1993

Atlas of Early American History L. Cappon (et al), Chicago, 1976

Atlas of North American Exploration: from Norse Voyages to the Race to the Pole William H. Goetzmann, Glyndwr Williams, New York, 1992

Atlas of the Civil War James M. McPherson, New York, 1994

Atlas of the North American Indian C. Waldman, M. Braun, New York, 1995

Atlas of Westward Expansion Alan Wexler, Molly Braun, New York, 1995

Civil War Newspaper Maps, a Historical Atlas David Bosse, Baltimore and London, 1993

Historical Atlas of Canada Donald Kerr and Deryck W. Holdsworth (eds.), Toronto, 1990

Historical Atlas of the American West Warren A. Beck and Ynez D. Haase, Norman, Oklahoma, 1989

Historical Atlas of New York E. Homberger, A. Hudson, New York, 1994

Historical Atlas of the United States: Centennial Edition National Geographic Society: Washington, 1988

Mapping America's Past: a Historical Atlas M.C. Carnes, P. Williams, J. A. Garraty, New York, 1997

Our United States...its History in Maps E.B. Wesley, Chicago, 1977

Penguin Historical Atlas of North America Eric Homberger, London,1995

The Settling of North America: the Atlas of the Great Migrations into North America from the Ice Age to the Present Helen Hornbeck Tanner (ed.), New York, 1995)

Other works:

America in 1492: the World of the Indian Peoples before the Arrival of Columbus Alvin M. Josephy, New York, 1992

An Introduction to American Archaeology (vols. 1 & 2) Englewood Cliffs, NJ, 1970

Battle Cry of Freedom: the Civil War Era James McPherson, Oxford, 1988

Documents of American History Henry Steele Commager, 1973

European and Native American Warfare 1675–1815 A. Starkey, London, 1998

Hispaniola; Caribbean Chiefdoms in the Age of Columbus S. M.Wilson, Tuscaloosa,1990

Native American Time: a Historical Time Line of Native America Lee Francis, New York, 1996

Oxford History of the American West Clyde A. Milner et al., Oxford and New York, 1994

Prehistory of North America, 3rd edn. J.D. Jennings, Mountain View, Calif., 1989

The American Century: the Rise and Decline of the United States as a World Power Donald W. White, New Haven, 1996

The Americans: Their Archaeology and Prehistory D. Snow London, 1976

The Fur Trader and the Indian L.O. Saum London, 1965

The Limits of Liberty Maldwyn A. Jones, Oxford/New York, 1983

The Market Revolution America: Social, Political and Religious Expressions, 1800–1880 M. Stokes, S. Conway, Charlottesville, 1996

The Slave Trade Hugh Thomas, London/New York, 1997

The Spanish Frontier in North America D.J. Weber, New Haven, 1992

The Maya Michael D. Coe, London, 1993

South America

Atlases:

Atlas of Ancient America Michael Coe, Dean Snow, Elizabeth Benson, Oxford and New York, 1993

Latin American History: a Teaching Atlas Cathryn L. Lombardi, John V. Lombardi, Kym L. Stoner, Madison, Wisconsin, 1983

Other works:

A History of Latin America: Empires and Sequels, 1450–1930 Peter John Bakewell, Gainesville, 1998

Anthropological Perspectives A. C. Roosevelt (ed.), Tucson and London, 1994

Ancient Mexico in the British Museum Colin McEwan, London, 1995

Ancient South America K. Bruhns, Cambridge 1994

Archaeology in the Lowland American Tropics P. W. Stahl (ed.), Cambridge, 1994

Cambridge History of Latin America Leslie Bethel (ed.), Cambridge, 1985

Chavin and the Origins of Andean Civilization R. L. Burger, London, 1992

Chiefdoms and Chieftaincy in the Americas E. M. Redmond (ed.), Malden Mass, 1997

Chieftains, Power and Trade: Regional Interaction in the Intermediate Area of the Americas C. H. Langebaek & F. C-Arroyo (eds.), Departamento de Antropologia, Universidad de los Andes: Bogota, Colombia, 1996

Moundbuilders of the Amazon. Geophysical Archaeology on Marajo Island, Brazil A. C. Roosevelt, New York, 1991

Parmana: Prehistoric Maize and Manioc Subsistence along the Amazon and Orinoco A. C. Roosevelt, New York, 1980

Prehistory of the Americas S. J. Fiedel, Cambridge, 1987

The Conquest of the Incas John Hemming, London, 1970

The Discoverie of the Large, Rich and Bewtiful Empire of Guiana by Sir Walter Ralegh N. L. Whitehead (ed.), Exploring Travel Series Vol. 1, Manchester University Press: Manchester, American Exploration and Travel Series Vol. 71, Oklahoma University Press: Norman, 1998

The Incas and Their Ancestors: The Archaeology of Peru M. E. Moseley, New York, 1992

The Meeting of Two Worlds: Europe and the Americas, 1492–1650 W. Bray (ed.), Proceedings of the British Academy 81, Oxford, 1993

The Penguin History of Latin America Edwin Williamson, London, 1992

Africa

Atlases:

An Atlas of African History J.D. Fage London, 1958

Atlas of African Affairs Ieuan LL. Griffiths, London and New York, 1994

Atlas of Ancient Egypt John Baines and Jaromir Malek, Oxford, 1996

Cultural Atlas of Africa Jocelyn Murray (ed.), Oxford, 1993

New Atlas of African History G.S.P. Freeman-Grenville, London, 1991

Penguin Historical Atlas of Ancient Egypt Bill Manley, London, 1996

Other works:

A History of West Africa (2 vols.) 3rd edn. J.F.A. Ajaya, M. Crowder, 1985

A Survey of West African History B.A. Ogot (ed.), London, 1974–1976

Africa and Africans in the Formation of the Atlantic World 1400–1680 John Thornton, Cambridge and New York, 1992

Africa and Asia: Mapping Two Continents Natalie Ettinger, Elspeth Huxley, Paul Hamilton, London, 1973

Africa in the Iron Age c.500 BC–AD 1400 R. Oliver, B. Fagan, Cambridge, 1975

Africa since 1800, 3rd edn. R. Oliver, A. Atmore, Cambridge, 1981

African Archaeology, 2nd edn. David W. Phillipson, Cambridge, 1993

An Economic History of Africa From Earliest Times to Partition P.L. Wickins, New York, 1981

Arab Seafaring in the Indian Ocean in Ancient and Medieval Times G.F. Hourani and J.Carswell, Princeton, 1995

Cambridge History of Africa J.D. Fage, R. Oliver (eds.), Cambridge, 1975–

Early Egypt: The Rise of Civilisation in the Nile Valley A.J. Spencer, London, 1993

Economic History of West Africa A.G. Hopkins, London, 1973

General History of Africa II: Ancient Civilizations of Africa G. Mokhtar (ed.), Paris and London, 1981

General History of Africa III: Africa from the Seventh to the Eleventh Century M. Elfasi (ed.), I. Hrbek (asst. ed.), Paris and London, 1981

General History of Africa VII: Africa under Colonial Domination 1880–1935 A.A. Boahen (ed.), Paris and London, 1981

Oxford History of South Africa (vols. 1 & 2) Oxford, 1969, 1971

The African Inheritance Ieuan L.L. Griffiths, London and New York, 1995

The Art and Architecture of Ancient Egypt, revised edn. W.S. Smith, London, 1981

The Changing Geography of Africa and the Middle East Graham P. Chapman and Kathleen M. Baker, London and New York, 1992

Wars and Imperial Conquest in Africa 1830–1914 B. Vandervort, London, 1998

West Africa under Colonial Rule M. Crowder, London, 1968

Europe

Atlases:

Atlas of Medieval Europe Angus Mackay, David Ditchburn (eds.), London, 1997

Atlas of the Classical World A.M. Van der Heydon, H.H. Scullard, London, 1959

Atlas of the Crusades Jonathon Riley-Smith, New York and Oxford, 1991

Atlas of the Greek World Peter Levi, Oxford, 1997

Atlas of the Roman World Tim Cornell, John Matthews, New York, 1982

Atlas Historyczny Polski Warsaw, 1967

Cultural Atlas of France John Ardagh and Colin Jones, Oxford, 1991

Cultural Atlas of Spain and Portugal Mary Vincent and R.A. Stradling, Oxford, 1994

Cultural Atlas of the Viking World J.Graham-Campbell (ed.), Oxford, 1994

Historical Atlas of East Central Europe: Volume I Paul Robert Magosci, Seattle and London, 1993

Penguin Historical Atlas of Ancient Greece Robert Morkot, London, 1996

Penguin Historical Atlas of Ancient Rome Chris Scarre, London, 1995

Penguin Historical Atlas of Russia John Channon with Robert Hudson, London, 1995

Penguin Historical Atlas of the Third Reich Richard Overy, London, 1996

Penguin Historical Atlas of the Vikings John Haywood, London, 1995

Russian History Atlas M. Gilbert, London, 1972

Times Atlas of European History London, 1994

Other works:

A History of Ancient Greece N. Demand, New York, 1996

A History of Business in Medieval Europe 1200–1550 E.H. Hunt and J. Murray, Cambridge, 1999

A Russian Economic History A. Kahan, Chicago, 1991

An Historical Geography of Western Europe before 1800, revised edn. C.T. Smith, London and New York

As the Romans Did: a Sourcebook in Roman Social History, 2nd ed. Jo-Ann Shelton, Oxford, 1997

Britain and Industrial Europe 1750–1870 W.O. Henderson, Liverpool, 1965

Britain as a Military Power 1688–1815 J. Black, London, 1999

Cambridge Economic History of Europe II: Trade and Industry in the Middle Ages, 2nd edn. A. Miller (ed.), Cambridge, 1987

Capetian France 987–1328 E. Hallam, London, 1980

Eighteenth Century Europe 2nd edn. J. Black, London, 1999

Eighteenth Century Europe: Tradition and Progress I. Woloch, London and New York, 1982

Enlightened Absolutism H.M. Scott (ed.), London, 1990

Europe in the Eighteenth Century, 2nd edn J. Black, London, 1999

Europe in the Fourteenth and Fifteenth Centuries D.Hay, London, 1966

Europe under Napoleon, 1799–1815 M.G. Broers, London, 1997

European Warfare 1453–1815 J. Black (ed.), London, 1999
Frederick II. A Medieval Emperor D.Abulafia, London, 1988
From Louis XIV to Napoleon: The Fate of a Great Power J. Black, London, 1999
From Tsar to Soviets C. Read, 1996
Gainful Pursuits: The Making of Industrial Europe 1600–1914 J. Goodman, K. Honeyman, London, 1988
Geography of the Soviet Union J.P. Cole, London, 1984
Germany and the Germans, after Unification John Ardagh, London, 1991
Germany in the Middle Ages 800–1056 T. Reuter, London, 1991
History of the Byzantine State G. Ostrogorsky, Oxford, 1969
History of the National Economy of Russia to the 1917 Revolution P.I. Lyaschenko, New York, 1949
Information USSR Oxford and New York, 1962
Ireland 1912–85 J.J. Lee, 1989
Louis XIV and the French Monarchy A. Lossky, London, 1995
Medieval England: Towns, Commerce and Crafts 1086–1348 E. Miller, J. Hatcher London, 1995
Medieval Trade in the Mediterranean World: Illustrative Documents R.S. Lopez and I.W. Raymond, reprinted New York, 1990
Money and its Use in Medieval Europe P. Spufford, Cambridge, 1988
Moorish Spain R. Fletcher, Phoenix, 1994
Napoleon and the Legacy of the French Revolution M. Lyons, London, 1994
Napoleon's Integration of Europe S.J. Woolf, London, 1991
National States and National Minorities C.A. Macartney, 1968
New Cambridge Medieval History, vol. V, c.1198–c.1300 David Abulafia (ed.), Cambridge, 1999
New Cambridge Medieval History, vol. VI, c.1300–c.1415 Michael Jones (ed.), Cambridge, 1999
New Cambridge Medieval History, vol. VII, c.1415–c.1500 Christopher Allmand Jones (ed.), Cambridge, 1998
Northern Europe in the Early Modern Period: the Baltic World 1492–1772 D. Kirby, London, 1990
Oxford Classical Dictionary, 3rd ed. Simon Hornblower and Antony Spawforth (eds.), Oxford, 1996
Oxford History of the Classical World J. Boardman (ed.), Oxford, 1989
Oxford Illustrated History of the Crusades J. Riley-Smith (ed.), Oxford, 1997
Oxford Illustrated History of the Vikings P. Sawyer (ed.) Oxford, 1997
Oxford Illustrated Prehistory of Europe B. Cunliffe, Oxford, 1994
Poverty and Capitalism in Pre-Industrial Europe C. Lis and H. Soly, Brighton, 1982
Roman Civilization (2 vols) 3rd ed. Naphtali Lewis and Meyer Reinhold (eds.), New York, 1990
Seventeenth-century Europe 1598–1700 T. Munck, London, 1990
Seventeenth–century Europe, 2nd ed. D.H. Pennington, London, 1989
Spain in the Middle Ages: from Frontier to Empire Angus Mackay, London, 1977
Textiles, Towns and Trade J.H. Munro, Aldershot, 1994
The British Revolution: British Politics 1880–1939 Robert Rhodes, London, 1978
The Cambridge Ancient History J.B. Bury, S.A. Cook, F.E. Adcock (eds.), Cambridge, 1923–; 2nd edn 1982–
The Civilization of Europe in the Renaissance J.R.Hale, London, 1993
The Creation of the Roman Frontier S.L. Dyson, Princeton, 1985
The Crusades: a Short History J.Riley -Smith, 1990
The Emergence of the Rus J. Shepherd, S. Franklin, 1996
The European Dynastic States 1494–1660 R. Bonney, Oxford, 1991
The German Hansa P.J. Dollinger, trans. D.S. Ault, S.H. Steinberg, London, 1970
The Habsburg Monarchy, 1618–1815 C. Ingrao, Cambridge, 1994
The Hundred Years War. England and France at War c.1300–c.1450 C.T. Allmand, Cambridge, 1988
The Huns E.A. Thompson, 1996
The Industrialization of Soviet Russia (3 vols.) R.W. Davis, Cambridge, 1989
The Italian City Republics, 3rd edn. D.Waley, London and New York, 1988
The Later Crusades 1274–1580: from Lyons to Alcazar N.Housley, Oxford, 1992
The Legacy of Rome: A New Appraisal Richard Jenkins (ed.) Oxford, 1992
The Making of Europe. Conquest, Colonization and Cultural Change 950–1350 R.Bartlett, London, 1993
The Making of Roman Italy Edward Togo Salmon, Ithaca, NY, 1982
The Mediterranean World in Late Antiquity AD 395–600 A.M. Cameron, London, 1993
The Merovingian Kingdoms 450–758 I.N. Wood, London, 1994
The Old European Order 1660–1800, 2nd ed. W. Doyle, Oxford, 1992
The Origins of the Second World War in Europe P.M.H. Bell, 1986
The Roman Empire, 27 BC–AD 476: A Study in Survival Chester G. Starr, New York, 1982
The State in Early Modern France J.B. Collins, Cambridge, 1995
The Struggle for Mastery in Germany, 1779–1850 B. Simms, London, 1998
The Thirty Years War Geoffrey Parker, London, 1984
The Transformation of the Roman World 400–900 L. Webster, M. Brown, London, 1997
The Two Cities. Medieval Europe 1050–1320 M.Barber, London and New York, 1992
The Wars of Napoleon C.J. Esdaile, London, 1995
The World in Depression 1929–1939 C. Kindleberger, 1973
Venice: A Maritime Republic F.C. Lane, Baltimore, 1973
War and Imperialism in Republican Rome 327–70 BC William V. Harris, Oxford, 1979
War in the Middle Ages P. Contamine, Oxford, 1984

West Asia:

Atlases:

Atlas of the Jewish World Nicholas de Lange, Oxford, 1984
Cultural Atlas of Mesopotamia and the Ancient Near East Michael Roaf, New York and Oxford, 1996
Historical Atlas of Islam William C. Brice (ed.), Leiden, 1981
Historical Atlas of the Middle East G.S.P. Freeman-Grenville, New York, 1993
Times Concise Atlas of the Bible James B. Pritchard (ed.), London, 1991

Other works:

A History of the Arab People A. Hourani, Harvard, 1991
A History of the Ottoman Empire to 1730 M.A. Cook (ed.), Cambridge, 1976
A Popular Dictionary of Islam Ian Richard Netton, Richmond, 1997
An Introduction to Islam David Waites, Cambridge, 1996
Arabia Without Sultans Fred Halliday, London, 1979
Cambridge Encyclopedia of The Middle East and North Africa Cambridge, 1988
Encyclopaedia of Islam (10 vols.) new edn. H.A.R. Gibb et al. (eds.), Leiden, 1960
Histoire de l'Empire Ottoman R. Mantran, Paris, 1989
History of the First World War B.H. Liddell Hart, London, 1979
Lords of Horizons: A History of the Ottoman Empire Jason Goodwin, Henry Hoh and Company, 1999
Middle East Sources: A MELCOM Guide to Middle Eastern and Islamic Books and Materials in the United Kingdom and Irish Libraries Ian Richard Netton, Richmond, 1998
Muhammed, Prophet and Statesman W. Montgomery Watt, London, 1961, 1967
Ottoman Warfare 1500–1600 R Murphy, London, 1999
Palestine and the Arab Israeli conflict C.D. Smith, 1994
The Age of the Crusades. The Near East from the Eleventh Century to 1517 P. M. Holt, London and New York
The Ancient Near East c. 3000–300 BC A.T.L. Kuhrt, London, 1995
The Arabs Peter Mansfield, London , 1997
The Birth of the Palestinian Refugee Problem 1947–1949 Benny Morris, Cambridge, 1988
The Cambridge History of Iran (vol. 3) E Yarshater (ed.) Cambridge, 1983
The Fifty Years War: Israel and the Arabs Ahron Bregman and Jihan el-Jahri, Penguin, London, 1996
The Lessons of Modern War: The Iran-Iraq War Anthony H. Cordesman and Abraham R. Wagner, Boulder and San Francisco, 1990
The Neolithic of the Near East J. Mellaart, London, 1975
The Ottoman Empire: The Classical Age 1300–1600 Halil Inalcik, London, 1973
The Ottoman Turks: an Introductory History to 1923 J. McCarthy, London, 1994
The Prophet and the Age of Caliphates: The Islamic Near East from the Sixth to the Eleventh Century Hugh Kennedy, London and New York, 1986
The Travels of Ibn Battuta AD 1325–1354 (4 vols.) Ibn Battuta trans. by H.A.R. Gibb and C.F. Beckingham, Cambridge, 1958–1984
The Venture of Islam (3 vols.) Marshall G.S. Hodgson, Chicago, 1974
The World of Islam Ernst J. Grube, London, 1966
The World of Islam Bernard Lewis, London, 1976

South and Southeast Asia

Atlases:

Historical Atlas of South Asia, 2nd edn. Joseph E. Schwartzberg, Oxford and New York, 1992
Historical Atlas of South-East Asia Jan M. Pluvier, Leiden, 1995
Historical Atlas of the Indian Peninsula C.C. Davies, London, 1959
Historical Atlas of the Vietnam War Harry G. Summers Jr., Boston and New York, 1995
Macmillan's Atlas of South-East Asia London, 1988

Other works:

A History of India M.A. Edwardes, London, 1961
A History of India Burton Stein, Oxford, 1998
A History of India Romila Thapar, London, 1967
A History of Malaya 1400–1959 J. Kennedy, London, 1967
A History of South-East Asia, 4th edn. D.G.E. Hall London, 1981
A History of Vedic India Z.A. Ragozin, Delhi, 1980
A New History of India S. Wolpert, Oxford, 1993
Cambridge Economic History of India, Vol. 1, c.1200–c.1750 Tapan Raycgaudhuri and Irfan Habib (eds.), Cambridge, 1981
Cambridge Economic History of India, Vol. 2, c.1757–c.1970 Dharma Kumar and Meghnad Desai (eds.), Cambridge, 1983
Early India and Pakistan to Ashoka M. Wheeler, London, 1968
In Search of Southeast Asia, revised edn. David Joel Steinberg, Honolulu, 1987
In Search of the Indo-Europeans: Language, Archaeology and Myth J.P. Mallory, London, 1994
India: A Modern History, new edn. Percival Spear, Ann Arbor, Michigan, 1972
New Cambridge History of India G. Johnson (ed.), Cambridge, 1989
Prehistoric India to 1000 BC S. Piggott, London, 1992
Prehistoric Thailand from Early Settlement to Sukhothai C.F.W. Higham, R. Thosarat, Bangkok, 1999
Prehistory of the Indo-Malay Archipelago P. Bellwood, Ryde, NSW, 1985
South-East Asia C.A. Fisher, London, 1964
Southeast Asia: An Introductory History, 2nd edn. M.E. Osborne
Southeast Asia: History, Culture, People, 5th revised edn. E. Graff, H.E. Hammond, Cambridge, 1980
Thailand: A Short History David Wyatt, New Haven, 1984
The Archaeology of Mainland Southeast Asia Charles Higham, Cambridge, 1989
The Archaeology of Mainland Southeast Asia from 1000 BC to the Fall of Angkor C.F.W. Higham, Cambridge, 1989
The Birth of Indian Civilisation B. and R. Allchin, London, 1968
The History of Post-War Southeast Asia: Independence Problems John F. Cady, Athens, Ohio, 1972
The Indianized states of Southeast Asia Georges Coedes, Honolulu, 1968
The Making of South-East Asia D.J.M. Tate, Kuala Lumpur, 1971
The Stone Age of Indonesia, revised edn. H.R. Van Heekeren, The Hague, 1972
The Traditional Trade of Asia C.F. Simkin, Oxford, 1968
The Vedic Age R.C. Majumdar, Bombay, 1951
The Wonder That Was India (2 vols.) 3rd revised edn. A.L. Basham, London, 1987
Trade and Civilization in the Indian Ocean: An Economic History of the rise of Islam to 1750 K.N. Chauduri, Cambridge, 1985
Vietnam S.C Tucker, London, 1999
War, Culture and Economy in Java 1677–1721 M.C. Ricklefs, The Hague, 1990

North and East Asia

Atlases:

Ajiarekishi chizu Matsui and Mori, Tokyo, 1965
Atlas of China Chiao-min Hsieh, USA, 1973
Cultural Atlas of China, C. Blunden and M. Elvin, Oxford, 1991
Historical and Commercial Atlas of China A. Herrmann, Harvard, 1935
Historical Atlas of China A. Herrmann, Edinburgh, 1966
Cultural Atlas of Japan, M. Collcutt, M. Jansen, Isao Kumakura Oxford, 1991
Nihon rekishi jiten Atlas Tokyo, 1959
Times Atlas of China P.J.M. Geelan D.C. Twitchett (eds.), London, 1974
Tubinger Atlas der Orients (various vols.) Wiesbaden, 1972-

Other works:

A Historical Geography of Russia H.Parker (ed.), London, 1968
A History of the Peoples of Siberia J. Forsyth, Cambridge, 1992
Cambridge Illustrated History of China P. B. Ebrey, Cambridge, 1996
Cambridge History of China D. Twitchett, M. Loewe (eds.), Cambridge, 1979–
China, Korea and Japan: The Rise of Civilization in East Asia, Gina L. Barnes London, 1993
The Early Civilization of China Yong Yap and A. Cotterel, London, 1975
Histoire du Parti Communiste Chinois J. Guillermaz, Paris, 1968, English translation 1972
Inner Asian Frontiers of China O. Lattimore, New York, 1951
An Introduction to Chinese History, B. Wiethoff London, 1975
Le Monde Chinois J. Gernet, Paris, 1969; English translation 1982
The Archaeology of Ancient China, 4th edn. K.C. Chang, New Haven, 1986
The Empire of the Steppes: A History of Central Asia R. Grousset, New Brunswick, NJ, 1970
World Prehistory, G. Clarke, Cambridge, 1977

Australasia and Oceania

Atlases:

Aboriginal Languages and Clans: An Historical Atlas of Western and Central Victoria J.D. Clark, Clayton, South Australia, 1988
Cultural Atlas of Australia New Zealand and the South Pacific Richard Nile and Christian Clerk, Oxford, 1996

Other works:

A Prehistory of Australia, New Guinea, and Sahul J.P. White and J.F. O'Connell, Sydney, 1982
Aboriginal Australians: Black Responses to White Dominance Richard Broome, Sydney, 1982
Australia Unveiled Günter Schilder, Amsterdam, 1976
Australian Civilisation Richard Nile (ed.), Melbourne, 1994
Blood on the Banner: Nationalist Struggles in the South Pacific D.Robie, London, 1989
Convict Workers: Reinterpreting Australian History Stephen Nicholas, Cambridge (UK), 1988
Culture and Democracy in the South Pacific Ron Crocombe et al. (eds.), Suva, Fiji, 1992
Dispossession: Black Australians and White Invaders Henry Reynolds (ed.), Sydney, 1989
Easter Island Studies Steven Roger Fischer (ed.), Oxford, 1993
Ethnicity, Class and Gender in Australia Gill Bottomley and Marie de Lepervanche (eds.), Sydney, 1991
European Vision and the South Pacific Bernard Smith, New Haven, Conn., 1992
Fatal Necessity: British Intervention in New Zealand Peter Adams, Auckland, 1977
Frontier: Aborigines, Settlers and the Land Henry Reynolds, Sydney, 1987
Historical Charts and Maps of New Zealand Peter B. Maling, Auckland, 1996
History of Australia John Malony, Ringwood, Victoria (Australia), 1987
History of New Zealand Keith A. Sinclair, Auckland, 1988
History of the Pacific Islands I.C.Campbell, Berkeley, 1989
Man's Conquest of the Pacific Peter Bellwood, Auckland, 1978
Native Lands: Prehistory and Environmental Usage in Australia and the South-West Pacific J. Dodson (ed.), Melbourne, 1992
New History of Australia Frank Crowley, Melbourne, 1974
New Zealand Politics in Perspective H. Gold, Auckland, 1985
Oxford History of Australia Geoffrey Bolton (ed.), Melbourne, 1994
Oxford History of New Zealand W.H. Oliver and B.R. Williams, Wellington, 1981
Oxford Illustrated History of New Zealand Keith Sinclair (ed.), Auckland, 1990
Pacific Navigation and Voyaging Ben F. Finney (ed.), Wellington, 1976
Social Change in the Pacific Islands A.D. Robillard (ed.), London, 1992
Sunda and Sahul: Prehistoric Studies in Southeast Asia, Melanesia and Australia J. Allen, J. Golson and R. Jones (eds.), London, 1977
The Australian Colonists K.S. Inglis, Melbourne, 1974
The Discovery of the Pacific Islands Andrew Sharp, Oxford, 1960
The Evolution of Highland Papua New Guinea Societies D.K. Feil, Cambridge, 1987
The Exploration of the Pacific J.C. Beaglehole, Stanford, 1966
The Journals of Captain James Cook on his Voyages of Discovery (4 vols.) Beaglehole, J.C. (ed.), Cambridge, 1955–1974
The Maori Population of New Zealand 1769–1971 Ian Pool, Auckland, 1977
The Pacific Islands: Politics, Economics and International Relations Te'o I.J. Fairburn et al., Honolulu, 1991
The Pacific Since Magellan O.H.K. Spate, Canberra, 1988
The People's History of Australia since 1788 Verity Burgman and Jenney Lee (eds.), Melbourne, 1988
The Polynesians Peter Bellwood, London, 1987
The Prehistoric Exploration and Colonisation of the Pacific Geoffrey Irwin, Cambridge, 1992
The Prehistory of Australia D.J. Mulvaney, Ringwood, Victoria (Australia), 1975
The Prehistory of Polynesia Jesse D. Jennings (ed.), Cambridge (USA), 1979
The Quiet Revolution: Turbulence and Transition in Contemporary New Zealand Colin James, Wellington, 1986
The South Pacific: An Introduction Ron Crocombe, Suva, Fiji, 1989 (revised edition)
The World of the First Australians: Aboriginal Traditional Life – Past and Present R.M. and C.H Berndt, Canberra, 1988
We, the Navigators: The Ancient Art of Land-finding in the Pacific David Lewis, Canberra, 1972

Chronologies

Chronology of the Ancient World E.J. Bickermann, London, 1968
Chronology of the Expanding World N. Williams, London, 1969
Chronology of the Modern World N. Williams, London, 1961
Encyclopedia of Dates and Events L.C. Pascoe (ed.), London, 1991

ACKNOWLEDGMENTS

The publisher would like to thank the following for their kind permission to reproduce the photographs.

A = Above, b = below, B = Bottom, C = Centre, L = Left, R = Right, T = Top.

1 **© 1996 Visual Language**.

2/3 **© 1996 Visual Language**.

5 **E.T. Archive**: British Library, London TC

10/11 **© Michael Holford**: British Museum, London.

12 **The Natural History Museum, London**: TRb, CA, BRA, CR, CB; **Science Photo Library**: John Reader TL.

13 **The Natural History Museum, London**: TCL, TR; **Science Photo Library**: John Reader TCR.

14 **DK Picture Library**: CL, BCL; **Professor Joseph E. Schwartzberg**: TRb; **Dr David Price Williams**: BRA.

15 **DK Picture Library**: CRA; Ashmolean Museum, Oxford TR; British Museum, London TL; **Eye Ubiquitous**: John Miles CRb.

16 **CM Dixon**: CR; **DK Picture Library**: CLL, BL, BCR; University Museum of Archaeology and Anthropology, Cambridge TL; **Dr David Price Williams**: CL.

17 **Ancient Art & Architecture Collection**: Ronald Sheridan TCR; **Coo-ee Historical Picture Library**: Ron Ryan BR; **DK Picture Library**: University Museum of Archaeology and Anthropology, Cambridge CL, CR; **© Michael Holford**: TCL.

18 **Ancient Art & Architecture Collection**: Ronald Sheridan TRb; **James Mellaant**: BR; **Scala, Florence**: Archaeological Museum, Belgrade CL; **The Utah Museum of Natural History, University of Utah**: BL.

19 **British Museum, London**: TCRb; **Robert Harding Picture Library**: Bildagentur Schuster / Schenk BR; **© Michael Holford**: Ankara Museum TCL; **Catherine Jarrige**: Centre de Recherches Archéologiques Indus-Baluchistan, Musée Guimet, Paris CRb.

20 **DK Picture Library**: CL(round-based shape); British Museum, London TL, CL(flat-based beaker); Museum of London CLA.

21 **Bridgeman Art Library, London / New York**: Photograph: Mrs Sally Greene TL; **DK Picture Library**: TR, BCL; British Museum, London BC.

22 **DK Picture Library**: TR; **Robert Harding Picture Library**: John G Ross BRA; Karachi Museum, Pakistan / Photograph: R Harding CL; **Smithsonian Institute**: Presented by Mrs Alice K Bache, Purchased from James Judge and Eugenia Rodriquez / Photograph: David Heald BL.

23 **James Davis Travel Photography**: TC; **Robert Harding Picture Library**: TRb, CR; **© Michael Holford**: British Museum, London CRb.

24 **British Museum, London**: CLb; **DK Picture Library**: British Museum, London BL; **Werner Forman Archive**: Ashmolean Museum, Oxford TL; **Hirmer Verlag München**: Iraq Museum, Baghdad CbL.

25 **Bridgeman Art Library, London / New York**: Ashmolean Museum, Oxford BRA; British Museum, London TRb; **DK Picture Library**: British Museum, London C, CR, BR; University Museum of Archaeology and Anthropology, Cambridge BCRA.

26 **AKG London / Erich Lessing**: BL; **Bridgeman Art Library, London / New York**: National Archaeological Museum, Athens BL(insert); **E.T. Archive**: National Museum, Copenhagen TRb; **National Museum of the American Indian**: Smithsonian Institute / Collected by MR Harrington / Photograph: David Heald CL.

27 **AKG London**: Archaeological Museum, Heraklion TL; **AKG London/ Erich Lessing**: BCL; **© Michael Holford**: Musée Cernuschi CRA; **DK Picture Library**: British Museum, London TR; **The University of Auckland**: Department of Anthropology / Excavated by Prof. R.C. Green CRb.

28 **Bridgeman Art Library, London / New York**: Musée du Louvre, Paris TL; **DK Picture Library**: British Museum, London CAL; **Friedrich-Schiller-Universität Jena / Hilprecht Collection of Near Eastern Antiquities**: Prof. Dr. Manfred Krebernik CbL; **Turkish Information Office, London**: BLA.

29 **© Michael Holford**: BRA; Ashmolean Museum, Oxford BR; **The Institute of Archaeology, Beijing**: Professor Zheng Zhen Xiang CRA.

30 **Werner Forman Archive**: Anthropology Museum, Veragruz University, Jalapa TR; **Robert Harding Picture Library**: BCL; **South American Pictures**: Kathy Jarvis CL.

31 **Bridgeman Art Library, London / New York**: Royal Albert Memorial Museum, Exeter BCL; **DK Picture Library**: British Museum, London TCL; **E.T. Archive**: British Museum, London CRA; Historical Museum of Armenia, Erevn TCRb; **Robert Harding Picture Library**: CRb.

32 **Bridgeman Art Library, London / New York**: Musée du Louvre, Paris / Photograph: Peter Willi CLL; **DK Picture Library**: British Library, London C; British Museum, London TL, TCR, BL, BCL; **© Michael Holford:** British Museum, London CL; Musée du Louvre, Paris CR.

33 **Bridgeman Art Library, London / New York**: Ashmolean Museum, Oxford CR(Athenian coin); British Museum, London TL, TCR; **DK Picture Library**: Ashmolean Museum, Oxford CRb; British Museum, London CL, C, CR(counting stick); **Robert Harding Picture Library**: Adam Woolfitt CbR; **© Michael Holford:** British Museum, London CR(Heracles); **Ch. Thioc, Musée de la Civilisation Gallo-Romaine, Lyon**: CLb.

34 **British Museum, London**: CL; **E.T. Archive**: TCR; **N.J. Saunders**: CLb.

35 **DK Picture Library**: Ashmolean Museum, Oxford CRb; British Museum, London TLb, CRA; **© Michael Holford:** British Museum, London TCLb; **Robert Harding Picture Library**: BCL; ACI TR.

36 **AKG London / Erich Lessing**: Iraq Museum, Baghdad TL; **Ancient Art & Architecture Collection**: Brian Wilson TCR; **Werner Forman Archive**: BL.

37 **AKG London**: BR; The Israel Museum, Jerusalem CRA; **AKG London / Erich Lessing**: National Museum of Archaeology, Naples CLA; **DK Picture Library**: British Museum, London CbR; **E.T. Archive**: Olympia Museum, Greece TC; **Werner Forman Archive**: Musées Royaux du Cinquantenaire, Brussels CbL.

38 **E.T. Archive**: British Museum, London CL; **Werner Forman Archive**: David Bernstein Collection, New York BL; **© Michael Holford:** British Museum, London BCR; **Tony Stone Images**: Robert Everts TCR.

39 **E.T. Archive**: TL; The Hermitage, Leningrad CRA; National Archaeological Museum, Naples TR; **Hutchison Library**: Jenny Pate CRb.

40 **E.T. Archive**: National Archaeological Museum, Naples CL; **Robert Harding Picture Library**: Archaeological Museum, Istanbul / Photograph: Christina Gascoigne TL; R Ashworth TCR; **Scala, Florence**: Museo Capitolini, Rome BL.

41 **British Museum, London**: CRb; **Robert Harding Picture Library**: CRA; **Réunion des Musées Nationaux Agence Photographique**: Musée des Arts Asiatique-Guimet, Paris C; **Scala, Florence**: Museo di Villa Giulia, Rome TCR; Museo Gregoriano Egizio, Vatican TCb.

42 **Axiom**: Guy Marks TC; **Bridgeman Art Library, London / New York**: British Museum, London BRA; **E.T. Archive**: Archaeological Museum, Lima CL; **Scala, Florence**: Museo della Civilta' Romana, Rome BCL.

43 **Axiom**: James Morris CR; **Robert Harding Picture Library**: TCRb; Richard Ashworth CRb; **Novosti (London)**: TCL.

44 **Bridgeman Art Library, London / New York**: British Museum, London TR; **CM Dixon**: CLb; **E.T. Archive**: Archaeological Museum of Merida CL; **Robert Harding Picture Library**: TL, CA.

45 **Ancient Art & Architecture Collection**: B Crip TR; J Powell: CRA; **Chris Scarre**: BC.

46 **Ancient Art & Architecture Collection**: Ronald Sheridan BL; **Bridgeman Art Library, London / New York**: British Museum, London CL; Fitzwilliam Museum, University of Cambridge TC.

47 **Bruce Coleman Ltd**: Fred Bruemmer TL; **Robert Harding Picture Library**: TC; **© Michael Holford:** British Museum, London BCL; Museo Prenestino CR; **Réunion des Musées Nationaux Agence Photographique**: Musée des Arts Asiatiques-Guimet, Paris / Photograph: Richard Lambert BR.

48 **Bridgeman Art Library, London / New York**: British Museum, London TCb; Galleria e Museo Estense, Modena CRb; National Museum of India, New Delhi BCA; **British Museum, London**: TL.

49 **CM Dixon**: Victoria & Albert Museum, London BR; **Werner Forman Archive**: TCR.

50 **AKG London / Erich Lessing**: Musée Lapidaire, Arles TC; **Werner Forman Archive**: Private Collection, New York CLb; **© Michael Holford:** British Museum, London CRb.

51 **DK Picture Library**: British Museum, London TR; **Werner Forman Archive**: CRb; **Sonia Halliday Photographs**: CR; **Robert Harding Picture Library**: CbL; Chinese Exhibition TCL.

52 **Ancient Art & Architecture Collection**: Ronald Sheridan TL; **Bridgeman Art Library, London / New York**: Private Collection TC; **© Michael Holford:** British Museum, London BR.

53 **AKG London / Erich Lessing**: National Museum, Budapest CRb; **Ancient Art & Architecture Collection**: Ronald Sheridan TC; **E.T. Archive**: Archaeological Museum, Madrid BL.

54 **Bridgeman Art Library, London / New York**: San Vitale, Ravenna TC; **Werner Forman Archive**: National Museum of Anthropology, Mexico BR; **© Michael Holford:** Museum of Mankind, London CbL.

55 **Werner Forman Archive**: Idemitsu Museum of Arts, Tokyo CRA; **Robert Harding Picture Library**: Bildagentur Schuster / Krauskopf TL; **© Michael Holford:** British Museum, London BR; **Leiden University Library, The Netherlands**: (Or. 3101) TCR.

56 **Ancient Art & Architecture Collection**: Ronald Sheridan TL; **Bridgeman Art Library, London / New York**: British Library, London (Or.6810 f.27v) CL; **Werner Forman Archive**: TC.

57 **AKG London**: Bibliothèque Nationale de France, Paris (Arabe 5847, fol.84) TL; **Robert Harding Picture Library**: BC; D Kraus TCL.

58 **DK Picture Library**: British Museum, London CRb; **Robert Harding Picture Library**: Gavin Hellier TC; **Tony Stone Images**: Robert Frerck CLb.

59 **Bodleian Library**: (Ms. Marsh 144 P.167) CR; **Bridgeman Art Library, London / New York**: British Library, London TL; **British Library, London**: TC; **DK Picture Library**: British Museum, London CLb; **E.T. Archive**: British Museum, London CRb.

60 **Bridgeman Art Library, London / New York**: Science Museum, London C; **Coo-ee Historical Picture Library**: BL; **Werner Forman Archive**: State Historiska Museum, Stockholm TL; **© Trustees of the National Museums of Scotland**: TCR.

61 **AKG London**: Bibliothèque Nationale, Paris (Arabe 5847, fol.119) BL.

62 **Axiom**: Chris Bradley CRb; **Bodleian Library**: Pocoche (Ms. fol. 3v-4r) CL; **Werner Forman Archive**: Maxwell Museum of Anthropology, Albuquerque, New Mexico BL; **Robert Harding Picture Library**: TC.

63 **Bridgeman Art Library, London / New York**: Bibliothèque Nationale de France, Paris (Fr 2630 f.111v) TC; **E.T. Archive**: National Palace Museum, Taiwan CR; **Robert Harding Picture Library**: CRb; **Hulton Getty:** (Ms. Bodleian 264) TL.

64 **Bridgeman Art Library, London / New York**: Château Roux, France TR; British Library, London (Roy 2A XX11 f.220) TL, (Add 42130 f.82) BC.

65 **E.T. Archive**: Bibliothèque Nationale de France, Paris TLb; **Robert Harding Picture Library**: C.

66 **DK Picture Library**: British Library, London BL; Museum of Mankind, London CL; **Robert Harding Picture Library**: Bodleian Library, Oxford TCR.

67 **Bridgeman Art Library, London / New York**: Bibliothèque Nationale de France, Paris CR; **DK Picture Library**: National Maritime Museum, London TR; **Robert Harding Picture Library**: BR; I Van Der Harst BCL; **© Michael Holford:** British Museum, London TL.

68 **Bridgeman Art Library, London / New York**: National Palace Museum, Taipei TL; Private Collection TR; **DK Picture Library**: British Library, London CL.

69 **Bridgeman Art Library, London / New York**: British Museum, London CR; Victoria & Albert Museum, London BR; **Werner Forman Archive**: Formerly Gulistan Imperial Library, Teheran CLA.

70 **Bridgeman Art Library, London / New York**: British Museum, London BL; **Werner Forman Archive**: University Library, Prague TC.

71 **Bridgeman Art Library, London / New York**: British Museum, London BL; **British Library, London**: (Harl.4379, fol.83v) TL; **Robert Harding Picture Library**: TR; MPH CR; Adam Woolfitt BR.

72 **Bridgeman Art Library, London / New York**: British Library, London (Harl 4380, f.22) BC; **Jean-Loup Charmet**: Musée d'Histoire de la Médecine, Lyon CLA; **DK Picture Library**: National Maritime Museum, London TL; **Scala, Florence**: State Archive, Lucca BL; **Science Photo Library**: John Burbridge BL(insert).

73 **Collections**: Liz Stares CA; **Katz Pictures**: The Mansell Collection / Time Inc. BLA; **Scala, Florence**: Galleria Sabauda, Torino TR.

74 **AKG London**: BC; **E.T. Archive**: TR; **Tony Stone Images**: Jerry Alexander CLb.

75 **AKG London**: TC; Pinacoteca Vaticana, Rome TL; **Ancient Art & Architecture Collection**: Ronald Sheridan BLA; **E.T. Archive**: CRb; **Sonia Halliday Photographs**: CAR.

76 **E.T. Archive**: Bibliothèque Nationale de France, Paris TL

77 **Bridgeman Art Library, London / New York**: Bibliothèque Nationale d France, Paris (Fr 2810 f.188) BCL; **E.T. Archive**: University Library, Istanbul BL; **Library of Congress, Washington, D.C.**: (GA 1124 1555 F.8 G&M RR Plate 43) BCR.

78 **Bridgeman Art Library, London / New York**: Kunsthistorisches Museum, Vienna TCR; **DK Picture Library**: BCL; **© Michael Holford:** British Museum, London BCR; **Peter Newark's Pictures**: CL.

79 **Bridgeman Art Library, London / New York**: Bibliothèque Nationale de France, Paris (Fr 2810, f.84) CRb; **DK Picture Library**: British Library, London TRb; **Sonia Halliday Photographs**: Topkapi Palace Museum, Istanbul TL.

80 **AKG London**: BL; **Bridgeman Art Library, London / New York**: British Library, London (Sloane 197 f.18) TL; **Werner Forman Archive**: Art Institute, Chicago BR.

81 **Bridgeman Art Library, London / New York**: Prado, Madrid / Index BC; **British Library, London**: C; Institut Amatller D'Art Hispànic, Barcelona: CR.

82 **Bridgeman Art Library, London / New York**: Château de Versailles, France / Giraudon TC; **Peter Newark's Pictures**: CLb.

83 **E.T. Archive**: Musée Guimet Paris TC; **Robert Harding Picture Library**: BCL; M Robertson CRb; **© Michael Holford:** Science Museum, London TCLb; **Royal Geographical Society Picture Library**: CR.

84 **Bridgeman Art Library, London / New York**: British Library, London BC; **DK Picture Library**: TL; **E.T. Archive:** National Maritime Museum, London CAR.

85 **AKG London**: CR; **DK Picture Library**: BL; **E.T. Archive**: Bibliothèque Nationale de France, Paris TCR; **Mary Evans Picture Library:** Cb; **Peter Newark's Pictures:** TL.

86 **DK Picture Library:** National Maritime Museum, London BCL; **Peter Newark's Pictures:** TC, CL.

87 **Bridgeman Art Library, London / New York**: Victoria & Albert Museum, London CRb; **British Library, London:** TC; **Werner Forman Archive:** British Museum, London BC; **National Maritime Museum, London:** TL.

88 **Bridgeman Art Library, London / New York**: Private Collection CA; **Hulton Getty**: TL; **Peter Newark's Pictures:** CR.

89 **The Granger Collection, New York:** TCR; **Hulton Getty:** BR; **Peter Newark's Pictures:** BL.

90 **Bridgeman Art Library, London / New York**: Private Collection CLb; **Image Select:** Ann Ronan TC; **Public Record Office Picture Library:** BCL; **Peter Newark's Pictures:** CL.

91 **Bridgeman Art Library, London / New York**: National Maritime Museum, London TL; Alexander Turnbull Library, National Library of New Zealand, Te Puna Mātauranga o Aotearoa CR; The Stapleton Collection BC; **DK Picture Library:** TCR.

92 **Mary Evans Picture Library:** TCR, CL; **Hulton Getty:** TL; **Library of Congress, Washington, D.C.:** C.

93 **Corbis:** Bettmann CA, CRA; **Mary Evans Picture Library:** CLb.

94 **Bridgeman Art Library, London / New York**: Historisches Museum der Stadt, Vienna TC; **Public Record Office Picture Library:** BC; **William L. Clements Library, University of Michigan** CL.

95 **AKG London:** BC; **British Library, London:** (Shelfmark No. 2443) TC; **Werner Forman Archive:** CD Wertheim Collection TL; **Peter Newark's Pictures:** CR.

96 **Jean-Loup Charmet:** CLb; **Mary Evans Picture Library:** TL, TCR, TR; **Hulton Getty:** BRA.

97 **Corbis:** BL; **Mary Evans Picture Library:** TCRb, TRb.

98 **Advertising Archives:** CL; **E.T. Archive:** BC; **Frank Spooner Pictures:** Roger Viollet TCR.

99 **AKG London:** TC; **Jean-Loup Charmet:** BC; **Corbis:** Bettmann / Underwood TL; **National Motor Museum, Beaulieu:** CR.

100 **Corbis:** Bettmann BCL; **DK Picture Library:** National Maritime Museum, London TL; **Mary Evans Picture Library:** CLA, BL.

101 **Corbis:** Bettmann CAL; **Peter Newark's Pictures:** CRb.

102 **Corbis:** Burs Can TCR; Hulton-Deutsch Collection BR; **Hulton Getty:** Keystone / Oscar Kersenbaum BC; **London Transport Museum:** CL.

103 **Hulton Getty:** TL, TR, BC.

104 **Rex Features:** TL.

105 - **Corbis:** UPI / Bettmann BL; **Topham Picturepoint:** C; Associated Press TLb.

106 **Robert Harding Picture Library:** David Lomax BC; **Hulton Getty:** TCR; **Tony Stone Images:** Earth Imaging CL.

107 **DK Picture Library:** TC, CR; **Hulton Getty:** TL; **Frank Spooner Pictures:** Cilo BC.

108 **Corbis:** Bettmann / UPI TL; **Hulton Getty:** BL; **Topham Picturepoint:** CA.

109 **Rex Features:** TC; Sipa-Press BL; **Topham Picturepoint:** A Young-Joon C.

110 **Robert Harding Picture Library:** R. Hanbury-Tenison BC; **Rex Features:** Sipa-Press TR; **Science Photo Library:** CNES, 1986 Distribution Spot Image CLA.

111 **Corbis:** Philippe Wojazer / Reuter BC; **Rex Features:** Setboun / Sipa-Press TL; **Frank Spooner Pictures:** Xinhua-Chine TCb; **Tony Stone Images:** Robert Mort CR.

112 **PowerStock Photolibrary / Zefa:** N Solitrenick CLA; **Rex Features:** TL; Alexandra Boulat BR; **Frank Spooner Pictures:** Gamma / Tom Kidd CLb.

113 **Hutchison Library:** Carlos Freire TC; **Panos Pictures:** Chris Stowers CbR.

114/115 **© 1996 Visual Language**.

117 **Robert Harding Picture Library:** Robert Frerck / Odyssey / Chicago BC; **Tony Stone Images:** Tom Bean Cb; Jake Rajas CRb.

118 **Bibliothèque Nationale de France, Paris:** BC; **Bridgeman Art Library, London / New York:** British Library, London BR; **Robert Harding Picture Library:** New York Historical Society TL; **Musée de L'Homme, Paris:** D Ponsard TCR.

119 **DK Picture Library:** C, BL, CRb; **Robert Harding Picture Library:** TCb; **Peter Newark's Pictures:** TLb.

120 **DK Picture Library:** CL; **E.T. Archive:** BL; **Werner Forman Archive:** Field Museum of Natural History, Chicago TL; **Robert Harding Picture Library:** Robert Frerck / Odyssey / Chicago TCR.

121 **Werner Forman Archive:** British Museum, London TC; Ohio State Museum BR.

122 **Bridgeman Art Library, London / New York:** British Museum, London TL; **James Davis Travel Photography:** Cb; **E.T. Archive:** CLb; **Robert Harding Picture Library:** Robert Frerck / Odyssey / Chicago BR; **© Michael Holford:** CAR; **Hutchison Library:** Edward Parker TCR.

123 **DK Picture Library:** Museum of Mankind, London TL; **Werner Forman Archive:** Arizona State Museum C; Museum of the American Indian, Heye Foundation, New York CR.

124 **Ancient Art & Architecture Collection:** Ronald Sheridan TR; **E.T. Archive:** Antochiw Collection Cb; National Library, Mexico TL; **Werner Forman Archive:** British Museum, London CA.

125 **Ancient Art & Architecture Collection:** G Tortoli TL; **Robert Harding Picture Library:** Mexican Museum of Natural History BR; **Peter Newark's Pictures:** CRA.

126 **E.T. Archive:** TC; **Peter Newark's Pictures:** TL, CR.

127 **Bridgeman Art Library, London / New York:** Trinity College, Cambridge BR; **Peter Newark's Pictures:** CLA, BC.

128 **Bridgeman Art Library, London / New York:** City of Bristol Museum and Art Gallery TL; **Corbis:** Bettmann TCR; **Peter Newark's Pictures:** BCL.

129 **Bridgeman Art Library, London / New York:** Photograph: D.F. Barry, Dakota TRb; **Mary Evans Picture Library:** BR; **Robert Harding Picture Library:** National Gallery of Art, Washington CR.

130 **Corbis:** Bettmann TR, C; **Mary Evans Picture Library:** TL.

131 **Corbis:** Bettmann BL; **Peter Newark's Pictures:** CRb; Alexander Gardener TC.

132 **Bridgeman Art Library, London / New York:** Liberty Island, New York TL; **Corbis:** Bettmann / UPI TCR; **Peter Newark's Pictures:** TRb, BR.

133 **AKG London:** Photograph: Agustin Victor Casasola, (1874-1938) TLb; **Peter Newark's Pictures:** CL.

134 **Corbis:** CAL, Cb, BL; Bettmann TL; **Hulton Getty:** TCR.

135 **Corbis:** TR; **Mary Evans Picture Library:** CRb; **Ronald Grant Archive:** CA, © Disney CRA; **Peter Newark's Pictures:** CbL.

136 **Corbis:** Grant Smith TCR; **Robert Harding Picture Library:** D Lomax BR; **Peter Newark's Pictures:** CRb; **Frank Spooner Pictures:** Hulton Getty Liaison TL.

137 **Corbis:** CLA; UPI TC, BL; **Redferns:** Elliot Landy CRb.

138 **Corbis:** Bettmann / UPI CL, C; **Rex Features:** JFK Library TL.

139 **Corbis:** Bettmann / UPI TCR, CR; **Rex Features:** Sipa-Press C.

140 **Robert Harding Picture Library:** Christopher Rennie CLb; **N.H.P.A.:** M Wendler Cb; **South American Pictures:** Tony Morrison BC.

142 **E.T. Archive:** Biblioteca Estense, Modena CL; **Mary Evans Picture Library:** TL; **Robert Harding Picture Library:** Cartes et Plans, Bibliothèque Nationale de France, Paris TC.

143 **Bridgeman Art Library, London / New York:** Royal Geographical Society, London BCR; **DK Picture Library:** BR; **Robert Harding Picture Library:** National Gallery, East Berlin CbR; **Royal Geographical Society Picture Library:** TLb.

144 **Bridgeman Art Library, London / New York:** British Museum, London BR; **E.T. Archive:** University Museum, Cuzco BL; **Robert Harding Picture Library:** Robert Frerck / Odyssey / Chicago TRb; **South American Pictures:** Tony Morrison TL.

145 **Ancient Art & Architecture Collection:** Mike Andrews BR; **Bridgeman Art Library, London / New York:** British Museum, London BC; **Werner Forman Archive:** David Bernstein Fine Art, New York CL.

146 **Bridgeman Art Library, London / New York:** British Museum, London BR; **Dumbarton Oaks Research Library and Collections, Washington, D.C.:** BC; **© Michael Holford:** Collection of Señor Mujica Gallo, Lima TL, BL; **South American Pictures:** Kimball Morrison CbL.

147 **Ancient Art & Architecture Collection:** Museo Oro del Peru, Lima / Photograph: R Sheridan CbR; **E.T. Archive:** Museo del Oro, Bogota CL; **Werner Forman Archive:** Museum fur Volkerkunde, Berlin BCA; **Robert Harding Picture Library:** BLA; **South American Pictures:** Tony Morrison TC.

148 **Jean-Loup Charmet:** TR; **E.T. Archive:** Archbishop Palace Museum Cuzco TL; **Mary Evans Picture Library:** BL; **Robert Harding Picture Library:** British Museum, London Cb; **South American Pictures:** CL.

149 **Bridgeman Art Library, London / New York:** Harold Samuel Collection, Corporation of London BC; **Jean-Loup Charmet:** Bibliothèque des Arts Decoratifs CL; **E.T. Archive:** BL; **Royal Geographical Society Picture Library:** CLA.

150 **AKG London:** TL, CL; **DK Picture Library:** TCR.

151 **Bridgeman Art Library, London / New York:** British Library, London CL; **DK Picture Library:** BRA; **Mary Evans Picture Library:** CR.

152 **Rex Features:** Sipa-Press / Arias TL; **Sygma:** A Balaguer TC; **Topham Picturepoint:** CR.

153 **Panos Pictures:** Michael Harvey Cb; **Rex Features:** Sipa-Press CRb; Sipa-Press / Poveda TR.

154 **Bruce Coleman Ltd:** Christer Fredriksson CLb; **Tony Stone Images**: Hugh Sitton CRb; **World Pictures:** BC.

156 **DK Picture Library:** TL; **E.T. Archive:** British Library, London BR; **Katz Pictures:** The Mansell Collection / Time Inc. CL.

157 **AKG London:** TR; **Bridgeman Art Library, London / New York:** Royal Geographical Society, London CbL; **Royal Geographical Society Picture Library:** TC, BL; **Topham Picturepoint:** BR.

158 **AKG London / Erich Lessing:** Egyptian Museum, Berlin, SMPK TL; **Robert Estall Photo Library:** David Coulson CRA; **Dr David Price Williams:** TCR.

159 **Axiom:** James Morris CR; **Robert Harding Picture Library:** Gavin Hellier CLb.

160 **Werner Forman Archive:** Courtesy Entwistle Gallery, London TL; **Sonia Halliday Photographs:** James Wellard CAR; **Dr David Price Williams:** CAL.

161 **AKG London / Jean-Louis Nou:** TR; **Ancient Art & Architecture Collection:** Ronald Sheridan TC; **Werner Forman Archive:** Cb.

162 **Ashmolean Museum, Oxford:** Hebreden Coin Room TL; **Werner Forman Archive:** TC; Tanzania National Museum, Dar Es Salaam TCb; **© Michael Holford:** British Museum, London TRB.

163 **Musée de L'Homme, Paris:** BCL.

164 **Bridgeman Art Library, London / New York:** British Library, London (Sloane 197 f.225v-6) TCb; **British Library, London:** TL, BC; **DK Picture Library:** CL.

165 **Axiom:** Chris Bradley TR; **Jean-Loup Charmet:** Bibliothèque de L'Arsenal, Paris BLA.

166 **Mary Evans Picture Library:** TL, CL, CRb; **Sonia Halliday Photographs:** Africana Library, Durban / Photograph: Jane Taylor BC.

167 **Chester Beatty Library, Dublin:** (Ms 1599 fols 1v-2r) TCb; **Corbis:** Bettmann BR.

168 **Corbis:** Bettmann CAL; UPI Photo TL.

169 **PA News Photo Library:** EPA Photo / Lusa / Joao Relvas CL; **Panos Pictures:** Betty Press BR.

171 **The J. Allan Cash Photolibrary:** BCR; **Bruce Coleman Ltd:** Dr Eckart Pott Cb; **World Pictures:** CRb.

172 **AKG London:** Postmuseum, Berlin BR; **DK Picture Library:** Danish National Museum CLb(Insert); Statens Historika Museum, Stockholm CLb; **© Michael Holford:** Science Museum, London TL.

173 **Bridgeman Art Library, London / New York:** British Library, London C; Hereford Cathedral TC; **British Library, London:** BL, BC; **DK Picture Library:** National Maritime Museum, London TR; **E.T. Archive:** Musée Carnavalet CR; **Ordnance Survey © Crown Copyright:** BR; **Royal Geographical Society Picture Library:** CLb.

174 **DK Picture Library:** CL; British Museum, London TC, CRb; **© Michael Holford:** British Museum, London TL; **Images Colour Library:** The Charles Walker Collection BR.

175 **Bridgeman Art Library, London / New York:** Archaeological Museum, Iraklion / Lauros-Giraudon BCL; **DK Picture Library:** Museum of London CR; **E.T. Archive:** Historical Museum, Sofia TC.

176 **Ancient Art & Architecture Collection:** Mike Andrews CLb; Dr S Coyne BC; **Bridgeman Art Library, London / New York:** British Museum, London TCR; **© Michael Holford**: British Museum, London TL.

177 **Ancient Art & Architecture Collection:** Ronald Sheridan BL; **DK Picture Library:** British Museum, London C; **Scala, Florence:** National Archaeological Museum, Madrid TL.

178 **Robert Harding Picture Library:** Robert Frerck / Odyssey / Chicago BC; **© Michael Holford:** British Museum, London TL; **Scala, Florence:** Musei Capitolini, Roma TC; Museo di Villa Giulia, Roma Cb.

179 **E.T. Archive:** CLA(Insert); **Robert Harding Picture Library:** Gascoigne BL; **© Michael Holford:** CbR; British Museum CLA.

180 **Werner Forman Archive:** TL; **Sonia Halliday Photographs:** BL; **© Michael Holford:** TCRb.

181 **Ancient Art & Architecture Collection:** Ronald Sheridan BR; **DK Picture Library:** TL; **Sonia Halliday Photographs:** The Hatay Museum, Antioch, Turkey BL; **© Michael Holford:** TC, CRb.

182 **Ancient Art & Architecture Collection:** Ronald Sheridan CbR; **DK Picture Library:** British Museum, London TL; **E.T. Archive:** San Apollinare Nuovo, Ravenna CLA; **Sonia Halliday Photographs:** TR.

183 **Bibliothèque Nationale de France, Paris:** BC; **E.T. Archive:** Medieval Museum, Rome TC; **© Michael Holford:** British Museum, London TLb.

184 **AKG London / Erich Lessing:** Musée du Louvre, Paris TL; **Bridgeman Art Library, London / New York:** Musée Goya, Castres (PF 2826, f.106r) / Photograph: Giraudon C; **E.T. Archive:** Palatine Chapel, Aachen CL.

185 **Ancient Art & Architecture Collection:** Ronald Sheridan BL; **Bridgeman Art Library, London / New York:** Musée Condé, Chantilly (PE 7887, Ms. 14) TLb; **© Michael Holford:** Statens Historiska Museum, Stockholm TC.

186 **AKG London:** Biblioteca Apostolica Vaticana, Rome TL; **E.T. Archive:** Templar Chapel, Cressac CL; **© Michael Holford:** Musée de Bayeaux C.

187 **Bridgeman Art Library, London / New York:** Private Collection BLA; **E.T. Archive:** Bibliothèque de L'Arsenal, Paris CbR; **Robert Harding Picture Library:** TRb.

188 **AKG London:** San Benedetto Monastery, Subiaco (Sacro Speco) TCRb; **Ancient Art & Architecture Collection:** Ronald Sheridan TL; **Bridgeman Art Library, London / New York:** British Library, London CL.

189 **AKG London:** CRb; **Robert Harding Picture Library:** K Gillham TC.

190 **Archiv der Hansestadt Lübeck:** TL; **Bridgeman Art Library, London / New York:** Bibliothèque Nationale de France, Paris (Fr 12420 f.71) BL.

191 **AKG London / Cameraphoto:** CRb; **E.T. Archive:** Bibliothèque Nationale de France, Paris TCRb; **Scala, Florence:** Museo Correr, Venezia TCLb; Santa Francesco, Prato TC.

192 **Bridgeman Art Library, London / New York:** Archives Nationales, Paris / Giraudon TL; Bibliothèque Nationale de France, Paris (Fr 2643 f.165v) TCb; **Robert Harding Picture Library:** Simon Harris BR.

193 **AKG London:** Burgerbibliothek, Bern (Mss hist.helv I, 1, fol.70) BL; **DK Picture Library:** Wallace Collection, London CL; **E.T. Archive:** TLb; National Gallery of Art, Budapest BR.

194 **AKG London:** National Museum, Stockholm TL; **Bridgeman Art Library, London / New York:** Musée de Sibiu, Rumania / Giraudon CLb; **E.T. Archive:** Capodimonte, Naples C.

195 **Bridgeman Art Library, London / New York:** British Library, London (Add 33733 f.9) C; Nationalmuseet, Copenhagen TL; **Mary Evans Picture Library:** CR.

196 **AKG London:** CL; Musée du Louvre, Paris TL; **Bridgeman Art Library, London / New York:** Private Collection BCR; **DK Picture Library**: BRA.

197 **AKG London:** Historische Museum der Stadt Wien, Vienna TR; Musée des Beaux-Arts, Arras BL; **Mary Evans Picture Library:** BCL; **Scala, Florence:** Museo Statale Russo, Leningrad C.

198 **Bridgeman Art Library, London / New York:** Private Collection / Giraudon BRA; The Stapleton Collection BR; Tretyakov Gallery, Moscow TL; By kind permission of the **Earl of Leicester and the Trustees of the Holkham Estate:** CLA.

199 **Bildarchiv Preußischer Kulturbesitz:** Kunstbibliothek Preußischer Kulturbesitz, Berlin CR; **Bridgeman Art Library, London / New York:** Musée Carnavalet, Paris BL.

200 **Bridgeman Art Library, London / New York:** Bibliothèque Nationale de France, Paris / Lauros-Giraudon TL; Musée du Louvre, Paris / Giraudon CLA; **Mary Evans Picture Library:** CLb.

201 **Bridgeman Art Library, London / New York:** Musée du Louvre, Paris / Giraudon TCR; **E.T. Archive:** Musée de Versailles CRb; **Mary Evans Picture Library:** BL.

202 **AKG London:** TR; Slg. E. Werner, Berlin TL.

203 **AKG London:** TCLb; **E.T. Archive:** Palazzo Pubblico, Siena BL; **Mary Evans Picture Library:** TLb, C.

204 **AKG London:** TCR; **Corbis:** Bettmann CLA; **DK Picture Library:** TL; **E.T. Archive:** BR.

205 **AKG London:** BL, BR; **DK Picture Library:** The Science Museum, London TR.

206 By kind permission of **The Trustees of The Imperial War Museum, London:** CLA, CR, CRb; **Topham Picturepoint:** TL.

207 **Corbis:** Bettmann TCb; **Hulton Getty:** CL; **Topham Picturepoint:** BR.

208 **Corbis:** Bettmann BR; **Hulton Getty:** CL; **Rex Features:** Sipa-Press TL.

209 **Hulton Getty:** CRA; **Topham Picturepoint:** CLb, BC.

210 **Bridgeman Art Library, London / New York:** The Stapleton Collection TL; **Corbis:** CLA; **Robert Hunt Library:** BC.

211 **Corbis:** UPI / Bettmann CLb; **Rex Features:** BL.

212 **AKG London:** TL; **Corbis:** Jerry Cooke CLb; **Hulton Getty:** Keystone Munich CLA.

213 **Corbis:** Bettmann BLA; **David King Collection:** TRb; **Topham Picturepoint:** CR.

214 **Panos Pictures:** Jeremy Hartley Cb; **Rex Features:** TL; Darryn Lyons BL; Pensjo CA.

215 **Rex Features:** Sipa-Press / Alexandra Boulat CLA.

216 **James Davis Travel Photography:** CLb; **Robert Harding Picture Library:** CRb, BC.

218 **Bibliothèque Nationale de France, Paris:** (Ms Arabe 5847.f.19) BL; **Bridgeman Art Library, London / New York:** Bibliothèque Nationale de Cartes et Plans, Paris TL; **British Library, London:** (Maps 856.(6.)) BR.

219 **Bridgeman Art Library, London / New York:** Bibliothèque Nationale de France, Paris TR; **E.T. Archive:** Naval Museum, Genoa TCb; Richmond Borough Council BC; **Koninklijke Bibliotheek, The Hague:** (76 F 5: fol. 1r) CR; **Royal Geographical Society Picture Library:** CRb, BL.

220 **Bridgeman Art Library, London / New York:** Ashmolean Museum, Oxford TCRb; British Museum, London C; Reconstruction by **Mrs James Mellaant:** CL; **Scala, Florence:** The Iraq Museum, Baghdad TL.

221 **Caroline Chapman:** TRb; **Robert Harding Picture Library:** CRb; **© Michael Holford:** British Museum, London CLb.

222 **AKG London / Erich Lessing:** British Museum, London BR; Musée du Louvre, Paris TCR; **Caroline Chapman:** CL; **Topham Picturepoint:** TL.

223 **British Museum, London:** TCb; **Robert Harding Picture Library:** CL, CR; **© Michael Holford:** British Museum, London TRb.

224 **Bridgeman Art Library, London / New York:** British Museum, London TCR; Private Collection / Ancient Art and Architecture Collection Ltd BL; **© Michael Holford:** British Museum, London TL.

225 **Ancient Art & Architecture Collection:** Ronald Sheridan CR; **Bibliothèque Nationale de France, Paris:** BR; **DK Picture Library:** British Museum, London CLb; **Werner Forman Archive:** Coptic Museum, Cairo TCb.

226 **Ancient Art & Architecture Collection:** Ronald Sheridan TC; **Bridgeman Art Library, London / New York:** Institute of Oriental Studies, St Petersburg (Ms.E-4/322a) / Giraudon CL; **British Library, London:** (Add 27261 f.363) CbL; **DK Picture Library:** British Museum, London TL.

227 **Bildarchiv Preußischer Kulturbesitz:** C; **Werner Forman Archive:** BR; **Robert Harding Picture Library:** Ellen Rooney BL.

228 **E.T. Archive:** Forrester / Wilkinson TL; Victoria & Albert Museum, London BC; **Robert Harding Picture Library:** TCR; **Peter Newark's Pictures:** BL.

229 **AKG London:** Bibliothèque Nationale de France, Paris (Add. 18866, fol.140) CLA; **Bildarchiv Preußischer Kulturbesitz:** Staatsbibliothek zu Berlin Preußischer Kulturbesitz Orientabteilung (Ms. Diez A.Fol.70) C; **Robert Harding Picture Library:** CLb.

230 **Bridgeman Art Library, London / New York:** Victoria & Albert Museum, London BR; **Sonia Halliday Photographs:** Topkapi Palace Museum, Istanbul (Ms. 3109) TL, (Ms. H1523 p.165A) CL.

231 **Werner Forman Archive:** CLb; **Sonia Halliday Photographs:** TL; Topkapi Palace Museum, Istanbul (Ms. H.1523 p.19A) C.

232 **AKG London:** TL; **Bridgeman Art Library, London / New York:** Château de Compiegne, Oise / Lauros-Giraudon BC; **Jean-Loup Charmet:** TCR; By kind permission of **The Trustees of The Imperial War Museum, London:** BR.

233 **Corbis:** Bettmann / UPI TR; **Hulton Getty:** BLA, BCL; **Royal Geographical Society Picture Library:** Capt. W.I. Shakespear CR.

234 **Hulton Getty:** BC; **Rex Features:** Sipa-Press TL; **Frank Spooner Pictures:** Halstead / Liaison C.

235 **Rex Features:** Sipa-Press C, CRb; **Frank Spooner Pictures:** Eslami Rad TRb; Van der Stockt BR.

236 **Eye Ubiquitous:** David Cumming BC; **Robert Harding Picture Library:** Thomas Laird Cb; **Tony Stone Images:** Hugh Sitton CLb.

238 **British Library, London:** CRA, BR; (Egerton 1018 fol.335) BL; **E.T. Archive:** British Library, London TCR; **Robert Harding Picture Library:** C; © Free Gallery of Art Washington BC; **The History of Cartography, University of Wisconsin:** Bharat Kala Bhavan, Varanasi TL; **Professor Joseph E. Schwartzberg:** CLb.

239 **British Library, London:** TRb; (Sloane 197, fol.395v-396) CA; **DK Picture Library:** CR, BRA; **Robert Harding Picture Library:** Jim Thompson Collection CRA; **Royal Geographical Society Picture Library:** CbL, BL, BC.

240 **British Museum, London:** BR; **Robert Harding Picture Library:** CLb; HRH Princess Chumbhot Collection BRA; Karachi Museum, Pakistan TL, TC; **Scala, Florence:** New Delhi Museum, India Cb.

241 **Bridgeman Art Library, London / New York:** Oriental Museum, Durham University CL; **Robert Harding Picture Library:** BR; Adam Woolfitt TCR.

242 **DK Picture Library:** Ashmolean Museum, Oxford BL; **Robert Harding Picture Library:** TL; Adam Woolfitt CbR; **© Michael Holford:** Musée Guimet, Paris CAL.

243 **British Library, London:** CbL; **Werner Forman Archive:** Private Collection TRb; **Robert Harding Picture Library:** BR; Gavin Hellier CR.

244 **Robert Harding Picture Library:** TL; Nigel Cameron CL; A Kennet TC, C; Adam Woolfitt BC; **Hutchison Library:** Christine Pemberton BCR.

245 **Robert Harding Picture Library:** TR, CA; Bangkok National Museum, Thailand BCL; Rolf Richardson BC.

246 **Ancient Art & Architecture Collection:** Chebel Sotun Palace, Isfahan / Photograph: Ronald Sheridan BCL; **Bridgeman Art Library, London / New York:** Metropolitan Museum of Art, New York TL; Private Collection / The Stapleton Collection CLb; **Robert Harding Picture Library:** TCR; Gavin Hellier CLA.

247 **Bridgeman Art Library, London / New York:** Private Collection / The Stapleton Collection CR, CLb; **British Library, London:** TR, BR.

248 **Bridgeman Art Library, London / New York:** Victoria & Albert Museum, London BC; **DK Picture Library:** British Library, London TCRb; **E.T. Archive:** India Office Library BR; Zoological Society of London TL.

249 **Bridgeman Art Library, London / New York:** British Library, London TLb, (As10 Vol.52 ff.3 4896.cat.201 i-iv) CR; **Mary Evans Picture Library:** BR.

250 **Corbis:** UPI BC; **Robert Harding Picture Library:** Alain Evrard TL; **Hulton Getty:** CLA.

251 **Hulton Getty:** CL; **Rex Features:** Tim Page TCR; **Topham Picturepoint:** CRA.

252 **Hulton Getty:** BC; Bert Hardy TL; **Frank Spooner Pictures:** Gamma CL.

253 **Robert Harding Picture Library:** J Bright BL; **Pictor International:** BCL; **Frank Spooner Pictures:** Olivier Duffau / Gamma TR; Gamma CRA; Xinhua-Chine / Gamma TC.

254 **Robert Harding Picture Library:** Cb, BC; Nigel Blythe CLb.

256 **British Library, London:** TL, CR, BR; **Werner Forman Archive:** Archaeological Museum, Teheran CRb; **Ninnaji Temple, Kyoto:** TRb.

257 **Fotomas Index:** CR; **Réunion des Musées Nationaux Agence Photographique:** Musée des Arts Asiatiques-Guimet, Paris / Photograph: Arnaudet CLb; **Royal Geographical Society Picture Library:** Compiled by T.G. Montgomerie from the work of Nain Singh BL.

258 **Bridgeman Art Library, London / New York:** British Museum, London TL; **Werner Forman Archive:** Art and History Museum, Shanghai BL; **Robert Harding Picture Library:** Gavin Hellier TCR.

259 **Bridgeman Art Library, London / New York:** Tomb of Qin Shi Huang Di, Xianyang, China BL; **DK Picture Library:** British Museum, London C; **E.T. Archive:** British Museum, London TR.

260 **Bridgeman Art Library, London / New York:** Private Collection BR; **DK Picture Library:** British Museum, London TL; **E.T. Archive:** British Museum, London TC.

261 **Bridgeman Art Library, London / New York:** Bonhams, London CR; **Werner Forman Archive:** TCR; **Peter Newark's Pictures:** Landesmuseum, Halle, Germany C.

262 **Ancient Art & Architecture Collection:** Ronald Sheridan TL; **Werner Forman Archive:** Christian Deydier, London BCL; **Collection of the National Palace Museum, Taiwan, Republic of China:** BL.

263 **Ancient Art & Architecture Collection:** Kadokawa TLb; Ronald Sheridan CAR, BCR; **Fotomas Index:** BRA.

264 **DK Picture Library:** National Museum of Scotland, Edinburgh TL; **E.T. Archive:** National Museum of Tokyo CL; **Robert Harding Picture Library:** Nigel Blythe BR.

265 **AKG London:** National Museum of Tokyo BL; **Ancient Art & Architecture Collection:** Ronald Sheridan TR; **E.T. Archive:** Forrester / Wilkinson CRb.

266 **Robert Harding Picture Library:** Michael J Howell TC; **Collection of the National Palace Museum, Taiwan, Republic of China:** TL; **Philadelphia Museum of Art, Pennsylvania:** Given by John T. Dorrance CR.

267 **Bridgeman Art Library, London / New York:** National Museum of India, New Delhi CLA; Private Collection CRb; **DK Picture Library:** National Maritime Museum, London CA; **Robert Harding Picture Library:** Gavin Hellier BL.

268 **Christie's Images:** TL; **E.T. Archive:** School of Oriental and African Studies, London Cb; **Peter Newark's Pictures:** TC.

269 **Bridgeman Art Library, London / New York:** Taylor Gallery, London BR; **Topham Picturepoint:** CLA.

270 **AKG London:** TL; **Bridgeman Art Library, London / New York:** British Museum, London CL; **E.T. Archive:** Postal Museum, Frankfurt Cb; **© Michael Holford:** Print by Kokyo BC.

271 **David King Collection:** CLb; **Smithsonian Institute:** Freer Gallery of Art / Arthur M Sackler Gallery Archive / Photograph: Hsun-Ling TC.

272 **Robert Hunt Library:** TL; **Rex Features:** Sipa-Press CL; **Topham Picturepoint:** Associated Press Photos TCR.

273 **Robert Hunt Library:** BR; **Topham Picturepoint:** TR.

274 **Corbis:** Bettmann / UPI BR; **E.T. Archive:** TC; **David King Collection:** CL; **Tony Stone Images:** TL.

275 **Rex Features:** Sipa-Press / Photograph: East News BL; Sipa-Press / Photograph: Ben Simmons CbR; **Frank Spooner Pictures:** Gamma / Photograph: Xinhua TR.

276 **Bruce Coleman Ltd:** Nicholas de Vore BC; **Robert Harding Picture Library:** Nick Servian CLb; **Planet Earth Pictures:** Frank Krahmer Cb.

278 **Bridgeman Art Library, London / New York:** Mitchell Library, State Library of New South Wales BR; **DK Picture Library:** Museum of Mankind, London TR; **E.T. Archive:** National Library, Canberra, Australia TL; **Maritiem Museum 'Prins Hendrik', Rotterdam, The Netherlands:** BCR.

279 **British Library, London:** CRA; **Coo-ee Historical Picture Library:** CLb, BL; **Mary Evans Picture Library:** TL.

280 **Bridgeman Art Library, London / New York:** British Museum, London TL; **Robert Harding Picture Library:** Richard Ashworth C; Robert Francis TR; David Holdsworth BL.

281 **Bridgeman Art Library, London / New York:** British Museum, London TC; Royal Geographical Society, London CR; **Peter Crawford:** TRb; **Robert Harding Picture Library:** Geoff Renner BRA.

282 **Coo-ee Historical Picture Library:** TL; **Corbis:** Gleason's Pictorial Drawing-Room Companion BC; **State Library of New South Wales:** TRb.

283 **Panos Pictures:** Penny Tweedie TL; **Tony Stone Images:** Paul Chesley CRb; **Topham Picturepoint:** CL.

284 **Bridgeman Art Library, London / New York:** National Library of Australia, Canberra BL; **Hulton Getty:** TCRb; **Tony Stone Images:** Warren Bolster TL.

285 **Hutchison Library:** CR; **Science Photo Library:** US Department of Energy TRb.

286 **Corbis:** Bettmann TL; **E.T. Archive:** BR; British Museum, London CbR.

287 **Corbis:** Underwood & Underwood CR; **Mary Evans Picture Library:** TR, BL; **Hulton Getty**: TCR;

Jacket:

Front **Bridgeman Art Library, London / New York:** British Library, London (Add 33733 f.9) CL; British Museum, London CLb; Hereford Cathedral, Hertfordshire Globe L; **DK Picture Library:** Globe R; British Museum, London CRb, BLA; **Werner Forman Archive:** Anthropology Museum, Veracruz University, Jalapa BRA; **Robert Harding Picture Library:** Simon Harris BL; **National Maritime Museum, London:** Globe C; Popperfoto BR; Rex Features: CR.

Back **Bridgeman Art Library, London / New York:** Tomb of Qin Shi Huang Di, Xianyang, China TR; **DK Picture Library:** British Museum, London CR; Museum of Mankind, London CL; **Rex Features:** Tim Rooke TL.

Front Flap **Bridgeman Art Library, London / New York:** Royal Geographical Society, London T; **Werner Forman Archive:** Idemitsu Museum of Arts, Tokyo B.

Endpapers **© 1996 Visual Language**.

Dorling Kindersley Photography:

David Ashby, Geoff Brighting, Tina Chambers, Andy Crawford, Geoff Dann, Mike Dunning, Lynton Gardiner, Steve Gorton, Peter Hayman, Chas Howson, Ivor Kerslake, Andrew McRobb, Gillie Newman, Nick Nicholls, Laurence Pordes, James Stevenson, Linda Whitman, Peter Wilson, John Woodcock.

Dorling Kindersley would like to thank:

Alice Whitehead at Bridgeman Art Library, Ute Krebs at AKG London, Caroline Haywood and all staff at E.T. Archive, Themis Halvantzi at Werner Forman Archive, Michael Holford, all at Robert Harding Picture Library and Mark Vivian at Mary Evans Picture Library for all their assistance with picture research.

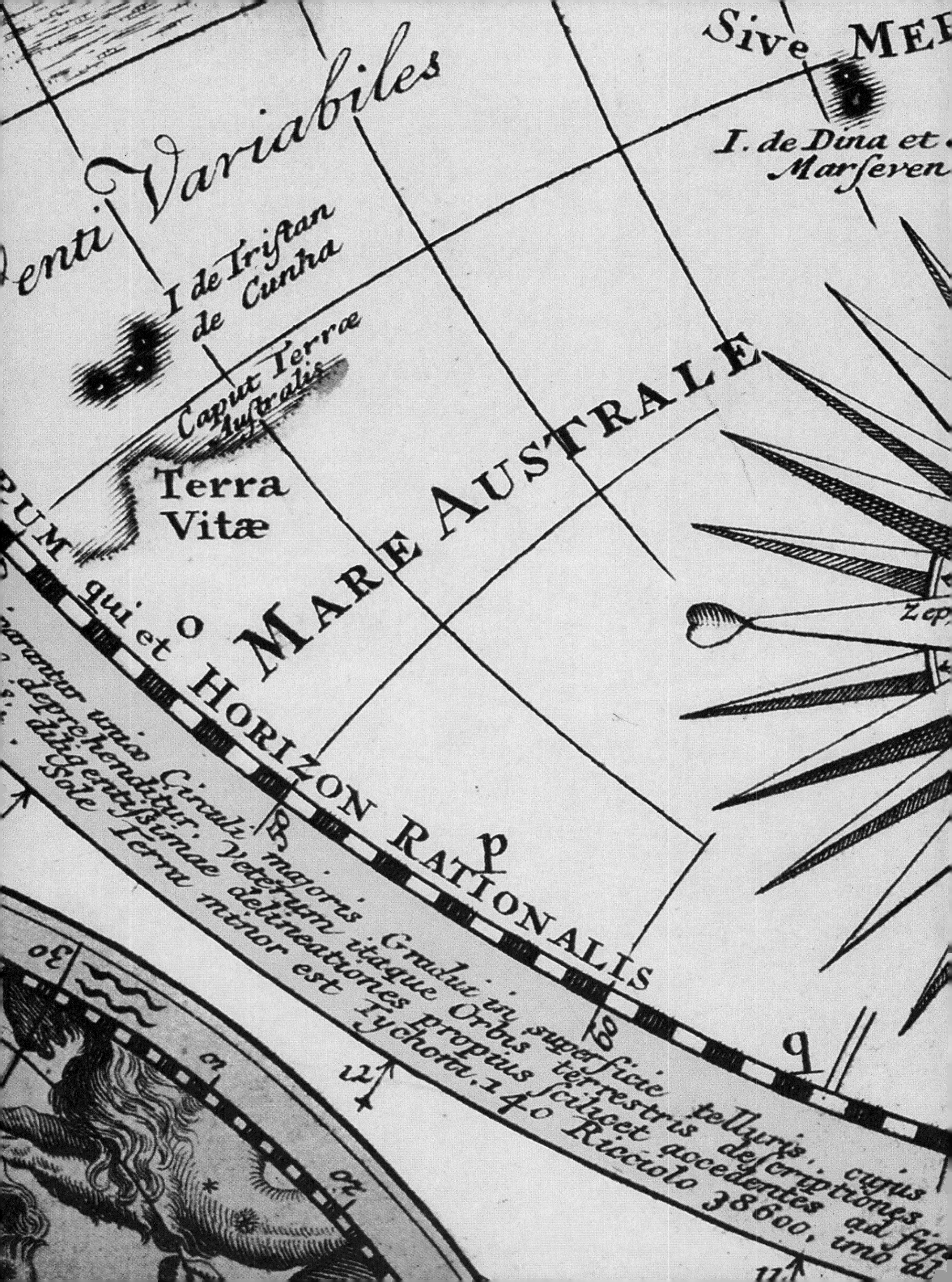

Sive MER

I. de Dina et
Marseven

enti Variabiles

I de Tristan
de Cunha

Caput Terræ
Australis

Terra
Vitæ

MARE AUSTRALE

UM qui et HORIZON RATIONALIS

Zep

p

q

variantur unio Circuli majoris. Gradui in superficie telluris, cujus
deprhenditur. Veterum itaque Orbis terrestris descriptiones ad fu
diligentissima delineationes propius accedentes ad
Sole Terra minor est Tychota, 140 scilicet Ricciolo 38600, imo

30

20

12

20